Cooking Temperatures

TOP STOVE

Simmering ....180°-200° F.
Boiling (sea level)........................212° F.
Soft-Ball Stage (Candies)..............234°-240° F.
Jelly Stage ....220°-222° F.

OVEN

Slow ....300°-325° F.
Moderate ....350°-375° F.
Hot ....400°-450° F.
Very Hot.............................475°-550° F.

BAKING

Meat and Poultry
        300°-325° F. (except Fresh Pork 350° F.)
Fish ....350°-400° F.
Egg and Cheese dishes ....350° F.
Custards, Soufflés......................325°-350° F.
Yeast Breads..........................375°-400° F.
Muffins, Coffee Cake, Cornbread............400° F.
Biscuits, Pastry ....450° F.
Layer Cakes ....350°-375° F.
Cup Cakes ....375°-400° F.
Fruit Cakes ....250°-300° F.
Angel and Sponge Cakes...............300°-375° F.

America's Cook Book

AMERICA'S
COOK BOOK

Compiled by

THE NEW YORK HERALD TRIBUNE
HOME INSTITUTE

CHARLES SCRIBNER'S SONS, NEW YORK

CHARLES SCRIBNER'S SONS, LTD., LONDON

1952

Foreword

WE FEEL SURE that you are going to enjoy cooking with this fourth revision of America's Cook Book, first developed by the HOME INSTITUTE of the New York *Herald Tribune* in 1937. Habits of family living are changing rapidly these days. Homemakers have less and less time to spend in the kitchen. With the watchwords of SPEED and EASE in mind, we have streamlined this new edition to meet a busy cook's requirements.

One new chapter offers a set of menus for Minute Meals based on the use of commercial food products which you may serve with an individual flair and interest. You will find here many "Quick Trick" food ideas developed by our home economists and in the testing laboratories of outstanding food companies.

Food freezing has made amazing strides in the past five years. Women enthusiastically endorse this method of preservation because it enables them to do weekly shopping; to prepare foods for several meals at one time; to store the finest quality vegetables and fruits, picked in their prime, for off-season eating and to save money by purchasing seasonal foods in quantity at reduced prices. Our section on home freezing gives the most up-to-date information available to us from the Bureau of Human Nutrition and Home Economics of the U. S. Department of Agriculture, representing the research conducted across the country. Directions are given for the freezing, storage and cooking of practically every food you will want to prepare in your kitchen. The purchase, use and care of the home freezer is discussed in a practical way.

Meat buying is a young homemaker's most difficult culinary problem, our readers tell us. In our chapter on meat cookery, you will note that we have used comprehensive but simple charts to aid in purchasing, preparing and cooking every cut of meat. Interesting ways of serving inexpensive meats are featured. More than forty additional charts on purchasing and preparing foods seek to give help where it is most needed by the inexperienced cook.

Other new chapters we have included emphasize the value of the pressure cooker as a time and penny saver with many family-favorite recipes; a chapter has been designed to help you entertain a crowd or to plan a club or church luncheon or supper, and a chapter brings the world into your kitchen via recipes from 38 countries.

We sincerely hope that this cook book can serve as a handbook to the beginner and a source of creative cooking to the experienced homemaker. You will find all phases of family food service here: meal planning, good nutrition for the family, methods of marketing, cooking and table service. We feel that its completeness and scientific accuracy may make it an important addition for schools, laboratories and hospitals.

Since this book first went to press in 1937, we have tested and retested and published more than 40,000 recipes. In this new edition you will find the best of these recipes chosen for your family use. Homemakers in every state of the union have contributed their best regional recipes. Foreign friends have supplied the international flavor to our foods through our visits to their kitchens in many countries and with their interviews here in the HOME INSTITUTE. Scientific research laboratories in universities and commercial food companies have been generous in sharing with us their very latest food knowledge and techniques for your benefit.

You will see that we have not changed our easy-to-follow basic pattern of writing these recipes. Hundreds of satisfied users concur that this book can be of real practical value to the beginning cook as well as to the experienced homemaker. In addition to the

❖❖

basic recipes given with new time-saving techniques, you will find
some of the finest gourmet dishes we could glean from well-
known cooks and chefs at home and abroad. In all there are more
than 3,500 recipes to give you a wide range of interesting foods for
your kitchen adventures.

Representing thirty-five years of research, these recipes have
been tested not only by our own home economists but by the
greatest of all cooking experts—the American homemaker.

We are especially grateful to the many faithful *Herald Tribune*
readers who have been kind enough to share with us their family's
favorite recipes. We are greatly indebted also to the heads of consumer service departments of countless food companies, college
professors and extension workers, government personnel and food
authorities for their enthusiastic cooperation in helping us to give
you the most modern and efficient food knowledge available to us
as we go to press.

Cooking is great fun—a creative adventure. We hope America's
Cook Book will help you to derive real satisfaction and enjoyment
from preparing good food for your family.

HARRIET JEAN ANDERSON
DIRECTOR OF THE HOME INSTITUTE

EUGENIA SHEPPARD
WOMEN'S FEATURE EDITOR
NEW YORK HERALD TRIBUNE

ACKNOWLEDGMENTS

Grateful acknowledgment is given here to the hundreds of *Herald Tribune* readers who have helped write this book by sharing with us their choice family recipes.

Acknowledgment is also made for the contributions of Elsie H. Dawson, Gladys Gilpin and Howard Reynolds of the Bureau of Human Nutrition and Home Economics, United States Agricultural Research Administration; Lura Jim Alkire and Stanley Schuler of the General Electric Company; Faith Fenton and Nancy K. Masterman of Cornell University; George Cook of the Long Island Institute of Technology and Donald K. Tressler of the U. S. Quartermaster Division to our section on home freezing and the purchase, use and care of the home freezer.

We are deeply grateful to the many leading home economists of food companies who have shared with us the results of their research in new food developments, especially Ellen Ann Dunham of General Foods Corporation, Ruth T. Andre of Pillsbury Mills, Inc., Janette Kelley of General Mills, Inc., Beth Baily McLean of Swift & Company, Esther Latzke of Armour & Company, Gwen Lam of the Wheat Flour Institute, Marye Dahnke of Kraft Foods Company, Rachel Reed of Borden Company, Elsie Stark of Best Foods, Gertrude Betten of National Dairy Products Company, June Bricker of Metropolitan Life Insurance Company, Mary Hinkle of Standard Brands, Inc., Ina Lindman of United Fruit Company, Helen Hamilton of Corn Products Refining Company, Jeanne Owen, Secretary of the Wine and Food Society, Kathryn Niles of the Poultry and Egg National Board, Rose Kerr of the United States Fish and Wildlife Service, Reba Staggs of the National Live Stock and Meat Board, Monica Clark of the American Meat Institute, Marietta Eichelberger of the Evaporated Milk Association.

Credit goes to The Kroger Company for their courtesy in arranging for the jacket illustration and to Hunt Foods, Inc., of Fullerton, California and Pillsbury Mills, Inc., for color illustrations in the text.

We are greatly indebted to the National Livestock and Meat Board, General Foods and the United States Department of Agriculture for permission to use their charts.

Full credit must be given to Clementine Paddleford, food editor of the *Herald Tribune,* for her invaluable contribution and help in the development of the new edition and to members of the HOME INSTITUTE staff: Frances Humm, Joyce Jones, Marilyn Laing, Anne Pappas, Beatrice Myers.

Contents

CONTENTS

For Better Eating

WHETHER you are a young bride enthusiastic about learning to cook and serve appealing, cooked-to-a-turn meals or an experienced homemaker interested in acquiring knowledge of new cooking techniques and recipes to add fillip to your daily menus—your goal is the same—to feed your family well.

This book has been planned to give you recipes that can be trusted to turn out well for the expert or the beginner, providing the directions are faithfully followed. The recipes have been gleaned from *Herald Tribune* readers in every state of the union and from many foreign countries, from research food laboratories in universities and commercial companies, from outstanding gourmets and authorities in the food world and from our own home economists. Each recipe has been carefully tested in our HOME INSTITUTE kitchens.

New methods of food processing and preserving are constantly being evolved. Every effort has been made to give you the most up-to-date information about cooking techniques, food products, canning and freezing food for the family. Here you will find help in menu planning, shopping, food preparation and serving.

Women today know that health is the cornerstone of happiness and that nutrition is the single most important factor affecting our health. College students of 1950 were taller, healthier and had more stamina than their parents who entered schools 30 years ago. In every instance this improvement has been attributed to better nutrition.

Don't let that word "nutrition" frighten you. Actually, it is simply a matter of eating and utilizing daily a wide variety of

I

❖❖

foods. Choosing, preparing and serving those foods for your family can be a stimulating, creative, soul-satisfying job.

Food reveals your personality as much as the way you act, what you wear and how you talk. Your feeling for beauty, your interest in the world around you, and your alertness to the newer developments of science are reflected in the type of meals you serve.

Enjoyment is the keynote to family food planning. Meals attractively served, combining color, flavor and texture, a pleasant atmosphere and stimulating conversation guarantee you the reputation of a successful hostess and an excellent cook.

The psychology of food is subtle but strong. Home-cooked food has a personal touch. A dish carefully prepared can convey more sentiment than you may feel like putting into words. Traditions strengthen family ties and certain foods for certain occasions will long be remembered. We venture to say that boys and girls growing up will remember affectionately Sunday brunches, picnics out-of-doors, birthday parties and the family's favorite dishes far longer than they will recall the ever-spotless house or a daily routine scrupulously kept. Food can form the basis of many fun-time gatherings for the family.

Meal Planning and Table Service

PLANNING three meals a day for your family is a boring task only if you choose to regard it that way. Consider it a challenging game with high stakes and you and your family will both benefit. You'll find that they'll appreciate your efforts and you yourself will gain a real feeling of satisfaction.

RULES OF THE FOOD GAME

1. More and more women are doing once-a-week shopping, so they plan their meals a week in advance. You may prefer to plan the menus, then make out your market list—or to shop, taking advantage of market surpluses and "specials" and build your menu around your market basket.
2. Plan your work so that you do not have a last-minute rush at meal time. You and your family will enjoy meals that have an air of leisure about them—difficult as you may think this is to accomplish.
3. Remember that the members of your family "eat with their eyes." The best nutrition-wise meal in the world is of no benefit unless the family enjoys it. Think of your meals as "patterns" on plates—balance colors, textures and flavors. Balance heavy and light courses—light dessert with full-course meal. Do not repeat the same food.
4. Your family will enjoy "surprises" in a meal—a new recipe for a casserole, a soup, a dessert. The meal may be built around

one interesting dish as the focal point. Use low-cost foods to balance the higher priced items.

5. Learn to make several sauces (store basic stocks in refrigerator ready for instant use) to add fillip to meats, fish, poultry and vegetables.
6. Learn to taste, season and taste again for that "perfect" flavor.
7. Learn to keep such garnishes as water cress, mushrooms (canned or fresh), parsley, chives, fresh herbs (a window herb garden is attractive and a pleasure to grow), pimiento and paprika on hand for attractive decorations. Garnishes make more difference than you may think in attaining eye-appeal.
7. Have a variety of table mats and cloths to add color and interest to your table.

DON'T FORGET BREAKFAST

THERE have been all kinds of surveys in the past five years conducted with school children, high school and college students and with professional men in the business world to determine the importance of breakfast in relation to health and work production. In every case, the importance of eating a good breakfast was emphasized. A sample might be as follows:

Fruit
(preferably with vitamin C)
Enriched cereal—cooked or prepared
Eggs in some form, occasionally with meat
Enriched bread toast
Milk or Coffee

PACKAGED FOODS IN YOUR MEALS

EACH week new food products are placed on the market aimed to make a homemaker's kitchen work simpler and quicker as well as to whet the family's appetite. Newspapers and magazines give you news of these foods and tell you where to buy them and how to serve them. So many products come prepared now that many hostesses find it convenient to stock an emergency shelf with several complete meals.

If you have a freezer or a frozen food refrigerator compartment, you may want to stock a frozen meal or two that can be served within a short period of time. The market abounds with frozen dishes that need only defrosting and heating.

DAILY FOOD PATTERN

YOU NEED not worry about specific food nutrients so long as you give your family a wide variety of foods. We have planned a nutrition-wise daily food pattern that will give your family all the "essentials" in a low-cost and a moderate plan. As you will note, the amounts are included for children and for pregnant and nursing mothers. Include these foods daily in your weekly food plan and add soups, appetizers, hot breads, desserts and other sweets as you wish. Once your family gets into the habit of these foods, you will realize how simple and easy meals planned around this pattern are to prepare and how appetizing they are to eat.

GOOD NUTRITION FOR YOUR MEALS

YOU NEED not know about the scientific side of nutrition to feed your family well. Nutrition is concerned with food and the ingredients of food—there are about 60 specific chemicals—needed by the body to prevent diseases and to maintain optimum health. Up-to-date nutritionists today tell us that it does not matter whether we get these 60 essential food chemicals from one food or another as long as we "eat it, use it, enjoy it and watch our weight." Eating a wide variety of foods daily with a high proportion of meats, poultry, fish, fruits, vegetables, milk, cheese, cream and ice cream is recommended.

Proteins, carbohydrates, fats, vitamins and minerals are the food nutrients needed by the body for energy, growth and the regulation of body processes. The unit used in measuring the amount of energy in food is called the Calorie. Foods vary in the amount of calories they contain. The chief sources of energy are proteins, carbohydrates and fats.

TABLE I

DAILY FOOD PATTERN

Number of Servings per Person per Week

GROUP	LOW-COST PLAN	MODERATE-COST PLAN
GROUP I		
Leafy, green and yellow vegetables	7 to 9 servings weekly	10 to 12 servings weekly

Choose from asparagus, green beans, broccoli, green peppers, okra, beet, dandelion, turnip and mustard greens, kale, collards, spinach, cabbage, corn, sweet potatoes, pumpkin, yellow turnips, squash, all raw salad greens.

GROUP	LOW-COST PLAN	MODERATE-COST PLAN
GROUP II		
Citrus fruits, tomatoes	*Children*—7 servings weekly *Pregnant and nursing women*—9 to 12 servings weekly *Other adults*—6 to 7 servings weekly	*Children*—8 to 9 servings weekly *Pregnant and nursing women*—12 to 15 servings weekly *Other adults*—7 to 9 servings weekly

Choose from oranges, grapefruit, lemons, tomatoes and pineapple. Use fresh, canned or frozen.

GROUP	LOW-COST PLAN	MODERATE-COST PLAN
GROUP III		
Potatoes and sweet potatoes	10 to 12 servings weekly	7 to 9 servings weekly

GROUP	LOW-COST PLAN	MODERATE-COST PLAN
GROUP IV		
Other vegetables and fruits	7 servings weekly	10 to 12 servings weekly

Choose fresh, frozen, canned or dried.

GROUP	LOW-COST PLAN	MODERATE-COST PLAN
GROUP V		
Milk, cheese, ice cream	*Children*—3½ cups daily *Pregnant women*— 1 quart plus daily *Nursing women*— 1½ quarts daily	*Children*—3½ to 4 cups daily *Pregnant women*— 1 quart plus daily *Nursing women*— 1½ quarts daily

1 quart milk equals 1 tall can evaporated milk plus the same amount of water. Or 10 to 12 tablespoons dry skim milk plus 2 tablespoons fat equals 1 quart fresh milk. 1 ounce cheese equals 1 8-ounce glass of milk. Cottage, farmer (American cheddar) and cream cheese have less calcium.

TABLE I—(*Continued*)
DAILY FOOD PATTERN
Number of Servings per Person per Week

GROUP	LOW-COST PLAN	MODERATE-COST PLAN
GROUP VI		
Meat, poultry, fish,	5 or 6 servings weekly	7 or 8 servings weekly
eggs	5 eggs weekly	7 eggs weekly
Dry beans, peas, nuts	2 to 4 servings weekly	1 to 2 servings weekly

Meats: Choose from all cuts of beef, veal, lamb, pork as well as the meat sundries such as liver, heart, kidney, and sweetbreads (all high in nutritive value; liver is recommended once or twice weekly). There is no difference in food value between expensive and inexpensive cuts of meat.

Poultry: Choose from chicken, turkey, duck, guinea hen and game birds bought fresh, frozen, smoked or canned.

Fish: Choose from fresh or salt water fish, fresh, frozen, canned or salted.

Eggs: There is no difference in food value between Grades A or B or between white and brown eggs.

GROUP	LOW-COST PLAN	MODERATE-COST PLAN
GROUP VII		
Flour, cereal, baked goods (Important to eat enriched, whole-grain, or restored)	Bread at every meal and also a cereal dish daily	At every meal

Nutritionists generally agree that there is little nutritional difference today between the enriched breads and cereals and the whole wheat or restored products, but it is important to eat one or the other.

GROUP	LOW-COST PLAN	MODERATE-COST PLAN
GROUP VIII		
Fats and oils	Throughout the week as desired. Butter or fortified margarine daily.	Throughout the week as desired. Butter or fortified margarine daily.

Butter, fortified margarine, peanut butter, nut butters, olive oil, salad oils.

GROUP	LOW-COST PLAN	MODERATE-COST PLAN
GROUP IX		
Sugar, syrup, preserves	Throughout week as desired	Throughout week as desired

In addition to the foods in the above groups, fish-liver oil or some other source of vitamin D should be allowed for small children, pregnant or nursing women, also for older children and adults who have little opportunity to be in sunshine.

There are also certain miscellaneous food items to be considered in the total food plan. The miscellaneous group includes such items as coffee, tea, cocoa, chocolate, iodized salt, pepper, other seasonings and flavorings, baking powder and soda, prepared puddings and gelatin. No quantities are suggested for these items, but allowance is made for their cost.

To measure the nutrients needed by members of the family, you should consider the age, size and activity of each member.

TABLE II

WHAT YOU NEED TO KNOW ABOUT FOOD NUTRIENTS

(For daily and weekly food planning, see guide on page 6)

Nutrients	Why They Are Necessary	Food Sources	How to Conserve in Storing and Cooking
PROTEINS (composed of amino acids)	Build and repair muscles, soft tissue, blood cells Precursors of hormones and enzymes Supply energy	Animal sources (made up of complete amino acids); milk, cheese, eggs, meat (especially liver and kidney), poultry, fish Vegetable sources: cereal products, legumes, and nuts. Soybeans and Brazil nuts contain complete amino acids	Storing: protein foods need storage in refrigerator or in cool dry place Cooking: high heat and long cooking toughens and coagulates proteins
CARBOHYDRATES Sugars Starches Cellulose	Supply quick and cheap energy Easily converted into excess fat in body Cellulose used for regulating—bulk of value in digestive tract	Animal sources: milk Vegetable sources: Sugars—sweets Starches — cereals, tubers and roots, legumes Cellulose — fresh, cooked, dried fruits, vegetables, whole wheat cereals, bran	Storage: cool dry place Cooking: no special problem
FATS, SOLIDS, OILS	Supply energy in concentrated form Easily converted into excess fat in body Regulate and protect: carry fat-soluble vitamins in body, contain essential fatty acids, helpful in food digestion	Animal sources: butter, cream, cheese, fat meats, fish, bacon, salt pork, egg yolk, milk Vegetable sources: corn, cottonseed, peanut, olive oils; margarines, hydrogenated fats; nuts, wheat germ, avocados	Storage: fats need to be stored in cool, dark place. (Watch odor absorption for rancidity) Cooking: never heat fats to smoking temperatures

8

MINERALS			
Calcium and Phosphorus	Build and repair bones, teeth, soft tissues, body fluids Regulate and protect: clotting of blood; functioning of heart, nerves, muscles, enzyme activity and utilization of iron	Animal: milk, cheese, fish Vegetable: green leafy vegetables, legumes, cabbage, broccoli, dried fruits	Storage: no special procedure necessary Cooking: minerals can be lost in cooking water. To minimize loss: 1. Use small amount of water and short cooking period for vegetables and fruits 2. Use any cooking water left over 3. Cook vegetables whole or in large pieces 4. Cook vegetables in skin when possible, as most minerals are near skin 5. Bake, steam and pancook to conserve minerals
IRON AND COPPER	Build and repair red blood cells Regulate and protect tissue function, carrying of oxygen, in maintaining neutrality	Animal: egg yolk, liver, heart, kidney, lean meat, fish and seafood, milk Vegetable: enriched grain products, fruits and fresh vegetables	
IODINE	Builds and repairs: needed for functioning of thyroid gland (protects from goiter) Regulates and protects use of carbohydrates	Animal: salt-water fish and shellfish Iodized salt Vegetable: fruits and vegetables (if iodine is in soil)	

9

Food as a whole nourishes the body in three ways: (1) it furnishes the body with fuels which supply *energy* for our activities; (2) food provides the materials for the *building* and *upkeep* of the body tissues; and (3) it supplies the substances for *regulating* body processes. A *nutrient* is a substance which takes part in any of these three functions in the body.

You will find a description of the food nutrients in Tables I and II, as well as a list of the food sources and brief suggestions for preserving these nutrients in storage and cooking.

YOUR MEAL GUIDE

"WHAT should I plan to eat?" That question comes over the HOME INSTITUTE telephones many times a day—for a family dinner, a company meal, a tea, a buffet,—the list grows long. Here we give some well-balanced menus that you may want to use as a springboard for your own imagination in planning meals your family will enjoy. For unusual foods we have given page references to individual recipes.

Breakfast Menus

Sparkling Orange Juice
Whole Wheat Dry or Cooked Cereal
Bacon and Eggs
Toast   Strawberry Jam
Coffee   Milk

Stewed Apricots
Cooked Enriched Cereal
Toasted Raisin Bread   Butter
Coffee   Milk

Half Grapefruit
Pancakes   Maple Syrup
Crisp Bacon Curls
Coffee   Milk

Chilled Fruit Compote
Scrambled Eggs, Frizzled Ham
White Mountain Muffins, p. 145   Jam
Coffee   Milk

Brunch Menus

Tray of Fresh Fruits
Waffles   Creamed Chicken
Hot Sweet Buns
Coffee   Milk

Grapefruit Basket of Fresh Fruits
Eggs Benedict, p. 115
Cornmeal Sticks, p. 147   Jam
Coffee   Milk

Iced Tomato Juice
Broiled Kidney & Bacon, p. 335
Scrambled Eggs
Toasted English Muffins
Plum Marmalade
Coffee   Tea

Orange in Sections
French Puffy Omelet, p. 120
Hard Rolls   Raspberry Conserve
Coffee   Milk

Luncheon Menus

Perch Tarts, p. 419
Watercress and Cucumber Salad with
Chiffonade Dressing, p. 618
Stir-n-roll Biscuits, p. 152
Butterscotch Pudding
Coffee   Tea   Milk

Spinach Roll with Meat Filling, p. 570
Egg Sauce, p. 464
Sliced Tomatoes   Muffins, p. 145
Lemon Pudding, p. 770
Coffee   Tea   Milk

Chicken Piquant in Pancake Shell,
p. 374
Tomato Aspic on Endive, p. 608
Maple Cake, p. 648
Coffee   Tea   Milk

Hot Tomato Bouillon
Pressed Chicken Pimiento, p. 609
Martha Washington Potato Rolls, p. 176
Sour Cream Pie, p. 750
Coffee   Tea   Milk

Noodles, Creole Style, p. 506
Avocado and Grapefruit Salad, p. 598
Hot French Bread
Nut Chiffon Cake, p. 675
Coffee   Tea   Milk

Frosted Grape Platter, p. 599
Hot Nut Muffins, p. 146
Delicate Sponge Cake, p. 670
Coffee   Tea   Milk

Consommé
Secret Salad, p. 595
Crisp Bacon-topped Cornbread, p. 158
Chocolate Cream Cake, p. 644
Coffee   Tea   Milk

Bisque à la Capetown, p. 443
Asparagus Macedoine Salad, p. 590
Buttered Biscuits, p. 149
Gourmet's Chocolate Cake, p. 644
Coffee   Tea   Milk

Tuna Stuffed Eggs, p. 123
Rice Salad, p. 592
Asparagus, p. 523
Herb Bread, p. 163
Hot Lemon Soufflé, p. 783
Coffee   Tea   Milk

Deviled Eggs, p. 123   Rice Salad, p. 597
Beet Pickles   Potato Chips
Cucumber Combination Salad, p. 593
Orange Coconut Cake, p. 634
Coffee   Tea   Milk

French Onion Soup, p. 242   Crackers
Sliced Ham, Turkey, Salami
Celery Curls   Green Pickle Relish
Whole Wheat Bread Sandwiches
Chocolate Indians, p. 694
Coffee   Tea   Milk

Asparagus Omelet, p. 524
Tomato Sauce, p. 469
Assorted Tea Sandwiches, p. 817
Vanilla Tapioca Cream, p. 771
Coffee   Tea   Milk

Chicken Lilly, p. 360
Endive Salad Fans, p. 588
Popovers, p. 140
Nut Torte, p. 668
Coffee   Tea   Milk

Stina's Macaroni Casserole, p. 501
Chicory and Tomatoes
Bacon Dressing, p. 587
Bran Muffins, p. 147
Raspberry Chiffon Pie, p. 754
Coffee   Tea   Milk

English Monkey, p. 134
(chafing-dish style)
Buttered Toast
Coffee   Tea   Milk

Ham Mousse, p. 610
Tomato and Cucumber Garnish
Finger Rolls, p. 169
Raspberry Sherbet, p. 803   Cookies
Coffee   Tea   Milk

Cream of Tomato Soup, p. 229
Baked Ham and Lettuce Sandwiches
Sweet Pickles   Ripe Olives
Fruit Bowl
Coffee   Tea   Milk

Dinner Menus

Planked Mackerel, p. 412
Potato Border, p. 564
Glazed Carrots, p. 538
Broccoli   Hollandaise Sauce, p. 473
Romaine Salad   French Dressing
Lemon Chiffon Pie, p. 755   Coffee

Tomato Juice
Shad Baked in Milk, p. 412
Duchess Potatoes, p. 564
Baked Squash, p. 572
Hearts of Lettuce
Pineapple Betty, p. 775   Coffee

Clear Borsch, p. 32
Crown Roast of Pork, p. 315   Potatoes
Buttered Peas and Carrots
Green Salad   Crescent Rolls, p. 170
Pears Crème de Menthe, p. 103
Cookies   Coffee

Fresh Cream of Mushroom Soup, p. 229
Broiled Shad Roe, p. 422
Melted Butter
Mashed Potatoes   Buttered Spinach
Mixed Green Salad
Cloverleaf Rolls, p. 170
Pineapple Meringue Cake, p. 663
Coffee

Filet of Sole en Papillote, p. 1025
Snap Beans with Tomatoes, p. 526
Cucumber Combination Salad, p. 593
Lemon Sherbet, p. 802   Coffee

Shrimp Cocktail, p. 216   Toast Sticks
Baked Ham, p. 321
Raisin Sauce, p. 476
Lima Beans   Corn on Cob
Cabbage Salad, p. 591
Garlic Rolls, p. 181
Fruit Platter   Cheese   Coffee

Chilled Melon Balls, p. 215
Duck in Wine Sauce, p. 376
Broccoli with Sautéed Tomatoes
Hot Rolls
Baked Sweet Potatoes
Avocado-Grapefruit Salad, p. 598
Peach Linzer Tartlets, p. 757   Coffee

Chicken Casserole, p. 366
Broiled Potatoes, p. 563   Buttered Peas
Spiced Cranberries, p. 950
Hot Biscuits, p. 169
Plain Chiffon Cake, p. 674   Coffee

Vegetable Juice Cocktail
Fresh Tuna Steaks, p. 428
Baked Potatoes
Asparagus, Hollandaise Sauce, p. 523
Pickled Mushrooms, p. 498
Pappy's Southern Rolls, p. 173
Grapefruit Baked Alaska, p. 813   Coffee

French Onion Soup, p. 242
Broiled Lobster Cordon Bleu, p. 437
Buttered Asparagus   Baked Potatoes
Sunday Nite Salad, p. 598 French Bread
Apple Fritters Parisian, p. 90
Coffee

Consommé
Steak and Kidney Pie, p. 284
Buttered Potatoes
Braised Dandelion Greens, p. 552
Tomato Aspic, p. 608   Popovers, p. 140
Fresh Fruit   Cheese
Coffee

Chilled Apple Juice
Pork Chops with Red Cabbage, p. 536
Boiled Rice, p. 507
Tossed Greens, French Dressing
Bran Muffins, p. 147
Lindy's Cheesecake, p. 666   Coffee

Minted Fruit Cup
Eggplant Stuffed with Shrimp, p. 351
Buttered Spinach
Sautéed Onions, p. 358
Hot Baking Powder Biscuits, p. 149
Blacksmith Chocolate Soufflé, p. 784
Coffee

Iced Cucumber Soup, p. 245
Planked Chicken, p. 358
Potato Rosettes, p. 564
Boiled Artichokes, p. 522
Finger Rolls, p. 169
Cream-filled Chocolate Eclairs, p. 759
Coffee

Onion Soup Chablis, p. 225
Apple Curry, p. 327
Boiled Rice, p. 507
Buttered Snap Beans
Sliced Tomatoes, Radishes, Celery
Lime Sherbert, p. 804   Coffee

Consommé
Beef Birds Cordon Bleu, p. 289
Potatoes Anna, p. 564
Buttered Zucchini
Asparagus Bavarian, p. 590
Fresh Fruit   Cheese   Coffee

Chilled Grapefruit Soup, p. 247
Baked Stuffed Fish, p. 411
Beet Greens Ring Filled with Fluffy
Mashed Patatoes, p. 564
Assorted Crisp Relishes
Magic Lemon Pie, p. 753   Coffee

Low-Cost Meals

Consommé
Baked Eggs in Rice, p. 119
Water Cress Salad
Cottage Pudding, p. 776
Cherry Sauce, p. 725
Coffee

Chicken Pilau, p. 372
Raw Vegetable Salad, p. 588
Glazed Apples, p. 87   Coffee

Hot Potato Soup, p. 230
Cold Salmon with Tartar Sauce, p. 477
Mixed Green Salad
Green Apple Pie, p. 743   Coffee

Grilled Hamburgers with Buns, p. 282
Corn on Cob
Green Salad   Sliced Tomatoes
Blackberries with Top Milk
Coffee

Sautéed Beef Liver, p. 338
Rice Pilaf, p. 502
Carrots in Chive Sauce, p. 538
Tomato Salad   French Dressing
Kumquat Snow, p. 763   Coffee

Shepherd's Pie, p. 327
Orange Mint Salad, p. 599
Bran Muffins, p. 147
Maple Rennet, p. 767   Coffee

Sautéed Pork Liver, p. 338
Onion Rings, p. 585
Buttered Kale   Mashed Potatoes
Toasted Garlic Rolls
Apple Scallop, p. 776   Coffee

Tomato Juice
Kidneys in Wine Sauce, p. 480
Baked Potatoes Fried Zucchini, p. 572
Pear Salad, p. 599
Chocolate Bread Pudding, p. 773
Coffee

Irish Stew with Dumplings, p. 1008
Buttered Peas   Boiled Potatoes
Cabbage Relish, p. 592
Chocolate Pudding, p. 769   Coffee

Spareribs with Sauerkraut, p. 316
Buttered Boiled Potatoes
Green Snap Beans
Waldorf Salad, p. 598
Black Plum Pie, p. 742   Coffee

Black Bean Soup, p. 227
Spinach Gnocchi, p. 1034
Lemon Sponge, p. 791   Crisp Cookies
Coffee

Cheese Soufflé, p. 135
Tossed Green Salad
Whole Wheat Muffins, p. 146
Brownies, p. 693   Coffee

Biscuit Meat Rolls, p. 296
Sautéed Sweet Corn, p. 544
Buttered Beets
Cauliflower and Pepper Salad, p. 593
Oatmeal Hermits, p. 689   Coffee

Creamed Salt Codfish, p. 429
Baked Potatoes   Buttered Beets
Tossed Green Salad
Spice Cake, p. 647   Coffee

Oven Dinners

Rice and Sausage Casserole, p. 512
Tomato-Stuffed Peppers, p. 562
Baking Powder Biscuits, p. 149
Stuffed Baked Apples, p. 86   Coffee

Beef Loaf, p. 287
Potatoes au Gratin, p. 565
Grapefruit and Apple Salad, p. 599
Hot Gingerbread, p. 649   Coffee

Pork Chops Casserole, p. 314
Broccoli au Gratin, p. 533
Tossed Salad
Corn Sticks, p. 147
Blackberry Roll, p. 778   Coffee

Ragout of Beef Casserole, p. 294
Crisp Relishes   Toasted Buns
Sour Cherry Cobbler, p. 779   Coffee

After-Theater Suppers

Assorted Cookies
Fruit Juice Punch, p. 195

Dainty Sandwiches, p. 817
Frosted Cup Cakes, p. 633   Coffee

Assorted Sandwiches
Pretzels
Pickled Beets   Stuffed Olives
Beer

Bouillon   Crisp Crackers
Frozen Fruit Salad, p. 616
Sweet Wafers   Coffee

Cocktail Parties

Parsley Butter Sandwiches, p. 201
Turnover Canapés, p. 199
Cheese Nut Balls, p. 199
Pickled Pearl Onions   Olives
Martini, p. 1077   Manhattan, p. 1078

Guava Cheese Sandwiches, p. 202
Crackers   Nut Bread Spread
Olives   Sweet Gherkins
Popcorn
Daiquiri, p. 1078 Tom Collins, p. 1079

Water Cress Butter Sandwiches
Pastry Canapés, p. 198
Avocado Spread, p. 202
Salted Pistachio Nuts
Planter's Punch, p. 1078

Lobster Butter Canapés, p. 200
Cocktail Sausages   Brazil Nuts
Cheese Puffs, p. 32
Dry Sherry   Orange Blossom, 1077

Bridge

Cream of Mushroom Soup, p. 229
Melba Toast
Frozen Tomato Salad, p. 616
Roquefort Cheese Biscuits, p. 150
Ambrosia, p. 763   Coffee

Frosted Citrus Juice Cup, p. 213
Oyster Casserole, p. 451
Asparagus, Butter Sauce, p. 523
Endive   Roquefort Cheese Dressing
Chocolate Soufflé, p. 782
Cookies   Coffee

Filled Cantaloupe Platter, p. 600
Thin Nut Butter Sandwiches, p. 200
Tea

Water Cress Butter Sandwiches, p. 201
Small Toasted Scones, p. 150
(split and spread with jelly)
Fruit Cake   Tea

Jellied Chicken Loaf, p. 609
Mixed Vegetable Salad, p. 588
Hot Cloverleaf Rolls, p. 170
Vanilla Ice Cream
Chocolate Mint Sauce, p. 729
Coffee

Hot Consommé
Chicken Terrapin, p. 372
Water Cress Salad
Butterhorn Rolls, p. 169
Ripe Olives
Fudge Cake, p. 644   Coffee

Early Morning Wedding Breakfast

Chilled Grapefruit
Fried Country Sausage Meat, p. 324
Scrambled Eggs, p. 117
Hashed Brown Potatoes, p. 565
Popovers, p. 140   Jam   Marmalade
Coffee

Chilled Melon Balls
Mixed Grill
(bacon, sausages, ham)
Waffles, p. 143   Syrup   Butter
Coffee

Late Morning Wedding Breakfast

Fruit Cup with Lime Ice, p. 762
Broiled Chicken
with Mushrooms, p. 356
Asparagus with
Hollandaise Sauce, p. 473
Parsley Buttered Potatoes
Assorted Relishes
Strawberry Ice Cream   Bride's Cake
Coffee

Jellied Madrilène, p. 1002
Lobster Newburg, p. 440
Buttered Lima Beans
Perfection Salad, p. 610
Hot Corn Muffins, p. 146   Jelly
Mint Parfait, p. 809   Bride's Cake
Coffee

Between-Meal Reception

Assorted Sandwiches and
Hors d'Oeuvres
Salted Nuts   Mints   Candies
Relish Tray
Raspberry Sherbet
Small Assorted Cakes   Bride's Cake
Punch   Coffee   Tea

Evening Wedding Dinners

Hot Beef Bouillon
Roast Turkey   Stuffing   Gravy
Buttered Green Peas
Mixed Green Salad
Salted Nuts   Mints   Candies
French Vanilla Ice Cream
Bride's Cake
Coffee

Honeydew Melon
Crown Roast of Lamb, p. 309
Mashed Sweet Potatoes   Lima Beans
Assorted Relishes
Salted Nuts   Mints   Candies
Raspberry Ice   Bride's Cake
Coffee

YOU AND YOUR WEIGHT

THERE is no magical way to control weight. Essentially it is a matter of eating enough, and only enough, of a nutritive diet to keep the body at normal weight. We need not count calories if we watch our weight and eat accordingly.

Physicians tell us that excess weight means that the food-calorie intake has been excessive *for that person* with his or her constitution and habits of exercise. Endocrine glands may make some differences, and fatness or leanness may be to some extent a family characteristic—but in the majority of people, overweight is due to overeating.

Records of life insurance companies show conclusively that underweight in young adults and overweight in older people are real health hazards. Correction of marked overweight or underweight belongs in the hands of a physician, but the optimal fatness for the older person is that which corresponds to the individual's height and to age 30 in the following standardized tables published by the United States Public Health Service. The height includes ordinary shoes and the weight includes ordinary indoor clothing. Medical authorities warn that in and after midde age, overweight increases the death rate and reduces life expectation.

TABLE III

WEIGHT FOR HEIGHT AS OF AGE 30

Height	Women	Men
4 ft. 8 in.	112	
4 ft. 9 in.	114	
4 ft. 10 in.	116	
4 ft. 11 in.	118	
5 ft. 0 in.	120	126
5 ft. 1 in.	122	128
5 ft. 2 in.	124	130
5 ft. 3 in.	127	133
5 ft. 4 in.	131	136
5 ft. 5 in.	134	140
5 ft. 6 in.	138	144
5 ft. 7 in.	142	148
5 ft. 8 in.	146	152
5 ft. 9 in.	150	156
5 ft. 10 in.	154	161
5 ft. 11 in.	157	166
6 ft. 0 in.	161	172
6 ft. 1 in.		178
6 ft. 2 in.		184
6 ft. 3 in.		190
6 ft. 4 in.		196
6 ft. 5 in.		201

Muscular exercises may be beneficial in a fair proportion of cases, physicians maintain, but it is apt to be an arduous process of weight reduction, especially as exercise is very likely to increase appetite. For the obese, increased muscular exercise may endanger the heart. As nutritionist M. S. Rose said, "the only form of exercise essential to the control of body weight is the exercise of intelligence."

When reducing weight, food should be considered not from the calorie angle alone, but as to what contribution it makes as a source of protein, needed minerals, and vitamins. Those foods which contain little food value other than fat or carbohydrate may be omitted.

A general guide for the number of calories needed by family members according to energy activity is found in the chart of Recommended Food Allowances issued by the National Research Bureau (page 24).

Nutritionists estimate that a decrease of 500 calories a day below the recommended number of calories will usually result in the loss of about 1 pound of body weight per week, as rapid a reduction as one should attempt unless under medical supervision.

The underweight person will, in general, be able to build his weight to standard by eating more calories and perhaps by eating six meals a day instead of three. Studies show that many women who try to attain a thin figure for reasons of fashion often develop tuberculosis. Underweight college women, who commonly thought of themselves as feeling well, were surprised to find that they felt more buoyant, tired less easily and were able to study better when their weight was brought up to normal.

The following food value tables of common foods will help you to plan your diets to suit your individual weight.

TABLE IV
FOOD VALUES OF MANY COMMON FOODS

NAME OF FOOD	AMOUNT OF ONE SERVING[1] MEASURE	WEIGHT Oz.	WEIGHT Gm.	NUTRITIVE VALUE—PER CENT OF MINIMUM DAILY ALLOWANCE FOR ADULT[2] PROTEIN	CALCIUM	PHOSPHORUS	IRON	VITAMIN A	THIAMINE	RIBOFLAVIN	NIACIN	ASCORBIC ACID	ENERGY VALUE TOTAL CALORIES	FIBER[2]
Milk and Milk Products														
Milk, fresh, whole..........	½ pint	8.7	244	12	38	30	2	7	8	20	3	0	168	—
Milk, whole, evaporated......	½ cup	4.4	122	12	40	32	2	12	6	22	3	0	168	—
Milk, fresh, skim...........	½ pint	8.8	246	12	39	31	2	1	9	20	2	0	86	—
Buttermilk................	½ pint	8.7	244	12	38	30	2	1	10	21	2	0	90	—
Cocoa, breakfast, made with milk, sweetened................	½ pint scant	7.5	210	11	30	34	7	6	6	11	2	0	218	+
Postum, made with milk, sweetened................	¾ cup	6.8	190	9	29	25	2	6	6	15	2	0	154	—
Butter................	1 tablespoon	.5	14	0	0	0	0	12	0	0	0	0	102	—
Cheese, American or Cheddar..	1¼ x 1 x 1 in.	.7	20	7	23	16	2	8	1	5	0	0	79	—
Cheese, cottage...........	3 tablespoons	1.8	50	14	6	18	2	2	1	7	1	0	51	—
Cream, light or coffee.......	2 tablespoons	1.0	30	1	4	3	0	5	1	2	0	0	63	—
Ice cream, vanilla.........	⅓ pint	4.8	134	7	17	16	11	16	6	11	2	0	279	—
Cereals and Breads														
Grape-nuts..............	¼ cup	1.0	28	4	2	12	16	*	24	2	14	*	106	+
Grape-nuts flakes.........	¾ cup	1.0	28	4	1	15	13	*	15	2	16	*	106	+
Corn Flakes.............	1 cup	1.0	28	3	0	2	5	*	12	1	5	*	106	+
40% bran flakes..........	¾ cup	1.0	28	5	2	25	18	*	15	3	27	*	103	++
Raisin bran.............	¾ cup	1.0	28	4	2	20	16	*	11	2	20	*	98	++
Cornmeal, yellow.........	¾ cup, cooked	1.0	28	3	0	5	3	2	4	1	3	0	100	+

18

Food	Measure												
Hominy grits	¾ cup, cooked	1.0	28	3	0	3	0	4	1	3	0	100	+
Macaroni	¾ cup, cooked	1.0	28	5	1	3	0	4	1	6	0	102	+
Oatmeal	¾ cup, cooked	1.0	28	6	2	15	0	17	2	3	0	111	+
Rice, brown	¾ cup, steamed	1.0	28	3	2	15	0	7	2	11	*	100	+
Rice, white	¾ cup, steamed	1.0	28	3	0	2	*	1	0	14	*	98	+
Bread, white, enriched	2 slices	1.8	28	8	4	9	*	12	4	11	0	131	+
Bread, whole wheat	2 slices	2.1	60	9	4	18	*	13	5	17	0	158	+
Muffins, bran flake	1 large	1.5	42	5	5	10	2	11	6	11	0	146	+
Meat, Poultry, Fish, Eggs													
Beef, lean	3 x 2 x ¾ in., broiled	3.5	100	28	2	30	1	13	11	45	0	194	–
Veal cutlet	3 x 2 x ¾ in., broiled	3.5	100	27	2	29	0	18	13	63	*	176	–
Liver, calf	4 x 2 x ½ in., broiled	3.2	90	24	1	109	608	36	149	162	*	122	–
Lamb chop	1 chop, broiled	3.0	85	24	1	27	0	17	11	42	0	195	–
Lamb, roast	3 x 2¾ x ½ in., roasted	3.5	100	26	1	27	0	20	13	50	*	230	–
Heart, lamb	2 slices, cooked	3.5	100	24	1	62	0	60	*	60	*	157	–
Kidney, lamb	1 kidney, cooked	3.5	100	24	2	65	25	30	105	65	*	100	–
Bacon	4 small slices, broiled	2.0	57	7	1	5	0	11	4	14	*	357	–
Ham, smoked	3 slices, boiled	3.5	100	24	1	25	0	78	10	38	0	384	–
Pork chop, lean	1 chop, broiled	3.2	91	23	2	20	0	120	11	50	*	213	–
Chicken	3¾ x 2 x ½ in., roasted	3.5	100	30	2	19	*	11	9	86	*	149	–
Cod, fresh	3¾ x 3 x ½ in., boiled	3.5	100	24	3	9	0	6	3	20	*	70	–
Mackerel	3½ x 3 x 1½ in., broiled	3.5	100	28	3	11	4	*	*	55	*	199	–
Salmon, red	3 x 2 x ¾ in., steamed	1.8	50	32	9	12	5	20	7	65	*	211	–
Oysters	⅓ cup	3.5	100	14	9	71	25	20	11	10	*	81	–
Eggs, whole	2	3.5	100	18	7	27	25	15	18	1	0	158	–
Egg whites	2	2.2	64	10	0	0	0	0	9	1	0	29	–
Egg yolks	2	1.3	36	8	7	27	25	15	9	0	0	129	–
Vegetables													
Asparagus, green	6 stalks	3.5	100	3	3	9	23	18	6	7	133	27	++
Beans, green, string, fresh	¾ cup cuts, cooked	3.5	100	3	9	11	38	8	6	5	83	43	++
Beans, green, string, canned	⅔ cup	3.5	100	1	4	14	25	3	3	3	13	19	+++
Beans, Lima, fresh	⅔ cup, cooked	3.5	100	11	8	23	13	30	8	9	100	131	+++
Beans, Lima, dried	¾ cup, cooked	1.9	54	16	5	41	1	28	20	8	0	184	+++
Beans, navy, dried	½ cup, cooked	1.2	35	12	7	36	0	18	6	5	0	123	+++
Soybeans, dried	½ cup, cooked	1.0	30	15	9	24	1	36	11	8	0	105	+++
Beets	⅔ cup cubes, cooked	3.5	100	2	2	10	6	3	3	6	50	45	+++
Beet greens	⅔ cup, cooked	3.5	100	3	**	32	375	5	15	10	150	33	+++
Broccoli	¾ cup, cooked	3.5	100	5	17	14	225	9	12	3	416	37	++
Brussels sprouts	1 cup scant, cooked	3.5	100	6	5	11	13	15	3		317	58	++

TABLE IV—(Continued)
FOOD VALUES OF MANY COMMON FOODS

Name of Food	Amount of One Serving — Measure	Weight Oz.	Weight Gm.	Nutritive Value—per cent of minimum daily allowance for adult — Pro-tein	Cal-cium	Phos-phorus	Iron	Vita-min A	Thia-mine	Ribo-flavin	Niacin	Ascorbic Acid	Energy Value — Total Calories	Fiber
Cabbage	1 cup, chopped	3.5	100	2	6	4	4	0	8	3	3	200	29	+++
Carrots	2⁄3 cup cubes, cooked	3.5	100	2	6	5	7	250	7	3	5	20	45	+++
Cauliflower	3⁄4 cup, cooked	3.5	100	3	3	10	11	1	15	6	6	250	32	++
Celery	2 hearts	3.5	100	2	7	5	5	0	3	2	2	17	22	++
Chard	1⁄2 cup, steamed	3.5	100	2	**	5	40	250	6	6	2	117	26	+++
Corn, yellow, fresh	2 ears, 6 in. long	3.5	100	5	1	16	5	15	14	7	17	33	108	++
Corn, yellow, canned	1⁄2 cup	4.0	113	3	1	8	5	5	2	3	8	17	77	+
Cucumber	7 slices	1.8	50	1	1	5	2	0	2	1	1	13	8	+
Dandelion greens	3⁄4 cup, cooked	3.5	100	4	25	9	31	300	19	7	8	120	52	+++
Kale	3⁄4 cup, cooked	3.5	100	6	30	8	22	400	15	20	8	333	50	+++
Lentils, dried	2⁄3 cup, cooked	1.6	45	16	6	22	38	1	23	7	14	0	157	+++
Lettuce, head	1⁄4 small head	1.8	50	1	2	2	3	1	4	1	1	13	9	++
Onions	2 small	3.5	100	2	4	6	5	0	3	1	1	50	49	++
Parsnips	2⁄3 cup cubes, cooked	3.5	100	2	8	11	7	0	8	5	2	73	84	+++
Peas, fresh	2⁄3 cup, cooked	3.5	100	10	3	16	19	25	40	10	20	83	102	+++
Peas, canned	2⁄3 cup	3.5	100	5	3	9	18	20	13	5	15	37	70	+++
Peas, dried, split	2⁄3 cup, cooked	1.6	45	16	4	24	27	4	39	7	14	0	160	+++
Peppers, green	1 medium	2.0	55	1	1	2	2	41	3	1	2	277	16	+
Potatoes, white	1 small	3.5	100	3	2	8	7	1	10	3	11	40	85	+
Rutabagas	2⁄3 cup cubes, cooked	3.5	100	2	7	6	4	3	7	3	5	150	41	++
Spinach, fresh	2⁄3 cup, cooked	3.5	100	3	**	7	34	450	10	13	7	167	25	++

The following table is printed sideways on the page. Column headings are not printed on this page; the first two numeric columns are the serving size in ounces (approx. 3.5 oz = 100 g). Values are transcribed as a best-effort reading.

Food	Measure	oz	g											rating
Spinach, canned	½ cup	3.5	100	3	**	4	16	16	2	4	3	70	28	++
Squash, summer	½ cup, cooked	3.5	100	1	2	2	4	325	5	3	10	67	19	+++
Squash, winter	½ cup, cooked	3.5	100	2	3	4	6	19	5	4	6	17	44	++
Sweet potatoes	1 small	3.5	100	3	4	7	8	100	10	4	8	50	125	+++
Tomatoes, fresh	1 small	3.5	100	1	2	4	6	125	8	2	6	73	23	+++
Tomatoes, canned	½ cup scant	3.5	100	1	2	4	6	25	7	2	6	50	22	+++
Tomato juice, canned	½ cup scant	3.5	100	1	1	2	4	23	5	2	6	60	23	+++
Turnips, white	⅔ cup cubes, cooked	3.5	100	2	5	5	5	0	5	3	6	100	34	++
Turnip greens	⅔ cup scant, cooked	3.5	100	4	34	7	24	450	10	23	7	333	38	+++
Fruits														
Apples	1 medium	3.5	100	0	1	1	3	2	3	1	2	20	65	++
Apricots, canned	2 halves with syrup	3.5	100	1	2	2	3	38	3	1	3	10	89	++
Apricots, dried	10 halves	1.2	35	3	4	6	18	61	3	3	11	7	102	+++
Bananas	1 medium	3.5	100	2	1	4	6	9	5	3	6	33	99	++
Blackberries	⅔ cup	3.5	100	2	4	5	9	2	3	4	*	23	63	++
Blueberries	⅔ cup	3.5	100	1	2	2	9	1	3	*	3	33	67	++
Cantaloupe	½ medium	10.7	300	2	6	6	11	67	13	3	17	267	60	+++
Cherries	¾ cup, stoned	3.5	100	1	2	3	5	4	5	7	1	27	68	++
Dates, cured	5, stoned	1.2	35	2	3	3	7	3	3	*	7	0	111	+
Figs, dried	3 small	1.2	35	1	11	5	11	0	2	1	5	0	106	+++
Grapefruit, fresh	½ small	5.3	150	2	4	4	5	0	6	1	4	217	66	++
Grapefruit, canned	½ cup scant	3.5	100	1	2	2	3	0	3	2	3	100	44	++
Grapefruit juice, canned	½ cup scant	3.5	100	1	3	2	3	0	4	1	2	140	52	*
Grapes, Concord	30 or ⅔ cup	4.5	125	3	3	4	8	0	6	2	4	17	97	+*
Lemon juice	2 tablespoons	1.0	28	0	1	0	0	0	1	1	0	43	9	++
Oranges	1 medium	5.3	150	2	7	5	6	7	12	0	3	217	76	+++
Orange juice, fresh	½ cup scant	3.5	100	1	4	3	4	4	7	2	3	150	54	*
Orange juice, canned	½ cup scant	3.5	100	4	4	3	4	3	7	2	3	140	55	*
Peaches, yellow, fresh	1 medium, stoned	3.5	100	1	1	3	6	50	4	3	9	23	51	++
Peaches, canned	1 half with syrup	3.5	100	1	1	2	4	11	4	3	7	13	76	++
Pears, fresh	1 medium	4.3	120	1	1	3	4	0	4	1	1	20	84	+++
Pears, canned	2 halves with syrup	3.5	100	0	2	1	2	1	6	2	2	7	76	++
Pineapple, fresh	2 slices, ½ in. thick	3.5	100	1	1	2	3	0	7	1	2	50	59	++
Pineapple, canned	1 slice with syrup	3.5	100	1	4	1	6	4	5	*	2	30	102	+
Pineapple juice, canned	½ cup scant	3.5	100	1	2	2	5	2	5	2	*	33	61	+
Plums	2 large, stoned	3.5	100	2	4	1	3	3	10	2	5	23	57	++
Prunes, dried	6 medium, stoned	1.8	50	1	2	3	9	9	6	3	9	0	150	+++
Raisins, seedless	⅓ cup	1.2	35	1	4	6	20	31	4	1	2	67	104	*
Raspberries, red	⅔ cup	3.5	100	1	5	6	13	0	3	*	5	50	67	+++
Rhubarb	½ cup scant, cooked	3.5	100	1	**	5	9	4	2	*	1		18	++

TABLE IV—(Continued)

FOOD VALUES OF MANY COMMON FOODS

Name of Food	Amount of One Serving — Measure	Weight Oz.	Weight Gm.	Nutritive Value — Pro-tein	Cal-cium	Phos-phorus	Iron	Vita-min A	Thia-mine	Ribo-flavin	Niacin	Ascorbic Acid	Energy Value Total Calories	Fibre
Strawberries	⅔ cup	3.5	100	1	3	4	9	1	3	2	2	183	40	++
Watermelon	6 in. diam. x ½ in.	7.0	200	1	2	3	4	3	6	4	4	47	63	++
Nuts														
Almonds	18 medium	.7	20	5	7	13	9	0*	5	3	9	0	128	+++
Coconut, Premium Shred	¼ cup	.7	20	1	0	4	4	*	1	1	28	*	117	+++
Peanuts, roasted	26	.7	20	8	2	11	4	0	4	2	32	0	121	+++
Pecans	17 halves	.7	20	3	2	9	5	2	10	1	2	0	149	+
Walnuts, English	12 halves	.7	20	4	2	10	4	0	9	1	2	0	140	+
Oils and Spreads														
Corn or cottonseed oil	1 tablespoon	.5	14	0	0	0	0	0	0*	0*	0*	0*	126	–
Margarine, vitamin A added	1 tablespoon	.5	13	0	0	0	0	6	*	*	*	*	95	–
Peanut butter	1 tablespoon	.5	15	6	2	8	3	0	3	1	24	0	94	+
Sugars and Syrups														
Corn syrup	1 tablespoon	.7	20	0	0	0	0	0	0	0	0	0	59	–
Honey	1 tablespoon	.7	20	0	0	0	2	0	0*	0*	0*	0*	64	–
Log Cabin Syrup	1 tablespoon	.7	20	0	1	1	4	*	*	*	*	*	56	–
Molasses	1 tablespoon	.7	20	0	7	1	13	0	2	2	0	0	44	–
Sugar	1 tablespoon	.5	15	0	0	0	0	0	0	0	0	0	60	–

22

Miscellaneous													
Cake, butter, 1 egg	2 x 2 x 1¾ in.	1.4	40	3	2	4	2	1	1	2	1	0	138	−
Cake, sponge, 6 eggs	4 x 1½ x 1 in.	1.0	28	2	2	4	3	2	2	2	1	0	84	−
Chocolate, unsweetened	1 square	1.0	28	5	5	32	9	0	2	*	*	*	181	+++
Chocolate fudge	1¼ x 1 x 1 in.	1.0	28	1	2	5	1	2	1	1	0	0	131	+
Prepared Chocolate pudding	½ cup	4.8	134	8	20	22	4	4	4	10	1	0	208	−
Quick tapioca cream	⅔ cup	4.8	136	9	21	20	5	7	6	12	1	0	192	−

Courtesy General Foods Corporation 1946 Food Chart

[1] Gives measure of food as prepared and weight of raw edible portions required per serving. Exceptions: prepared foods where weights are for the ready to serve product.

[2] Ratings for fiber are relative: − indicates little or none; + some; ++ a good source; +++ an excellent source; * indicates values not determined; ** indicates calcium not nutritionally available.

23

TABLE V

RECOMMENDED DAILY DIETARY ALLOWANCES[1]

REVISED 1948

FOOD AND NUTRITION BOARD, NATIONAL RESEARCH COUNCIL

	CALORIES[2]	PROTEIN, GM.	CALCIUM, GM.	IRON, MG.	VITAMIN A, I.U.	THIAMINE, MG.	RIBO-FLAVIN, MG.	NIACIN (Nicotinic Acid), MG.	ASCORBIC ACID, MG.	VITAMIN D, I.U.
Man (154 lb, 70 kg.)										
Sedentary	2400	70	1.0	12	5000	1.2	1.8	12	75	[3]
Physically active	3000	70	1.0	12	5000	1.5	1.8	15	75	[3]
With heavy work	4500	70	1.0	12	5000	1.8	1.8	18	75	[3]
Woman (123 lb, 56 kg.)										
Sedentary	2000	60	1.0	12	5000	1.0	1.5	10	70	[3]
Moderately active	2400	60	1.0	12	5000	1.2	1.5	12	70	[3]
Very active	3000	60	1.0	12	5000	1.5	1.5	15	70	[3]
Pregnancy (latter half)	2400[4]	85	1.5	15	6000	1.5	2.5	15	100	400
Lactation	3000	100	2.0	15	8000	1.5	3.0	15	150	400
Children up to 12 years[5]										
Under 1 yr.[6]	110/2.2 lb. (1 kg.)	3.5/2.2 lb. (1 kg.)	1.0	6	1500	0.4	0.6	4	30	400
1–3 yrs. (27 lb., 12 kg.)	1200	40	1.0	7	2000	0.6	0.9	6	35	400
4–6 yrs. (42 lb., 19 kg.)	1600	50	1.0	8	2500	0.8	1.2	8	50	400
7–9 yrs. (58 lb., 26 kg.)	2000	60	1.0	10	3500	1.0	1.5	10	60	400
10–12 yrs. (78 lb., 35 kg.)	2500	70	1.2	12	4500	1.2	1.8	12	75	400

Children over 12 yrs.[5]									
Girls, 13–15 yrs. (108 lb, 49 kg.)	2600	80	1.3	15	5000	1.3	2.0	13	80	400
16–20 yrs. (122 lb, 55 kg.)	2400	75	1.0	15	5000	1.2	1.8	12	80	400
Boys, 13–15 yrs. (108 lb, 49 kg.)	3200	85	1.4	15	5000	1.5	2.0	15	90	400
16–20 yrs. (141 lb, 64 kg.)	3800	100	1.4	15	6000	1.7	2.5	17	100	400

[1] Objectives toward which to aim in planning practical dietaries: The recommended allowances can be attained with a good variety of common foods which will also provide other minerals and vitamins for which requirements are less well known.

[2] Calorie allowances must be adjusted up or down to meet specific needs. The calorie values in the table are therefore not applicable to all individuals but rather represent group averages. The proper calorie allowance is that which over an extended period will maintain body weight or rate of growth at the level most conducive to well-being.

[3] The need for supplemental vitamin D by vigorous adults leading a normal life seems to be minimum. For persons working at night and for nuns and others whose habits shield them from the sunlight, as well as for elderly persons, the ingestion of small amounts of vitamin D is desirable. The value of

[4] During the latter part of pregnancy the calorie allowance should increase to approximately 20 percent above the preceding level. The value of 2400 calories represents the allowance for pregnant, sedentary women.

[5] Allowances for children are based on the needs for the middle year in each group (as 2, 5, 8, etc.) and are for moderate activity and for average weight at the middle year of the age group.

[6] Needs for infants increase from month to month with size and activity. The amounts given are for approximately 6 to 8 months. The dietary requirements for some of the nutrients such as protein and calcium are less if derived largely from human milk.

25

TABLE SETTING AND SERVICE

SOCIETY has changed rules of table service to meet the needs and whims of succeeding generations. For, conventional as most of us are at heart, we like the zest that comes with some display of originality in our table settings. But the basic facts of forks and spoons and rules of serving have altered very little—because table customs, like social customs, are nothing more nor less than convenient and expedient rules to facilitate finer living and entertaining and to maintain beauty and orderliness.

The costliest table equipment can look out of place on a carelessly set table. Linen, silver and china should conform to a fundamental rule of alignment: the crease of the cloth should run precisely down the center of the table; threads of place mats parallel to the edge. Allow 20 to 24 inches between the centers of adjacent covers for adequate elbow room. The linen space and the number of pieces of silver, glass and china used by one person are commonly called the cover or service.

One rule that is pretty well standardized is that a formal dinner requires an allover cloth of white damask with a felt or baize undercloth for protection; or, an allover cloth of Madeira linen or exquisite filet lace, laid, usually, on the bare, polished table.

TABLE VI

TABLE SETTING AND SERVICE

MEAL	SILVER	CHINA	GLASS
Breakfast Fruit	Teaspoon or fruit spoon	Serving plate (may be lunch size or smaller)	Fruit juice glass or dish on serving plate
Cereal	Dessert spoon	Cereal dish on serving plate	
Eggs or Meat	Lunch knife and fork	Lunch plate	
Toast or bread	Butter knife	Bread and butter plate	
Beverage	Teaspoon	Coffee cup and saucer	Water glass (tumbler)

TABLE VI—(*Continued*)

TABLE SETTING AND SERVICE

MEAL	SILVER	CHINA	GLASS
Luncheon Fruit or Soup	Teaspoon or fruit spoon Teaspoon or bouillon spoon	Place plate Soup cup and saucer or rimless soup plate on place plate	Fruit cocktail glass with matching plate on place plate
Bread	Butter knife	Bread and butter plate (remove after salad course)	
Entrée (meat and vegetables)	Lunch knife and fork	(Place plate removed) Lunch plate	
Salad	Salad or lunch fork	If separate course at the formal lunch, serve with place plate	Choice of glass or china salad plate
Dessert	Dessert spoon and fork brought in with dessert plate	Dessert plate or dish of china or glass	Finger bowl and plate with doily brought in with dessert
Beverage	Teaspoon	Cup and saucer	Water glass or goblet
Dinner Oysters or Fruit	Oyster fork Teaspoon or fruit spoon	Place plate	Oyster or fruit plate (may be of china) on place plate
Soup	Dinner soup spoon	Soup plate on place plate	
Bread or rolls	Butter knife (omit at formal meal)	Bread and butter plate (omit at formal meal), remove after salad course	
Fish or entrée	Fish knife and fork or dessert knife and fork	Fish or entrée plate on place plate	
Roast	Dinner knife and fork	(Place plate removed) Dinner plate	
Salad	Salad fork	Salad plate on place plate at formal meal	May be on small glass or china plate if served with main course at informal meal

TABLE VI—(*Continued*)

TABLE SETTING AND SERVICE

MEAL	SILVER	CHINA	GLASS
Dinner (*Continued*) Dessert	Dessert spoon and fork brought in with dessert plate	Dessert plate (on place plate at strictly formal meal)	May be of glass if dessert is cold, glass finger bowl and doily rest on dessert plate unless brought in with fruit course
Fruit	Fruit knife and fork brought in with finger bowl		Fruit plate with finger bowl and doily
Beverage	Coffee spoon	Demitasse cups and saucers	Water goblet, Claret and Champagne glasses

28

Easy Minute Meals

In our time-pressed world today, speed and convenience become our daily watchwords—even in the kitchen. Our mothers and grandmothers customarily spent six and eight hours in meal preparation alone. Few of us today have more than a third of that time to give. Fortunately, food manufacturers and producers have co-operated to an amazing degree since World War II in developing lines of prepared foods that may be eaten "as is" from the package or with only a minimum of kitchen preparation.

In this chapter, our goal has been to give you suggestions for short-order meals. You will need to vary them to suit the individual tastes of your family, and as new products come on the market, you may be able to make even speedier substitutions.

The efficient modern cook or hostess is learning to make commercial food products an important part of her menu planning. With resourcefulness and imagination, she gives her own stamp to them by serving unusual food combinations, with attractive garnishes, in glamorous table settings.

For you who need to do a lot of baking for your family, we are including basic dry mixes which you may make up and store to be used at your convenience in speedy fashion. These can accompany the varied and delicious commercial mixes upon your pantry shelf.

30-MINUTE MENUS

We have planned the following menus so that you can prepare them from start to finish in about 30 minutes if you use the commercial products that are available on the market. For you who

29

may want to prepare some of the dishes in your own kitchen, we
have included several recipes in this chapter.

Commercial sauces, soups, and dishes made with gelatin are
particularly adaptable for short-order meals. You will find many
dinners in the can or the frozen food package that you need only
heat or that may serve as a basic ingredient to which "stretchers"
of meat, fish, eggs, cheese, rice or macaroni products may be
added.

Boula
Planked Hamburgers
Julienne Beans
Savory Mashed Potatoes
Grapefruit-Apple Salad
Angel Food Cake à la Mode

Tomato-Pea Soup
Frank-Fritters in Rolls
Buttered Broccoli (frozen)
Wilted Lettuce Salad
Crushed Pineapple Sundae

Corned Beef and Tomatoes with
Cheese Sauce
Buttered Cabbage   Boiled Potatoes
Tossed Green Salad
Clabbered Cream with Strawberries

Apricot Nectar
Ham with Sour Sauce
Buttered Lima Beans
(frozen or canned)
Mashed Potatoes
Quick Tomato Aspic
Maple Sundae

Clams on Half Shell—Marinara Sauce
Savory Chicken Livers on Rice
Broiled Tomato Halves
Hot French Bread with Garlic Butter
Crisp Radishes, Celery, Cauliflowerettes
Broiled Grapefruit

Jiffy Curry on Spaghetti
Buttered String Beans (frozen)
Sliced Tomatoes
Whole Wheat Bread
Fresh Pears with Cheese

Boula
Spaghetti with Wine Sauce
Grilled Tomatoes   French Bread
Fresh Spinach Salad with
Bacon Dressing
Lemon Ice

Crab Meat Cocktail
Vegetable Rabbit
Tossed Salad
Cherries Jubilee

Chicken Soup
Mint Meat Patties
Buttered Carrots   Buttered Potato Balls
Mixed Green Salad
Sponge Cake—Whipped Cream and
Fruit

Borsch
Minute Steaks
French Fried Potatoes (frozen)
Buttered Spinach (fresh or frozen)
Lettuce with Russian Dressing
Mousse au Chocolat

Melon
Beef Curry on Rice
Green Salad with Grapefruit Sections
Macaroons (commercial)

Consommé with Sherry
Pinwheel Ham Casserole
High-shine Golden Yams
Tomato-Cucumber Salad
Cherries Jubilee

Italian Spaghetti with Salami
Buttered Zucchini   Bread Sticks
Tossed Chef's Salad
Fresh Fruit and Cheese

Pineapple Juice
Shrimp Creole on Rice
Sautéed Green Pepper Squares
Lettuce and Chicory—Prepared
Garlic Dressing
Butterscotch Pudding

Borsch
Beef Stew with Biscuit Topping
Wilted Lettuce
Frozen Strawberries and Pineapple

Frosted Fruit Juice
Broiled Liver Sausage with Mexi-corn
Garden Fresh Salad
French Quickie Dessert

Chicken Soup
Curry Fried Pork Sandwiches
Tomato Salad
Applesauce Meringues

Boula
Eggs Ragù
Mixed Vegetables (frozen)
Jiffy Tomato Aspic
Fruit Cocktail Upside-Down Cake

Shrimp Cocktail—Marinara Sauce
Eggs Goldenrod
Peas and Carrots (frozen)
Tomato Salad
Ribbon Cake

Cream of Asparagus Soup
Broiled Liver Sausage
Spiced Yams with Peaches
Tossed Salad
Chocolate Puff Soufflé

Corned Beef 'n Tomatoes—Easy
Cheese Sauce
French Fried Potatoes (frozen)
Buttered Broccoli (frozen)
Cottage Cheese and Olive Salad
Broiled Grapefruit

Shrimp Creole on Rice
Lettuce, Radish, Cucumber Salad
Canned Blueberries with Sour Cream

Vegetable Juice Cocktail
Crab and Shrimp Newburg on
Canned Noodles
Mixed Vegetables (frozen)
Whole Wheat Muffins
Coconut-Vanilla Pudding

Fruit Cup
Salmon Steak Dinner
Buttered Peas (frozen)
Celery and Radishes
Chocolate Waffles—Whipped Cream

Beef Claret Bouillon
Pinwheel Ham Casserole
Mashed Potatoes
Lettuce with French Dressing
Peach Melba

Vegetable Juice Cocktail
Chicken Casserole
Lettuce and Radish Salad
Popovers (ready-mix)
Pineapple-Rhubarb Surprise

Grape Juice Cocktail
Corned Beef and Cabbage
Currant Jelly-Horseradish Sauce
Boiled Potatoes   Relish Tray
Fruit Compote

Chilled Pineapple Juice
Mint Meat Patties
Sautéed Corn and Green Peppers
Grilled Tomatoes
Broiled Grapefruit

Jellied Consommé
Salmon Steak Dinner
Broiled Stuffed Tomatoes
Asparagus Tips (frozen)—Easy
Cheese Sauce
Lemon Meringue Tarts

Tomato-Pea Soup
Spiced Ham—Pineapple Kabobs
High-shine Golden Yams
Tossed Green Salad
Cookie Twins

CHEESE PUFFS

⅛ pound grated processed   ¼ cup butter
  cheese   ½ cup flour

Mix and blend cheese, butter and flour. Shape into small balls and
bake on a greased baking sheet in a moderate oven (375° F.) 20 minutes, or until done. Approximate yield: 20 puffs.

QUICK SOUPS

Chicken Soup—Combine 1 can cream of chicken soup and 1 can of
chicken soup with rice. Add equal amount of water, ¼ teaspoon curry
powder and ¼ cup white wine. Heat thoroughly. Yield: 4 to 6 portions.

Tomato-Pea Soup—Combine 1 can condensed tomato soup and 1 can
condensed green pea soup. Add 1½ cans milk and 2 teaspoons Worcestershire sauce. Heat thoroughly. Stir in ½ cup Sherry. Yield: 4 to 6
portions.

Borsch—Combine 1 can of consommé, ⅔ to 1 cup beet juice (from
canned beets) and ½ cup finely-chopped beets. Heat and serve with
sour cream. Yield: 3 to 4 portions.

Boula—Combine and heat 1 can each pea and turtle soups, and 2 tablespoons chopped chives. Add 3 tablespoons Madeira and garnish with
whipped cream or sour cream sprinkled with grated Parmesan cheese.
Yield: 4 portions.

QUICK BREADS

Florida Biscuits—Add 2 teaspoons grated orange rind to standard biscuit mixture; use half milk, half orange juice for liquid. Dip a half
lump of loaf sugar in orange juice. Then press into the top of each
cut-out biscuit. When baked this makes a sweet glaze.

QUICK MAIN DISHES

Chicken Casserole—Turn 1 can of chicken à la king into greased
casserole. Top with 1 package frozen spinach or broccoli, cooked and
seasoned, and grated Parmesan cheese. Bake in moderate oven (375° F.)
15 to 20 minutes. Yield: 2 to 3 portions.

Crab and Shrimp Newburg—Combine 1 cup canned crabmeat, 1 cup
canned shrimp, 1 cup Medium White Sauce (page 125) and heat. Add
1 tablespoon Sherry. Yield: 2 to 3 portions.

Spaghetti with Wine Sauce—Cook 1 8-ounce package spaghetti. Melt ½ cup butter or margarine; add 1 clove of garlic, minced, salt and pepper to taste, ½ cup red wine, ¼ teaspoon each orégano and basil. Simmer 5 minutes. Pour over hot spaghetti and toss. Yield: 4 portions.

Vegetable Rabbit—Add 1 cup canned cream-style corn to 1 can condensed cream of asparagus soup. Blend well and add 1 cup grated cheese, ½ teaspoon dry mustard, ½ teaspoon Worcestershire sauce, salt and pepper to taste. Heat, stirring constantly, over low heat, until piping hot. Serve over hot toast squares or crisp canned noodles. Yield: 4 portions.

Creamed Chipped Beef—Add 1 can chipped beef and 1 small can mushroom stems and pieces to 1 can cream of mushroom soup. Then add a little white wine and season with grated cheese, minced parsley, salt and pepper. Heat and serve in toast cups. Yield: 3 to 4 portions.

Jiffy Curry—To 2 cups Medium White Sauce (page 125) add 1 teaspoon curry powder, salt and pepper to taste, and 1 pound liverwurst, cubed. Reheat thoroughly. Serve over 1 8-ounce package spaghetti or macaroni, cooked. Yield: 4 portions.

Eggs Goldenrod—Dice 6 hard-cooked eggs. Add to 1 can condensed cream of mushroom soup thinned with ½ cup milk. Season with ½ teaspoon salt, ¼ teaspoon Tabasco. Heat thoroughly. Serve on rusks or toast. Yield: 4 portions.

Frank-Fritters—Split frankfurters lengthwise and spread inside with prepared mustard. Press together. Dip into Cover Batter (page 787) and fry in deep hot fat (365° F.) until browned. Serve two per portion.

Meat Loaf—To save time, make any meat loaf into *individual* loaves. Cuts baking time in half.

Poultry Casserole—Top a casserole of plain cooked spaghetti with a jar of sliced turkey or chicken. Cover with a can of cream of mushroom soup and bake in a moderate oven (350° F.) 25 minutes.

Beef Stew with Biscuit Topping—Pour a can of beef stew in a shallow casserole, cover with a thin layer of biscuit dough to which grated onion has been added. Bake in a hot oven (425° F.) until biscuits are done and stew is heated through.

Creamed Salmon—Add 1 can salmon, flaked, and ½ cup diced ripe olives to 2 cups Cheese Sauce (page 470). Serve over toast or toasted English muffins. Yield: 3 to 4 portions.

LONDON BROIL

Broil large flank steak 5 minutes on each side, placed 3 inches from source of heat. Brush with melted butter. Salt and pepper to taste. To serve, cut in thin slices diagonally across the grain. Serve with Red Wine Mushroom Sauce (page 481).

CORNED BEEF AND CABBAGE

1 small head of cabbage
1 12-ounce can corned beef, sliced
butter or margarine
1 tablespoon lemon juice
salt
pepper

Cut cabbage into thick wedges and place in large kettle with small amount of boiling, salted water. Place corned beef in a strainer, suspended over top of cooking kettle but not in contact with the water. Cook 8 to 10 minutes. The steam from the cabbage will heat the corned beef. Season cabbage with melted fat, lemon juice, salt and pepper. Serve on warm platter with corned beef slices. Yield: 4 portions.

SALMON STEAK DINNER

6 salmon steaks, 1-inch thick
juice of 1 lemon
¼ teaspoon paprika
½ teaspoon pepper
½ teaspoon salt
½ cup butter, melted
1 small clove of garlic, minced
1 tablespoon finely chopped shallots
1 tablespoon finely chopped onion
1 tablespoon finely chopped parsley
1 tablespoon chopped fresh dill
2 tablespoons white wine
grated Swiss cheese

Preheat broiler at 400° to 425° F., greasing the grill well. Sprinkle lemon juice over the steaks and season. Brush with melted butter and broil 5 to 8 minutes on each side, or until steaks are lightly browned and tender, basting frequently. Combine rest of ingredients with remaining melted butter, simmer 5 minutes and serve over steaks sprinkled with Swiss cheese. Accompany with whole tomatoes, the centers scooped out and mixed with canned whole-kernel corn, finely grated green pepper and minced onion, sautéed in butter or bacon fat. Add the stuffed tomatoes the last 10 minutes of broiling time. Cucumber slices marinated in French dressing will add a crisp touch. Yield: 4 portions.

BEEF CURRY ON RICE

2½ cups Medium White Sauce   ½ teaspoon curry powder
   (page 125)   3 cups boiled rice
1 5-ounce glass dried beef

Make white sauce. Add dried beef, broken in small pieces, and curry
powder (more may be added if desired). Serve hot over freshly boiled
rice. Yield: 4 to 5 portions. Dried Beef Curry may be served over toast
points or hot canned shoestring potatoes. A fresh green vegetable or
salad is a good accompaniment.

BROILED LIVER SAUSAGE

½ pound liver sausage (cut   butter or drippings
   ¼ inch thick, 8 slices)   sliced onions (optional)
2 whole tomatoes

Remove casing from liver sausage. Place the slices of liver sausage on
the broiler pan with tomatoes that have been cut in half and brushed
with butter or drippings. Place the broiler pan at least 3 inches from
the heat unit. Broil for about 8 minutes. The liver sausage need not be
turned. Onion slices may be broiled with the tomatoes if desired. Serve
onions on top of tomatoes. Yield: 4 portions.

Broiled Liver Sausage with Mexican Corn—To 1 can Mexican corn
add salt and pepper to taste. Spread in broiler pan and heat for a few
minutes 4 inches below heat unit. Place ½ pound Braunschweiger liver
sausage, sliced, on rack. Broil about 4 minutes. Needs no turning.
Yield: 4 portions.

SHRIMP CREOLE

¼ cup chopped celery   pinch of thyme
½ cup chopped onion   2 5-ounce cans shrimp
3 tablespoons salad oil   2½ cups cooked rice (quick-cook-
½ cup water   ing or leftover rice may be
1 can condensed tomato soup   used)
1 teaspoon wine vinegar

Sauté celery and onion in heated salad oil until onion is golden. Add
water, soup, vinegar and thyme and simmer 12 to 15 minutes. Add
shrimp and reheat. Serve over rice. Yield: 4 portions.

SAVORY CHICKEN LIVERS

3 tablespoons butter or   salt and pepper to taste
    margarine   ⅛ teaspoon rosemary
1 pound chicken livers   ½ cup white wine

Melt butter; when bubbling add chicken livers and season with salt, pepper and rosemary. Cook until well browned, stirring occasionally. Add wine and simmer 10 minutes. Serve over rice. Yield: 4 portions.

CORNED BEEF 'N TOMATOES

4 fresh tomatoes   salt and pepper
1 can corned beef hash (2 cups) Easy Cheese Sauce (page 42)

Scoop out pulp from inside of tomatoes. Save. Combine corned beef hash with tomato pulp. Add salt and pepper to taste. Stuff hash mixture into the tomatoes. Set in a baking dish. Bake in a moderately hot over (400° F.) for about 15 minutes. Remove from oven. Top each serving with Easy Cheese Sauce. Serve at once. Yield: 4 portions.

EGGS RAGU

1 8-ounce can Ragu or mush-   8 eggs
    room sauce   salt and pepper to taste

Pour sauce into large skillet, dilute with half a can of liquid (broth, milk, tomato juice, water, etc.). Break eggs one by one into saucer and slide gently into skillet. Cover well, and when eggs are done, serve. Yield: 4 portions.

PINWHEEL HAM CASSEROLE

1 can condensed mushroom soup   1½ cups peas, canned
1⅓ cups evaporated milk   2 cups biscuit mix
1½ cups ham, diced   8 stuffed olives, sliced
                ¾ cup grated cheese

In a saucepan, combine soup with ⅔ cup milk and beat until smooth. Add ham and peas and pour into baking dish. Place in hot oven (425° F.) until bubbly. Combine biscuit mix with balance of milk (⅔ cup) and stir just enough to blend. Turn out on lightly floured board and knead lightly a few times. Roll into rectangle (8 x 12 inches). Sprinkle layer with olives and cheese. Start at long side and roll up like jelly roll and cut into 1 inch slices. Arrange slices on top of meat-vegetable mixture. Bake in hot oven (425° F.) 20 minutes or until pinwheels are done to a golden brown. Yield: 6 portions.

HAM WITH SOUR SAUCE

4 slices precooked canned ham
  or Canadian bacon*
1 tablespoon meat fat
1 tablespoon flour
½ cup drained juice from
  canned pineapple
2 tablespoons prepared mustard
¾ cup drained canned pineapple
  cubes
⅔ cup of 1 inch squares green
  pepper (optional)

Brown ham on both sides. Remove to a hot platter. In same pan blend in the flour until smooth. Stir in pineapple juice. Cook until thickened on low heat, stirring constantly. Mix in prepared mustard. Add pineapple and green pepper. When hot, but while peppers are still crisp, spoon over ham slices. Yield: 2 portions.

QUICK ITALIAN SPAGHETTI WITH SALAMI

3 tablespoons butter or bacon
  drippings
1 cup chopped onions
1 cup sliced mushrooms
1 tablespoon flour
½ pound salami (cut half into
  8 very thin slices and grind
  or chop remainder)
1½ cups tomato juice
1 cup water
1½ tablespoons Worcestershire
  sauce
¼ teaspoon pepper
2 tablespoons minced parsley
¼ cup chopped green pepper
6–8 ounces uncooked spaghetti

Melt butter, add onions and mushrooms and brown lightly. Blend in flour, add chopped salami. Add tomato juice diluted with water and seasonings. Simmer 25 minutes. Add parsley and green pepper and simmer 5 minutes more. Meanwhile, cook spaghetti in boiling water until tender (about 15 minutes). Drain and rinse with boiling water. To serve, make a ring of spaghetti on chop plate and pour sauce in center. Encircle with sliced salami. Yield: 4 portions.

MINT MEAT PATTIES

1 pound hamburger meat
¼ cup chopped fresh mint
1 teaspoon salt
pinch of pepper and nutmeg
2 slices white bread, crusts
  removed
½ cup sour cream
¼ cup bacon fat

Combine meat, mint, salt, pepper and nutmeg. Soften bread in sour cream 10 minutes. Blend with meat mixture. Shape into small patties and brown in bacon fat. Approximate yield: 12 patties.

* Smoked pork shoulder butt may also be used. Simmer first in hot water a few minutes. Drain. Then continue above directions.

CURRY FRIED PORK SANDWICHES

¼ cup vinegar
4 to 6 slices cooked pork
3 tablespoons flour
2 teaspoons curry powder

½ teaspoon salt
1 tablespoon shortening
4 slices bread
butter or margarine

Pour vinegar over pork. Let stand 15 to 30 minutes. Combine flour, curry powder and salt. Drain pork slices and dip in flour mixture. Fry in melted shortening until crisp. Place between slices of buttered bread. Serve hot. Yield: 2 sandwiches.

SPICED HAM—POTATO KABOBS

Cut 1 12-ounce tin of ham into 9 cubes. Score each cube on sides. Insert on skewer, alternating with small cooked potatoes. Baste with your favorite barbecue sauce and place under moderate broiler for 8 to 10 minutes, turning and basting with additional sauce throughout the broiling period.

Spiced Ham—Pineapple Kabobs—Proceed in same manner as above, substituting pineapple chunks for potatoes. Baste with glaze of equal parts of brown sugar and pineapple syrup.

PLANKED HAMBURGERS

1 pound hamburger meat
¼ cup minced onion
½ cup dry bread crumbs
1 teaspoon Worcestershire sauce
1 teaspoon prepared mustard

2 tablespoons prepared horseradish
¼ cup evaporated milk
1 teaspoon salt
¼ teaspoon pepper

Combine meat, onion, bread crumbs, Worcestershire sauce, mustard, horseradish, milk, salt and pepper. Shape into 8 cakes. Place in pre-heated broiler (375° F.) with fresh or canned mushrooms stuffed with processed snappy cheese and bacon, sprinkled with bread crumbs. Add 4 slices of canned pineapple, topped with 4 canned apricots. Broil 10 to 15 minutes, turning hamburgers. Transfer to pre-heated individual planks and divide 1 pound julienne-style green beans, cooked and seasoned, into four portions. Decorate edge with border of mashed and seasoned potatoes (quick-cooking) forced through a pastry tube. Brown potatoes under broiler with temperature raised to 550° F. for 3 to 5 minutes. Yield: 4 portions.

STUFFED GREEN PEPPERS

6 medium-sized green peppers
1 cup finely chopped onion
1 clove of garlic, minced
¼ cup butter
½ pound hamburger meat
1 cup cooked rice (quick cooking)

2 eggs, slightly beaten
¼ cup minced parsley
2 tablespoons ketchup
1¼ teaspoons salt
¼ teaspoon pepper
pinch of orégano and chili powder

1 8-ounce can tomato sauce

Slice off tops of green peppers; remove seeds and wash. Parboil in boiling salted water about 10 minutes. Drain and cool. Sauté onion and garlic in butter until tender. Combine with meat, rice, eggs, parsley, ketchup, salt, pepper, orégano and chili. Pack lightly into peppers. Stand upright in greased baking dish. Pour tomato sauce around peppers. Bake in moderate oven (375° F.) about 20 minutes. Serve with sauce in the pan. Yield: 6 portions.

QUICK MACARONI CASSEROLE

2 cans macaroni with tomato sauce

2 tablespoons butter or margarine

¼ pound dried beef or ½ pound liverwurst or baloney, sliced

Heat macaroni and turn into casserole; sauté meat in butter until crisp and arrange around edge of casserole. Approximate yield: 6 portions.

LAMB CHOPS—FIESTA STYLE

4 medium zucchini squash
8 rib or loin chops or 4 shoulder chops, cut ¾ inch thick
salt and pepper

2 large tomatoes, cut in half
4 large mushrooms
¼ cup butter or margarine, melted

Wash squash, slice and simmer until tender. Set regulator to broil. Place chops on broiler rack. Insert broiler pan and rack so the top of the chops is 2 inches from the heat. When one side is browned, season and turn. Place tomatoes cut side up on broiler rack and top with a mushroom button. Arrange squash slices on rack. Brush tomatoes, mushrooms and squash with melted butter. Continue broiling until chops are done and vegetables are lightly browned. Yield: 4 servings.

JIFFY STUFFED PEPPERS

4 medium-sized green peppers   grated cheese *or* bread crumbs

1 can of any of the following: spaghetti with meat sauce, spaghetti
in tomato sauce with cheese, macaroni in cheese sauce, macaroni
in tomato sauce, chili con carne or beef stew

Cut tops off peppers, remove seeds; cook in boiling water to cover for
5 minutes or until tender. Drain. Heap canned mixture into the
peppers. Sprinkle with grated cheese or bread crumbs. Bake in moderate oven (350° F.) 20 minutes or until piping hot. Yield: 2 portions.

HAM BALLS IN SOUR CREAM GRAVY

1 pound ground cooked ham	1 egg
¼ cup chopped onion	2 tablespoons flour
4 tablespoons fat	½ cup water
¼ teaspoon pepper	1 cup sour cream

Panfry onion in fat in skillet. Remove and combine with ham, pepper
and egg. Shape mixture into balls and brown in hot fat. When evenly
browned remove from pan onto platter. Combine flour with remaining fat in skillet. Add water and sour cream and cook slowly. Pour
over ham balls and serve. Yield: 4 to 6 portions.

HAM WITH SHERRY

Place a 2-pound slice of ham in a shallow baking dish and cover with
⅓ cup medium dry Sherry. Bake ½ hour in moderate oven (350° F.).
Arrange canned cling peach halves, one to a person, over the ham.
Baste with Sherry and continue baking another ½ hour.

QUICKIE CHEESE RABBIT (RAREBIT)

1 10-oz. can cream of chicken soup	½ teaspoon Worcestershire sauce
¼ cup milk	⅛ teaspoon cayenne
¼ teaspoon dry mustard	½ pound sharp Cheddar cheese, shredded

Combine soup, milk, mustard, Worcestershire sauce and cayenne and
heat over low heat or in top of double boiler set over hot water. Add
cheese and stir until smooth and well blended. Serve over toast topped
with slices of cooked ham. Yield: 1¾ cups.

Variation—Add chopped ripe or pimiento olives and top with chopped
chives.

GLAZED CARROTS AND PINEAPPLE CHUNKS

1 No. 2 can sliced carrots*   1 tablespoon cornstarch
½ cup pineapple chunks   ½ teaspoon salt
½ cup pineapple juice   1 tablespoon butter or margarine

Drain carrots and pineapple. Reserve ½ cup carrot liquor and combine
with ½ cup pineapple juice; gradually stir into cornstarch and salt in a
saucepan. Cook, stirring constantly, until mixture thickens and clears.
Add butter and stir until blended. Add carrots and pineapple; combine
carefully. Heat thoroughly. Yield: 4 portions.

SWEET-SOUR BEANS

½ cup vinegar   3 tablespoons flour
⅔ cup sugar   ⅛ teaspoon salt
2 cans red kidney beans

Mix together vinegar, sugar, flour and salt. Add to beans and cook,
stirring occasionally until thickened. Yield: 4 portions.

SPICED YAMS WITH PEACHES

1½ cups mashed canned yams   ¼ teaspoon powdered cloves
1 teaspoon lemon juice   6 canned peach halves
2 tablespoons brown sugar   1 tablespoon butter or margarine

Mix yams, lemon juice, sugar and cloves; whip until fluffy. Drain
peach halves. Arrange in buttered dish and pile high with yam mixture. Dot with butter. Bake 20 minutes in hot oven (400° F.). Serve
hot. Yield: 6 portions.

HIGH-SHINE GOLDEN YAMS

1 large can yams   ¼ cup orange juice
¼ cup sugar   ¼ teaspoon salt
2 teaspoons cornstarch   1 tablespoon butter or margarine
¾ cup syrup from canned yams   3 slices lemon

Drain yams; arrange in greased baking dish. Mix sugar and cornstarch; blend with canned yam syrup and stir until smooth. Cook
gently over medium heat until mixture thickens, becomes clear. Add
remaining ingredients. Pour over yams. Bake 15 minutes in a moderate oven (350° F.), basting occasionally. Yield: 4 to 6 portions.

* Diced or shoestring carrots may be substituted.

QUICK SAUCES

Easy Cheese Sauce—Melt ½ pound processed American cheese over hot water. When melted stir in ½ cup milk (fresh or diluted evaporated). Serve hot over meat and vegetables.

Marinara Cocktail Sauce—Combine 1 can Marinara sauce, 2 tablespoons horseradish and Tabasco sauce to taste. Serve on shrimp, clam, crab meat cocktail.

Currant Jelly-Horseradish Sauce—Whip together with a fork equal portions of currant jelly and horseradish. Serve with hot or cold sliced smoked beef tongue or corned beef.

Tangy Oyster Sauce—Combine ½ cup tomato sauce, ½ cup chili sauce, 4 teaspoons sweet pickle relish, 4 teaspoons horseradish, dash of Tabasco and 1 teaspoon of Worcestershire sauce. Heat thoroughly. Serve hot over fried oysters or chilled over oysters in cocktail. Yield: 1 cup sauce.

CANNED SOUP SAUCES

Cream of Mushroom—Use with tuna fish, scallops, ham, vegetables.

Cream of Tomato—Use with fish cakes, fried fish fillets, ground beef.

Cream of Asparagus—Use with salmon.

Cream of Chicken—Use with tuna fish, mushrooms.

QUICK SALADS

Tomato Salad—Make four lengthwise slices (not all the way through) in tomato. Insert a scored cucumber slice in each cut place. Top with dressing of sour cream thinned with a little vinegar and seasoned with salt and pepper.

Jiffy Tomato Aspic—Heat 1 cup tomato juice or vegetable juice cocktail; add to 1 package lemon-flavored gelatin and stir until thoroughly blended. Add 1 more cup of juice. Pour into lightly oiled mold or molds and chill. Yield: 4 portions.

Deviled Celery—Mix 1 small can of deviled tongue with 1 package cream cheese and 1 can jellied cranberry sauce or whole cranberry sauce. Chill. Stuff chilled crisp celery with chilled mixture, pressing through pastry tube. Yield: 6 portions of 1 stalk of celery, stuffed.

QUICK DESSERTS

Cake—Top ready-made angel food or sponge cake with almost defrosted frozen fruit and, if desired, whipped cream; or top with sauce made with pudding mix, using twice the amount of milk called for on the package.

Cake—Top prepared cake mixes with fresh, frozen or canned fruits and whipped cream; or softened cream cheese, ice cream, applesauce or pudding sauce.

Fruit—Serve chilled canned or almost defrosted frozen fruits, such as apricots, peaches, blueberries with sour cream and a sprinkling of grated nutmeg.

Broiled Grapefruit—Sprinkle brown sugar over grapefruit halves and broil, or broil without sugar and pour a little Sherry over each before serving.

Pudding Mixes—Add variety to mixes by adding coconut, bananas, 2 tablespoons of marmalade and ½ cup heavy cream, whipped, or whipped cream flavored with peppermint or rum flavoring.

Applesauce Meringue—Top applesauce with meringue and bake.

Sundaes—Make quick sundaes by topping ice cream with jam, maple syrup, honey, or canned berries, sliced fruits, or crushed pineapple.

Lemon Ice—Sprinkle cinnamon drops over lemon ice.

Rum Topping—Add rum flavoring to whipped cream to use as a delicious topping for canned peaches, apricots, ready-made cakes.

Jelly Frosting—Beat ½ cup bright-colored jelly with 1 egg white until stiff and firm. Spread between and on top of layers.

Cottage Cheese Topping—Combine 1 cup creamed cottage cheese and 2 to 3 tablespoons sour cream or sweet cream gradually and beat until fluffy. More cream may be added, depending upon the moistness of the cottage cheese. Add a few grains of salt if desired. Serve on sour cherry tarts or pies, berry pies or cobblers, baked peaches, fruit salad desserts, upside-down cakes, gingerbread, fruit gelatin, etc. Tint if desired. Yield: 8 to 10 portions.

APRICOT SAUCE

2 tablespoons butter	1 cup apricot juice
1 tablespoon cornstarch	1 tablespoon apricot brandy

Melt butter, blend with cornstarch. Gradually add apricot juice stirring until thick and clear. Remove from stove; add apricot brandy.

COFFEE SUNDAE SAUCE

2 tablespoons instant coffee
1 tablespoon flour
dash of salt

1 cup light corn syrup
¾ cup light cream
2 tablespoons butter or margarine

Combine coffee, flour and salt in a saucepan. Add corn syrup gradually, stirring constantly. Add cream and butter. Simmer 5 minutes, or until thickened, stirring constantly. Cool. Then serve on ice cream (vanilla or coffee flavor), on creamy desserts or cream puffs. Yield: 1½ cups sauce.

COOKIE TWINS

Put several chocolate pieces or shaved semi-sweet chocolate between two cookies, bottom sides together. Place on a baking sheet in a moderate oven (350° F.) until the chocolate melts.

MOUSSE AU CHOCOLAT

½ 6-ounce package chocolate
    pieces

3 eggs, separated
1 teaspoon vanilla

Melt chocolate pieces over hot water. Remove from heat and beat in egg yolks one at a time. Add vanilla. Beat egg whites until stiff, but not dry; gently fold into chocolate mixture. Spoon into sherbet glasses, and chill. Serve garnished with cream or soft vanilla ice cream. Yield: 4 portions.

CHOCOLATE PUFF SOUFFLÉ

½ 6-ounce package chocolate
    pieces
1 cup milk

3 tablespoons sugar
dash of salt
1 teaspoon vanilla

3 eggs

Melt chocolate pieces and milk over hot water; beat with egg beater until smooth. Add sugar, salt, vanilla and eggs. Beat with egg beater one minute. Cover and cook over boiling water for 20 minutes without lifting the cover. Remove from heat and serve immediately with cream. Yield: 6 portions.

PINEAPPLE-RHUBARB SURPRISE

2 cups diced rhubarb	1 tablespoon butter or margarine
1 9-oz. can crushed pineapple	1 cup soft bread crumbs
½ cup brown sugar, firmly packed	8 marshmallows

Cook rhubarb and pineapple together about 10 minutes, until rhubarb is tender. Add sugar, butter and crumbs. Pour into a buttered baking dish and top with marshmallows. Bake in a moderate oven (350° F.) about 20 minutes. Yield: 6 portions.

RIBBON CAKE

1 6-inch round angel food cake	1 cup heavy cream, whipped and sweetened
½ pint chocolate ice cream	
½ pint peppermint ice cream	½ cup shredded coconut, lightly toasted

Split cake crosswise into three layers. Slightly soften ice creams and spread chocolate ice cream on bottom layer. Put middle layer of cake into place and spread this with peppermint ice cream. Replace top of cake. Cover entire cake with whipped, sweetened cream and sprinkle with toasted coconut. Place in freezer for 20 minutes or longer. Any two flavors of ice cream that taste well together may be used. Yield: 6 to 8 portions.

RIO CREAM

1 tablespoon instant coffee	2 cups milk
1 package vanilla pudding	½ cup cream, whipped

Combine coffee and pudding powder in a saucepan. Add milk gradually, blending well. Cook and stir over medium heat until mixture comes to a boil and is thickened. Turn into bowl, cover, and chill well. Then beat slowly with rotary egg beater and fold in whipped cream. Turn into sherbet glasses. Garnish with ladyfinger strips, coconut and maraschino cherries with stems. Yield: 5 portions.

FRENCH QUICKIE DESSERT

Cut left-over bread or cake in oblongs, wedges or cubes. Place one cup corn syrup and one teaspoon water in shallow dish or pie plate. Dip bread or cake in syrup, lift out with fork or slotted spoon. Immediately roll in one or several of the following: Shredded coconut, chopped nuts, finely crushed cornflakes, coating all sides of the cake. If desired, garnish with slivered gum drops, shaved chocolate, chocolate chips or colored candy sprinkles. Place on greased baking sheet and bake in moderately hot oven (375° F.) 8 to 10 minutes.

CLABBERED CREAM AND STRAWBERRIES

1 pint sour cream	2 cups strawberries, washed,
1 cup cottage cheese	drained dry and hulled
1 tablespoon sugar	

Combine cream, cottage cheese and sugar. Beat with a spoon until blended. Just before serving stir in berries. Serve with toasted crackers or split hot biscuits. Yield: 4 cups.

CHEESE BOWL

¾ cup creamed cottage cheese	1 tablespoon sour cream
¼ pound Roquefort cheese,	few drops Worcestershire sauce
sieved	crackers
	fruit

Mix cottage cheese, Roquefort cheese and sour cream just enough to blend. Add Worcestershire sauce to taste. Serve in bowl. Pass crackers and fruit. Yield: 1 generous cup cheese, 6 portions.

CHERRIES JUBILEE

1 No. 2 can pitted Bing cherries	1 tablespoon cornstarch
or	1 tablespoon cold water
1 package frozen cherries	4 to 5 tablespoons Kirsch, heated
¾ cup cherry syrup	ice cream

Drain cherries. Heat syrup from cherries in saucepan and boil 5 minutes. Blend cornstarch with water; add to syrup and continue cooking until mixture clears. Pour over cherries. Ignite Kirsch and pour 1 tablespoon over each portion. Serve flaming over ice cream. When using frozen cherries, thicken the syrup in package with cornstarch blended with water. Yield: 4 to 5 portions.

FRUIT COCKTAIL UPSIDE-DOWN CAKE

Coat bottom of buttered 2-quart fruit mold with 3 tablespoons brown sugar and arrange drained fruit from ½ can (No. 2½) fruit cocktail in bottom. Cover with cake batter made from a package of white cake mix and bake according to directions on package for loaf cake. Serve warm with rum-flavored whipped cream to which remaining half of fruit cocktail is added. Yield: 8 portions.

MAKE-YOUR-OWN MIX

9 cups sifted all-purpose flour   ¼ cup double-acting baking
1 tablespoon salt   powder
         2 cups hydrogenated lard

Combine sifted flour, salt and baking powder. Stir well. Sift into a large bowl. Add hydrogenated lard. Use finger tips or pastry blender to distribute lard throughout dry ingredients until the mixture resembles coarse cornmeal. The Make-Your-Own Mix is now ready to use or store in a closed canister on your pantry shelf. Approximate yield: 13 cups.

EGG ROLL

2 cups Make-Your-Own Mix   ⅓ cup salad dressing
   (page 47) (do not pack)   1 teaspoon salt
½ cup milk   ¼ teaspoon white pepper
6 hard-cooked eggs   1 teaspoon prepared mustard
½ cup chopped celery   2 teaspoons horseradish
1 tablespoon chopped parsley

Combine Mix and milk to make biscuit dough. Turn onto waxed paper. Knead 6 times. Chop eggs. Add celery and seasonings. Blend together. Roll out dough on a lightly floured pastry cloth or board into 8 x 12 inch rectangle. Spread egg filling evenly over dough to within 1 inch of edges. Roll up as for jelly roll. Press ends together to hold in filling. Place on baking sheet. Bake in hot oven (450° F.) 20 to 25 minutes. Cut into slices. Serve hot with creamed peas, or mushroom or cheese sauce. Yield: 6 portions.

FRANCISCAN MEAT PIE

2 cups Make-Your-Own Mix
(do not pack)
½ cup milk
2 cups ground cooked veal or
beef

1 can condensed cream of mushroom soup
⅔ cup shredded cheese
1 cup drained cooked tomatoes

Combine Mix and milk to make a biscuit dough. Turn onto waxed
paper. Knead 6 times. Roll out the dough on a lightly floured pastry
cloth or board to fit a 9-inch pie pan. Fill with meat mixed with mushroom soup. Sprinkle with cheese. Top with tomatoes. Bake in hot
over (450° F.) 25 to 30 minutes. Serve hot. Yield: 4 portions.

MODIFIED PIZZA

2 cups Make-Your-Own Mix
(page 47) (do not pack)
½ cup milk
1 pound pure pork sausage
meat

⅛ teaspoon thyme
½ clove garlic, finely chopped
1 cup shredded cheese
1 cup drained cooked whole
tomatoes

Combine Mix and milk to make a dough. Turn onto waxed paper.
Knead 6 times. Roll out dough on a lightly floured pastry cloth or
board to fit a shallow 9-inch cake or pie pan. Brown sausage meat in
skillet. Pour off drippings. Add thyme and garlic to sausage. Spread
filling over dough. Cover with cheese, then top with tomatoes. Bake
in hot oven (450° F.) about 25 minutes. Serve hot, cut into wedges.
Yield: 6 portions.

CHOCOLATE BARS

1 egg
1 tablespoon water
1 teaspoon vanilla
½ cup granulated sugar
½ cup brown sugar, firmly
packed

1½ cups Make-Your-Own Mix
(page 47) (do not pack)
½ cup chopped nuts
½ cup moist coconut
1 6-oz. package chocolate pieces

In mixing bowl, beat egg, water and vanilla. Beat in sugars. Stir in the
Mix, nuts, coconut and chocolate pieces. Spread in prepared cake pan
(11½ x 7⅜ x 1½ inches or 9 x 9 x 1¾ inches). Bake in moderate oven
(350° F.) about 25 minutes. Cool. Cut into bars. Approximate yield:
24 bars.

COCONUT BARS

2 cups Make-Your-Own Mix
    (page 47) (do not pack)
1½ cups brown sugar, firmly
    packed

1 cup shredded coconut
1 cup chopped nuts
2 eggs, beaten
1 teaspoon vanilla

Blend Mix, brown sugar, coconut and nuts. Add eggs and vanilla. Mix to blend thoroughly. The batter is very stiff. Spread batter in prepared baking pan (11½ x 7⅞ x 1½ inches). Bake in a moderate oven (350° F.) 25 to 30 minutes. Cut into bars. Approximate yield: 24 bars.

TWO-EGG CAKE MIX

3⅓ cups hydrogenated
    shortening (1½ pounds)
7⅔ cups granulated sugar
    (3¼ pounds)
12¾ cups sifted cake flour
    (2¾ pounds) or

11 cups sifted all-purpose flour
    (2¾ pounds)
5 tablespoons double-acting
    baking powder
3 tablespoons salt

To make mix by hand: Place shortening at room temperature in round-bottom bowl, 3- to 4-quart capacity. Cream with wooden spoon until soft (75 strokes). Add 4 cups sugar, 1 cup at a time; cream well after each addition (150 strokes). The mixture should be light and fluffy. Sift together 3 times flour, baking powder, salt and remaining 3⅔ cups of sugar. Add 2 cups sifted ingredients to shortening-sugar mixture. Blend with pastry blender, two knives or finger-tips. Turn mixture into dry ingredients. Blend until like cornmeal. Be sure all ingredients are well blended.

To make mix by electric mixer: Place shortening at room temperature in largest mixer bowl. Cream ½ minute at medium speed. Scrape sides and bottom of bowl. Cream another ½ minute at same speed. Add 4 cups sugar, 1 cup at a time. Cream 1 minute at medium speed after each addition. Sift together 3 times flour, baking powder, salt and remaining 3⅔ cups sugar. Continue mixing as above.

To store mix: Measure mix into six equal lots. Spoon it lightly into measuring cup. Each lot should measure 3½ cups. Place each lot in a quart glass jar. Cover and store in a cool, *dark* place; or place in a metal can, cover and store in a cool place.

TWO-EGG CAKE BATTER

3½ cups mix   1 teaspoon vanilla extract
2 eggs   ¾ cup milk

Have basic mix, eggs and milk at room temperature. Place mix in a
2-quart bowl. Make a well in the center of the mix. Combine ingredients as follows:— *With Spoon:* Add eggs, vanilla and ½ cup of
milk to mix. Beat mixture for 1½ minutes (150 strokes) or until batter
is fairly smooth. Add remainder of milk. Beat mixture for 1½ minutes
(150 strokes). Batter should be smooth and free of lumps. *With Electric Mixer:* Add eggs, vanilla and all the milk to the mix. Beat 1 minute
at low speed. Run spoon or rubber scraper around sides and bottom of
bowl to be sure that ingredients are mixed. Beat mixture for 2 minutes
longer at same speed. Batter should be smooth and free of lumps. Pour
into prepared pans and bake in moderate oven (350° F.); cup cakes
30 minutes, layer cake 35 minutes, loaf cake 40 to 50 minutes. Yield:
1 square cake (8 x 8 x 2 inches *or* 9 x 9 x 1¾ inches), or 1 loaf cake
(10 x 5 x 3 inches), or 1 sheet cake (11½ x 7⅜ x 1½ inches), or 2 8-inch
layers, or approximately 14 cup cakes.
White Cake—Use ¾ cup unbeaten egg whites (whites of 3 medium-
sized eggs) instead of whole egg. Mix batter as directed.
Spice Cake—Add 1 teaspoon cinnamon, ½ teaspoon allspice and ½
teaspoon ground cloves. Mix batter as directed.
Orange Cake—Add 1 teaspoon of grated orange rind to mix. Use
½ teaspoon lemon extract in place of vanilla. Mix batter as directed.
Rich Chocolate Cake—Increase milk to 1 cup. Stir liquid into mix
until just blended. Add 3 squares of melted unsweetened chocolate and
blend into mixture. Continue mixing batter as directed.

DRY MIXES

Following are some recipes for dry mixes—modern time-and-trouble
savers. They can be made when convenient, stored in the cupboard,
used as needed. They are inexpensive when you think how much milk
they put into your foods.

BISCUIT MIX

8 cups sifted flour   3 teaspoons salt
1 cup dry milk, whole or nonfat 1 cup fat (a kind that needs no
¼ cup baking powder   refrigeration)

Sift dry ingredients together three times; cut or rub in fat until thoroughly mixed.
Lift Mix lightly into glass jars or tin cans. Do not pack. Close tightly
and store on shelf.

USE THE BISCUIT MIX FOR—

Biscuits—To 1 cup Mix, add about ⅓ cup water or fluid milk—enough to make a soft dough. Turn onto a lightly floured board or pastry cloth and knead a few times. Pat or roll to the desired thickness and cut with a floured cutter. Bake in a hot oven (450° F.) 12 to 15 minutes. Makes 6 medium-sized biscuits.

Shortcakes—To 1 cup Mix, add 1 tablespoon sugar; cut in 1 tablespoon fat. Add water or fluid milk (about ⅓ cup) to make a soft dough.

Roll ¼ inch thick and cut. Brush half the pieces with melted fat, and cover each with one of the remaining pieces. Bake in a hot oven (425° F.) 12 to 15 minutes. Makes 6 medium-sized shortcakes.

QUICK BREAD MIX

6 cups sifted flour	2 teaspoons salt
1 cup dry milk, whole or nonfat	½ cup sugar
¼ cup baking powder	¾ cup fat (a kind that needs no refrigeration)

For added milk value: Use 2 cups milk powder, in place of amount given above.

Sift dry ingredients together three times; cut or rub in fat until thoroughly mixed.

Lift Mix lightly into glass jars or tin cans. Do not pack. Close tightly and store on shelf.

USE THE QUICK BREAD MIX FOR—

Muffins—To 1 cup Mix, add ⅓ cup water or fluid milk and 1 beaten egg. Fill greased muffin pans two-thirds full. Bake in hot oven (400° to 425° F.) about 20 minutes. Makes 5 small muffins.

Waffles—To 1 cup Mix, add ¾ cup water or fluid milk and 1 beaten egg yolk. Fold in 1 beaten egg white. Bake in hot waffle iron. Makes 2 large waffles.

Griddlecakes—To 1 cup Mix, add ⅔ to 1 cup water or fluid milk and 1 beaten egg. Drop batter by spoonfuls onto a hot greased griddle. Cook slowly until surface is covered with bubbles, turn, and brown on bottom. Makes 7 medium-sized griddlecakes.

VARIATIONS WITH COMMERCIAL CAKE MIXES

Quick Hot Fudge Pudding—Prepare White, Yellow or Devil's Food Cake Mix as directed on package. Then fold 1 cup chopped nuts into half the batter. Pour into prepared square pan (9 x 9 x 1¾ inches). Sprinkle over top a mixture of 1 cup brown sugar (packed in cup) and 4 tablespoons cocoa. Pour over batter 1¾ cups hot water. Bake 40 to 45 minutes in moderate oven (350° F.). Serve warm with cream. Pour other half of batter into prepared 8- or 9-inch layer pan. Bake according to recipe on package. Cool and frost as desired for another meal.

Party "Short" Cake—Prepare White, Yellow or Spice Cake Mix as directed on package. Bake as directed. Allow cake to cool. Split layer crosswise to make 2 thin layers. Spoon between layers about 1½ cups sweetened prepared fruit—fresh, frozen or drained canned fruit such as berries, peaches, bananas, etc. Spread over top ½ cup heavy cream, whipped. Serve at once, or keep in refrigerator until serving time. Ice remaining layer as desired, and save for another meal.

Easter Layer Cake—Prepare White Cake Mix as directed on package. Divide into 3 parts. Use ⅓ for white layer. Color ⅓ pink with a few drops of red food coloring. Color ⅓ yellow or other desired color. Pour batter into three prepared 8-inch layer pans. Bake about 18 minutes in moderate oven (350° F.). Spread orange marmalade between layers. Frost top and sides with Orange Butter Icing (page 709).

Lemon Surprise Cake—Prepare 1 package lemon pie filling following package directions. Spread filling in oblong pan (13 x 9½ x 2 inches). Let stand while making cake batter. Make White Cake Mix batter according to directions on package. Pour over lemon filling. Bake 35 to 40 minutes in moderate oven (350° F.). Sift confectioners' sugar over the top. Serve warm or cold. If served cold, lemon filling will be stiffer.

Chocolate Banana Cream Cake—Prepare Devil's Food Cake Mix as directed on package. Bake as directed. Split one of the warm layers in half crosswise to make 2 thin layers. Put layers together with sweetened whipped cream and sliced bananas in the middle. Place more whipped cream and sliced bananas on top. Frost remaining layer as desired and save for another meal.

For Recipe Success

No RECIPE, no matter how carefully tested and written, will give perfect results if it falls into careless hands. An experienced cook will automatically take these steps:

1. *Assemble the ingredients* for the recipe. Use those suggested; they are best suited for the dish to be made. For best results in baking, butter, eggs and milk should not be too cold. Let them stand at room temperature a short time before they are used.

2. *Assemble the equipment* needed for measuring, mixing, cooking, or baking—spoons, cups, bowls, pans, etc. If baking pans are to be used, prepare them as directed in the recipe. In the section "The Well-Equipped Kitchen," useful equipment is listed.

3. *Pre-heat oven* for correct temperature stated.

4. *Follow the recipe accurately*.

HOW TO FOLLOW A RECIPE

USE LEVEL measurements. They are the basis of all modern recipes. Standard measuring cups and sets of measuring spoons will eliminate guesswork and simplify one of the most important steps in following a recipe. Some measuring cups designed for liquid have an extra rim about the one-cup mark, but should not be used for measuring those ingredients which must be leveled off.

Home Economists throughout the country have worked with the American Standards Association, 70 East 45th Street, to encourage manufacturers of measuring and baking utensils to con-

form to standards so that all equipment will be identical. Look
for the initials AS on the equipment you buy. In this cookbook
we have used the pan measurements recommended by the American Standards Association in specifying the pan sizes for you to
use with the recipes.

To Measure Flour. Always sift all flours, except whole wheat
and bran, once before measuring. To measure one cup of flour,
pile sifted flour lightly into measuring cup with scoop or
spoon, then level off top gently with spatula or straight edge of
knife.

Never Pack Flour into Cup and Do Not Shake Cup. For portions
as ¼ or ⅓ cup of flour, or less, it is easier to measure by tablespoons (see table of equivalents, page 80). Stir whole grain flours
and meals with a fork or spoon, but do not sift before measuring.

To Measure Fats. With bulk shortening, measure by tablespoons
for amounts of ¼ cup or less. To measure a spoonful of fat, pack
it solidly into spoon, then level off with spatula or knife. To
measure by cup, pack the shortening in so solidly that it will hold
the shape of the cup when turned out; then level off. For fractions of cup, pack solidly or level off at the desired fraction mark
or use the *water displacement method.* For example, for ½ cup
of shortening, fill cup half full of cold water, add shortening until
the water reaches the top of the cup, then drain off water. The
remaining shortening measures the correct amount. This method
may be used for any fraction of a cup. *To measure from a pound
print* is an easy matter if one is familiar with the relation between
pound and cup. One pound print is equivalent to 2 cups. One-
half pound equals 1 cup; a ¼-pound stick equals ½ cup.

To Measure Sugar. For white sugar, fill the cup and level off as
for flour. Never heap the cup nor scant the measure. For brown
sugar, pack it into the cup firmly. If lumpy, roll and sift before
measuring.

To Measure Baking Powder. Baking powder is a delicate leavening agent and should be measured accurately. Too much or too
little may give definitely inferior results in baking.

Level off teaspoon with a spatula or edge of knife. *Never level
off on the rounded edge of the can.* If ½- and ¼-teaspoons are
not available, measure one level teaspoon and subdivide it.

To Measure Liquids. Measuring cups for liquids have the one-cup
mark below the brim; fill with liquid to the one-cup mark, bring
the cup to eye level for accurate measurement. For fractions of a
cup, fill carefully to the desired mark. To measure by spoonfuls,
fill them brimming full. Sticky liquids such as molasses, honey
and syrups should be poured from the container into a greased cup
or spoon, or dipped out with another spoon.

Follow Technique Given.

Cook or Bake as Directed. The way a finished product is handled
is important. Directions for removing from the pan, molding,
chilling, etc., are incorporated in the recipes in this book.

HOW TO REDUCE RECIPES

MOST of the basic recipes given in this book are for six, and many
of them can be reduced very easily to serve two, three or four by
using only ⅓, ½ or ⅔ of the amount of each ingredient listed.

HOW TO INCREASE A RECIPE

FOR THE average homemaker, it is usually unwise to make more
than twice the recipe at a single time. If an even larger amount
is required, more time and trouble will be saved by making a
double batch the number of times necessary than by struggling
with the greater quantities of ingredients in household-size equipment.

When a recipe is doubled, the amounts of all ingredients should
be multiplied by two. The cooking time, however, is not always

increased, for usually the larger quantity is baked in two pans instead of one, or a larger pan of no greater depth.

YOUR WELL-EQUIPPED KITCHEN

FOR YOU to function as an efficient cook you will need certain tools. Here we give you a list of kitchen utensils for food preparation and dish washing designed to serve as a guide for equipping your own kitchen according to your individual needs. These lists have been developed from the experience of homemakers in a recent survey. Utensils used at least once a week in at least half of the homes are starred (*). These make up a minimum set. A recommended set includes the other pieces used once a week or more by at least a quarter of the women. If you have still others that you use often, they belong in your set.

TOOLS FOR FOOD PREPARATION AND DISHWASHING

*1 beater, rotary
*1 bottle and jar opener
*1 can opener (for tin cans)
*1 colander
*1 cutting board
 1 flour sifter
 1 food chopper (crank type)
 1 food mincer (blade type)
 1 food press
*1 fork, 2 tines, long handle
 1 grater and shredder set
*1 knife, bread or slicing, 8-inch blade
*1 knife, butcher, 7- or 8-inch blade
*1 knife, case
*1 knife, paring
*1 knife sharpener
*1 ladle
*1 measure, 1 cup
*1 measure, 1 pint
*1 measure, 1 quart
*1 set measures, ¼-, ⅓-, ½-, and 1-cup
*1 mixing bowl, 1 pint

*1 mixing bowl, 1 quart
*1 mixing bowl, 2 quart
*1 mixing bowl, 4 quart
*1 orange or fruit juicer or reamer
*1 pan, round, 12-inch
*1 potato or food masher
*1 rolling pin
*1 spatula, 7-inch blade
*1 spoon, basting, long handle
*1 spoon, perforated mixing, long handle
*1 spoon, wooden, 11-inch
 1 spoon, wooden, 15-inch
*1 set spoons, measuring
*1 strainer, medium size, medium mesh
*1 turner, pancake, long handle
*1 dish drainer
*1 dishpan
*1 sink strainer
*1 pan to fit under dish drainer or second dishpan
*1 vegetable brush

PANS FOR RANGE-TOP AND OVEN USE

*1 coffee maker, size and type to suit
  family
*1 double boiler
*1 fry pan, 10- to 12-inch diameter
*1 fry pan, 8-inch diameter
 1 griddle
*1 kettle with lid, 8-quart
*1 saucepan, 1-quart
 1 saucepan, 3-cup to 3-quart capacity
  as needed
*1 saucepan, 3-quart
*1 saucepan or saucepot, 4-quart
 1 teakettle
*1 teapot

1 baking pan, about 10 by 14 inches
1 bread pan
*2 cake pans, layer, 8- or 9-inch
1 cake pan, square, 8- or 9-inch
*1 casserole with lid
*1 cooky sheet
1 cooky sheet (additional)
*1 cooling rack
1 cooling rack (additional)
*6 custard cups
1 muffin pan, 8- to 12-cup
*2 pie pans
*1 pudding pan, 9-inch
1 roaster

Cookery Methods

To HELP you follow accurately the recipes in this book, we have assembled here definitions and explanations for the use of ingredients, processes and techniques of cooking.

COOKING AND BAKING IN HIGH ALTITUDES

AT HIGH altitudes the following adjustments are needed in cooking: (1) increased length of time for cooking foods by boiling; and (2) increased temperatures for processing the pressure cooker, as well as changes in finish temperatures for candies and icings. Adjustments, too, have to be made in cake, cookie and doughnut recipes in order to give a top-flight product.

The higher the elevation, the lower the temperature of boiling water. In fact, on some of the highest mountain peaks, water will boil when only lukewarm.

A general rule a homemaker may follow for cooking vegetables in boiling water is to increase the cooking time. See table on page 59.

A pressure cooker is a "must" for canning low-acid vegetables and meats at high elevations. The higher the elevation, the more pressure will be needed in the cooker to bring the temperature up to where it will be comparable with sea level.

The temperature within the cooker may be increased 2° F. by raising the pressure one pound. Caution must be taken when increasing pressures beyond 15 pounds, as cookers frequently exhaust in high elevations at 17 or 18 pounds pressure. Almost all vegetables and meats are now processed at 10 pounds at sea level, therefore adjustments may be safely made by increasing pressures

TABLE VII

TIMETABLE FOR COOKING VEGETABLES BY BOILING AT HIGH ALTITUDES [1]

VEGETABLE	HOW PREPARED FOR COOKING	HIGH ALTITUDE COOKING TIME LARAMIE, WYOMING
		(Minutes)
Beans, green and wax	Cut into 1" pieces	45–50
Beets (old)	Left whole	210–240 (3½–4 hrs.)
Beets (new)	Left whole	135–150 (2¼–2½ hrs.)
Broccoli	Buds and 3" of stalk	8–9
Brussels Sprouts	Sprouts 1⅜" x ⅞"	20
Cabbage (white)	Shredded	13–15
Cabbage (green)	Shredded	9–10
Carrots (old)	Cut into thirds, lengthwise,	35–45
Carrots (new)	sliced across	32–41
Cauliflower	Separated into flowerettes	20–24
Chard	Large leaves with midrib	20–22
Kale and Mustard Greens	Midrib and stem removed	5–7
Onions (yellow)	Partially quartered	45–55
Parsnips	Cut in thirds, lengthwise, and across once	30–38
Peas (immature)	Shelled	10–15
Peas (mature)	Shelled	25–30
Potatoes (Irish)	Peeled thin, cut in halves lengthwise	(varied) 32–44
Rutabagas	Cut lengthwise in slices ½" thick	(Jan. Tests) 32–38
Spinach	Stems discarded in older leaves	(Dec. Tests) 10–12
Squash, Hubbard	Pared, cut in 2" x 3" cubes	20–25
Sweet Potatoes	Cut crosswise once and lengthwise in halves	23–30
Turnips (old)	Pared, cut in ¾" cubes	20–30
Turnips (new)	Pared, cut in ¾" cubes	17–23

NOTE: Water must be boiling rapidly when vegetables are put in, for comparable results with time table.

[1] Chart prepared by Emma J. Thiessen, Home Economics Research Associate, University of Wyoming, Laramie.

at 7200 feet to an equivalent 15 pounds without danger of exhausting the steam.

For specific information about pressure cooking and formulae for doughnuts, cakes, etc., consult your county agent for the State University Extension Service.

DEFINITIONS OF FOOD INGREDIENTS

Bouillon Cube—A small cube of dried meat, chicken or vegetable extract and seasonings; used with water to make bouillon.

Bread Crumbs—(1) **Dry bread crumbs** are fine, rolled and sometimes sifted. Used for coating foods and for buttered crumbs. (2) **Soft bread crumbs** are crumbled or shredded. Used for bread puddings, fondues, stuffings.

Caramel—Sugar melted over dry heat, used for coloring and flavoring.

Cider—The juice pressed from fresh apples; used as a beverage and for making vinegar.

Condiment—Something taken with food to season or improve its flavor.

Cracklings—The crisp residue left after rendering fat.

Cream—The portion of milk which rises to the surface of milk on standing or is separated from it by centrifugal force. **Light cream** is coffee or table cream. It contains not less than 18 per cent milk fat. **Medium cream** is light whipping cream. It contains at least 30 per cent but less than 36 per cent milk fat. **Heavy cream** is heavy whipping cream and contains not less than 36 per cent milk fat, usually 36 to 40 per cent. **Homogenized cream** is medium or light cream that has been mechanically treated to reduce the size of the fat globules. It seldom whips.

Drippings—The fat and juices which drop from roasting meat.

Egg Whites, Stiffly Beaten—Whites beaten until stiff but not dry, (see Beat, page 63) so peaks form which "tail" when beater is lifted from bowl and fall over.

Egg Yolks, Well Beaten—Yolks beaten until thick and lemon-colored. (See Beat, page 63.)

Enriched Foods (restored, fortified)—Staple foods such as bread, cereals, flour, milk, margarine and salt to which nutritional essentials (vitamins and minerals) have been added or restored.

Fat—General term for solid and liquid edible fats.

Fillet—Long, thin, boneless strip of lean meat or fish.

Gelatin—A purified protein formed, by continuous simmering, from collagen found in the connective tissues and bones of animals. Marketed as granulated, unflavored gelatin and flavored gelatin with sugar, fruit acids, flavor and coloring, etc.

Herb Bouquet—A bunch of mixed herbs tied together in a small bag, used for seasoning meats, stuffings and soups.

Hydrogenated Fat—Made from refined, bleached oils solidified to a plastic state by the addition of hydrogen.

Junket Tablet—Small tablets containing rennin, an enzyme substance that coagulates milk at lukewarm temperatures (40°–42° C.) or (104°–107.6° F.). Rennin or rennet tablets are prepared commercially from the lining of a calf's stomach.

Legumes—Vegetables which bear their fruit or seeds in pods, such as peas, beans, lentils and soybeans.

Marinade—Seasoned mixture used to give flavor to meats or salads.

Meat—Broadly, includes the flesh of mammals, poultry, game, fish and shellfish. **Aged** or **ripened meat** (mainly beef, some lamb and game) has been stored (just above freezing 38° F.) from 15 to 30 days to increase tenderness and add flavor by a natural breakdown of tissues by enzymes and microorganisms.

Meat Extract — A concentrated meat in paste or liquid (often called Glacé Viande) form to use in flavoring sauces, soups, gravies and stews. For family-size recipes, use ½ to 1 teaspoon unless otherwise stated.

Oil—Edible fats that are liquid at room temperature.

Paste—A smooth mixture of flour and water used to thicken a liquid.

Poultry — Includes all domestic fowls (chickens, ducks, geese and turkey). **Dressed** (New York dressed) **poultry,** as purchased, have been bled and picked. **Drawn poultry** have had head, feet and viscera removed. **Table-dressed** poultry are ready for cooking without additional cleaning; split, disjointed or whole. **Oven-dressed poultry** are whole and ready for the roaster or kettle. **Pan-dressed poultry** are disjointed or cut in pieces for serving and ready for the cooking pan.

Roux—A smooth uncooked mixture of flour and butter or other fat used to thicken sauces and soups.

Seasoning—See **Condiment.**

Shortening—A general term given to any fat used for making a product short or tender, as in breads, cakes, cookies and pastries, etc.

Spice—See section on herbs.

Sugars (commonly used)—Obtained from sugar cane and sugar beet. (1) **White crystal sugars,** classified according to size of crystals, are 99.7 per cent sucrose. **Sugar** (standard granulated sugar), with crystals that vary in size, is used generally in baking, cooking, and sweetening. **Berry** or **fruit sugar,** with very fine crystals, goes into solution quickly and may be used to sweeten fresh fruits, cocktails, etc. **Powdered sugars,** pulverized sugar of various degrees of fineness, are usually mixed with cornstarch or tricalcium phosphate. The higher the number of X's after a confectioners' or powdered sugar, the finer the crystals. **Confectioners' sugar** (XXXX) is most commonly used in uncooked frostings. (2) **Special forms of sugar** are: **Cube or tablet sugar,** a refined white crystal sugar mixed with high-purity sucrose syrup, compressed and dried in cubes or tablet form. **Coarse sugar,** a dry refined white crystal sugar with large crystals, is often colored and used for decorative purposes. **Brown sugars** are obtained in refining raw cane sugar, are moist with a very minute crystalline structure and contain from 75 to 99.7 per cent sucrose, and not more than 4.5 per cent ash and 6 per cent water. Light and dark brown sugars are the two most commonly used. Keep well covered.

Maple sugar, a solid product obtained by evaporating maple sap or maple syrup, consists mostly of sucrose with some invert sugar and ash; used largely for flavor. **Corn sugar,** a crystallized dextrose, is obtained by hydrolizing cornstarch with acid. It is less sweet than sugar. Often used in sugar solutions and candies to prevent them from becoming grainy.

Syrups—from sugar cane. (1) **Cane syrup,** the concentrated sap of sugar cane, contains not more than 30 per cent water and 2.5 per cent ash. A table syrup. (2) **Molasses,** the mother liquor from which cane sugar has crystallized, is usually marketed as: (a) **Table molasses,** light in color, containing more sugars and less ash than cooking molasses. (b) **Cooking molasses** is dark in color and high in iron. **Barbados molasses** is specially treated cooking molasses; resembles cane syrup. (3) **Refiners' syrup,** the residual product obtained in refining raw cane sugar which has been clarified and decolorized, is a solution of sucrose and invert sugars (dextrose and levulose) containing not more than 25 per cent water. It is used for flavoring corn syrup. (4) **Sorghum syrup,** the clarified and concentrated juice of the sugar sorghum containing about 30 per cent water, is used for the table and in cooking. (5) **Maple syrup,** the concentrated form of maple tree sap or maple sugar solution, is a table syrup containing about 35 per cent water. (6) **Corn syrup (unmixed),** a liquid from a partial hydrolysis of cornstarch by acid, alkali, enzymatic catalysts, is neutralized, clarified and concentrated to a syrup generally about 25 per cent water. Marketed as: **Light corn syrup,** a clarified and colorless syrup less sweet than cane syrup; it is used in cooking. **Dark corn syrup,** a mixture of corn syrup and refiners' sugar, used as table syrup and for cooking and for its darker color and distinctive flavor. (7) **Honey,** The nectar of plants, gathered, modified, stored and concentrated by honey bees, contains about 25 per cent water and largely levulose and dextrose (invert sugars). In cookery, honey implies extracted or strained honey.

Tapioca—from the flour obtained from the cassava root; marketed usually as: (a) **Pearl tapioca,** in the form of shell-covered pellets, made by cooking tapioca flour and water on a heated metal surface; requires long cooking. (b) **Quick-cooking tapioca,** made by grinding the pearl or native flake tapioca, or by crushing the cooked tapioca dough; used in most recipes.

Vinegars—an alcoholic and subsequent acetous fermentation of different products. **Cider vinegar** from the juice of apples is the most generally used vinegar. **Wine, malt** or **sugar** vinegar is from the juice of grapes, malt or sugar solutions respectively. **Spirit** or **distilled vinegar** (white) is from dilute distilled alcohol.

Wines—See section on wines.

STEPS IN PREPARATION AND COOKERY PROCESSES

Bake—To cook by dry heat, usually done in oven; called roasting when applied to meats.

Barbecue—To roast meat on spit or rack over coals, usually basting with highly seasoned sauce.

Baste—To moisten foods, usually meat, while cooking. Melted fat, meat drippings, water and fat, water, or special sauce may be used to add flavor and prevent the surface from drying.

Beat—To make a mixture smooth or to incorporate air by a brisk regular movement that lifts the mixture up and over. A mechanical mixer or a rotary movement of the wrist is used for beating. **To beat eggs: whole**—Beat in bowl or cup enough to mix yolk and white thoroughly.

Whole, well beaten—Beat with rotary egg beater in small bowl until eggs are light and foamy.

Blanch—(1) To remove skins from fruit or nuts by allowing them to stand in boiling water or steam from 1 to 5 minutes, then draining, rinsing in cold water and slipping off skins. (2) To inactivate enzymes and shrink food for canning, freezing and drying.

Boil—To cook in liquid, usually at the boiling temperature. The boiling point is reached when bubbles rise continuously and break at the surface.

Braise—To brown meat or vegetables in small amount of hot fat, and then cook slowly in closely covered utensil, adding a very small amount of liquid or cooking in meat juices.

Bread—To cover with bread crumbs preparatory to cooking. See **Coat.**

Broil—To cook directly under a flame or red hot heating unit, or over an open fire or grill.

Candy—To cook fruit in heavy syrup until transparent, then drain and dry; to cook vegetables with sugar or syrup to glaze.

Caramelize—To melt sugar slowly over low heat until it develops characteristic flavor and golden brown color.

Chop—To cut into small pieces with a sharp knife or cutter.

Coat—To dip food into flour until all sides are evenly covered. To dip food into bread crumbs alone, or into slightly beaten egg or milk, then in seasoned crumbs.

Coddle—To cook slowly and gently just below the boiling point; eggs and fruit are coddled.

Combine—To mix together all ingredients.

Cook—To prepare food by application of heat in any form, such as direct, dry or moist heat, radiant or electronic.

Cream—To make soft, smooth and creamy by rubbing with back of spoon or other utensil; usually applied to fat and sugar.

Crisp—To make firm and brittle in very cold water, a moist, cold place, a moderate oven or by frying.

Cube—To cut into small cubes or solids of six equal square sides.

Cut—(1) To divide food in pieces with knife or scissors. (2) To combine fat with dry ingredients using two knives, a fork or blender.

Devil—To prepare with hot seasoning as pepper, mustard, etc.

Dice—To cut into small cubes. See **Cube.**

Dissolve—To cause a liquid and a dry substance to pass into a solution.

Dot—To scatter small bits, as butter, over surface of food.

Dredge—To coat with some dry ingredient, as seasoned flour or sugar.

Dust—To sprinkle or coat lightly with flour or sugar.

Fireless Cooking—To cook by means of stored heat in insulated oven or fireless cooker.

Fold (cut and fold)—To combine ingredients by cutting vertically down through the mixture with spatula or spoon, and gently lifting a portion of the mixture to a new spot, at the same time turning the bowl to cut and fold in a new spot.

Fricassee—To cook by braising. Applied to such foods as poultry, game and meats cut into pieces.

Fry—(1) To cook in small amount of fat, also called sauté or panfry; (2) to cook, immersed, in a deep layer of hot fat, also called deep-fat frying; (3) to cook, partly immersed, in a 1- to 2-inch layer of fat.

Garnish—To decorate.

Glacé—To make smooth and glossy with icing; to coat with jams or jellies or a thin syrup cooked to the crack stage.

Grate—To wear away into small particles by rubbing on a grater.

Grill—See **Broil.**

Grind—To reduce to particles by cutting, crushing or friction.

Julienne—To cut vegetables into match-like strips.

Knead—To work and press dough with balls of the hands, followed by a folding, stretching and rolling motion.

Lard—To place strips of fat, called lardoons, on top of meat, to insert them in gashes on sides of meat, or to insert them into lean meat by means of a larding needle or skewer; this is done to add fat and to prevent dryness.

Marinate—To let food stand in an oil-acid mixture to season.

Mask—To cover completely, usually with mayonnaise or thick sauce.

Melt—To liquefy by heat.

Mince—To cut or chop into very fine pieces.

Mix—To combine ingredients into one mass, usually by stirring.

Panbroil—To cook uncovered in a hot frying pan, pouring off fat as it accumulates. Pan is ungreased or rubbed lightly with fat to prevent sticking of food.

Panfry—To cook in small amount of fat. See **Fry.**

Parboil—See **Precook.**

Parch—To dry and brown with dry heat; applied to grains, as corn.

Pare—To cut away outside covering.

Pasteurize—To partially sterilize a liquid at a temperature (140°–180° F.) which destroys certain pathogenic organisms and arrests fermentation.

Peel—To strip off outer covering.

Plank—To broil or bake meat or fish on a plank.

Poach—To cook gently in hot liquid, usually below boiling point, so shape of food is retained.

Pot Roast—To cook by braising.

Precook—To cook food partially in a liquid below the boiling point. See **Simmer.**

Render—To free fat from connective tissue by heating in top of double boiler, covered, over hot water.

Roast—To cook by dry heat, usually in an oven. See **Bake.**

Salt—To apply salt; to cure or season with salt.

Sauté—To fry in small amount of fat. See **Fry.**

Scald—(1) To bring to a temperature just below the boiling point. To scald milk, heat, covered, over boiling water. (2) To dip poultry in moderately hot, not boiling, water, to loosen feathers before plucking.

Scallop—To bake a food, usually cut in pieces, in a casserole with sauce or other liquid. The top is usually covered with crumbs. Food and sauce may be mixed together or arranged in alternate layers.

Score—To cut a surface ⅛ inch deep several times in two different directions.

Scramble—To prepare by stirring while cooking.

Sear—To brown surface of meat quickly by intense heat.

Shirr—To break (eggs) into a dish with cream and crumbs and bake.

Sift—To put one or more dry ingredients through a sieve or fine strainer once or several times; use 2 squares of paper or 2 bowls, sifting from one to the other.

Simmer—To cook in liquid below the boiling point—about 185–200° F.

Skewer—To fasten meat or poultry with long pin of wood or metal to keep it in shape during cooking.

Steam—To cook in steam.

Steep—To soak in a liquid below the boiling point to extract color, flavor or other qualities.

Sterilize—To destroy microorganisms. In cooking, usually done by boiling in water or subjecting to steam for at least 20 minutes.

Stew—To simmer slowly in just enough liquid to cover until tender.

Stir—To mix ingredients with a circular motion until blended.

Toast—To brown by direct heat breads, nuts or marshmallows.

Whip—To beat rapidly, as eggs, cream, gelatin, with whisk or rotary beater to incorporate air and produce expansion.

DEFINITIONS OF PREPARED PRODUCTS

Appetizer—A small, individual portion of food or drink, served before or as the first course of a meal.

Aspic—A savory meat jelly made with gelatin used to garnish meat or fish, or to make a mold of meat, fish, etc.

Batter—A mixture of flour, liquid, etc., of such consistency that it can be beaten and stirred, poured or dropped from a spoon.

Bisque—A rich cream soup made from a purée, or a frozen ice cream with nuts in it.

Bombe Glacé—A melon or round mold layered with one kind of ice cream and filled with another ice cream or an ice.

Bouillabaisse—Several varieties of fish and shellfish cooked like a stew and often with white wine added.

Canapé—An appetizer made of fried or toasted bread spread with some highly seasoned food.

Cobbler—A type of deep-dish fruit pie made with rich biscuit dough, with top and side crusts, or with top crust only.

Cocktail—An appetizer. May be liquid (vegetable or fruit juice or alcoholic beverage) or solid (fruits or shellfish with sauce).

Compote—Several kinds of fruit stewed in syrup.

Consommé—A clear soup made usually from a combination of meat stock.

Cream Sauce—A white sauce made with cream.

Croquettes—A mixture of cooked and chopped ingredients, as fish, meat, cheese, etc., held together by a thick sauce, shaped—usually in cones —dipped in egg and crumbs and fried.

Croustade—A case for creamed meat or fish, made from bread, and fried or brushed with butter and browned in oven.

Croutons—Small cubes of fried or toasted bread served with soup.

Curry—Special blend of herbs and spices used to flavor stews.

Custard—A cooked or baked mixture of eggs and milk.

Cutlet — A small piece of meat, usually veal, cut from leg or ribs, for broiling or frying; or a mixture, usually of fish, held together by a thick white sauce, shaped and cooked like a meat cutlet.

Deep-dish Pie—A fruit pie with top crust only, baked in a deep dish.

Dough—A mixture of flour, liquid, etc., of such consistency that it can be handled or kneaded; may be soft or barely stiff enough to handle.

Éclair—A small oblong pastry filled with custard or whipped cream.

Entrée—A small portion of food that is served as a separate course before the heavy course of a formal dinner; in informal meals the chief dish of the main course may be called an entrée.

Fondant—Sugar syrup cooked to soft ball stage (234° F.), cooled and kneaded to smooth creaminess.

Fondue—A light, fluffy baked food made with eggs, cheese and milk and thickened with bread or cracker crumbs.

Frappé — Diluted sweetened fruit juice frozen to a mushy consistency and served in glasses.

Fritters — A mixture of chopped fruit, vegetable, fish or meat with a batter; or pieces of fruit, vegetable or fish enclosed in a batter, dropped by spoonfuls into hot fat and fried.

Goulash—A thick Hungarian stew made from beef or veal, flavored with vegetables and paprika.

Ice Cream—A frozen product made from cream or a combination of milk and cream, sweetened and flavored. **Plain, American** or **Philadelphia ice cream** contains only thin cream, sweetening and flavoring. **French ice cream** is made from a combination of rich custard with cream added. **Bisque ice cream** is usually higher in fat than plain ice cream with the addition of dried macaroon or sponge cake crumbs, or marshmallows. **Parfait** or **New York ice cream** is high in fat with sufficient egg yolks used to produce a distinct yellow color. **Mousse** is frozen whipped cream, sweetened and flavored. **Pudding** is a high-fat ice cream, with eggs, nuts and fruits added and highly flavored or seasoned. **Neapolitan ice cream** is a layered brick of two or more ice creams variously colored and flavored, or a combination of ice creams and an ice.

Ice—A frozen mixture of fruit juice, sugar and water, which may or may not contain gelatin or egg white.

Infusion—The liquid extract obtained by steeping a substance, as coffee, herbs, etc., in a liquid.

Junket—A dessert of milk coagulated by rennet, sweetened and flavored. Called rennet desserts.

Kisses—Small meringues.

Macaroons — Small cakes made from egg whites, sugar, almond paste or powdered almonds.

Macédoine—A mixture, usually of vegetables or fruit.

Marguerite—A saltine covered with mixture of boiled frosting and nuts or coconut and baked in the oven until browned.

Meringue—A stiffly beaten mixture of egg whites and sugar used to cover the top of a pie, usually browned in the oven, or made into small cakes and baked.

Mignon Fillets—Small tender cross-section cuts of meat, usually from beef tenderloin.

Mocha—A flavor from coffee infusion or a combination of coffee and chocolate.

Mousse—See **Ice Cream.**

Pancakes—Flat batter cakes baked on a griddle on top of stove. Also called **Griddle cakes.**

Parfait—See **Ice Cream.** The term also may signify ice cream with syrup and sometimes fruit or nuts served in a (tall) parfait glass.

Patty—A patty shell filled with a creamed mixture of chicken, fish.

Patty Shell — A small container made from puff paste.

Pilau—Rice stewed with meat, poultry or fish, spices, etc.

Purée—A heavy, smooth, very thick liquid made by rubbing cooked foods through a sieve.

Rabbit or **Rarebit—Welsh rabbit.** A combination of medium white sauce, egg yolk or whole egg, seasonings and cheese.

Ragout—A highly seasoned thick stew.

Ravioli—A savory meat or vegetable mixture enclosed in noodle dough and cooked in boiling water.

Relish—A highly flavored or seasoned food used with other foods to make them more palatable or to stimulate appetite.

Rissole—A savory meat mixture enclosed in rich pastry and fried in deep fat.

Sherbet—A frozen fruit juice mixture similar to an ice, with egg white, gelatin or milk added to decrease the size of crystals. For **milk sherbet** milk is used in place of all or part of water.

Soufflé—A delicately spongy hot baked dish made from a sweet or savory mixture, as cheese, meat, fish, vegetables, fruit or chocolate, made light by gently folding in egg whites beaten until stiff but not dry.

Stock—The liquid in which meat, poultry, fish or vegetables have been cooked.

Timbale—An unsweetened custard combined with minced vegetable, chicken or fish, molded and baked.

Timbale Case—A small case of batter fried in deep fat on a special iron. Used with cream mixtures and desserts.

Torte — A rich single layer cake usually made from crumbs, eggs and nuts and topped with fruit and whipped cream.

Tutti-frutti—Mixed fruit.

White Sauce—A mixture of fat, starch (usually flour) and milk or part milk and stock, seasoned and cooked until smooth and creamy. To use rice flour, see page 77.

TABLE VIII

TERMS COMMONLY USED TO DESCRIBE OVEN TEMPERATURES [1]

Term	Temperatures
	Degrees F.
Very slow	250 to 275
Slow	300 to 325
Moderate	350 to 375
Hot	400 to 450
Very hot	475 to 525

[1] When oven is equipped with an automatic heat control, set regulator at desired temperature before oven is lighted. If food does not bake satisfactorily in the time indicated in recipes, thermostat may need adjusting. Call the local range dealer to make the necessary adjustment.

A portable oven thermometer of reliable make will register the temperature of the oven accurately, and should be used if possible when the oven has no regulator. Place thermometer at one side and toward the front of the rack on which food will be baked, turning it so it may be read quickly when the oven door is opened. To test the accuracy of a mercury thermometer, heat it in hot water deep enough to cover the bulb. When the water has boiled about one minute, at sea level the thermometer should read 212° F.

TABLE IX

BAKING TEMPERATURES AND TIME FOR PREHEATED OVEN [1]

BATTERS AND DOUGH

FOOD	TEMPERA-TURE	TIME (APPROXIMATE)	FOOD	TEMPERA-TURE	TIME (APPROXIMATE)
	Degrees F.	*Minutes*		*Degrees F.*	*Minutes*
Breads—Quick			Cakes, without fat		
Baking Powder			Angel Food	300–350 or	45–60
Biscuits	450	12–15		375–30 min	
Coffee Cake	400	30	Sponge Cake	300–350 or	45–60
Cornbread	400	30–35		375–30 min	
Fruit or Nut Bread	350–375	55–70			
			Jelly Roll	350	20
Muffins	400–425	20–25	Cookies		
Popovers	450 }	15 }	Drop	350–400	8–15
	then 350 }	20–30 }	Rolled	375	8–10
Breads—Yeast	400 }	15 }	Sliced	400	8
Bread		30–40 }	Macaroons	300	30
	then 375 }		Meringues	275	45–60
			Ladyfingers	350	10–12
Coffee Bread	375	35–45			
Rolls—Plain	400–425	15–25	Brownies	325–350	25–30
Fancy	375	25–30			
Cakes, with fat			Pastry		
Cup	375	15–25	Pie Shells	450	12–15
Layer	350–375	25–35	Tarts	450	12–15
Square (Deep)	350	40–45	Turnovers	450	15
Loaf (Deep)	325–350	1–1¼ hr.	Puff Pastry	450–500	5–8
Chocolate					
Layer	350	25–35			
Square	325	60	Pies		
Fruitcake (2″			One-crust (un-	450 }	15
thick)			baked) Custard	then 350 }	25–30
(steamed 1 hr.			type		
—then baked)		15 min.	Meringues on	325 or	20
Light	250	per lb.	cooked fillings	350	15
		30 min.			
		per lb.	Two-crust Fruit	425 or	30–40
Rich	250	40 min.	Pies (Apple pies		
	275–300	per lb.	10–20 minutes	450 }	10 }
			longer.)	then 350 }	20–30 }
(entirely baked)					
Gingerbread	350	30	Deep-dish Pies	450 }	10 }
				then 350 }	30–35 }
Upside-Down			Meat Pies	450 }	15 }
Cake	350	50	Pastry	then 350 }	30 }
Tortes			Biscuit top	450	12–15
Layer	350	20	Puff shells		
Deep	350	50	Cream Puffs and	450 }	15 }
Pound Cake	275–325	1–2 hr.	Eclairs	then 350 }	20–25 }

[1] A preheated oven is one that has been heated to the desired temperature before the food is placed in it. Many quick breads may be baked successfully by starting in a cold oven. It is not recommended that yeast breads be baked by this method. When possible, follow the directions of the range manufacturer for each type of product. In general, add 5 to 20 minutes to the total baking time indicated for each product above; the time will vary with the type of food to be baked, the size of pan, the fuel used and the construction of the oven. This method of baking is comparatively new and all research workers are not always in agreement.

DEEP-FAT FRYING

FATS such as lard, the hydrogenated fats, corn oil and cottonseed oil are commonly used for deep-fat frying, for they can be heated to a temperature high enough for this purpose without smoking or burning. If a fat contains foreign particles such as flour or crumbs, it will smoke at a lower temperature than normal and each time it is heated it will smoke at a still lower temperature. Fat absorption increases as the smoking point of the fat is lowered. Since fat at the smoking temperature is undesirable for deep-fat frying, the selection of the fat and the care given it are important. Do not heat the fat to smoking. After it has been used, to reclaim it cook sliced potatoes in it to absorb flavors and strain through cheesecloth or a fine sieve to remove foreign particles. Fats smoke at a lower temperature when these are not removed.

Desirable equipment includes a flat-bottomed, straight-sided heavy kettle with a small frying surface and deep enough to prevent the fat from boiling over. A frying basket, a large strainer, a skimmer or a flat wire egg whisk should be used to lower the food into the fat and to lift it out. A shallow pan lined with absorbent paper or paper toweling should be ready to receive the food as it is taken from the kettle. A flat thermometer with a metal clip on the back is a great convenience.

New on the market are electric deep fat fryers which automatically control the temperature of the fat by means of a thermostat. With these fryers, foods can be cooked at the correct temperature under the smoking point. Acrid odors and smoke are greatly reduced.

Procedure. Fill the kettle about two-thirds full of fat. If a thermometer is used, hook the clip over the side of the kettle, so the bulb will be about halfway below the surface of the fat. Heat the fat to the desired temperature. When the right degree is reached, lower food gently into the hot fat. As soon as the food rises to the surface of the fat, turn it at once and several times during cooking so it will keep its shape and brown evenly. When a golden brown, lift the food from the fat, drain over the kettle, then transfer it to the paper-lined pan so the excess fat will be absorbed.

TABLE X

TEMPERATURE [1] AND TIME FOR DEEP–FAT FRYING

Kind of Food	Tempera-ture of Fat	Cooking Time (Approx.)	Kind of Food	Tempera-ture of Fat	Cooking Time (Approx.)
	Degrees F.	Minutes		Degrees F.	Minutes
Uncooked mixtures	350–370	1–5	Oysters, clams, scallops	375–380	2–5
Doughnuts	360–370	2–3			
Fritters	350–365	2–5			
Timbale cases	360–370	1–1½	Wet, cold foods	380–390	2–6
Chicken, young	350–365	10[2]	Meats, cutlets or steaks	380–390	4–6
Cooked mixtures	365–380		Vegetables		
Codfish balls	365–380	1–5	Eggplant	380	2–4
Croquettes	365–380	1–5	Onion rings	380	4–6
Fried pies	370	3–4	Potatoes, chips	380	3–5
Crabs, soft shell	375	3–4	French-fried	380	3–5
Fish (small, fillets)	370	3–6	Shoestring or		
Frogs' legs	375–380	3–4	Julienne	380–390	2–4

[1] When a fat thermometer is not available, the temperature of the fat may be tested by dropping a 1-inch cube of stale bread into the hot fat. If bread browns in 60 to 70 seconds, it is hot enough for uncooked mixtures (350°–370°F.); if it browns in 40 to 50 seconds, it is right for cooked mixtures (365°–380°F.); and if it browns in 20 to 30 seconds, it is hot enough for wet, cold foods (380°–390°F.).
When fat smokes, it has been overheated and changed, and it is no longer as desirable for deep-fat frying.
[2] Then bake 20–40 minutes (325°–350°F.). For older chickens, precook before frying.

The frying time depends upon the kind of food, the size of the pieces and the temperature of the fat. Use the temperature and timetable below as a guide.

Do not fry too much at one time, for the temperature of the fat is lowered as the food goes in; if it cools off too much, the food will require longer cooking and may be grease soaked. Adjust heat to keep the fat near the desired temperature.

Shallow-fat Frying. Many foods may be successfully fried in smaller amounts of fat. Use enough fat to cover the bottom of the kettle with a 1- to 2-inch layer, and fry as directed. Since it is more difficult to measure the temperature with a small amount of fat, frying should be watched carefully.

BATTERS AND DOUGHS

FLOUR forms the backbone of every batter or dough. Wheat flour is the most widely used.

Kinds of flours. White or wheat flour is derived from the inner part of the wheat grain. Depending upon when and where the wheat has been grown and how the flour has been milled, we have bread flour, pastry and cake flours, all-purpose or general-purpose flour and whole wheat, entire wheat, or graham flour.

Bread flour comes from "hard" or spring wheat. Real bread flour is almost entirely restricted to the commercial bakery field. It is seldom available to the housewife, who prefers a good all-purpose flour.

Pastry and cake flours contain more starch and less gluten than bread flour; these flours are less suitable for yeast breads. Cake flours are usually finer and more uniform than pastry flours.

All-purpose flour is a term interchangeable with general-purpose and family flour. For all-around use, all-purpose flour is suitable for most batters and doughs, including yeast breads. It is not generally recommended for angel food and sponge cakes.

Whole wheat, entire wheat, and graham flours are terms used for flour ground from the whole wheat grain. This flour contains all the constituents of the cleaned grain in their natural proportions and is richer in minerals than white flour (unless enriched) from which the outer, mineral-containing husks have been removed.

Bran is a by-product of whole wheat flour, consisting of the cellulose or outer husk and some of the endosperm.

Enriched flour for home baking is prepared voluntarily by millers in accordance with state laws. The term "enriched" means (as we go to press) added thiamine, riboflavin, niacin (part of the Vitamin B complex) and iron, and to some flours, in addition, calcium and Vitamin D.

Self-rising flours contain salt and a leavening agent. If substituted for flour in a quick bread recipe, the salt and baking powder should be omitted. If used in yeast bread recipes, a shorter rising period is allowed. Most self-rising flours are accompanied by complete directions.

Rye flour lacks glutenin, the protein that makes for elasticity. Rye flour can be used alone in yeast breads, but makes a lighter, more porous loaf when combined with one-half wheat flour.

Corn flour is a by-product of the new process method of making cornmeal. It may be made by grinding and bolting cornmeal until the granules are as fine as those of wheat flour.

Buckwheat flour is made from the finely ground buckwheat kernel. It may be used alone or with wheat flour in making griddle cakes and waffles. Self-rising buckwheat flours are on the market and popular for quickly made griddle cakes.

Soybean flour comes from the soybean and is milled with or without the seed coat. Like the soybean, it is high in protein and fat, vitamins B_1, B_2, calcium and iron. Soy flour made from the "pressed cake" has most of the fat removed.

Rice flour is milled from the original rice kernel and is very fine and white. It is used largely in fancy cakes, cookies and quick breads. It is often used to replace wheat flour in special diets when an allergy to wheat flour exists.

GRAIN PRODUCTS OTHER THAN FLOUR

CORNSTARCH is the starch refined from the endosperm of corn.

Cornmeal contains no gluten and is made by grinding corn to various degrees of fineness. "Old process" or "water ground" cornmeal is usually the product of white corn. It retains much of the skin and germ and for that reason becomes rancid more quickly. "New process" cornmeal is the product of either white or yellow corn; the skin and germ are largely removed.

Hominy is corn with the hulls and germs removed, left whole or broken into particles. *Pearl hominy* is whole grain hominy with the hulls removed by machinery. *Granulated hominy* is a ground form of hominy. *Hominy grits* are broken grains.

Oatmeal is a cereal sometimes used in breads in combination with flour. It consists of the bulk of the germ and considerable parts of the outer layers of the kernel. Rolled oats—made by rolling the steamed kernels so that they are flattened—is consumed extensively as a breakfast food.

Rice is the white starchy endosperm of the rice grain. It is sold either uncoated or coated. *Coated rice* has been treated with a harmless coating of glucose and talc. *Brown rice*, also called hulled rice, is the grain from which only the hull has been removed. Brown rice contains endosperm, bran coats, polish and germ. *Converted rice* is white rice with the vitamins and water-soluble minerals retained by a manufacturing process which forces them into the heart of the grain. *Quick-cooking rice* has been partially cooked in the commercial process and requires only a limited number of minutes to cook.

Wheat germ is the fat-containing portion of the wheat kernel. The germ is flattened and then sifted out as an oily yellowish flake.

LEAVENING AGENTS

LEAVENING agents make the product light and affect the grain and texture as they expand with heat.

Chemical leavens are of two general kinds: (1) baking powders, (2) baking soda with sour milk or molasses.

(1) *Baking Powders* sold under different trade names are of three types: the tartrate, the phosphate, and the S.A.S. phosphate or double-acting baking powder. The tartrate liberates gas speedily when it comes in contact with the liquid in a recipe. The phosphate acts a little slower than the tartrate. The double-acting baking powder acts slowly until heated.

It is customary to use slightly larger amounts of the tartrate and phosphate powders than of the double-acting type. In general, one uses 1½ teaspoons of the first two powders to 1 cup of flour, and only 1 teaspoon of the double-acting (follow directions included with specific brands).

Refrigeration retards the reaction of baking powder in a batter.

(2) *Baking Soda and Sour Milk or Molasses.* ½ teaspoon of baking soda to 1 cup sour milk or ½ cup molasses gives as much leavening power as 2 teaspoons baking powder. In other words, that amount will leaven 2 cups of flour. Baking soda should be mixed and sifted with the flour and supplemented with the additional baking powder needed to leaven the amount of flour called for in the recipe. If added to the liquid, much of the gas escapes as soon as the two are combined. Unless milk is fully soured, it is sometimes best to use ¼ teaspoon of soda and add 1 teaspoon of baking powder for each cup of sour milk used.

Yeast grows best at a temperature of 80° to 85° F. It is commonly used as either compressed yeast or dry granular yeast (see page 77).

Liquid is essential to a batter or dough mixture. The amount used in proportion to the flour determines the thickness or stiffness of the batter or dough. Milk, if substituted for water in a recipe, may stiffen the mixture because of the small amount of solids the milk contains. Usually a tablespoon extra of milk to each cup of water called for should be allowed. Evaporated milk may be substituted for whole, fresh milk when diluted in proper proportions. Condensed milk contains sugar and therefore cannot be substituted for whole milk without making adjustment in the amount of sugar. Molasses and honey, because of their small water content, can only be substituted for sugar if a comparable change is made in the amount of liquid (page 78).

Shortening is so named because of its ability to render the mixture "short" or more tender. Butter, lard, vegetable oils, margarine, hydrogenated fats, bacon, salt pork fat and suet are commonly used. Lard has a greater shortening power than most fats. Oils must be combined somewhat differently in a mixture if good results are to be obtained. In most recipes the solid fats are used interchangeably.

SUBSTITUTIONS AND BASIC PROPORTIONS

Flour Substitutions

For 1 cup flour (all-purpose flour) use:
```
Cake or pastry flour .......................1 cup + 2 tablespoons
Bran ....................................½ cup + ½ cup flour
Cornmeal ......................⅓ or ½ cup + ⅔ or ½ cup flour
Rice flour ..........................½ or 1 cup + ½ or no flour
Rye .................................½ or 1 cup + ½ or no flour
Soybean ......................¼ or ⅓ cup + ¾ or ⅔ cup flour
Whole wheat flour ........................½ cup + ½ cup flour
```
For 1 cup cake or pastry flour use:
```
All-purpose flour .............⅞ cup or 1 cup minus 2 tablespoons
```

Leavening Proportions

½ to 1 package dry granular or cake of yeast, depending on the length of time allowed for rising, will leaven 3 cups sifted flour

1½ teaspoons baking powder [1] will leaven 1 cup sifted flour

---

[1] Baking powders vary as to type. These are compromise proportions and should give satisfactory results with all types of powders. The leavening produced by neutralizing ½ teaspoon baking soda with an acid (sour milk, molasses, cream of tartar, etc.) is equivalent to the leavening of 1½ teaspoons baking powder.

½ teaspoon baking soda and 1 teaspoon cream of tartar will leaven
1 cup sifted flour and is equal to 1½ teaspoons baking powder
½ teaspoon baking soda will neutralize 1 cup sour milk or buttermilk and leaven 1 cup flour
½ teaspoon baking soda will neutralize ½ to 1 cup molasses and
leaven 1 cup sifted flour.
Baking powder, in proper proportion, is often added to recipes calling for baking soda and sour milk or molasses if a need for additional leavening is indicated.

Milk Substitutions

For 1 cup fresh sweet milk use:
Evaporated ....½ cup + ½ cup water
Condensed ....Contains added sugar; keep for special uses.
Dried whole milk...4 tablespoons + 1 cup water
Dried skim milk....3 tablespoons + 1 cup water
Sour milk or
buttermilk ....1 cup + ½ teaspoon baking soda
Skim ....1 cup + 2 teaspoons fat
Water ....1 cup or 1 scant cup
Fruit juice ....1 cup

Sugar and Syrup Substitutions

For 1 cup granulated sugar, in most recipes, use:

Maple sugar .... 1 cup, shaved and firmly packed
Brown sugar .... 1 cup, firmly packed
Honey [2] .... ¾ cup for sweetness; reduce liquid
Sorghum [2] ....1½ cups "   "   "   "
Syrups [2]
Corn .... 2 cups "   "   "   "
Maple ....1½ cups "   "   "   "

It is best to use syrups only in recipes developed for them.
In general, when substituting liquid sugars for sugar, use up to ½
sugar called for and reduce liquid by ¼. Full substitution may be
made in fruit and beverages, quick breads and yeast breads.

[1] Substitute sugars and syrups by weight when possible. Measure syrups and honey in lightly greased cup. If brown sugar is hard and lumpy, heat in slow oven or in top of double boiler.
[2] Honey, syrups and sorghum are not ordinarily used to replace all the sugar in a recipe, especially in cakes. They vary in sweetness; they contain liquid and it is necessary to adjust for same. With honey, reduce liquid 3⅓ tablespoons for each cup honey used; for the others, reduce liquid about ¼ cup.

Shortening Substitutions

For 1 cup butter in most recipes,[3] use:

Hydrogenated fats ....⅞ to 1 cup
Lard ....⅞ cup
Margarine ....1 cup
Oils ....Best to use recipes developed
for this type of fat

Bacon fat ....⅞ cup, clarified [4]
Chicken fat ....⅞ cup, clarified [4]
Cottonseed, corn, nut oil ....⅞ cup (solid or liquid)
Suet ....½ cup + salt [4]

For 1 cup cream, use:

Cream, light (20%)—about ....3 tablespoons butter plus ⅞
cup milk
Cream, heavy (40%)—about ....⅓ cup butter plus ¾ cup milk

Egg Substitutions

1 whole fresh egg.....2 yolks or 2 whites
2 tablespoons dried whole-egg powder and
2½ tablespoons water
2 fresh egg yolks .....3 tablespoons dried egg yolks and 2 tablespoons water
2 egg whites ....2 tablespoons egg white (powdered) plus
¼ cup lukewarm water

Chocolate and Cocoa Substitutions

For 1 square chocolate (1 oz.) in batters and doughs use:
3–4 tablespoons cocoa. In cake and cookie mixtures, add 1 teaspoon
shortening. It may also be necessary to reduce the flour or increase liquid slightly.

For 1 cup liquid in beverages use:
¼ to ½ square chocolate, or
2 to 3 teaspoons cocoa

METHODS OF RECONSTITUTION

Dried Whole Egg. Add a little water (lukewarm) to the dried
egg. Stir and blend until a medium thick paste is formed

---

[3] For cakes very high in fat, it is sometimes necessary to reduce amount of lard or
hydrogenated fats by about 2 tablespoons per cup.
[4] Increase the liquid in recipes high in sugar and fat 2 to 4 tablespoons.

and there are no lumps of egg powder. Gradually add the remainder of the water and stir or beat with an egg beater until the mixture is smooth. For custards, mix the dried egg with the sugar before reconstitution.

Dried Egg Yolk. Reconstitute same as whole egg.

Dried Egg White. Sprinkle the powder onto lukewarm water and let stand 15 minutes; then stir. If egg white is not entirely dissolved, let it stand longer, stirring occasionally.

Dry Whole Milk. Sprinkle the powder over the surface of lukewarm water. Beat the mixture with an egg beater or shake in a jar. For custards or puddings, mix the milk powder with the sugar before reconstitution; for white sauces or cream soups, first mix the milk powder with flour or blend with melted fat.

TABLE XI

EQUIVALENT MEASURES AND WEIGHTS

MEASURES (LEVEL)		WEIGHTS [1]	
STANDARD	EQUIVALENT	OUNCES	GRAMS
Dash	Less than 1/8 teaspoon		
1 teaspoon	1/3 tablespoon		
1 tablespoon	3 teaspoons	1/2 (fluid)	
1/4 cup	4 tablespoons		
1/3 cup	5 1/3 tablespoons		
1 cup	16 tablespoons	8	226.8
1 cup	236.5 cubic centimeters (cc.)		
1 pint	2 cups	16	453.6
1 quart	2 pints	32	907.2
1 gallon	4 quarts	128	
1 liter	1.05 quarts (U. S. liquid)		
1 liter	.905 quart (U. S. dry)		
1 liter	1000 cubic centimeters (cc.)		

[1] One ounce equals 28.35 grams; one kilogram equals 1000 grams or 2.2 lb.

Storage of Dried Eggs and Dried Milk. Store dried egg and milk products in tightly closed containers in a cool, dry place, preferably in the refrigerator. They will retain their high nutritive value, color, flavor and cooking qualities under favorable storage conditions. When exposed to air and heat they deteriorate quickly.

TABLE XII

THICKENING POWERS OF STARCHES AND PROTEINS [1]

SAUCES		PUDDINGS		CUSTARDS	
INGREDIENTS	AMOUNTS (AP-PROX.)	INGREDIENTS	AMOUNTS (AP-PROX.)	INGREDIENTS	AMOUNTS (AP-PROX.)
(1 cup milk)	*T.*[3]	*(1 cup milk)*	*T.*[3]	*(1 cup milk)*	*number*
Flour[2]—thin	1	Flour—creamy	2–2½	Sauce or baked cup custard—soft	
medium	2	molded	3–4	Eggs—whole	1–1½
thick	3–4	Cornstarch—		yolks	2
Dry bread crumbs	1 cup	creamy	1	whites	2–3
—thick		molded	1¼–1½	Baked cup custard	
(fondue)		Cornmeal—		Eggs—whole	1–1½
Tapioca—quick-		molded	2–3	Large baked cus-	
cooking—thick	3–4	Rice flour	.	tard	
(omelets, soufflés,		creamy	1	Eggs—whole	1½–2
croquettes)	¾–2	molded	1¼–1½	yolks	3–4
Pearl has half the		Arrowroot—		whites	3–4
thickening power	2 T.	creamy	1	Pie filling cus-	
of quick cooking.		molded	1¼–1½	tard—molded	
		Potato—creamy	2	Eggs—whole	1½–2
		Tapioca—quick-		yolks	3–4
		cooking—			
		creamy	¾–1¼		
		pearl—creamy	2	Gelatin—molded	½ T.
		Rice—creamy	1–2	(dessert or aspic)	

[1] In many recipes starch and egg are used together. This table can serve as a guide in making dishes, such as wheatless or eggless puddings and sauces, for special diets.

[2] All-purpose flour; for pastry or cake flour, add approximately ⅛ teaspoon for every 1 tablespoon of all-purpose flour. Browned flour has approximately one-half the thickening power of the original flour.

[3] *T.* stands for tablespoon.

FRESH FRUITS—FRESH VEGETABLES [1]

KIND	PURCHASING UNIT	EQUIVALENT PER LB. [2] (APPROX.)
Apples [3]	lb.	2–3; 3c. (diced); 1½ c. (sauce)
Apricots	doz., lb.	8–16; 2½ c. (cooked)
Avocados	per fruit	2 med.; 1½-2 c. (cubed)
Bananas	lb., hand	3 med.; 2 c. (sliced); 10–15
Berries	pt., qt.	2–4 c.
Cherries	lb., qt.	3 c. (stemmed); 2–2¾ c. (pitted)
Cranberries	lb., qt.	4 c.; 4 c. (sauce)
Grapefruit	per fruit, lb.	1 med.; 1⅓ c. (pulp); 1 c. (juice)
Grapes	lb.	1 bunch; 1 qt.
Lemons	doz., lb.	4–5; ¾ c. (juice)
Limes	doz.	7–9
Melons		
Cantaloupe	2 lb.	2–3 [4]
Casaba	6–10 lb.	6–8 [4]
Honey Dew	5 lb.	4–5 [4]
Watermelon	5–50 lb.	3–20 [4]
Oranges [5]	doz., lb.	2–3 c.; 1⅓ c. (pulp); 1 c. (juice)
Peaches	doz., lb.	4–8; 2½ c. (sliced)
Pears	doz., lb.	3–5; 2½ c. (cooked)
Persimmons	fruit	3
Pineapple	fruit	2–3 c. (cubed)
Plums	doz., lb.	12–20; 2 c. (cooked)
Rhubarb	lb.	4–8; 3½ c. (diced); 2 c. (cooked)
Tangerines	doz.	4–6
Asparagus	lb.	16–20 stalks
Beans, Lima, in pod	lb.	⅔ c. shelled
Beans, Lima, shelled	lb.	2 c.
Beans, snap	lb.	3 c. (1 inch)
Beets	lb. bunch	2 c. diced
Carrots	lb. bunch	4 c. diced or 6 small
Cauliflower	head (12 oz.)	1 small
Celery	bunch	½ lb. medium
Peas, in pod	lb.	1 c. shelled
Potatoes, sweet	lb.	3 medium
Potatoes, white	lb.	3–4 medium

[1] Only the more commonly used are included.
[2] C., cup; doz., dozen; lb., pound; med., medium; pt., pint; qt., quart.
[3] *Excellent eating or table apples:* Baldwin, Cortland, Delicious, Gravenstein, Grimes Golden, Jonathan, McIntosh, Northern Spy, Spitzenberg, Wealthy, Winesap.
Excellent baking apples: Baldwin, Gravenstein, McIntosh, Pippin, Spitzenberg.
Excellent pie and sauce apples: Baldwin, Gravenstein, Pippin, Rhode Island Greening, Spitzenberg, Winesap.
[4] Portions.
[5] Oranges. The navel oranges are in season from November to May: the Valencias from May to November. The kumquats, Mandarins and Satsumas are distinct types of citrus fruit; they are smaller than the orange.

FOOD–PURCHASING GUIDE
APPROXIMATE EQUIVALENTS PER POUND OF SOME COMMON FOOD MATERIALS

FOOD	CUPS	FOOD	CUPS
Beverages		**Fruits, dried—**(*Continued*)	
Coffee, ground	5–5½	Pears, halves	25–30[1]
Tea	6–6½	Prunes, whole	30–40[1]
		cooked	3–4
Cereals		Raisins	3–3½
Barley, pearl	2		
Corn, hominy grits	2½–3	**Milk and Cream**	
Oats, rolled	4	Fresh (1 pint)	2
Rice	2–2¼	Condensed (15 oz. can)	1¾
Wheat, cracked	2¼	Evaporated (14½ oz. can)	1½
cream of	2½–2¾	Powdered	3
		Cream (1 pint)	2
Cheese, grated	4–4½		
		Nuts [2]	
Chocolate, grated	4	In shell (meat)	2
Cocoa	4½	Shelled, chopped	4
		Coconut, shredded	5
Fats, solid or liquid	2	fresh, shredded	2–3
Flours		**Pastes**	
Barley	2	Macaroni, broken	5
Buckwheat	4½	Spaghetti, broken	5–6
Cornmeal	3	Vermicelli, broken	5
Rice	3¾–4	Noodles, broken	5–6
Rye	4½–5		
Soybean	7½–8	**Starches**	
Wheat, all-purpose	4	Arrowroot	4
cake or pastry	4½	Cornstarch	3
		Tapioca, quick-cooking	2½–3
Fruits, candied			
Angelica, stalks	9–11[1]	**Sugars**	
Cherries	140–180[1]	Granulated	2–2¼
Citron, sliced	4	Berry or fruit	2¼
Fruit peels, sliced	4	Powdered xx	2½–2¾
Ginger	1½–2	Confectioners' xxxx	3½
Pineapple, rings	6–8	Brown, firmly packed	2
		Loaf or tablet, cube	180–220[1]
Fruits, dried			
Apples, cooked	10	**Syrups**	
Apricots, cooked	5	Cane	1⅓–1½
Currants	3	Corn	1⅓–1½
Dates, unpitted	60[1]	Honey, strained	1½
chopped	3	Maple	1½
Figs, whole	20–50[1]	Molasses	1½
chopped	3	Sorghum	1½
Peaches, cooked	6		

[1] Measured by count.
[2] Almonds, peanuts, pecans, English walnuts. Other nuts vary in size and weight; one fresh coconut used.

Many dried foods may become infested with certain pantry insect pests, especially during warehouse storage. Milk powders, in particular, are susceptible. If infected they can be salvaged by heating the packages in a slow oven (140° F.) about 30 minutes. Heating destroys the insects and their eggs and does not affect the quality of milk. Always transfer the heated powders to metal or glass containers.

Fruits

ARDENT fruit lovers staunchly believe that no improvement can be made on the fresh, ripened fruit as an appetizer or as a dessert. We Americans like fruits with our meat course—broiled pineapple or grapefruit with baked ham, apple rings with pork, minted pears with lamb. Green seedless grapes with filet of sole are a favorite of the French and so are black cherries or orange sections with duck.

Fruits are splendid sources of Vitamin C. The citrus fruits—oranges, grapefruit, limes, lemons, tangerines and kumquats—are especially rich in this vitamin, as are also strawberries, tomatoes and cantaloupes. To preserve the highest amount of the vitamin, cut these fruits just before serving; do not let them stand long even in the refrigerator.

Citrus juices will help fruits that darken on exposure to air to retain their natural color; immerse fruits in juice or sprinkle liberally over them.

Fruits today may be purchased fresh, canned, dried or quick-frozen. Learn to read the labels to be assured of good value and follow directions for preparation.

APPLESAUCE

4 tart cooking apples   ½ cup water (about)
¼ cup sugar

Pare, quarter and core juicy apples; cut in eighths, if desired; add just enough water to steam fruit and keep from burning. Bring to a boil and cook slowly, covered, 20 to 30 minutes, or until tender; add sugar and simmer just long enough to dissolve sugar; serve hot or cold. If apples lack flavor, add dash of grated lemon or orange rind, or 1 to 3 teaspoons lemon juice. Approximate yield: 4 portions.

Strained Applesauce—It is not necessary to pare apples; remove all bruised spots. Cook apples until soft, then force through sieve; add sugar and simmer to dissolve sugar.

Spiced Applesauce—Substitute 5 tablespoons brown sugar for granulated sugar in Strained Applesauce and add ¼ teaspoon mace, dash of cinnamon and grated lemon rind.

Rosy Applesauce—Cook 2 tablespoons cinnamon candies with apples.

BAKED APPLES

Select firm apples such as Jonathans or McIntoshes. Wash and core 6 medium-sized tart apples and place in baking dish; fill each cavity with 2 tablespoons brown, granulated, or maple sugar, dash each of cinnamon and nutmeg and ½ teaspoon butter. Cover bottom of pan with boiling water and bake, covered, in moderately hot oven (375°–400° F.) 30 to 40 minutes, or until apples are soft; if baked uncovered, baste occasionally with syrup in pan. Remove apples, boil syrup until thick and pour over apples. Serve hot or cold with cream.

BAKED STUFFED APPLES

Use recipe for Baked Apples (above); fill cavities with one of the following mixtures and bake as directed: brown sugar, ginger, raisins and nuts; brown sugar, cinnamon, chopped dates or figs; chopped preserved ginger, watermelon rind, quince, cranberry or currant jelly.

BAKED GLAZED APPLES

8 large apples	**¼ lemon**
1 cup sugar	**water**

Select large tart apples that hold their shape when baked; wash, cut off thin slice on blossom end and reserve; then peel about ⅓ of each apple from cut end. Place apples, stem ends down, in shallow baking pan, add ½ cup sugar, lemon and water to cover ⅓ of apples, place shallow baking pan over top and cook slowly on top of range about 15 minutes, or until ends are just soft but not mushy; then turn on pared side and cook about 10 minutes, or until just soft; then transfer apples, peeled side up, to second pan; strain juice. To glaze apples, sprinkle part of remaining ½ cup sugar over tops and baste with liquid; place under moderately hot broiler (375° F.) for 10 to 15 minutes, or until apples are delicately glazed, sprinkling frequently with sugar and basting with liquid in pan. If apples brown too quickly, place reserved slices over tops for protection. Yield: 8 portions.

With Coffee Cream—Use recipe for Baked Glazed Apples and chill. Combine 1 egg and 1 egg yolk with 3 tablespoons each of sugar and flour. Beat well and stir in 1 package gelatin and 2 teaspoons coffee flavoring or 100% instant coffee. Slowly add ¾ cup hot milk. Heat to boiling. Chill until syrupy. Beat 1 egg white until stiff but not dry and flavor with rum. Gently fold into egg-gelatin mixture with 2 tablespoons whipped cream. Fill pastry bag with cream mixture and fill centers of apples and pipe edges on top. Pour syrup over apples and sprinkle with sliced blanched almonds, toasted.

TART APPLES

Core apples, slice in rings about ¼ inch thick and fry in hot deep fat (375°–380° F.) 2 to 3 minutes, or until browned. Drain on absorbent paper and sprinkle with sugar; serve as garnish with meat, especially pork, ham, duck or goose.

NUT CRUSTED APPLES

6 baking apples	⅓ cup dry bread crumbs
6 tablespoons apricot preserves	⅓ cup brown sugar
1 egg white, lightly beaten	⅓ cup chopped nuts
	1 cup water

Wash and core apples. Place 1 tablespoon of apricot preserves in the center of each. Brush apples with egg white lightly beaten. Coat with mixture of crumbs, brown sugar and nuts. Place in baking pan with 1 cup of water in bottom of pan. Bake in a moderate oven (350° F.) until apples are tender, about 45 to 60 minutes. Approximate yield: 6 portions.

GLAZED SIMMERED APPLES

4 large apples, peeled and cored	grated rind of 1 orange
¾ cup sugar	5 tablespoons apple or red currant
2 teaspoons orange flower water	jelly
2 cups water	whipped cream

Rinse apples in lemon juice and water. Combine sugar, orange flower water, water, rind and jelly. Simmer apples in syrup until tender. Remove apples and boil syrup until thick for sauce, if desired. Drain and serve hot or cold, garnished with cream, topped with jelly. Yield: 4 portions.

Cinnamon Glazed Simmered Apples—Omit orange flower water and orange rind; add 2 teaspoons red cinnamon drops to syrup in which apples are simmered. Top with candy.

Apple Rings—Cut pared and cored apples crosswise in ¾-inch thick slices; cook in syrup, colored and flavored with cinnamon candy, until soft, basting frequently. Remove with ladle and boil syrup until thick; fill rings with jellied syrup.

Green Mint Glazed Apples—Substitute 2 to 3 drops oil of peppermint or spearmint and a small amount of green vegetable coloring for cinnamon drops. Top with mint jelly.

CIDER SPICED APPLES

4 medium-sized cooking apples	6 whole cloves
2 cups cider	4 whole allspice
1½ cups sugar	¼ teaspoon ginger
1 stick (2 inch) cinnamon	¼ teaspoon nutmeg
1½ tablespoons lemon juice	

Peel, core and quarter apples and drop in cold water. Boil cider, 1 cup sugar and spices 10 minutes; add drained apples, a few at a time, and cook until soft but not broken; remove pieces to serving dish as soon as soft; add remaining ½ cup sugar and lemon juice to syrup and boil until thick. Strain out spices and pour over fruit. This makes a piquant accompaniment to pork, ham or poultry dishes. Approximate yield: 4 portions.

APPLE AVOCADO SALAD

6 fully ripe avocados	mayonnaise
6 red apples	whole salted almonds
½ cup chopped almonds	thin slices unpared red apple
	chicory

Halve avocados lengthwise and remove pits, but do not pare. Brush cut surface with lemon juice. Core, pare and dice apples; combine with chopped almonds and enough mayonnaise to hold ingredients together. Fill avocados with this mixture. Garnish with whole almonds, apple slices and chicory. Yield: 6 salads.

PIONEER APPLES

8 to 10 tart apples   ⅓ cup firmly packed brown sugar
3 tablespoons butter   ⅛ teaspoon salt

Pare, core and quarter apples, then slice in eighths. Melt butter in large
heavy frying pan, add apples, cover and cook slowly until they are
nearly soft, or 10 to 15 minutes, depending upon the apples. Sprinkle
brown sugar and salt over them and cook, uncovered, 10 to 15 minutes
longer. Approximate yield: 6 portions.

APPLE SOUFFLÉ

5 to 6 apples   4 eggs, beaten
2 tablespoons sugar   1 cup milk
                12 slices zwieback

Peel, core and slice apples. Mix with 1 tablespoon sugar. Combine
eggs, milk and remaining tablespoon sugar. Grease baking dish, place
a layer of zwieback on bottom, next a layer of apples, then part of
egg-milk mixture. Repeat until dish is filled and cover with egg-milk
mixture. Cover and bake in a moderate oven (350° F.) 45 minutes,
or until apples are tender. Approximate yield: 6 portions.

HOBGOBLINS

large prunes   1 10-ounce package dates
12 medium-sized red apples   6 marshmallows
6 whole figs   blanched almonds
1 cup seedless raisins   toothpicks
                butcher's wooden skewers

Wash and dry prunes, apples, figs, raisins and dates. Press 6 prunes
into shape for heads, using skewer to mold depression for eyes and
mouth, into which press bits of marshmallow. Make a gash and push
in blanched almond for nose. Cut pieces from another prune for
pointed ears; pin to heads with pieces of toothpick. Slit figs lengthwise
and fatten with prunes or other figs for bodies. For women, connect
head to marshmallow neck and fig body with toothpick. Attach to
apple for skirt; insert 3 skewers so figure will stand. Use dates for
shoes. Make arms by slipping raisins over toothpicks with piece of
marshmallow at end and bend to comical curves after attaching to
body. For men, omit fig body, use marshmallow slice for collar and
apple for body. Skewer several dates for long legs. Bits of marshmallow in front of apple make fine buttons. Yield: 12 hobgoblins.

APPLE FRITTERS PARISIAN

4 firm apples (Jonathans or   1 egg
    McIntoshes)   3 tablespoons flour
½ cup confectioners' sugar   ¼ cup milk
½ cup water   deep fat
½ cup brandy or rum

Core and peel apples. Cut into slices ⅓-inch thick. Marinate slices for
1 hour in sauce made by combining confectioners' sugar, water and
brandy or rum. Dry slightly, dip slices into thin batter made by blending egg, flour and milk, stirred until smooth. Fry slices in deep, hot
fat (375° F.) until golden brown. Drain on absorbent paper. Sprinkle
with granulated sugar and glaze quickly under the broiler. Serve hot
in a napkin for dessert. Yield: 8 portions.

APRICOTS

Fresh apricots can be used interchangeably with peaches in fruit cups,
salads, desserts, pastries, etc. To remove the skin, immerse fruit in
boiling water about ½ minute to loosen skin, then plunge into cold
water to keep fruit firm.

APRICOT MOLD

1½ cups hot stewed apricots   ½ teaspoon cinnamon
1 14½-oz. can evaporated milk   ½ teaspoon ginger
½ cup water   ½ teaspoon salt
½ cup firmly packed brown   2 eggs, slightly beaten
    sugar, or to taste   orange marmalade

Rub apricots through a coarse sieve. Add milk and ½ cup juice from
apricots, or water. Add sugar, stir until dissolved, then add spices and
eggs. Turn into greased custard cups, place in a pan of hot water and
bake in a moderate oven (375° F.) 30 minutes or until firm. Cool,
unmold onto serving plates. Serve with bitter orange marmalade
diluted to sauce consistency with hot water. Approximate yield:
6 portions.

AVOCADO SAVORY SPREAD

1 cup mashed avocado   1½ teaspoons Worcestershire
1 teaspoon olive oil   sauce
2 teaspoons minced onion   2½ dozen potato chips

Combine avocado, oil, onion and Worcestershire sauce. Blend well
and spread on potato chips. Approximate yield: 2½ dozen.

AVOCADOS

Avocados must be ripe to be edible; when the flesh yields slightly to pressure of finger, they are ripe. Peel ripe fruit and cut in half to remove large seed; rub with lemon juice to prevent darkening. Serve ½ fruit, or sliced or diced fruit, with lemon; in combination with other fruits or with vegetables, lobster, crabmeat, mixed with salad dressing, as in appetizers or salads. Or mash peeled ripe avocados to a paste, season with salt and lemon or grapefruit juice, and use as spread for canapés; or use avocado pulp in sherbets, ice creams and other desserts.

BAKED AVOCADOS

3 ripe avocados
  (4 cups mashed)
1 cup confectioners' sugar

3 tablespoons lemon juice
¼ teaspoon salt

Scoop avocado pulp from shells. Mash and put through a sieve. Combine with lemon juice, salt and sugar in a buttered baking dish and bake in a moderate oven (350° F.) 30 minutes, or until brown crust forms on top. Approximate yield: 6 desserts.

AVOCADO SUPREME

3 avocados
1 No. 2 can pineapple and
  juice

¼ cup grated coconut
2 tablespoons slivered blanched
  almonds, toasted

Cut avocados in half and remove pits. Scoop out pulp or cut in cubes. Cut pineapple into one-inch cubes. Toss pineapple, juice and avocado together. Place in sherbet glasses, or heap into avocado shells or arrange in layers on platter of crisp lettuce. Chill thoroughly. Garnish with layer of coconut and slivered almonds. Approximate yield: 6 portions.

MIXED AVOCADO COCKTAIL

2 medium-sized cucumbers,
  peeled and diced

2 medium-sized avocados, diced
¾ cup French dressing
water cress

Marinate the diced cucumbers and avocados for 2 hours in the dressing. At serving time arrange them attractively in glasses. Pour the dressing over them and sprinkle crisp water cress leaves on top. Approximate yield: 6 to 8 portions.

❖❖

CHICKEN SALAD ON AVOCADO

2 avocados   1 cup halved and seeded white
4 teaspoons lemon juice   grapes
½ cup mayonnaise   ¼ cup slivered almonds
2 cups cubed chicken   ½ teaspoon salt
                  ⅛ teaspoon pepper

Cut avocados in half. Remove seeds and scoop out some of the avocado
pulp. Mash pulp and add 1½ teaspoons lemon juice. Blend in mayonnaise. Sprinkle avocado halves with 1½ teaspoons lemon juice. Combine chicken, grapes, almonds, 1 teaspoon lemon juice, salt and pepper.
Add ¾ of the mayonnaise mixture to chicken mixture. Fill avocado
halves and garnish with a spoonful of mayonnaise mixture and grapes.
Serve on lettuce. Yield: 4 portions.

BANANAS

Store ripe bananas in cool but not cold place until ready to use; the
standard yellow banana is ripe when color deepens, skin becomes shaded
or speckled with brown, and green color disappears from tips. Serve
bananas whole or sliced with a wedge of lemon, or serve sliced with
sugar and cream; or serve in fruit cups and salads, sprinkling fruit
with lemon juice to prevent discoloration.

BAKED BANANAS

Bake 4 medium or large bananas in moderate oven (350° F.) about
20 minutes, or until skins split open. Remove fruit carefully, dust with
powdered sugar and cinnamon, and sprinkle with pineapple, lemon, or
maraschino cherry juice, or ginger syrup. Or sprinkle finely-chopped
walnuts, crumbled macaroons, or bits of marmalade over bananas.
Yield: 4 portions.

BANANA SCALLOPS

6 bananas, peeled   1½ teaspoons salt
1 egg, slightly beaten   ½ cup dry bread crumbs

Cut bananas in 1-inch slices and dip in mixture of egg and salt; drain,
then roll in crumbs. Fry in hot deep fat (375° F.) 1 to 2 minutes, or
until brown; drain on unglazed paper; serve very hot. Yield: 6 portions.

GLAZED BAKED BANANAS

Peel 4 bananas and place in buttered baking dish, whole or cut in halves lengthwise; sprinkle with lemon juice and bake in moderate oven (350° F.) 20 minutes, sprinkling sugar over fruit 5 minutes before removing from oven to glaze tops. Before serving, sprinkle with nuts or crumbs, if desired. For variety, bake bananas in cranberry sauce, using 1⅓ cups sauce. Yield: 4 portions.

FRIED BANANAS

Cut peeled bananas in halves crosswise, then lengthwise. Sprinkle with orange or lemon juice and dredge with seasoned flour. Sauté in butter until a delicate brown and sprinkle with brown or powdered sugar. To serve with pork, sauté in sausage or pork drippings.

BANANA CREAM

½ cup sugar
juice of 1 orange

6 bananas, sliced thin
1 cup heavy cream, whipped

guava jelly or strawberry jam

Combine sugar and orange juice and marinate bananas in mixture in refrigerator for 30 minutes. Drain, cover with whipped cream and dot with jelly or jam. Yield: 6 portions.

BANANA BOB

Select short, fat bananas for this dish and peel them. Insert a slender wooden stick through the banana the long way and wrap a slice of bacon around the banana. Broil until the bacon is crisp.

BANANA NUT STICKS

Cut bananas into finger lengths, dip in lemon juice and then roll in finely-chopped nuts.

BANANA CUTLETS

6 medium-ripe bananas
⅓ cup lemon juice (about)

1 cup crushed corn flakes
3 tablespoons butter

lettuce

Peel bananas and cut in halves crosswise. Dip in lemon juice, then roll in corn flake crumbs. Sauté in butter until golden brown. Serve on lettuce. Yield: 6 portions.

BANANA SOUFFLÉ

2 tablespoons butter
2 tablespoons flour
½ cup milk
dash of salt

2 tablespoons powdered sugar
3 eggs, separated
6 ripe bananas
¼ cup granulated sugar

Melt butter, blend in flour and add milk slowly. Cook over low heat, stirring constantly, until sauce is thick and smooth. Add salt and sugar and cool. Beat in egg yolks, one at a time. Remove one narrow strip of skin from bananas, taking care not to break the seal at the ends. Remove pulp and rub through sieve into sauce. Mix well after each addition to prevent darkening. Fold mixture into stiffly-beaten egg whites. Fill skins and bake in hot oven (400° F.) 10 minutes. Sprinkle lightly with sugar and return to oven until sugar appears to melt. Serve at once with whipped cream. Yield: 6 portions.

BANANAS NEWBURG

Sprinkle brown sugar over Fried Bananas (page 93); add just enough Sherry to make a sauce and simmer a few minutes. Serve hot as meat accompaniment.

BERRIES

Spread berries on flat surface and remove soft or moldy fruit; place in colander, wash by dipping quickly in cold water, drain; stem or hull. Sprinkle with berry or fruit sugar, or powdered sugar, if extra sweetness is desired; if fruit is sour, mix and let stand ½ to 1 hour before serving; add lemon juice to bland fruit for flavor and tartness. Large perfect strawberries are sometimes served whole: wash but do not remove hulls; arrange 8 to 12 around a mound of powdered sugar. If fruit is stored overnight, pick over to remove soft berries but do not wash. Spread out on tray, cover and place in refrigerator. One quart berries makes 4 to 5 portions.

STEWED BERRIES

Use 1 quart berries; wash, drain and sort; add ½ to 1 cup boiling water and ½ to 1 cup sugar and cook, covered, 10 to 15 minutes, or until tender, adding sugar when nearly done. For blueberries, cook syrup of sugar, water and a small amount of lemon juice and add fruit to hot syrup. Approximate yield: 1 quart sauce.

CRANBERRY SAUCE

1 pound (4 cups) cranberries   1½ cups sugar
                        2 cups water

Pick over and wash cranberries in colander; drain. Place berries, sugar and water in deep saucepan and bring to a boil; cover and cook slowly about 10 minutes, or until skins are broken. Skim and cool. Approximate yield: 4 cups sauce, or 8 to 12 portions.

Jellied Cranberry Sauce—Use 2 cups sugar and cook about 20 minutes; pour into large mold.

Cranberry Jelly—Increase sugar to 2 cups. Boil cranberries and water about 20 minutes, or until skins are broken; force through sieve. Bring pulp to a boil, add sugar and boil 3 to 5 minutes, stirring until sugar is dissolved. Skim and pour into one large or several small molds; or pour into jelly glasses. To keep jelly for some time, seal jars with paraffin. Approximate yield: 1 large mold, or 4 (8-ounce) glasses.

Cranberry Applesauce—Combine 2 cups cranberries, 2 cups sliced apples, ¾ cup water and 1 cup sugar. Cover and cook slowly until fruit is tender, about 20 minutes. Cool slightly and then beat with wire whip until fluffy. Approximate yield: 3 cups sauce.

SPICED CRANBERRIES

2½ cups sugar   1 teaspoon whole cloves
½ cup water   2 tablespoons lemon juice
2 2-inch sticks cinnamon   1 tablespoon grated lemon rind
                        4 cups cranberries

Combine sugar, water, spices, lemon juice and rind and boil 5 minutes. Add cranberries and cook slowly, without stirring, until all the skins pop open. Seal in sterilized jars. Yield: 1 quart.

RASPBERRY AMBROSIA

¼ pound marshmallows   juice of ½ lemon
1½ cups fresh raspberries   1 cup heavy cream
                        grated fresh coconut

Quarter marshmallows. Mix well with raspberries and lemon juice and chill. Whip cream until it begins to thicken and fold in just before serving. Sprinkle with coconut. Approximate yield: 6 portions.

BLACKBERRY PUFFS

1 cup sifted all-purpose flour
dash of salt
1 teaspoon double-acting
   baking powder

1 egg, beaten
½ cup milk
1 cup blackberries, hulled

Sift flour, salt and baking powder. Combine egg and milk and stir in. Stir in blackberries. Drop by spoonfuls into hot fat (375° F.) and fry until brown. Drain on unglazed paper. Dust with sugar and serve with Lemon Sauce (page 727). Approximate yield: 6 portions.

STEWED CHERRIES

Use sour or sweet cherries; wash, stem and pit, if desired. If not pitted, prick each with a pin. Cook in a small amount of water until nearly tender. Sweeten to taste and cook about 2 minutes. Serve with meat or as a dessert. For a delicious ice cream sauce, use Bing or dark cherries. Thicken slightly with cornstarch, add sugar to make a sweet sauce and flavor with brandy or Kirsch.

CHERRIES

Select cherries that are not over-ripe, cracked, or shriveled; leave stems on until ready to use. They can be kept in refrigerator for a week or more if perfectly fresh. Wash and dry large cherries, using absorbent paper or cloth, and serve with stems on; or serve, pitted, with other fruits in cups, salads and desserts. Pitted large black cherries stuffed with nuts or a cream cheese make an attractive salad.

FRESH FRUIT COMPOTE

2 grapefruits
3 oranges
1 pint strawberries
2 bananas
1 small bunch grapes
2 cups melon balls

5 or 6 dates
1½ teaspoons cornstarch
1 tablespoon cold water
1 12-ounce can apricot nectar
2 tablespoons diced candied
   ginger

2 tablespoons brandy

Section grapefruits, oranges; hull and slice strawberries and bananas. Skin and pit grapes and scoop out melon balls. Finely cut dates and combine all fruits. Chill. Dissolve cornstarch in cold water and add apricot nectar. Cook, stirring constantly, until thickened. Add ginger. Cool. Stir in brandy and chill well. Pour over fruits and top with fresh sprigs of mint and red maraschino cherries. Yield: 6 portions

CITRUS FRUITS

(Kumquats, oranges, grapefruit, lemons, limes, tangerines)

Citrus fruits should be selected for quality and size; large fancy fruits are attractive but expensive and not necessarily of better quality; fruits that are thin-skinned and heavy for their size are juicy and not pithy. They should be firm, not soft or flabby, with no soft spots or evidence of decay. Most of the citrus fruits on the market have been picked green and ripened in storage under favorable conditions.

Citrus fruits are valued for their vitamin and mineral content and for the tang and flavor they add to other foods. The vitamin content varies with the kind of fruit and conditions of storage. When juice is strained through a fine sieve, some of the food value is lost; it is wise to use a reamer or extractor that will remove the seeds and membrane, but permit the pulp to pass through. The frozen concentrate yields vitamin-high orange juice.

GRAPEFRUIT, ORANGE, OR LEMON BASKETS

A basket may be made from two halves of fruit; cut fruit in half cross-wise, remove sections, membranes and core; pink or scallop edge of one half and cut ¾-inch band through center of other half, and insert as handle in filled basket. Use for fruit cup.

To make a basket with attached handle use whole fruit. With a sharp toothpick mark the strip for the handle (¾ inch wide) over the blossom end. Then cut the remaining skin on the upper half of the fruit, on each side of the handle. Remove the pulp carefully from the entire fruit. Pink or scallop the edges of the skin and fill with sections of the fruit. Chill.

BROILED GRAPEFRUIT

Prepare grapefruit halves (above), but do not remove pithy centers. Sprinkle each half with 1 teaspoon sugar and dot with ½ teaspoon butter. Place fruit in shallow pan on broiling rack so that fruit is about 4 inches below flame or 3 inches below electric unit, and cook in pre-heated broiler with door slightly ajar about 15 minutes, or until skin begins to brown and fruit is heated through; serve hot. Or sprinkle each half with 1 tablespoon brown sugar and 1 tablespoon wine, and broil as above; garnish with a cherry and serve hot or cold.

GRAPEFRUIT AND ORANGE SECTIONS

Wash and dry fruit; hold over bowl to catch all juice and with sharp knife remove rind and white skin, cutting round and round as in paring an apple. Loosen sections by cutting on either side of membrane; lift out segment and remove seeds if present. Chill and serve plain or sweetened with sugar, honey or maple syrup, or serve as fruit cup or salad.

GRAPEFRUIT WITH GINGER

Remove centers, seeds and membranes from grapefruit halves; shred pulp fine with silver fork. To each half, add ½ teaspoon powdered sugar, 1 teaspoon grated coconut and 1 tablespoon each diced Canton ginger and ginger syrup, and mix well. Place halves in covered dish and bury in ice, or chill very thoroughly in refrigerator.

BAKED GRAPEFRUIT PUDDING

1 No. 2 can grapefruit	3 teaspoons baking powder
½ cup firmly packed brown	¼ teaspoon salt
sugar	3 tablespoons shortening
1 tablespoon melted butter	1 egg, slightly beaten
1½ cups sifted all-purpose flour	⅓ cup milk

Turn grapefruit into greased 8-inch square baking pan. Mix sugar, butter and 1 tablespoon flour; sprinkle over grapefruit. Mix and sift together remaining flour, baking powder and salt. Cut in shortening. Combine egg and milk. Add to flour mixture, mixing quickly to form a soft dough. Turn onto grapefruit and bake in hot oven (425° F.) 25 to 30 minutes. Serve in squares bottom side up, with or without cream. Approximate yield: 6 portions.

LEMONS

A ripe lemon has a lower acid content and poorer keeping qualities than an under-ripe fruit. Lemon juice is more easily extracted if lemon is rolled until softened, or dropped into boiling water for a few seconds before cutting in half.

For lemon slices for tea, wash, slice thin and remove seeds. Serve slices cut in halves or in thirds and garnished with chopped mint leaves or parsley, thin pimiento strips or whole cloves placed through slice. For serrated edge, use a special cutter, or cut with sharp knife. For lemon wedges, wash and cut lemon in quarters lengthwise and remove seeds; cut each wedge in half, if desired.

LIMES

Limes should be used green, for they lose their refreshing flavor on turning yellow. Limes are perishable and should be kept in refrigerator; they can be substituted for lemons.

TANGERINES

Tangerines, mandarins, King of Siam and satsuma oranges are less used types of citrus fruits popular in many markets. They are smaller in size than the navel or Valencia orange, and are graded as to size. The tangerine is popular as a table fruit; the skin is peeled and the sections are separated easily.

FLOATING ORANGES

4 oranges	½ cup granulated sugar
½ cup powdered sugar	½ cup pistachio nuts
½ cup white wine	1 cup white seedless grapes,
1 cup water or white wine	halved
½ cup orange juice	juice of 1 lemon or lime

Peel oranges, removing white tissue; slice very thin. Sprinkle with powdered sugar and add white wine. Cook water (or an equal quantity of white wine), orange juice and granulated sugar to a fairly thick syrup, about 15 minutes. Add pistachio nuts, grapes and lemon juice to syrup. Chill. Then add oranges and juice and chill for several hours. Serve in a large bowl with plenty of syrup so the orange slices float. Yield: 6 portions.

GRAPES

Grapes are an excellent fruit for table use; select compact bunches with firm, well-formed fruits that cling tightly to the stems. Wash and drain. For dessert, cut bunches and serve with fruit knives for removing seeds or with spoons for removing seeds and skins from mouth, if desired; for fruit cups and salads, cut in halves, lengthwise, and remove seeds; the skins may be removed, if desired.

KUMQUATS

Kumquats are very small oblong citrus fruits, orange in color. The entire fruit is edible; the rind is sweet and the pulp is acid. To serve fruit, wash, dry, cut in quarters or slices, and remove seeds; serve with bland fruit or with salads.

MELONS

Melons are of many types including muskmelons (cantaloupes, etc.) and watermelons; sweetness and flavor develop as the melon ripens. Melons are choicest when fully matured; they yield to pressure at blossom ends and the stems are readily pulled out. Wash melons and chill thoroughly; before serving, cut muskmelons in halves, lengthwise or crosswise, and remove seeds; cut larger melons in slices, lengthwise; cut watermelons in slices crosswise, in half circles, or in wedge-shaped pieces. Serve melons with wedge-shaped pieces of lemon or lime, or with salt; serve watermelon with salt. To store, wrap cut pieces of melon in waxed paper.

PAPAYA

Papaya or tropical papaw resembles the muskmelon and is best when fully ripened. Wash and chill thoroughly in refrigerator; just before serving, cut in wedge-shaped pieces and remove seeds; the many small gelatinously coated blade seeds have a pleasant mustard-like taste and some should be served with the fruit. Serve with wedge-shaped pieces of lemon or lime, or with salt or sugar.

MANGOES

Mangoes vary in quality; the best ones have a single small seed stone, surrounded by soft, juicy, aromatic, non-fibrous flesh. Mangoes may be eaten in various ways: cut through skin, circle fashion, around each end, then cut through skin lengthwise from circle to circle, turn back wide band of skin on one side and eat with spoon; cut through skin, X-fashion, on opposite sides of fruit, turn back corners and eat with spoon; cut open lengthwise, remove stone and eat in same way as a cantaloupe. Mangoes are also canned, preserved and used in making East-Indian chutney. One small mango makes 1 portion.

PEACHES

Choose large, plump peaches; they are superior in flavor to the small and flat fruit. The yellow-fleshed, freestone peaches are most generally eaten raw; the clingstone variety is popular for canning and preserving; it is firm, retains its shape and develops a rich, full flavor on cooking. Use ripe peaches that yield to pressure of the finger and are creamy or yellow on under side; peel off skin, slice and sprinkle with a small amount of sugar to keep from discoloring, and serve at once. Sliced peaches may be sweetened with honey. (If skin does not come off readily, drop into boiling water for ½ minute, then into cold water.) Peaches are delicious in many fruit combinations, in fruit cups or salad. They can be broiled, baked, or cooked as compote.

NECTARINES

Nectarines are a delicious fruit, much like the peach; they have peach-like pits and smooth, downless, plum-like skins. They can be substituted for peaches, but are more expensive.

JELLY GLAZED PEACHES

6 ripe peaches, peeled   ¼ cup raspberry jelly
½ cup currant jelly   12 blanched almonds (optional)

Place whole peaches in serving dish. Melt jellies together and pour over fruit and turn to cover. Sprinkle with almonds. Chill and serve on a plate, one peach to a portion, with French vanilla ice cream. Approximate yield: 6 portions.

BAKED PEACHES

Peel 6 large peaches, cut in halves and remove stones; fill each cavity with 1 teaspoon sugar, ¼ teaspoon butter, a few drops of lemon juice and a sprinkling of nutmeg. Bake in moderate oven (350° F.) about 20 minutes; serve hot or cold with cream, as a dessert. For variety, cover with meringue as for pie, sprinkle with coconut and bake as directed. Yield: 6 to 12 portions.

SPICED PEACHES

7 pounds (about 35 medium-   whole cloves
    sized) peaches   1 pint mild vinegar
mace   5 pounds sugar (11¼ cups)
         ⅔ cup broken cinnamon sticks

Peel peaches and stick into each a blade of mace and 2 whole cloves. Cover peach peelings with sufficient water to give 1 cup of liquid when cooked and drained. Prepare syrup by cooking together the peach syrup, vinegar, sugar, cinnamon and ⅓ cup of whole cloves. Place peaches, about 6 or 8 at a time, into the syrup and cook slowly until tender but not soft. Remove peaches carefully to hot sterilized jars, cook down syrup until rather thick and fill jars to overflowing. Divide the spices evenly among the jars for a dark, spicy product or omit for a milder, lighter colored one. Seal at once. Approximate yield: 4 quarts.

BRANDIED PEACHES

Select firm, unblemished peaches. Peel and place in layers in a jar. A crock or bean pot with a loosely fitting cover is the most convenient to use. Cover each layer of peaches with granulated sugar, filling all crevices between the peaches. When the jar is full, place a plate on the top of the peaches inside the jar and weight it. Cover to keep out the dust and let stand until the next day. Next morning the peaches will have shrunk to about one-half their size and there will be a quantity of syrup present. Add more peaches and sugar to refill the jar. Keep this up for a week, until, after standing overnight, the jar remains full. Cover it, but do not seal for about six weeks. Keep the peaches submerged in the syrup at all times. Place the crock in a pan as the syrup may run over. During the fermentation period the crock should not be exposed to extremes of heat or cold. If any scum forms on the surface, remove it. At the end of the six weeks, it is safe to seal the jar. If a crock or bean pot is used, pour a layer of hot paraffin directly on peaches and syrup before storing. Store in cool place. Yield: 8 pounds peaches (about 40 small) will fill a 1 gallon crock.

BROILED PEACHES POACHED IN WINE

Select large ripe peaches; cut in half, remove stone. Place peach halves cut side up on baking pan and sprinkle with brown sugar. Slash peach flesh here and there and fill center with wine. Drip melted butter on edges of peach and brown under broiler. When sugar begins to brown and wine is hot, slip each peach half onto a large grape leaf and serve with spoons.

FRENCH FRIED PEARS

1 cup sifted all-purpose flour	3 eggs, well beaten
1½ teaspoons baking powder	1 cup milk
½ teaspoon salt	6 large ripe pears
1 teaspoon sugar	Lemon Sauce (page 727)

Sift flour, baking powder, salt and sugar. Combine eggs and milk; add to flour mixture, stirring until smooth. Pare, halve and core pears; dip into batter, covering pears completely, and fry in hot fat (360° F.) 2 minutes, or until browned; drain on unglazed paper. Serve with lemon juice, lemon sauce or rum sauce. Yield: 6 portions. Peach and apricot halves may be fried in the same way.

BAKED PEARS

Pare, halve and core large firm pears; place in baking dish and fill hollows with one of the following mixtures: brown or granulated sugar and butter; brown or granulated sugar, chopped preserved ginger and ginger syrup; raisins, chopped nuts, dash of cinnamon, grape juice and bits of butter; orange or grapefruit marmalade, or any tart marmalade. Cover bottom of pan with water, and bake, covered, in moderate oven (350° F.) about 20 minutes, or until tender. Serve warm or cold with cream. If baked whole, cut off thin slice on blossom end, stand upright in pan, sprinkle sugar over tops, dot with butter and bake about 30 minutes.

PEAR COMPOTE PARISIENNE

Use recipe for Pears Crème de Menthe below; omit coloring and flavoring and add chopped rind and juice of 1 lemon and 1 orange. Remove tender but firm pear halves to large serving dish, top with whipped cream and sprinkle with chocolate decorettes or sweet chocolate, grated; serve as dessert. Yield: 6 portions.

PEARS CRÈME DE MENTHE

1½ cups sugar	green vegetable coloring
1 cup water	3 tablespoons Crème de Menthe
	6 pears

Boil sugar and water 5 minutes; add coloring to give desired green and flavor with Crème de Menthe. Add pears, peeled, halved and cored, bring to a boil and cook about 15 minutes, or until tender, transparent and tinted an emerald green; drain and serve hot or cold with lamb or mutton. Bartlett, Seckel or winter pears may be used. Yield: 6 portions.

PERSIMMONS

The Japanese persimmon is green, hard and puckery when picked; as it ripens, it loses its astringency and hardness and becomes soft and sweet. To serve raw, wash, cut off flower end, cut in half and serve one whole or half to a person; the inner soft flesh is eaten with a spoon. Garnish with a tiny sprig of mint placed in the center of each half, if desired. Pieces of persimmon may be used as garnish on fruit salads or desserts; it is delicious served with orange or grapefruit.

PERSIMMON MOUSSE

1½ cups ripe persimmon pulp   ¼ cup sugar (about)
¼ cup diced orange   dash of salt
½ cup diced canned pineapple   1 tablespoon lemon juice
                1 cup evaporated milk, whipped

Select four to six very ripe persimmons. Wash, dry, cut away from
stem. Carefully strip off thin skin, quarter, discarding pit and any
black specks. Put pulp through a sieve and measure. Combine persimmon pulp, orange, pineapple, sugar, salt and lemon juice; gently
blend, not to destroy the delicate persimmon flavor. Fold in whipped
milk. Pour into a refrigerator tray, setting the control for lowest temperature. Freeze. Approximate yield: 6 portions.

PINEAPPLE

Square-shouldered pineapples are slightly more economical than long
tapering ones. Spines pull easily from ripe fruit; wash and cut around
crown, or twist top leaves until crown comes off. Stand upright on
board and with sharp, long-bladed knife, cut off rind, working from
top down; remove "eyes" with small pointed knife. Cut in pieces or
shred, sprinkle with sugar and place in refrigerator to chill thoroughly;
sugar will dissolve in the juice as it stands. One medium-sized pineapple makes 5 to 6 portions.

Pineapple Rings—Lay pared pineapple on side on board and cut in
½- to ¾-inch slices; if "eyes" have not been removed, cut them out
from each slice; remove hard core.

Pineapple Wedges or Cubes—Cut pineapple slices in wedge-shaped
pieces or cubes, removing core.

Pineapple Spears or Sticks—Stand pared pineapple upright on board,
remove "eyes" and cut in half lengthwise, then in quarters. Remove
core from each piece, cut in ½- to ¾-inch strips and divide each in half.

Shredded Pineapple—Stand pared pineapple upright on board and
remove eyes; put fork through top and hold firmly with left hand.
With another fork in right hand, scrape pulp from core, cutting it off
with knife, if necessary.

BRANDIED PLUM SAUCE

Stew washed plums or prunes in water to cover about 10 minutes, or
until soft, adding sugar to taste when half done; to 1½ cups sauce, add
2 tablespoons brandy and serve on ice cream or other desserts.

PINEAPPLE CONES

Wash and dry pineapple; cut or twist off crown. With sharp knife, cut around each "eye" to core, making a pointed piece; pull resulting wedge-shaped piece away from core; or loosen and pull out wedge-shaped piece with a sharp-tined, strong fork. Leave rind on each piece and arrange 6 to 8 pieces on each plate around a mound of confectioners' sugar.

PLUM SURPRISE

2 large oranges   ¼ cup honey
12 plums   ½ cup shredded coconut
                1 cup heavy cream, whipped

Peel oranges and cut each in 6 slices. Cut plums in quarters, removing pits; roll in honey, then in coconut. Arrange a slice of orange on each of 6 dessert plates; place 4 plum quarters on top and top with cream. Cover with orange slice, top with cream and garnish dish with 4 plum quarters. Yield: 6 portions.

BAKED QUINCES

Use ripe quinces, deep yellow in color; wash, pare, cut in halves, remove cores and place, hollow side up, in buttered baking pan or heat-proof dish. Boil peelings and cores in water to cover for 20 minutes; drain liquid. Fill each half with ½ tablespoon sugar, place one orange slice on top, pour 2 tablespoons quince liquid over fruit and bake, covered, in slow oven (300° F.) 3 hours, or until soft and a deep red. Remove cover, dust thickly with macaroon crumbs, dot with butter and brown quickly in hot oven (400° F.) 5 minutes. Allow one quince per portion.

DRIED FRUITS

Dried fruits with a tough skin are generally soaked in water 2 to 12 hours to plump before cooking, using 3 to 4 cups water to each cup of fruit; if hot (not boiling) water is used, the fruit is plump in 2 to 3 hours. Fruits with thin skin and soft flesh need not be soaked.

Cook dried fruits slowly in the water in which they have been soaked; cover and simmer (do not boil), until fruit is plump and tender, adding sugar to taste when nearly done.

POMEGRANATES WITH HONEY

Wash 1 pomegranate and cut off a portion of the rind. Break the fruit in half and then in sections. With the fingers or a spoon shuck out the ruby-like seeds, discarding the membrane. Mix the seeds with 1 teaspoon of honey and ¼ cup coarsely cut nut meats. Chill and serve in stemmed sherbet glasses. Approximate yield: 2 portions.

STEWED APRICOTS

Pick over apricots and wash thoroughly; soak in hot water to cover for 2 hours; simmer, covered, 15 to 20 minutes, or until tender; add sugar to taste when nearly done. Allow 4 to 6 apricot halves per portion.

STEWED RHUBARB

Cut off leaves and stem end and wash 1 pound rhubarb. Peel old rhubarb stalks but do not peel young tender stalks, as the peels turn pink on cooking; cut in 1 inch pieces. Add ¼ cup water and ½ cup sugar and simmer, covered, 25 to 30 minutes, or until tender. Add a dash of cinnamon, if desired. Approximate yield: 4 portions.

STEWED PRUNES

Soak prunes covered with boiling water 1 hour or until plump. Simmer plumped prunes 15 to 20 minutes, or until tender, adding sugar to taste when nearly done. A few drops of lemon juice or a piece of orange rind may be cooked with fruit for flavor. Large partially plump or fancy prunes may be prepared without cooking; wash well, cover with boiling water and let stand, covered, in warm place 2 to 3 hours; they are plump and delicate; add sugar, if desired. Prunes soaked in Claret overnight, cooked until tender and chilled thoroughly, make an attractive dessert. Allow 6 to 8 prunes per portion.

Cereals

NOT MANY of us pause to give thanks for our morning breakfast cereal. We take it as much for granted as the orange juice and toast that accompany it. Thanks to Ceres, goddess of agriculture, we have a nutritious and inexpensive food available in many forms such as wheat, oats, rye, corn, barley and rice, either the whole or cracked grain, flaked, rolled, processed and ready-to-serve.

Storage of Cereals. With so many varieties from which to choose, several kinds of cereal can be kept on hand to be used as needed. Bulk cereals should be stored in airtight containers in a cool, dry place. Packaged cereals, when tightly covered, keep well in their original containers. In warm weather, it is wise to purchase cereals in small amounts because the fat in cereals, which contains the germ, readily turns rancid; and there is always the possibility that weevils may develop from eggs laid in raw cereals.

Cereals in the Diet. Cereals are valuable in the diet as an economical source of energy, minerals and vitamins (thiamine, riboflavin and niacin). They also supply proteins, though not of as good quality as the proteins of milk and meat. When cereals are used with milk, however, the proteins of the milk make up any deficiency in the cereal grains.

The "instant" cereals for infants and young children are especially nutritious, because they are enriched with added vitamins and minerals, too, chiefly in the form of calcium and iron.

Cooking of Cereals. Quick-cooking cereals are decided timesavers. Experiments seem to prove that the quick-cooking cereals retain the food value of the untreated grain.

Left-over Cereals. They can be used economically in many appetizing dishes. Cooked cereals may be substituted for part of the flour in quick breads; they may be added to steamed pudding mixtures, meat loaves, croquettes; when thick enough, they can be molded, sliced and fried and served with bacon or syrup, or made into individual molds, chilled and served with a sweet dessert sauce.

SERVICE SUGGESTIONS FOR COOKED CEREALS
(Allow ½ to ⅔ cup per portion)

Just before serving, stir in dried fruits such as sliced dates, figs, apricots, prunes, raisins or plumped currants (page 106).

Top servings with canned or cooked fruits such as apples, apricots, peaches, pears, pineapple, berries or cherries—sliced, diced or whole.

Serve with fresh fruit such as apricots, bananas, peaches or berries. Place fruit in bottom of dish and in alternate layers with cereal or sprinkle over serving.

Serve with a sprinkling of prepared cereals such as flaked cereals, grape-nuts, whole bran, bran flakes or wheat germ.

Turn creamy cereal into individual molds and chill. Unmold and serve cold with fruit sauce or fresh fruit and cream.

SCRAPPLE

Add small pieces of fresh pork to cornmeal while cooking mush, using from 1 to 2 cups pork to 1 cup cornmeal; season highly with salt and pepper. Add powdered herbs or sage, if desired. Mold in loaf pan rinsed with cold water and cover to prevent crust from forming; chill overnight. When ready to use, cut in ¼ inch slices and sauté in bacon fat or butter until crisp and nicely browned on both sides; serve as main breakfast dish on a cold morning. Before sautéing, slices may be dipped in cornmeal, or in slightly beaten egg diluted with 1 tablespoon water, then in fine dry crumbs or cornmeal. Yield: 8 to 10 portions.

Salmon Scrapple—To 4 cups hot cornmeal mush, add 2 cups (1 can) flaked salmon. Season with salt and pepper and pour into mold. Left-over fish may be used instead of salmon.

Chestnut Scrapple—Cook mush, using 1 cup cornmeal and ½ cup hominy. While hot, stir in 2 cups blanched, ground chestnuts.

Tomato and Nut Scrapple—To 2 cups hot cornmeal mush, add ¾ cup chopped nuts and ½ cup chili sauce.

FRIED CORNMEAL MUSH

Pack cooked cereal such as cornmeal, oatmeal, or finely ground wheat cereal in straight-sided loaf pan rinsed with cold water; mush must be thick to mold. Cover to prevent crust from forming. When firm and cold, cut in ¼ inch slices and sauté in bacon fat or butter until crisp and nicely browned on both sides. Serve hot with butter and syrup, honey or jelly, or with crisp bacon or small sausages. For a crisper crust, dip slices in cornmeal, then sauté. Two cups of mush will yield about 4 portions.

SPECIAL CEREAL DISHES

STRAINED CEREALS, gruels and cereal jelly, the latter served hot or cold, plain or sweetened, with cream or milk, or a simple sauce, are valuable adjuncts to the diets of infants, convalescents, semi-invalids and old people. Arrowroot, generically not a cereal, is often included in the diets of infants and invalids. It may be used in the proportion of 2 tablespoons of arrowroot to 1½ cups of liquid, in blanc mange and many simple puddings.

OATMEAL JELLY

½ cup oatmeal   3 cups boiling water
1 teaspoon salt   1 cup whole milk

Add oatmeal and salt to water and boil 5 minutes, stirring constantly; then cook over boiling water 4 hours. Add milk and strain through fine sieve; turn into mold rinsed with cold water. When cold, unmold and serve with sugar and milk or cream, if desired. If preferred hot, reheat; it will be a very thick purée. Quick-cooking oats may be used for speed. Approximate yield: 4 portions.

OATMEAL GRUEL

Use recipe for Oatmeal Jelly (page 110); when cooked, strain through fine sieve and add hot milk or light cream as desired. One to 2 tablespoons Sherry or Port added to gruel make it delicious.

READY-TO-SERVE CEREALS

Ready-to-serve cereals have been precooked and they may be flaked, toasted, shredded, puffed, or coarsely ground; they may be made from a cereal such as corn, rice and wheat, or a mixture of products. They should be served fresh and crisp. Damp weather often causes dry cereals to become limp. To crisp dry cereals, spread on shallow baking pan and heat in moderate oven (350° F.) about 5 minutes. Serve with cream or rich milk and sugar; fresh or stewed fruit may be served with cereal. Allow ⅔ to 1 cup or 1 individual package a portion.

Some ready-to-serve cereals such as shredded wheat, krumbles or grape-nuts, may be served as hot cereals; crush, moisten with hot milk or water, and heat over boiling water 5 to 10 minutes.

Eggs, Milk and Cheese

IN THE old saying, "an apple a day, keeps the doctor away," "egg" could very well be substituted for "apple," because the egg rates so high in food value; it contains valuable proteins, vitamins, fat and minerals. It is impossible here to give all the delicious and tantalizing ways of cooking eggs—but you can carry on from these few simple, basic recipes.

Egg lore—You can read about egg buying in our section What To Buy. Store eggs unwashed in refrigerator. For best cooking results, remove from refrigerator one-half hour before using, so that eggs will be at room temperature. Eggs can be stored several weeks in a water-glass solution (wash before storing). For poaching, cooking or frying, fresh eggs are generally preferred. Best results are obtained in omelets with eggs two to three days old.

To get fluffy long-standing egg whites, add a dash of salt and ¼ teaspoon of cream of tartar to each two egg whites while beating. Be sure to have at room temperature. When directions call for stiffly beaten whites, beat until egg whites stand in peaks and tail slightly. Do not beat until dry and no longer shiny. Use immediately.

DRIED EGGS

DRIED whole eggs, apart from use as an ingredient in cooked dishes, can be served as scrambled eggs, using 3 parts water to 1 part egg powder. They should be well seasoned and turned constantly. Care in storage is necessary, since powdered eggs tend to deteriorate quickly. Cover well and keep in the refrigerator once they are opened.

Today, powdered whole eggs and egg yolks are used by bakers and candy manufacturers. Powdered egg whites are also important commercially. They are a handy item on the emergency shelf, for camping trips and general cooking.

COOKING WITH DRIED EGGS

DRIED WHOLE EGGS can be used in two ways. They may be reconstituted by adding water (see table below), then used in recipes just as shell eggs are used. This method is recommended for light, delicate butter cakes (page 628), omelets and scrambled eggs. Or they may be added in powdered form with the dry ingredients. Use dried eggs this way in making quick breads, popovers (page 140), griddle cakes and cookies. But remember to increase slightly the amount of liquid called for in any standard recipe. This must be done accurately. Add to the recipe just the amount of water required to reconstitute the number of eggs used in each recipe.

TABLE XIII
DRIED WHOLE EGGS FOR SHELL EGGS

Shell Eggs	equal	Whole Egg Powder	plus	Water
1		2 tablespoons		2½ tablespoons
2		¼ cup		5 tablespoons
3		6 tablespoons		½ cup
4		½ cup		⅔ cup
5		½ cup plus 2 tablespoons		¾ cup
6		¾ cup		1 cup less 1 tablespoon
7		¾ cup plus 2 tablespoons		1 cup plus 2 tablespoons
8		1 cup		1¼ cups

To cook dried whole eggs or yolks to add to salads, scalloped or creamed dishes, heat the reconstituted eggs over hot water. Season, cover and steam until firm. Cut into cubes and use like hard-cooked eggs.

When dried eggs have been mixed with water, they will keep no longer than fresh eggs removed from the shell.

Dried egg whites, now available chiefly for commercial use in bakeries, etc., can be reconstituted and whipped light to use in sponge cakes, angel food cakes, soufflés, meringues, etc.

CUSTARD WITH DRIED EGGS

6 tablespoons dried whole-egg powder, firmly packed
¼ cup sugar
¼ teaspoon salt
3 cups milk
½ cup water
1 teaspoon vanilla or almond extract
nutmeg

Sift together dried whole-egg powder, sugar and salt. Combine milk, water and flavoring. Add liquid to egg mixture, small amount at a time, and beat until smooth. Pour into custard cups. Sprinkle with nutmeg. Place in pan of hot water and bake in slow oven (325° F.) 40 to 50 minutes, or until knife inserted in the center comes out clean. Approximate yield: 6 portions.

LAYER CAKE WITH DRIED EGGS

⅔ cup shortening
1 cup sugar
6 tablespoons dried whole-egg powder, firmly packed
2 cups sifted cake flour
3 teaspoons double-acting baking powder
1 teaspoon salt
½ cup milk
7 tablespoons water
1 teaspoon vanilla

Cream shortening, gradually add sugar and cream until light and fluffy. Stir in dried whole eggs and blend thoroughly. Sift together dry ingredients. Add alternately with combined milk, water and vanilla to egg mixture. Stir only until batter is smooth. Pour into two prepared 8-inch cake pans. Bake in moderate oven (375° F.) 25 to 30 minutes. Frost as desired. Yield: 1 layer cake (8-inch).

SOFT–COOKED EGGS

Slip eggs from spoon into pan of boiling water. Water must cover eggs. Cover pan and just simmer for 3 to 5 minutes, depending on desired consistency.

To prevent cracking—Allow eggs to stand at room temperature for 30 minutes or place eggs in lukewarm water for about 5 minutes before cooking.

POPOVERS WITH DRIED EGGS

1 cup milk
1 tablespoon shortening, melted
7 tablespoons water

1 cup flour
6 tablespoons dried whole-egg powder, firmly packed

½ teaspoon salt

Preheat oven to 450° F. Combine milk, shortening and water. Sift together remaining ingredients. Combine with liquid ingredients and beat with rotary egg beater for 2 minutes or until batter is smooth. Preheat well-greased custard cups or popover pans. Fill cups ⅓ full of batter. Bake in hot oven (450° F.) 15 minutes, reduce oven temperature to 350° F. and continue baking 20 to 25 minutes. Yield: 8 to 10.

OMELET WITH DRIED EGGS

1 cup water
¾ cup dried whole-egg powder, firmly packed
⅓ cup milk

½ teaspoon salt
dash of pepper
¼ teaspoon Worcestershire sauce
2 tablespoons ham or bacon fat

Add water gradually to dried eggs, beating constantly with rotary egg beater. Add milk and seasonings and continue to beat until smooth. Melt fat in skillet, add egg mixture and cook over low heat. Lift edges and tip pan during cooking to allow uncovered egg to run underneath until omelet is cooked through and lightly browned. Yield: 4 to 6 portions. Variation: Add 1 tablespoon finely chopped onion, green pepper or celery; ½ cup grated cheese or 1 teaspoon dried herbs, crumbled; or 1 cup chopped cooked meat such as smoked turkey or chicken, or cooked vegetables to the egg before it is cooked.

CODDLED EGGS

Use enough water to cover eggs; bring to a boil, then turn off or remove from heat. Carefully slip each egg into water with a tablespoon, cover kettle and let stand 7 to 10 minutes, depending on desired consistency.

HARD–COOKED EGGS

Follow directions for soft-cooked eggs (see above); cook below boiling point for 15 to 20 minutes, then plunge eggs into cold water to prevent or reduce the formation of the dark ring likely to appear where the egg white and yolk meet. The shell is peeled easily from quickly cooled eggs, or eggs cooked in salted water, using 1 tablespoon salt to each quart of water.

MOLDED CHOPPED EGGS

4 hard-cooked eggs, chopped   ¼ teaspoon pepper
salt   ¼ cup butter, melted

Combine chopped eggs with salt to taste, pepper and butter; put in well-greased individual molds and press firmly. Cover with waxed paper and chill; this makes a pleasing garnish for many salads. Approximate yield: 4 small molds.

POACHED EGGS

Oil bottom of heavy shallow pan. Add 1 tablespoon salt to each quart of water and bring to a boil. Break egg first into small dish, then from dish quickly slip into boiling water; cover, reduce heat and let stand 3 to 5 minutes, or until white is firm and a white film covers the yolk. Remove eggs with skimmer or perforated spatula or spoon, and place on hot buttered toast and season with salt and pepper; serve at once.

To keep eggs round, cook in a greased egg poacher or slip eggs into greased rings placed on bottom of pan.

To poach eggs in the shape of balls, sometimes called the French method, use a large deep pan and stir the boiling salted and acidulated water with a circular motion until a vortex is formed, then drop egg into hollow, reduce heat and stir enough to keep water in circular motion. Only one egg can be poached at a time. Let stand in warm water until ready for serving.

Eggs may be poached in milk (scalded), tomato sauce, meat or vegetable stock. Use as little liquid as possible and pour liquid, slightly thickened, over eggs.

Eggs with Corned Beef Hash—Form patties of Corned Beef Hash and arrange on serving plate; place a hot poached egg on each and garnish with parsley or water cress.

Chicken and Eggs—Mix together equal amounts of chopped cooked chicken and fried mushrooms; season and heat thoroughly. Heap on slices of buttered toast and place a poached egg on each.

Eggs Benedict—Split English muffin or use 3-inch bread rounds; toast, butter and cover each with a thin slice of broiled ham cut to fit. Place poached egg on top and serve with Hollandaise Sauce (page 473). Mushroom caps that have been broiled with butter may be added.

POACHED EGG SOUFFLÉ

3 tablespoons butter	dash cayenne pepper
3 tablespoons flour	½ teaspoon dry mustard
¾ cup milk	4 egg yolks, beaten
4 tablespoons Parmesan cheese	5 egg whites, beaten
2 ounces Camembert cheese	6 teaspoons sour cream
½ teaspoon salt	6 eggs

bread crumbs

Melt butter and gradually stir in flour. Slowly add milk, stirring constantly, and cook until smooth and thickened. Add Parmesan cheese and Camembert cheese that has been put through a strainer, salt, pepper, mustard and egg yolks. Mix and let stand over hot water until cheese is melted. Remove from heat. Carefully fold in egg whites which have been beaten stiff but not dry. Lightly grease bottom of a 1-quart baking dish and sprinkle with a thin layer of dry bread crumbs. Pour in one-half of cheese mixture and make 6 depressions with the back of a spoon. In each depression place a teaspoon of sour cream and an uncooked egg. Cover with remaining cheese mixture and top with a light layer of dry bread crumbs. Bake in a slow oven (325° F.) 45 minutes or until done. Approximate yield: 6 portions.

TABASCO EGGS

1 cup light cream	1 teaspoon butter
8 drops Tabasco sauce	1 teaspoon chopped chives
½ teaspoon salt	5 eggs

5 slices buttered hot toast

Scald cream with Tabasco, salt, butter and chives; drop eggs, one at a time, into hot cream mixture, basting, but not stirring, until whites are firm. Serve on toast. Yield: 5 portions.

BURGUNDY EGGS

4 eggs, poached	¼ cup grated cheese
¼ cup dry bread crumbs	salt and paprika

½ cup Brown Sauce (page 467)

Place poached eggs in buttered shallow baking dish which has been dusted with 2 tablespoons each crumbs and cheese, salt and paprika. Pour sauce over eggs and dust with remaining 2 tablespoons each crumbs and cheese. Place under preheated broiler about 5 minutes, or until cheese is melted. Yield: 4 portions.

POACHED EGGS WITH LOBSTER SAUCE

3 tablespoons butter
3 tablespoons flour
½ cup light chicken or fish
    stock
½ teaspoon salt
dash cayenne pepper

¼ cup light cream
1 can lobster or 1 small, cooked
    lobster (1 pound)
1 egg yolk
1 tablespoon milk
2 teaspoons chopped parsley

6 poached eggs

Melt butter and slowly stir in flour. Gradually add chicken or fish stock, stirring constantly. Cook until smooth and thickened. Add seasonings and cream, lobster, and egg yolk mixed with milk. Combine and bring to a boil. Add parsley and serve over eggs poached 3½ minutes. Yield: 6 portions.

SCRAMBLED EGGS

4 eggs
½ teaspoon salt

⅛ teaspoon pepper
¼ cup milk or light cream

4 teaspoons butter

Beat eggs until whites and yolks are well mixed; add salt and pepper and stir in milk. Melt butter in frying pan, saucepan, or top part of double boiler; add egg mixture and cook over low heat or boiling water, stirring constantly to move the cooked portion from the bottom and sides of pan, this forming soft, creamy flakes. Serve at once; if left in pan, eggs continue to cook. For a custard type of scrambled eggs, stir mixture constantly until thick but not dry and firm. Serve with broiled mushrooms or bacon, or sausage if desired. To increase recipe, use 1 tablespoon milk and 1 teaspoon butter for each egg. Approximate yield: 4 portions.

Chipped Beef Scramble—Add 2 tablespoons chipped beef to egg-milk mixture; chopped fried sausage may be substituted for beef.

Egg with Mushroom Soup—Substitute ½ cup undiluted mushroom soup and ¼ cup warm water for milk; serve with crisp slices of bacon.

Spinach Scrambled Eggs—Add ½ cup drained, seasoned chopped spinach to egg-milk mixture as it begins to cook.

Celery Scrambled Eggs—Cook ½ cup diced celery in 2 tablespoons butter or bacon fat until lightly browned; add egg-milk mixture and scramble.

Eggs Ranchero—Cook ½ small onion, minced, and ¼ cup minced green pepper in butter until lightly browned. Add egg-milk mixture and scramble; turn into hot dish and sprinkle with 2 tablespoons grated American cheese.

FRIED EGGS

Melt 1 tablespoon butter or bacon fat or ham drippings in frying pan for each egg; break egg into small dish and then slip from dish into pan. Cook slowly until firm, spooning fat over eggs to cook the tops; or cover and cook for 3 to 5 minutes, or until tops are cooked by steam and yolks covered by a white film. To cook eggs on both sides, omit basting, turn with pancake turner or broad spatula when white is partially firm and cook until set. Sprinkle with salt and pepper.

BACON AND EGGS

Slowly panbroil slices of bacon until crisp; remove and drain on absorbent paper. Drain excess fat from frying pan, slip eggs into pan and cook slowly until firm, basting occasionally with fat in pan.

HAM AND EGGS

Panbroil slice of ham in hot frying pan; remove to hot platter. Slip eggs into pan and cook slowly until firm, basting occasionally with fat in pan; arrange around ham. Or serve each egg on a slice of broiled tomato or pineapple and arrange around ham.

FRENCH FRIED EGGS

Heat about 2 tablespoons fat in a small frying pan. Slip egg from saucer into pan, tilting it so that fat is deep; with spoon or knife, curl the white up around the yolk, making a nest with a white ruffle, to keep yolk soft.

BAKED OR SHIRRED EGGS

Place 1 tablespoon cream in a buttered ramekin or custard cup; break an egg into each, sprinkle with salt and pepper and place on baking sheet or in shallow pan. Bake in moderate oven (350° F.) for 15 to 20 minutes, or until eggs are firm.

Baked Eggs au Gratin—Sprinkle seasoned, buttered bread crumbs over eggs before baking.

Baked Eggs with Cheese—Sprinkle grated cheese over eggs before baking; or sprinkle lightly with bread crumbs, then with cheese.

Baked Eggs à la Bercy—Line ramekins (small individual heatproof dishes) with thin slices of cooked pork sausage; substitute 1 tablespoon tomato sauce flavored with onion for cream and sprinkle with buttered bread crumbs.

Baked Eggs à la Rossini—Line ramekins with slices of sautéed chicken livers; substitute 1 tablespoon Cider and Truffle Sauce for cream and sprinkle with buttered bread crumbs.

BAKED EGGS IN BACON RINGS

6 slices bacon	6 eggs	6 tea rusks

Partially panbroil bacon and fit around sides of muffin pans, using one slice for each cup; break one egg into each cup and bake in moderate oven (350° F.) about 12 minutes, or until eggs are firm. Serve immediately on hot buttered tea rusks. Yield: 6 portions.

BAKED EGGS IN MACARONI

1 tablespoon butter	½ cup grated cheese
1 tablespoon flour	1 teaspoon salt
1 cup milk, or ½ cup evaporated milk diluted with ½ cup water	¼ teaspoon pepper
	2 cups hot cooked macaroni
	4 eggs

Melt butter and stir in flour; gradually add milk, stirring constantly until smooth and thickened. Cook 1 minute. Add cheese and seasonings and cook until cheese is melted. Place macaroni in buttered baking dish; cover with cheese sauce, make four hollows and drop an egg in each depression. Bake in moderate oven (350° F.) about 15 minutes, or until eggs are firm. Yield: 4 portions.

BAKED EGGS IN RICE

3 cups hot cooked rice	6 eggs
½ cup grated cheese	2 tablespoons butter
	salt and pepper

Pack rice in well-greased individual ring molds; let stand about ½ hour, then unmold. Sprinkle cheese over rice and place in moderate oven (375° F.) until cheese is melted. Drop an egg in center of each, dot with butter and season with salt and pepper. Return to oven and bake for 15 to 20 minutes, or until eggs are firm. Yield: 6 portions.

BAKED TOMATO AND EGG

Grease muffin pans and put one thick slice of unpeeled tomato in each cup; season with salt and pepper. Break one egg in each prepared cup and again season with salt and pepper; place a small piece of butter on top of each egg. Bake in moderate oven (350° F.) about 15 minutes, or until egg is firm. Serve on rounds of toast and garnish with parsley; 1 or 2 eggs on tomatoes make an unusual, quickly prepared summer dish. If desired, use one tomato for each egg; peel, cut off top, scoop out centers; sprinkle with salt; break egg into each.

FLUFFY OMELET

4 eggs, separated

¼ cup milk

½ teaspoon salt

1 tablespoon butter

dash of pepper

parsley

Beat egg yolks until thick and lemon-colored; add seasonings and milk; fold into egg whites which have been beaten stiff but not dry. Turn into buttered, hot 9-inch frying or omelet pan and cook over low heat 3 to 5 minutes, or until omelet puffs up and is browned on bottom. (Test by raising edge of omelet with spatula.) Place in moderate oven (350° F.) 5 to 10 minutes, or until top springs back when pressed with finger. Cut about 1 inch incisions at opposite sides and crease down through center in line with cuts; then fold carefully on crease by slipping spatula under half of omelet to fold over. Slip onto hot platter and garnish with parsley; if an omelet pan is used, merely fold over; omelet will shrink slightly when removed from pan. Serve at once. Approximate yield: 6 portions.

Cheese Omelet—Add 1 tablespoon Worcestershire sauce, ¼ cup grated cheese and 2 tablespoons chopped parsley to egg yolk-milk mixture; or omit parsley and sprinkle grated cheese over omelet while it is cooking.

Cottage Cheese Omelet—Add from ½ to 1 cup cottage cheese and 2 tablespoons finely chopped pimiento to egg yolk-milk mixture.

Rice Omelet—Add ¼ cup cooked rice and dash of tomato ketchup to egg yolk-milk mixture.

Bacon or Ham Omelet—Sprinkle about ¼ cup chopped broiled bacon or minced ham over omelet while it is cooking, or sprinkle over omelet just before folding.

Marmalade Omelet—Heat ¼ cup orange or grapefruit marmalade, or any tart jelly or jam, and spread over omelet just before folding; dust top with confectioners' sugar, if desired.

Chicken Omelet—Sprinkle 1 cup diced cooked chicken over omelet just before folding, or fold and serve creamed chicken over omelet.

Mushroom Omelet—Sauté ½ pound mushrooms, sliced, in 2 tablespoons butter. Serve around omelet.

Apricot Omelet—Omit pepper and add 1½ teaspoons grated orange rind; substitute orange juice and 1½ teaspoons lemon juice for milk. Spread ¼ cup cooked apricot pulp over omelet just before folding; dust top with 1 tablespoon confectioners' sugar. Use canned or dried apricots. Approximate yield: 4 portions.

Bacon and Cheese Omelet—Add ½ cup bran flakes to milk and let stand while beating egg yolks; substitute ½ teaspoon nutmeg for pepper; add ½ cup diced, panbroiled Canadian bacon to egg yolk-milk mixture. Sprinkle ¼ cup grated cheese over partially cooked omelet when placing it in oven. Garnish omelet with slices of panbroiled Canadian bacon. Approximate yield: 5 portions.

LAMB KIDNEY OMELET

Skin and slice 2 lamb kidneys; soak in cold water 30 minutes. Drain; sauté in 2 tablespoons butter. Prepare Fluffy Omelet (page 120), spreading kidneys over top just before folding omelet. Sprinkle minced chives over top. Yield: 4 portions.

NEVER-FAIL OMELET

2 tablespoons quick-cooking tapioca	¾ cup milk
	1 tablespoon butter or margarine
¾ teaspoon salt	4 egg whites
⅛ teaspoon pepper	4 egg yolks

Combine tapioca, salt, pepper and milk in saucepan. Place over medium heat and cook until mixture comes to a full boil, stirring constantly. Add butter. Remove from heat and allow to cool slightly while beating eggs. Beat egg whites until stiff. Beat egg yolks until thick and lemon-colored. Add tapioca mixture to egg yolks and mix well. Fold into egg whites. Turn into hot, buttered, 10-inch skillet. Cook over low heat 3 minutes. Then bake in moderate oven (350° F.) 15 to 18 minutes. Omelet is sufficiently cooked when a knife inserted comes out clean. Cut across at right angles to handle of pan, being careful not to cut all the way through. Fold from handle to opposite side and serve on hot platter. Yield: 4 to 6 portions.

FRENCH OMELET

4 eggs	2 teaspoons cold water
2 tablespoons butter	½ teaspoon salt
	dash of pepper

Use a pan of cast iron or cast aluminum for best results. Heat and test it with a very small amount of butter. The butter should foam but not brown when pan is at the right temperature. Beat eggs with cold water, salt and pepper. Add butter to hot pan, then the egg mixture and cook over moderate heat. As omelet cooks, lift edges toward center and tip pan so that the uncooked mixture flows under the cooked portion. When bottom is browned, sprinkle parsley over top. Fold over and slip onto hot platter. Serve at once. Yield: 4 portions.

Herb Omelet—Just before adding eggs to the pan, place 1 tablespoon freshly chopped parsley and chives (fresh tarragon and fresh thyme may be used if desired) in the pan with 1 teaspoon chopped onion and garlic mixed. Pour on the egg mixture and finish as in recipe above.

Chopped Spinach and Sour Cream Omelet—Mix 3 tablespoons cooked, chopped spinach with parsley and 1 tablespoon sour cream to moisten and a little salt and pepper; then fill into the French Omelet before folding over.

Spanish Omelet—Serve omelet with Spanish Sauce (page 470); serve sauce around or over omelet. Approximate yield: 4 portions.

Vegetable Omelet—Place ½ cup bread crumbs and 3 tablespoons butter in frying pan and sauté until crisp and brown, stirring constantly. Add browned crumbs with ½ cup finely grated carrots and 2 teaspoons minced parsley to omelet mixture. Melt 1 tablespoon additional butter in frying pan, add omelet-vegetable mixture and cook as directed. Serve with Cheese Sauce (page 470). Approximate yield: 4 portions.

Rum Omelet—Omit water and pepper and use ⅛ teaspoon salt; add 1½ teaspoons powdered sugar and 1⅓ tablespoons rum to beaten eggs; cook as directed. Pour 4 tablespoons rum around omelet on platter; ignite rum and serve at once. Sprinkle omelet with sugar, if desired. Approximate yield: 3 portions.

DEVILED EGGS

4 hard-cooked eggs
2 tablespoons grated cheese
¼ teaspoon dry mustard

salt and cayenne
1 teaspoon vinegar
1 tablespoon butter, melted
milk

Cut eggs in halves lengthwise. Remove yolks, mash or force through sieve, and add cheese, seasonings, vinegar, butter and enough milk to moisten. Fill egg whites and put halves together; wrap in waxed paper and chill, if served cold! Yield: 4 stuffed eggs.

Eggs Stuffed with Ham—Cut hard-cooked eggs in halves lengthwise; remove yolks, mash and mix with an equal amount of minced ham. Season and moisten with mayonnaise. Pile into egg whites.

Tuna Stuffed Eggs—Use 6 hard-cooked eggs. Combine mashed yolks with 1 7-ounce can tuna fish, mashed, ¼ cup creamed butter and season with black pepper and cayenne. Combine 2 cups cooked pea purée, salt, pepper and curry powder to taste. Pile egg yolk-tuna mixture in six egg halves; pile pea-purée mixture in remaining halves. Yield: 6 portions.

Deviled Egg Garnish—Combine mashed egg yolks with 1 tablespoon mayonnaise, few drops Tabasco sauce, ½ teaspoon horseradish, 1½ tablespoons lemon juice and 1 tablespoon minced celery. Refill whites, leaving surface roughened, and serve filled half as garnish.

Hot Filled Eggs—Sauté ¾ cup chopped mushrooms and 2 teaspoons parsley in 1 tablespoon butter; then combine with mashed egg yolks and 2 tablespoons chili sauce; season with ½ teaspoon salt and cayenne. Heap mixture into whites and arrange in greased baking dish; pour one can of tomato sauce over eggs and sprinkle with 2 tablespoons grated Parmesan cheese. Bake in hot oven (425° F.) about 15 minutes, or until heated. Approximate yield: 4 portions.

SOUTHERN CHICKEN CUSTARD

1 cup strong chicken broth
1 cup light cream

6 egg yolks, or 3 eggs, beaten
salt and pepper

Scald broth and cream and stir into egg yolks; season to taste with salt and pepper and pour into custard cups. Set cups in pan of hot water and bake in moderate oven (350° F.) about 40 minutes, or until knife inserted in center comes out clean. Serve warm with water cress sandwiches as a luncheon or Sunday night supper dish. Approximate yield: 6 portions.

EGG FRITTERS CARMELITE

4 hard-cooked eggs   cayenne
2 slices liverwurst, ¼ inch   1 egg, beaten
   thick   ¼ cup dry bread crumbs
salt   3 tablespoons butter

Cut shelled eggs in half lengthwise. Remove yolks and rub through strainer. Mash liverwurst, combine with egg yolks and season with salt and cayenne to taste. Blend well and refill eggs. Press two halves together. Dip filled eggs into beaten egg. Roll in bread crumbs. Sauté breaded eggs in hot butter until golden brown. Serve hot topped with Hollandaise Sauce (page 473). Approximate yield: 4 portions. Eggs may be stuffed with tuna fish instead of liverwurst, if desired.

CREAMED EGGS

6 hard-cooked eggs   2 tablespoons tomato ketchup
2 cups Medium White Sauce   6 slices hot buttered toast
   (page 125)

Cut eggs lengthwise in eighths; heat gently in white sauce seasoned with ketchup; serve on toast. Approximate yield: 6 portions.

Eggs Goldenrod—Cut hard-cooked eggs lengthwise in halves; cut egg whites in long slices and add to sauce. Serve on slices of hot toast. Force egg yolks through sieve and scatter over whites; garnish with toast points.

Eggs à la King—Add 1 cup sliced cooked mushrooms, ½ cup peas and 1 canned pimiento, cut in strips, to creamed eggs and heat thoroughly. On each round of hot buttered toast, place a slice of tomato, fresh or broiled, and pour creamed mixture over all; garnish with parsley.

Fricassee Eggs—Place small slices of broiled bacon or boiled ham on hot toast; arrange sliced eggs, sautéed in 3 tablespoons butter, on top and pour sauce over all; garnish with parsley.

Eggs Delmonico—Substitute Cream Sauce for white sauce; sauté 8 mushroom caps, sliced, in 1 tablespoon butter and add to sauce with 1 canned pimiento, cut in strips. Add sliced eggs and ½ to 1 cup grated American cheese and cook over hot water until cheese is melted, stirring constantly.

MILK

THAT milk is a splendid source of food value cannot be overemphasized. Cheap compared to other essential foods, it should be used daily by the whole family. A pint a day is recommended for adults, a quart for children. Part of this can be used in cooking. There are few rules for the use of milk. It scorches easily, so heat in a double boiler or place over low heat. A cover will prevent the scum from forming. Store covered in the coldest part of the refrigerator.

THIN WHITE SAUCE

1 tablespoon butter
1 tablespoon flour
½ teaspoon salt
⅛ teaspoon pepper
1 cup milk, rich milk or light
cream

Use as base for cream soups, thin cheese sauce and other sauces.

Medium White Sauce—Same recipe as Thin White Sauce, using 2 tablespoons butter and 2 tablespoons flour. Use for gravies, creamed dishes and scalloped dishes. Substitute stock for all or part of milk in meat gravies.

Thick White Sauce—Same recipe as Thin White Sauce, using 4 tablespoons butter and 4 tablespoons flour. Use for soufflés and croquettes.

METHODS FOR MAKING WHITE SAUCE AND GRAVIES

Method I—Melt butter and then stir in flour until smooth. Gradually add milk and stir constantly until mixture boils and thickens. Then cook about 3 minutes longer, stirring occasionally. Add seasonings. Place over hot water to keep hot and cover tightly to prevent skin forming on top. Yield: 1 cup.

Method II—Use when the amount of fat is less than the flour or when no fat is used. Heat about ¾ of milk in double boiler. Stir cold milk into flour to make a smooth paste; stir gradually into hot liquid. Stirring constantly, bring to a boil and cook until thickened. Return to double boiler and cook 3 minutes, stirring occasionally. Yield: 1 cup.

DRIED MILK

DRIED milk is convenient to use; it is as nutritious as the fresh milk; it can be stored on the shelf for instant use; and best of all for penny watchers—it saves on the food bill. Dry milk products are put up in two forms: nonfat dry milk solids (commonly called nonfat dry milk), and whole dry milk. Only water is removed from the skim and the whole milk to make these powdered milks. A pound package—about 4 cups—equals 4 quarts whole or skim fresh milk. *Two and one-half tablespoons of butter added to a quart of the reconstituted skim milk equals one quart fresh milk (2 teaspoons per cup).*

Easy to Measure and Mix: Open container; stir powder with spoon. Measure as you would baking powder. Sift dry ingredients for cakes and breads; stir into flour for gravy or sauce; or mix with cornstarch and sugar for puddings.

To mix, place powder on top of water in bowl or jar. Beat with a rotary beater or shake in a covered container until smooth. Mixing is speeded by having the water warm (not hot).

You can use milk powder in any recipe calling for milk. Follow the table below. For example, if you need 1 cup of milk, measure ¼ cup milk powder and 1 cup water. Mix the dry powder with the dry ingredients and add the water with the other liquids, or make the powder into fluid milk. You may add milk powder to fluid milk and milk beverages to put extra nourishment into them. Use as much as ½ to ¾ cup of milk powder to 1 cup of liquid in preparing soups, cereals and other foods.

Baking Tip: In baking, an extra amount of milk powder gives added nourishment and a richer browning.

This table shows how much milk powder to use to replace various amounts of bottled milk.

For	Use
1 quart milk	1 cup powder, 4 cups water
1 pint milk	½ cup powder, 2 cups water
1 cup milk	¼ cup powder, 1 cup water
½ cup milk	2 tablespoons powder, ½ cup water
¼ cup milk	1 tablespoon powder, ¼ cup water

HOW TO STORE

STORE milk powder in a cool dry place, preferably not warmer than 75° F. It will keep this way on a shelf several months. The nonfat dry milk keeps somewhat better than the whole milk powder.

If you put milk powder in the refrigerator, transfer it to an airtight jar or can.

Whenever these products are stored, be sure to keep the container tightly covered. Close it right after use. Milk powder takes up moisture and gets lumpy if exposed long to air.

Fluid milk made from milk powder and water needs to be kept cool, clean, and covered, just like any other fluid milk. Keep it in the refrigerator, if it is not used right after mixing.

WHITE SAUCE MADE WITH DRIED MILK

INGREDIENTS	THIN	MEDIUM	THICK
Fluid milk or water ....cup	1	1	1
Dry milk, whole or nonfat ....cup	¼	¼	¼
Flour ....tablespoons	1	2	3
Salt ....teaspoon	¼	¼	¼
Fat ....tablespoons	1	2	3

For added milk value: In medium white sauce use ½ cup milk powder and 1 tablespoon flour, in place of amounts given above. In thick sauce use ½ cup milk powder and 2 tablespoons flour.

Method 1—Pour liquid into a pan. Add dry ingredients. Beat until smooth. Add fat and cook over low heat or boiling water until thickened, stirring constantly.

Method 2—Melt fat. Remove from heat and blend in flour, then milk powder and salt. Add liquid all at once and stir until mixed. Cook as in Method 1. This method is for medium and thick white sauces only, since they have enough fat to moisten the dry ingredients.

Makes 1 cup.

Cheese Sauce—Add ½ cup grated cheese to white sauce after it is cooked. Stir until cheese is melted.

Parsley Sauce—To 1 cup medium white sauce add 2 or more tablespoons finely chopped parsley. Season with a few drops onion juice.

Egg Sauce—To 1 cup medium white sauce add 1 or 2 hard-cooked eggs, coarsely chopped.

MILK POWDER SPECIALS

Some things that milk-in-a-bottle can't do are easy for dry milk products. You can have extra milk in cooked cereals without extra liquid . . . a dessert topping much lower in calories than whipped cream . . . a milk-rich candy without long cooking. This means added calcium, vitamins, and protein where you least expect to find them.

COOKED BREAKFAST CEREAL

Put into a saucepan or top of double boiler enough uncooked breakfast cereal to make six servings when cooked. Add ¼ to ½ cup milk powder and mix well.

Add water or fluid milk and salt in the proportions indicated on the package. Stir until smooth. Cook over low heat or boiling water until done, stirring often.

Serve as usual.

WHIPPED TOPPING

½ cup water   ½ cup *nonfat* milk powder
1 tablespoon lemon juice   2 tablespoons sugar
                    ¼ teaspoon vanilla

Put water and lemon juice into a bowl and add the nonfat milk powder.

Beat with a rotary beater until stiff. Beat in sugar and vanilla.

Chill and use as you would whipped cream.

Makes about 2½ cups topping.

TUTTI-FRUTTI

1 cup sugar   ¼ cup raisins
½ cup water   ¼ cup chopped candied or well
¼ teaspoon salt   drained maraschino cherries
½ tablespoon corn syrup   ¼ cup broken nut meats
1 teaspoon table fat   ½ cup dry milk, whole or nonfat
                    ½ teaspoon vanilla

Combine sugar, water, salt, and corn syrup in a saucepan. Boil until the syrup forms a firm ball in cold water. If you use a candy thermometer, cook the syrup to 248° F.

Add fat, fruit, and nuts, and cool to lukewarm without stirring.

Add milk powder and vanilla. Stir until thoroughly mixed and creamy.

Quickly turn the candy into a greased pan, and when firm enough, cut in squares.

CHEESE

CHEESE in any language—"käse," "ost," "fromage," "formaggio," "queso"—stands for hospitality. It is one of the most widely used foods, being found alike in the cottage of the peasant and on the tables of large mansions.

As a food, cheese is very concentrated. A pound of average American or "store" cheese is equivalent in protein and butterfat value to a gallon of milk. Most cheeses are made from cows' milk, but some, like Roquefort, are made from sheep's milk, while goats' milk cheese is popular in the Scandinavian countries.

Cheese, rightly used, takes an important place in cookery. High temperatures and overcooking toughen cheese, so it should be cooked at low temperature over hot water, or in a slow to moderate oven when it is an ingredient in a baked dish.

French and Italian cooks have recognized the unique flavor that cheese gives to cooked dishes, since they use it liberally not only in soufflés and omelets, but on onion soup, spaghetti and even a chicken casserole. Grated Parmesan and Gruyère cheese are the favorites with continental cooks.

Buying Cheese. Always choose a reliable dealer, one who makes a quick turnover. The unprocessed or "natural" cheeses, as they are called, will keep fresh much longer if bought in one piece and not sliced. The processed or pasteurized cheeses should be kept in their original wrappings to prevent drying out and the growth of molds.

Storing Cheese. To keep the cut surface of "natural" hard cheese from drying, it can be rubbed with butter. Or, if the cheese is being used every day, tie a double thickness of waxed paper around it and hold firmly in place with string or a rubber band. If cheese drys out, soak in a small amount of milk.

The best place to store cheese is in a covered dish in a cool, dry room, or in the refrigerator. Soft cheeses, such as cream cheese and cottage cheese, are just as perishable as milk. They should be eaten fresh and stored the same way as milk—covered and in the refrigerator. For finest flavor, cheese should be at room temperature.

COMMON USES FOR POPULAR CHEESES

American Cheddar—An all-purpose cheese used in cooking for soufflés, fondues; used in sandwiches, or with desserts.

Blue (Bleu)—Use on cheese tray, with crackers or with salads.

Bel Paese—Serve with fruit or crackers.

Brick—Use for sandwiches, with cold cuts or on cheese tray.

Brie—Serve with fruit or in sandwiches.

Camembert—A dessert cheese. Serve it with fruit.

Chantelle—Slice and serve with cold cuts or with fruit and crackers.

Cream—Often used as recipe ingredient, with sandwich filling mixtures, or served with desserts.

Edam—Serve with fruit; cut off top and scoop out from center as used.

Gouda—Good with fruit or in salad.

Gorgonzola—Serve with fruit or add to tossed salad.

Liederkranz—Serve with crackers as accompaniment to fruit or salad.

Limburger—Good for sandwiches, particularly snack sandwiches on pumpernickel or other dark bread to serve with beer.

Muenster—Good for dark bread sandwiches or for canapés.

Neufchatel—Use as sandwich spread, with crackers, salad.

Parmesan—Use grated in soufflé, in spaghetti sauce or in soup.

Swiss—Use with plate of cold cuts or in sandwiches.

Processed Cheeses—Should be kept in original wrapper or re-wrap in waxed paper or aluminum foil and stored in covered dish in refrigerator.

Other Cheeses—Should be properly wrapped in waxed paper or aluminum foil and stored in covered dish. Grate all ends of cheese and store in jar with tight lid in refrigerator. If very dry, soak a short time in small quantity of milk before using in soufflés, etc.

Grating Cheese—When using cheese for cooking, slice or cut into small pieces and grate on either coarse or fine grater.

TABLE XIV

CHEESE

TYPE OF CHEESE	VARIETY [1]	PURCHASING UNIT	DESCRIPTION [2]	USE
Unripened Soft	Cottage or Smier-kase	8 oz. jar, pound (2 c.)	Domestic; from skimmed milk; acid or rennin added; white color, mild	Sandwich spread, relish, salad, dessert
	Cream	3 oz. package, pound	Domestic; extra cream added; white color, smooth texture, mild	Sandwich spread, with crackers, salad
	Neufchatel	2½–3 oz. package	French; from whole or skimmed milk, may be slightly ripened; resembles cream cheese; with peppers added called Pimiento Cheese	
Semi-hard	Mysost or Primost	Pound	Scandinavian; from whey; light brown; sweet	Sandwiches, with crackers
Hard	Gjetost	Pound	Norwegian; from goats' milk; dark brown; strong	
Ripened (by desirable mold or bacteria) Soft	Brie	Pound	French; mold ripened; interior soft and creamy, pronounced odor, flavor	Sandwich spread, with crackers, dessert
	Camembert	1⅓ oz. portions, 8 oz. round wooden box	French; mold ripened; ⅛-inch rind; interior very soft and waxy; sharp bitter flavor	
	Liederkranz	4 oz. package	Domestic; bacteria ripened; strong flavor and odor resembling Limburger	Sandwiches, with crackers, relish
	Limburger	8 oz. package, 14 oz. brick, pound	Belgian, domestic; bacteria ripened; strong odor and flavor	
Semi-hard	American	8 oz. package, grated 2–4 oz. package, pound	Domestic "store cheese"; Cheddar type; bacteria ripened; smooth texture, mild to sharp	All purpose and cooking cheese, grated[3]
	Brick	8 oz. package, pound	Domestic; bacteria ripened; rather elastic texture, many holes or "eyes," strong, sweetish	Sandwiches, relish, dessert

131

TABLE XIV—(*Continued*)

CHEESE

TYPE OF CHEESE	VARIETY [1]	PURCHASING UNIT	DESCRIPTION [2]	USE
Semi-hard (cont'd)	Gorgonzola	Pound	Italian; mold ripened; interior mottled blue-green, rich, strong flavor	Sandwiches, relish, dessert
	Münster	Pound	German; bacteria ripened; generally flavored with anise or caraway	
	Roquefort (Blue cheese)	1¼ oz. portions, 8 oz. package, pound	French; from sheep's milk; mold ripened; mottled blue-green interior American; cow's milk	Sandwiches, salads, salad dressings, with crackers
	Stilton	Pound	English; mold ripened; brown crinkled surface, light interior, blue-green veins, sharp, rich flavor	
Ripened (by desirable bacteria only) Hard	Cheddar	8 oz. package, pound	English (original); process widely used; yellow or white color, mild to sharp flavor	All purpose, grated[3]
	Cheshire	Pound	English; usually highly colored; sharp, strong	Sandwiches, relish, grated[3]
	Edam	Whole— 1½-2-3 lb.	Dutch; flattened spherical shape; outside colored red; salty, nut-like flavor	Sandwiches, with crackers, dessert
	Gouda	Whole— 15 oz.	Dutch; like Edam in shape, color and flavor	
	Parmesan	Pound, grated — jar, package— 2-4 oz.	Italian; granular, too hard to slice; interior green-yellow, flavor rather mild	Flavoring for soups, entrées, etc.
	Pineapple	Whole — 10-18-26-60 oz.	Domestic; highly colored; characteristic pineapple shape; flavor of Cheddar	Sandwiches, with crackers, dessert
	Swiss Emmenthal Gruyère	1⅓ oz. portions, 8 oz. pkge., lb.	Swiss; light yellow color, characteristic holes or "eyes," mild flavor	Sandwiches, with crackers, dessert

[1] A number of cheese spreads made from such varieties as American, Cheddar, Roquefort, Cream, Limburger, etc.—with or without additional seasonings—are packed in small cartons or glass jars.
[2] Unless otherwise specified all varieties listed are rennet cheeses made from cows' milk.
[3] One pound cheese, grated, measures 4 to 4½ cups.

YOGURT

Buy a "starter" of 2 to 4 tablespoons of yogurt from a health store, dairy or drugstore. Let stand covered for 3 hours at room temperature. Place in top of a double boiler. Add 1 quart skim or whole milk. Heat the milk to 120° F. (check by a candy thermometer). Cool a bit, then set top of double boiler over hot water and keep milk at 90° to 105° F. for 2 to 3 hours or until mixture thickens like a custard. Chill and refrigerate. Yogurt will keep about 5 days refrigerated. A portion of it may be used as a "starter" for the next batch. Made with skim milk, yogurt is low in calories. Use in salad dressings, on fruits, garnish for desserts or soups. Yield: 1 quart.

COTTAGE CHEESE

Use sour or clabbered milk, skim or whole, or use buttermilk; heat slowly over hot water until lukewarm (95° F.) and casein begins to coagulate. Let stand in warm place a few minutes for curd to collect before turning mass into cheesecloth-lined strainer; drain thoroughly and if milk is very sour, pour cold water over curd; bring ends of cloth together and hang until all whey is removed. Moisten with cream or butter and season with salt. One quart milk makes 1 cup.

To make cottage cheese from sweet milk, heat milk to lukewarm, then stir in rennet tablet, powdered and dissolved in small amount of milk, using 1 tablet to 1 quart milk, and let stand in warm place until set. Break curd and drain as above.

WELSH RABBIT

1 cup Thin White Sauce	¼ teaspoon dry mustard
(page 125)	2 cups (½ lb.) grated cheese
4 slices hot buttered toast	

Prepare sauce, add mustard and cheese, and heat over boiling water until cheese is melted and mixture smooth, stirring constantly. Serve at once on toast. Approximate yield: 4 portions.

Sardine Rabbit—Arrange sardines (1 tin) on 4 pieces of hot buttered toast; place under hot broiler for 2 to 3 minutes. Pour rabbit over slices and serve at once.

Tuna Fish Rabbit—Prepare rabbit, using ¼ cup grated cheese; reduce salt to ⅛ teaspoon and substitute 1 teaspoon Worcestershire sauce for mustard. Add ⅓ cup coarsely flaked canned tuna fish and cook about 5 minutes, or until fish is thoroughly heated.

Tomato Rabbit—Substitute 1 can condensed tomato soup for 1 cup white sauce; add 1 cup grated cheese, 1 canned pimiento, cut in strips, and 2 tablespoons minced green pepper and cook until cheese is melted. Serve on toast with 2 strips of crisp bacon across each slice.

Welsh Rabbit Sandwiches—Allow rabbit to cool. Spread one slice of bread with cold rabbit; spread second slice with butter, sprinkle with finely sliced or shredded Bermuda onion and put slices together.

CREAMY WELSH RABBIT

½ teaspoon dry mustard
1⅓ cups (1 can) evaporated
   milk

1 pound Old English cheese,
   chopped
⅔ cup ale

hot buttered toast

Blend mustard with a little evaporated milk and add remaining milk and cheese; cook over boiling water until cheese is just melted, stirring constantly; stir in ale. Serve at once over toast. Yield: 6 portions.

CHEESE RABBIT WITH BEER

4 cups (1 lb.) grated American
   cheese
1 tablespoon butter

1 cup beer
2 egg yolks, slightly beaten
6 slices hot toast

dash of paprika

Put grated cheese and butter in top of double boiler and melt slowly. When about ¼ of cheese is melted, add ½ cup beer slowly and cook until all cheese is melted, stirring constantly. Stir remaining ½ cup beer into egg yolks; add slowly to cheese-beer mixture, stirring constantly, and cook until thick and smooth. Serve at once on slices of toast and sprinkle with paprika. Approximate yield: 6 portions.

ENGLISH MONKEY

1 cup milk
1 cup dry bread crumbs
1 cup grated sharp American
   cheese
½ teaspoon salt

¼ teaspoon paprika
⅛ teaspoon dry mustard
½ teaspoon Worcestershire sauce
1 egg, slightly beaten
4 slices hot buttered toast

Cook milk, crumbs and cheese over boiling water until cheese is melted; add seasonings and Worcestershire sauce, stir in egg and cook about 1 minute, stirring constantly. Pour over toast. Yield: 4 portions.

CHEESE SOUFFLÉ

¼ cup butter	1 teaspoon salt
¼ cup flour	⅛ teaspoon paprika
1 cup milk	½ teaspoon mustard
1 cup grated American cheese	4 eggs, separated

Melt butter and stir in flour; gradually add milk and cook about 5 minutes, stirring constantly until mixture thickens; add cheese and seasonings, stirring until it is melted, and remove from heat. Gradually stir in well-beaten egg yolks and fold in stiffly beaten egg whites; turn into greased casserole or baking dish and put in pan of hot water; bake in moderate oven (350° F.) 50 to 60 minutes, or until delicately browned and firm to touch. Serve at once. Garnish with parsley, if desired. Approximate yield: 6 portions.

Cheese–Chive Soufflé—Add ½ teaspoon minced chives and 1 teaspoon minced parsley when folding in beaten egg white.

Cheese and Mushroom Soufflé—Chop fine ¼ pound mushrooms, cook slowly in butter about 2 minutes; proceed as for cheese soufflé.

Tomato Cheese Soufflé—Substitute 1 cup tomato juice for cup of milk.

FRENCH CHEESE SOUFFLÉ

3 tablespoons butter	3 tablespoons grated Parmesan cheese
3 tablespoons flour	2 sections Gruyère cheese
½ teaspoon salt	1 teaspoon dry mustard
dash of cayenne	4 egg yolks
¾ cup milk	5 egg whites

Melt butter, remove from heat and stir in flour, salt and cayenne. Gradually add milk and stir constantly until it is smooth and thickened, but do not boil. Remove from heat and stir in grated Parmesan cheese and Gruyère cheese, which has been put through a strainer, and mustard. Add egg yolks beaten until thick and lemon-colored and carefully fold in egg whites beaten stiff but not dry. Pour into soufflé dish with bottom only greased. Bake in slow oven (325° F.) 45 minutes. Approximate yield: 6 portions.

CORN AND CHEESE SOUFFLÉ

¼ cup butter
¼ cup flour
1 cup milk
1 cup grated American cheese
2 cups whole kernel corn

1 teaspoon salt
dash of paprika
few drops Tabasco sauce
1 pimiento, cut in strips
4 eggs, separated

Melt butter and stir in flour; gradually add milk and cook about 5 minutes, stirring constantly until mixture is thickened; add cheese, stirring until it is melted; add corn, seasonings and pimiento and remove from heat. Gradually stir in well-beaten egg yolks and fold in stiffly beaten egg whites; turn into buttered baking dish and set in pan of hot water; bake in moderate oven (350° F.) 50 to 60 minutes, or until delicately browned and firm. Yield: 6 to 8 large portions.

MOLDED CHEESE SOUFFLÉ

Prepare white sauce, using ⅓ cup each butter and flour, 1½ cups milk, ¾ teaspoon salt and dash of cayenne. Beat in 3 egg yolks, one at a time. Fold in stiffly beaten egg whites. Sprinkle ⅔ cup grated cheese into 4 ramekins, well greased on bottoms; fill each two-thirds full with egg-mixture. Place in pan of hot water; bake in moderate oven (375° F.) 20 minutes, or until firm. Unmold. Yield: 4 portions.

OLIVE-CHEESE CUSTARD

5 slices bread, crusts removed
2 tablespoons butter
1 cup grated American cheese
½ cup sliced stuffed olives

3 eggs, slightly beaten
⅛ teaspoon dry mustard
⅓ cup olive liquor
2 cups milk, scalded

Spread bread with 1 tablespoon butter; cut in cubes and scatter ⅓ over bottom of greased casserole. Arrange alternate layers of ⅓ cup cheese and ¼ cup olives over bread cubes; repeat. Then cover with remaining bread cubes and top with remaining ⅓ cup cheese; dot with remaining butter. Combine eggs, mustard and olive liquor; gradually stir in hot milk. Pour over mixture in casserole and bake in slow oven (300° F.) about 1 hour, or until knife inserted comes out clean. Serve as main luncheon dish. Approximate yield: 6 portions.

CHEESE FONDUE

1½ cups milk
2 cups soft bread crumbs
1½ cups grated American cheese
1 teaspoon salt

⅛ teaspoon paprika
dash of cayenne
1 tablespoon butter, melted
3 eggs, separated

Pour milk over bread crumbs and let stand until milk is absorbed; add cheese, seasonings, butter and well-beaten egg yolks, mixing lightly. Fold in egg whites beaten stiff but not dry; turn into greased baking dish and bake in moderate oven (350° F.) 30 to 45 minutes, or until a knife inserted in center comes out clean. Serve at once. Approximate yield: 6 portions.

CHEESE-HALIBUT CASSEROLE

1 pound fresh halibut
1 cup fine noodles
2 cups Thin White Sauce
    (page 125)

2 cups grated American cheese
½ teaspoon Worcestershire sauce
2 tablespoons lemon juice
¼ cup buttered bread crumbs

Cook halibut 10 to 15 minutes; drain, remove skin and bones and flake. Cook noodles in boiling salted water about 10 minutes; drain. Prepare white sauce; add 1 cup cheese, Worcestershire sauce and lemon juice and cook until cheese is melted and sauce is smooth, stirring constantly. Line greased casserole with ½ of remaining cheese; add layers of noodles, fish and sauce, using ½ of each amount; repeat. Top with remaining ½ cup cheese and sprinkle buttered crumbs over all. Bake in slow oven (300° F.) about ½ hour. Approximate yield: 4 portions.

CHEESE CROQUETTES

1 cup grated American cheese
dash of paprika
1 teaspoon grated onion
1 tablespoon finely minced
    parsley

2 cups Thick White Sauce
    (page 125)
dry bread crumbs
1 egg, slightly beaten
1 tablespoon water

Add cheese, paprika, onion and parsley to white sauce in top of double boiler and heat over hot water until cheese is melted; turn out on well-greased platter and cool. Shape into small cylinders, cones, or balls; roll in crumbs, dip in combined egg and water and roll again in crumbs. Fry in hot deep fat (380° F.) about 1 minute, or until golden brown, or fry in shallow fat in skillet, turning frequently to brown evenly. Serve with a sauce such as tomato or cream sauce flavored with anchovy paste. Approximate yield: 10 croquettes.

Cheese and Ham Cutlets—Reduce white sauce to 1½ cups, season with ¼ teaspoon dry mustard and salt and pepper to taste. Add ½ cup chopped cooked ham and reduce cheese to ½ cup. Shape into small cutlets. Chill coated cutlets thoroughly before frying.

Cheese and Nut Balls—Reduce white sauce to 1½ cups, season to taste. Add ½ to 1 cup coarsely chopped nuts to cheese mixture. Shape into small balls. Chill coated balls thoroughly before frying.

Cheese and Celery Croquettes—Reduce white sauce to 1½ cups. Cook slowly about 5 minutes 1 cup chopped celery in 6 tablespoons butter used for white sauce, stirring to cook evenly. Proceed as for Cheese Croquettes.

CHEESE AND SPINACH ROLL

1 quart cooked, chopped spinach
1 tablespoon butter, melted
1 cup grated cheese
1 cup cooked rice
1 teaspoon salt

⅛ teaspoon pepper
2 tablespoons ketchup
1 tablespoon horseradish
2 hard-cooked eggs
sprigs of parsley

Mix thoroughly spinach, butter, cheese, rice and seasonings; shape into roll and bake in greased pan in slow oven (325° F.) 20 minutes. Serve hot, garnished with hard-cooked eggs and parsley; Tomato Sauce may be served with roll. Approximate yield: 6 portions.

Breads

WILL YOU ever forget those days when the heavenly aroma of freshly baking bread wafted through the house with undeviating regularity? Our mothers and grandmothers gained their reputations as "the best cook in town" on the breads they baked for the family table—fluffy, tender biscuits, fragrant nut loaves, crisp thin corn sticks, cinnamon brown still-hot doughnuts, and the culinary climax—slices of golden crusty bread spread to the very edges with creamy butter. They found breadmaking a very rewarding and satisfying experience.

Today we can duplicate this experience of quick and yeast bread-making with the same satisfaction, time-pressed as we are, because new methods have been developed to speed and ease the task.

"Quick" breads have gained their name because they are made with a quick-acting leavening such as baking powder, sour milk and soda, and steam, instead of the slower yeast. Biscuits, muffins, nut loaves, corn breads are baked in the oven. Pancakes and waffles take to the griddle. Fritters and doughnuts receive the hot fat treatment.

Yeast breads, too, have been speeded up by improved quick methods and the new fast yeasts that cut rising time. You will truly enjoy making a wide variety of breads. They are especially welcome in the holidays.

Our HOME INSTITUTE staff has developed many of these recipes. Others have been given to us by bread-loving readers. Some we have gained in our travels around the world. A few we have requested from the famous testing kitchens of the big milling companies.

Here they are—as carefully tested and as simply written as we could make them to help you make the breads your family will extol to the skies.

QUICK BREADS
POPOVERS

POPOVERS that won't "pop" can break the heart of their maker. Often the difficulty lies not with the recipe or the mixing, but with the baking. Since popovers, like cream puffs, tend to rise quickly in the oven, it is fairly easy to make the mistake of removing them before they are fully baked. Leave them in the oven, at the correct temperature, for the full baking time to be sure they stay "popped." *Grease bottom of pan only*. Ungreased sides allow popover to cling and grow tall.

POPOVERS

1 cup sifted all-purpose flour	2 eggs
½ teaspoon salt	1 cup milk

Grease bottom of oven custard cups or heavy iron muffin tins. Beat all the ingredients together in a bowl with a rotary beater until smooth. Pour into greased cups (¾ full) and bake in hot oven (425° F.) until golden brown, 35 to 40 minutes or until the popovers are firm. Serve at once. To vary, add a few grains of paprika, dried sage, crushed mint, or other herbs or spices. Yield: 8 popovers.

GRIDDLE CAKES AND WAFFLES

THE PERFECT griddle cake is golden brown and tender. A good waffle is light, porous and crisp enough to be eaten with the fingers when the mood strikes.

Griddle cakes may be baked best on a heavy griddle—soapstone is ideal. Modern griddles require no seasoning or greasing; follow manufacturer's directions.

Do's and Don'ts with Griddle Cakes:

1. Heat griddle while making batter. To test: sprinkle a few drops of water on surface; when they "skate around," griddle is ready.

2. Pour batter from a narrow-mouthed pitcher or drop from tip of large spoon in separated lots to allow for slight spreading.
3. For thick cakes, make a thick batter (add a little flour).
4. For thin cakes, make a thin batter (add a little milk).
5. Turn cakes when they puff and begin to bubble to brown on other side. Do not let break before turning.
6. Pancakes may be placed between folds of a warm towel in warm oven to keep hot or when making a quantity for dessert.
7. Batter may be kept in refrigerator for several days.
8. Prepared flours, such as buckwheat and other types, are quick and convenient to use.

GRIDDLE CAKES

2 cups sifted all-purpose flour	1 tablespoon sugar
3 teaspoons baking powder	2 eggs, well beaten
½ teaspoon salt	1½ cups milk (scant)
2 tablespoons shortening, melted	

Mix and sift dry ingredients. Combine egg and milk; add flour mixture and beat only until smooth; add shortening. Bake on ungreased or lightly greased hot griddle. For a thick cake, use 1 to 1⅓ cups milk; do not overbeat batter. Approximate yield: 24 small griddle cakes.

Blueberry Pancakes—Add 1 cup fresh or drained, canned blueberries to batter. Bake slowly on greased, hot griddle. Spread with butter, sprinkle with brown sugar and roll; or serve plain with blueberry hard sauce. (See Strawberry Hard Sauce, page 732.)

Apple Pancakes—Add 1 cup finely chopped apples to batter. Bake slowly on greased, hot griddle. Spread with butter, sprinkle generously with freshly shaved maple sugar or with brown sugar and roll. Serve hot on platter with bacon, sausages or pork roast.

Pineapple Pancakes—Add 1 cup drained, crushed pineapple to batter. Bake slowly on greased, hot griddle. Serve with butter and honey.

Cherry or Peach Griddle Cakes—Add 1 cup drained, chopped cherries or peaches, fresh or canned, to batter. Bake slowly on greased, hot griddle. Serve hot with butter and a syrup of cherry juice and sugar.

Jelly-filled Pancakes—Butter hot griddle cakes, spread with a tart jelly or jam and roll tightly, or serve rolled, buttered cakes with a sauce made by beating together equal amounts of whipped cream and jelly which has been beaten with a fork until smooth.

Sour Milk Griddle Cakes—Substitute 1 teaspoon baking soda for baking powder and 2 cups sour milk or butter milk (scant) for sweet milk.

Cornmeal Griddle Cakes—Substitute ¾ cup cornmeal for ¾ cup flour and dark molasses for sugar.

Rice Griddle Cakes—Substitute 1 cup boiled rice for 1 cup flour and reduce the milk to 1 cup. Add rice to egg-milk mixture.

Corn Griddle Cakes—Reduce milk to 1 cup and add 2 cups fresh corn cut from cob or drained, canned corn. Add ¼ teaspoon paprika.

Buckwheat Cakes—Substitute 1 cup buckwheat flour for 1 cup flour, increase sugar and shortening to 3 tablespoons each and increase milk if necessary.

OLDFASHIONED BUCKWHEAT CAKES

2 cups buckwheat flour
½ cup sifted all-purpose flour
1½ teaspoons salt
1 tablespoon sugar (optional)
½ cup warm water

1 pkg. dry granular yeast or
1 cake compressed yeast
1¾ cups warm (not hot) water
½ teaspoon baking soda

Blend flours, salt and sugar. Sprinkle or crumble yeast into warm (not hot) water (for yeast cake, use lukewarm water) and let stand until dissolved (5 minutes). Add to flour mixture and mix thoroughly. Allow to rise 6 to 8 hours until light (if too light, stir several times). Just before baking, add baking soda to ½ cup warm water and add to batter. Stir just enough to mix, no more. Bake at once on hot griddle. Yield: 1 dozen pancakes.

GERMAN POTATO PANCAKES

3 eggs, separated
1 teaspoon salt
1 tablespoon sugar
3 cups grated raw potatoes

3 cups milk
2½ cups sifted all-purpose flour
1 tablespoon shortening, melted

To well-beaten egg yolks add salt, sugar and milk. Gradually add flour and shortening, beating well. Stir in grated potatoes; fold in stiffly beaten egg whites. Bake at once on greased hot griddle. Finely chopped onions are sometimes put on top of batter on griddle. Serve hot with meat. Approximate yield: 2 dozen pancakes.

WAFFLES

MODERN waffle irons require no greasing and some do not require tempering (follow manufacturer's directions). Heat while mixing the batter. If not thermostatically controlled, heat until drops of water dropped on the griddle "skid" across. The waffle batter should only partly fill each compartment to prevent overflow. Cook until steaming stops. Lift waffle off griddle with fork. Serve with soft butter, maple or other syrups, or sauces.

WAFFLES

2 cups sifted all-purpose flour	3 eggs, separated
3 teaspoons baking powder	1¼ cups milk
1 teaspoon salt	¼ cup shortening, melted

Sift together dry ingredients. Combine well-beaten egg yolks and milk and add to flour mixture, beating until smooth; add shortening. Gently fold in egg whites beaten stiff but not dry. Bake in hot waffle iron. Approximate yield: 6 waffles.

Sour Milk Waffles—Substitute ¾ teaspoon soda for baking powder and 1½ cups sour milk or buttermilk for sweet milk.

Ham Waffles—Sprinkle 2 tablespoons finely diced cooked ham over batter of each waffle before closing iron.

Nut Waffles—Add ½ cup chopped nuts to batter, or sprinkle nuts over batter of each waffle before closing iron.

Cheese Waffles—Add 1 cup grated American cheese to batter before folding in beaten egg whites.

Lemon or Orange Waffles—Add 2 teaspoons grated lemon or orange rind to egg yolk-milk mixture. Serve with butter and orange or grapefruit marmalade, or top with ice cream and Orange Sauce. To serve with a fruit salad, substitute 3 tablespoons lemon or ½ cup orange juice for an equal quantity of milk.

Coconut Waffles—Add 1 cup shredded coconut to batter, or sprinkle coconut over batter of each waffle before closing iron.

Cornmeal Waffles—Substitute 1 cup cornmeal for 1 cup sifted flour and add 1 tablespoon sugar to dry ingredients. Use 2 eggs.

CREAM WAFFLES

2 cups sifted all-purpose flour	1 tablespoon sugar
½ teaspoon baking soda	2 eggs, separated
½ teaspoon salt	2 cups heavy sour cream

Sift together dry ingredients. Combine well-beaten egg yolks and cream; add to flour mixture, beating until smooth. Fold in egg whites beaten stiff but not dry. Bake in hot waffle iron. Yield: 6 waffles.

GINGERBREAD WAFFLES

2 cups sifted all-purpose flour	2 eggs, separated
¾ teaspoon baking soda	1 cup molasses
½ teaspoon salt	½ cup sour milk or buttermilk
2 teaspoons ginger	⅓ cup shortening, melted

Sift together dry ingredients. Combine well-beaten egg yolks and molasses; add to flour mixture alternately with sour milk, beating until smooth; add shortening and gently fold in egg whites beaten stiff but not dry. Bake in moderately hot waffle iron, removing tender waffle from iron in quarters. Serve hot with applesauce and bacon, or serve as a dessert with whipped cream flavored with molasses or ice cream with fresh fruit. Approximate yield: 8 waffles.

MUFFINS

MUFFINS are an American favorite for every meal of the day. Rounded, golden brown, crunchy crusted and tender inside, the muffin adds a welcome touch as a breakfast treat, as the hot bread for luncheon or supper.

Do's and Don'ts for Muffin Making:

1. Set oven for correct temperature (usually 400° F., moderately hot).
2. Assemble ingredients and utensils.
3. Grease muffin cups well.
4. Sift dry ingredients into mixing bowl.
5. Measure and add soft shortening (no more melting shortening), unbeaten egg and milk.

6. Mix together with pastry blender or blending fork. Use a quick cutting-in motion.
7. Stir with blender until ingredients are just mixed, the flour moistened. The batter will be lumpy.
8. Fill greased muffin tins ⅔ full.
9. Bake until golden brown. Immediately remove from tins. Use a sharp knife or spatula to help loosen them.

Peaks and tunnels in muffins are caused by overstirring or too stiff a batter. Heaviness or toughness is likely due to wrong proportions or to insufficient leavening.

SWEET MUFFINS

1½ cups sifted all-purpose flour   ½ teaspoon salt
2 teaspoons double-acting   ¼ cup soft shortening
   baking powder   1 egg
½ cup sugar   ⅓ cup milk

Sift together dry ingredients into mixing bowl. With a pastry blender or blending fork cut in soft shortening until just blended. Add egg and milk and *stir only until* ingredients are blended. Fill well-greased muffin pans ⅔ full and bake in moderately hot oven (400° F.) 20 or 25 minutes. Serve immediately. Yield: 12 medium-sized muffins.

Pecan Orange Muffins—Add ¾ teaspoon grated orange rind, ¾ cup chopped pecan meats to above recipe, and use ¼ cup milk and ¼ cup orange juice, instead of ⅓ cup milk.

ONE BOWL PLAIN MUFFINS

2 cups sifted all-purpose flour   3 tablespoons sugar
3 teaspoons double-acting   ¼ cup soft shortening
   baking powder   1 egg
½ teaspoon salt   1 cup milk

Sift together the dry ingredients in a mixing bowl. Add soft shortening with a blending fork or pastry blender. Mix *only enough* to blend ingredients. Add egg and milk, and *stir just enough* to blend ingredients (batter will be lumpy). Fill well-greased muffin tins ⅔ full. Bake in 400° F. oven 20 to 25 minutes or until golden brown. Serve immediately. Yield: 1 dozen medium-sized muffins.

Blueberry Muffins—Add 1 cup fresh blueberries or huckleberries to sifted dry ingredients.

Cherry Muffins—Add ¾ cup drained, chopped cherries, fresh or canned, to muffin batter.

Cranberry Muffins—Add ¾ cup chopped cranberries mixed with 3 tablespoons sugar to sifted dry ingredients.

Dried Fruit Muffins—Add to sifted dry ingredients ½ cup of one of the following fruits, whole, sliced or chopped: raisins, currants, dates, figs, prunes, apricots, peaches, or a combination of prunes and raisins.

Nut Muffins—Add ½ cup coarsely chopped nuts to sifted dry ingredients.

Bacon or Ham Muffins—Reduce sugar to 2 tablespoons and add ⅓ cup coarsely chopped crisp bacon or finely cut boiled ham to sifted dry ingredients.

Cheese Muffins—Add dash of paprika and ⅔ cup grated American cheese to sifted dry ingredients. Sprinkle additional grated cheese over tops of muffins and bake in hot oven (400° F.) about 30 minutes.

Sour Milk Muffins—Reduce baking powder to 1 teaspoon, add ½ teaspoon baking soda and substitute thick sour milk or buttermilk for sweet milk.

Sweet Cream Muffins—Increase salt to ¾ teaspoon, substitute 1¼ cups heavy cream for milk and shortening.

Sour Cream Muffins—Reduce baking powder to 1 teaspoon and add ½ teaspoon baking soda, increase salt to ¾ teaspoon and substitute 1¼ cups heavy sour cream for milk and shortening.

Whole Wheat Muffins—Substitute brown for granular sugar, and 1 cup unsifted whole wheat or graham flour for 1 cup all-purpose flour, adding it to sifted dry ingredients; increase salt to ¾ teaspoon.

Cornmeal Muffins—Substitute 1 cup cornmeal for 1 cup flour; sugar may be omitted, if desired.

Maple Sugar Muffins—Substitute ¼ cup grated dark maple sugar for granular or substitute ½ cup maple syrup for ½ cup milk.

BRAN MUFFINS

Sift 1 cup flour with 3½ teaspoons baking powder and ½ teaspoon salt into mixing bowl. Stir in 2 tablespoons brown or white sugar and 1 cup bran. Combine 1 egg, beaten, ⅔ cup milk and 2 tablespoons soft fat. Add to dry ingredients and mix quickly. Turn into prepared muffin pans and bake in hot oven (400° F.) 20 to 25 minutes. Raisins or chopped dried prunes may be added if desired. Approximate yield: 12 small muffins.

STICKY BUNS

Mix together ½ cup firmly packed brown sugar, 2 tablespoons cinnamon, 1 cup chopped nut meats and 2 tablespoons butter, melted; add ½ to Plain Muffins batter (page 145). Fill prepared muffin pans ½ full and sprinkle remaining sugar-nut mixture over tops; bake as directed. Approximate yield: 1½ dozen muffins.

CORN BREAD STICKS

1½ cups sifted all-purpose flour	2 tablespoons sugar
¾ cup yellow cornmeal	1 egg, well beaten
3 teaspoons baking powder	1 cup milk
1½ teaspoons salt	¼ cup melted shortening

Sift together flour, cornmeal, baking powder, salt and sugar. Combine egg, milk and shortening and add dry ingredients. Stir only enough to moisten mixture. Fill well-greased corn stick pans ¾ full. Bake in hot oven (425° F.) 25 minutes. Yield: 14 corn bread sticks.

HUSH PUPPIES

3 cups cornmeal	1 tablespoon flour
2 teaspoons double-acting baking powder	1 egg, beaten
1½ teaspoons salt	2 cups milk
	⅓ cup chopped onion

Mix cornmeal, baking powder, flour and salt together in a bowl, add egg, milk and onion; blend. Mold into small cakes and fry in deep hot fat (375° F.) until golden brown. (Cakes may be fried in one inch deep fat in frying pan; turn to brown on both sides.) Drain on absorbent paper. Serve hot. Especially good with fried shrimp, fish or hamburgers. Yield: 8 portions.

CORNMEAL GEMS

2 cups yellow cornmeal	2 cups milk, scalded
¾ teaspoon salt	2 tablespoons shortening
2 tablespoons sugar	2 eggs, well beaten

Mix together dry ingredients and stir into scalded milk; add shortening and cool; stir in eggs. Fill greased, small muffin pans ⅔ full. Bake in hot oven (400° F.) 20 to 25 minutes. Approximate yield: 2 dozen gems.

BAKING POWDER BISCUITS

WHERE you live probably determines a "good" baking powder biscuit. If you live in the South, no doubt you like a flat biscuit; Northerners favor the tall, puffy biscuit. You will want them to be symmetrical in shape, doubled in size, flaky and tender. Here is the procedure our HOME INSTITUTE staff follows:

Steps in Making Baking Powder Biscuits:

1. Read your recipe. Pre-heat the oven for 450° F. (hot oven).
2. Assemble ingredients and utensils.
3. Sift flour and measure all dry ingredients into sifter.
4. Sift dry ingredients into mixing bowl. Measure shortening and cut into flour mixture with pastry blender until finely blended. The mixture should be like a "meal," not too finely mixed.
5. Stir in most of the milk at beginning. Flours differ in absorption. Use enough to make a soft but not sticky dough when rolled out. Too much milk makes a dough too sticky; not enough, too dry a dough.
6. Shape into a flat round ball on floured board and knead (fold dough over and press lightly with heel of hand about five times). Handle lightly and quickly. A tough biscuit is caused by too much handling.
7. Roll or pat out dough ¼ inch thick for thin crunchy biscuits; ½ inch for thick, soft biscuits.

8. Cut close together with floured biscuit cutter. For variation cut in squares with a knife. Place close together on greased baking sheet for soft sides; an inch apart for crusty sides. An aluminum or shiny pan prevents heavy browning on bottom of biscuits.

9. Bake in center of heated oven until golden brown. Serve at once.

BAKING POWDER BISCUITS

2 cups sifted all-purpose flour	1 teaspoon salt
3 teaspoons baking powder	¼ cup shortening

⅔ to ¾ cup milk

Sift together dry ingredients; cut in shortening until well mixed and add milk, stirring quickly until a soft but not sticky dough is formed. Turn out on lightly floured or cloth-covered board and knead gently to shape into smooth ball; roll lightly or pat ½ to 1 inch thick and cut with floured biscuit cutter. Place on lightly greased baking sheet, ½ inch apart for a biscuit with crusty sides and close together for a tall, soft biscuit; bake in hot oven (450° F.) 12 to 15 minutes. Approximate yield: 12 biscuits (2 inches), or 18 to 24 biscuits (1¾ inches).

For a less short biscuit, reduce fat to 2 tablespoons; for a richer biscuit, increase fat to 6 tablespoons and reduce the milk to ½ or ⅔ cup.

Nut Biscuits—Add ½ cup chopped black walnuts to flour-shortening mixture. Other nut meats may be used, if desired.

Orange Tea Biscuits—Press a small lump of sugar dipped in orange juice into top of each biscuit, sprinkle with grated orange rind and bake as directed.

Christmas Biscuits—Use 6 tablespoons fat; add 2 tablespoons chopped green pepper to flour-shortening mixture. Cut rolled dough with star-shaped cutter and serve as bread or with a salad.

Cheese Biscuits—Add ½ cup grated American cheese to dry ingredients; reduce milk to ⅔ cup and add to 1 slightly beaten egg. Brush biscuits with milk or melted butter just before removing from oven. Serve as bread, with a salad, or as tea biscuits. Approximate yield: 2 dozen small biscuits.

Soda Biscuits—Substitute ½ teaspoon baking soda for baking powder and thick sour milk or buttermilk for sweet milk.

Roquefort Cheese Biscuits—Add a dash of cayenne and ¼ cup Roquefort cheese, crumbled, to dry ingredients. Cut dough with 1¾-inch biscuit cutter; brush tops of biscuits with 2 tablespoons melted butter before baking. Approximate yield: 18 to 20 small biscuits.

Chive Biscuits—Add ¼ cup freshly chopped chives to flour-shortening mixture. Serve with a meat dish or a green salad.

Drop Biscuits—Increase milk to 1 cup (scant) and drop mixture from teaspoon on lightly greased baking sheet or muffin pans. Bake in hot oven (450° F.) 12 to 15 minutes.

Whole Wheat Biscuits—Substitute 1 cup unsifted whole wheat or graham flour for 1 cup all-purpose flour and use ¾ teaspoon salt.

Corn Biscuits—Increase salt to 1 teaspoon, reduce milk to ½ cup (scant) and add ⅔ cup grated fresh corn or drained, canned corn to milk. Brush tops of unbaked biscuits with melted butter. Bake in hot oven (450° F.) 12 to 15 minutes.

Savory Biscuits—Roll dough ¼ inch thick, cut with floured 1½-inch biscuit cutter and spread ½ of rounds with concentrated beef and vegetable extract; cover with remaining rounds, press edges together lightly. Bake as directed and serve with consommé, main course or green salad. Approximate yield: 2 dozen small biscuits.

Scottish Tea Scones—Divide dough in half; roll each into a round piece ½ inch thick and cut in quarters. Bake slowly on greased, hot griddle about 20 minutes, turning frequently for even browning; split open, butter and place in oven to melt butter. Yield: 8 scones.

Mint Biscuits—Add ¼ cup finely chopped mint to flour-shortening mixture. Excellent to serve with lamb dishes or to top an old-fashioned lamb pie.

Water Cress Biscuits—Add ¼ cup finely chopped water cress to flour-shortening mixture. Serve with meat stews and salads.

Scotch Cream Scones—Increase the salt to 1 teaspoon, use ½ cup shortening instead of ¼ cup; and beat together 2 eggs and ½ cup (scant) cream (use instead of ¾ cup milk). Turn out on lightly floured board and divide into 2 equal parts; roll each into round piece, 6½ inches in diameter, and cut in quarters. Place in lightly greased round baking pans, brush tops with melted butter and bake 12–15 minutes in 450° F. oven. Or roll dough lightly into sheet ½-inch thick; cut in diamond-shaped pieces with floured knife; brush with melted shortening and sprinkle with additional sugar. Yield: 8 large scones or 16 diamond-shaped scones.

Cream Biscuits—Add 1 tablespoon sugar and sift with dry ingredients, and substitute 1 cup medium cream (scant) for shortening and sweet milk.

FILLED BISCUITS

1 recipe Whole Wheat Biscuits	½ cup honey
(page 150)	2 tablespoons butter
	½ cup chopped raisins

Roll biscuit dough ¼ inch thick and cut with floured 1½-inch biscuit cutter. Spread filling of honey, butter and raisins on ½ of rounds, using 1 teaspoon on each; cover with remaining rounds and press edges together with a fork. Bake as directed. Yield: 1 dozen small biscuits.

APPLE COFFEE CAKE

Use recipe for Drop Biscuit Dough (page 150); sift ¼ cup sugar with dry ingredients and add 1 egg, beaten, to ¾ cup milk. Spread dough in well-buttered 9-inch square pan. Pare and slice thin 3 tart apples; press slices in rows into dough. Prepare topping of ¼ cup butter, creamed, ½ cup firmly packed brown sugar, ½ teaspoon cinnamon and dash of nutmeg; spread over top. Bake in hot oven (400° F.) about 40 minutes. Yield: 9 square pieces.

CHERRY ROLLS

1 recipe Cream Biscuits	½ cup chopped pecans
(above)	5 tablespoons brown sugar
6 tablespoons butter, melted	12 maraschino cherries, chopped

Prepare biscuit dough and roll into rectangle ¼ inch thick; brush with 2 tablespoons melted butter, sprinkle with nuts, roll as for jelly roll and cut in 1 inch slices. Put 1 teaspoon of remaining butter and 1 teaspoon brown sugar in each of 12 muffin tins and arrange cherries on mixture; place slice of cherry roll on top and press down well. Bake in hot oven (400° F.) 15 to 20 minutes. Yield: 1 dozen rolls.

Pecan Rolls—Sprinkle ½ cup chopped pecans over butter-sugar mixture spread on rolled dough.

Cinnamon Rolls—Substitute ½ cup granulated sugar for brown sugar and add 1 teaspoon cinnamon. If desired, sprinkle ½ cup currants over butter-sugar mixture when spread on rolled dough.

BUTTERSCOTCH ROLLS

1 recipe Baking Powder Biscuits   **⅓ cup butter**
  (page 149)   **⅓ cup firmly packed brown sugar**

Prepare biscuit dough and roll into rectangle ¼ inch thick; spread with creamed mixture of butter and brown sugar. Roll as for jelly roll and cut in 1 inch slices; place slices in greased pan or muffin pans and bake in hot oven (450° F.) 10 to 15 minutes. Approximate yield: 10 rolls.

Maple Nut Pinwheels—Spread rolled dough with softened butter and sprinkle with ½ cup each maple sugar and chopped walnuts; spread tops of slices with butter.

Date Rolls—Brush rolled dough with melted butter and sprinkle with ½ cup ground dates; brush tops of slices with butter.

Orange Tea Rolls—Brush rolled dough with melted butter and sprinkle with ¼ cup sugar and ½ cup finely chopped, candied orange peel; brush tops of slices with butter. Spread Lemon Icing on top of cooled baked rolls.

Orange Marmalade Rolls—Brush rolled dough with melted butter and spread with ½ cup of a thick, tart orange marmalade, or any other tart marmalade, jam or jelly; brush tops of slices with butter.

Cheese Pinwheels—Brush rolled dough with melted butter and sprinkle with 1 cup grated American cheese; brush tops of slices with butter. If desired, add ½ cup grated cheese to flour-shortening mixture and sprinkle remaining ½ cup cheese over rolled dough. Ground pecans may be added if desired.

STIR-N-ROLL BISCUITS

2 cups sifted all-purpose flour   **1 teaspoon salt**
3 teaspoons double-action   **⅓ cup salad oil**
  baking powder   **⅔ cup milk**

Sift together dry ingredients into bowl. Pour oil and milk into a measuring cup but don't stir together. Pour liquid all at once into the flour. Stir with a fork until mixture cleans sides of bowl and rounds up into a ball. Smooth up by kneading dough about 10 times without additional flour. With the dough on waxed paper, press out ¼ inch thick with hands, or roll out between waxed papers. For higher biscuits, roll dough ½ inch thick. Cut with unfloured biscuit cutter. Bake 10 to 12 minutes on ungreased cookie sheet in very hot oven (475° F.) Approximate yield: 16 medium biscuits.

BACON BISCUITS

2 cups sifted all-purpose flour
4 teaspoons baking powder
1 teaspoon salt
½ teaspoon dry mustard
4 tablespoons chilled bacon fat

⅔ cup buttermilk (about)
1 egg, beaten
raw bacon cut in 1-inch squares
cheese cut in 1-inch squares
dry mustard
cayenne

Sift together flour, baking powder, salt and mustard. Cut in bacon fat. Add buttermilk to make a soft but not sticky dough. Place in waxed paper and chill ½ hour. Roll out to ½ inch thickness and cut into small rounds with 1½-inch cookie cutter. Place half the rounds on greased cookie sheet. Brush with egg. On each, place bacon square and cheese. Sprinkle with mustard and cayenne. Top with another round of biscuit dough. Brush with egg. Bake in moderately hot oven (375° F.) 15 to 20 minutes. Yield: 1 dozen biscuits.

QUICK LOAF BREADS

You'll enjoy making the so-called quick breads for supper, for tea and for delicious paper-thin sandwiches. To slice smoothly, allow the bread to stand 24 hours well wrapped before cutting.

The mixing procedure is similar to that of muffins. The same caution applies—do not overbeat. Stir only enough to mix and moisten all the ingredients. Use the small or medium-sized loaf pans; too deep a pan lengthens the baking period and drys out the loaf. Cool, uncovered before storing.

NUT BREAD

2 cups sifted all-purpose flour
3 teaspoons baking powder
¼ teaspoon salt

¼ cup sugar
1 cup chopped nuts
2 eggs, well beaten
1 cup milk

Sift flour, baking powder, salt and sugar together. Add nuts. Combine eggs and milk and add to dry ingredients. Mix only enough to moisten flour. Turn into a greased 9½ x 5¼ x 2¾-inch loaf pan and spread to sides; bake in a moderate oven (350° F.) 40 to 45 minutes, or until done. Cool and cut (fresh or day old) into thin slices. Spread with creamed butter and a sandwich filling. Yield: 1 loaf.

Orange Sandwich Bread—Substitute 1 cup finely chopped, candied orange peel for nuts, or use ½ cup each chopped nuts and candied orange or grapefruit peel.

Fruit Nut Bread—Reduce nuts to ½ cup and add 1 cup of one of the following fruits: raisins, currants, sliced dates or dried apricots.

Spiced Fruit Bread—Increase sugar to ¾ cup and substitute 1 cup currants and ½ cup raisins for nuts. Sift the following spices with dry ingredients: ¾ teaspoon cinnamon and ¼ teaspoon each mace, cloves, ginger and nutmeg.

Quick Whole Wheat Bread—Substitute 1½ cups unsifted entire wheat or graham flour for 1½ cups all-purpose flour; use ¼ cup firmly packed brown sugar for granulated sugar.

Black Walnut Bread—Substitute ½ cup chopped black walnuts and 1 cup chopped dates for 1 cup nuts in recipe for Whole Wheat Bread.

BRAN BREAD

1½ cups sifted all-purpose flour	½ cup chopped raisins
4½ teaspoons baking powder	1 egg, well beaten
1 teaspoon salt	¾ cup milk
½ cup sugar	¼ cup molasses
1½ cups bran	¼ cup shortening, melted

Sift together flour, baking powder, salt and sugar; stir in bran and raisins. Combine egg, milk and molasses; add to flour mixture, stirring only until mixed; add shortening. Turn into greased loaf pan and bake in moderate oven (350° F.) about 1 hour. Yield: 1 loaf, 8½ x 4½ x 2½ inches.

BANANA BREAD

1¾ cups sifted all-purpose flour	⅓ cup shortening
1 teaspoon baking soda	⅔ cup sugar
2 teaspoons cream of tartar	2 eggs, well beaten
½ teaspoon salt	1 cup banana pulp

Sift together flour, baking soda, cream of tartar and salt. Cream shortening well and beat in sugar. Add eggs, mixing well. Mash ripe bananas, as soon as peeled, with a silver fork (3 to 4 ripe bananas yield 1 cup). Add flour alternately with banana, mixing well after each addition. Turn into greased loaf pan and bake in moderate oven (350° F.) 1 hour or until done. Yield: 1 loaf, 8½ x 4½ x 2½ inches.

CEREAL BREAD

1½ cups sifted all-purpose flour
¼ cup cornmeal
2½ teaspoons baking powder
¾ teaspoon baking soda
½ teaspoon salt

¼ cup sugar
1 cup bran
½ cup quick-cooking oats
1½ cups sour milk or buttermilk
1 tablespoon shortening, melted

Sift together flour, cornmeal, baking powder, soda, salt and sugar; stir in bran and oatmeal; add sour milk and shortening, stirring only until mixed. Turn into greased loaf pan and bake in moderate oven (350° F.) 45 to 50 minutes. Yield: 1 loaf, 9½ x 5¼ x 2¾ inches.

ORANGE BREAD

1½ cups sifted all-purpose flour
2½ teaspoons baking powder
½ teaspoon salt
½ cup minced candied orange peel

2 tablespoons shortening
¼ cup sugar
1 egg
½ cup milk
¼ cup orange juice

Sift together flour, baking powder and salt; stir in candied orange peel. Cream shortening; gradually add sugar, creaming until well mixed, and beat in egg. Add flour mixture alternately with milk, beating well after each addition; stir in orange juice. Turn into greased loaf pan and bake in moderate oven (350° F.) 45 to 60 minutes. Yield: 1 loaf, 8½ x 4½ x 2½ inches.

APRICOT ALMOND BREAD

1½ cups dried apricots
½ cup almonds, chopped
3 tablespoons shortening
¾ cup granulated sugar
1 egg, beaten

2½ cups sifted all-purpose flour
5 teaspoons double-acting baking powder
½ teaspoon salt
¾ cup milk

Wash apricots, cover with water and cook 5 minutes. Drain, cool and chop. Combine with chopped almonds. Cream shortening and sugar. Add egg. Mix and sift dry ingredients and add apricots and nuts. Add alternately to first mixture with milk. Pour into greased loaf pan. Bake in a moderate oven (350° F.) 45 to 55 minutes. Yield: 1 loaf.

BANANA WALNUT BREAD

⅔ cup soft butter or margarine

1 cup sugar

2½ cups sifted all-purpose flour

1 teaspoon double-acting
  baking powder

1 teaspoon soda

½ teaspoon salt

2 eggs, beaten

1⅓ cups ripe mashed bananas

½ cup sour cream or buttermilk

1½ cups chopped walnuts

Cream butter or margarine and sugar together in mixing bowl. Sift flour with dry ingredients, not once but 4 times. Place bowl with butter and sugar under electric mixer; add 1 beaten egg with about 1 tablespoon of the sifted flour mixture, beat until smooth at low speed; add second beaten egg with 1 tablespoon of the sifted flour mixture and beat again until smooth. Add mashed bananas and beat again. Add sour cream or buttermilk alternately with the balance of the flour mixture. Remove bowl from the electric mixer and stir in the chopped walnuts. Place batter in 2-pound loaf pan or in 2 pans of 1-pound size, these oiled and lined with waxed paper. Bake about 1¼ hours in a moderate oven (350° F.) for the 1 large loaf or 1 hour for 2 loaves. Let cool slightly before removing. Yield: 1 2-pound loaf or 2 of the 1-pound size.

RICH NUT BREAD

3 cups sifted all-purpose flour

3 tablespoons white or brown
  sugar

5 teaspoons double-acting
  baking powder

1 teaspoon salt

1 cup chopped nuts

1 cup seedless raisins

1½ cups milk, warmed

¾ cup molasses

Mix dry ingredients and add raisins and nuts. Mix warm milk and molasses and cool. Add to flour and beat well. Turn into two well-greased loaf pans (8 x 4½ x 2½) and bake in moderate oven (350° F.) 35 minutes, or until done. Yield: 2 small loaves.

CARAWAY LOAF

2 cups prepared biscuit mix

½ teaspoon baking soda

2 tablespoons sugar

1 tablespoon caraway seeds

½ cup seedless raisins

1 cup buttermilk or sour milk

Mix together dry ingredients, caraway seeds and raisins; add buttermilk, stirring only until mixed. Turn into greased loaf pan and bake in moderate oven (350° F.) about 40 minutes. Yield: 1 loaf, 8½ x 4½ x 2½ inches.

BOSTON BROWN BREAD

1 cup sifted rye flour
1 cup cornmeal
1½ teaspoons baking soda
1 teaspoon salt

1 cup graham flour
¾ cup molasses
2 cups thick sour milk or
   buttermilk

Sift together rye flour, cornmeal, soda and salt; stir in graham flour; mix liquids and add to dry ingredients, stirring only until mixed. Fill well-greased molds ⅔ full, place greased covers on molds and steam 2 to 3 hours, depending upon size. Remove covers and bake in moderate oven (350° F.) about 15 minutes, or until tops are dry. To substitute sweet for sour milk, reduce amount to 1¾ cups, reduce soda to ½ teaspoon and add 4 teaspoons baking powder. Approximate yield: 2 large loaves.

Prune and Raisin Bread—Add ½ cup chopped uncooked prunes and ¼ cup chopped raisins to flour mixture. Approximate yield: 3 large loaves.

STEAMED BROWN BREAD

1 cup sifted all-purpose flour
2 teaspoons double-acting
   baking powder
1 teaspoon baking soda
1 teaspoon salt

2½ cups graham flour
1 cup raisins
1 egg, well beaten
¾ cup honey
2 cups sour milk or buttermilk

Sift all-purpose flour, baking powder, soda and salt; stir in graham flour and raisins. Combine egg, honey and sour milk; add to flour-raisin mixture, stirring until mixed. Fill large or small molds ⅔ full and cover tightly with greased lids. Steam large molds 4 hours, small molds 3 hours. Remove immediately from molds. Approximate yield: 2 large or 4 small loaves.

SHORTBREAD

1 cup butter or margarine   10 tablespoons sugar
2½ cups sifted all-purpose flour

Cream butter, gradually add sugar. Cream until light and fluffy. Blend in flour. Chill. Place dough on lightly floured board and roll ½ inch thick. Cut into strip ½ inch wide and 3 inches long. Bake in slow oven (300° F.) 25 minutes. Approximate yield: 2½ dozen sticks.

CRISP, BACON-TOPPED CORNBREAD

1½ cups sifted all-purpose
    flour
¾ cup cornmeal
3 teaspoons double-acting
    baking powder

1½ teaspoons salt
2 tablespoons sugar
1 egg, well beaten
1 cup milk
¼ cup melted shortening

6 slices cooked bacon

Sift together flour, cornmeal, baking powder, salt and sugar. Combine egg, well beaten, milk and shortening. Add dry ingredients. Stir to moisten well and turn into a greased jelly roll pan (16 x 1 x 9) and sprinkle with cooked bacon, crumbled. Bake about 25 minutes in a hot oven (425° F.), or until lightly browned. Yield: 8 portions.

CORN BREAD

¾ cup sifted all-purpose flour
1½ cups yellow cornmeal
4 teaspoons baking powder
1 teaspoon salt

2 tablespoons sugar
2 eggs, well beaten
1¼ cups milk
¼ cup shortening, melted

Sift together dry ingredients. Combine eggs and milk and add to flour mixture, stirring until mixed; stir in shortening. Turn into greased pan, 11½ x 7⅜ x 1½ inches, and bake in hot oven (400° F.) about 30 minutes. Sugar may be omitted, if desired. Yield: 6 squares (4 inches).

RICE SPOON BREAD

3 tablespoons white cornmeal
1 tablespoon flour
1 teaspoon salt
1 tablespoon sugar

1 cup boiling water
1 cup cooked rice
1 tablespoon shortening, melted
2 eggs, separated

1 cup milk

Mix together dry ingredients; stir into boiling water and cook over hot water until thick, stirring occasionally. Stir in rice and shortening and add beaten egg yolks and milk; fold in stiffly beaten egg whites. Turn into greased baking dish, place in shallow pan of hot water and bake in moderate oven (350° F.) 35 to 40 minutes. Serve from baking dish. Approximate yield: 6 portions.

VIRGINIA SPOON BREAD

1 cup cornmeal   2 cups milk, scalded
1 teaspoon salt   2½ teaspoons baking powder
          2 eggs, separated

Gradually stir cornmeal into salted hot milk and cook over hot water until thick and smooth, stirring occasionally; cool slightly. Stir in baking powder and well-beaten egg yolks and fold in stiffly beaten egg whites. Turn into greased casserole or 9-inch square pan. Bake in moderate oven (375° F.) about 35 minutes, or until firm and crust is brown. Serve from baking dish. Yield: 8 to 12 portions.

SALLY LUNN

2 cups sifted all-purpose flour   3 tablespoons sugar
3 teaspoons double-acting   2 eggs, separated
   baking powder   ½ cup milk
½ teaspoon salt   ½ cup shortening, melted

Sift dry ingredients. Combine beaten egg yolks and milk and add to flour mixture, stirring only until mixed. Add shortening; fold in stiffly beaten egg whites. Turn into greased 9-inch square pan. Bake in moderate oven (350° F.) about ½ hour. Yield: 9 squares (3 inches).

JOHNNY CAKE

Use recipe for Corn Bread (page 158); reduce baking powder to 1½ teaspoons and add ¾ teaspoon baking soda; substitute sour milk or buttermilk for sweet milk. Bake in greased 8 x 8 x 2-inch pan in moderate to hot oven (375°–400° F.) about 40 minutes. Approximate yield: 8 portions.

YEAST BREADS

WE ARE sure that you will find the little time and effort that bread-making takes more than repays you when you see the beaming family faces around the table as you serve the freshly baked loaf, golden brown, tender, crunchy outside, soft and yeasty inside —a real treat when spread thickly with soft butter.

We have made every effort to make breadmaking seem as simple and as easy as it really is in these pages. You will see here standard recipes, taking a trifle longer but guaranteeing excellent results if the directions are followed, as well as "quick" methods for the time-pressed cook.

FLOURS

FIRST choice of flours is the hard wheat or bread flour used by bakers. The all-purpose enriched flour, a blend of hard and soft wheats, is more commonly used at home. The following recipes have been developed using all-purpose enriched flour. When whole wheat, graham, rye, corn and other cereals are substituted for part of the all-purpose flour, see page 77 for substitutions.

YEAST

YEAST is available generally in the *dry granular package* and in the *compressed cake*. The dry granular needs no refrigeration. Check for expiration date on package for best results. Use like compressed yeast in a recipe (1 package dry yeast equals 1 cake compressed). Follow directions on package or *add to each package ¼ cup warm, not hot, water* (95° F.) and *let stand without stirring for 5 minutes*. If the recipe calls for milk or some other liquid, use the ¼ cup water and subtract that amount from the total liquid called for in the dough. Stir thoroughly before adding to the liquid mixture.

Compressed or moist yeast is perishable and can be stored in the refrigerator for 1 to 2 weeks and about 4 months in a freezer. It is sold in ⅗-ounce and ⅔-ounce size cakes. *Crumble into ¼ cup lukewarm water* (80° F.) *or other liquid and let stand about 5 minutes. Stir until dissolved.*

You will get superior bread by giving it time to rise slowly. Allow about 4 to 5 hours before baking. The yeast content can be increased in any recipe to cut the rising time, but better results are generally obtained with the slower method.

LIQUIDS

LIQUIDS added to yeast, alone or in combination, include water, which produces a wheaty flavored bread with a crisp crust, and milk, which gives a softer crumb, better keeping qualities, and higher nutritive value than water (scald milk and cool to luke-warm). Potato water adds a characteristic flavor, hastens the action of the yeast, and gives a coarser texture to the bread.

OTHER BREADMAKING INGREDIENTS

Sugar adds flavor and color to crust, helps yeast to produce leavening gas, but will retard action of yeast if used in too great a quantity. *Shortening* improves flavor, makes bread more tender, extends keeping qualities and causes bread to brown well. Butter or other shortenings, alone or in mixture, may be used. *Salt* gives flavor. Too much salt retards action of yeast.

STEPS IN MAKING PERFECT BREAD EASILY

1. Read recipe. Assemble necessary ingredients and utensils.
2. Sift flour before measuring. Measure accurately. Follow recipe directions for mixing. Have liquid at right temperature for the yeast. Dry granular yeast requires a slightly higher temperature (95°–105° F.) than does the compressed yeast cake (85° F.). Test by dropping on wrist; should not feel hot or cold.
3. Let yeast stand in liquid 5 minutes. Stir until dissolved. Add shortening and egg if called for. Mix in ½ of flour, beat with spoon, then use hand for remaining flour and work well. When dough gets stiff enough so it begins to leave sides of bowl, turn out on lightly floured board in a round ball to knead.
4. *Knead* by folding dough over toward you. Then push down away from you with the heel of the hand, using a rolling motion. Give dough a quarter turn, repeat until dough is smooth and elastic, and doesn't stick to board. (If dough sticks to the board badly in beginning, use a small amount of additional flour.) Kneading time will take 5 to 10 minutes.
5. Shape into a ball and place in a lightly greased bowl. Cover with a clean damp cloth and allow to rise in a draft-free warm place (80° to 85° F.) until doubled in bulk, or light enough to

hold the impression when pressed with a finger (1½ to 2 hours). Caution: *Do not let yeast doughs rise more than double their shape*. The bread will fall, become coarse and be dry when baked.

6. *Punch down* in the center. Thrust fist into center of dough, pull edges into center, and turn dough completely over in bowl. Cover and let rise again until *almost double* (30 to 45 minutes).
7. Remove dough to board. Divide for loaves, cover and let rest a few minutes. Knead until smooth and shape into a loaf. Place in greased loaf pan with sealed edge down.
8. Bake according to directions in recipe. The bread is done when the crust is well browned, shrinks from sides of pan and sounds hollow when tapped.

NOTE: To reduce time by one hour, add extra package or cake of yeast. Yeasty flavor is not due to too much yeast, but to too-high temperatures during rising.

RECIPE FOR WHITE BREAD

For 2 Loaves	*For 4 Loaves*
¼ cup warm, not hot, water (cool to lukewarm for compressed yeast)	½ cup warm, not hot, water (cool to lukewarm for compressed yeast)
1 pkg. dry granular yeast or 1 cake compressed yeast	2 pkgs. dry granular yeast or 2 cakes compressed yeast
1¾ cups lukewarm liquid	3½ cups lukewarm liquid
2 tablespoons sugar	4 tablespoons sugar
1 tablespoon salt	2 tablespoons salt
2 tablespoons shortening	4 tablespoons shortening
6 to 6¼ cups sifted all-purpose flour	12 to 12½ cups (about 3 quarts) all-purpose flour

Measure water into large mixing bowl. (Cool to lukewarm for compressed yeast.) Sprinkle or crumble in yeast. Let stand for 5 minutes. Stir until dissolved. Add remaining liquid (scalded and cooled to lukewarm), sugar and salt and stir to dissolve completely. Add shortening. Stir in ½ of flour, beat until smooth and elastic. Add remaining flour. See directions on page 161 for mixing, kneading, rising. Mold the loaves and place in greased 9 x 5 x 3-inch bread loaf pans. Let rise again and bake in hot oven (425° F.) 25 to 30 minutes.

MODIFICATIONS OF WHITE BREAD

Prepare dough for 2 loaves. Before kneading, remove half to another bowl. Add ingredients in one of the variations, mix well, knead, proceed as for bread.

Nut Bread—Add 1 cup coarsely chopped nuts.

Date or Raisin Bread—Add 1 cup cut-up dates or raisins.

Cracked Wheat Bread—Add 2 tablespoons honey and 1 cup cracked wheat. Bake at 375° F.

Whole Wheat Bread—Add ¼ cup molasses, ¾ cup whole wheat flour. Bake at 375° F.

Whole Wheat Prune Bread—Add ½ tablespoon grated orange rind to dough; knead ½ cup chopped prunes into light dough, mold.

Salt-Free Bread—Increase sugar to 6 tablespoons and shortening to 6 tablespoons. Let rise only half the time (without salt it rises twice as fast) and shape into loaves at first rising. Let rise again and bake at 400° F. for 25 to 30 minutes. Yield: 2 loaves.

Herb Bread—Use milk as liquid and increase sugar to ¼ cup. Add 2 well-beaten eggs, 1 teaspoon nutmeg, 2 teaspoons dried sage, crumbled, and 4 teaspoons caraway seeds before flour is added. Bake in hot oven (400° F.) about 40 minutes. Yield: 2 loaves (1 lb. each).

ANADAMA BREAD

½ cup yellow cornmeal
2 cups boiling water
2 tablespoons shortening
½ cup dark molasses

1 teaspoon salt
1 envelope dry granular yeast
½ cup warm, not hot, water
5 cups bread flour (about)

Stir the corn meal slowly into the boiling water in top of double boiler and let steam very slowly over boiling water for 1 hour. Add shortening, molasses and salt. Cool. When lukewarm, add the yeast which has been dissolved in the warm, not hot, water. Add enough flour to make a regular stiff bread dough. Knead on a lightly floured board for 10 minutes. Form into a ball, lightly grease the top, place in a bowl and let stand covered in a warm place until it rises to more than double its size, about 2 hours. Shape into 2 loaves and place in bread pans and let rise until light. Bake in hot oven (400° F.) 1 hour, or until done. Yield: 2 loaves of bread.

MOLASSES RAISIN BREAD

¼ cup warm, not hot, water
1 package dry granular yeast
¾ cup milk, scalded and cooled
1 teaspoon salt
⅓ cup molasses
1 egg, slightly beaten

3 to 3½ cups sifted all-purpose
    flour
¼ cup melted shortening
1 teaspoon grated lemon rind
½ teaspoon almond extract
1 cup chopped raisins

Dissolve yeast in warm, not hot, water (about 95° to 105° F.). Add warm milk, salt, molasses and egg and blend. Add half the flour; beat thoroughly. Add melted shortening, lemon rind, almond extract and raisins. Add rest of flour gradually, beating well after each addition until mixture will not cling to bowl and breaks from spoon. Place in greased bowl, brush surface with melted shortening, cover and let rise in warm place (80° to 85° F.) until double in bulk. Punch down dough and let rise again. Shape bread and place in greased bread pan, 9 x 4½ inches. Cover and let rise until doubled in volume. Bake in moderate oven (350° F.) about 1 hour. Yield: 1 loaf. *Note:* This bread may be sliced thin and used for tea or for sandwiches.

THE NO-KNEAD METHOD

Making bread by the no-knead method saves time and labor and gives a bread of fair quality. There are several differences between the standard method and the no-knead method. First, it is an egg bread and more yeast is used; second, the flour is gradually added and the dough beaten well between each addition; third, when the ingredients are combined the dough is ready to shape. At this point in the process the dough can be refrigerated for 2 hours or more, or it can be shaped immediately. If dough has been refrigerated, then the approximate rising time to double in bulk will be 2 hours. However, if it is shaped immediately, it will take about 1 hour to rise.

QUICK NO-KNEAD BREAD

½ cup warm, not hot, water
   (cool to lukewarm for cake
   yeast)
3 pkgs. dry granular yeast or
   3 cakes compressed yeast
1½ cups scalded milk, cooled to
   lukewarm

½ cup shortening
¼ cup sugar
2 tablespoons salt
3 eggs, beaten
8-8½ cups sifted all-purpose
   enriched flour

Place water in a large mixing bowl (cool to lukewarm for compressed yeast). Scatter or crumble yeast in water. Let stand without stirring for 5 minutes. Add scalded milk that has been cooled to lukewarm, shortening, sugar and salt. Stir until yeast is dissolved. Blend in eggs. Gradually add sifted flour and stir until dough is thoroughly mixed. It is softer than a kneaded dough. Place in a large greased bowl and cover. Store dough in refrigerator or cold place at least 2 hours. Shape dough (chilled or unchilled) into 3 loaves on well-floured board; place in greased loaf pan (9 x 5 x 3 inches), and cover. Allow dough to rise in warm place (80° to 85° F.) until double in bulk: about 2 hours for chilled dough, 1 hour for unchilled dough. Bake in moderate oven (375° F.) 1 hour. Yield: 3 loaves.

Nut Bread—Add 1½ cups chopped nuts with the eggs and blend.

Cheese Bread—Add 3 cups grated cheese with eggs and blend.

BASIC BEATEN BATTER (YEAST-LEAVENED)

¼ cup warm, not hot, water
   (cool to lukewarm for compressed yeast)
1 pkg. dry granular yeast or
   1 cake compressed yeast
1 cup milk
¼ cup sugar

1 teaspoon salt
½ cup shortening
3¼ cups sifted all-purpose flour
   (about)
1 egg*
½ teaspoon vanilla extract (if
   desired)

Soften yeast in warm water (cool to lukewarm for cake yeast). Scald milk. Add sugar, salt and shortening. Cool to lukewarm. Add 2 cups flour and beat well. Add softened yeast, egg and vanilla extract. Beat well. Add more flour to make a stiff batter. Beat thoroughly until smooth. Cover and let rise until bubbly (about 1 hour). Use with different toppings to make coffee cakes and puff rolls. Yield: 2 8-inch square or 9-inch round coffee cakes or about 2½ dozen 2-inch puffs.

MODIFICATIONS OF BASIC BEATEN BATTER

The following modifications call for one-half the recipe of the Basic Beaten Batter. We found that making a full recipe, and using one-half for rolls, etc., and the other half for any of these modifications gave best results. If you want to prepare just one-half recipe of Basic Beaten Batter, use full amount of yeast and warm, not hot, water (cool to lukewarm for cake yeast). Reduce milk to 6 tablespoons.

Fruit Puffs—Prepare muffin pans by putting ½ teaspoon melted butter or margarine in each. Cover with about 1 teaspoon Cinnamon Sugar (page 724) and arrange fruit in each pan. (1 cup pitted cherries or sliced peaches may be used.) When ½ Basic Beaten Batter is light, stir down and drop in muffin cups filling about ½ full. Let rise until light (about 30 minutes). Bake in moderate oven (375° F.) 20 to 25 minutes. Approximate yield: 12 3-inch puffs.

Orange Blossoms—When ½ Basic Beaten Batter is light, stir down. Drop by spoonfuls into greased muffin pans, filling muffin cups ⅓ full. Over each muffin cup sprinkle about 1 teaspoon Orange Sugar (page 724) and ½ teaspoon chopped nuts. Let rise until light (about 30 minutes). Bake in moderate oven (375° F.) 20 to 25 minutes. Approximate yield: 16 2-inch puffs.

* For richer batter use two eggs.

Marmalade Coffee Cake—Prepare 8-inch square pan by spreading with 2 tablespoons melted butter or margarine and ½ cup orange marmalade. When ½ Basic Beaten Batter is light, stir down. Spread over marmalade. Let rise until light (about 30 minutes). Bake in moderate oven (375° F.) about 30 minutes. Turn out upside down. Yield: 1 coffee cake.

Cranberry Upside-down Coffee Cake—Prepare 9-inch round pan by spreading with 2 tablespoons melted butter or margarine, and adding 2 cups raw cranberries. Combine 1 cup sugar and 1 tablespoon flour and sprinkle over cranberries. When ½ Basic Beaten Batter is light, stir down. Spread over fruit mixture. Let rise until light (about 30 minutes). Bake in moderate oven (375° F.) about 30 minutes. Turn out upside down. Yield: 1 coffee cake.

Crumble Squares—Combine ¼ cup enriched flour, ¼ cup enriched bread crumbs, 2 tablespoons sugar, and ½ teaspoon cinnamon. Cut or rub in 2 tablespoons butter or margarine until mixture is crumbly. When ½ Basic Beaten Batter is light, stir down. Spread evenly into greased 8-inch square pan. Sprinkle with crumb mixture. Make squares by pressing lines into batter with floured fingertips. Let rise until light (about 30 minutes). Bake in moderate oven (375° F.) about 30 minutes. Yield: 9 2½-inch squares or 16 2-inch squares.

Hot Cross Squares—Add ½ teaspoon cinnamon and ¼ teaspoon allspice with flour to ½ recipe Basic Beaten Batter. When batter is light, add 1 cup currants and stir down. Follow procedure for Crumble Squares. Make cross on each square with Confectioners' Sugar Icing (page 719).

Apricot Coffee Cake—When ½ Basic Beaten Batter is light, stir down. Melt ¼ cup butter or margarine in 8-inch square pan. Sprinkle with ¼ cup sugar. Arrange 1 cup cooked apricots in pan and top with basic batter. Sprinkle with brown sugar. Let rise until light (about 30 minutes). Bake in moderate oven (375° F.) about 30 minutes. Yield: 16 2-inch squares.

Butterscotch Coconut Topping—Combine ¼ cup brown sugar with ¼ cup grated coconut. Add 1 tablespoon melted butter or margarine and mix until well blended. Sprinkle over ½ recipe of Basic Beaten Batter. Let rise until light (about 30 minutes). Bake in moderate oven (375° F.) about 30 minutes. Yield: 16 2-inch squares.

SPICY NUT COFFEE CAKE

1 pkg. prepared hot roll mix
¾ cup lukewarm water
1 egg
1 teaspoon cinnamon
¾ teaspoon nutmeg

½ cup raisins
¼ cup candied cherry halves
¼ cup sugar
3 tablespoons butter
¼ cup all-purpose flour

¼ cup chopped nut meats

Place yeast from roll mix package in mixing bowl; add water and stir until completely dissolved. Blend in egg, ½ teaspoon cinnamon, ½ teaspoon nutmeg, raisins, cherry halves and 2 tablespoons sugar. Add contents of hot roll mix and stir until dough is well blended. Grease top of dough lightly, cover with waxed paper and let rise in warm place (85° F.) until doubled, about 1 hour. Divide dough into 6 portions and shape into balls. Arrange in a circle in bottom of greased 8-inch tube pan. Prick top of dough with fork and brush with 1 tablespoon melted butter. Combine remaining butter, remaining sugar, flour, nut meats and remaining cinnamon and nutmeg; sprinkle over dough. Let rise in warm place until doubled. Bake in moderate oven (375° F.) 30 minutes. Yield: 8 portions.

STANDARD ROLLS

1 or 2 pkgs. dry granular yeast
   or cakes compressed yeast
½ cup warm, not hot, water
   (cooled to lukewarm for
   compressed yeast)

1½ cups milk, scalded
2 teaspoons salt
¼ cup sugar
⅓ cup shortening
6 cups sifted all-purpose flour
   (about)

Follow standard method of mixing, kneading and rising on pages 161–162. Shape as desired and place in greased pans. Brush with melted shortening, cover and let rise in warm place until double in bulk (about 1 hour). Bake in hot oven (400° to 425° F.) 15 to 20 minutes. Yield: 3 to 4 dozen rolls.

TYPES OF STANDARD ROLLS

Biscuits—Cut off small, uniform pieces; fold sides under until top is smooth and dough is round. For crusty biscuits, place balls 1 inch apart; for tall, soft biscuits, place close together.

Twists—Roll dough ½ inch thick, cut in narrow strips and roll with palm of hand into 8 inch strips; twist from ends in opposite directions, then bring ends together. Place in greased pan 1 inch apart; brush with egg yolk diluted with 1 tablespoon milk.

Finger Rolls—Shape small pieces of dough into balls; roll with hand on unfloured board to desired thickness, keeping them smooth and uniform in size. Place 1 inch apart.

Parker House Rolls—Roll dough ¼ inch thick, cut with floured 2-inch biscuit cutter and make crease just off center of each round with dull end of knife. Brush with melted shortening; fold each over so that top overlaps bottom. Press edges together at ends of crease. Place rolls 1 inch apart.

Bread Sticks—Roll dough ½ inch thick; cut in ½ inch strips and roll with palm of hand into long, smooth rolls, the thickness of a pencil. Cut in 6 to 9 inch lengths and place in greased pan 1 inch apart. Let rise until double in bulk. When nearly baked, reduce heat to 350° F.; bake until dry and crisp.

Butterhorns—Roll dough into 8 or 9 inch circle about ¼ inch thick; cut into 10 or 12 pie-shaped pieces. Dip each wedge in melted butter and roll as for jelly roll, beginning with wide edge. Place on buttered baking sheet with points on top.

Clover Leaf Rolls—Shape very small pieces into balls, dip in melted shortening and place 3 in each section of greased muffin pan.

Crescents—Roll dough ¼ inch thick; with floured, sharp knife cut in about 3 inch squares; then cut each square in half diagonally. Brush with melted shortening and roll each triangle from base to point; press point down firmly and bring two ends almost together to form crescent. Place on greased baking sheet about 1 inch apart; brush tops with egg white, beaten slightly with 2 tablespoons water.

Bowknot Rolls—Roll dough about ¼ inch thick and cut in strips about 6 inches long and 1 inch across. Roll each strip and tie in single knots. Place on greased baking sheet, cover with a towel. Let rise until double in bulk. Bake in moderate oven (375° F.) 20 to 25 minutes.

MODIFICATIONS OF STANDARD ROLLS
(Use recipe on page 169)

Whole Wheat Rolls—Use 3 cups whole wheat flour and about 3 cups sifted all-purpose flour.

Cinnamon Rolls—Use ½ recipe; roll raised dough ½ inch thick, brush with melted butter and sprinkle with mixture of 6 tablespoons sugar, 1 teaspoon cinnamon and ½ cup currants; roll as for jelly roll and cut in 1 inch slices. Place close together in greased pan, brush with melted butter and let rise until double in bulk.

Butterscotch Pecan Rolls—Use ½ recipe; roll light dough ½ inch thick, brush with melted butter and sprinkle with ½ cup brown sugar; roll as for jelly roll and cut in 1 inch slices. Cream together 6 table-spoons butter and ½ cup brown sugar, spread in bottom of pan and sprinkle ½ cup pecan nuts over top; place slices of roll on mixture and brush tops with melted butter.

REFRIGERATOR ROLLS

Use recipe for Standard Rolls (page 169) or Sweet Rolls (page 171). Store in refrigerator, if desired. From 1½ to 2 hours before baking, re-move desired quantity, shape at once and let rise until double in bulk. Bake as directed for rolls. Approximate yield: 3 to 4 dozen rolls.

Ring Rolls—Roll dough out on a lightly floured board about ⅓ inch thick and cut with floured doughnut cutter (or two cookie cutters, one smaller in diameter than the other). Place on a greased pan, spread with melted butter; cover with a towel and allow to rise in warm place until doubled in bulk. Bake in hot oven (400° F.) 18 to 20 minutes.

Braided Rolls—Roll dough about ½ inch thick and cut in strips ½ inch wide and 7 inches long. Place 3 strips together and braid. Press ends together. Cover and allow to double before baking.

Snails—Roll dough in palm of hands into thin strips 10 inches long and ½ inch thick. Place one end on a greased baking sheet and coil around end. Brush with beaten egg white. Sprinkle with ground almonds. Bake in moderate oven (350° F.). Remove from oven, sprinkle with sifted confectioners' sugar and cool before serving.

Leaflet Rolls—Roll well-chilled refrigerator dough into an oblong shape ¼ inch thick. Spread with melted butter. Cut into 8 strips, about 1¾ inches wide. Lay one strip on top of other and cut through the layers to form squares. Turn the squares and place each in a greased muffin tin with the edges pointed upward (use 1¾ inch muffin tins). Cover and allow to double before baking.

BASIC SWEET DOUGH

¼ cup warm, not hot, water
  (cool to lukewarm for compressed yeast)
2 pkgs. dry granular yeast or
  2 cakes compressed yeast
1 cup milk
½ cup sugar

2 teaspoons salt
¼ cup shortening
5 cups sifted all-purpose flour
  (about)
2 eggs
1 teaspoon grated lemon rind (if
  desired)

Soften yeast in warm water. (Cool to lukewarm for cake yeast.) Scald milk. Add sugar, salt and shortening. Cool to lukewarm. Add flour to make a thick batter. Mix well. Add softened yeast, eggs and lemon rind. Beat well. Add enough more flour to make a soft dough. Turn out on lightly floured board and knead until smooth and satiny. Place in greased bowl, cover and let rise in warm place until doubled (about 1½ hours). When light, punch down. Let rest 10 minutes. Shape into tea rings, rolls or coffee cakes. Let rise until doubled (about 45 minutes). Bake in moderate oven (350° F.) 20 to 30 minutes. Yield: 2 or 3 coffee cakes, or approximately 3½ dozen rolls.

MODIFICATIONS OF BASIC SWEET DOUGH

The following modifications call for one-third to one-half the recipe of the Basic Sweet Dough. We found that making a full recipe, and using two-thirds to one-half for rolls, etc., and the other one-third or one-half for any of these modifications gave best results. If you want to prepare just one-half recipe of Basic Sweet Dough, use full amount of yeast and warm, not hot, water (cool to lukewarm for cake yeast). Reduce milk to 6 tablespoons.

Whirligig Rolls—When one-third to one-half recipe Basic Sweet Dough is light, punch down and let rest 10 minutes. Roll dough into slender roll about ¾ inch in diameter. Cut into 5 pieces, about 8 inches long. In greased 9-inch round pan, lay pieces of dough in shape of spokes of wheel, rolling each piece loosely toward center. Let each roll overlap its neighbor slightly. Brush with Honey Topping (page 720). Let rise until doubled (about 45 minutes). Bake in moderate oven (350° F.) 25 to 30 minutes. Yield: 5 rolls.

Fan Coffee Cake—When one-third to one-half recipe Basic Sweet Dough is light, punch down and let rest 10 minutes. Roll out to square 12 x 12 inches. Brush with melted butter or margarine and sprinkle with Cinnamon Sugar (page 724). Fold in half. Brush top surface with melted butter or margarine, sprinkle with Cinnamon Sugar and fold over again to make small square. Roll out into square 12 x 12 inches, brush with melted butter or margarine and sprinkle with Cinnamon Sugar. Fold over to form a triangle. Put on greased baking sheet. With sharp knife or scissors slash strips tapering from long edge of triangle toward point leaving uncut near point (about 8 slashes). Separate loose ends of strips and lay on side. Brush with melted butter or margarine. Let rise until doubled (about 45 minutes). Bake in moderate oven (350° F.) 25 to 30 minutes. When cool, frost with Confectioners' Sugar Icing (page 719) and sprinkle with chopped nuts, if desired. Yield: 1 coffee cake.

Cinnamon Blossom Coffee Cake—When one-third to one-half recipe Basic Sweet Dough is light, punch down and let rest 10 minutes. Pat or roll into a rectangular sheet about ½ inch thick and 8 inches wide. Sprinkle Sugar Crunch Filling (page 724) evenly over dough. Roll up like jelly roll, sealing edge. With a sharp knife, make five diagonal cuts through the roll. Arrange five sections in a circle on greased baking sheet, with edges touching each other. Place the remaining section in the center. Let rise until doubled (about 45 minutes). Bake in moderate oven (350° F.) 25 to 30 minutes. When cool, frost with Confectioners' Sugar Icing (page 719). Yield: 1 coffee cake.

Carrousel Coffee Cake—When one-third to one-half recipe Basic Sweet Dough is light, punch down and let rest 10 minutes. Roll out in rectangular sheet 9 x 18 inches. Spread with melted butter or margarine and sprinkle with Cinnamon Sugar. Fold over in thirds making sheet 9 x 6 inches. Cut into strips 1 inch wide and 6 inches long. Roll one strip starting at narrow end. Stand on edge in center of greased baking sheet. Roll remaining strips in similar manner rolling only half of strip, leaving about 2-inch end. Stand these half rolls on edge around center roll with unrolled end toward center. Let rise until doubled (about 45 minutes). Bake in moderate oven (350° F.) 25 to 30 minutes. When cool, frost with Sugar Icing (page 719). Yield: 1 coffee cake.

Kris Kringle's Tree—When one-third to one-half recipe Basic Sweet Dough is light, punch down and let rest 10 minutes. Roll or stretch out to square sheet a scant half inch thick. Brush one diagonal half of the dough with 2 tablespoons melted butter or margarine. Sprinkle this half with ¼ cup sugar, ¼ cup chopped cherries, and ¼ cup chopped nuts (if desired). Fold the unspread half over the sugar-and-fruit covered half to form a triangle. Press edges firmly together. Place on greased baking sheet. With scissors or sharp knife cut dough from two opposite edges of triangle toward center. Cut almost to center making cuts about an inch apart. Twist each cut slightly. Place a small twist of dough at base to form "trunk." Cover and let rise until doubled (about 45 minutes). Bake in moderate oven (350° F.) 25 to 30 minutes. If desired, frost with Confectioners' Sugar Icing (page 719) and garnish with colored fruits, candies or sugar. Yield: 1 coffee cake.

PAPPY'S SOUTHERN ROLLS

1 cake of compressed yeast or	½ cup shortening, melted
1 package granular yeast	⅓ cup milk (room temperature)
⅓ cup warm, not hot, water	1 tablespoon sugar
(cool to lukewarm for cake	1 teaspoon salt
yeast)	3 cups sifted all-purpose flour
3 eggs	¼ pound butter or margarine

Dissolve yeast in warm, not hot, water (cool to lukewarm for cake yeast) for 10 minutes. Drop eggs into mixing bowl, add melted shortening, milk, dissolved yeast, sugar and salt. Beat well and begin working in the flour. Knead continuously in the bowl until it's a good dough, smooth and elastic. Cover and let rest in warm place 45 minutes or until double in bulk. Punch down dough. Cut off small pieces about the size of a walnut. Place in greased muffin pans. Let rise in a warm place until roll is as high as the pan. Bake in a hot oven (400° F.) for 8 to 12 minutes. Brush with butter. Yield: 2 dozen rolls.

MOM'S JAM SURPRISE ROLLS

1 pkg. dry, granular yeast or
   1 cake compressed yeast
¼ cup warm, not hot, water
   (cool to lukewarm for cake
   yeast)
½ cup and 1 tablespoon sugar
¼ cup scalded milk
4 cups unsifted all-purpose
   flour
1½ teaspoons salt
1 teaspoon grated lemon rind
2 teaspoons vanilla

¼ teaspoon finely crushed
   cardamom seed
3 egg yolks
1¼ cups sour cream
½ cup apricot jam (about)
¼ cup butter
¼ cup margarine
¼ pound walnuts or pecans,
   ground
2 tablespoons sugar
1 cup confectioners' sugar
¼ cup light cream

Dissolve yeast in warm, not hot, water (cool to lukewarm for cake yeast) for 10 minutes. Add 1 tablespoon sugar and the milk, stirring until well blended. Add ½ cup flour, beating in well. Cover bowl, set in warm place and let rise 15 minutes.

Meanwhile sift 3½ cups flour, ½ cup sugar and salt. Add lemon rind, 1½ teaspoons vanilla, cardamom seed, egg yolks and sour cream. Pour mixture into risen sponge and beat 5 minutes until very smooth. Turn sponge into a large greased bowl and cover, but not too tightly. Set aside in a warm place to rise for 2 hours. Rising period may be shortened 30 minutes by preheating oven to 70° F.; then off with the heat and in goes the sponge. After its full rising the dough is divided into two parts; half may be refrigerated and the rolls made up a day or two later. Turn dough to well-floured board and roll to ¼ inch thickness; cut into 3-inch squares. Place 1 teaspoon thick apricot jam in center of each square. Pinch four corners together over jam. Now pinch protruding four corners together to form a ball, rounding smoothly.

Melt butter and margarine and dip each roll into the lukewarm shortening, then into ground nuts combined with 2 tablespoons sugar. Place rolls cut-side down into 10 x 2 inch deep pie plates.

Cover rolls with clean cloth and allow to rise in a warm place 1½ hours or until more than double in bulk. Bake 15 minutes in a 375° F. oven; reduce heat to 350° F. and bake 25 to 30 minutes longer. While still warm, drizzle on sugar icing in a spiral starting at center of cake-like array, working outward. To make frosting, combine confectioners' sugar with cream and remaining ½ teaspoon vanilla. Around the border there should be a double drizzle. Yield: 32 rolls.

PHILADELPHIA CINNAMON BUNS

1¼ cups milk	¾ cup sugar
¼ cup warm, not hot, water	2 eggs
1 pkg. dry, granular yeast	¼ cup butter or margarine
5 cups sifted all-purpose flour	½ cup brown sugar
1½ teaspoons salt	2 teaspoons cinnamon
1 tablespoon sugar	½ cup black walnut meats
½ cup shortening	½ cup raisins or currants

1 cup dark or light corn syrup

Scald milk, cool to lukewarm. Dissolve yeast in warm, not hot, water for 10 minutes and combine with milk. Make a sponge by adding 2 cups flour, salt and 1 tablespoon sugar, beating until smooth. Set aside in a warm place. Beat shortening until light, whip in ¾ cup sugar and add eggs one at a time, beating each in thoroughly. When the sponge is bubbly, gradually beat in shortening mixture, then knead in remaining 3 cups flour. Cover, let rise in a warm place until double in bulk.

Divide and roll each portion of the dough to ¼ inch thickness. Spread with softened butter or margarine, sprinkle with a mixture of brown sugar and cinnamon. Scatter on the nuts and raisins or currants and dribble with a part of the syrup. Roll as a jelly roll and cut in 1½ inch lengths. Stand buns in two deep 9-inch pans that have been well buttered and filled with syrup to a depth of ¼ inch. Cover and let rise until double in bulk. Bake in a moderate oven (350° F.) 45 minutes. Turn out of pans immediately. Yield: 2 dozen.

CINNAMON BOWKNOTS

1 cup milk	1 cake yeast or 1 package
⅔ cup shortening	granular yeast
⅔ cup sugar	½ cup warm, not hot, water
1 teaspoon salt	½ cup butter or margarine
2 eggs	2 cups sugar
4½ cups all-purpose flour	2 teaspoons cinnamon

Scald milk, add shortening, sugar and salt. Cool to lukewarm, add eggs and one cup flour. Beat smooth. Add yeast which has been dissolved in the water. Beat well, add remainder of flour and mix to a smooth dough just stiff enough to handle. Lightly grease top of dough, cover and allow to rise until double in bulk. Punch down and place covered in refrigerator to chill 2 hours. Turn to floured board. Roll out ¼ inch thick and cut into strips ½ inch wide, 12 inches long. Dip in butter, then into sugar-cinnamon mix. Tie into bowknots. Place in muffin tins, bake in (375° F.) oven 15 to 20 minutes. Yield: 30 rolls.

NO-KNEAD WATER-RISING TWISTS

½ cup shortening
3 tablespoons sugar
1½ teaspoons salt
1 teaspoon vanilla
½ cup scalded milk*
2 cakes compressed yeast,
   crumbled (or 2 envelopes

dry granular yeast dissolved
   in ¼ cup warm water)
3 cups sifted all-purpose flour
3 eggs
¾ cup chopped nuts (any kind)
½ cup sugar
1 teaspoon cinnamon

Combine shortening, sugar, salt, vanilla and milk. Add crumbled compressed yeast or dissolved dry yeast; mix well. Blend in 1½ cups flour and beat until smooth. Cover and let rest for 15 minutes. Add eggs, one at a time, beating well after each addition. Blend in remaining flour and mix thoroughly. The dough will be quite soft. Let rise in only one of two ways: *Either* (1) set covered dough in warm place about ½ hour; *or* (2) tie dough in a tea towel, allowing space for dough to rise. Then place in a large mixing bowl and fill with water (75° to 80° F.). Let stand until dough rises to top of water, about 45 minutes. Remove from water. The dough will be soft and moist. Divide dough into small pieces. Roll each piece in combined nuts, sugar and cinnamon-mixture. Stretch to about 8 inch length. Twist into desired shape. Place on greased cookie sheet. Let stand for 5 minutes. Bake in moderate oven (375° F.) 12 to 15 minutes. Yield: 24.

MARTHA WASHINGTON'S POTATO ROLLS

2 large potatoes
1 teaspoon salt
2 tablespoons sugar
3 tablespoons butter
1½ cups potato water

½ cup milk, scalded
1 pkg. dry granular yeast or
   1 cake compressed yeast
¼ cup warm, not hot, water
7 cups sifted all-purpose flour

Cook potatoes, drain and save water. Mash potatoes and add salt, sugar and butter, beating well; add potato water and hot milk, and cool. When lukewarm, add yeast dissolved in warm water and stir in 4 cups flour, beating well; add enough remaining flour to make a dough stiff enough to knead. Knead until smooth and elastic; brush top with melted butter and place in greased large mixing bowl; cover and let rise 5 hours, or until doubled in bulk. Place on board and pat ½ inch thick; pinch off small pieces and shape into small rolls. Place in greased pan and let rise until more than doubled in bulk; bake in hot oven (400° F.) 20 minutes, or until done. Yield: 48 rolls.

*If dry yeast is used, decrease milk to ¼ cup.

HARD ROLLS

1 pkg. granular yeast or	¼ cup sugar
cake compressed yeast	1 teaspoon salt
¼ cup warm, not hot, water	1 tablespoon butter
(cooled to lukewarm for	1 tablespoon lard
compressed yeast)	1 cup boiling water

4 cups sifted all-purpose flour

Sprinkle or crumble yeast on warm, not hot, water (lukewarm if compressed yeast is used) and let stand 5 minutes without stirring. Stir to dissolve. Add sugar, salt and shortening to boiling water and mix well; when lukewarm add to yeast and beat in flour. Knead dough lightly 5 minutes; place in bowl greased with butter, cover and let rise in a warm draft-free place. When doubled in bulk, pat out on board, about ½ inch thick, and cut in small, narrow strips; place strips 2 inches apart on baking sheet, cover and let rise until very light. Brush with butter and bake in slow oven (300° F.) 40 minutes; then increase heat to moderate (375° F.) and bake 10 minutes longer; slow baking is essential. Yield: 2½ dozen rolls.

RAISED MUFFINS

To ½ recipe for Sweet Rolls (page 171), add 1 egg and flour enough to make a stiff dough which can be beaten thoroughly but not kneaded. When doubled in bulk, fill greased muffin pans ½ full, brush with melted shortening, cover and let rise until doubled in bulk. Sprinkle chopped nuts over top and bake in hot oven (400°–425° F.) 15 to 20 minutes. Approximate yield: 2 to 2½ dozen muffins.

ENGLISH HOT CROSS BUNS

1 recipe Standard Rolls	¼ cup chopped, candied orange
(page 169)	peel
3 eggs	2 tablespoons milk
½ cup seeded raisins	½ cup confectioner's sugar
½ cup currants	(about)
¼ cup shredded citron	

Prepare dough by standard method, adding 2 slightly beaten eggs before adding the flour. When double in bulk add the fruit, knead lightly and shape or cut into large biscuits; place in greased pan, 1 inch apart, cover and let rise in warm place until doubled in bulk. Make a deep cross in center of each and brush over with remaining egg yolk mixed with milk; bake in moderate to hot oven (375°–400° F.) about 20 minutes. While warm, glaze slightly with remaining egg white beaten with confectioners' sugar. Yield: 3 dozen buns.

EASTER BABA

¾ cup hot milk   ¼ cup warm, not hot, water
½ cup sugar   4½ cups all-purpose flour
½ teaspoon salt   ¾ cup butter, melted and cooled
1 package dry granular yeast   6 eggs, slightly beaten

In a large mixing bowl combine the milk, sugar and salt. Cool to lukewarm. Dissolve yeast in warm, not hot, water. Add to milk mixture
with 1 cup of flour. Beat until smooth; cover and let rise in warm place
until spongy and double in bulk. Beat in butter, eggs and remaining
flour, adding just enough to make a dough which is slightly sticky, but
which can be easily handled. Cover and let rise in warm place until
doubled in bulk. Punch down dough. Knead gently on lightly floured
board until smooth and elastic. Place in a greased large ring mold (3-
quart). Cover and allow to rise until doubled in bulk. Bake in moderate oven (350° F.) about 35 to 40 minutes. The baba ring can be
served hot, or with the slices toasted, with rum-flavored Fruit Apricot
Sauce or the whole baba may be brandy- or rum-soaked and served
cold with stewed fruits and whipped cream. Yield: 12 portions.

EASTER FLOWER COFFEE CAKE

1 pkg. dry granular yeast   1 egg, beaten
¼ cup warm, not hot, water   ½ teaspoon grated lemon rind
½ cup milk, scalded and cooled   2 tablespoons soft butter
¼ cup sugar   ¼ cup sugar
1 teaspoon salt   2 teaspoons cinnamon
2 tablespoons melted shortening   ¼ cup chopped nuts
2½ cups sifted all-purpose flour   confectioners' sugar

Dissolve yeast in warm water in a large mixing bowl. Add milk, sugar,
salt and shortening and stir until mixed. Work enough flour into the
dough to make a soft dough. Knead until smooth and elastic. Place in
greased bowl, cover and let rise until double in bulk (about 2 hours).
Punch down, stir in egg and lemon rind before adding remaining flour.
Roll dough into large narrow sheet (8 x 12 inches). Brush with butter.
Combine sugar, cinnamon and nuts and sprinkle over dough. Roll up
like jelly roll and seal edge. Cut in 1 inch slices. Place seven of the
slices ½ inch apart in a circle on a greased baking sheet. Arrange the
remaining five slices in the center of the first circle, letting the slices
overlap. Cover and let rise until double in bulk (30 to 40 minutes).
Bake in moderate oven (350° F.) 25 to 30 minutes. When slightly cool,
brush lightly with confectioners' sugar mixed with water and sprinkle
with chopped nuts. Yield: 1 large coffee cake.

KUCHEN

¼ cup warm, not hot, water
   (cooled to lukewarm for
   compressed yeast)
1 pkg. dry granular yeast or
   1 cake compressed yeast
1¼ cups milk, scalded, cooled
1¼ teaspoons salt

1 cup sugar
3 egg yolks, well beaten
6 cups sifted all-purpose flour
   (about)
¾ cup shortening, melted
1 egg white, slightly beaten
1 tablespoon water

Follow standard method of mixing, kneading and rising on page 161. Add egg yolks to liquid mixture before first addition of the flour. When dough is double in bulk and is ready for shaping, roll into rectangle, ½-inch thick and fit into 2 greased square pans or 1 large pan; cover and let rise in warm place until double in bulk. Then brush with mixture of egg white and water, or sprinkle with chopped nut meats or currants if desired, and bake in moderately hot oven (375°–400° F.) 20 to 25 minutes. Yield: 2 square (9-inch) cakes.

AMERICAN BRIOCHE

Use recipe for Kuchen (page 179); reduce sugar to ½ cup, use whole eggs instead of egg yolks and flavor with ½ teaspoon grated lemon rind or a dash of crushed cardamon seeds; add flour, as necessary, to make a soft dough. When dough is double in bulk, shape or cut down, cover and place in refrigerator overnight. To shape, roll dough into long, rectangular piece, ¼ inch thick, brush with melted butter, fold lengthwise toward center to make 3 layers and cut in ¾ inch slices; cover and let rise until double in bulk. Twist ends of each piece in opposite directions, shape in a coil and place in greased pan; cover and again let rise until double in bulk. Brush with mixture of egg white and water and bake in moderate oven (375°–400° F.) about 20 minutes. Approximate yield: 2 dozen brioches.

TEA RING

Use recipe for Kuchen (page 179); flavor with 1 teaspoon almond extract. When dough has doubled in bulk and is ready for shaping, roll into rectangular sheet, ⅓ inch thick, and brush with ¼ cup melted butter; sprinkle with ⅓ cup chopped, blanched almonds, roll lengthwise, place on greased baking sheet and join ends to form a ring. With scissors, cut 1½ inch slices on slant almost to center, turning each slice partly on its side with pointed end at bottom; cover and again let rise until double in bulk. Then brush with milk mixed with egg yolk, sprinkle with additional chopped almonds and bake in moderately hot oven (375°–400° F.) about 25 minutes. Approximate yield: 1 large ring.

ENGLISH MUFFINS

1 pkg. dry granular yeast or   1 tablespoon salt
   1 cake compressed yeast   1 tablespoon sugar
1 cup warm, not hot, water   4 cups sifted all-purpose flour
½ cup milk   3 tablespoons shortening

Soften yeast in ¼ cup warm, not hot, water (cool to lukewarm for compressed yeast). Combine milk, remaining water, salt and sugar in top of double boiler. Heat to lukewarm. Add yeast. Stir in 2 cups of flour and blend until smooth. Return to top part of double boiler, cover, and let rise until doubled in bulk (30 to 45 minutes) over warm (not hot) water. Add shortening (slightly softened) and remaining flour. Knead until smooth and elastic. Let rise again over warm water until doubled in bulk (1 to 1½ hours). Place dough on lightly floured board. Roll ¼ inch thick. Cut with flour cutter 3½ inches in diameter. Cover with towel and let stand until light. Bake 15 minutes on hot greased griddle, turning several times during cooking. When cool, split and toast muffins. Yield: 12 muffins.

STOLLEN

1 pkg. dry granular yeast   3½ cups sifted all-purpose flour
¼ cup warm, not hot, water   ¼ cup soft shortening
¾ cup milk (scalded and cooled   ¼ cup chopped citron
   to lukewarm)   1 cup raisins
¼ cup sugar   ½ cup chopped blanched
1 teaspoon salt   almonds (lightly toasted)
1 egg (or 2 egg yolks plus   ½ teaspoon grated lemon rind
   1 tablespoon water)   ¼ cup of butter

Follow general directions for mixing, kneading and rising (page 161). Add egg before flour and fat. Remove from bowl onto lightly floured board. Flatten into a circle, pressing out all air. Place citron, raisins, almonds and lemon rind in center of circle. Fold edges toward center, covering all the fruit mixture. Then knead until fruits and nuts are evenly distributed through the dough. Round up on lightly floured board and let stand 15 minutes. Roll out to form an oval (about 15 inches long and 9 inches wide). With a rolling pin, press lengthwise down center. Spread with soft butter. Fold lengthwise through center so top and bottom edges are even. Press creased edge down with palm of hand, but do not press open edges together. Place on lightly greased heavy baking sheet. Brush top with soft butter. Cover and let rise until double in bulk (about 1 hour). Bake 30 to 35 minutes in a moderate oven (375° F.). Brush with Lemon Icing (page 710).

GARLIC BREAD

Cut Vienna or sandwich loaf in ½ inch thick slices, leaving bread intact at bottom. Spread slices with Garlic Butter (page 200). Cover lightly with paper bag to hold slices together. Heat in moderate oven (350° F.) 15 minutes, or until heated through. Place loaf, covered, on heated platter and serve in place of hot rolls.

GARLIC ROLLS

Cut fresh bread into thin slices and trim off the crusts. Spread with Garlic Butter (page 200), then roll up and fasten with toothpicks. Dust with cayenne pepper and brown in a hot oven (375° F.). Serve hot.

SWEET TOAST

Use thin slices of bread toasted quickly; remove crusts, cut in strips, triangles or other shapes and spread with butter. Sprinkle with one of the following mixtures and place in broiler to melt sugar. Serve hot for breakfast or afternoon tea.

Cinnamon Toast—Add ½ teaspoon cinnamon to ¼ cup granulated or brown sugar, or use crushed maple sugar.

Orange Toast—Add ½ tablespoon grated orange rind and 2 tablespoons orange juice to ¼ cup sugar. For variation add a dash of cinnamon.

Honey Cinnamon Toast—Mix equal amounts of hot strained honey and butter and spread on dry toast; sprinkle with cinnamon.

Nutbread Tea Crisps—Mix ¼ cup each brown sugar and butter, and spread on 6 nutbread slices. Brown in hot oven (400° F.) about 5 minutes, or until mixture becomes syrupy. Yield: 6 portions.

MELBA TOAST

Cut stale bread in ⅛ inch slices; arrange on baking sheet and bake in slow oven (300°–325° F.) 15 to 20 minutes, or until evenly browned and crisp, turning several times for uniform toasting and drying.

MILK TOAST

Sprinkle hot buttered toast lightly with salt and serve with scalded milk, allowing ½ cup for each slice; pour hot milk over toast in cereal bowl or soup plate, or serve milk in hot pitcher.

CREAM TOAST

Serve hot buttered toast with Thin White Sauce (page 125) made with part light cream or rich milk; allow ½ cup sauce for each slice.

FRENCH TOAST

2 eggs, slightly beaten   **1 cup milk**
¼ teaspoon salt   **6 slices bread**
               2 tablespoons fat

Mix together eggs, salt and milk in deep plate or bowl; dip bread into mixture and sauté in butter, bacon drippings or pork fat in heavy frying pan, turning with spatula to brown both sides; add more fat if necessary to keep slices from sticking. Or fry in hot deep fat (380°–390° F.) 1 to 2 minutes, or until browned. Add 1 to 2 tablespoons sugar to egg-milk mixture for a sweet toast. Yield: 6 slices.

JELLY TOAST ROLLS

Cut crusts from 12 slices fresh bread. Spread lightly with jelly. Roll as for jelly roll and fasten with toothpicks. Place on baking sheet, seam side down; cover with damp cloth until ready to serve. Toast under medium broiler heat, turning until evenly browned. Yield: 6 portions.

CROUTONS

Cut stale bread in ⅓ inch slices and remove crusts; spread with softened butter, cut in ⅓ inch strips, then cut across to make cubes. Bake in slow oven (300°–325° F.) 15 to 20 minutes, stirring occasionally to brown evenly; sauté unbuttered cubes in small amount of butter, turning frequently to brown evenly; or fry unbuttered cubes in hot deep fat (375°–390° F.) about 40 seconds and drain on unglazed paper. Serve with soup.

CRUMBS

Soft Bread Crumbs—Use day-old but soft bread and remove crusts; crumble between fingers, tear out with fork, grate, put through coarse sieve, or cut in cubes or squares. Use for stuffings, puddings and the like.

Dry Bread or Cracker Crumbs—Use dry bread or crackers; dry, but do not brown, in slow oven (300° F.) if not crisp; roll, crush or grind, and sift. Use to coat food or to top scalloped or baked dishes. Store crumbs in covered ventilated container in dry place.

Buttered Crumbs—Mix melted butter with sifted dry bread crumbs, allowing 2 tablespoons butter to ½ cup crumbs. Use as covering for scalloped and baked dishes; or sprinkle browned and seasoned buttered crumbs over vegetables; sauté crumbs in butter or brown buttered crumbs in oven, stirring frequently.

RUSKS OR ZWIEBACK

Cut leftover or stale sweet buns in halves crosswise and bake in slow oven (250°–275° F.) ¾ to 1 hour, or until evenly browned and dry throughout, turning occasionally.

CROUSTADES

Cut stale bread in 1½ to 2 inch slices, remove crusts and cut in rectangles, squares, triangles, diamonds or rounds of desired size. With point of sharp knife cut down around shape, ¼ to ½ inch from edge, and remove center to within ¼ to ½ inch of bottom, leaving a shell-like case. Brush with melted butter and place in moderate oven (350° F.) 15 to 20 minutes, or until browned and crisp, turning occasionally; or fry in hot deep fat (375°–390° F.) about 1 minute, or until delicately browned, and drain on unglazed paper. Heat in oven just before filling with creamed mixture. Use as patty shells.

Beverages

People the world over choose a cup of coffee or tea as an early morning bracer, as a meal accompaniment or as an excuse to have a good chat. Good fellowship and fun surround the serving of these beverages. They deserve to be made carefully and served attractively with a choice of good foods—coffee cake, a doughnut, hot buttered toast, desserts—whatever your desire.

We mustn't forget the value of milk as a beverage and its importance in the daily diet—a quart for youngsters and at least a pint for adults. Cocoa and chocolate are delicious and nutritious; teamed with milk they offer rich refreshment. Fruit juices rate high with family members and seldom need "doctoring" except in a punch, perhaps.

TEA

You may be a black or green tea enthusiast. If the former, you prefer fermented or black tea; if the latter, you like green tea that has not been subjected to fermentation. Or if your taste runs to a modified version of the two, you champion the semi-fermented tea known as Oolong.

Most tea as purchased is a blend of several grades and varieties and the price may be influenced by a greater or less preponderance of fine quality tea mixed or blended with teas of poorer grade and quality.

HOW TO MAKE A GOOD CUP OF TEA

Begin with a spotlessly clean pot. Use one to two teaspoons tea leaves for each cup of freshly boiling water; use tea bags or tea leaves directly from tightly covered canister. Fill earthenware, china, or glass pot, or pitcher with boiling water; drain when heated thoroughly. Place tea in pot, add freshly boiling water, cover and steep in warm place one to three minutes. Stir once. Pour through strainer into preheated serving pot or directly into cups. For strong tea, increase the amount of tea used.

ICED TEA

PREPARE strong tea, using 1½ teaspoons leaves for each cup. Pour hot tea over cracked ice in tall glasses. If served in quantity, pour hot tea over block of ice in large pitcher. Iced tea, cooled quickly, is clearer and more sparkling than tea which is cooled slowly, then iced or chilled. Garnish glass with slice of lemon or orange. If iced tea appears cloudy, just add a few drops of boiling water.

SPICED ICED TEA

2 cups sugar	1 teaspoon allspice
2 cups water	1½ cups strained orange juice
4 rounded teaspoons black tea	¾ cup strained lemon juice
5 mint leaves	4 quarts iced water

Boil sugar and water 5 minutes; add tea, mint and spice; cover lightly and let stand 10 minutes; strain and add fruit juices. Pour over cracked ice, add the water and serve in tall glasses with additional ice. Approximate yield: 15 to 20 glasses.

COFFEE

ANY ONE of several methods may be used to make good coffee. It is important to match the right grind of coffee with the corresponding method. With the filter or drip method of making coffee, a fine grind is used; percolating requires an all-purpose or steel-cut grind; the boiling method takes steel-cut or more coarsely ground coffee.

HOW TO MAKE GOOD COFFEE EVERY TIME

THERE are a few basic rules that apply to all types of coffee makers. By following them, you can be assured of delicious coffee every time.

Make certain that your coffee pot is sparkling clean. Scrub thoroughly after each use. Occasionally wash with a solution of baking soda. Be sure the coffee is fresh and the proper grind for your coffee maker.

Here are the proper measuremnts: For each serving, use one Standard Coffee Measure (or its equivalent, two level measuring tablespoonfuls) to each three-quarters of a measuring cup of fresh, cold water. Water that is warm or that has been pre-heated gives the coffee a flat taste. Bring cold water to a full rolling boil before it comes in contact with the coffee. Coffee experts agree that coffee itself should never be boiled. For best results, have the coffee maker at least three-quarters full. Serve coffee as soon as possible after brewing. If necessary to have it stand, place over hot water or on asbestos pad over low heat. Cold coffee cannot be reheated without loss of flavor. Coffee grounds should not be re-used.

VACUUM METHOD

Measure required amount of fresh cold water into lower bowl; place on heat. Place filter into upper bowl, and add measured quantity of finely ground coffee, but *do not* insert in lower bowl.[1] When water in lower bowl boils actively, reduce heat. (If electricity is used, turn it off.) Insert upper bowl with a slight twist to insure a tight seal. When the water has risen into upper bowl (some water will always remain in the lower bowl) stir water and coffee thoroughly. In two to three minutes (depending on grind—finer grinds require the shorter time) turn off heat. (If electricity is used, remove coffee maker from unit.) When all coffee has been drawn into lower bowl, remove upper bowl and serve. Cloth filters should be washed in cold water immediately after being used and *kept immersed in cold water* until used again. Never use soap in washing cloth filters.

[1] If you have a vacuum maker with a vented stem (a small hole in the side of the tube above the hot water line) the pot may be completely assembled before placing on heat. In this type of vacuum maker the water in the lower bowl will not start to rise until the water boils. When water starts to rise, reduce heat and follow the regular procedure.

DRIP METHOD

Preheat pot by scalding with hot water. Measure required amount of ground coffee into coffee basket. Measure required amount of fresh boiling water into upper container, then cover. When dripping is completed, remove upper section immediately. Stir brew and serve.

PERCOLATOR METHOD

Measure required amount of fresh cold water into percolator and place on heat. When water boils, remove from heat. Measure required amount of ground coffee into basket and insert basket into percolator. Cover, return to heat and allow to percolate slowly for six to eight minutes. Remove coffee basket and serve.

DEMITASSE

Prepare strong coffee, using 3 to 4 tablespoons coffee for 1 cup boiling water; the drip method is generally used. Serve hot in small cups; after-dinner coffee or demitasse is usually served black.

CREOLE COFFEE

¼ cup coffee, drip-grind   2 cups boiling water
1 tablespoon cocoa or chocolate

Place a drip coffeepot in a pan of very hot water. Place coffee, mixed with cocoa, in middle section of pot (French-type drip coffeepot), which is kept scalding hot. Pour boiling water, one tablespoon at a time at three-to-four-minute intervals, over the coffee, covering pot between intervals. When dripped through, serve with sugar to taste. Approximate yield: 2 cups. Note: This cannot be properly made without a French-type drip coffeepot.

CAFÉ ESPRESSO

⅓ cup coffee, drip-grind   1 egg white
5 (or 4) cups boiling water   2 tablespoons sugar
¼ pint heavy cream

Prepare strong drip coffee by the usual method. Beat egg white until foamy. Beat in sugar. Whip cream lightly but not until stiff. Fold the two together and top each cup of coffee with fluffy white caps. Place the lump of sugar in cup before pouring coffee. Loaf sugar may be omitted. Approximate yield: 6 portions.

ICED COFFEE

Prepare coffee twice the usual strength. Pour hot coffee over cracked ice in tall glasses, or over block of ice in large pitcher. Serve with plain or whipped cream and sugar or serve black.

SPICY COFFEE COOLER

20 whole cloves	**1 cup powdered sugar**
1 stick (5-inch) cinnamon	**1 tablespoon granulated sugar**
½ cup ground coffee	**1 cup heavy cream, whipped**
7 cups water, boiling or cold	**cinnamon**

Add cloves, stick cinnamon and coffee to water and brew as usual; strain and add powdered sugar. Pour into tall glasses half filled with crushed ice; top with sweetened cream and dust with cinnamon. Approximate yield: 6 portions.

FROSTED COFFEE

Half fill 6 tall glasses with chipped ice; pour hot strong coffee over ice until glasses are three-fourths full, and top each with a heaping tablespoon of vanilla ice cream. Use 1 quart coffee for 6 glasses.

CHOCOLATE AND COCOA

CHOCOLATE and cocoa are derived from the seeds of *Theobroma cacao*, a tropical evergreen tree. Some of the fat is extracted from chocolate to make cocoa. The starch in chocolate and cocoa must be cooked, for a few minutes, before adding milk to the beverage. Chocolate, whether for use in a beverage or in cooking, should always be melted over low heat, preferably in the top part of a double boiler over hot water. It is more easily removed from the pan in which it is heated if the pan is rubbed with butter first.

HOT CHOCOLATE

2 squares bitter chocolate	**dash of salt**
1 cup cold water	**3 tablespoons sugar**
	3 cups milk

Heat together chocolate and water, stirring until chocolate is melted and blended; add salt and sugar and boil 4 minutes, stirring constantly. Place pan over hot water, gradually stir in milk and heat thoroughly. When ready to serve, beat with rotary beater until light and frothy. Approximate yield: 6 portions.

PARTY CHOCOLATE

⅓ cup heavy cream, whipped   4 cups milk, scalded
¾ cup Jiffy Chocolate Syrup
    (page 191)

Fold cream into cold chocolate syrup; serve 1 heaping tablespoon in each serving cup and fill with hot milk, stirring well; serve at once. This makes an attractive, simple and convenient drink to serve at bridge or after-theatre parties. Yield: 6 to 8 medium-sized cups.

FRENCH OR SWISS CHOCOLATE

3 squares bitter chocolate   1 cup water
½ cup sugar   4 cups milk, scalded

Grate chocolate, add sugar and water and cook gently over boiling water 15 minutes or longer; stir in hot milk and serve at once. Approximate yield: 6 portions.

MEXICAN CHOCOLATE

The outstanding flavor of Mexican chocolate is cinnamon. This chocolate may be purchased in Mexican stores and some Mexican restaurants. It comes in rounds, each round divided into quarters. Heat as many cups of milk as there are people to serve, and add one quarter of chocolate for each cup. When the chocolate is dissolved in the hot milk, beat with a rotary egg beater until it is foaming. If Mexican chocolate cannot be obtained, use recipe below.

NEW MEXICAN CHOCOLATE

3 squares bitter chocolate, grated   ¼ cup firmly packed brown
1 cup cold water   sugar
½ teaspoon cinnamon   3 cups milk
1 teaspoon vanilla   1 egg white
pinch of salt   ½ cup heavy cream, whipped

Mix chocolate and water. Cook over very low heat 1 hour, stirring frequently. Add cinnamon, vanilla and salt. Dissolve sugar in 1 cup milk and add. Heat remaining milk to scalding point and add. Beat egg white until stiff and fold into cream. Add to chocolate, remove from heat and beat with Mexican chocolate mixer or egg beater until well blended. Approximate yield: 6 portions.

ICED RUSSIAN CHOCOLATE

Mix ½ cup cold black coffee, ¼ cup chocolate syrup and 1 cup boiling water. Pour over cracked ice and serve in a tall glass garnished with whipped cream.

CHOCOLATE ORIENTALE

4 cups ginger ale   ½ pint vanilla ice cream
½ cup cocoa or chocolate malt-
 flavored powder

Pour the ginger ale into shaker. Then add the prepared chocolate powder. Add the ice cream and shake vigorously. Pour into tall glasses and serve. Yield: 6 portions.

CHOCOLATE CREAM NECTAR

2 1-oz. squares bitter chocolate 3 cups milk
½ cup coffee   1 teaspoon vanilla
1 cup sugar   whipped cream

Heat chocolate and coffee together, stirring until chocolate is melted and blended. Cook 2 minutes, stirring constantly. Add sugar and milk and cook slowly 5 minutes. Flavor with vanilla and serve with a spoonful of whipped cream in each cup. Approximate yield: 6 portions.

COCOA

¼ to ⅓ cup sugar   dash of salt
6 tablespoons cocoa   1 cup water
       5 cups milk

Combine sugar, cocoa and salt in saucepan; stir in water and boil 2 minutes, stirring until thickened. Add milk and heat slowly until scalded and just below the boiling point; cover and keep hot over hot water; just before serving, beat with rotary beater until frothy. Serve with whipped cream or marshmallow, if desired. Approximate yield: 1½ quarts, or 6 portions.

ICED MINT COCOA

Use recipe for Cocoa (page 190), increase sugar to 1 cup and add 3 sprigs crushed mint to cocoa, sugar and water; strain hot cocoa and chill. Add 1 teaspoon vanilla and pour into tall glasses, half filled with crushed ice. Top each glass with whipped cream and garnish with a mint spray. Approximate yield: 6 glasses.

JIFFY CHOCOLATE SYRUP

6 squares bitter chocolate   1 cup boiling water
1⅓ cups (1 can) sweetened   ⅓ cup sugar
   condensed milk   dash of salt
       1 teaspoon vanilla

Melt chocolate over boiling water, remove and gradually stir in condensed milk, then hot water and sugar, stirring until sugar is dissolved; add salt and vanilla, chill and store in covered container in refrigerator. Use for iced or hot chocolate, allowing 2 tablespoons syrup for 1 cup milk. Approximate yield: 2⅔ cups syrup.

ICED CHOCOLATE OR COCOA

Use 2 tablespoons Jiffy Chocolate Syrup (page 191) to 1 cup milk; beat with rotary beater or shake until frothy and pour over cracked ice in tall glasses. Flavor with cinnamon, ginger, a drop of peppermint extract, or crushed mint leaves, and serve with whipped cream, if desired. Yield: 1 large glass.

ICED CHOCOLATE MOCHA

1 cup hot strong coffee   ½ cup Jiffy Chocolate Syrup
3 cups milk   (page 191)
    ¼ cup heavy cream, whipped

Combine hot coffee, milk and chocolate syrup; beat with rotary beater until frothy; cool. Pour over chopped ice in small glasses and top with whipped cream. Approximate yield: 6 portions.

FROSTED CHOCOLATE

Use 2 tablespoons Jiffy Chocolate Syrup (page 191) to 1 cup milk, chilled; beat with rotary beater or shake well and pour into tall glass. Add small scoop of chocolate or coffee ice cream, stir slightly with spoon and serve at once. Yield: 1 tall glass.

CHOCOLATE SODA

Use recipe for Frosted Chocolate (page 191); substitute ½ cup carbonated water for ½ cup milk, and stir only enough to mix; do not beat.

EGGNOG

1 egg, well beaten	1 cup chilled rich milk, or ½ cup
2 teaspoons sugar or	milk and ½ cup light cream
2 tablespoons honey	¼ teaspoon vanilla
	Dash of nutmeg

Beat egg with sugar; beat in milk and vanilla and serve cold in tall glass; sprinkle lightly with nutmeg. For a more fluffy eggnog, separate egg and beat egg white until stiff but not dry. Beat egg yolk until light; beat in sugar, milk, flavoring; fold in white. Yield: 1 tall glass.

MODIFICATIONS OF EGGNOG

Fruit Eggnog—Flavor Eggnog (see above) with 2 tablespoons fruit pulp instead of vanilla and nutmeg, or flavor with 1 tablespoon fruit juice, such as grape juice, orange juice or cherry juice.

Chocolate Eggnog—Flavor Eggnog (see above) with 2 tablespoons Jiffy Chocolate Syrup (page 191), omitting sugar.

Sherry Eggnog—Flavor Eggnog (see above) with 2 tablespoons Sherry or any desired wine. For eggnog with brandy, whiskey or rum, see wine section.

FRUIT FIZZES

Combine equal amounts of fruit juice and ginger ale, or use charged water and syrup. Add the carbonated beverage just before serving and pour over ice cubes to serve.

COFFEE MILK SHAKES

To prepare shakes, mix ingredients by shaking in cocktail shaker or beating with rotary beater. Pour over cracked ice in tall glasses and serve at once; if permitted to stand until ice melts, they become too diluted. Each recipe yields approximately 6 portions.

Coffee-Egg Milk Shake—Use 3 cups cold strong coffee, 3 eggs, well beaten, 6 cups chilled milk, 6 tablespoons cream, sugar to taste and dash of salt. Add enough iced carbonated water to each glass to foam mixture to the top.

Coffee-Chocolate Milk Shake—Use 1½ cups cold strong coffee, ¾ cup Jiffy Chocolate Syrup (page 191) and 7 cups milk. Top each glass with 1 tablespoon whipped cream, if desired.

Iced Coffee Shake—Use 3 cups cold strong coffee, 3 drops almond extract, 2 cups chilled milk, 2 cups soda water and powdered sugar to taste. Top each glass with sweetened whipped cream and dust with cinnamon.

ORANGE MILK SHAKE

2½ cups orange juice	½ teaspoon salt
1½ cups grapefruit juice	¼ teaspoon almond extract
1 cup evaporated milk	¼ cup sugar
1 cup water	1 cup cracked ice

Combine all ingredients as listed, in a shaker; shake until well mixed. Yield: 6 tall glasses.

GINGER ALE CREAM

⅓ cup lemon juice	½ cup light cream
1 banana, mashed	½ pint orange ice
½ cup sugar	1 pint ginger ale, chilled
	1 orange, sliced

Combine lemon juice, banana and sugar and chill; stir in cream, add orange ice and ginger ale, mix well and serve at once. Decorate with orange slices. Approximate yield: 4 cups.

ORGEAT

1 stick cinnamon	¾ cup (4 ounces) almonds
2 quarts milk	¼ cup sugar
	2 tablespoons rose water

Add cinnamon to milk and bring gradually to boiling point. Remove cinnamon and allow milk to cool. Blanch the almonds and grind and pound to a paste in a mortar. Add the rose water to the chopped almonds and add milk, mixing well. Sweeten the milk to taste and heat under boiling for a minute or two but no longer. Strain the drink through a fine sieve or cheesecloth to remove almonds and chill. Yield: 6 portions.

SUGAR SYRUP

Boil equal amount of sugar and water 5 minutes, pour into a hot sterilized jar, cover, chill and use for sweetening fresh fruit or beverages.

LEMONADE

6 lemons (1 cup and 2 table-   1 cup Sugar Syrup (page 193)
    spoons juice)   3½ cups water

Squeeze juice from lemons; add to syrup and dilute with water, adding more syrup if a sweeter drink is desired; pour over cracked ice in tall glasses and garnish with mint leaves, orange slices, fresh berries or pineapple sticks. Approximate yield: 6 tall glasses.

MODIFICATIONS OF LEMONADE

Limeade—Use 1 cup lime juice, 1 cup Sugar Syrup (page 193) and 3½ cups water.

Orangeade—Use juice of 4 oranges and 1 lemon, 1 cup Sugar Syrup (page 193) and 3½ cups water.

RASPBERRY MINT CRUSH

2 cups sugar   1 cup red raspberries
3 cups boiling water   1 bunch mint
    2 cups lime juice

Dissolve sugar in hot water and chill; add berries, crushed with mint, and lime juice and chill 2 to 3 hours in refrigerator. Strain and pour over cracked ice in small glasses and serve with additional mint leaves. Approximate yield: 1½ quarts, or 12 small glasses.

TEA PUNCH

To 1 cup strong tea infusion, add 1 cup sweetened strawberry juice, ½ cup orange juice and 3 tablespoons lemon juice; chill. Just before serving, add 1 cup chilled, pale dry ginger ale. Pour into chilled glasses and garnish with berries. Yield: 6 punch-cup portions.

MINT JULEP ICED TEA

To 2 cups tea infusion, add 1 bunch mint, crushed, 6 tablespoons lemon juice, 1 cup orange juice, ¾ cup sugar and 3 whole cloves; chill several hours. When ready to serve, strain and add 1 pint white grape juice, ¼ cup each diced pineapple and sliced maraschino cherries, 1 orange sliced thin, then cut in eighths, and 1 quart carbonated water. Pour into tall glasses half filled with cracked ice and top with sprig of fresh mint. Or pour over block of ice in punch bowl and serve from bowl. Approximate yield: 10 tall glasses or 25 punch-cup portions.

RHUBARB-TEA PUNCH

To 1 cup tea infusion, add 6 tablespoons lemon juice, ¾ cup sugar, 1 small bunch fresh mint, 2 cups slightly sweetened, stewed rhubarb and 1 stick (2 inches) cinnamon; chill. When ready to serve, remove cinnamon and add 1 quart cracked ice, 1 orange, thinly sliced, 1 quart chilled ginger ale and 1 pint carbonated water. Yield: 12 tall glasses.

APRICOT PUNCH

½ pound dried apricots	3 tablespoons lemon juice
½ cup sugar	1 cup sweet cider
1 cup orange juice	1½ to 2 quarts iced water
candied cherries	

Soak apricots 1 hour in boiling water to cover, then stew in water in which they were soaked 15 minutes, or until soft; add sugar and cook 5 minutes longer; put through potato ricer or coarse sieve. Combine orange and lemon juice and cider, pour over apricots and stir thoroughly; strain and dilute with iced water to taste. Garnish with candied cherries. Yield: 8 to 10 glasses.

PINEAPPLE LIME PUNCH

2 cups currant jelly	1 cup orange juice
2 cups boiling water	2 cups strained lime juice
2 cups pineapple juice	1 quart ginger ale

Beat currant jelly with rotary beater until frothy; add hot water and continue beating until jelly is dissolved; add fruit juices and chill. Before serving, add ginger ale and pour over a large piece of ice. Approximate yield: 3 quarts, or 24 small glasses.

MULLED CIDER

¾ cup firmly packed brown sugar	1 teaspoon allspice
	3 sticks cinnamon
¼ teaspoon salt	dash of nutmeg
1 teaspoon cloves	2 quarts sweet cider

Thoroughly mix brown sugar, salt and spices; add to sweet cider and simmer 10 minutes; strain through cheesecloth and reheat. This is best served steaming hot in earthen mugs. Approximate yield: 8 portions.

GINGER PUNCH

1 quart cider	3 sprigs of mint, crushed
½ cup shredded pineapple	1 quart ginger ale
1 orange, sliced thin	1 pint carbonated water

Mix cider and fruit. Add mint and chill. Before serving add remaining ingredients. Yield: 20 punch-cup portions.

Appetizers for Meals or Parties

An APPETIZER must not only create a desire for more, but it must, without taking the edge off his appetite, make a guest feel that there is something very elegant in store for him later. Many will serve as accompaniments to soups, juices and cocktails. In the following section are recipes developed and tested in our HOME INSTITUTE kitchens for canapés, hors d'œuvres and cocktails, designed to please amateur or professional.

CANAPÉS

CANAPÉS are little mouthfuls of savory food spread on a firm, edible base. Because of their festive appearance, canapés often take the place of sandwiches at cocktail and buffet parties.

BREAD CANAPÉ BASES

Use thin slices of bread cut ¼ inch thick; remove crusts and cut in small shapes such as rounds, triangles, crescents, stars, squares, diamonds, hearts, oblongs and strips; toast or sauté in butter on one side only. Use as base for canapés; spread mixture over untoasted surface and garnish as desired. When bread is used for rolled canapés, remove crusts from very thin slices, cut in halves or smaller pieces, spread with filling, roll, fasten with toothpicks and toast in broiler, or sauté in butter, turning to brown evenly.

PREPARED CANAPÉ BASES

A variety of ready-to-use canapé bases made of bread, cracker or pastry mixtures can be purchased; these may be as simple or elaborate as you like. Thin crackers or wafers of many varieties, flaked or shredded cereals, corn and potato chips make simple, attractive bases. To crisp or freshen, place in moderate oven (350° F.) about 10 minutes before using, spreading them over bottom of pan.

PASTRY CANAPÉ BASES

Use recipe for Plain Pastry (page 736) or its modifications; roll ⅛ inch thick and cut in small shapes as desired. For variety, sprinkle shapes lightly before baking with celery, caraway, coriander, cardamon or fennel seeds; cayenne, paprika, curry powder, mustard, allspice or mace; or grated cheese or chopped nuts; or spread with peanut butter. Roll Puff Paste ⅛ inch thick; cut in small rounds, put two together to make small patty cases and bake as directed. Fill with seasoned caviar, fish or meat, fruit or cheese spread (pages 201–204), or any canapé filling. Puff pastry, rolled ¼ inch thick, may be cut in small shapes, baked and used as desired with canapé spreads or fillings. Fill miniature Puff Shells with canapé fillings such as butter, fish, meat, cheese or fruit spreads (pages 199–204).

CANAPÉ CHEESE PASTRY BASE

¾ cup sifted all-purpose flour   **½ cup butter**
⅛ teaspoon salt   **1 6-oz. package cream cheese**
1 tablespoon cold water

Mix flour and salt; cut in butter and cheese with pastry blender or two knives. Stir in water, then chill thoroughly. When ready to use, roll very thin, cut in rounds or oblongs and bake in hot oven (450° F.) about 6 minutes, or until lightly browned. This dough may be kept covered in refrigerator several days and used a little at a time. Use as canapé base, top with fillings (pages 199–204 or see recipes, page 205) or serve plain. Approximate yield: 2½ cups dough, or 100 canapé bases.

CHEESE PASTRY CANAPÉS

Use recipe for Canapé Cheese Pastries (page 198); sprinkle chopped nuts, caraway or poppy seeds, or cinnamon and sugar over baked pastries while they are still hot. Approximate yield: 100 canapés.

PASTRY CHEESE STICKS

Use ½ recipe for Plain Pastry (page 736) and ⅓ cup grated cheese. Roll dough ¼ inch thick and sprinkle one-half with grated cheese, leaving a ½-inch margin around the edges; fold in half, press edges together and roll ¼ inch thick; repeat three times. Then cut in strips about ½ inch wide; place on ungreased baking sheet and chill. Bake in very hot oven (500° F.) about 10 minutes. Leftover pastry may be used for cheese sticks. Yield: 16 sticks.

TURNOVER CANAPÉS

½ recipe Plain Pastry   1 hard-cooked egg, chopped
  (page 736)   2 tablespoons minced parsley
1 cooked chicken liver, minced ¼ teaspoon curry powder
2 slices broiled bacon, crumbled   salt
                       paprika

Prepare Plain Pastry or one of modifications; roll ⅛ inch thick and cut in 2-inch squares. Mix together chicken liver, bacon, egg, parsley and curry powder; season with salt and paprika. Place 1 teaspoon of mixture in center of each square, fold pastry over into a triangle and press edges together with floured fork. Fry in hot deep fat (370° F.) 3 to 5 minutes, or until golden brown. Garnish with parsley if desired. These canapés may be made with caviar flavored with lemon juice. Approximate yield: 2 dozen canapés.

HOT CHEESE NUT BALLS

2 teaspoons flour   1 cup grated American cheese
⅛ teaspoon cayenne   1 egg white, stiffly beaten
½ teaspoon salt   ¼ cup finely chopped nuts

Mix flour, cayenne, salt and grated cheese. Fold egg white lightly into cheese mixture until well blended. Form into small balls and roll in chopped nuts. Fry in hot deep fat (375° F.) until golden brown. Drain on absorbent paper. Serve hot on cocktail picks as an appetizer or with salad. Approximate yield: 15 balls.

CANAPÉ BUTTERS

To prepare any one of the following butters, beat the ingredients into ¼ cup butter, creamed; store in covered container in cold place until ready to use. If hard, leave in room temperature about 1 hour, or cream enough to soften before spreading on canapé base.

Anchovy Butter—Use 1 tablespoon anchovy paste, ½ teaspoon lemon juice and dash of paprika.

Caviar Butter—Use 1 2-oz. can caviar, mashed with soft butter.

Cheese Butter—Use ¼ cup soft snappy cheese.

Chili Butter—Use 2 tablespoons chili sauce.

Chives Butter—Use 1 tablespoon finely minced chives and 1 teaspoon lemon or lime juice, or a few drops of tarragon vinegar.

Chutney Butter—Use 1 tablespoon chutney.

Egg Butter—Use 2 hard-cooked egg yolks, finely mashed, ½ teaspoon lemon juice and dash of Tabasco sauce; season with salt and cayenne.

Garlic Butter—Allow one clove of garlic to stand 2 hours in ½ cup of butter; remove garlic before using as spread. Or mince fine and add to butter as spread.

Green Savory Butter—Mix together 3 tablespoons spinach purée, 1 tablespoon anchovy paste, 1 teaspoon capers, dash of paprika and salt to taste; force through sieve.

Herb Butter—Use ½ teaspoon dried tarragon and 1 tablespoon chopped chives or ½ teaspoon tarragon and ½ teaspoon dried rosemary. Rub together and let stand 20 minutes before using.

Honey Butter—Use equal amounts of honey and butter. Stir until well blended. Use on hot biscuits, waffles and griddle cakes.

Horseradish Butter—Use 2 tablespoons horseradish.

Ketchup Butter—Use 2 tablespoons ketchup.

Lemon Butter—Use a few gratings lemon rind and 2 teaspoons lemon juice. Lime or orange rind and juice may be substituted for lemon.

Lobster Butter—Use 1 tablespoon lobster paste, ½ teaspoon lemon juice and dash each of paprika and dry mustard.

Mint Butter—Use 2 tablespoons finely chopped mint leaves and 1 teaspoon lemon juice. Color a delicate green with vegetable coloring.

Mustard Butter—Use 1 tablespoon prepared mustard.

Nut Butter—Use 2 tablespoons finely ground nuts; season with salt.

Olive Butter—Use 1 tablespoon olive paste and ¼ teaspoon lemon juice.

Onion Butter—Use 1 teaspoon onion juice.

Parmesan Butter—Use 2 tablespoons Parmesan cheese.

Parsley Butter—Use 2 tablespoons finely cut parsley and 1 teaspoon lemon juice.

Peanut Butter—Use ¼ cup peanut butter and 1 teaspoon honey; season with salt.

Pimiento Butter—Use 2 tablespoons mashed pimiento and 1 teaspoon finely chopped pickles.

Roquefort Butter—Use 1 tablespoon Roquefort cheese.

Salmon Butter—Use 1 tablespoon salmon paste, 1 teaspoon lemon juice and dash of cayenne.

Sardine Butter—Use 1 tablespoon sardine paste, ½ teaspoon each lemon and onion juice, and dash of paprika.

Shredded Lobster or Crabmeat Butter—Use 1 cup finely shredded lobster or crabmeat.

Shrimp Butter—Use 1 cup shrimp. Rub through fine sieve. Add ½ teaspoon lemon juice and a dash of paprika or cayenne. Salt to taste.

Water Cress Butter—Use 2 tablespoons finely chopped water cress, 1 teaspoon lemon juice and a few drops Worcestershire sauce.

Worcestershire Butter—Use ¼ teaspoon Worcestershire sauce.

WINE BUTTER

To ⅓ cup butter creamed until soft, add 3 tablespoons Burgundy or Claret a little at a time and stir until it disappears. Add a pinch of salt and dash of cayenne. Rub bread lightly with clove of garlic and spread with wine butter. Bake in hot oven (400° F.) 10 minutes.

CHEESE SPREADS

Cheese-Caviar Spread—Moisten cream cheese with cream; shape into tiny balls and roll in caviar. Serve on small crackers, buttered lightly.

Cheese-Onion Spread—Mix ½ package (1½ oz.) cream cheese with 1 tablespoon minced onion and season with salt; add light cream to moisten. Serve on crackers or toast rounds. Sprinkle lightly with paprika or place sprig of parsley in center. Or spread on slices of dried beef, roll tightly and cut in 1-inch lengths.

Chili-Cheese Spread—Mix 1 3-oz. package cream cheese with enough chili sauce to moisten. Serve on crisp potato chips.

Dill Canapés—Soften cream cheese with sour cream and season with finely chopped fresh dill, salt and pepper. Or mix chopped dill with the least possible amount of unsweetened butter or thick cream. Spread the mixture on long, thin slices of smoked salmon, roll them up and spear them with toothpicks. Serve chilled.

Ham Balls—Combine 1 cup cottage cheese, ½ cup deviled ham, 1 tablespoon prepared horseradish, ¼ cup sour cream, ¼ teaspoon salt and dash of pepper. Form into balls and roll in ½ cup chopped water cress and 2 tablespoons chopped chives.

Horseradish Spread—Combine 1 3-oz. package of cream cheese with 1½ teaspoons drained horseradish, ½ teaspoon scraped onion and ⅛ teaspoon salt. Blend thoroughly and spread on toast rounds and top with bacon.

Pistachio Canapé Spread—Combine 1 3-oz. package of Roquefort cheese and cream cheese with 1 tablespoon heavy cream, 1 teaspoon minced onion, 2 tablespoons chopped ripe olives, and ½ cup blanched pistachio nuts. Mix well and chill. Spread on rye wafers.

Roquefort-Chives Spread—Mix Roquefort cheese with enough French dressing to moisten; season with chopped chives. Serve on crisp crackers, potato or corn chips.

FRUIT SPREADS

Avocado-Onion Spread—Season mashed avocados with minced onion, salt and dash of Tabasco sauce. Serve on toasted bread rounds.

Avocado Spread—Season mashed avocado with lemon, lime or grapefruit juice, and salt. Spread on toast rounds or crackers. Garnish with sprig of parsley, or place thin slice of tomato on toast and cover with spread.

Date Spread—Stuff dates with marshmallow cream which has been mixed sparingly with powdered coffee.

Guava-Cheese Spread—Spread bread or crackers with cream cheese, then with guava jelly; sprinkle chopped nuts over top.

Pine Aigrettes—Chop 6 slices of canned pineapple, or four of fresh pineapple, and set to drain. Add 2 tablespoons of grated American cheese, ⅛ teaspoon each of salt and pepper, 1 teaspoon of sugar, 2 teaspoons of toasted crumbs and the stiffly beaten white of an egg. Mix lightly, then heap on bread rounds and brown in the oven, but do not dry out or burn. Serve at once.

FISH SPREADS

Anchovy-Cheese Spread—Mix 1 part anchovy paste with 2 parts cream cheese. Spread on crackers. Garnish each with ½ anchovy or caper.

Caviar-Egg Spread—Mix 2 tablespoons caviar with 2 hard-cooked eggs, minced; moisten with mayonnaise. Serve on toast rounds.

Caviar Spread—Mix 3 tablespoons caviar, 2 tablespoons finely chopped white onions and 1½ teaspoons lemon juice. Serve on toast points. Garnish with hard-cooked egg, daisy style.

Deviled Crabmeat Spread—Add 1 cup flaked crabmeat, 1 tablespoon each butter and onion juice, 1 teaspoon Worcestershire sauce and ¼ teaspoon mustard to ¼ cup Thick White Sauce (page 125), and heat thoroughly. Season with salt and pepper and serve hot on crackers.

Kippered Herring Spread—Mix 1 cup mashed kippered herring, ½ cup minced cucumber and 2 drops onion juice. Serve on toast rounds.

Shrimp Spread—Mix finely chopped shrimp with lemon juice and Tabasco sauce and season with salt and pepper. Spread on toast rounds and garnish each with section of pickled walnut.

Tuna Fish Spread—Mix ½ cup shredded tuna fish, 1 tablespoon lemon juice and 1 teaspoon grated onion with mayonnaise to moisten. Spread on toast squares and garnish with a half slice of lemon.

MEAT SPREADS

Ham-Cheese Spread—Mix 1 cup finely chopped, cold boiled ham, ¼ cup grated American cheese, ½ teaspoon grated onion and 1 teaspoon ketchup. Spread on crackers and place in center of each a bit of Fluffy Horseradish Sauce (page 477). Sprinkle with paprika.

Deviled Ham Spread—Mix 1 cup deviled ham, 2 hard-cooked eggs, chopped, and 1 tablespoon horseradish. Spread on toast rounds and garnish with water cress.

Pâté de Fois Gras Spread—Mix 3 tablespoons pâté de foie gras with ¼ cup cream and season to taste. Rub through sieve and spread on toast fingers. Garnish with parsley.

Chicken Liver Spread—Mix ½ cup chopped, cooked chicken livers with 2 hard-cooked eggs, chopped, and 1 teaspoon minced onion; season to taste and moisten with cream. Spread on crisp crackers and garnish each with parsley.

Liverwurst Spread—Remove skin from ½ pound liverwurst; mash well and add 1 teaspoon lemon juice, ½ teaspoon Worcestershire sauce and dash of paprika. Moisten with cream. Spread on toast rounds and garnish with Onion Butter (page 200).

CANAPÉ CRÊPES

½ cup sifted flour
½ teaspoon salt

2 egg yolks, beaten
1 cup water

Mix flour and salt. Combine egg yolks and water; gradually add to flour, beating until smooth. Bake on greased hot griddle or frying pan (see French Pancakes, page 1043). Cool, spread with a canapé filling and roll lightly. Approximate yield: 20 very thin, small crêpes or canapé bases.

CRÊPES CAVIAR

1 recipe Canapé Crêpes
   (page 204)

1 cup heavy cream, whipped
1 4-oz. can caviar
dash of Tabasco sauce

Prepare crêpes. Mix together cream, caviar and Tabasco; spread layer on each cooled crêpe and roll lightly. Yield: 20 crêpe canapés.

STINGEREES

6 tablespoons mincemeat
1 tablespoon chutney
1 tablespoon rum

6 French pancakes
3 tablespoons melted butter
paprika

Heat mincemeat and chutney together. Remove from heat and add rum. Place a spoonful of mixture in hot pancakes and roll. Brush with butter, sprinkle with paprika and place under broiler 1 minute. Yield: 6 portions.

CAVIAR RISSOLETTES

Roll Puff Paste (page 759) ¼ inch thick and cut in small rounds. Place 1 teaspoon caviar, seasoned with lemon juice, in the center of each; moisten edges and cover with a second round; press edges together. Fry in hot deep fat (370° F.) 3 to 4 minutes, or until delicately browned. Drain on absorbent paper.

ALMOND PARMESAN FINGERS

3 tablespoons chopped blanched
  almonds
3 tablespoons butter
6 tablespoons grated Parmesan
  cheese

3 tablespoons heavy cream
3 tablespoons minced parsley
salt and pepper
12 buttered toast strips

Sauté almonds in butter until golden brown. Mix cheese, cream and parsley and add salt and pepper to taste; spread on toast strips. Sprinkle tops with almonds and place in hot oven to heat thoroughly before serving. Yield: 1 dozen canapés.

ANCHOVY–EGG CANAPÉS

Drain 1 4-oz. can anchovy fillets, then marinate with mixture of 3 tablespoons each lemon and onion juice and dash of cayenne for ½ hour. Drain and arrange fillets on 12 toast rounds; border with 1 hard-cooked egg, finely minced, dust with paprika and garnish with water cress. Yield: 1 dozen canapés.

ASPARAGUS CANAPÉS

12 thin slices bread
6 thin slices boiled ham
prepared mustard

12 asparagus tips, cooked or
  canned
mayonnaise

Trim crusts from bread; cut slices of ham in halves, then trim to fit bread slices and spread with mustard. Dip asparagus in mayonnaise, place one tip at end of prepared slice of bread and roll as for jelly roll; spear with a toothpick at each end. Place on broiler rack in preheated broiler and turn to toast evenly. Yield: 1 dozen canapés.

SMOKED FISH CANAPÉS

Arrange thin strips of smoked salmon and smoked herring on toast fingers. Decorate edge of toast with Anchovy Butter (page 200) and sprinkle with chopped parsley.

LOBSTER CANAPÉS

8 buttered toast rounds
tartar sauce
1 cup chopped cooked lobster
¼ cup chopped sautéed
  mushrooms
salt and paprika

2 tablespoons grated Parmesan
  cheese
1 teaspoon horseradish
mayonnaise
stuffed olives, sliced
water cress

Spread untoasted sides of bread with tartar sauce and cover with mixture of lobster meat and chopped mushrooms; sprinkle lightly with salt and paprika and chill. Mix cheese and horseradish and add enough mayonnaise to make a creamy mixture; press through pastry bag to form border around edge of canapés. Place an olive slice garnished with a sprig of water cress in center of each canapé. Yield: 8 canapés.

HORS D'ŒUVRES

HORS D'ŒUVRES may be as simple or intricate as desired, but they are meant only to stimulate the appetite for the remainder of the meal, and should never become the dominant course. All the hot hors d'œuvres are served piping hot, of course, and the crisp, raw vegetables arctic cold.

VERY, VERY ENGLISH

2 small marrowbones
6 rounds anchovy-buttered
  toast

salt and white pepper
1 teaspoon lemon juice
minced parsley

Place marrowbones in a little water and boil until heated through. Remove marrow from bones and pile hot on toast rounds. Dust lightly with salt and pepper, sprinkle each one with lemon juice and a bit of parsley and serve them very hot. Yield: 6 savories.

RUSSIAN EGGS

2 envelopes plain gelatin
½ cup cold water
2 cups chicken stock or bouillon
salt and pepper

2 tablespoons Sherry
2 tablespoons lemon juice
6 Deviled Eggs (page 123)
12 slices of tomatoes

Soften gelatin in water about 5 minutes; add to boiling hot stock and stir until dissolved. Add seasonings, Sherry and lemon juice; season to taste; chill. Place ½ deviled egg, cut side up, in each cup or mold and pour slightly thickened gelatin mixture over egg. Chill until firm. Unmold and serve each on slice of tomato. Yield: 1 dozen portions.

AVOCADO CANAPÉ

Carve tiny balls of avocado with a small French scoop and pile lightly on a thick slice of red tomato. Mash the pulp that is left in the shells of the pear and add cream cheese and a little lime juice to give the right consistency. Then pipe this green butter around the edge of the tomato to hold the balls in place. Cover the top of the balls with a sauce made of chili sauce and grated horseradish to season highly.

MAKE–IN–A–MINUTE APPETIZERS

Cut canned pork or ham into inch cubes; stick with toothpicks. May be alternated on appetizer plate with cheese cubes, olives, pickles, etc.

COCKTAIL PORKWICHES

Cut canned pork or ham into paper-thin slices, then into 1½-inch squares. Cut cheese into pieces the same size, then put two slices pork together with a slice of cheese in center like a sandwich. Place under broiler until lightly browned and cheese is soft. Serve on toothpicks.

APPETIZER KABOBS

Fill toothpicks with alternating pieces: small cube canned pork or ham, pickle slice, cube cheese, pickled onion.

QUICK PORK 'N HAM CANAPÉS

Place thin squares of canned pork and ham thinly sliced on buttered rye bread; top each with a half teaspoonful cream cheese or whipped cream mixed with a little horseradish.

STUFFED EGG APPETIZERS

Caviar Monte Carlo—Cut hard-cooked eggs in halves lengthwise and remove yolks. Fill whites with mixture made by combining egg yolks with cheese, water cress, onion juice and mayonnaise to moisten. Serve each half on slice of salami; garnish with water cress.

Crab Meat-Stuffed Eggs—Cut 6 hard-cooked eggs in halves lengthwise and remove yolks. Fill whites with mixture made by combining minced egg yolks with 1 teaspoon dry mustard, 1 cup flaked crab meat, 1 cup finely chopped celery, 2 tablespoons chopped green pepper and ¾ cup mayonnaise. Garnish with tomatoes and parsley.

Harlequin-Stuffed Eggs—Cut 6 hard-cooked eggs in halves lengthwise; remove yolks and force through sieve. Mix together 2 cooked carrots, shredded, 2 cooked beets, shredded, 1 cup string beans, shredded, and ⅓ cup mayonnaise; season to taste and pile into whites. Sprinkle with yolks; dust with paprika.

VEGETABLE APPETIZER BASES

Use vegetables such as tomatoes, cucumbers, large mild onions, celery, French endive, lettuce, new cabbage, radishes, raw or cooked young carrots, cooked small beets and artichoke hearts, and broiled mushroom caps; use vegetable cutter for fancy shapes. Cut firm tomatoes, onions and cucumbers in thin slices and tender celery stalks in short lengths, shredded and placed in ice water to curl; cut medium-sized crisp round radishes and cooked beets in halves crosswise and hollow out centers to make cups; cut small carrots and mild white winter radishes in halves lengthwise and crosswise and hollow out to make troughs; separate tender small leaves of endive, lettuce and early red cabbage. Crisp raw vegetables (pages 583–584), and marinate cooked vegetables in French dressing; then drain and dry; spread or fill with a savory filling, garnish as desired, and place on crisp lettuce or water cress; roll leaves around filling and fasten with toothpicks. Arrange on tray or platter as assorted hors d'œuvres, or separately on plates.

STUFFED CELERY

Use only the crisp, tender white stalks of 1 bunch celery; wash and leave tips of leaves on stalks, or remove leaves from coarser stalks and crisp in ice water. Dry on absorbent paper or clean towel before stuffing. Fill grooves with one of the following mixtures. Chill thoroughly before serving. Approximate yield: 10 stalks.

Cheese-Stuffed Celery—For filling, use ½ package (1½-oz.) cream cheese, 2 tablespoons mayonnaise, 4 stuffed olives, chopped, 2 tablespoons minced nuts and ¼ teaspoon salt.

Roquefort-Stuffed Celery—For filling, use ¼ pound Roquefort cheese, 1 tablespoon ketchup, 1 tablespoon mayonnaise, ½ teaspoon salt and dash each of cayenne and sugar.

Egg-Stuffed Celery—For filling, use 2 hard-cooked eggs, finely chopped, and 4 tablespoons mayonnaise, seasoned with salt and pepper. Sprinkle lightly with paprika or minced parsley. Serve very crisp.

ENDIVE APPETIZER

6 endive leaves	seasonings
2 tablespoons caviar	1 3-oz. package cream cheese
2 lemon wedges	mayonnaise

Fill endive with caviar and arrange three blades on each plate, meeting at the center on a lemon wedge. Season cheese highly and moisten with mayonnaise; shape in balls and arrange 3 on each plate between endive blades. Yield: 2 portions.

TOMATO–LIVER PASTE CUPS

Use 6 small tomatoes; cut off stem ends, scoop out centers to form cups and turn upside down to drain. Then stuff with Chicken Liver Spread (page 203). Serve on lettuce and garnish tops with strips of tomato. Yield: 6 portions.

SMOKED SALMON ROLLS

Mix caviar with a little lemon juice, cream and chopped fresh dill. Spread on thin slices of smoked salmon. Roll as for jelly roll and spear with a toothpick.

BACON TARTLETS

Cook very small tarts of cheese pastry (see Pastries and Pies). When pastry is cool, sprinkle a few bread crumbs in the bottom of each tart shell and fill with the following mixture: finely chop 3 slices crisp bacon; combine with 1 egg, 1 egg yolk, ¼ cup cream, salt, pepper and a little dry mustard and beat well. Fill the tart shells with mixture and bake until firm in a slow oven (325° F.) 10 minutes. Sprinkle with paprika and serve very hot. Approximate yield: 6 tartlets.

STUFFED BEETS

6 tiny cooked beets	2 sweet pickles, chopped
¼ cup French dressing	dash of dry mustard
1 hard-cooked egg, chopped	dash of salt
	dash of pepper

Marinate beets for several hours in French dressing. Scoop out part of the inside and fill with paste made by mixing together remaining ingredients. Yield: 6 portions.

EGG TOMATO APPETIZER

Use 6 small tomatoes; peel, cut off stem ends, scoop out centers and turn upside down to drain. Fill with Caviar-Egg Spread (page 203) and place on toast rounds spread with Worcestershire Butter (page 201); garnish with mixed mayonnaise and caviar. Yield: 6 portions.

FRANKFURTER SAVORY

Broil cocktail frankfurters; slit halfway down on one side. Spread with mixture of prepared mustard and horseradish, using these in the proportion of 1 tablespoon prepared mustard to ½ teaspoon horseradish. Fasten with toothpicks.

HAM AND FIG ROLLS

Wrap fresh figs in boiled ham slices and fasten with a toothpick. Serve chilled.

SAUSAGE–STUFFED PRUNES

Use large prunes, cooked or steamed until soft but not mushy; remove pits. Insert a tiny cocktail sausage in each. Place in well buttered baking dish and bake in very hot oven (450° F.) until sausages begin to brown. Cool slightly before serving on toothpicks.

PRUNE AND OLIVE APPETIZERS

Remove pits from large prunes, steamed until almost tender, and fill each with small stuffed olive; wrap each in a small strip of bacon and fasten with toothpick. Broil until bacon is crisp, turning to crisp all sides. Serve warm.

PEARL ONION APPETIZERS

Cut bacon slices in thirds; place a pickled pearl onion in each piece, roll, fasten with toothpick. Broil until bacon is crisp. Serve warm.

CHEESE AND BACON ROLLS

Take as many slices of bacon as there are guests to be served and use American cheese. Cut cheese in 1-inch cubes, roll strip of bacon around each and fasten with toothpicks. Broil quickly, turning often to crisp bacon and prevent cheese from melting. Serve at once on toothpicks.

CHEESE BEEF ROLLS

1 cup cottage cheese
2 tablespoons chili sauce

Worcestershire sauce
salt and pepper
12 small slices dried beef

Mix together cottage cheese, chili sauce and few drops of Worcestershire sauce; season to taste. Spread on dried beef, roll tightly and fasten with toothpicks. Yield: 1 dozen rolls.

PIMIENTO CHEESE ROLLS

Use ½ cup pimiento cheese for filling; spread 12 thin slices bread with mayonnaise, using 3 tablespoons; cover with cheese and top with dried beef. Roll, cut each in half and fasten with toothpicks. Toast under broiler and serve hot. Yield: 2 dozen rolls.

CELERY CHEESE BALLS

1 cup finely chopped celery
1 3-oz. package cream cheese
¼ teaspoon salt

dash of pepper
2 tablespoons finely chopped
parsley
paprika

Mix together celery, cheese and seasonings; shape in small balls. Roll balls in parsley and sprinkle lightly with paprika; pimiento cream cheese may be used if desired. Yield: 1 dozen small balls.

CUCUMBER CHEESE SLICES

1 medium-sized cucumber
salt
16-oz. package cream cheese
2 tablespoons chopped onion
¼ cup chopped green pepper

paprika, salt and pepper
Worcestershire sauce
French dressing
lettuce
pimiento
mayonnaise

Cut cucumber in half crosswise; pare and remove seeds, leaving center hollow. Sprinkle salt around inside; drain before filling. Mix together cheese, onion and green pepper and add enough paprika to make a reddish color. Season with salt, pepper and a few drops Worcestershire sauce; pack firmly into cucumber shells. Marinate in a little French dressing and place in refrigerator to chill. Cut in slices, ¼ inch thick; place 3 slices on small bed of crisp, shredded lettuce. Garnish with strips of pimiento and mayonnaise. Approximate yield: 6 portions.

CALIFORNIA SALAD—HORS D'ŒUVRES

Use chilled fruits and vegetables; cut avocado pear in small slices, red tomatoes in tiny pie-shaped pieces and tiny string beans in 1-inch pieces. Marinate with French dressing seasoned with Worcestershire sauce and a few scrapings of onion. Drain after standing; then arrange in individual lettuce nests on a large platter, sprinkle sparsely with pinhead sized balls made of snappy cheese and serve with well-seasoned mayonnaise. Cantaloupe may be substituted for the avocado.

APPLE ANTIPASTO

On each serving plate arrange thin, unpeeled apple slices, strips of green pepper, a mound of cole slaw, a pimiento, one or two sardines, stuffed pickled onions, black olives and stuffed olives. Serve olive oil and wine vinegar in cruets to accompany the antipasto.

CHICKEN LIVER HORS D'ŒUVRES

6 chicken livers   **2 tablespoons finely chopped**
2 tablespoons prepared mustard   **olives**
                6 slices bacon, cut in halves
                ¼ cup dry bread crumbs

Rinse chicken livers in cold water and cut each in half; spread with mixture of mustard and olives. Wrap bacon around each piece, fasten with a toothpick and roll in crumbs. Bake in hot oven (425° F.) 10 to 15 minutes. Yield: 1 dozen portions.

COCKTAILS

COCKTAIL APPETIZERS include the juices of many fruits and vegetables, as well as mixed fruits, vegetables, seafood and meats. With the exception of the juices, some of which may be served hot, cocktails are at their best chilled.

FROSTED GRAPE JUICE COCKTAIL

Mix 2 cups grape juice and 3 tablespoons lemon juice and chill thoroughly. Just before serving, frost cocktail glasses by dipping rims in 3 tablespoons lemon juice, then dipping immediately in sugar. Add 1 pint chilled ginger ale to chilled fruit juices and pour at once into prepared glasses. Approximate yield: 6 portions.

FROSTED CITRUS JUICE CUP

Mix 2 cups orange juice, 1 cup grapefruit juice and 1½ tablespoons lemon juice and chill thoroughly. Just before serving, frost cocktail glasses by dipping rims in 3 tablespoons orange juice, then dipping immediately in sugar. Add 1 pint chilled ginger ale to chilled fruit juices and pour at once into prepared glasses. Yield: 6 portions.

CITRUS JUICE COCKTAIL

Fill 12 glasses half-full of crushed ice. Place mixture of 1 cup grapefruit juice, ½ cup orange juice, 3 tablespoons lemon juice, ⅔ cup Sugar Syrup (page 193) and dash of salt in cocktail shaker; add 1½ cups carbonated water and shake thoroughly. Pour into iced glasses, garnish each with sprig of fresh mint and ¼ teaspoon Sherry jelly. Serve at once. Yield: 1 dozen portions.

SPICED FRUIT JUICE COCKTAIL

Mix 1 cup orange juice, ½ cup pineapple juice, ⅓ cup Sugar Syrup (page 193), ⅔ cup water, ½ teaspoon grated lemon rind, ½ teaspoon nutmeg, ¼ teaspoon cinnamon and 3 whole cloves. Chill 3 hours. Strain, add 1½ pints sweet cider and stir briskly. Serve in glasses with cracked ice. Approximate yield: 6 portions.

CIDER MINT COCKTAIL

Mix 2 cups sweet cider, ½ cup pineapple juice and ½ cup orange juice; strain and chill. Serve in cocktail glasses and garnish each with a sprig of mint. Approximate yield: 6 portions.

TOMATO CUP

Heat to boiling point 2 cups canned tomato juice, ½ cup sugar, 2 lemons, sliced, ¼ teaspoon cinnamon, ⅛ teaspoon nutmeg and 6 whole cloves; strain and chill. Add ½ cup lemon juice and 2 cups iced water. Serve, thoroughly chilled, in cocktail glasses with bits of candied ginger. Approximate yield: 6 portions.

BEET JUICE COCKTAIL

Mix 1 cup liquor from canned beets, ⅓ cup lemon juice, 1½ cups water, ½ teaspoon salt and dash of cayenne; chill. Serve very cold in cocktail glasses. Approximate yield: 6 portions.

CLAM JUICE COCKTAIL

To 4 cups Clam Broth (page 277) (or canned juice) add 3 tablespoons lemon juice, 3 tablespoons ketchup, ¼ teaspoon Worcestershire sauce, ¼ teaspoon salt and ½ teaspoon celery salt; chill. Shake in cocktail shaker and serve; several drops Tabasco sauce may be substituted for Worcestershire sauce. Approximate yield: 8 portions.

CLAM AND TOMATO COCKTAIL

Combine 1½ cups each clam broth (or juice) and tomato juice; season with salt and pepper and chill thoroughly. Serve in cocktail glasses and garnish each with ½ thin slice of lemon. Yield: 6 portions.

FRUIT CUP COCKTAILS

For fresh or canned fruit combination cocktails, use ½ cup of mixture. Serve in cocktail glasses, sherbet glasses, glass bowls or orange cups.

Grapefruit-Ginger Cocktail—Mix 2 cups each diced grapefruit and fresh pineapple, and 1 tablespoon each preserved ginger and ginger syrup. Decorate each glass with a green cherry.

Orange Fruit Cocktail—Mix sections of oranges, halved strawberries and white grapes; chill. Before serving, top with Hot Jelly Sauce (page 727).

Pineapple-Mint Cocktail—Mix wedges of fresh pineapple, cubes of mint jelly and thin slices of preserved kumquats and spiced crab apples with fruit juices. Chill thoroughly.

Cape Cod Cocktail—Mix 2 canned apricot halves, diced, 1 large banana, sliced, ⅔ cup canned Cranberry Sauce. Chill and serve in sherbet glasses.

Peach Cocktail—Place 1 fresh or canned peach, peeled and diced, in each of 6 cocktail glasses; sprinkle with powdered sugar and pour mixture of ¾ cup grape juice, ¼ cup lemon juice and ¾ cup cracked ice over fruit. Garnish with mint leaves and serve at once.

GRAPE–FILLED AVOCADOS

1½ pounds red grapes, seeded
and halved (3 cups)

3 ripe avocados
lemon juice
Madeira wine

Cut grapes in halves, lengthwise, and remove seeds. Cut avocados in halves, remove large stone, and rub fruit with lemon juice to prevent darkening. Chill. Pile grapes into avocado halves, pour wine over. Serve as an appetizer. Yield: 6 portions.

AVOCADO–GRAPEFRUIT COCKTAIL

Peel and cut 2 small ripe avocados; mix with 1½ cups drained, canned grapefruit, or sections from 1 large fresh grapefruit, cubed, and chill. Add ¾ teaspoon tomato ketchup, 1 teaspoon Worcestershire sauce and 1 teaspoon lemon juice to ¾ cup heavy cream, whipped; mix ½ of sauce with fruit. Serve very cold in cocktail glasses and top with remaining sauce. Approximate yield: 6 portions.

MELON CUP COCKTAILS

As a cocktail, cantaloupe is splendid, either alone or in combination with other fruits. Shape fleshy part into balls, using a vegetable ball cutter, or cut in cubes. The following combinations will make about 6 portions each.

Melon-Mint Cocktail—Mix 3 cups cantaloupe cubes (about 2 small melons) with 24 after-dinner mints, broken; chill.

Cantaloupe Fruit Cup—Mix 1½ cups each cantaloupe cubes and diced pineapple with ⅓ cup pineapple juice and 1½ tablespoons lemon juice. Serve in cocktail glasses; garnish with green grapes.

Grape-Melon Cocktail—Mix 1 cup seedless grapes, 1 cup diced honeydew melon, cubed sections from 1 medium-sized orange, 2 tablespoons lemon juice and 1 tablespoon sugar; chill. Serve in sherbet glasses.

Raspberry-Melon Cup—Cover 1½ cups fresh raspberries with 1 cup sugar and chill about 1 hour; then force through coarse sieve. Heap 3 cups chilled, diced watermelon in cocktail glasses and pour raspberry purée over melon.

Watermelon Cup—Sprinkle juice from 2 limes and 3 tablespoons chopped mint leaves over 3 cups watermelon cubes or balls; chill. Serve in sherbet glasses and garnish each with sprig of mint.

LOUIS' COCKTAIL SAUCE

½ cup tomato ketchup	4 teaspoons horseradish
½ cup chili sauce	dash of Tabasco
4 teaspoons sweet pickle relish	1 teaspoon Worcestershire sauce

Mix all ingredients together and chill thoroughly. Serve with shrimp, oysters or clams. Garnish with water cress. Approximate yield: 1 cup.

OYSTERS OR CLAMS ON HALF SHELL

Use small medium-sized oysters or hard-shelled clams, allowing 5 or 6 to each portion. See page 446 for directions for cleaning and opening shells. Serve on deeper halves of the shells and arrange on plate or shallow glass bowl filled with finely shaved ice. Place small glass of Louis' Cocktail Sauce in center and garnish with 3 small radish roses or wedge-shaped pieces of lemon.

EPICUREAN OYSTER COCKTAIL

Thoroughly chill 30 oysters. Place 1 tablespoon minced celery in bottom of each of 6 chilled cocktail glasses and lay 5 oysters on top; top with Epicurean Cocktail Sauce (page 218) and garnish with a strip each of green pepper and pimiento. Yield: 6 portions.

OYSTERS IN GAY NIGHTIES

18 oysters on half shell	3 egg whites, stiffly beaten
2 tablespoons butter	½ cup chopped, crisp bacon
salt and pepper	1 pimiento, cut in strips
1 tablespoon drained horseradish	1 bunch water cress

Remove oysters from shell, drain and saute in butter until the edges curl. Return to shells and season with salt and pepper. Add horseradish to egg whites; season with salt and pepper. Heap meringue on oysters, make a depression in the center; place under low broiler heat 3 minutes or until golden brown. Fill depression with bacon and garnish with pimiento and water cress sprigs. Serve as appetizer. Yield: 6 portions.

CRAB COCKTAILS

Crab Meat Cocktail—Mix 1½ cups flaked crab meat with ½ cup ketchup and ⅓ cup finely minced, sour mustard pickles. Chill thoroughly and serve in cocktail glasses. Approximate yield: 6 portions.

Piquant Crab Cocktail—Mix 1½ cups flaked crab meat with Piquant Sauce (page 218). Approximate yield: 6 portions.

LOBSTER OR SHRIMP COCKTAIL

Cut cooked lobster in pieces; remove intestinal vein from cooked shrimp and break in pieces, allowing about ¼ cup per portion. Chill thoroughly and serve in cocktail glasses with any cocktail sauce (page 217) or with highly seasoned mayonnaise.

QUEENSLAND LOBSTER COCKTAIL

2 lobster tails
juice of 1 lemon
1¼ teaspoons Worcestershire
    sauce

¼ cup tomato chili sauce
¼ cup liquid (lobster water)
¼ cup heavy cream, whipped

Boil 2 lobster tails (page 438), adding the juice of 1 lemon. Cool lobster
in same liquid and refrigerate 2 hours. Combine Worcestershire sauce,
chili sauce, and ¼ cup liquid lobster was cooked in. Blend and fold in
heavy cream, whipped very stiff, and chunks of the lobster meat removed from the shells. Serve in fish cocktail glasses garnished with
water cress and a wedge of lemon. Yield: 4 portions.

PICK 'N DIP

1 cup mayonnaise
1 tablespoon anchovy paste
½ teaspoon dry mustard
½ teaspoon Tabasco
¼ teaspoon garlic salt
2 tablespoons tarragon vinegar
3 hard-cooked eggs, finely
    chopped

3 tablespoons finely chopped,
    stuffed olives
3 tablespoons finely chopped
    gherkins
1 tablespoon chopped parsley
1 teaspoon finely chopped onion
2 12-oz. rock lobster tails

Blend mayonnaise, anchovy paste, mustard, Tabasco and garlic salt. Stir
in vinegar, eggs, olives, gherkins, parsley and onion. Mix well. Yield:
2 cups sauce. Boil lobster tails according to basic recipe (see page 438).
Remove meat, chill and cube, saving one shell to serve sauce in. Place
a toothpick in each cube and arrange around sauce-filled shell. Decorate
platter with water cress or parsley. Approximate yield: 24 appetizers.

SHRIMP-GRAPEFRUIT COCKTAIL

Use 1 No. 1 can shrimp and sections from 1 medium-sized grapefruit;
arrange in alternate layers in cocktail glasses. Top with ¼ cup mayonnaise seasoned with 4 drops Tabasco sauce. Yield: 6 portions.

COCKTAIL SAUCES

In general, 1 cup sauce will be enough for 4 to 6 cocktails.

Celery Cocktail Relish—Mix ½ cup ketchup, ½ cup lemon juice,
1 tablespoon Worcestershire sauce, ½ teaspoon Tabasco sauce, 2 teaspoons horseradish, 6 tablespoons minced celery, 3 tablespoons grated
onion and ¼ teaspoon salt. Chill thoroughly. Yield: 1½ cups sauce.

Chili-Ketchup Sauce—Mix ½ cup chili sauce, ¼ cup ketchup, few drops Tabasco sauce, 1 tablespoon horseradish, ½ tablespoon minced celery, 2 teaspoons minced green peppers, 2 teaspoons minced pimiento, ½ teaspoon salt and dash of pepper; chill. Yield: 1 cup sauce.

Cocktail Dressing—Mix together 3 tablespoons lemon juice, 6 tablespoons ketchup, 1 tablespoon horseradish, 1 teaspoon Worcestershire sauce and 4 drops Tabasco sauce; add salt and celery salt to taste. Chill well before serving with shellfish. Approximate yield: ⅔ cup sauce.

Cocktail Sauce—Mix together 1 tablespoon lemon juice, ¼ cup ketchup, 2 teaspoons horseradish, 3 drops Worcestershire sauce and ½ teaspoon salt; chill well. Approximate yield: ⅓ cup sauce.

Cucumber Relish—Pare and grate 1 medium-sized cucumber; mix with ½ cup chili sauce, 1 teaspoon onion juice, 3 tablespoons lemon juice, dash of pepper and Tabasco sauce. Yield: 1¾ cups sauce.

Epicurean Cocktail Sauce—Mix 3 tablespoons lemon juice, 3 tablespoons ketchup, 1 tablespoon horseradish, 3 drops Tabasco sauce, 1 teaspoon minced onion and ½ teaspoon salt; chill thoroughly before using. Approximate yield: ½ cup sauce.

Mayonnaise Cocktail Sauce—Combine 1 cup mayonnaise, 2 tablespoons ketchup, 2 tablespoons chili sauce, 1 tablespoon tarragon vinegar and 1 teaspoon lemon juice. Serve with chilled shrimp, crab meat or lobster. Approximate yield: 1¼ cups sauce.

Piquant Sauce—Combine ⅓ cup ketchup, 1 teaspoon onion juice, ½ teaspoon Tabasco sauce, ½ teaspoon salt and ⅛ teaspoon cayenne; chill thoroughly before serving with fish. Yield: ⅓ cup sauce.

Tomato Cream Sauce—Fold ¼ cup heavy cream, whipped, into ½ cup tomato sauce or condensed tomato soup and add ½ teaspoon lemon juice; beat well just before serving. This is very good served on orange sections arranged in a cocktail glass. Yield: 1 cup sauce.

Soups

PROBABLY there is no other dish on the menu so truly international in character as soup. From faraway places come exotic, refreshing clear soups, hearty vegetable soups, flavorful chowders and velvet smooth cream soups—all of them contributing their goodness and flavor to the American table.

Soup cookery should be unhurried, with frequent tasting for proper seasoning and simmering temperature to bring out the best in flavor.

The more substantial soups can be served as the main dish of a luncheon or supper, followed, perhaps, by a crisp salad and light dessert. The lighter soups stimulate the appetite and usually precede a hearty main dish.

SOUPS WITH STOCK

SOUP STOCK is of two kinds—brown or white. Brown soup stock is made from the lean meat of beef, cracked bones and a small amount of fat. White soup stock is made from chicken or veal or both. A light fish stock is obtained from the fleshy portions and trimmings of fish or shellfish, while vegetable stock—from strained cooked vegetables—may be light or dark depending upon added ingredients.

Bouillon is a clear soup made from brown soup stock, having beef only as the meat ingredient.

Consommé, a clear soup, is made from brown soup stock, but has veal and chicken with beef to give it its meaty flavor.

Broth is the liquid resulting from meat simmered slowly in

water and is not as highly clarified (cleared) or as delicately seasoned as either bouillon or consommé.

PREPARING SOUP STOCK

SHANK OF BEEF or knuckle of veal is an economical cut for soup. The meat is cut in small pieces to draw out the flavor and the bones are cracked to loosen the marrow. Long, slow cooking is essential to form gelatin from the connective and cartilaginous tissue and to develop a rich, meaty flavor. Vegetables may be added at the beginning or during the last hour of cooking, depending upon the strength of flavor desired. If vegetables are to be served in the soup, they should be cooked until just tender.

Removing Fat from Soup. For clear broth or soup, strain through a fine sieve or cheesecloth; the meat and vegetable residue may be used in making croquettes or escalloped dishes. Skim off as much fat as possible from the stock with a shallow spoon, then gently float absorbent paper over the surface to remove flecks of fat. Or skim off the hard layer of fat that forms on top of cold soup.

To Clarify Soup. Add slightly beaten egg white and crushed shell to cold stock (1 white to 4 cups) and heat slowly to boiling, stirring constantly. Remove from heat and allow to stand 10 minutes. Strain through 2 thicknesses of damp cheesecloth or a fine sieve.

When soup is oversalted, add a few slices of peeled raw potato while it is simmering. Remove after a few minutes.

Vegetable soups may be made from water in which vegetables have been cooked or soup stock. When vegetables are forced through a sieve, the liquid combined with the pulp forms a purée.

Cream soups have a thin white sauce base with cooked vegetable or pulp, finely chopped meat or fish added; light stock combined with the milk improves the flavor.

SOUP GARNISHES

Clear Soups. Consommé or bouillon and similar clear soups may be garnished with a teaspoon of finely minced parsley, chives, julienned carrots, string beans or okra, finely diced cooked carrots, little snips of puff paste, thin slices of cooked button mushrooms, rice, vermicelli, alphabet macaroni, tapioca, a thin sliver of lemon, small cubes of custard or small meat, egg or cereal dumplings.

Purées and Thick Soups. Garnish with thin strips of lemon, croutons, cooked vegetables and minced parsley.

Cream Soups. Color contrast is introduced by adding diced cooked vegetables, minced chives, parsley, paprika, pimiento and croutons. Bisques require nothing more than a spoonful of salted whipped cream with a halo of paprika or finely minced parsley.

Soup Accompaniments. Melba toast, cheese straws, varieties of crisp crackers, toast and toast sticks, croutons, bread sticks and pastry strips add crispness.

BROWN SOUP STOCK (BOUILLON)

4 pounds shin of beef	4 whole cloves
2½ quarts cold water	⅓ teaspoon peppercorns
¼ cup diced carrot	1 bay leaf
¼ cup diced celery	2 sprigs thyme
¼ cup diced onion	1 sprig marjoram
¼ cup diced turnip	2 sprigs parsley

2 teaspoons salt

Use soup bone from hind or fore shank; wipe and cut lean beef in small cubes and crack marrowbone. Brown about ½ of meat in marrow from bone, or in 2 tablespoons fat; add with remaining meat and bone to cold water, heat slowly to boiling and simmer 10 minutes. Skim thoroughly, cover and simmer 3 hours, removing the scum as it forms; add vegetables and seasonings and cook 30 minutes longer. Strain stock through fine sieve or several thicknesses of cheesecloth and cool quickly; when cold, remove fat, heat and clear, if necessary (page 220). Brown soup stock served as clear soup is usually called bouillon. Use less seasonings for a more delicate stock, or vary seasonings and vegetables as desired. Yield: 2 quarts stock.

White Stock—Substitute 4 pounds knuckle of veal or veal scraps, or fowl (largely bones), or a combination of both, for beef. Add 1 leek, other vegetables and seasonings, as desired.

Lamb or Mutton Stock—Substitute 4 pounds lamb or mutton for beef; use bones and trimmings from leg, shoulder, neck or ribs.

FISH STOCK (FUMET)

bones, fins and head of fish
3½ cups water
½ cup dry white wine
6 peppercorns

bouquet garni (parsley, chives, marjoram and chervil—fresh preferred)
1 carrot
1 onion

Put all ingredients in a heavy pan. Simmer until liquid is reduced by one-third. Strain for use.

BEEF BROTH

Use 3 to 4 pounds of beef, shin, neck or chuck; cut in pieces and crack bone. Add 1 quart cold water, bring slowly to a boil, skim and simmer, covered, about 4 hours, adding ½ teaspoon salt after 2 hours of cooking. Strain as for clear soup (page 220); reheat and serve in hot cups, or chill and serve as a jelly. Approximate yield: 2 cups broth.

CHICKEN BROTH

Use 3- to 4-pound dressed fowl; clean, remove skin and fat and cut in pieces; cover with 2 quarts cold water. Heat slowly to boiling point, skim and simmer, covered, 3 hours, or until tender, adding 1 teaspoon salt after 2 hours of cooking. Strain as for clear soup (page 220); season to taste and serve hot. If desired, 2 tablespoons sago, tapioca, rice, or barley soaked overnight, may be cooked with broth. Meat cut from bones may be used in salad or creamed and used as shortcake. Yield: 1 quart broth.

MUTTON BROTH WITH BARLEY

Prepare broth or stock as directed on page 220, using 2 pounds breast of mutton, cut in pieces, 3 quarts cold water, 2 tablespoons pearl barley, 3 tablespoons chopped celery, 1 cup sliced onions, 2 cups diced carrots, 1 teaspoon salt, ½ teaspoon pepper and 1 bay leaf. Strain and skim fat. Yield: 2 quarts broth.

MINESTRA

¼ clove garlic, chopped	⅛ teaspoon pepper
3 tablespoons oil	½ cup shelled peas
½ cup chopped onion	½ cup diced green beans
½ cup chopped celery	2 tablespoons uncooked rice
1 cup diced carrot	2 bay leaves
2 teaspoons tomato paste	2 tomatoes, sliced
3 cups light beef stock	3 tablespoons grated Gruyère
1 teaspoon salt	cheese

Cook garlic in oil about 2 minutes. Add onions, celery and carrots. Simmer 6 minutes. Add tomato paste, beef stock, salt and pepper. Bring slowly to boiling. Add peas, beans, rice and bay leaves. Simmer until vegetables are tender, not mushy. Add tomatoes and cheese. Simmer 2 minutes. Add more salt and pepper, if desired. Serve very hot with a bowl of grated cheese. Approximate yield: 6 portions.

TURKEY BONE SOUP

bones of 1 turkey	1 teaspoon chopped onion
2 quarts cold water	1 sprig parsley
1 carrot, sliced	¼ bay leaf
1 stalk celery, chopped	3 peppercorns
	½ teaspoon salt

Place all ingredients in large kettle, bring to a boil and simmer, covered, 2 hours; strain. Approximate yield: 1½ quarts soup.

CLEAR TOMATO SOUP

¼ cup diced celery	½ teaspoon peppercorns
¼ cup diced carrot	3 whole cloves
¼ cup diced onion	⅛ teaspoon dried thyme
¼ cup diced, uncooked ham	1 small bay leaf
2 tablespoons fat	¾ teaspoon salt
2 sprigs parsley	¼ teaspoon pepper
4 cups canned tomatoes	1 quart meat stock (page 221)

Cook celery, carrots, onions and ham in fat for 5 minutes; add parsley, tomatoes, spices and seasonings, bring to a boil, cover and simmer 1 hour. Strain carefully; add hot meat stock. Approximate yield: 1½ quarts soup.

CONSOMMÉ

Use recipe for Brown Soup Stock (page 221); substitute 2 pounds lean beef, cut in 1 inch cubes, 1 pound marrowbone, cracked, and 2 pounds knuckle of veal, cut in pieces, for shin of beef. Sauté vegetables in 1 tablespoon butter until lightly browned before adding to stock; chicken stock or chicken bones may be added to soup kettle. Approximate yield: 2 quarts consommé.

Consommé Bordeaux—Boil 3 cups consommé and ¼-inch stick cinnamon about 5 minutes; add ⅔ cup hot water and 1 cup Claret, and pour mixture slowly over 1 well-beaten egg yolk. Fold in stiffly beaten egg white and serve immediately in bouillon cups. Approximate yield: 6 portions.

Consommé Royale—Pour hot consommé into bouillon cups. Place fancy shapes or tiny dice of Custard Royale (page 249) in each portion.

Julienne Consommé—To 1 quart hot consommé add about 2 tablespoons each shredded and cooked carrots, celery, string beans and turnips, and 1 tablespoon minced onion or leeks. Yield: 6 portions.

Two-toned Jellied Consommé—Prepare dark and light-colored jellied consommé mixtures; pour into shallow pans to make a 1-inch thick layer of each; chill in refrigerator until firm. Cut layers in 1 inch cubes and arrange light and dark cubes in bouillon cups.

For dark jellied consommé, use recipe for Jellied Madrilène (page 1002).

For light jellied consommé, use 3 cups clam broth or a similar canned broth, dash of pepper, 2 envelopes plain gelatin and ¼ cup cold water; prepare as for Jellied Madrilène.

QUICK BOUILLON OR CONSOMMÉ

For quick stock, bouillon or consommé, use one of the following prepared soups or extracts: canned light soup directly from can; canned condensed soup diluted with an equal volume of water; 1 or 2 bouillon cubes dissolved in 1 cup boiling water; 1 to 2 teaspoons beef extract or meat concentrate dissolved in 1 cup boiling water.

Beef Claret Bouillon—Heat 2½ cups beef bouillon to boiling point. Remove from heat and add ¾ cup Claret. Serve in bouillon cups and garnish with chopped parsley. Yield: 6 portions.

Chilled Bouillon—Chill thoroughly 2½ cups beef bouillon; add 1½ tablespoons lemon juice and season with salt, if needed. Pour over ice cubes in cocktail glasses. Approximate yield: 6 portions.

Jellied Bouillon—To 3 cups bouillon use 1 envelope plain gelatin. Soften gelatin in ¼ cup cold bouillon 5 minutes; add 1 cup boiling hot soup and stir until gelatin is dissolved. Then add remaining cold soup, season to taste and pour into bowl; chill until firm or jellied. Arrange by spoonfuls irregularly, in bouillon cups. Serve with lemon wedges. Approximate yield: 6 portions.

ONION SOUP CHABLIS

1 pound small white onions	1 cup Chablis
½ cup butter	1 teaspoon salt
3 cups chicken broth or	dash of black pepper
consommé	1 cup cream

Cook onions, sliced very thin, in butter until soft and transparent, but not brown. Add chicken broth or consommé and simmer until mixture is reduced almost two-thirds. Add Chablis, salt and pepper. Bring to boil and simmer about 10 minutes. Stir in cream, heat and serve in an earthenware tureen, garnish liberally with freshly grated Swiss cheese. Approximate yield: 6 portions.

POT AU FEU

2½ pounds lean beef	1½ cups diced celery
1 small soupbone, cracked	2½ cups diced potatoes
2 quarts water	2 cups diced turnips
1 slice beef liver, diced	2 tablespoons shredded parsley
2½ cups diced carrots	2 teaspoons salt
4 small white onions, sliced	pepper
	crisp toast

Cut beef in pieces, add with soupbone to water, bring slowly to a boil and simmer, covered, 4½ hours. Add liver, vegetables and salt, bring to boil and simmer, covered, 1½ hours longer. Remove beef and bone; cut meat in small pieces and return to soup. Let stand until cold and fat hardens on top; remove fat and reheat soup; season with pepper and additional salt, if needed. This soup is thick and like a purée. Serve hot with squares of crisp toast; any appetizing vegetable in season may be added. Other meats such as veal, lamb, or chicken may be substituted for beef. Add a clove, bay leaf, peppercorn or other herbs for flavoring. Approximate yield: 2½ quarts.

CURRY SOUP

2 medium onions, sliced	4 cups veal broth
2 tablespoons butter	salt
2 tablespoons flour	dash of cayenne
2 teaspoons curry powder	2 cups diced cooked veal

Sauté onions in butter until lightly browned; stir in flour and curry powder, gradually add veal broth; cook 5 minutes, stirring until smooth and thickened. Season with salt and cayenne and add veal. Approximate yield: 6 portions.

SCOTCH BROTH WITH RICE

Bring to a boil 1 shoulder lamb bone, 2 quarts cold water, ½ onion, sliced, ½ teaspoon salt and ¼ teaspoon pepper; skim, cover and cook slowly 2½ hours; strain. Add 2 tablespoons rice and cook 10 minutes, then add ½ cup finely diced carrots and cook 20 minutes longer. Just before serving, add ¼ cup finely minced lamb and sprinkle with finely chopped parsley. Approximate yield: 1½ quarts broth.

SPRING VEGETABLE SOUP

4 young carrots, diced	¼ pound spinach, chopped
3 stalks celery, diced	½ cup chopped parsley
1 tablespoon minced onion	6 okra, sliced
2 quarts boiling water	½ teaspoon salt
	pepper

Add carrots, celery and onion to boiling water and cook, covered, 10 minutes; add remaining vegetables and salt and cook 20 minutes longer; season with pepper and additional salt, if needed. Yield: 6 cups.

LIVER SOUP

½ pound calf's liver, chopped	1 teaspoon salt
1 cup chopped mushrooms	1 quart bouillon
2 teaspoons chopped parsley	1 tablespoon flour
3 tablespoons butter	1 cup light cream

Sauté liver, mushrooms and parsley in 2 tablespoons butter 5 minutes; add salt and bouillon and simmer, covered, 20 minutes, or until tender. Brown flour in remaining 1 tablespoon butter and add small amount of soup mixture, stirring until smooth and thickened; then stir this into remainder of soup; add cream and cook over low heat 5 minutes longer, stirring occasionally. Approximate yield: 8 portions.

BLACK BEAN SOUP

1 cup dried black beans	⅛ teaspoon celery salt
1 quart cold water	⅛ teaspoon dry mustard
½ onion, sliced	dash of cayenne
1 stalk celery, diced	2 teaspoons flour
2 tablespoons butter	1 hard-cooked egg, sliced
¼ teaspoon salt	1 lemon, sliced

Wash and soak beans overnight in cold water (or use quick-cooking type). Sauté onion and celery in 1 tablespoon butter until lightly browned; add to beans, bring to a boil and simmer, covered, 3 hours, or until beans are soft, adding more water as it boils away. Rub through sieve; reheat and add well-mixed seasonings. Melt remaining 1 tablespoon butter and stir in flour; gradually add strained soup mixture and cook 3 minutes, stirring constantly until smooth and thickened. Turn into serving dishes and garnish with thin slices of egg and lemon. From 1 to 2 tablespoons Sherry may be added just before serving. Yield: 4 portions.

CORN AND CHICKEN SOUP

1 cup canned corn	2 cups hot milk
½ cup minced celery	2 egg yolks, slightly beaten
1 cup minced cold chicken	2 tablespoons butter
4 cups chicken stock	salt and pepper
	croutons

Heat corn and force through coarse sieve; add pulp, celery and chicken to stock, bring to a boil and simmer, covered, 15 minutes. Gradually stir hot milk into egg yolks; add to soup mixture and cook 2 minutes, stirring constantly; add butter and season to taste with salt and pepper. Serve with croutons. Yield: 8 portions.

CLAM BROTH

Scrub 1 quart clams in shells and wash in several waters until free from sand; place in large kettle. Add 2 cups water, cover tightly and cook slowly over low heat about 6 to 10 minutes, or until shells open; then remove from broth and serve clams hot on the half shell, or remove from shells and use as desired. When liquor has settled, strain carefully through cheesecloth; add water or milk to make 1 quart broth, season with paprika or celery salt and heat. Serve hot or cold with or without whipped cream and dash of paprika, with crisp water wafers or crackers. Approximate yield: 6 portions.

CREAM OF VEGETABLE SOUP

2 cups vegetable pulp and   3 to 4 cups Thin White Sauce
    liquid or purée   (page 125)
salt, pepper and paprika

Dice or slice vegetables and cook until soft in just enough boiling salted water to cover, using ½ teaspoon salt to 1 quart water; force through sieve. Add to white sauce, heat thoroughly and season to taste; beat with rotary beater before serving. Light stock can be substituted for ½ the milk or cream. Sprinkle with paprika or serve with whipped cream, grated cheese, chopped parsley or croutons as desired. Approximate yield: 6 portions.

Cream of Carrot Soup—Use 2 cups cooked carrot pulp and liquid, and 4 cups thin white sauce.

Cream of Celery Soup—Use 2 cups finely diced celery and 1 slice onion. If cooked in 1 cup milk, cook over boiling water; remove onion. It is not necessary to force celery through sieve unless coarse large pieces are used. Add celery and liquid to 3 cups thin white sauce. Season with celery salt.

Cream of Corn Soup—Use 2½ cups (No. 2 can) corn and 1 slice onion; cook in 2 cups milk over boiling water. Remove onion and force through sieve. Add pulp and liquid to 3 cups thin white sauce. Serve sprinkled with popped corn, if desired.

Cream of Onion Soup—Use 5 medium-sized white onions or 18 green onions. Cut white onions in slices and cook in water to cover until soft; force through sieve and add with 1 cup milk to 3 cups thin white sauce. Add 2 tablespoons grated cheese and stir until melted and smooth. If green onions are used, remove outside skins, cook and force through sieve; cook onion hearts separately and add to soup.

Cream of Spinach Soup—Use 1 pound spinach or 1½ cups cooked spinach; chop and force cooked spinach through sieve. Add with 1 teaspoon scraped onion and 1 cup stock or milk to 3 cups thin white sauce. Stir into 1 beaten egg yolk and heat 2 minutes. Season with dash of nutmeg.

Cream of Pea Soup—Use 2½ cups (No. 2 can) peas; add ½ teaspoon scraped onion and cook in liquor from can about 10 minutes. Force through sieve and add with 1 cup milk or stock to 3 cups thin white sauce. Beat well with rotary beater before serving.

Cream of Chicken Soup—Substitute 1 to 1½ cups minced chicken for vegetable pulp and 1 to 2 cups chicken stock for an equal amount of milk in thin white sauce. Approximate yield: 6 portions.

Alsatian Chicken Soup—Serve with Alsatian Dumplings, preparing ½ recipe (page 248). Yield: 6 portions.

CREAM OF CRAB SOUP

1 1-lb. can crab meat	⅛ teaspoon allspice
3 hard-cooked eggs	1½ quarts milk, scalded
2 teaspoons salt	1 tablespoon butter
1 teaspoon dry mustard	2 small lemons, sliced thin
	toasted crackers

Chop crab meat and eggs and stir in seasonings; add to hot milk and cook over boiling water or low heat 10 minutes; add butter. Place lemon slices in hot tureen, pour soup over slices and serve with toasted crackers. Approximate yield: 10 portions.

CREAM OF TOMATO SOUP

3 cups canned or stewed tomatoes	3 cups Thin White Sauce (page 125)
⅓ cup minced onion	salt and pepper
	paprika

Cook tomatoes and onion 10 minutes; force through sieve and reheat. Just before serving, stir hot tomato pulp and juice gradually into hot white sauce, season to taste and serve at once. Light stock may be substituted for ½ the milk in white sauce. If soup curdles, beat with rotary beater until smooth. Approximate yield: 6 portions.

CREAM OF MUSHROOM SOUP

¼ pound mushrooms, or stems from ½ pound	2 tablespoons flour
¼ cup butter	1 quart milk, scalded
	salt and pepper
	cayenne

Wash and chop mushrooms; sauté in butter in heavy pan 5 minutes. Stir in flour; gradually add milk and cook 5 minutes, stirring until mixture thickens; add seasonings and strain, if desired. Approximate yield: 6 portions.

CREAM OF GREEN BEAN SOUP

2 cups finely cut string beans
1 tablespoon minced onion
3 tablespoons butter
1 teaspoon salt
dash of pepper

dash of cayenne
2 tablespoons flour
2 cups boiling water
2 cups (14½-oz. can) evaporated milk

¼ cup grated American cheese

Add beans and onion to butter and season; simmer, covered, about 20 minutes, or until soft, stirring occasionally. Stir flour into vegetables, gradually add water and cook 5 minutes, stirring constantly until thickened and smooth; add evaporated milk and heat thoroughly. Sprinkle grated cheese over portions. Approximate yield: 6 portions.

POTATO SOUP

8 medium-sized potatoes
2 medium-sized onions, minced
2 tablespoons butter
2 teaspoons salt
¼ teaspoon pepper

3 cups potato water
1 egg, slightly beaten
1 cup heavy cream
⅛ teaspoon nutmeg
chopped parsley

Peel and dice potatoes and cook in water to cover until tender; drain and reserve 3 cups of the liquid; force potatoes through ricer or sieve. Sauté onions in butter until lightly browned; season with salt and pepper. Add with riced potatoes to reserved potato water; then add egg, cream and nutmeg mixture and heat 3 minutes, stirring constantly. Serve hot garnished with chopped parsley. Approximate yield: 6 large portions.

LOVE APPLE SOUP

3 tablespoons butter
⅓ cup minced onion
2 tablespoons flour
1 teaspoon minced parsley

½ teaspoon sugar
dash of pepper
1 teaspoon salt
3 cups sieved tomatoes

Melt butter, add onion and brown lightly. Blend in flour, parsley and seasonings. Gradually add tomatoes, stirring until thick and smooth. Simmer 15 minutes. Serve hot. Approximate yield: 4 portions.

CHESTNUT SOUP

3 to 4 dozen chestnuts
¼ cup diced fat bacon
1 large potato, quartered

1 to 2 medium carrots, halved
1 bay leaf
salt and pepper

To shell chestnuts, cover with cold water, add salt and boil 20 minutes. Peel chestnuts, add remaining ingredients and cover with 1 pint water. Allow to simmer until chestnuts are tender. Rub chestnuts, potato and carrots through coarse sieve. Thin purée to desired soup consistency with stock, stirring well; simmer 2 minutes. Serve with croutons. Yield: 6 portions.

CHESTNUT AND APPLE SOUP

1 pound chestnuts
3 tablespoons butter
1 onion, sliced
1 sliced apple, skin on

½ teaspoon minced garlic
1 quart stock
½ cup light cream
1 teaspoon flour

Cover chestnuts with cold water and bring to a boil. Simmer 20 minutes, drain and remove skins. Combine butter, onion, apple and garlic and simmer 5 minutes. Add chestnuts and stock. Bring to a boil and simmer until soft. Rub through a fine strainer. Gradually add cream to flour and stir into chestnut mixture. Bring to a boil. Garnish with slices of fried apple. Approximate yield: 6 portions.

CREAM OF ONION SOUP

1 teaspoon minced garlic
4 finely sliced onions
3 tablespoons butter
4 tablespoons flour
2½ cups chicken stock
⅛ teaspoon nutmeg
1 teaspoon salt

⅛ teaspoon crushed cardamon
    seeds
⅛ teaspoon black pepper
1 cup light cream
3 tablespoons sour cream
¼ cup finely sliced blanched
    scallions

Combine garlic, onion and butter and simmer until onions are soft but not brown. Remove from heat and add flour. Gradually add stock and cook over low heat, stirring constantly until mixture comes to a boil. Add nutmeg, salt, cardamon seeds, and pepper. Simmer 5 minutes. Rub through strainer. Add cream and sour cream and reheat slowly. Garnish with scallions. Approximate yield: 6 portions.

FRENCH CREAM OF MUSHROOM SOUP

2¼ cups finely chopped mushrooms
6 tablespoons minced onion
½ clove garlic, minced
3 tablespoons fat
6 tablespoons flour

¾ teaspoon meat extract
4½ cups stock
2 bay leaves
2 teaspoons salt
¼ teaspoon pepper
1¼ cups light cream

Combine mushrooms, onion, garlic and fat and simmer 8 minutes.
Remove from heat and stir in flour and meat concentrate. Gradually
add stock. Cook over low heat, stirring constantly until mixture comes
to a boil. Add bay leaves, salt and pepper and simmer about 10 minutes. Remove bay leaves and add cream. Serve with croutons. Approximate yield: 6 portions.

CREAM OF PEA SOUP

3 tablespoons butter
¼ clove garlic, minced
1 apple, sliced
¼ cup chopped onion
1½ cups shelled peas
6 tablespoons water

1 teaspoon salt
⅛ teaspoon pepper
2½ cups beef stock
2 tablespoons flour
¾ cup light cream
4 tablespoons cooked peas

Combine butter, garlic, apple and onion and simmer 3 minutes. Add
peas, water, salt and pepper and cook slowly until mushy. Gradually
add a paste of ¼ cup stock and flour to remaining stock and vegetable
mixture. Cook over low heat, stirring constantly until mixture comes to
a boil. Rub through a strainer. Add cream and garnish with peas.
Approximate yield: 6 portions.

SALMON BISQUE

Prepare 4 cups Thin White Sauce (page 125—substitute light soup or
fish stock for half of milk or cream, if desired), sautéing 1 small onion,
minced, in the butter 5 minutes. Add 1 cup canned or cooked salmon,
rubbed through a fine sieve, ¼ cup cooked peas and heat thoroughly.
Top servings with ¼ cup heavy cream, whipped and flavored with
1 teaspoon minced red sweet pepper. Yield: 6 portions.

Fish Bisque—Substitute codfish or haddock for salmon; cook 1 to 1½
pounds fish with ½ cup each diced carrots and celery, 1 sliced onion and
water to cover. Drain and rub through sieve, removing skin and bones
from fish; use stock for part of milk in white sauce and omit peas.

Mushroom and Clam Bisque—Substitute ½ pound mushrooms, finely chopped and sautéed in 3 tablespoons butter, for salmon; use 2 cups clam broth for 2 cups milk in preparing white sauce; flavor with dash of nutmeg and top each serving with whipped cream.

Tomato Bisque—Cook 2 cups canned tomatoes, ¼ cup rice, 2 cups water and 2 teaspoons concentrated beef extract about 20 minutes, or until rice is tender; rub through sieve. Prepare 2 cups thin white sauce, sautéing 1 small minced onion in the butter 5 minutes. Add tomato mixture and serve at once.

LOBSTER BISQUE

1 2½-lb. lobster, broiled	6 tablespoons butter
2 cups fish stock	¼ cup flour
1 quart milk	1 teaspoon salt
	paprika

Remove lobster meat and cut in cubes; break body and claws, cover with fish stock, bring slowly to a boil and simmer 10 minutes; drain, add stock to milk and scald. Melt ¼ cup butter and stir in flour; gradually stir in hot liquid and cook 5 minutes, stirring until smooth and thickened. Add seasonings and lobster meat and heat thoroughly. Serve with remaining 2 tablespoons butter, placing 1 teaspoon in each dish. Approximate yield: 6 portions.

OYSTER STEW

1 pint oysters	¼ teaspoon Worcestershire sauce
3 tablespoons butter	3 cups milk, scalded
½ teaspoon salt	1 cup light cream
dash of pepper	paprika
	crackers or oysterettes

Pick over oysters, remove bits of shell, drain and reserve liquor; add oysters to melted butter, season with salt, pepper and Worcestershire sauce and cook 2 minutes, or until oysters are plump and edges begin to curl. Add hot milk and oyster liquor and heat to boiling but do not boil. Sprinkle with paprika and serve at once with crackers. Approximate yield: 4 portions.

Scallop Stew—Substitute 1 pound of scallops for oysters. Mince and add to milk mixture.

BISQUE OF SHRIMP BRETONNE

2 pounds raw shrimp	3 tablespoons butter
¼ cup chopped mushrooms	salt and cayenne
2 tablespoons chopped onion	2 cups chicken or veal stock
2 tablespoons chopped celery	1 cup white wine (Rhine or
1 tablespoon chopped carrot	Sauterne)

1 cup light cream

Remove shells and veins of shrimp and chop fine; cook with vegetables in butter over low heat 2 minutes; add seasonings and stock and simmer about 10 minutes, or until tender and soft; force through sieve. Add wine and cream to purée and heat almost to boiling point; serve immediately. Approximate yield: 8 portions.

SPINACH PURÉE

½ pound spinach (frozen or	2 sprigs parsley
fresh)	1 bay leaf
¼ teaspoon salt	3 tablespoons butter
2 cups milk	3 tablespoons flour
2 slices onion	paprika

¼ cup light cream

Wash spinach, add salt and cook, covered, over low heat about 10 minutes, stirring occasionally to prevent burning; chop very fine or force through sieve. Scald milk with onion, parsley and bay leaf; strain. Make roux of butter and flour, gradually add hot milk and cook 3 minutes, stirring until smooth and thickened. Add spinach, season to taste, reheat and add cream. Approximate yield: 6 portions.

CARROT PURÉE

2 large carrots, sliced	3 cups beef stock or bouillon
1½ cups boiling water	¼ cup rice

salt and pepper

Cook carrots in boiling water until soft, drain and reserve stock; force carrots through sieve. Heat carrot and beef stock to boiling, add rice and cook slowly 20 minutes, or until rice is tender. Add carrot purée, season to taste and simmer 5 minutes longer. Approximate yield: 6 portions.

SPLIT PEA SOUP

1 pound dried split peas	1 carrot, sliced
3 quarts cold water	1 stalk celery, chopped
1 large onion	1 ham bone
	salt and pepper

Wash peas, add cold water, vegetables and ham bone and simmer about 3 hours, or until mixture is thick. Force through a coarse sieve and season to taste with salt and pepper. Dilute as desired with milk or cream. Serve with toast. Note: When using quick-cooking dried peas, follow cooking directions given. Approximate yield: 6 portions.

PEA SOUP ST. GERMAINE

1 ham bone, or ¼ pound ham	½ teaspoon salt
3 cups water	⅛ teaspoon pepper
4 cups shelled peas	1 teaspoon sugar
3 small carrots, sliced	1 quart milk
½ cup chopped onion	2 tablespoons butter

Heat ham bone and water to boiling point and simmer 1 hour; add vegetables and seasonings, bring to a boil and simmer ½ hour longer. Remove bone and force vegetables through sieve; add milk and butter, bring to a boil and serve. Approximate yield: 8 portions.

MANHATTAN CLAM CHOWDER

⅓ cup minced onion	2 teaspoons salt
½ clove garlic, minced	1 pint fresh clams, minced, or
¼ cup chopped celery	1 No. 1 can minced clams
2 tablespoons minced green pepper	1½ cups tomato juice
	dash of cayenne
2 tablespoons butter	dash of sage
2 large potatoes, diced	¼ teaspoon dried thyme
2½ cups boiling water	4 pilot or hard crackers

Sauté onions, garlic, celery and green pepper in butter in large saucepan about 4 minutes; add potatoes, boiling water and salt and boil until potatoes are tender. Heat fresh clams and clam liquor to boiling point, add with tomato juice, cayenne, sage and thyme to soup mixture and again bring to a boil. Pour chowder over plain or crumbled crackers in serving bowls. Approximate yield: 4 portions.

NEW ENGLAND CLAM CHOWDER

½ pound salt pork, diced
½ cup minced onion
3 cups boiling water
3 cups diced potatoes

⅛ teaspoon pepper
1 quart fresh clams, minced, or
  2 No. 1 cans minced clams
3 cups milk, scalded
6 pilot or hard crackers

Fry salt pork and onions until lightly browned; add water, potatoes and pepper and boil about 15 minutes, or until potatoes are tender. Heat fresh clams and clam liquor to boiling, add with milk to soup mixture and again bring to a boil. Pour chowder over plain or crumbled crackers in serving bowls. Approximate yield: 6 portions.

New England Fish Chowder—Substitute 2¼ pounds cod, haddock, pickerel or whitefish for clams. Cover with salted cold water, or fish stock, bring slowly to a boil and simmer, covered, 10 minutes; drain, reserving stock; remove meat from skin and bones and flake.

Crab Chowder—Substitute 3 tablespoons fat for salt pork and 3 cups flaked crab meat for clams. Thicken, if desired, with 1½ tablespoons flour mixed with 1½ tablespoons butter; gradually add stock, stirring constantly; cook 5 minutes; season.

Oyster Chowder—Substitute 1 quart oysters for clams and use 4 cups diced potatoes; add oysters to boiling hot soup mixture and cook 2 minutes, or until plump and edges begin to curl.

FISH CHOWDER

2 pounds haddock or cod
1½-inch cube fat salt pork,
  diced
1 medium onion, chopped
4 cups diced potatoes
2 cups boiling water

1 quart milk, scalded
1 cup light cream, scalded
1 tablespoon salt
⅛ teaspoon pepper
6 crackers, split
2 tablespoons butter

Wash fish, cover with salted cold water, bring slowly to a boil and simmer, covered, 5 minutes; drain, reserving stock, and remove skin and bones from fish. Fry salt pork in large kettle until golden brown; remove and drain on absorbent paper. Sauté onion in pork drippings, add potatoes and boiling water and boil about 5 minutes; then add fish and stock, bring to a boil and simmer about 15 minutes. Add milk, cream and seasonings and heat thoroughly; then add crackers and butter, sprinkle cracklings over chowder and serve at once. Approximate yield: 8 portions.

KENNEBUNK LOBSTER CHOWDER

1 1½-lb. lobster, boiled
5 tablespoons butter
1 cup cold water
lobster liver
3 cups milk
2 crackers, crumbled fine
1 cup light cream
1 teaspoon salt
2 slices onion
¼ teaspoon paprika
½ clove garlic
1 tablespoon minced parsley
1 teaspoon Worcestershire sauce

Cook lobster according to method given on page 438 and cut meat in cubes; cover shell with cold water and simmer 10 minutes; strain and reserve stock. Scald milk and cream with onion and garlic; then strain. Cream butter and mix well with liver and cracker crumbs; gradually add scalded milk and cream, stirring until smooth; add lobster and stock, salt, paprika, parsley and Worcestershire sauce; heat thoroughly. Approximate yield: 6 portions.

CLAM AND OYSTER CHOWDER

3 tablespoons butter
1 dozen clams, cut up
1 teaspoon minced onion
3 cups light cream
1 teaspoon minced scallion
1 teaspoon salt
1 teaspoon minced garlic
few grains of cayenne
1 dozen oysters, cut up
4 teaspoons butter
¼ cup chopped parsley

Combine butter, onion, scallion and garlic and simmer 2 minutes. Add oysters, clams, cream, salt and cayenne. Bring very slowly to boiling. Add butter and parsley. Simmer 3 minutes and serve. Approximate yield: 6 portions.

CORN–CRAB MEAT CHOWDER

2 tablespoons chopped onion
dash of pepper
2 tablespoons minced green
dash of paprika
   pepper
1½ cups boiling water
2 tablespoons fat
1½ cups canned corn
½ cup diced raw potatoes
½ cup flaked crab meat
½ teaspoon salt
1½ cups milk

Sauté onion and green pepper in fat in large saucepan 5 minutes; add potatoes, seasonings and boiling water and boil until potatoes are tender. Add corn, crab meat and milk, bring to a boil and serve at once. Approximate yield: 6 portions.

VEGETABLE CHOWDER

2 cups canned or fresh corn
2 cups chopped celery
½ green pepper, cut in fine
    strips
1 onion, thinly sliced
1 cup canned or fresh tomatoes
1 tablespoon salt

⅛ teaspoon pepper
2½ cups cold water
¼ cup butter
3 tablespoons flour
2 cups milk, scalded
½ cup grated cheese
½ cup chopped pimiento

¼ teaspoon paprika

Place corn, celery, green pepper, onion, tomatoes, salt and pepper in kettle; add cold water, bring to a boil, cover and simmer ½ hour. Melt butter and stir in flour; gradually add milk and cook 5 minutes, stirring constantly until smooth and thickened; add to vegetable mixture. Add cheese, pimiento and paprika, stirring until cheese is melted. Approximate yield: 8 portions.

CORN CHOWDER

1 ounce salt pork, diced
⅓ cup chopped onion
1⅓ cups (No. 1 can) corn
2 cups boiling water

1 quart milk
¾ cup mashed potatoes
salt and pepper
6 crackers

Fry salt pork until lightly brown; remove and sauté onion in drippings. Add corn and water and cook 10 minutes. Then add milk, potatoes and onions and heat thoroughly. Season to taste. Pour over crisp crackers and sprinkle cracklings over top, or add crumbled crackers to chowder just before serving. Approximate yield: 6 portions.

PHILADELPHIA PEPPERPOT

¾ pound fresh tripe, finely
    cubed
2 pounds knuckle of veal
3 quarts cold water
3 green peppers, chopped

3 medium onions, chopped
3 medium beets, chopped
3 tablespoons butter
1½ teaspoons salt
⅓ cup rice

1½ cups canned tomatoes

Slowly heat tripe, knuckle of veal and water to boiling and simmer 10 minutes; skim thoroughly, cover and simmer 3 hours. Sauté vegetables in butter until lightly browned and add salt; add with washed rice to soup mixture and simmer, covered, 30 minutes; add tomatoes and cook 10 minutes longer. Remove bone and cool; skim and reheat before serving. Approximate yield: 8 portions.

MOCK MULLIGATAWNY SOUP

½ clove garlic
1 tablespoon chicken fat or
  drippings
¾ teaspoon curry powder
1 can condensed vegetable soup

1 can water
2 tablespoons chicken gravy or
  1 bouillon cube (chicken)
2 tablespoons applesauce
¾ cup leftover diced chicken
1 teaspoon lemon juice

Sauté garlic in fat until color begins to change; remove garlic and blend in curry powder. Mix together soup, water, gravy and applesauce, bring to a boil and purée, using a coarse sieve. Add curry mixture and diced chicken and simmer 5 minutes. Add lemon juice and serve in soup plates with plenty of freshly boiled rice. If desired, omit garlic and add ½ cup chopped onion or leeks, increasing fat to 2 tablespoons. Force through sieve with other vegetables. Yield: 4 portions.

BOUILLABAISSE AU BISTRO

1 2½-pound lobster
1 pound whitefish
1 pound striped bass
1 pound red snapper
1 pound eel or other fish
⅔ cup olive oil
2 medium-sized onions, finely
  chopped
2 small white leeks, finely
  chopped
3 carrots, finely chopped
3 tomatoes, sectioned

2 bay leaves
bouquet garni or fresh herbs
1 clove of garlic, crushed
2 or 3 fish heads and bones
3 tablespoons flour
salt and black pepper
1 quart fish stock
1 quart mussels, cleaned
pinch of saffron
3 tablespoons butter
3 tablespoons flour
1 tablespoon chopped parsley

Remove skin, wash and cut fish into 2-inch pieces. Cut up lobster. Heat ⅓ cup olive oil and lightly brown onion, leeks and carrots. Add tomatoes, bay leaves, bouquet garni, garlic, fish bones and heads and lobster with shells. Add fish stock or wine and simmer, covered, about 15 minutes. Strain, reserving lobster shells, meat and fish stock. Heat ⅓ cup olive oil in second deep saucepan. Add mussels in shells, pieces of fish and sprinkle with parsley. Cook 5 minutes, stirring frequently. Add hot strained sauce, lobster and shells; thicken with butter blended with flour. Add saffron and season to taste. Cook 7 to 10 minutes longer and serve in soup plates with additional sauce in side dish, accompanied by white wine and garlic French bread. Yield: 8 portions.

CHICKEN GUMBO

1 3-lb. fowl, dressed	1 tablespoon salt
1 pound beef (shoulder, chuck or brisket)	2 dozen (1 pt.) oysters
¼ cup fat	pepper
1 small onion, sliced	dash of paprika
1½ quarts boiling water	½ teaspoon filé powder, or
	1½ teaspoons sassafras leaves

Cut chicken in pieces; cut beef in small pieces; sauté in fat in large heavy kettle until browned, adding onion the last 10 minutes of cooking. Add water, bring to a boil, cover and simmer 2 to 4 hours, or until meat is tender, adding salt when half done. Cut chicken from bones and return it to soup stock; add oysters with their liquor and cook until edges of oysters curl. Add additional salt, if needed, pepper to taste and paprika; stir in filé and serve at once in hot soup bowls. Approximate yield: 6 portions.

WATER CRESS SOUP

3 tablespoons butter	2 medium potatoes, diced
2 bunches water cress, chopped	3 cups canned chicken soup
⅓ cup minced onion	salt and pepper
1 bay leaf	½ teaspoon paprika
pinch of dried thyme	¼ cup light cream

Melt butter. Add water cress, onion, bay leaf and thyme. When cress is limp, add potatoes and soup to cover. Simmer until potatoes are very tender, then force mixture through a sieve. Add seasonings and cream. Heat and serve garnished with chopped parsley. Approximate yield: 6 portions.

OXTAIL CLARET SOUP

1 can condensed oxtail soup	rind of 1 lemon
1 cup water	½ teaspoon onion juice
⅛ teaspoon salt	½ cup Claret
dash of cayenne	1 tablespoon chopped parsley

Heat to boiling point soup, water, seasonings, lemon rind cut off thinly in one long strip, and onion juice and simmer 5 minutes; remove rind, add Claret and parsley and heat thoroughly. Approximate yield: 4 portions.

NEW ORLEANS GUMBO

12 hard shelled crabs, or	1 bay leaf
2 cups crab meat	1 sprig thyme
3 tablespoons butter	2 cups oyster liquor
1 medium onion, minced	1½ quarts water
6 large tomatoes, peeled	1 tablespoon filé powder, or
1 quart okra, sliced	3 tablespoons sassafras leaves

cooked rice

Clean and remove meat from crabs (see Fish and Shellfish); leave meat from claws whole; sauté in butter in large heavy saucepan about 10 minutes, add onion and cook until lightly browned. Add vegetables and herbs and cook 10 minutes, stirring frequently; add oyster liquor and water, bring to a boil and simmer about ½ hour, stirring occasionally. When ready to serve, add filé. Serve in large soup plates with rice. Approximate yield: 8 portions.

CHICKEN CORDIALE

6 cups canned chicken broth	½ teaspoon salt
6 eggs	¼ teaspoon pepper
5 tablespoons lemon juice	2 tablespoons Sherry

Strain chicken broth if it contains rice; bring to a boil over low heat. Beat eggs thoroughly, add lemon juice, salt and pepper and continue to beat until mixture is light and frothy; gradually beat in boiling broth and add Sherry. Pour into thin china bowls and serve at once. This soup is equally delicious when chilled. Approximate yield: 6 portions.

WHITE WINE SOUP

3 eggs, separated	2 cups hot water
1 tablespoon cake flour	2 slices lemon
5 tablespoons sugar	2 cups white wine (Rhine or
dash of salt	Sauterne)
dash of mace	zwieback

Beat egg yolks slightly and stir in flour, ¼ cup sugar and seasonings; gradually add hot water, add lemon and cook about 2 minutes, stirring constantly; add wine and heat to boiling point but do not boil. Pour soup into hot tureen and drop stiffly beaten egg whites, mixed with remaining 1 tablespoon sugar, by spoonfuls into hot soup; cover tureen immediately so that the steam will set the whites. Serve hot with zwieback, ladyfingers or sugar croutons. Yield: 6 portions.

For a frothy wine soup, stir 2 teaspoons flour into the slightly frothy whole eggs, then beat into hot soup mixture, beating with wire whisk until frothy and foamy; do not boil soup after adding eggs.

FRENCH ONION SOUP

12 small white onions, thickly
   sliced
3 tablespoons butter
1 tablespoon oil
½ teaspoon minced garlic
1 teaspoon meat concentrate
1 teaspoon potato or all-purpose
   flour

1¾ cups light stock
½ cup dry white wine or flat
   leftover champagne
salt
black pepper
grated Parmesan cheese

Lightly brown onions in 2 tablespoons hot butter and oil. Add garlic but do not cook. Stir in meat concentrate. Sprinkle potato flour over mixture. Gradually add stock, stirring constantly, and wine. Stir over heat until soup begins to boil. Season with salt and black pepper and simmer for 10 minutes. Add remaining butter bit by bit. Add cheese and simmer 5 minutes. Pour into individual bowls, sprinkle with cheese and dot with butter, and serve with garlic bread. Approximate yield: 2 portions.

ACADIAN TURTLE SOUP

1 pound veal bones
1 onion, sliced
1 carrot, sliced
1 tablespoon margarine
2 tablespoons flour
4 cups beef or turtle stock, cold
5 cups tomatoes

3 whole cloves
salt and pepper
1 cup cooked fresh turtle meat
   or canned turtle meat
¼ cup Sherry
½ lemon, sliced
1 hard-cooked egg, chopped

Wipe bones with a damp cloth and then crack. Brown bones, onion and carrot very slowly in margarine in heavy kettle. Add flour, and stir until blended. Add cold beef or turtle stock, tomatoes, cloves and salt and pepper to taste. Heat slowly to boiling, skim thoroughly, cover and simmer 2 hours. Strain stock through a fine sieve or several thicknesses of cheesecloth and cool quickly. When cold, remove fat and, if necessary, clarify soup (see page 220). Add turtle meat and Sherry, bring to a boil and serve garnished with a thin slice of lemon and a sprinkling of chopped egg on each serving. Approximate yield: 1 quart soup.

MOCK OYSTER SOUP

Scald 2½ cups milk with 2 slices onion. Add 1 cup sieved cooked salsify (oyster plant) and ½ teaspoon salt and cook in double boiler 30 minutes. Remove onion; strain if desired. Add 2 tablespoons butter and dash of pepper. Approximate yield: 4 portions.

PARMESAN POTAGE

4 cups hot water
4 bouillon cubes
3 tablespoons grated Parmesan
  cheese

1 cup soft bread crumbs
2 eggs, slightly beaten
salt and pepper
dash of nutmeg

Pour hot water over bouillon cubes, stirring until dissolved; mix together cheese and crumbs; stir into eggs. Gradually add hot bouillon, season to taste with salt and pepper and simmer 8 minutes, stirring constantly. Just before serving, add nutmeg and beat thoroughly. Approximate yield: 6 portions.

COLD BUTTERMILK SOUP

½ pound shrimp, cooked and
  chopped
½ medium-sized cucumber,
  finely diced
1 quart buttermilk

1 tablespoon minced fresh dill
1 tablespoon prepared mustard
1 teaspoon salt
1 teaspoon sugar

Mix together shrimp, cucumber and seasonings; stir in buttermilk and chill thoroughly. Approximate yield: 6 portions.

VICHYSSOISE

4 leeks (1½ cups)
½ cup chopped onion
1 tablespoon butter
1 quart boiling water
5 medium potatoes

1 tablespoon salt
2 cups milk
2 cups light cream
1 cup heavy cream
chopped chives

Clean and chop the white parts of leeks to make 1½ cups and combine with chopped onion. Melt butter in saucepan, add leeks and onion; cook gently until they are soft but not brown. Add boiling water, peeled and chopped potatoes and salt. Cook until potatoes are well done, about 30 minutes. Strain through a fine sieve or food mill. Return the purée to the pan, add milk and light cream. Bring back to the boil and then strain through a very fine sieve. Cool, stirring occasionally. When cold, strain again and add heavy cream. Mix well and chill before serving. For a bright garnish and more flavor, sprinkle with chopped chives. Approximate yield: 9 to 10 portions.

ICED CHICKEN AND CURRY SOUP

2 tablespoons butter
1 onion, chopped fine
1 small apple, sliced
2 teaspoons curry powder
¼ cup all-purpose flour
½ cup pea purée
salt

chili powder
cayenne
1½ cups strong chicken or game
  stock
1½ cups light cream
⅔ cup diced chicken or game
  white meat

Melt butter in a skillet, add onion and apple and cook slowly, without browning, until quite soft. Add curry powder and cook slowly 5 to 6 minutes, stirring occasionally. Stir in flour and pea purée slowly; add salt, chili powder and cayenne to taste. Stir in stock until smooth. Bring soup to a boil, stirring constantly, and force through a fine sieve. Cool. Add cream and meat. Serve in bowls surrounded by crushed ice. Note: This soup can be served hot. Yield: 6 portions.

FROSTED SHERRY SOUP

1½ cups water
½ cup sugar
1 2-inch stick cinnamon
2 cups grape juice
2 cups pineapple juice

1½ teaspoons grated lemon rind
3 tablespoons quick-cooking
  tapioca
1 cup fresh raspberries
½ cup Sherry

Heat water, sugar and cinnamon to boiling point and simmer 5 minutes; add fruit juices and lemon rind and bring to a boil. Gradually stir in tapioca and bring to a brisk boil, stirring constantly; then simmer over low heat or boiling water 5 minutes, stirring occasionally. Cool slightly, stir in raspberries and chill thoroughly; add Sherry just before serving. Approximate yield: 6 portions.

ICED AVOCADO SOUP

6 tablespoons flour
5 cups chicken stock
2 avocados, mashed
¾ cup light cream

dash of crushed coriander seed
1 teaspoon salt
3 black peppercorns, crushed
3 white peppercorns, crushed
red caviar

Mix flour and ¼ cup chicken stock to a smooth paste. Gradually add remaining chicken stock and bring to a boil, stirring constantly. Add mashed avocados to mixture and force through sieve. Chill thoroughly. Add cream, coriander seed, salt and peppercorns. Stir well before serving. Garnish with red caviar. Serve ice cold. Approximate yield: 6 portions.

COLD RED RASPBERRY SOUP

1 cup boiling water	2 tablespoons cold water
1 quart fresh raspberries	¼ cup sugar
1 tablespoon cornstarch	6 tablespoons orange juice

½ cup Sherry

Add boiling water to berries and cook, covered, 10 minutes, or until tender. Force berries through sieve. Mix cornstarch with cold water. Add with berry purée and sugar to hot juice. Cook over low heat, stirring until mixture begins to thicken; simmer, covered, 10 minutes. Cool slightly and add orange juice. Add Sherry just before serving. Serve very cold. Garnish with mint leaves. Yield: 4 portions.

JELLIED TOMATO BOUILLON

6 fresh tomatoes, sliced	1¾ cups water
1 onion, sliced	½ teaspoon salt
2 stalks celery, chopped	1 teaspoon sugar
¼ green pepper, chopped	4 whole cloves
1 tablespoon chopped parsley	1 bay leaf

1 envelope plain gelatin

Bring to a boil vegetables, 1½ cups water and seasonings and simmer, covered, 20 minutes; strain. Soften gelatin in remaining ¼ cup cold water; add to hot tomato liquid, stirring until dissolved, and chill until firm. Arrange by spoonfuls in bouillon cups. If desired, use 2 cups stewed tomatoes and reduce water to ¼ cup. Yield: 6 portions.

ICED CUCUMBER SOUP

¼ cup finely chopped onion	4 tablespoons flour
2 cups peeled, sliced cucumbers	1½ cups light chicken stock
¼ cup water	1 cup light cream
1 teaspoon salt	1 tablespoon finely chopped
⅛ teaspoon pepper	fresh mint

finely shredded peeled cucumber

Combine onion, cucumbers, water, salt and pepper and cook until very tender. Combine flour and ¼ cup stock. Gradually add to remaining stock and vegetables. Cook over low heat, stirring constantly until mixture comes to a boil. Force through a sieve. Add cream and mint. Chill thoroughly. Add cucumber and serve very cold surrounded by crushed ice. Approximate yield: 3 portions.

ICED BROCCOLI SOUP

1 onion, finely sliced
1 carrot, finely sliced
1 small stalk of celery, finely
  sliced
salt and cayenne
1 bunch of broccoli, cut up
3 cups chicken stock

2 tablespoons flour
¼ cup cold water
1 cup light cream
1 tablespoon finely chopped chives
1 teaspoon finely chopped
  rosemary

Place onion, carrot and celery in pan with a little water. Season to taste with salt and cayenne and simmer until almost tender. Bring broccoli to a boil in cold water, simmer 5 to 6 minutes and drain. Add broccoli to onion, carrot and celery. Pour on stock. Add a little extra seasoning and simmer until broccoli is just tender. Add flour mixed with cold water. Bring to a boil once more, stirring constantly. Force through fine sieve. Place in refrigerator or stir over ice until very cold. Add cream with chives and rosemary and serve in glass bowls surrounded by crushed ice. Yield: 4 portions.

ICED TOMATO SOUP

4 tomatoes, sliced thin
2 small white onions, sliced thin
½ teaspoon minced garlic
¼ cup water
4 tablespoons tomato paste
4 tablespoons flour

1¾ cups water or light stock
1 teaspoon salt
⅛ teaspoon pepper
1 cup light cream
1 tablespoon chopped fresh dill
1 shredded tomato

Combine tomatoes, onions, garlic and water. Cook over low heat until tomatoes are very tender, about 10 minutes. Add tomato paste and cook 3 minutes longer. Stir in paste of flour and ½ cup water and gradually add remaining 1¼ cups water, salt and pepper. Cook, stirring constantly until mixture comes to a boil. Force through fine strainer. Cool. Add cream and let stand in refrigerator until very cold. Add dill and tomato. Serve ice cold in bowls surrounded by crushed ice. Approximate yield: 3 to 4 portions.

CHILLED GRAPEFRUIT SOUP

2 cups diced grapefruit sections	1 cinnamon stick
2 cups hot water	1 blade of mace
3 tablespoons lemon juice	2 tablespoons cornstarch
1 teaspoon grated lemon rind	¼ cup cold water
2 tablespoons sugar	½ cup currant or raspberry jelly

½ cup red wine

Cook grapefruit in hot water until soft. Force through a coarse strainer and return to saucepan. Add lemon juice and rind, sugar, cinnamon and mace. Blend together and add cornstarch and cold water. Cook, stirring constantly, until thick and clear. Add jelly and stir until dissolved. Cool. Remove cinnamon and mace. Add wine to soup and chill. Serve in bouillon cups with bits of cracked ice and garnish with a cherry. Approximate yield: 4 portions.

SOUP GARNISHES

GARNISH MEAT BALLS

½ cup minced cooked meat	few drops onion juice
⅛ teaspoon salt	1 teaspoon lemon juice
dash of pepper	1 egg yolk (about)
⅛ teaspoon dried thyme	1 tablespoon flour

1 tablespoon fat

Use any kind of cooked meat; mix with seasonings, lemon juice and just enough egg yolk to moisten. Shape in balls about ¾ inch in diameter; roll in flour and sauté in fat until lightly browned. Add to hot soup just before serving. Approximate yield: 1 dozen small balls.

MARROW BALLS

2 tablespoons dry bread crumbs	1 teaspoon grated lemon rind
2 teaspoons beef marrow	dash of salt
1 tablespoon chopped parsley	dash of pepper

1 egg white (about)

Combine bread crumbs, beef marrow, parsley, lemon rind and seasonings; add enough egg white to moisten; shape in small balls the size of marbles. Drop into hot soup; when cooked, balls rise to surface. Approximate yield: 1½ dozen small balls.

CHICKEN TIMBALE BALLS

1½ cups finely chopped chicken | 1 teaspoon onion juice
½ teaspoon salt | 1 tablespoon lemon juice
⅛ teaspoon paprika | 1 egg yolk (about)
dash of dried thyme | ¼ cup flour

Combine chicken, seasonings, lemon juice and just enough egg yolk to moisten; shape in tiny balls, roll in flour and cook in boiling consommé 5 minutes. Serve 3 balls in each cup. Approximate yield: 1½ dozen balls.

EGG BALLS

2 hard-cooked egg yolks | 1 egg white (about)
¼ teaspoon salt | 1 tablespoon flour
dash of pepper | 2 tablespoons fat

Force egg yolks through sieve, add seasonings and enough egg white to moisten. Shape in small balls about ¾ inch in diameter; roll in flour and sauté in fat until lightly browned. Add to soup just before serving. Approximate yield: 10 small balls.

CHEESE PUFF BALLS

½ cup grated Parmesan cheese | dash of cayenne or paprika
1 tablespoon flour | 2 egg whites, stiffly beaten
¼ teaspoon salt | 3 tablespoons cracker crumbs

Mix cheese, flour, salt and pepper and fold into egg whites; if too crumbly to mold, add a few drops of milk. Shape in small balls, roll in crumbs and fry in hot deep fat (375° F.) about 1 minute, or until golden brown; drain on absorbent paper. Yield: 1½ dozen balls.

ALSATIAN DUMPLINGS

½ cup butter | ¾ cup all-purpose flour
1 egg, separated | ¼ teaspoon salt
1 egg yolk | dash of pepper
dash of nutmeg

Cream butter until soft and beat in egg yolks; gradually stir in flour and seasonings and fold in stiffly beaten egg white. Shape in small balls 1 inch in diameter, drop into boiling salted water and simmer, covered, 5 to 8 minutes; do not let dumplings boil. Put in hot tureen and pour hot soup over them; or cook dumplings in boiling hot bouillon or consommé. Approximate yield: 1½ dozen dumplings.

CUSTARD ROYALE

2 egg yolks	dash of pepper
1 egg	dash of cayenne
⅛ teaspoon salt	½ cup beef stock or consommé

Beat egg yolks and egg; add seasonings and stock. Pour layer, ½ inch thick, into 7-inch pie pan or shallow small pan; place in pan of hot water and bake in moderate oven (350° F.) about 20 minutes, or until knife inserted comes out clean. When cold, cut in fancy shapes or tiny dice. Yield: 1 layer (7-inch) custard, ½ inch thick, or enough for 1 dozen portions of soup.

Vegetable Egg Cubes—Heat 1 cup canned peas in liquid, drain and force through ricer or sieve; add to egg and stock and season with a dash of salt, celery salt, paprika and nutmeg. Pour layer into greased shallow pan, about ¾ inch thick. Bake in slow oven (300° F.) 45 minutes, or until mixture is firm. Cool. Cut in cubes and serve in thin soup. Approximate yield: Enough for 10 to 12 portions of soup.

Meat

IF YOU are a bride or simply unaccustomed to shopping or cooking meats, you may approach the meat counter puzzled and bewildered. Other women may order various cuts unknown to you in an authoritative manner. In a panic you may find yourself calling for the well-known but expensive steak or veal cutlet.

Meat has no mystery if you will take a few minutes to study our charts and to learn what the cuts are and how you can cook them. In this way, you'll find yourself buying a variety of meat cuts that will give you many delicious dishes, at the same time saving countless pennies on your meat bill. The expensive cuts will have the advantage of tenderness, possibly will be more juicy and have better fat-marbling, but you will have the same nutritional value from the cheaper cuts, and if you have patience and use a bit of imagination in their preparation, you will be amazed at the mouth-watering results.

GUIDES TO MEAT BUYING

WHEN you buy meat you will need to notice the markings on the meat, indicated by a purple stamp in harmless vegetable coloring, and the appearance of the meat itself.

Most of the meat now sold to homemakers in meat shops is federally graded carrying the initials "U. S." These initials indicate that the meat was packed in federal inspected plants or in other plants which met federal requirements. New grades most useful for the homemaker to know are for beef, veal and calf—Prime, Choice, Good, Commercial and Utility; and for lamb and mutton—Prime,

Choice, Good and Utility. Here is what these federal beef grades stand for:

Prime—Excellent quality, with a wide selection of cuts suitable for broiling and roasting.

Choice—High quality, usually leaner than Prime, with many cuts which can be broiled or roasted.

Good—Relatively tender meat, from higher quality young animals, with a high ratio of lean to fat, providing consumers with economical meat dishes.

Commercial—Meat from mature animals, with a more pronounced beef flavor than Good. These cuts require different methods of cooking because of less natural tenderness. This grade provides economical meat dishes.

Utility—Cut has little fat and a high percentage of lean meat; suitable for pot roasts, stews and ragouts. Classified as a cheaper cut.

Federal grades have never been established for pork, which does not vary so widely in quality as other meats.

AGING OF MEAT

THE TWO meats most frequently aged are high quality beef and mutton. Sometimes high quality lamb is also aged. Aging does not improve veal or pork. Suitable meat for aging must have a fairly thick covering of fat to prevent discoloration of the lean and to prevent drying out. The usual period of aging is from three to six weeks at temperatures from 34° to 38° F. Those who like aged meats usually prefer to buy it already aged at their retail markets.

WAYS OF COOKING MEAT

EVERY grade and cut of meat can be made delicious and tempting if you will follow a few rules of meat cookery.

Meats are tender, less-tender or tough, depending upon their cut, grade of meat and age of animal. In most cases, the tenderness of the meat determines the way you will cook it. In general, tender cuts are best cooked by *dry heat methods*, such as roasting, broiling, panbroiling and frying. Less-tender cuts of meat are made tender by cooking with *moist heat*, such as braising and cooking in liquid where the meat is surrounded by either steam or hot liquid. Usually long cooking is required unless pressure is used. Braising is the method by which pot roasts and Swiss steaks are cooked. Large cuts and stews are cooked in large amounts of liquid.

Exceptions to this rule are found in cooking pork and veal. Chops, steaks and cutlets need to be cooked well done. They are better braised or fried—not broiled or panbroiled. Braising or panfrying cooks them to the well-done stage without drying them out.

THE NEW WAY OF MEAT COOKERY

LABORATORY tests have proved beyond a doubt that high temperatures cause 15 to 20 per cent shrinkage in meats, poor appearance and loss of palatability, as well as nutritive losses. Low cooking temperatures save meat whether roasting, broiling, frying, braising or cooking in liquid.

Meat is more tender, juicier and more flavorful when cooked at uniform low temperatures. Less fuel is required, too, particularly in roasting. You'll find you need to do less watching and "fussing." You'll have better carving results.

USING A MEAT THERMOMETER

WHEN meat is cooked *exactly* to the right degree of doneness, it is juicy, flavorful and there is more meat to serve than when it is overdone, shrunken and dried out. Your meat thermometer is the most accurate guide to the degree of doneness, especially when you are roasting meats. Cooking time is only an approximate guide.

If you like your meat medium, rare or well done, the thermometer will eliminate all the guesswork by recording the internal temperature of the meat. You may have any degree of doneness desired.

To use in a roast: Insert meat thermometer in meat so that its bulb is in the center of the largest muscle of the roast. (Be careful not to jamb the thermometer against a bone, or you may run the danger of breaking it. In case this happens, remove the thermometer if possible, or cut away the meat around it. The mercury in the thermometer does not injure the meat.) When it indicates the desired degree of doneness (rare, medium or well done) for the particular kind of meat, the meat should be removed from the heat. Meat continues to cook after it is removed and the temperature may rise 15° to 20° F. if it is cooked to the rare stage. A meat thermometer can be used to indicate doneness in thick steaks; it is more difficult to use in thin steaks.

COOKING FROZEN MEATS

THE PALATABILITY of meats is not affected by freezing. Frozen meats may be cooked, thawed or frozen, by the same methods used for fresh meats. The cooking time is slightly less for frozen meats that have been thawed than for unfrozen meats. In cooking frozen meats, additional cooking time must be allowed for thawing the meat and raising its temperature to the usual one of unfrozen meats. For frozen roasts add about 10 minutes per pound to the time given for comparable unfrozen roasts (Table XV); for frozen steaks and chops add about 10 minutes to the time given for the unfrozen cuts (Table XV). Insert the meat thermometer into the frozen roast after the meat is partially thawed. Thawing of meats may be done at room temperature or in the refrigerator, wrapped or uncovered. They should be cooked soon after defrosting to prevent excessive loss of juices. Frozen meat thawed has approximately the same keeping quality as fresh meat.

Meat Cuts and How to Cook Them
BEEF CHART

Retail Cuts

Ground Beef
— Roast or Broil —

Heel of Round
— Braise or Simmer —

Hind Shank
— Soup or Simmer —

Rolled Flank
— Braise —

Flank Stew
— Stew —

Flank Steak
— Braise —

Flank Steak Fillets

Plate Boiling Beef

Rolled Plate
— Simmer or Braise —

Short Ribs

Beef Brisket

Corned Beef
— Simmer —

Knuckle Soup Bone

Cross Cut Fore Shank
— Soup or Braise —

English Cut

Arm Pot Roast
— Braise —

Arm Steak

Rolled Neck

Boneless Neck
— Braise or Stew —

Wholesale Cuts

ROUND
RUMP
LOIN END
SHORT LOIN
FLANK
PLATE
RIB
BRISKET
SHANK
CHUCK

Retail Cuts

Round Steak **Top Round** **Bottom Round**
— Braise — (Swiss Steak)

Rolled Rump **Rump Roast**
— Braise or Roast —

Sirloin Steak **Pin Bone Sirloin Steak**
— Broil or Panbroil —

Porterhouse Steak **T Bone Steak** **Club Steak**
— Broil or Panbroil —

Standing Rib Roast **Rolled Rib Roast**
— Roast —

Rib Steak
— Broil —

Blade Steak **Blade Pot Roast**

Triangle Pot-Roast **Boneless Chuck Pot-Roast** **Shoulder Fillet**
— Braise —

254

TABLE XV

BEEF-PURCHASING GUIDE

| Retail Cut | Average Size | | Qualities and Description | Method of Cookery | Portions per Cut or Weight per Portion[1] |
	Thickness	Weight			
	Inches	*Pounds*			
Steaks—tender			Very tender, juicy; excellent flavor, choice cuts	Dry heat.	½–1 lb. per portion
Porterhouse	1–2	2–4	T-bone, eye muscle, tenderloin, and flank end. Tenderloin becomes smaller toward shoulder	Broil, pan-broil, plank Fry	3–5
Club steak	1–2	1½–3	Rib-bone and large eye muscle, no tenderloin		2–3
Sirloin	1–2	2¼–5	Large, derives name from shape of bone; small tenderloin, more connective tissue and fat		3–6
Rib steak			Contains rib eye and may contain rib bone		
Minute steak	½–¾	¾–1	Any small tender steak		1, or 2 small
Steaks—less tender			Less tender, but juicy and well-flavored in young, choice beef	Dry heat, for cuts from better grade of young animals:	½–1 lb. per portion
Top round steak	1	1¾–2	The large and most tender muscle of leg used for individual small steaks		3–4
Round steak (full cut)	½–1		One of the less tender sections; lean—little waste; av. wt., 2–2½ lb.	Broil, pan-broil, fry	4
Top sirloin steak	1	1½	Triangular muscle, no bone, fairly tender and juicy		2
Flank steak	½	1¾–2	Large coarse muscle, fibers running lengthwise; boneless, some fat, scored across fibers	Moist heat for cuts from less choice or older animals:	3–4
Chuck steak	1	2	More bone and fibers run in various directions; low in fat	Braise	2–3
Roasts—tender			Tender, juicy, good flavor	Dry heat: Roast	½–¾ lb. per portion

TABLE XV—(*Continued*)

BEEF-PURCHASING GUIDE

Retail Cut	Average Size Thick-ness	Average Size Weight	Qualities and Description	Method of Cookery	Portions[1] per Cut or Weight per Portion
Rib roast —(1st 6 ribs)	*Inches*	*Pounds*	Choicest cuts of fore-quarter; large eye mus-cle and rib-bone muscle become smaller and coarser nearer shoulder blade	Dry heat: Roast	
Standing	1 rib	3½			4
Rolled		2½			
Standing	2 ribs	6½			6
Rolled		5			
Standing	3 ribs	9½			
Rolled		8			8–10
Blade rib roast (7–8th rib)	2 ribs	10¾	Large section of shoulder blade bone, also called chuck end of rib roast		8–10
Rolled		7			
Roasts—less tender			Less tender but of good quality; juicy and well flavored in young, choice beef	Dry heat for cuts from better grade of young beef: Roast	½–¾ lb. per portion
Round-bot-tom	3–8	5–13	Two smaller muscles from outside of leg; little fat; not as choice as top round		6–12
Top sirloin	2–4	4–7	Triangular muscle sepa-rating rump from round; no waste	Moist heat for cuts from less choice or older ani-mals: Braise, pot-roast	4–8
Rump (bone-less)		4	Hip-bone removed		4–6
Cross rib roast	4–8	4–8	Cut made across ribs at right angles to chuck rib roast and chuck roast, with round bone and cross sections of ribs		4–8
Top chuck		5–6	Top chuck roast has shoulder bone, connec-tive tissue; low in fat		5–6
Chuck	2–4	4–8	Shoulder blade and back-bone; fibers run in dif-ferent directions; con-nective tissue, high in bone		3–6
Tenderloin Fillet Mignon		4–6 3 per lb.	Muscle usually not re-moved from a choice loin; usually from an inferior loin; no bone and fat; price per lb. high, but no waste	Dry heat: Roast, broil	⅓ lb. per portion

TABLE XV—(*Continued*)

BEEF-PURCHASING GUIDE

RETAIL CUT	AVERAGE SIZE		QUALITIES AND DESCRIPTION	METHOD OF COOKERY	PORTIONS[1] PER CUT OR WEIGHT PER PORTION
	THICK-NESS	WEIGHT			
	Inches	*Pounds*			
Miscellaneous Stews, etc.			Less tender and tough cuts	Moist heat, long slow cooking:	½–¾ lb. per portion
Boneless stew meat		any weight	Chuck, flank steak, heel or round	Stew, simmer	⅓ lb. per portion
Chuck			Good quality meat; very good for stew		½ lb. per portion
Ground meat			Neck, shank, brisket, heel of round, flank	Hamburg, broil, pan-broil meat loaf	⅓ lb. per portion
Flank			Entire flank with steak; about ½ fat and cartilage; one of cheapest cuts	Braise, stew, grind; corned	¾ lb. per portion
Heel of round (horse-shoe cut)			Weighs 4–6 lb.; lean, boneless; not used in New York	Pot roast, stew, grind	½ lb. per portion
Brisket Boneless	3–6	2½–5	If unboned it contains breast bone and ribs; much fat; poor for stew	Corned; simmer, grind	¾ lb. per portion
Plate	3–6	3–6	Includes corner piece, thick plate and navel; fat and lean in alternate layers; poor for stew	Simmer; corned	¾ lb. per portion
Neck		any weight	Many bones and little meat, poor cut for stew	Simmer; soup, mincemeat	¾ lb. per portion

[1] This column shows number of portions in retail cuts or the usual weights of one portion; in roasts and other large cuts it is economy to plan for leftovers.

TIME-TABLE FOR COOKING BEEF

TABLE XVI

CUT	ROASTED AT 300° F. OVEN TEMPERATURE		BROILED [1]		BRAISED	COOKED IN LIQUID
	MEAT THERMOMETER READING	TIME	MEAT THERMOMETER READING	TOTAL TIME	TOTAL TIME	TOTAL TIME
	Degrees F.	Min./lb.	Degrees F.	Min.	Hrs.	Hrs.
Standing Ribs Rare	140	18–20	—	—	—	—
Medium	160	22–25	—	—	—	—
Well	170	27–30	—	—	—	—
Rolled Ribs	170	Add 10–15	—	—	—	—
Blade, 3rd to 5th Rib (*high quality only*)	150–170	25–30	—	—	—	—
Rump (*high quality only*)	150–170	25–30	—	—	—	—
Tenderloin	140–170	20–25	—	—	—	—
Beef Loaf	160–170	25–30	—	—	—	—
Steaks 1 inch Rare Medium	— —	— —	140 160	15–20 20–30	— —	— —
1½ inch Rare Medium	— —	— —	140 160	25–35 35–50	— —	— —
2 inch Rare Medium	— —	— —	140 160	30–40 50–70	— —	— —
Beef Patties—1 inch Rare Medium	— —	— —	140 160	12–15 18–20	— —	— —
Pot-Roasts Arm or Blade Rump	— —	— —	— —	— —	3–4 3–4	— —
Swiss Steak	—	—	—	—	2–3	—
Corned Beef	—	—	—	—	—	3½–5
Fresh Beef	—	—	—	—	3–4	3–4
Stew	—	—	—	—	—	2–3

[1] Panbroiling or griddle-broiling requires approximately one-half the time for broiling.

BEEF AND ITS COOKING METHODS

HIGH quality beef has a smooth covering of firm, creamy white fat evenly distributed over the exterior. The lean of this beef should be uniform and bright. The color may range from pale red to deep blood red. It is well marbled with creamy white fat. The texture of the lean is firm, velvety in appearance and fine in grain. The bones in young beef are reddish and porous; in older animals, white and flinty.

Different grades and cuts of beef vary greatly in tenderness. This is why it is necessary to select beef cuts with the cooking methods in mind, or adapt the cooking method to the cut selected.

All of the thick cuts of Choice and Good grades of beef, excepting the outside round, the outside chuck and the neck, are tender enough to be cooked by dry heat, especially if low temperatures are used. On the other hand, most cuts of Utility grade beef are best if cooked by moist heat. With Commercial beef, the grade next to Good, the tender cuts—rib, short loin and sirloin—are cooked by dry heat methods, as roasting, broiling, panbroiling and frying; while the less-tender cuts are cooked by moist heat methods, as braising and cooking in liquid.

Less-tender meat may be ground and then cooked by the same methods as the tender cuts—roasting, broiling, panbroiling or frying. Less-tender steaks may be made tender by pounding, scoring, cubing, etc. Beef is cooked rare, medium and well done.

VEAL AND ITS COOKING METHODS

VEAL has very little fat. In high quality veal, the fat is clear, firm and white. The lean is light pink with no marbling. The texture of the lean is very fine, fairly firm—though not so firm as beef— and velvety in appearance. Since veal is the young of beef, the bones are porous and soft, with a reddish tinge; the ends of some of them are still in the cartilage stage.

Most wholesale veal cuts are very much like those of beef, except

Meat Cuts and How to Cook Them
VEAL CHART

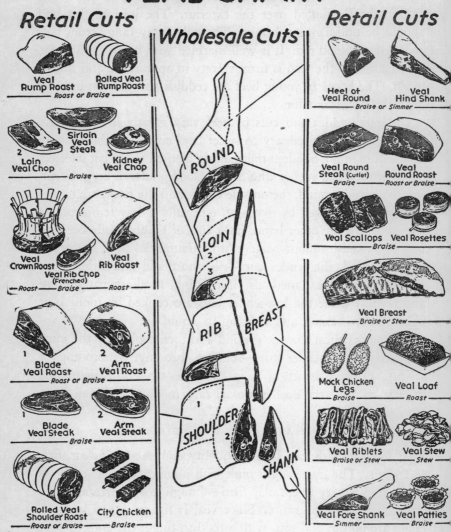

Retail Cuts

Veal Rump Roast
Rolled Veal Rump Roast
— Roast or Braise —

Loin Veal Chop
Sirloin Veal Steak 1
Kidney Veal Chop 3
2
— Braise —

Veal Crown Roast
Veal Rib Chop (Frenched)
Veal Rib Roast
— Roast — Braise — Roast —

Blade Veal Roast 1
Arm Veal Roast 2
— Roast or Braise —

Blade Veal Steak 1
Arm Veal Steak 2
— Braise —

Rolled Veal Shoulder Roast
City Chicken
— Roast or Braise — Braise —

Wholesale Cuts

ROUND
LOIN 1 2 3
RIB
BREAST
SHOULDER 1 2
SHANK

Retail Cuts

Heel of Veal Round
Veal Hind Shank
— Braise or Simmer —

Veal Round Steak (Cutlet)
Veal Round Roast
— Braise — Roast or Braise —

Veal Scallops
Veal Rosettes
— Braise —

Veal Breast
— Braise or Stew —

Mock Chicken Legs
Veal Loaf
— Braise — Roast —

Veal Riblets
Veal Stew
— Braise or Stew — Stew —

Veal Fore Shank
Veal Patties
— Simmer — Braise —

260

TABLE XVII
VEAL-PURCHASING GUIDE

Retail Cut	Average Size		Qualities and Description	Method[1] of Cookery	Portions[2] per Cut or Weight per Portion
	Thickness	Weight			
	Inches	*Pounds*			
Chops and steaks				Veal is lacking in fat and high in connective tissue; it generally requires long slow cooking in moist heat to make it tender. Low temp.; well done: Braise	½–¾ lb. per portion
Steak or cutlet	1–2	1¼–2½	Choice flavor; most economical cut; from leg		3–6
Loin and kidney chops	¾–1	3 per lb.	Very choice, with or without kidney attached; corresponds to porterhouse		2–3
Rib chops	¾–1	3 per lb.	Choice, lean, fine-grained with connective tissue; one-rib chops		2–3
Shoulder chops	¾–1	2 per lb.	Fine flavor; bone; muscle grain in different directions		2
Roasts Leg without rump	Whole	15–17 10–12	Good flavor; sold in different weights; little waste without rump	Dry heat at low temp. when fat is added; well done: Roast	½–¾ lb. per portion
Loin (kidney)	Split	3½	Choice, with or without kidney; flank included in larger carcass		3–4
Rib or hotel rack	8 ribs	3	Rather thin for roasting; eye muscle small		2–3
Shoulder (boned)		6–7	Fine flavor; more satisfactory if boned	Moist heat at low temp. for tougher cuts: Braise, pot-roast	6–8
Rump		5½–6	Good flavor; large irregular bone, often removed and rolled		5–6
Breast (pocket)		4–5	Fair quality; often contains flank		4–6
Miscellaneous Stews, etc.			Less tender and tough cuts	Moist heat, long slow cooking: Stew, simmer	½–¾ lb. per portion
Boneless stew		any weight	Shoulder good for stew; cut in 1- to 1½-inch pieces		¼–⅓ lb. per portion
Breast		any weight	See Breast (above)	Braise; stew, simmer, grind	½ lb. per portion
Heel of round		any weight	Solid meat, coarse	Braise; stew, simmer, grind	⅓–½ lb. per portion

TABLE XVII—(*Continued*)

VEAL-PURCHASING GUIDE

Retail Cut	Average Size		Qualities and Description	Method of Cookery[1]	Portions[2] per Cut or Weight per Portion
	Thickness	Weight			
	Inches	*Pounds*			
Shanks (knuckle)		3	Little meat and much bone and gristle, gelatinous; fore and hind shanks	Stew, simmer, grind; pressed	1 lb. per portion
Neck		any weight	Little meat; poor for stew	Stew; soup	½–¾ lb. per portion

[1] Veal is lacking in fat; to broil or roast, rub surface well with fat and use lower temperature than for beef.
[2] This column shows number of portions in retail cuts or the usual weight of one portion.

they are considerably smaller, consequently the retail cuts made from them are smaller. In general, veal cuts are from one-third to one-half the size of comparable cuts of beef. The cuts from the loin of veal are called loin chops instead of steaks, as they are in beef. The loin of veal is also sold as a roast. The chops from the rib section are known as rib chops.

Veal has certain characteristics which make its cooking somewhat different from that of the other meats. It lacks fat and, while it is tender, it has considerable connective tissue which means that it requires long, slow cooking. Veal is delicate in color, becoming lighter when cooked. It also has a fine delicate flavor. Cooking methods which intensify color and make the flavor more pronounced should be used. The best methods of cooking veal are roasting, frying and braising. Veal is also cooked in liquid for stews. Veal chops, steaks and cutlets are best if fried or braised. Rich, colorful sauces and gravies are delicious with veal. For broiling or panbroiling, only loin and rib chops from high quality heavy veal should be used; and a lower cooking temperature than that for beef and lamb is advisable. Always cook veal to the well-done stage.

TABLE XVIII

TIME-TABLE FOR COOKING VEAL

| CUT | ROASTED AT 300° F. OVEN TEMPERATURE | | BROILED | | BRAISED | COOKED IN LIQUID |
	MEAT THER-MOMETER READING	TIME	MEAT THER-MOMETER READING	TOTAL TIME	TOTAL TIME	TOTAL TIME
	Degrees F.	Min./lb.	Degrees F.	Min.	Hrs.	Hrs.
Leg	170	25	—	—	—	—
Loin	170	30–35	Veal is seldom broiled	—	—	—
Rack	170	30–35	—	—	—	—
Shoulder Whole	170	25	—	—	—	—
Rolled	170	40–45	—	—	—	—
Cushion	170	30–35	—	—	—	—
Breast Stuffed	170	40–45	—	—	1½–2	
Rolled	170	40–45	—	—	1½–2	—
Loaf	170	25–30	—	—	—	—
Birds	—	—	—	—	¾–1	—
Chops	—	—	—	—	¾–1	—
Steaks	—	—	—	—	¾–1	—
Stew	—	—	—	—	—	2–2½

Meat Cuts and How to Cook Them
LAMB CHART

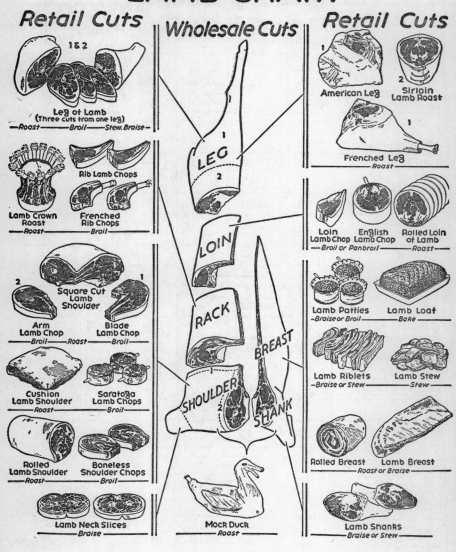

Retail Cuts

1 & 2

Leg of Lamb
(Three cuts from one leg)
— Roast — Broil — Stew, Braise —

Rib Lamb Chops

Lamb Crown Roast
— Roast —

Frenched Rib Chops
— Broil —

Square Cut Lamb Shoulder

2 **Arm Lamb Chop**
— Broil — Roast —

1 **Blade Lamb Chop**
— Broil —

Cushion Lamb Shoulder
— Roast —

Saratoga Lamb Chops
— Broil —

Rolled Lamb Shoulder
— Roast —

Boneless Shoulder Chops
— Broil —

Lamb Neck Slices
— Braise —

Wholesale Cuts

LEG 1 2

LOIN

RACK

BREAST

SHOULDER 1 2

SHANK

Mock Duck
— Roast —

Retail Cuts

1 **American Leg**

2 **Sirloin Lamb Roast**

1 **Frenched Leg**
— Roast —

Loin Lamb Chop **English Lamb Chop**
— Broil or Panbroil —

Rolled Loin of Lamb
— Roast —

Lamb Patties
— Braise or Broil —

Lamb Loaf
— Bake —

Lamb Riblets
— Braise or Stew —

Lamb Stew
— Stew —

Rolled Breast **Lamb Breast**
— Roast or Braise —

Lamb Shanks
— Braise or Stew —

TABLE XIX

LAMB AND MUTTON

Retail Cut	Average Size: Thickness	Average Size: Weight	Qualities and Description	Method of Cookery	Portions[1] per Cut or Weight per Portion
	Inches	*Pounds*			
Lamb chops				Dry heat. Broil, pan-broil, plank, fry	1–2 chops per portion
Loin	¾–1	¼–⅓	Tender, juicy; corresponds to porterhouse in beef; little waste; little bone, more lean than rib		
Double loin	1½–2	⅔–¾	English lamb chop cut entire width of loin—not split—boned, skewered and kidney half on top		
Rib	¾–1	¼–⅓	Tender, juicy; one rib. Frenched chop—meat scraped from end of bone, cut off or wrapped		1–2 chops per portion
Double rib	1½–2	⅔–¾	Two ribs in double chop		
Hip	¾–1	⅓–½	When leg is too large, loin end may be cut into chops		
Shoulder	¾–1	⅓–½	Less tender; good flavor; fibers in different directions; for Saratoga chops, shoulder is boned, rolled, skewered and sliced	Dry heat. Broil, pan-broil, plank, fry	1–2 chops per portion
Mutton chops			Mutton should be aged 2 to 5 weeks; coarser fibered and stronger flavored than lamb	Dry heat; Broil, pan-broil	1–2 chops per portion
Loin	¾–1	⅓–½	Aged 4 weeks, see lamb loin chops		
Double loin or English mutton chops	2	1	Aged 4–5 weeks; tender and delicious		
Rib	¾–1	⅓–½	Aged 4 weeks		
Double rib	1½–2	⅔–¾	Aged 4–5 weeks		
Roasts—Lamb				Dry heat: Roast	½–¾ lb. per portion
Loin (saddle)	Single	4	Tender, choice; little waste		5
Loin	Double	7–8	See loin, single		8–10
Rib (hotel rack)	Double	5–6	Tender, juicy; bone to lean meat high		4–5

TABLE XIX—(*Continued*)
LAMB AND MUTTON

Retail Cut	Average Size		Qualities and Description	Method of Cookery	Portions[1] per Cut or Weight per Portion
	Thickness	Weight			
Roasts—Lamb (cont.)	*Inches*	*Pounds*			
Crown, lamb	14–16 ribs	4–6	Both sides of ribs; vertebræ removed, rib ends Frenched, ends sewed with ribs outside		4–6
Leg	Whole	6–8	Choice, little bone and fat; corresponds to rump, round and shank of beef		7–8
Square chuck	Split	5–7	Slightly less tender, good flavor, more bone	Moist heat: Braise, stew, simmer	4–6
Mock Duck			Shoulder and fore shank; bones removed; molded, sewed into shape of duck	Roast (dry heat); braise (moist heat)	
Breast (with pocket)	Whole	2–4	Less tender, coarser grained; much fat and bone; pocket made at flank end, or breastbone is removed	Braise, stew, simmer, roast	3–6
Roasts— Mutton Loin (saddle)	Single	5–6	Aged 5 weeks, see lamb, loin roast	Dry heat: Roast	½–¾ lb. per portion
	Double	10–12	Aged 5 weeks		
Leg		10–12	Aged 5 weeks; less tender than lamb	Moist heat: Braise, simmer	
Miscellaneous: Stews, etc.			Less tender, coarser grained; high in extractives	Moist heat, slow cooking: stew, simmer	½–¾ lb. per portion
Lamb and mutton chuck	Cut in 1–1½-inch pieces	any weight	Excellent flavor, good quality; fat and lean; much bone	Pot-roast, stew, simmer, grind	½–¾ lb. per portion
Neck			Less tender, good flavor; much gristle	Simmer, stew, soup, grind	
Shank			Much bone, lean meat	(Broil, fry), stew, grind	
Flank			Separated from breast; like flank and plate of beef	Stew	
Breast			More fat than chuck; like brisket of beef	Stew, grind	
Ground Meat		any weight	Lean portions of chuck, neck, shank and breast	Patty (wrapped with bacon), broil, fry lamb loaf: Roast	⅓–½ lb. per pox

[1] This column shows number of portions in retail cuts or the usual weights of one portion.

266

LAMB AND ITS COOKING METHODS

HIGH quality lamb has a smooth covering of clear, white, brittle fat over most of the exterior. The lean is pinkish red in color; in yearling lamb and mutton it is a deeper red. The texture of the lean is fine grained and velvety in appearance.

The bones are porous and reddish in color. In older lamb and mutton they become hard and white. In young lamb, the fore feet when broken off expose eight well-defined ridges, known as the *break joint*. In yearlings, the break joint is hard and white instead of porous, moist and reddish. This joint cannot be broken by the time the mutton stage is reached. The break joint is a sure and simple way, therefore, of identifying lamb; however, about 90 per cent of the sheep in this country are marketed as lambs.

The thin, paper-like covering over the outside of the lamb carcass is known as the *fell*. It does not affect the flavor unless the lamb has been aged for some time. Under normal conditions, the fell should not be removed from the leg, since this cut keeps its shape better, cooks in less time and is juicier when the fell is left on. Chops, however, will be more desirable if the fell is removed before cooking.

Most cuts of high quality lamb are tender, therefore roasting, broiling and panbroiling or griddle-broiling are the cooking methods most used.

The neck, shanks and breasts may be prepared for braising or cut into small pieces for stew, which is cooked in liquid. The meat from these cuts also may be ground for patties or loaf, then cooked by dry heat. Most cuts of Utility lamb are best if cooked by moist heat. Lamb is cooked medium or well done. If cooked so that it is still slightly pink on the inside, there will be less shrinkage and the meat will be very juicy and delicious.

Lamb should be served very hot or cold, but it should never be served lukewarm.

TABLE XX

TIMETABLE FOR COOKING LAMB

CUT	ROASTED AT 300° F. OVEN TEMPERATURE		BROILED [1]		BRAISED	COOKED IN LIQUID
	MEAT THERMOMETER READING	TIME	MEAT THERMOMETER READING	TOTAL TIME	TIME	TIME
	Degrees F.	Min./lb.	Degrees F.	Min.	Hrs.	Hrs.
Leg	175–180	30–35	—	—	—	—
Shoulder Whole	175–180	30–35	—	—	—	—
Rolled	175–180	40–45	—	—	—	—
Cushion	175–180	30–35	—	—	—	—
Breast Stuffed	175–180	30–35	—	—	1½–2	—
Rolled	175–180	30–35	—	—	1½–2	—
Lamb Loaf	175–180	30–35	—	—	—	—
Chops 1 inch	—	—	170	12	—	—
1½ inch	—	—	170	18	—	—
2 inch	—	—	170	22	—	—
Lamb Patties—1 inch	—	—	—	15–18	—	—
Neck Slices	—	—	—	—	1	—
Shanks	—	—	—	—	1½	—
Stew	—	—	—	—	—	1½–2

[1] Panbroiling or griddle-broiling requires approximately one-half the time for broiling.

Meat Cuts and How to Cook Them
PORK CHART

Retail Cuts

2 Sirloin Pork Roast
— Roast —

Pork Tenderloin
Frenched and Whole
— Broil or Braise —

2 to 5 Canadian Style Bacon
— Broil —

3 Loin Chop

4 Rib Pork Chop

Frenched Rib Chop

2 to 5 Butterfly Chop
— Broil or Braise —

1, 2 Loin Roast
Ham End

3, 4 Loin Roast
Center Cut

5 Loin Roast
Shoulder End

4 Crown Pork Roast
— Roast —

Fat Back
— Lard - Salt Pork —

Lard
— Shortening —

Blade Pork Steaks
— Braise —

Smoked Cottage Roll
— Bake or Panbroil —

Boston Style Butt

Rolled Boston Style Butt
— Roast —

Wholesale Cuts

HAM

LOIN
1 2 3 4 5

SIDE

SPARE RIBS

BUTT

PICNIC

JOWL

Retail Cuts

Half Ham Butt End

Half Ham Shank End
— Bake or Simmer —

Ham Butt Slice

Center Ham Slice
— Broil or Panbroil —

Fresh Ham Roast

Rolled Fresh Ham Roast
— Roast —

Bacon

Salt Pork
— Broil - Panbroil or Seasoning —

Spareribs
— Simmer - Braise or Roast —

Fresh Picnic Shoulder
— Roast —

Smoked Picnic Shoulder
— Bake or Simmer —

Cushion Style Picnic Shoulder

Rolled Picnic Shoulder
— Roast —

Fresh Shoulder Hock
— Simmer —

Arm Pork Steak
— Braise —

Bacon Square
— Seasoning · Panbroil —

269

TABLE XXI

FRESH AND CURED PORK

RETAIL CUT	AVERAGE SIZE		QUALITIES AND DESCRIPTION	METHOD OF COOKERY	PORTIONS[1] PER CUT OR WEIGHT PER PORTION
	THICK-NESS	WEIGHT			
	Inches	Pounds			
Pork chops and steaks			Tender, fine grain, juicy; choice cuts	Pork is tender and low in connective tissue, yet it is cooked until well done by moist heat and not broiled	⅓–¾ lb. per portion
Center loin chops	½–¾	⅓	Excellent flavor; lean; tenderloin is sometimes removed; more lean than rib chop	Moist heat: Braise	1–2 chops
Rib chops	½–¾	⅓	Tender, juicy, good flavor; large muscle and rib bone; every other thin chop contains no rib		
Double rib chop	1½	⅔–¾	See rib chops; one bone to chop		1
Sausage meats		any weight	70 per cent lean; lean trimmings, shoulder, butt, shank, hock		¼ lb. per portion
Fresh ham steak	½	1	Less tender; solid meat; corresponds to round of beef		2
End loin chops	½	⅓	Tender, juicy, little fat; tenderloin tapers; single or double		1–2 chops
Shoulder chops	½–¾	⅓–½	Coarser than loin with more bone and fat; well flavored; inexpensive		1
Roasts Crown roast (Ribs)	16 ribs	6–8	Rib section of two loins having same number of ribs; rib ends Frenched, backbone removed and ends sewed, with ribs outside	Dry heat: Roast	⅓–½ lb. per portion or 10–12
Loin roast	Whole	10–12	Choice; see center loin chops		⅓–½ lb. per portion
Boston butt	Whole	2–6	Tender, high in lean, well streaked with fat; bone may be removed and meat rolled		3–5

[1] This column shows number of portions in retail cuts or the usual weight of one portion.

270

TABLE XXI—(*Continued*)
FRESH AND CURED PORK

Retail Cut	Average Size Thickness	Average Size Weight	Qualities and Description	Method of Cookery	Portions[1] per Cut or Weight per Portion
Roasts—Cont. Fresh ham	*Inches* Whole	*Pounds* 8–12	Regular or skinned, tender, juicy, layer of fat on outside; little waste	Dry heat: Roast	8–10
Shoulder	Whole	8–12	Skinned, N. Y. style, tender; coarser, good flavor; may be boned, rolled and cut into roasts		6–9
Picnic		4–6	Lower end of shoulder; bone removed, skin cut off and edges of two flat pieces sewed together; good flavor, lean		3–5
Spareribs		1½–2	Half sheet (consists of lower or belly ribs), lean and fat, good flavor, much bone	Roast, braise, simmer	2–3
Tenderloin[2]		½–¾	Short round muscle beneath backbone; very tender, juicy, excellent flavor; may be smoked	Roast, braise	¼–⅓ lb. per portion
Frenched		4–6 to 1 loin	Tenderloin cut in 2-inch pieces and flattened	Braise	1–2 patties
Stews Lean trimmings		any weight	From back, butt, neck, etc.	Moist heat, long, slow cooking: Stew, simmer, pickle	¼–⅓ lb. per portion
Shoulder hock		½–¾	Less tender and little meat but of good flavor; bone, skin		1 lb. per portion
Knuckles Shank		½–¾ 1½–2½	Less tender		
Fat back			1 to 3 inch thick layer of fat covering loin, cut in thin slices	Fry, wrapped around lean meat, larding	
Cured pork Sliced ham	¼–1	1–3	Cuts from center cut more expensive than from butt or shank ends; little waste in center cuts	Dry heat: Broil, pan-broil, fry, roast	¼–⅓ lb. per portion
Ham No. 1		12–14	Skinned, excess fat is trimmed; short, thick, stocky with small shank; flesh firm, fine, well marbled	Simmer, roast, braise	¼–⅓ lb. per portion

TABLE XXI—(*Continued*)

FRESH AND CURED PORK

Retail Cut	Average Size		Qualities and Description	Method of Cookery	Portions[1] per Cut or Weight per Portion
	Thick-ness	Weight			
Cured pork—Continued Ham No. 2	*Inches*	*Pounds* 12–14	Regular, not skinned; may show excessive amount of fat, otherwise like No. 1	Simmer, roast, braise	¼–⅓ lb. per portion
Smoked butts		1½–3	Boneless, prepared from Boston butt without the blade bone		3–5
Smoked pic-nics	Whole	4–8	Shoulder; sometimes bottom or shank end of shoulder cut off and cured. Palatable and costs less per pound than ham	Simmer	5–8
Sliced bacon		20–30 slices per lb.	Choice bacon, evenly streaked lean and beef; other quality bacon also sliced	Broil, pan-broil, bake	1–4 slices per portion
Bacon strip No. 1	Whole	4–8	Belly strips below spareribs; side pork		
Bacon strip No. 2		4–10	Less choice bacon; jowl (bacon squares)		
Canadian bacon			Prepared from ham-end cut of pork loin; boned and cured		
Salt Pork			Fat back (see fresh pork); belly, jowl	Fry, simmer, larding, wrapped around meat	¼ lb. per portion

PORK AND ITS COOKING METHODS

THE FAT of pork indicates quality and is largely responsible for the desirable flavor of this meat. In high quality pork, the exterior is well covered with a layer of fairly firm white fat. The color of the lean of young pork is grayish pink, turning to a delicate rose color in older animals. The lean is well-marbled with fat. The

TABLE XXII

TIMETABLE FOR COOKING PORK

| CUT | Roasted at 300°–350° F. Oven Temperature [1] | | Broiled | | Braised | Cooked in Liquid |
	Meat Thermometer Reading	Time	Meat Thermometer Reading	Total Time	Total Time	Time
	Degrees F.	Min./lb.	Degrees F.	Min.	Hrs.	Min./lb.
FRESH			Fresh Pork is never broiled			
Loin Center	185	35–40		—	—	—
Whole	185	15–20	—	—	—	—
Ends	185	45–50	—	—	—	—
Shoulder Rolled	185	40–45	—	—	—	—
Cushion	185	35–40	—	—	—	—
Boston Butt	185	45–50	—	—	—	—
Leg or Ham	185	30–35	—	—	—	—
Chops	—	—	—	—	¾–1	—
Steaks	—	—	—	—	¾–1	—
Spareribs	—	30–35	—	—	1½	30
Pork and Ham Loaf	—	30–35	—	—	—	—
SMOKED						
Ham Large	160–170	15–18	—	—	—	—
Medium	160–170	18–22	—	—	—	18–20
Small	160–170	22–25	—	—	—	—
Half	160–170	25–30	—	—	—	25
Ham Loaf	160–170	30–35	—	—	—	—

[1] 350° F. oven temperature is recommended for fresh pork and 300° F. oven temperature for smoked pork

TABLE XXII—(*Continued*)
TIMETABLE FOR COOKING PORK

| CUT | ROASTED AT 300°–350° F. OVEN TEMPERATURE [1] | | BROILED | | BRAISED | COOKED IN LIQUID |
	MEAT THERMOMETER READING	TIME	MEAT THERMOMETER READING	TOTAL TIME	TOTAL TIME	TIME
SMOKED— (Continued) Ham Slice	*Degrees F.*	*Min./lb.*	*Degrees F.*	*Min.*	*Hrs.*	*Min./lb.*
½ inch	—	—	160–170	15–20	—	—
1 inch	—	—	160–170	20–30	—	—
Picnic	170	35	—	—	—	35–45
Shoulder Butt	170	35	—	—	—	—
Bacon	—	—	—	4–5	—	—

[1] 350° F. oven temperature is recommended for fresh pork and 300° F. oven temperature for smoked pork

texture of the lean is firm and fine grained. The bones are porous and pinkish in color, since pork is usually young.

Some cuts are in demand as fresh pork, while others are in greatest demand as cured pork. Many pork cuts are sold both fresh and cured.

All cuts of pork are tender, therefore all large or chunky cuts, both fresh and cured, may be cooked by roasting. Fresh pork is usually roasted at 350° F., and cured pork at 300° F.

Pork chops, cutlets, sliced fresh ham or shoulder, and sliced pork liver are best if cooked by braising, rather than by broiling, panbroiling or griddle-broiling. Braising cooks them well done without drying them out. They may also be cooked by frying. Sliced cured ham and bacon may be broiled, panbroiled or griddle-broiled. Ham also may be panfried, and bacon may be panfried, deep-fat fried or oven-cooked (on a rack in an open roasting pan, at 325° F.). Pork should always be cooked well done. The

TABLE XXIII
VARIETY MEATS

Kind	Retail Cut	Average Weight	Qualities and Description	Method of Cookery	Portions (Approx.)
		Pounds		Precook to make firm and to keep fresh	
Beef	Brains (single or in pairs)	½–¾	Very tender, delicate flavor; rich in vitamins, protein and fat; no bones; spoil quickly	Dry heat: Broil fry (precooked)	¼ lb. per portion
Calf		½			
Lamb		¼		Moist heat: simmer; creamed, scrambled, baked	
Pork		¼			
Pork	Head (split)	3–5	Medium tender; good flavor; high in protein and fat	Moist heat, slow cooking: simmer, head-cheese	
	Feet	½–1	Little meat, much bone and gelatin-yielding substance	Simmer; pickled, jellied	1–2 feet
Beef	Heart	4	Less tender, muscular and compact; no bone; veal, lamb and pork hearts more tender than beef; an inexpensive meat with little waste	Moist heat, long, slow cooking: Braise; stuffed, baked, simmer, corned, pickled	¼ lb. per portion
Calf		½			
Lamb		½			
Pork		¼			
Beef	Kidneys	1	Tender, rich in flavor, high in vitamins; spoil quickly; veal and lamb kidneys may be cut with chops	Braise, simmer: Broil, fry	¼ lb. per portion
Veal		¾			
Lamb		3 oz.–¼		Broil, fry	
Pork		⅛		Braise, simmer	
Beef	Liver (sold by the pound)	7–12	Beef liver less tender; rich in vitamins and iron; spoils quickly; calf's liver choicest; lamb or pig's liver substituted for calf's liver; pig's liver must come from inspected animals	Moist heat: Braise, bake Dry heat: Broil, fry Moist heat: Braise, bake	¼ lb. per portion
Calf		1½–4			
Lamb		¾–1			
Pork		1½–3			
Calf	Sweetbreads Heart Throat	½–1	Thymus gland; very tender, almost white; delicate flavor; heart sweetbread round, more compact and slightly choicer than throat sweetbread; expensive, spoil quickly	Moist heat: Precook Dry heat: Broil, bake Moist heat: Precook, creamed, scrambled, salads	½–1 pair per portion
	Pancreas	¼	Similar to thymus sweetbread		

TABLE XXIII—(*Continued*)

VARIETY MEATS

KIND	RETAIL CUT	AVERAGE WEIGHT	QUALITIES AND DESCRIPTION	METHOD OF COOKERY	PORTIONS (APPROX.)
		Pounds			
Beef	Tail (oxtail)	1–2	Less tender; good flavor; mostly bone	Stew, simmer, braise, soup	
Beef	Tongue Fresh, smoked, pickled, canned	4–6	Less tender; long, coarse fibers; muscular; little waste	Moist heat, long slow cooking until tender, remove skin, simmer, braise; pickled, baked	¼ lb. per portion
Calf Lamb Pork	Fresh, canned Pickled Pickled, canned or smoked	1–2 ¼–⅓ ½	More tender and delicately flavored than beef tongue		
Beef	Tripe Fresh Pickled Plain Honeycomb	8–10 6½ 1½	Less tender; rubbery muscle — lining of beef's stomach; plain—lining of first stomach; honeycomb—lining of second stomach, more delicate	Precook to make tender. Moist heat, long slow cooking: simmer, stew; pickled, corned	¼ lb. per portion

cooked lean of fresh pork should be grayish white without even a tinge of pink.

VARIETY MEATS AND THEIR COOKING METHODS

VARIETY meats is the term used to designate the following edible portions of meat animals: Liver, heart, kidney, tongue, tripe, brains, and sweetbreads. Liver, heart, kidney and tongue are very flavorful, while brains, sweetbreads and tripe are very delicate in flavor.

Most of the variety meats are slightly more perishable than other meats and should not be purchased far ahead unless given special care. Liver, heart, kidney, brains, and sweetbreads are always purchased fresh. Tongue may be purchased fresh, pickled, corned or smoked. Tripe may be purchased fresh, pickled or canned. Fresh tripe is partly cooked before selling.

Variety meats, like all meats, are cooked according to their

TABLE XXIV

TIMETABLE FOR COOKING VARIETY MEATS

KIND	BROILED	BRAISED [1]		COOKED IN LIQUID	
	Total Time	Total Time		Total Time	
	Min.	*Min.*	*Hrs.*	*Hrs.*	*Min.*
Liver					
Beef					
3- to 4-lb. piece	—	—	2–2½	—	—
Sliced	—	20–25	—	—	—
Veal (Calf)—sliced	8–10	—	—	—	—
Pork					
Whole (3 to 3½ lbs.)	—	—	1½–2	—	—
Sliced	—	20–25	—	—	—
Lamb—sliced	8–10	—	—	—	—
Kidney					
Beef	—	—	—	1–1½	—
Veal (Calf)	10–12	—	—	¾–1	—
Pork	10–12	—	—	¾–1	—
Lamb	10–12	—	—	¾–1	—
Heart					
Beef					
Whole	—	—	3–4	3–4	—
Sliced	—	—	1½–2	—	—
Veal (Calf)					
Whole	—	—	2½–3	2½–3	—
Pork	—	—	2½–3	2½–3	—
Lamb	—	—	2½–3	2½–3	—
Tongue					
Beef	—	—	—	3–4	—
Veal (Calf)	—	—	—	2–3	—
Pork } usually sold Lamb } ready-to-serve					
Tripe					
Beef	10–15 [2]	—	—	1–1½	—

[1] On top of range or in a 300°F. oven.
[2] Time required after precooking in water.

TABLE XXIV—(*Continued*)
TIMETABLE FOR COOKING VARIETY MEATS

KIND	BROILED	BRAISED [1]		COOKED IN LIQUID	
	Total Time	Total Time		Total Time	
	Min.	Min.	Hrs.	Hrs.	Min.
Sweetbreads					
Beef	10–15 [2]	20–25	—	—	15–20
Veal (Calf)	10–15 [2]	20–25	—	—	15–20
Lamb	10–15 [2]	20–25	—	—	15–20
Brains					
Beef	10–15 [2]	20–25	—	—	15–20
Veal (Calf)	10–15 [2]	20–25	—	—	15–20
Pork	10–15 [2]	20–25	—	—	15–20
Lamb	10–15 [2]	20–25	—	—	15–20

[1] On top of range or in a 300° F. oven.
[2] Time required after precooking in water.

tenderness. Liver and kidney from young animals, brains and sweetbreads are tender. Tongue, heart, tripe, beef kidneys and beef liver are less tender and need long, slow cooking in moisture. Pork liver also is at its best when braised.

Variety meats are usually cooked well done, with the possible exception of veal liver which may be served medium. Variety meats from pork are always cooked well done.

CARE OF MEAT IN THE HOME

FRESH, cooked, smoked or frozen meats require proper storage in the refrigerator if they are to be in a desirable condition when used.

Unwrap fresh meat when delivered, wipe or scrape off, but do not wash, place on clean plate or in shallow bowl, cover top *lightly* with a piece of waxed paper and store in the refrigerator in coldest section. A slight drying of the cut surface will retard bacterial action. Steaks, chops and roasts should be used within a week (preferably 3 days); ground meats, meat sundries, drawn and disjointed poultry should be used within 2 days unless kept at 38° F. or lower. Store cooked meats covered to prevent drying out of the surface; use within a few days. Cooked meat should be ground shortly before using. Store smoked ham and bacon, wrapped in cellophane or waxed paper (as purchased) in a cold, dark place. Remove only the amount to be cooked and do not allow the remaining meat to stand exposed and at room temperature while preparing the meal. Uncut boiled or baked hams can be held safely 10 days at 36°–38° F.; slab bacon, 14 days; sliced bacon should not be held more than a week at the usual refrigerator temperature. Frozen meat should be held solidly frozen in the freezing unit or in a home freezer.

CARVING

PRACTICE alone brings perfection in the art of carving. Sharp tools are essential and more important than the size of the knife. An 8- to 9-inch carver is usual for carving roasts and certain game. A 5- to 7-inch blade is recommended for small hams, meat loaves and steaks. To prevent scratching the surface of a silver platter or a valuable china platter, and to prevent slipping, the roast, steak or fowl should rest on a wooden carving board, cut to fit the inner circumference of the platter.

Meat should be cut across the grain. A roast consisting of a number of chops from the loin is carved to serve one chop to each person. A standing rib or rolled roast is placed with cut surface on platter and meat is carved horizontally in ⅛- to ¼-inch slices. A whole ham or a leg of lamb is usually placed on platter, fat side uppermost, with bone end to the left of the carver; the meat is sliced at right angles to the platter, commencing from the choice, center section and slicing outwards. A crown roast of lamb is readily separated into individual chops, and care is taken to serve portions of the dressing which fills the center of the roast with each portion of meat served.

BEEF

BROILED STEAK

Select a tender steak 1 to 2 inches thick. (See Beef-Purchasing Guide for information on the different kinds of steak to use and their relative weights.) Allow ½ to ¾ pound per portion. Trim off excess fat and cut through the fat edge in several places to prevent curling. In broiling, the meat is cooked by direct or radiant heat from a gas flame, an electric element or hot coals. Whatever the source of heat or type of broiler, the broiling should be done at a moderate temperature. With the range type of broiler, which cooks one side of the meat at a time, preheat the broiler, if desired, to shorten the cooking time. With oven door closed, heat broiler to moderate by using the thermostat. With some types, turn it to broil and regulate heat by hand; with others turn it to 350° F.

Place steak on greased rack of broiler pan with top surface of thick steak (1½ to 2 inches) 3 inches or more from heat, of thin steak (1 inch or less) about 2 inches. Broil until surface is brown and steak is about half done, leaving broiler door ajar or open, if necessary, to maintain a moderate temperature. Season and turn carefully to avoid loss of juice by inserting a large fork into the fat, or by turning steak with a vegetable tong or turner. When browned, season, remove to heated platter or sizzling platter, spread with butter and garnish as desired. (See Table XVI, p. 258, for approximate time for broiling the different kinds of steaks, 1 to 2 inches thick, to rare and to medium.)

Combination Broiling and Roasting—For quantity broiling use this method; it is also good for thick steaks cooked well done. Sear meat in hot broiler (500° F.) on both sides, allowing about 5 minutes for each side. Season, turn and transfer (meat and broiler pan) to slow oven (250° F.) to finish cooking (without turning). This method takes somewhat longer than constant temperature broiling but requires little attention after searing. Season and serve hot on heated platter.

SAVORY BROILED STEAK

Rub 2 tablespoons dry mustard into thick porterhouse steak and broil as directed (page 280). Remove to hot platter, spread with butter and sprinkle with salt and pepper; surround with Sautéed Onions (page 558).

FILET MIGNON

Fillets are cut from the tenderloin of beef and are usually from 1 to 2 inches thick. Broil or panbroil (pages 280, 282) to the desired degree of doneness (page 257); spread with softened butter, sprinkle with salt and pepper and serve with broiled mushroom caps or sautéed chopped mushrooms, French fried or sautéed onions, or broiled tomatoes.

PLANKED STEAK

Broil or panbroil a tender steak about 2 inches thick and until seared on both sides (pages 280–282), allowing 10, 15 or 25 minutes, according to desired degree of doneness; then place on heated plank brushed with butter or oil and border edge of plank with Duchess Potatoes (page 564), or Mashed Potatoes (page 564) brushed with melted butter, milk or diluted egg yolk. Place in moderate oven (350°–375° F.) and bake about 10 minutes, or until steak is cooked and potatoes browned. Spread softened butter over steak, season with salt, pepper and minced parsley and arrange hot vegetables around meat. Choose vegetables with contrasting color and texture and with a pleasing blend of flavors.

SERVICE SUGGESTIONS FOR PLANKED STEAK

Borders—
  Mashed Irish and sweet potatoes in various forms.
  Bananas, halved lengthwise, grilled pineapple slices.
  Cooked apple or peach quarters or apricot halves.
  Mashed squash, turnip.

Vegetable Combinations—
  Buttered peas, carrot strips and cauliflower flowerets.
  Broiled mushrom caps, string beans, diced beets.
  Buttered string beans, stuffed onions, grilled tomatoes.
  Buttered cauliflower, diced carrots, spinach.
  Stuffed green peppers, diced turnips, kidney beans.
  Buttered asparagus, diced beets, lima beans.
  Stuffed tomatoes, buttered young carrots, French fried onion rings.
  French fried eggplant, grilled tomatoes, buttered Brussels sprouts.
  Stuffed mushroom caps, beet greens, kernel corn.

To Season a New Plank

Use a hardwood plank (oak, hickory or pine) about one inch thick. Soak in cold water overnight. Rub thoroughly with oil or suet. Warm slowly to heat thoroughly (250° for one hour). Edges should be protected with oil. To clean plank, scrape, wash and rinse and allow to dry slowly. Always use a plank oiled and preheated.

PANBROILED STEAK

Use a heavy iron frying pan; it need not be preheated. If meat is lean rub pan lightly with suet. Sear tender steak quickly on both sides, then cook more slowly to the desired degree of doneness (page 257); turn steak once for even cooking, being careful not to pierce lean meat with fork. If fat accumulates, pour off to avoid frying meat. Remove steak to hot platter, spread with softened butter, sprinkle with salt and pepper and garnish as desired. Allow ½ to ¾ pound per portion.

MINUTE STEAK

Minute steaks are small individual steaks from ¼ to ½ inch thick. If cut from the top chuck, they contain the blade bone and make attractive steaks. Any small and thin tender cut may be called a minute steak. Panbroil steaks quickly (see above), allowing 4 to 5 minutes for entire cooking; spread with softened butter and sprinkle with salt and pepper after turning to sear other side. If cooked longer, steaks become dry and tough.

CAMPFIRE HAMBURGS

Season 1½ pounds lean beef, ground, with ¾ teaspoon salt and ¼ teaspoon pepper; shape into 12 very thin round cakes the size of the round rolls used. Sauté 1 cup chopped onions in 2 tablespoons butter until browned; stir in 1 tablespoon prepared horseradish mustard. Spread mixture over 6 meat cakes; cover with remaining cakes and press together. Broil over glowing coals or in broiler until well browned (page 257). Serve between buttered halves of 6 rolls. Yield: 6 portions.

FRIED HAMBURG

Season 1 pound round steak, ground, with ½ teaspoon salt and ¼ teaspoon pepper, and shape into flat patties. Fry in hot deep fat (380° F.) for 5 to 8 minutes, or until browned, and serve immediately. Approximate yield: 6 patties.

GRILLED HAMBURG

Use lean beef, ground; shape lightly into large steak or flat cakes about 1 inch thick and broil (page 257). Turn when seared on one side; brown, spread with butter, season and serve at once.

HAMBURG ON ONION SLICES

Place 6 slices Bermuda or white onion, ½ inch thick, in pie plate, sprinkle with salt and pepper and pour 2 tablespoons melted butter over them; cover and bake in moderate oven (350° F.) about ½ hour, or until nearly soft. Mix together lightly 1 pound lean beef, ground, 2 tablespoons ground suet, ½ cup soft bread crumbs, 1 tablespoon chopped parsley, ½ teaspoon salt and ⅛ teaspoon pepper; shape into 6 cakes, wrap each with a slice of bacon and fasten with a toothpick. Place cakes on onion slices and broil (page 257), turning once. Yield: 6 portions.

PLANKED HAMBURG STEAK

Mix 1 pound lean beef, ground, with 2 tablespoons lemon juice, ½ teaspoon salt and ¼ teaspoon pepper; shape lightly into large steak about 1¼ inches thick and broil (page 257) just enough to sear both sides. Transfer to heated and greased plank, spread with softened butter and season with salt and pepper; border edge of plank with mashed potatoes brushed with egg yolk mixed with 1 tablespoon milk. Place in moderate oven (350°–375° F.) and bake until meat is done and potatoes are browned. Arrange seasoned hot vegetables around meat. Approximate yield: 4 portions.

MEAT BALLS

Season 1 pound beef, ground, and ¼ pound fresh or salt pork, ground, with ½ teaspoon salt, ⅛ teaspoon pepper and 1 small onion, chopped and sautéed in 1 tablespoon butter; add ½ cup bread crumbs and ⅓ cup milk and mix thoroughly. Shape into cakes, roll in flour and sauté in 2 tablespoons fat until well browned. Approximate yield: 1 dozen balls, or 6 portions.

MEAT BALLS AND VEGETABLE CASSEROLE

Grind together ½ pound beef and ½ pound each veal and fresh pork; season with 1 teaspoon salt, ⅛ teaspoon pepper and ½ small onion, minced, and mix with ½ cup applesauce, ½ cup soft bread crumbs and 1 egg or 2 egg yolks. Shape into balls, roll in flour and brown in 2 tablespoons fat; then place in casserole. To drippings in frying pan add the following vegetables: 2 cups canned tomatoes; 4 medium-sized potatoes and 1 small carrot, each diced; ½ small onion, 1 stalk celery and 1 green pepper, each minced. Bring to a boil and turn out over meat balls; bake in moderate oven (350° F.) about 45 minutes. Approximate yield: 6 portions.

BEEF PATTIES AND BACON

Season 1 pound lean beef, ground, with 1 tablespoon minced onion, ½ teaspoon salt and ¼ teaspoon pepper; add ¼ cup bread crumbs and ⅓ cup milk, and mix thoroughly. Shape into patties, wrap each with a slice of bacon and fasten with toothpick; broil or panbroil (page 282). Approximate yield: 6 patties.

BEEF AND PORK PATTIES

Mix together ½ pound each beef, ground, and sausage meat; shape into 8 thin patties. Place layer of sliced apples between 2 patties and press together. Brown on both sides, then reduce temperature and cook slowly until apples are soft and meat is well done. Yield: 4 patties.

MEAT PUFFS WITH MUSHROOM SAUCE

1½ pounds lean beef, ground
1½ medium-sized onions, grated
1½ cups soft bread crumbs
2 eggs, well beaten
½ to ¾ teaspoon salt

¼ teaspoon pepper
dash of paprika
¼ cup flour
¼ cup fat
1 can condensed mushroom soup
½ cup water

Combine meat, onions, bread crumbs, eggs and seasonings; form lightly into small balls and sprinkle with flour. Brown in fat; add mushroom soup and water, cover and simmer 10 minutes. Yield: 6 portions.

STEAK AND KIDNEY PIE

1 pound top round steak
1 pound beef kidney
1 clove of garlic
4 medium-sized onions, sliced
2¼ cups water
½ pound mushrooms, sliced

1 green pepper, diced
3 potatoes, peeled and diced
2 tablespoons flour
2 teaspoons salt
few grains of pepper
½ recipe Rich Pastry (page 739)

Remove fat from steak and kidneys. Sauté garlic in drippings until brown. Remove garlic. Cut steak and kidneys into thin strips. Sauté lightly with onions. Add 2 cups water. Cover and simmer 1 hour. Add mushrooms, green pepper and potatoes and cook until potatoes are tender. Combine flour, salt and pepper and mix to a smooth paste with ¼ cup water for gravy thickening. Cool. Place in baking dish and top with pastry. Bake in hot oven (400° F.) about 20 minutes, or until crust is brown. Yield: 6 portions.

SWISS STEAK

2 pounds beef, 1 inch thick   2 tablespoons fat
⅓ cup flour   3 slices onion
1 teaspoon salt   ½ cup water
⅛ teaspoon pepper   1 cup tomato juice

Use round, chuck or shoulder beef; dredge with mixture of flour, salt and pepper and pound into steak with wooden potato masher or meat pounder. Brown in hot fat in heavy frying pan or Dutch oven, add onion, water and tomato juice, cover and simmer 1 hour, or until meat is very tender, turning occasionally. For oven cooking, place seared meat, vegetables, and liquid in casserole, and bake, covered, in moderate oven (350° F.) about 1 hour. If a thicker steak (2 to 2½ inches) is used, simmer meat about 2 hours. Yield: 6 portions.

STUFFED FLANK STEAK

2 pounds flank steak   Bread-Ham Stuffing (page 489)
1 teaspoon salt   flour
⅛ teaspoon pepper   3 tablespoons chopped suet
⅛ teaspoon ginger   ½ cup boiling water

Have butcher score flank steak; season with salt, pepper and ginger. Spread stuffing evenly over steak and roll with grain; tie or skewer and sprinkle with flour. Sauté meat roll in suet until well browned, then add water, cover tightly and simmer about 2 hours, or until meat is very tender, turning occasionally. To serve, remove thread, place on hot platter and garnish as desired; cut in slices across grain. Approximate yield: 6 portions.

SCRAMBLED BEEF

1 pound beef, ground   1 dill pickle, chopped
3 tablespoons minced onions   ½ teaspoon salt
¼ cup chopped cooked beets   ⅛ teaspoon pepper
1½ teaspoons chopped mixed   1 egg
    sweet pickles   3 tablespoons butter

Mix together beef, vegetables, pickles, seasonings and egg; sauté in 2 tablespoons butter in heavy frying pan until browned; add remaining 1 tablespoon butter just before removing from heat. Approximate yield: 4 portions.

FRENCH FRIED STEAKS

1½ pounds round steak   salt and pepper

Cut steak in pieces for serving, about 3 inches square; score both sides
with sharp knife and trim off all connective tissue. Fry in hot deep fat
(390° F.) 4 to 6 minutes; drain on unglazed paper, sprinkle with
salt and pepper and serve at once on hot platter with a border of
French Fried Potatoes (page 267). Approximate yield: 6 portions.

STANDING RIB ROAST

Use a 1- to 3-rib roast according to number to be served, allowing about
one-half pound per portion. (For information on average weights of
ribs and other cuts suitable for roasting, see Beef-Purchasing Guide.)
To estimate the approximate time needed for roasting, weigh the
meat. Let stand at room temperature 30 minutes or longer. Season with
salt and pepper if desired. Place fat side up in open shallow pan;
a rack is not necessary—the chine bone and rib ends keep the roast
out of the drippings. Insert a meat thermometer into the largest
muscle so that the bulb is in center, not touching fat or bone.

Roast (uncovered) in a slow to moderately slow oven (300° F.):
use 325° F. for small roast (1 rib weighs about 2 pounds); 300° F.
for larger roasts. Basting is not necessary; the fat as it melts bastes the
meat. Roast until the meat thermometer registers the desired degree
of doneness (page 257). For large roast allow per pound (approximately): 18 to 20 minutes for rare meat (140° F.); 22 to 25 minutes for
medium (160° F.); and 27 to 30 minutes for well done meat (170° F.).
For small roast allow per pound: 33 minutes for rare meat; 45 minutes
for medium; and 50 minutes for meat well done. *If a large roast,
cooked rare or medium well done, is to stand 20 to 30 minutes or longer
before serving, remove it from the oven when the meat thermometer
is several degrees below the desired temperature; cooking in center
continues after the roast is removed from the oven.* Place on heated
platter with Browned Potatoes (page 566) and serve with Brown Gravy
(page 291). Serve with one or several vegetables buttered, baked or
scalloped.

ROLLED ROAST WITH YORKSHIRE PUDDING

Use a rolled rib roast. The size will vary with the number to be served.
Place roast, fat side up, on rack in pan and insert meat thermometer
through fat covering; allow 10 to 15 minutes longer per pound for
each degree of doneness, as above. Turn occasionally to cook evenly.
Serve with squares of Yorkshire Pudding and Brown Gravy (page 291).

Yorkshire Pudding—Mix 1 cup sifted flour and ½ teaspoon salt; add gradually 1 cup milk beating until smooth after each addition. Add 2 eggs, one at a time, and beat with rotary beater until smooth and creamy. Cover with towel and chill for 2 hours. Pour into sizzling hot, shallow pan containing ¼ cup hot beef dripping and bake in hot oven (425° F.) 25 to 30 minutes. Cut in squares and serve at once with hot roast. Approximate yield: 6 portions.

ROAST BEEF TENDERLOIN

The fillet or tenderloin is a long narrow strip of tender lean meat weighing from 4 to 6 pounds; have it larded by butcher or lard with salt pork (page 64), or place strips of pork on top. Sprinkle with salt and pepper, allowing ½ teaspoon salt per pound of meat. Place on rack in pan and insert meat thermometer. Roast at 300° to 325° F. (page 257), allowing 20 to 25 minutes per pound, according to the desired degree of doneness. Serve with Brown or Mushroom Sauce (page 467). Allow about ⅓ pound per portion.

BEEF LOAF

1½ pounds beef, ground   1½ tablespoons minced onion
¾ teaspoon salt   1½ cups soft bread crumbs
¼ teaspoon pepper   ½ cup water
                  Tomato Sauce (page 469)

If beef is lean, add ¼ pound suet or fat pork. Combine ingredients lightly but thoroughly and turn into greased loaf pan, 8½ x 4½ x 2½ inches. Bake in slow to moderate oven (325°–350° F.) 30 to 45 minutes. Serve with tomato sauce. Approximate yield: 6 portions.

ITALIAN HAMBURG LOAF

1 pound lean beef, ground   1 small onion, minced
½ pound cheese, grated   1 teaspoon salt
1 green pepper, chopped   pepper
                  4 eggs, well beaten

Mix thoroughly all ingredients and shape into loaf. Bake in slow to moderate oven (325°–350° F.) 45 to 50 minutes. Approximate yield: 1 medium-sized loaf, or enough for 6 portions.

THREE-LAYERED DINNER

¼ cup diced onion
1 teaspoon minced garlic
3 tablespoons butter or
    margarine
½ pound ground beef
½ cup canned tomato sauce
½ teaspoon salt

⅛ teaspoon pepper
pinch of orégano
1 pound elbow macaroni
1½ cups grated American cheese
1 12-ounce package frozen or
    fresh asparagus
¾ cup milk

1 egg, beaten

Sauté onion and garlic in 2 tablespoons butter until tender. Add meat
and cook, stirring constantly, until browned. Stir in tomato sauce, salt,
pepper and orégano. Simmer a few minutes. Spread on bottom of
greased 2-quart casserole. Cook macaroni in boiling salted water until
tender. Drain. Add cheese and toss gently. Place on top of meat mixture. Cook asparagus in boiling salted water until just tender. Drain
and arrange over macaroni. Dot with remaining butter. Combine milk
and egg and pour into casserole. Bake in moderate oven (350° F.)
about 35 minutes, or until custard is set. Carefully unmold from casserole by inverting the dish over the serving platter. Garnish with
parsley, if desired. Serve in pie-shaped wedges. Yield: 4 portions.

AMERICAN CHOP SUEY

4 ounces egg noodles
1½ cups canned tomatoes
½ cup grated cheese
1 large onion, sliced

¼ cup oil
½ pound lean beef, chopped
1 stalk celery
soy sauce

salt and pepper

Cook noodles in large amount of boiling salted water 10 minutes, or
until soft; drain and return to kettle; then add tomatoes and cheese,
and stir until cheese is melted. Sauté onion in oil until slightly yellow,
add chopped beef and stir until well browned; add celery cut in thin
long strips. Add to noodle-cheese mixture, season to taste with soy
sauce, salt and pepper and heat thoroughly; serve with additional soy
sauce, if desired. Approximate yield: 4 to 6 portions.

MEAT LOAF WITH CHILI SAUCE

1 pound beef, ground
½ pound pork, ground
½ pound veal, ground
4 slices bread
½ cup warm water

1 medium-sized onion, minced
2 teaspoons salt
¼ teaspoon pepper
2 eggs
1 cup chili sauce

Mix meats thoroughly with bread softened in warm water, seasonings and eggs; pack into greased loaf pan, 8½ x 4½ x 2½ inches, and cover with chili sauce. Bake in slow to moderate oven (325°–350° F.) about 50 minutes. Approximate yield: 8 portions.

BEEF BIRDS CORDON BLEU

6 thin slices round steak
6 chicken livers
6 tablespoons butter
1 teaspoon sugar
½ clove of garlic, minced
2 tablespoons chopped parsley
3 mushrooms, sliced
1 cup chopped apple

2 ounces chopped cooked ham
salt and pepper
3 tablespoons cooking Sherry
½ teaspoon tomato paste
2 teaspoons potato flour
1 teaspoon meat glaze
1¼ cups stock
¼ cup dry red wine

1 teaspoon currant jelly

Trim off fat from meat. Place each slice between two pieces of waxed paper and pound with a wooden mallet until very thin. Sprinkle chicken livers with sugar and brown in 2 tablespoons butter; slice. Add more butter to pan and add garlic, parsley and mushrooms. Sauté 2 minutes. Add apples and cook 5 minutes. Combine with livers and ham and season. Spread a tablespoonful of mixture on each slice of beef. Roll carefully and tie ends with string. Brown rolls quickly in remaining butter. Heat Sherry, ignite and pour over beef birds. Remove meat from pan to a warm place. Add to pan the tomato paste, potato flour and meat glaze. Stir until smooth; then add stock, wine, salt and pepper. Stir until it comes to a boil. Add jelly. Return beef birds to the pan. Cover and simmer until tender, about 45 minutes. Approximate yield: 6 portions.

CREOLE BEEF WITH NOODLES

1 pound lean beef, ground
3 tablespoons fat
2 cups hot water
1 teaspoon salt

1 cup diced celery
¾ cup diced onion
1 cup tomato purée, or condensed
   tomato soup
4 ounces noodles

Sauté meat in fat until well browned, stirring occasionally; then add water, cover and simmer 20 minutes. Add salt, vegetables and purée and cook 20 minutes longer, or until vegetables are tender and mixture has the consistency of thick sauce. Cook noodles in boiling salted water 10 minutes, or until soft; drain, place in well-buttered ring mold and keep hot. To serve, unmold noodles on hot chop or round plate and fill center with meat-vegetable mixture. Approximate yield: 4 to 6 portions.

POT ROAST

4 to 6 pounds beef
¼ cup flour
2 teaspoons salt
⅛ teaspoon pepper

¼ cup chopped suet, or 3 tablespoons beef fat
water
2 cups brown gravy

Use a compact piece of meat, solid or rolled, weighing from 4 to 6 pounds; choose meat from top, bottom, eye or heel of round, rump, chuck, shoulder arm or clod (see Beef-Purchasing Guide). Dredge meat with mixture of flour and seasonings. Flour is optional; it intensifies browning. Brown meat slowly on all sides in hot suet in heavy kettle or Dutch oven. Add about 2 tablespoons water, cover tightly and simmer on top of range or in slow oven (300° F.) until tender and well done, turning meat occasionally and adding small amounts of water, as needed, to prevent meat from burning and to cook it uniformly. Just enough water should be added to form the steam needed to soften the connective tissue. Allow 3 to 4 hours for large roast (page 257). An ideal pot roast is well browned, moist, juicy and flavorful. A rack or trivet may be placed under the browned meat, if desired. Soluble meat nutrients will adhere to the rack and some of the flavor is lost. Remove meat to heated platter and serve with a brown gravy made from the drippings and meat juices. Approximate yield: 8–12 portions.

BROWN GRAVY

Skim off excess fat from liquid in roaster or pan. For each cup of gravy, use 2 tablespoons each flour and drippings and 1 cup liquid (water, stock or part milk). Stir flour into fat and cook until lightly browned; gradually stir in liquid and cook 5 minutes, stirring until smooth and thickened; season to taste with salt and pepper; strain, if desired. Milk makes the gravy lighter in color and gives it flavor; a small amount of sweet or sour cream may also be added for flavor.

Pan Gravy—Skim off fat from liquid in roaster or broiler. If time permits, pour drippings (fat and liquid) into a bowl or cup and cool quickly. The fat will rise to the top and can be removed. Add 3 tablespoons of water to pan, stir and boil to loosen the meat nutrients which stick to pan. Concentrate the liquid, add the meat juice and heat. Season and serve in heated bowl or pour over steak. The liquid contains meat extractives, salts and proteins, and adds flavor to the meat and color to the pan gravy.

MODIFICATIONS OF POT ROAST

(Use recipe, page 290)

Italian Pot Roast—Use 1½ pounds chuck, rolled and tied, and sear in 3 tablespoons olive oil; add 3½ cups (No. 2 can) tomatoes, 1 teaspoon salt, ¼ teaspoon pepper, ¼ clove garlic, ½ bay leaf and 1 whole clove, cover tightly and simmer 3 hours, or until tender. Remove garlic; thicken gravy, if desired, by stirring in a thin mixture of flour and water and cook about 3 minutes. Approximate yield: 6 portions.

Cape Cod Pot Roast—Brown meat slowly on all sides in 2 to 3 tablespoons fat. Season and place in Dutch oven or deep-well cooker; add 2 cups cranberry sauce, ¼ cup water, 4 whole cloves and 1 stick (1 inch) cinnamon, and cover; simmer 3 hours, or until meat is tender, turning when half done. Strain liquor in cooler and use for gravy.

Pot Roast with Vegetables—Vegetables such as carrots, celery, onions, potatoes, tomatoes and turnips, whole, quartered, sliced or diced, may be added to the roast when nearly done and cooked until just tender; if cooked whole, turn occasionally to cover with juice.

SAUERBRATEN (SPICED STEAMED BEEF)

3 pounds beef, round or rump
1 teaspoon salt
¼ teaspoon pepper
1 tablespoon dry mustard
½ teaspoon thyme
1 leaf sage
parsley ·
1 tablespoon chopped onion
1 cup water

1 bouillon cube, or 1 tablespoon
   meat extract
½ cup tarragon vinegar
3 tablespoons butter
3 tablespoons flour
6 oz. can tomato paste
1 tablespoon Madeira
1 recipe Potato Dumplings
   (page 492)

Place beef in a small earthenware crock with close fitting lid. Mix together seasonings, water, bouillon cube and vinegar and pour over meat; cover securely and leave in a cool place for several days, turning daily. On fourth day, draw off liquor and use for sauce; sauté meat in butter in heavy frying pan until lightly browned; remove meat, stir flour into drippings, add spiced liquor gradually and cook until thickened, stirring constantly. Place meat in gravy and simmer, covered, about 3 hours, or until meat is tender. Remove meat, cut in thick slices and arrange on platter; pour hot sauce mixed with tomato paste and Madeira over meat, and decorate platter with potato dumplings and parsley. Approximate yield: 6 portions.

BEEF À LA MODE

Lard a 4-pound piece of round or chuck roll with salt pork, using a larding needle or inserting ¼-inch strips of salt pork into meat (page 64). Season with salt and pepper, dredge with flour and brown in 3 tablespoons chopped suet or beef drippings; half cover with hot water and simmer, covered, about 4 hours, or until meat is tender; add ½ cup peas and ½ cup each diced carrots, celery and onions, ½ hour before meat is done, adding water, if necessary. Place meat on hot platter with vegetables arranged around meat and serve with Brown Gravy (page 291). Allow about ½ pound meat per portion.

COOKED BEEF

Choose cut containing some fat such as brisket, plate, chuck or larded round. Add water to half cover meat and simmer, covered, until meat is tender; a 4 pound piece of beef will require from 3 to 4 hours. Add salt when half done, allowing ½ teaspoon per pound; add more water, if necessary. Serve hot or cold; if served cold, chill meat in stock to reduce shrinkage and increase flavor. Use stock for gravy, skimming off as much excess fat as possible (page 291). Or serve with Horse-radish Sauce (page 477). For a brown stock, sear meat on all sides before simmering. Allow about ½ pound meat per portion.

BRAISED STUFFED FLANK

1 cup vinegar
2 tablespoons chopped green
   pepper
2 teaspoons salt
1 teaspoon dry mustard
1 teaspoon sugar

½ clove garlic
1 flank steak
Celery-Bread stuffing (page 485)
2 tablespoons butter
boiling water
2 tablespoons flour

¼ cup cold water

Cook vinegar, green pepper and seasonings 5 minutes; cool, pour
over steak and allow to stand in refrigerator 3 to 4 hours, turning meat
several times; then remove steak from marinade and pound until thin.
Cover with stuffing, roll compactly and tie securely; sauté in butter until
well browned, add 1½ cups hot water and bake, covered, in slow oven
(300°–325° F.) about 2 hours, or until meat is tender. Remove steak
to heated platter and garnish as desired; add enough hot water to
stock to make 2 cups, thicken with paste made from 2 tablespoons
flour and ¼ cup cold water and serve gravy in heated bowl with
steak. Approximate yield: 6 portions.

SPICED MOLDED BEEF

2 pounds round steak
1 veal knuckle, cracked
1 small bunch soup greens
1 tablespoon vinegar
water
1 teaspoon salt

dash of celery salt
¼ teaspoon dry mustard
½ teaspoon allspice
½ teaspoon cloves
½ teaspoon mace
2 tomatoes

pickle fans

Cut steak in 1 inch cubes and place in large kettle with bone, soup
greens and vinegar; add just enough water to cover and simmer,
covered, 3 hours, or until meat is very tender. Allow meat to partially
cool in stock; remove meat and chop coarsely; skim fat from stock and
strain. Add seasonings and spices to stock and bring to a boil; add
meat and heat thoroughly, then chill. When slightly thickened, stir to
distribute meat, turn into mold and chill until firm. To serve, unmold
on serving platter, garnish with sliced or quartered tomatoes and pickle
fans. Approximate yield: 6 portions.

BEEF WITH POTATO DUMPLINGS

2½ pounds breast of beef, boned
 and rolled
1 teaspoon salt

2 tablespoons fat
4 cups boiling water
2 cups small white onions

Potato Dumplings (page 492)

Rub meat with salt and brown in fat; add hot water and simmer, covered, 1½ hours; add onions and continue cooking, uncovered, ½ hour, or until meat is tender. Place meat on hot platter with onions around it; cook dumplings in stock and arrange among onions. Approximate yield: 6 portions.

RAGOUT OF BEEF CASSEROLE

2 cups dried lima beans
1 pound chuck beef
3 tablespoons flour
1 teaspoon salt
¼ teaspoon paprika

dash of mace
2 tablespoons bacon fat
2 small onions, diced
1 large carrot, cut in strips
1 cup stewed tomatoes, seasoned

Wash and soak lima beans overnight in water to cover. Cook 30 minutes. Cut beef in 1 inch cubes, roll in flour mixed with seasonings and sauté in fat until well browned, adding onions when partially browned. Arrange beans and meat and onion mixture in alternate layers in heated 2-quart casserole, sprinkling carrot strips over each layer. Pour tomatoes over all, add hot water to barely cover and bake, covered, in moderate (350° F.) about 2½ hours. Approximate yield: 6 portions.

MADRAS CURRY

1½ tablespoons curry powder
½ cup water
3 medium-sized onions, ground
½ clove garlic, ground
¼ cup fat

1½ pounds beef, mutton, pork
 or fowl
hot water
1 teaspoon salt
⅛ teaspoon pepper

Add curry powder (soaked in water), onions and garlic to fat and cook, stirring constantly, until mixture becomes dark brown and begins to stick to bottom of pan. Cut meat in 1 inch cubes (if fowl is used, cut as for stew); add to curry mixture and fry slowly about 10 minutes, or until browned, stirring constantly. Add hot water to cover and seasonings and simmer, covered, 1 hour, or until meat is tender and stock has cooked down to a thick gravy. Approximate yield: 6 portions.

CANADIAN MEAT PIE

1½ pounds round steak
3 lamb kidneys
1 medium-sized onion, sliced
1⅓ cups hot water
1 tablespoon Worcestershire
 sauce

1 teaspoon salt
⅛ teaspoon pepper
2½ tablespoons butter
2 tablespoons flour
½ recipe Plain Pastry (page 736)

Wipe steak; trim off fat, chop and use as drippings; cut lean meat in 1 inch cubes. Split kidneys in halves lengthwise, remove tubes and fat and soak in cold salted water ½ hour; cut in small pieces. Sauté onion in beef fat in large frying pan or heavy kettle until lightly browned; add steak and brown slightly, stirring constantly. Add hot water and seasonings, cover and simmer about 1 hour, or until tender. Sauté kidneys in 1 tablespoon butter 10 minutes, turning frequently, and add to meat; drain off stock and thicken with roux made from flour and remaining 1½ tablespoons butter. Put meat-kidney mixture in greased casserole and pour half of gravy over top; cover with pastry, moistening rim with water to make crust adhere, then prick crust with fork, or make several incisions to permit escape of steam. Bake in hot oven (400° F.) about 20 minutes, or until crust is browned; serve with remaining hot gravy. Approximate yield: 6 portions.

The original English pie used suet in the pastry. Covered tightly with paper, it was steamed or baked for about 4 hours.

SNOW-CAPPED MEAT LOAVES

1½ cups mashed potatoes
1 pound lean ground beef
½ cup rolled oats (quick or
 old-fashioned, uncooked)

1 egg, beaten
⅔ cup tomato juice
¼ cup chopped onion
1½ teaspoons salt

¼ teaspoon pepper

Grease with butter or margarine six medium-sized custard cups. Place ¼ cup of the mashed potatoes in the bottom of each custard cup. Combine remaining ingredients thoroughly; pack on top of the mashed potatoes. Bake in a moderate oven (350° F.) 50 to 55 minutes. Let stand 10 minutes before turning out. Serve immediately.

HAMBURG DUMPLING STEW

1½ pounds lean beef, ground
1½ teaspoons salt
⅛ teaspoon pepper
1 teaspoon onion juice
⅓ cup fat

1 tablespoon flour
2 cups hot water
1 cup tomato soup
1 tablespoon chili sauce
1 recipe Dumplings (page 492)

Mix beef with salt, pepper and onion juice, shape lightly into small cakes and sear in hot fat until well browned; remove cakes. Stir flour into drippings in pan, add water, tomato soup and chili sauce, and bring to a boil. Return cakes to pan and drop 1 tablespoon dumpling mixture on top of each, cover closely and cook 12 to 15 minutes. Approximate yield: 6 portions.

BISCUIT MEAT ROLLS

1½ medium-sized onions, thinly sliced
3 tablespoons fat
1½ pounds lean beef, ground
1½ teaspoons salt

¼ teaspoon pepper
3 tablespoons water (about)
1 recipe Baking Powder Biscuits (page 149)
1 recipe Tomato Sauce (page 469)

Sauté onions in fat until lightly browned, add meat mixed with seasonings and brown, stirring constantly; moisten with water. Roll biscuit dough into a rectangle, ¼ inch thick; cover with meat mixture, roll as for jelly roll and cut in 6 slices. Place slices on greased baking pan and bake in hot oven (400° F.) about 25 minutes; serve with tomato sauce. Yield: 6 portions.

CORNED BEEF

Use a 4-pound solid piece of corned beef such as fancy brisket, navel, flank or neck; wash under running water to remove outside brine and tie securely. Soak if very salty. Cover with cold water and cook at simmering temperature from 3 to 4 hours, or until meat is tender. Cool slightly in stock; then remove to hot platter and serve with Horseradish Sauce (page 477) or Mustard Sauce (page 475). Approximate yield: 8 portions.

Pressed Corned Beef—Cool cooked beef in stock to increase flavor and reduce shrinkage. Drain, cover and place heavy weight on top to press meat.

New England Boiled Dinner—Skim excess fat off liquid and add the following vegetables to corned beef ½ hour before meat is cooked: 1 medium-sized yellow turnip, pared and quartered; 6 parsnips, pared and cut in halves lengthwise; 6 small carrots, scraped; 6 medium-sized potatoes, pared; 1 medium-sized cabbage, quartered and cored. Place hot meat in center of large platter and arrange vegetables, including 6 beets, cooked and buttered, around meat.

Glazed Corned Beef—Drain cooked corned beef, place in baking pan, cover with ⅓ cup brown sugar and stick with 6 whole cloves. Bake in moderate oven (350° F.) about ½ hour, or until glazed. Slice for serving.

Corned Beef and Cabbage—About 20 minutes before meat is cooked, remove enough stock to cook the cabbage. Skim off excess fat, add 1 medium-sized cabbage, sliced, and boil, uncovered, 15 to 20 minutes, or until cabbage is just tender. Place meat on hot platter; drain cabbage, arrange around meat and sprinkle with salt and paprika.

MOLDED CORNED BEEF

1½ tablespoons gelatin	1 cup diced celery
⅓ cup cold water	¾ cup cooked peas
2 cups boiling water	½ cup diced pickled beets
2 bouillon cubes	¼ cup sliced radishes
¼ teaspoon Worcestershire sauce	1 12-oz. can corned, beef, chopped
½ teaspoon salt	lettuce

Soften gelatin in cold water; add hot water and bouillon cubes, stirring until dissolved, and season with Worcestershire sauce and salt; chill. When mixture begins to thicken, add celery, peas, beets, radishes and corned beef; mold as desired and chill until firm. Unmold and serve on lettuce. Approximate yield: 6 portions.

CREAMED DRIED BEEF

2 cups Medium White Sauce (page 125)	¼ to ½ pound dried beef, shredded and scalded
	buttered hot toast

Prepare white sauce, omitting salt. Scald shredded beef if salty, add to sauce and heat slowly about 10 minutes. Serve on toast or with hot baked potatoes as desired. One egg or 2 egg yolks, slightly beaten and mixed with a small amount of hot sauce, may be stirred into creamed beef just before serving. Approximate yield: 6 portions.

Frizzled Dried Beef—Sauté shredded beef in butter about 5 minutes, or until curled; then prepare white sauce, adding flour and milk to meat in pan.

Dried Beef and Almonds—Prepare creamed beef with egg yolks; add ½ cup toasted blanched almonds and serve on hot whole wheat biscuits, split and buttered. Garnish with sliced stuffed olives.

DRIED BEEF AND CORN

2½ cups whole kernel corn
1 2½-oz. jar dried beef, shredded
2 tablespoons butter

3 tablespoons flour
1 can cream of mushroom soup
buttered hot toast, or biscuits, halved, toasted and buttered

Drain corn and reserve liquid for gravy. Sauté corn and shredded beef in butter until slightly browned and dry; stir in flour and continue browning. Gradually add soup and liquid from corn and cook about 5 minutes, stirring until thickened. Serve on hot toast or biscuits. Approximate yield: 6 portions.

VEAL
BRAISED VEAL CHOPS

Use rib, loin or shoulder chops, ½ to ¾ inches thick. Dredge in flour if desired. Brown slowly on both sides in a small amount of fat. Season with salt and pepper. Add a small amount of water (1 to 2 tablespoons); cover and simmer until tender, turning frequently. Add more liquid as needed. Sour cream may be added for flavor when partially done; or tomato juice may be used as liquid. Allow 45 to 60 minutes for total cooking. Serve with Brown or Pan Gravy (page 291).

WIENER SCHNITZEL

1½ pounds veal steak, ½ inch thick
1½ teaspoons salt
⅓ cup flour

1 egg, slightly beaten
1 tablespoon water
¾ cup dry bread crumbs
lemon slices

Cut veal in 6 pieces and flatten with meat pounder; rub with salt, roll in flour, dip in egg mixed with water and roll in crumbs. If chilled before cooking, coating will stick to meat. Brown in small amount of hot fat; cover and simmer 30 minutes, or until tender, adding just enough water (1 tablespoon), as needed, to steam the meat. Turn meat frequently for uniform cooking. Serve with lemon slices. Yield: 4 to 6 portions.

VEAL STEAK MADEIRA

Sauté 2 pounds veal steak (1 inch thick) in 2 tablespoons fat until browned, then cover and cook slowly 45 minutes, or until tender, adding a very small amount of water as needed and turning meat frequently. Place on hot platter, sprinkle with salt and pepper and spread with 2 tablespoons butter; pour Madeira Scallion Sauce (page 479) over and around steaks. Approximate yield: 6 portions.

VEAL EN BROCHETTE

Cut 1 pound veal steak, ½ inch thick, ½ pound fat fresh pork, sliced thin, in 2 inch squares. Arrange alternate squares of veal and pork on small skewers, using about 4 veal and 3 pork pieces for each. Roll in seasoned flour and sauté in 3 tablespoons fat in heavy frying pan, turning to brown all sides; then cover and cook slowly ½ hour, or until tender, turning frequently. Serve with Brown Gravy (page 291). Approximate yield: 6 portions.

JELLY–GLAZED VEAL SAUTÉ

Cut 1½ pounds veal steak in 1 inch cubes and roll in seasoned flour. Sauté in 3 tablespoons fat until browned, then simmer, covered, about ½ hour, turning frequently. Heat ½ cup currant jelly until it melts and add ½ cup boiling water; pour over meat and cook until slightly glazed, stirring constantly. Serve on heated platter around a mound of boiled or steamed rice. Approximate yield: 6 portions.

VEAL KNOTS

1½ pounds veal steak, ½ inch thick	⅓ cup butter
	½ bay leaf
flour, seasoned	⅓ cup white wine

Cut veal steak in thin strips about 1 inch wide and 8 inches long; roll in seasoned flour and tie each strip in a knot. Sauté in butter until well browned, add bay leaf and simmer, covered, 30 minutes, turning occasionally. Add wine, heat just to the boiling point, season with salt and pepper to taste and serve at once. Yield: 6 portions.

BREADED VEAL CUTLETS

Use 2 pounds veal steak, ½ inch thick; wipe with damp cloth and cut in pieces for serving. Sprinkle with salt and pepper; roll in flour, dip in 1 egg, beaten slightly with 1 tablespoon water, and roll in fine bread or cracker crumbs. Chill thoroughly. Sauté slowly in ¼ cup fat until well browned, cover and simmer 30 minutes, adding just enough water as needed to steam meat. Turn meat several times. Serve with Cream Sauce (page 466) or a tomato sauce. Yield: 8 portions.

RICE AND VEAL CUTLETS

¾ pound veal, ground	6 stuffed olives, minced
6 tablespoons fat	1 teaspoon salt
2 cups cooked rice	1 egg, beaten
1 cup Thick White Sauce	1 cup dry bread crumbs
(page 125)	Frontier Sauce (page 471)

Sauté veal in 2 tablespoons fat until well browned, stirring to brown evenly; mix with rice, white sauce, olives, salt and egg and cool. Shape in cutlets and roll in crumbs; sauté in remaining ¼ cup fat in heavy frying pan until lightly browned; cover and cook slowly 10 minutes. Serve with Frontier Sauce. Leftover cooked veal, ground, may be used in this recipe. Approximate yield: 6 portions.

VEAL ROAST

Use loin, rib or rack or leg of veal for roasting, allowing about one-half pound per portion. For information on retail cuts suitable for roasting see Veal-Purchasing Guide. Veal, high in connective tissue, is cooked until well done. It requires long, slow cooking to soften the connective tissue. Because veal is lacking in fat, it should not be seared. To increase its juiciness and flavor, lard (page 64) with strip of salt pork, suet or bacon, place slices of salt pork or bacon over top, or brush with bacon drippings or other fat. Season with salt and pepper. Insert meat thermometer so that bulb is in the center of the thickest muscle. Place fat side up on rack in shallow pan.

Roast (uncovered) in a slow oven (300° F.) until the meat thermometer registers 170° F. If sufficiently larded, basting with drippings or additional fat is not necessary. When done remove roast to heated platter and serve with Brown Gravy (page 291), using milk for part of liquid or adding sour cream to gravy.

POT ROAST OF VEAL

Select a solid piece of veal from shoulder, chuck or leg weighing from 3 to 5 pounds; wipe, sprinkle with salt and pepper and dredge with flour. Brown on all sides in heavy frying pan or Dutch oven, using suet or bacon fat; add ½ cup hot water, cover and simmer for 2 to 2½ hours, or until meat is tender, turning occasionally. A low rack may be placed in bottom of kettle after meat is seared. Vegetables such as potatoes, carrots and onions may be added ½ to ¾ hour before meat is done; turn vegetables to brown all sides. Place roast on hot platter and surround with vegetables; serve with Brown Gravy (page 291) made from drippings in pan. Yield: 6 to 8 portions.

STUFFED VEAL SHOULDER

Have butcher remove bones from 5-pound shoulder of veal; wipe with damp cloth. Fill cavity with Nut-Prune Stuffing (page 486), roll and sew or tie in place. Place on rack in roasting pan and roast in moderately slow oven (300° F.) until done; allow 40 to 45 minutes per pound; baste twice with melted fat, using ¼ cup. Yield: 6 to 8 portions.

VEAL BIRDS

1½ pounds veal steak, ½ inch thick
1 cube (1 inch) fat salt pork
½ cup soft bread crumbs
1 egg yolk
meat stock
salt and pepper
1 tablespoon Worcestershire sauce, or 1 tablespoon lemon juice
flour
3 tablespoons butter
1 cup light cream

Wipe veal, cut off skin and fat and remove bone; pound meat until thin and cut into individual servings. Grind veal trimmings and pork; mix with bread crumbs and egg, moisten with stock and add ¼ teaspoon salt, dash of pepper and Worcestershire sauce. Spread stuffing over each piece of veal, to within ⅛ inch of edge, roll and fasten with toothpicks. Sprinkle with salt and pepper, roll in flour and sauté in butter, turning to brown all sides; add cream and simmer, covered, about ½ hour, or until tender, turning several times. A small amount of leftover jam, jelly or marmalade may be added to gravy if desired. Serve hot with creamy gravy in pan; thicken and add more cream, if necessary. Approximate yield: 6 portions, or 1 dozen meat rolls.

VEAL LOAF

2 pounds veal
¼ pound salt pork
1 cup bread crumbs
1 teaspoon minced onion
1 tablespoon lemon juice
1½ teaspoons salt
⅛ teaspoon pepper
1 egg, separated
1 cup milk or stock
2 tablespoons butter
¼ cup hot water

Use veal from shoulder or rump and grind with salt pork; add crumbs, onion, lemon juice, seasonings, egg yolk and milk and mix thoroughly. Pack in greased loaf pan, brush top with slightly beaten egg white and bake, uncovered, in moderate oven (350° F.) about 1 hour, basting occasionally with mixture of butter and hot water. Serve hot or cold. Yield: 1 loaf, 8½ x 4½ x 2½ inches, or 8 portions.

ANCHOVY LEG OF VEAL

leg of veal (6 pounds)
6 anchovy fillets
1 clove garlic, sliced
salt and pepper
6 whole cloves

1 medium-sized onion, sliced
1 bay leaf
½ cup butter
¼ cup dry bread crumbs
½ cup heavy cream

Trim and wipe leg of veal; make small incisions over surface and fill with strips of anchovies and garlic. Sprinkle with salt and pepper and stick with cloves; allow to stand 1 hour. Place, fat side up, on rack in roasting pan. Insert a meat thermometer into meat with bulb in center of largest muscle (page 252). Arrange onion slices over top and crush bay leaf over all. Pour ¼ cup butter (melted) over meat. Roast in slow oven (300°–325° F.) until nearly done (160°–165° F.), allowing about 22 minutes per pound. Baste occasionally with drippings in pan or additional fat. When nearly done, turn meat over, dust with crumbs and pour remaining ¼ cup butter (melted) over meat. Roast about 20 minutes longer, or until meat is well done (170° F.) and crumbs browned. Pour cream over meat about 10 minutes before removing it from oven. Place on heated platter. Thicken drippings and cream if desired with a smooth paste made of 1 tablespoon flour and 2 tablespoons milk or water; serve with meat. Approximate yield: 12 portions.

VEAL BIRDS IN CASSEROLE

Use Mushroom Stuffing (page 487) in preparing the Veal Birds (above). Brown each veal roll on all sides in 2 tablespoons bacon fat. Place in greased casserole or baking pan, cover and bake in slow oven (300°–325° F.) about 1 hour, basting occasionally with mixture of 2 additional tablespoons bacon drippings and ¼ cup hot water. Serve with Brown Gravy made from drippings in pan (page 291). Approximate yield: 6 portions, or 1 dozen Veal Birds.

PRUNE–STUFFED VEAL BIRDS

Substitute cooked and pitted large prunes for stuffing in recipe for Veal Birds (above), using 1 prune for each roll; substitute 3 tablespoons butter and ⅓ cup stock for cream. Place sautéed rolls in casserole, pour ¼ cup of butter-stock mixture over them, cover and bake in slow oven (300°–325° F.) about 1 hour, or until tender, basting several times with remaining butter and stock. Serve with pan gravy poured over birds. Approximate yield: 6 portions.

BRAISED VEAL WITH BACON

Panbroil 8 slices bacon until crisp; remove and keep hot; sauté 1½ pounds veal steak (dredged with seasoned flour) in drippings. Add ¼ cup hot water and simmer, covered, ½ hour; add 1 cup sour cream, sprinkle with 1 teaspoon paprika and simmer 15 minutes longer. Serve on hot platter with cream gravy thickened slightly, if desired, in a heated bowl. Yield: 6 portions.

VEAL "SCHNITZEL"

Cut 1½ pounds veal steak, ½ inch thick, in 6 pieces; dredge with seasoned flour, sauté in ¼ cup butter until browned, cover and simmer 15 minutes. Add 3 tomatoes, peeled and cut in sections, and 1 cup sour cream and simmer 15 minutes; then add ⅓ cup chopped mushrooms, sprinkle with 6 tablespoons Parmesan cheese and simmer 15 minutes longer. Approximate yield: 6 portions.

SIMMERED VEAL

Use neck, shoulder, breast, ends of ribs or knuckle; wipe and add water to barely cover meat. Simmer, covered, 1 to 2 hours, according to thickness of piece or until meat is tender, adding ½ teaspoon salt per pound when half done. Dredge with flour, sauté in fat and serve with Brown Gravy (page 291), or use as "boiled" veal in stews, fricassees or leftover veal dishes.

VEAL STEW

2 pounds neck of veal, cut in pieces	⅛ teaspoon pepper
water	2 cups canned peas
⅛ teaspoon thyme	3 tablespoons flour
6 medium-sized potatoes, diced	3 tablespoons cold water
6 medium-sized carrots, diced	½ recipe Baking Powder Biscuits
1½ teaspoons salt	(page 149)

Wash veal and cover with water; add thyme and simmer, covered, 2 hours, or until tender. Add potatoes, carrots and seasonings and cook ½ hour longer; add peas and thicken with a smooth paste of flour and water. Prepare and bake biscuits; split and cover with veal stew. Approximate yield: 6 portions.

STEAMED VEAL STRIPS

Cut 1 pound veal shoulder in strips. Run 1 cup brown rice through meat chopper; place half in steamer. Add veal, sprinkle with salt and pepper and cover with remaining rice. Cover steamer and cook over rapidly boiling water about 1 hour or until done. Place each piece of meat with rice on platter. Serve with any seasoning sauce. Yield: 4 portions.

PIQUANT HEAD OF VEAL

1 head of veal, cut in half	2 tablespoons fat
2 quarts water	2 tablespoons flour
2 tablespoons salt	½ cup chopped onion
2 cups white wine	salt and pepper to taste
¼ cup chopped onion	2 tablespoons capers or chopped
10 peppercorns	anchovies
3 tablespoons chopped parsley	1 tablespoon cider vinegar
4 bay leaves	1 tablespoon Madeira, optional

Wash head and place in boiling salted water with wine, onion, peppercorns, parsley and bay leaves. Cover and simmer about 2 hours, or until meat is tender. Remove head from stock, remove meat from bone and cut in ½ inch pieces. Melt fat, add flour and onions and sauté until lightly browned. Add about 2 cups broth in which meat was cooked. Salt and pepper to taste. Simmer ½ hour. Add meat to sauce and bring to a boil. Add capers or anchovies, cider vinegar and wine. Approximate yield: 4 portions.

SWISS VEAL TONGUE

3 veal tongues	1 tablespoon salt
water	1 bay leaf
	3 peppercorns

Wash tongues. Place in pan and cover with boiling water. Add salt, bay leaf and peppercorns. Cook until tips of tongues can readily be pierced with a fork (about 2 hours). Dip meat into cold water and remove skins. Reheat tongues in plain Brown Sauce (page 467), Mustard, or Anchovy Sauce (pages 475–479) before serving. Mashed turnips, squash or mashed potatoes go well with this dish. Approximate yield: 6 to 8 portions.

Calf's Tongue Diable—Split cooked tongue in half lengthwise; rub with seasoned Onion Butter (page 200); add 1 cup broth. Bake in moderate oven (350° F.) 15 minutes. Spread with sour cream; heat.

BOHEMIAN LUNG OF VEAL

1 pair of veal lungs
1 quart water
1½ teaspoons salt
1 parsnip
1 carrot
4 celery stalks
1 small onion
2 tablespoons vinegar
6 peppercorns
6 whole allspice
½ cup shortening

½ cup flour
1 tablespoon brown sugar
¼ cup chopped onion
2 tablespoons chopped parsley
2 anchovy fillets, chopped
1 teaspoon lemon juice
1 tablespoon grated lemon rind
½ teaspoon vinegar
salt and pepper to taste
pinch thyme
1 bay leaf

Wash lungs and place in water to cover with salt. Add vegetables, vinegar, peppercorns and allspice. Simmer about 2 hours or until meat is tender. Cool and slice fine. Melt shortening, stir in flour and sugar. Add onion and parsley and cook until brown. Gradually add 2 to 3 cups broth in which meat was cooked, anchovies, lemon juice, lemon rind, vinegar, salt, pepper, thyme, bay leaf, and meat. Simmer about 15 minutes. If desired, ½ cup sour cream may be added to gravy before serving. Serve with dumplings or noodles and a green salad. Approximate yield: 6 to 8 portions.

VEGETABLE VEAL PIE

1½ pounds veal
6 tablespoons flour
1 teaspoon salt
dash of pepper
3 tablespoons fat
water

¾ cup diced celery
¾ cup diced carrots
4 small onions, sliced
2 tablespoons cold water
Baking Powder Biscuits
  (page 149)

Use veal from shoulder, chuck or breast; cut in 1 inch pieces. Dredge with ¼ cup flour mixed with salt and pepper and sauté in fat until well browned, stirring frequently. Cover with water and simmer, covered, 1½ hours, or until tender, adding vegetables last ½ hour of cooking. Thicken with a smooth paste made of remaining 2 tablespoons flour and cold water; turn into heated individual casseroles or 1 large one. Roll biscuit dough ½ inch thick, cut with cutter and place biscuits on top. Bake in hot oven (450° F.) about 15 minutes, or until browned. Approximate yield: 6 portions.

PRESSED VEAL

2½ pounds veal   2 teaspoons salt
½ pound pork   ¼ teaspoon pepper
boiling water   1 slice onion
                    1 stalk celery

Use veal from chuck, breast, or neck, and fat fresh pork from side, back, or shoulder; wipe with damp cloth and place in kettle. Cover with boiling water and cook 5 minutes; skim and simmer, covered, about 2 hours, or until meat is very tender, adding salt and pepper when half done. Remove meat from bones and put through food chopper with onion and celery; return to stock and cook until thick but moist, stirring constantly; pack in loaf pan (8½ x 4½ x 2½ inches) and chill thoroughly. Unmold and cut in slices for serving; this makes an excellent luncheon or picnic meat. Yield: 1 loaf, or 8 to 10 portions.

JELLIED VEAL

Prepare aspic, using 2 envelopes plain gelatin, ½ cup water, 2 cups veal stock, 3 tablespoons sugar, ½ cup vinegar, 3 tablespoons lemon juice and 1 teaspoon salt. When slightly thickened, fold in 3 cups ground cooked veal and 3 tablespoons parsley. Pour into oiled shallow pan. Yield: 6 portions.

LAMB AND MUTTON

BROILED LAMB OR MUTTON CHOPS

Select single or double chops of uniform thickness from loin, ribs or shoulder (Lamb and Mutton Purchasing Guide). Remove fell or outer skin and excess fat; slash edges. Preheat broiler with oven door closed to moderate (350° F.). Place chops on rack of broiler pan with top surface of thick chops (1½ to 2 inches) about 3 inches from heat; of thin chops (1 inch) about 2 inches. Broil at moderate heat until surface is brown and chops are about half done. Leave broiler door ajar or open, as necessary, to maintain a moderate temperature. Season and turn to brown other side. See Table XX, page 267, for approximate time. When browned, season and remove to heated platter. Lamb chops are cooked medium to well done; mutton usually well done. Garnish with parsley, curly endive or water cress. Serve with Mint Sauce (page 476), Butter and Lemon Sauce (page 472), Horseradish Sauce (page 465), or mint jelly.

Frenched Lamp Chops—Use rib chops; scrape meat and fat down from end of rib; cut off or wrap flank end around meat and fasten with toothpicks. Broil or panbroil; place paper frill on end of each bone, if desired.

Broiled Lamb Chops with Orange Slices—When chops are half done, sprinkle with salt and pepper and place an orange slice on each; brush with melted butter and finish broiling. Place on heated platter and garnish with parsley.

LAMB CHOPS WITH MUSHROOMS

6 lamb chops
½ pound large mushrooms
1 egg, slightly beaten

fine cracker crumbs
3 tablespoons butter
buttered hot toast
parsley

Broil or panbroil chops, allowing 12 to 20 minutes. While chops are broiling, wash mushrooms, dry and cut in halves lengthwise through caps and stems. Dip each half in egg, roll in crumbs and fry slowly in butter in heavy frying pan about 10 minutes, or until golden brown, turning frequently; remove and keep hot. Serve broiled chops on buttered toast, placing mushrooms over each chop so as to completely cover it. Garnish with parsley. Approximate yield: 6 portions.

PANBROILED LAMB OR MUTTON CHOPS

Remove superfluous fat from each chop, place in heavy frying pan and brown slowly on both sides, turning thick chops on edge to brown fat. Cook to desired degree of doneness (page 267), allowing time as for broiling (page 267). Turn chops occasionally and pour off fat as it accumulates to broil and not fry meat. Very thick chops, when browned, may be placed in slow oven (300°–325° F.) to finish cooking. Sprinkle with salt and pepper, place on heated platter, garnish as desired and serve at once.

PLANKED LAMB CHOPS WITH PINEAPPLE

Brown 6 chops on both sides, then place each on a slice of cooked pineapple arranged on a greased hot plank; brush with butter and sprinkle with salt and pepper. Bake in moderate oven (375° F.) to desired degree of doneness, allowing time as for broiling (page 267); baste once with melted butter. Drain 1 cup diced, canned pineapple and sauté in 2 tablespoons butter until lightly browned; heap on chops just before serving and garnish with fresh mint. Substitute broiled sliced tomatoes for diced pineapple, if desired, placing 1 slice on each chop. Yield: 6 portions.

LAMB EN BROCHETTE

1½ pounds lamb, ½ inch thick	pepper
6 slices canned pineapple	⅓ cup butter, melted
salt	¾ cup fine cracker crumbs
	6 slices whole wheat toast

Choose steak from shoulder or leg; cut meat and pineapple in 1 inch squares. Alternate pieces on skewers and sprinkle with salt and pepper; dip in melted butter and roll in crumbs. Broil under moderate heat (page 267); turn often; serve on toast. Yield: 6 portions.

BROILED LAMB PATTIES

1⅓ pounds lean lamb or mutton	6 slices bacon
1 teaspoon salt	6 slices tomatoes
¼ teaspoon pepper	melted butter

Use lean meat from breast, neck, shank or shoulder for grinding; season and shape into patties about 1 inch thick; wrap a strip of bacon around each and fasten with small skewers or toothpicks. Broil as directed (page 267); when browned on both sides, top each with a slice of tomato, brush with butter and continue broiling until tomato is browned. Yield: 6 portions.

ROAST LEG OF LAMB

Select leg of lamb, with or without part of loin. Do not remove fell (thin papery covering); it does not flavor the meat, it shortens the roasting time, and helps to keep the meat juicy. Rub with salt and pepper. Place fat side up on rack in an open roasting pan. Insert a meat thermometer into the thick muscle with bulb in center. Roast in a slow oven (300° F.) until the meat thermometer registers medium done (175°–180° F.). Roast small legs, shoulders and breasts at 325°–350° F. Basting is not necessary if leg has a fat covering; the fat bastes as it melts. Allow from 30 to 35 minutes per pound (page 267). Place on heated platter and garnish as desired. Serve with gravy made from drippings in pan (page 291) and Currant Orange Sauce (page 475) or Mint Sauce (page 476). Allow about ¾ pound per portion.

JELLY-GLAZED ROAST LAMB

Rub leg or shoulder of lamb, boned and rolled, with 1 bunch of mint, finely chopped, and sprinkle with salt and pepper. Roast as directed (above), basting meat frequently the last hour of roasting with ½ cup grape jelly dissolved in ½ cup hot water. Serve on heated platter with gravy made by thickening liquor in pan with a smooth mixture of 2 tablespoons flour and ¼ cup water.

ROAST LAMB WITH VEGETABLE STUFFING

Have butcher remove bone from leg. Fill cavity with Vegetable Stuffing (page 486); sew or tie securely. Prepare and roast as directed (page 267). Serve with gravy made from drippings. Whole breast of lamb may be used instead of leg; bone, stuff and roast as directed.

CROWN ROAST OF LAMB

1 crown of lamb or mutton   salt and pepper
                    chopped onion

The crown of lamb is prepared by the butcher from the rack and usually contains from 12 to 15 ribs; wipe with damp cloth and sprinkle with salt and pepper. Season ground meat prepared from trimmings with salt, pepper and chopped onion and place in crown of roast; tie a strip of salt pork around the end of each rib to prevent it from charring. Roast as for Leg of Lamb (page 267); it will take from 1½ to 2 hours. Remove salt pork and cover ends of ribs with paper frills; place on heated platter and garnish as desired. Serve with brown gravy made from drippings (page 291). If prepared without filling, place a small bowl or glass in crown to keep meat in shape during roasting. To serve, fill center of crown with vegetables such as mashed potatoes or potato balls, peas, or peas and diced carrots, or whole cauliflower, sprinkled with crumbs sautéed in butter. Allow 2 ribs to 1 portion.

STUFFED SHOULDER OF LAMB

Select a shoulder weighing 3 to 4 pounds and have it boned; use bone for stock. Wipe meat, sprinkle inside of pocket with salt and pepper and stuff with Bread Stuffing (page 484); roll and sew edges together or fasten with skewers. Rub surface with salt and pepper and dredge lightly with flour; place in roasting pan or on rack in open pan. Roast as directed (page 267), allowing 30 to 35 minutes per pound. Serve hot with Brown Gravy (page 291). Approximate yield: 6 portions.

SAUSAGE-STUFFED MUTTON CHOPS

2 navel oranges   6 link sausages
6 mutton chops   ¾ teaspoon salt

Grate rind from oranges and cut each into 3 thick slices. Bone chops and wrap each around a sausage; fasten securely with skewers. Place orange slices in greased baking pan with a stuffed chop on each and sprinkle with salt and grated orange rind. Bake in slow to moderate oven (325°–350° F.) 45 to 60 minutes. Yield: 6 portions.

BRAISED BREAST OF MUTTON

Breast may be cooked with or without boning; if shank is included, have butcher remove bone and excess fat and roll meat. Wipe meat with damp cloth, rub surface with salt and pepper and brown on all sides in a small amount of fat. Add 1 cup hot water and bake, covered, in slow oven (300° F.) 2 to 3 hours, or until meat is tender; add 1 small onion, sliced, the last half hour and bake uncovered. Serve with Brown Gravy made from drippings in pan (page 291). The boned breast may be stuffed with Celery Stuffing (page 485), if desired. Leg of mutton, with or without boning, may be braised in this way; additional vegetables such as carrots and turnips may be added. Allow ½ to ¾ pound per portion.

ITALIAN LAMB CUTLETS

6 lamb chops, ¼ inch thick
1 tablespoon chopped parsley
1 blade mace
6 tablespoons butter
1½ cups milk
½ cup dry bread crumbs
2 egg yolks

1 tablespoon water
1 tablespoon flour
1 tablespoon lemon juice
½ teaspoon salt
dash of pepper
3 cups green peas, cooked and
  seasoned

Use shoulder lamb chops (arm or blade). Add with parsley, mace and 2 tablespoons butter to milk and simmer, covered, 1 hour; drain and reserve milk mixture for gravy. Roll each chop in crumbs, dip in mixture of 1 egg yolk, slightly beaten with water, and roll again in crumbs; sauté in 2 tablespoons butter until browned on both sides and remove to heated platter. Gradually add milk to mixture of remaining 2 tablespoons butter and flour, stirring constantly, and cook 5 minutes, stirring until thickened; gradually stir into remaining egg yolk, slightly beaten; add lemon juice, seasonings; strain and pour over cutlets. Serve with well-seasoned peas. Yield: 6 portions.

LAMB CHOP CASSEROLE

12 small lamb chops
6 small tomatoes, peeled
6 small apples, peeled and cored

6 onions, peeled
18 raw potato balls
boiling water

Panbroil lamb chops until lightly browned; place 2 chops, 1 tomato, 1 apple, 1 onion and 3 potato balls in each of 6 heated individual casseroles. Add about 3 tablespoons water to each casserole, cover and bake in moderate oven (350° F.) about 45 minutes. Yield: 6 portions.

LAMB AND LIMA BEAN CASSEROLE

1½ pounds lamb or mutton
¼ cup flour
3 tablespoons drippings or
    bacon fat

1 cup water
1 teaspoon salt
⅛ teaspoon pepper
2 cups stewed tomatoes

2 cups fresh lima beans

Use meat from neck or breast; cut in 1 inch cubes, roll in flour and sauté in drippings until browned; add water and seasonings and simmer about 2 hours, or until meat is tender. Add tomatoes and beans, heat and turn into casserole; bake, covered, in moderate oven (350° F.) about ½ hour, or until beans are tender. Approximate yield: 6 portions.

COOKED LAMB OR MUTTON

Select a cut from shoulder or breast of lamb or mutton, or leg of mutton and trim. Cover meat with water and simmer, covered, until meat is tender, adding ½ teaspoon salt per pound of meat when half done. Simmer smaller cuts for 1½ to 2 hours; simmer leg for 3 to 3½ hours; use stock for soup. For variation add 1 bay leaf, 1 sprig of thyme and 2 peppercorns with salt to stock. Serve hot with Caper Sauce (page 478), or with brown gravy made from stock (page 291). Allow ½ to ¾ pound per portion.

YORKSHIRE LAMB HOTPOT

6 lamb shoulder chops
1½ tablespoons butter
4 cups milk, scalded
12 small white onions
12 small potatoes

½ teaspoon salt
⅛ teaspoon black pepper
2 tablespoons butter
2 tablespoons flour
parsley

Trim off excess fat from chops and brown in butter in heavy frying pan; add milk, onions, potatoes, salt and pepper, cover and simmer about ½ hour, or until vegetables are tender. Arrange chops, onions and potatoes on heated platter and serve with gravy made by gradually adding liquid in pan to roux of butter and flour, stirring constantly; garnish with parsley. Yield: 6 portions.

PORK—FRESH AND CURED

BRAISED PORK CHOPS

Use rib, loin or shoulder chops ¾ to 1 inch thick. Dredge chops in flour, if desired. Brown chops quickly on both sides in a heavy frying pan; if fat, hold fat edge down to cook out enough fat to grease pan; if lean, add about 1 tablespoon fat. Season, reduce heat, cover and cook slowly until chops are tender, turning occasionally. Do not add water. Allow 45 to 60 minutes for total braising.

Pork Chops with Orange—Braise chops as above. When done place on rack of broiler pan, top each chop with a slice of orange, brush with melted butter and broil until orange is browned lightly.

DEVILED PORK FILLETS

2 pork tenderloins, each cut in 6 pieces	1½ teaspoons Worcestershire sauce
salt and pepper	1 teaspoon prepared mustard
3 tablespoons butter	¼ teaspoon onion salt
2 tablespoons chili sauce	¼ teaspoon paprika
2 tablespoons ketchup	⅓ cup boiling water

Flatten pieces of tenderloin, sprinkle with salt and pepper and sauté in butter until browned and almost tender; then place in baking pan; add remaining ingredients to drippings and pour over meat. Bake in moderate oven (350° F.) 20 to 30 minutes. Yield: 6 portions.

FRENCHED PORK TENDERLOIN FILLETS

Cut tenderloin crosswise in 2 inch pieces; place each between pieces of waxed paper and flatten with wooden masher, mallet or back of meat tenderer. Sprinkle with salt, pepper and flour, sauté in butter until well browned. Add ½ cup light cream; simmer, covered, ½ hour, or until tender. Allow 1 to 2 pieces per portion.

TENDERLOIN ROLLS

2 pork tenderloins (about)	Potato Stuffing (page 489)
salt and pepper	6 strips bacon

Cut each tenderloin in 3 pieces about 4 inches long; split each lengthwise, being careful not to cut through; spread open, place between pieces of waxed paper and flatten with mallet. Sprinkle with salt and pepper, cover with stuffing, roll and tie securely; place in uncovered baking pan with bacon strip on each. Bake in slow to moderate oven (325°–350° F.) about 1 hour, or until tender. Yield: 6 portions.

CRANBERRY PORK CHOPS

6 pork chops   4 cups cranberries, ground
½ teaspoon salt   ¾ cup honey
                    ½ teaspoon cloves

Brown chops quickly on both sides in hot fat and sprinkle with salt;
place 3 chops in greased baking dish. Combine cranberries, honey and
cloves; spread ½ over chops in dish. Arrange remaining 3 chops on
top and cover with remaining cranberry mixture. Cover and bake in
slow to moderate oven (325°–350° F.) about 1½ hours. Yield: 6
portions.

PORK CHOPS WITH SAVORY STUFFING

6 loin chops, 1 inch thick   ¼ teaspoon paprika
1½ teaspoons salt   1½ cups milk, scalded
                Celery Stuffing (page 485)

Brown chops in heavy frying pan; place in large casserole, season with
salt and paprika and add hot milk. Bake, covered, in moderate oven
(350° F.) about 45 minutes. Cover each chop with stuffing and bake,
uncovered, ½ hour longer, or until stuffing is browned and milk
absorbed by chops. Yield: 6 portions.

PORK CHOPS WITH RED CABBAGE

4 thick pork chops   ½ lemon, chopped
all-purpose flour   ½ cup red wine
salt and pepper   ½ teaspoon caraway seeds
ginger   1 small head red cabbage,
mace   shredded
3 tablespoons drippings   2 tablespoons brown sugar
½ cup diced onion   2 tablespoons vinegar

Dredge chops with flour seasoned with salt, pepper, ginger and mace;
brown on both sides in 1 tablespoon drippings. Add onion, cover and
simmer until onion is lightly browned. Add lemon, wine and caraway
seeds. Cover and simmer 15 minutes, turning once or twice. Wilt cabbage in remaining drippings; add sugar, vinegar, salt and pepper, and
cover. Simmer 10 minutes. Spread over chops and simmer until tender.
Yield: 4 portions.

PORK CHOPS CASSEROLE

6 pork chops, ½ inch thick
1 teaspoon salt
⅛ teaspoon pepper
4 medium-sized sour apples,
  peeled and sliced
4 medium-sized sweet potatoes,
  peeled and sliced

1 cup water
1 teaspoon Worcestershire sauce
few drops Tabasco sauce
4 strips bacon
1 medium-sized onion, chopped

Brown chops in hot frying pan; place in casserole, sprinkle with half the salt and pepper and place apples and potatoes in layers on chops. Sprinkle with remaining salt and pepper and add water mixed with Worcestershire sauce and Tabasco. Fry bacon, remove and brown onion in bacon fat. Spread onions over mixture in casserole and arrange bacon strips on top; cover and bake in moderate oven (350° F.) about 1½ hours. Yield: 6 portions.

PORK CHOPS

Wipe 6 pork shoulder chops with damp cloth, sprinkle with salt and pepper and dust lightly with flour; sear quickly in hot fat in heavy pan or Dutch oven. Add ¼ teaspoon dried savory, 1 cup water, tomato juice or milk, and 1 small onion, minced; cover tightly and cook at simmering temperature on top of stove until tender, turning frequently; or bake, covered, in slow oven (300°–325° F.) about 40 minutes. Remove chops to heated platter, add liquid to drippings in pan to make 2 cups and thicken with a smooth mixture of 3 tablespoons flour and 3 tablespoons water. Season to taste and serve over chops. Yield: 6 portions.

ROAST PORK

Select cut from loin, ham, shoulder or butt (see Table XXI for information on cuts). Pork is always cooked thoroughly to the well-done stage. Wipe off roast, rub with salt and pepper. Place fat side up on rack in open roasting pan. A rack is not necessary for a loin roast. Insert a meat thermometer into the largest muscle so that the bulb is in the center and not touching fat or bone. Roast in a slow to moderate oven (300°–350° F.) until well done (meat thermometer registers 185° F. for interior of roast), or allow 30 to 40 minutes per pound (see Table XXII, page 273). Remove to heated platter and serve with gravy made from drippings (page 291). Allow ⅓ to ½ pound per portion.

CROWN PORK ROAST

Use rib section of two pork loins; see Crown Roast of Lamb (page 270) for directions. A 16 rib roast of pork will weigh about 4½ pounds. Sprinkle inside lightly with salt and pepper and fill center with Cranberry Stuffing (page 485). Roast in moderate oven (350° F.) until done, allowing 30 to 40 minutes per pound (page 30). Transfer to a hot platter, decorate tops of ribs with paper frills and garnish with radish roses and parsley. Use other stuffing as desired, or roast plain and fill center with mashed potatoes when ready to serve. Serve with gravy made from drippings (page 291). Approximate yield: 10 portions.

BAKED PORK TENDERLOIN

Split tenderloin lengthwise, being careful not to cut through; spread open, place between pieces of waxed paper and flatten with mallet. Sprinkle with salt and pepper, cover with 1 cup Bread Stuffing (page 484) mixed with ½ cup chopped apple, roll and tie securely; place in uncovered pan. Roast at 350° F., allowing 50 to 60 minutes. Serve with Cream or Brown Gravy (page 291). Approximate yield: 5 portions.

STUFFED FRESH HAM

1 fresh ham, 6 to 8 pounds   Mushroom Stuffing (page 487)
salt and pepper   2 cups sweet cider

Have ham boned at market; wipe with damp cloth and sprinkle lightly with salt and pepper. Fill with stuffing, roll and tie securely; place fat side up in uncovered roasting pan and insert meat thermometer into center of leg. Roast as directed (page 271), pouring cider over ham after ½ hour of baking; baste frequently with drippings and allow from 3 to 3½ hours for roasting or 30 to 35 minutes per pound. Serve with gravy made from drippings (page 291). Approximate yield: 12 portions.

BAKED SPARERIBS

Have butcher crack sheet or half sheet of spareribs through center to make carving easier. Wipe with damp cloth and sprinkle with salt and pepper; flour may be sprinkled lightly over surface. Place in shallow baking pan and roast as for Pork Roast (page 271), allowing about 1 hour for sheet of ribs and 1½ hours if stuffed and put together in pairs. Serve with Brown Gravy made from drippings in pan (page 291). Allow from ½ to ¾ pound per portion.

Stuffed Spareribs—Use two whole or half sheets of spareribs, or if one sheet is used have it cracked along both sides so that ends may be folded up over center piece. Place stuffing over sheet or center of sheet, using Onion Stuffing (page 487), Bread-Ham Stuffing (page 489) or any desired stuffing; put sheets together or fold sides up over center and sew together or tie.

Baked Spareribs with Sauerkraut—Serve baked spareribs with cooked sauerkraut (page 537). If desired, place sauerkraut over ribs when baked ¾ hour, cover and bake about ½ hour longer, adding a small amount of hot water if sauerkraut is dry. Use about 1 quart sauerkraut with 3 pounds spareribs.

SPARERIBS AND SAUERKRAUT

3 pounds spareribs, cut in pieces   water
½ teaspoon salt   4 cups sauerkraut, drained

Wipe spareribs, place in large kettle, add salt, cover with water and simmer, covered, ½ hour. Add sauerkraut, bring to a boil and cook, uncovered, ½ hour. Drain slightly and serve on heated platter. Approximate yield: 6 portions.

BARBECUED SPARERIBS

3 pounds spareribs   3 tablespoons horseradish
⅓ cup water   3 tablespoons Worcestershire
¾ cup vinegar   sauce
⅓ cup butter   ½ teaspoon salt
⅓ cup chili sauce   dash of cayenne

Crack rib bones across middle. Arrange sheets with meaty side up in large shallow pan. Place in preheated hot oven (450° F.) 20 minutes to sear meat. Reduce heat quickly to moderately slow (300°–325° F.), baste generously with hot barbecue sauce made by combining remaining ingredients and roast slowly until ribs are well done (1 hour), brown and crisp, basting occasionally with sauce and turning sheets several times. Serve on heated platter with barbecue sauce poured over meat. Approximate yield: 6 portions.

ROAST SUCKLING PIG

1 suckling pig, about 10 lb.   hot water
Sage or Onion Stuffing   ¼ cup butter
    (page 487)   1 bunch water cress
carrot   1 small red apple
salt   2 cranberries

Choose suckling pig not more than 5 or 6 weeks old; have butcher clean it thoroughly; rinse inside and dry. Fill inside loosely with stuffing, then sew securely, tie legs in place and put pig in kneeling position or with forelegs ahead and hindlegs back in roasting pan. Place raw carrot in mouth to keep it open. Sprinkle with salt, pour about 1 cup hot water in bottom of pan and lay a piece of cooking parchment or greased heavy paper over pig. Roast in moderately slow oven (325°–350° F.) about 3½ hours, basting frequently with butter, hot water and drippings to keep skin from cracking. Remove paper ½ hour before meat is done. Baste with dripping and dust with flour to brown surface. Put pig in kneeling position on hot platter on bed of water cress; place apple in mouth and cranberries in eye sockets. To carve pig, cut at right angles to backbone down to the bone, making cuts about 1 inch apart. Run the knife along the backbone and under meat to loosen, then lift off each piece onto a heated platter or plate. Approximate yield: 10 portions.

BROILED HAM

Cut rind off slice of smoked ham and cut edges of fat in several places to prevent curling; lay on rack in broiling pan and broil at moderate heat (350° F.) 10 to 30 minutes according to thickness of slice, turning frequently. Allow 10 minutes for slice ¼ inch thick; 15 to 20 minutes for slice ½ to ¾ inch thick; and 20 to 30 minutes for slice 1 inch thick. Tenderized ham slices require from ⅓ to ½ less time. Serve with broiled pineapple and sweet potato slices, or with sautéed apples if desired. Allow ¼ to ⅓ pound per portion.

FRIED HAM

Trim rind off slice of smoked ham. Rub moderately hot heavy frying pan with ham fat and brown slice on both sides. Reduce heat and cover; cook slowly until tender, turning several times. Allow about 10 minutes for slice ¼ inch thick; 15 to 20 minutes for slice ½ to ¾ inch thick; and 20 to 30 minutes for slice 1 inch thick.

HAM WITH CREAM GRAVY

Brown 1 large slice of smoked ham, ¾ inch thick, on both sides and pour off fat; cover ham with 2 cups Thin White Sauce (page 125) seasoned only with 1 teaspoon sugar and ½ teaspoon dry mustard and simmer, covered, 1½ hours, turning occasionally. Add milk as needed to keep ham nearly covered. Approximate yield: 6 portions.

HAM CUTLETS WITH APPLE RINGS

3 slices ham, ½ inch thick	¾ cup pineapple juice
6 tablespoons brown sugar	3 apples, cored
3 tablespoons bread crumbs	3 tablespoons fat

Cut slices of ham in halves; precook 10 minutes and place over bottom of baking pan. Cover pieces with brown sugar and sprinkle with bread crumbs; pour pineapple juice over all. Bake, uncovered, in moderate oven (350° F.) about 25 minutes, basting occasionally. Cut apples in rings and sauté in fat until lightly browned; serve with ham. Add French fried onions, if desired. Yield: 6 portions.

Ham Cutlets with Apricots—Substitute 1½ cups dried apricots for apples; soak apricots in hot water 20 minutes, place around ham slices in baking pan and bake as directed.

Ham Cutlets with Pineapple—Substitute 6 canned pineapple slices for apples. Arrange slices on top of ham when nearly done. Sprinkle with additional brown sugar, dot with 2 tablespoons butter and continue baking about 15 minutes, or until pineapple is glazed.

BAKED HAM WITH GINGER PEARS

1 cup water	½ cup chopped preserved ginger
½ cup granulated sugar	3 pears
1½ teaspoons grated lemon rind	1 slice ham, 2½ pounds
3 tablespoons lemon juice	¼ cup firmly packed brown sugar

Mix together water, granulated sugar, lemon rind and juice, and ginger; boil 5 minutes; add pears, pared, halved and cored, and cook 5 minutes longer. Place ham in large casserole, rub well with brown sugar, pour ½ of pear-ginger syrup around it and bake in moderate oven (350° F.) about 20 minutes, basting frequently with syrup; arrange pear halves around ham and continue baking for 20 to 25 minutes. Approximate yield: 6 portions.

HAM LOAF

1½ pounds lean smoked ham,
   ground
¾ pound lean fresh pork, ground
1½ cups soft bread crumbs
1½ teaspoons Worcestershire
   sauce

⅛ teaspoon pepper
1 egg
1 cup milk
flour
6 medium-sized potatoes

Mix together meats, crumbs, seasonings, egg and milk; shape in loaf, place in greased roaster and sprinkle with flour. Place potatoes, parboiled 10 minutes, around roast and bake in moderate oven (350° F.) about 1 hour, or until browned, turning potatoes several times during baking. Approximate yield: 6 portions.

HAM, COUNTRY STYLE

Brown 1 large slice of ham, 1½ inches thick, on both sides; add 1 large onion, chopped, 6 carrots, sliced, 2 tablespoons raisins, 6 thin strips orange peel and 1 cup water, cover and simmer 1½ hours. Mix 1 tablespoon flour and ½ cup orange juice to a smooth paste; add to ham and liquid and cook 5 minutes, stirring until thickened. Serve immediately. Approximate yield: 6 portions.

BARBECUED HAM AU VIN

8 to 10 small slices ham, ½ inch
   thick
1½ tablespoons prepared
   mustard
½ teaspoon black pepper

¼ cup vinegar
1½ tablespoons flour
1 cup water
½ cup red or white wine
1 teaspoon sugar

If ham is strongly cured, soak in milk or water 2 hours before preparation; dry slices. Spread each slice with mustard on both sides and sprinkle with pepper. Rub heavy frying pan with ham fat and brown slices on both sides. Add vinegar, cover and simmer about 20 minutes; remove ham to hot platter. Stir flour into drippings in pan; gradually add water and cook and stir until sauce is smooth; add wine and sugar and simmer 5 minutes longer. Strain sauce over ham and serve at once. Approximate yield: 8 to 10 portions.

SPANISH HAM

1 large slice smoked ham, ¾ inch thick	1 tablespoon flour
	2 teaspoons dry mustard
3 tablespoons brown sugar	boiling water
	¼ cup milk

Spread ham with mixture of sugar, flour and mustard, place in heavy frying pan and pour ¾ cup boiling water over it; cover and simmer 1 hour, turning occasionally. Add water as needed and pour milk over ham 10 minutes before serving. If ham is salty or strongly cured, pre-cook for 10 minutes before using. Yield: 6 portions.

UPSIDE-DOWN HAM LOAF

3 tablespoons butter	½ pound fresh lean pork, ground
5 tablespoons brown sugar	½ cup soft bread crumbs
3 slices canned pineapple, halved	¼ teaspoon pepper
1 pound lean smoked ham, ground	2 eggs, beaten
	¼ cup milk

Melt butter in loaf pan and add brown sugar, stirring until dissolved; add pineapple and sauté 5 minutes, or until slightly browned. Mix meats with remaining ingredients; spread in pan over pineapple sections and press down. Bake in moderate oven (350° F.) about 1 hour. Turn out on hot platter with pineapple on top. Yield: 6 portions.

"BOILED" HAM

Scrub high-grade smoked ham with stiff brush or scrape thoroughly, rinse and place, rind side up, in large kettle; soak strongly cured hams several hours or overnight, then cook. Add water to cover and simmer, partially covered, 25 to 30 minutes per pound, or until meat is tender. To use meat thermometer, insert as for Baked Ham (page 321), place ham in kettle so thermometer extends above water and can be read, and simmer until it registers 170° F. for inside of meat (tenderized hams, 160° F.). If served cold, cool ham in stock overnight in cool place, then peel off rind; if served hot, let it stand in stock until ready to serve. A 12 pound ham requires from 5 to 6 hours; water should be kept below boiling point at simmering temperature (about 180° F.).

BAKED HAM

Place well scrubbed, high-grade smoked ham, rind side up, in uncovered roaster or pan; make an incision through rind with pointed knife or steel skewer and insert meat thermometer so that bulb is in the center of the thickest part of ham. Bake, uncovered, in slow oven (300° F.) until thermometer registers 160°–170° F. for inside of ham, or allow 20 to 30 minutes per pound, according to size and part of ham baked; large hams require 15 to 18 minutes; average or 10 to 12 pound hams, 18 to 22 minutes; and half hams, about 25 to 30 minutes per pound. Allow from 35 to 40 minutes per pound for shank ends and picnic butts. One half hour before meat is done, remove rind from ham, cover with about 1½ cups brown sugar, stick whole cloves into surface (1 inch apart) and pour ¼ cup cider or vinegar over ham; continue baking, basting twice with drippings. Serve hot with Raisin Sauce (page 476) or any desired sauce. Allow ¼ to ⅓ pound per portion.

TENDER HAMS

If a ham is a special process ham and graded "tender" by the packer, it should be prepared according to directions on the label or by following the general directions for cooking ham. These hams may be simmered until tender or baked without precooking. Warm the ham to room temperature if taken from the refrigerator. These special hams should be cooked to an internal temperature of 160° F. Allow 15 to 22 minutes per pound according to size: For 15 pounds and over, 15 minutes; 12 to 15 pounds, 17 minutes; 10 to 12 pounds, 18 minutes; under 10 pounds, 20 minutes; half hams, 22 minutes.

BAKED VIRGINIA HAM

1 Virginia ham, about 8 pounds	¼ cup whole cloves
1½ cups flour	1 quart sweet cider
water	¾ cup lemon juice
1 cup firmly packed brown sugar	½ cup orange juice

Soak strongly cured ham 24 hours, drain and dry. Mix flour with water to make a smooth thick paste; rub over ham, wrap in cheesecloth and sew tightly. Cover with water and simmer 3 hours. Cool ham overnight in stock; drain and remove cloth, dough and rind and place in uncovered baking pan or roaster. Rub surface with brown sugar, stud with cloves and pour cider over all. Bake in moderate slow oven (300°–325° F.) 1½ to 2 hours; baste occasionally with cider in pan; pour lemon and orange juice over ham the last half hour. Serve with sauce made from juices in pan. Yield: 20 portions.

CRANBERRY–GLAZED HAM

1 smoked ham, 8 to 10 pounds   1 quart Cranberry Sauce
2 dozen long-stemmed whole   (page 95)
   cloves

Precook well-scrubbed ham 1 hour (page 320); drain, wrap in cooking parchment and place in baking pan or roaster. Bake, uncovered, in slow oven (300° F.) about 2½ hours; remove paper and rind, score fat with sharp knife, stud with cloves and return to baking pan. Strain cranberry sauce and pour half over ham; bake 1 hour longer and pour remaining sauce over ham just before serving. Approximate yield: 25 to 30 portions.

DIRECTIONS FOR SCORING HAM

After ham is almost done, remove from oven and with a sharp paring knife remove all rind carefully. Don't break or tear the fat. Pour off all drippings to save for seasoning and panfrying later. Turn the oven to hot (400° F.). Now mark off one-inch spaces with toothpicks at both sides of ham. With a long thin knife, start at the butt end and cut from one marker to the one on the other side, making a diagonal cut. Don't cut too deep—about ⅛ inch is enough. Continue making cuts an inch apart on the same slant as the first cut, until the entire surface is scored. Plan the slant of the second set of diagonal lines, cutting across ham surface to make uniform diamonds. Cut from one toothpick marker on one side to the selected marker at opposite side.

A little planning makes this scoring in diamond shapes a work of art. The slashes should be uniformly deep, but don't cut too deep or the surface will split open.

Glazing—Next, drizzle honey over the entire scored surface. Then sift brown sugar uniformly over the honey. Return the ham (on the rack in the open pan) to the hot oven. Bake 15 to 20 minutes until beautifully glossy and brown. If necessary, add more honey and sifted sugar to any spots that do not brown uniformly. This glazing process requires close attention but professionally perfect results are well worth the effort. See page 321 for other glazes.

BARBECUED HAM

6 thin slices boiled ham   ¼ teaspoon dry mustard
2 tablespoons butter   dash of salt
1 tablespoon vinegar   dash of pepper

Sauté ham in butter until slightly browned; spread with mixture of vinegar and seasonings, and cook 2 minutes longer. Yield: 6 portions.

BROILED BACON

Place thin slices of bacon on rack in broiling pan and broil at moderate heat (350° F.) until light brown and crisp, turning frequently. Or place on rack, in dripping pan, and bake in moderate oven (350° F.) until light brown and crisp, turning frequently.

PANBROILED BACON

Place bacon in cold frying pan so that slices are straight and do not overlap. Cook slowly until light brown and crisp, turning frequently and pouring off fat from pan as it accumulates. Remove slices as soon as crisp to absorbent or unglazed paper and keep hot.

Bacon Curls—Panbroil thin slices of bacon, shaping each slice with two forks into a spiral or curl as it browns. Drain on absorbent paper.

Canadian Bacon—Canadian-style bacon is also called English or Irish bacon; panbroil thin slices; if very lean, fry bacon in its own fat or in a small amount of butter.

Fried Bacon and Pineapple Rings—Panbroil bacon and drain; dip cooked pineapple slices in seasoned flour and sauté in bacon fat until browned. Serve two slices of crisp bacon with each pineapple ring.

IRISH BACON ROLLS

12 slices Irish or Canadian   **½ recipe Raisin and Nut Stuffing**
bacon, ¼ inch thick   **(page 486)**
                    ¾ cup tomato juice

Spread slices of bacon with stuffing, roll and hold in place with toothpicks; place rolls in cupcake pans, laying one in each section. Pour 1 tablespoon tomato juice over each and bake in moderate oven (350° F.) 45 minutes. Yield: 12 rolls or 6 portions.

FRIED SALT PORK

Use mild-flavored salt pork; cut in thin slices and gash rind in several places. Fry in heavy frying pan at moderate heat until crisp and browned, turning frequently and removing fat as it accumulates; drain and keep hot on hot plate. Serve with Medium White Sauce made with pork drippings instead of butter (page 125). Slices may be rolled in mixture of equal parts cornmeal and flour before frying, if desired. Crisp pieces of pork and part of pork drippings may be used for flavoring green vegetables and soups. Allow ¼ pound pork and ¼ cup white sauce for an average portion.

FRIED SAUSAGE CAKES

Shape sausage meat into flat cakes; panbroil 20 to 30 minutes, pouring off fat as it accumulates; drain on absorbent paper; or bake, uncovered, in moderate oven (350° F.) about ½ hour. One pound makes 8 cakes.

FRIED COUNTRY SAUSAGE MEAT

3¾ pounds lean pork, ground
1¼ pounds fat pork, ground
3½ teaspoons salt
1 teaspoon black pepper
1 to 2 teaspoons powdered sage

Mix lean and fat pork thoroughly; stir in seasonings and store in refrigerator at least 12 hours before using. Panbroil or fry until thoroughly cooked. Approximate yield: 5 pounds sausage meat.

SAUSAGE LOAF

1 pound sausage meat
1 pound lean beef, ground
½ cup dry bread crumbs
1 teaspoon salt
¼ teaspoon pepper
1 teaspoon sage
2 eggs, beaten
¼ cup light cream

Mix all ingredients thoroughly; shape into loaf and bake, uncovered, in moderate oven (350° F.) about 1 hour. This may be served with a cream sauce. Approximate yield: 1 loaf, 8½ x 4½ x 2½ inches, or 6 portions.

SAUSAGE BISCUITS

2 cups prepared biscuit mix
milk or water
18 or 20 Vienna or cocktail sausages, cooked

Combine biscuit mix and milk as directed on package; roll ¼ inch thick and cut in 3 inch rounds; place sausage on each and fold over. Bake in hot oven (450° F.) about 15 minutes. Approximate yield: 18 small biscuits.

To cook over campfire coals, measure ⅓ cup mix into individual paper cups and add liquid to make a soft dough; put sausage on end of green stick or fork and dip it into dough until well coated. Toast slowly over campfire coals until a delicate brown; allow 10 to 12 minutes.

SAUSAGES

Separate link sausages and prick with fork, panbroil or bake as for Fried Sausage Cakes (page 324); or place sausage links and 2 tablespoons water in a cold frying-pan. Cover and cook slowly 8 to 10 minutes. Remove cover and brown links. Remove links. Serve on toast fingers with fried bananas, apples or pineapples, with fried or scrambled eggs, or with griddle cakes or waffles.

FRANKFURTERS OR WIENERS

Frankfurters or wieners may be simmered, broiled or fried. Drop into boiling water, cover and simmer 5 to 10 minutes; split and broil in moderately hot broiler 8 to 10 minutes; or split and fry in small amount of butter or other fat until browned on both sides. Spread with ketchup or mustard and serve in split and buttered long rolls, if desired.

BROILED STUFFED FRANKFURTERS

6 frankfurters   6 strips bacon
              Bread Stuffing (page 484)

Split frankfurters lengthwise; open and spread with stuffing; close, wrap each with bacon and fasten with toothpicks. Broil under medium heat 8 to 10 minutes, turning frequently to brown and crisp bacon. Yield: 6 portions.

FRANKFURTER CASSEROLE

8 frankfurters   3 cups canned tomatoes
1 medium-sized onion, minced   3 cups diced, cooked carrots
¼ cup butter   3 tablespoons ketchup
⅓ cup flour   salt and pepper

Split frankfurters and arrange, split side down, in greased casserole. Sauté onion in butter until slightly browned, stir in flour; gradually stir in tomatoes and cook until thickened. Add carrots and ketchup and season to taste with salt and pepper; pour over frankfurters and bake in moderate oven (350° F.) about ½ hour. Yield: 6 portions.

CURRY OF LAMB OR MUTTON

2 pounds lean lamb	¼ cup flour
2 teaspoons salt	2 teaspoons curry powder
⅛ teaspoon pepper	3 cups hot lamb stock
6 tablespoons butter	3 tablespoons lemon juice
1 cup water	¼ cup shredded coconut
1½ cups chopped onion	4 cups hot cooked rice, seasoned

Use meat from shoulder, chuck or breast; cut in 1 inch squares, sprinkle with salt and pepper and sauté slowly in 2 tablespoons butter in large pan (or Dutch oven) until lightly browned, turning frequently. Add water and simmer, covered, 1 hour. Sauté onions slowly in remaining ¼ cup butter until light yellow, stir in flour and brown slightly; add curry powder, then add stock gradually and cook until thickened, stirring constantly. Pour over meat and mix well; cover and simmer about ½ hour, or until meat is tender; add lemon juice and coconut. Arrange border of rice on round or chop plate and fill center with curried meat. If desired, 3 cups hot water and 2 beef bouillon cubes may be substituted for stock.

CURRY OF VEAL

1 small onion, chopped	2 tablespoons curry powder
2 tablespoons chopped green pepper	2 cups veal stock
	salt and pepper
3 tablespoons fat	2 cups diced, cooked veal
3 tablespoons flour	2 cups Boiled Rice (page 507)

Sauté onion and green pepper in fat slowly 10 minutes; stir in flour and curry powder and add stock gradually, stirring until thickened. Season to taste, add veal, cover and simmer about 5 minutes. Serve over boiled rice. Approximate yield: 6 portions.

MOCK CHICKEN CURRY

1½ pounds breast or neck of veal	2 tablespoons flour
water	½ teaspoon curry powder
1 teaspoon salt	¼ cup cold water
	1 tablespoon chopped parsley
3 cups boiled rice	

Wipe veal and cut in small pieces; cover with water and simmer, covered, about 2 hours, or until tender, adding salt when half done. Thicken stock with a smooth paste of flour, curry powder and water. Add parsley and serve with a border of rice. Yield: 6 portions.

APPLE CURRY

1 pound stewing lamb, without bone	1 teaspoon paprika
	½ teaspoon powdered ginger
3 tablespoons fat	¼ teaspoon sugar
¾ cup finely chopped onion	¼ teaspoon chili powder
1 clove garlic, minced	1 6-ounce can tomato paste
1 teaspoon curry powder (more optional)	2 cups chopped apple
	salt to taste

Cut lamb in 1-inch pieces. Melt fat in skillet and sauté onion and garlic until golden brown. Add curry powder, paprika, ginger, sugar and chili powder; cook until brown. Add lamb and brown on all sides. Add tomato paste and enough boiling water to cover. Cover and cook 20 minutes, or until meat is tender. Add apple and salt to taste; cook 10 minutes longer. Yield: 4 servings.

LEFTOVER MEATS
SHEPHERD'S PIE

1½ cups seasoned vegetables	celery salt
1½ cups diced cold meat	1 cup gravy
¼ teaspoon salt	2 cups hot Mashed Potatoes
dash of pepper	(page 564)

Use leftover cooked vegetables such as diced carrots and celery, lima beans and sliced onions; heat and put in greased hot casserole. Use leftover cooked meat such as beef, veal, lamb or pork; season, heat in gravy and turn out over vegetables. Cover with layer of mashed potatoes and bake in hot oven (425° F.) about 15 minutes, or until potatoes are browned. Approximate yield: 6 portions.

HAM AND CHEESE PIE

1 cup sliced, cooked carrots	1¼ cups Medium White Sauce
1 cup sliced, cooked potatoes	(page 125)
1 tablespoon minced celery	⅛ teaspoon paprika
1½ cups coarsely chopped boiled ham	½ recipe Cheese Pastry
	(page 198)

Arrange the 3 vegetables and ham in layers in greased 8 inch casserole. Prepare white sauce, omitting salt and adding paprika; add to filled casserole. Cover with pastry rolled ⅛ inch thick; moisten edge of casserole with water; press down crust and prick with fork to permit escape of steam. Bake in hot oven (425° F.) about 25 minutes. Approximate yield: 6 portions.

MEAT FRITTERS

2 cups sifted all-purpose flour   1½ cups milk
2 teaspoons baking powder   2 tablespoons cranberry juice
1 teaspoon salt   ¾ cup diced, cooked meat
1 tablespoon sugar   1 slice broiled bacon, chopped
1 egg, beaten   1 tablespoon chopped celery

Sift together dry ingredients; gradually add combined egg, milk and cranberry juice, beating until smooth; stir in meat, bacon and celery. Drop from tablespoon into hot deep fat (365°–375° F.) and fry 2 to 3 minutes, or until golden brown; serve hot. Any leftover meat may be used. Approximate yield: 20 fritters.

PORK LOAF

1½ cups dry bread crumbs   2 apples, pared, cored and minced
½ cup milk   1 medium-sized onion, minced
2 eggs, beaten   ½ teaspoon salt
3 cups ground, cooked pork   dash of pepper
⅛ teaspoon thyme

Mix crumbs, milk and eggs and allow to stand ½ hour. Mix together pork, apples and onion, or put through food chopper; stir in seasonings and soaked crumbs and pack into loaf pan. Bake in moderate oven (350° F.) about 35 minutes. Yield: 1 loaf, 8½ x 4½ x 2½ inches, or 8 portions.

HAM TIMBALES

¾ cup milk, scalded   ¼ cup soft bread crumbs
2 eggs, slightly beaten   1½ cups ground, boiled ham
1 tablespoon fat   dash of paprika
Tomato Sauce (page 469)

Stir milk gradually into beaten eggs, add fat, bread crumbs, ham and paprika and turn into well-buttered heated custard cups or timbale molds. Place molds in pan of hot water and bake in moderate oven (350° F.) about ½ hour, or until knife inserted comes out clean. Serve with tomato sauce. Approximate yield: 6 portions.

MEAT CROQUETTES

2 cups ground, cooked meat	1 teaspoon ketchup
1 cup Thick White Sauce	flour
(page 125)	1 egg, slightly beaten
1 teaspoon chopped onion or	1 tablespoon milk or water
parsley	dry bread crumbs

Use any leftover cooked meat such as beef, veal, lamb, mutton, pork, chicken or turkey. Prepare white sauce, substituting ½ cup meat stock for ½ cup milk, if desired; stir in meat and seasonings and chill thoroughly. Shape in pyramids, cylinders, balls or small cutlets; roll in flour, then dip in egg mixed with milk and roll in crumbs; chill. Fry in hot deep fat (365°–385° F.) 2 to 5 minutes, or until browned. Approximate yield: 1 dozen small croquettes.

PORK WITH MUSHROOM SAUCE

2 tablespoons fat	salt and pepper
3 tablespoons flour	4 hard-cooked eggs, chopped
½ cup water	2 cups diced, cooked pork
2 cups condensed mushroom	1 tablespoon chopped parsley
soup	paprika

Mix fat and flour in large frying pan; gradually stir in water and soup and cook until thickened; season with salt and pepper to taste, add eggs, pork and parsley and turn into greased baking dish. Sprinkle with paprika and bake in hot oven (400° F.) about 10 minutes; or cook over low heat in frying pan about 15 minutes to heat thoroughly. Serve in baking dish or heated deep platter. Approximate yield: 6 portions.

PORK AND APPLE CASSEROLE

6 medium-sized apples	¾ teaspoon salt
⅓ cup water	⅓ cup firmly packed brown sugar
2 cups diced, cooked pork	¾ cup soft bread crumbs

Peel, core and slice apples; add water and cook, covered, until soft. Place half of pork in bottom of casserole, sprinkle with ¼ teaspoon salt and add half of applesauce and brown sugar; repeat, using remaining ingredients. Top with bread crumbs and bake in moderate oven (350° F.) about ½ hour. Approximate yield: 6 portions.

LAMB SOUFFLÉ

1 cup Thick White Sauce (page 125)

2 eggs, separated
1½ cups cold minced lamb

Remove white sauce from heat and stir in beaten yolks and lamb; cool slightly, then fold in stiffly beaten egg whites. Turn into medium baking dish with bottom greased; place in pan of hot water; bake in moderate oven (350° F.) 45 to 50 minutes, or until delicately browned and firm to touch; serve at once. Approximate yield: 6 portions.

BAKED HAM AND EGG MOLDS

2 cups finely ground cooked ham, tongue or corned beef
2 cups grated American cheese

6 eggs
1 tablespoon butter
paprika

Combine ham and cheese; line greased large muffin pans, using ⅔ of mixture. Break an egg carefully into each cup; place a narrow bar made of remaining ham-cheese mixture across center of each cup. Bake in moderate oven (350° F.) about 15 minutes; remove from oven, dot each egg yolk with butter, sprinkle with paprika and bake 10 minutes longer, or until eggs are firm. Yield: 6 portions .

PINEAPPLE VEAL PATTIES

2 cups chopped, cooked veal
⅔ cup fine cracker crumbs
½ teaspoon salt
1 teaspoon minced onion
1 egg, slightly beaten

6 slices canned pineapple
3 tablespoons butter
5 tablespoons brown sugar
⅛ teaspoon cloves
¼ cup pineapple juice

Mix together veal, crumbs, salt, onion and egg; shape in 6 patties, put one on each pineapple slice and place in greased baking dish. Heat butter, sugar, cloves and pineapple juice and pour over patties. Bake, covered, in moderate oven (350° F.) about 40 minutes, basting occasionally. Yield: 6 portions.

ROAST VEAL CUTLETS

2 cups ground, cooked veal
2 cups cooked rice
1 cup Thick White Sauce (page 125)
6 stuffed olives, minced

1 teapoon salt
1 egg, beaten
1 cup dry bread crumbs
¼ cup fat
Tomato Sauce (page 469)

Thoroughly mix veal with rice, white sauce, olives, salt and egg. Shape in cutlets and roll in bread crumbs. Sauté in fat in heavy frying pan until lightly browned on both sides; cover pan and cook slowly 10 minutes. Serve with tomato sauce. Yield: 6 portions.

MEAT SHORTCAKE

Prepare Baking Powder Biscuits (page 149); split and spread with butter. Put halves together with hot creamed meat between and over tops. Garnish with sliced egg and serve hot. To cream the meat, prepare 1½ cups Medium White Sauce (page 125); add ½ cup leftover gravy, 2 teaspoons Worcestershire sauce, 2 cups diced cooked beef, veal, lamb or pork; heat thoroughly and keep hot. Yield: 6 portions.

MOCK SWEETBREADS

1 pound cooked veal	½ cup milk
¼ pound salt pork	½ teaspoon salt
⅔ cup soft bread crumbs	⅛ teaspoon pepper
⅓ cup flour	1 tablespoon butter
1 egg, beaten	½ cup water

Grind leftover veal and pork; mix with crumbs, flour, egg, milk, salt and pepper and shape into 8 oval patties. Place in baking dish, dot with butter and pour water around meat. Cover and bake in moderate oven (350° F.) about 40 minutes, basting twice. Yield: 8 patties.

CORNED BEEF HASH

2¼ cups chopped, cooked corned beef or 1 can (12 oz.)	¼ cup chopped onion
2¼ cups chopped, cooked potatoes	⅓ cup stock, cream or rich milk
	salt and pepper
	2 tablespoons butter or margarine
	parsley

Mix together beef, potatoes, onion and stock and season to taste. Add to butter in hot frying pan, spreading evenly over bottom; cook slowly until browned on bottom. Fold over as for omelet, serve on hot platter and garnish with parsley. Yield: 6 portions.

CORNED BEEF HASH WITH EGG

Use recipe for Corned Beef Hash (above), or use 2 cans (1¼ lbs.) corned beef hash. Chill beef-potato-stock mixture or canned hash 1 hour; then divide into 6 equal parts, shape into balls with back of a spoon and make a depression or deep well in top of each. Place in greased baking pan or casserole and break an egg into each depression; dot with butter and sprinkle with salt and pepper. Bake, covered, in slow oven (325° F.) 25 to 30 minutes, or until eggs are set. Serve on hot platter and garnish with parsley. Yield: 6 portions.

SOUTHERN BEEF HASH

Use recipe for Corned Beef Hash (page 331); substitute roast beef for corned beef and add 1 cooked beet, chopped, to mixture; use 1 egg, slightly beaten with 1 tablespoon milk for liquid. Brown as directed. Approximate yield: 6 portions.

HAM CASSEROLE

¼ pound American cheese, chopped
1½ cups Thin White Sauce (page 125)

2 cups Boiled Macaroni (page 499)
1½ cups chopped, cooked ham
4 hard-cooked eggs, sliced
½ cup bread crumbs, buttered

Add cheese to white sauce and stir until cheese is melted. Put 1 cup macaroni in bottom of greased casserole, sprinkle with ¾ cup ham, cover with layer of egg slices and pour ½ of cheese sauce over top. Repeat, arranging remaining ingredients in layers; cover with buttered crumbs. Bake in moderate oven (350° F.) about ½ hour, or until crumbs are well browned. Approximate yield: 6 portions.

LAMB WITH OLIVES

½ recipe Baking Powder Biscuits (page 149)

2 cups lamb gravy
6 slices cooked lamb
½ cup sliced, stuffed olives

Prepare biscuit dough and bake biscuits as directed. Heat lamb gravy, adding water if too thick; add lamb and olives and heat thoroughly. Arrange on heated platter and border with hot biscuits; serve at once. Yield: 6 portions.

VEAL TERRAPIN

1 cup Thin White Sauce (page 125)
3 cups chopped cooked veal

3 hard-cooked eggs, chopped
1 teaspoon lemon juice
1 tablespoon Worcestershire sauce
3 cups Cooked Rice (page 507)

Prepare white sauce with thin cream or evaporated milk; add veal and egg and heat thoroughly. Just before serving, add lemon juice and Worcestershire sauce; serve with a border of rice. Yield: 6 portions.

VARIETY MEATS

COOKED BRAINS

Brains of calf, lamb, pork and beef may be used (see Table XXIII, for information); wash, remove membrane and soak in cold salted water about ½ hour. Rinse, cover with water, add 1 teaspoon salt and 1 tablespoon vinegar or lemon juice, cover and simmer 20 to 25 minutes. Drain and serve with Drawn Butter (page 471) or Lemon Butter (page 200). To slice and sauté brains, plunge cooked brains into cold water to make firm, then drain, dry and place under light weight. Allow 1 pair small brains per portion.

SCRAMBLED BRAINS

brains, cooked (page 333)	1 tablespoon Worcestershire sauce
4 hard-cooked eggs, chopped	2 tablespoons ketchup
¼ cup butter	1 teaspoon salt
2 eggs, slightly beaten	¼ teaspoon pepper
buttered hot toast	

Use 1 pair of beef brains, 2 pairs calves' or pork brains, or 4 pairs lambs' brains; cut brains in small cubes and add with cooked eggs to melted butter in large frying pan. Mix beaten eggs with seasonings, pour over brain mixture and cook slowly, stirring enough to scramble. Serve on toast. Approximate yield: 6 portions.

BRAINS À LA KING

3 calves' brains, cooked (page 333)	2 tablespoons butter
1 green pepper, chopped	1 pimiento, chopped
¼ cup diced celery	1 cup Medium White Sauce (page 125)
2 tablespoons grated onion	salt and pepper
6 slices toast or patty shells	

Cut brains in small cubes. Sauté green pepper, celery and onion in butter until lightly browned; add with brains and pimiento to white sauce, heat and season to taste. Serve on toast or in patty shells. One half cup chopped mushrooms may be substituted for green pepper, celery and onion; sauté in butter and add to white sauce. Sprinkle servings with paprika. Yield: 6 portions.

BRAINS AND BACON

3 calves' brains, cooked   1 teaspoon salt
   (page 333)   ¼ teaspoon pepper
¾ cup milk   ¼ cup flour
             6 slices bacon

Cut each half of brains in 3 or 4 slices, dip in milk and drain 2 minutes; then dredge with seasoned flour. Panbroil bacon until crisp; drain on absorbent paper and keep warm. Sauté prepared brain slices slowly in bacon fat until well browned on both sides; serve with broiled bacon. Yield: 6 portions.

BRAISED CALVES' HEARTS

Remove veins and arteries from 2 calves' hearts, wash in warm water and cut crosswise in ½ inch slices. Wipe dry, sprinkle with salt, pepper and flour and brown on both sides in bacon fat; add ½ cup water, tomato juice or sour cream, cover and simmer about 1 hour, or until tender, turning frequently. Serve with crisp bacon and broiled tomatoes. Approximate yield: 6 portions.

COOKED HEART

Use beef, calf, lamb or pork heart, remove large arteries and veins and wash thoroughly in warm water. Soak beef heart in buttermilk or sour milk overnight, if desired. Nearly cover with water to which 1 teaspoon of salt for each quart of water has been added. Simmer, covered, 3 to 4 hours for beef, 2½ to 3 hours for calf, lamb and pork heart. Remove gristle and fat, slice crosswise and serve with gravy made from stock (page 291); or chop and serve on buttered hot toast. Allow about ½ pound heart per portion.

STUFFED CALVES' HEARTS

Prepare 2 calves' hearts for cooking. Fill cavities with plain Bread Stuffing (page 484), highly seasoned with sage; sew and tie securely. Roll in seasoned flour, sear in hot fat until well browned and place in deep baking dish. Pour 1 cup water into frying pan, bring to a boil and pour over hearts, adding additional water to half cover meat; cover and bake in slow oven (325° F.) about 2 hours, or until tender. Place heart on hot platter and serve with gravy made from stock (page 291). Carve crosswise in ½ inch slices. Approximate yield: 6 portions.

STUFFED HEART WITH FRUIT

Sprinkle cavity of prepared beef heart with salt and fill with mixture of ½ cup dried prunes, soaked and pitted, and ½ cup dried apricots, soaked. Brown in fat, add water to half cover and bake, covered, at 325° F. 2½ to 3½ hours. Approximate yield: 8 portions.

HEART WITH VEGETABLE STUFFING

Stuff 1 beef or 2 calves' hearts with Vegetable Stuffing (page 486). Sear and bake as directed above, adding ½ pound mushrooms, peeled, to liquor in casserole the last 15 minutes of baking. Arrange mushrooms around heart and serve with gravy made from stock.

BROILED KIDNEYS

Use beef, veal, lamb, mutton or pork kidneys; wash, remove outer membrane; split in halves lengthwise, remove white centers, fat and tubes. Marinate in French dressing. Rinse, drain and dry thoroughly between absorbent paper or cheesecloth. If old or very large, cover with cold water and simmer, covered, about 1 hour, changing water several times during cooking; drain. Dip halves in French dressing, place on well-greased broiler and broil under moderate heat 10 to 15 minutes, browning on both sides. Place on hot platter, dot with butter and garnish with sprigs of parsley or water cress, or with lemon slices as desired. Veal or lamb kidneys are choicest. Allow about ½ beef kidney, 1 veal or small pork kidney, or 1½ to 2 lamb or mutton kidneys for each portion.

MUTTON KIDNEYS EN BROCHETTE

9 mutton kidneys	⅓ cup olive oil
1½ teaspoons salt	3 large tomatoes, quartered
¼ teaspoon pepper	3 tablespoons butter, melted
	bacon, broiled

Prepare kidneys as for broiling (above). Season with salt and pepper and dip in oil or melted butter; arrange kidney halves alternately with tomato quarters on skewers. Broil about 15 minutes, turning to brown all sides. Place on hot platter, pour melted butter over each and serve with crisp bacon. Approximate yield: 6 portions.

HEADCHEESE

1 small hog's head with ears and tongue	3 whole cloves
water	1 tiny bunch mixed herbs
salt	paprika and sage
onion	cloves and allspice
	½ cup vinegar

Let butcher scrape and clean head, split and remove eyes and brain; then scrape ears, scrub tongue and rinse all thoroughly. Cover with cold water, add 1 tablespoon salt, onion stuck with whole cloves and herbs, and simmer, covered, 2 to 3 hours, or until very tender; cool in stock. Place cooled meat in colander to drain; strip meat from bones, cut ears in slices and tongue in oblongs, squares and triangles, 1 inch or more in length. Season meat to taste with salt, paprika, sage, cloves and allspice and add vinegar, mixing thoroughly. Pack tightly in molds or bowls, interspersing layers of meat with slices of ears and bits of tongue; cover with rinsed plate or cover and place heavy weight on top. In 2 or 3 days the headcheese is ready for use; cut in thin slices and serve with chili sauce, chutney or prepared mustard as desired. To serve hot, dip slices in egg, then roll in fine crumbs and fry in small amount of fat. Allow 2 to 3 slices per portion.

RAGOUT OF KIDNEYS

6 veal or 9 lamb kidneys	1½ teaspoons salt
3 tablespoons flour	¼ teaspoon pepper
3 tablespoons butter	¼ cup currant jelly
1½ cups stock	⅔ cup red wine

Prepare kidneys for cooking. (See Broiled Kidneys.) Drain and slice thin. Stir flour into butter and brown slightly; gradually add stock and cook 5 minutes, stirring until thickened. Add kidneys and seasonings, cover and simmer about 1 hour, or until tender; add jelly, beaten slightly with fork, and wine; heat and serve at once. Wine may be omitted and 1½ teaspoons horseradish and 1½ tablespoons lemon juice added with jelly. Yield: 6 portions.

BRAISED LAMB KIDNEYS

Use recipe for Sweetbreads Velouté (page 342), substituting 9 lamb kidneys for sweetbreads. Prepare kidneys as for broiling; cut in small pieces and mix with lemon juice. Add to browned onions and sauté slowly about 5 minutes, then add flour, stock, mushrooms, seasonings and Sherry as directed. Serve on buttered hot toast. Yield: 6 portions.

OLD-FASHIONED KIDNEY STEW

3 beef kidneys	2 teaspoons minced onion
3 tablespoons butter	¾ teaspoon salt
¼ cup flour	⅛ teaspoon pepper
2 cups water	3 cups hot boiled rice
	toast strips

Prepare kidneys (page 335) and cut into sections. Sauté in butter 3 minutes; add flour and cook 2 minutes longer, or until well browned, stirring constantly. Add water, onion and seasonings, cover and simmer 1 to 1½ hours, or until tender. Serve on rice and garnish with toast strips. Approximate yield: 6 portions.

BREADED KIDNEYS

9 lamb or 6 veal kidneys	¼ teaspoon salt
1 egg, slightly beaten	¼ teaspoon mace
1 tablespoon water	fine cracker crumbs
½ teaspoon minced onion	2 tablespoons butter, melted
	water

Prepare kidneys for cooking; drain and dry thoroughly. Dip each half in egg mixed with water, onion and seasonings and roll in crumbs; chill. Brown in butter; add just enough water to steam, cover and simmer about 20 minutes, turning several times. Fry breaded kidneys in deep fat if desired. Place, cut side down, in greased casserole or baking pan and baste with butter. Bake, uncovered, in very hot oven (450° F.) about 20 minutes. Serve hot in casserole or remove to heated platter. Approximate yield: 6 portions.

BAKED LIVER WITH APPLES

1 pound liver, sliced thin	½ teaspoon salt
2 large sour apples, pared and chopped	dash of pepper
	6 slices bacon, cut in pieces
1 medium-sized onion, chopped	½ cup water

Use beef, veal, pork or lamb liver. Place in greased casserole. Cover with mixture of apple, onion, salt and pepper; top with pieces of bacon and pour water over all. Bake, covered, in moderate oven (350° F.) about 45 minutes, removing cover the last 15 minutes of baking. Approximate yield: 6 portions.

BROILED LIVER

12 small slices calf's liver,	melted butter
½ inch thick	salt and pepper

Brush liver with butter, sprinkle with salt and pepper and place on greased broiler. Broil 8 to 10 minutes, turning to brown both sides; brush with butter and serve on hot platter; marinate in French dressing before broiling, if desired. Yield: 6 portions.

FRIED LIVER

1½ pounds calf's liver,	dash of pepper
½ inch thick slices	¼ cup flour
milk	3 tablespoons fat
1 teaspoon salt	butter

Dip liver in milk, roll in seasoned flour and sauté in fat 5 to 8 minutes, or until browned on both sides. Spread with butter; sprinkle with parsley, if desired. Approximate yield: 6 portions.

CALF'S LIVER SPANISH STYLE

Brush Broiled Liver (above) with Maître d'Hôtel Butter (page 472) and serve with broiled slices of tomatoes and Bermuda onions, or serve with lemon wedges. Yield: 6 portions.

LIVER AND BACON

Broil or fry slowly 6 slices bacon, drain on absorbent paper and keep warm; fry liver in bacon fat (above) and serve with crisp bacon.

LIVER LOAF WITH PAN GRAVY

1½ pounds beef liver	2 cups soft bread crumbs
1½ cups boiling water	2 eggs, slightly beaten
1 slice salt pork, ¼ inch thick	salt and pepper
1 medium-sized onion	2 tablespoons flour
¼ cup chopped parsley	1½ cups cold water

Wash liver if necessary, cover with boiling water and let stand 10 minutes; drain. Grind with 1 slice salt pork and onion; add parsley, crumbs, eggs, 1 teaspoon salt and ¼ teaspoon pepper and mix thoroughly. Press into baking pan, 8½ x 4½ x 2½ inches, and bake in moderate oven (350° F.) about 1 hour, or until browned; remove loaf to hot platter. Stir flour into drippings and brown; gradually add water and cook 5 minutes, stirring until thickened; season to taste and pour over loaf. Yield: 1 loaf, or enough for 6 portions.

SAVORY LIVER

1½ pounds beef or pork liver, sliced thin	2 tablespoons flour
¼ cup chopped onion	¾ teaspoon salt
2 teaspoons chopped parsley	dash of pepper
2 tablespoons butter	3 tablespoons vinegar
	2½ cups bouillon

Sauté liver, onion and parsley in butter in frying pan until lightly browned, turning liver to brown both sides; remove liver, stir in flour, seasonings and vinegar; gradually add bouillon, stirring and cooking until well mixed. Place liver in gravy and cook, covered, 15 minutes, turning once. Approximate yield: 6 portions.

PARSLIED LIVER AND GRAVY

Use beef or pork liver. Cut 1½ pounds liver in 1 inch cubes; cover with water mixed with 3 tablespoons vinegar and let stand ½ hour; drain and dry thoroughly. Sauté in 3 tablespoons bacon fat; add just enough water to steam meat, cover and simmer 10 to 15 minutes, or until tender; remove to serving dish. Brown 1 small onion, sliced, in 2 tablespoons butter; stir in 2 tablespoons flour; gradually add 1½ cups milk and cook 5 minutes, stirring until thickened. Season with salt and pepper, pour over liver and sprinkle 2 teaspoons chopped parsley over top.

CALF'S LIVER PIQUANT

Fry 1½ pounds sliced calf's liver in ¼ cup butter as directed (page 338) and remove to hot platter. Stir 1 tablespoon flour into fat in pan; gradually add 1½ cups water and cook 5 minutes, stirring until thickened. Add 1 tablespoon mushroom ketchup, 1 teaspoon Worcestershire sauce, 1 teaspoon lemon juice, ½ cup chopped stuffed olives and 3 hardcooked eggs, chopped, and heat thoroughly; serve over liver.

COOKED LIVER

Wash liver thoroughly, cover with water and simmer, covered, until tender, adding ½ teaspoon salt per pound when half done. Cook ¼ inch slices 5 to 15 minutes; solid pieces of 2 or more pounds 1 to 1½ hours. Grind and use for sandwich fillings, croquettes, baked loaves and molded dishes; cube or dice and use for creamed dishes.

LIVER CASSEROLE

4 strips lean bacon	1 green pepper, chopped
1 pound veal, lamb or chicken livers, cubed	¼ cup chopped onion
	2 green apples, cut in eighths
1 cup sliced okra	½ teaspoon salt
1 cup fresh lima beans	⅛ teaspoon pepper
1 cup chopped celery	2 cups bouillon

6 1-inch cubes apple jelly

Cut bacon in pieces and fry in large frying pan until crisp; add liver, vegetables, apples, seasonings and bouillon and heat thoroughly. Turn into greased casserole, cover and bake in slow oven (250° F.) about 2 hours; add cubes of jelly just before serving. Yield: 6 portions.

BRAISED OXTAIL

1 oxtail (2 lb.)	1 teaspoon celery salt
flour	4 whole cloves
¼ cup fat	1 bay leaf
1 cup water	4 medium-sized carrots, diced
1 cup canned tomatoes	½ cup chopped onion
1 teaspoon salt	1 clove garlic, chopped
⅛ teaspoon pepper	1 cup sliced mushrooms

⅓ cup Sherry or lemon juice

Wash oxtail, dry and cut in 2 inch lengths; roll in flour and sauté in 2 tablespoons fat until well browned. Add water, tomatoes and seasonings, bring to a boil and simmer, covered, about 3 hours, or until tender. Sauté carrots, onions and garlic in remaining 2 tablespoons fat until slightly browned; add to meat and cook ½ hour longer, adding mushrooms and Sherry the last 10 minutes of cooking. Serve at once. Approximate yield: 6 portions.

PIGS' FEET

Wash, scrape and rinse pigs' feet; cover with cold water and simmer, covered, 3 to 4 hours, or until tender, adding ½ teaspoon salt per quart when partially cooked. Cool slightly in stock; strain and reserve stock for soup. Serve pigs' feet hot with brown gravy made from stock, or cold with Vinegar Sauce (page 474).

To pickle boiled pigs' feet, cover with hot vinegar, plain or spiced, and allow to stand in mixture 2 or more days; to brown cooked pigs' feet, sprinkle with salt, pepper and flour and sauté in small amount of fat; to fry cooked pigs' feet, roll in flour, dip in egg, roll in fine crumbs and cook in hot deep fat (365°–380°) 2 to 5 minutes.

PRECOOKED SWEETBREADS

Sweetbreads consist of the thymus gland of the calf: the gland is divided into two distinct parts, sold separately or as a pair; the breast sweetbread, or the round and compact half, is slightly choicer than the throat sweetbread. Sweetbreads spoil quickly and should be washed and put in cold water if not cooked at once. Cover with salted acidulated water (1 teaspoon salt and 1 tablespoon vinegar to each quart of water); simmer, covered, 15 minutes; drain and cover with cold water to whiten and keep flesh firm. When cool enough to handle, remove membrane and tubes, then broil, sauté, cream or prepare as desired. Allow ½ to 1 pair sweetbreads per portion.

BROILED SWEETBREADS

Precook 3 pairs sweetbreads (page 341); split in halves crosswise, sprinkle with salt and pepper and broil 10 to 15 minutes, turning to brown both sides. Spread with Lemon Butter (page 200) and serve at once. Approximate yield: 6 portions.

SAUTÉED SWEETBREADS

Precook 3 pairs of sweetbreads (page 341); split each crosswise, sprinkle with salt and pepper and sauté in 2 tablespoons fat until delicately browned. Spread with lemon butter made by creaming ¼ cup butter and beating in 1 tablespoon lemon juice. Yield: 6 portions.

SWEETBREAD SUPPER PLATE

Serve Sautéed Sweetbreads (see above) with Baked Tomatoes with Olive Stuffing (page 578) and plain sandwiches or buttered hot baking powder biscuits or rolls.

BRAISED SWEETBREADS

Use 2 pairs sweetbreads (page 341); cut lengthwise in slices, ¼ inch thick, and sauté in 2 tablespoons butter. Add 1 cup brown gravy made with meat stock (page 291), 1 tablespoon ketchup, 2 teaspoons each chopped onion and parsley, ⅛ teaspoon salt and dash of pepper, and cook slowly 10 to 15 minutes; add ¼ cup Sherry, bring just to a boil and serve at once. Approximate yield: 6 portions.

SWEETBREADS EN BROCHETTE

Precook sweetbreads and cut in 1 inch squares; cut slices of bacon in 1 inch squares. Arrange 5 pieces of bacon and 4 of sweetbreads alternately on small skewers beginning and ending with bacon. Broil as for sweetbreads (page 341) until bacon is crisp and browned. Fat salt pork may be substituted for bacon. To crisp bacon or pork, spread pieces on skewers during broiling, or partially broil slices before cutting them into squares. Allow about ½ sweetbread and 1 slice bacon for each skewer.

FRIED SWEETBREADS AND BACON

Roll 1 inch squares of sweetbreads (precooked) in flour, dip in egg mixed with 1 tablespoon water and roll in fine bread crumbs. Arrange pieces on small skewers, alternately with 1 inch squares of sliced bacon, using about 4 sweetbreads and 3 bacon squares for each. Fry in hot deep fat (380°–390° F.) 4 to 6 minutes, or until browned. Drain on absorbent paper and arrange in a circle around mound of buttered peas. Allow about ½ sweetbread for each skewer.

SWEETBREADS VELOUTÉ

3 pairs sweetbreads	1 cup chopped fresh mushrooms
3 tablespoons lemon juice	½ teaspoon salt
1 small onion, thinly sliced	¼ teaspoon pepper
2 tablespoons fat	¼ teaspoon Worcestershire sauce
1 tablespoon flour	2 tablespoons Sherry or Madeira
1 cup meat stock	buttered hot toast

Precook sweetbreads (page 341), cut in cubes and mix with lemon juice. Sauté onion in fat until slightly browned, stir in flour, add stock and cook until thickened, stirring constantly. Add mushrooms, salt and pepper, cover and simmer 10 minutes; add sweetbreads and lemon juice, Worcestershire sauce and Sherry and simmer 5 minutes. Serve on hot toast. Approximate yield: 6 portions.

CREAMED SWEETBREADS

Precook 3 pairs sweetbreads (page 341) and separate into small pieces; add to 2 cups Medium White Sauce (page 125) made with rich milk and heat thoroughly. Stir in 1 egg yolk, slightly beaten, just before serving, if desired. Serve on buttered hot toast or waffle sections, or in warm Patty Cases or Croustades (page 183); sprinkle finely minced parsley or paprika over top. Yield: 6 portions.

Creamed Sweetbreads and Oysters—Substitute oysters for half of sweetbreads; heat oysters in their own liquor until edges curl and add to creamed sweetbreads. Serve in patty shells.

Sweetbreads and Veal—Substitute diced veal or chicken for half of sweetbreads. Serve wtih buttered asparagus tips or sautéed mushroom caps.

SWEETBREADS NEWBURG

3 pairs sweetbreads, precooked (page 341)
2 eggs, separated

1 cup heavy cream
1 cup Thick White Sauce (page 125)

2 teaspoons Sherry

Cut sweetbreads in small pieces or dice. Mix together slightly beaten egg yolks and cream; stir into white sauce, add sweetbreads and heat thoroughly. Fold in stiffly beaten egg whites and Sherry and serve at once. Diced breast of chicken or veal may be substituted for half of the sweetbreads. Approximate yield: 6 portions.

SWEETBREAD TIMBALES

1½ pairs sweetbreads
¼ teaspoon grated onion
1 cup soft bread crumbs
½ cup milk

1 teaspoon salt
dash of white pepper
6 mushrooms, chopped
3 eggs, separated

Medium White Sauce (page 125)

Precook sweetbreads (page 341); chop and season with onion. Heat crumbs in milk until thick; stir in seasonings, mushrooms, sweetbreads and slightly beaten egg yolks. Fold into stiffly beaten egg whites and turn into well-buttered custard cups or molds. Place in pan of hot water and bake in moderate oven (350° F.) about 30 minutes, or until firm. Serve with well seasoned white sauce. Yield: 6 timbales.

COOKED FRESH TONGUE

Use beef, veal, lamb or pork tongue. For information on weights, see table on Fancy Cuts and Sundries. Scrub thoroughly in warm water. Cover with water and simmer, covered, until tender, adding about ½ teaspoon salt per pound when half done: allow 3 to 4 hours for beef tongue; 2 to 3 hours for veal tongue; 1 to 1½ hours for lamb tongue; 1½ to 2 hours for pork tongue. Plunge into cold water to loosen skin. Remove skin and root end. Serve whole or sliced with a tart sauce such as Tartar Sauce (page 477) or Horseradish Sauce (page 477). If served cold, chill tongue in the stock; it will be more juicy. Allow ¼ to ⅓ pound per portion. Veal tongue will serve 3 to 6; lamb and pork, 1 to 2.

VIRGINIA COOKED TONGUE

1 beef tongue	½ cup firmly packed brown sugar
1 teaspoon salt	1 cup cooked cranberries
1 cup tongue stock	1 tablespoon whole cloves
	½ lemon, sliced

Cook tongue until tender. Remove skin and roots and simmer in mixture of remaining ingredients 15 to 20 minutes. Serve whole or sliced with sauce in which it was cooked. Approximate yield: 10 portions.

SLICED LAMBS' TONGUES

Wash and cook 4 fresh lambs' tongues until tender (page 343), adding 1 teaspoon salt, 1-inch piece stick cinnamon, 1 small bay leaf, 3 whole cloves stuck in 1 slice onion and about 3 tablespoons lemon juice when half done; cool in stock. Place on platter, surround with hearts of lettuce and serve with Tartar Sauce (page 477). Yield: 6 portions.

COOKED CURED BEEF TONGUE

Scrub smoked, pickled or corned tongue in warm water; soak corned tongue, if very salty, in cold water several hours or overnight before cooking. Cover with cold water and simmer, covered, 3 to 4 hours, or until tender. Cook in stock until cold enough to handle. Plunge tongue in cold water, skin and trim root end. Serve hot or cold, with a savory sauce. Yield: 6 to 8 portions.

SPICED TONGUE

1 fresh or smoked beef tongue	¼ teaspoon black pepper
water	½ teaspoon allspice
2 tablespoons flour	12 whole cloves
2 tablespoons butter	2 bay leaves
1 quart tongue stock	1 medium-sized onion, finely
½ teaspoon salt	chopped
	1 carrot, diced

Scrub fresh tongue, cover with water and simmer, covered, 2 hours; remove skin and trim roots. Mix together butter and flour in saucepan; gradually stir in stock and cook until thickened; add salt, pepper, spices and tongue and simmer 1½ hours, or until tender, adding vegetables ½ hour before meat is done. Serve hot or cold with or without gravy. Yield: 6 to 8 portions.

TONGUE AND MUSHROOMS

1 6½-oz. can tongue or
   1 small tongue, cooked
2 cups mushroom caps
2 tablespoons butter

1½ cups Medium White Sauce
   (page 125)
buttered hot toast
1 tablespoon chopped parsley

Use canned or cooked tongue; cut in cubes. Sauté mushrooms in butter about 5 minutes, stirring to cook evenly; add with tongue to white sauce and heat thoroughly. Serve on buttered toast and sprinkle with parsley. Approximate yield: 6 portions.

CRUSTED TONGUE SUPREME

1 smoked tongue
2 eggs, beaten
1½ cups soft bread crumbs
1 cup Port
Chestnut Balls (page 495)

1 small onion, chopped
2 stalks celery, chopped
2 tablespoons butter
1 small can (No. 1) tomato paste
small sprig of thyme

Cook tongue 3 to 4 hours, or until tender (page 343); skin and cut away roots. Make paste of eggs and crumbs and spread over tongue; place in baking pan and bake in moderate oven (350° F.) about ½ hour, basting every 10 minutes with wine. Remove to hot platter and garnish with chestnut balls; reserve stock for sauce. Sauté onion and celery in butter about 10 minutes, stirring frequently: add tomato paste and thyme, stir in wine-tongue stock and bring to a boil; strain, season, if necessary, and serve sauce with crusted tongue. Approximate yield: 8 portions.

TONGUE CROQUETTES

Use 1 cup chopped, cooked tongue and 1 cup chopped, blanched almonds for meat in recipe for Meat Croquettes (page 329) and omit onion and ketchup. Cooked chicken, turkey or pork may be used instead of tongue. Approximate yield: 1 dozen small croquettes.

STEWED TRIPE

Choose cleaned honeycomb tripe, fresh, corned or pickled. Wash, cover with cold water and bring slowly to a boil; then drain, cover with boiling water and simmer, covered, 1 to 2 hours, or until tender; add ½ teaspoon salt per pound (to fresh tripe only) when half done. Serve with Tomato Sauce (page 469), a savory sauce, or sautéed apple slices. Allow ¼ pound tripe per portion.

TRIPE À LA GENEVA

1½ to 2 pounds honeycomb
   beef tripe
1 cup soft bread crumbs
1½ cups oil or fat

1 cup canned tomatoes
1 teaspoon salt
½ cup stock
½ cup grated cheese

Clean tripe and cook in salted water until tender (1 to 1½ hours). Slice meat in strips ¼ inch wide and 2 inches long. Lightly brown bread crumbs in oil. Add meat, tomatoes, salt and about ½ cup water or stock. Simmer 5 minutes. Stir cheese into mixture. Serve with parsley and panroast potatoes. Approximate yield: 6 to 8 portions.

TRIPE IN SOUR GRAVY

2 pounds honeycomb tripe, cut
   in pieces
2 cups water
¼ cup vinegar
1 medium-sized onion, minced
½ clove garlic, crushed

4 whole cloves, crushed
⅛ teaspoon allspice
⅛ teaspoon marjoram
dash of pepper
1 tablespoon flour
1 tablespoon sugar

2 tablespoons butter

Cook tripe until tender in salted water (page 345); dran and add water, vinegar, onion, garlic, spices, marjoram and pepper and cook 10 minutes. Stir flour and sugar in butter and cook until browned; add to tripe stock and cook 3 minutes, stirring constantly. Approximate yield: 6 portions.

CURRIED BEEF TRIPE

1½ pounds beef tripe, cut in
   pieces
6 cups cold water
1 teaspoon salt
1 medium-sized onion, sliced
6 tablespoons flour

6 tablespoons fat
1½ cups tripe stock
2 tablespoons curry powder
1 teaspoon paprika
1 teaspoon brown sugar
4 cups Boiled Rice (page 507)

Put tripe in cold water and cook until tender (page 345), adding salt and onion when nearly done. Stir flour into fat in saucepan, gradually stir in stock, curry powder, paprika and sugar and cook 5 minutes, stirring until thickened. Arrange cooked tripe over hot rice and pour sauce over all; serve immediately. Yield: 6 portions.

BAKED TRIPE

1 pound honeycomb tripe
2 onions, chopped
2 tablespoons butter

½ teaspoon salt
dash of pepper
1 tablespoon flour
2 cups milk

Cut tripe in 1 inch pieces, cover with water, bring to a boil; drain. Cover with boiling water and simmer, covered, 1 to 2 hours, or until tender; drain. Sauté onions in butter until lightly browned; turn into heavy casserole. Place tripe on top, sprinkle with salt, pepper and flour; add milk. Cover and bake in moderate oven (350° F.) 2 hours. Serve with a highly seasoned sauce. Yield: 4 portions.

Poultry

TODAY's chicken is a "super-duper." Scientific breeding, feeding and management, and marketing are making the bird a cross-country favorite because it is meatier, better prepared for immediate cooking and more tender than its ancestors.

Nutritionally, poultry compares favorably with other lean meat in proteins and minerals. Chicken livers have many of the excellent qualities of liver. Dark meat is somewhat richer than white in both vitamins and minerals.

WHEN YOU BUY CHICKEN

YOU WILL want to know the meaning of some of the terms used by producers and market men when you buy the "dressed" poultry.

New York dressed or *dressed*. Both terms mean that the blood and feathers have been removed. The bird has *not* been drawn, and the head and feet have *not* been cut off.

Ready-to-cook, drawn, or *eviscerated*. Chicken prepared in this way has had the entrails removed, the head and feet cut off, and the giblets cleaned. It is a good idea to look for pin feathers and to singe the bird, if necessary. Most frozen chicken is marketed ready to cook and needs little, if any, further cleaning, other than washing.

"Cut-up" chicken. As the name implies, has been cut into pieces for serving. Most cuts are usually made at the joints. You can also buy separate parts of a chicken. Breasts and thighs cost most, wings and backs less, and parts may be had in any quantity.

There is usually a difference in cost among the three ways of preparing chicken for sale. You may expect to pay more for chicken that is ready to cook. More labor is required in preparing the bird for sale, and there is less waste to the consumer since the feet, head and entrails have been discarded.

HOW TO JUDGE QUALITY

LIVE and dressed poultry are graded the same as other food products into A, B, and C grades. The higher the grade, the more meat there is on the carcass and the better the quality, as a rule. An A-grade dressed chicken will have a well-rounded breast and thighs. On young chickens the breastbone will be long and straight and flexible. The skin will have relatively few tears, and few, if any, pin feathers. Most housewives prefer a bird with yellow skin. In buying chicken, it is best to ask the poultryman or market man to supply you with the class of poultry desired; that is, broiler or fryer, roaster, or stewing chicken; then check the quality.

HOW MUCH TO BUY

WHEN you buy live chicken you need to figure that the bird will lose from 25 to 35 percent of the live weight when blood, feathers, feet, head and entrails are removed.

New York dressed or dressed poultry will lose about 20 percent of its weight when it is drawn.

All poultry loses some weight in cooking, but proper methods will keep cooking losses at a minimum.

When buying: **Broilers**—Allow one bird to a person if the birds are small (1 to 1¼ pounds dressed). If birds are large, allow from one-fourth to one-half bird to a person. Do not broil a bird that weighs more than 3 pounds dressed.

Fryers—Allow one chicken for two persons unless the bird is small; then you will need more. For small servings, allow from ¾ to 1 pound to a person.

Roasting Chicken—Allow from ¾ to 1 pound to a person if the bird is ready-to-cook.

Stewing or Fricassee Chicken—Allow from ½ to ¾ pound to a person, depending on how the meat is to be served.

Four or five pounds of cut-up chicken made into chicken pie serves from 6 to 8 persons. Some recipes call for cupfuls of cooked meat separated from the bones. The yield of such meat varies with the size of the bird. The larger the bird, the greater the proportion of meat to bone. Usually from ¾ to 1 cup of cooked lean meat may be obtained from each pound of ready-to-cook or cut-up chicken.

FROZEN POULTRY

To COOK frozen poultry, defrost or cook it from the frozen state.

To Defrost—Follow package directions, or thaw in original wrappings in the refrigerator. Allow 2 to 3 days for large birds, 12 to 24 hours for small birds.

Thaw small birds in wrappings before an electric fan. Allow 1½ to 4 hours for a chicken.

Roast thawed poultry as soon after defrosting as possible. Cook exactly like fresh poultry.

To Roast from Frozen State—Increase roasting period for fresh birds by one and one-half times.

If stuffing is desired, remove bird from oven and stuff when thawed enough to handle easily.

For Turkey Roll or Log—Start roasting from frozen or defrosted state. Leave roll in original foil and place on rack in shallow open pan with folded edge of foil on top. Roast 4½-pound frozen roll for 4 hours at 325° F., or defrosted roll for 3 to 3½ hours; roast 2-pound frozen roll for 3 to 3½ hours, or defrosted roll for 2 to 2½ hours. Tighten foil promptly on removal from oven. To serve hot, let stand 15 to 20 minutes in wrap before slicing. To serve cold, leave in wrappings and refrigerate overnight.

CANNED AND SMOKED POULTRY

READY-TO-HEAT or to eat cold, canned and glassed chicken and turkey products have grown tremendously in variety and distribution since the past war.

Among the many fine quality canned poultry products are chicken fricassee, whole chicken, boned chicken, boned turkey,

TABLE XXV

POULTRY—PURCHASING GUIDE

Kind and Market Class	Average Weight (Dressed)	Age	Qualities and Description	Method of Cookery	Portions (Approx.)
	Pounds	*Months*			
Chicken—tender			Young, tender pliable cartilage at end of breastbone: short legs, sharp, short claws, pinfeathers	Dry heat, Broil (rubbed with oil), panbroil, bake	½–1 lb. per portion
Squab, broilers	¾–1¼	2–2½	Small broilers, little fat; similar to young pigeon; either sex		1
Broilers	1½–2½	2½–3½	Small muscles, little fat, delicate flavor		2
Fryers	2½–3½	3½–5	Larger muscles, more meat and fat, pinfeathers	Panfry, braise, fry in deep fat	3–4
Roasters	3½–5	5–8	Plump, young, more fat and connective tissue, pinfeathers	Roast (rubbed with fat), fry, braise	4–5
Capons	6–9	6–10	Castrated males; tender, fleshy, excellent flavor; size of mature bird with fine qualities of young bird	Roast, braise	5–8
Chicken—less tender				Moist heat at low temperature, long slow cooking: Braise, stew, simmer, steam	½–¾ lb. per portion
Fowls (hens)	4–6	Over 9	Thicker connective tissue between muscle fibers, fine flavor		5–7
Stags (young males)	4–7	8–10	Spurs developing, tough, stringy flesh, bony		5–8
Cocks	4–7	Over 10	Tough, darker flesh, stronger flavor; less fat than hen, long hairs, bony		5–8
Ducks			Higher in fat than chicken; all dark meat; little flesh on bones	Dry heat, Broil, plank, roast	¾–1 lb. per portion
Duckling	2–4	2½–3½	Soft windpipe; pliable breastbone cartilage, tender		2–4

TABLE XXV—(*Continued*)
POULTRY—PURCHASING GUIDE

Kind and Market Class	Average Weight (Dressed)	Age	Qualities and Description	Method of Cookery	Portions (Approx.)
	Pounds	*Months*			
Light	3–5	6–8	Fine flavor; small amount of meat to bone		3–5
Heavy	5–6	Over 12	Hard windpipe, longer neck; greater amount of meat to bone; less delicately flavored	Moist heat: Braise, stew	4–6
Geese			Contain more fat than any other poultry; short legs; all dark meat	Dry heat: Roast (outside surface pricked if very fat)	1–1½ lb. per portion
Young	8–12	Under 12	Tender, thick, firm breast; pliable breastbone cartilage and bill, soft, yellow feet		1–1½ lb. per portion
Heavy	Over 12	Over 12	Less tender, more meat on bone, usually very fat, longer neck	Moist heat, slow cooking: Braise, stew	
Turkey			Largest eating bird, little fat; light and dark meat; full breast	Dry heat Broil, bake	½–1 lb. per portion
Broilers	3–4	3–5	Young, tender, lean; either sex; black legs and feet		2–4
Turkey—small	5–10	6–9	Young, tender; abundant meat on breast and legs	Broil, fry, roast	6–8
Roasters Hens or toms	8–16	6	Plump, young, more meat, fat and connective tissue	Roast	¾–1 lb. per portion
Old turkey hens and toms	18–25	Over 12	Tough, good flavor, more connective tissue, moderately fat, much meat on bone, broad, full breast	Moist heat, slow cooking: Stew, simmer, steam	½–¾ lb. per portion
Pigeons Squabs	½–1½	1	Very tender, plump, milky delicate flesh; old has more purplish flesh, little fat	Dry heat: Broil, panbroil, roast, plank	1
Guinea hen	2–4	7	Tender, thick white breast, lean, gamy	Panfry, roast, braise	2–3

chicken à la king, chicken or turken and noodles, chicken giblets and noodles, chicken sandwich spread, chicken soup. Specialty items such as wild turkey, pheasant, and guinea hen are also canned.

Smoked turkey is a cooked specialty sold in some markets fresh or frozen. It may be purchased as a whole or half bird.

TABLE XXVI

TIMETABLE FOR ROASTING POULTRY, GAME BIRDS, DUCKS

Kind	Dressed Weight	Ready-to-Cook Weight	Oven Temperature	Total Cooking Time
	Pounds	*Pounds*	*Degree F.*	*Hours*
Chicken		1½ to 2½	325	1½ to 2½
"		2½ to 3½	325	2½ to 3
"		3½ to 4¾	325	3 to 3½
"	3½ to 5		325–350	1¾ to 2
"	6 to 9		325–350	2½ to 3
Duck (light)	5 to 6		325–350	2 to 2½
Goose (young)	8 to 12		300–325	3 to 4
Grouse			325–350	50 to 60 mins.
Guinea (young)	2 to 3½		325–350	1½ to 2
Pheasant (young)	2 to 2½		300–325	1½ to 2
Pigeon (young)	1½		325–350	45 to 60 mins.
Turkey (young)		2 to 5	350	2½ to 3½
" "		5 to 8	325	3½ to 4
" "		8 to 12	325	4 to 4½
" "		12 to 16	300	4½ to 5
" "		16 to 20	300	5 to 5½
" "		20 to 24	300	5½ to 6
" "	6 to 10		300–325	3 to 3½
" "	10 to 16		275–300	3½ to 5½
" "	18 to 24		250–300	6½ to 7½
" "	24 to 30		250–300	8 to 9
(Half)	5 to 8		300–325	1½ to 2
(Wild)	9 to 14		250–300	3½ to 4½
Waterfowl (ducks)	½ to 2½		325–350	½ to 2

TABLE XXVII

TIMETABLE FOR BROILING, BRAISING, SIMMERING GAME

WILD DUCK, VENISON, SQUIRREL, RABBIT, RACCOON, OPOSSUM, MUSKRAT

KIND RETAIL CUTS	APPROXIMATE SIZE		METHOD OF COOKING	TEMPERATURE OF BROILER OR DEGREE OF HEAT	COOKING TIME (APPROXIMATE)	
	THICKNESS	WEIGHT			RARE	MEDIUM WELL DONE
	Inches	*Pounds*			*Minutes*	*Minutes*
Duck, coot (Young)	Quarter		Braise			35–40
(Old)						1–1¼ hrs.
Game Mammals Venison steaks	½–¾		Broil	Constant 350°F.	8–10	15–20
Steaks, old	½–¾		Braise			1–1½ hrs.
Rump, Arm	Solid	1½–2				1½–2 hrs.
Squirrel, Rabbit	Split	¾–1½	Broil	Constant 350°F.		30–45
Old	Pieces	1½–2	Braise			1–1½ hrs.
Raccoon (Young)	Split	5–7	Broil	Constant 350°F.		
(Old)		8–12	Braise			1½–2 hrs.
Opossum (Young)	Split	1½–2	Broil	Constant 350°F.		45–60
(Old)	Pieces	3–3½	Braise			1½–2 hrs.
Muskrat	Split	12–14 oz.	Broil	Constant 350°F.		30–40
	Pieces	1–1¼	Braise			1–1½ hrs.

TABLE XXVIII

TIMETABLE FOR ROASTING WATERFOWL, GAME MAMMALS

KIND RETAIL CUT	WEIGHT (AP-PROX.)	OVEN TEMPER-ATURE	TEST FOR DONENESS		COOKING TIME (APPROXIMATE)	
			STAGE	INTERNAL TEMP.	PER POUND	TOTAL TIME
	Pounds	*Degree F.*		*Degree F.*	*Minutes*	
American Coot	6–12 oz.	325–350	Well done	—	—	½–1 hr.
Mammals (game)	—	—	Rare	170–175	30–35	60–70 mins.
Venison, rib	2	300–325	Medium	175–180	40–45	1¼–1½ hrs.
Squirrel, rabbit	1¼–2	300–325	Well done	—	—	1½–2 hrs.
Raccoon	8–10	300–325	"	—	—	2½–4 hrs.
Opossum	1½–2	300–350	"	—	—	2–2½ hrs.
Muskrat	1–1½	300–350	"	—	—	1–1½ hrs.

HOW TO PREPARE AND COOK CHICKEN

Most chicken, before it is cooked, must be inspected carefully for pin-feathers. Boxed or wrapped frozen, eviscerated poultry probably requires the least attention.

Remove pinfeathers with a stout pair of tweezers or grip pinfeathers between a paring knife and your thumb. Be careful not to tear the skin—if chicken is to be cooked whole—as many homemakers believe that an uncut skin helps to hold in the juice during the roasting process. An uncut skin greatly improves the appearance of the bird.

If necessary, singe the bird over a gas flame or hot coals to remove hair and down on the carcass. Or light 2 tablespoons of wood alcohol which has been poured into a platter in the sink. Turn the bird until all the hairs are singed. With this method, you need to use caution to keep the flame confined to the sink.

Cut out the oil sac on the back near the tail if the oil sac has not been removed. Wash the outside of the bird with warm water and soda. Work soda into the skin until it is clean. After the bird is drawn, wash the inside. Rinse *thoroughly* and *dry* inside and out with paper towels so that the bird will be easy to handle.

Cut-up chicken should also be checked for pinfeathers, then washed and dried.

Clean and wash the giblets.

Poultry is a *very perishable food* and must be kept cold before cooking and kept chilled after cooking if not eaten at once.

HOW TO PREPARE CHICKEN FOR BROILING

Select plump young chickens, 8–12 weeks old and weighing from 1 to 2½ pounds. Remove the shanks at the hock or knee joint. Cut off the head but leave the neck attached to the body. If you are using shears or tin snips for cutting, place the bird on the table with the neck toward you and the back of the bird toward your cutting hand. Reverse the position of the bird if you are using a knife. Cut just through the bones down each side of the backbone from the tail to the shoulder. Lay open the body cavity, cut around the vent, and carefully loosen the intestines, crop, windpipe, liver and other organs, and remove them together with the backbone and the neck. Cut through the cartilage at the front end of the brown-colored breastbone. The breastbone can then be snapped out by pressing from underneath. Split the bird by cutting through the breast meat. Nick wings to prevent curling in cooking. Cut off the wings at the first joint. Large birds are usually halved.

HOW TO BROIL CHICKEN

Grease broiler rack and adjust rack so chicken will be about 4 inches from heat. Preheat broiler at 350° F. Brush both sides of the chicken with melted fat; season with salt and pepper. Place chicken on rack with the skin-side down. Baste five or six times during broiling. Turn pieces when they are brown and about half-done. Broil pieces until they are tender to the bone and evenly browned. Small broilers will require 30 to 40 minutes; larger broilers, from 40 to 50 minutes. To test for doneness, cut into the thickest part of the thigh; when juice is no longer pink and flesh is tender, the meat is done.

Combination Broiling and Roasting—Broil until partly done and finish cooking in a moderately slow oven (325°–350° F.). Allow a little more time for this method than for broiling.

Broiling Frozen Chicken—Table- or oven-dressed broiler halves, solidly frozen, may be broiled without thawing. Proceed as for thawed or unfrozen broilers, placing broilers (top surface) 5 or 6 inches from heat. Allow 1½ times the time needed for unfrozen broilers.

Broiled Chicken Barbecue—Baste frequently with a barbecue sauce while broiling.

BROILERS TARTARE

Split, wash and dry 3 broilers (about 1½ lb. each); sprinkle with salt and pepper and sauté in ½ cup butter until browned on both sides. Add 6 sprigs parsley, chopped, 4 scallions, chopped, ¼ clove garlic, minced, and ¾ pound mushrooms, diced; cover and cook slowly until chicken is tender, turning occasionally; allow 30 to 40 minutes for cooking. Remove chicken, roll in fine bread crumbs and place under hot broiler until crumbs are browned, turning frequently. Serve with Brown Sauce made from drippings and vegetables in pan and giblet stock (page 364). Yield: 6 portions.

MIXED CHICKEN GRILL

3 1½- to 2-lb. broilers	**3 tablespoons grated American**
salt and pepper	**cheese**
6 slices eggplant	**6 small sweet potatoes, boiled**
1 egg, beaten	**½ cup butter, melted**
2 tablespoons water	**6 slices tomatoes**
½ cup dry bread crumbs	**6 slices bacon**

Split, wash and dry broilers; sprinkle with salt and pepper and place, skin-side down, on greased rack of broiler. Sprinkle eggplant with salt and pepper, dip in egg mixed with water, roll in mixture of crumbs and cheese and place on rack; place potatoes on rack. Brush all with melted butter, place in moderate broiler (350° F.) and broil 15 to 20 minutes, or until browned; turn, brush with butter and continue broiling about 15 minutes, placing tomatoes on eggplant and bacon on rack about 10 minutes before removing from broiler; turn tomatoes and bacon to brown both sides. Approximate yield: 6 portions.

BROILED CHICKEN FILLETS

Fillets of chicken consist of the breast meat; the upper or longer muscle is called the "large fillet" and the lower or smaller muscle, the "filet mignon." To remove solid meat on one side, cut with sharp pointed knife or poultry shears through skin along entire keel of breast and pull skin from breast; cut down close along side of breastbone and, with knife and fingers, scrape and push meat from breastbone, collar bone, wing joint, along wishbone and the entire length of breast, cutting it away from the wing joint; remove tendons and sinews and separate solid meat into the two fillets; remove fillets on other side of breast in the same way. Marinate fillets in Lemon Butter (page 200) and broil as for Broiled Chicken (page 356); allow about 20 minutes for total broiling and baste several times with lemon butter. Sprinkle with salt and pepper and serve with broiled mushroom caps page 556) or fried asparagus tips (page 525) and cream gravy. Allow 1 whole fillet per portion.

PLANKED CHICKEN

Split, wash and dry 3 medium-sized broilers; sprinkle with salt and pepper and spread with half of savory butter made by mixing ½ cup butter with 1 teaspoon each minced onion, parsley and pimiento, and 1 tablespoon lemon juice. Broil or bake (pages 356–361) 20 minutes, basting with remaining ¼ cup savory butter when turning chicken. Arrange chicken, skin-side up, in center of greased heated plank. Place 6 potatoes, baked and stuffed (page 563) and 6 buttered cooked artichokes (page 522) alternately around outside of plank, and individual portions of buttered cooked carrot sticks between chicken and border. Place in moderately hot oven (350°–375° F.) 10 minutes, or until chicken is done and vegetables are browned. Fill spaces with parsley or water cress and serve at once. Approximate yield: 6 portions.

HOW TO PREPARE CHICKEN FOR FRYING

Clean and wash the bird or the cut-up parts as previously directed (page 355). Prepare the bird as for broiling (page 356) and halve it. Cut each half into four or six pieces by disjointing the bird. Many small pieces are desirable, cook faster, and make more servings than do large pieces.

HOW TO FRY CHICKEN

Use a heavy frying pan large enough to hold pieces without crowding. Place cooking oil or fat in pan to depth of 1 inch. Heat to frying temperature (never let fat become so hot it smokes). Shake pieces of chicken in paper bag to which seasoned flour has been added or roll pieces in seasoned flour, and place pieces in hot fat. Lower heat so pieces will brown slowly. Brown pieces on one side; turn and finish browning on other side. Small pieces may be done at this point. Remove them to a warm place. If you have doubt about the tenderness of other pieces, add 3 tablespoons of water to frying pan, cover and continue cooking 15 or 20 minutes. You may want to remove the cover the last 5 minutes in order to crisp the chicken. Allow ½ hour for broilers; ¾ hour for small fryers; 1 hour for fryers weighing more than 3 pounds. When the pieces are fork-tender, remove to warm place and serve with gravy made from drippings in pan, giblet stock and rich milk or light cream. Allow ¾ pound per portion.

SMOTHERED CHICKEN

Brown young chicken as directed for Fried Chicken (page 359), then cover with light cream, bring to a boil, turn into casserole and bake, covered, in slow oven (300° F.) ½ to ¾ hour, or until tender. Serve from casserole. Allow ¾ pound per portion.

MARYLAND FRIED CHICKEN

1 young chicken (3 lb.)	**4 tablespoons water**
salt and pepper	**1 cup dry bread crumbs**
1 cup flour	**¼ cup butter or margarine**
2 eggs, slightly beaten	**¼ cup pork fat**

Cream Gravy (page 363)

Cut chicken in pieces for serving, wash and dry. Season with salt and pepper, roll in flour, dip in slightly beaten eggs, diluted with water, and roll in crumbs. Sauté in butter and pork fat in heavy frying pan until browned on all sides; cover and place in slow oven (300° F.) ½ to ¾ hour, or until tender. If chicken weighs more than 3 pounds, add ½ cup hot water to pan in oven. Serve with cream gravy made from drippings in pan, substituting light cream for milk. Yield: 6 portions.

BATTER-FRIED CHICKEN

Use recipe for Southern Fried Chicken (page 359); substitute Cover Batter (page 487) for well-seasoned flour. Dip each piece of chicken in batter and proceed as directed. Approximate yield: 6 portions.

CHICKEN SAUTÉ

1 fryer chicken, cut in pieces	salt to taste
3 tablespoons butter	1 clove of garlic, minced
3 shallots, chopped	½ cup white wine
1 bay leaf	2½ tablespoons chowchow
pinch of thyme	½ cup light cream

Brown chicken in butter, browning well. Add seasonings and white wine. Cover and simmer 25 to 35 minutes, or until chicken is tender; remove to warming oven. Add chowchow and cream to sauce in skillet. Blend and cook 3 to 5 minutes, or until sauce is thickened, stirring constantly. Pour over chicken. Garnish with parsley if desired. Approximate yield: 4 portions.

CHICKEN LILLY

1 tender young chicken	8 fresh mushrooms, sliced
1 teaspoon salt	4 tomatoes, peeled, quartered
dash of pepper	2 shallots, chopped
½ cup flour	⅓ cup Sherry
3 tablespoons butter	1 teaspoon minced parsley

Cut chicken in four pieces. Shake in paper bag with salt, pepper and flour. Sauté slowly in butter. Add mushrooms, tomatoes, shallots and Sherry. Cover and cook slowly 30 minutes. Add parsley. Yield: 2 portions.

COMPANY CHICKEN CASSEROLE

1 3-pound chicken, cut up	1½ teaspoons double-acting
½ cup seasoned flour	baking powder
½ cup cooking oil or shortening	4 eggs
1½ cups sifted all-purpose flour	1½ cups milk
1 teaspoon salt	3 tablespoons melted butter

Keep the wings, back, neck and giblets for soup. Coat the meaty pieces of chicken with flour. Brown in hot shortening in heavy pan. Drain chicken on absorbent paper. Save the drippings in the pan for gravy. For batter, sift flour, salt and baking powder together. Beat eggs very light, then stir in milk and melted butter. Stir the egg mixture into dry ingredients slowly, to prevent flour from lumping. Then beat batter until smooth. Pour into greased, heavy 10-inch baking dish 3 inches deep. Arrange pieces of browned chicken on top. Bake in 350° F. oven 1 hour, or until batter is golden brown. Serve with gravy made by blending 3 tablespoons drippings with 3 tablespoons flour and adding 2 cups water. Season and simmer 3 to 4 minutes, stirring constantly. Yield: 6 to 8 portions.

SOUTHERN FRIED CHICKEN

Cut 2 frying chickens in pieces for serving, wash and dry. Roll in well-seasoned flour and fry in hot deep fat (350°–365° F.) about 10 minutes, or until browned, turning frequently. Remove to covered frying pan or Dutch oven and cook at simmering temperature on top of range or bake slowly (300°–325° F.) 20 to 25 minutes, or until tender, turning frequently. Simmer fowl until almost tender before frying. Serve with giblet gravy (page 364). Yield: 6 portions.

PREPARING POULTRY FOR ROASTING

SINGE and pick the pinfeathers from bird, clean and dry thoroughly as directed on page 355.

Stuffing. Choice of stuffing depends on the type of poultry or game. The mild, sweet flavor of chicken or turkey should not be masked by too strong a flavor in the stuffing. Simple bread, vegetable, oyster, sausage or crisp nut stuffings are well liked with the blander poultry. The flesh of duck or goose is naturally fat and requires a dry stuffing since the dressing tends to soak up moisture and fat during the roasting; fruit or sharply seasoned stuffings are preferred. The cavity should be packed loosely enough to allow for slight expansion during the cooking. A little stuffing in the neck gives a plump, well rounded contour. Draw the skin over the back and close the openings by sewing with string, or insert skewers and lace with string.

Trussing. Fold the wings back and press the tips against the back. Press thighs close to body, tie the ends of the legs together with string and bring it down around the tailpiece, leaving two ends. Then turn bird over on breast and bring each end of string forward over the front and tip of one of the wings and across the back to the other wing, and tie ends securely in the middle of the back. Remove all string and skewers before serving.

ROAST CHICKEN

Choose a young, well-fatted chicken 5 to 9 months old, weighing 3½ to 5 pounds; capons are usually 6 to 10 months old and weigh 6 to 9 pounds (Poultry-Purchasing Guide). Oven-dress as directed (pages 355–356). Rub inside with salt. Stuff, truss and rub with melted butter or oil. Salt is likely to cause the skin to blister.

Place breast down on V-shaped roaster or flat rack in open pan; roast in slow oven (325° F.) until tender, allowing for unstuffed weight (smaller chicken), 24 to 30 minutes per pound; for stuffed weight, 35 to 50 minutes. For capons and heavier chickens, allow 20 to 25 minutes per pound. When half done, turn breast up and finish roasting. Baste frequently with drippings in pan or additional fat. Chicken may also be roasted by being placed upright on roaster rack. Use a square of cheesecloth large enough to cover breast and drumsticks. Dip cloth into melted butter or shortening before covering the chicken and baste occasionally. Bake according to time and temperatures given above. A meat thermometer inserted into the heaviest part of the thigh will register 185° F. when chicken is well done. If both joints of leg can be broken or moved easily, the chicken is done. Place chicken on heated platter and garnish as desired. Serve with chicken gravy with or without the giblets (page 363). Allow about ¾ pound (unstuffed weight) per portion.

Roast Chicken, Country Style—Prepare older and less tender chicken as for roasting. Roast in moderately slow oven (325°–350° F.) until lightly browned (about half done). Pour ¼ cup boiling water in pan, cover and bake until tender. Basting is not necessary. If a crisp crust is desired, open vent in cover of pan or remove cover the last half hour of baking. Serve with Chicken Gravy (page 363).

Jelly-Glazed Roast Chicken—Roast prepared chicken, country style (above). When removing cover, spread with ½ cup currant or any other tart jelly (beaten with fork until thin) and continue roasting, uncovered, until done, basting several times with jelly mixture.

STUFFED FRYERS

Two stuffed fryers take less time to roast than one large roasting chicken. Fryer meat when oven-roasted is very delicate in flavor and fork tender. Both the stuffing and gravy help to stretch servings. Allow ¾ to 1 quart bread crumb stuffing for a chicken 3 to 4 pounds "dressed weight" or 2¼ to 3 pounds ready-to-cook weight. Roast between 1½ to 2 hours in a 350° F. oven.

ROASTED BONED CHICKEN

Use a freshly killed, dry picked and undrawn chicken or capon with unbroken skin (an undrawn bird is firmer to work with); turkey, guinea hen, squabs and game birds are frequently boned, while a duck or goose is more difficult to bone without breaking the skin. The skin and flesh should be removed in one piece. Lay bird, breast down, on board and with a sharp-pointed knife or poultry shears cut down center back from neck to tail. With back of pointed knife and with fingers, scrape and push flesh from backbone to and from each shoulder blade and around each wing joint, pull out tendons and continue along entire backbone, forward across ribs. Turn bird over and scrape and push flesh from wishbone and collarbone and remove crop and windpipe; scrape flesh from breastbone and down to the vent, being careful not to break the skin or cut the membrane holding the entrails in place. Scrape flesh from thigh and leg bones, pulling it back over end of leg, flesh side out; then turn flesh back, skin side out, as you would a glove which was pulled off wrong side out. Repeat process with other leg and with wings, breaking bone at tip end joint of wing in large birds and cutting wings off close to body in smaller birds; remove carcass and put skin and flesh back in shape. Stuff lightly with Chicken or Veal Forcemeat (page 489), filling wings and legs first, then body, leaving space enough for stuffing to swell. Sew together along back, truss, pressing thighs and wings close to body, and bake as for Roast Chicken (page 362); add about 5 minutes per pound for roasting. For glazed surface, brush with 1/3 cup grape jelly, slightly beaten, 1/2 hour before chicken is done, basting several times with jelly and drippings in pan. Remove giblets, clean and cook with bones and trimmings for stock. Serve hot or cold. To carve, remove legs and wings as for roast chicken and cut across legs and body.

To serve cold as pressed chicken, wrap the roasted bird firmly in a cloth, weight it and store in refrigerator overnight. Unwrap and slice thin; serve as hors d'oeuvres or sliced meat.

CHICKEN GRAVY

Use butter or drippings from roast chicken; to 4 tablespoons fat add 4 tablespoons flour and brown slightly, stirring constantly; gradually add 2 cups chicken stock and water and cook 5 minutes, stirring until thickened. Use milk or light cream for part of stock, if desired; season to taste with salt and pepper. Gravy may be prepared in this way for any roasted bird. Approximate yield: 2 cups gravy, or 6 portions.

GIBLET GRAVY

Add finely chopped cooked, steamed or baked giblets (page 365) to 1 to 2 cups Chicken Gravy (page 363). Yield: 1½ to 2½ cups gravy.

BAKED MARYLAND CHICKEN

Use 2 frying chickens weighing about 2½ pounds each; disjoint, cut in pieces for serving, wash and dry. Roll in seasoned flour, dip in egg, beaten slightly with 2 tablespoons water, and roll in coarse bread crumbs; place close together in well-greased pan or casserole. Bake, uncovered, in moderately hot oven (370°–400° F.) 45 to 60 minutes, or until tender, basting frequently with hot mixture of ⅓ cup butter, 2 tablespoons water and 1 teaspoon lemon juice. Serve with gravy made from giblet stock and cream (page 363). The crusty crumb covering serves as a dressing. Yield: 6 portions.

DEVILED CHICKEN

1 3-lb. frying chicken	1 teaspoon salt
⅓ cup butter or margarine	pepper
2 teaspoons Worcestershire sauce	dash of cayenne
1 teaspoon dry mustard	2 cups soft bread crumbs,
1 tablespoon minced parsley	buttered

Disjoint chicken, cut in pieces for serving, wash and dry; spread with butter mixed with seasonings and place in well-greased pan or casserole. Cover with crumbs and bake, covered, in moderately slow oven (325°–350° F.) 1 to 1½ hours or until tender. Serve with chicken gravy or cream sauce (page 363), as desired. Giblets, simmered or cooked until partially done, may be prepared in this way; reduce time to ½ hour. Yield: 4 portions.

OVEN–GRILLED BROILERS

Split, wash and dry broilers; sprinkle with salt and pepper. Heat ½ inch layer of fat (part butter) in baking pan. Place broilers, skin-side down, in hot fat. Bake, uncovered, in hot oven (400° F.) about ½ hour, or until tender, turning when half done; baste each side occasionally with fat in pan. Allow about ¾ pound per portion.

STEWED CHICKEN

Clean and wash fowl and leave whole or cut in pieces; place in large kettle, add water to cover and simmer, covered, 2 to 3 hours, or until tender, adding ½ teaspoon salt per pound after first hour of cooking. Serve with Chicken Gravy made from stock (page 363) or with Dumplings (page 492). Allow ½ to ¾ pound per portion.

COOKED GIBLETS

Clean giblets (heart, gizzard and liver); cover heart and gizzard with cold water and simmer, covered, until tender, or for ¾ to 1 hour, adding liver and ½ teaspoon salt the last 20 minutes of cooking. The neck cut off near the body and the tips of wings may be cooked with giblets to make a rich stock; chop meat and giblets and add to gravy or dressing and use stock for gravy or to moisten stuffing.

CHICKEN FRICASSEE

Cut up fowl and cook as for Stewed Chicken (above); roll pieces in well-seasoned flour and sauté in butter, bacon or pork fat in heavy frying pan until browned. Remove to hot platter; thicken 1½ cups stock with roux of 2 tablespoons each butter and flour, add ½ cup cream, bring to boiling point and pour over chicken. Serve with spaghetti, rice or hot baking powder biscuits.

CHICKEN AND SWEETBREAD CASSEROLE

¼ pound mushrooms, sliced
1 tablespoon chopped onion
3 tablespoons butter
¼ cup flour
1 cup chicken stock
½ cup milk
½ cup light cream
3 cups diced cooked chicken
½ cup chopped cooked sweetbreads (page 341)
⅜ cup blanched almonds
1 teaspoon salt
dash of pepper
¼ cup dry bread crumbs, buttered

Sauté mushrooms and onion in butter until lightly browned; stir in flour, add stock and milk gradually and cook, stirring until thickened. Add cream, chicken, sweetbreads, almonds, salt and pepper and bring to a boil; turn into greased hot casserole or individual baking dishes and cover with crumbs. Bake in moderate oven (350° F.) about 20 minutes, or until heated thoroughly and crumbs are browned. Approximate yield: 6 portions.

BROWN FRICASSEE

Dredge pieces of fowl in seasoned flour, brown on all sides in butter, bacon or pork fat; add water to almost cover and simmer, covered, 1 to 3 hours, or until tender. Prepare gravy from stock. Serve chicken on hot platter with gravy poured over top.

CHICKEN CREOLE

1 3-lb. fowl, cut in pieces
salt and pepper
¼ pound bacon, cut in 1 inch cubes
1 thin slice ham, cut in 6 pieces
½ cup chopped onion

7 medium tomatoes
1 tablespoon chopped parsley
½ teaspoon thyme
2 cups sliced okra
1½ quarts boiling water
3 cups Boiled Rice (page 507)

Season prepared chicken with 1 teaspoon salt and sprinkle with pepper. Panbroil bacon in large heavy frying pan or Dutch oven until crisp and remove pieces; slowly fry ham and chicken in drippings until browned, adding onion when turning to brown other side; pour off all but 3 tablespoons drippings. Add bacon, 1 chopped tomato or ½ cup cooked tomato, parsley, thyme, ½ cup okra and hot water, and simmer, covered, 1½ hours; add remaining 1½ cups okra and cook ½ hour longer, adding more water if necessary. Place remaining 6 whole tomatoes on top and cook, covered, 15 minutes, or until just tender. Place mixture in a tureen, arranging tomatoes on top; serve with hot rice. Yield: 6 portions.

CHICKEN CASSEROLE

1 2½-pound chicken, dressed
1 lemon, halved
2 tablespoons butter or chicken fat
2 tablespoons Sherry
12 small white onions
12 small carrots
12 small turnips, cut in 1-inch pieces

1 stalk of celery
4 mushrooms, quartered
1 teaspoon meat extract
2 tablespoons flour
1½ cups chicken stock
salt
pepper
1 bay leaf or sprig of fresh tarragon

Truss chicken. Rub with lemon and brown slowly in hot butter. When brown, ignite Sherry and pour over chicken. Remove chicken and add onions, carrots, turnips and celery to pan. Brown evenly and add mushrooms. Cook 1 minute and remove pan from heat. Stir in meat extract and flour and blend well. Gradually add stock, stirring constantly. Add salt and pepper to taste and stir over heat until the sauce comes to a boil. Chicken may be added either whole, placed breast-side down, and cooked slowly 1 hour, or it may be disjointed and cooked 35 minutes. Add bay leaf or sprig of tarragon and cover during cooking. Yield: 4 to 6 portions.

CHICKEN BRUNSWICK STEW

2 3-pound chickens
2 tablespoons salt
2 cups whole grain corn
5 medium onions, chopped
1 pound okra, sliced
2 large green peppers, chopped

5 large ripe tomatoes, peeled and
  chopped
½ pound salt pork, sliced
2 pounds lima beans
1 teaspoon Tabasco sauce
½ teaspoon black pepper

Place whole, cleaned chickens in deep kettle with water to cover and add salt. Simmer 1½ to 2 hours, or until meat begins to separate from the bones. Add corn, onion, okra, peppers, tomatoes, salt pork, lima beans, Tabasco and pepper. Reduce heat to slow simmering and cook 2 to 2½ hours longer. The stew should be of mushy consistency. Remove chicken bones and serve with Corn Bread (page 158) or Biscuits (page 149). Yield: 10 portions.

FAMOUS CHICKEN CURRY

2 3½-lb. fowls, cut in pieces
1½ quarts boiling water
1 teaspoon salt
1 cup minced onion
6 stalks celery, minced
2 apples, minced
½ cup olive oil
¼ cup curry powder
¼ teaspoon pepper
½ teaspoon ginger

½ teaspoon Tabasco sauce
1 tablespoon Worcestershire sauce
¼ cup flour
½ cup cold water
1 fresh coconut
2 cups heavy cream
3 egg yolks, well beaten
6 cups boiled rice, molded in
  ring (page 507)

Add cleaned chicken to boiling water and simmer until tender, adding salt when half done; reserve stock, pick meat from bones and cut in smaller pieces. Sauté onion, celery and apple in olive oil until slightly browned; stir in curry powder and simmer 5 minutes; add remaining seasonings and chicken stock (1 quart) and cook 20 minutes; stir in flour mixed with water and cook 5 minutes, stirring until thickened. Drain milk from coconut and add with chicken to vegetable-curry mixture, remove from heat and let stand 3 hours. When ready to serve, add cream and egg yolks and heat thoroughly, stirring constantly. Serve in hot rice ring with shredded fresh coconut. Use large relish tray for a more elaborate service; fill each section with an accompaniment such as chutney, shredded fresh coconut, chopped peanuts, chopped hard-cooked egg yolks, chopped cooked egg whites, chopped crisp bacon or tiny circles of fried onion. Yield: 8 portions.

LUNCHEON CHICKEN

thinly sliced smoked ham or
   Canadian bacon
hot toast, buttered

sliced cooked chicken, duck,
   goose, turkey or guinea hen
Mushroom Sauce (page 467)

Broil or panbroil ham (page 317), cut in pieces and place on buttered hot toast; place slices of chicken on top and serve sauce over all. Any leftover meat may be used to make a luncheon or supper dish.

CHICKEN WITH NOODLES

1 large fowl, cut in pieces
6 cups cooked noodles
   (page 499)
½ pound mushrooms, sliced
½ teaspoon salt
dash of pepper

3 tablespoons butter
1 cup chicken broth
1 cup milk, scalded
½ cup dry bread crumbs,
   buttered

Cook chicken until tender (page 364) and remove meat from bones. Place hot noodles, chicken and mushrooms in alternate layers in greased hot casserole, using ½ of each; repeat layers with remaining amounts. Add salt, pepper and butter to hot broth and milk and pour over filled casserole; cover with crumbs and bake, uncovered, in moderate oven (350° F.) about 20 minutes. Yield: 6 to 8 portions.

CHICKEN PIE

1 4-lb. fowl, cut in pieces
1 onion, sliced
¾ cup diced celery
2 tablespoons minced parsley
½ pound mushrooms, sliced
¼ cup butter or margarine

3 tablespoons flour
salt and pepper
rosemary (optional)
1 hard-cooked egg, sliced
1 recipe Baking Powder Biscuits
   (page 125)

Cook fowl until tender (page 364); remove from stock and separate meat from bones. Add onion, celery and parsley to stock and simmer ½ hour; strain. Sauté mushrooms in butter 5 minutes, stirring frequently; stir in flour, gradually add 2 cups stock, cook until thickened and season to taste; add chicken, bring to a boil and turn into lightly greased hot casserole. Cover with egg slices and arrange rounds of baking powder biscuit dough on top. Bake in hot oven (425° F.) 15 to 20 minutes. Approximate yield: 6 portions.

Chicken Pie with Pastry—Line a deep pie pan or individual pans with pastry, fill with chicken mixture, top with pastry and bake at 450° F. about 30 minutes.

JELLIED CHICKEN LOAF

1 4-lb. fowl, cut in pieces	2 stalks celery
1½ quarts boiling water	1 small onion
2 teaspoons salt	1 envelope plain gelatin
⅛ teaspoon pepper	¼ cup cold water
1 carrot	olive oil

Add fowl to hot water and simmer until tender, adding seasonings and vegetables after first hour of cooking (page 364); remove meat, boil down stock to about 2 cups and strain through wet cheesecloth. Soften gelatin in cold water 5 minutes; add to hot stock, stirring until dissolved, then cool. Pick chicken from bones, chop fine, add to stock-gelatin mixture and cool; when slightly thickened, turn into mold or loaf pan, lightly greased with olive oil; chill until firm. When ready to serve, unmold on cold platter and garnish with parsley, water cress or radish roses, as desired. Yield: 1 loaf, 8½ x 4½ x 2½ inches, or 8 portions.

Pressed Chicken—Boil down chicken stock about one-third, strain and add to chicken, mixing thoroughly; pack into greased loaf pan, place same size pan on top; hold down with light weight. Chill until cold; slice and serve. Approximate yield: 6 portions.

Quick-layered Chicken—Substitute 3 cups coarsely chopped cooked chicken and 2 cups hot chicken broth or canned chicken soup for fowl and stock; use 2 hard-cooked eggs, sliced, and ½ cup sliced stuffed olives. Pour a thin layer of gelatin-stock mixture in bottom of lightly greased mold or loaf pan and chill; when firm, arrange egg and olive slices in attractive design on layer, cover with enough gelatin mixture to anchor design and chill until firm. Place one-half of chicken over this, pour gelatin over top and chill until firm. Repeat layers with remaining amounts, pouring gelatin over all; chill until firm. To serve, unmold on crisp lettuce on cold platter and slice. Approximate yield: 1 loaf, 8½ x 4½ x 2½ inches, or 8 portions.

KINSLEY'S CHICKEN CROQUETTES

Prepare recipe for Meat Croquettes (page 329), using ground chicken for meat; add ¼ cup sliced mushrooms sautéed in 1 tablespoon butter, 1½ tablespoons lemon juice, 2 tablespoons Sherry and a dash of nutmeg to croquette mixture and mix thoroughly. Shape and fry as for croquettes; serve with a savory sauce. Yield 12 croquettes.

CHICKEN SOUFFLÉ

1 cup milk
3 tablespoons quick-cooking
   tapioca
1 teaspoon salt
⅛ teaspoon pepper

¼ cup grated American cheese
1 cup chopped cooked chicken
3 eggs, separated
1 to 3 teaspoons Angostura bitters
paprika

Cook milk and tapioca over rapidly boiling water 8 to 10 minutes, stirring frequently; add salt, pepper, cheese and chicken and stir until cheese is melted. Cool slightly, then stir in well-beaten egg yolks and bitters; fold in egg whites beaten stiff but not dry, turn into casserole with bottom greased and sprinkle with paprika. Place in pan of hot water and bake in moderate oven (350° F.) 40 to 50 minutes, or until delicately browned and firm in center. Approximate yield: 6 portions.

CHICKEN–OYSTER SHORTCAKE

1 recipe Corn Bread (page 158)
2 cups Medium White Sauce
   (page 125)
2 cups diced cooked chicken

8 oysters
butter
dash of paprika
pimiento

Bake corn bread in 11½ x 7⅜ x 1½-inch pan as directed. When bread is nearly baked, prepare white sauce, add chicken and heat thoroughly. Cut oysters in halves and sauté in ½ tablespoon butter about 3 minutes; add to creamed chicken, season with additional salt and pepper, if needed, add paprika and keep hot. Cut hot corn bread in 4-inch squares, split and spread with butter; then put chicken-oyster filling between pieces and on top of corn bread; garnish with pimiento. Yield: 6 portions.

CREAMED CHICKEN EN CASSEROLE

2½ cups sliced cooked chicken
2 tablespoons chopped pimiento
3 cups Thin White Sauce
   (page 125)

½ cup dry bread crumbs,
   buttered
cooked broccoli (page 533)
grated cheese

Add chicken and pimiento to white sauce and bring to a boil; turn into greased casserole, sprinkle with ¼ cup crumbs and bake in moderate oven (350° F.) 15 minutes; place broccoli on top, sprinkle with grated cheese and remaining ¼ cup crumbs and continue baking 10 minutes, or until browned. Yield: 6 portions.

SOUTHERN CHICKEN ROLL

1¼ cups diced cooked chicken
⅓ cup minced ripe olives
1 teaspoon minced onion
1 tablespoon minced pimiento

⅛ teaspoon paprika
1 recipe Baking Powder Biscuits
   (page 149)
6 pimiento strips

Chicken Gravy (page 363)

Mix together chicken, olives, onion, pimiento and paprika. Prepare biscuit dough, increasing shortening to ⅓ cup; roll ¼ inch thick and spread with chicken mixture. Roll and place, seam side down, in greased pan; bake in hot oven (425° F.) 15 to 20 minutes. Remove to hot platter, place pimiento strips across roll and serve with gravy or cream sauce. Approximate yield: 6 portions.

CHICKEN LOAF WITH MUSHROOM SAUCE

2 cups cooked chicken
1 cup peas
½ cup cooked diced carrots
1 cup soft bread crumbs
½ cup milk

2 egg yolks
1 teaspoon salt
1½ teaspoons onion juice
1 teaspoon lemon juice
Mushroom Sauce (page 467)

Put cold leftover chicken and vegetables through food chopper; mix with crumbs, milk, egg yolks, salt, onion and lemon juice and pack into greased loaf pan. Bake in moderate oven (350° F.) about 40 minutes. Unmold on hot platter, slice and serve with mushroom sauce. Yield: 1 loaf, 8½ x 4½ x 2½ inches, or 6 portions.

CHICKEN À LA KING

2 cups Medium White Sauce
   (page 125)
1 cup light cream
1 cup sliced mushrooms
1 green pepper, minced

3 tablespoons butter
1 pimiento, cut in thin strips
2 cups diced cooked chicken
salt and pepper
2 egg yolks, slightly beaten

Prepare sauce with 1 cup milk and 1 cup chicken stock, add cream and bring to a boil. Sauté mushrooms and green peppers in butter 10 minutes, stirring frequently; add with pimiento and chicken to sauce, season to taste with salt and pepper and simmer about 5 minutes; stir into egg yolks and cook 1 minute, stirring constantly. Serve at once on hot toast or rusks; or serve in patty shells. For variation add one of the following: 1 wine glass Sherry; 1 teaspoon lemon juice and ¼ cup chopped stuffed olives. Yield: 6 portions.

CHICKEN TERRAPIN

3 cups diced cooked chicken
½ cup chicken stock
1 cup Thick White Sauce
(page 125)

¼ cup Sherry
1 hard-cooked egg
buttered hot toast
minced parsley (optional)

Simmer chicken, covered, in broth about 10 minutes, then add to white sauce; gradually stir in Sherry, add grated egg yolk and simmer 5 minutes. Serve on toast and garnish with diced egg white. Diced parboiled sweetbreads may be substituted for part of chicken and creamed mixture may be served in timbale or patty shells. Sprinkle with parsley. Approximate yield: 6 portions.

CHICKEN PILAU

1 cup rice
2 quarts boiling water
1 3½-lb. stewing chicken, cut
in pieces
2 teaspoons salt

¼ teaspoon pepper
1 onion, chopped
2 stalks celery, chopped
2 tomatoes, sliced
6 tablespoons butter

Drop rice into boiling water in large saucepan, add chicken and simmer, covered, 1½ to 2 hours, or until chicken is almost done, adding salt and pepper after first hour of cooking. For quick-cooking rice, add last 20 minutes cooking time. Brown onion, celery and tomatoes in butter; add to chicken and continue cooking ½ hour. Approximate yield: 6 portions.

CHICKEN WITH ALMONDS

1 tablespoon minced onion
3 tablespoons butter
½ cup white wine, Sauterne,
or Rhine
1 cup chicken stock
1 cup Medium White Sauce
(page 125)
1 whole clove

¼ bay leaf
3 cups diced cooked chicken
or 1 can boned chicken
¼ cup raisins
½ cup shredded blanched almonds
¼ cup Sherry
3 egg yolks, slightly beaten
½ cup heavy cream

buttered toast

Sauté onion in butter until slightly browned; add wine, chicken stock, white sauce and seasonings and cook 5 minutes, stirring until smooth. Add chicken, raisins and almonds and heat thoroughly; add Sherry and egg yolks mixed with cream and cook 1 minute, stirring constantly. (In Peru they add a dash of cumin seed to this dish.) Serve at once on toast. Approximate yield: 8 portions.

CHICKEN–MUSHROOM RICE RING

1 pound mushrooms
water
¼ cup butter, melted
3 tablespoons flour
1½ cups chicken stock
2 cups diced cooked chicken
1 tablespoon lemon juice

few drops onion juice
½ teaspoon salt
dash of pepper
¼ cup shredded pimiento
2 egg yolks, slightly beaten
3 cups hot boiled rice, molded
 in ring (page 507)

Remove stems and peelings from mushrooms, cover with water and simmer 5 to 10 minutes; strain through cheesecloth. Slice mushroom caps and sauté in butter 5 minutes; sift flour over the mushrooms and stir carefully with fork until butter absorbs flour. Gradually add mushroom and chicken stocks and cook, stirring until thickened; add chicken, seasonings, pimiento and egg yolks and cook 2 minutes, stirring constantly. Serve at once in molded ring of hot rice. Pile fluffy rice into well-buttered ring mold and keep hot until ready to serve. To unmold, invert on heated chop plate. Approximate yield: 6 portions.

TROPICAL CHICKEN

2 cups cubed white meat of
 chicken
2 cups medium white sauce
½ cup chopped, sautéed fresh
 mushrooms
¼ cup chopped green pepper

¼ cup chopped almonds
1 teaspoon Worcestershire sauce
dash of black pepper
dash of nutmeg
3 pineapples, halved lengthwise
½ cup chopped pineapple

Parmesan cheese

Combine chicken, white sauce, mushrooms, green pepper, almonds, Worcestershire sauce, pepper and nutmeg in saucepan and heat. With grapefruit knife scoop out pineapples to within ½ inch of edges. Dice ½ cup pineapple. Combine with chicken and pile into pineapple shells. Sprinkle with Parmesan cheese and paprika. Place pineapples under broiler for 10 minutes or until golden brown. Protect leaves with aluminum foil. Arrange on tray and fill center with slices of avocado, tomato and onion rings. Yield: 6 portions.

CHICKEN AND VEGETABLE BAKE

¼ cup non-fat dry milk
¼ cup flour
½ teaspoon ground sage
½ teaspoon paprika
⅛ teaspoon pepper
1 teaspoon salt

1¼ cups water
1¼ cups milk
2 cups cubed cooked chicken
2 cups cooked peas
12 small white onions
¼ cup sliced ripe olives

Combine milk powder, flour, sage, paprika, pepper and salt; sprinkle on surface of water and milk poured into top of double boiler. Beat with rotary beater until smooth. Cook over boiling water, stirring constantly until thickened. Stir in remaining ingredients. Cook for an additional 5 to 8 minutes. Pour into six 5-inch diameter casseroles. Cover with Biscuit dough (page 149). Bake in a hot oven (425° F.) 12 to 15 minutes. Yield: 6 portions.

CHICKEN PIQUANT IN A PANCAKE SHELL

Chicken Piquant

2 tablespoons chicken fat,
 butter or margarine
¼ cup flour
2 cups chicken broth or milk
1½ teaspoons salt

½ cup diced cooked celery
½ cup diced cooked carrots
1½ cups diced cooked or canned
 chicken

Melt fat in saucepan; stir in flour. Add broth and salt. Cook until thickened. Add celery, carrots and chicken and simmer gently 15 minutes, stirring occasionally.

Pancake Shell

½ cup pancake ready-mix
1 egg

¼ cup milk
2 tablespoons shortening, melted

Combine all ingredients, beating with rotary egg beater until smooth. Lightly grease sides and bottom of a 9- or 10-inch frying pan and heat until very hot. Pour in the batter, immediately rolling the pan until sides and bottom are evenly coated. Cook pancake over moderate heat until dry on the top. Prick bottom of pancake in several places.

Bake in moderately hot oven (400° F.) for 5 minutes or until edge is brown. To remove pancake from pan, run a knife around edge, tilt pan and very gently slide pancake on a serving dish. Fill with Chicken Piquant. Yield: 6 portions.

CHICKEN LIVERS CONSADINE

1 pound small white onions	2 tablespoons flour
½ teaspoon salt	1 teaspoon meat extract
2 cups water	⅓ cup Sherry
1 pound chicken livers	⅛ teaspoon pepper
¼ cup butter or margarine	½ teaspoon dry mustard
1 tablespoon capers and liquid	

Cook onions in salted water until tender. Drain and reserve 1 cup onion liquid. Sauté chicken livers in 2 tablespoons butter until almost cooked. Melt remaining butter, stir in flour and brown lightly. Gradually add onion liquid. Add meat extract, Sherry, pepper and mustard. Cook, stirring constantly, until smooth and thickened. Add onions, livers and capers. Bring to a boil. Serve on cooked noodles or Hominy Ring. Approximate yield: 6 portions.

DUCKLING

Duckling is now sold on most markets "New York Dressed," weighing about 5 to 7 pounds and Quick-Frozen Eviscerated, weighing 3½ to 5 pounds. Scientific breeding and feeding are producing plump and meaty birds.

BROILED DUCKLING

Have poultry dealer prepare duck for broiling by removing backbone and keel from breast bone. Place duck skin-side down on ungreased pan in preheated broiler (350° F.) 4 to 5 inches from source of heat. Broil for a total of 20 to 25 minutes, turning pieces when golden brown. Baste if desired. (For more detailed directions, see How to Broil Chicken, page 356.)

HOW TO ROAST DUCKLING

Prepare duck for cooking as directed for chicken on page 361. Place duck breast-side up, on a rack in a shallow pan in oven. Duck roasted at 325° F. for 1½ to 2 hours, or until a meat thermometer inserted in the stuffing records an interior temperature of 165° F. will be moderately well done but juicy and delicious. Allow 18 minutes per pound for dressed weight (5 to 7 pounds). For very well done duck, the interior temperature should read about 185° F. Allow 22 to 25 minutes per pound. For ducklings with drawn weight of 3½ to 5 pounds, allow 25 minutes per pound for medium well done; 30 to 35 minutes per pound for very well done.

❖❖❖

HOW TO BRAISE DUCKLING

To braise duck, prepare as for roasting and cut in quarters. Place skin-side up in rack in shallow baking pan. Roast in slow oven, 325° F., for 1 hour. Meanwhile cook giblets and prepare desired sauce, using duck broth or fruit juice. Transfer duck to covered pan. Pour sauce over duck and cover tightly. Continue baking in sauce until duck is tender, about 30 minutes longer. For a brown finish, brush duck with 1 teaspoon kitchen bouquet and 2 tablespoons of honey before cooking in sauce.

HOW TO SKIN DUCKLING

With sharp pointed knife, cut the skin from the neck to the vent, first along breast of duck, then along backbone. Loosen the skin by running knife underneath, close to flesh of duck. Peel skin back as it is loosened, cutting the skin where necessary but keeping the flesh intact.

It is really easy and simple to remove the skin since there is a solid layer of fat between skin and flesh, but if you prefer, ask your meat dealer to skin the duck for you.

DUCK IN WINE SAUCE

1 5–6-pound duckling	2 sprigs parsley
2 tablespoons duck fat	1 small bay leaf
½ clove garlic, minced	⅛ teaspoon thyme
2 tablespoons flour	1 teaspoon salt
2 cups red wine	8 small white onions
8 mushrooms, sliced	8 small carrots

Remove skin and fat from duck. Cut duck into serving-size pieces. Cook skin and fat with giblets and neck. Drain off liquid. Allow fat to rise to top, then pour it off. Melt 2 tablespoons duck fat in large frying pan. Brown the pieces of duck in fat over moderate heat. Remove duck to 9-inch casserole. Add garlic to fat and cook 1 minute. Stir in flour. Add wine, mushrooms, parsley, bay leaf, thyme and salt. Bring to boil, stirring constantly, until sauce thickens. Place peeled onions, trimmed carrots and duck giblets in casserole with duck. Top with sauce. Cover tightly. Bake in moderate oven (350° F.) until duck and vegetables are tender, about 1 hour and 15 minutes. Yield: 4 portions.

BRAISED DUCK IN BLACK CHERRY SAUCE

1 5–6-pound duckling	½ teaspoon salt
¼ cup fat	1 bay leaf
1 tablespoon duck fat	⅛ teaspoon marjoram
1 tablespoon minced onion	1 No. 2 can black cherries
1½ cups duck broth	2 tablespoons cornstarch

Have duck cut in quarters. Brown duck in fat in heavy saucepan; roast uncovered in moderate oven (325° F.). Meanwhile cook giblets. Drain off liquid. Allow fat to rise to top and pour it off. Place 1 tablespoon fat in saucepan. Add onion. Cook over low heat about 3 minutes. Add duck broth, salt, bay leaf and marjoram. Drain cherries. Combine ½ cup cherry juice and cornstarch. Stir into hot broth. Cook, stirring constantly, until sauce thickens and boils. Remove bay leaf. Add cherries and heat thoroughly. Serve hot over braised duck quarters. If desired, substitute ½ cup red wine for ½ cup broth. Yield: 4 portions.

DUCK WITH ORANGE

1 5-pound duck	1½ cups chicken stock
1 tablespoon butter	juice of 1 orange
3 tablespoons Sherry	salt and pepper
1 mushroom, finely chopped	1 tablespoon red currant jelly
½ teaspoon minced garlic	(blackberry, raspberry, grape
grated rind of 1 orange	or guava may be substituted)
2 tablespoons flour	3 tablespoons red wine
½ teaspoon meat concentrate	1 bay leaf

2 oranges, cut in sections

Wash duck and split in half. Remove and disjoint legs; cut in halves. Cut rest of duck into thirds. Brown in hot butter. Drain off all fat except 3 tablespoons. Heat and ignite Sherry; pour over duck while flaming and shake pan until flame burns out. Remove duck and keep warm. To duck drippings and wine add mushroom, garlic and orange rind. Sauté 2 to 3 minutes, remove from heat and stir in flour and meat concentrate. Gradually add stock; return to heat and when sauce begins to boil, add orange juice, salt and pepper to taste, jelly and red wine. Add duck, placing skin-side down in pan, and bay leaf. Cook over low heat or bake in moderate oven (350° F.) 45 minutes. Remove bay leaf. Serve in hot casserole. Pour sauce over duck and garnish with orange sections and sliced, sautéed duck liver. Approximate yield: 4 portions.

ROAST GOOSE

Choose young goose, 8 to 10 pounds in weight; singe, clean, cut off neck at body, wash and dry. Rub inside with salt and outside with salt and pepper and if desired, a clove of garlic. Fill cavities loosely with Celery Stuffing (page 485) or a fruit stuffing; sew or skewer cut surfaces together, fold skin back over neck and fasten with skewer. Truss and place on roasting rack. Prick skin well with sharp fork to let fat run out. Roast as directed for Roast Chicken (page 361), allowing 25 to 30 minutes per pound for total roasting. (See chart on page 353.) Place on hot platter; garnish as desired and serve with gravy made from 4 tablespoons each drippings and flour and 2 cups giblet stock. Goose fat drippings may be used in many baking recipes. Allow 1 to 1¼ pounds per portion.

SALMIS OF GOOSE

4 cups sliced cooked goose	**2 cups goose gravy**
2 tablespoons lemon juice	**12 ripe olives, sliced**
2 tablespoons Worcestershire	**¼ cup Sherry**
sauce	**buttered hot toast**

Add goose, lemon juice and Worcestershire sauce to gravy and simmer about 20 minutes. Add olives and Sherry, heat thoroughly and serve at once on toast. Leftover vegetables such as carrots and peas may be added to the dish. Approximate yield: 6 portions.

HOW TO BROIL A SMALL TURKEY

Use a young turkey weighing 2 to 4 pounds. Have turkey split in half lengthwise for broiling. Break drumstick, hip and wing joints to keep bird flat during broiling. For frozen turkeys increase cooking time one and one-half times.

Flatten Halves—Skewer leg to body. Fold wing tip back under wing. Skewer wing flat against cut edge of backbone. Season each half turkey with about ¼ teaspoon salt and a sprinkling of pepper. Place turkey in broiler pan (not on rack). Brush with melted fat, place skin-side down.

Broil Slowly—Place in broiler 5 to 7 inches under heat source. Regulate heat or pan position so that turkey just begins to brown lightly in 10 minutes (350° F.). Cook slowly. Turn and brush with fat two or three times during broiling to brown and cook evenly. Total cooking time, 50 to 60 minutes for 2½ pound ready-to-cook turkey. The turkey is done when meat on the thickest part of the drumstick cuts easily and there is no pink color visible. Serve on warm platter with pan drippings poured over turkey. If giblets are served with broiled turkey, coat the liver and precooked heart and gizzard with fat, season and broil.

Lemon Barbecued Small Turkey—Place prepared turkey halves in broiling pan. Rub both sides of turkey with cut lemon, squeezing lemon to obtain plenty of juice. Brush with melted fat. Sprinkle with a mixture of 1 teaspoon each of salt and sugar, ¼ teaspoon paprika and ⅛ teaspoon black pepper for each half. Place skin-side down in broiler (not on rack). Follow directions for broiling (see above).

HOW TO ROAST A SMALL TURKEY

Young turkeys of any size may be roasted. Stuff turkey *just before roasting.* Stuffing prepared in advance must be refrigerated. Allow 1 cup stuffing per pound ready-to-cook weight.

Rub cavity of bird with ½ to 1 teaspoon salt. Stuff body and wishbone cavities *lightly.* Close by placing skewers across the body opening and lacing shut with cord. Tie drumsticks securely to tail. Fasten neck skin to back with skewer. Shape wings "akimbo" style, bringing tips onto back. Brush skin with melted fat. Poultry seasoning or other herbs may be sprinkled over the surface. Place trussed bird, breast down, on a rack at least ½ inch high in a shallow open pan. Lay fat-moistened thin cloth (large enough to drape down the sides) over top of turkey. Roast at low temperature (see timetable). *Do not sear. Do not add water. Do not cover.* Turn bird breast-side up when about three-quarters done. Roast until tender (see timetable). If cloth dries during cooking, moisten cloth with fat from bottom of pan.

TABLE XXIX

TIMETABLE FOR ROASTING SMALL TURKEYS

Ready-to-Cook Weight (drawn)	Oven Temperature	Total Cooking Time [1] (hours)
2 to 4 pounds	350° F.	2½ to 3
4 to 6 pounds	325° F.	3 to 3½
6 to 8 pounds	325° F.	3½ to 4

[1] These times are approximate. Roasting time will vary slightly with individual birds.

HOW TO FRY A SMALL TURKEY

A young turkey weighing 2 to 4 pounds ready-to-cook weight is suitable for frying. It is usually disjointed and cut up.

For each pound of turkey, blend ¼ cup flour, 1 teaspoon paprika, ¾ teaspoon salt and ⅛ teaspoon pepper (⅛ teaspoon poultry seasoning optional) in a paper bag. Shake turkey, 2 or 3 pieces at a time, in bag to coat evenly. Save any leftover flour for gravy.

Heat ½ inch of cooking fat in a skillet until a drop of water just sizzles. Start browning meaty pieces first, slipping less meaty pieces in between as turkey browns. To brown evenly, turn as necessary with kitchen tongs or two spoons. This browning takes 15 to 20 minutes. Reduce heat, cover tightly and cook slowly until tender, 30 minutes for 2 pound ready-to-cook weight, 40 to 50 minutes for 4 pound ready-to-cook weight. If pan cannot be covered tightly, add 1 to 2 tablespoons water and cover. The liver and precooked heart, gizzard and neck may be floured and browned with turkey the last 15 minutes. Uncover last few minutes to recrisp skin. The turkey is done when meat on the thickest part of the drumstick cuts easily and there is no pink color visible. Lift turkey to a warm platter. If desired, prepare gravy with pan drippings.

HOW TO OVEN-FRY SMALL TURKEY

This method is excellent when two or more turkeys are being fried.

Coat the cut-up turkey with seasoned flour. Brown in at least ½ inch layer of fat in a heavy skillet. If a large quantity of turkey is prepared, it may be deep-fat browned. Place golden-browned turkey, one layer deep, in a shallow pan. For each 2 pounds of turkey, spoon a mixture of 2 tablespoons of melted butter and 2 tablespoons of broth or milk over the turkey. Continue the cooking in a moderate oven (350° F.) until turkey is tender, 50 to 60 minutes. Turn once to crisp evenly. During the cooking, broth or milk may be drizzled over turkey if it appears dry.

HOW TO ROAST HALF AND QUARTER TURKEYS

Prepare for oven same as whole turkey except skewer skin to meat along cut edges; tie end of drumstick to tail; lay wing flat over white meat and tie cord around breast end to hold wing down; place skin-side down on flat rack. Grease with cooking fat and cover with fat-moistened cheesecloth. Set oven for 325° F. Allow 3 to 3½ hours total roasting time for 3½ to 5 pounds, ready-to-cook weight; 3½ to 4 hours for 5 to 8 pounds; 4 to 4½ hours for 8 to 12 pounds. When three-fourths done, turn skin side up. Allow about ⅔ cup stuffing per serving. Press lightly into greased pan or casserole, or put in "bag" of aluminum foil. Cover, or not, as desired. Bake during last 1 to 1½ hours of turkey roasting time. Pour ½ cup hot water into pan, baste stuffing with some of the drippings, leaving enough in pan for gravy.

ROAST TURKEY

Choose a young turkey weighing 10 to 16 pounds. Dress, clean and stuff, using 8 to 14 cups stuffing; proceed as directed (page 378), allowing 18 to 25 minutes per pound according to age of bird and method used (see chart on page 353). Baste, if desired, with mixture of butter and hot water or with drippings in pan; hot cider may be used instead of water. Slices of bread arranged over parts which brown faster than others will insure an even browning. Make turkey gravy (page 363). Allow ¾ to 1 pound per portion.

TURKEY FRICASSEE

Cut up old turkey tom or hen in pieces for frying; roll in seasoned flour and sauté in fat in heavy frying pan or Dutch oven until browned on all sides. Add hot water to half cover and simmer, covered, 3 to 4 hours, or until tender. Thicken stock with roux of butter and flour and season to taste. Serve turkey on hot platter or in large bowl with gravy poured over top. If desired, add vegetables such as sliced carrots, celery and onions to turkey the last 20 to 30 minutes of cooking. Allow about ¾ pound turkey per portion.

STEWED TURKEY

Clean and wash old hen or tom turkey; leave whole or cut in pieces; add boiling water to half cover, bring to a boil and simmer, tightly covered, 3 to 5 hours, or until tender, adding ½ teaspoon salt per pound after first hour of cooking. Serve with gravy made from stock and with dumplings or biscuits, or use in salads, soufflés, creamed or baked dishes. To cook in pressure cooker, see directions for cooking ham in pressure cooker (page 968); allow 10 to 15 minutes per pound for whole turkey at 10 pound pressure. Allow ½ to ¾ pound per portion.

TURKEY CASSEROLE

Use an old turkey; prepare and sauté pieces as for Turkey Fricassee (above); place browned pieces in casserole, cover with milk and bake, covered, in slow oven (300° to 325° F.) 4 to 5 hours, or until tender. Thicken gravy, if desired, with a smooth paste made of flour and water or milk. Allow ¾ pound per portion.

RAGOUT OF TURKEY

1 tablespoon flour
2 tablespoons butter
1 to 1½ cups gravy or stock
¼ teaspoon salt
pinch of nutmeg

½ teaspoon Worcestershire sauce
3 cups cooked turkey
1 tablespoon cranberry or
　currant jelly
¼ cup Sherry or Madeira
toast or rusks

Brown flour in butter, stirring constantly; stir in gravy or stock and cook until thickened; season with salt, nutmeg and Worcestershire sauce. Add turkey and cook 10 minutes, or until thoroughly heated. Stir in jelly and Sherry, bring to a boil and turn at once into covered dish; serve on hot toast. Approximate yield: 6 portions.

TURKEY MOUSSE

1½ tablespoons gelatin
2 tablespoons cold water
1 cup hot chicken broth or stock
salt, celery salt and paprika

1 tablespoon chopped olives
1 cup chopped cooked turkey
1 cup heavy cream, whipped
2 egg whites, stiffly beaten

Soften gelatin in water 5 minutes, add hot broth, stirring until dissolved; season to taste and cool. When slightly thickened, beat with rotary beater until frothy; add olives and turkey and fold in cream and egg whites. Turn into greased loaf pan or mold and chill thoroughly in refrigerator. Unmold on chilled platter or plate and serve cut in slices. Approximate yield: 1 loaf, 8½ x 4½ x 2½ inches, or 6 portions.

TURKEY ROULETTES

1 recipe Baking Powder Biscuits
　(page 149)
1 cup ground cooked turkey
½ teaspoon salt

¼ teaspoon pepper
2 tablespoons cream or stock
2 cups turkey gravy or Medium
　White Sauce (page 125)

Roll biscuit dough ⅛ inch thick and cut in 3 inch squares. Spread squares with turkey mixed with seasonings and cream; moisten edges with water, roll like a jelly roll and place, seam down, in baking pan. Bake in hot oven (425° to 450° F.) 15 to 20 minutes and serve with hot gravy or sauce. Approximate yield: 12 roulettes or 6 portions.

TURKEY CHARTREUSE

Line bottom and sides of buttered mold with seasoned boiled rice. Mix finely chopped leftover turkey with an equal amount of dressing, season with salt, paprika, onion juice and chopped parsley and moisten with giblet gravy. Pack into center of mold and cover with rice; cover tightly and steam 1 hour. A 1½-quart mold makes 6 portions.

SCALLOPED TURKEY

4 oz. egg noodles, cooked   1½ cups diced cooked turkey
  (page 499)   1½ cups Thin White Sauce
1 cup cooked diced celery   (page 125)
              ¼ cup grated cheese

Arrange noodles, celery and turkey in alternate layers in greased casserole; pour white sauce over all and sprinkle with cheese. Bake in moderate oven (350° F.) about 25 minutes, or until top is browned. Approximate yield: 6 portions.

TURKEY LOAF

2 cups Thick White Sauce   ½ cup dry bread crumbs
  (page 125)   2 cups diced cooked turkey
1 cup turkey stock or chicken   3 tablespoons minced pimiento
  bouillon   ¼ cup chopped celery
              3 eggs, beaten

Prepare white sauce, add stock, crumbs, turkey, pimiento, celery and eggs and mix well; turn into greased baking dish. Bake, uncovered, in moderate oven (350° F.) about 35 minutes; let stand 2 to 3 minutes, loosen sides with spatula and turn out on hot platter. Garnish with cooked and well-seasoned mushroom caps and parsley, if desired, or serve Mushroom Cream Sauce (page 466) over sliced loaf. Leftover or canned chicken may be used in place of turkey. Yield: 6 portions.

TURKEY CROQUETTES

Prepare recipe for Meat Croquettes (page 329) with 3 cups diced cooked turkey. Shape and fry as directed. Serve with Mushroom or Parsley Sauce (pages 466 or 464). Approximate yield: 1 dozen small croquettes, or 6 portions.

RUSSIAN TURKEY PIE

½ cup white wine	½ pound bacon, finely ground
1 tablespoon vinegar	½ cup dry bread crumbs
½ cup water	¼ cup chopped onion
¼ cup chopped onion	½ teaspoon capers
5 strips of lemon rind	¼ teaspoon nutmeg
1 tablespoon chopped parsley	⅛ teaspoon dill seeds
1 bay leaf	½ teaspoon salt
1 teaspoon salt	pepper
2 to 3 peppercorns	1 egg
sliced cooked turkey	1 recipe Plain Pastry (page 736)

Measure wine, vinegar, water, onion, rind, parsley, bay leaf, salt and peppercorns into saucepan. Cover and simmer about 5 minutes. Pour over sliced turkey to steep while preparing rest of recipe. Combine bacon, bread crumbs, onions, capers, nutmeg, dill, salt and pepper. Fry in skillet until slightly brown. Pour off excess fat. Stir in slightly beaten egg. Make pastry for 2-crust 9-inch pie. Line pie pan with pastry. Spread the bacon mixture on the bottom crust. Lay the slices of the wine-soaked turkey on the bacon mixture. Cover with top crust. Bake in hot oven (450° F.) 15 to 20 minutes, or until brown. Strain wine and herb mixture. Pour part of it over pie before serving and use remainder for gravy. Approximate yield: 8 portions.

TURKEY DIVAN

8 stalks broccoli	2 tablespoons flour
3 tablespoons melted margarine or butter	1 cup evaporated milk
	2 egg yolks
2 tablespoons Parmesan cheese	salt and pepper
5 tablespoons Sherry	¼ cup Sherry
4 slices (about 2 pounds) cooked turkey or chicken or fillet of haddock or sole	

Cook broccoli and arrange in shallow oblong baking dish. Sprinkle with 1 tablespoon melted margarine and 3 tablespoons Sherry. Arrange slices of turkey, chicken, fillet of haddock or sole on top of broccoli. Sprinkle with 1 tablespoon cheese and 2 tablespoons Sherry. Melt 2 tablespoons margarine in top of double boiler, add flour and blend. Gradually add evaporated milk and continue stirring until thickened. When slightly cool beat in egg yolks, add seasoning to taste and blend in ¼ cup Sherry and 1 tablespoon cheese. Pour over turkey. Bake in moderate oven (325° F.) for about 20 minutes. Yield: 4 servings.

TURKEY WITH CHERRY SAUCE

1 cup canned pitted cherries and juice	½ teaspoon ginger 1 teaspoon lemon juice
4 whole cloves	thinly sliced cooked turkey
½ teaspoon allspice	4 tablespoons butter
	½ cup Madeira

Heat cherries with spices and lemon juice and rub through a sieve. Re-heat the liquid. Heat turkey in the butter. Pour Madeira over turkey and serve hot with cherry sauce. Approximate yield: 4 portions.

QUICK-FROZEN SMOKED TURKEY

Defrosting—In refrigerator, defrosting requires 2 to 3 days. At room temperature, allow 1 hour per pound of bird.

Keeping Cautions—If refrigerator space does not permit storing the bird whole, separate at movable joints, wrap well in waxed paper and keep in the refrigerator. Will retain the fresh smoked flavor for 2 to 3 weeks.

Serving Suggestions

Appetizer—Slice wafer thin and serve on bread triangles spread with mayonnaise. Make cornucopias of thin slices, secure with toothpicks and fill with cottage cheese and chives or potato salad. Grind leftover turkey, mix with mayonnaise, chopped onion and olives and spread on crackers.

Buffet—Slice wafer thin and serve both light and dark meat for cold buffet menu. Garnish meat platter with spiced fruit, individual fruit salads, relishes or tiny individual lime gelatin molds, flavored with horseradish.

Main Dish—Serve thin slices heated with barbecue sauce or on toast with asparagus and cheese sauce. Serve bite-size pieces in hot dishes, such as scalloped peas with mushrooms, noodles with cheese, or potatoes. Also use with creamed sweetbreads and in turkey soufflé.

Salad—Cut turkey into bite-size pieces and combine with salad in-gredients to use in tomato cups or sandwiches. Use also in molded gelatin salads.

COOKING SMOKED TURKEY

Wash bird thoroughly. Soak overnight in enough cold water to cover. Wipe dry throughout. Stuff bird if desired, but omit salt in stuffing. Truss bird (see page 361) and place on V-shaped rack breast-side up in a slow oven (250° F.). Turn the bird for even cooking. Do not baste with pan dripping as it is likely to be too strong. Use a mixture of brown sugar and vinegar, flavored with a dash of cloves and mustard. At this temperature, a young 10-pound turkey will require about 4½ hours. If the bird is an older smoked turkey, wash thoroughly and cook in water, whole or in pieces. Simmer, do not boil. A sliced onion and several stalks of celery may be added to the broth. Cooking time will range from 4 to 5 hours. Cool bird in broth. Serve baked or boiled smoked turkey in thin slices, hot or cold.

ROAST SQUAB WITH RICE PILAU

6 slices bacon, diced	4 cups chicken stock
¾ cup chopped celery	4 eggs, beaten
1 onion, chopped	salt and pepper
1 cup rice	mustard-pickle juice

4 squabs, dressed

Fry bacon until crisp. Remove bacon, add chopped celery and onion to drippings and sauté until brown. Cook rice in chicken stock until tender and add bacon and onion and celery mixture. Add eggs, stirring well so that heat of rice may cook eggs. Season to taste. Stuff squabs with mixture and make mounds of remainder on which to place squabs. Bake in moderately hot oven (350°–375° F.) 35 to 60 minutes, basting frequently with mustard-pickle juice. Approximate yield: 4 portions.

PLANKED SQUAB

Prepare and broil squab or young pigeon on one side as for Broiled Squab (above); place, broiled-side down, on greased hot plank and brush with melted butter. Arrange border of creamy mashed potatoes around edge of plank, brush with beaten egg and bake in hot oven (450° F.) 10 minutes, or until potatoes and squab are browned. Allow ½ jumbo or 1 small pigeon per portion.

BROILED SQUAB ON TOAST

Dress squabs, split down the back and spread open; rub meat with lemon juice, brush with melted butter or bacon fat and sprinkle with salt and pepper. Broil in moderately hot broiler (350° F.) 15 to 20 minutes, turning to brown both sides. Serve on hot toast, buttered and spread with Squab Giblet Paste. Allow ½ jumbo king squab or 1 whole small squab per portion.

Squab Giblet Paste—Simmer giblets of 3 squabs in water to cover for 15 minutes, or until tender; mash, season to taste with salt and paprika and add 1 tablespoon Worcestershire sauce and 2 tablespoons of any tart jelly. Young chicken livers may be prepared in this way and used as spread for sandwiches.

FRIED GUINEA BREASTS

Use breasts from young guinea chickens; sprinkle with salt and pepper and sauté in butter or bacon drippings in heavy frying pan about 20 minutes, or until browned and tender. Place on hot platter and serve with buttered mushroom caps and sauce made from drippings in pan and cream. Allow 1 breast per portion.

ROAST GUINEA HEN

Singe, clean, wash and dry young guinea fowl; rub cavity with butter, sprinkle with salt and place 1 medium-sized onion, quartered, and 1 green pepper, quartered and seeds removed, in cavity. Truss and place on rack in baking pan, breast down; lay 2 thin strips salt pork over back. Roast as directed for Roast Chicken (page 361). When half done, turn on its back, sprinkle with salt, pepper and flour, place salt pork pieces over breast, brush with butter and roast 30 minutes longer, or until tender; allow 35 to 45 minutes per pound for total roasting. Remove vegetables from inside, place bird on hot platter and serve with giblet gravy made from drippings in pan and giblet stock, with ground or chopped giblets and ¼ cup currant jelly added to gravy. Stuff with highly flavored stuffing, if desired. Allow about 1 pound per portion.

GAME

GAME birds and mammals are prepared like domestic poultry and mammals for cooking and eating, but require slightly different handling directly following slaughter. Game flavor is increased by aging or ripening; those who like their game "high" will age it from 1 to 2 weeks or even longer. However, much of the game lacks a protective fat covering and is not ideal for long aging. Birds are "high" when the tail feathers can be plucked easily. Most people prefer the flavor of game slightly under the "high" stage. Birds are plucked by hand and singed only when necessary. Woodcock is the only commonly consumed game bird that is not drawn (entrails removed) before cooking since the whole bird is considered a delicacy. All birds should be washed well inside and out, rinsed under running water and drained well before stuffing and roasting.

There are several important steps between bagging game and eating the kill. One which baffles the inexperienced is how to get the bird out of its feathers. Grouse and small birds sometimes are skinned. For many game birds, however, great care is taken to keep the skin intact. The problem then is to remove feathers, pinfeathers and down. The paraffin method is recommended by many sportsmen for waterfowl.

Paraffin Method. Have the bird well chilled but not frozen. Melt paraffin over boiling water. It takes about 2 pounds of paraffin for 4 ducks if a deep, narrow container is used. Pull out the heavy back, tail and wing feathers and cut off the wings at the first joint. Dip the bird (feathers and all) in the melted paraffin. There must be enough paraffin to cover thoroughly. The more large feathers left on the bird the more paraffin required. Coat thoroughly. Then immediately plunge the paraffin-encrusted bird into ice water for 1 to 30 minutes, or until the paraffin hardens all the way through. Remove from the ice water and peel off the feathers with the paraffin.

GAME COOKERY

FUNDAMENTALLY all meats are cooked in the same way at a constant temperature (moderately low) to the desired degree of doneness. But unless the meat is of good quality to begin with, the cooked game will not be palatable. Much of the success of a game dish depends upon the handling of the animal in the field when killed. Thorough bleeding, removal of entrails as quickly as possible, rapid cooling, keeping the game cold and protecting it from contamination en route from the hunt; finishing the cleaning and dressing in the home, followed by proper aging and storing of the dressed carcass—all are as important as the actual cooking of the game. Before cooking a carcass or piece of meat, it should be checked for any spots that may be stale or sour from contact with entrails, and the offending spot should be cut away. All fat should be removed from meat that is "strong" or fishy. Game is less fat than domestic meats and requires generous additions of butter, bacon, salt pork, drippings, oils or other fats, especially when cooked by dry heat.

Young, tender and quality game retains its natural and distinctive game flavor and is best when cooked by dry heat as in broiling, roasting or frying. Older and less tender game requires long slow cooking by moist heat, as in braising and stewing, to make it palatable. To cook game birds, squirrels and rabbits, follow the directions and recipes given for cooking poultry; for large game and small game mammals, follow directions and recipes for meat cookery. With few exceptions all game should be cooked to the medium done stage; it should be savory, juicy and tender— not dry, tasteless and tough.

A greased cloth over the carcasses of birds and small mammals and frequent bastings during roasting will help keep the skin or outer surface moist and tender. Game flavor can be enhanced, supplemented or modified by a wise choice and use of condiments, sauces, spices, herbs and vegetables.

Serving. A small carving knife, 5- to 7-inch blade, is used for carving game. Duck shears are also used to split small birds and to sever limbs. A medium-sized roast bird is split in half, lengthwise, or in four portions, lengthwise and again transversely. The breast alone of small wild duck is used; one thick fillet, or slice, is cut off each side, or both fillets are divided lengthwise in two. Young pigeons are served whole, or split lengthwise in half. Pheasant is usually roasted and carved at the table. One small pheasant (1½ to 2 lb. each) will serve two people; a 3 lb. pheasant yields four small or three generous portions. The breast alone is used, or slices of the breast and the legs are served. If stuffing is used, a spoonful of stuffing is served with each portion.

WILD DUCKS AND WILD GEESE

Serve at least one small duck to each person. From here on cooking is a matter of personal preference and depends upon whether you like birds rare or well done and whether you wish them stuffed or not. If you do not use a dressing for wild ducks and geese, place one-quarter onion and half an apple inside with a strip or two of bacon over the breast.

BROILED WILD DUCKS OR COOTS

Both duck and coot meat is dark and likely to be dry. Select the less gamy, young and plump birds. Split each dressed bird in half and flatten breastbone; leave small ducks whole. Rub with cut surface of onion or garlic, lemon or lime and brush with oil or melted fat 30 minutes before broiling. Broil at moderately slow heat (325°–350° F.) (page 364): for rare ducks allow 15 to 25 minutes; for medium done ducks or coots, 20 to 35 minutes. Season, arrange on heated platter, brush with melted butter and garnish with parsley sprigs and lemon or lime wedges. Serve with fluffy rice, buttered peas and diced turnips, fruit salad, cornsticks and a tart jelly, or serve with your favorite combinations. Allow ½ large or 1 small bird per portion.

Combined Broiling and Roasting—For quantity serving, broil to brown both sides and finish by roasting in a slow oven (300° to 325° F.) until done. It will take a little longer than for broiling.

Barbecued Ducks or Coots—Baste with a barbecue sauce during broiling. Use a highly seasoned sauce for "strong" or fishy birds.

ROAST WILD GOOSE OR DUCK

Use young and plump birds. The Canada goose is probably the best known of six or more different varieties. Geese are long-lived; when old they are "strong" and tough; only the young should be roasted. Undressed, they average 8 to 13 pounds. They are usually not fat. Prepare, stuff and truss wild goose or duck, following directions given for roasting domestic waterfowl (pages 375–378). Roast under tender and done to the desired degree of doneness, basting occasionally with drippings or a mixture of butter and hot water. Goose or ducks may be covered with slices of bacon or salt pork or with a greased cloth to keep skin moist. Roast goose in a slow oven (300° to 325° F.) until well done, allowing 18 to 20 minutes per pound. For rare ducks roast them in a hot oven (450° F.) 15 to 20 minutes, basting every 5 minutes with a mixture of butter and water. Red juice will ooze out on carving. For medium done ducks, roast them in a moderate oven (325° to 350° F.) for ½ to 2 hours, or until tender. Serve with gravy made from drippings, brown or wild rice, vegetables, a green salad, tart jelly and a hot bread. Allow 1 to 1½ pounds per portion.

BROILED GROUSE

Singe grouse, clean, split down back, wipe thoroughly with wet cloth and press flat. Brush both sides with olive oil, sprinkle with salt and place, skin-side down, on greased broiler. Broil birds in moderate broiler (350° F.) about 15 minutes, turning once; place slice of bacon over each bird when browned on both sides and continue broiling until bacon is crisp. Allow 1 grouse per portion.

ROAST GROUSE

Singe grouse, clean, wash or wipe with damp cloth and dry. Rub cavities and outside with salt and fill with Sage Stuffing (page 485); do not sew opening together but place thin slices of fat salt pork over fronts of birds, fasten with toothpicks and place on rack in roasting pan. Roast in moderately slow oven (325°–350° F.), or until birds are tender. Brush surfaces with cooking oil, dredge lightly with flour and bake 15 minutes longer, or until browned. Arrange grouse in center of hot large platter, arrange fluffy rice at ends and sides of platter with broiled mushroom caps placed on top. Garnish with crystallized, red apple halves.

BROILED WILD BIRDS

Young upland game birds such as the quail, baby pheasant, red leg partridge, English partridge, Scotch or snow grouse, Norwegian ptarmigan and snipe, may be broiled in the same way as domestic broilers (page 356). Split dressed birds (plucked, not skinned) down back with breast intact, or leave whole. Rub well with oil or melted butter. Broil at moderate heat (350° F.) with top surface 3 to 4 inches from heat, basting frequently with additional fat and turning to cook evenly. For approximate time for broiling each see Timetable XXVII, page 354. Spread with butter, season and serve on buttered slices of toast or toast points. Allow 1 small bird per portion.

BROILED WOODCOCK

The woodcock is not drawn by the English and American connoisseurs, who consider the entrails edible; the entrails shrivel on cooking and are easily removed. Clean birds, blanket with thin slices of fat salt pork and broil at moderate heat (350° F.) about 15 minutes, turning frequently. Serve on toast with Rice Croquettes (page 510) and currant or wild plum jelly; allow 1 bird per portion.

BROILED QUAIL

Clean quails and split down back; brush with olive oil or Lemon Butter (page 200) and sprinkle with salt and pepper. Broil as for grouse (page 391), allowing about 10 minutes for broiling. Serve on buttered hot toast with spicy, stuffed melon mangoes or with Mushroom Cream Sauce (page 465) and broiled tomatoes. Allow 1 quail per portion.

ROAST WILD BIRDS

Fill oven-dressed plucked young birds with a mild-seasoned stuffing, (bread, wild or brown rice, oyster or mushroom) and truss as for chicken (page 361). Wrap bacon strips around lean birds or protect well with a greased cloth. Wrapping the legs with strips of greased cloth will help to keep them from becoming dry and too brown. Place breast down on greased rack in shallow pan and roast in a slow to moderate oven (300° to 350° F.) until done, turning them when half done, and basting frequently with an unsalted fat, or a mixture of melted butter and water. For approximate time for roasting each bird, see Timetable XXVII, page 354. Brush well with butter or oil, season and remove to heated large platter. Pile fluffy rice at ends and sides of platter with broiled mushroom caps placed on top. Garnish with crystallized red apple halves, baked green pepper cups stuffed with creamed corn and sprigs of water cress. Or garnish as desired. Allow 1 small bird per portion.

OVEN–GRILLED BIRDS

Use young, tender, oven-dressed birds; split in half or leave whole. Proceed as for Oven-Grilled Pheasant (page 394), baking until tender and done. Fat should cover one-third of birds. Allow 15 to 20 minutes for baking. Birds should be juicy and tender. Serve at once on buttered hot toast with spicy stuffed melon mangoes or with Mushroom Cream Sauce (page 465) and broiled tomatoes.

HAZEL HEN IN CREAM SAUCE

2 hazel hens, cleaned	2 tablespoons light cream
3 tablespoons melted butter	½ cup lemon juice

Rub hens with olive oil and roast in moderate oven (325°–350° F.) 45 to 60 minutes, basting frequently with a sauce made of the melted butter, cream and lemon juice. The meat should have a pink tinge when done. Pour sauce over bird for serving. Approximate yield: 2 portions. Serve with hearts of artichoke, small browned potatoes and tomato or a green salad.

PARTRIDGE, HUNTER'S STYLE

1 partridge	2 small carrots, sliced
1 cup chopped cabbage	1 onion, sliced
3 slices sautéed bacon,	mixed herbs
crumbled	½ to 1 teaspoon salt
3 to 4 large cabbage leaves	dash of pepper

Clean partridge. Mix chopped cabbage and bacon bits and stuff bird. Wrap securely in cabbage leaves, place in pan with 1 inch of boiling water, add remaining ingredients, cover and simmer without removing cover for 1½ hours. Serve bird covered with liquid and vegetables. Approximate yield: 1 portion.

PTARMIGAN EN CASSEROLE

2 ptarmigans (about 1¼	peel of ½ lemon
pounds each), dressed	1 dozen juniper berries
5 tablespoons butter, melted	¼ cup white wine
peel of ½ orange	2 tablespoons hot brandy

Sear birds in 3 tablespoons butter, turning constantly until golden brown, or about 20 minutes. Then place in casserole with butter from frying pan, adding two tablespoons more melted butter, orange and lemon peel and juniper berries. Sprinkle with a white wine and cook in slow oven (300° F.) 15 minutes, basting lightly. Just before serving, lift the ptarmigans out of the casserole, and pour burnt brandy on top of the birds. Cover with the juniper gravy. Yield: 2 to 4 portions.

ROAST WILD TURKEY

The wild turkey is the largest of American upland game birds; it is a highly prized and delicious meat. Young hens average 8 pounds; young toms, 12 pounds, undressed. Follow method used for preparing, stuffing, trussing and roasting domestic turkey (page 379).

PARTRIDGE OR QUAIL PIE

3 partridges or quail	3 tablespoons flour
½ pound veal steak	2 cups stock or water
1 teaspoon salt	2 whole cloves
⅛ teaspoon pepper	1 cup sliced mushrooms
¼ cup bacon drippings	1 tablespoon chopped parsley
6 slices bacon, halved	½ cup Sherry

½ recipe Plain Pastry (page 736)

Clean and split birds down the back; cut veal in six strips; sprinkle all with salt and pepper and sauté in drippings in heavy frying pan until lightly browned. Put birds in casserole, cover with veal and bacon pieces over top. Stir flour into drippings in pan, gradually add stock and stir and cook until thickened; add cloves and pour over meat in casserole. Bake, covered, in moderate oven (350° F.) 1 hour, or until tender; then place mushrooms on top, sprinkle with parsley and pour Sherry over all. Adjust pastry crust over casserole, cutting gashes in crust to permit escape of steam; bake in hot oven (450° F.) 15 to 20 minutes, or until browned. Approximate yield: 6 portions.

OVEN–GRILLED PHEASANT

1 pheasant	salt
¾ to 1 cup butter and other fat	pepper, paprika
	celery or onion salt

Use a young pheasant weighing 2 to 2½ pounds. Cut dressed bird in half or quarters. Measure butter and other fat (equal amount of each is most desirable) into a shallow baking pan and heat in very hot oven (450°–500° F.). Place pheasant, skin-side down, in sizzling hot fat (not smoking) and bake 21 to 25 minutes, basting every 5 minutes with fat in pan and turning when browned on top and half done. Remove to hot platter, season and garnish with broiled tangerine or orange sections, water cress, parsley sprigs or tender celery leaves. Serve at once with creamed potatoes, buttered asparagus or broccoli, tossed green salad, hot biscuits and a tart jelly, if desired. Approximate yield: 2 to 4 portions.

ROAST PHEASANT

Choose young hens for roasting weighing about 2½ pounds each when dressed. Prepare as for Roast Chicken (page 361), brush inside with olive oil or butter, sprinkle with salt, fill lightly with stuffing (page 484), sew together and truss; or place 2-inch square steak and 2 mushrooms in cavity of each bird. Brush with butter, sprinkle with salt and pepper and roast, breast down, in slow oven (300° to 325° F.) about 1½ hours, or until tender, basting frequently with mixture of butter and hot water to prevent skin from becoming hard and turning when half done. Or cover birds completely with thin slices of fat salt pork or greased cloth, basting occasionally with drippings in pan. Place on hot platter; make gravy from drippings in pan and giblet stock, skimming off excess fat; serve in bowl. Allow 1 pheasant for 3 to 4 portions.

SMOTHERED PHEASANT

Cut pheasant in pieces for serving; roll in seasoned flour and sauté in 3 tablespoons butter until well browned. Add 1 cup light cream and simmer, covered, ½ to ¾ hour, or until tender, adding milk if necessary and turning occasionally; or bake, covered, in slow to moderate oven (325°–350° F.) ½ to 1 hour. Serve meat on hot platter with gravy made from cream in pan. One pheasant makes 3 to 4 portions.

CASSEROLE OF PHEASANT IN WINE

2 medium-sized pheasants	2 onions, quartered, or
salt and pepper	2 cups cooked wild rice
2 stalks celery	2 tablespoons olive oil
2 small carrots	½ cup diced ham
1 apple, quartered	½ cup Sauterne
1 teaspoon butter	

Wash birds well. Season, stuff with celery, carrots, apple and onions, or with the mixture of rice, olive oil and ham. Put Sauterne and butter in a tightly covered casserole or small roaster; place in a moderate oven (350° F.) 15 minutes. Place birds in casserole and bake, covered, in moderate oven (350° F.) 1 hour or until tender and browned. Serve with any drippings as sauce. Approximate yield: 4 to 6 portions.

BRAISED PHEASANT

Clean pheasant, disjoint and cut in pieces to serve; roll in seasoned flour, sauté in bacon drippings in heavy frying pan. Add 4 slices bacon, chopped; 4 small carrots; 4 stalks celery, cut in 2 inch pieces; 1 large onion, chopped; 1 shallot; 1 sprig thyme, crushed; 1 bay leaf, crushed; 2 tablespoons chopped parsley and 1 cup game stock or water, and simmer, covered, ½ to 1 hour, adding 1 cup shelled and blanched chestnuts (page 543) 10 minutes before meat is done. Yield: 4 portions.

SQUIRREL, RABBIT (COTTONTAIL)

Fresh from the forest or field, dressed with care and cleanliness, held for a day or two in the refrigerator, squirrel and cottontails make delicious eating and taste much like chicken. When broiled, roasted, fried or stewed in the same way as chicken, they can readily pass for chicken. The fox and gray squirrel are small, the dressed carcass ranging in weight from ¾ to 1⅔ pounds; the cottontail is heavier, with an average of 1 to 2 pounds (dressed). The best way to learn to skin and dress a squirrel or rabbit is to watch a skilled hunter at work. Rabbits, in particular, are susceptible to infections. By hunting rabbits after the first heavy frost, by shooting only the lively ones and with care and cleanliness in dressing them, any danger of possible infection is greatly reduced. The snowshoe hares and jack rabbits are larger than the cottontail; they are rangy, more gamy and are usually soaked in weak brine or vinegar solution to reduce their gaminess.

ROAST RABBIT OR SQUIRREL

Rub inside of an oven-dressed rabbit or squirrel with salt and pepper, fill with stuffing, sew or lace edges together and truss. Brush generously with butter, bacon or beef drippings, season and place (underside down) with legs outstretched, or on side, on greased rack in shallow roasting pan. Cover with greased cloth and roast in slow oven (300°–325° F.) 1½ to 2 hours, or until well done, basting frequently with melted fat. Remove to heated platter and arrange crisp bacon slices over meat to cover up the prominent ribs; garnish with parsley sprigs or curly endive. Serve hot with gravy made from drippings in pan. To serve, cut carcass in half along backbone and breastbone with heavy shears, and cut each half in two. Allow ½ to 1 pound per portion.

BROILED SQUIRREL OR RABBIT

Follow recipes given for broiled chicken (page 356). Cut each in half, brush generously with a mixture of melted butter and lemon juice. Broil as directed, allowing 30 to 45 minutes to cook until well done.

FRIED RABBIT

2 2½- to 3-lb. young rabbits	salt
2 egg yolks, slightly beaten	½ cup fat
3 cups light cream	1 tablespoon parsley
1¼ cups flour	2 teaspoons currant jelly

Wipe dressed rabbits with a damp cloth and cut in pieces for serving. Combine egg yolks and 1 cup cream, gradually stir in 1 cup flour, add 1 teaspoon salt and beat until smooth. Dip pieces of rabbit into batter and fry in fat in heavy frying pan about 15 minutes, or until well browned on all sides. Reduce heat and cook, uncovered, over low heat or in slow oven 30 to 40 minutes, or until tender, turning frequently. Serve on hot platter with cream gravy. Prepare gravy from drippings in pan, using remaining ¼ cup flour and 2 cups cream; season to taste and add chopped parsley and currant jelly. Yield: 6 to 8 portions.

Fried Rabbit with Orange Sauce—Reduce flour to 2 tablespoons, omit cream and use ¼ cup water, 1 cup orange juice; ⅛ teaspoon salt, ½ teaspoon grated orange rind, and 1 tablespoon brown sugar.

HASENPFEFFER

3-pound rabbit	½ teaspoon salt
1 cup vinegar	⅛ teaspoon pepper
1 onion, sliced	1 bay leaf
1 cup water	¼ cup shortening
	1 cup sour cream

Cut rabbit into serving pieces. Add vinegar, onion, water, salt, pepper and bay leaf. Let stand for two days. Remove meat, coat each piece with shortening, fry until brown. Add sour cream to vinegar solution in which rabbit was soaked. Pour over rabbit. Cook slowly for 2½ hours. Thicken gravy and serve. Yield: 4 portions.

STEWED RABBIT

3-pound rabbit	2 whole cloves
¼ cup shortening	2 tablespoons flour
1 teaspoon salt	1 cup sour cream
½ teaspoon pepper	3 slices bacon

Cut rabbit into serving pieces. Coat each piece with shortening, fry until brown. Place half the meat in bottom of pan, sprinkle with half the seasonings, flour and sour cream. Repeat with second half of meat, seasonings, flour and sour cream. Top with bacon. Cover. Simmer slowly for 2½ hours. Yield: 4 portions.

VENISON

The term "venison" applies broadly to the flesh of all animals with the peculiar type of horns called antlers. Usage has limited it largely to deer or elk flesh. The actual cookery of venison differs very little, if at all, from domestic-meat cookery. (See Meat Section, page 250 and on.) It should be cooked medium to well done—a wise rule to follow in cookery of game in general. Tender cuts of young animals are cooked by dry heat—roasted, broiled or fried. Tough cuts are cooked slowly by moist heat—braising, pot roasts, stews, casserole dishes. Venison is likely to be lean and fats have to be added generously to keep meat moist and juicy.

ROAST VENISON

Use a 3 to 5 pound piece of loin, round or shoulder from a young deer, elk, or caribou. Lard it with salt pork strips if very lean or cover with slices of bacon or salt pork. Place on rack in shallow pan. Insert meat thermometer with bulb in center of meat. Roast in slow oven (300°–325° F.) until medium to well done, or until meat thermometer registers 175°–180° F. Allow 35 to 45 minutes per pound (Table XXVII, page 354). Serve with gravy made from drippings in pan. Allow ½ to ¾ pound per portion.

ALASKAN VENISON ROAST

4 pound roast of venison	1 teaspoon salt
salt pork	¼ teaspoon pepper
1 apple, peeled and sliced	¼ teaspoon allspice
1 onion, sliced	2 bay leaves, crumbled

2 sprigs of rosemary

Wipe meat with a damp cloth. With a wide knife make gashes in roast about two inches apart and half the thickness of the roast. Place a slice of salt pork, thin slice of apple and slice of onion in each gash. Top with another slice of onion. Sprinkle the top with salt, pepper, allspice, bay leaves and rosemary. Insert meat thermometer into thick muscle with bulb in center. Place the meat on a rack in an oven roaster. Roast, uncovered, in slow oven (300°–325° F.) 2 to 3 hours, or until the internal temperature of the meat has reached 170° F. Venison should be roasted medium done. Allow 30 to 35 minutes to the pound. To serve, remove the spices and place meat on a hot platter. The gravy may be thickened, if desired. Approximate yield: 8 servings.

BROILED VENISON

Use tender cuts from loin or leg, about ½ to ¾ inch thick. Brush
with olive oil and broil as for lamb chops (page 306), allowing 10 to 20
minutes; season with salt and pepper and serve with Lemon Butter
(page 200). To panfry, brush hot frying pan with fat and fry, uncovered, turning frequently to cook evenly. If venison is strong, marinate
in oil and lemon juice or French dressing for 1 hour before broiling.
Allow ½ to ¾ pound per portion.

VENISON CUTLETS

Use tender cuts from loin, about ½ to ¾ inch thick; marinate in oil
and grape juice for 1 hour. Drain, sprinkle with salt and pepper, roll
in flour, dip in slightly beaten egg and roll in dry bread crumbs. Sauté
in butter 10 to 12 minutes, turning frequently. Place meat on hot platter;
add ¼ cup currant jelly to drippings, stir, bring to a boil and pour
over steak. Allow ½ to ¾ pound per portion.

BRAISED VENISON

Use a 6 pound cut of venison from the lower end of leg or shoulder
clod. Wipe with damp cloth and lard with fat salt pork; rub with
well-seasoned flour. Sauté in ½ cup fat until well browned, turning frequently. Add ½ cup hot water and 1 tablespoon vinegar and simmer,
covered, 2 to 2½ hours, or until tender, turning frequently and adding
small amounts of water, if necessary, from time to time. One-half
hour before meat is done, cover with mixture of ½ cup chopped
celery; 1 onion, chopped; 1 carrot, sliced; 1 tart apple, chopped, and
1 tablespoon lemon juice. Serve on hot platter; add more water to
gravy if cooked down, and pour over meat. Serve with elderberry and
grape or wine jelly. Approximate yield: 8 to 10 portions.

BROILED REINDEER STEAKS

Preheat broiling pan and compartment to moderate (350° F.). Dust
reindeer steaks or chops lightly with flour and brush surface evenly
with melted fat. Place 2 inches from source of heat. Broil 3 to 5 minutes,
season and turn. Brush surface of second side evenly with fat. Broil
3 to 5 minutes. Season and serve immediately. If too gamy, marinate in
French dressing or oil and lemon juice.

REINDEER ROAST

7 pounds reindeer rib roast,   3 cups Apple or Cranberry
    boned   Stuffing (page 485)
salt, pepper   bacon drippings

Place meat flat. Season lightly and spread evenly with stuffing. Roll as for jelly roll. Tie securely with white string. Place on rack in shallow baking pan. Insert meat thermometer with bulb in center of roll; brush with drippings. Roast in slow oven (325° F.) until meat thermometer reaches 170°–175° F. Allow 35 to 40 minutes per pound.

REINDEER STEW

1 cup diced salt pork   2 tablespoons chopped green
⅓ cup flour   pepper
½ teaspoon salt   1 tablespoon chopped parsley
⅛ teaspoon pepper   1 quart water
2 pounds reindeer meat, cut in   2 teaspoons salt
    cubes   ½ teaspoon dried savory
1 cup chopped celery   1 bay leaf
½ cup chopped onion   2 cups diced potatoes

Fry salt pork until crisp and remove from fat. Combine flour, salt and pepper. Roll meat in flour mixture. Brown well in fat. Remove meat. Simmer celery, onion, green pepper and parsley in remaining fat until soft. Add meat, water, salt, savory and bay leaf. Cover and simmer until meat is almost tender (about 1½ hours). Add crisp salt pork and potatoes. Cook until potatoes are tender. Yield: 6 portions.

Fish and Shellfish

AMERICANS can take a tip from Europeans and learn the art of fish cookery as well as the enjoyment of fish in daily meals. Just as with wines, each country has its own specialties of fish. A delicate sauce gives an individual flavor to sole Marguery, a favorite dish of the French. Fish becomes the food focus at the Swedish Smorgasbord; and fried in oil with a touch of garlic, it is welcomed by South Americans.

Actually there are more than 180 varieties of fish in American markets. A good cook can look upon fish as one of the greatest food challenges today, because of the possibilities it offers as the basis of many gourmet dishes.

Fish today may be bought fresh, frozen or canned, either dressed or drawn—whole, whole split, or in pieces as fillets or steaks.

Dressed fish means that the scales, fins, tail, head and entrails have been removed.

Drawn fish have scales and entrails only removed.

If you are purchasing a fish to bake whole, request the fish dealer to "run the fins." This means removing all the fine fin bones within the flesh. You may also have the blood line removed when buying whole fish. If it has not been removed, do so by scraping it out under running water before storing since this is the main source of "fishy" odors.

Quick-frozen fish and shellfish come cleaned, trimmed and ready for use. Cook fish the day it is purchased unless it is held frozen.

If you have a home freezer or a freezing compartment in which fish may be held frozen, it can be held as well at home as in the market. Follow the manufacturer's directions on the package for cooking. If thawed, frozen fish may be cooked like fresh fish. Fish may be thawed completely or only partially before cooking. To thaw, place it in the refrigerator in the unopened container. This requires about 6 to 10 hours. With slow thawing there is less leakage. Fish may be cooked unthawed. If cooked unthawed, more time is required for cooking.

Canned fish such as salmon, tuna and sardines, are ready to use as they come from the can. Many kinds of fish are sold canned or in bulk, pickled in oil or vinegar and spices. Dried fish, either salted or smoked, are sold both packaged and in bulk. Dried fish such as cod, mackerel, haddock, hake and finnan haddie, are soaked in cold water from ½ to 12 hours before cooking, depending upon the degree of saltiness. Soak flesh-side down, so the salt can settle to the bottom of the pan; change the water several times if fish is very salty.

Among the smoked varieties of fish are salmon, sturgeon, cod, ciscoes, sablefish, mackerel, butterfish, whitefish, halibut and herring. Delicately smoked sturgeon and salmon are eaten as appetizers without further cooking—or the fish may be soaked to soften the tissues and then cooked as desired.

Fresh fish should be used as soon as possible after purchasing since they deteriorate rapidly unless held in the refrigerator. To hold, wrap tightly in waxed or parchment paper and place in the coldest part of the refrigerator.

To Clean a Fish. If the fish has not been scaled, remove scales first. Scrape from tail to head against the scales with the back of a short, blunt knife, holding it flat and slanting. If the fish is large, make a slit in the belly from under the gills to about halfway down the body cavity just through the skin. Remove the entrails without breaking the membrane holding them, if possible. With

small fish, such as flounder, smelt and sardines, the entrails are
found close to the head and can be removed easily along with the
head. If you remove the head with the gills, cut straight through
the backbone, just behind the gills. The fins can be clipped off with
scissors or you can "run the fins." To do this cut down the center
of the back through the skin about ½ inch deep on either side of
the fins. The fins and all the fine fin bones along the back can
then be lifted out in one piece in many fish.

To Skin a Fish. Clean the fish. "Run the fins," place the fish on a
board or paper. Cut the skin across the body where it meets the
tail and loosen it enough to grasp a piece firmly. With the fingers
dipped in salt to prevent slipping, work the edge of the skin loose
from the flesh along one side from tail to head, then pull gently
to strip the skin. In the same manner, strip the skin from the
other side. The blunt edge of a knife may be helpful.

To skin flat fish such as flounder, remove the fins and cut away
the fillets (see page 403). Place the fillets skin-side down on the
board. With a sharp knife cut the flesh free of the skin, working
from tail to head. To do this, press the knife against the skin,
drawing the flesh free.

To Bone a Fish. Split the scaled fish on belly-side and remove the
entrails. Lay flat on a board. Begin at the tail and with a sharp
knife cut the flesh close to the bone along one side, pressing against
the bone with the knife; then turn fish over to loosen the flesh on
the other side. With a knife or scissors and fingers, remove the
long backbone. Use tweezers or a short-bladed knife to pick out
as many of the small bones as possible. Fish with many fine bones,
such as shad and herring, are not usually boned completely except
commercially, since the task is long and arduous. Save all bones
to cook for stock. (See page 414.)

To Fillet a Fish. Fillets of fish are boneless, solid slices of meat
(with or without the skin) cut away from each side of the backbone. Bone fish (see directions above) and remove flesh in one

long strip. Feel the fillets to detect and then remove any small bones left in the flesh. (See page 412 for cooking directions.)

To Steak a Fish. Fish four pounds and over are best for steaking. To prepare steaks, cut across the fish through the backbone to make slices ½ to 1½ inches thick. Skin should be left on steaks whenever possible to hold the meat together and keep the juices in during cooking. The bone may be removed from steaks but usually it is left in.

To Split a Fish. Drawn, small whole fish from one to three pounds can merely be split before cooking. Split the fish in half lengthwise, cutting through the rib bones at either side of the back-bone. The appearance of the fish when served whole will be better if you do not cut through the back skin. After broiling, the bones will lift out easily in one piece. This is a simple way to prepare and serve fish.

To Prepare a Fish for Baking. Any dressed or drawn whole fish up to six pounds may be used for baking. The body cavity should be rinsed thoroughly. Drain the fish well and, if you wish, fill it with a savory stuffing (see page 488). Bake fish according to method given on page 406.

To Serve a Baked Whole Fish. If fish is stuffed, remove skewers or thread used to hold in stuffing and garnish attractively with parsley, water cress, lemon or lime wedges, tomato or cucumber slices, radish roses, pickles or other relishes. Button onions or olives may be placed in eye cavities and a sprig of green in the mouth. Place platter with head to the left of the carver. To serve, cut flesh along one side of backbone in slices about 2 inches thick; the flesh is easily removed from the bone. Serve stuffing with each portion. If the fish is large, turn the platter to serve the other side. If the fish has no bones, cut across and through it into steak portions.

Sauces to Serve with Fish. Proper cooking and careful seasoning
of fish are very important. Equally important is the preparation of
the sauce to serve with it. It is the sauce which points up the flavor
of the fish and gives it the finishing touch. The type of sauce to
serve is dependent to a large extent on the fish itself. The delicate
flavor of sole or flounder is best enhanced with a sauce of subtle
appeal. Fish with more pronounced flavors, such as salmon or
mackerel, are improved with a more robust sauce. There are many
sauces and garnishes to serve with fish. Famous chefs have made
their reputation on sauces alone. Creamy rich Hollandaise or a
smooth Béarnaise sauce will do wonders with poached fillet of sole
or flounder.

Mayonnaise with a touch of sour cream turns cold salmon into
a superb dish, while a white wine sauce, using the court bouillon,
is excellent with some of the white fish. A Hollandaise sauce with
a liberal amount of dry mustard blended into it for added tang
is a perfect accompaniment for poached mackerel.

Then there are the savory butters to add new flavor combinations to fish dishes. Maître d'hôtel butter with its tart lemon
flavor or the nutty taste of browned butter is equally good with
sole and other white fish. Strongly flavored garlic butter is perfect
with broiled cod or mackerel. (See Sauces, page 473.)

Fish Garnishes. Lemon or lime slices, plain or dipped in minced
parsley or paprika, are used to garnish many kinds of fish. Parsley,
water cress or lettuce, the latter with cold fish, makes a suitable
green garnish. Garnishes that add color and point up the flavor are
paprika, minced hard-cooked eggs, capers and bright relishes.
Fried, baked and broiled fish are garnished with lemon or lime sections, lemon cups filled with tartar sauce, lemon butter sprinkled
with minced parsley and cooked vegetables.

Button mushrooms sautéed in butter with fillets of flounder,
tiny onions cooked in butter and tossed in chopped parsley around
halibut and cod steaks, wedges of skinned tomato cooked in olive

oil with a touch of garlic for mackerel, cucumbers cut up into olive shapes and cooked in butter with fresh salmon—all of these add interest and glamor to the service of fish.

Try a bed of cooked, chopped spinach mixed with crushed garlic and sour cream under the fillet of sole, or a garnish of cooked shrimp—even succulent seedless grapes or blanched almonds. To garnish fish attractively, never hesitate to try new combinations of color and texture, with special emphasis on subtle blending of flavor well seasoned with a dash of imagination.

Fish Cookery. Each variety of fish and shellfish has a distinct flavor brought out when cooked by one of the basic methods which follow. Most people overcook fish. The connective tissue in fish is largely collagen which is readily converted into gelatin with moist heat; so fish should be cooked only long enough to develop the flavor and coagulate the protein.

Only overcooked fish is flavorless, dry, tough or rubbery. Improper storage before cooking also affects the flavor of fish.

Fish Odors. Fish odors present in the house usually result from overcooking. When steaming or poaching, use a cover to keep the odors in the pan. Odors that cling to the hands after handling fish can be removed by rubbing moistened hands with dry salt followed by warm soapy water. Finish up the job by rubbing the hands with the rind of a freshly squeezed lemon. Dishes and utensils used to cook fish should be soaked in salt water for 20 to 30 minutes before washing in hot soapy water. Broiler pans and skillets, etc., should be put to soak immediately in hot salted water.

TABLE XXX
FRESH SHELLFISH

KIND	AVERAGE SIZE	SOURCE[1] AND SEASON	MARKET UNIT[3]	DESCRIPTION	METHOD OF COOKERY
Abalone[2]	Muscle 2–4 in. wide 3–4 in. thick	P Mar. to Jan.	Sliced, steak	Central muscle of sea-snail; white, solid flesh	Chowder, fry
Clams[2]	Small, medium, large	A, P All year	In shell—by count Shucked—pint	Bivalve mollusk; small meat, delicate flavor	Half shell, chowder, steam, broil, roast
Crabs[2] Soft shell	3½–7 in. wide	A,P,G,I All year May to Sept.	Alive—by count	Crustacean; short, broad, flattened shells; large jointed legs and claws, sweet, delicate meat	Boil, (hard shell), cocktail, salad, (soft shell) broil, fry, deep-fat fry
Crayfish	4–12	I Sept. to Apr.	Sold as lobster tails	Lobster-like crustacean; but without claws	Boil, salads, creamed dishes
Frogs' legs[3]	2–4 oz. per pair	All states	By count, 6 to a serving	Hind legs used; delicate like chicken	Fry, broil
Lobster[2]	1–2½ lb.	A, G, P All year	Alive—by pound	Crustacean; shells mottled green, turn red on boiling; delicate flavor	Boil, cocktail, salad, broil, bake
Oysters[2]	Varies with species	A, P "R" mos.	In shell — by count Shucked—pint, cup	Bivalve mollusk; meat gray-white, tender; characteristic flavor	Half shell, soup, fry, broil
Bay mussels	2–4 in.	A, P	In shell — by count Shucked—pt.	Bivalve mollusk similar to clams and oysters	Steam, chowder, bake
Scallops[2] Bay Sea	½ in. 1½ in.	A, P, G Sept. to Mar.	Pound	Bivalve mollusk; only hard muscle used	Fry, cream, bake, saute, broil
Shrimps[2]	1–3	A, P, G All year	Pound 1 lb. = 1 pt. 1 lb. = 15	Crustacean; green-gray, flesh turns pink when cooked	Cocktail, salad, boil, broil, bake
(Snails) Periwinckle Winkle Conch	Variable	All year	By pound By count By count	Flavor rather like oyster, univalve mollusk	Boil, stew, saute

[1] The following abbreviations are used to denote source: A, Atlantic Coast; P, Pacific Coast; G, Gulf Coast—all salt-water fish; I, interior waters—fresh-water fish.
[2] Also available in canned or frozen forms. The majority are available frozen all year.
[3] Not a shellfish.

TABLE XXXI

FISH—FRESH AND SALT WATER [1]

KIND	AVERAGE SIZE	SOURCE[2] AND SEASON	MARKET UNIT[3] POUND	DESCRIPTION	METHOD OF COOKERY
	Pounds				
Bass Black	½–5	I All year	Whole, split, fillet, steak	White, flaky flesh	Broil, fry, bake, steam
Rock or Striped	3–15	A All year	Fillet, steak, whole		
Sea	½–4	A Summer	Whole, fillet, split		
Bluefish	1–4	A, G All year	Whole, split, fillet	Firm, sweet flesh	Broil, plank, bake, fry, steam
Butterfish	¼–1	A All year	Whole	Delicate flavor	Broil, fry, bake
Carp[3]	2–7	I All year	Whole, fillet, split	Rich meated; flavor often poor in summer	Bake, steam, fry
Catfish[3]	1–35 up	I All year	Whole, fillet	Firm, flaky flesh, red or white	Fry, bake, broil
Cod[3]	6–75	A, P All year	Whole, fillet, steak	Firm, white flesh; lean; mild flavor	Broil, bake, steam
Eel[3]	2½–3 ft.	A, I All year	Whole	Long, slender; tender	Fry, broil, steam
Flounder	1–5	A, P All year	Whole, fillet	Firm, white flesh	Broil, bake, fry, steam
Grouper	2–100	A, G, P All year	Fillet, steak, whole	Firm, white, rather coarse flesh; lean	Broil, bake, steam
Haddock[3]	1–8	A All year	Whole, split, fillet, steak	Firm, white, flaky flesh; lean	Broil, bake, steam
Hake[3]	2–8	A, P All year	Whole, fillet, steak	Like cod; lean	Broil, bake, steam
Halibut[3]	10–80	A, P All year	Steak, fillet	Firm, white flesh; medium	Broil, bake, steam
Herring[3]	¼–1	A, P Apr. to Nov.	Whole, split	Good flavor; cheap; small canned as sardines	Bake, broil, steam, fry
Mackerel[3]	½–1½	A May to Nov.	Whole, fillet, steak	Firm flesh, good flavor; few bones	Bake, broil, steam, fry
King Spanish	10 2–7	Nov. to May			

TABLE XXXI—(*Continued*)
FISH—FRESH AND SALT WATER [1]

Kind	Average Size	Source[2] and Season	Market Unit[3] Pound	Description	Method of Cookery
	Pounds				
Mullet	½–5	A, P All year	Whole, fillet	Firm flesh	Broil, bake steam
Perch White Yellow	½–3	I All year All year	Whole	Firm, white flesh; yellow poorer quality, bony, lean	Broil, bake, fry
Pike[3] Pickerel	6–40 2–8	I All year	Steak, whole, fillet	Firm, flaky	Broil, fry, bake
Pompano	½–2	A, G Winter	Whole	Fine flavor	Bake, broil, fry
Red Snapper Rose Fish	10–20 ½–1	G All year A All year	Fillet, whole fillet	White flesh; good flavor	Broil, bake; steam
Salmon[3] Penobscot	10–17	A Apr. to Sept.	Fillet, steaks, whole	Pink, flaky	Broil, bake, steam
Chinook	20–22	P May to Oct.		Deep salmon color, flaky	
Sockeye	7–20			Deep red; firm; good texture	
Coho	6–8			Pale to deep pink; firm	
Pink	4			Pale pink; soft; sweet	
Chum	9–11			White to yellow; soft	
Shad[3]	4	A Jan. to June Roe best early	Whole, fillet boned	Sweet, white; many small bones	Bake, plank broil, steam
Sheepshead	4–15	A, I Nov. to March	Whole	Coarse flesh	Broil, bake, steam
Scup (Porgy)	½–2	All year	Whole, split, fillet	Lean, moist, mild flavored	Bake, steam, fry, broil
Smelt	⅕	A, P Sept. to May	Whole	Delicate flavor	Fry, broil
Sole, Lemon	3–6	A, P All year	Fillet	Delicate flavor	Broil, bake, steam

TABLE XXXI—(*Continued*)
FISH—FRESH AND SALT WATER [1]

KIND	AVERAGE SIZE	SOURCE[2] AND SEASON	MARKET UNIT[3] POUND	DESCRIPTION	METHOD OF COOKERY
	Pounds				
Sturgeon[3]	20–200	A, P I Mar. to Jan.	Steak	Solid, meaty fish	Broil, bake, steam
Swordfish	90–300	A, P June to Oct.	Steak	Firm, flaky flesh; definite flavor	Fry, broil, bake, steam
Trout Rainbow Brook Lake	1–6 1–12 2–20	I All year All year Apr. to Nov.	Whole, fillet, split	Tender, pinkish, delicate flesh; medium	Fry, broil Bake, broil
Tuna[3]	30 up	A, P Apr. to Nov.	Steak	Yellow to pink; firm flesh, gamy flavor	Bake, broil, fry
Weakfish	1–6	A All year	Whole	White, flaky flesh; lean	Broil, bake, steam
Whitefish	½–5	I Apr. to Dec.	Whole, fillet, split	White, sweet flesh; flavor like halibut	Bake, plank, broil, steam
Whiting[3]	½–2	A, P, G May to Dec.	Whole, split, fillet	White, fine-textured flesh; no fine bones	Broil, bake, steam, fry

[1] Frozen fish which compares favorably with fresh-caught fish is available in many sections of the country. Fillets and steaks of cod, salmon, mackerel, sole, haddock, etc., are popular frozen varieties.
[2] The following abbreviations are used to denote source: A, Atlantic Coast; P, Pacific Coast; G, Gulf Coast—all salt-water fish; I, interior waters—fresh-water fish.
[3] Also available in one or more of the following forms: canned, smoked, dried, salted, pickled.

BAKED FISH

Baked fish should be juicy and tender with the full rich natural flavor. Any variety may be baked, but use a fish that is dressed or drawn (see page 401). Request the fish dealer to leave the head on or not as you choose. Know the weight of the fish, for accurate cooking.

Fat or lean fish may be used; select a fish weighing 3 to 5 pounds and prepare the fish for stuffing, with or without head and tail; bone if desired (page 403). Rub inside with salt, fill with any desired stuffing (pages 484–493) and sew edges together; place, underside down, on greased rack or greased heavy paper in shallow pan, arranging fish in "S" shape or circle. Rub outside with salt and, if fish is lean, brush with melted fat and lay strips of bacon or fat salt pork over top, or cut several slits in each side and insert a strip of salt pork in each slit. Bake fish, uncovered, in moderately hot oven (375°–400° F.), allowing 10 to 16 minutes per pound. Flesh shrinks slightly from skin and bone when done. Baste occasionally with melted fat if fish seems dry. Place on hot platter, garnish with lemon slices. tomato wedges or parsley and serve with any desired sauce. Allow ½ pound fish per portion.

BAKED STUFFED FISH

1 3-lb. fish, dressed or drawn	¼ teaspoon thyme or marjoram
3 cups soft bread crumbs	½ medium-sized onion, minced
½ teaspoon salt	⅓ cup butter, melted
⅛ teaspoon pepper	strips of bacon or salt pork

Prepare fish for stuffing. Rub inside with salt. Mix bread crumbs with ½ teaspoon salt, pepper, thyme and onion; add butter slowly, tossing lightly with a fork until blended. Fill fish with stuffing and sew edges together. Place, underside down, on greased rack or greased heavy paper in shallow pan, arranging fish in "S" shape or circle. Rub outside with salt and if fish is lean, brush with melted fat. Lay strips of bacon or fat salt pork over top, or cut several slits in each side and insert a strip of salt pork in each slit. Bake fish, uncovered in moderately hot oven (375° F.), allowing 10 to 16 minutes a pound. Flesh shrinks slightly from skin and bone when done. Allow ½ pound fish a portion.

STUFFED BAKED STRIPED BASS

1 5-pound striped bass	2 tablespoons butter
3 small white onions, sliced thin	1 teaspoon finely chopped parsley
4 stalks tender white celery	dash of pepper and salt
4 slices bacon, chopped fine	1 cup dry white wine
½ green pepper, chopped	2 teaspoons butter

Clean and split bass, but do not detach halves, so that fish will retain its shape; remove backbone. Place onions, celery cut in thin strips, bacon and green pepper into saucepan and sauté until light brown. Add butter and cook over low heat, adding parsley. Blend well and add dash of black pepper. Wipe fish clean and salt and pepper well. Spread filling inside between halves, fold fish over and place in well-buttered casserole. Pour wine over fish and place the 2 teaspoons butter in bits over top. Bake in medium hot oven (400° F.) for 35 to 40 minutes or until fish is tender, basting frequently with the wine. Serve with own sauce. Serve with marinated cucumbers. Yield: 4 portions.

BAKED FISH FILLETS OR STEAKS

Use fillets or steaks ½ to 1 inch thick; cut into serving-size pieces or leave whole. Dip in solution of 1 cup milk and 1 tablespoon salt, roll in fine bread crumbs and place in a greased shallow baking pan. Pour melted butter over fish. Bake in moderately hot oven (375°–400° F.) until done, allowing 15 to 30 minutes. Place on hot platter and serve immediately, garnished with parsley and lemon or lime wedges and serve with Almond Butter (page 472) or any desired tart sauce. Allow 2 to 3 servings to the pound for steaks; 3 servings for fillets.

Baked Fillets with Bacon—Omit melted butter and lay strips of bacon over breaded fillets. Serve with lemon slices and parsley.

Baked Fillet of Sole—Omit milk and bread crumbs. Sprinkle fillets with salt and pepper and brush with Butter and Lemon Sauce (page 472), basting several times with the butter. Serve with lime wedges. This method can be used with any fillets.

Fillets Baked in Milk—Omit milk and bread crumbs, sprinkle fillets with salt and pepper and add enough milk to cover.

Fillets Baked in Tomato Sauce—Omit milk and crumbs, sprinkle lightly with salt and pepper, cover with Tomato Sauce (page 469). Creole Sauce (page 470) or Cheese Sauce (page 470) may be substituted for tomato sauce.

QUICK OVEN GRILLED FILLETS

Prepare fillets as for Baked Fish Fillets (page 412). Bake, uncovered, in very hot oven (500°–550° F.) 10 to 12 minutes, depending on thickness of fish. The crumbs are crisp and brown, the fillets have the characteristic flavor of fish fried in deep fat, and the cooking odor of fish is practically eliminated.

PLANKED FISH *

Use whole fish, split fish, or fillets or steaks ½ to 1 inch thick. Dry fish thoroughly, season both sides with salt and pepper and brush with oil or melted fat. Place, skin-side down, on oiled hot plank or ovenware platter and bake in hot oven (400° F.) 15 to 30 minutes or until done, basting frequently. Remove from oven, border with Mashed Potatoes (page 564) or Duchess Potatoes (page 564), brush with melted butter, milk, or diluted egg yolk and brown in oven or under broiler. Garnish with parsley and serve at once. Other vegetables, such as string beans, lima beans, tomato slices or small Stuffed Tomatoes (page 578), may be used with the potatoes. Allow ⅓ to ½ pound fish per portion.

* See page 281 on how to season a plank.

BAKED STUFFED FILLETS

Place large fillet in greased baking dish, season with salt, pepper and lemon juice and cover with desired stuffing; place second fillet over stuffing and brush with melted butter, or cover with buttered crumbs. Bake, uncovered, in moderate oven (350°–400° F.) about 30 to 40 minutes, basting with melted butter. Allow ⅓ pound fish per portion.

STUFFED FILLETS OF HADDOCK

Place haddock fillet (1 lb.) in greased ovenproof baking dish. Cover with layer of thinly sliced onions, top with layer of sliced tomatoes, season with salt, pepper and minced parsley and dot with butter or margarine. Place fillet on top, season and brush with butter. Bake in moderately hot oven (375°–400° F.) about 30 minutes. Sprinkle with grated cheese; place under moderate broiler to brown cheese. Yield: 6 portions.

BROILED FISH

Properly broiled fish should be golden brown, juicy and tender when ready to serve. Broiling is a quick method of preparing fish and is ideal for last minute meals. Any small whole fish, fillet, steak or split fish can be broiled. Use a moderately hot broiler (375°–400° F.). Rinse, drain well and brush fish with butter. Place it on greased rack 2 to 4 inches from source of heat: small fish near heat, larger fish farther removed. Broil until browned, turning as needed to cook fish. Baste liberally while broiling. Butter, shortening, margarine or oil may be used. If you wish, give a final basting, a minute before done, with a tablespoon of wine. Garlic and herbs, when used, are added shortly before removing the fish from the broiler. Serve immediately.

To Broil Fish Fillets—Place the well-buttered fillet, skin down, on broiler rack two inches from the source of heat and broil 5 to 10 minutes. Do not turn fillets while broiling.

To Broil Whole Fish—Place buttered, dressed whole fish on broiler rack 3 to 6 inches from source of heat for different fish. Broil one side 3 to 5 minutes, season, turn, baste with fat, finish broiling.

To Broil Split Fish—Place buttered whole split fish, skin down, on broiler rack 2 to 3 inches from source of heat and broil (without turning) 6 to 8 minutes. Mackerel requires a total of 10 minutes.

To Broil Fish Steaks—Brush steaks of cod, salmon, swordfish, tuna, halibut and striped bass ½ to 1 inch thick, with fat and place on broiler rack 2 inches from source of heat; turn after 3 to 4 minutes of broiling. Broil a total of 6 to 9 minutes.

POACHED FISH

Wrap fish steaks, fillets or small fish in cheesecloth or cooking parchment paper or place, one layer deep, in wire basket. Lower fish into kettle and cover with hot, not boiling, water, adding ½ teaspoon salt and ½ tablespoon lemon juice or vinegar for each quart used. Simmer, covered, until fish is done. Allow from 5 to 10 minutes per pound or simmer until fish flakes when tested with a fork. Drain and use stock as part of liquid for Court Bouillon (below). Serve fish on hot platter with a cream sauce (page 466) or a butter sauce (page 471); or serve cold with mayonnaise, Hollandaise Sauce (page 473) or Tartar Sauce (page 477); or use fish in a salad. Allow ½ pound whole or ⅓ pound sliced fish per portion; one pound makes 2 cups flaked fish.

For additional flavor, add thin slices of salt pork, onion, celery, parsley, whole cloves, thyme, bay leaf and peppercorns to kettle of hot water.

COURT BOUILLON

½ cup chopped carrots	2 whole cloves
½ cup chopped onion	1 bay leaf
½ cup chopped celery	1 tablespoon salt
2 sprigs parsley	¼ cup vinegar
2 tablespoons butter	fish trimmings
6 peppercorns	(heads, fins, tails, bones)

3 quarts water

Sauté vegetables in butter 3 minutes; turn into large kettle, add remaining ingredients with fish trimmings placed in cheesecloth bag for added flavor. Cover and heat slowly to boiling; simmer 5 minutes. Use for cooking fish and shellfish or as base for sauces, gravies and chowder. Approximate yield: 3 quarts bouillon.

FISH WITH DILL SAUCE

4 pounds fillet of cod or haddock	4 tablespoons minced fresh dill
Court Bouillon (above)	3 tablespoons butter

2 tablespoons flour

Poach fish in Court Bouillon (above); drain, reserving 2 cups stock. Add dill to stock and simmer about 15 minutes. Melt butter; remove from heat and stir in flour. Add hot liquid gradually and cook 5 minutes, stirring constantly. Pour over fish and serve at once. One tablespoon minced dried dill or 1 teaspoon seeds may be used. Yield: 6 portions.

STEAMED FISH

Any fish or shellfish can be steamed successfully. This method of cooking develops the fine flavor and gives a juicy, tender product.

For successful steaming, know the weight of the fish and calculate accurately the steaming time for best results. Wrap the fish in cheesecloth or muslin so that it can be removed from the rack of steamer easily without breaking. Or place (one layer deep) on rack.

Cover steamer tightly and calculate accurately the cooking time after the water has returned to a rolling boil. Allow 10 to 12 minutes per pound, or steam until fish flakes when tested. Season with salt and pepper when done, serve immediately. When steaming large fish you may find it expedient to use your roaster or canning water bath. Use a rack that keeps the fish well out of the water.

STUFFED TURBOTS OF FISH

½ cup sliced mushrooms	½ cup corn bread crumbs
2 tablespoons fat	⅓ cup milk, heated
1 teaspoon salt	3 fish fillets, haddock or cod
⅛ teaspoon pepper	2 tablespoons butter
1 cup soft bread crumbs	Butter Lemon Sauce (page 472)

Sauté mushrooms in hot fat 2 minutes, or until delicately browned; add salt, pepper, crumbs and milk; mix thoroughly. Cut fillets in strips about 1½ inches wide and place them around the inside of greased muffin pans; fill centers with stuffing and cover with oiled paper. Bake in moderate oven (350° F.) 20 minutes, then remove paper, dot with butter and continue baking 10 minutes, or until delicately browned. Serve with lemon butter or lemon slices. Yield: 6 portions.

PANFRIED FISH

Leave heads and tails on small fish, if desired. Cut larger fish into 1 inch slices or steaks, or use fillets. Roll in salted flour, cornmeal or bread crumbs. Fry in a small amount of hot (not smoking) fat; when brown on one side, turn and brown on other. Cook 5 to 10 minutes, or until done. Avoid overcooking or allowing fish to stand after cooking since it will become dry and tough. Use pancake turner or broad spatula for turning fish. Garnish with slices of tomato, cucumber and lemon and serve with Maître d'Hôtel Butter (page 472) or any desired sauce. Allow ⅓ to ½ pound per portion.

FRIED FISH

Select some small drawn fish such as smelt or sardines or fillets; cut fish fillets in individual portions. Rinse in cold water and drain on absorbent paper. Roll in salted flour, cornmeal or dry bread crumbs and arrange in frying basket, one layer deep. Fry in hot deep fat (370° F.) 3 to 5 minutes, according to type and thickness of fish. Allow ⅓ pound a portion.

FISH FILLETS WITH PARMESAN

1 cup grated Parmesan cheese
2 egg yolks, well beaten
dash of cayenne
6 small fillets of sole or haddock
salt and pepper

2 tablespoons butter
2 tablespoons flour
1½ cups milk
1 tablespoon heavy cream
1 teaspoon lemon juice

Mix ½ cup cheese with egg yolks; add cayenne. Season fillets with salt and pepper; spread with egg-cheese mixture, place in greased pan and cover with greased paper or moistened parchment paper; bake in moderate oven (350° F.) 15 minutes. Melt butter and stir in flour off the heat; add milk gradually, stirring constantly, and cook until thickened, then add cream and lemon juice. Remove paper from top of fillets, cover with the sauce, sprinkle with remaining cheese and bake 8 to 10 minutes longer, or until cheese is browned. If baked too long, sauce will separate. Approximate yield: 6 portions.

MACKEREL WITH MUSTARD HOLLANDAISE

8 mackerel fillets (skin left on)
2 tablespoons lemon juice
2 tablespoons melted butter

2 tablespoons oil
1 teaspoon minced garlic
6 tomatoes, skins removed

Rinse mackerel in cold water. Drain on absorbent paper. Place in greased heatproof baking dish. Combine lemon juice and butter and pour over fish. Cover with waxed paper and tuck in around the edges. Bake in hot oven (400° F.) 20 minutes. Heat oil in skillet. Add garlic and cook slowly 1 minute. Slice tomatoes ½ inch thick and add to garlic and oil. Cook briskly 2 minutes. Arrange on bottom of hot serving platter. Place mackerel on tomatoes and top with Mustard Hollandaise Sauce (page 473). Yield: 8 portions.

MACKEREL IN RED WINE

6 fillets mackerel
1 cup sliced mushrooms
2 tablespoons butter, melted
3 tablespoons Sherry
1 teaspoon salt
⅛ teaspoon pepper
3 tablespoons flour
¾ cup red wine

¾ cup stock
2 tablespoons chopped fresh dill
1 teaspoon minced garlic
2 tablespoons minced onion
4 tablespoons light cream
2 tablespoons grated cheese
2 tablespoons shredded blanched
    almonds

2 tablespoons butter

Arrange fillets in greased heatproof dish. Combine mushrooms and melted butter and simmer 3 minutes. Add Sherry, salt and pepper and simmer 2 minutes. Remove from heat. Stir in flour and gradually add red wine and stock. Cook over low heat, stirring constantly, until mixture comes to a boil. Add dill, garlic, onion and cream. Pour over mackerel. Sprinkle with cheese and almonds and dot with butter. Bake in moderate oven (350° F.) 25 to 30 minutes. Yield: 6 portions.

SALMON TROUT IN WHITE WINE

2 pounds salmon trout
1 teaspoon salt
½ teaspoon paprika
2 tablespoons lemon juice
bacon strips
½ cup white wine

½ cup water
2 tablespoons butter
¼ cup flour
1 cup light cream
2 tablespoons minced parsley
¼ teaspoon nutmeg

dash of pepper

Wipe fish with damp cloth. Remove head and tail. Cut crosswise slits in fish at 2 inch intervals and fill each with salt, paprika and lemon juice. Place fish in shallow baking pan, cover with bacon strips, add wine and water. Cover and bake in a moderately hot oven (400° F.), 15 minutes. Remove cover and bake 15 minutes longer. Place fish on hot platter. Melt butter, add flour and stir until well blended. Gradually add cream and enough of the liquid remaining in the baking pan to give the desired consistency. Add parsley, nutmeg and pepper and serve with the fish. Yield: 6 portions.

HADDOCK À LA CRÈME

2 pounds haddock fillets
6 tablespoons flour
1 teaspoon salt
⅛ teaspoon pepper
3 tablespoons butter

6 anchovy fillets, chopped
1½ tablespoons minced parsley
¾ teaspoon grated onion
½ cup light cream
¼ cup milk

Cut haddock in pieces for serving and roll in mixture of flour, salt and pepper. Melt butter, add anchovies and cook slowly for 2 minutes; then add haddock and brown lightly. Place in greased casserole, add parsley, onion, cream and milk; bake in a moderately hot oven (400° F.) 20 to 25 minutes, basting occasionally. Approximate yield: 6 portions.

FILLET OF POMPANO FLORIDA

4 fillets of pompano or other
    fish with skin removed
2 large oranges
1 recipe Mornay Sauce (omit
    cheese) (page 469)

½ teaspoon salt
dash of pepper
1 shallot, chopped
⅓ cup white wine
⅓ cup dry Sherry

1 tablespoon butter

Wash and dry fish. Peel the outside rind of 2 oranges and cut peeling into very thin julienne strips. Place fish, julienne of orange, salt, pepper, shallot, white wine and any fish stock from package, in a saucepan. Let simmer 10 minutes. Remove fish to serving dish and keep hot. Cook the liquid until reduced to a third of its original quantity. Add the Mornay Sauce made without cheese and stir until smooth. Season sauce and add Sherry and butter. Garnish fish with orange sections and pour sauce over top. Brown if desired under broiler. Yield: 4 portions.

GLOUCESTER TAVERN PERCH TURBANS

Wrap 12 small ocean perch fillets (fresh or frozen) turban style around 12 medium-sized cooked shrimp and fasten with a toothpick. Place fillets in a saucepan and add 1 cup boiling water. Poach in simmering water 5 to 8 minutes, or until perch is tender. Serve with a sauce made by combining 1 cup thick white sauce, ¼ cup light cream, 6 finely-diced shrimp sautéed in butter, and 1½ tablespoons Sherry. Season to taste and pour over turbans. Yield: 4 portions.

PERCH TARTS

1 1-pound package frozen perch fillets	2½ tablespoons flour
3 tablespoons butter or margarine	1 teaspoon salt
	⅛ teaspoon pepper
⅔ cup chopped onions	⅛ teaspoon powdered sage
½ cup diced celery	1 teaspoon finely chopped dill
	1 cup milk
6 baked 3½-inch tart shells	

Cut frozen or thawed block of fish into 1-inch cubes. Melt butter in saucepan. Add onions and celery and sauté about 5 minutes, or until tender but not browned. Add flour and seasonings and stir until blended. Then add milk gradually and cook over medium heat until mixture is thickened, stirring constantly. Add cubes of fish, cover, and cook over low heat 10 to 12 minutes, stirring occasionally. Turn into tart shells. Yield: 6 portions.

FISH KEBABS

1 1-pound package frozen perch fillets	1 whole clove
½ cup ketchup	2 tablespoons butter or margarine, melted
½ teaspoon salt	

Cut fish into 1-inch cubes and thaw 1½ hours. Marinate 1 hour in mixture of ketchup, salt and clove. Arrange cubes of fish on skewers. Brush fish with melted butter. Place on baking sheet and broil under medium heat 5 or 6 minutes, or until fish is easily flaked with a fork; turn once. Garnish with lemon wedges and serve at once. Yield: 4 portions.

FILLET OF SOLE

1 tablespoon minced shallots	2 cups fish stock or
4 medium-sized tomatoes, diced	Court Bouillon (page 414)
1½ cups minced mushrooms	¾ cup white wine
1 tablespoon minced parsley	2 pounds lemon sole or flounder
3 tablespoons butter	fillets

Sauté shallots, tomatoes, mushrooms and parsley lightly in butter; add fish stock or court bouillon and white wine. Add fillets and simmer gently 5 to 8 minutes or until fish is done. Remove fillets to hot platter and keep hot. Continue cooking liquid until it is reduced to half its original volume; then pour over fish and garnish with parsley and lemon slices. Approximate yield: 6 portions.

ROLLED FISH FILLETS IN WINE SAUCE

5 tablespoons butter or
  margarine
½ cup sliced mushrooms
½ cup finely diced carrots
¼ cup finely diced green pepper
½ cup finely diced onions
1¼ teaspoons salt

pinch of white pepper
½ cup dry white wine
¼ cup chopped parsley
¼ cup chopped mushrooms
¼ teaspoon dried sweet basil
¼ teaspoon dried marjoram
2 cups soft bread crumbs

4 fillets of flounder

Sauté in 2 tablespoons butter sliced mushrooms, carrots, green pepper
and onion 5 minutes. Season with ½ teaspoon salt and white pepper.
Place in shallow greased baking dish with wine. Melt 2 tablespoons
butter in skillet. Add parsley, chopped mushrooms and herbs. Sauté a
few minutes; add bread crumbs, ¾ teaspoon salt and pepper. Toss
lightly until well mixed. Place a spoonful in center of each fish fillet;
roll fish and secure with toothpick. Place over vegetables in baking
dish. Dot with remaining butter. Bake in hot oven (400° F.) 15 minutes. Serve with bread crumbs browned in butter. Approximate yield:
4 portions.

FILLET OF SOLE WITH GRAPE SAUCE

6 lemon sole fillets
2 cups cold water
1 tablespoon lemon juice
½ cup dry white wine
¼ cup water
8 peppercorns

1 bay leaf
¼ teaspoon salt
Grape Sauce (page 421)
2 tablespoons grated Cheddar
  cheese
1 tablespoon butter

Rinse fish in cold water and lemon juice. Drain on absorbent paper.
Place in greased heatproof baking dish. Pour combined wine and ¼
cup water over fillets. Add peppercorns, bay leaf and salt to liquid.
Cover with waxed paper and tuck in edges. Bake in moderate oven
(350° F.) 15 to 20 minutes or until done; drain stock to use in grape
sauce and top with grape sauce. Sprinkle with cheese, dot with butter
and brown under broiler just before serving. Approximate yield: 6
portions.

GRAPE SAUCE FOR SOLE

3 tablespoons butter
3 tablespoons flour
¼ teaspoon salt
dash of cayenne
¾ cup fish stock
½ cup light cream

2 tablespoons finely chopped
   fresh tomato
1 tablespoon finely chopped
   parsley
½ cup white seedless grapes,
   skins removed

Melt butter. Add flour, off the heat, with salt and cayenne and blend well. Strain stock from baked fish to measure ¾ cup. Gradually add stock and cream to flour mixture, stirring constantly. Heat to boiling and add tomato, parsley and grapes. Yield: 2 cups sauce.

FISH PUDDING

1 pound fish
2 cups water
1 bay leaf
2 peppercorns
1 small onion, sliced
1 small carrot, sliced
¼ cup butter

¼ cup flour
1 teaspoon salt
⅛ teaspoon pepper
½ teaspoon dry mustard
1 cup milk
1 cup fish stock
½ cup buttered crumbs

Cook fish, if fresh or frozen, 10 minutes in water with bay leaf, peppercorns, onion and carrot; drain, reserving stock, and separate fish into large flakes, removing skin and bones. Make a roux of butter and flour, add seasonings. Gradually add milk and stock and cook until smooth and thickened, stirring constantly. Mix with fish; turn into greased casserole and top with crumbs; bake in moderate oven (350° F.) 20 to 30 minutes, or until thoroughly heated and crumbs are browned. Approximate yield: 6 portions.

FRIED EEL

Select a live or freshly killed eel; the average eel is 2½ to 3 feet long. Remove head; then loosen skin at top and with strong quick jerk, pull it back over entire body. Cut fish open, clean, wash thoroughly and cut in 3 inch lengths; dry, dip in slightly beaten egg and roll in dry bread crumbs or cornmeal. Fry in hot deep fat (375°–380° F.) 2 to 5 minutes; or panfry in a small amount of fat 4 to 6 minutes, turning occasionally; drain and serve with Vinaigrette Sauce (page 478) or Cucumber Sauce (page 478).

EEL IN ASPIC

Prepare eel as for Fried Eel (see above); cook 3 inch lengths in Court Bouillon (page 414) about 8 to 10 minutes; drain and chill, then place in oblong mold. Prepare an aspic, using plain gelatin and highly seasoned fish stock for liquid; flavor with 1 tablespoon brandy; chill. When slightly thickened, pour over fish to fill mold and chill until firm. When ready to serve, unmold on cold platter and serve with Horseradish Sauce (page 465) or Parsley Caper Sauce (page 468). Serve at a bridge or after-theater spread, or as hors d'œuvres.

PARBOILED ROE OR MILT

The shad roe (eggs) is highly prized and weighs from ½ to 1¼ pounds. The roe from other fish are satisfactory and less expensive. The roe is in two sections. The salted roe of the sturgeon is called caviar. The milt of the male fish is prepared in the same way as the roe of the female fish; the large vein in the center is usually removed.

Wash roe and drop into boiling, salted, acidulated water, using ½ teaspoon salt and 1 tablespoon lemon juice or vinegar to 1 quart water; simmer shad or small roe 5 minutes and larger roe 8 to 10 minutes. Drain, cover with cold water and drain again; after carefully removing membrane, broil, fry, bake, scallop or mash and add to fish sauce. The shad roe, which is small, need not be parboiled. One shad roe makes 1 to 2 portions; or allow ¼ to ⅓ pound roe per portion.

BROILED SHAD ROE

Use 3 shad roe; brush with butter or margarine. Place on rack in broiler pan 2 inches from source of heat. Broil in moderately hot broiler (375°–400° F.) 4 minutes, season with salt and pepper. Turn and broil 5 to 8 minutes longer. Season and sprinkle with finely chopped parsley or Maître d'Hôtel Butter (page 472). Serve immediately with wedges of lemon. Approximate yield: 6 portions.

SIX-HOUR SHAD

Have 1 large shad split and head and tail removed. Slip knife under and remove backbone. Grease outside of fish well with soft butter. Wrap in oiled parchment paper so that fish is entirely covered. Lay in shallow pan and bake in slow oven (300° F.) about 6 hours. Bones will almost entirely disappear.

COD TONGUES

½ pound cod tongues	pinch of pepper
¼ cup flour	2 tablespoons minced onion
4 tablespoons butter, melted	¼ teaspoon minced garlic
2 tablespoons white wine	3 tablespoons oil
½ teaspoon salt	5 tomatoes, sliced

Hollandaise Sauce (page 473)

Dredge cod tongues in flour. Brown quickly on each side in 2 table-spoons butter. Add remaining butter, wine, salt and pepper. Cover and simmer 8 minutes. Add onion and garlic to hot oil and cook briskly 2 minutes. Add tomatoes and cook 3 minutes. Arrange on heat-proof serving dish and place cod tongues over tomatoes. Cover with Hollandaise Sauce and brown quickly under the broiler. Approximate yield: 6 portions.

FISH SHASLIK

bacon strips, cut in half	pieces of fillet of sole
cubes of salmon	cooked lobster
scallops	minced garlic
large shrimp	melted butter

3 tablespoons Sherry

Wrap bacon around pieces of fish. Thread on skewers in the order listed. Season with salt, pepper and garlic; broil over charcoal grill 10 to 15 minutes. Brush with butter. Heat Sherry, ignite and pour over shaslik. Serve with a bowl of Hollandaise Sauce (page 473).

COOKED OR CANNED FISH

CREAMED FISH

1½ cups flaked fish, cooked or canned	1½ cups Medium White Sauce (page 125)

Heat fish in white sauce; add more seasonings, if desired. Serve on toast, crisp crackers or in patty shells. Yield: 6 portions.

Creamed Fish with Eggs—Use 1 cup flaked fish and 2 hard-cooked eggs, chopped.

Fish au Gratin—Turn creamed fish into greased casserole and cover with ½ cup buttered crumbs; bake in hot oven (450° F.) about 10 minutes, or until crumbs are browned. One-fourth to ½ cup grated cheese may be mixed with crumbs, if desired.

Creamed Fish in Noodle Ring—Prepare Noodle Ring (page 506). Turn out on hot serving plate, place creamed fish in center and garnish with parsley. Spaghetti Mold (page 499) or Spinach Ring (page 569) may be used with creamed fish. Yield: 6 to 8 portions.

FISH SOUFFLÉ

4 tablespoons butter	dash of pepper
4 tablespoons flour	1¾ cups cooked fish or 1 6-oz.
1½ cups milk	can fish
1 teaspoon onion juice	3 eggs, separated
½ teaspoon salt	Cream Caper Sauce (page 466)

Melt butter and stir in flour off the heat; gradually add milk, stirring constantly. Cook until smooth and thickened. Add seasonings and fish. Remove from heat and add egg yolks, beaten. Mix and carefully fold in egg whites beaten stiff but not dry. Turn into casserole with bottom only greased and bake in slow oven (325° F.) 45 to 60 minutes or until inserted knife comes out clean. Serve at once with Cream Caper Sauce. Approximate yield: 6 portions.

DEVILED SEAFOOD

2½ cups flaked seafood	½ cup shredded pimiento
1½ cups cooked macaroni	¼ cup cubed American cheese
1 tablespoon prepared mustard	1½ tablespoons bread crumbs
2 cups Medium White Sauce	1½ tablespoons butter or
(page 125)	margarine

Combine seafood, macaroni and mustard. Blend pimiento and cheese with white sauce. Combine with other mixture. Place in greased sea shells or individual casseroles. Top with bread crumbs, dot with butter. Bake in moderate oven (350° F.) 20 to 25 minutes. Yield: 8 portions.

FINNAN HADDIE RABBIT

6 slices buttered toast	1½ cups Cheese Sauce (page 470)
1 jar finnan haddie	paprika

Spread toast with finnan haddie as it comes from the jar. Cover with cheese sauce and sprinkle with paprika. Yield: 6 portions.

FISH POTATO PUFF

2 cups flaked fish, cooked or
   canned
2 cups seasoned mashed potatoes
1 teaspoon salt
1 tablespoon lemon juice
few drops Tabasco sauce

2 tablespoons chopped celery
2 tablespoons chopped parsley
1 tablespoon minced green pepper
1 teaspoon minced onion
2 tablespoons butter
3 eggs, separated

Combine fish, potatoes, salt, lemon juice and Tabasco. Sauté celery, parsley, pepper and onion in butter until tender; add to fish mixture. Add well-beaten egg yolks and beat until very light; then fold in the egg whites, beaten stiff but not dry, and pile lightly in baking dish with bottom only greased. Bake in moderate oven (350° F.) 30 to 40 minutes, or until firm and lightly browned. Approximate yield: 6 portions.

BAKED TUNA FISH WITH BRAZIL NUTS

1 cup finely chopped Brazil nuts
½ teaspoon Worcestershire sauce
2 cups Medium White Sauce
   (page 125)

2 pimientos
1 13-oz. can tuna fish, flaked
6 whole Brazil nuts

Add nuts and Worcestershire sauce to white sauce. Cut six strips of pimiento and reserve for garnishing; cut remaining pimiento into small pieces and add to white sauce; fold in tuna fish and heat thoroughly. Turn into greased casserole, arrange pimiento strips and whole nuts on top; cover and bake in moderate oven (350° F.) about 15 minutes. Approximate yield: 6 portions.

SALMON AND PICKLE LOAF

1 1-lb. can salmon
¾ cup dry bread crumbs
¾ cup milk
½ cup coarsely chopped sweet
   pickles
2 eggs, slightly beaten

1½ teaspoons salt
1½ tablespoons melted butter
1 teaspoon minced onion
1½ cups Medium White Sauce
   (page 125)
2 hard-cooked eggs, sliced

6 stuffed olives, sliced

Flake salmon, add crumbs, milk, pickles, eggs, salt and melted butter; mix well. Pack into greased loaf pan in a shallow pan of hot water and bake in moderate oven (350° F.) about 30 minutes, or until loaf becomes firm. Turn out on hot platter, add onion to white sauce and pour over loaf. Arrange egg slices on top with olive slice on top of each. Serve hot. Approximate yield: 6 portions.

HOT SALMON MOUSSE

1 pound raw salmon	1¼ cups heavy cream
4 egg whites, slightly beaten	½ teaspoon salt
pinch of pepper	

Skin and bone salmon and put through food chopper. Gradually beat in egg whites. Place bowl of salmon on crushed ice and gradually beat in cream. Add salt and pepper. Pour into well-greased individual ring molds. Place in pan of hot water and bake in moderate oven (350° F.) 15 minutes or until just firm. Turn onto serving plate. Pour Hollandaise Sauce (page 473) over each mold. Yield: 6 portions.

TUNA FISH PIE

4 medium-sized carrots, diced	1 cup Thin White Sauce
3 medium-sized potatoes, diced	(page 125)
3 medium-sized onions, sliced	½ recipe Baking Powder Bicuits
1 can (No. 1 tall) tuna, flaked	(page 149)

Cook vegetables in boiling salted water 10 minutes, or until just tender; drain and combine with tuna fish. Add white sauce, turn into greased baking dish and cover with biscuit dough, rolled ¼ inch thick. Bake in moderately hot oven (375° F.) 20 minutes. Salmon or any cooked fish may be substituted for tuna. Approximate yield: 4 portions.

SALMON ROLL FARCI

2 cups canned salmon	dash of pepper
¼ cup soft bread crumbs	paprika
2 tablespoons onion juice	3 tablespoons butter, melted
1 tablespoon minced parsley	2 eggs, beaten
½ teaspoon salt	1 hard-cooked egg, sliced
½ teaspoon celery salt	6 stuffed olives, sliced

Drain salmon and free from skin and bones; mash with fork, and add crumbs, seasonings, 2 tablespoons butter and beaten eggs; mix well. Turn out on lightly floured waxed paper and form into rectangle about ½ inch thick. Place sliced egg and olives on top, then roll up lengthwise; place seam side down, in greased baking dish and brush with remaining melted butter. Bake in moderate oven (350° F.) 30 minutes, or until delicately browned. Serve hot with Tomato Sauce (page 469), adding 2 tablespoons chopped pickles; or serve cold with mayonnaise seasoned with 2 tablespoons chili sauce. Substitute tuna fish for salmon, if desired. Approximate yield: 6 portions.

SALMON CROQUETTES

2 tablespoons butter
5 tablespoons flour
½ cup milk
1 cup flaked salmon, canned or
  cooked

2 eggs
1 cup dry bread crumbs
⅓ cup fine cracker crumbs

Melt butter, add flour and blend; stir in milk gradually and cook 5 minutes, or until thick and smooth. Add salmon, 1 egg, well beaten, and bread crumbs; mix thoroughly and chill. Form into croquette shapes; dip in 1 egg, slightly beaten, and roll in crumbs; chill. Fry in hot deep fat (370° F.) 3 to 5 minutes, or until browned. Tuna or any cooked fish may be substituted for salmon. Yield: 4 portions.

SALMON CAKES

2 cups drained, canned salmon
1 large onion, chopped fine
1 cup thick tomato pulp
½ teaspoon salt

dash of pepper
1 teaspoon thyme
3 eggs, separated
¼ cup butter

Free salmon from skin and bones and flake; mix with onion, tomato and seasonings. Stir in well-beaten egg yolks; fold in stiffly beaten egg whites. Drop by tablespoons on buttered hot griddle or heavy frying pan and fry until nicely browned on both sides. Yield: 6 portions.

SWORDFISH

5 slices swordfish, 1 inch thick
1 cup olive oil
2 sprigs parsley, chopped
½ teaspoon thyme
2 bay leaves
2 scallions, sliced
8 peppercorns

2 cups bread crumbs
1 cup freshly grated Parmesan
  cheese
2 teaspoons salt
1 teaspoon pepper
¼ cup minced parsley
½ teaspoon orégano

lemon wedges

Cut each swordfish steak in half. Combine olive oil, chopped parsley, thyme, bay leaves, scallions and peppercorns in a bowl. Add fish and allow to stand two hours, turning occasionally. Drain off oil and strain to remove herbs and reserve. Combine bread crumbs, cheese, salt, pepper, parsley and orégano. Coat fish steaks with this crumb mixture. Place in oiled shallow baking pan. Sprinkle lightly with the reserved olive oil. Cover with greased waxed paper. Bake in moderate oven (375° F.) 30 to 45 minutes, or until done, basting occasionally with the oil in the pan. Serve with lemon wedges. Yield: 6 to 10 portions.

TUNA STEAKS

To Broil Fresh Tuna Steak—Dry flesh thoroughly, dust with flour and baste with butter, margarine, shortening or oil. Place steaks on preheated broiler pan two inches from source of heat. Broil at full flame or 550° F. for four minutes on each side. When done, garnish with chopped parsley and lemon wedges and serve immediately.

To Panfry Fresh Tuna Steak—Dry flesh thoroughly, dust with flour. Melt two tablespoons of butter or margarine in frying pan. Do not permit pan to reach smoking point. Place tuna steaks in pan and fry for four minutes on each side. A tablespoon of minced onion gives an added impact to the flavor. When done, remove tuna steak from pan. Add to juices in pan two tablespoons of dry wine or vinegar, turning off flame under pan immediately after adding wine or vinegar. Allow mixture to stand for a moment, then pour it over the steak. Serve immediately.

ROAST TUNA FISH

3 slices tuna fish, 1 inch thick (about 3 pounds)
6 fillets of anchovy, chopped
½ cup minced onion
½ cup chopped scallions
½ cup vinegar
¼ cup lemon juice
½ cup melted butter
2 bay leaves
1 teaspoon salt
¼ teaspoon pepper
1 tablespoon capers

Skin and bone tuna; wash and drain well on absorbent paper; place on rack in roasting pan. Mix anchovy, onion, scallions, vinegar, lemon juice, butter, bay leaves, salt and pepper and pour over tuna. Roast in hot oven (400° F.) about 16 minutes, basting often. Place tuna slices on platter. Add capers to sauce, pour over tuna. Yield: 6 portions.

BROILED TUNA FISH WITH SAUCE BRETONNE

3 slices fresh tuna fish, 1 inch thick (about 3 pounds)
½ cup olive oil
1 teaspoon salt
¼ teaspoon pepper
buttered dry bread crumbs

Skin and bone tuna; wash and drain well on absorbent paper; dry and place on rack in broiler pan. Mix olive oil, salt and pepper and pour over tuna. Broil under broiler, preheated to 550° F., 4 minutes, basting once. (See page 413.) Turn and broil about 5 minutes longer, basting once. Sprinkle bread crumbs over tuna and let brown. Serve with Sauce Bretonne (see page 481). Approximate yield: 6 portions.

TUNA AND HAM SUPREME

3 slices fresh tuna fish, 1 inch   2¼ cups white wine
    thick (about 3 pounds)   1 teaspoon salt
6 slices bacon, chopped   ¼ teaspoon pepper
6 fillets of anchovy, chopped   6 slices boiled ham

Skin and bone tuna; wash and drain well on absorbent paper. Mix bacon, anchovies, wine, salt and pepper and bring to boiling. Add ham and tuna and simmer, covered, 10 to 15 minutes. Place ham and tuna on serving platter, pour wine sauce over. Yield: 6 portions.

SALT FISH

Remove rusty-looking portions of salt fish and thin black membrane found on inside. Soak, flesh-side down, in large amount of cold water for several hours, according to size and saltiness of fish. Drain, place flesh-side up in pan, cover with fresh water and heat slowly to boiling. Drain, add fresh water and simmer until just tender. Finish cooking by broiling, baking, creaming, etc., as desired. Allow ⅓ to ½ pound per portion; 1 pound fish without waste yields about 2 cups flaked fish.

CREAMED SALT CODFISH

1½ cups shredded salt codfish   1½ cups Medium White Sauce
water   (page 125)

Cover codfish with water and heat slowly to boiling point; repeat once or twice if fish is hard and very salty. Add fish to white sauce; heat thoroughly. Serve on toast or baked potatoes. Yield: 6 portions.

KIPPERED HERRING

Kippered herring is salted, smoked and partially cooked and requires little cooking. To prepare fish, cover with cold water and bring to a boil. Dry and panfry or broil. To prepare canned fish, place in greased shallow pan or on cooking parchment paper and brush with butter and lemon juice. Bake in moderately hot oven (375° F.) about 10 minutes. Serve with lemon and melted butter.

POACHED FINNAN HADDIE

Finnan haddie or smoked haddock is salted, smoked and only partially cured; it will not keep for any length of time unless stored in refrigerator. Cover with milk or water, bring slowly to a boil and let stand over hot water about 20 minutes. Allow ¼ pound per portion.

BROILED SALT MACKEREL

Soak salt mackerel fillets in cold water 12 hours; drain, wipe and place, skin-side down, on greased rack of broiler. Brush with melted butter and broil 8 to 10 minutes (page 413). Sprinkle chopped parsley over fish, serve with butter and lemon wedges. Allow 1/4 pound per portion.

DROP CODFISH CAKES

1 pound salt codfish
3 cups hot mashed potatoes

dash of pepper
1 egg, beaten

Rinse codfish well in cold water and let soak 2 hours if very salty; drain, add fresh water, bring to a boil and simmer 15 minutes. Drain, shred and add to mashed potatoes; then add pepper and egg and beat well. Drop by spoonfuls into hot deep fat (365°–380° F.) and fry 1 to 5 minutes, or until golden brown; drain on absorbent paper. Yield: 6 portions.

HERRING AND POTATO CASSEROLE

1 pound salt herring
6 medium-sized cooked potatoes

2 medium-sized onions, sliced
1/4 cup soft bread crumbs
2 tablespoons butter

Soak herring overnight; drain and cut into bits, removing entrails and as many bones as possible. Place herring, potatoes and onions in layers in greased casserole, beginning and ending with potatoes; sprinkle with bread crumbs and dot with butter. Bake in hot oven (425° F.) 25 to 30 minutes. Approximate yield: 6 portions.

SHELLFISH

Shellfish include oysters, clams, scallops, abalone, sea mussels, snails, lobsters, crabs, shrimp and crayfish. They are high in nutritive value, supplying protein and minerals, chiefly iron, phosphorus, iodine, copper and vitamin B.

Frogs, terrapin and turtle are grouped here with shellfish although generically they do not belong with them.

Selection and Storage. Shellfish should be strictly fresh when purchased, since they deteriorate rapidly. Oysters, clams and mussels should be alive when purchased. This is indicated by a tightly closed shell. If any of the shells remain open when touched, they should be discarded. Lobsters and crabs, too, should be actively alive when purchased.

Lobsters, alive, should be stored in a cool place—never directly on ice. Oysters, clams and mussels in the shell also should be stored in a cool place, while scallops or shucked clams and oysters should be well covered and placed in the coldest part of the refrigerator.

Clams may be purchased as soft or hard shell, in the shell, shucked (shell removed) or canned. *Soft shell clams* are usually bought as small, medium or large size. With shell removed, the entire clam is edible. Clams are popular for broth, steaming, chowders, frying, etc. *Hard shell clams* have good keeping qualities and may be purchased as littlenecks (small), cherrystones (medium). They yield about one-half cup of clam juice and one-half cup of pulp from one dozen. Chowder clams (large) yield about two-thirds cup of juice and one-third cup clam pulp from six. Hard shell clams are served raw on the half shell and are sometimes steamed and used for chowders. *Razor or Long Clams* are found on the west coast and are used for soups and chowders and are also used for commercially canned clams.

Old Fashioned New England Clam Bake

Clam Chowder (page 236)
Clams with Melted Butter (page 432)
Onions   Corn on Cob   Sweet Potato
Sausage (page 432)   Fish (page 432)   Stuffing (page 484)
Small Lobster with Melted Butter
Warm Brown Bread (page 157)
Watermelon
Coffee

The chowder and stuffing can be prepared at home and carried to the "bake" ready to heat and serve. Take the chowder in a large kettle and the dressing in a pan wrapped in a double thickness of paper.

How to Prepare the Fire. A clam bake requires a special type of fire. This must be started and burning hard for two hours or more before the bake is laid. This is how it is done: Gather large flat stones (6 inches thick), wood and seaweed. Make a rectangular pyre, intermingling stones with wood. Light the fire and let it burn hard until the stones are white hot.

How to Prepare the Food. While the stones are heating, cut the fish in suitable serving portions, season and wrap securely in metal foil or parchment paper. (Bluefish, swordfish, cod or striped bass are often used.) Remove all but the inner husks of the corn and wrap each ear in paper. Wrap each onion in paper after it is peeled and seasoned. Wrap each serving of sausage. Wash and wrap each sweet potato in paper. Wash lobsters and use as they are caught. Wash clams well.

Procedure. When the wood fire has burned low, which may take two hours, and the stones are fiery hot, scrape off all the dying embers. Then move quickly before stones have time to cool. Spread seaweed generously over the hot stones and place a large wire net over them. Dump all the clams onto the net, follow with individual packages of wrapped corn, onions, fish, sausages and stuffing in this order. If the stuffing is wrapped in cheesecloth, place it on a shallow pan. Add on top the sweet potatoes and lobsters. Quickly cover with a heavy canvas. Fasten the corners down well with stones or stakes to prevent the continually rising steam from billowing the canvas, which allows the heat to escape. It may be necessary to lift the canvas occasionally to let some of the heat escape. Experience only can tell you when. Bake for about one hour if the stones are very hot. If you have not worked fast to keep the heat in, more time may be required.

STEAMED CLAMS

Soft shelled clams are best for steaming; fresh clams are tightly closed or close when touched. Scrub with brush and wash in running water until free from sand; place in large kettle and add about ½ cup boiling water to 1 peck (8 quarts) of clams. Cover tightly and simmer 6 to 10 minutes, or until shells open. Remove clams to hot platter; cover with napkins to keep hot; pour clam broth into glasses and serve with clams. Serve with dishes of melted butter, seasoned with lemon juice, salt and pepper. To eat clams, remove from shells and dip into butter, eating all but neck. Allow 6 to 12 clams for one portion.

CLAM FRITTERS

8 large shucked clams	3 tablespoons milk
¼ cup clam liquor	1 cup sifted all-purpose flour
1 egg, slightly beaten	3 teaspoons baking powder
3 tablespoons melted butter	½ teaspoon salt
⅛ teaspoon pepper	

Put clams through food chopper; add clam liquor, egg, butter and milk. Sift dry ingredients and add to clam mixture, stirring until smooth. Drop by spoonfuls into hot fat (375° F.) and cook 2 to 3 minutes or until brown. Drain on absorbent paper. Yield: 6 portions.

CLAM AND CHICKEN PIE

1 3- to 4-lb. young chicken	1 tablespoon butter
1 teaspoon salt	1 cup chopped celery
dash of cayenne	1 tablespoon flour
1 pint clams	½ cup milk
2 hard-cooked eggs, diced	½ recipe Plain Pastry (page 736)

Clean chicken and cut as for fricassee (page 365). Cover with boiling water and simmer, covered, 1 hour, or until almost tender. Add seasonings, clams, eggs, butter and celery. Mix flour and milk to a smooth paste; add to clam-chicken mixture and cook 5 minutes, stirring occasionally. Turn into baking dish. Cover with pastry, rolled thin, and slash top to permit escape of steam. Bake in hot oven (450° F.) 15 minutes; then reduce heat to moderate (350° F.) and bake 20 minutes longer. Approximate yield: 6 portions.

SUNDAY NIGHT SUPPER CLAMS

1 dozen large clams	½ cup dry Sherry
2 tablespoons margarine	6 slices hot buttered toast,
½ teaspoon flour	halved
cayenne	chopped parsley

Scrub clams with brush and wash under running water, until free from sand. Plunge into boiling water 2 to 3 minutes. Drain and open. Use only the round, plump part. Melt margarine in a pan. Sauté clams in margarine about 1 minute on each side. Stir in flour and cayenne; add Sherry, bring to a boil, cover and simmer 5 minutes. Serve on hot buttered toast with a sprinkle of parsley. Approximate yield: 6 portions.

CLAM RAMEKINS

½ cup minced onion	⅛ teaspoon black pepper
¼ cup butter	3 tablespoons flour
2 cups boiling water	1 quart milk
2 large potatoes, diced	½ cup button mushrooms
1 tablespoon salt	1 pint clams, finely chopped

Sauté onion in butter 5 minutes, or until light yellow; add boiling water, potatoes, salt and pepper and cook over low heat 15 to 20 minutes, or until tender, stirring occasionally. Mix flour and ¼ cup milk to a smooth paste; add remaining milk gradually, mixing until smooth. Add with mushrooms and clams and cook 5 minutes, stirring occasionally. Turn into 6 greased individual ramekins and bake in moderate oven (350° F.) 15 to 20 minutes, or until browned. To make Clam Pie, cover with biscuit dough (page 149) and bake as for biscuits.

CRABS

Crabs may be bought as soft or hard shell. Soft shell crabs when cleaned and cooked are edible, shell and all. Hard shell crabs must be cooked and the meat extracted before eating.

Crabs have a hard shell except during the molting season in the spring and summer; between the shedding of the old shell and the hardening of the new shell, they have a soft shell and are called soft shell crabs. Oyster crabs are found in the oyster shell; they are very small and eaten whole in oyster stews. Hard shell crabs are boiled like lobster; soft shell crabs are generally broiled or panfried.

Wash crabs free from dirt and marsh grass; drop, headfirst, into rapidly boiling salted water, using 1 tablespoon salt to each quart of water; cover and boil, allowing 10 minutes to the pound; the shell turns a strawberry pink and the meat a milky white. Plunge into cold water and when cool enough to handle, break off claws and apron or tail. Working at the tail end, force upper and lower shells apart. Remove or scrape away the spongy fibrous material between the two halves of the body and between the sides of the top shell and the body (gills, sand bags and intestines). Flake meat from bony tissue; crack claws and pull out meat with pick or pointed knife. Use as desired in hot or cold dishes. Approximate yield: ½ cup flaked meat from ½ lb. crab.

BROILED SOFT SHELL CRABS

Clean crabs, dip in melted butter, sprinkle with lemon juice, salt, pepper and cayenne; roll in flour or bread crumbs. Broil under moderate heat 8 to 10 minutes, turning once. Allow 1 to 2 crabs per portion.

FRIED SOFT SHELL CRABS

Soft shell crabs should be alive when purchased; place, face down, on a board. The back tapers to a point on each side; take hold of one point and pull the soft shell back, scraping out the fibrous spongy material underneath; treat other side the same way. Cut off ¼ inch slice just behind eyes. Turn crab face up, pull off apron, scrape off spongy portion beneath and wash in cold water.

Sprinkle prepared crabs with salt and pepper; dip in slightly beaten egg, then roll in fine, dry bread crumbs. Fry in hot deep fat (375° F.) 3 to 4 minutes, or until golden brown, or panfry in hot fat over direct heat, allowing 3 to 4 minutes cooking time on each side. Drain on unglazed paper and serve with lemon. Allow 1 to 2 crabs per portion.

STUFFED CRABS AND MUSHROOMS

1 cup sliced fresh mushrooms	1 cup flaked, cooked crab meat
2 tablespoons butter	1½ tablespoons lemon juice
1 tablespoon flour	1 teaspoon capers
½ teaspoon salt	1 teaspoon chopped parsley
½ cup heavy cream	2 egg whites, stiffly beaten

Sauté mushrooms in butter and cook 5 minutes; remove mushrooms and stir in flour; add salt and cream and cook 5 minutes, stirring until thickened. Add mushrooms, crab meat and seasonings and cook over moderate heat 5 minutes longer. Fold gently into egg whites; turn into crab shells or small ramekins. Bake in moderate oven (350° F.) 20 minutes, or until browned. Approximate yield: 6 portions.

CRAB ROYAL

3 tablespoons butter	⅔ cup milk
3 tablespoons flour	⅔ cup chicken stock
½ teaspoon salt	2 cups flaked, cooked crab meat
⅛ teaspoon paprika	½ cup sliced, cooked mushrooms
1 egg, beaten	

Make a roux of butter, flour and seasonings; add liquid slowly, stirring constantly, and cook over moderate heat until mixture thickens. Add crab meat and well-drained mushrooms; add slowly to egg and heat thoroughly, stirring constantly. Serve hot. Yield: 6 portions.

CRABURGERS

1 1-lb. can crab meat	1 teaspoon Worcestershire sauce
2 eggs	1 teaspoon chopped parsley
1 teaspoon salt	1 teaspoon minced chives
⅛ teaspoon pepper	2 tablespoons mayonnaise
1 teaspoon dry mustard	½ cup flour
dry bread crumbs	

Flake crab meat, removing stiff bony tissue. Add 1 egg, slightly beaten, seasonings and mayonnaise, mixing lightly with fork. Form into small cakes, roll in flour, dip in remaining egg, slightly beaten, and roll in bread crumbs. Fry in small amount of butter about 6 minutes, turning to brown both sides. Serve on biscuits flavored with curry, mushroom or cheese. Approximate yield: 6 portions.

CRAB MEAT BACON ROLLS

1 cup flaked, cooked crab meat	¼ teaspoon salt
1 egg, slightly beaten	⅛ teaspoon pepper
½ cup tomato juice	1½ teaspoons chopped parsley
1 cup soft bread crumbs	1 teaspoon chopped celery leaves

12 slices bacon

Combine crab meat, egg, tomato juice, bread crumbs and seasonings, mixing well. Shape into 12 rolls of finger length. Spiral each roll with a strip of bacon and fasten with toothpick. Place on broiler rack and broil until bacon is crisp, turning frequently. Yield: 6 portions.

MOCK CRAB SOUFFLÉ

3 eggs, separated	1 cup grated cheese
2 cups Thick White Sauce	2 cups flaked, cooked crab meat
(page 125)	1 cup coarse dry bread crumbs

1 tablespoon butter

Beat yolks until thick and lemon colored; add white sauce gradually, mixing well, then cheese and crab meat. Sauté crumbs in butter and add to crab mixture; fold in egg whites beaten stiff but not dry. Turn into greased casserole, place in pan of hot water and bake in moderate oven (350° F.) 50 minutes. Approximate yield: 8 portions.

SOUTHERN CRAB CAKES

2 cups flaked, cooked crab meat	dash of pepper
¼ teaspoon salt	1 egg

flour

Mix crab meat, salt, pepper and egg; shape into small cakes and dredge lightly with flour. Fry in hot deep fat (375°–380° F.) for 2 to 3 minutes, or until golden brown. Serve with Tartar Sauce (page 477) or cole slaw. Approximate yield: 6 portions.

RICE AND CRAB MEAT

2 tablespoons minced onion	1 cup cooked rice
2 tablespoons butter	1 cup flaked, cooked crab meat
½ cup light cream	½ cup chili sauce

toast points

Sauté onion in butter 2 minutes. Add cream, rice and crab meat and heat slowly in saucepan or chafing dish until almost boiling; add chili sauce. Serve on toast points. Approximate yield: 4 portions.

CRAB MEAT AND POTATO CASSEROLE

4 cups seasoned mashed potatoes   ½ cup buttered crumbs
2 cups flaked, cooked crab meat   parsley
1 cup Medium White Sauce
    (page 125)

Line 1 large or 6 individual casseroles with mashed potatoes; bake in hot oven (400° F.) 10 minutes, or until slightly browned. Fill with combined crab meat and white sauce. Sprinkle with crumbs and return dish to oven for 15 minutes, or until crumbs are browned. Serve with parsley garnish. Approximate yield: 6 portions.

CRAB FLAKE MOUSSE

2 envelopes plain gelatin   1 cup mayonnaise
1 cup cold water   1 cup heavy cream, whipped
1 cup boiling water   2 cups flaked, cooked crab meat
              pimiento strips

Soften gelatin in cold water 5 minutes; add boiling water, stir until dissolved and chill until slightly thickened. Fold in mayonnaise and cream; add crab meat. Turn into molds, garnish with tiny strips of pimiento and chill until firm. Unmold on serving platter. Approximate yield: 6 to 8 portions.

BOILED LOBSTER IN SHELL

Serve boiled lobster hot or cold; leave claws intact, cut open and remove stomach and dark vein. Garnish with crisp water cress or lettuce and lemon. Serve with hot melted butter or with Caper Sauce (page 478). Serve one small lobster per portion.

BROILED LOBSTER CORDON BLEU

2 live lobsters (1¾ pounds each) 1 tablespoon paprika
⅓ cup clam broth   2 tablespoons butter, melted
2 tablespoons Sherry wine   ¼ teaspoon salt
¼ cup bread crumbs   dash of pepper

Prepare lobster for broiling (page 438). Fill the cavity in the head with the dressing made as follows: Pour clam broth and Sherry over crumbs. Blend paprika with butter and seasonings. Combine with crumbs. Place stuffed lobsters on oiled broiler pan and broil 16 to 18 minutes with flesh-side up. Serve with melted butter and section of lemon. Garnish with claws. Yield: 4 portions.

STEAMED LOBSTER

Place live lobsters in steamer. Cover tightly and steam 20–40 minutes, depending on size. Keep water in steamer boiling very rapidly.

BOILED LOBSTER

Lobsters should be bought alive. "Chicken" lobsters (small) weigh within one ounce of one pound, "Mediums" weigh 18 ounces to 1¼ pounds and "Selects" (large) weigh anything over 1¼ pounds (Fresh Shellfish table). A live lobster is speckled green and should be active. Grab it just behind the claws or pick it up with vegetable tongs; straighten tail and plunge it headfirst into a large kettle nearly full of rapidly boiling salted water, using one tablespoon salt for each quart of water. Cover and boil rapidly 5 to 7 minutes to the pound, counting the cooking time after the water returns to boiling. With tongs or long-handled spoon remove lobster and drop into cold water. When cold enough to handle, twist off claws, reserving small claws to use as garnish; crack large claws with a nutcracker or hammer; pick out meat with fork, or if lobster is served in shell, place cracked claws beside the body. Turn lobster over on back; cut lengthwise from head to end of tail and discard stomach or "lady"—a small sac just back of head; the dark vein which runs to end of tail should come out with stomach, and if it does not, remove it piece by piece. The tail meat can be pulled out in one piece; remove meat from body in large pieces. The liver or green part is edible and highly prized, as well as the coral in the female lobster. The spongy tissue or lungs found under the claws and the shell are discarded.

Cut lobster meat with a silver or a stainless steel knife, as other metal discolors the meat; use scissors to cut away thin shell under tail. Chill lobster meat; if packed in ice it will keep about a week. Use in cocktails, salads or in hot dishes, as desired. Approximate yield: 1 medium-sized lobster (1½ to 2 lb.) yields 2 to 4 portions.

BROILED LIVE LOBSTER

When possible have the fish dealer split the live lobster. To kill the lobster, insert a sharp knife between the body and tail shells; this severs the spinal cord. Place on back and make deep cut lengthwise from head to end of tail; open and remove stomach, dark vein (page 438) and liver. Season liver with salt, pepper, grated onion, lemon juice and fine bread crumbs and replace in lobster cavity. Crack large claws and lay lobster as flat as possible, flesh side up, on broiler. Brush meat with melted butter and sprinkle lightly with salt and pepper. Broil slowly under moderate heat (350° F.), meat side up, until delicately browned. Allow 12–14 minutes for smaller lobsters; 16–18 minutes for heavier ones. Allow ¾ to 1 pound lobster in shell per portion.

LOBSTER FARCI

6 1-lb. lobsters	salt and pepper
2 cups milk	lemon juice
1 cup light cream	2 tablespoons Sherry
¼ cup butter	½ cup buttered dry bread crumbs
2 tablespoons flour	hard-cooked egg yolk, riced
chopped parsley	

Boil live lobsters and remove meat (page 438), keeping shells intact; clean shells. Slip the tail shells into the upper part of the body shell, making containers for the farci. Cut lobster meat in about ¾-inch cubes. Scald milk and cream in a double boiler; gradually add to roux of 2 tablespoons butter and flour and cook 5 minutes, stirring constantly until smooth and thickened. Season to taste with salt, pepper, lemon juice and a little mace, if desired; add lobster meat and heat thoroughly, then add Sherry and turn into shells. Sprinkle with bread crumbs, egg yolk and parsley; dot with remaining 2 tablespoons butter and brown under broiler; use small lobster claws as garnish. Yield: 6 portions.

PLANKED LOBSTER

1 1½-pound live lobster	2 cups Duchess Potatoes (page
½ teaspoon salt	564)
dash of cayenne	lemon
½ teaspoon Worcestershire sauce	parsley
4 tablespoons melted butter	2 Stuffed Tomatoes (page 578)
cucumber slices	

Split lobster as for broiling (page 438). Remove liver, mix with seasonings and sauté in 2 tablespoons butter 3 minutes. Brush remaining butter over lobster meat, spread with liver mixture and place on oiled hot plank. Bake in hot oven (450° F.) 15 minutes. Loosen meat and crack claws. Garnish plank with ribbon of Duchess Potatoes and return to oven for 10 minutes, or until potatoes are browned. Garnish with lemon sections and parsley and serve with corn-stuffed tomatoes arranged on cucumber slices. Yield: 2 portions.

LOBSTER STEW

1 1¼-pound lobster, boiled	1 slice onion
3 tablespoons butter	1 teaspoon salt
1 quart milk	paprika

Cut lobster meat in small pieces and sauté lightly in butter but do not brown. Scald milk with onion; remove onion, add milk to lobster meat and season with salt and paprika. If desired, rub liver or coral through a sieve and add to stew. Approximate yield: 6 portions.

LOBSTER NEWBURG

2 cups cubed lobster meat	1 cup light cream
2 tablespoons butter	½ teaspoon salt
¼ cup Sherry	cayenne
2 tablespoons brandy	nutmeg
3 egg yolks, slightly beaten	6 slices toast

Cook lobster in butter 3 minutes; add liquors and cook 1 minute longer. Mix egg yolks and cream, add to lobster and cook just until mixture thickens, stirring constantly; if overcooked, sauce will curdle. Remove from heat immediately, season with salt, cayenne and nutmeg and serve on toast or crackers, or in patty shells. Yield: 6 portions.

LOBSTER AND CRAB NEWBURG

1 cooked lobster (1½ pounds), or 2 cups cubed lobster meat	2 tablespoons butter
	2 tablespoons grated Parmesan cheese
1 cup cooked crab meat	
3 tablespoons Sherry	salt
3 tablespoons brandy	cayenne
4 egg yolks	1 teaspoon paprika
1 cup light cream	

Remove lobster meat from shell and cut into large pieces. Mix with crab meat and let stand with 2 tablespoons Sherry and 2 tablespoons brandy 15 to 20 minutes. Place eggs, butter, cheese, salt, cayenne, paprika and remaining Sherry and brandy in top of double boiler over hot water. Place over low heat and gradually add cream, stirring constantly until it thickens or just coats spoon. (If mixture curdles pour immediately into cold bowl and beat with whisk or rotary beater.) Add lobster and crab meat, turn into casserole and serve immediately. Yield: 6 portions.

FRIED LOBSTER

1 lobster, boiled (page 438)	½ cup dry bread crumbs
salt and paprika	1 egg, well beaten
juice of 1 lemon	Tartar Sauce (page 477)

Remove lobster meat from shell, tail and claws, cutting tail meat in quarters; sprinkle with salt, paprika and lemon juice. Dip in crumbs, then in egg and again in crumbs; fry in hot deep fat (380° F.) 2 minutes. Drain on absorbent paper; serve with Tartar Sauce. Approximate yield: 2 to 3 portions.

MERRYMOUNT LOBSTER

3 cups broken lobster meat, canned or boiled	¼ teaspoon pepper
	dash of cayenne
2 cups light cream	1 teaspoon prepared mustard
1 cup soft bread crumbs	½ teaspoon lemon juice
2 eggs, slightly beaten	2 tablespoons butter
1 teaspoon salt	1 cup buttered cracker crumbs

Heat lobster meat, cream and bread crumbs almost to boiling; stir gradually into the eggs; add salt, pepper and cayenne and cook over hot water 5 minutes, or until slightly thickened, stirring constantly. Add remaining seasonings and butter; turn into greased ramekins and top with buttered crumbs. Bake in moderate oven (375° F.) 10 minutes, or until crumbs are browned. Approximate yield: 8 portions.

LOBSTER CUTLETS

1 cup Thick White Sauce (page 125)	½ teaspoon salt
	1 teaspoon lemon juice
2 cups cubed lobster meat, canned or boiled	1 tablespoon minced parsley
	dash of paprika
½ cup soft bread crumbs	2 eggs, slightly beaten
dry bread crumbs	

Mix white sauce, lobster and crumbs; add salt, lemon juice, parsley and paprika, mixing well; chill. When stiff enough to handle, shape into cutlets, dip in eggs, then in crumbs; chill. Fry in hot deep fat (385° F.) about 2 minutes, or until golden brown. Approximate yield: 6 portions.

BAKED LOBSTER

Prepare lobster as for broiling (page 438). Dot meat with butter and sprinkle with salt, pepper and ¼ cup dry bread crumbs, buttered. Place on rack in roasting pan, cover and bake in hot oven (425° F.) 35 minutes, basting once with melted butter. The meat will be tender and juicy. Allow 1 pound lobster per portion.

LOBSTER WITH ANCHOVY SAUCE

1 1¼-pound lobster	4 teaspoons anchovy paste
2 tablespoons butter	½ teaspoon salt
2 tablespoons flour	1½ tablespoons lemon juice
1 cup water	3 slices toast

Boil or steam lobster (page 438); remove meat from shell in as large pieces as possible. Make a roux of butter and flour; add water and stir constantly, cooking until mixture thickens. Add anchovy paste, mixing well; add salt, lemon juice and lobster meat and simmer 5 minutes. Serve on toast. Yield: 2 portions.

LOBSTER TAILS

The so-called lobster tails which have come on the American market within recent years are actually classified as spiny lobsters or Crustaceans, and are grown in Pacific and African waters as well as off the coast of Cuba and Florida. Known by the Latin names of *Jasus Lalandii* for the foreign variety and of *Pellanauras Argus* for our American types, they are chiefly esteemed for their tender, solid flesh and the ease with which they are prepared for boiling or broiling. Lobster tails are marketed frozen in sizes weighing from 5 to 18 ounces; the meat is also sold canned. Allow ⅓ of a pound for an average portion.

TIMETABLE FOR PREPARING LOBSTER TAILS
(IN MINUTES)

WEIGHT	4 oz.	5 oz.	6 oz.	7 oz.	8 oz.	9 oz.	10 oz.	11 oz.	12 oz.	13 oz.	14 oz.	15 oz.	16 oz.
BOILING:													
Thawed	5	6	7	8	9	10	11	12	13	14	15	16	17
Frozen	7	8	9	10	11	12	13	14	15	16	17	18	19
PRESSURE COOKING (at 15 pounds)	3	3	3	3	4	4	4	5	5	5	5	5	5
BROILING:													
Shell side	5	5	5	5	5	5	5	5	5	5	5	5	5
Flesh side	6	6	6	7	7	7	8	8	8	9	9	9	9
BAKING IN FOIL	25	25	25	25	25	30	30	30	30	35	35	35	35

LOBSTER TAILS

How to Broil—Thaw. Cut under-shell around edges and remove. Grasp tail in both hands and bend backwards toward shell side to crack and prevent curling; or insert skewer to keep tail flat. Arrange shell-side up on rack of broiler pan. Place 5 inches below heater unit or flame, preheated to moderate (350° to 375° F.) or medium temperature. Broil 5 minutes. Turn, spread with butter, and broil according to timetable. Serve in shell with melted butter and lemon wedges.

How to Bake in Foil—Thaw. Cut under-shell around edge and remove. Fold each tail securely into piece of foil cut 4 inches longer than length of tail. Place on baking pan in hot oven (450° F.) and bake according to timetable above.

BOILED LOBSTER TAILS

lobster tails	¼ cup white wine
salt	1 small onion, chopped
bay leaf	dash of cayenne

Place lobster tails in saucepan and cover with boiling water. Add 1 tablespoon salt and 1 bay leaf for each quart of water. Add wine, onion and cayenne. Cover and bring to a boil. When water reboils, lower heat and begin counting time, following timetable on page 442. Remove and serve immediately with any desired sauce or chill and serve cold.

Note: To remove meat easily, drain off hot water, drench with cold, and cut through under-shell with kitchen scissors. Insert fingers between shell and meat and pull firmly. In recipes calling for diced, boiled lobster, chill meat to dice easily.

BISQUE À LA CAPETOWN

1 medium-sized onion, sliced	¼ teaspoon nutmeg
1 quart of milk	¼ teaspoon celery salt
4 tablespoons melted butter	1½ cups (12 oz.) boiled, flaked
4 tablespoons flour	lobster tail meat
1 teaspoon salt	chopped pimientos
⅛ teaspoon pepper	½ cup cream
additional salt	

Add onion to milk and heat in top of double boiler. Combine melted butter, flour, salt, pepper, nutmeg and celery salt in 2-quart saucepan. Strain onion from milk. Stir milk into flour mixture gradually. When thickened slightly, add lobster meat and pimientos. Simmer 10 minutes. Add cream and additional salt, if desired. Yield: 6 servings.

CHILLED COCKTAIL IN SHELL

4 4-oz. lobster tails	2 tablespoons mayonnaise
¼ cup tomato catsup	1 teaspoon prepared horseradish
2 tablespoons lemon juice	⅛ teaspoon celery salt
1 tablespoon vinegar	3 drops Tabasco

Boil lobster tails according to directions (page 442). Remove meat, chill, dice; refill individual shells. Top with a sauce of catsup, lemon juice, vinegar, mayonnaise, horseradish, celery salt and Tabasco. Serve icy cold with lemon wedges. Yield: 4 servings.

LOBSTER TAIL NEWBURG

4 tablespoons melted butter
¼ cup Sherry or Marsala
2 cups diced, boiled lobster
meat

¼ teaspoon salt
½ teaspoon paprika
4 egg yolks, slightly beaten
1 cup thin cream

2 drops Tabasco

To melted butter, add Sherry or Marsala, lobster meat, salt and paprika. Mix lightly. Cover. Cook over hot water 3 minutes. Mix eggs and cream thoroughly. Stir gradually into mixture. Add Tabasco. Continue cooking, stirring gently about 3 minutes, or until sauce thickens slightly. Garnish with sprigs of parsley. Serve at once with toast points. Yield: 4 to 5 servings.

THERMIDOR AFRIKAANS

4 tablespoons melted butter
4 tablespoons flour
1 teaspoon salt
1 teaspoon paprika
½ teaspoon dry mustard
¼ teaspoon nutmeg
1½ cups hot milk and drained,
canned mushroom liquor

½ cup cream
4 (6 oz.) diced, boiled lobster
tails
½ cup drained canned mushrooms
2 tablespoons Sherry
1 cup soft bread crumbs
2 tablespoons butter, melted

Make cream sauce of melted butter, flour, salt, paprika, mustard, nutmeg, milk and mushroom liquor, and cream. Mix in lobster meat and Sherry. Refill shells. Combine bread crumbs and butter. Sprinkle over filled shells. Brown lightly under broiler. Garnish with lemon wedges. Yield: 4 servings.

Omelet Filling—Halve recipe. Omit bread crumbs and extra butter. Spread on omelet before folding.

LOBSTER TAILS WITH DIAVOLO SAUCE

¼ cup olive oil
2 cloves garlic, minced fine
⅛ teaspoon cayenne
1 teaspoon orégano

1 teaspoon salt
⅛ teaspoon pepper
1 tablespoon chopped parsley
1 No. 2 can tomatoes

4 lobster tails

Heat olive oil in saucepan and add garlic; lightly brown. Add cayenne, orégano, salt, pepper, chopped parsley and tomatoes. Simmer 30 minutes. Prepare lobster tails by splitting in half lengthwise in shell. Remove dark vein. Place in greased casserole and pour sauce over tails. Bake in moderate oven (350° F.) 30 minutes. Yield: 4 portions.

MUSSELS

Mussels are purchased alive as small, medium and large (see table on Fresh Shellfish). They are entirely edible except for the small black beard, or byssus, which can serve as a handle for lifting the mussel from the shell. Overcooking mussels will cause them to lose their shape and fall apart. Scrub; discard all open shells. Steam 2 minutes only, or until the shells open. Allow 6 to 12 mussels per portion.

MUSSELS BAKED WITH CHEESE

42 steamed mussels	1 teaspoon grated onion
½ teaspoon salt	½ pound sliced bacon
dash of pepper	½ cup grated Parmesan cheese

Spread mussels in shallow baking pan and sprinkle with salt, pepper and onion. Panfry bacon until almost crisp; place on top of mussels, about ¼ inch apart; sprinkle cheese between strips. Bake in moderate oven (350° F.) 15 minutes. Approximate yield: 6 portions.

SCRAMBLED EGGS WITH MUSSELS

30 steamed mussels	6 eggs, slightly beaten
¾ teaspoon salt	6 tablespoons light cream
dash of pepper	½ cup soft bread crumbs
1 tablespoon butter, melted	

Chop mussels fine and season with salt and pepper. Mix together eggs, cream and bread crumbs; add to melted butter in frying pan and cook over low heat until mixture begins to thicken, stirring constantly. Add mussels and scramble slowly. Yield: 6 portions.

MUSSELS À LA MARINIÈRE

42 steamed mussels	dash of thyme
½ small onion	1½ tablespoons tarragon vinegar
2 sprigs parsley	1 tablespoon butter
1 stalk celery	½ teaspoon salt
drop of Tabasco	

Scrub mussels well; place in saucepan with onion, parsley, celery and thyme, cover and cook over low heat 2 to 5 minutes until shells open. Remove beards and serve mussels on half shell in soup plates; add remaining ingredients to juice in saucepan; heat thoroughly and strain. Serve in small bowls as a sauce for the mussels. Yield: 6 portions.

FRENCH MUSSELS

5 pounds mussels	1 bay leaf
2 quarts cold water	3 peppercorns
2 tablespoons dry mustard	½ teaspoon salt
1 onion, finely sliced	1 tablespoon butter, melted
¼ clove garlic, minced	1 tablespoon flour
2 tablespoons oil	3 egg yolks, beaten
1 cup dry white wine	½ cup light cream
3 tablespoons water	3 tablespoons coarsely chopped parsley

Soak mussels in combined water and mustard 15 minutes. Drain and scrub shells. Discard any that are open. Lightly brown onion and garlic in hot oil. Add wine, water, mussels, bay leaf, peppercorns and salt. Bring slowly to boiling. Cover and shake over the fire until all mussels are open. Strain and reserve liquid. Carefully remove top shells from mussels and arrange on hot serving plate. Combine butter and flour. Gradually add reserved liquid. Bring to boiling and simmer 5 minutes. Combine well-beaten egg yolks, cream and parsley. Gradually add hot liquid mixture. Pour over mussels. Yield: 6 portions.

OYSTERS

Oysters are purchased as small, medium and large. They may be purchased frozen as well as fresh, in the shell or shucked. Cook them only until plump and the edges begin to curl. Overcooking results in tough and rubbery oysters. Whenever possible add them as the last ingredient in a recipe.

OPENING AND CLEANING OYSTERS

Scrub shells thoroughly and rinse in cold water. To remove sand from oysters, clams and mussels, allow to stand for 2 or 3 hours in water with a handful of cornmeal sprinkled over the surface. Insert a strong blunt knife between the shells at the joint of the thick end. Twist knife to pry open. Run knife around until the muscle holding the shells together is cut. Cut muscle under oyster and turn out with liquor into a bowl. Strain liquor before using; examine oysters closely and remove pieces of shell. Use as desired (see table, page 407). There are about 14 small, 10 medium or 8 or 9 large oysters to 1 cup. Oysters can be bought in cans. Allow about ⅔ cup per portion; or 9 to 10 small, 6 to 7 medium or 5 to 6 large oysters per portion.

OYSTERS BRÛLOT

24 oysters   ⅓ cup rum

Dry oysters carefully; place in four shallow cocktail glasses imbedded in ice. Heat rum (do not boil). Pour over oysters and ignite just before serving. Garnish with lemon wedges. Yield: 4 portions.

OYSTERS COOKED IN SHELL

Scrub oysters well and rinse in cold water. Set in baking pan, deep shell down, and bake in hot oven (450° F.) 10 minutes, or until shells open. Season with a little butter, salt and pepper and serve on the half shell at once.

SAUTÉED OYSTERS

Drain oysters and dry thoroughly. Roll in fine bread or cracker crumbs. Fry on well-greased hot griddle or frying pan 1 minute on each side, turning to brown both sides. Serve on toast.

PANNED OYSTERS

Place oysters in shallow baking pan, add a very small amount of oyster liquor. Bake in hot oven (425° F.) 3 to 5 minutes, or just until they are plump and hot. Serve on buttered toast softened with hot oyster liquor.

GRILLED OR BROILED OYSTERS

18 shucked large oysters   dry bread crumbs
2 eggs, slightly beaten   ¼ cup butter, melted
½ teaspoon salt   3 to 4 slices buttered toast
⅛ teaspoon pepper   6 slices lemon
                    parsley

Drain oysters and dry thoroughly. Dip in eggs seasoned with salt and pepper, roll in crumbs and place on greased broiler. Pour a drop or two of butter on each oyster and broil under moderate heat 1 minute, or until browned. Turn, pour another drop of butter on each oyster and broil 1 minute. Serve on toast, garnished with lemon slice and parsley. Approximate yield: 3 to 4 portions.

OVEN GRILLED OYSTERS

Prepare oysters as for Grilled or Broiled Oysters (above) and place in greased shallow pan. Bake in hot oven (400° F.) 10 minutes, or until browned. Serve with crisp bacon strips.

PANBROILED OYSTERS

2 quarts large oysters	¼ cup butter, melted
½ teaspoon salt	8 to 10 strips of toast
⅛ teaspoon cayenne	¼ cup Sherry

Drain oysters and dry thoroughly; sprinkle both sides lightly with salt and cayenne. Fry in greased, hot frying pan 2 minutes, or until plump, turning them once. Dip in melted butter and place on toast strips. Pour a teaspoon of Sherry over each strip and serve immediately. Approximate yield: 8 to 10 portions.

FRIED OYSTERS

1 quart large oysters	2 eggs, slightly beaten
	dry bread crumbs

Dry oysters between pieces of absorbent paper or on a clean towel. Dip in egg, roll in crumbs; chill. Fry in deep hot fat (375°–380° F.) 2 to 3 minutes, or until golden brown. Serve with shredded cabbage salad. Approximate yield: 6 portions.

MARYLAND FRIED OYSTERS

1 pint of oysters, drained	1 tablespoon milk
flour	salt and pepper
1 egg, beaten	1 cup sifted dry bread crumbs

Roll oysters in flour, shaking off excess. Combine beaten egg, milk, salt and pepper. Dip oysters in egg mixture and roll in crumbs. Fry in deep fat (375° F.) or in frying pan filled with fat ⅛-inch deep. Turn to brown evenly on both sides. Drain on absorbent paper. Serve at once with lemon sections, Tartar Sauce (page 477) or Tangy Oyster Sauce (page 465). Yield: 4 to 6 portions.

CREAMED OYSTERS

3 cups oysters	6 patty shells
2 cups Medium White Sauce	1 teaspoon chopped parsley
(page 125)	or paprika

Examine oysters for bits of shell; heat in their own liquor about 3 minutes, or until plump and edges begin to curl; add to hot white sauce. Serve in patty shells with a sprinkle of parsley or paprika. Or serve in buttered croustades. Yield: 6 portions.

OYSTERS BENEDICT

6 thin slices boiled ham	3 English muffins
1 square inch ham fat	1 recipe Hollandaise Sauce
1 pint small oysters, drained	(page 473)
6 thin strips pimiento	

Sauté ham in fat 3 or 4 minutes, or until hot and lightly browned. Remove from pan, add oysters and sauté 2 minutes, or until plump and edges curl. Split and toast muffins; place slice of ham and 4 oysters on each half. Serve with Hollandaise Sauce and garnish with pimiento. Approximate yield: 6 portions.

OYSTER BÉCHAMEL

1 quart oysters	¼ teaspoon paprika
1 cup oyster liquor	dash of nutmeg
3 tablespoons butter	½ cup light cream
3 tablespoons flour	2 egg yolks, slightly beaten
½ teaspoon salt	toast, pastry or crackers
	parsley

Heat oysters in liquor 3 to 5 minutes, or until plump and edges begin to curl; drain, saving liquor. Make a roux of butter and flour and add seasonings; add oyster liquor gradually and cook 5 minutes, stirring constantly until smooth and thickened. Add cream slowly, beating sauce until glossy; add oysters and heat thoroughly. Add small amount to egg yolks, mixing well; return to oyster mixture and cook 1 minute longer, stirring constantly. Serve on toast. Garnish with parsley. Yield: 6 portions.

SAVORY BAKED OYSTERS

1 quart large oysters	dash of paprika
3 tablespoons olive oil	½ teaspoon curry powder
3 tablespoons lemon juice	1 tablespoon horseradish
½ teaspoon salt	2 cups buttered crumbs
12 slices crisp broiled bacon	

Drain oysters thoroughly. Mix olive oil, lemon juice and seasoning; add oysters and marinate 30 minutes. Dry between sheets of absorbent paper, roll in crumbs and place in long shallow baking pan; bake in hot oven (425° F.) 15 to 20 minutes, or until puffed and crisp. Serve with bacon strips. Approximate yield: 6 portions.

DEVILED OYSTERS

1 onion, finely chopped	dash of cayenne
¼ cup butter	½ teaspoon Worcestershire sauce
1 quart oysters, chopped	2 eggs, well beaten
1 tablespoon chopped parsley	½ cup cracker crumbs
¼ cup dry bread crumbs	

Sauté onion in 3 tablespoons butter 3 minutes, or until tender; add oysters, parsley, cayenne and Worcestershire sauce and simmer 1 minute; add to eggs. Add cracker crumbs and turn into shells or small ramekins. Sprinkle with bread crumbs and dot with remaining tablespoon butter; bake in hot oven (425° F.) 15 minutes or until browned. Approximate yield: 6 portions.

BOHEMIAN OYSTERS

1 tablespoon bacon drippings	½ teaspoon Worcestershire sauce
1 tablespoon cornstarch	1 egg yolk, beaten
1 cup milk	3 dozen oysters
1 cup oyster liquor	1 package fine noodles, cooked
½ teaspoon salt	½ pound Cheddar cheese, grated
dash of Tabasco	black pepper

Melt drippings in saucepan, add cornstarch and mix to a smooth paste. Add milk, oyster liquor and salt. Cook over low heat, stirring constantly until thickened. Cover and let cook 5 minutes longer. Add Tabasco sauce and Worcestershire sauce. Pour a little of mixture into egg yolk and then return to saucepan. Remove from heat. Place drained oysters in a hot skillet and cook for 5 minutes, stirring frequently to prevent burning. Add sauce and stir to absorb browned oyster flavor. Place ⅓ of noodles in the bottom of a greased casserole, add ⅓ oyster mixture, sprinkle with ⅓ grated cheese. Continue until all ingredients are used. Sprinkle with cheese and pepper. Bake in a moderate oven (350° F.) 15 minutes. Yield: 6 servings.

BAKED OYSTERS À PARIS

2 dozen oysters	dash of Tabasco
½ cup melted butter	1 tablespoon chopped chives
1 tablespoon lemon juice	salt and pepper

Wash oysters in shell, place in baking pan (deep shell down) and bake in 400° F. oven for about 15 minutes or until shells open. Remove upper shell. Combine butter, lemon juice, Tabasco, chives, salt and pepper. Spoon sauce over hot oysters and serve immediately. Yield: 4 portions.

OYSTER CASSEROLE

1 cup chopped mushrooms	1½ pints oysters
8 to 10 small whole mushrooms	1 cup milk
½ cup butter	½ cup light cream
1 cup fine cracker crumbs	paprika

Sauté all mushrooms in 2 tablespoons butter 2 minutes. Line bottom of greased casserole with ⅓ of crumbs, add a layer of chopped mushrooms and dot with 1 tablespoon butter; add another layer of crumbs, then oysters, remaining chopped mushrooms and a final layer of crumbs. Pour milk, cream and remaining 5 tablespoons butter, melted, over top. Bake in moderate oven (350° F.) 25 minutes. Stand whole mushrooms upright in crumbs, sprinkle with paprika and place under moderate broiler heat about 5 minutes. Approximate yield: 6 portions.

FRIED OYSTER PIES

½ recipe Plain Pastry	6 large oysters
(page 736)	salt and pepper

Place pastry on lightly floured board and roll ⅛ inch thick; cut in twelve 3-inch rounds. Place one oyster on each of 6 rounds; season and top with remaining 6 rounds and press edges together with a fork dipped in flour. Fry in hot deep fat (380° F.) 3 to 5 minutes, or until golden brown. Approximate yield: 6 portions.

OYSTERS ROCKEFELLER

8 oysters on half shell	4 tablespoons sour cream
5 tablespoons sour cream	2 tablespoons grated cheese
⅛ teaspoon salt	¼ teaspoon salt
dash of cayenne	dash of pepper
¼ teaspoon crushed garlic	¼ cup grated Cheddar cheese
1 cup finely chopped raw	2 tablespoons dry bread crumbs
spinach	2 tablespoons butter

Cut muscle joining oyster to shell. Carefully lift out oyster. Combine sour cream, salt, cayenne and garlic; blend well. Place a spoonful of sour cream mixture in each shell. Replace oyster. Combine spinach, sour cream, cheese, salt and pepper. Blend well and place a spoonful on each oyster. Sprinkle with cheese and top with bread crumbs, dot with butter, place on rock salt on shallow baking pan and brown under broiler. Approximate yield: 4 portions.

SCALLOPED OYSTERS

1 cup soft bread crumbs	dash of pepper
1½ cups fine cracker crumbs	dash of nutmeg
¾ cup butter, melted	2 tablespoons chopped parsley
1 quart oysters	½ cup oyster liquor
1 teaspoon salt	¼ cup milk

Mix bread crumbs, cracker crumbs and butter; line bottom of greased casserole with half of crumbs; arrange oysters in three layers, sprinkling each layer with seasonings; add oyster liquor and milk and top with remaining crumbs. Bake in moderate oven (350° F.) 1 hour, or until mixture is puffed and browned. Yield: 6 portions.

BAKED OYSTERS AND NOODLES

1 12-oz. box frozen oysters, or	½ teaspoon paprika
1½ cups oysters	2 tablespoons flour
¼ cup butter	1¼ cups milk
½ teaspoon salt	2 cups broken noodles
dash of pepper	½ cup buttered bread crumbs

Allow oysters to thaw a little. Sauté oysters in butter about 10 minutes, or until plump and edges begin to curl, then add seasonings; remove oysters and stir flour into mixture in pan. Gradually add milk, stirring until thick and smooth. Cook noodles in large amount of rapidly boiling salted water about 10 minutes, or until tender; drain and arrange half of them in greased casserole. Cover with oysters, then add remaining noodles. Pour sauce over top and sprinkle with crumbs; bake in hot oven (450° F.) 15 minutes. Approximate yield: 6 portions.

HOT CURRIED OYSTERS

Combine 1 cup heavy sour cream, 4 teaspoons lemon juice, 2 teaspoons onion juice and 1 teaspoon curry powder; chill several hours. Add 2 tablespoons lemon juice and ⅛ teaspoon Tabasco sauce to 2 dozen oysters. Heat sauce, add oysters and simmer 2 minutes, or until oysters are plump and edges curl. Serve with rice. Yield: 6 portions.

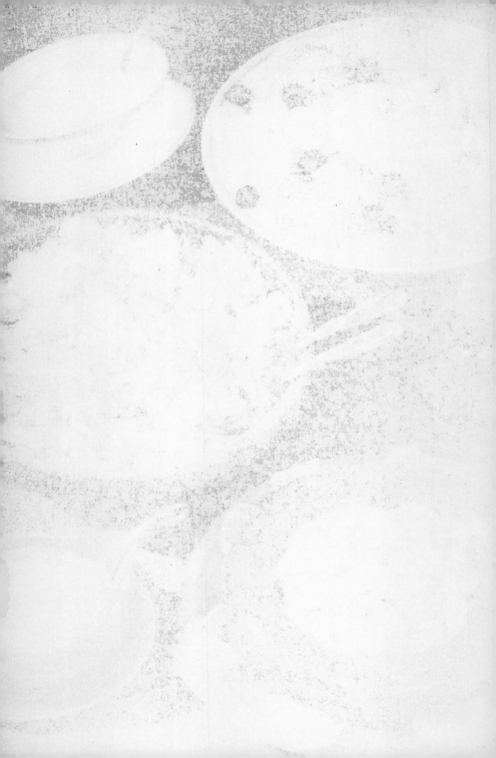

OYSTER CUTLETS

1 quart oysters	¼ teaspoon salt
1 cup oyster liquor	dash of cayenne
1 cup light cream	1 tablespoon minced parsley
¼ cup butter	2 eggs
½ cup flour	dry bread crumbs

Heat oysters in liquor 3 to 5 minutes; drain, add liquor to cream and chop oysters fine. Make a roux of butter and flour, then add liquor-cream mixture slowly and cook 5 minutes, stirring constantly until thick and smooth. Add seasonings and oysters; then stir in 1 egg, slightly beaten, and cook 1 minute longer. Turn out on large plate and chill. Shape into cutlets, dip in remaining egg, beaten, and roll in crumbs. Fry in hot deep fat (380° F.) 2 to 3 minutes. Yield: 6 portions.

SCALLOPS

Scallops are always bought shucked, either fresh or frozen. Bay scallops are small (¼ to ½ inch in diameter). Sea scallops are larger (½ to 1½ inches in diameter). They may be panfried, steamed, baked or broiled and are excellent in chowder. Leftover cooked scallops may be used as a cocktail served with Louis' Cocktail Sauce (page 215).

BROILED OR SAUTÉED SCALLOPS

2 pounds (1 qt.) scallops	dry bread crumbs
1 cup milk	2 tablespoons butter

Wash and pick over scallops; dip in milk and roll in bread crumbs. Place one layer deep in greased shallow pan, dot with butter and broil 3 minutes, or until browned, turning frequently. Serve with melted butter and lemon juice. Approximate yield: 6 portions.

To sauté scallops, prepare as for broiling and fry on well-greased hot griddle or frying pan 3 minutes, or until browned, turning frequently.

SCALLOPS AU GRATIN

2 pounds (1 qt.) scallops	½ cup finely chopped celery
1 cup buttered dry crumbs	1 cup light cream
1 teaspoon salt	2 tablespoons grated Parmesan
½ cup minced green pepper	cheese

Rinse and drain scallops; cover with cold water, heat slowly to boiling and drain. Line a greased baking dish with a thin layer of bread crumbs. Add scallops in layers, sprinkling each layer with salt, green pepper and celery until all scallops are used. Add cream. Top with remaining crumbs, mixed with cheese, and bake in moderate oven (350° F.) 30 minutes. Approximate yield: 6 portions.

SAVORY SCALLOPS

1 pound (1 pt.) scallops	1 egg, slightly beaten
½ cup Medium Cream Sauce	½ teaspoon salt
(page 466)	dash of cayenne
½ cup canned tomatoes	½ teaspoon dry mustard
1 cup grated cheese	6 toast squares

Wash scallops, cover with cold water, heat slowly to boiling and drain. Mix cream sauce, tomatoes and cheese and heat until cheese is melted; add slowly to egg, mixing well. Add seasonings and scallops and cook over hot water 5 minutes, stirring occasionally. Serve on toast. Approximate yield: 6 portions.

SCALLOPS AND MUSHROOMS

1 pound (1 pt.) scallops	¾ cup evaporated milk
¼ pound mushrooms	½ teaspoon salt
2 tablespoons butter	dash of pepper
1 tablespoon flour	½ teaspoon Worcestershire sauce
1 sweet red pepper, shredded	6 slices toast

Rinse scallops, cover with cold water, heat slowly to boiling and drain. Rinse and slice mushrooms; sauté in butter 5 minutes; stir in flour off the heat; add red pepper. Gradually add milk and cook 5 minutes, or until thickened, stirring constantly. Add scallops and remaining seasonings and heat thoroughly; serve on toast. Yield: 6 portions.

FRIED SEA SCALLOPS

2 pounds (1 qt.) scallops	½ cup flour
2 eggs, slightly beaten	1 teaspoon salt
	dash of paprika

Wash scallops, drain and dry between folds of absorbent paper. Dip in egg, then in seasoned flour. Fry in hot deep fat (375° F.) 2 to 3 minutes, or until golden brown; drain on unglazed paper. Serve with Tartar Sauce (page 477). Approximate yield: 6 portions.

SHRIMP

Shrimp are sold by the pound and will vary in number from 15 to 65, depending on the size. Large shrimp are often called prawns. Store them wrapped tightly on ice or in the coldest part of the refrigerator.

BOILED SHRIMP

Wash shrimp in cold water and drop into rapidly boiling salted water; add 2 bay leaves, a stalk of celery, a dash of thyme and a sprig of parsley, cover tightly and cook 5 minutes. Drain and cover with cold water to chill; then drain, remove shells and vein (the black line running along the back); prepare as desired. Shrimp may be cooked without the addition of vegetables. Shrimp may be shelled and cleaned before cooking. This is thought by many to be the easiest way to clean them. One pound fresh shrimp yields about 2 cups cooked shrimp. Canned shrimp may be used in any recipe. Allow 1½ pounds for 6 portions (see table on Fresh Shellfish).

CREAMED SHRIMP

1½ pounds fresh shrimp   6 slices toast or patty shells
2 cups Medium White Sauce
  (page 125)

Cook and prepare fresh shrimp (above); mix with white sauce. Heat thoroughly and season with additional salt and pepper, if desired. Serve on toast or in patty shells. Yield: 6 portions.

BROILED FRESH SHRIMP

1½ pounds fresh shrimp   4 tablespoons butter or oil
salt   Black Butter Sauce (page 472)

Remove all shells from shrimp except the last segment and tail. Remove vein (above). Dip uncooked shrimp into seasoned melted butter; place in moderately hot broiler (375°–400° F.) 2 inches from source of heat. Broil 4 to 6 minutes, depending on size of shrimp. Season and serve with Black Butter Sauce for dunking. Yield: 4 to 6 portions.

FRIED SHRIMP

2 pounds jumbo shrimp, shelled   2 tablespoons minced parsley
  and veins removed   1 teaspoon salt
2 eggs, beaten   ½ teaspoon dried basil
1 cup bread crumbs   ¼ teaspoon pepper
½ cup grated Parmesan cheese   olive oil and salad oil

Dip shrimp in beaten eggs. Roll in the combined bread crumbs, cheese, parsley, salt, basil and pepper. Allow to stand for 5 minutes. Place equal amounts of olive oil and salad oil in a heavy skillet to make a layer 1-inch deep. Heat until hot but not smoking. Add just enough shrimp to fill the pan; fry until golden brown on all sides. Cook remaining shrimp in the same manner. Drain on absorbent paper. Approximate yield: 4 portions.

BUTTERFLY SHRIMP

2 eggs, beaten	⅛ teaspoon white pepper
2 tablespoons milk	5 tablespoons flour
1 teaspoon salt	1 pound shrimp

Combine eggs, milk, salt and pepper. Beat in flour until smooth. Remove shells from shrimp, leaving tails on. Make a shallow cut along the back. With the point of a knife lift out the vein. Split each shrimp lengthwise almost all the way through; spread and flatten each. Dip into batter; fry in deep fat at 350° F. until golden brown. Drain on absorbent paper. Yield: 2 portions.

CURRIED SHRIMP

1½ pounds fresh shrimp	dash of pepper
3 cups shrimp stock	3 tablespoons flour
3 chicken bouillon cubes	3 tablespoons butter
½ tablespoon curry powder	3 cups hot, cooked rice
½ teaspoon salt	3 hard-cooked eggs

Cook and prepare shrimp (page 455), saving stock. To 3 cups strained shrimp stock, add bouillon cubes and stir until dissolved; moisten curry powder with a little water and add to stock with salt and pepper, mixing well. Stir flour into melted butter; gradually stir in seasoned stock and cook over low heat until smooth and slightly thickened; then add shrimp. Pack hot rice into greased ring mold and bake in moderate oven (350° F.) 15 minutes; unmold on platter, pour shrimp mixture in center and garnish with sliced eggs. Approximate yield: 6 portions.

SHRIMP AND OYSTER DELIGHT

1 pound fresh shrimp	1 cup flaked cooked crab meat
2 dozen large shucked oysters	2 cups Thin Cream Sauce (page 466)
6 mushrooms, peeled and sliced	
½ green pepper, diced	½ cup chopped pimiento
2 tablespoons butter	10 slices toast

Wash shrimp, drop into boiling water and cook 5 minutes. Plunge into cold water, remove shell and black vein along the back. Heat oysters in their liquor 3 to 5 minutes, or until plump and edges begin to curl; drain. Sauté mushrooms and green pepper in butter 5 minutes. Add fish, cream sauce and pimiento; heat thoroughly. Serve on toast. Approximate yield: 10 portions.

CHARLESTON SHRIMP

1½ pounds fresh shrimp   dash of pepper
1 teaspoon salt   ¾ cup butter, melted

Remove shells and veins (page 455); add with seasonings to melted butter, cover and cook over low heat 10 minutes, stirring occasionally. Serve with hot hominy grits or rice, if desired. Approximate yield: 6 portions.

STEWED SHRIMP À LA CREOLE

2 tablespoons butter   1 teaspoon fresh thyme or
1 tablespoon flour   ½ teaspoon dried thyme
2 onions, finely chopped   2 teaspoons fresh parsley, chopped
2 pounds peeled shrimp, raw,   or 1 teaspoon dried
   frozen or canned   1 bay leaf or ½ teaspoon
6 tomatoes or 1¼ cups canned   powdered
1 cup water   ½ teaspoon garlic salt
1 green pepper, diced   salt and pepper to taste

Melt butter, add flour gradually and cook to light brown. Add onions and sauté until golden. Add shrimp and mix well. Let cool slightly, add tomatoes and water, green pepper and seasonings. Cook, stirring frequently, 10 minutes. Serve over rice in soup plates. Approximate yield: 6 portions.

CORN AND SHRIMP SOUFFLÉ

6 large ears corn   2 teaspoons sugar
3 eggs, separated   1 tablespoon melted butter
½ teaspoon salt   1½ pounds fresh shrimp, cooked

Scrape corn kernels from cob and stir into well-beaten egg yolks; add seasonings, melted butter and shrimp; fold in stiffly beaten egg whites. Turn into greased soufflé dish, cover and place in pan of hot water; bake in slow oven (300° F.) 1 hour, or until firm. Remove cover the last 15 minutes of baking to brown top. Yield: 6 portions.

FRIED SHRIMP

Remove shells and veins from shrimp (page 455), season with salt and pepper, dip in milk and roll in cornmeal. Fry in hot deep fat (380° F.) 2 to 3 minutes, or until golden brown. Drain on absorbent paper and serve at once on squares of buttered toast; garnish with parsley sprigs and olives. Allow 6 to 8 shrimp per person.

SHRIMP PIE

1½ pounds fillet of haddock (or other white fish)
1 medium-sized onion, minced
½ cup dry bread crumbs
½ teaspoon salt
⅛ teaspoon pepper
¾ cup heavy sour cream

1½ pounds fresh shrimp, cooked (page 455)
1 cup cooked peas
1 recipe Plain Pastry (page 736)
1 egg yolk
3 tablespoons butter
1 tablespoon flour

1 cup water

Rinse fish; wrap in cheesecloth, drop into boiling salted water and simmer 5 minutes; drain, remove cloth and mince with fork. Add onion, bread crumbs, seasoning and ½ cup sour cream. Place fish mixture, shrimp and peas in alternate layers in 6 small casseroles; top with pastry, cutting a small hole in center of each. Brush pastry with slightly beaten egg yolk; bake in hot oven (450° F.) 12 to 15 minutes. Melt butter and add flour off the heat; gradually add water, stirring constantly, add remaining ¼ cup sour cream; cook over low heat 5 minutes, or until thick and smooth. When pies are baked, pour sauce into pies through center opening in top crust. Yield: 6 portions.

SHRIMP JAMBALAYA

1 cup finely diced onion
2 cloves of garlic, minced
3 tablespoons butter
2 tablespoons minced parsley
1 bay leaf
⅛ teaspoon dried thyme

1 tablespoon flour
¼ teaspoon chili powder
3 large tomatoes, chopped
4½ cups chicken broth or water
salt to taste
1 cup rice, washed

2 pounds uncooked shrimp

Sauté onion and garlic in butter until tender, about 10 minutes. Add parsley, bay leaf and thyme. Stir in flour and chili powder. Add chopped tomatoes with juice. Simmer 10 minutes, stirring frequently. Add chicken broth; season lightly with salt; bring to a boil. Sprinkle in rice. Cover and simmer 25 minutes, stirring occasionally. Remove shells and veins from shrimp. Add to rice mixture. Cook, covered, 15 minutes. Serve with a tossed green salad. Approximate yield: 6 portions.

SHRIMP TEMPURA

1 teaspoon almond butter or peanut butter	½ teaspoon salt
2 eggs	dash of pepper
1 tablespoon cornstarch	1½ pounds fresh shrimp, cooked (page 455)

Cream nut butter; separate one egg and add one-half of the white to nut butter, beating until smooth. Beat remaining egg white, yolk and second egg; stir in cornstarch, then nut butter and seasoning, beating until smooth. Dip shrimp in this batter and fry in hot deep fat (380° F.) 2-3 minutes, or until browned. Drain on unglazed paper and garnish with parsley or water cress. Approximate yield: 6 portions.

SHRIMP AND RICE CASSEROLE

½ pound sharp cheese	2½ cups cooked rice
½ cup evaporated milk	1½ pounds fresh shrimp, cooked (page 455)
½ teaspoon salt	
dash of pepper	1 cup buttered bread crumbs

Grind cheese or cut in small pieces; melt over hot water. Gradually stir in milk, beating until smooth; then add seasonings. Pour half of cheese sauce into greased casserole; place half of rice over sauce, cover with shrimp and top with remaining rice. Pour remaining cheese sauce over all and top with crumbs; bake in moderate oven (350° F.) 15-20 minutes. For canned shrimp, use 1½ cups or 1½ cans (No. 1). Approximate yield: 6 to 8 portions.

SHRIMP CREOLE

1 pound fresh shrimp	¼ teaspoon meat extract
6 tablespoons butter	¼ teaspoon tomato paste
4 mushrooms, finely sliced	½ teaspoon salt
2 tablespoons Marsala wine	pinch of chili powder
2 tablespoons minced red pepper	few grains of cayenne
2 tablespoons minced green pepper	1 cup light cream
	¼ cup heavy sour cream
2 onions, sliced	

Shell shrimp and remove vein. Cook in 3 tablespoons hot butter 2 minutes. Remove shrimp. Add 1 tablespoon butter and mushrooms. Cook briskly 2 minutes and add Marsala and red and green pepper. Cook briskly until liquid has evaporated. Add 1 tablespoon butter, meat extract, tomato paste, salt, chili powder and cayenne. Gradually stir in cream and sour cream. Brown onions in remaining butter. Add with shrimp to sauce. Simmer over low heat until heated through. Serve with Rice Pilaf (page 509). Yield: 6 portions.

FROGS' LEGS

The hind legs of the frog are the only part that is eaten; they are considered a delicacy. Cut legs from body, wash and turn the skin down; it can be pulled off like a glove. Allow 4 to 6 legs per portion.

FRIED FROGS' LEGS

12 pair large frogs' legs
1 teaspoon salt
pepper

3 tablespoons lemon juice
1 egg, slightly beaten
dry bread crumbs

Skin frogs' legs; marinate in mixture of salt, pepper and lemon juice about 1 hour. Dip quickly in egg, roll in crumbs and chill. Fry in hot deep fat (385° F.) 3 minutes, or until brown. Yield: 4 to 6 portions.

FROGS' LEGS IN WINE

1 pound frogs' legs
salt, pepper and nutmeg
1 teaspoon minced onion
2 tablespoons chopped chives
½ cup chopped mushrooms
1 truffle, chopped
1 tablespoon capers

¼ cup butter
1 cup white wine (Rhine or Sauterne)
½ cup brown stock
1 tablespoon chopped fresh parsley, chervil and tarragon leaves

Skin frogs' legs and season with salt, pepper and nutmeg. Sauté frogs' legs, onion, chives, mushrooms, truffle and capers in butter 5 minutes, or until lightly browned. Add wine and simmer 10 minutes, or until wine is almost evaporated. Add brown stock, heat thoroughly and sprinkle with herbs. Approximate yield: 2 to 3 portions.

FRICASSEE OF FROGS' LEGS

12 pair large frogs' legs
2 cups milk
6 tablespoons flour
1 teaspoon salt

dash of pepper
½ cup butter
¾ cup heavy cream
2 tablespoons chopped parsley

Skin frogs' legs, cover with milk and soak 15 minutes; drain. Mix 2 tablespoons flour with salt and pepper, dredge legs and sauté in butter 3 minutes, or until browned, turning frequently. Remove from frying pan. Stir in remaining flour; add cream gradually and cook over low heat 5 minutes, stirring constantly, until sauce is smooth and slightly thickened. Add frogs' legs, cook gently 3 minutes longer and add parsley. Approximate yield: 4 to 6 portions.

STUFFED FRESH SNAILS

1 pound snails (2½ dozen)   ¼ cup chopped parsley
Court Bouillon (page 414)   1 teaspoon minced onion
¼ cup butter   minced garlic

Preparing snails is tedious and difficult; they may be coaxed from their shells by a sprinkling of salt, then washed; or they may be soaked in salt water several hours, washed in several waters and boiled about ½ hour. Remove snails from shells and boil in Court Bouillon about 4 hours; wash shells and dry thoroughly. Return cooked snails to shells and force paste made of butter and seasonings into opening of each. Place in baking pan and bake in moderately hot oven (375° F.) about 20 minutes, or until heated through. Serve with an oyster fork or snail pick, picking up each snail with a clamp, or holding it with the corner of a napkin. Approximate yield: 6 portions.

CANNED SNAILS

Canned snails are imported and sold as a delicacy; they come in special cartons with two containers. One holds the cooked snails and the other the washed and polished shells. The family-size can contains 2 dozen snails. Place snails in shells and prepare as Stuffed Fresh Snails (see above). Or substitute a filling of equal parts butter and ground filberts, mixed together in a bowl which has been rubbed lightly with garlic. Yield: 2 dozen snails or 4 to 6 portions.

BOILED TURTLE AND TERRAPIN

Snapping turtles and soft shell turtles or tortoises should be alive when purchased. Sever the head with an axe and cover with cold water; or hang, neck down, on a hook until the blood has stopped dripping. Wash carefully, drop into boiling salted water and cook 10 minutes; drain and cover with cold water; then drain, pull out nails and rub black skin from legs. Cover again with boiling water and simmer, covered, ½ to ¾ hour, or until shell separates easily and the legs can be dented; cool in water. Place turtle on its back, and working from the tail end, loosen and remove under-shell. The gall bladder, a sac near the head, and the intestines should be carefully removed and discarded. The eggs, if any, the heart and the liver should be dropped in water. Use for stews, creamed dishes or for croquettes, saving juice.

The diamond-back Chesapeake and the Long Island terrapin are considered the choicest. They weigh around 3 pounds each. To cook live terrapin, wash, pick up with tongs and plunge, headfirst, into boiling salted water; cook 10 minutes, drain and cover with cold water; then drain, pull out nails and rub dark skin from legs. Cover again with boiling salted water and cook, covered, ½ to ¾ hour, or until legs are tender. Prepare meat as for turtle, saving the small intestines.

TURTLE À LA KING

6 hard-cooked eggs
2 tablespoons butter
2 cups light cream
½ teaspoon salt

dash each of pepper, allspice, nutmeg
2 cups chopped, cooked turtle meat

Remove egg yolks from whites and force yolks through sieve; then cream yolks with butter. Scald cream over hot water, add seasonings and beat in egg yolk-butter mixture. Add turtle, cover and cook 10 minutes, or until thoroughly heated. Serve very hot in individual metal saucepans; garnish with white of eggs. Yield: 6 portions.

TERRAPIN WITH MUSHROOMS

2 cups chopped, cooked terrapin
2 cups Medium White Sauce
   (page 125)

½ pound mushrooms, peeled and chopped
2 tablespoons white wine
6 slices toast

Combine terrapin, white sauce and mushrooms; cook 10 minutes. Add wine and serve at once on toast. Yield: 6 portions.

Meat, Fish and Vegetable Sauces

THE preparation of sauces was considered truly an art in the Middle Ages. A *saucier* or master of sauces presided over that department of the menu. But diligence and practice rather than a title make a perfect sauce—perfection that comes with the mastery of simple sauces before attempting the more complex.

If you learn how to make the foundation sauces, you can add to your cooking skill by using your own ingenuity and imagination in creating new sauces.

Making of Sauces. The smooth consistency of a sauce starts with the proper blending of the flour with the liquid. In most sauces, flour, plain or browned, is mixed with fat into a roux. When adding flour to melted fat, turn heat low for white sauce, or use medium heat for brown sauce, stirring to brown evenly.

In sauces where cold or hot liquid is used, the liquid is added slowly to the roux and cooked, with constant stirring, until the sauce is smooth and thickened; or the paste is added gradually to the hot liquid and cooked with constant stirring until thickened. When the sauce is made in advance, it should be placed over hot water and covered to prevent skin from forming over top. If it becomes too thick, additional liquid can be added.

Other substances besides flour, such as cornstarch, rice flour, or potato flour, can be used to thicken sauces; their relative thickening powers are given in Table XII (page 81). Recipes that call for meat stock can be made with bouillon cubes or meat extract and hot water or canned soups for part or all of stock.

Sauces high in butter and eggs, such as Hollandaise, require careful technique to be made without separating. The recipes should be followed exactly. If the sauce separates, place the saucepan immediately on crushed ice and beat vigorously. This usually brings the sauce back to a smooth, velvety consistency.

When making sauces of this type, beat or stir with a whisk, rather than a rotary beater. Some cooks prefer to place the ingredients in an earthenware bowl and place it over a pan of hot water for cooking. For light sauces, use a glass or enamel pan.

Sauces of the Hollandaise type are likely to separate on standing and should be served at once.

Wine sauces should be made with infinite care to retain as much of the fine flavor and bouquet of the wine as possible. Boiling and prolonged heating dissipate the flavor of the wine, hence the sauce should never be allowed to boil or stand for long after the wine is added.

FOUNDATION WHITE SAUCE

2 tablespoons butter
2 tablespoons flour
1 cup milk
½ teaspoon salt
⅛ teaspoon pepper

Melt butter and stir in flour off the heat; gradually stir in milk and stir constantly until mixture boils and thickens; cook about 3 minutes longer, stirring occasionally; add seasonings. Place over hot water to keep hot and cover tightly to prevent crust from forming. Use for sauces, creamed or scalloped vegetables, fish or meat. For other methods of combining white sauce, see page 125. Approximate yield: 1 cup sauce.

Parsley Sauce—Add 2 to 4 tablespoons chopped parsley.

Egg Sauce—Add 2 diced, hard-cooked eggs; add more salt if desired. Serve with cooked fish. Approximate yield: 1½ cups sauce.

Green Pea Sauce—Add 1 tablespoon chopped pimiento and ½ cup cooked or canned peas. Serve with salmon loaf or omelet. Approximate yield: 1½ cups sauce.

Pimiento-Parsley Sauce—Add ½ cup diced pimiento and 2 to 4 tablespoons chopped parsley. Serve with cooked fish or egg dishes. Approximate yield: 1½ cups sauce.

Celery Sauce—Substitute ½ cup celery water and 1 chicken bouillon cube for ½ cup milk. Add 1 cup diced, cooked celery and 2 tablespoons chopped parsley. Three tablespoons whipped cream may be added to sauce if desired. Approximate yield: 2 cups sauce.

Horseradish Sauce—Add ¼ cup grated horseradish, drained, and ⅛ to ¼ teaspoon dry mustard, if desired. Serve with cooked beef, corned beef or ham. Approximate yield: 1¼ cups sauce.

Mustard Sauce—Add 2 teaspoons prepared mustard. Serve with broiled fillet of haddock.

Cheese Sauce—Add ½ to 1 cup grated American cheese and a dash of paprika; stir over low heat until cheese is melted. Serve with rice, macaroni, fish or eggs, fried eggplant or zucchini. Approximate yield: 1½ cups sauce.

Worcestershire Cheese Sauce—Add ¼ cup grated American cheese and 1½ teaspoons Worcestershire sauce; cook over low heat until cheese is melted.

Golden Malaga Sauce—Add 1 egg yolk and cook 2 minutes; then add ½ cup peeled white grapes, seeded and cut. Serve with broiled fish fillets or cooked white fish. Approximate yield: 1½ cups sauce.

Sauce Alexandra—Add ¾ cup cooked asparagus cut in small pieces. Serve with green pea timbales or cheese soufflé. Yield: 1¾ cups sauce.

Shrimp Sauce—Add ½ to 1 cup canned or cooked shrimps, cut in small pieces. Serve with omelet or cooked fish. One tablespoon white wine may be added, if desired. Approximate yield: 1¾ cups sauce.

Oyster Sauce—Simmer ½ cup small oysters in the oyster liquor 3 minutes, or until plump and edges begin to curl; add to hot sauce and serve at once. Serve with omelets or fish timbales. Yield: 1½ cups.

Olive Sauce—Prepare 1½ cups White Sauce (page 464); add mixture of 1 egg, slightly beaten, and ¼ cup light cream and cook over hot water 2 minutes, stirring constantly. Add ⅓ cup chopped ripe olives. Serve with sweetbread cutlets, tongue or cooked beef. Yield: 2 cups sauce.

TURKEY–MUSHROOM SAUCE

2 tablespoons butter   1½ cups diced, cooked turkey
3 tablespoons flour   4 hard-cooked eggs, sliced
1 can cream of mushroom soup salt and pepper

Melt butter in saucepan and stir in flour; add mushroom soup and
stir until thickened. Add turkey and eggs and season to taste. Serve
over slices of Turkey Loaf (page 383). Leftover chicken, goose or duck
may be substituted for turkey. Yield: 3 cups sauce.

CREAM SAUCE

Substitute light cream for milk in White Sauce (page 464). Serve with
baked or boiled fish, meat loaves, croquettes, etc. Approximate yield:
1 cup sauce.

Savory Cream Sauce—Add 1 teaspoon each chopped onion, parsley,
pimiento and celery. Serve with pork or lamb.

Cream Horseradish Sauce—Add ½ cup drained, grated horseradish
and a dash of cayenne. Serve with pot roast, ham, lamb or venison.
Approximate yield: 1½ cups sauce.

Cream Caper Sauce—Add 2 to 4 tablespoons chopped capers and additional salt to taste. Serve with fish.

Russian Cream Sauce—Add ½ cup diced American cheese, ¾ cup
chopped, stuffed olives, 2 teaspoons Worcestershire sauce, 3 tablespoons
chili sauce and a dash of Tabasco. Serve very hot on flaked crab meat
or veal cutlet. Approximate yield: 2 cups sauce.

Yellow Cream Sauce—Add 1 slightly beaten egg yolk to ¼ cup light
cream; stir into cream sauce. Approximate yield: 1⅓ cups sauce.

Mushroom Cream Sauce—Add ⅓ cup chopped or sliced cooked
mushrooms. Approximate yield: 1⅓ cups sauce.

Pineapple Cream Sauce—Add ¼ cup light cream and ½ cup drained,
crushed pineapple. Serve with fish. Yield: 1¾ cups sauce.

Cream Gravy—Substitute 2 tablespoons meat drippings for butter.
Serve with broiled ham or pork tenderloin.

BROWN SAUCE

2 tablespoons butter or fat   1 cup beef stock
3 tablespoons flour   ½ teaspoon salt
dash of pepper

Melt butter, stir in flour and cook until browned, stirring constantly; gradually add stock, stirring until mixture boils and thickens, then cook about 3 minutes longer, stirring occasionally; add seasoning. Canned beef bouillon or 1 cup water and 1 beef bouillon cube or 2 teaspoons beef extract may be substituted for beef stock, if desired. Approximate yield: 1 cup sauce.

Pan Gravy—Substitute drippings for butter and use water or stock. Add 2 tablespoons sour cream if desired and milk for part of liquid.

Mushroom Sauce—Sauté 1 dozen medium-sized mushrooms or ½ cup whole button mushrooms in butter before flour is added; add few drops Worcestershire sauce.

Savory Mustard Sauce—Add 2 tablespoons prepared horseradish and 2 tablespoons prepared mustard.

Mexican Sauce—Add ½ teaspoon kitchen bouquet, ½ cup tomato ketchup, 1 tablespoon each minced onion and green pepper sautéed lightly in butter; season to taste with salt, paprika and celery salt. Serve with fish, meat or omelets. Yield: 1½ cups sauce.

Sour Sauce—Add 2 tablespoons chopped cucumber pickles or cucumber relish. Serve with meat or fish.

Piquant Sauce—Simmer for 5 minutes ½ tablespoon each minced onion and chopped capers, 2 tablespoons vinegar, ½ teaspoon sugar, dash each of salt and paprika. Add to sauce; then add 2 tablespoons thick chili sauce or chopped sweet pickle. Serve hot with tongue, beef, veal or fish. Approximate yield: 1½ cups sauce.

Bordelaise Sauce—Add ½ cup Tomato Sauce (page 469), 1 tablespoon Sherry and 3 or 4 slices meat marrow. Heat thoroughly. Serve with steak. Approximate yield: 1½ cups sauce.

VELOUTÉ SAUCE

2 tablespoons butter   1 cup chicken or veal stock
2 tablespoons flour   ¼ teaspoon salt
dash of white pepper

Melt butter and stir in flour off the heat; gradually stir in stock, stirring constantly until mixture boils and thickens, then cook about 3 minutes longer, stirring occasionally; add seasonings. Serve with croquettes, baked or broiled fish. Approximate yield: 1 cup sauce.

Soubise Sauce—Cook 2 cups sliced white onions in boiling water 5 minutes; drain and again cook in boiling water about 15 minutes, or until soft; drain and force through sieve. Add pulp to sauce; then stir in ½ cup light cream and heat thoroughly. Serve with pork or mutton dishes, veal chops or hard-cooked eggs. Yield: 2 cups sauce.

Allemande Sauce—Add 1 egg yolk, well beaten, 1 tablespoon mushroom liquor, 1 teaspoon lemon juice and 3 tablespoons grated Parmesan cheese. Serve at once with chicken or ham patties, croquettes, fish or meat loaves. Approximate yield: 1¼ cups sauce.

Parsley-Caper Sauce—Add ¼ teaspoon parsley and 1 teaspoon capers. Serve with vegetables.

BÉCHAMEL SAUCE

1 slice onion	1 cup chicken stock
1 slice carrot	2 tablespoons flour
½ bay leaf	2 tablespoons butter, melted
sprig of parsley	½ cup light cream
6 peppercorns	½ teaspoon salt
	½ teaspoon pepper

Add onion, carrot, bay leaf, parsley and peppercorns to chicken stock and simmer 20 minutes; strain and, if necessary, add water to make ½ cup. Stir flour into melted butter, then add hot stock and cream gradually and cook 5 minutes, or until thick and smooth, stirring constantly; add seasonings. Serve on chicken timbales, croquettes, mousse, or fried chicken. Approximate yield: 1 cup sauce.

Yellow Béchamel Sauce—Stir sauce into slightly beaten egg yolk. Serve with ham or veal loaves or patties.

Béchamel Mayonnaise—Add 1 cup mayonnaise to hot sauce and serve at once with fish. Approximate yield: 2 cups sauce.

Ravigote Sauce—Add 1 teaspoon each chopped chives, parsley, tarragon, shallots and 1 tablespoon tarragon vinegar. Serve with cooked fowl and crab meat.

Olive-Almond Sauce—Add ⅓ cup blanched shredded almonds, 8 olives, stoned and cut in quarters, ½ tablespoon lemon juice and a dash of cayenne. Serve with cooked or baked fish or with chicken entrées. Approximate yield: 1½ cups sauce.

Normandy Sauce—Substitute fish stock or Court Bouillon (page 414) for chicken stock; stir sauce into 1 slightly beaten egg yolk, add 1 tablespoon lemon juice and a dash of cayenne. Serve with fish mousse, timbales or soufflé.

Anchovy Béchamel Sauce—Add 1 teaspoon anchovy paste to 1 cup sauce and heat thoroughly. Serve with fish or serve as a foundation sauce with leftover fish, adding about ½ cup fish to 1 cup sauce. Serve in patty shells or timbale cases.

MORNAY SAUCE

3 tablespoons butter
3 tablespoons flour
½ teaspoon salt
dash of cayenne

½ teaspoon dry mustard
1 cup milk
2 tablespoons grated Gruyère
    cheese

2 tablespoons light cream

Melt butter and blend in flour, salt, cayenne and mustard. Gradually add milk, stirring constantly. Cook 1 minute. Add cheese and cream. Simmer until cheese is melted. Serve over gnocchi. Sprinkle with cheese, dot with butter and brown under broiler. Yield: 6 to 8 portions.

TOMATO SAUCE

1 No. 2 can tomatoes
½ teaspoon salt
¼ teaspoon pepper

1 onion, sliced
2 tablespoons butter
2 tablespoons flour

Cook tomatoes with seasonings and onion 10 minutes; force through sieve—there should be 1 cup. Melt butter and stir in flour; gradually stir in strained tomato and stir until mixture boils and thickens, then cook about 3 minutes longer, stirring occasionally. Use with vegetables, meat loaves or fish. Four medium-sized fresh tomatoes and ½ cup water, cooked and strained, or 1 cup tomato juice may be substituted for canned tomatoes. Approximate yield: 1 cup sauce.

Tomato Sherry Sauce—Add ¼ cup Sherry. Yield: 1¼ cups sauce.

Tomato-Cheese Sauce—Add ½ cup grated cheese and 1 teaspoon prepared mustard; cook until cheese is melted.

FRENCH TOMATO SAUCE

1 tablespoon fat, melted
1 tablespoon flour
½ teaspoon salt
dash of cayenne

1 tablespoon tomato paste
1 cup light stock or water
¼ clove garlic, finely minced
salt and pepper to taste

Combine fat, flour, salt and cayenne. Stir in tomato paste and stock. Cook over low heat, stirring constantly, until it comes to a boil. Add garlic, salt and pepper. Cook over low heat until thickened. Approximate yield: 1 cup sauce.

SPANISH SAUCE

1 tablespoon minced onion	2 tablespoons fat
1 tablespoon minced green pepper	2 cups stewed tomatoes
	½ teaspoon salt
dash of pepper	

Slowly cook onion and green pepper in fat about 5 minutes; add tomatoes, salt and pepper and simmer until sauce is thick. Approximate yield: 1½ cups sauce.

CHEESE SAUCE

2 tablespoons butter, melted	1 cup milk
3 tablespoons flour	2 tablespoons light cream
½ teaspoon salt	2 tablespoons grated Parmesan
dash of cayenne	cheese
½ teaspoon dry mustard	

Combine butter, flour, salt and cayenne. Gradually stir in milk. Cook over low heat, stirring constantly, until sauce comes to a boil. Add cream, cheese and mustard and blend well. Simmer until thickened, about 3 minutes. Approximate yield: 1 cup sauce.

CREOLE SAUCE

2 tablespoons minced onion	salt and pepper
4 tablespoons minced green pepper	2 tomatoes or ½ cup canned tomatoes
2 tablespoons butter	¼ cup sliced mushrooms
3 tablespoons flour	1 cup bouillon

Sauté onion and pepper in butter 5 minutes; add flour and seasonings and stir until browned; add tomatoes and mushrooms and cook 2 minutes; then gradually add bouillon and heat to boiling. Serve with omelets, spaghetti and fish. Approximate yield: 2 cups sauce.

FRONTIER SAUCE

3 tablespoons flour	dash of Tabasco
2 tablespoons butter	¾ cup tomato juice
½ teaspoon salt	¼ cup liquid drained from stewed
½ teaspoon paprika	or canned mushrooms
2 tablespoons heavy cream	

Stir flour into melted butter; add seasonings and Tabasco, then add tomato juice and mushroom liquor gradually and cook 5 minutes, stirring constantly until smooth and thick. Add cream and blend. Serve on macaroni or spaghetti. Approximate yield: 1¼ cups sauce.

DRAWN BUTTER SAUCE

4 tablespoons flour   **2 cups boiling water**
⅓ cup butter   **¼ teaspoon salt**

Stir flour into 4 tablespoons butter melted, add water, gradually and cook 5 minutes, or until thick and smooth, stirring constantly. When ready to serve, add salt and remaining butter, beating well. Serve with green vegetables, fried or broiled fish or shellfish. Yield: 2 cups.

Anchovy Drawn Butter—Season to taste with anchovy paste.

Caper Drawn Butter—Add ⅓ cup capers.

Drawn Butter with Egg—Add 2 hard-cooked eggs, sliced.

Maître d'Hôtel Sauce—Add 1 tablespoon lemon juice and 1 tablespoon chopped parsley; add slowly to 2 egg yolks, slightly beaten, mixing well. Season to taste with salt and pepper. Serve with shellfish.

ANCHOVY BUTTER

¼ cup butter   **dash of pepper**
2 teaspoons minced parsley   **1 teaspoon anchovy paste**
½ teaspoon salt   **1 teaspoon prepared mustard**
1½ tablespoons lemon juice

Cream butter until soft; add parsley, seasonings and lemon juice, beating until fluffy. Spread on steak or broiled fish just before serving. Yield: ⅓ cup sauce.

STEAK BUTTER

¼ clove garlic   **1 teaspoon lemon juice**
½ cup butter   **1 teaspoon finely minced**
½ teaspoon hickory salt   **tarragon (or basil, savory,**
dash of pepper   **dill or sage)**
1 teaspoon finely minced chives

Rub a shallow bowl with cut side of garlic; discard garlic. Place the butter in the bowl and cream it until it is like mayonnaise in consistency. Work in remaining ingredients, blending thoroughly. Do not chill. Spread on hot steak, chops, broiled kidneys, hamburgers, broiled lobster or broiled chicken immediately before serving. Approximate yield: ½ cup sauce.

BUTTER AND LEMON SAUCE

Melt ¼ cup butter, add 1½ tablespoons lemon juice and serve over cooked broccoli, lamb chops or fish. Approximate yield: ⅓ cup sauce.

BLACK BUTTER SAUCE

4 tablespoons butter or margarine   **4 tablespoons lemon juice or vinegar**

Brown butter in frying pan until golden, add vinegar and mix. Serve at once over meat or brains. Approximate yield: ½ cup.

DILL SAUCE FOR COLD FISH

2 eggs   **1 tablespoon minced fresh dill**
¼ cup olive oil   **½ cup light cream**
dash of salt   **½ teaspoon lemon juice or**
dash of pepper   **Worcestershire sauce**

Beat eggs and add remaining ingredients, beating until blended. Approximate yield: 1 cup sauce.

ALMOND BUTTER

Sauté ¼ cup shredded blanched almonds in ¼ cup butter until delicately browned, stirring constantly. Serve with fish. Approximate yield: ⅓ cup sauce.

CRUMB SAUCE

½ cup melted butter   **1 teaspoon minced chives**
5 tablespoons dry bread crumbs   **salt and pepper**

Mix butter, bread crumbs and chives; season to taste with salt and pepper. Sauté until browned and serve hot with asparagus, baked onion or cauliflower. Approximate yield: ¾ cup sauce.

MAÎTRE D'HÔTEL BUTTER

¼ cup butter   **½ teaspoon salt**
2 teaspoons minced parsley   **dash of pepper**
                1½ tablespoons lemon juice

Cream butter until soft; add parsley, seasonings and lemon juice, beating until fluffy. Spread on broiled steak, chicken or fish just before serving. For lemon butter, omit parsley. Yield: ⅓ cup sauce.

SAVORY BUTTERS
(Use recipe for Maître d'Hôtel Butter (above)

Shrimp Butter—Omit parsley and lemon juice; add ¼ cup minced, cooked or canned shrimp. Approximate yield: ½ cup sauce.

Lobster Coral Butter—Omit parsley and lemon juice; add 1 lobster coral rubbed to a paste. Approximate yield: ⅓ cup sauce.

Anchovy-Roquefort Butter—Use ¼ cup butter, 1 teaspoon each vinegar, anchovy paste and prepared mustard, and 2 teaspoons Roquefort cheese. Serve with broiled fish. Approximate yield: ⅓ cup sauce.

For additional butters for meats and fish, see Appetizers (pages 200 and 201).

HOLLANDAISE SAUCE

¾ cup butter
1½ tablespoons lemon juice

3 egg yolks, well beaten
dash of salt
dash of cayenne

Divide butter into 3 pieces; put 1 piece in top of small double boiler, add lemon juice and egg yolks. Place over hot water (not boiling) and cook slowly, beating constantly with wire whisk or beater. When butter is melted, add second piece of butter and, as mixture thickens, add the third piece and cook until thickened, stirring constantly. Remove immediately from water, add salt and cayenne and serve at once. Serve with vegetables, fish and shellfish. If sauce has a tendency to curdle, place on crushed ice, stirring vigorously. Yield: ¾ cup sauce.

Hollandaise Sauce with Water—Slowly stir in ½ cup boiling water after the last addition of butter and cook 1 minute, stirring constantly.

Cucumber Hollandaise—Add 1½ cups drained, chopped cucumber. Serve with fish and shellfish.

Béarnaise Sauce—Add 1 teaspoon onion juice, 1 teaspoon each chopped tarragon and parsley, and 1 tablespoon tarragon vinegar. Serve with baked or broiled or cooked fish.

Mousseline Chutney Sauce—Add ½ cup heavy cream, whipped, and 1 tablespoon finely cut chutney. Serve with Asiatic Supper Plate (page 514). Approximate yield: 1¼ cups sauce.

Mustard Hollandaise—Add 1 tablespoon dry mustard and substitute 1½ tablespoons tarragon vinegar for lemon juice. Serve with fish.

Tomato Hollandaise—Add 2 teaspoons tomato paste and substitute 1 tablespoon tarragon vinegar for the lemon juice. Especially good with fish. Yield: ¾ cup sauce.

EASY HOLLANDAISE

1 cup butter or margarine	**¼ cup lemon juice**
2 eggs	**½ teaspoon salt**
	dash of cayenne

Melt butter over hot water. Beat in remaining ingredients with a rotary beater. Continue beating until thick. Remove at once from over hot water. Serve with artichokes, fish or broccoli. Yield: 1½ cups.

COLD HOLLANDAISE SAUCE

⅓ cup butter or margarine	**¼ teaspoon salt**
4 egg yolks	**2 tablespoons tarragon vinegar**
	¼ cup seasoned stock

Melt butter in top of double boiler over hot water. Add remaining ingredients. Cook over hot water, stirring constantly, until thickened. Cool. Serve cold. Approximate yield: ¾ cup.

SAVORY CIDER SAUCE

1 tablespoon minced onion	**2 tablespoons flour**
1 tablespoon chopped green	**1 cup cider**
pepper	**1 to 2 teaspoons mustard relish**
2 tablespoons pork fat	**6 drops kitchen bouquet**

Sauté onion and green pepper in fat until slightly browned, then remove from heat and add flour; cook until browned. Stir in cider gradually and cook 5 minutes, stirring constantly until smooth and creamy. Add relish; color with kitchen bouquet, if desired. Serve with cooked, baked or grilled ham, or baked eggs. Approximate yield: 1 cup sauce.

VINEGAR SAUCE

1 cup vinegar	**½ bay leaf**
1 tablespoon brown sugar	**1 ½-inch stick cinnamon**
2 whole cloves	**2 whole allspice**
1 blade mace	**¼ teaspoon salt**
	dash of paprika

Simmer vinegar, sugar, spices and seasonings 8 minutes; strain. Serve hot or cold with pigs' feet or pork dishes. Yield: ¾ cup sauce.

FLUFFY MUSTARD SAUCE

¼ cup firmly packed brown
    sugar
2 tablespoons dry mustard
3 eggs, separated

½ cup vinegar
½ cup consommé
½ teaspoon salt
dash of pepper

Mix sugar, mustard and beaten egg yolks in top of small double boiler; add vinegar and consommé and heat thoroughly; add seasonings. Fold into stiffly beaten egg whites and continue cooking about 5 minutes. Serve with ham, beef or fish. Approximate yield: 2½ cups sauce.

WESTERN BARBECUE SAUCE

1 gallon tomato purée or
    ketchup
1 cup vinegar
1 cup brown sugar
1 tablespoon salt
4 cloves garlic, mashed

2 tablespoons celery seed
1 5-ounce bottle Worcestershire
    sauce
Red-hot sauce to taste
1 tablespoon curry powder
    (optional)

2 tablespoons Tabasco

Place tomato purée or ketchup in pot; add remaining ingredients. Simmer until mixture is reduced to three quarts. Yield: 3 quarts.

BARBECUE SAUCE

½ cup butter
1½ cups hot water
2 tablespoons vinegar
¼ teaspoon salt
dash of black pepper
dash of red pepper
¼ teaspoon paprika

¼ teaspoon chili powder
1 teaspoon sugar
2 teaspoons prepared mustard
¼ teaspoon Worcestershire sauce
few drops Tabasco sauce
1 teaspoon minced onion
clove of garlic

Mix ingredients and heat to boiling point; remove garlic. Dip meats in sauce before broiling or roasting, or use to baste during roasting. Approximate yield: 2 cups sauce.

CURRANT ORANGE SAUCE

1 cup currant jelly   ½ cup orange juice

½ cup minced mint leaves

Break jelly into small pieces with fork; add orange juice and mint leaves and let stand 1 hour in refrigerator before serving. Serve with chicken, duck, game, lamb or veal. Yield: 1½ cups sauce.

ORANGE SAUCE

2 tablespoons flour
2 tablespoons butter or
  drippings
¼ cup water

1 cup orange juice
⅛ teaspoon salt
½ teaspoon grated orange rind
1 tablespoon brown sugar

Stir flour into melted butter; gradually add water and orange juice
and cook 5 minutes, stirring until thickened; season with salt, orange
rind and sugar. Serve with game or fowl. Yield: 1½ cups sauce.

MINT SAUCE

½ cup vinegar
1½ cups water
½ cup chopped fresh mint

¼ cup lemon juice
2 tablespoons sugar
½ teaspoon salt

Simmer vinegar, 1 cup of water and ¼ cup of mint until reduced to
½ of original quantity; remove from heat and strain through a fine
strainer. Add remaining water, lemon juice, sugar and salt; chill
thoroughly, then add remaining mint leaves. Serve with lamb. Approximate yield: 1⅓ cups sauce.

BLACK CHERRY SAUCE FOR DUCK

Melt 2 tablespoons butter in heavy pan. Add 2 tablespoons flaming
Marsala wine. Add a few sliced mushrooms and a little crushed garlic.
Cook 1 minute and then stir in 1 teaspoon meat extract. Remove from
heat and stir in 2½ teaspoons potato flour. Pour on 1¼ cups beef
stock. Stir over heat until it comes to a boil, then add ½ cup cherry
juice (from can), 2 tablespoons red wine, 1½ cups pitted black cherries
and salt and pepper to taste. Add a bay leaf. Simmer sauce down to a
creamy consistency and just before serving, add to it the sautéed liver
of the duck, diced. Serve over duck. Yield: 2 cups sauce.

RAISIN SAUCE FOR HAM

¾ cup raisins
1 cup water
4 or 5 whole cloves
¾ cup brown sugar
2 teaspoons cornstarch

¼ teaspoon salt
dash of pepper
1 tablespoon butter
1 tablespoon vinegar or lemon
  juice

Wash raisins, cover with water, add the cloves and simmer 10 minutes.
Add mixture of sugar, cornstarch, salt and pepper. Cook and stir until
slightly thickened and add the remaining ingredients. Simmer until
ready to serve. Approximate yield: 2 cups sauce.

SECRET MUSTARD SAUCE

2 egg yolks
1 cup milk
1 tablespoon flour

1 tablespoon dry mustard
¾ cup sugar
½ cup vinegar

Beat the egg yolks with the milk. Add mixture of flour, mustard and sugar and cook over hot water until thickened. Gradually stir in the vinegar and heat thoroughly. Yield: 1½ cups sauce.

GINGERSNAP SAUCE

4 gingersnaps, crushed
¼ cup seedless raisins
½ cup brown sugar

1 cup hot water
¼ cup vinegar
1 lemon, thinly sliced

Mix ingredients, bring to a boil and simmer about 15 minutes, or until lemon slices are transparent, stirring frequently; serve hot as a meat sauce. Approximate yield: 1¼ cups sauce.

TARTAR SAUCE

1 tablespoon chopped capers
1 tablespoon chopped olives

1 tablespoon chopped parsley
1 tablespoon chopped pickles

1 cup mayonnaise

Combine ingredients just before serving. Serve with fish, hot or cold, or as dressing for fish salads. Yield: 1¼ cups sauce.

FLUFFY HORSERADISH SAUCE

½ cup heavy cream
4 to 6 tablespoons prepared
  horseradish

½ teaspoon salt
dash of pepper
dash of paprika (optional)

Whip cream until stiff; fold in horseradish and seasonings. Serve with baked ham, roast or cooked beef, or fish. One tablespoon chopped blanched almonds may be added, if desired. Sour cream may be substituted for sweet cream. Mix it with remaining ingredients. Yield: ¾ cup sauce.

Cucumber Sauce—Substitute 1 medium-sized cucumber, chopped and drained, for horseradish and add 1 tablespoon vinegar. Approximate yield: 1¾ cups sauce.

CAPER SAUCE

1 teaspoon dry mustard
1 teaspoon sugar
1 teaspoon salt
2 egg yolks
3 tablespoons lemon juice

½ cup salad oil
1 small red pepper, minced
1 teaspoon onion juice
1 tablespoon chopped capers
1 tablespoon chopped pickles

Add mustard, sugar and salt to egg yolks; beat thoroughly. Add lemon juice and beat again, then add the oil gradually, drop by drop at first. The mixture should be thick and creamy. Just before serving, add remaining ingredients. Approximate yield: 1 cup sauce.

VINAIGRETTE SAUCE

½ cup French Dressing (page 618)
1 tablespoon chopped green pepper

1 teaspoon chopped chives
1 teaspoon chopped parsley
1 teaspoon chopped capers
1 tablespoon chopped pickles

Combine ingredients in order given; stir vigorously before serving. Serve with beef or lamb. Approximate yield: ⅔ cup sauce.

CUCUMBER SAUCE

1 teaspoon salt
¼ teaspoon dry mustard
3 tablespoons vinegar

1 teaspoon minced onion
1 cup evaporated milk
2 teaspoons minced parsley

½ cup finely diced cucumber

Combine salt, mustard, vinegar and onion and stir slowly into milk. Just before serving, add parsley and cucumber. Serve with fish, hot or cold, or corned beef. Approximate yield: 1½ cups sauce.

SOUR CREAM SAUCE

2 tablespoons vinegar
1 tablespoon sugar
1 teaspoon salt

¼ teaspoon paprika
1 teaspoon dry mustard
1 cup heavy sour cream

Mix together vinegar, sugar and seasonings; add gradually to cream, beating lightly. Serve with cold tongue or tenderloin. Approximate yield: 1½ cups sauce.

SAUCE POULETTE

1 tablespoon chopped onion	1 cup chicken stock
1 teaspoon chopped shallots	¼ cup light cream
1 cup sliced mushrooms	salt
3 tablespoons butter	½ cup Sherry
3 tablespoons flour	1 teaspoon lemon juice

Sauté vegetables in butter about 5 minutes, stirring constantly; stir in flour, gradually add stock and cream and cook 5 minutes, stirring until thickened. Season to taste, add Sherry and lemon juice, bring to a boil and serve at once with broiled chicken, game, fish or veal cutlets. Approximate yield: 2 cups sauce.

DEMI-GLACÉ SAUCE

Put into heavy pan 3 tablespoons cooking oil, add a little finely sliced onion, carrot and celery (about 2 tablespoons). Cook a few moments, remove from heat and add 3 tablespoons flour. Brown flour slowly and carefully to a dark brown color. Then add 3 chopped mushrooms, 1 sliced tomato and 1 teaspoon tomato paste. Pour on 2 cups strong beef stock. Bring to boiling and add 1 tablespoon apple jelly, 2 tablespoons red wine, 1 tablespoon Sherry and ½ teaspoon meat extract. Add 1 bay leaf, salt and pepper and boil down to a creamy consistency. Strain. Serve with chicken. Approximate yield: 2½ cups sauce.

MADEIRA SCALLION SAUCE

1 dozen scallions, finely chopped	¼ teaspoon salt
	dash of pepper
3 tablespoons butter	2 teaspoons ketchup
2 tablespoons flour	1 teaspoon minced parsley
¾ cup hot water	3 tablespoons Madeira wine

Sauté scallions in butter about 5 minutes, add flour off the heat and brown slightly, stirring constantly; gradually add water and cook 5 minutes, stirring until thickened. Add seasonings, ketchup, parsley, and Madeira, bring to a boil and serve at once with veal or other meat dishes. Approximate yield: 1¼ cups sauce.

ANCHOVY SAUCE

2 teaspoons anchovy paste	1 cup melted butter
⅓ cup dry Sherry	

Dissolve anchovy paste in melted butter; gradually stir in Sherry. Heat to boiling point and simmer 5 minutes, or until sauce thickens slightly, stirring vigorously. Serve with cold halibut, panned oysters, veal or pork chops, cooked or baked chicken. Yield: 1⅓ cups sauce.

WHITE WINE SAUCE

3 tablespoons flour
3 tablespoons butter
¾ cup water

¼ cup white wine
1 cup milk
¼ teaspoon salt
1 tablespoon Sherry

Stir flour into melted butter and blend well. Gradually add water, wine and milk and cook 5 minutes, stirring constantly until mixture is smooth and thickened; add salt and Sherry. A dash of cayenne may be added, if desired. Serve with fish. Approximate yield: 2 cups sauce.

TIREAU SAUCE

1 cup Port or Bordeaux
1 2-inch stick cinnamon
6 almonds, blanched and
    pounded to a paste

6 whole cloves
¼ cup firmly packed brown
    sugar
rind of 1 lemon (yellow only)
1 cup currant jelly

Combine wine, cinnamon, almonds, cloves, sugar and lemon rind; simmer 15 minutes; strain. Add currant jelly and heat to boiling point, stirring constantly. Serve with lamb, mutton or venison. Approximate yield: 2 cups sauce.

SAUCE CHASSEUR

1 cup finely cut mushrooms
1 tablespoon olive oil
2 shallots, chopped
½ cup white wine (Rhine
    or Sauterne)

1 cup bouillon
1 tablespoon tomato paste
¼ cup butter
1 teaspoon chopped parsley
1 teaspoon chopped tarragon

Sauté mushrooms in oil until browned; add shallots and cook 2 minutes. Stir in wine and bouillon; then add tomato paste and mix thoroughly. Blend in butter; add parsley and tarragon. Serve at once with baked or broiled fish. Approximate yield: 2½ cups sauce.

CREAMY EGG SAUCE

4 hard-cooked egg yolks
¼ teaspoon salt
¼ teaspoon paprika

½ cup butter, creamed
2 tablespoons heavy cream
2 teaspoons lemon juice

Rub egg yolks to a paste; add salt and paprika; gradually work in creamed butter, cream and lemon juice. Spread over hot asparagus or cauliflower. Approximate yield: 1 cup sauce.

JELLY WINE SAUCE

2 tablespoons butter, melted
2 tablespoons flour
1 cup water
½ teaspoon salt

¼ cup currant jelly
¼ cup Port
2 teaspoons lemon juice
4 maraschino cherries, chopped

Mix butter and flour until smooth, gradually add water and cook 4 minutes, stirring until thickened. Add remaining ingredients and cook 1 minute, stirring constantly. Serve with venison and other game. Approximate yield: 1½ cups sauce.

RED WINE MUSHROOM SAUCE

2 cups sliced or chopped fresh
    mushrooms
¼ cup butter or meat drippings
2 tablespoons grated onion
2 tablespoons grated carrot

1 bay leaf
4 whole cloves
4½ tablespoons flour
2 cups meat stock or consommé
salt and pepper

3 tablespoons red wine

Brown mushrooms in butter or meat drippings. Add grated onion, carrot, bay leaf and cloves. Simmer over low heat until browned. Add flour, stirring until well blended. Cook, stirring over low heat, until flour browns. Remove from heat. Gradually stir in meat stock or consommé. Season to taste with salt and pepper; cook until thick and smooth. Remove bay leaf and cloves. Add red wine and heat. Serve over steak. Yield: 1¾ cups sauce.

SAUCE BRETONNE

2 medium-sized onions, sliced
1 tablespoon butter
¾ cup white wine
2 8-ounce cans tomato sauce

½ teaspoon chili powder
½ teaspoon salt
⅛ teaspoon pepper
dash of cayenne

Sauté onions in butter until browned. Add wine, cover and simmer until wine is half gone. Add tomato sauce and seasonings, blend well and simmer 7 minutes. Serve with baked or broiled fish. Approximate yield: 2 cups sauce.

SAUCE À LA SCHOENBERG

1 tablespoon flour	1 small bay leaf
2 tablespoons butter	1 whole clove
½ teaspoon salt	½ teaspoon minced parsley
⅛ teaspoon pepper	1 teaspoon Cognac
2 scallions, finely minced	2 tablespoons white wine
2 cups chicken broth	⅓ cup canned mushrooms
3 tablespoons tomato juice	1 egg yolk, beaten
½ cup heavy cream	

Stir flour into 1 tablespoon butter melted; cook 2 minutes, or until lightly browned. Add seasonings, scallions, chicken broth and tomato juice, bay leaf, clove and parsley, and simmer 10 minutes, stirring occasionally. Strain and add Cognac, wine and mushrooms sautéed in remaining tablespoon butter. Combine egg yolk and cream; stir into hot sauce and heat thoroughly. Serve with halibut, sea bass, flounder and sole, chicken breasts and white-fleshed game birds. Approximate yield: 2 cups sauce.

MAYONNAISE SAUCE

Beat 3 egg yolks with 2 tablespoons tarragon vinegar, 1 tablespoon sour cream, salt and cayenne and ½ teaspoon dry mustard. Very slowly beat in 1½ cups salad oil. When mayonnaise is thick, add ½ teaspoon lemon juice and 2 or 3 tablespoons thin cream. Serve with cold lobster or salmon or with green salads. A little finely shredded raw tomato and cucumber may be added if desired. Yield: 2 cups sauce.

LOBSTER MAYONNAISE

1 cup finely diced carrots	3 cups cooked rice
1 cup finely diced string beans	½ cup French dressing
1 cup finely diced cucumber	2 2- to 2½-pound lobsters, cooked
2 tomatoes, diced	½ cup mayonnaise

Cook carrots and beans in small amount of boiling salted water until tender. Drain and chill. Combine with cucumber, tomatoes, rice and French dressing and arrange on serving plate. Remove meat from lobster shells and slice. Carefully arrange on top of rice mixture. Pour mayonnaise over lobster. Approximate yield: 6 portions.

VEGETABLE COMBINATION FISH SAUCE

⅓ cup diced cucumber
1 tablespoon minced green
   pepper
1 tablespoon ground raw carrot
⅓ cup minced celery
¼ teaspoon grated onion

¼ teaspoon minced parsley
3 stuffed olives, ground
⅓ teaspoon salt
⅛ teaspoon pepper
1 cup heavy cream
1 tablespoon vinegar

Mix the vegetables, olives and seasonings and chill thoroughly. When
ready to serve, drain vegetable mixture. Whip cream stiff and add
vinegar gradually; fold vegetable mixture into cream and vinegar and
stir up lightly. Serve large spoonful with each portion. Approximate
yield: 6 portions.

ANCHOVY–EGG SAUCE

2 hard-cooked eggs, chopped
3 anchovies, chopped
3 stuffed olives, chopped
½ teaspoon onion juice

2 egg yolks, beaten
1 teaspoon dry mustard
½ teaspoon salt
dash of paprika

3 tablespoons lemon juice

Mix hard-cooked eggs and anchovies thoroughly. Add remaining ingredients, beating until well mixed. Serve cold with fish. One to 2
tablespoons chow-chow may be added, if desired. Approximate yield:
6 portions.

Stuffing, Dumplings and Relishes

STUFFING is much more than a mere padding or extender for meat, poultry, game or fish. It complements and modifies strong and "gamy" flavors and offers pleasing contrast of texture.

There are many varieties of stuffings. Most stuffings swell slightly on cooking and should not be tightly packed into the cavity of a bird, roast or fish. In general allow ¾ to 1 cup dressing per pound of poultry, New York dressed weight, or 1½ cups per pound full-drawn weight, to fill cavity and neck.

Just when a particular stuffing should be used is a matter of individual taste. It is generally agreed that fat birds, such as goose, require a tart, fruit stuffing. Mild-flavored poultry and meats combine well with a highly seasoned or a simple stuffing. Sometimes onions and celery are stuffed into strong-flavored game birds to absorb and modify the flavor, then discarded.

BREAD STUFFING

3 cups soft bread crumbs or cubes	⅛ teaspoon pepper
	¼ teaspoon thyme or marjoram
½ teaspoon salt	½ medium-sized onion, minced
⅓ cup butter, melted	

Mix bread crumbs, seasonings and onion; add butter slowly, tossing lightly with a fork until blended. For a more subtle blend of flavors, cook onion and seasonings in butter about 10 minutes; add bread and cook until lightly browned, tossing with fork to brown evenly and mix well. Approximate yield: 3½ cups stuffing, or enough for 1 bird or fish (5 lb.).

Celery Stuffing—Substitute 1 cup finely chopped celery for 1 cup bread crumbs. Use stalks and tender leaves of celery.

Corn Stuffing—Substitute 1 cup corn kernels for 1 cup bread crumbs; increase salt to 1 teaspoon.

Sage Stuffing—Substitute 1 tablespoon dried sage leaves, crumbled, for thyme or marjoram; if desired, add 1 onion, minced.

Dill Pickle Stuffing—Omit thyme and marjoram and add ¼ cup chopped dill pickles and 1 tablespoon minced parsley. Or reduce onion to 1 tablespoon and add 1 tablespoon capers. This is a delicious stuffing for fish. Approximate yield: 3½ cups, or enough for 2 fish (3 lb.).

Sausage Stuffing—Use 1½ loaves stale bread. Remove heavy crust and dip bread in hot water; squeeze to remove all excess moisture and crumble. Sauté 1 lb. sausage 5 to 8 minutes, drain, add to bread with 2 onions, chopped, and 1 green pepper, minced. Season. Add preserved cherries for variety. Yield: stuffing for 12- to 16-lb. bird.

CRANBERRY STUFFING

2 cups cranberries, ground	¼ teaspoon pepper
½ cup butter	1 tablespoon crumbled dried sage
½ cup sugar	2 teaspoons crumbled dried thyme
8 cups soft bread crumbs	½ cup chopped celery
or cubes	3 tablespoons minced parsley
2 teaspoons salt	1 cup water

Cook cranberries in butter slowly about 5 minutes, then stir in sugar. Mix together crumbs, seasonings, celery and parsley; add with water to cranberry mixture and cook about 8 minutes, or until blended, stirring constantly. Approximate yield: 6 cups stuffing, or enough for large pork crown roast.

CRANBERRY STUFFING FOR REINDEER

½ cup finely chopped suet	2 cups dry bread crumbs
1 quart cranberries, chopped	1½ teaspoons salt
1½ cups sugar	¼ teaspoon pepper

Cook suet in skillet until crisp. Add cranberries, stir in sugar and cook until cranberries are clear. Add remaining ingredients. Lightly toss together to combine. Approximate yield: 6 cups stuffing.

APPLE STUFFING FOR REINDEER

½ cup diced salt pork
1 cup chopped celery
1 cup chopped onion
½ cup chopped parsley

4 cups diced apples
1 cup sugar
2 cups dry bread crumbs
1½ teaspoons salt

¼ teaspoon pepper

Fry salt pork until crisp. Remove all cracklings. Add celery, onion and parsley to fat; cook until vegetables are tender. Remove from fat; add apples. Sprinkle with sugar. Cover and cook until tender. Add cracklings, vegetables, remaining ingredients and blend well. Approximate yield: 5 cups stuffing.

NUT–PRUNE STUFFING

¼ cup chopped walnuts
¼ cup butter
¾ cup chopped, stewed prunes

3 cups soft bread crumbs
1 tablespoon chopped parsley
½ teaspoon salt

dash of pepper

Sauté nuts in butter in large heavy pan until lightly browned; remove from heat and add remaining ingredients, stirring enough to mix well. One egg, slightly beaten, may be added. Approximate yield: 4 cups.

Raisin-Nut Stuffing—Add ½ teaspoon dried sage and substitute chopped seeded raisins for prunes.

VEGETABLE STUFFING

1 medium onion, minced
¼ cup chopped celery
2 tablespoons chopped green
   pepper
2 tablespoons bacon fat

1 cup soft bread crumbs
1 teaspoon salt
¼ teaspoon paprika
¼ teaspoon crumbled dried sage
¼ teaspoon poultry seasoning

1 carrot, grated

Cook onion, celery and green pepper in bacon fat until softened but not browned; remove from heat and add bread crumbs, seasonings and grated carrot, stirring until well mixed; add more fat if mixture is dry. Use as meat stuffing. Approximate yield: 2 cups stuffing, or enough for 1 leg of lamb, boned.

ONION STUFFING

2 cups hot water or stock	4 teaspoons dried sage
6 cups soft bread crumbs	2 teaspoons poultry seasoning
2 eggs, beaten	4 medium onions, chopped
1 teaspoon salt	½ cup drippings
½ teaspoon pepper	½ cup chopped celery tops
½ teaspoon nutmeg	¼ cup chopped parsley
	½ cup raisins

Pour hot water over bread crumbs; add eggs and seasonings. Sauté onions in drippings until lightly browned, stirring constantly; add celery tops, parsley and raisins and mix thoroughly with seasoned crumbs. Fill cavity loosely with stuffing. Approximate yield: 8 cups stuffing, or enough for a 10-pound suckling pig.

CHESTNUT STUFFING

2 pounds chestnuts	⅛ teaspoon pepper
1 cup cracker crumbs	¼ cup butter, melted
1 teaspoon salt	½ cup heavy cream

Cook shelled chestnuts (page 543); force through ricer and add remaining ingredients, mixing lightly. Approximate yield: 3½ cups stuffing, or enough for 1 bird (5 lb.).

MUSHROOM STUFFING

⅓ cup mushrooms, chopped	½ teaspoon grated onion
2 tablespoons butter	¼ teaspoon salt
½ cup dry bread crumbs	dash of paprika
2 tablespoons minced parsley	½ teaspoon poultry seasoning

Sauté mushrooms in butter about 5 minutes, stirring constantly; add remaining ingredients and mix well. Yield: ¾ cup stuffing.

OYSTER–MUSHROOM STUFFING

2 cups soft bread crumbs	2 teaspoons salt
¾ cup chopped celery leaves	⅛ teaspoon paprika
3 tablespoons diced bacon	1 tablespoon Worcestershire
1 quart oysters, cut in pieces	sauce
¼ pound mushrooms, chopped	2 tablespoons ketchup

Mix ingredients by tossing together lightly with a fork; lightly fill cavity. Use for wild or domestic turkey. Approximate yield: 6 cups stuffing, or enough for an 8- to 10-pound bird.

CORN STUFFING

12 slices bacon, chopped
1 cup chopped onion
1½ cups chopped celery
1 cup chopped green pepper
6 tablespoons bacon fat
2 cups dry bread crumbs

8 cups cooked or canned whole
   kernel corn
½ teaspoon nutmeg or dried sage
1½ teaspoons salt
1 teaspoon black pepper
1 cup light cream

Fry bacon until crisp and drain on absorbent paper. Cook onion, celery and green pepper in bacon fat until tender and yellow. Combine all ingredients. Fill bird. Approximate yield: 10 cups stuffing.

WILD RICE AND MUSHROOM STUFFING

⅓ cup chopped onion
¼ cup butter
1 cup chopped mushrooms

¼ pound sausage meat
3 cups cooked wild rice (page
   511)

1 teaspoon salt

Sauté onion in 2 tablespoons butter 5 minutes, or until lightly browned, and remove from pan; add remaining 2 tablespoons butter and mushrooms and cook 5 minutes, then remove from pan. Fry sausage meat until lightly browned, stirring constantly; remove from heat and stir in onion and mushrooms; add wild rice and salt, mixing lightly. This makes a light loose stuffing. Approximate yield: 5 cups stuffing, or enough for 1 goose (10 lb.).

SAVORY WILD RICE STUFFING

1 cup diced onion
1 cup diced celery
½ cup fat
1½ teaspoons salt

½ teaspoon black pepper
¼ teaspoon nutmeg
½ teaspoon dried thyme
2½ cups cooked wild rice
   (page 511)

Simmer onion and celery in fat until tender and yellow but not brown. Add seasonings. Mix with wild rice. Yield: 7 cups.

Filé and Oyster Stuffing—Substitute 2 tablespoons filé powder for the nutmeg. Simmer 2 dozen oysters until plump in the fat that was used to cook the vegetables. Add to stuffing mixture.

BROWN RICE DRESSING

2 cups brown rice
1 medium onion, minced
1 cup minced celery
2 tablespoons butter

turkey giblets, cooked and
ground
½ teaspoon poultry seasoning
½ teaspoon dried thyme
pepper

Cook brown rice until tender (see page 508); drain and rinse with cold water. Sauté onion and celery lightly in butter; add rice, giblets and seasonings, mixing well. Yield: 6 cups, or enough for 1 turkey (10 lb.).

MASHED POTATO STUFFING

12 strips of bacon
3 cups chopped onions
2 cups chopped celery
18 medium potatoes
½ cup butter or margarine

1½ cups evaporated milk,
undiluted
4 tablespoons minced parsley
2 teaspoons salt
1 teaspoon pepper

Fry bacon until crisp and drain on absorbent paper. Cook onions and celery in bacon fat until tender and yellow. Peel and cook potatoes; add butter, milk, parsley, salt and pepper and mash. Combine all ingredients. Stuff the bird lightly. Approximate yield: 8 cups stuffing.

CHICKEN OR VEAL FORCEMEAT

1 pound boneless chicken or veal
½ cup fine bread crumbs
1 teaspoon salt
⅛ teaspoon pepper
dash of cayenne

1 teaspoon minced parsley
2 tablespoons lemon juice
3 tablespoons butter, melted
1 egg, slightly beaten
stock or water

Use breast and thighs of chicken or round of veal; put 3 times through food chopper. Stir in crumbs and seasonings; add remaining ingredients and beat until very light, adding stock if mixture seems dry. Use as stuffing for poultry or veal birds. Approximate yield: 3 cups forcemeat, or enough for 1 bird (6 lb.).

BREAD–HAM STUFFING

1 tablespoon grated onion
3 tablespoons butter
1 cup soft bread crumbs

1 slice boiled ham, minced
1 teaspoon chopped parsley
dash of salt and pepper

Sauté onion in butter until lightly browned; add remaining ingredients and cook about 2 minutes. Yield: 1¼ cups stuffing.

SWEET POTATO AND ORANGE STUFFING

8 large sweet potatoes or yams
2 tablespoons grated orange rind
1½ tablespoons grated lemon rind
¼ cup brandy or Sherry
3 large oranges
½ cup chopped onion
½ cup butter or margarine
salt and pepper

Cook peeled potatoes in boiling salted water until they can just be pierced with a fork—they must not be too soft. Rice potatoes. Add grated rinds and Sherry or brandy. Cut oranges in half and scoop pulp out with a small spoon and add to potato mixture. Cook onion in butter until tender and yellow. Add with salt and pepper, being careful not to mash the potatoes. Season to taste. Stuff the bird lightly—do not pack down. Approximate yield: 5 to 6 cups stuffing.

OLD SWISS STUFFING

½ loaf stale bread
½ cup soft butter
½ cup chopped apple
½ cup chopped celery
1 tablespoon minced onion
½ cup raisins
½ cup chopped walnuts
2 tablespoons currant jelly
½ teaspoon salt
⅛ teaspoon pepper
dash of paprika
1 teaspoon lemon juice

Crumble bread and rub in butter; add remaining ingredients, mixing well. Yield: 4½ cups stuffing, or enough for 1 fowl (6 lb.).

WALNUT STUFFING

1 loaf white or whole wheat bread, sliced
butter or margarine
12 small pork sausages
1 cup chopped onions
1 cup sliced mushrooms
1 cup sliced ripe olives
chopped giblets
1½ teaspoons salt
4 tablespoons minced parsley
½ teaspoon pepper
¼ teaspoon nutmeg
2 cups chopped walnuts

Toast bread. Butter and cut into small cubes while still warm. Cook the sausages and cut into half-inch pieces. Cook onions and mushrooms in ½ cup of the sausage fat 5 minutes. Combine all ingredients. Stuff the bird lightly. Approximate yield: 12 cups stuffing.

CUCUMBER STUFFING

2 slices bacon	1 cup soft bread crumbs
1 small onion	dash of salt
½ cup mushrooms	dash of pepper
2 cups chopped cucumbers	1 tablespoon butter, melted

2 eggs, slightly beaten

Chop together bacon, onion and mushrooms; add remaining ingredients and mix well. For a dry, light stuffing, omit eggs and increase butter to 3 tablespoons. Yield: 3 cups, or enough for large fish.

STUFFING FOR SQUAB

2 small chicken livers	¼ teaspoon chopped garlic
1 squab liver	1 tablespoon chopped cooked
2 tablespoons butter	ham
2 mushrooms, sliced	1 tablespoon chopped parsley

1 tablespoon chopped chives

Brown chicken and squab livers quickly in hot butter. Remove from the pan, then add the sliced mushrooms and garlic. Cook over low heat 2 minutes, add ham. Slice the livers and return to the pan with the chopped herbs. Mix well. Stuff squab lightly.

PECAN SHRIMP DRESSING

½ cup minced onion	1 teaspoon salt
1 cup diced celery	3 cups cooked brown rice
½ cup butter or margarine	1 cup coarsely chopped pecans
chopped turkey giblets	3 cups cooked shrimp, cut in
4 tablespoons minced parsley	half crosswise

Cook the onion and celery in fat until tender and yellow. Combine with remaining ingredients. Approximate yield: 7 cups dressing.

CHARLESTON CRAB MEAT DRESSING

4 slices bacon	2 eggs, lightly beaten
1 cup chopped onion	3 cups dry bread crumbs
1½ cups chopped celery	½ cup dry Sherry
1 pound fresh or canned	1 teaspoon salt
crab meat	½ teaspoon pepper

¼ teaspoon nutmeg

Fry bacon until crisp, drain on absorbent paper and crumble. Cook onion and celery in bacon fat until tender and yellow. Combine all ingredients, mixing with a fork. Approximate yield: 7 cups dressing.

CATALONIAN STUFFING

chopped turkey liver
1 pound pork sausage
½ pound prunes, soaked,
   pitted and chopped
½ pound dried peaches or apricots, soaked and chopped
1 cup broken walnut meats

1 pound lean ham, chopped
½ cup dry Sherry
¼ teaspoon thyme
¼ teaspoon marjoram
¼ teaspoon basil
2 tablespoons minced parsley
2 teaspoons salt

¼ teaspoon pepper

Cook liver and sausage 10 minutes. Add remaining ingredients and toss together lightly. Yield: 8 cups or enough for 12-pound turkey.

ITALIAN DRESSING

8 skinned pork sausages
½ pound prunes, soaked and
   pitted
1 pound chestnuts, boiled,
   skinned and chopped
½ pound ham, chopped

chopped giblets
1 cup pitted black olives
¼ cup honey
½ cup dry white wine
3 tablespoons oil
1 cup grated cheese

2 eggs, beaten

Cook all ingredients except cheese and eggs in oil 10 minutes. Stir in cheese and eggs. Approximate yield: 10 cups dressing.

DUMPLINGS

2 cups sifted all-purpose flour
4 teaspoons baking powder

1 teaspoon salt
1 tablespoon shortening

1 cup milk

Sift together dry ingredients. Cut in fat; add milk, stirring quickly to make a soft dough. Drop by small spoonfuls on top of boiling stew. Cover and cook 12 to 15 minutes. Serve at once with hot stew. Approximate yield: 6 portions, or 12 dumplings.

POTATO DUMPLINGS

1 cup mashed potatoes
1 cup sifted all-purpose flour
3 teaspoons baking powder
1½ teaspoons salt

¼ cup minced onion
1 tablespoon grated
   Parmesan cheese
1 tablespoon butter, melted

3 egg yolks, beaten

Combine all ingredients. Shape into balls, using tablespoon, and drop into boiling salted water. Cover and cook 12 minutes. Serve with meat such as Sauerbraten (page 292). Yield: 16 dumplings.

RELISHES

Most of us prefer the spicy tang of a relish to supplement the fine flavor of the food it embellishes.

Relishes include simple or elaborate combinations of fruits and vegetables, tart or sweet, and usually spiced, as well as crisp vegetables such as celery curls, carrot sticks and radishes. The latter are used as garnishes or appetizers and their preparation is described in the section on Salads (page 583). The molded relishes are distinctly cold meat accompaniments. With meats and fish, savory relishes such as Apple Pepper Relish (page 957) and Beet and Cabbage Relish (page 956) are appropriate choices. See Appetizers (pages 197 to 218), ices in Frozen Desserts and pickles and relishes in Canning and Preserving for additional relishes.

CRANBERRY CITRUS RELISH

4 cups cranberries   1 lemon
1 orange   1 lime
                    1 cup sugar

Pick over and wash cranberries and put through food chopper, using fine knife. Wash orange, lemon and lime, slice and remove seeds and put through food chopper; mix with sugar and cranberries. Chill in refrigerator several hours before serving, or pour into hot sterilized jelly glasses and seal immediately with layer of paraffin. Store for a limited time only in refrigerator. Excellent with meats. Approximate yield: 1 quart relish.

UNCOOKED CONSERVE

3 small lemons   1 15-oz. package seeded raisins
1 medium orange   1⅓ cups honey

Put lemons, orange and raisins through grinder twice; add honey and mix well. Turn into jars; store in refrigerator. Yield: 4 8-ounce jars.

BRANDIED AND SPICED FRUIT

Use commercially canned whole or halved fruit, drain syrup and to each cup of syrup, heated to boiling, add 2 tablespoons brandy. Stir well, pour over fruit in jar, reseal and store in refrigerator 3 days.

To Spice: To each cup of syrup add 2 inches of stick cinnamon, 6 whole cloves, a few allspice and 2 tablespoons vinegar. Heat to boiling and pour over fruit. Seal and keep in refrigerator 3 days before using.

BRANDIED PEACHES

1 No. 2½ can peach halves	2 tablespoons butter, melted
2 tablespoons chopped crystal- lized ginger	3 tablespoons peach or apricot brandy

Place drained peach halves, cut side down, in baking pan; sprinkle with ginger and pour melted butter and fruit brandy over top. Bake in moderate oven (350° F.) 5 minutes and serve as meat accompaniment. Approximate yield: 6 portions.

SPICED FIGS

1 pound dried figs	3 cups sugar
2 cups vinegar	2 tablespoons whole cloves
	1 3-inch stick cinnamon

Wash figs carefully, cut in half, cover with cold water and let soak overnight. Combine with remaining ingredients and simmer 1 hour, stirring frequently. Fill hot sterilized jars and seal. Yield: 3 8-ounce jars.

SPICED PRUNES

1 pound prunes	2 teaspoons whole clove
4 cups water	1 teaspoon whole allspice
2 lemons	2 peppercorns
4 blades mace	1½ cups sugar
	½ cup vinegar

Rinse prunes thoroughly and let stand overnight in water or simmer gently in water until plump; do not drain. Extract juice of lemons and chop rinds. Tie spices in a cheesecloth bag and add with lemon rind to prunes; simmer 1 hour. Remove spice bag, add sugar, lemon juice and vinegar and boil 5 minutes. Approximate yield: 4 cups.

PICKLED PEACH IN ASPIC

1 envelope plain gelatin
¼ cup cold water
1¼ cups boiling water
¼ cup lemon juice

¼ cup brandied or pickled
   peach syrup
6 brandied or pickled peach
   halves

lettuce

Soften gelatin in cold water; add hot water, stirring until dissolved, and cool slightly. Add lemon juice and peach syrup; chill until slightly thickened. Place a peach half in each individual mold, fill with gelatin and chill until firm. Unmold on crisp lettuce and serve with a platter of assorted cold meats. Yield: 6 portions.

ORANGE BAKED PEACHES

8 canned cling peach halves
whole cloves
dash of allspice
1 teaspoon grated orange rind
½ cup orange juice

2 tablespoons firmly packed
   brown sugar
pinch of salt
2 tablespoons rum, brandy or
   Sherry

sour cream

Arrange peach halves in shallow baking pan. Stud with cloves and sprinkle with allspice and orange rind. Combine orange juice, sugar and salt and simmer until slightly thickened. Add rum and pour over peaches. Bake in moderate oven (350° F.) about 20 minutes, basting occasionally. Serve warm or chilled with sour cream. Approximate yield: 8 portions.

CHESTNUT BALLS

1 pound chestnuts
½ cup soft bread crumbs

1 egg, beaten
¼ cup water

salt and pepper

Shell and blanch chestnuts (page 543) and cook in boiling salted water about 20 minutes, or until tender; or steam 45 minutes. Drain and force through coarse sieve; add crumbs, egg and water and cook over slow fire until mixture is almost dry and holds together. Season to taste and roll into balls. A celery leaf may be inserted in each ball, if desired. Serve as a meat or fish accompaniment. Yield: 12 balls.

SPICED BLUEBERRY MOLDS

3 cups canned unsweetened
blueberries
2 tablespoons sugar
1 stick cinnamon
1 teaspoon whole allspice

1 teaspoon whole cloves
1½ tablespoons plain gelatin
½ cup cold water
dash of salt
2 tablespoons vinegar

¼ cup lemon juice

Bring blueberries, sugar and spices to a boil and simmer 10 minutes, stirring constantly; force through a fine strainer to remove pulp and spices; measure and, if necessary, add water to make 2 cups. Soften gelatin in cold water 5 minutes; add to boiling hot fruit mixture and stir until gelatin is dissolved. Stir in salt, vinegar and lemon juice and pour into small individual molds; chill until firm. One quart fresh blueberries may be used; sort, wash and steam in double boiler about 20 minutes, adding spices after steaming 10 minutes. Then proceed as directed. Approximate yield: 10 small molds or portions.

MINTED QUICK CRANBERRY SAUCE

2 cups sugar
2 cups water
4 cups fresh cranberries

2 tablespoons finely chopped
fresh mint, or
¼ to ½ teaspoon mint extract

Boil sugar and water 5 minutes. Add cranberries, cover and boil without stirring until all the skins pop open. Remove from heat and stir in finely chopped mint or mint extract. Allow sauce to remain in saucepan until cool. Approximate yield: 1 quart.

SPICED BEET RELISH

1 tablespoon mixed whole
spices
1 cup water

1 cup vinegar
½ cup sugar
1 bunch small beets

1 cup sweet pickle relish

For mixed whole spices, use allspice, stick cinnamon, cloves and mustard seeds; tie in cheesecloth bag and drop into water-vinegar-sugar mixture. Wash beets, pare and chop fine; add to the spice mixture and cook until tender, adding water if liquid cooks away. Approximate yield: 4 cups relish.

LEMON PEPPER RELISH

2 green peppers   1½ teaspoons grated lemon
⅓ cup lemon juice   rind
                   ⅔ cup sugar

Cut peppers in quarters and remove white membrane and seeds; put through food chopper, using fine knife, and combine with remaining ingredients. Cook, stirring constantly, until liquid is absorbed and mixture becomes thick; chill. Serve with hot or cold meat. Approximate yield: 1 cup relish.

VEGETABLE RELISH

3 onions, chopped   3 large, sweet red peppers,
2 tablespoons butter   shredded
2 medium tomatoes, sliced   ½ teaspoon salt
                   ⅛ teaspoon pepper

Sauté onions in butter until lightly browned; add tomatoes, peppers and seasonings and cook slowly 30 minutes, or until peppers are tender. Serve hot or cold. Approximate yield: 2 cups relish.

HORSERADISH AND BEET RELISH

2 cups diced or shredded cooked   ½ cup prepared horseradish,
   beets   drained
½ cup sugar   2 tablespoons onion juice
                   ½ cup vinegar

Lightly toss together all ingredients and bring to boiling. Serve hot or cold with meat or fish dishes. Excellent if allowed to stand overnight. Approximate yield: 3½ cups relish.

FRUITS IN MUSTARD SAUCE

2 tablespoons cornstarch   ½ teaspoon salt
½ tablespoon mustard   ½ teaspoon paprika
½ teaspoon turmeric   1 teaspoon celery seed
½ cup vinegar   1 teaspoon curry powder
½ cup brown sugar   1½ cups vinegar
                   1 No. 2 can fruit salad, drained

Combine cornstarch, mustard, turmeric and vinegar. Combine brown sugar, seasonings and vinegar and bring to a boil. Stir in cornstarch mixture and cook, stirring constantly until mixture thickens. Stir in the fruits and cook 2 to 3 minutes. Approximate yield: 1 quart relish.

MINT AND ONION RELISH

1 cup sliced scallions
¾ cup chopped mint leaves

1 tablespoon light brown sugar
½ cup vinegar

Slice scallions, using some of the green part. Combine mint leaves, sugar and vinegar; heat, stirring until sugar dissolves. Chill. Add onions and chill again until onions are crisp. Approximate yield: 1 cup.

FROZEN HORSERADISH RELISH

½ cup heavy cream
½ cup prepared horseradish, drained

¼ teaspoon salt
½ teaspoon lemon juice
1 tablespoon chopped parsley

Whip cream; gently fold in remaining ingredients. Turn into freezing tray of automatic refrigerator with temperature control set at coldest point. Freeze 2 to 4 hours, or until frozen to the desired consistency, stirring once during freezing. Yield: 1¼ cups relish.

MUSHROOM RELISH

2 cups small button mushrooms
1 teaspoon salt
1 teaspoon peppercorns

2 bay leaves
1 clove garlic, sliced
vinegar

1 sprig tarragon

Wipe mushrooms well with a damp cloth. Add seasonings and garlic. Heat vinegar with tarragon, pour over mushrooms and let stand for three days. Approximate yield: 1 pint relish.

PICKLED MUSHROOMS

1 clove garlic
¾ cup salad oil
¼ cup olive oil
½ cup lemon juice
1 medium onion, chopped

1 teaspoon salt
¼ teaspoon pepper
½ teaspoon dry mustard
3 bay leaves
2 4-oz. cans button mushrooms

Rub mixing bowl with cut clove of garlic, pour in oils and lemon juice. Add onion, salt, pepper, mustard and bay leaves. Drain mushrooms and add to sauce. Put in covered jar to store. Be sure the sauce is sufficient to cover mushrooms. Let stand 24 hours in refrigerator. Before serving, drain mushrooms, lay on paper towel, insert toothpicks. Approximate yield: about 80 marinated mushroom buttons.

Macaroni, Noodles and Rice

MACARONI, spaghetti, vermicelli and noodles are the more commonly used Italian pastes. Macaroni and spaghetti, the tubular forms, vary in size; spaghetti is the smaller; vermicelli, a solid length, is the smallest in thickness. Macaroni is also shaped into small forms, including elbows, shells, twists, rosettes and alphabet letters. The egg noodles have egg added to the paste. They are usually made into thin bands varying in width and are often made at home for use in soups, as a vegetable or as the basis of many dishes.

The time for cooking pastes varies slightly. Most of them are cooked in 9 to 12 minutes; they are better if not overcooked. As cereal foods, pastes are cheap sources of starch and proteins and are valuable foods. The Italians have taught us to use them with tomato paste, savory sauces containing onions, peppers and garlic and to serve them with grated cheese or a cheese sauce. As extenders of meat, chicken, eggs and other foods, macaroni products deserve an important place in menu making.

BOILED MACARONI OR SPAGHETTI

Break sticks of macaroni or spaghetti in 1- to 2-inch pieces, or use elbow macaroni, shells or other small shapes; drop into large quantity of rapidly boiling salted water using about 2 quarts water and 2 teaspoons salt for 1 cup macaroni. Boil 9 to 12 minutes, or until tender; directions on package give definite cooking time for that product. Drain in strainer. Macaroni and spaghetti double in bulk on cooking. Allow 1½ to 2 ounces uncooked macaroni or spaghetti a portion.

Reheat with butter or serve with a sauce made with cheese or a combination of cheeses, cream (sweet or sour), can of condensed soup, bouillon or a canned prepared sauce. Some of these pastes are also canned with a sauce ready to heat and serve. In most recipes, macaroni, spaghetti, vermicelli, noodles may be used interchangeably.

To serve whole or unbroken, boil spaghetti in long pieces by placing ends in boiling salted water and coiling as they soften. For vermicelli and noodles use directions above.

BAKED MACARONI AND CHEESE

1 8-oz. package macaroni	1½ to 2 cups grated cheese
2 cups Medium White Sauce (page 125)	½ cup dry bread crumbs, buttered

Boil macaroni (see above); put in greased casserole in alternate layers with sauce and grated cheese. Pour white sauce over top and cover with buttered crumbs; bake in moderate oven (375° F.) 20 to 25 minutes, or until crumbs are browned. Spaghetti may be used in place of macaroni. Approximate yield: 4 to 6 portions.

Macaroni with Tomato Sauce—Substitute Tomato Sauce (page 469) for white sauce.

Macaroni with Ham—Substitute ½ pound boiled ham, finely chopped, for cheese. Season layers of ham with a little finely chopped onion and dot with butter.

Scalloped Sausage and Macaroni—Substitute 1½ to 2 cups chopped, cooked sausage for cheese.

Macaroni à la King—Line bottom and sides of greased casserole with cooked macaroni; fill center with Chicken à la King (page 371); top with macaroni.

Macaroni-Broccoli Casserole—Substitute 2 cups chopped, cooked broccoli for cheese; add ¾ cup mayonnaise to white sauce.

NUT SAVORY MACARONI

2 cups elbow macaroni	2 cups canned tomatoes
1 cup grated American cheese	1 teaspoon salt
1 cup chopped walnuts	¼ teaspoon pepper
½ tablespoon minced onion	

Cook macaroni (page 499); arrange in greased casserole in alternate layers with cheese and nuts. Season tomatoes with salt and pepper and add onion; pour over macaroni, cover and bake in moderate oven (350° F.) 20 to 30 minutes, or until cheese is melted. Yield: 6 portions.

BAKED MACARONI, CREOLE STYLE

1½ cups macaroni	1½ teaspoons sugar
3 tablespoons minced onion	1½ teaspoons salt
3 tablespoons butter	¼ teaspoon pepper
1 green pepper, chopped	¾ pound country sausage
3 cups canned tomatoes	⅓ cup dry bread crumbs

Cook macaroni (page 499). Sauté onion in butter 5 minutes; add green pepper, tomatoes, sugar, salt and pepper and simmer 15 minutes. Form sausage into 6 flat patties. Place half of macaroni in casserole; lay patties on top and cover with remaining macaroni. Add tomato mixture, sprinkle with bread crumbs and bake in moderate oven (375° F.) 45 minutes. Approximate yield: 6 portions.

STINA'S MACARONI CASSEROLE

1 14½-oz. can evaporated milk	1 8-oz. package macaroni, cooked
¼ pound sharp cheese	1 cup light sour cream
½ teaspoon dry mustard	1 tablespoon minced chives
1 teaspoon Worcestershire sauce	crushed corn flakes or buttered
salt and pepper	bread crumbs

Heat evaporated milk, cheese, mustard, Worcestershire sauce, salt and pepper over hot water until cheese is melted and mixture is thick. Add macaroni and turn into greased baking dish. Pour over sour cream and sprinkle with cut chives, if desired, and cover with corn flakes. Bake in moderate oven (350° F.) about 45 minutes. Approximate yield: 6 portions.

SALAMIED MACARONI

1 large onion, finely chopped	1 6-oz. can tomato paste
1 large green pepper, finely chopped	1 cup water
1 clove garlic, minced	marjoram, thyme, sweet basil
6 tablespoons olive oil	1 pound mushrooms, sliced
1 pound pork, ground	1 8-oz. package elbow macaroni
½ pound Italian salami, ground	¼ pound grated Parmesan cheese

Sauté onion, pepper and garlic lightly in ¼ cup olive oil; add pork and salami and sauté 5 minutes. Stir in tomato paste and water, add herbs and simmer slowly about 2 to 4 hours, adding mushrooms, sautéed in remaining 2 tablespoons oil, 15 minutes before sauce is done. Cook macaroni (page 499); arrange on hot platter in layers with sauce; sprinkle generously with cheese. Approximate yield: 6 to 8 portions.

MACARONI LOAF

2 cups cooked macaroni	1 teaspoon salt
2 tablespoons chopped pimiento	½ teaspoon paprika
¾ cup finely diced cheese	2 tablespoons butter, melted
1 tablespoon minced onion	2 eggs, well beaten
1 cup dry bread crumbs	1½ cups canned tomatoes

Mix all ingredients together thoroughly, turn into greased loaf pan and bake in moderate oven (350° F.) about 40 minutes. Approximate yield: 6 portions.

MACARONI CHEESE TIMBALES

1½ cups cooked, broken macaroni	½ teaspoon Worcestershire sauce
2 eggs, well beaten	1½ cups grated American cheese
½ teaspoon salt	
dash of pepper	1¾ cups milk
6 cooked mushroom caps	

Divide macaroni equally among six buttered custard cups. Mix together eggs, seasonings, 1 cup grated cheese and 1½ cups milk; pour over macaroni in custard cups. Place cups in pan of hot water and bake in moderate oven (350° F.) 30 minutes, or until firm. When ready to serve, unmold on hot platter, garnish each timbale with a mushroom cap and serve with cheese sauce. For sauce, cook remaining ½ cup cheese and ¼ cup milk in double boiler until cheese is melted; season with additional salt and pepper. Yield: 6 portions.

MACARONI AND CHEESE CROQUETTES

2 cups elbow macaroni	1 cup grated cheese
3 tablespoons chopped, cooked bacon	1 teaspoon onion juice
1 teaspoon chopped parsley	1 cup Thick White Sauce (page 125)

Cook elbow or broken macaroni (page 499); put through food chopper; add bacon and parsley. Add cheese and onion juice to white sauce and blend with macaroni. Spread out on platter, cool, shape into croquettes and fry in hot deep fat (365°–380° F.) 3 to 5 minutes. Serve with game and fowl. Approximate yield: 6 portions.

SPAGHETTI, FRONTIER STYLE

1 8-oz. package spaghetti
1 small onion, finely chopped
1 clove garlic, minced
2 tablespoons butter
4 pimientos, minced
1 green pepper, finely chopped

1 cup diced, cooked chicken
½ cup canned mushrooms
1 No. 2½ can tomatoes
¼ teaspoon pepper
Frontier Sauce (page 470)
¼ cup grated Parmesan cheese

Cook unbroken spaghetti (page 499). Sauté onion and garlic in butter until delicately browned. Add pimientos, green pepper, chicken, mushrooms, tomatoes and pepper. Add to spaghetti, mix lightly by lifting with two forks. Turn into greased casserole, cover with Frontier Sauce (page 470), sprinkle with cheese, cover and bake in moderate oven (350° F.) 30 to 40 minutes. Approximate yield: 6 portions.

SPAGHETTI WITH CLAMS

4 ounces spaghetti
1 dozen large clams
¾ cup chopped celery

2 cups Medium White Sauce
(page 125)
¼ cup buttered bread crumbs
1 tablespoon grated cheese

Cook spaghetti (page 499). Cut clams in half, remove necks; arrange spaghetti, clams, celery and white sauce in alternate layers in greased baking dish. Mix crumbs with cheese, sprinkle over top and bake in hot oven (400° F.) 15 to 20 minutes. Yield: 6 portions.

ITALIAN DELIGHT

4 ounces spaghetti
2 cups chopped corned beef
1 small onion, minced
¼ cup butter
¾ cup canned mushrooms

1 cup canned red kidney beans
½ teaspoon salt
⅛ teaspoon pepper
1 cup canned condensed tomato
soup
¾ cup grated American cheese

Cook spaghetti (page 499). Sauté corned beef and onion in butter 8 minutes, stirring frequently. Arrange half of spaghetti in greased casserole, then layers of ½ the meat, mushrooms and beans; season with salt and pepper. Repeat layers in reverse order, having spaghetti on top; pour soup over spaghetti, sprinkle with cheese and bake in moderately hot oven (375° F.) about 30 minutes. Yield: 6 portions.

SPAGHETTI WITH TOMATO SAUCE

½ pound chopped round steak
½ cup dried mushrooms, rinsed
1 small dried hot red pepper
½ cup olive oil
½ clove garlic, chopped

1 No. 2½ can Italian tomatoes, strained
½ cup tomato paste
salt and pepper
1 8-oz. package spaghetti

Sauté lightly meat, mushrooms and red pepper in olive oil 10 minutes; add garlic and tomatoes and simmer 40 minutes. Add tomato paste, season to taste with salt and pepper and simmer 10 minutes longer. Cook unbroken spaghetti (page 499), turn out on hot platter and cover with sauce. Approximate yield: 6 portions.

SPAGHETTI DELECTABLE

1 8-oz. package spaghetti
1⅓ cups canned tomatoes
salt, pepper, celery salt
1 onion, sliced

1 tablespoon fat
3 strips lean bacon
6 lamb kidneys
2 tablespoons butter

Cook spaghetti (page 499) and turn into greased baking dish. Strain tomatoes, season to taste with salt, pepper and celery salt; add onion which has been sautéed in fat 2 minutes and pour over spaghetti. Cut bacon strips in halves and arrange around edge of dish. Remove outer skin from each kidney, cut in halves, removing tubes; arrange halves, cut side up, on spaghetti and dot with butter. Bake in moderate oven (375° F.) about 40 minutes, or until kidneys are cooked. Approximate yield: 6 portions.

VERMICELLI WITH ANCHOVIES

1 8-oz. package vermicelli
1 tablespoon chopped parsley
2 tablespoons melted butter
1 teaspoon grated onion

2 tablespoons grated Parmesan cheese
1½ cups Medium White Sauce (page 125)

9 anchovy fillets

Cook vermicelli (page 499); turn into greased casserole. Add parsley, butter, onion and cheese to white sauce; pour over vermicelli, arrange anchovies on top and bake in moderate oven (375° F.) about 25 minutes, or until lightly browned. Approximate yield: 6 portions.

BASIC NOODLE RECIPE

3 eggs, beaten
1 tablespoon melted shortening
 or oil

2½ cups sifted all-purpose flour
½ teaspoon salt

Combine eggs and shortening. Sift flour and salt; stir into egg mixture. Turn onto lightly floured board. Knead for one minute. Divide dough in half. Roll out into paper-thin sheets; let stand about one hour. Roll up as for jelly roll; slice into ¼ inch strips. Unroll and hang over a taut string or arrange on waxed paper on a flat pan. Allow to dry until noodles are crisp. Store covered in glass jars. Yield: 8 ounces.

GREEN NOODLES

2 eggs, beaten
¼ cup cooked spinach, finely
 chopped

1 tablespoon melted shortening
2 cups sifted all-purpose flour
½ teaspoon salt

Combine eggs, spinach and shortening. Sift together flour and salt; stir into egg mixture. Turn onto lightly floured board. Knead for one minute. Divide dough in half. Roll out into paper-thin sheets; let stand about one hour. Roll as for jelly roll; slice in ¼ inch strips. Unroll and hang over taut string, or arrange on waxed paper on a flat pan. Dry until noodles are crisp. Yield: 8 ounces.

BOILED NOODLES

For cooking commercial or homemade noodles, follow directions for Boiled Macaroni and Spaghetti (page 499); boil about 10 minutes. Allow 1½ to 2 ounces uncooked noodles a portion.

FRIED NOODLES

Cook noodles in boiling, salted water until just soft enough to bend. Drain and dry on absorbent paper. Heat deep fat to 375° F. Swirl forkful of noodles in it until browned. Drain on paper towels.

NOODLE OMELET

3 tablespoons milk
½ teaspoon salt
dash of pepper

3 eggs, slightly beaten
3 cups cooked noodles (page 499)
3 tablespoons butter or margarine

Add milk and seasonings to eggs. Sauté noodles in butter until lightly browned, pour in egg mixture and cook like French Omelet (page 122). Fold in half; serve on hot platter with topping of cinnamon and sugar, if desired. Approximate yield: 6 portions.

NOODLES IN COTTAGE CHEESE AND GARLIC

1 8-oz. package noodles, cooked 1 clove garlic, finely minced
1 cup cottage cheese 1 onion, chopped
1 cup light sour cream 1 tablespoon Worcestershire sauce
½ teaspoon salt

Mix together noodles, cheese, cream, garlic, onion and seasonings. Place in greased 1½ quart casserole. Bake in moderate oven (350° F.) 30 minutes. Top each serving with additional sour cream and sprinkle with grated Cheddar cheese. Yield: 6 portions.

NOODLE RING

4 ounces flat noodles ½ cup light cream
3 eggs, separated ¼ cup grated cheese
½ cup milk ½ teaspoon salt
dash of pepper

Cook noodles (page 499). Beat egg yolks until thick and light, add milk and cream, noodles, cheese and seasonings; fold in stiffly beaten whites. Turn into well greased 8-inch ring mold, place in pan of hot water and bake in moderate oven (350° F.) about 1 hour. Turn out on round serving plate and fill with well-seasoned creamed chicken, mushrooms or fish, as desired. Approximate yield: 4 to 6 portions.

NOODLES, CREOLE STYLE

6 ounces broad noodles 1 green pepper, chopped
4 okra pods 6 tomatoes, peeled and quartered
1 medium-sized onion, chopped 1 cup cut green string beans
2 tablespoons butter or 1 teaspoon salt
  margarine

Parboil noodles in boiling salted water; drain. Wash okra, remove both ends, cut in ¼ inch pieces and blanch. Sauté onion in butter until lightly browned; add okra, pepper, tomatoes and beans; simmer 20 minutes. Add noodles and salt and cook about 10 minutes, or until tender, adding more water if necessary. Approximate yield: 6 portions.

CHEESE NOODLE CASSEROLE

½ pound bacon, diced	½ teaspoon salt
1½ cups cooked wide noodles	¼ teaspoon pepper
1 cup cottage cheese	¼ teaspoon paprika
½ cup buttered bread crumbs	

Panbroil bacon until crisp. Combine bacon, noodles, cheese and seasonings, mixing well. Turn into greased casserole, sprinkle with crumbs and bake in moderate oven (375° F.) 20 minutes. Approximate yield: 4 to 6 portions.

POPPY SEED NOODLES

1 8-oz. package broad noodles, cooked and drained	1 tablespoon butter
	grated rind of one orange
3 tablespoons poppy seeds	grated rind of one lemon
½ cup slivered blanched almonds, toasted	1 cup heavy sour cream (optional)
salt and pepper	

Combine noodles, poppy seeds, almonds, butter and rinds and toss together lightly. Turn into buttered casserole and dot with butter or top with cream; season. Bake in moderate oven (350° F.) 20 minutes, or until thoroughly heated. Yield: 6 portions.

FLUFFY BOILED RICE

1 cup rice	3 teaspoons salt
8 to 10 cups boiling water	

Wash rice thoroughly. Add salt to boiling water in deep saucepan; add rice slowly so boiling does not stop. If water is very hard, add 1 teaspoon lemon juice or 1 tablespoon vinegar to keep rice white. Boil gently, without stirring, 14 to 18 minutes, depending upon variety, or until rice is entirely tender when pressed between fingers. Drain into sieve, rinse with hot water, place in sieve or strainer and keep over hot water until ready to use. Serve as a cereal or in place of potatoes; or form mound on serving plate and cover with creamed fish, meat or vegetables. Water in which rice is cooked may be substituted for part of liquid in making sauces and soups. Approximate yield: 4 cups cooked rice, or 6 portions.

BOILED BROWN RICE

¾ cup brown rice   1 teaspoon salt
                  4½ cups boiling water

Wash rice thoroughly; drain. Add salt to boiling water; add rice slowly.
Cover and cook over very low heat 40 to 60 minutes, or until all liquid
is absorbed. Uncover and let stand over low heat for rice to dry and
fluff; turn from kettle and serve as desired. Meat or chicken stock may
be used in place of water. Approximate yield: 3⅔ cups cooked rice, or
6 portions.

ITALIAN RICE

Sauté 1 cup washed rice in ⅓ cup butter about 5 minutes, or until delicately browned, stirring constantly. Add 2 cups canned tomatoes, season to taste with salt, pepper and onion salt; boil about 5 minutes. Add
2 cups water or stock as necessary, cover and simmer 25 to 30 minutes,
or until liquid has been almost entirely absorbed by rice. Serve with
mild-flavored meat or fish. Approximate yield: 6 portions.

BROWNED WHITE RICE

3 tablespoons fat or salad oil   3 cups boiling water
¾ cup rice, washed   1¼ teaspoons salt

Melt fat in a skillet. Add rice and sauté, stirring constantly until golden
brown. Stir in boiling water gradually, then salt. Cover and simmer
about 15 to 20 minutes without stirring, or until rice is dry and flaky.
Approximate yield: 3½ cups rice, or 6 portions.

SPANISH RICE

1 cup rice   ½ cup finely chopped green
2 tablespoons fat   pepper
1 cup canned tomatoes   3 cups boiling water
2 large onions, sliced   1 teaspoon salt
                  ½ teaspoon chili powder

Wash rice; sauté in fat until lightly browned. Add remaining ingredients and simmer 15 to 20 minutes, or until rice is tender. Approximate yield: 6 portions. Good with chicken or liver dishes.

SAUTÉED RICE WITH GREEN PEPPERS

Sauté ½ green pepper, chopped, in 2 tablespoons butter until browned; add 3 cups cooked rice, season to taste with salt and pepper and continue cooking until rice is thoroughly heated and lightly browned. Approximate yield: 6 portions.

BAKED RICE AND CHEESE

½ teaspoon Worcestershire sauce
dash of thyme
2 cups Medium White Sauce
    (page 125)

2 cups cooked rice
1 cup grated American cheese
¼ cup buttered crumbs

Add Worcestershire sauce and thyme to white sauce. Arrange layer of rice in bottom of greased casserole, cover with part of sauce and sprinkle generously with cheese; repeat until all is used. Top with buttered crumbs and bake in moderate oven (350° F.) 15 to 20 minutes, or until cheese is melted. Approximate yield: 6 portions.

RICE PILAF

1 cup rice
1 quart stock
3 tablespoons oil
¼ clove garlic, minced

1 teaspoon salt
¼ teaspoon pepper
3 tablespoons shredded blanched
    almonds

Combine rice, stock, oil, garlic, salt and pepper. Bring to boiling and add almonds. Pour into 1½ quart casserole. Stock should be 2 inches over rice layer. Cover and bake in moderate oven (350° F.) 20 to 25 minutes, or until rice is tender. Serve with chicken, lamb, shrimp or crab, as desired. Approximate yield: 6 portions.

SPANISH RICE AND OYSTER PIE

Prepare Spanish Rice (page 508), substituting 1 can condensed tomato soup for canned tomatoes, and cook over low heat until all moisture is absorbed. Remove from heat and blend with 2 slightly beaten eggs. Line bottom and sides of greased pie pan with ⅔ of rice mixture. Prepare Creamed Oysters (page 448), using Thick White Sauce (page 125). Add ½ pound sliced, cooked mushrooms, 2 tablespoons cracker crumbs, 1 tablespoon chopped parsley, ¼ teaspoon Worcestershire sauce and 2 well-beaten eggs. Turn into tomato-rice crust, use remaining crust mixture to top the pie and bake in hot oven (400° F.) 20 minutes. Approximate yield: 6 portions.

LOUISIANA SHRIMP WITH RICE

1 small onion, chopped	2 cups cooked rice
3 tablespoons butter	1½ cups cooked shrimp, sliced in
1 cup strained, canned tomatoes	half lengthwise
1 cup chicken stock	salt, pepper and paprika

Sauté onion in butter 5 minutes; add remaining ingredients, seasoning to taste with salt, pepper and paprika and heat thoroughly. Lobster or other cooked fish may be substituted. Yield: 6 portions.

RICE CROQUETTES

2 cups cooked rice	3 tablespoons grated American
½ cup Thick White Sauce	cheese
(page 125)	1 teaspoon salt
1 egg, separated	⅛ teaspoon cayenne
	dry bread crumbs

Combine rice, white sauce, well-beaten egg yolk, cheese, salt and cayenne. Spread out on platter, cool and shape into small croquettes. Dip into beaten egg white, then into bread crumbs and fry in hot deep fat (365°–380° F.) 2 to 4 minutes, or until golden brown. Approximate yield: 6 portions.

BROWN RICE BALLS

1 cup brown rice	1 cup tomato pulp
2 onion slices	1 cup cooked flaked salmon
1 bay leaf	salt and pepper
¼ cup chopped onion	2 eggs
2 tablespoons fat	dry bread crumbs

Steam rice (see page 507) in water to which onion slices and bay leaf have been added. Sauté chopped onion in fat until lightly browned; add tomato pulp, salmon and seasonings and cook until lightly browned and somewhat dry. Mix rice with 1 beaten egg, cool and form into small balls. Remove centers from balls with spoon or sharp knife, fill with salmon mixture, then close opening with additional rice mixture. Roll in 1 beaten egg, then in bread crumbs and fry in hot deep fat (370° F.) 3 to 5 minutes. Approximate yield: 6 portions.

BROWN RICE WITH CHEESE

2 cups cooked brown rice   2 eggs, slightly beaten
  (page 508)   2 cups grated cheese
3 cups milk, scalded   1 teaspoon salt
¼ teaspoon paprika

Mix ingredients together thoroughly, turn into buttered custard cups, set in pan of hot water and bake in moderate oven (350° F.) 30 to 35 minutes, or until custards are firm. Garnish with very thin rings of sweet red pepper, if desired, and serve at once. Yield: 6 portions.

STEEPED WILD RICE

Pour a teakettle of boiling water over 1 cup wild rice and let stand while next kettle is heating. Drain. Repeat five times. Add 2 tablespoons salt to sixth kettle of water. Drain, add 1 tablespoon melted butter. Especially nice to serve with game.

POPPED WILD RICE

Place about 2 tablespoons at a time of wild rice in strainer in small frying basket. Place in hot deep fat (380° F.) about 3 minutes or until grains pop open. May be served on day after frying; turn into shallow baking pan and heat in oven. Serve with pheasant, wild duck or other game. One 1-lb. package makes 8 to 10 portions.

BOILED WILD RICE

¾ cup wild rice   3 cups boiling water
½ teaspoon salt   2 teaspoons butter

Wash rice thoroughly in cold water several times. Add salt to boiling water, then add rice slowly so water continues to boil. Do not stir; shake kettle to prevent rice from sticking. Cook 25 to 45 minutes, or until rice is tender and water entirely absorbed; add butter. Serve in place of potatoes with beef or game. Approximate yield: 6 portions.

BAKED WILD RICE WITH MUSHROOMS

1 cup wild rice   ¼ cup butter
½ pound mushrooms   ½ teaspoon salt
⅛ teaspoon pepper

Cook rice (above). Peel and slice mushrooms, reserving smaller ones for garnish, and sauté in butter until lightly browned. Add to rice, mixing lightly; season with salt and pepper and turn into greased casserole. Garnish with small whole mushrooms and bake in moderate oven (350° F.) 25 minutes, or until thoroughly heated. Approximate yield: 6 portions.

LEMON RICE

3 tablespoons sugar   1 tablespoon grated lemon rind
3 tablespoons lemon juice   4 cups cooked rice

Mix sugar, lemon juice and rind. Pour over rice. Serve hot or cold.
Approximate yield: 6 portions.

WILD RICE CORDON BLEU

2 cups wild rice   ½ cup white raisins, soaked in dry
4 cups strong duck or game   white wine
   stock   ½ cup split blanched almonds
2 bay leaves   ¼ cup finely chopped onion
rock salt   6 slices fat bacon, shredded and
freshly cracked black pepper   crisply fried
1 teaspoon crushed garlic   2 tablespoons chopped chives
½ cup raisins, soaked in brandy ¼ cup grated Parmesan cheese
            ⅓ cup butter or margarine

Wash rice; put in pan and cover with stock. Add bay leaves and season
well with salt and pepper. Bring to a boil slowly and add garlic,
drained raisins and almonds. Cook onions slowly in bacon fat 2 minutes; add to rice mixture with bacon and chives. Cover and cook in
moderate oven (350° F.) 25 to 30 minutes. Remove from oven and,
with a fork, stir in half of Parmesan cheese and butter. Place in serving
dish and sprinkle liberally with more grated Parmesan cheese. Yield:
4 to 6 portions.

RICE AND SAUSAGE CASSEROLE

¾ pound link sausage   3 tablespoons chopped celery
2 tablespoons hot water   leaves
1½ cups coarse cracker crumbs   1½ tablespoons chopped onion
1½ cups hot cooked rice   1½ teaspoons salt
1½ cups canned tomato   ¼ teaspoon pepper
¼ cup chopped green pepper   2 tablespoons butter

Cut sausage into small pieces and fry until delicately browned, stirring
constantly; add water. Combine crumbs, rice, tomato, green pepper,
celery leaves, onion and seasonings, mixing lightly; add sausage. Turn
into greased casserole, dot with butter and bake in moderate oven
(375° F.) 30 minutes. Approximate yield: 6 portions.

RICE CREAM WITH STRAWBERRIES

¾ cup rice
3 cups milk
5 egg yolks
6 tablespoons sugar
1 envelope plain gelatin
1½ cups hot milk
2 tablespoons lemon juice

2 tablespoons heavy cream,
   whipped
5 tablespoons grape jelly
1 tablespoon guava jelly
2 tablespoons Sherry
1 tablespoon Curaçao
2 cups strawberries, hulled

Combine rice and milk and cook over low heat until rice is tender, adding more milk if necessary. Beat egg yolks until thick and lemon-colored. Gradually beat in sugar. Stir in gelatin. Gradually stir in hot milk. Cook over low heat until slightly thickened, stirring constantly. Combine rice mixture and custard. Chill until slightly thickened. Add lemon juice. Fold in whipped cream and pour into lightly greased 8-inch ring mold. Let stand in refrigerator until firm. Combine jellies and cook until syrupy. Cool. Stir in Sherry and Curaçao. Pour over strawberries. Turn rice ring onto serving dish. Fill with strawberries and top with whipped cream. Yield: 6 to 8 portions.

MAYONNAISE POACHED EGGS

6 eggs
1½ cups rice
½ cup green peas, cooked
½ cup diced cooked carrots
1 teaspoon salt
½ teaspoon pepper
1 tablespoon vinegar
3 tablespoons salad oil
3 egg yolks

½ teaspoon salt
dash of pepper
½ teaspoon dry mustard
1 tablespoon tarragon vinegar
¾ cup salad oil
2 tablespoons sour cream
2 tablespoons heavy cream
1 tablespoon chopped parsley
1 tomato, shredded

¼ cucumber, shredded

Poach eggs for 3½ minutes. Remove from hot water and let stand in cold water until cold. Cook rice in boiling salted water 15 to 20 minutes, or until done. Drain and rinse in cold water. Add peas and carrots and season with salt, pepper, vinegar and oil. Mix and arrange on a platter or dish. Place eggs on rice and garnish with mayonnaise made by putting egg yolks in mixing bowl with salt, pepper, dry mustard, and vinegar and slowly beating in ¾ cup oil. Add sour cream, heavy cream, parsley, shredded tomato and cucumber. Blend well and pour over eggs. Yield: 6 portions.

ASIATIC SUPPER PLATE

3 cups cooked rice (page 507) paprika
½ cup shredded coconut parsley
½ cup chopped, blanched 12 stuffed olives
   almonds Mousseline Chutney Sauce
12 slices chicken, roast or canned (page 473)

Combine hot cooked rice with coconut and almonds. Place serving of
rice in center of each of 6 hot serving plates, flank with slices of chicken.
Sprinkle rice with paprika, garnish with parsley and olives and serve
with Mousseline chutney sauce. Approximate yield: 6 portions.

Vegetables

CRISP, colorful vegetables, cooked just to fork tenderness, dripping with butter and seasoned a bit with salt and pepper, offer appetizing appeal to any eater in the family. A lot has been said about the several methods of vegetable cookery. We give you here numerous ways of serving them in order to add variety to your menus.

For some reason, women in the past have generally been poor vegetable cooks. Overcooking, bad seasoning and lack of imagination in serving have been the chief weakness. The situation is changing today as cooks realize the boundless possibilities of color, interest and food value offered by vegetable gardens.

For high nutritive value, serve vegetables as fresh as possible, even raw, frequently, if they can be prepared that way. Research shows that the most advantageous way to retain the vitamins in vegetables is to cook them with no water in a heavy covered pan. Pressure cooking is the second recommended method (see pages 958–961). They will retain more nutrients when baked or boiled in the skin, than when peeled, diced or sliced, and cooked. Any vegetable juices left over should be stored in a refrigerator jar for soups or sauces. Vitamin value is lost when vegetables stand too long, cooked or uncooked.

General rules for storage. Soft-textured vegetables usually need to be washed, the imperfect spots removed and stored in the covered hydrator in the refrigerator. Plastic bags may also be used. Cauliflower, artichokes, Brussels sprouts, cabbage, and broccoli may need preliminary soaking in salted water to remove

TABLE XXXII

TIMETABLE FOR COOKING VEGETABLES
(APPROXIMATE) [1]

VEGETABLE[2]	BOILING[3]	STEAMING[4]	PRESSURE SAUCEPAN[5]	BAKING[6]
	Minutes	*Minutes*	*Minutes*	*Minutes*
Artichokes, French (whole).....	35–45		10–12	
Jerusalem (pared, whole)..........	25–35	35	4–10	30–60
Asparagus (whole or butts).....	10–30	12–30	½–2	
(tips)	5–15	7–15	½–1½	
Beans, Lima (fresh)...........	20–30	25–35	1–3	
Lima, kidney (dried)....	2–3 hr		25	
Beans, Green, wax (whole, pieces)....	15–30	20–35	1½–3	
(shredded)..	10–20	15–25	1–2	
Beans, soybeans[7]	20–30	25–35	2–3	
soybeans, navy (dried) ..	2–3 hr		40	
Beets, young (small, whole)....	30–45	40–60	5–10	40–60
mature (small, whole) ...	45–90	50–90	10–18	1–2 hr
Beet greens....................	5–15		3	
Broccoli (stalks and buds)......	8–20	15–20	1½–3	
Brussels sprouts (whole)........	8–18	10–20	1–2	
Cabbage, green (quarters)......	10–15	15	2–3	
green (shredded).....	3–10	8–12	½–1½	
Cabbage, red (shredded).......	8–12	10–15	½–1½	
Carrots, young (whole)........	15–25	20–30	3–5	35–45
young (sliced)........	10–20	15–25	1½–3	30–40
Carrots, mature (whole)........	20–30	40–50	10–15	60
mature (sliced)........	15–20	25–30	2–3	
Cauliflower (whole)...........	20–30	25–30	3½–5	
(flowerets)	8–15	10–20	1½–3	
Celeriac (sliced or diced).......	15–20	25	2	
Celery (diced)................	15–20	25–30	2–3	
Chard, Swiss.................	10–20	15–25	1½–3	
Chinese cabbage (sliced).......	8–10		3	
Collards.......................	10–15	20–30		
Corn, on cob................	5–15	10–15	1½–3	
Cucumbers (whole)............	10–15	20		20–25
(sliced)	5–6		1	
Dandelion greens..............	15–25		2½–3	
Dasheen (whole, with skin).....	15–30			
Eggplant (sliced)..............	10–20	15–20	¼–1	
Endive, curly..................	15–20			
Kale........................	10–20		2	
Kohlrabi (sliced, quarters).....	20–25	30	4	
Leeks (white part of bunch)....	15–20		2–3	
Lentils, green, yellow (dried) ...	2–3 hr		15	
Mushrooms (own juice)........	5		2–5	
Mustard greens................	15–20		5	
Okra (sliced)..................	10–20	20	3	
Onions, green (scallions).......	8–15	15–20	2–3	
mature (quarters, whole)	30–35	35–40	5–7	50–60
Parsnips (quarters, whole)......	20–40	30–45	4–10	30–45
Peas, green...................	8–20	10–20	1	
green, split, yellow (dried)	2–3 hr		15	
Peppers, green, parboiled (whole)	2–10			25–30

TABLE XXXII—(*Continued*)

TIMETABLE FOR COOKING VEGETABLES (Approximate)[1]

VEGETABLE[2]	BOILING[3]	STEAMING[4]	PRESSURE SAUCEPAN[5]	BAKING[6]
	Minutes	*Minutes*	*Minutes*	*Minutes*
Potatoes, Irish (medium, whole)	25–40	30–45	8–11	45–60
Irish (quartered).....	15–25	20–30	3–5	
Potatoes, sweet (whole)........	25–35	30–35	5–8	30–45
sweet (quartered).....	15–25	25–30	6	
Rutabagas (sliced, diced).......	20–30	35–40	5–8	
Salsify or oyster plant (sliced, cubed)...................	20–25		5–15	
Spinach....................	3–10		2	
Squash, winter, Hubbard (pieces)	20–30	25–40	10–12	40–60
winter, Acorn (halves)..	10–20	20–30	6–8	60
summer (sliced, halves).	10–20		2–8	30
Tomatoes....................	7–15		½–1	15–30
Turnips, (whole, halves).......	20–30		8–12	
(slices, cubes).........	15–20	20–25	1½–3	
Turnip greens................	15–25		2–5	

[1] Data based on Vegetable Cookery Chart in Handbook of Food in Preparation, page 41, American Home Economics Association.
[2] Cook vegetables until just tender; they should not be soft and mushy. Test with a sharp tined fork or knife point.
[3] Boil vegetables, in general, in a minimum amount of water in a covered container. The vegetable is cooked largely by steam and from water in the food; the cooking period is shortened.
[4] To steam vegetables keep water boiling in lower part of steamer and do not let it boil dry. Salt before or after steaming.
[5] Follow instructions given with pressure saucepan. Rapid cooling of cooker is advised for almost all fresh vegetables. At 15 pounds pressure vegetables are steamed at 250°F; for a short time.
[6] A vegetable is baked whole in its own skin at a moderate heat (350°–375°F.); or sliced or cut up and baked in a covered casserole at moderate heat.
[7] Cook soybean pods 3 minutes before shelling.

insects from the tightly flowered heads. More than one change of water is frequently necessary. Thick-skinned vegetables, such as turnips, potatoes, etc., should be stored unwashed in a cool, dry, dark storage bin. Leave one inch of stem on beets and carrots.

DIRECTIONS AND TIMETABLE FOR COOKING FROZEN VEGETABLES IN PRESSURE SAUCEPANS

1. Remove vegetable from package and allow to stand at room temperature until thawed just enough to separate—about ½ hour. (Spinach may be cut into ½ inch cubes while still frozen. Corn on the cob should be completely thawed.)
2. Place water (see amount below) and ½ teaspoon salt in pressure saucepan. Add vegetable. Cover saucepan and proceed as directed

by manufacturer, using cooking time given below. Start counting
time the moment control indicates that the *pressure is at 15 pounds*.
3. When cooking time is up, remove from heat and set saucepan in
pan of cold water until control indicates that the pressure has been
reduced enough to remove the cover.
4. Season with butter or margarine, salt, and pepper.
5. *Serve immediately.*

TABLE XXXIII

PRODUCT	AMOUNT OF WATER	COOKING TIME *
Asparagus spears	¼ cup	1–2 minutes
Asparagus cuts	¼ cup	1–2 minutes
Broccoli	¼ cup	1–2 minutes
Broccoli cuts	¼ cup	1–2 minutes
Brussels sprouts	¼ cup	1–2 minutes
Cauliflower	¼ cup	½–1 minute
Corn, whole kernel	¼ cup	½–1 minute
Corn on the cob	⅓ cup	1½–2 minutes
Green beans, cut	¼ cup	2–3 minutes
Green beans, French style	¼ cup	½–1 minute
Green peas	¼ cup	½–1 minute
Lima beans, small	½ cup	1–2 minutes
Lima beans, Fordhook	½ cup	1–2 minutes
Mixed vegetables	¼ cup	1–2 minutes
Peas and carrots	¼ cup	½–1 minute
Spinach	¼ cup	½–1 minute
Spinach, chopped	¼ cup	½–1 minute
Wax beans	¼ cup	1–2 minutes

* Time after 15-pound pressure has been reached.

VEGETABLE COMBINATIONS

Interesting combinations of color, flavor and texture may be obtained
by using two or more vegetables. This is an ideal way to use leftover
cooked vegetables, but smaller amounts of raw vegetables may be
freshly cooked and served together. Unless the vegetables chosen cook
in the same way and in approximately the same time, cook them separately and reheat together just before serving. Vegetable combinations
may be used with only a seasoning of salt, pepper and melted butter,
or creamed as Creamed Vegetables (page 521), Vegetables au Gratin
(page 521), Scalloped Vegetables (page 520) or in Vegetable Soufflé
(page 521).

Some suggested combinations from which two or more vegetables may
be chosen are:

Beans, green—with mushrooms, onions, tomatoes, celery.
Beans, lima—with corn, tomatoes, onions.
Brussels sprouts—with chestnuts, celery.
Cabbage—with lima beans, green peppers, tomatoes.
Carrots—with peas, onions, celery.
Cauliflower—with corn, mushrooms.
Celery—with peas, beans, parsnips, mushrooms.
Corn—with tomatoes, eggplant, green peppers.
Eggplant—with tomatoes, green peppers, mushrooms.
Parsnips—with tomatoes, celery.
Peas—with carrots, onions, celery, potatoes, cucumbers, turnips.
Peas—with scallions, mushrooms, garlic.
Potatoes—with peas, onions.
Spinach—as ring or nest for almost any vegetable.
Spinach—with chopped garlic.
Squash—with tomatoes, corn.
Tomatoes—with beans, onions, mushrooms, corn, eggplant, parsnips, green peppers, cabbage.
Turnips—with peas.

WATERLESS COOKED VEGETABLES

Recent research shows that more food value in vegetables is saved when they are cooked without water or with a very small amount of water for long-cooking vegetables. This is possible because most vegetables contain sufficient water to convert to steam in the cooking process. A heavy pan must be used with a tight-fitting cover. Allow ½ teaspoon salt to each pound of vegetables (add a tablespoon or two of water with vegetables taking a long time to cook), cover tightly, and use high heat for the first two or three minutes, then reduce to very low heat. Shaking the pan occasionally will help to prevent sticking and burning.

COOKING IN PARCHMENT

Moisten a square of parchment paper large enough to enfold the vegetables. Place prepared vegetables in center, add seasonings and butter or margarine if desired, gather ends up and tie to make a watertight bag so that steam and water cannot enter. Place bag or bags in a pan of boiling water or in a pressure cooker (adding ½ cup of water to cooker). The paper may be washed, dried and re-used. Several vegetables at once may be cooked in the same kettle with this method.

BOILED VEGETABLES

Prepare vegetables and boil in different amounts of water according to type. For amounts to use for each one, see individual recipes or Time-table for Boiling Vegetables (page 516). With almost no water or a small amount, add ½ teaspoon salt per pound of vegetable; with water to cover, add ½ teaspoon salt per quart of water; and with a large amount of water, add 1 teaspoon salt per quart of water. To serve, drain, if necessary, add 1 to 2 tablespoons butter per cup of cooked vegetable and salt and pepper to taste. The water in which vegetables are cooked contains soluble minerals and should be saved from all but the strongly flavored vegetables; boil down and use in sauces or soups.

STEAMED VEGETABLES

Steaming conserves most of the nutriments of the vegetables. Many mild-flavored vegetables, such as carrots, beets, parsnips, potatoes, spinach, squash, sweet potatoes and wax beans, can be cooked by steaming. Prepare vegetables and place in perforated part of steamer or put in strainer or colander, place over hot water and cover tightly. Steam until vegetables are just tender, allowing ¼ to ⅓ longer than the time indicated in table for boiling (page 516). Salt just before or after cooking, adding ⅓ to ½ teaspoon salt for each pound. Season and serve as a boiled vegetable.

PANNED VEGETABLES FRENCH STYLE

Prepare vegetables as usual for cooking. Allow 1 tablespoon of forti-fied margarine for each vegetable serving; place in saucepan with tight-fitting cover. Add vegetables and season with salt and pepper. Cover vegetables with wet lettuce leaves (big outer leaves can be used). Cover saucepan and cook over low heat until vegetables are tender. Shake occasionally to prevent sticking. Allow approximately normal cooking time. Discard lettuce leaves and serve vegetables at once. This method is an adaptation of an old French way of preparing vegetables and is especially good with green beans, zucchini, onions, corn, cabbage, spinach, greens and squash.

SCALLOPED VEGETABLES

Use 2 to 3 cups cooked vegetables; arrange layer of hot cooked vege-tables in bottom of greased casserole, cover with layer of Medium White Sauce (page 125), Cream Sauce (page 466), or Cheese Sauce (page 470); repeat until all vegetables and sauce are used. Top with ½ cup buttered crumbs and bake in moderate oven (375° F.) 10 to 15 minutes, or until crumbs are browned. Layers of sliced hard-cooked eggs may be included, if desired. Yield: 4 to 6 portions.

CREAMED VEGETABLES

2 to 3 cups cooked vegetables   1 to 1½ cups Medium White
  (whole, sliced or diced)   Sauce (page 125)

Small vegetables such as peas and lima beans are used whole; others should be sliced or diced. Use one vegetable alone or a combination of two or more. Heat thoroughly in white sauce; serve plain, on toast, in patty cases or in rice or spaghetti ring. Cream Sauce (page 466) or Cheese Sauce (page 470) may be substituted for white sauce; additional seasonings such as chopped parsley or pimiento may be added, if desired. Approximate yield: 4 to 6 portions.

Vegetables Au Gratin—Turn Creamed Vegetables (see above) into greased casserole; sprinkle with ½ cup buttered crumbs and bake in moderately hot oven (375° F.) 10 to 15 minutes, or until crumbs are browned. One-fourth to ½ cup grated cheese may be mixed with crumbs, if desired. Approximate yield: 4 to 6 portions.

VEGETABLE SOUFFLÉ

3 eggs, separated   ¼ to ½ teaspoon minced onion
½ to 1 cup Thick White Sauce   1 cup drained cooked vegetables
  (page 125), seasoned   (minced, mashed, puréed)

Beat yolks until thick and lemon colored, stir into white sauce and add vegetables. Fold in stiffly beaten egg whites and turn into ungreased casserole. Bake in moderate oven (325° to 350° F.) 30 to 45 minutes. Vegetable may be increased to 2 cups, if desired. Serve at once with Cream Sauce (page 466) or Cheese Sauce (page 470) if desired. Yield: 4 to 6 portions.

UPSIDE–DOWN VEGETABLE SQUARES

2 cups sifted all-purpose flour   4 cups cooked vegetables
3 teaspoons baking powder   (carrots, peas, celery,
½ teaspoon salt   lima beans)
¼ cup shortening   ¼ cup vegetable stock
1 egg, well beaten   2 tablespoons butter
1 cup milk   Mushroom Sauce (page 466)

Sift together dry ingredients; cut in shortening. Combine egg and milk; add to dry ingredients, stirring until mixed. Arrange hot seasoned vegetables in bottom of greased shallow baking pan, add vegetable stock, dot with butter and cover with dough. Bake in hot oven (425° F.) 20 to 25 minutes. Turn out on hot serving plate with vegetables on top and serve with mushroom sauce. Yield: 6 portions.

VEGETABLE SHORTCAKES

Serve Creamed Vegetables (page 521) between halves and over tops of 6 buttered hot baking powder biscuits or squares of hot corn bread. Sprinkle with paprika and garnish with parsley. Approximate yield: 4 to 6 portions.

BOILED JERUSALEM ARTICHOKES

Jerusalem artichokes are tubers like the potato, but sweeter and more watery. Scrub with brush, pare as thin as possible, or pare after cooking. Drop in rapidly boiling water to cover and cook, covered, 15 to 25 minutes, or until tender. Drain, season with melted butter, or pickle with vinegar. Jerusalem artichokes may also be eaten raw with salt, like radishes. Allow 1 to 1¼ pounds for 6 portions.

BOILED FRENCH OR GLOBE ARTICHOKES

Wash artichokes; remove discolored outer leaves, cut off stem about ½ inch below base of leaves. Drop into rapidly boiling, salted, acidulated water to cover and cook, covered, 35 to 45 minutes, or until tender (test by inserting fork into center); drain upside down. Cook with a clove of garlic for flavor, if desired. Serve whole or in half with individual dishes of melted butter, mayonnaise, French Dressing (page 618), Hollandaise Sauce (page 473), or Black Butter Sauce (page 472). To eat: pull off a leaf, dip large end in sauce and eat only the white fleshy part, discarding the rest. When all leaves are eaten, cut or scoop out and discard hairy growth or "choke" from the choice bottom or heart; then eat heart with fork. When only ½ artichoke is served, the choke is usually removed before serving. Allow ½ to 1 medium-sized artichoke per portion.

ITALIAN ARTICHOKES

3 small artichokes
3 tablespoons olive oil
salt and pepper
6 eggs, slightly beaten
grated Parmesan cheese

Wash artichokes, trim off prickly ends, removing tough upper portions of petals; cut in halves, remove chokes and cut lengthwise in thin strips; cook in oil until wilted and somewhat softened. Season with salt and pepper, cover and cook slowly about 20 minutes, or until artichokes are tender, adding a little water, if necessary, to keep from browning. Add eggs and cook until eggs are firm, stirring frequently. Sprinkle with cheese and serve at once. Approximate yield: 6 portions.

STUFFED ARTICHOKES

6 medium-sized artichokes	1½ cups chopped cooked chicken
1½ tablespoons chopped green pepper	2 eggs, slightly beaten
	¾ teaspoon celery salt
3 tablespoons butter	salt and pepper
¾ cup dry bread crumbs	1½ cups chicken stock

Cream Sauce (page 466)

Boil artichokes (page 522) until almost tender; spread leaves and remove chokes. Cook green pepper in butter until soft but not browned, add crumbs, chicken and eggs, season with celery salt, salt and pepper and moisten with ½ cup stock. Fill artichokes with chicken mixture, tie so they will not spread; place in casserole and pour remaining stock around them. Cover and bake in moderate oven (375° F.) about 40 minutes. Serve with cream sauce, using part cream and liquid remaining in pan for sauce. Approximate yield: 6 portions.

BOILED ASPARAGUS

Use only tips and tender part of stalks and snap or cut off tough end; the tough white ends may be pared, cut in pieces and creamed or used in soups. Scrub with brush, wash and remove scales, if desired. To cook whole, tie firmly in bunches for serving and stand upright in a deep pan (top part of double boiler, coffee pot, or a special asparagus cooker); add boiling water to cover about 2 inches of ends and cook, covered, 10 to 20 minutes, or until tender. Lift bunches from kettle; drain, untie and serve hot, stalks parallel, with melted butter, or desired vegetable sauce poured over top. To cook tough ends, cut in 1 inch lengths, and cook, covered, in boiling salted water to cover 15 to 20 minutes. Drain, season and serve as desired. Allow 5 to 7 stalks or ¼ pound per portion; 1 pound, cut in pieces, yields 2 cups cooked asparagus.

ASPARAGUS TIPS

Arrange 5 to 7 tips on each of 6 pieces of buttered or plain hot toast and serve in one of the following ways:

Asparagus à la Jean—Serve with sauce of ½ cup melted butter, 2 tablespoons chopped pecans, 1 teaspoon lemon juice, ¼ teaspoon salt and dash of pepper.

Asparagus Hollandaise—Cook asparagus stalks separately from tips; mash stalks, mix with 3 tablespoons melted butter or Hollandaise Sauce (page 473) and spread on toast before arranging tips. Serve with melted butter or Hollandaise sauce.

Asparagus Parisienne—Serve with sauce made as follows: put ½ head chicory or French endive, 1 small onion and 1 small head lettuce through food chopper, using coarse knife. Add to 1 cup thin Velouté Sauce (page 467) and simmer gently 15 to 20 minutes.

Asparagus Vinaigrette—Serve hot cooked asparagus with following sauce: combine 1 teaspoon salt, ½ teaspoon black pepper, ½ teaspoon coarsely crushed black and white peppercorns, ½ teaspoon dry mustard, ¼ teaspoon sugar, ½ teaspoon lemon juice, 2 drops Worcestershire sauce, 1 tablespoon tarragon vinegar, 1 tablespoon cider vinegar, 10 tablespoons soybean oil. Then add very slowly, over ice, ¼ cup heavy cream, 2 tablespoons chopped mixed fresh herbs, 1 tablespoon finely chopped green olives, 1 finely chopped hard-cooked egg and 4 tablespoons finely chopped fresh tomato pulp. Serve this sauce separately surrounded by crushed ice.

ASPARAGUS LOAF

4 eggs, well beaten
½ cup chopped cooked chicken or sweetbreads

1 cup Thick White Sauce (page 125)
asparagus tips

Add eggs and chicken to white sauce; turn into greased baking dish that has been lined with asparagus tips, set in pan of hot water and bake in slow oven (300° F.) 30 to 40 minutes, or until center is firm. Serve with cream sauce. Approximate yield: 6 portions.

ASPARAGUS OMELET

1½ cups cooked asparagus, cut up
¼ cup bread crumbs
3 tablespoons grated Parmesan cheese

1 tablespoon minced parsley
salt and pepper to taste
⅛ teaspoon basil
2 eggs

Combine asparagus with bread crumbs, cheese, parsley, salt, pepper and basil. Beat eggs slightly and add to asparagus mixture. Heat 1 tablespoon olive oil in 8-inch frying pan. Pour in asparagus mixture. Cook slowly until lightly browned on one side. Turn over with a wide spatula and cook until browned. Serve hot or cold. Yield: 2 portions.

FRENCH FRIED ASPARAGUS

1 bunch asparagus   ½ cup grated American cheese
1 cup Thick White Sauce   1 egg, beaten
   (page 125)   1 tablespoon water
              ½ cup dry bread crumbs

Steam asparagus (page 520), cool and roll each stalk in sauce, then in grated cheese and let stand until cold. Dip coated asparagus in mixture of egg and water, roll in crumbs and fry in hot deep fat (380° F.) for 4 to 6 minutes, or until delicately browned. Approximate yield: 4 to 6 portions.

ASPARAGUS WITH WALNUTS

2 cups croutons   3 cups cooked asparagus, cut
2 cups black or English walnuts   in small pieces
6 tablespoons butter or   4 cups Medium White Sauce
   margarine   (page 125)
              ¾ cup grated cheese

Brown croutons and nuts in butter. Place a layer of asparagus, a layer of croutons and nuts and of white sauce in baking dish; repeat. Top with cheese. Brown in hot oven (400° F.) 20 minutes. Approximate yield: 6 to 8 portions.

BOILED SNAP BEANS

Use either green or wax (yellow) beans. Break off both ends, pull off strings, if present, and leave whole; cut or break into 1 inch pieces, or cut in julienne strips. Cook, covered, in small amount of boiling salted water 15 to 30 minutes, or until just tender. Drain and season. Small bits of bacon, salt pork or ham may be cooked with beans, if desired. Allow ¼ pound per portion; one pound, cut in pieces, yields approximately 3 cups cooked beans.

Sautéed Snap Beans—Cut 1½ pounds beans in julienne strips, boil and drain. Sauté in ¼ cup butter 5 minutes, stirring frequently; season to taste with salt and pepper. Approximate yield: 6 portions.

Snap Beans with Garlic—Add 1 small clove garlic to water in which beans are cooked. Season with butter, salt and pepper.

SNAP BEANS WITH BACON

1 pound snap beans, cut in julienne strips	1 tablespoon chopped parsley
1 slice bacon or lean salt pork	1 teaspoon grated onion
1 small clove garlic	½ teaspoon dried savory crumbled
2 tablespoons butter	salt and pepper

Cook beans, covered, in ½ cup boiling water with bacon or pork and garlic. When tender, remove the garlic, chop the pork and add to the drained beans. Melt butter and add remaining ingredients. Pour over hot beans. Approximate yield: 6 portions.

SNAP BEANS AND MUSHROOMS

1 pound snap beans	2 teaspoons minced onion
1 cup canned sliced mushrooms	

Break off ends of beans, pull off strings, if present, and cut or break in 1 inch pieces. Add ½ cup boiling salted water. Add onion. Cover and cook 15 to 20 minutes. Meanwhile sauté mushrooms in a little butter until golden brown. Drain beans, if necessary; add mushrooms. Season to taste with butter, salt and pepper. Yield: 4 portions.

SNAP BEANS WITH TOMATOES

2 medium onions, chopped	2 whole cloves
2 tablespoons butter	1 tablespoon minced parsley
2 cups canned tomatoes	2 teaspoons sugar
1 teaspoon salt	1 pound snap beans, cut in
¼ teaspoon pepper	1½ inch pieces

Sauté onion in butter 5 minutes, or until lightly browned. Add tomatoes, seasonings and sugar and bring to a boil. Add beans and cook 15 to 30 minutes, or until beans are tender. Yield: 6 portions.

DEVILED SNAP BEANS

¼ cup butter or margarine	¼ teaspoon salt
1 teaspoon prepared mustard	⅛ teaspoon pepper
1 teaspoon Worcestershire sauce	dash of cayenne
	4 cups cooked snap beans

Cream butter until soft. Stir in seasonings. Blend with hot beans. Approximate yield: 6 portions.

BOILED LIMA BEANS

Shell beans and wash in cold water. Cook, covered, in small amount of boiling salted water 15 to 30 minutes, or until just tender. Drain and season with salt, pepper and butter or cream, as desired. Allow ½ to ¾ pound beans in shell, or ¼ to ⅓ pound shelled beans per portion.

COOKED DRIED BEANS

These include a number of varieties such as the pea or navy, kidney, Lima (large and baby), yellow-eye, black-eye or cowpea and soy bean. Pick over beans, rejecting bad ones. Wash thoroughly in several waters. New processing makes overnight soaking of beans unnecessary; such beans are labeled "quick-cooking." Follow directions on the package for preparation.

Sometimes it's convenient to soak beans overnight. If not, here's a short-soak method. To 2 cups of dry beans, add 6 cups of water, boil 2 minutes, remove from heat and let soak an hour. Then simmer beans 2 to 3 hours in the same water to conserve minerals and vitamins, and to prevent beans from breaking and becoming mushy.

A pound of beans, usually about 2 cups, will serve 6 to 8 portions, 12 servings in a hearty bean soup.

LIMA BEAN LOAF

2 cups cooked Lima beans	¼ teaspoon pepper
1 cup dry bread crumbs	¼ cup chopped onion
2 tablespoons melted butter	½ cup chopped nut meats
2 tablespoons chopped green pepper	2 eggs, well beaten
	½ cup light cream
½ teaspoon salt	parsley

Combine ingredients, mixing thoroughly. Turn into well-greased loaf pan and bake in moderate oven (350° F.) about 1 hour, basting frequently with meat stock or hot water in which a little butter has been melted. Garnish with parsley. Approximate yield: 6 portions.

DRIED LIMA BEANS WITH TOMATOES

Wash 1 pound Lima beans, soak overnight; simmer until tender; drain. Sauté 1 small onion, chopped, in ¼ cup cooking oil or bacon fat until faintly browned; add ½ teaspoon salt, dash each of sugar and cayenne and ½ small green pepper, cleaned and diced. Add beans, tossing until all are covered with oil. Place in shallow casserole, filling it half full. Top with 3½ cups canned tomatoes, sprinkle lightly with salt and pepper and grated Parmesan cheese. Bake in moderate oven (350° F.) 35 minutes. Yield: 6 to 8 portions.

BARBECUED LIMAS

2 cups dried Lima beans	**1 medium onion, grated**
½ teaspoon salt	**1 tablespoon chili powder**
small piece salt pork	**2 tablespoons molasses**
2 tablespoons prepared mustard	

Wash beans. Soak in water 6 to 8 hours. Add salt, bring to a boil and simmer 45 minutes. Drain beans; reserve stock. Rinse salt pork with warm water and add with beans to bean pot or casserole. Mix bean stock with remaining ingredients and add to beans, mixing well. Add more water if needed to cover beans; bake, covered, in moderate oven (350° F.) 2 hours, removing cover the last ½ hour to brown. Yield: 6 portions.

NEW ENGLAND BAKED BEANS

1 quart pea or navy beans	**¼ cup dark molasses**
½ pound fat salt pork	**½ teaspoon dry mustard**
2 teaspoons salt	**½ teaspoon Worcestershire sauce**
1 tablespoon brown sugar	**boiling water**

Wash, soak and cook beans (Cooked Dried Beans, page 527). Turn beans into bean pot. Pour boiling water over pork, scrape rind until white, score in ½ inch strips and press into top of beans, leaving only rind exposed. Mix salt, brown sugar, molasses, mustard and Worcestershire sauce; add 1 cup boiling water and pour over beans. Add more water to cover beans, if necessary. Cover and bake in slow oven (250° to 300° F.) 6 to 8 hours, adding water as needed to keep beans just covered; uncover during last ½ hour to brown pork and beans. One small onion may be placed in bottom of bean pot. Yield: 8 portions.

Baked Lima Beans—Substitute dried Lima beans for pea beans.

Baked Kidney Beans—Substitute dried kidney beans for pea beans; substitute ½ cup tomato ketchup for water, if desired.

Idaho Baked Beans—Add ½ green or red pepper, finely chopped.

St. Johnsbury Maple Beans—Substitute ½ cup maple syrup or 3 tablespoons maple sugar for brown sugar and molasses.

Lima Beans and Sausage—Arrange parboiled beans and uncooked sausage in alternate layers; substitute 1 can tomato soup for molasses and part of water.

TERRACE BAKED BEANS

2 quarts canned baked beans	¼ cup honey
(8 8-ounce cans)	2 to 4 tablespoons horseradish
1 cup chili sauce	2 teaspoons Worcestershire sauce
1 cup ketchup	8 slices bacon, broiled

Combine beans, chili sauce, ketchup, honey, horseradish, and Worcestershire sauce. Turn into a casserole, heat and garnish with bacon slices. Yield: 12 portions.

PORK AND BEANS HAWAIIAN

1 pound navy beans	½ cup brown sugar
1 pound salt pork, diced	½ teaspoon pepper
2 tablespoons minced onion	1 No. 2½ can drained sliced
2 tablespoons prepared mustard	pineapple
½ cup vinegar	salt

Wash, soak and cook beans (page 527) with pork and onion until almost tender, but not quite done. Mix mustard, vinegar, sugar and pepper with the beans. Arrange in alternate layers with sliced pineapple in a greased casserole. Add salt if necessary. Cover and bake about 3 hours in a slow oven (300° F.). Uncover last 30 minutes to brown. Approximate yield: 6 portions.

RED BEANS

3 cups dried kidney beans	1 tablespoon chopped water cress
2 onions, chopped	or parsley
1 clove garlic, chopped	2 pounds ham, cut in 1-inch
½ bay leaf	cubes
salt	

Wash, soak and simmer beans (page 527) with onions, garlic, bay leaf, water cress or parsley ½ hour. Add ham and continue cooking 2 to 3 hours, or until beans and ham are tender, adding water as necessary to have a rich red gravy with the beans and ham. Add salt to taste, according to saltiness of ham. Approximate yield: 10 portions.

CHILI CON CARNE

1 onion, diced   1 pound ground beef
1 tablespoon fat   2 cups canned red kidney beans
2 cups canned tomatoes   ½ teaspoon chili powder
1 teaspoon salt

Sauté onion in fat until browned; add tomatoes, meat, beans and seasonings; cover and simmer 20 minutes, adding water if mixture seems dry. Approximate yield: 6 portions.

Lima Bean Chili—Substitute canned Lima beans for red kidney beans.

Economy Stew—Sauté 3 tablespoons chopped green pepper with onion; omit chili powder. Turn into greased casserole, sprinkle with ¼ cup each buttered crumbs and grated cheese; bake in hot oven (400° F.) about 10 minutes, or until cheese and crumbs are browned.

LENTIL CURRY

Boil 1 pound red lentils (page 529); force through sieve. Sauté 4 sliced large onions in ½ cup bacon drippings about 5 minutes, or until lightly browned; remove from fat. Mix 4 tablespoons curry powder in 2 tablespoons cold water and add to fat; then add lentils and heat thoroughly. Serve over Boiled Rice (page 507) and top with onions. Approximate yield: 8 portions.

BOILED DRIED LENTILS

Prepare as Boiled Dried Beans (page 527); lentils may be substituted for dried beans or dried peas in almost any recipe.

SAVORY LENTILS

2 cups dried lentils   2 teaspoons salt
1 teaspoon minced onion   ¼ teaspoon pepper
1 teaspoon chopped parsley   1 tablespoon vinegar or lemon
2 tablespoons drippings   juice
2 strips bacon, cut in pieces

Soak washed lentils in boiling water to cover for 1 hour. Add onion, parsley, drippings, salt and pepper. Cover, bring to boil and simmer 1 to 2 hours, or until tender. Add lemon juice. Pour into individual ramekins, adding sufficient water from the lentils to moisten. Top with two pieces of bacon and brown under a broiler. Yield: 6 portions.

BAKED LENTILS

1 pound dried lentils	1½ teaspoons salt
1 medium onion, chopped	⅛ teaspoon pepper
3 tablespoons chopped celery	½ clove garlic
18 small sausages	

Soak lentils and cook in boiling water 1 hour (see above), adding onion, celery, salt and pepper to water; drain. Rub casserole with garlic and grease lightly; turn lentils into casserole, arrange sausages over top and broil at moderate heat until sausages are browned and cooked through, turning them to brown. Serve with brown bread. Yield: 6 portions.

BOILED BLACK–EYED PEAS

Soak 1 pound dried black-eyed peas overnight, or for 1 hour in hot water. Add sufficient water to make 5 cups. Add ¼ pound salt pork or 4 strips of bacon cut in pieces, or some bacon fat, 1 large onion, chopped, 2 teaspoons salt or salt to taste, and ⅛ teaspoon black pepper. Cover and simmer 1½ hours or until well done, adding more water if necessary. Approximate yield: 4 portions.

BOILED DRIED PEAS

Prepare as Boiled Dried Beans (page 527). Dried peas may be substituted in practically all recipes calling for dried beans, although molasses is omitted in baked dried peas.

HOPPING JOHN

1 cup dried peas, soaked	1 cup rice
1 to 2 pounds ham knuckle	½ teaspoon salt
dash of pepper	

Boil dried peas (see above), cooking ham knuckle with peas; when peas are almost tender, remove ham, add rice and seasonings and boil gently about 20 minutes, or until rice is soft and liquid has almost evaporated. Serve on hot platter garnished with ham slices. Approximate yield: 6 portions.

BRAISED BEETS

Pare and shred 1 pound beets into heavy saucepan. Add 3 tablespoons butter; cover tightly and simmer 3 to 5 minutes, stirring several times. Season with salt and pepper and serve hot. Approximate yield: 4 portions.

TEN–MINUTE BEETS

Thinly peel 1 pound fresh beets, then shred them on a coarse grater. Bring ½ cup water and ½ teaspoon salt to a rolling boil and add 1 tablespoon vinegar and the shredded beets. Cover tightly and simmer 10 minutes. Yield: 4 to 6 portions.

BOILED BEETS

Cut off all but about 2 inches of tops of beets; wash thoroughly. If tops are young and tender, they may be washed and cooked separately as greens; tiny beets are often cooked with leaves attached. For young beets, with or without tops, cook, covered, in boiling salted water to cover 30 to 45 minutes, or until tender. For mature beets, use a large amount of water and cook 45 to 90 minutes. When beets are tender, plunge into cold water and rub off skins. Serve small beets whole and slice or dice large beets; reheat and season as desired. Allow ¼ to ⅓ pound topped beets per portion; 1 pound yields about 2 cups diced, cooked beets.

Use 2 bunches or 1½ to 2 pounds beets for 6 portions; cook and serve whole, sliced or diced in one of the following ways:

Vinegar Beets—Combine ⅓ cup each water and vinegar, ½ teaspoon salt, ⅛ teaspoon pepper and 1 teaspoon sugar; pour over 3 cups sliced hot beets and let stand until cold.

Deviled Beets—Heat 3 tablespoons melted butter, 2 tablespoons vinegar, ½ teaspoon salt, ¼ teaspoon each paprika and dry mustard, 1 tablespoon powdered sugar and 1 teaspoon Worcestershire sauce; pour over 3 cups diced, cooked beets and serve hot.

Sliced Beets in Sour Sauce—Use 2 tablespoons each butter and flour, and ¾ cup beet stock, and prepare as for Medium White Sauce (page 125); add ½ teaspoon salt, dash of pepper, 2 tablespoons sugar and ¼ cup vinegar and bring to a boil; pour hot sauce over sliced beets.

Harvard Beets—Use 3 tablespoons butter, 2¼ teaspoons cornstarch, ½ teaspoon salt, 2¼ tablespoons sugar, ¼ cup vinegar and ½ cup beet stock and prepare as for Medium White Sauce (page 125); add 6 to 8 medium-sized beets and heat thoroughly.

Beets in Orange Sauce—Use 1 tablespoon each butter and flour, ⅛ teaspoon salt, dash of paprika, ½ tablespoon brown sugar and ¼ cup water; prepare as for White Sauce (page 125). Add ⅛ teaspoon grated orange rind, ½ cup orange juice and 3 cups sliced beets and heat thoroughly.

RUSSIAN BEETS

2 bunches small young beets	¼ teaspoon salt
1 tablespoon butter	dash of pepper
¼ cup light cream	

Wash and remove stems from beets. Bake in a slow oven (325° F.) 1 hour and 20 minutes, or until tender. Remove skins; chop fine; add butter, salt, pepper and cream. Heat and serve. Yield: 4 portions.

BEETS WITH CLARET SAUCE

2 bunches beets, freshly cooked	dash of nutmeg
2 tablespoons butter	salt and pepper
1 tablespoon flour	¼ cup beet stock
1 teaspoon sugar	¼ cup Claret

Rub skins from beets; cut into julienne strips or, if very small, cut in half. Melt butter, blend in flour and then add sugar and seasonings. Gradually add stock and wine and cook over low heat until thickened. Add beets, cover and cook over very low heat to heat thoroughly, or place in top of double boiler over hot water until ready to serve. Yield: 6 portions.

BEET CUPS

6 medium-sized beets	1 tablespoon chopped onion
1 cup chopped, cooked beet greens	½ teaspoon salt
1 hard-cooked egg, chopped	¼ teaspoon pepper
1 slice bacon, diced	1 tablespoon butter, melted
	parsley

Boil beets (page 532); cut in halves and scoop out centers; pink edges, if desired. Chop centers and mix with greens and egg. Panbroil bacon and add to beet greens with onion, salt, pepper and butter. Heap mixture into beet cups; garnish with parsley. Serve hot. Yield 6 portions.

BOILED BROCCOLI

Soak broccoli in cold water 15 to 30 minutes; drain. Cut off all large leaves; peel woody outer skin of main stem. If stems are large, split into pieces for serving. Cook, covered, in a small amount of boiling salted water, 8 to 20 minutes, or until just tender. Or tie in a bunch, stand upright in bottom of double boiler and cook in a small amount of salted water with top of double boiler inverted for cover. Drain; season with salt, pepper and melted butter. Or serve with Cheese Sauce (page 470), Butter and Lemon Sauce (page 472), Hollandaise Sauce (page 473), or Crumb Sauce (page 472). Allow about ½ pound per portion.

Italian Broccoli—Cook broccoli until almost tender; drain and sauté lightly in hot olive oil until delicately browned. Sprinkle with grated Parmesan cheese.

Broccoli and Chicken Divan—Arrange broccoli in greased casserole, cover with layer of cooked chicken, then with Cream Sauce (page 470) flavored with 2 tablespoons Sherry, and sprinkle with grated Parmesan cheese. Bake in moderate oven (350° F.) 10 to 15 minutes, or until cheese is browned. (Cooked broccoli may be arranged on individual plates, covered with sauce, browned under broiler.)

Broccoli with Béarnaise Sauce—Arrange cooked broccoli on a hot serving dish and pour over Béarnaise Sauce (page 473), or Maître d'Hôtel Sauce (page 472).

ITALIAN SOUFFLÉ

Use recipe for Vegetable Soufflé (page 521), using ¾ cup chopped, cooked broccoli and ¼ cup grated Parmesan cheese.

BROCCOLI WITH SAUTÉED TOMATOES

4 or 5 tomatoes, peeled	cayenne
2 tablespoons hot cooking oil	1 tablespoon tarragon vinegar
chopped fresh marjoram or	1 tablespoon light cream
dried marjoram and fresh	1 teaspoon tomato paste
parsley	2 tablespoons butter
1 bunch broccoli, cooked	½ teaspoon meat extract
2 egg yolks	1 tablespoon chopped fresh herbs
salt	drop of lemon juice

1 clove of garlic, minced

Slice tomatoes thick and cook quickly in hot oil. Sprinkle with marjoram to taste. Arrange on a serving dish, place sprigs of cooked broccoli on top and pour over the following sauce: Beat egg yolks with salt, cayenne and vinegar; add cream and tomato paste. Place in top of double boiler over hot water and beat with a whisk until sauce begins to thicken. Add butter bit by bit. Lastly add meat extract, herbs, lemon juice and garlic; blend. Pour over broccoli and tomatoes and serve. Yield: 4 to 6 portions.

BOILED BRUSSELS SPROUTS

Remove wilted leaves and let stand about 30 minutes, head down, in cold salted water (1 teaspoon to 1 quart); wash well. Cook, covered, in a small amount of boiling salted water 10 to 20 minutes, or until just tender. Drain, toss in seasoned butter and serve as desired. Allow 1 quart (1¼ to 1½ pounds) for 6 portions.

BRUSSELS SPROUTS LYONNAISE

Sauté 1 medium-sized onion, diced, in 3 tablespoons bacon fat; add ¼ cup bouillon and 1 quart Boiled Brussels Sprouts (see above); season to taste with salt and paprika. Simmer, stirring frequently, until bouillon has evaporated; sprinkle with 3 tablespoons chopped parsley and serve very hot. Approximate yield: 6 portions.

BOILED CABBAGE

Remove outer wilted leaves; cut in quarters, or chop or shred as desired. Cook, covered, in small amount of boiling salted water—green quartered, 10 to 15 minutes; green shredded, 3 to 10 minutes; red shredded, 8 to 12 minutes, or until just tender. To preserve color of red cabbage, add a small amount of vinegar or an apple, peeled and quartered. Overcooking develops a strong, undesirable flavor. Drain, season and serve as desired. Allow about 2 pounds cabbage for 6 portions. One pound yields about 3½ cups shredded raw cabbage, or 2½ cups cooked.

Buttered Cabbage—To each cup boiled cabbage, add 1½ tablespoons melted butter, stirring until cabbage is well coated with butter.

Sautéed Cabbage—Panbroil 2 slices bacon, diced, until crisp; add 3 cups boiled cabbage and continue cooking until cabbage is lightly browned. Serve with melted butter and vinegar; garnish with sliced hard-cooked eggs. Approximate yield: 6 portions.

Norwegian Creamed Cabbage—To 3 cups shredded, cooked cabbage, add ½ cup sour cream and ½ teaspoon caraway seeds; season to taste with salt and pepper. Cook over hot water 10 minutes. Approximate yield: 6 portions.

German Cabbage—Reheat 4 cups cooked, shredded cabbage with 2 tablespoons butter, 1 tablespoon chopped onion, 2 tablespoons vinegar and 1 tablespoon sugar. Approximate yield: 6 portions.

Dutch Cabbage—To 1 medium-sized head cabbage, shredded and cooked, add mixture of 2 beaten eggs, 1 tablespoon melted butter, ½ teaspoon salt, dash of pepper and ¼ cup heavy cream. Turn into greased casserole and bake in moderately hot oven (375° F.) about 20 minutes, or until lightly browned. Approximate yield: 6 portions.

New England Cabbage—Panbroil 18 small link sausages until crisp and brown; remove sausages and pour off all but 2 tablespoons fat. Add 3 cups shredded, cooked cabbage and sauté 5 minutes or until lightly browned, stirring constantly. Serve on hot platter; garnish with sausages. Approximate yield: 6 portions.

Red Cabbage and Apple—Shred fine ¼ head red cabbage and grate 1 apple. Place in heavy saucepan, add 3 tablespoons butter, cover tightly and simmer 5 minutes, stirring several times. Season with salt and pepper, a dash of sugar and 1 teaspoon lemon juice. Approximate yield: 4 portions.

BAKED RED CABBAGE

1 small head red cabbage	2 tablespoons sugar
½ cup seedless grapes	¾ teaspoon salt
2 cooking apples, pared and sliced	⅓ cup Claret
1 small onion, chopped	¾ tablespoon butter
	¾ tablespoon flour

Shred and boil cabbage (page 535); drain, reserving 1 cup liquid. Place layer of cabbage in buttered baking dish. Combine grapes, apples, onion, sugar and salt and arrange in alternate layers with cabbage, making top layer cabbage. Add cabbage liquid and Claret and dot with butter. Cover and bake in moderately hot oven (375° F.) 1 hour. Shake flour over top, mix lightly with fork and bake 15 minutes longer. Approximate yield: 6 portions

STUFFED CABBAGE LEAVES

1½ pounds veal	⅓ cup butter
3 sprigs fresh dill	½ cup heavy sour cream
¾ cup rice	½ cup milk
3 tablespoons minced onion	salt and pepper
12 large cabbage leaves	1 tablespoon ketchup

Stew meat, dill and rice in water to cover until meat is tender; reserve broth, cool and grind meat and add to rice and onion. Wilt cabbage leaves by pouring boiling water over them; fill each with veal-rice mixture, fold over and tie securely. Brown cabbage rolls in butter on all sides, place in lightly greased casserole, pour reserved broth over them, cover and bake in moderately slow oven (325° F.) about 1 hour. Combine sour cream, milk, seasonings and ketchup, heat and use as sauce to serve with rolls. Yield: 6 portions.

CABBAGE AND TOMATO CASSEROLE

1 small onion, minced
¼ cup butter
1 cup Tomato Sauce (page 469)
3 cups cooked cabbage

1 cup grated American cheese
1 cup dry bread crumbs
2 tablespoons chopped green
   pepper

Sauté onion in 2 tablespoons butter 5 minutes; add to tomato sauce. Arrange alternate layers of cabbage and sauce in greased casserole, sprinkling each layer of cabbage with cheese, crumbs and green pepper. Top with crumbs, dot with remaining butter and bake in hot oven (400° F.) about 25 minutes, or until thoroughly heated and slightly browned. Approximate yield: 6 portions.

HOT CABBAGE SLAW

1 tablespoon butter
½ cup water
1 medium young cabbage,
   diced
¼ teaspoon salt

dash of pepper
2 egg yolks
¾ cup sugar
½ cup vinegar
1 cup light cream

Heat butter to a froth, then add water, cabbage, salt and pepper. Cook until cabbage is tender but not soft, about 10 minutes, stirring occasionally. Combine egg yolks, sugar, vinegar and cream just before serving and pour over the cabbage. Heat to boiling but do not boil. Serve at once. Approximate yield: 6 portions.

SAUERKRAUT

Drain sauerkraut, cover with boiling water and cook, uncovered, ½ hour; drain and season with salt, pepper and butter. Reheat canned sauerkraut and season to taste. Use 4 cups sauerkraut for 6 portions.

BOILED CARROTS

Cut off tops, scrape, wash and cut in strips or slices, or dice; if young carrots are to be served whole, skins may be left on and scraped off after cooking. Cook, covered, in small amount of boiling salted water until just tender: for young carrots—whole, 18 to 20 minutes; strips, slices or diced, 10 to 20 minutes; for mature carrots—whole, 20 to 30 minutes; sliced, 15 to 20 minutes. Drain, season and serve as desired. Allow ½ pound carrots per portion. One pound topped carrots yields about 2½ cups raw, or 2 cups cooked, diced carrots.

Riced Carrots—Put 6 medium cooked carrots through potato ricer, add 2 tablespoons butter and season to taste with salt and pepper. Approximate yield: 6 portions.

Glazed Carrots—Cook ½ cup brown sugar, ¼ cup butter and ¼ cup hot water together 5 minutes. Brush syrup over 24 small cooked whole carrots and bake in moderate oven (375° F.) about 20 minutes, or until browned, basting occasionally with remaining syrup. Approximate yield: 6 portions.

Carrots with Peanut Butter—Add 1 tablespoon peanut butter to 1 cup Medium White Sauce (page 125); combine with 2 cups cooked, diced carrots. Approximate yield: 6 portions.

Carrots à la Bourguignonne—Sauté 2 diced onions in 2 tablespoons butter 5 minutes. Roll 12 carrots, sliced lengthwise, in ¼ cup flour; add to onions and cook until flour is browned. Add 1 cup bouillon, season with salt and pepper to taste and simmer 30 minutes. Approximate yield: 6 portions.

CARROTS IN CHIVE SAUCE

8 medium carrots, scraped	1 bay leaf
1 cup light beef or chicken	1 slice lemon
stock	½ cup water
½ teaspoon salt	3 teaspoons chopped chives
dash of pepper	1 egg yolk, beaten

3 tablespoons light cream

Slice carrots ¼ inch thick. Bring to boil in beef or chicken stock. Add salt, pepper, bay leaf, lemon and cook until carrots are tender. Add ½ cup water and chives. Remove from heat and add egg yolk mixed with cream. Return to heat and cook until sauce begins to thicken, but do not boil. Yield: 4 portions.

CARROT-POTATO PANCAKES

2 large carrots, grated	¼ cup flour
3 medium-sized potatoes, grated	3 eggs, slightly beaten
1 onion, minced	1½ teaspoons salt
½ cup milk	¼ teaspoon pepper

sour cream

Combine carrots, potatoes and onion. Beat in milk, flour, eggs, salt and pepper. Drop by tablespoonfuls onto hot greased griddle. Brown on both sides. Serve with sour cream. Yield: 12 pancakes.

BOILED CAULIFLOWER

Remove leaves and stalk; separate into flowerets, if desired. Soak about 20 minutes, head down, in cold salted water (1 teaspoon to 1 quart). Cook, covered, in small amount of boiling salted water 20 to 30 minutes whole, 8 to 15 minutes for flowerets, or until just tender; drain. Serve with melted butter, Cheese Sauce (page 470), Cream Sauce (page 466) or Hollandaise Sauce (page 472). Allow 2 small or 1 large head for 6 portions. A 2-pound head yields 3 cups cooked cauliflower.

Cauliflower stems, which are often discarded, may be peeled, diced and cooked until tender. Serve as Creamed Vegetables (page 521) or Vegetables au Gratin (page 521). Use 3 cups diced cauliflower and 1½ cups sauce for 6 portions.

Cauliflower Polonaise—Spread Crumb Sauce (page 472) over top of cauliflower; place in hot oven (425° F.) long enough to brown crumbs.

Curried Cauliflower—To 1 cup Brown Sauce (page 467) add 1 small onion sautéed in fat for 5 minutes, ½ teaspoon curry powder and few drops kitchen bouquet. Serve over cauliflower.

Cauliflower à la Creole—Add 1 teaspoon prepared mustard and 1 tablespoon sautéed minced onion to Tomato Sauce (page 469). Heat 1 medium head cooked cauliflower, separated into flowerets, in sauce 5 minutes. Approximate yield: 6 portions.

Cauliflower with Mustard Sauce—Add 2 tablespoons piccalilli to Mustard Sauce (page 465). Serve over whole cooked cauliflower.

French Fried Cauliflower—Dip cauliflower flowerets into Cover Batter (page 787) and fry in hot deep fat (380° F.) 3 to 4 minutes, or until delicately browned.

CAULIFLOWER FRITTERS

1 cup sifted all-purpose flour	¾ cup chopped, cooked
1½ teaspoons baking powder	cauliflower
½ teaspoon salt	1 egg, beaten
dash of mace	½ cup milk
2 tablespoons butter, melted	

Mix and sift dry ingredients; add cauliflower. Combine egg, milk and melted butter; add to flour mixture and mix until smooth. Drop by spoonfuls into hot deep fat (350° to 365° F.) and fry 3 to 5 minutes, or until golden brown; drain. Approximate yield: 6 portions.

CAULIFLOWER BROWNED WITH CHEESE

1 large head cooked cauliflower   ¼ teaspoon paprika
¼ cup Parmesan cheese, grated   ½ dozen browned almonds

Sprinkle cauliflower with cheese, then with paprika. Place under broiler grill until lightly browned, 5 to 8 minutes. When ready to serve, stick quarters of browned almonds into the flower. Approximate yield: 6 portions.

CAULIFLOWER MILANESE

1 medium-sized head   ⅛ teaspoon pepper
   cauliflower   2 tablespoons tomato purée
salt   2 tablespoons finely chopped,
1½ cups cauliflower stock   cooked salt pork
1 bouillon cube   1 cup grated Swiss cheese
3 tablespoons butter   salad oil
3 tablespoons flour   3 tablespoons finely chopped
½ cup cream   mushrooms

Remove leaves and stalk of cauliflower; separate into flowerets. Soak 20 minutes in cold salted water; drain. Cook covered in a small amount of boiling salted water 7 minutes. Drain and save 1½ cups cauliflower stock; dissolve bouillon cube in it. Melt butter, add flour; gradually stir in cream, cauliflower stock and cook until thickened. Then add pepper, tomato purée, salt pork and ¾ cup cheese. Grease a deep baking dish generously with salad oil; place flowerets in dish; add sauce and sprinkle with remaining cheese. Bake in moderate oven (375° F.) 25 to 30 minutes, until lightly browned. Yield: 6 portions.

CAULIFLOWER AND MUSHROOMS

2 small heads cauliflower   3 mushrooms, sliced
1 tablespoon butter   3 teaspoons chopped fresh mint
2 tablespoons flour   1 egg yolk, beaten
1¼ cups cauliflower stock   2 tablespoons light cream
    toast strips

Divide cauliflower into flowerets and boil until tender (page 539). Drain and reserve stock. Melt butter and stir in flour off the heat. Gradually add stock, stirring constantly until smooth and thickened. Add cauliflower and mushrooms and simmer until mushrooms are tender. Add mint and egg yolk mixed with cream, stirring until heated thoroughly. Serve over toast strips. Yield: 6 portions.

STUFFED CAULIFLOWER

1 large head cauliflower   6 mushrooms, chopped
1 teaspoon capers   1½ cups Cream Sauce (page 466)
½ cup soft bread crumbs   ½ cup grated American cheese

Boil whole cauliflower (page 539) until almost tender; place in baking
dish in which it is to be served, cutting thin slice off top, if necessary,
to keep it level; remove center stalk and small portion of stems. Stuff
with mixture of capers, bread crumbs and mushrooms moistened with
a little cream sauce. Pour remaining sauce over all, sprinkle thickly
with cheese and bake in moderate oven (350° F.) about 20 minutes,
or until browned. Approximate yield: 6 portions.

BOILED CELERIAC

Celeriac, celery root or knob celery, is a variety of celery with a large
turnip-like root. It is often served raw, sliced and seasoned with salt
and vinegar as a relish. To cook, cut away leaves and root fibers, pare
and slice or dice. Cook as celery 15 to 20 minutes, or until just tender;
drain. Serve with seasonings and melted butter, with Hollandaise
Sauce (page 473), or as Creamed Vegetables (page 521). Allow 3 to 4
roots for 6 portions.

ALSATIAN CELERY ROOT

1 celery root, pared and sliced   ¼ cup vinegar
   lengthwise in thin strips   ½ teaspoon salt
¾ cup water   ⅛ teaspoon pepper

Put celery root with remaining ingredients in a covered saucepan and
cook until tender. Cool, drain and serve cold as a relish. Approximate yield: 6 portions.

BOILED CELERY

Cut off roots and leaves, separate stalks and scrub thoroughly with
brush; scrape outer stalks to remove coarse fibers; cut in pieces of desired size, usually from 1 to 4 inches, splitting wider stalks. Cook,
covered, in a small amount of boiling salted water 15 to 20 minutes, or
until tender. Serve with melted butter, adding a little chopped parsley
and pimiento, if desired, to improve the color, or with Cream Sauce
(page 466). Allow ½ small bunch per portion; a 1½ pound bunch
yields about 3 cups raw, or 2 cups cooked celery.

False Braised Celery—Use 3 bunches celery; cut stalks in halves lengthwise. To 1 cup Velouté Sauce (page 467), add 1 tablespoon brandy and serve over boiled celery. Yield: 6 portions.

BRAISED CELERY

Cut celery stalks in 3- to 4-inch lengths; prepare 36 to 40 lengths. Sauté in 3 tablespoons butter in heavy frying pan until delicately browned and somewhat tender, stirring occasionally. Add ¾ cup meat stock or ¾ cup water and 1 bouillon cube and continue cooking until celery is tender and stock reduced to about ¼ cup. Approximate yield: 6 portions.

FRENCH FRIED CELERY

Cut celery stalks in 3 inch lengths, allowing 4 lengths per portion; parboil and drain. Marinate 5 minutes in vinegar and salt (¼ teaspoon salt to ½ cup vinegar); dry thoroughly. Dip in Cover Batter (page 787) and fry in hot deep fat (380° F.) 3 to 5 minutes, or until golden brown. Serve with Tomato Sauce (page 469) with veal or fish.

CELERY FARCI

celery stalks	½ cup mayonnaise
¼ pound Roquefort cheese	juice of 1 lemon
½ pound cream cheese	1 teaspoon Worcestershire sauce
	paprika

Use only the short, tender, white stalks of the celery. Break stalks apart. Wash. Leave tips of leaves on stalks. Curl in ice water. Dry. Blend the cheeses and mayonnaise with a silver fork. Add lemon juice and Worcestershire sauce. Fill celery with cheese mixture; garnish with paprika and chill thoroughly. Approximate yield: 2 cups.

CELERY AU DIABLE

1 cup mashed avocado	½ teaspoon Tabasco sauce
2 tablespoons horseradish, drained	salt to taste
	celery stalks

Combine avocado, horseradish and Tabasco sauce. Season to taste. Fill celery stalks. Chill thoroughly. Approximate yield: 6 portions.

BOILED CHAYOTE

Chayotes are a type of squash grown chiefly in Mexico and South America. They are pear-shaped, chalky white to pale green in color with white, firm, non-fibrous flesh and one large edible seed. Slice crosswise through seed in ¾ inch slices; pare before or after cooking. Cook, covered, in small amount of boiling salted water about 20 minutes, or until just tender; drain. Serve with melted butter, Cream Sauce (page 466) or Tomato Sauce (page 469). Allow 1 chayote weighing 1 pound for 4 to 6 portions.

FRIED CHAYOTE

Dip slices of boiled chayote (see above) in beaten egg and crumbs; sauté until delicately browned. For fritters, dip pieces in Cover Batter (page 787) and fry in hot deep fat (370° F.) 3 to 5 minutes, or until delicately browned. Drain on unglazed paper and serve hot with Savory Cream Sauce (page 466).

BAKED CHAYOTE

Arrange sliced, cooked chayote (see above) in greased casserole, cover with 1 cup Medium White Sauce (page 125) seasoned with dash of nutmeg; sprinkle with ¼ cup soft bread crumbs mixed with ¼ cup grated American cheese. Bake in hot oven (400° F.) 10 minutes. Approximate yield: 6 portions.

CHESTNUTS

Shell and Blanch Chestnuts—Prick or slit well, place nuts in pan, mix with oil, using about 1 teaspoon for each cup of nuts, and bake in very hot oven (450° F.) about 20 minutes. When cool enough to handle, remove shells and skins with sharp knife. Or cut slits in each nut, put in heavy frying pan, mix with oil to just coat shells and shake over heat about 10 minutes. Or cut slits in each shell and boil in water to cover 20 minutes; peel off shells and skins.

Boiled Chestnuts—Cover blanched nuts with boiling salted water and simmer, covered, 8 to 20 minutes, or until just tender; drain. Mash or rice and season with salt, pepper and butter, or serve with White Sauce (page 125), or use in Stuffings (page 487). Allow 1½ to 2 pounds chestnuts for 6 portions.

STEWED CORN

Cut corn from cob with sharp knife. Add small amount of milk or water, cover and simmer 5 or 6 minutes, or until corn is just tender. Season to taste with salt, pepper and butter. Allow about ⅓ to ½ cup cut corn per portion.

BOILED CORN ON THE COB

Remove husks, cut off undeveloped tip and strip off silk. Cook, covered, in water to cover 5 to 10 minutes, or until just tender. Do not salt water, because salt tends to make corn tough; for mature corn, add ½ teaspoon sugar per quart water. Lift corn from water with fork or kitchen tongs, place on platter covered with napkin and draw corners of napkin over corn; or cut corn from cob before serving. Serve with salt, pepper and butter. Allow 1 to 2 ears per portion. Four medium-sized ears yield 1 cup corn, cut from cob.

SAUTÉED SWEET CORN

Sauté 2½ cups cut corn in 2 tablespoons fat about 5 or 6 minutes, or until delicately browned, stirring constantly. Season to taste with salt and pepper, add ¼ cup light cream, heat thoroughly and serve at once. Approximate yield: 6 portions.

ROAST CORN

Place ears of corn with the husk on in a hot oven (400° F.) and bake 15 minutes, or until corn is tender. Remove husks and serve corn with seasoned butter.

MEXICAN CORN SAUTÉ

1 No. 2 can corn	1 tablespoon chopped green
2 tablespoons butter	pepper
1 tablespoon chopped pimiento	½ teaspoon salt
1 teaspoon chili powder	

Heat corn in butter, add remaining ingredients and simmer 10 to 15 minutes, stirring frequently. Serve hot. Yield: 6 portions.

BARBECUE CORN

Husk 6 ears corn; wrap each ear with 1 slice lean bacon, securing bacon with toothpicks. Broil very slowly, turning ears frequently until bacon is crisp. This is especially good done on sticks over a camp fire. Approximate yield: 6 portions.

CORN PUFFS

1 cup corn (leftover)	pinch of salt
1 egg, separated	2 tablespoons margarine, melted

Combine corn and beaten egg yolk. Fold in stiffly beaten egg white and salt. Drop by spoonfuls onto hot greased griddle. Lightly brown on both sides. Approximate yield: 12 puffs.

SQUAW CORN

3 slices bacon, diced
1 No. 2 can corn
½ teaspoon salt

dash of pepper
3 eggs, slightly beaten
6 buttered toast rounds

Panbroil bacon until crisp, add corn and heat thoroughly. Add seasonings to eggs and pour over corn. Cook slowly, stirring occasionally until eggs are cooked. Serve on toast. Yield: 6 portions.

BAKED CORN WITH GREEN PEPPERS

2 cups canned corn
¾ cup soft bread crumbs
2 tablespoons butter, melted
1 egg

⅓ cup minced green pepper
1 teaspoon Worcestershire sauce
½ teaspoon salt
⅛ teaspoon pepper

Mix together corn, bread crumbs, butter, egg, green pepper, Worcestershire sauce, salt and pepper; turn into greased casserole; bake in moderate oven (350° F.) 20 minutes. Approximate yield: 6 portions.

SUCCOTASH

Combine 1½ cups each cut corn and Lima beans, freshly cooked or canned. Reheat with 2 tablespoons butter, salt, pepper and ½ cup top milk or light cream. Approximate yield: 6 portions.

SCALLOPED CORN

¼ cup yellow cornmeal
1½ teaspoons salt
3 tablespoons brown sugar
3 tablespoons butter

¾ cup milk, scalded
1 egg, well beaten
4 cups fresh or canned corn
¼ cup minced pimiento
12 slices broiled bacon

Combine cornmeal, salt and brown sugar. Add butter to milk and add slowly to cornmeal, mixing well; add egg, corn and pimiento; turn into greased casserole and bake in slow oven (325° F.) about 1 hour, or until browned. Stir frequently during first 20 minutes of baking to prevent meal from settling. Serve hot with bacon. Approximate yield: 6 portions.

SUCCOTASH PIQUANT

5 shallots or scallions, finely sliced
3 tablespoons butter
2 tablespoons flour
¾ cup Lima bean stock
1½ cups cooked Lima beans

1½ cups fresh or canned corn
¾ teaspoon salt
dash of pepper
1 tablespoon finely chopped parsley

Sauté shallots in butter until yellow, stir in flour, add bean stock gradually and cook 2 minutes, stirring frequently. Add Lima beans, corn, salt and pepper and simmer about 10 minutes. Add parsley and serve. Approximate yield: 6 portions.

CORN PUDDING

2 cups milk or light cream
2 cups canned corn
2 tablespoons melted butter
3 eggs, well beaten

1 tablespoon sugar
1 teaspoon salt
¼ teaspoon pepper

Add milk, corn, butter, sugar and seasonings to eggs. Turn into greased casserole and bake in moderate oven (350° F.) about 45 minutes, or until pudding is firm. One-fourth cup chopped green pepper or pimiento, ½ cup cheese, or ½ cup minced ham or chopped mushrooms may be added for variety, if desired. Yield: 6 portions.

CORN AND SAUSAGE FRITTERS

1 cup sifted all-purpose flour
1 teaspoon baking powder
1 teaspoon salt
⅛ teaspoon pepper

⅛ teaspoon paprika
2 cups sausage meat
2 cups canned corn, drained
2 eggs, separated

Sift together dry ingredients; combine with sausage meat and corn, add beaten egg yolks and mix well. Beat egg whites until stiff, then fold into mixture. Drop by spoonfuls into hot fat (350°–365° F.) and fry 2 to 5 minutes, or until golden brown on all sides; drain on absorbent paper. Serve hot with Pimiento-Parsley Sauce (page 465); ground cooked frankfurters or leftover meat may be used instead of sausage meat. Approximate yield: 6 portions.

CORN FRITTERS

1¾ cups sifted all-purpose flour　1 cup drained canned corn, or
2 teaspoons baking powder　　　　grated fresh corn
¾ teaspoon salt　　　　　　　　　1 egg, beaten
¾ cup milk　　　　　　　　　　　1 tablespoon melted fat

Sift together dry ingredients. Mix milk, corn, egg and fat; add to dry ingredients, mixing well. Fry in hot deep fat (350°–365° F.) 2 to 5 minutes, or until golden brown; drain on absorbent paper. Or fry spoonfuls in a small amount of fat. Serve hot with syrup or tart jelly. Approximate yield: 8 fritters.

BOILED FRENCH ENDIVE OR CHICORY

Chicory or the French or Belgian endive consists of blanched broad leaves, packed close together to form solid, elongated heads. Wash thoroughly, wind cord around each head, drop into a small amount of boiling salted water and cook, covered, 10 to 20 minutes, or until just tender. Drain in sieve for ½ hour, or until thoroughly drained. Untie and sauté slowly in butter 10 minutes, turning several times. Season with salt and pepper. Allow 1½ pounds chicory and 3 to 4 tablespoons butter for 6 portions.

BOILED CUCUMBERS

Pare cucumbers and cut into quarters lengthwise or into thick slices. Cook, covered, in small amount of salted water 5 to 15 minutes; cucumbers are stewed rather than boiled. Chicken or veal stock may be substituted for water, if desired. Drain, arrange on slices of hot buttered toast and cover with sauce made from butter, flour and cucumber stock, following directions for Foundation White Sauce (page 125). Allow ½ medium-sized or ⅓ large cucumber per portion; a medium-sized cucumber yields about 1½ cups sliced cucumber.

Stewed Cucumbers, 1839 Style—Cut 6 small cucumbers into thick slices, dredge with flour and sauté in 2 tablespoons butter until delicately browned. Add 1 cup rich stock or thin gravy and season to taste with salt and pepper; add 1 tablespoon sugar and 1 tablespoon ketchup. Cover and simmer gently 10 to 20 minutes.

Cucumber Sauté—Cook cucumbers, cut in quarters, about 5 minutes. Drain, roll in flour and sauté in butter 10 to 15 minutes, or until cucumbers are tender. Arrange on slices of toast and cover with Tomato Sauce (page 469).

Creamed Cucumbers—To 1 cup Velouté Sauce (page 467) add a few grains chopped raw ginger root and 2 tablespoons finely chopped cooked ham; combine with 2 cups sliced or 12 quarters of cooked cucumbers.

BAKED CUCUMBERS

12 small cucumbers

2 tablespoons butter

2 tablespoons flour

¾ teaspoon salt

1 cup milk

¼ cup grated Parmesan cheese

¼ cup dry bread crumbs

¾ teaspoon paprika

Pare cucumbers and steam until tender. Place in buttered casserole. Melt butter, blend in flour and salt and gradually add milk, stirring until thick and smooth. Turn over cucumbers. Mix cheese, crumbs and paprika and sprinkle over top of dish. Bake in moderate oven (350° F.) 25 to 30 minutes, or until nicely browned. Approximate yield: 6 portions.

LOBSTER IN CUCUMBER BOAT

1 tablespoon minced onion

2 tablespoons drippings

1 cup cooked rice

3 tablespoons tomato juice

½ pound lobster meat, finely diced

1 tablespoon tomato ketchup

½ teaspoon Worcestershire sauce

salt, pepper, celery salt

3 cucumbers, cut lengthwise, partially hollowed out

2 tablespoons butter

2 tablespoons flour

1½ cups broth

1 hard-cooked egg, chopped

1 tablespoon capers

Sauté onion in drippings until tender, add rice and cook until fat is absorbed. Stir in tomato juice, lobster meat, tomato ketchup, Worcestershire sauce, salt, pepper and celery salt. Turn into cucumber cavities and place in a well-greased baking dish. Melt butter and blend in flour; gradually add broth, stirring constantly until mixture thickens. Pour around cucumber boats. Bake in moderate oven (350° F.) 25 to 30 minutes, or until cucumbers are tender. Add hard-cooked egg and capers to sauce before serving. Yield: 6 portions.

DASHEEN

Dasheens are white-fleshed vegetables with brown fibrous coats and are grown chiefly in Trinidad. They may be prepared in almost any of the methods given for potatoes (page 562); rice before mashing. In general, they cook in a shorter time than the potato—15 to 30 minutes for boiled dasheen. Cooked dasheens are creamy to light violet in color and have a mealy texture and nut-like flavor. Allow about ¼ pound per portion.

STEWED EGGPLANT

Pare eggplant; cut in slices or cubes. Cook, covered, in small amount of salted water 10 to 20 minutes, or until just tender; drain and reheat in Tomato Sauce (page 469). Allow ⅓ small eggplant per portion.

SAUTÉED EGGPLANT

Pare, cut in ¼ inch slices, sprinkle with salt and pepper, dredge with flour and sauté in hot fat about 15 minutes, or until crisp and delicately browned, turning occasionally. One medium-sized eggplant yields 10 to 12 slices.

EGGPLANT AND BACON

Stew ½ inch slices of eggplant 5 minutes; drain, place in greased baking dish, sprinkle with salt and pepper and dot with butter. Cover each slice with thick slice of fresh tomato, season again and sprinkle with bread crumbs. Lay a strip of bacon across each tomato slice and bake in moderate oven (350° F.) 20 minutes, or until bacon is crisp.

EGGPLANT STUFFED WITH CHICKEN LIVERS

2 eggplants, split lengthwise
1 teaspoon salt
4 tablespoons oil
4 chicken livers, chopped
2 tablespoons butter
3 large onions, finely chopped
1 cup mushrooms, chopped
1 tablespoon tomato paste

1 tablespoon flour
3 tomatoes, skinned and chopped
½ teaspoon salt
dash of pepper
2 tablespoons chopped mixed
    herbs
dry bread crumbs
grated cheese

Sprinkle eggplant halves with salt and let stand in water 30 minutes. Drain; simmer, covered, in 3 tablespoons oil until tender. Scoop out center and chop fine. Add chicken livers that have been browned in butter. Add onions, mushrooms and remaining oil to butter and cook about 5 minutes, or until tender. Add tomato paste mixed with flour, tomatoes, salt, pepper, herbs, chicken livers and eggplant. Thoroughly heat and fill eggplant shells. Sprinkle with bread crumbs and grated cheese. Place under broiler until crumbs are brown. Yield: 4 portions.

SAUTÉED EGGPLANT

1 large eggplant, peeled
oil

salt and pepper to taste
2 tablespoons chopped parsley

¼ cup grated Parmesan cheese

Cut eggplant into ½-inch slices crosswise. Cover with hot water; let stand 5 minutes. Drain. Sauté in hot oil until soft and light brown. Drain on absorbent paper. Sprinkle with seasonings, parsley and cheese. Yield: 4 portions.

EGGPLANT MEAT PIE

¾ pound lean shoulder of lamb,
  coarsely ground
1½ cups diced onions
¼ cup fat

1 teaspoon salt
⅛ teaspoon allspice
1 eggplant
1 8-ounce can tomato sauce

1 tablespoon grated Parmesan Cheese

Sauté lamb and onions in fat until onions are tender. Then add salt and allspice. Cut eggplant in ¼-inch slices crosswise. Arrange half the slices in greased shallow baking pan (7 x 11 x 2 inches). Place a spoonful of meat mixture on top of each slice and top each with an eggplant slice. Sprinkle with salt. Cover with tomato sauce; top with Parmesan cheese. Bake in moderate oven (350° F.), basting occasionally with the sauce, 1 hour, or until eggplant is tender. Approximate yield: 6 portions.

STUFFED EGGPLANT

1 large eggplant
¼ pound cooked ham, diced
1 cup dry bread crumbs

¼ cup chopped onion
2 tablespoons butter
1 tablespoon chopped celery

salt and pepper

Cut eggplant in half lengthwise and parboil 15 minutes. Scoop out pulp to within ½ inch of skin; chop pulp fine, add ham, ¾ cup bread crumbs, onion, 1 tablespoon butter and celery; season to taste with salt and pepper. Fill shell with the mixture, sprinkle top thickly with remaining crumbs, seasoned and browned in remaining butter. Bake in hot oven (400° F.) 15 minutes. Yield: 4 to 6 portions.

Nut-stuffed Eggplant—For stuffing, mash removed pulp and combine with 2 cups soft bread crumbs, ½ cup chopped nut meats, ⅛ teaspoon pepper, 1 tablespoon each finely chopped parsley and onion, ¼ teaspoon marjoram and 1 beaten egg. Bake in moderate oven (375° F.) about 30 minutes, basting occasionally with mixture of ¼ cup water and 2 tablespoons melted butter. Yield: 4 to 6 portions.

Shrimp-stuffed Eggplant—For stuffing, chop removed pulp and combine with 1 cup chopped, cooked shrimp, 1 Bermuda onion, chopped and sautéed in 2 tablespoons butter, 1 tablespoon chopped parsley, ½ cup coarse cracker crumbs and 1 egg yolk; season to taste with salt and pepper. Bake in moderate oven (375° F.) 20 to 30 minutes.

FRENCH FRIED EGGPLANT

1 large eggplant	1 egg
salt and pepper	2 tablespoons milk or water
¼ cup flour	¼ cup dry bread crumbs

Pare eggplant and cut in ¼ inch slices crosswise. Sprinkle with salt and pepper, dredge with flour, then dip in egg which has been combined with milk or water. Roll in crumbs until completely covered, then fry in hot fat (380° F.) 2 to 4 minutes, or until a golden brown on both sides. Drain and season. Yield: 6 portions.

BOILED FENNEL

The young leaves of the garden variety of fennel are used generally mixed with salad greens and for garnishing. To cook as a vegetable, wash thoroughly, tie leaves in bunches and cook, covered, in small amount of boiling salted water 10 to 15 minutes, or until just tender. Drain, untie and place in hot serving dish; sprinkle with salt and pepper and pour melted butter over leaves. Add a little lemon juice to butter if vegetable is too sweet.

The Italian or Florence fennel is much like unbleached celery. Wash, scrape and cut bulb and stalk in 1 inch slices. Cook, covered, in small amount of boiling salted water 15 to 20 minutes, or until just tender. Season as above. Allow 1 medium-sized fennel for 1 portion.

BOILED GREENS

The term "greens" includes a number of plant leaves used as food. Those used most generally are the more delicate Swiss chard, spinach and lettuce, cooking directions for which are given under their respective headings, and the stronger flavored beet tops, chicory or curly endive, dandelion, escarole or scarola, kale, mustard and turnip greens.

To cook greens, cut off roots, discard imperfect leaves and wash thoroughly in 5 or 6 waters to remove dirt and insects, lifting greens from water each time. Cook, covered, in small amount of boiling salted water until just tender: beet greens, 5 to 15 minutes; dandelion greens and kale, 10 to 20 minutes; curly endive, escarole or scarola, 15 to 20 minutes; mustard greens, 15 to 20 minutes; turnip greens, 15 to 25 minutes. If greens are very young and tender, cook as spinach (page 568). Drain, chop, if necessary, and add desired seasonings, usually salt, pepper and butter and often vinegar, lemon juice or a little cream. Small pieces of bacon or salt pork may be cooked and served with greens. Greens may be prepared as Creamed or Scalloped Vegetables (page 520). Allow ¼ to ⅓ pound greens per portion.

FIDDLEHEAD GREENS

Fiddlehead greens are the tops of ferns known as fiddlehead. They are picked before they begin to uncurl.

Wash greens well and soak in cold water with a little salt 15 or 20 minutes. Drain. Cook, covered, in a small amount of boiling water 15 to 20 minutes, or until tender. Drain, season with salt, pepper and butter and serve. One quart serves six. They taste something like asparagus but have a more solid texture. Allow 1 pound for 3 portions.

BAKED DANDELION GREENS

2 pounds dandelion greens	1 cup milk
6 tablespoons flour	½ teaspoon salt
5 tablespoons melted fat	⅛ teaspoon pepper
(preferably bacon fat)	4 tablespoons grated cheese
¾ cup dry bread crumbs	

Wash and chop the greens. Arrange in layers in greased baking dish, sprinkling flour between layers. Mix fat, milk, salt and pepper and pour over greens. Combine grated cheese and bread crumbs and sprinkle over top. Bake in moderate oven (350° F.) 30 minutes or until tender. Yield: 6 portions.

BRAISED DANDELION GREENS

1 clove garlic, finely diced	1 teaspoon salt
¼ cup bacon fat	pinch of pepper
3 quarts dandelion greens	¼ cup vinegar

Sauté garlic in bacon fat until lightly browned. Chop and add dandelion greens, salt, pepper and vinegar. Cover and cook over low heat, stirring occasionally, until greens are wilted. Top with bread crumbs browned in butter. Approximate yield: 4 portions.

BEET GREEN RING

3 strips bacon, chopped
3 cups finely chopped, cooked
  beet tops
2 cups thick White Sauce
  (page 125)

3 teaspoons grated onion
1 teaspoon Worcestershire sauce
¼ teaspoon ginger
¼ teaspoon nutmeg
1 teaspon salt

2 eggs, separated

Fry bacon and add, with fat, to greens. Add white sauce, onion, Worcestershire sauce and seasonings, and mix thoroughly. Add beaten egg yolks, fold in beaten whites. Pour in greased ring mold and bake in a moderate oven (350° F.) about 30 minutes. Unmold onto platter and fill center with creamed mushrooms. Yield: 6 portions.

BEET GREENS WITH SOUR CREAM

4 cups chopped, cooked beet
  greens
2 teaspoons minced onion
⅓ cup sour cream

2½ tablespoons horseradish,
  drained
¾ teaspoon salt
⅛ teaspoon pepper

Combine all ingredients, heat thoroughly. Yield: 6 portions.

SCALLOPED KALE

Combine 1½ pounds kale, cooked and chopped (Greens, page 551), with chopped hard-cooked egg; add stock or gravy to moisten. Arrange alternate layers of the kale and grated cheese in 6 greased ramekins, sprinkle with buttered crumbs and bake in hot oven (400° F.) 10 to 15 minutes. Approximate yield: 6 portions.

CREAMED KALE

2 pounds kale, cooked
2 tablespoons bacon fat
3 tablespoons butter or
  margarine
3 tablespoons flour
1 cup milk

1 cup grated American cheese
1 teaspoon salt
pinch of pepper
1 tablespoon crumbled cooked
  bacon

Chop kale medium fine. Mix with bacon fat. Melt butter in saucepan, remove from heat and stir in flour. Gradually add milk and cook, stirring constantly, until thickened. Add cheese, salt and pepper. Stir until cheese is melted. Blend with kale. Sprinkle with bacon. Approximate yield: 6 to 8 portions.

KALE WITH EGG SAUCE

3 tablespoons shortening
3 tablespoons flour
2 cups milk
½ teaspoon salt

⅛ teaspoon pepper
2 hard-cooked eggs, chopped
1 teaspoon minced parsley
4 pounds kale, cooked
paprika

Melt shortening and stir in flour. Gradually add milk and cook until thickened. Add salt, pepper, eggs and parsley. Heat thoroughly. Pour sauce over the hot kale and sprinkle with paprika. Approximate yield: 6 to 8 portions.

SAVORY KALE

1 pound kale
2 cloves garlic, halved
½ teaspoon salt
dash of pepper

¼ teaspoon crumbled, dried
    marjoram
2 tablespoons tarragon vinegar
¼ cup olive oil

Separate leaves from tough stems. Place kale leaves in pan with garlic. Sprinkle with salt, pepper and marjoram. Pour 1 tablespoon vinegar over all. Cover and cook 12 to 15 minutes, or until just tender. Combine oil and remaining vinegar and pour over kale before serving. Yield: 4 portions.

BOILED KOHLRABI

Cut off leaves, wash, pare and cut into ½ inch cubes or ¼ inch slices. Cook, covered, in small amount of boiling salted water 25 to 35 minutes, or until just tender. Drain; season with salt, pepper and butter, or serve with Medium White Sauce (page 125) or Hollandaise Sauce (page 473), or prepare as Scalloped Vegetables (page 520). Allow 1 medium kohlrabi for each portion.

BOILED LEEKS

Cut off green tops to within 1½ to 2 inches of white part. Cook, covered, in small amount of boiling salted water 15 to 20 minutes, or until just tender; drain. Serve with melted butter or as Creamed Vegetables (page 521). Allow 4 bunches for 6 portions.

BRAISED LEEKS

4 bunches leeks
1 medium-sized onion, sliced
2 tablespoons butter
2 cups meat stock or bouillon

2 whole cloves
1 bay leaf
½ teaspoon salt
dash of pepper

Prepare leeks as for Boiled Leeks (above). Sauté onion in butter 3 minutes, or until lightly browned; add leeks, stock and seasonings. Cover and simmer about 30 minutes, or until leeks are tender and stock has almost evaporated. Approximate yield: 6 portions.

BOILED LETTUCE

Remove wilted leaves from leaf or head lettuce, wash under running water and cut heads in quarters. Cook heads, covered, in small amount of salted water and leaves in no additional water 5 to 10 minutes, or until just tender. Drain and season with salt, pepper and butter, or with chopped crisp bacon. Allow 2 medium heads for 6 portions.

STEWED MUSHROOMS

Trim off discolored end of stalks, clean by brushing or wash quickly in cold water. If skin is thick and coarse, peel with silver knife; do not peel young tender caps. If stems are solid and tender, cut off and cook with caps. Discarded stems and peelings may be cooked separately in very small amount of water and used in soups and sauces.

Stew mushrooms, covered, in almost no water 5 to 8 minutes. Meat stock or thin cream may be substituted for water, if desired. Season with salt, pepper and butter; serve with the juices on hot toast, or combine with white sauce as Creamed Vegetables (page 521). Mushrooms may be first sautéed in butter 3 minutes, then simmered 3 to 5 minutes in their own juices. Allow 1 pound for 6 portions.

SAUTÉED MUSHROOMS

Use mushroom caps, whole or cut in pieces. Allow 2 tablespoons butter for ½ pound mushrooms. Sauté slowly 6 to 10 minutes, or until just tender, turning frequently.

Russian Mushrooms—Turn whole mushroom caps, sautéed 3 minutes, into greased casserole, cover with sour cream, sprinkle with grated cheese and bake in moderate oven (350° F.) 8 to 10 minutes, or until cheese is melted and browned.

Mushroom and Cheese Casserole—Combine 1½ pounds sautéed mushrooms with 1 cup Medium White Sauce (page 125). Add 1 tablespoon chopped chives, 2 tablespoons pimiento, cut in strips, 1 tablespoon pimiento liquor, 1 tablespoon chopped mint and ¼ teaspoon dry mustard. Turn into greased casserole, cover with 1 cup grated cheese and 2 tablespoons buttered bread crumbs; bake in moderate oven (375° F.) 10 to 15 minutes, or until cheese bubbles and begins to brown. Approximate yield: 6 portions.

Mushrooms in Red Sauce—To 1 pound mushrooms sautéed 3 minutes add the following sauce: Force 1 cup canned red kidney beans through coarse sieve; add 1 teaspoon onion juice, ½ teaspoon chili powder mixed with 1 tablespoon water, ¼ clove garlic and boil 5 minutes; remove garlic. Add ¾ cup red wine, ½ teaspoon salt and ⅛ teaspoon pepper. Turn into greased casserole, cover with 1 cup buttered bread crumbs and bake in hot oven (425° F.) about 10 minutes, or until crumbs are browned. Approximate yield: 6 portions.

BROILED MUSHROOMS

Use 1½ dozen large mushroom caps. Brush with butter or oil and sprinkle with salt and pepper and a dash of nutmeg, if desired. Place on broiler, cap side up, about 3 inches below heat or broiling unit and broil 8 to 10 minutes. Serve on buttered toast. Yield: 6 portions.

BAKED MUSHROOMS

Prepare 1½ pounds large mushrooms; place in shallow baking dish, season with 1½ teaspoons salt and a dash of pepper, dot with 3 tablespoons butter and add ½ cup light cream or top milk. Bake in hot oven (400°–425° F.) 10 to 15 minutes. Yield: 6 portions.

STUFFED MUSHROOMS

12 large mushrooms	2 tablespoons butter
2 cups cold water	1 tablespoon dry bread crumbs
⅓ cup vinegar or lemon juice	¼ teaspoon salt
1 tablespoon chopped parsley	⅛ teaspoon mace
pinch of caraway seeds	2 egg yolks, slightly beaten

Wash mushrooms, remove stems and drop caps into water-vinegar mixture for 10 minutes; drain. Chop stems fine, mix with parsley and caraway seeds and sauté lightly in butter. Stir in crumbs, salt and mace and remove from heat; add egg yolks and pile lightly into inverted mushroom caps. Place in shallow buttered pan and bake in hot oven (400° F.) 15 minutes, or until browned. Yield: 6 portions.

STUFFED MUSHROOMS ITALIAN STYLE

1 pound mushrooms
2 tablespoons butter
1 clove garlic, minced
¼ cup minced onion
2 tablespoons grated Parmesan
  cheese

salt and pepper to taste
pinch of orégano
½ cup ground beef
2 tablespoons dry bread crumbs
¼ cup olive oil

Select 12 of the largest mushrooms, wash, remove stems and reserve. Chop stems with remaining mushrooms. Sauté in butter 5 minutes. Add garlic, onion, cheese, salt and pepper, orégano, ground beef, bread crumbs and 1 tablespoon olive oil. Mix until well blended. With a spatula or knife, fill the 12 mushrooms with this stuffing, packing in gently. Pour 1 tablespoon olive oil in shallow baking pan. Arrange stuffed mushrooms in pan and dribble 2 tablespoons olive oil over tops. Bake in moderate oven (375° F.) about 25 minutes. Yield: 12 mushrooms.

MUSHROOM AND HAM SOUFFLÉ

2 cups Thick White Sauce
  (page 125)
⅓ cup grated American cheese
¾ cup minced celery
1½ tablespoons minced pimiento

1 cup mushrooms, cooked
¾ cup chopped boiled ham
4 eggs, separated
¾ teaspoon curry powder
1½ teaspoons grated onion

To white sauce add cheese, celery, pimiento, mushrooms, ham, well-beaten egg yolks, curry powder and onion. Mix well; then fold in egg whites beaten stiffly but not dry. Turn into a greased casserole and place in a pan of hot water. Bake in moderate oven (350° F.) about 30 to 45 minutes, or until nicely browned. Yield: 6 portions.

BOILED OKRA

Cut off stems and wash well. Leave small pods whole; cut large ones in ½ inch slices. Cook, covered, in small amount of boiling salted water 10 to 20 minutes, or until just tender. Drain, season with salt, pepper, butter and vinegar, if desired. Serve as a vegetable or with Boiled Rice (page 507). Allow 1 to 1½ pounds for 6 portions.

SOUTHERN GUMBO

3 onions, sliced
3 tablespoons butter or bacon
   drippings
1 cup cut corn

2 green peppers, chopped
18 small okra pods
5 large tomatoes, peeled

Sauté onions in butter 2 minutes; add peppers and continue cooking 3 minutes. Add okra which has been washed and stemmed and tomatoes; cover and cook about 10 minutes, stirring frequently. Add corn and cook about 10 minutes longer, or until mixture is quite dry. Approximate yield: 6 portions.

BOILED ONIONS

12 medium-sized onions or 6
   large onions

salt and pepper
2 tablespoons butter

Wash and peel onions. Boil, covered, in small amount of water 20 to 35 minutes, or until tender. If very strong in flavor, drain after cooking 10 minutes, cover with fresh boiling water and cook until tender. Drain; season with salt, pepper and butter. If desired, add 1½ cups top milk or light cream and heat thoroughly. Yield: 6 portions.

SAUTÉED ONIONS

12 medium-sized onions
¼ cup fat

½ teaspoon salt
⅛ teaspoon pepper

Wash and peel onions. Slice very thin and soak in cold water 30 minutes. Drain and dry. Sauté in fat 20 minutes, or until faintly yellow and tender, stirring frequently. Season with salt and pepper. Approximate yield: 6 portions.

SCALLIONS À LA KING

2 bunches scallions
¾ cup mushrooms
2 tablespoons butter
1 cup Medium White Sauce
   (page 125)

1 pimiento, shredded
1 tablespoon chopped parsley
½ teaspoon salt
dash of celery salt
dash of pepper

Cut roots and tip ends from scallions and wash well. Cook in small amount of boiling salted water until tender, about 8 to 15 minutes; then drain. Wash and peel mushrooms, cut in halves and sauté in butter 5 minutes; add to white sauce and stir in remaining ingredients. Pour over scallions and serve on toast points, if desired. Yield: 6 portions.

GRILLED ONIONS

3 large mild onions   ½ cup butter, melted
½ cup boiling water   salt and pepper

Wash and peel onions; cut in slices ¼ inch thick. Place slices in baking pan, 1 layer deep. Add water and bake in moderate oven (350° F.) 15 minutes. Drain, dip in melted butter, sprinkle with salt and pepper, and broil under moderate heat 5 minutes on each side. Serve at once. Yield: 6 portions.

GLAZED ONIONS

1½ pounds small white onions   1 tablespoon sugar
2 tablespoons butter   salt and pepper
½ cup water   1 tablespoon flour

Wash and peel onions. Melt butter in a frying pan, add onions, water and sugar. Season with salt and pepper and simmer gently 15 minutes, or until tender. Add a smooth paste of flour and 2 additional tablespoons water, mixing well. Cover and bake in moderate oven (375° F.) 20 minutes. Yield: 6 portions.

STUFFED ONIONS

6 large onions   ½ teaspoon salt
1 cup chopped celery   ¾ cup grated cheese
⅓ cup chopped nuts   water cress
              red and green pepper slices

Parboil onions 20 minutes; remove a small portion from center; fill with a mixture of celery, nuts and salt. Place in baking pan, top with cheese and bake in moderate oven (350° F.) 15 minutes. Garnish with water cress and pepper slices. Yield: 6 portions.

FRENCH FRIED ONION RINGS

4 large mild onions   ½ cup flour
½ cup milk   ¼ teaspoon salt
              dash of pepper

Wash and peel onions; slice ¼ inch thick and separate slices into rings. Dip into milk and then into flour seasoned with salt and pepper. Fry in hot fat (380° F.) 4 to 6 minutes, or until lightly browned; drain on absorbent paper. Yield: 6 portions.

DEVILED ONIONS

Chop 6 large boiled onions (page 558) very fine, add mashed yolks of 3 hard-cooked eggs, ½ teaspoon salt, 1½ tablespoons chopped parsley and 1 cup Medium White Sauce (page 125). Turn into 6 greased ramekins and sprinkle with buttered dry crumbs. Brown under medium broiler heat.

BOILED PARSNIPS

12 medium-sized young	salt and pepper
parsnips	¼ cup butter
dash of nutmeg (optional)	

Wash and scrape parsnips, and cook, covered, in small amount of boiling salted water 20 to 40 minutes, or until just tender. Drain, cut in half and each half in quarters. If core is fibrous, cut it out before serving. Season with salt, pepper, butter and nutmeg. If desired, cut parsnips into inch cubes and add 1 cup Medium or Thin White Sauce (page 125). Approximate yield: 6 portions.

FRANCONIA PARSNIPS

Cut boiled parsnips (page 560) lengthwise in 8 wedges, place in greased baking pan, brush with melted fat and sprinkle liberally with brown sugar and dry mustard. Bake in moderate oven (400° F.) 20 minutes. Allow 2 medium parsnips per portion.

PARSNIP SAUTÉ

| 1½ pounds parsnips | 2 tablespoons butter |

Cook parsnips, covered, in small amount of boiling water 20 to 40 minutes, or until tender. Drain. Slip off skins, slice lengthwise and sauté in butter until lightly browned. Approximate yield: 6 portions.

FRENCH FRIED PARSNIPS

Cut boiled parsnips (see page 560) crosswise in ½ inch slices. Dip in slightly beaten egg, then flour, or dip in Cover Batter (page 787); fry in hot deep fat (380° F.) 3 to 5 minutes, or until lightly browned. Drain on absorbent paper; salt lightly and serve at once. Allow 2 medium-sized parsnips per portion.

BOILED PEAS

Have peas as fresh as possible and shell just before cooking since flavor decreases rapidly after shelling. Cook, covered, in a small amount of boiling salted water 8 to 20 minutes, or until just tender. With mature peas ¼ teaspoon sugar per pound of peas may be added to water, if desired. A sprig of mint cooked with peas will add flavor. There should be almost no water left after cooking. Season with salt, pepper and butter or cream, or use as Creamed Vegetables (page 521). Allow ½ pound peas in the pod per portion. One pound peas yields about 1 cup cooked, shelled peas.

COUNTRY STYLE PEAS

3 small carrots, diced
½ cup shredded cabbage
2 tablespoons melted butter
1 teaspoon salt
¼ teaspoon pepper
¼ teaspoon Worcestershire sauce
1 cup chicken bouillon
2 cups shelled peas
¼ head lettuce, finely shredded

Add carrots and cabbage to melted butter, cook 2 minutes, add seasonings, bouillon and peas. Cover and simmer about 30 minutes, adding lettuce during last 5 minutes. Yield: 6 portions.

PEAS NEW ORLEANS

3 cups shelled peas
8 shallots
¾ cup diced ham
¾ cup water
1 tablespoon sugar
salt and pepper

Combine all ingredients in heavy saucepan with tight lid. Bring to a boil and simmer slowly 20 to 30 minutes, or until peas are tender. Yield: 6 portions.

FRENCH FRIED PEPPER RINGS

4 large green peppers
1 egg
1 tablespoon water
½ cup dry bread crumbs
1 teaspoon salt

Wash peppers, cut in thin slices and remove seeds and membranes. Dip in egg combined with water, then in crumbs to which salt has been added. Fry a few at a time in hot deep fat (380° F.) 3 to 5 minutes, or until nicely browned. Drain on absorbent paper; serve with broiled steak. Approximate yield: 6 portions.

STUFFED GREEN PEPPERS

2 cups cooked chicken	½ teaspoon salt
¼ cup seedless raisins	⅛ teaspoon pepper
1 cup cooked rice	1 teaspoon chili powder
1 tablespoon melted butter	¼ cup grated cheese
2 eggs, well beaten	6 green peppers

Combine chicken, raisins, rice, butter, eggs and seasonings and stir in cheese. Cut thin slice from stem end of peppers, or cut in half lengthwise, remove seeds and parboil, covered, in small amount of boiling salted water 2 to 10 minutes. Stuff peppers with chicken mixture and bake in moderate oven (375° F.) 25 to 30 minutes. Serve with Medium White Sauce (page 125). Yield: 6 portions.

Tomato-stuffed Peppers—For stuffing, mix 1 tablespoon chopped onion, 2 tablespoons chopped parsley, 1 cup soft bread crumbs, 2 tablespoons melted butter and ½ cup canned tomatoes; dot with butter.

Cheese-Nut-stuffed Peppers—For stuffing, add ½ cup grated cheese, 1½ tablespoons melted butter, 1 teaspoon minced parsley, ¼ cup finely chopped celery, ¼ cup chopped, blanched almonds and 3 hard-cooked eggs chopped, to 1 cup Thick White Sauce (page 125); season to taste with salt and paprika. Sprinkle stuffed peppers with ½ cup grated cheese.

Corn-stuffed Peppers—Use 3 cups seasoned corn, cooked or fresh; dot with 3 tablespoons butter.

Hash-stuffed Peppers—Use 2 to 3 cups corned beef hash.

Unique Stuffed Peppers—For stuffing, combine 1 can condensed mock turtle soup, 2 tablespoons chopped onion and 1½ cups soft bread crumbs; sprinkle stuffed peppers with ½ cup buttered crumbs.

Delicious Stuffed Peppers—For stuffing, combine 1⅓ cups soft cottage cheese, 2 well-beaten eggs, ¼ teaspoon onion juice, ⅛ teaspoon paprika and enough crushed corn flakes to make mixture firm enough to handle. Pour 1 cup Tomato Sauce (page 469) or Spanish Sauce (page 470) around stuffed peppers.

POTATOES FOR BOILING AND BAKING

White or Irish potatoes differ in their cooking qualities. Good boiling potatoes cook uniformly and hold their shape; they are not choice for baking. Good baking potatoes such as the Idaho are mealy when baked. Certain kinds of potatoes are good for both boiling and baking and these are the most satisfactory to buy for the small family. New or young potatoes are less mealy when cooked and are, therefore, better boiled than baked.

BOILED POTATOES

Select uniform potatoes. Scrub, wash, rinse and pare before or after cooking; if uneven in size, cut in uniform pieces. Cover whole potatoes with boiling salted water and cook, covered, 25 to 40 minutes, or until just tender; if quartered, allow 15 to 25 minutes. Drain; peel, if boiled with jackets, and place, uncovered, in warm place, or shake over heat to dry and make mealy. Or cook potatoes in a small amount of water in a tightly covered heavy saucepan. The potato water contains soluble minerals and vitamins and should be used in making gravies and soups. Allow 1½ to 2 pounds for 6 portions, or 1 medium-sized potato for 1 portion.

BAKED POTATOES

Select uniform, medium-sized to large potatoes; scrub, remove blemishes, rinse, prick and dry. Place in shallow baking pan or on rack; rub with melted fat for a soft skin. Bake in hot oven (450° F.) 45 to 60 minutes; to test, pick up with cloth and squeeze; if soft, they are done. Squeeze baked potatoes to break skin, or cut gashes in top of potato to allow escape of steam. Serve in hot open dish, plain or with a square of butter in opening of each. Allow 1 potato per portion.

BAKED POTATO SURPRISE

Cut small slices from ends (lengthwise) of 6 medium potatoes. With an apple corer, cut hole through the center of each. Fill holes with carrots, diced or cut in strips; plug ends with potato slices. Rub with butter and bake (page 563).

POTATOES ON THE HALF SHELL

Bake 6 medium-sized potatoes (page 563); cut a slice from top of each and scoop out inside. Mash thoroughly, add 3 tablespoons butter, ½ teaspoon salt, ¼ teaspoon white pepper and about ¼ cup hot milk; beat until light and fluffy. If desired, add 2 teaspoons finely minced chives, parsley or onion; or fold in 1 stiffly beaten egg white. Pile lightly into shells and bake 5 to 8 minutes longer to reheat and brown lightly. Tops may be sprinkled with grated cheese or brushed lightly with slightly beaten egg yolk. Yield: 6 portions.

Stuffed Pimiento Potatoes—Bake 3 large potatoes and cut in halves lengthwise. To fluffy potato filling add 2 tablespoons each grated cheese and chopped pimiento. Or substitute 2 tablespoons chopped pimiento-stuffed olives for pimiento and omit cheese.

Stuffed Waldorf Potatoes—Put 3 hard-cooked egg yolks through coarse sieve and add with ¼ cup grated cheese to fluffy potato filling. Brush tops with melted butter and sprinkle with paprika.

Potatoes Martinique—Beat 1 slightly beaten egg yolk into fluffy potato filling and fold in stiffly beaten egg white. Shape between 2 buttered tablespoons and place on greased baking sheet. Bake in moderately hot oven (375° F.) 20 minutes, or until delicately browned.

MASHED POTATOES

Pare and boil 6 medium-sized potatoes (page 563); drain and shake over heat to dry. Force through ricer or mash well with wire or wooden masher. Add 3 tablespoons butter and ⅓ to ½ cup hot milk, beating until light and fluffy; add more milk if not as moist as desired; season to taste with salt and pepper. Keep over hot water until ready to serve. Pile lightly in hot serving dish, dot with butter and sprinkle lightly with paprika. Boil potatoes with jackets if more convenient; then peel, mash and season. Approximate yield: 4 cups or 6 portions.

Duchess Potatoes—To 2 cups mashed potatoes, add dash of paprika and 1½ beaten egg yolks; beat thoroughly. Shape into mounds on greased baking dish or shallow pan, or force through pastry bag to make rosettes or other fancy shapes. Brush with remaining ½ egg yolk and place under broiler or in very hot oven (450° F.) and brown lightly. Approximate yield: 6 small portions.

Potato Border—A fluting of mashed potatoes or Duchess Potatoes is sometimes served around planked meat or fish. Force mixture through pastry tube, or shape with spoons to make a border of potato around meat or fish on a hot greased plank (page 279); brush with melted butter or milk and brown lightly under broiler or in very hot oven.

Savory Mashed Potatoes—To 2 cups plain mashed potatoes add 1 tablespoon minced water cress, 1 teaspoon minced mint leaves and dash of white pepper.

Potato Casserole—To 4 cups moist mashed potatoes add 2 well-beaten egg yolks; fold in 2 stiffly beaten egg whites. Turn into greased casserole and bake in moderately hot oven (375°–400° F.) 15 to 20 minutes, or until lightly browned. Approximate yield: 6 portions.

Potatoes Anna—To 2 cups mashed potatoes, add 3 well-beaten egg yolks; stir in ¾ cup grated cheese and fold in 3 stiffly beaten egg whites. Pile in greased casserole and bake in moderately hot oven (375°–400° F.) 15 to 20 minutes, or until browned, or turn into greased, heavy muffin pans and bake 10 to 15 minutes. Approximate yield: 6 portions.

SCALLOPED POTATOES

6 medium-sized potatoes	flour
salt and pepper	2 teaspoons butter
	3 cups milk

Pare potatoes and slice thin; place half in buttered baking dish, sprinkle with salt and pepper and sprinkle with flour. Repeat, add butter to hot milk and pour over potatoes. Bake, covered, in moderate oven (375° F.) ½ hour, then uncover and bake 10 to 15 minutes longer, or until a delicately brown crust has formed on top. If milk boils over, uncover and bake at lower temperature (350° F.). One tablespoon chopped onion may be added. Yield: 6 portions.

Scalloped Potatoes and Ham—Add 1 cup chopped cooked ham, sprinkling ½ cup over each layer of potatoes.

Baked Creamed Potatoes—Use 6 cooked potatoes, diced, and 1½ cups Medium White Sauce (page 125). Cover each layer of potatoes with white sauce and sprinkle mixture of 1½ tablespoons each dry bread crumbs and grated cheese over top. Dice 2 hard-cooked eggs and sprinkle over each layer of potatoes, if desired. Bake 15 to 20 minutes.

Baked Potatoes au Gratin—Use 4 cups cubed cooked potatoes, 1 small onion, chopped, sautéed lightly and mixed with 2 pimientos, chopped, and 2 cups Medium White Sauce (page 125) mixed with 1 cup grated cheese. Arrange in layers and top with ¼ cup buttered, dry bread crumbs; bake 15 to 20 minutes.

VENETIAN POTATOES

2 pounds small potatoes	1 bunch parsley
2 cloves garlic	2 tablespoons oil
1 medium onion	2 tablespoons fat

Wash and peel potatoes. Boil in salted water until almost tender; drain. Finely chop garlic, onion and parsley and add to potatoes; sauté in hot oil and fat over a low heat until potatoes are lightly browned. Approximate yield: 6 portions.

HASHED BROWN POTATOES

Add 3 cups finely chopped boiled potatoes to 3 tablespoons fat in hot frying pan, sprinkle with 1 teaspoon salt and ¼ teaspoon each pepper and paprika, add ¼ cup milk and cook slowly without stirring until browned on under side; then turn with broad spatula to brown other side. Fold in half like an omelet and serve on hot platter. The potatoes are brown and crusty on outside and soft in center. Chopped parsley may be cooked with potatoes. Yield: 6 portions.

PERSILLADE NEW POTATOES

1½ pounds small new potatoes   ¼ cup butter, melted
2 tablespoons lemon juice   ⅓ cup finely chopped parsley

Wash, scrape and boil new potatoes (page 563); drain. Pour mixture of lemon juice and butter over potatoes, then roll in parsley. Approximate yield: 6 portions.

POTATO BALLS

With a French cutter or melon scoop, cut potato balls out of pared large potatoes. Boil (page 563) until just done, drain and serve with parsley butter or in Cream or White Sauce (pages 466 and 125). Boil scraps of potatoes, drain and mash, or use for soups. Allow about 8 balls per portion.

BRAISED POTATO BALLS

Crisp 3 cups potato balls by letting them stand for 1 hour in cold water; drain, add to 3 tablespoons butter in heavy frying pan, cover and cook slowly about 45 minutes, shaking pan occasionally to cook evenly. Just before removing from fire, add 1½ teaspoons salt and 1½ tablespoons parsley. Approximate yield: 6 portions.

RICED POTATOES

Pare potatoes and boil or steam (page 563); drain and shake dry over heat; force through potato ricer or coarse strainer. Pile lightly in hot serving dish and sprinkle with paprika; if steamed, sprinkle with salt. Allow 1 medium potato per portion.

FRANCONIA OR BROWNED POTATOES

Pare 6 medium-sized potatoes and cook in boiling salted water 15 minutes; drain and place in pan in which meat is roasting. Bake about 40 minutes, or until tender and lightly browned, basting with drippings in pan or turning occasionally to brown all sides. Serve on platter with roast. Yield: 6 portions.

BROILED POTATOES

Pare 6 medium-sized potatoes and cook in boiling salted water 15 minutes; drain and cut in ¼ to ½ inch slices. Brush with melted butter and broil until tender, turning once and brushing again with melted butter to brown other side. Just before removing, sprinkle with grated cheese and heat long enough to melt cheese. Allow 1 potato per portion.

GERMAN FRIED POTATOES

Pare and thinly slice 7 medium-sized potatoes and place in heavy frying pan with 3 tablespoons melted fat; sprinkle with ¾ teaspoon salt and a dash of pepper. Sauté slowly about 15 minutes, or until evenly browned, turning occasionally; then cover and cook 15 minutes longer, or until tender. Approximate yield: 6 portions.

POTATOES O'BRIEN

Add 3 cups diced cooked potatoes (page 563) and 2 tablespoons each minced pimiento, green pepper and onion to 3 tablespoons melted fat in heavy frying pan; sprinkle with 1 teaspoon salt and dash of pepper and sauté until delicately browned, stirring occasionally. Approximate yield: 6 portions.

FRENCH FRIED POTATOES

Wash and pare small potatoes and cut lengthwise into strips about ⅜ inch thick; soak in cold water ½ to 1 hour. Drain, dry between towels or paper towels and place just enough in bottom of frying basket or sieve to cover sparsely. Immerse in hot deep fat (380° F.) and cook 3 to 5 minutes, or until a golden brown, keeping potatoes in motion. Hold basket over kettle for fat to drip, then turn out on absorbent paper to drain. Sprinkle with salt and serve hot. Allow 1 to 2 potatoes per portion.

Potato Chips—Slice pared potatoes very thin, using a sharp knife, vegetable slicer or one of the slicing machines. Separate chilled and thoroughly dried slices, place loosely in bottom of frying basket and fry, keeping potatoes in motion.

Potato Crisps—Slice pared potatoes with lattice vegetable slicer. Soak, dry thoroughly and fry.

Shoestring or Julienne Potatoes—Cut pared potato in matchlike sticks. Soak, dry thoroughly and fry.

Oven Fried Potatoes—Prepare potatoes as for French Fried (see above); place in greased shallow baking pan to make thin layer and brush with oil or melted fat, turning to cover all sides. Bake in hot oven (450° F.) 20 to 30 minutes, or until browned, turning occasionally. Drain on absorbent paper, season and serve hot. Allow 1 to 2 potatoes per portion.

PUFFED POTATO SLICES

Select medium-sized Idaho potatoes of uniform size; pare and cut on slant in even thin slices about ⅛ inch thick. Dry between towels and fry, a few at a time, in medium-hot deep fat (275°–300° F.) 5 minutes, keeping potatoes in motion; then lift basket and plunge quickly into very hot deep fat (400°–425° F.) 1 to 2 minutes, or until puffed and browned, keeping potatoes in motion. They should puff at once when dropped into the kettle of hot fat. Hold basket over kettle for fat to drip, then turn out on absorbent paper to drain. Sprinkle with salt and serve at once. These are attractive on a luncheon or supper plate. The type of potato and the quick change from a medium-hot to a very hot fat are important in making slices puff. Allow 1 potato per portion.

POTATO OR HOMINY CROQUETTES

To 3 cups riced hot potatoes (page 563) add 3 tablespoons melted butter, 2 egg yolks, ½ teaspoon salt, dash of cayenne and 1 tablespoon minced parsley; beat thoroughly and shape into croquettes. Fry in hot deep fat (365°–380° F.) 3 to 5 minutes, or until delicately browned. Or use 1½ cups hominy for potatoes. Yield: 6 portions.

BOILED SPINACH

Remove roots, tough stems and wilted leaves from 2 pounds spinach. Wash 3 times in large quantities of cold water, or until all trace of sand has disappeared. Lift spinach from last rinsing water, drain slightly and place in large kettle. Cover and cook over medium heat 8 to 10 minutes, or until tender. Drain if necessary; chop spinach, add ½ to 1 teaspoon salt, dash of pepper and ¼ cup butter. Place in hot serving dish and garnish with lemon sections or slices of hard-cooked egg. Approximate yield: 6 portions.

Spinach with Grapefruit—Cook spinach as above. Sauté lightly 6 sections of grapefruit (membrane removed) in 3 tablespoons butter and add to spinach. Heat 1 minute and serve very hot.

Spinach with Chopped Garlic—Cook spinach as above. Melt ¼ cup fat and add 1 teaspoon finely chopped garlic. Cook 1 minute over low heat. Add drained spinach and cover pan tightly. Cook over fairly high heat for 5 to 10 minutes, shaking pan frequently.

Travis House Spinach—Cook spinach as above; drain, chop fine and add 1 cup heavy cream, 1 tablespoon butter, 1 teaspoon salt and ¼ teaspoon pepper. Reheat and serve at once. Yield: 6 portions.

SPINACH AND CHEESE SOUFFLÉ

Use recipe for Vegetable Soufflé (page 521), using 1 cup finely chopped spinach for vegetable; add 1 teaspoon chopped onion, sautéed in small amount of butter, and ½ cup grated cheese to Medium White Sauce (page 125). Approximate yield: 6 portions.

SPINACH CASSEROLE

1 pound spinach	½ cup butter, melted
6 medium-sized potatoes	1 teaspoon salt
3 eggs, well beaten	dash of pepper

Pick over spinach; wash thoroughly, drain and chop very fine. Pare and grate potatoes and add eggs, butter and seasonings; put half in greased casserole. Cover with spinach and top with remaining potato mixture. Bake in moderate oven (350° F.) 1¼ hours, or until potatoes are done. Approximate yield: 6 portions.

SPINACH TIMBALES

1 cup finely chopped, cooked spinach	2 tablespoons butter, melted
½ teaspoon salt	2 eggs, well beaten
1 teaspoon onion juice	1¼ cups milk
	Tomato Sauce (page 469)
	parsley

Combine spinach, seasonings, butter, eggs and milk; turn into greased small molds, set in pan of hot water and bake in moderate oven (350° F.) 30 minutes. Unmold, serve at once with tomato sauce and garnish with parsley. Approximate yield: 4 to 6 portions.

SPINACH RING

1 small onion, minced	2 cups Thick White Sauce
2 tablespoons butter	(page 125)
3 cups chopped, cooked spinach	2 eggs, separated
½ cup soft bread crumbs	salt, pepper and paprika

Sauté onion in butter 3 minutes; remove from heat and add spinach, crumbs, white sauce and slightly beaten egg yolks, mixing well. Season to taste and fold in stiffly beaten egg whites. Turn into greased ring mold, place in pan of hot water and bake in moderate oven (375° F.) 30 minutes, or until firm. Unmold on hot plate and serve at once. Center may be filled with creamed chicken, ham or any roast meat. Approximate yield: 6 portions.

SPINACH ROLL

4 eggs, separated
⅓ cup soft bread crumbs
¼ cup milk
2 teaspoons butter, melted
¾ teaspoon salt
¼ teaspoon black pepper
¼ teaspoon nutmeg

⅛ teaspoon cloves
1 tablespoon grated Parmesan
    cheese
2 tablespoons minced parsley
2 tablespoons finely diced onion
3 cups cooked spinach, finely
    chopped
meat filling

Beat egg yolks until light. Soak crumbs in milk and add to egg with butter, ½ teaspoon salt, pepper, spices, cheese, parsley, onion and spinach. Beat egg whites with remaining salt until stiff. Fold into spinach mixture. Pour into 10 x 14 inch shallow pan which has been oiled and lined with waxed paper. Bake in moderate oven (375° F.) 12 to 15 minutes. Invert pan over waxed paper on a board. Peel off oiled paper. Spread with Meat Filling and roll as for jelly roll. Serve sliced with Egg Sauce (page 464). Approximate yield: 6 portions.

Meat Filling

3 tablespoons drippings
½ pound ground beef
4 large mushrooms, finely diced
1 tablespoon grated onion

1 tablespoon chopped chives
½ teaspoon salt
¼ teaspoon pepper
pinch of nutmeg
salt

Heat drippings in a pan. Add beef, mushrooms, onion, chives, salt, pepper and nutmeg. Cook, stirring occasionally, until meat is browned. Add more salt, if necessary.

SPINACH STEW

1 cup diced onion
¼ cup oil
2 cups hot water
1 cup rice, washed

1 tablespoon chopped dill
1 tablespoon chopped parsley
1 pound spinach, washed
2 teaspoons salt
¼ teaspoon pepper

Sauté onion in oil until tender. Add water and bring to a boil. Sprinkle in rice, dill and parsley. Add spinach and seasonings. Simmer, covered, 25 minutes. Yield: 1 quart.

BOILED SUMMER SQUASH

Summer squash includes a variety such as the white disk-shaped, the yellow-long and crooked-necked, and the green or green-striped cylindrical which are known as vegetable marrows or Italian squash. Wash but do not pare if skin is tender; slice, add a very small amount of boiling water and cook, covered, 10 to 20 minutes. Drain, mash and season with salt, pepper and butter, or sprinkle slices with salt and pepper and add melted butter. Allow about ⅓ pound per portion. To sauté squash, cut in ½ inch slices, dip in well-seasoned flour and sauté in butter and garlic 10 to 15 minutes, or until browned.

For **creamed summer squash,** add 3 tablespoons butter and ⅓ cup heavy cream to cooked squash (3 to 4 pounds); season to taste.

BAKED ACORN SQUASH

3 acorn squash	**2 tablespoons butter**
1½ teaspoon salt	**3 cooking apples**
⅛ teaspoon pepper	**2 tablespoons sugar**
	12 link sausages

Wash and split squash lengthwise, scrape out seeds and pulp, sprinkle with salt and pepper and dot with butter. Peel and core apples; cut in halves and place a half in the hollow of each piece of squash. Sprinkle with sugar and place in baking pan; add a little water. Cover and bake in hot oven (400° F.) 45 minutes to 1 hour. Brown sausages in frying pan and place 2 on each piece of squash around apple; return to oven and bake 15 minutes longer. Approximate yield: 6 portions.

BOILED WINTER SQUASH

Use Hubbard, acorn or Des Moines squash; wash, cut in halves and remove seeds and stringy portions. Cut off rind and cut in pieces; cook in small amount of boiling, salted water, covered: Acorn, 10 to 20 minutes; Hubbard, 20 to 30 minutes. Drain thoroughly, mash and season with salt, pepper and butter or cream; or use for pie, fritters, etc. Boil pumpkin in same way. Allow about ½ pound squash as purchased, per portion; or ½ cup mashed squash seasoned with about 2 teaspoons butter or heavy cream.

BAKED WINTER SQUASH

Prepare squash as for Boiled Winter Squash (page 571), but do not remove rind, cutting in pieces for serving; place in shallow pan, spread with softened butter and sprinkle with salt and pepper. Bake in moderate oven (375° F.) 40 to 60 minutes, or until soft; if baked at a higher temperature (400° F.), cover the first 30 minutes of baking. Allow about ½ pound squash per portion.

FRIED ZUCCHINI

Wash 2 medium-sized Italian squash, or zucchini, and cut in ¼-inch slices. Sauté slowly in ¼ cup butter in heavy frying pan about 10 minutes, stirring constantly; cover and simmer 5 minutes, stirring occasionally. Cook with 1 clove garlic, finely sliced, or 1 teaspoon finely chopped onion; or 4 skinned sliced tomatoes may be added, if desired. Approximate yield: 6 portions.

ZUCCHINI FLORENTINE

2 pounds zucchini	2 cups canned tomatoes
⅔ cup minced onion	½ teaspoon salt
2 tablespoons butter	dash of pepper
½ cup grated sharp cheese	

Wash zucchini and cut, without peeling, in ¼-inch slices. Sauté onion in butter until golden; add zucchini and cook over low heat 5 minutes, stirring frequently. Add tomatoes, salt and pepper and simmer, covered, 5 minutes longer. Place in greased casserole, cover with grated cheese and bake in moderate oven (375° F.) about 20 minutes, or until cheese browns. Yield: 6 portions.

ZUCCHINI AND TOMATOES

3 small zucchini	1 tablespoon oil
1 tablespoon butter	4 tomatoes, skinned and sliced
2 tablespoons water	4 tablespoons hot oil
½ teaspoon salt	dash of salt
dash of pepper	dash of pepper
1 teaspoon minced garlic	grated Parmesan cheese
	butter

Cut off top of zucchini, wash and cut in 1-inch slices. Place in pan with butter, water, salt and pepper. Add garlic, cooked 1 minute in hot oil, cover and cook slowly until tender. Add tomatoes, cooked 2 minutes in hot oil; add salt and pepper and arrange in heatproof flat dish. Sprinkle with grated cheese, dot with butter and brown quickly under broiler. Yield: 4 portions.

PUMPKIN CAKES WITH BACON

Use canned or cooked pumpkin; for directions for cooking pumpkin, see Boiled Winter Squash (page 572). To 2 cups mashed pumpkin add ½ teaspoon salt, dash of paprika, 1 teaspoon sugar, 1 teaspoon ketchup, ¼ cup milk and 2 tablespoons melted butter; shape into patties. Fry 6 to 12 strips of bacon (page 323); drain on absorbent paper and keep hot; pour off all but 2 tablespoons of the bacon drippings in pan. Sauté patties in bacon fat and serve with crisp bacon. Approximate yield: 6 portions or 12 small patties.

BRAISED RADISHES

Wash, pare and slice 2 bunches of radishes and parboil 10 minutes; drain and sauté slowly in butter 5 minutes; add ¼ cup light cream and simmer, covered, 5 minutes. Approximate yield: 6 portions.

BOILED SALSIFY OR OYSTER PLANT

Scrub, wash and scrape salsify, dropping at once into acidulated water to prevent discoloration; use 1 tablespoon vinegar for 1 quart water. Drain, cut in slices, cube, or leave whole and add a small amount of salted water; boil, covered, 20 to 25 minutes, or until tender. Drain and serve seasoned with butter or cream, with Medium White Sauce (page 125), or mashed or chopped in fritters. Allow about 2 pounds for 6 portions.

FRIED SALSIFY

Boil whole salsify (see above); drain, cut in half lengthwise and roll in seasoned flour. Sauté slowly in fat about 10 minutes, or until well browned. Serve hot. Allow 1½ to 2 pounds salsify for 6 portions.

MOCK OYSTERS

To 2 cups mashed, cooked salsify (see above), add 1 egg, beaten, ½ teaspoon salt, dash of paprika and 1 tablespoon melted butter. Shape into small patties, roll in dry bread crumbs or cornmeal and sauté slowly in butter about 10 minutes, or until well browned. Or fry in hot deep fat (380° F.) about 2 minutes. Approximate yield: 6 portions or 12 small patties.

BOILED SWEET POTATOES

Sweet potatoes and yams are usually cooked with skins on. Scrub, wash and rinse; cook whole in boiling salted water, covered, 25 to 35 minutes; or quartered, 15 to 25 minutes, or until tender. Drain, peel and serve plain, mashed, candied or fried, as desired. Allow 1 medium potato per portion.

CANDIED SWEET POTATOES

6 medium-sized sweet potatoes　　**1 cup firmly packed brown**
⅓ cup water　　　　　　　　　　　　　**sugar**
　　　　　　　2 tablespoons butter

Wash potatoes and boil until tender; drain, peel and cut in halves lengthwise. Bring water and sugar to a boil; dip potatoes into syrup and place in greased baking pan; dot with butter and add remaining syrup. Bake in hot oven (400° F.) 20 minutes, basting occasionally with syrup. Approximate yield: 6 portions.

Sherried Sweet Potatoes—Follow recipe for Candied Sweet Potatoes, omitting water and substituting ½ cup Sherry. Pour syrup over potatoes, then bake. One-fourth cup sweet cider or wine vinegar may be used instead of Sherry.

Honeyed Sweet Potatoes—Place sliced potatoes in greased baking dish and cover with a mixture of 1 cup honey and ⅓ cup butter, melted. Bake in moderate oven (350° F.) 30 minutes, turning potatoes once and basting several times with honey in pan.

MASHED SWEET POTATOES

Boil 6 medium-sized sweet potatoes (page 573); peel and force through ricer or mash with fork. Add 3 tablespoons butter, ½ teaspoon salt, dash each of pepper and nutmeg and about ⅓ cup hot milk or light cream; beat until light and fluffy; add more milk if not as moist as desired. Keep hot over hot water until ready to serve. Approximate yield: 6 portions, or 4 cups mashed potatoes.

Crusted Mashed Sweet Potatoes—Turn mashed sweet potatoes into shallow baking pan, dot with butter and sprinkle with sugar. Bake in moderate oven (350° F.) 30 minutes. The sugar will form a thin crisp crust.

Sweet Potatoes in Orange Cases—Cut a ½ inch slice from tops of 6 oranges. Scoop out pulp and beat ½ cup of orange pulp into hot mashed potatoes. Fill orange shells with potato mixture and bake in moderate oven (350° F.) 20 minutes. Top each serving with a slice of orange and garnish with a cranberry.

Maple Sweet Potatoes—Add 1 teaspoon grated orange rind to mashed sweet potatoes; turn into greased baking dish and top with 2 tablespoons melted butter mixed with 2 tablespoons maple syrup. Bake in moderate oven (350° F.) 25 minutes.

Sweet Potato Cutlets—Add ½ cup finely chopped pecans to mashed potatoes and shape into 12 round, flat patties. Roll in ground pecans, place in greased baking pan and dot with butter. Bake in hot oven (450° F.) 20 minutes. Serve with Mushroom Sauce (page 466), if desired. Or shape mashed potatoes into cones and stick blanched almonds, split in halves, into cones and bake as directed.

SWEET POTATO PONE

3 large sweet potatoes
2 cups boiling water
1 teaspoon salt
¼ teaspoon pepper
2 teaspoons allspice
¼ cup butter
¼ cup brown sugar

Pare and grate potatoes; add boiling water and mix well. Add remaining ingredients and beat well; turn into greased, shallow baking pan and bake in moderate oven (350° F.) 1 hour, or until crusty and browned. Approximate yield: 6 portions.

SWEET POTATOES AND CRANBERRIES

6 large sweet potatoes
1½ cups canned cranberry
  sauce
3 tablespoons butter
⅓ cup firmly packed brown
  sugar
1 teaspoon salt
½ cup chopped nuts

Boil sweet potatoes (page 573), peel and cut in halves lengthwise; scoop out halves slightly. Place 6 halves in greased baking dish, fill centers with cranberry sauce and top with remaining halves. Melt butter, add sugar, salt and nuts; spread over potatoes. Bake in a moderate oven (350° F.) 20 to 25 minutes, or until lightly browned. Approximate yield: 6 portions.

SWEET POTATO PUFF

6 medium sweet potatoes
2 eggs, well beaten
¼ cup flour
1 teaspoon baking powder
salt and pepper
2 tablespoons butter
parsley

Cook sweet potatoes in boiling water until tender. Drain, peel and put through potato ricer into the beaten eggs; blend lightly. Sift into this mixture flour and baking powder, mix and season to taste with salt and pepper. Melt butter in pan and add potato mixture. When lightly browned on the bottom, fold over and slip onto a hot platter. Serve with Mushroom Sauce (page 466). Approximate yield: 6 portions.

SWEET POTATO CROQUETTES

4 medium sweet potatoes	2 tablespoons brown sugar
2 tablespoons butter	dry bread crumbs
1 teaspoon salt	1 egg, slightly beaten
¼ teaspoon white pepper	1 tablespoon water

Boil or bake sweet potatoes (pages 573–576); peel and mash; add butter, salt, pepper and sugar and beat until fluffy; chill. Shape into patties or cylinders and roll in crumbs. Dip in mixture of egg and water and roll again in crumbs; chill. Fry in hot deep fat (375° F.) 3 to 4 minutes, or until golden brown. Drain on absorbent paper and serve hot. Leftover baked, boiled or mashed sweet potatoes may be used. Croquettes can be basted with butter and browned in a hot oven (400° F.). Approximate yield: 6 portions, or 12 patties.

Sweet Potato Puffs—Substitute 1 egg, beaten, for butter in croquette mixture; shape in balls and roll in crushed corn flakes. Fry in hot deep fat.

Sweet Potato and Almond Croquettes—Add ½ cup chopped, blanched almonds to croquette mixture before shaping.

Candied Sweet Potato Balls—Use canned sweet potatoes or yams; mash, mixing with juice in can, and season with salt and pepper. Shape around a marshmallow, roll in crushed corn flakes and fry in hot deep fat. Serve on platter of chicken. Allow 2 cups mashed potatoes for 6 portions.

BAKED SWEET POTATOES OR YAMS

Choose potatoes of uniform size and shape; wash, scrub and rinse. Bake in hot oven (400° F.) 35 to 40 minutes, or until soft. Prick skin to permit escape of steam; serve at once. Rub washed potatoes with fat if a soft skin is desired. Allow 1 medium potato per portion.

BAKED STUFFED SWEET POTATOES

Bake sweet potatoes (see above); cut large potatoes in halves lengthwise, or cut a slice from one end of medium-sized potatoes. Scoop out inside, leaving a shell; mash, season as for mashed potatoes and beat until very light and fluffy, adding milk to make a moist potato. Pile lightly in shells, sprinkle with paprika and bake in hot oven (450° F.) about 10 minutes, or until browned. Allow ½ large or 1 medium-sized potato per portion.

Sweet Potatoes with Bacon—Top each stuffed half with a strip of bacon and bake in hot oven (450° F.) 12 minutes, or until bacon is light brown and crisp.

Sweet Potatoes with Pineapple—Use 3 large baked sweet potatoes; to contents add 2 tablespoons butter, 3 tablespoons orange juice and salt to taste, beating well. Stir in 3 tablespoons chopped nuts and ½ cup drained crushed pineapple. Fill shells, top each with a marshmallow and brown under broiler.

SWEET POTATOES AND APPLES

6 medium sweet potatoes	½ cup sugar
3 medium apples	¼ cup butter
1 cup water	

Wash and boil sweet potatoes (page 573); drain, peel and cut in ½-inch slices. Pare and slice apples; place alternate layers of potato and apple in greased casserole, sprinkling each layer of apple with sugar, and dotting each layer of potato with butter. Add water, cover and bake in moderate oven (350° F.) 30 minutes; remove cover and bake 15 minutes longer to brown top. Approximate yield: 6 portions.

BOILED SWISS CHARD

Wash young chard thoroughly; if wilted, soak in cold water until crisp. Cook, covered, in almost no water (the water which clings to the leaves is usually sufficient) 10 to 15 minutes, or until just tender. There should be almost no liquid remaining when chard is tender. Chop, add butter and other seasonings. With older chard, the white stalks are often cut into 1-inch pieces and cooked and served as asparagus; the leaves are cooked as above. Allow about ¼ to ⅓ pound per portion.

CONCORDIA CHARD

Cook leaves and stalks separately (see above). Chop leaves, season and press into ring mold. Unmold on round plate, fill center with creamed stalks (Creamed Vegetables, page 521); garnish with paprika.

STEWED TOMATOES

Blanch firm ripe tomatoes in boiling water 1 minute; drain, slip off skins and remove stem ends. Cut in quarters and cook, covered, in their own juice or with very small amount of water 5 to 17 minutes, or until tender. Season with salt, pepper and sugar; add small amount of onion sautéed in 1 tablespoon butter, if desired. One-half cup bread or cracker crumbs may be used for thickening, or tomatoes may be served with croutons. Canned tomatoes may be substituted for the fresh. Allow ½ to ⅔ cup stewed tomatoes per portion.

STUFFED TOMATOES

6 firm, ripe tomatoes	1 teaspoon minced onion,
salt and pepper	sautéed
soft bread crumbs	½ cup dry bread crumbs,
	buttered

Wash tomatoes, remove stem ends and scoop out center pulp, leaving a shell ¼ inch thick; sprinkle with salt. Chop pulp and mix with an equal amount of soft bread crumbs; add sautéed onion and season to taste. Fill tomatoes with stuffing and place in greased baking dish; sprinkle with buttered crumbs and bake in moderate oven (375° F.) 20 minutes. Serve with Cheese Sauce (page 470), Mushroom Sauce (page 466) or melted butter. Yield: 6 portions.

Tomatoes with Celery—For stuffing, mix together 1½ cups chopped celery, ½ small onion, finely chopped, ¼ cup grated cheese, 1 tablespoon quick-cooking tapioca, 1 teaspoon salt and dash of pepper.

Tomatoes with Crab Meat—For stuffing, combine 1 cup flaked crab meat, ½ cup dry bread crumbs, ¼ cup light cream, ½ teaspoon dry mustard, 1 teaspoon Worcestershire sauce and 1 teaspoon Sherry. Season to taste with salt, pepper and paprika.

Tomatoes with Macaroni or Rice—For stuffing, sauté 2 cups cooked elbow macaroni or rice in ¼ cup olive oil 5 minutes, or until oil is absorbed. Season with salt, pepper, paprika and thyme and stir in 2 tablespoons chopped chives.

Tomatoes with Mushrooms and Corn—For stuffing, sauté 1 teaspoon chopped onion in 2 tablespoons butter; add 2 tablespoons chopped green pepper, 1 cup mushrooms, peeled and sliced, 1 cup kernel corn, ¼ cup water and 1 egg, slightly beaten. Season to taste with salt, pepper and celery salt.

Tomatoes with Okra and Peppers—For stuffing, wash 12 okra pods and slice; parboil 5 minutes and drain. Mix with 1 finely chopped green pepper, 3 tablespoons dry bread crumbs, 1 tablespoon butter, melted, and ½ teaspoon minced onion. Season to taste with salt, pepper and paprika.

Tomatoes with Olives—For stuffing, mix 1 cup Medium White Sauce (page 125) with 12 olives, sliced, 2 hard-cooked eggs, diced, 2 slices crisp bacon, chopped, dash of cayenne and ½ teaspoon curry powder. Serve with Cheese Sauce (page 470).

Tomatoes with Oysters—Sprinkle tomato shells with celery salt and minced onion; fill with 1 or 2 oysters marinated in French dressing; cover with buttered crumbs and bake in moderate oven (350° F.) 20 minutes. Use as garnish for roast or game.

Tomatoes with Spinach—For stuffing, chop 2 cups cooked spinach; season with 1 tablespoon melted butter, ½ teaspoon salt and ½ onion, minced. Serve with Egg or Oyster Sauce (pages 464–465).

BROILED TOMATOES WITH OLIVE SAUCE

Wash 6 medium-sized tomatoes and cut in halves crosswise; brush cut surfaces with 2 tablespoons melted butter and sprinkle with salt, pepper and ⅓ cup dry bread crumbs. Grated cheese may be added, if desired. Broil under moderate heat 2 minutes, or until lightly browned. Serve with Olive Sauce (page 465). Allow 1 tomato per portion.

FRIED TOMATOES

Wash firm, ripe or green tomatoes, remove stem ends and cut each crosswise in 3 or 4 slices. Dip in seasoned flour and fry in hot bacon drippings or butter about 2 minutes, turning to brown both sides. Serve at once. If desired, add 1 tablespoon flour to fat left in pan, mix until smooth and add ¾ cup milk or light cream; cook 5 minutes, or until smooth and slightly thickened, stirring constantly; serve on tomatoes. Allow 1 tomato per portion.

SCALLOPED TOMATOES

1 No. 2½ can tomatoes	1 small onion, sliced
1 medium-sized cucumber,	½ cup buttered cracker crumbs
pared and sliced	salt and pepper
½ cup grated cheese	

Place layer of tomatoes in 6 buttered individual baking dishes or large casserole; add half of cucumber, onion and crumbs and season with salt and pepper. Repeat with half of remaining tomatoes and remaining cucumber, onion and crumbs; top with remaining tomatoes and sprinkle with cheese. Bake in moderate oven (375° F.) 30 to 40 minutes. Approximate yield: 6 portions.

CUP–BAKED TOMATOES

6 medium-sized tomatoes	1 cup Medium White Sauce
salt and paprika	(page 125)
1 tablespoon powdered sugar	¼ cup horseradish, drained
2 tablespoons butter	¼ teaspoon dry mustard

Wash tomatoes, remove stem ends and place in greased individual custard cups. Cut a cross in the center top, sprinkle with salt, paprika and sugar and dot with butter. Bake in hot oven (400° F.) for 20 minutes. Season white sauce with remaining ingredients and serve over tomatoes in cups. Yield: 6 portions.

TOMATO FRITTERS

Wash 6 firm, ripe or green tomatoes; remove stem ends and cut each crosswise in 4 slices. Dip each slice in Cover Batter (page 787) and fry in hot deep fat (375° F.) 2 to 3 minutes, or until delicately browned; drain on absorbent paper and serve at once. Allow 1 tomato per portion.

BAKED TOMATOES AND SQUASH

1 large yellow summer squash	6 slices fresh tomatoes
salt	2 medium onions, sliced
pepper	2 tablespoons butter

Wash squash, cut in half and remove seeds; place in buttered baking dish and sprinkle with salt and pepper. Place tomato and onion slices on top, sprinkle with salt and pepper and dot with butter. Cover and bake in moderate oven (350° F.) 45 minutes, or until squash is tender. Yield: 6 portions.

TAMALE PIE

½ pound salt pork, diced	½ cup olive oil
1 medium-sized onion, sliced	1 tablespoon chili powder
1 No. 2 can tomatoes	½ can (No. 2) hominy, chopped
1 cup canned corn	1 egg, slightly beaten
½ cup yellow cornmeal	½ cup milk
1 teaspoon salt	1 cup chopped olives

Fry salt pork; add onion and brown slightly. Boil tomatoes, corn, cornmeal and salt 5 minutes, stirring constantly; add salt pork and onion, oil, chili powder and hominy, stirring well, then cool. Combine egg and milk and stir into tomato-corn mixture; add olives and turn into casserole; bake, covered, in moderate oven (350° F.) about 1 hour. Leftover meats may be added to this dish. Yield: 6 to 9 portions.

TOMATO CAKES

8 medium-sized tomatoes	½ teaspoon salt
4 eggs, well beaten	dash of pepper
3 tablespoons butter, melted	¼ cup cracker crumbs

Blanch, skin and cook tomatoes (page 577); cool. Combine remaining ingredients and add tomatoes, mixing well. Drop by spoonfuls on hot greased griddle; brown on both sides. Serve hot. Yield: 6 portions.

BOILED TURNIPS OR RUTABAGAS

Use either medium-sized white turnips or the larger stronger-flavored yellow turnips or rutabagas. Scrub, scrape or pare, cut in large pieces, slice or dice. Small turnips may be cooked whole, if desired. Cook, whole or halved, covered, in small amount of boiling salted water 20 to 30 minutes, or sliced or cubed 15 to 20 minutes, or until just tender. Drain, mash, season with salt, pepper and butter; or serve as Creamed Vegetables (page 521). Allow 2 pounds (2 bunches) for 6 portions.

TURNIP CUPS WITH PEAS

Wash, pare and boil 6 small turnips (see above). Cut a slice from root end of each and scoop out centers; fill with 2 cups buttered peas (page 561) and brush cups with melted butter. Place in shallow pan in moderate oven (350° F.) 10 minutes or until hot. Yield: 6 portions.

TURNIPS NEWBURG

Add 3 hard-cooked egg yolks, thoroughly mashed, to 2 cups Thin White Sauce (page 125) and cook and stir until smooth. Stir in 1 teaspoon anchovy paste and add dash each of paprika, cayenne and mace; add 3 cups cooked diced turnips, heat thoroughly and serve on buttered toast rounds. Approximate yield: 6 portions.

TURNIPS WITH SAUCE POULETTE

Omit Sherry in Sauce Poulette (page 479), stir in 1 slightly beaten egg yolk and cook 1 minute. Add 12 boiled small turnips or 2 cups quartered large turnips, heat thoroughly and serve at once.

GLAZED TURNIPS

8 small turnips	salt
3 tablespoons butter	1½ teaspoons sugar
1 cup bouillon	1 blade mace

Wash and pare turnips; cut in large cubes and boil about 5 minutes; drain and add to melted butter in saucepan. Add bouillon, salt, sugar and mace and bring to boil; cover and simmer about 15 minutes, or until turnips are tender. Uncover and cook until sauce is reduced to a glaze. Approximate yield: 6 portions.

NEW ENGLAND BOILED DINNER

1 head cabbage, quartered	4 medium potatoes, peeled
1 pound peas, shelled	4 onions, peeled
1 bunch small carrots, scraped	ham stock
1 large turnip, quartered	ham
	dumplings

Combine all ingredients and simmer in ham stock, covered, 25 to 30 minutes, or until vegetables are tender. Serve on hot platter with ham and dumplings. Yield: 4 portions.

GARDEN CASSEROLE

1 cup cooked diced celery	2 cups Medium Cream Sauce
1 cup cooked string beans	(page 125)
1 cup cooked cubed potatoes	1 tablespoon chopped parsley
1 cup cooked cubed carrots	1 tablespoon chopped chives
1 cup cooked cauliflower	or onion
1 tablespoon ketchup	½ cup crushed corn flakes
2 tablespoons grated cheese	or cracker crumbs
¼ teaspoon thyme	1 tablespoon butter or margarine

Drain well and combine the cooked vegetables; add the ketchup, cheese and thyme to the cream sauce. Place a layer of vegetables in a well-greased casserole and sprinkle with parsley and chives, then add a layer of cream sauce. Repeat until all is used. Sprinkle crushed corn flakes on the top and dot with butter; bake in moderate oven (350° F.) 30 minutes. Approximate yield: 6 portions.

Salads and Salad Dressings

SALADS have been compared to gardens—a delight to the eye and refreshing to the spirit. Effectively arranged and contrasted in color, flavor and texture, they can become an artistic masterpiece—a picture of fruit or vegetable color against a background of crisp salad green.

Almost anything edible goes into salad these days. You may serve the crisp salad greens dressed with a blend of olive oil and vinegar as a first course, California style, or with fruits or vegetables as a main course, or as a dessert.

Whatever your choice, have the ingredients cold and crisp, the plates chilled and the dressing tart. Use your imagination in the selection of ingredients and make the salad the pièce de résistance of your meal.

How to Make a Perfect Green Salad. Wash, dry thoroughly and chill salad greens. Use only a small amount of each. Lettuce—both blanched and green—romaine, chicory, both French and Italian, endive, water cress, field salad. Just before serving, break dry, crisp greens into garlic-rubbed wooden salad bowl. Sprinkle sparingly with olive oil directly from the can or cruet. Ideally, each piece of salad green should be just coated and there should be no excess. Mix salt and herb-flavored pure wine vinegar in the wooden salad spoon. Add freshly ground pepper and sprinkle over salad and toss gently until just mixed.

Slices of onion, radish, green pepper, finely chopped chives and fresh tarragon may be tossed with greens and whole ripe olives added. Or place whole scallions at one end of bowl and serve with individual portions.

A wooden fork and spoon crush tender leaves less than metal utensils, although, if gently handled, the leaves are never bruised as they are tossed lightly in the bowl with the dressing.

Herbs in Salads. Besides parsley, chives, mint and mustard greens, most green or vegetable salads are improved with a sprinkling of finely chopped salad herbs. Chervil may be used in place of parsley; sprigs of peppergrass, sorrel, anise and basil add subtle and distinctive flavors; burnet suggests mild cucumber. Tarragon and dill—the latter particularly good with potato salad—are compatible with some meat and fish salads. Lemon balm, rue, rosemary and tender young nasturtium leaves and buds may be combined with fruit salads or crushed and infused in the oil dressing that accompanies the salad.

Salad Accompaniments. The most popular accompaniments include crisp crackers, Melba toast, pulled bread, crisp French or Italian bread, bread sticks and tiny cucumber sandwiches or thin bread and butter cut into finger lengths. Cheese may be spread on crackers or shaped into balls, but it is never used in addition to a cheese dressing. When wine is served with salad, it is customary to pass cheese at the same time, to offset the slightly acid flavor of the dressing.

CRISP VEGETABLES, GARNISHES

Carrot Straws—Wash and scrape or pare tender young carrots and cut in quarters, then in smaller strips, or cut in narrow strips, about 3 inches long. Place on plate, cover with damp cloth and chill for an hour before serving.

Carrot Curls—Cut young, cleaned carrots in half lengthwise; cut in paper-thin slices. Roll each slice and place, close together, in ice water to curl.

Carrot Orchids—Use 4 carrot curls for each orchid; place flat in water and chill slightly. Secure wider ends of each carrot together with a toothpick. Place sprig of parsley or water cress in center. Place in water and chill. Use to garnish meat or large appetizer platters.

California Poppies—Use only thick carrots. Trim leaf end into rounded points and cut into 1 to 1½ inch pieces. Then pare thinly the entire surface, continuously to the center, keeping the spiral paring intact. Chill in ice water. Draw a piece of parsley through to be a center and a stem.

Celery Curls—Select large tender stalks of celery; cut in 3-inch lengths and slit each length in narrow parallel strips almost to the end. Place in water, add a quantity of chipped ice; as the slit celery chills the ends will curl. If desired, cut both ends of celery almost to center of piece, and when chilled, both ends will curl.

Corn Stalks—Scrape or peel large carrots and slice. Cut out small hole in center of carrot. Make celery curls but shred celery from both ends to center. Chill in ice water after placing through center of carrot slice.

Cucumber Slices—Pare cucumber; with a four-tined fork, score the cucumber lengthwise, then cut in very thin slices; chill in ice water to crisp. Drain and sprinkle lightly with finely chopped parsley. When skin is tender, cut in slices without removing it; the rim is decorative.

Cucumber Strips—Pare cucumber and cut in half; remove seeds and cut solid portion into narrow strips about 3 inches long. Place on plate, cover with damp cloth and chill for 1 hour before serving.

Cucumber Cornucopias—Pare cucumber; cut in paper-thin slices and with a sharp knife make an incision from the rim of each slice to the center. Bring one cut edge inside the other to form a cornucopia. Hold in place with a toothpick. Garnish with a sliver of carrot.

Pickle Fans—Cut small gherkins or sweet pickles in thin slices to—but not through—the end. Spread as a fan.

Calla Lily—Cut unpared cucumbers into very thin crosswise slices. Fold edge of one slice together at bottom. Insert a small strip of raw carrot for the stamen. Wrap a second slice of cucumber over open side and secure at bottom with toothpicks. Crisp in ice water before serving. Variation: Use slices of pared turnip in place of cucumber.

Onion Rings—Select large, mild onions—Bermuda or Spanish onions. Peel and cut in thin slices crosswise and place in ice water. When thoroughly chilled and crisp, loosen rings with a fork and drain well; serve with carrot strips, radish roses, or other crisp vegetables.

Onion Slices—Peel and slice small white onions. Cover with equal amounts of vinegar and water. Add cucumber slices, if desired; let stand 1 hour. Drain and sprinkle with salt and pepper.

Radish Fans—Select firm, rather long radishes and wash well. With a thin sharp knife, cut thin slices crosswise almost through the radish. Chill in ice water; as they chill the slices spread, fan shaped.

Radish Roses—Select firm round radishes, uniform in size, with no blemishes; wash and cut tops, leaving about 1 inch of stem on each. Cut a thin slice from root end of each. With a sharp thin knife, cut uniform thin strips of the red peel almost through to the stems. Place radishes in ice water; as they chill, the peel will curl back like petals.

Radish Pinwheels—Slice radish crosswise into very thin slices. Cut small slits in another radish, starting at top and working around and around to the stem end. In each slit place slice of radish. Chill.

Tomato Roses—Wash tomatoes and pare thickly through outer skin layer as you would an apple. Discard center, roll tomato peel around finger to form rose. Fill center with cream cheese or water cress.

Narcissus—Slice white turnips ¼-inch thick. Make a cardboard pattern of a narcissus opened flat. Place on turnip slice and cut around petals with a sharp knife. Run a pastry wheel or score lightly with sharp knife down center of each petal. Cut additional slices of turnip ⅜-inch thick and from these cut round pieces, ½ inch in diameter. Dig out center at one end to make "cups." Fasten one of these to each flower with a toothpick, leaving long end of pick on underside of flower to secure to stem. Use thick stems from spinach bunches for base of flowers. Crisp narcissus in ice water. When ready to use, dry and touch outer edge of cup and tips of petals with paprika. Place flowers in center of cluster of water cress.

CALIFORNIA SPECIAL

Break 3 quarts of crisp greens into bowl and sprinkle with 6 tablespoons of salad oil, 1 tablespoon of Worcestershire sauce, freshly ground black pepper and salt to taste, ½ cup Parmesan and Roquefort cheese cut in small cubes. Break 1 uncooked egg into the greens and over it pour the juice of 3 lemons and 1 pint of crisp croutons which have been marinated in 6 tablespoons of olive oil flavored with garlic. Toss all ingredients together lightly and serve. Yield: 6 portions.

SALAD GREENS

The most commonly used salad greens are lettuce (leaf, Boston—butter head type, Iceberg, or Simpson), romaine, chicory or French or Belgian endive, curly endive, water cress, escarole, parsley, tender spinach and dandelion leaves, Chinese or celery cabbage, tender cabbage leaves, fennel, salad chervil and nasturtium leaves. Remove all wilted leaves and wash thoroughly to remove sand; heads are more easily cleaned if core is removed and water is permitted to run down through head. Drain thoroughly and wrap in cloth, or place in vegetable container or bag, and chill until ready to use. Use many of these alone or in combination in bowl or on salad plate, or use as garnish. Always break, never cut, salad greens. Marinate with an acid dressing or serve with a French, mayonnaise or cooked dressing. Use one of the following salad green combinations.

Lettuce and water cress.
Lettuce, curly endive, spinach.
Lettuce, romaine, and chicory (French endive).
Lettuce, romaine, water cress, chicory, sliced green pepper.
Lettuce, sliced cucumbers and radishes, chopped scallions, slices of garlic, green pepper rings.
Lettuce, romaine, chicory, endive, escarole, chopped onion and garlic.
Curly endive, chopped pimiento.
Chicory, endive, tomato sections, thinly sliced raw mushrooms.
Romaine, sliced radishes and cucumbers.
Romaine, chopped pimiento, green pepper, green and ripe olives.
Romaine, dandelion greens, water cress, sliced radishes, minced scallions.
Dandelion greens, chicory, garlic and diced crisp bacon.
Crisp endive to dip in French dressing, dunking style.

CHICORY WITH BACON DRESSING

Allow 1 slice of bacon or ½ slice plus 1 teaspoon bacon fat per person. Cut bacon into small pieces. Fry until crisp and add vinegar, about 1 tablespoon per person. Set aside to keep warm. Break washed and crisp chicory, dandelion greens or garden lettuce in 2-inch pieces into a salad bowl. Heap on top finely chopped onion sprinkled well with sugar. Chill thoroughly. Just before serving, pour slightly warm bacon fat and vinegar over the greens and toss lightly.

WILTED LETTUCE

2 medium heads lettuce	dash of pepper
1 teaspoon sugar	4 to 6 slices bacon
½ teaspoon salt	¼ cup vinegar
	1 hard-cooked egg, chopped

Wash, drain and shred lettuce into a hot serving bowl; sprinkle with sugar, salt and pepper; mix with fork and let stand about 10 minutes to wilt slightly. Cut bacon in small pieces and fry until crisp; add vinegar, bring to a boil and pour over lettuce, mixing lightly with fork. Sprinkle with egg and serve at once. Approximate yield: 6 portions.

ENDIVE SALAD FANS

2 bunches endive	6 sprigs parsley
1 avocado	¼ cup French dressing

Wash endive stalks and separate spikes. Arrange 6 spikes in fan formation to cover half of the salad plate. Cut avocado in half lengthwise, remove seeds and peel halves, then slice crosswise. Lay 2 of these fan-shaped slices, 1 overlapping the other, across the tips of the converging endive points. In each endive spike, close to the avocado, place a tiny sprig of parsley. Serve with dressing. Yield: 6 portions.

STUFFED ENDIVE SALAD

1 3-oz package cream cheese	⅛ teaspoon salt
3 tablespoons ketchup	4 stalks endive
8 stuffed olives, chopped	French dressing

Mix the cream cheese, ketchup, olives and salt well and stuff crisp leaves of endive with the mixture. Serve 3 or 4 leaves to a person. Serve with French dressing. Approximate yield: 6 portions.

VEGETABLE COMBINATION SALAD

Raw, freshly cooked or canned vegetables may be used in many combinations in salads. They may be mixed, or marinated and served in salad bowl, or arranged as individual salads (page 583). Allow ⅔ cup per portion.

Raw Vegetable Salad—Marinate separately for 30 minutes equal amounts of grated raw carrots, beets and cucumber in French dressing. Place separately in small lettuce cups arranged 3 on each salad plate and serve with French dressing.

Raw Cauliflower Salad—Thinly slice crisp, uncooked cauliflower flowerets and marinate in French dressing ½ hour. Drain, add sliced celery heart, chopped red sweet pepper and sweet pickles, salt, pepper and onion juice and mix thoroughly. Pack in small molds; unmold on bed of crisp lettuce and garnish with rings of green and red pepper. Serve with mayonnaise.

Cooked Vegetable Salad—Mix equal amounts of cooked peas, string beans, cut in strips, diced carrots and diced cauliflower, asparagus tips, cubed, a clove of garlic or onion slices; sprinkle with salt and marinate in French dressing 1 hour in refrigerator. Drain off excess dressing and remove garlic or onion. Arrange in lettuce cups on salad plates.

Halloween Salad—Lightly mix canned kernel corn, cooked shredded string beans, cubed cooked potatoes and hard-cooked eggs, chopped; season to taste with minced onion, salt and pepper and fold in mayonnaise. Serve in lettuce cups, garnish with tomato slices and sprinkle with grated cooked egg yolk.

Macedoine Salad—Marinate separately with French dressing, cooked cauliflower, separated into small pieces, cooked peas and diced carrots. Drain and combine vegetables, arrange on crisp lettuce leaves and sprinkle with sliced stuffed olives. Serve with French dressing.

Picnic Salad—Lightly mix canned kidney beans, diced celery, chopped green pepper and sliced hard-cooked eggs with mayonnaise to moisten. Season with salt and pepper and serve on crisp lettuce.

ARTICHOKE SALAD

Cut 6 chilled Cooked Artichokes (page 522) in halves and remove the chokes; place 2 halves on individual salad plates and serve, cut side up, with mayonnaise. Approximate yield: 6 salads.

ASPARAGUS SALADS

Use cooked or canned asparagus tips; drain and chill. They may be marinated in French or any other dressing 1 hour before serving. Serve on crisp lettuce or other greens. Allow 4 to 6 tips per portion.

Asparagus Tip Salad—Marinate tips in French dressing, arrange in bundles in green pepper rings, or with thin strips of pimiento over top, or arrange like spokes of a wheel with ends at center and with tiny crisp hearts of lettuce leaves between tips. Serve with French dressing, Chiffonade Dressing (page 618), mayonnaise or Thousand Island Dressing (page 623).

Goldenrod Asparagus Salad—Cut off whites, lengthwise, from opposite sides of hard-cooked eggs, then cut each egg in 3 lengthwise slices. Remove yolks and force through fine sieve. Put 4 asparagus tips through each oval ring of egg white and place on crisp lettuce or water cress. Garnish with egg yolk and sprinkle lightly with paprika, salt and pepper. Serve with French dressing.

ASPARAGUS BAVARIAN

1 envelope plain gelatin	¼ teaspoon salt
¼ cup cold water	¼ teaspoon white pepper
1 cup canned asparagus liquid	¼ teaspoon onion juice
1 14½-oz. can of cut asparagus	½ pimiento, chopped (canned)
spears, drained and sieved	¼ teaspoon Worcestershire sauce

1 cup heavy cream

Soak gelatin in cold water, dissolve in hot asparagus liquid. Chill until slightly thickened, add sieved asparagus and the seasonings. Whip cream until stiff and fold into gelatin mixture. Chill well before serving. Yield: 6 to 8 portions.

ASPARAGUS MACEDOINE SALAD

2 cups cooked asparagus	¼ cup French dressing
(1 inch pieces)	lettuce
6 radishes, sliced	green pepper
4 scallions, sliced	mayonnaise
4 tablespoons chopped water	18 cooked asparagus tips
cress	

Mix together cooked asparagus, radishes, scallions and water cress; moisten with French dressing. Arrange nests of lettuce leaves on individual salad plates and heap with vegetable mixture. Cap the mound of salad with rings of green pepper, add a tablespoon of mayonnaise and place 3 asparagus tips upright in the center. Yield: 6 portions.

BEAN SALADS

Use cooked or canned green or waxed string beans, Lima, navy or kidney beans. Chill thoroughly and marinate in French dressing ½ to 1 hour before serving, if desired. Allow ½ to ⅔ cup per portion.

String Bean-Pimiento Salad—Lightly mix together 3 cups shredded string beans, 1 pimiento, cut in slender strips, and dash each of salt and pepper. Serve in crisp lettuce cups with ⅓ cup Cooked Salad Dressing (page 624) mixed with 2 tablespoons chow chow. Yield: 6 salads.

Lima Bean Salad—Mix together 3 cups Lima beans, 1 cup chopped celery, 1 tablespoon minced onion, 3 tablespoons India relish, ½ teaspoon salt and mayonnaise to moisten. Serve on crisp lettuce, garnish with slices of hard-cooked eggs and sprinkle with paprika. Approximate yield: 6 salads.

Baked Bean and Bacon Salad—Mix together 2 cups baked beans, 6 slices crisp bacon, diced, ½ cup diced cooked beets, 2 stalks celery, chopped, 2 tablespoons minced sweet pickle, 1 tablespoon ketchup and Cooked Salad Dressing (page 624) to moisten. Serve in lettuce cups. Approximate yield: 6 salads.

Kidney Bean and Apple Salad—Mix together 2¼ cups drained, cooked kidney beans, ¼ cup diced tart apple, ½ cup chopped cabbage, ½ teaspoon salt and mayonnaise to moisten. Serve on crisp salad greens. Approximate yield: 6 salads.

BEET SALADS

Beet Salad—Marinate 6 medium-sized beets, sliced, and 1 small onion, sliced, in ⅓ cup French dressing 1 hour. Arrange on crisp lettuce and serve with ⅓ cup mayonnaise mixed with 1 tablespoon horseradish. Approximate yield: 6 salads.

Beet Cup—Use 6 medium-sized cooked or canned beets; cut a slice from end of each so that they will stand; then scoop out centers from stem ends, leaving thin walls. Marinate in French dressing, if desired. Chop removed beet and mix with an equal amount of minced cabbage and 3 tablespoons chopped walnuts. Season lightly with salt and paprika and moisten wtih mayonnaise. Pile into beet cups, place each on crisp lettuce leaves and garnish with 3 capers. Yield: 6 salads.

CABBAGE SALADS

Remove wilted leaves from firm head of cabbage; cut in half or thirds, then cut in fine shreds and soak in ice or very cold water ½ hour or until crisp. Drain and dry between towels or absorbent paper; wrap and let stand in refrigerator until ready to use. Serve salads in large bowl. One pound cabbage makes about 3½ cups shredded cabbage. Allow ½ to ⅔ cup shredded cabbage per portion.

Coleslaw—Mix 3 cups crisped and dried shredded cabbage with 1 cup Cooked Salad Dressing (page 624), or Sour Cream Dressing (page 624), adding salt and pepper to taste and a few caraway seeds, if desired. Approximate yield: 6 portions.

Red Cabbage and Celery Salad—Mix together 2½ cups crisp and dried shredded cabbage, ½ cup cubed celery and 1 tablespoon minced onion. Add Sour Cream Dressing (page 624) and salt and pepper, stirring lightly with fork. Yield: 6 portions.

Virginia Coleslaw—Put small head of cabbage through food chopper, add 2 teaspoons salt, mix well and let stand 1 hour; drain. Grind 2 small green peppers (seeded) and add to cabbage. Combine ¼ teaspoon each of pepper and paprika, 3 tablespoons sugar, 2 tablespoons lemon juice and 3 to 4 tablespoons heavy cream; pour over cabbage and mix lightly. Equal amounts of green and red cabbage may be used. Approximate yield: 6 portions.

Cabbage Relish Salad—Mix 3 cups crisped and dried shredded cabbage, ½ cucumber, diced, ½ green pepper, finely shredded, ¼ cup chopped celery and 1 tablespoon minced onion; add mixture of ½ cup vinegar, 1 teaspoon salt and ⅛ teaspoon pepper and mix lightly with fork. Marinate in refrigerator for 1 hour. Just before serving, add ½ cup light cream. Approximate yield: 6 portions.

Hot Slaw—Place 4 cups shredded cabbage in flat-bottomed saucepan, add 1 teaspoon salt, ⅛ teaspoon pepper, 1 cup light cream and 2 tablespoons vinegar and heat thoroughly, stirring lightly with fork. Serve immediately. Approximate yield: 6 portions.

NEW YORK COLESLAW

1 2-pound cabbage, shredded	2 tablespoons sugar
2 carrots, grated	¼ teaspoon dry mustard
1 small onion, grated	⅔ cup water
3 stalks celery, minced	⅓ cup vinegar
2 tablespoons flour	1 egg, slightly beaten
¼ teaspoon salt	2 teaspoons sour cream

Toss shredded cabbage, grated carrots, grated onion and minced celery. Make a dressing by mixing flour, salt, sugar, and dry mustard. Stir to a smooth paste with water and vinegar. Add egg, slightly beaten, and stir over low heat until mixture thickens. Remove from heat and add sour cream. Garnish with green pepper rings. Chill. Serve over slaw. Approximate yield: 6 portions.

CARROT SALADS

Use raw, cooked or canned carrots; chop, cube, slice thinly, cut in matchlike strips, grate or shred. Serve plain, in combination with other vegetables, or with fruit, meat or fish. Allow ⅔ cup per portion.

Carrot and Raisin Salad—Mix grated raw carrots with seedless raisins, using ¼ cup raisins to 1 cup carrots; add French dressing or mayonnaise to moisten. Serve on crisp lettuce, water cress or shredded romaine. Cubes of apple or pineapple or chopped nuts may be added.

CAULIFLOWER SALADS

Cauliflower may be used raw or cooked in many combinations. Select small heads, remove leaves and blemishes; wash and soak in cold water ½ hour and dry well. Separate flowerets, cut in large pieces or slice, shred, or chop; slice or chop stems fine. If cooked, marinate in French dressing in refrigerator ½ hour.

Cauliflower and Green Pepper Salad—Combine 1 cup shredded raw cauliflower, ½ cup diced celery, 3 tablespoons minced green pepper, 2 tablespoons chopped sweet pickle, dash of salt and ¼ cup French dressing; chill ½ hour. Place on salad plates on nest of shredded lettuce, garnish with tomato sections and serve with additional dressing. Approximate yield: 6 salads.

CUCUMBER COMBINATION SALAD

Chill 1 large cucumber; pare with a fluted knife and slice thinly. Add 1 cup sliced celery hearts, ½ cup broken pecan meats and ⅓ cup shredded red and green peppers. Moisten with mayonnaise mixed with whipped cream. Arrange in mounds on thick slices of tomatoes. Set in nests of lettuce leaves and sprinkle each with 1 teaspoon finely chopped Bermuda onion. Approximate yield: 6 salads.

STUFFED CUCUMBER CUPS

Wash 3 small cucumbers and score lengthwise with a fork; cut in halves crosswise, cut off ends and hollow out centers, discarding seeds, and save pulp. Sprinkle insides with salt and pepper and chill 20 minutes. Fill cups with mixture of 1 3-oz. package cream cheese, finely chopped cucumber pulp, ⅛ teaspoon each salt and paprika, and 1 teaspoon lemon juice. Garnish with bit of pimiento and serve on beds of fresh water cress with French dressing. Yield: 6 salads.

STUFFED CUCUMBER SALAD

Select 2 medium-sized cucumbers, cut in half crosswise, pare thinly and scoop out the seeds, leaving the entire centers hollow; sprinkle with salt, pepper and Worcestershire sauce and chill 20 minutes. Combine 2 3-oz. packages cream cheese, ¼ cup each chopped onion and green pepper; season with salt and paprika; stuff firmly into cucumber shells. Put shells together, fasten with toothpicks and roll in French dressing; chill. To serve, cut in ¼ inch slices, place on shredded crisp lettuce and garnish with strips of pimiento; pour French dressing over salad. Approximate yield: 6 to 8 salads.

STUFFED GREEN PEPPER SALAD

Wash 2 large green peppers, cut off tops and remove seeds and centers; chop tops for filling. Mash 2 3-oz. packages cream cheese to a paste with ⅓ cup mayonnaise. Add ¼ cup stuffed Spanish olives, chopped, chopped green pepper tops, ½ teaspoon salt and dash of pepper and mix thoroughly. Pack into green peppers and chill. Slice thin and arrange on bed of crisp lettuce. Serve with Russian dressing (page 623). Approximate yield: 6 portions.

POTATO SALAD

3 cups diced hot potatoes	1 teaspoon salt
2 hard-cooked eggs, chopped	dash of pepper
½ cup diced cucumbers	2 tablespoons sugar
½ cup diced celery	2 tablespoons vinegar
2 tablespoons minced onion	½ cup mayonnaise or Cooked

Salad Dressing (page 624)

Mix all ingredients thoroughly and chill; sugar may be omitted, and one or several of the following vegetables may be substituted for cucumbers or celery or both: diced radishes, chopped cabbage, minced pimientos, chopped green peppers or chopped sweet pickles. Yield: 6 portions.

POTATO–BACON SALAD

4 cups diced hot potatoes	1 pimiento, chopped
8 slices crisp bacon, crumbled	2 tablespoons chopped chives
12 stuffed olives, chopped	½ cup French dressing

Mix all ingredients thoroughly and let stand until cold. Serve in salad bowl lined with salad leaves, if desired. Yield: 6 portions.

PARTY POTATO SALAD

6 large potatoes (2 quarts
   diced cooked)
½ cup mayonnaise
½ cup cooked peas
½ cup diced, cooked carrots
2 apples, pared and diced
2 stalks celery, diced

2 dill pickles, finely chopped
1 tablespoon chopped parsley
1 tablespoon chopped, fresh dill
½ cup heavy sour cream
5 tablespoons cider vinegar
   or lemon juice
1 tablespoon salt

Wash potatoes and place in boiling, salted water. Cook until tender. While still warm, peel and dice and blend with mayonnaise. Cover and chill several hours. Add remaining ingredients and blend. Approximate yield: 8 to 10 portions.

HOT POTATO SALAD RING

Boil 6 medium-sized potatoes in their skins; peel and dice into salad bowl rubbed with garlic. Add ½ cup minced celery, 1 small onion, minced, 1 green pepper, minced, and 1 cup hot Cooked Sour Cream Dressing (page 624) and mix thoroughly. Season to taste and arrange, ring shape, on large chop plate. In center of ring, serve a tomato sauce made by cooking until thick 1⅓ cups canned tomatoes, 1 onion, minced, 1 teaspoon minced chives, ¼ teaspoon salt and a dash of paprika. Approximate yield: 6 portions.

SECRET SALAD

3 pounds potatoes
¼ cup finely diced bacon
¼ cup chopped onion
1 tablespoon flour
2 teaspoons salt

1¼ tablespoons sugar
¼ teaspoon pepper
⅔ cup cider vinegar
⅓ cup water
½ teaspoon celery seed

3 tablespoons chopped parsley

Cook potatoes in jackets until tender. Cool, peel, thinly slice. Fry bacon until crisp, add chopped onion; cook 1 minute. Blend flour, salt, sugar and pepper. Stir in vinegar and water. Cook 10 minutes, stirring well. Pour over sliced potatoes, add celery seed and parsley; mix, serve warm. Yield: 6 portions.

STUFFED TOMATO SALADS

Wash medium-sized, firm, ripe tomatoes; peel, if desired, and scoop out centers. Sprinkle insides with salt, invert and chill in refrigerator. Fill with stuffing, serve on crisp salad greens with salad dressing and garnish as desired. The following fruit, vegetable, fish, or meat stuffings may be used:

Avocado Stuffing—Mix together diced avocado, chicory or French endive and celery hearts; moisten with French dressing.

Orange Stuffing—Mix together diced orange sections, chopped tomato pulp, drained, and minced onion or chives; moisten with dressing.

Pineapple-Cabbage Stuffing—Mix shredded fresh pineapple and cabbage and chopped tomato pulp, drained; moisten with mayonnaise.

Pineapple-Cheese Stuffing—Mix together finely chopped fresh or canned pineapple and tomato pulp, drained, minced scallion and water cress and cream cheese; moisten with mayonnaise.

Carrot-Olive Stuffing—Mix together grated raw carrot, minced stuffed olives, tomato pulp and cream cheese; moisten with cream and serve with salt and pepper.

Corn and Green Pepper Stuffing—Mix together cooked kernel corn, diced celery, tomato pulp, drained, and minced green pepper and pimiento; sprinkle with salt and marinate in French dressing. Top filled tomatoes with frankfurters, boiled, skinned, sliced and sautéed in butter, if desired.

Crab Meat Stuffing—Mix flaked crab meat, diced celery, chopped tomato pulp, minced pimiento and capers. Moisten with mayonnaise.

Chicken Stuffing—Substitute diced chicken and cucumber for crab meat and celery, and omit capers in crab meat stuffing.

Cottage Cheese-Chive Stuffing—Mix together cottage cheese and minced chives; moisten with dressing and season to taste.

Cucumber and Celery Stuffing—Mix together diced cucumber and celery, chopped tomato pulp and scraped onion. Moisten with dressing and season.

EASTER SALAD

6 hard-cooked eggs	½ teaspoon salt
1 tablespoon softened butter	⅛ teaspoon black pepper
2 teaspoons lemon juice	1 tablespoon French dressing
¾ teaspoon dry mustard	water cress
1 teaspoon Worcestershire sauce	1 pound cooked asparagus tips
	pimiento

Remove shells from hard-cooked eggs and cut eggs in halves horizontally. Remove yolks. Press yolks through a sieve and combine with butter, lemon juice, dry mustard, Worcestershire sauce, salt, pepper and French dressing. Beat until smooth and refill whites, reserving a portion. Fit together. Cut one end of egg into star shape with a sharp knife and decorate with reserved egg yolks portion forced through a pastry tube. Place on a bed of water cress with 1 pound cooked asparagus tips and garnish with strips of canned pimiento. Yield: 6 portions.

RICE SALAD

1 cup rice	1 small cucumber, diced
2 quarts boiling water	2 tomatoes, skinned and
1 teaspoon salt	quartered
1 cup cooked peas	½ cup lobster, shrimp or crab
1 cup diced cooked carrots	meat (optional)

Gradually add rice to boiling water with salt. Cook covered 12 to 15 minutes, stirring occasionally. Drain and rinse in colander with cold water. Drain thoroughly. Lightly toss together with peas, carrots, cucumbers, tomatoes and fish, if desired. Mix with French dressing. Serve with bundles of cooked asparagus or a bunch of fresh water cress and surround with stuffed eggs. Yield: 3 cups rice salad.

CAMELBACK MOUNTAIN SALAD BOWL

Make a garlic French dressing by whipping together 2 raw eggs, ½ cup garlic oil and ½ cup lemon juice. Marinate 2 hours in this dressing, small whole cooked carrots, slices of cooked potatoes, whole cooked green beans and cooked peas. Line a large salad bowl with romaine lettuce and in the center arrange the vegetables. Garnish with tomato wedges, cucumber rings, slices of avocado, ripe olives and capers. Serve with Herb Mayonnaise (page 622).

SUNDAY NIGHT SALAD BOWL

1 clove garlic, halved	3 tomatoes, cut in small pieces
1 bunch water cress	1 bunch scallions, chopped
1 bunch chicory	3 tablespoons Roquefort cheese,
1 small head lettuce	crumbled
5 radishes, thinly sliced	3 slices crisp bacon, chopped
3 stalks celery, chopped	½ cup Anchovy Dressing (page
1 raw carrot, thinly sliced	618)
2 stalks chicory, thinly sliced	salt and pepper to taste

Rub a large salad bowl with both halves of the garlic. With fingers break the greens (water cress, chicory, lettuce) into small pieces into bowl; add other ingredients and mix thoroughly. Doing this properly requires about 5 minutes. Marinate with ½ cup dressing and serve with additional dressing in bowl. Approximate yield: 6 portions.

FRUIT SALADS

Fresh, cooked or canned fruits are used in many combinations in salads. Choose firm, perfect fruit. Prepare fruit that discolors, such as apples, avocados, bananas and peaches, just before serving, or dip in lemon juice to prevent discoloration. Pare, peel or leave skin on; scoop out to make cups, halve, quarter, slice, remove sections or dice. Marinate if desired; chill and drain. Serve in salad bowl, or on individual plates on a salad green. Allow about ½ cup fruit per salad.

Waldorf Salad—Combine diced apples, celery and mayonnaise or Cooked Salad Dressing (page 624); add walnuts just before serving.

Avocado and Grapefruit Salad—Peel avocados and slice lengthwise; marinate in French dressing ½ hour. Place 4 slices alternately with 3 sections of grapefruit on 5 crisp stalks of chicory or French endive on each salad plate. Serve with Cream Mayonnaise (page 621), or use tomatoes or cucumbers and French dressing with avocados.

Avocado-Persimmon Salad—Substitute persimmons for grapefruit in salad above; arrange on beds of water cress on salad plate or in individual wooden bowls and serve with French dressing.

Summer Salad—Peel avocados, cut in halves lengthwise, remove large stones and cut crosswise in about ¾-inch slices; marinate in French dressing or lemon juice. Place 2 slices together to form ring on crisp lettuce leaves and fill center with mixture of chopped beets and celery. Serve with French dressing.

Banana Glacé Fruit Salad—Slice bananas and sprinkle with lemon juice; arrange on crisp romaine, sprinkle with minced glacé fruit and top with Cream Mayonnaise (page 621).

Ginger-Fruit Salad—Combine diced orange sections and canned pineapple, sliced bananas, seedless or seeded, halved grapes, chopped candied ginger and nut meats and Lime French Dressing (page 619). Serve in crisp lettuce cups.

Grapefruit and Apple Salad—Alternate wedges of grapefruit sections and red apples (unpeeled) on crisp lettuce. Serve with Fruit French Dressing (page 618) or with French dressing diluted with grapefruit juice.

Grapefruit, Pineapple, Apricot Salad—Place sliced pineapple on crisp lettuce; build wedges of grapefruit sections around pineapple; place apricot half, hollow side up, in center and fill with mixture of chopped celery and dates. Serve with Fruit French Dressing (page 618).

Orange and Onion Salad—Pare and slice seedless oranges crosswise; place 2 slices on crisp salad green on each plate and top with a thin slice of Bermuda onion. Serve with French dressing. For **Orange Mint Salad,** omit onion, add chopped mint to French dressing and serve on crisp lettuce, garnished with sprigs of mint.

Peach Salad—Mix together diced canned pineapple, fresh peaches and celery, blanched almonds and Cream Mayonnaise (page 621); serve in lettuce cups.

Pear Salad—Place drained canned pear half, cut side down, on bed of crisp lettuce on salad plate; stick with blanched sliced almonds and garnish with sliced maraschino cherries. Serve with French dressing mixed with melted currant jelly.

Dessert Salad—Combine cantaloupe balls or cubes, diced bananas, quartered marshmallows, pecan halves and Cooked Salad Dressing (page 624). Serve on crisp lettuce.

FRUIT PLATTERS FOR BRIDGE

Use large silver platter or glass tray; fill center depression with chipped ice and embed crisp lettuce cups in it for each fruit. Fill cups individually with the following or similar fruits:

Frosted Grapes—Dip small clusters of grapes in slightly beaten egg white; when nearly dry, shake fine granulated sugar over them.

Pear Slices—Cut ripe Bartlett pears in thin slices and dip in heavy ginger syrup just before placing in lettuce cup.

Orange Bowls—Cut seedless oranges in halves, leaving a pointed elevated side for a handle. Remove pulp in sections; mix with crystalized cherries, bits of marrons glacés and blanched almonds; sprinkle with powdered sugar and maraschino liqueur. Fill bowls and half bury them in cracked ice.

Filled Cantaloupe—Cut small melons in halves, remove seeds, embed in ice and fill with clusters of cherries and fragments of ice.

Strawberries and Pineapple Cones—Dip unhulled large strawberries and pineapple cones (page 105) in powdered sugar.

Frosted Currants—Plumb currants (page 106); while slightly damp, roll in powdered sugar. Use to top any fruit salad bowl.

Apricot Bursts—Remove stones from large ripe apricots, opening only enough to remove stones and not breaking skins unnecessarily. Fill centers of pitted lichee nuts or pitted dates with a wedge of Roquefort or sharp cheese, slip one into each apricot and press together lightly, leaving nut barely visible.

Watermelon Chips—Cut watermelon into small strips ¼ inch thick. Garnish with a sprig of water cress.

PERSIMMON SALAD

4 large ripe persimmons	4 teaspoons chopped pistachio
lettuce	nuts
¾ cup diced canned pears	4 teaspoons chopped English
½ cup sliced canned peaches	walnuts
¾ cup seedless grapes	1 cup Honey Cream Dressing
½ cup diced fresh pineapple	(page 622)

Select ripe persimmons; wash and cut in quarters at the small end, leaving an uncut portion at the stem end so that the quarters may be spread apart but will remain attached. Do not peel persimmons if you wish to preserve the natural shape of fruit; if it is fully ripe, it is very easy to cut pulp away from skin with fork while eating it. Place a persimmon in center of bed of lettuce on salad plate; spread apart and fill center with mixture of remaining fruits. Sprinkle 1 teaspoon each of pistachio and English walnuts on top of each and serve salad dressing on side. Yield: 4 salads.

MINTED FRUIT SALAD

¾ cup diced fresh pineapple   1½ cups ginger ale
¾ cup sliced bananas   ½ cup lemon juice
¾ cup cubed oranges or peaches   ¼ bunch mint, minced
¾ cup diced cantaloupe   lettuce
¾ cup marshmallows, quartered   cantaloupe balls
1½ tablespoons powdered sugar   mint sprigs

Lightly combine pineapple, bananas, oranges or peaches, cantaloupe, marshmallows and sugar. Mix ginger ale and lemon juice and pour over fruits; chill about 2 hours in refrigerator. To serve, drain off ginger ale, lightly mix mint into fruits and serve on lettuce; garnish with cantaloupe balls and sprigs of mint. Yield: 6 salads.

APRICOT SALAD

6 large ripe apricots   4 tablespoons chopped olives
2 cups diced celery   mayonnaise
½ cup broken nuts   salt and pepper

Wash, stone and cut apricots in halves; fill halves with mixture of celery, nuts, olives, mayonnaise to moisten and salt and pepper to taste. Serve 2 halves on bed of crisp salad greens on individual plate or arrange salads on platter or chop plate. Yield: 6 salads.

CANTALOUPE WALDORF SALAD

2 cups diced cantaloupe   ½ cup chopped nuts
1 cup diced apples   lettuce
1 cup diced fresh peaches   1 cup Cream Mayonnaise (page
1 cup minced celery   621)
¼ cup French dressing   finely chopped fresh mint

Combine fruits and celery; marinate in French dressing 10 minutes. Drain off excess dressing, add nuts and serve on crisp lettuce on individual plates. Top with cream mayonnaise and sprinkle with mint. Yield: 6 salads.

ORANGE AND BLACK OLIVE SALAD

4 navel oranges   ½ cup ripe olives, sliced
2 onions, thinly sliced   pimiento rings
lettuce   ½ cup French dressing, chilled

Peel oranges, removing all membrane; slice thin. Arrange in alternate layers with onions on lettuce. Sprinkle with olives. Garnish with pimiento. Chill; serve with dressing. Yield: 4 to 6 portions.

VALENTINE FRUIT SALAD

1 No. 2½ can pears   1 No. 2½ can sliced pineapple
½ cup red cinnamon drops   ½ cup chopped nuts
3 tablespoons vinegar   1½ cups Cream Mayonnaise
lettuce   (page 621)

Drain pears; to pear syrup add cinnamon drops and vinegar and bring
to a boil. Trim each pear half into heart shape and simmer in syrup
20 minutes; chill. Place pear half, hollow side down, on crisp lettuce
arranged on individual plates. Cut pineapple in small sections and
arrange around pears. Sprinkle nuts around edge of salad to give lacy
effect. Serve mayonnaise in separate bowl. Yield: 8 salads.

KUMQUAT FRUIT SALAD

1 cup orange sections (page 98) ½ cup heavy cream, whipped
3 preserved kumquats, sliced   dash of salt
2 large tart apples   lettuce
juice and grated rind of 1 lemon 2 teaspoons chopped pistachio
½ cup mayonnaise   nuts

Cut orange sections in half lengthwise. Combine with kumquat slices.
Pare, core and cut apples into thin strips and toss as soon as cut with
other fruit and lemon juice to prevent discoloring. Add lemon rind to
mayonnaise and fold in cream. Add more salt if necessary. Just before
serving, fold ½ of the dressing into the fruit so that each piece is
coated with it. Serve in crisp lettuce cups garnished wtih remaining
mayonnaise and chopped pistachio nuts. Yield: 6 portions.

LAITUE AUX CRÊPES

½ cup cottage cheese   5 tablespoons mayonnaise,
½ cup grated cheese   highly seasoned
1 cup raisins   large lettuce leaves

Cream cheeses together. Combine with raisins and mayonnaise. Spread
thickly on large lettuce leaves and roll up. Allow two lettuce rolls to a
serving. Or use 1 3-oz. package cream cheese, 2 tablespoons Roquefort cheese, salt, pepper, Worcestershire sauce and mayonnaise for
spread. Approximate yield: 1¼ cups of spread.

MEAT, CHICKEN AND FISH SALADS

Use well-seasoned cooked meat or poultry, or use cooked or canned fish. Remove bone, skin, fat and gristle from meat and poultry; cut in ¼ to ½ inch cubes; cut or flake fish. Toss lightly with mayonnaise or Cooked Salad Dressing (page 624), seasoning to taste as desired. Chill, serve in salad bowl or individual plates. Garnish with crisp greens and additional dressing, cooked or raw vegetables, fruit. Macaroni, etc., may be substituted for part of meat, chicken or fish, if desired. Additional flavor may be given to meat and poultry salads by marinating with a little French dressing before mixing. Allow 3 cups ingredients and about ¾ cup dressing for 6 portions.

MEAT SALADS

Ham and Cheese Salad—Use 1 cup diced ham, 1 cup diced cheese, 1 small onion, diced, ½ cup diced celery. Garnish with slices of tomato and hard-cooked eggs.

New England Salad—Use ¾ cup diced corned beef, cooked or canned, 1 cup each diced cooked beets and potatoes, ½ cup chopped celery, 1 tablespoon minced onion, ½ teaspoon salt and 2 hard-cooked eggs, coarsely chopped.

Rosy Veal Salad—Marinate 2 cups diced veal in ¾ cup red wine vinegar for ½ hour. Add ½ pound water chestnuts, peeled and diced, heart leaves of 1 head curly chicory and ½ bunch water cress; sprinkle with chives.

Veal Salad—Use 1½ cups diced veal, ¾ cup diced celery, 2 hard-cooked eggs, chopped, and 8 stuffed olives, sliced. Veal may be substituted for all or part of the chicken in any recipe for chicken salad.

Sweetbread Salad—Use 1 cup diced sweetbreads, 1 cup diced celery and 1 cup diced cucumber.

Sweetbread and Orange Salad—Use 1½ cups diced sweetbreads, 1 cup diced orange and ½ cup diced celery.

Tongue and Vegetable Salad—Use 1½ cups each diced cooked tongue and finely shredded cabbage, 1 large carrot, shredded, ⅜ cup diced sweet pickles, ½ teaspoon salt and enough Savory Mayonnaise (page 623) to moisten.

CHICKEN SALADS

Chicken and Asparagus Salad—Use 1½ cups diced chicken, 1 cup asparagus tips, 2 tablespoons minced green pepper and ¼ cup chopped cabbage.

Chicken and Cabbage Salad—Use 2 cups shredded cabbage, ½ cup diced chicken, ½ cup diced ham and ¼ cup minced pimiento.

Chicken Salad—Use 2 cups diced chicken, ½ cup chopped celery, ½ cup diced cucumbers and 2 tablespoons capers.

Chicken and Mushroom Salad—Use 2 cups chicken, ½ cup sautéed mushrooms, ½ cup diced celery; garnish with grapefruit sections.

Chicken and Olive Salad—Use 2 cups diced chicken, ¾ cup diced celery, ⅓ cup sliced stuffed olives. Garnish with hard-cooked eggs.

Chicken and Pineapple Salad—Use 2 cups diced chicken, 1 cup diced fresh pineapple and 12 ripe olives, diced.

Chicken and Sweetbread Salad—Use 1 cup each diced chicken and sweetbreads, ½ cup celery, 3 hard-cooked eggs, sliced, and 3 stuffed olives, sliced.

Chicken and Tomato Salad—Use 1 cup diced chicken, ½ cup diced, crisp bacon and 1 cup diced tomato.

Chicken and Tongue Salad—Use 1 cup diced chicken, 1 cup diced tongue, ½ cup diced celery and ½ cup sliced stuffed olives.

Chicken and Vegetable Salad—Use 1½ cups diced chicken and 1½ cups mixed vegetables—cooked peas and Lima beans, diced cucumber and celery.

Duck and Orange Salad—Use 1½ cups diced duck, 1¼ cups diced oranges and ¼ cup diced celery.

Turkey and Chestnut Salad—Use 1 cup diced turkey, ½ cup chopped, boiled chestnuts (page 543), 1 cup diced celery, 2 hard-cooked eggs, chopped, and 10 stuffed olives, chopped.

FISH SALADS

Crab and Marcaroni Salad—Use 1½ cups flaked crab meat, 1 cup cooked elbow macaroni, ½ cup diced celery, 2 tablespoons chopped green pepper, 1 tablespoon chopped pimiento and 2 teaspoons chopped sweet pickles. Season with salt and few drops of Tabasco sauce.

Fish and Apple Salad—Use 1½ cups flaked fish (tuna, crab, salmon, shrimp or white fish) and 1½ cups diced tart apple.

Fish and Cucumber Salad—Use 1½ cups flaked fish, ½ cup each diced cucumber and celery, 2 slices minced Bermuda onion, 6 chopped radishes and ½ small head lettuce, shredded.

Mold of Salmon Salad—Use 1 1-pound can flaked salmon, 1 cup diced celery, 1 cup diced cucumber, ½ cup chopped ripe olives, 1 teaspoon onion juice, ½ teaspoon salt, ⅛ teaspoon pepper and ¾ cup mayonnaise. Serve on crisp lettuce, arranging it in heart shapes with spoon and spatula. Edge each heart with mayonnaise, marking border with a fork, and garnish with red arrow cut from pimiento.

Herring Salad—Use 2 salt herrings, flaked, 1 cup cooked potato cubes, 8 sliced olives, 1 small onion, grated, 2 hard-cooked eggs, chopped, and 1 tablespoon capers. Substitute French dressing for mayonnaise.

Lobster Salad—Use 2½ cups lobster and ½ cup diced celery. Garnish with lobster claws. Marinate in French dressing before combining with mayonnaise. Garnish with sliced hard-cooked eggs and caviar.

Sardine and Potato Salad—Use 8 sardines, flaked, 2 cups diced potatoes, 1 small onion, diced, 2 tablespoons chopped parsley and 2 tablespoons chopped dill pickle. Mix with French dressing.

Seafood Salad—Use 1½ cups flaked crab meat, 1 cup cooked shrimp marinated 20 minutes in 2 tablespoons French dressing. Add 1 cup diced celery, 2 tablespoons capers, 1 tablespoon chopped green pepper and 3 tablespoons pickle relish.

Shrimp and Asparagus Salad—Arrange 3 or 4 asparagus tips and 3 or 4 cooked whole shrimp on salad plates. Top with Savory Mayonnaise (page 623).

Shrimp and Grapefruit Salad—Use 1 cup shrimp, 1 cup broken grapefruit sections, ⅓ cup diced cucumber and ¾ cup diced celery. Garnish with pimiento strips.

Pavlova Salad—Use 1½ cups flaked crab meat, ½ cup diced cucumber, ½ cup diced tomato and 1 hard-cooked egg, chopped. Mix with Russian Dressing (page 623).

Tuna-Spinach Salad—Use 1½ cups chopped raw spinach, marinated ½ hour in ⅓ cup French dressing, 1½ cups flaked tuna fish and 1 small onion, minced. Serve with French dressing with a garnish of stuffed olive slices.

DELICES FLORIDEN

3 avocados
½ cup flaked smoked salmon
½ cup flaked tuna fish
2 anchovy fillets, minced
½ cup diced celery

½ cup diced apple
½ cup diced tomato
French dressing
lettuce
1 hard-cooked egg, sliced
caviar

Cut avocados in half lengthwise; remove stone. Marinate fish, celery, apple and tomato in French dressing ½ hour. Heap shells with mixture. Serve on crisp lettuce and garnish with a slice of hard-cooked egg and a little caviar. Yield: 6 portions.

COTTAGE CHEESE SALAD

2 cups cottage cheese
salt and pepper

light cream
6 lettuce leaves
¾ cup French dressing

Season cottage cheese to taste with salt and pepper; add cream until of desired consistency. Two tablespoons chopped onion may be added, if desired. Serve on lettuce with French dressing. Cottage cheese and grated American cheese may be used in equal amounts, if desired. Yield: 6 portions.

Cottage Cheese and Chive Salad—Add ¼ cup finely cut chives to cheese; substitute mayonnaise for cream.

Cottage Cheese and Cucumber Salad—Add 1½ tablespoons minced pimiento, 2 teaspoons horseradish and ¼ cup chili sauce to 1 cup cottage cheese. Slice 1 large cucumber, arrange on lettuce and top with mound of cheese mixture.

Cottage Cheese and Raisin Salad—Add ½ cup seedless raisins and ¼ cup chopped green pepper to 1½ cups cottage cheese; substitute mayonnaise for cream.

Cottage Cheese and Olive Salad—Add 24 stuffed olives to 1½ cups cottage cheese; serve with Cooked Salad Dressing (page 624), garnishing with additional sliced olives.

Cottage Cheese and Strawberry Salad—Combine 1½ cups cottage cheese lightly with 1 cup fresh strawberries and 2 teaspoons chopped mint. Substitute diced orange sections for berries.

CHEESE BALLS

Mix softened cream cheese, or cream cheese spread, with chopped pickles, nuts, olives, green pepper, pimiento, pineapple or preserved ginger, using ¼ to ⅓ cup to 1 3-oz. package cheese. Shape into small balls, or form into long roll, chill and slice. Arrange 3 balls or slices on crisp lettuce or water cress and serve with French dressing. Or use tiny balls as a garnish for fish, vegetable or tart fruit salads.

TOMATO LOAF SALAD

3 cups tomato juice	1 cup chopped, cooked ham
1 small onion, grated	1 teaspoon prepared mustard
1 teaspoon sugar	mayonnaise
salt and pepper	1 cup cream cheese
2 envelopes plain gelatin	2 tablespoons sour cream
½ cup cold water	½ teaspoon salt
lettuce and water cress	

Simmer tomato juice, onion and sugar 5 minutes; add salt and pepper to taste. Soften gelatin in cold water 5 minutes, then dissolve in hot tomato juice; cool. Mix ham with mustard and moisten well with mayonnaise; blend cheese, sour cream and salt. Pour ⅓ of dissolved gelatin into loaf mold, lightly brushed with oil, and chill until firm. Cover with ham mixture, add ⅓ of gelatin and again chill. Cover with cheese mixture, add last of gelatin; chill until firm. Unmold on large platter, garnish with lettuce and water cress; serve with additional mayonnaise. Approximate yield: 8 portions.

MOLDED CUCUMBER SALAD

1 package lime-flavored gelatin	dash each pepper, paprika
1½ cups water	1 cucumber, finely chopped
1 tablespoon vinegar	lettuce
1 teaspoon scraped onion	Cooked Salad Dressing (page
½ teaspoon salt	624)

Dissolve gelatin in water according to package directions; add vinegar and seasonings; chill. When slightly thickened, fold in cucumber. Turn into square pan and chill until firm. Cut in squares and serve on crisp lettuce with dressing. Approximate yield: 4 to 6 portions.

GOLDEN GLOW SALAD

1 package lemon-flavored   ¼ teaspoon salt
    gelatin   ¾ cup grapefruit sections
2 cups water   ¾ cup grated raw carrots
1½ teaspoons vinegar   lettuce
                       mayonnaise

Dissolve gelatin in water according to package directions, add vinegar
and salt; chill. When slightly thickened, fold in grapefruit and carrots.
Turn into 6 individual molds; chill until firm. Unmold on crisp
lettuce and garnish with mayonnaise. Yield: 6 salads.

TOMATO ASPIC

2 cups canned tomatoes   2 whole cloves
¾ cup water   ¼ teaspoon peppercorns
1 stalk celery, chopped   blade of mace
2 carrots, sliced   ¼ teaspoon salt
2 tablespoons chopped onion   dash of pepper
½ small green pepper, chopped   1½ tablespoons plain gelatin
                  1 tablespoon lemon juice

Put tomatoes and ½ cup water in saucepan and add vegetables and
seasonings; bring to boiling point and simmer 15 minutes; strain.
Soften gelatin in remaining ¼ cup cold water about 5 minutes; add
hot tomato juice, stirring until gelatin is dissolved; add lemon juice.
Pour into individual molds; chill until firm. Unmold on crisp lettuce
and garnish with mayonnaise. One to 2 cups mixed cooked vegetables or diced hard-cooked egg may be added, if desired, or plain
aspic may be molded in 1 large or 6 small ring molds and served with
chicken, fish or vegetable salad heaped in center. Approximate yield:
6 to 8 salads.

JELLIED TOMATO RINGS

Prepare Tomato Aspic (see above), adding 1 cup flaked, canned crab
meat, 2 tablespoons chopped sweet pickles and 2 tablespoons lemon
juice. When gelatin is slightly thickened, turn into individual ring
molds; chill until firm. Unmold on crisp lettuce, fill centers with crab
meat salad. Approximate yield: 4 to 6 salads.

CHINESE CHICKEN SALAD

2 envelopes plain gelatin
¼ cup cold water
1½ cups boiling chicken stock
½ teaspoon salt
⅛ teaspoon paprika
1 cup canned pineapple juice
2½ cups minced cooked chicken

1½ cups drained diced pine-
　apple
1 cup shredded, toasted
　almonds
lettuce and chicory
Mustard Cream Mayonnaise
　(page 622)

Soften gelatin in cold water 5 minutes; dissolve in boiling stock, add seasonings and pineapple juice; chill. When slightly thickened, fold in chicken, pineapple and almonds. Turn into large mold; chill until firm. Unmold on large platter, garnish with lettuce and chicory and serve with mayonnaise. Approximate yield: 8 salads.

PRESSED CHICKEN PIMIENTO

2 3-pound chickens
2 envelopes plain gelatin
3 or 4 canned pimientos, sliced
2 hard-cooked eggs, sliced

3 cups boiling chicken stock
¼ cup cold water
¼ cup white wine
1 teaspoon salt
⅛ teaspoon black pepper

Simmer chicken in just enough water to cover. Remove skin and separate meat from bones. Slice breast meat; chop balance and chill. Skim fat from broth and boil until reduced to 3 cups; season well with salt and pepper; strain. Soften gelatin in cold water, add to condensed broth and wine and stir until dissolved. Cover bottom of a 2-quart loaf pan or mold, rinsed with cold water, with ⅛ inch layer of prepared broth and chill until set. Arrange pimiento slices and sliced eggs in fancy design, then add sliced white meat to make an even layer. Cover lightly with broth and chill until firm. Cool, then chill remaining broth until syrupy. Add remaining chicken, pimientos and chopped eggs to broth and pack into mold. Chill until firm. Unmold on platter and garnish with water cress and chicory on which hard-cooked eggs and asparagus are arranged. Yield: 8 portions.

PERFECTION SALAD

1 envelope plain gelatin
2 tablespoons cold water
1 cup boiling water
2 tablespoons sugar
1½ teaspoons salt
dash of pepper
¾ cup canned pineapple juice

¼ cup vinegar
1 cup shredded cabbage
¾ cup diced celery
1 tablespoon chopped green
  pepper
¼ cup chopped stuffed olives
lettuce
mayonnaise

Soften gelatin in cold water 5 minutes, add boiling water and stir until gelatin is dissolved. Add sugar, ½ teaspoon salt, pepper and pineapple juice; chill. Add vinegar and remaining salt to vegetables and olives. When gelatin has thickened slightly, fold in vegetables. Turn into individual molds; chill. Unmold on crisp lettuce. Yield: 6 salads.

HAM MOUSSE

1½ tablespoons plain gelatin
2 tablespoons cold water
2 egg yolks, slightly beaten
½ teaspoon salt
dash of paprika and cayenne
½ teaspoon dry mustard
1 cup chicken bouillon

1 cup milk
2 cups chopped cooked ham
½ teaspoon onion juice
1 teaspoon vinegar
1 tablespoon chopped parsley
½ cup heavy cream, whipped
water cress

Soften gelatin in cold water 5 minutes. Combine egg yolks and seasonings in top part of double boiler; add bouillon and milk and cook over hot water 5 or 6 minutes, or until thickened, stirring constantly. Add to gelatin, and stir until dissolved; then add ham, onion juice, vinegar and parsley; chill. When slightly thickened, fold in cream. Turn into loaf mold; chill until firm. Unmold on serving platter, garnish with water cress and serve with mayonnaise. Approximate yield: 6 portions.

CHICKEN SALAD IN CRANBERRY MOLD

1 can cranberry jelly (2 cups)
1 cup orange juice
1 envelope plain gelatin
1 cup diced celery

1 tablespoon shredded orange
  rind
salt
3 cups chicken salad

Break up cranberry jelly and put in top of double boiler with ¼ cup hot orange juice. Soften gelatin in remaining orange juice, then stir over hot water until dissolved. Add to cranberry with celery, orange rind and salt. Pour into a ring mold. Chill until firm. Unmold and fill center with chicken salad. Yield: 6 portions.

SPICED FRUIT SALAD

6 cloves	2 cups diced pickled peaches,
1½ cups water	drained
1 package lemon-flavored	lettuce
gelatin	crushed or ground peanuts
¾ cup pickled peach juice	Cream Mayonnaise (page 621)

Boil cloves in water 5 minutes; strain and use 1 cup to dissolve gelatin according to package directions; add peach juice and chill. When slightly thickened, fold in peaches. Turn into individual molds, chill until firm. Unmold on crisp lettuce and garnish with crushed peanuts and mayonnaise. Pickled pears may be substituted for peaches, if desired. Approximate yield: 6 salads.

MOLDED TUNA FISH SALAD

1 envelope plain gelatin	¾ cup milk
¼ cup cold water	1½ tablespoons melted butter
1½ teaspoons salt	4 tablespoons lemon juice
1½ teaspoons prepared mustard	1 cup flaked tuna fish
dash of cayenne	lettuce
2 egg yolks, slightly beaten	Cucumber Cream Dressing
	(page 627)

Soften gelatin in cold water 5 minutes. Combine seasonings, egg yolks and milk in top of double boiler and cook over hot water 6 to 8 minutes, or until thickened, stirring constantly. Add butter, lemon juice and gelatin, stirring until gelatin is dissolved. Remove from heat and fold in tuna fish. Turn into fish mold; chill until firm. Unmold on bed of crisp lettuce and serve with cucumber cream dressing. Salmon, shrimp or crab meat may be substituted. Yield: 4 to 6 portions.

JELLIED GINGER PEARS

1 package lemon-flavored	1 cup diced pears
gelatin	⅓ cup chopped nuts
1 cup water	2 tablespoons chopped crystal-
1 cup ginger ale	lized ginger
½ cup seeded and halved white	lettuce
grapes	Cream Mayonnaise (page 621)

Dissolve gelatin in water according to package directions, add ginger ale and chill. When slighty thickened, fold in fruit, nuts and 1 tablespoon ginger. Turn into individual molds; chill until firm. Unmold on crisp lettuce; garnish with mayonnaise to which remaining ginger has been added. Approximate yield: 6 salads.

JELLIED CRANBERRY SALAD

1 envelope plain gelatin   ¼ cup sugar
2 tablespoons cold water   1 cup chopped raw cranberries
1½ cups boiling water   ½ cup diced celery
2 tablespoons vinegar   lettuce
¼ teaspoon salt   mayonnaise

Soften gelatin in cold water 5 minutes. Add to boiling water, stirring until dissolved; add vinegar, salt and sugar; chill. When slightly thickened, fold in cranberries and celery. Turn into mold and chill. Unmold on crisp lettuce and garnish with mayonnaise. Approximate yield: 6 portions.

MELON RING WITH WINE DRESSING

3 cantaloupes   ½ cup lemon juice
3 cups strawberries   ¼ teaspoon salt
2 cups fresh or canned pine-   ½ cup sugar
   apple   ¼ cup Sherry

Cut chilled melons in half crosswise, remove seeds carefully and cut slice from bottom of each half, leaving a ring-shaped piece. Pare carefully and place on serving plate. Wash and hull 2 cups of strawberries and cut in half lengthwise. Cut pineapple in pieces of similar size, mix carefully with strawberries and heap into centers of melon rings. Wash remaining berries without hulling and use as garnish, arranging a few around each salad. For wine dressing combine lemon juice, salt and sugar, stirring until sugar is dissolved. Add Sherry and serve in a separate bowl with melon salads. Approximate yield: 6 portions.

PINEAPPLE AND CHEESE SALAD

1 package lemon-flavored   ½ cup grated American cheese
   gelatin   ½ cup heavy cream, whipped
1 cup water   chicory
1 small can shredded pineapple   mayonnaise

Dissolve gelatin in water according to package directions; chill. When slightly thickened, fold in pineapple, cheese and whipped cream. Turn into individual molds; chill until firm. Unmold and garnish with chicory and mayonnaise. Or take large ring mold and fill center with Chicken Salad (page 604) or Fish Salad (page 605). Approximate yield: 6 salads.

JEWEL RELISH JELLY

1 envelope plain gelatin	12 maraschino cherries, sliced
2 tablespoons cold water	1 cup diced orange
1 cup orange juice	6 sweet pickles, diced
½ cup maraschino cherry	12 stuffed olives, sliced
juice	water cress
	mayonnaise

Soften gelatin in cold water 5 minutes; heat orange and cherry juices to boiling, add to gelatin and stir until dissolved; chill. When slightly thickened, fold in cherries, orange, pickles and olives. Turn into individual molds; chill until firm. Unmold on water cress; garnish with mayonnaise. Approximate yield: 6 salads.

GINGER ALE FRUIT SALAD

1 envelope plain gelatin	½ cup sliced and seeded white
2 tablespoons cold water	grapes
½ cup boiling water	½ cup diced canned pineapple
1 tablespoon sugar	1 tablespoon chopped preserved
dash of salt	ginger
1 cup ginger ale	½ cup diced celery
2 tablespoons lemon juice	¼ cup chopped pecans
½ cup heavy cream, whipped	lettuce
	mayonnaise

Soften gelatin in cold water; add boiling water and stir until gelatin is dissolved. Add sugar, salt, ginger ale and lemon juice; chill. When slightly thickened, fold in cream, fruits, ginger, celery and nuts. Turn into individual molds; chill. Unmold on crisp lettuce; garnish with mayonnaise. Approximate yield: 6 salads.

MOLDED CHERRY NUT SALAD

1 envelope plain gelatin	¼ cup lemon juice
2 tablespoons cold water	1 cup ginger ale
½ cup boiling water	½ cup canned white cherries
2 teaspoons sugar	¼ cup pecans
dash of salt	lettuce
	mayonnaise

Soften gelatin in cold water 5 minutes and dissolve in boiling water. Add sugar, salt, lemon juice and ginger ale; chill. When slightly thickened, fold in cherries that have been pitted and stuffed with pecans. Turn into individual molds; chill until firm. Unmold on crisp lettuce and garnish with mayonnaise. Yield: 6 salads.

APPLE SURPRISE SALAD

1 package raspberry-flavored
   gelatin
2 cups water
½ cup chopped celery
½ cup diced apples
½ cup chopped dates
1 cup drained, crushed pineapple
¼ cup chopped nuts
mayonnaise
½ cup heavy cream, whipped
lettuce

Dissolve gelatin in water according to package directions; cool. Combine celery, fruits, nuts and 2 tablespoons mayonnaise. When gelatin is thickened slightly, fold in fruit mixture and whipped cream. Turn into mold; chill until firm. Unmold on crisp lettuce; garnish with additional mayonnaise. Approximate yield: 6 portions.

ROQUEFORT CHEESE MOUSSE

1 envelope plain gelatin
¼ cup cold water
1 cup boiling water
1 teaspoon salt
¼ pound Roquefort cheese
1 green pepper, minced
4 stuffed olives, minced
1 teaspoon minced onion
1 cup heavy cream, whipped
½ cup finely chopped celery
1 cup apple (pared and cut in
   thin strips)
French dressing
pimiento
olive rings

Soften gelatin in cold water; add boiling water, stirring until dissolved. Add salt and chill. Mash cheese and combine with green pepper, olive and onion. When gelatin mixture begins to thicken, fold in cheese mixture and cream. Pour into a ring mold which has been rinsed in cold water and chill until firm. Unmold, and in the center pile the celery and apples which have been tossed together in the French dressing. Garnish with bits of pimiento, olive rings. Or use 1 3-oz. package cream cheese and 1 oz. Roquefort or blue cheese and substitute 1 cup minced cucumber or green pepper, if desired. Approximate yield: 6 portions.

FROZEN NIPPY CHEESE SALAD

1 3½-oz. package sharp cheese
½ cup sweet or sour cream
8 to 10 green olives, chopped
lettuce
mayonnaise

Mash cheese and mix with cream. Add olives and blend. Turn into 6 small paper cups, place in freezing compartment of automatic refrigerator and freeze 2 to 3 hours, or until firm. Unmold. Serve on crisp lettuce; garnish with mayonnaise. Yield: 6 portions.

CHEESE AND CRESS MOUSSE

1 envelope plain gelatin	½ pound cream cheese
⅓ cup cold water	¼ cup pimiento, cut in strips
1 cup hot water	½ cup coarsely chopped water
1 teaspoon salt	cress
¼ teaspoon pepper	1 cup heavy cream
few drops onion juice	1 tablespoon lemon juice
¼ teaspoon dry mustard	

Dissolve gelatin in cold water; let stand 5 minutes. Add hot water and seasonings and stir until dissolved. Chill until slightly thickened. Then beat with rotary beater until fluffy. Mash and fold in cheese; stir in pimiento strips and chopped cress. Whip cream and fold into mixture. Pour into 1 large or individual molds; chill until firm. Serve on a bed of water cress. Yield: 8 portions.

FROZEN VEGETABLE SALAD

1 envelope plain gelatin	3 tablespoons chopped green
¼ cup cold water	peppers
¾ cup mayonnaise	2 tablespoons minced onions
¼ cup heavy cream, whipped	1 teaspoon salt
¾ cup diced tomatoes	¼ teaspoon paprika
¾ cup sliced cucumbers	2 tablespoons lemon juice
¾ cup diced celery	lettuce

Soften gelatin in cold water; dissolve over hot water and mix with mayonnaise. Fold in whipped cream, vegetables and seasonings. Turn into freezing tray of automatic refrigerator and freeze 2 to 3 hours, or until firm. Or turn into mold and pack in ice and salt. Cut into squares and serve on lettuce with additional mayonnaise. Approximate yield: 6 portions.

Frozen Chicken or Shrimp Salad—Substitute 1 cup diced, cooked chicken or shrimp for sliced cucumbers.

FROZEN CREAM CHEESE SALAD

½ pound cream cheese   ½ cup chopped nuts
1 cup heavy cream   ½ teaspoon salt
2 pimientos, minced   ¼ teaspoon paprika
                              lettuce

Break up cheese with fork, add cream, pimientos, nuts and seasonings, mixing until smooth and creamy. Turn into freezing tray of automatic refrigerator and freeze 2 to 3 hours, or until firm. Unmold, slice and serve on crisp lettuce with desired dressing. Yield: 8 portions.

FROZEN TOMATO SALAD

6 firm small tomatoes   2 tablespoons chopped pimiento
1 cup cottage cheese   ½ teaspoon salt
½ cup chopped cucumber   1 cup Cooked Salad Dressing
2 tablespoons minced onion   (page 624)
3 tablespoons chopped green   1 cup heavy cream, whipped
  pepper   lettuce

Wash and peel tomatoes, remove stem ends and scoop out center to form cups. Stuff with mixture of cheese, cucumber, onion, pepper, pimiento, salt and 3 tablespoons salad dressing. Fit into freezing tray of automatic refrigerator, cut side down, taking care not to spill filling. Mix remaining salad dressing with whipped cream and pour around tomatoes, almost covering them. Freeze about 2 hours, but do not allow to freeze too hard. Cut in squares so that each portion is a stuffed tomato in a square of frozen dressing. Serve on lettuce and top with more dressing. Yield: 6 salads.

FROZEN FRUIT SALAD

3½ tablespoons flour   ⅓ cup lemon juice
3 tablespoons sugar   ¼ cup orange sections
1 teaspoon salt   ¼ cup cherries
⅓ teaspoon paprika   ¼ cup pineapple
few grains of cayenne   ¼ cup sliced banana
2 egg yolks, well beaten   1 cup heavy cream, whipped
⅔ cup milk   lettuce
1 tablespoon melted butter   mayonnaise

Mix flour, sugar and seasonings in top of double boiler; add egg yolks, gradually stir in milk and cook over hot water, stirring constantly, until mixture thickens; add butter and lemon juice, turn into bowl, beat 2 minutes, then cool. Cut fruits into small pieces and add to mixture; fold in whipped cream. Turn into tray and freeze 3 to 4 hours. Cut in slices and top with mayonnaise. Yield: 6 portions.

SALAD DRESSINGS

SALAD dressings are of two main types—the *uncooked,* which include simple oil and acid mixtures like French dressing, mayonnaise and modifications of the two, and *cooked* dressings, usually thickened with egg or flour or some ingredient that acts as a permanent binder.

Ingredients. Pure or virgin olive oil is bright and limpid with no trace of strong odor or flavor. Inferior olive oil, usually made from overripe olives, is dark and strongly flavored. Other vegetable oils are used successfully for salad dressings; they should be mild and sweet. They may be mixed with olive oil in any desired proportion.

Vinegar supplies tartness and adds piquancy to a salad, but a poor vinegar or one that is too strong will destroy the natural food flavors. Good cider or wine vinegars make the best dressings. Tarragon vinegar adds a unique flavor which is enjoyed by many. The proportion of oil to vinegar is approximately 4 of oil to 1 of vinegar.

Choice of Dressing. A light salad accompanying a substantial meal requires a light, delicate dressing. A substantial dressing may accompany a hearty salad when it forms the main dish at a meal. But at a meal otherwise high in fat, simple dressings are preferred to those rich in oil or cream. Too much dressing may ruin a salad, so it is a wise hostess who seasons salads lightly with dressing, providing additional dressing as needed.

Storage of Salad Dressings. Since oil or fat is the basic ingredient in most dressings, it is necessary to store them in a moderately cold place, preferably in the refrigerator. However, a dressing such as mayonnaise should never be frozen, as it will separate. If it separates, add it slowly to 1 egg yolk as directed for mayonnaise.

FRENCH DRESSING

1 small onion or 1 clove garlic, sliced	⅛ teaspoon pepper
¼ cup vinegar or lemon juice	¼ teaspoon paprika
¾ teaspoon salt	1 tablespoon sugar
	¾ cup salad oil

Add onion to vinegar, let stand 20 minutes; strain. Combine salt, pepper, paprika and sugar in jar or large bottle; add vinegar and oil, cover closely and shake vigorously, or make in bowl and beat with rotary egg beater. French dressing may be made in larger amounts and stored in the refrigerator. Always shake or beat again just before serving. Approximate yield: 1 cup dressing.

MODIFICATIONS OF FRENCH DRESSING
(Use ½ above recipe)

Anchovy Dressing—Cream 2 teaspoons anchovy paste with seasonings; add 1 tablespoon each of chopped parsley and onion.

Cheese and Egg Dressing—Add 1 tablespoon each chopped parsley and pimiento, 4 tablespoons chopped American cheese and 1 hard-cooked egg, chopped.

Chiffonade Dressing—Add 1 tablespoon each of chopped green pepper, pimiento, olives and cucumber pickle and 1 hard-cooked egg, chopped.

Chutney French Dressing—Add 2 tablespoons chopped chutney.

Cream French Dressing—Add 2 tablespoons sweet or sour cream.

Curry French Dressing—Add ¼ teaspoon curry powder with salt.

Fruit French Dressing—Add a dash each of nutmeg and marjoram and ¼ teaspoon chervil to dry ingredients. Use lemon juice instead of vinegar.

Fruit Juice French Dressing—Omit onion; use 1½ tablespoons fruit juice alone or in combination, such as: grapefruit, orange, pineapple, grape, apricot, raspberry, etc., and ½ tablespoon lemon or lime juice for vinegar.

Horseradish Dressing—Add 1 tablespoon prepared horseradish.

Italian Dressing—Add 1 tablespoon tomato conserve or ketchup and 1 small green pepper, minced.

Lime French Dressing—Omit onion; use equal parts lime and lemon juice, or 3 tablespoons lime and 1 of lemon juice for vinegar.

Mint Dressing—Add 1 tablespoon chopped fresh mint.

Miramar Dressing—Add 3 anchovy fillets, chopped, 1 hard-cooked egg, chopped, and ½ teaspoon chopped chives. Yield: 1 cup dressing.

Mustard French Dressing—Add 1 teaspoon dry mustard and dash of cayenne to dry ingredients.

Olive French Dressing—Add ¼ cup chopped, stuffed olives.

Piquant Dressing—Add 1 tablespoon chopped olives and ½ teaspoon each chopped capers and pimiento.

Roquefort French Dressing—Cream ¼ cup soft Roquefort cheese with 2 tablespoons dressing; add remaining dressing gradually.

Spanish French Dressing—Add ½ teaspoon chili powder and ½ teaspoon dry mustard to dry ingredients.

Spiced French Dressing—Add 1 tablespoon prepared horseradish to 1 tablespoon vinegar; add ¼ teaspoon dry mustard, ½ teaspoon chopped chives, 1 shallot, finely chopped, and 1 tablespoon chopped parsley to dry ingredients.

Swiss Dressing—Add ¼ teaspoon dry mustard, ¼ cup grated cheese and ¼ teaspoon Worcestershire sauce to dry ingredients.

Tart French Dressing—Omit sugar, add ½ teaspoon dry mustard to dry ingredients; increase vinegar or lemon juice to 3 tablespoons.

YELENA'S FRENCH DRESSING

1 clove garlic, halved	¾ teaspoon curry powder
2 teaspoons salt	½ teaspoon paprika
1 tablespoon sugar	½ cup vinegar
½ teaspoon dry mustard	½ cup olive oil
1 teaspoon celery seed	½ cup salad oil
Roquefort cheese (optional)	

Mix ingredients in order given. Place in shaker and shake vigorously, or beat in bowl with rotary egg beater until mixture is well combined. Approximate yield: 1½ cups dressing.

HERB DRESSING

6 rosemary leaves
⅛ teaspoon thyme
⅛ teaspoon marjoram

salt
½ clove garlic
½ cup salad oil

¼ cup vinegar

Crush herbs and add to remaining ingredients in jar or bowl. Shake vigorously or beat and let stand 2 hours before serving. Shake again before using. Approximate yield: ¾ cup dressing.

SPECIAL FRENCH DRESSING

1 whole clove
1 teaspoon salt
2 teaspoons sugar
1 teaspoon dry mustard

dash of Tabasco
½ teaspoon paprika
1 cup lemon juice
1½ cups olive oil

½ cup tiny pearl onions

Mix ingredients in order given. Place in shaker and shake vigorously, or beat in bowl with rotary egg beater, until mixture is well combined. Approximate yield: 2½ cups dressing.

CENTURY FRENCH DRESSING

½ cup sugar
1 cup water
½ cup lemon juice
½ teaspoon salt
2 teaspoons celery salt

½ teaspoon white pepper
½ cup vinegar
2 cups olive oil or other salad
oil
1 cup ketchup

1 large onion, grated

Boil sugar and water 10 minutes, add lemon juice and boil 5 minutes longer; cool. Add remaining ingredients and beat until thick. Always shake thoroughly to emulsify before using. Yield: 1 quart dressing.

MINT DRESSING

1 cup salad oil
⅓ cup cider vinegar
1½ teaspoons salt

pinch of white pepper
1½ tablespoons chopped mint
leaves

1 teaspoon minced shallots

Combine all ingredients in a pint jar with a lid. Chill. Before serving, shake thoroughly. Serve over fresh fruit salads. Approximate yield: 1¼ cups dressing.

MAYONNAISE

1 egg yolk
½ to 1 teaspoon salt
½ teaspoon dry mustard
¼ teaspoon paprika

dash of cayenne
2 tablespoons vinegar or lemon
    juice
1 cup salad oil

Put egg yolk and seasonings into small bowl and beat thoroughly; add 1 tablespoon vinegar and beat again. Gradually beat in oil, adding ½ teaspoon at a time until ¼ cup is used; then add 1 to 2 tablespoons at a time. As mixture thickens, add remaining vinegar. If oil is added too rapidly, mayonnaise will curdle. To remedy this, at once beat curdled mixture gradually into a second egg yolk and continue as above. Keep mayonnaise in a moderately cold place. Too much heat or freezing will cause oil to separate and come to the top; if this happens, skim oil off. Serve mayonnaise with all types of salads. Approximate yield: 1¼ cups mayonnaise.

MODIFICATIONS OF MAYONNAISE

(Use ½ above recipe)

Banana Nut Mayonnaise—Combine 1 small mashed banana and 2 tablespoons peanut butter with mayonnaise. If too thick, thin with a little cream. Serve with fruit salad. Approximate yield: 1 cup.

Cheese Mayonnaise—Thin ½ cup mayonnaise with 1 tablespoon thin cream, fold in ⅓ cup grated American cheese; season to taste with salt and paprika. Serve with fruit salads. Approximate yield: 1 cup.

Chili Mayonnaise—Add ¼ cup chili sauce, 2 tablespoons vinegar, 1 tablespoon Worcestershire sauce and ½ tablespoon chopped chives. Serve with fish salads. Approximate yield: 1 cup dressing.

Cream Mayonnaise—Fold mayonnaise into ⅓ cup heavy cream, whipped. Serve with fruit or vegetable salads. Approximate yield: ¾ cup dressing.

Cream Cheese Mayonnaise—Cream 1 3-oz. package cream cheese and add 2 tablespoons Roquefort or Camembert cheese. Combine with mayonnaise, thinning with cream to desired consistency. Serve with grapefruit salad. Approximate yield: 1¼ cups dressing.

Crispy Mayonnaise Dressing—Add ⅓ cup crisp chopped celery and cucumbers and 1½ tablespoons sour or sweet heavy cream. Serve with avocado salads, garnishing with pimiento strips. Yield: 1 cup.

Frozen Mayonnaise—Mix mayonnaise, ¼ cup heavy cream, whipped, 1 tablespoon lemon or lime juice and 1 tablespoon sugar. Turn into small molds and freeze in automatic refrigerator. Serve with fruit salad. Approximate yield: 6 small molds.

Ham Dressing—Add ¼ cup tomato juice and 2 tablespoons chopped or potted Virginia ham. Serve with artichoke salad. Yield: 1 cup.

Herb Mayonnaise—To 1 cup mayonnaise, add 3 tablespoons red wine, and 3 tablespoons combined finely chopped parsley, fresh mint, chives and fresh tarragon. Blend with 2 tablespoons minced onion and ½ cup creamed cottage cheese. Serve with green salads. Approximate yield: 2 cups dressing.

Honey Cream Dressing—Blend ¼ teaspoon dry mustard with 1 tablespoon honey and ½ teaspoon lemon juice. Add to mayonnaise; season to taste with salt and fold into ½ cup heavy cream, whipped. Serve with fruit salads. Approximate yield: 1 cup dressing.

Marmalade Dressing—Add 3 tablespoons orange marmalade. Serve with fruit salad. Approximate yield: ¾ cup dressing.

Mustard Cream Mayonnaise—Add ¼ cup prepared mustard to mayonnaise; fold into ½ cup heavy cream, whipped. Serve with meat and vegetable salads. Approximate yield: 1½ cups dressing.

Pickle Mayonnaise—Add ½ tablespoon each ketchup and minced parsley, 1 tablespoon each minced sweet pickles, cucumbers and pickled beets. Serve with meat, vegetable or egg salads. Yield: ¾ cup.

Pimiento Cheese Dressing—Add ¼ cup pimiento cheese spread, a dash of salt and 1 hard-cooked egg, finely chopped. Serve with vegetable salads. Approximate yield: 1 cup dressing.

Pimiento-Mustard Dressing—Combine 2 tablespoons minced pimiento, ¼ teaspoon dry mustard and a dash each of salt, pepper and paprika. Add to mayonnaise, thinning with 1 teaspoon vinegar and a little cream or evaporated milk. Serve with meat or vegetable salads. Approximate yield: ⅔ cup dressing.

Piquant Mayonnaise—Rub a bowl with ½ clove garlic; add 2 tablespoons each minced green pepper and pimiento, ¼ cup each minced celery, dill pickle, chili sauce and ketchup; add mayonnaise and combine gently. Serve with green salads. Yield: 1½ cups dressing.

Ravigote Mayonnaise—Mix and chop 1 tablespoon cooked spinach, 2 teaspoons capers, ¼ small onion, 2 tablespoons each parsley and water cress and 2 anchovy fillets. Force mixture through very fine sieve and add to mayonnaise. Serve with fish and vegetable salads. Approximate yield: 1 cup dressing.

Roquefort Cheese Dressing—Work ½ pound Roquefort or Bleu cheese into 1½ cups mayonnaise, add ½ cup French dressing, 1 clove of garlic, minced, 1 tablespoon lemon juice, 3 teaspoons dry mustard, white pepper to taste, 2 teaspoons Worcestershire sauce and ¾ teaspoon sugar, blending well. Allow to stand 12 hours to mellow and blend. Just before serving, add ¼ pound Roquefort cheese coarsely crumbled to give little matters for the teeth to touch. Serve with tomato salads. Yield: 1 pint dressing.

Roquefort Sour Cream Dressing—Add 1½ tablespoons minced green onion, ¼ cup minced parsley, 1 clove minced garlic, 1 tablespoon anchovy paste, ½ cup sour cream, ¼ cup wine vinegar, 1 tablespoon lemon juice, and ¼ pound Roquefort or Bleu cheese. Serve with green salads. Yield: 1 pint dressing.

Russian Dressing—Add 2 teaspoons each chopped green pepper, pimiento and chives, ½ teaspoon paprika, 3 tablespoons chili sauce and 1 hard-cooked egg yolk, sieved. Serve with crisp head lettuce. Approximate yield: 1 cup dressing.

Savory Mayonnaise—Add ⅛ teaspoon each dry mustard, paprika and Worcestershire sauce. Serve with vegetable, meat or fish salads.

Thousand Island Dressing—Add 2 tablespoons chili sauce, ½ tablespoon ketchup, ½ tablespoon each vinegar, chives, chopped green peppers and chopped pimientos, and ½ teaspoon paprika. Serve with vegetable salads. Approximate yield: 1 cup dressing.

Cucumber-Tomato Dressing—Add 3 tablespoons each of shredded cucumber and shredded tomato (using the firm outside part); blend carefully. Serve with cold lobster or salmon. Yield: ¾ cup dressing.

CURRY MAYONNAISE

1 tablespoon curry powder	¼ cup cider vinegar
¼ cup tarragon vinegar	1 teaspoon sugar

Mayonnaise (page 621)

Cook curry powder, vinegars and sugar in top of double boiler until smooth, stirring occasionally; chill. When cold, add curry mixture to mayonnaise, according to taste, and blend. Serve with meat, fish, chicken, egg or vegetable salads.

ORANGE CREAM CHEESE DRESSING

Blend 1 3-oz. package cream cheese and 3 tablespoons orange juice. Add 1 tablespoon sugar, ½ teaspoon orange rind and dash of salt. Serve with fruit salad. Also excellent as sauce for hot gingerbread.

ORANGE DRESSING

¼ cup sugar	dash of paprika
1 tablespoon flour	1 cup orange juice
½ teaspoon dry mustard	¼ cup lemon juice
½ teaspoon salt	2 tablespoons butter, melted

Combine dry ingredients in top of double boiler, add fruit juices and cook over hot water 5 to 7 minutes, or until mixture thickens, stirring constantly; add butter; chill. Serve with fruit salads. Yield: 1½ cups dressing.

COOKED SOUR CREAM DRESSING

1 teaspoon dry mustard	1 egg yolk, beaten
1 teaspoon salt	⅓ cup vinegar
2 teaspoons flour	1 tablespoon melted butter
2 teaspoons sugar	½ cup heavy sour cream,
dash of cayenne	whipped

Combine dry ingredients in top of double boiler, add egg and vinegar and cook over hot water 7 to 8 minutes, or until smooth and thick, stirring constantly; add butter. Cool and fold into sour cream. Serve with meat, poultry and vegetable salads. Approximate yield: ¾ cup dressing.

COOKED SALAD DRESSING

2 tablespoons flour	dash of paprika
1½ teaspoons salt	2 egg yolks, well beaten
½ teaspoon dry mustard	1¼ cups scalded milk
1 tablespoon sugar	⅓ cup vinegar
2 tablespoons melted butter	

Combine flour, salt, mustard, sugar and paprika in top of double boiler; add egg yolks and mix well. Stir in milk gradually, place over hot water and cook 7 to 10 minutes, or until thickened, stirring constantly. Remove from heat, stir in vinegar and butter; chill. Thin with milk or fruit juices before using. One-half to 1 cup heavy cream, whipped, may be folded into chilled dressing, if desired. Approximate yield: 1½ cups dressing.

LEMON–HONEY DRESSING

1 egg, beaten	3 tablespoons milk
¼ cup lemon juice	1 cup cottage cheese
½ cup honey	dash of salt
	dash of mace

Combine egg, lemon juice and honey in top of double boiler and cook over hot water until mixture thickens, stirring constantly; cool. Stir milk into cottage cheese, beat until smooth, add salt and mace and blend with cooked mixture. Serve with fruit salads. Approximate yield: 1½ cups dressing.

COOKED OIL DRESSING

1½ teaspoons dry mustard	2 eggs, slightly beaten
1 teaspoon salt	2 tablespoons salad oil
1¾ teaspoons powdered sugar	⅓ cup vinegar, diluted with
few grains of cayenne	cold water to make ½ cup

Combine dry ingredients in top of double boiler; slowly add eggs and oil, stirring constantly; then add diluted vinegar. Cook over boiling water until mixture begins to thicken. Strain and cool. Serve with any salad. Approximate yield: ¾ cup dressing.

HOT OIL SALAD DRESSING

1 teaspoon salt	2 tablespoons salad oil
1 tablespoon sugar	1 hard-cooked egg, minced
½ to 1 teaspoon dry mustard	2 cucumbers, sliced and pared
⅓ cup vinegar	paprika

Combine salt, sugar and mustard; add vinegar and oil and heat to boiling point; add egg. Pour over sliced cucumbers or lettuce, dust with paprika and serve at once. Approximate yield: ¾ cup dressing.

BUTTERMILK DRESSING

½ clove garlic	1 teaspoon salt
½ green pepper, minced	½ teaspoon paprika
3 radishes, minced	¼ cup lemon juice
2 hard-cooked egg yolks, mashed	6 tablespoons cottage cheese
	½ cup buttermilk

Rub bowl lightly with garlic. In it combine green pepper, radishes and egg yolks. Add salt, paprika, and lemon juice, then cottage cheese and buttermilk and beat thoroughly until mixture is blended. Serve with vegetable salads. Yield: 1½ cups dressing.

HONEY–WHIPPED CREAM DRESSING

1 cup heavy cream
2 tablespoons strained honey

dash of salt
1 tablespoon lemon juice

Whip cream, gradually beating in honey and salt; then add lemon juice. Serve with fruit salads. Approximate yield: 1½ cups dressing.

HORSERADISH CREAM DRESSING

1 teaspoon salt
½ teaspoon sugar
½ teaspoon dry mustard
¼ teaspoon paprika or
dash of cayenne

3 tablespoons grated horseradish
1 tablespoon tarragon vinegar
1 tablespoon red wine vinegar
1 tablespoon lemon juice

1 cup heavy cream, whipped

Mix seasonings, horseradish, vinegars and lemon juice; beat into cream. Serve with green salad. Approximate yield: 1½ cups dressing.

SNAPPY CREAM DRESSING

¼ cup chili sauce
1 teaspoon lemon juice

1 teaspoon prepared horseradish
1¼ teaspoons salt

½ cup heavy cream, whipped

Combine chili sauce, lemon juice, horseradish and salt; fold into cream. Serve with asparagus salad. Yield: ¾ cup dressing.

QUICK SOUR CREAM DRESSING

¾ cup heavy sour cream
3 tablespoons vinegar

½ teaspoon salt
3 tablespoons sugar

dash of paprika

Beat cream, vinegar and seasonings together until ingredients are well combined and mixture is thick. Serve with vegetable salad. Approximate yield: 1 cup dressing.

FRUIT SALAD DRESSING

1 tablespoon orange juice
1 tablespoon lemon juice
1 tablespoon pineapple juice

1 tablespoon maraschino cherry
juice
6 maraschino cherries, minced

1 cup heavy cream, whipped

Fold juices and cherries into cream. Serve with fruit salads. Approximate yield: 1½ cups dressing.

CUCUMBER CREAM DRESSING

2 tablespoons vinegar	1 cup diced cucumber
2 tablespoons sugar	1 cup heavy cream, whipped

Add vinegar and sugar to cucumber; fold into cream. Serve with meat or chicken salads. Approximate yield: 2 cups dressing.

SHERBET DRESSING

Stir ½ cup finely chopped pecans into 1 pint Lemon Sherbet (page 802) and serve at once with fruit or cabbage salads. Orange or pineapple sherbet and almonds, walnuts or pistachio nuts may be used, if desired. Approximate yield: 2½ cups dressing.

FROZEN TOMATO DRESSING

1 quart tomatoes (fresh or canned)	1 tablespoon chopped green pepper
1 slice onion	3 cups water
3 whole cloves	⅔ teaspoon salt
1 bay leaf	2 tablespoons sugar
dash of cayenne	¼ cup lemon juice
1 cup finely minced celery	

Simmer tomatoes, onion, seasonings and 2 cups water about 30 minutes; put through sieve, add salt, sugar, lemon juice and remaining water. Turn into freezing tray of automatic refrigerator with temperature control set at coldest point. Freeze to a mush and add celery. Do not freeze too hard. Serve with vegetable salad. Yield: 6 to 8 portions.

LEMON PEANUT DRESSING

2 tablespoons peanut butter	¼ teaspoon drained horseradish
2 tablespoons heavy cream	½ teaspoon powdered sugar
2 tablespoons lemon juice	¼ teaspoon paprika
¼ teaspoon salt	

Cream peanut butter; add remaining ingredients and beat until very light. Serve with green salads. Yield: ½ cup dressing.

RED WINE DRESSING

1 teaspoon sugar	1 clove garlic
¾ teaspoon salt	¾ cup salad oil
1 teaspoon Worcestershire sauce	¼ cup Claret or Burgundy
½ teaspoon dry mustard	¼ cup red wine vinegar
¼ cup ketchup	

Measure ingredients into jar and shake thoroughly. Shake before using. Approximate yield: 1½ cups dressing.

Cakes

Judging by the number of reader requests we receive each week for recipes, cakes are the most popular American dessert. Perhaps it is because cakes combine beauty and artistry with palate-satisfying sweetness. Today new methods of cake making speed the process and give lighter, finer grained and consistently better results. Even a beginner can be proud of her endeavors in the cake-baking field, be it a high golden chiffon, a light-as-a-cloud angel or a rich, moist chocolate devil's food.

Cake mixes, too, have been developed to a high degree of excellence in the testing kitchens of commercial companies so that a uniform product is assured if the directions are followed. See page 52 for some ideas for using these mixes in a novel fashion.

Frostings for the cake are almost without number. Readers have sent their favorite recipes to us for years—we believe that the ones we have included in this chapter represent a cross-country list of family favorites.

So follow the directions carefully, use the right size pans, be sure your oven thermostat is working correctly, and we will predict that you will soon gain a glamorous reputation as a "wonderful cakemaker."

DO'S AND DON'TS FOR CAKEMAKING

1. Assemble all tools needed for your cakemaking. Prepare the pans for baking before combining ingredients. Set the oven at the correct temperature. (Have oven thermostat checked frequently by utility service department or check yourself with portable oven thermometer.)

628

2. Be sure to follow directions carefully. Cake recipes are carefully balanced, and careless measuring can cause inferior results. All measurements are level in these recipes.

3. Have all ingredients at room temperature. This is especially important for eggs, which will not whip to full volume when cold, and for fats that are to be creamed.

4. Flour should be sifted before measuring; then lightly fill the cup to the desired level with a spoon. Do not shake cup. Level off with a knife. Sift the flour again with the dry ingredients as the recipe directs. Waxed paper is helpful in the sifting process. Use cake flour when directed for fine-textured results. Use only the amount of flour called for.

5. Sugar should be fine-grained for a fine-textured cake, but cane or beet sugar may be used. Follow directions for using brown sugar, packing firmly in cup.

6. In these recipes we have used the double-acting baking powders (Calumet, Clabber Girl, Davis OK, K.C.). If you choose to use a tartrate (Royal or Schilling) or a phosphate (Rumford, Dr. Price, Davis Phosphate), sprinkle it over the batter during the last minute of beating and bake *immediately* so that the leavening power will not be lost.

7. You will note in some of our recipes that we call for measured eggs because this is the most accurate way of using eggs. When cup measure is not specified, use medium-sized eggs.

8. Hydrogenated shortenings will insure consistently good baking results and are easy to use. Butter may be substituted for part of the shortening for the real butter flavor prized by many cake bakers. The water displacement method is the easiest way to measure fats (see page 54). When a pound of butter is divided into four sticks, each stick equals ½ cup or 4 ounces.

9. Liquids include milk—sour, buttermilk, and reconstituted dry milk powder—water, coffee or fruit juices. A cup of sour milk may be made from fresh milk by adding a tablespoon

of vinegar and letting it stand five minutes. See page 78 for other susbtitutions.

10. It is well to become acquainted with these terms so that you will know how to follow the steps of cakemaking.

To stir means to blend ingredients in a circular motion with a spoon.

To beat means to blend ingredients rapidly in a circular motion to incorporate air. A slotted spoon is helpful. A rotary beater may be called for.

To whip means to incorporate as much air as possible in order to make a light, fluffy mixture as for whipped cream. A rotary beater or a wire whisk may be used for whipping.

To cream refers to working the fat and sugar in a recipe with the back of the spoon to blend to a smooth, creamy mixture.

To fold is to combine two prepared mixtures; for example, egg whites beaten until stiff combined with a cake batter.

REASONS FOR CAKE FAILURE

TROUBLE	THIS MAY BE WHY
Coarse, dry texture	Batter overmixed Too much baking powder Oven too hot
Peaked, cracked top	Too much flour Not enough liquid in batter Oven too hot Cake baked too high in oven
Poor volume	Not enough baking powder Not enough mixing Too much liquid Not enough flour
Heavy layer on bottom	Too much liquid Too much egg Not enough flour Batter not mixed enough

Lightly spoon the lighter onto the surface of the heavier and fold it in with a cutting motion, bringing the bottom mixture up with a rounding motion. A rubber or plastic scraper is effective as a tool. The mixture should be lightly blended and the action done gently to incorporate as much air as possible.

Cakes are usually referred to as "butter cakes" or as sponge cakes (cakes without butter); their methods of mixing differ somewhat.

STANDARD METHOD OF MIXING A BUTTER CAKE

USE INGREDIENTS at room temperature (in hot weather ingredients should be cool). (1) Sift flour, measure and sift again with dry ingredients. Measure flavoring into specified liquid. Melt chocolate, if called for in recipe. (2) Cream shortening and sugar until smooth and fluffy. (With electric mixer, use medium speed.) (3) Beat in whole eggs or yolks. Add chocolate if called for in recipe. Beat mixture until well blended. (With mixer, use medium speed.) (4) Stir in dry ingredients alternately with liquid in recipe. (With mixer, use low speed, adding flour and liquid at the same time.) (5) Stir enough to make batter smooth. Beware of overstirring when using mixer, since this will cause reduced cake volume. Blend in fruits, nuts, etc., if called for in recipe. (6) Fold in stiffly beaten egg whites by hand. Turn into prepared cake pans.

QUICK PASTRY-BLEND METHOD

SIFT flour, measure and sift with dry ingredients directly into mixing bowl. Add softened hydrogenated shortening (must be used with this method) and two-thirds of the liquid in the recipe (if all-purpose flour is used, add all the liquid). Beat at medium speed in electric mixer for 2 minutes, scraping down the batter in the bowl constantly or beat with a spoon for 2 minutes (150 strokes). Add remaining liquid and *unbeaten eggs* (yolks or whites). Beat 2 minutes more (scraping bowl frequently in electric mixer). Turn into prepared cake pans.

Pans and Their Preparation for Baking. Choose the size and shape of pan to fit the type of cake to be baked. Prepare the pans before mixing the batter. Do not grease or butter the sides of pan; the cake tends to have a greater volume and flatter top if the sides are not buttered. For easy removal of cake, prepare bottom in one of the following ways: rub with pancoat made by creaming until smooth two parts shortening with one of flour; or grease, then line bottom with waxed or heavy paper and butter top.

Baking of Cakes. Place pan as near the center of oven as possible. When baking several layers at once, never place one pan directly over another. Stagger pans in the oven to get best distribution of heat. Allow clearance around each pan. Bake in carefully controlled preheated oven (350° to 375° F.). Since control of temperature in cake baking is very important, unless you know your oven regulator is carefully adjusted, check it with a tested oven thermometer.

Test for Doneness. When nearly done, open the oven door just enough to test the cake quickly. If the surface springs back when touched lightly, the cake is done. If the impression of the finger remains, bake longer and test again. Another test is to insert a wooden pick or cake tester into the center. When it comes out clean, the cake is done. Cakes are generally overbaked when they shrink from the sides of the pan. Allow the cake to stand in the pan on rack only until it begins to shrink from the sides. Remove cake to rack; if warm cake is placed on a plate or board, the bottom becomes wet and soggy. Frost the cake as soon as it is cool. Brush off loose crumbs before frosting.

ONE–EGG CAKE

2 cups sifted cake flour	1 cup sugar
3 teaspoons baking powder	1 teaspoon vanilla
¼ teaspoon salt	1 egg
⅓ cup butter or other fat	⅔ cup milk

Mix and sift flour, baking powder and salt. Cream butter until soft and smooth and gradually add sugar, beating until fluffy; beat in vanilla and egg. Add flour alternately with milk, beating until smooth after each addition. Turn into prepared pan or pans and bake: in 8-inch square pan in moderate oven (350° F.) about 35 to 40 minutes; in 2 layer pans (8 inch) or in muffin pans in moderate oven (375° F.) about 25 to 30 minutes.

Boston Cream Pie—Spread Cream Filling (page 720) between layers, sift confectioners' sugar over top and cut in wedges. Approximate yield: 8 portions.

Washington Pie—Spread raspberry or loganberry jam between layers, sift confectioners' sugar over top and cut in wedges. Approximate yield: 8 portions.

Blueberry Tea Cakes—Turn half of batter into prepared 9-inch square pan, cover with 1½ cups fresh blueberries or huckleberries and turn remaining batter over top; bake as directed. Sprinkle with powdered sugar, cut in 3 inch squares and serve warm with butter for tea or supper. Yield: 9 square portions (3 inch).

CUP CAKES

Any butter cake recipe can be baked in cup cake or muffin pans. Fill prepared medium-sized cup cake pans ⅔ full of batter. Bake in moderate oven (375° F.) 18 to 25 minutes. Batter for a 2 layer cake (8 inch) yields 14 cup cakes; for a 2 layer cake (9 inch) yields 20 cup cakes.

SOUR CREAM CAKE

2 cups sifted cake flour	1 egg, beaten
¾ teaspoon baking soda	1 cup sugar
⅛ teaspoon salt	1 cup sour cream
¼ teaspoon nutmeg	1 teaspoon vanilla

Sift together dry ingredients. Beat egg and sugar together until light; stir in sour cream and vanilla. Turn into prepared loaf pan (8½ x 4½ x 2½ inches) and bake in a moderate oven (350° F.) about 50 minutes. Yield: 1 loaf.

ALASKA BLUEBERRY CAKE

3 tablespoons butter or
  margarine
1 cup sugar
1 egg, beaten

1¾ cups sifted cake flour
2 teaspoons baking powder
¼ teaspoon salt
1½ cups blueberries

¾ cup milk

Cream butter, add sugar gradually, add egg and blend well. Sift
flour, baking powder and salt together. Mix part of the flour and
blueberries. Add flour and milk alternately to egg mixture. Add
blueberries. Pour into 2 prepared 8-inch layer cake pans. Bake in
moderate oven (350° F.) 25 to 30 minutes. Serve warm with whipped
cream. Approximate yield: 2 layers (8 inch).

TWO–EGG CAKE

2 cups sifted cake flour
2½ teaspoons baking powder
¼ teaspoon salt
½ cup butter or other fat

1 cup sugar
1 teaspoon vanilla or other
  flavoring
2 eggs

⅔ cup milk

Sift together flour, baking powder and salt. Cream shortening until
soft and smooth and gradually add sugar, beating until fluffy; add
flavoring and beat in eggs, one at a time. Add flour mixture alternately
with milk, beating until smooth after each addition. Turn into prepared pan or pans and bake: in square pan in moderate oven (350° F.)
for 35 to 45 minutes; in 2 layer pans or in muffin pans in moderate oven
(375° F.) about 25 minutes. Yield: 1 square (8 inch), 2 layers (8 or 9
inch), or 20 cup cakes.

Orange Coconut Cake—Flavor with 1 tablespoon grated orange rind
instead of vanilla; substitute orange juice for milk and fold in ½ cup
grated coconut before folding in egg whites. Put layers together and
cover cake with Orange Seven Minute Frosting (page 711); decorate
cake with 1 cup shredded coconut. Yield: 2 layers (8 or 9 inch).

Spiced Layer Cake—Add 1 teaspoon cinnamon and ¼ teaspoon each
cloves and nutmeg to dry ingredients. Put layers together and cover
cake with Mocha Frosting (page 709). Yield: 2 layers (9 inch).

Marble Layer Cake—Divide batter into two parts and add 1 square
chocolate, melted, to one part. Put by spoonfuls into 2 prepared layer
pans, alternately light and dark mixtures. When baked, put layers
together with cover cake with Chocolate Butter Frosting (page 709).
Yield: 2 layers (9 inch).

Walnut Mocha Cake—Substitute strong coffee for milk and add ¾ cup broken walnut meats. Bake in prepared square pan in moderate oven (350° F.) 35 to 40 minutes. Yield: 1 square cake (8 inch).

Lemon Dessert Cake—Put layers together with Lemon Cream Filling (page 722) or with Gentlemen's Favorite Filling (page 723). Cover top and sides with Fluffy Lemon Frosting (½ recipe, page 711).

Tutti-Frutti Cup Cakes—Prepare cake batter and bake as directed for cup cakes. When cool, cover tops and sides with orange marmalade; roll in toasted coconut and place on cooky sheet. Top with meringue made by beating 2 tablespoons sugar into 1 stiffly beaten egg white. Bake in moderate oven (350° F.) about 15 minutes, or until meringue is delicately browned. Approximate yield: 14 cup cakes.

BURNT SUGAR CAKE

2 cups sugar	½ teaspoon salt
1 cup boiling water	¾ cup butter or other fat
3 cups sifted cake flour	1 teaspoon vanilla
4 teaspoons baking powder	2 eggs, separated

Melt ½ cup sugar in heavy pan over low heat, stirring until liquid becomes golden brown. Remove from heat and gradually stir in boiling water; then simmer until caramel is dissolved; cool. Sift flour, baking powder and salt. Cream butter until soft and smooth; gradually add remaining 1½ cups sugar, beating until very fluffy; beat in flavoring and well-beaten egg yolks. Add flour alternately with caramel syrup, beating until smooth after each addition; fold in thoroughly egg whites beaten stiff but not dry. Bake in 2 prepared layer pans in moderate oven (375° F.) about 25 to 30 minutes, or in muffin pans, 18 to 25 minutes. Put layers together and cover cake with Caramel Fudge Frosting (page 717) or Burnt Sugar Frosting (page 711). Yield: 2 layers (9 inch), or 30 cup cakes.

MIX-EASY CAKE

2 cups sifted cake flour	½ cup fat (hydrogenated)
3 teaspoons baking powder	1 cup milk
1 teaspoon salt	1 teaspoon vanilla
1 cup sugar	½ cup eggs (2 medium)

Sift together flour, baking powder, salt and sugar. Add shortening, milk and flavoring. Beat vigorously with spoon for 2 minutes by clock (150 strokes per minute); or mix with electric mixer at slow to medium speed for 2 minutes. Add eggs and continue beating 2 more minutes. Pour batter into 2 prepared round 8-inch layer pans. Bake in moderate oven (375° F.) 25 to 35 minutes. Yield: 2 layers (8 inch).

BANANA CAKE

2 cups sifted cake flour   1½ cups sugar
½ teaspoon baking powder   1 teaspoon vanilla
¾ teaspoon baking soda   1 teaspoon lemon extract
¼ teaspoon salt   2 eggs
½ cup butter or other fat   1 cup mashed bananas (2 or 3)
              ¼ cup sour milk or buttermilk

Sift together flour, baking powder, soda and salt. Cream butter until
soft and smooth; gradually add sugar, beating until very fluffy. Beat
in flavoring, eggs and bananas. Add flour alternately with sour milk,
beating until smooth after each addition. Turn into prepared layer
pans and bake in moderate oven (350° F.) 30 to 35 minutes. Put
layers together and cover cake with Sea Foam Frosting (page 711).
Yield: 2 round 9 inch layers (1¼ inches thick).

THREE–EGG CAKE

2 cups sifted cake flour   1¼ cups sugar
1½ teaspoons baking powder   1 teaspoon vanilla
¼ teaspoon salt   3 eggs, separated
⅔ cup butter or other fat   ½ cup milk

Sift together flour, baking powder and salt. Cream butter until soft
and smooth; gradually add 1 cup sugar, beating until light and fluffy;
beat in vanilla and well-beaten egg yolks. Add flour alternately with
milk, beating until smooth after each addition. Beat egg whites until
stiff and gradually beat in remaining ¼ cup sugar; fold thoroughly
into cake batter. Turn into prepared pan or pans and bake: in square
pan in moderate oven (350° F.) about 1 hour; in 2 layer pans or in
muffin pans in moderate oven (375° F.) 20 to 25 minutes. Yield: 1
square (9 inch), 2 layers (9 inch), or 30 cup cakes.

Marble Nut Cake—Divide batter into two parts. To one half add
mixture of ½ teaspoon cinnamon, ¼ teaspoon allspice, ⅛ teaspoon each
cloves, mace and nutmeg and 1 tablespoon dark molasses; to other half
add ¼ cup chopped nuts. Put by tablespoons into prepared 11½ x 7⅜
x 1½-inch pan or 2 round 9-inch layers, alternating spice and nut mixtures. Bake in moderate oven (350° F.): layers 30 to 35 minutes; oblong
cake, 40 to 45 minutes.

Fruit Loaf Cake—Add ¾ cup seedless raisins, currants or sliced
citron to the butter-sugar-egg mixture and beat thoroughly. Yield:
1 loaf, 9½ x 5¼ x 2¾ inches.

MARASCHINO CHERRY CAKE

3 cups sifted cake flour   1½ cups sugar
3 teaspoons baking powder   1 teaspoon vanilla
¼ teaspoon salt   3 eggs, separated
⅔ cup butter or other fat   1 cup milk
¾ cup maraschino cherries

Sift together flour, baking powder and salt. Cream butter until
soft and smooth; gradually add sugar, beating until very fluffy; beat
in vanilla and well-beaten egg yolks. Add flour alternately with milk,
beating until smooth after each addition. Add cherries, drained and
dried on absorbent paper, and fold in egg whites beaten stiff but not
dry. Turn into 3 prepared 8-inch layer pans and bake in moderate
oven (375° F.) 25 to 30 minutes. Put layers together and cover cake
with Boiled Frosting (page 712). Yield: 3 layers.

Tower Bride's Cake—Omit maraschino cherries. Turn batter into 4
prepared round layer pans, graduated in size from 9 to 3 inches in
diameter, and bake in moderate oven (375° F.) 20 to 25 minutes. Put
together and cover with Boiled Frosting (page 712). Approximate
yield: 4-layer tiered cake.

Almond Cherry Loaf—Add ½ cup finely chopped almonds to butter-
sugar-egg mixture and reduce cherries to ½ cup, finely chopped. Turn
batter into two prepared loaf pans and bake in moderate oven (350°
F.) about 1 hour. Spread Butter Frosting (page 709) over cakes and
decorate with blanched almonds. Yield: 2 loaves (8½ x 4½ x 2½
inches).

Black Walnut Cake Squares—Substitute ½ cup chopped black walnuts for maraschino cherries. Bake in prepared 13¼ x 8¾ x 1¾-inch
cake pan. When cold spread with Chocolate Butter Frosting (page
709); sprinkle ½ cup chopped black walnuts over top. Yield: 24 squares.

OLD-FASHIONED NUT LOAF

2 cups sifted cake flour   1 cup sugar
3 teaspoons baking powder   1 teaspoon vanilla
½ teaspoon salt   3 eggs
⅔ cup butter or other fat   1 cup finely chopped walnuts
½ cup milk

Sift together flour, baking powder and salt. Cream butter until soft
and smooth; gradually add sugar, beating until light and fluffy. Add
vanilla and beat in thoroughly 1 egg at a time; add nuts and beat well.
Add flour alternately with milk, beating until smooth after each addition. Turn into prepared loaf pan and bake in moderate oven (350°
F.) about 1¼ hours. Yield: 1 loaf (8½ x 4½ x 2½ inches).

FOUR–EGG CAKE

3 cups sifted all-purpose flour   1½ cups sugar
4½ teaspoons baking powder   4 eggs, separated
½ teaspoon salt   1 teaspoon vanilla
1 cup butter or other fat   1 cup milk

Sift flour, baking powder and salt together three times. Cream butter until creamy and smooth; gradually beat in the sugar and beat until very light and fluffy. Beat in egg yolks, one at a time; add vanilla. Add flour alternately with milk, beating until smooth after each addition. Fold in egg whites beaten until stiff but not dry. Turn into prepared 9-inch spring form pan, or an 11½ x 7⅜ x 1½-inch pan. Bake in slow to moderate oven (325° to 350° F.) until done: spring form, about 1 hour; oblong pan, 35 to 45 minutes. Yield: 1 cake, or 16 portions.

LOAF CAKE

3⅓ cups sifted cake flour   1¾ cups sugar
5 teaspoons baking powder   ½ teaspoon vanilla
½ teaspoon salt   4 eggs
¾ cup butter or other fat   1 cup milk (scant)

Sift together flour, baking powder and salt. Cream shortening until soft and smooth; gradually add sugar, beating until very fluffy; add flavoring and beat in eggs, one at a time. Add flour alternately with milk, beating until smooth after each addition. Turn into 2 prepared loaf pans and bake in moderate oven (350° F.) about 1 hour. Yield: 2 loaves (8½ x 4½ x 2½ inches).

MOM'S LAYERS

4 eggs, separated   3 tablespoons water
1 cup sugar   1 cup sifted flour
1½ tablespoons cornstarch   1¼ teaspoons baking powder

Beat egg yolks until thick. Add sugar very slowly, beating until well blended. Stir in cornstarch mixed smooth with water. Sift flour 3 or 4 times with baking powder and stir into egg yolks, but do not beat. Fold in stiffly beaten egg whites. Spread in two paper-lined 8-inch layer cake pans. Bake in hot oven (450° F.) 8 to 10 minutes. Cool and put together with Jelly Frosting (page 43).

CAKE RING

2 cups sifted cake flour
1½ teaspoons baking powder
½ teaspoon salt
1 cup butter

1¼ cups sugar
1 teaspoon vanilla
4 eggs
½ cup milk

Sift together flour, baking powder and salt. Cream butter until smooth; gradually add sugar, beating until fluffy; add vanilla and beat in thoroughly one egg at a time. Add flour alternately with milk, beating until smooth. Bake in prepared 10-inch tube pan in slow oven (325° F.) 60 to 70 minutes. Frost, if desired. Yield: 1 cake (10 inch).

ALMOND PASTE

2 cups sugar   2 eggs
                2 cups ground almonds

To make almond paste, blend sugar, eggs and ground almonds and mix to a smooth paste. Cover and store in refrigerator.

DELICATE WHITE CAKE
(4 Egg Whites)

2 cups sifted cake flour
2 teaspoons baking powder
¼ teaspoon salt
½ cup butter or other fat

1⅓ cups sugar
½ teaspoon vanilla
⅔ cup milk
4 egg whites

Sift together flour, baking powder and salt. Cream butter until smooth and gradually add 1 cup sugar, beating until fluffy; add flavoring. Add flour alternately with milk, beating until smooth. Beat egg whites until foamy, gradually beat in remaining ⅓ cup sugar; fold into cake batter. Turn into 2 prepared layer pans or square pan and bake: layers, in moderate oven (375° F.) about 25 to 30 minutes; in square pan in moderate oven (350° F.) 30 to 35 minutes. Yield: 2 layers (8 inch), or 1 square (8 inch), or 14 cup cakes.

ALLEGRETTI PECAN CAKE

1 recipe Delicate White Cake
    (page 639)
1 cup finely chopped pecans

1 recipe Fluffy Marshmallow
    Frosting (page 711)
Bittersweet Veneer (page 714)

Prepare cake batter; carefully fold in nuts and bake in 2 prepared 8-inch layer pans. Put layers together and spread sides and top of cake with frosting. When frosting is firm but not hard, pour bittersweet veneer over top, allowing veneer to run over edge and drip down on sides.

SILVER CAKE
(6 Egg Whites)

3 cups sifted cake flour
3½ teaspoons baking powder
¾ teaspoon salt
¾ cup butter or other fat
2 cups powdered sugar

½ teaspoon rose or almond
  extract
½ cup milk
½ cup water
6 egg whites, stiffly beaten

Sift together flour, baking powder and salt. Cream butter until soft and smooth and gradually add sugar, beating until very fluffy, add flavoring. Add flour alternately with combined milk and water, beating until smooth after each addition; fold in thoroughly the stiffly beaten egg whites. Turn into prepared layer pans or paper-lined, 8-inch tube pan and bake: in layers in moderate oven (375° F.) 30 to 35 minutes; in tube pan in moderate oven (350° F.) about 55 minutes. Yield: 3 layers (9-inch), or 1 tube cake.

Lady Baltimore Cake—Put layers together and cover top with Lady Baltimore Frosting (page 714). Yield: 3 layer (9-inch) cake.

FAVORITE WHITE CAKE
(3 Egg Whites)

Use recipe for Two-egg Cake (page 634); change sugar to 1⅛ cups; substitute 3 stiffly beaten egg whites for 2 whole eggs and fold thoroughly into batter. Yield: 1 square (8 inch), 2 layers (8 inch), or 14 medium cup cakes.

SIMPLE WHITE CAKE
(2 Egg Whites)

Use recipe for One-egg Cake (page 633); substitute 2 stiffly beaten egg whites for 1 whole egg and fold thoroughly into batter. Yield: 1 square (8 inch), 2 layers (8 inch), or 14 medium cup cakes.

Baby Baltimore Cakes—Bake in greased muffin pans. Cut each cake in 3 slices; put together with Fruit-nut Filling (page 722) and spread Boiled Frosting (page 713) over cakes. Approximate yield: 2 dozen cup cakes.

Lord Baltimore Cake—Put layers together and cover top with Lord Baltimore Frosting (page 711). Yield: 3 layer (8-inch) cake.

GOLD CAKE

(8 Egg Yolks)

1¾ cups sifted cake flour
3 teaspoons baking powder
¼ teaspoon salt
½ cup butter or other fat

1 cup sugar
1 tablespoon grated orange rind
8 egg yolks
½ cup milk

Sift together flour, baking powder and salt. Cream butter until soft and smooth and gradually add sugar, beating until very fluffy; add orange rind. Beat egg yolks until very thick and light colored and add to butter-sugar mixture, beating thoroughly. Add flour alternately with milk, beating until smooth after each addition. Turn into 3 prepared layer pans or muffin pans and bake in moderate oven (375° F.) 25 to 30 minutes. Yield: 3 layers (8 inch), or 24 cup cakes.

QUICK GOLD CAKE

2 cups sifted cake flour
2 teaspoons baking powder
¾ teaspoon salt
1 cup sugar

½ cup shortening
5 egg yolks, unbeaten
¾ cup milk
1 teaspoon vanilla

Sift together dry ingredients. Cream shortening until soft. Add dry ingredients and egg yolks and half of milk. Mix until all flour is dampened. Then beat 2 minutes with electric beater. Add remaining milk and vanilla and beat 1 minute longer—or count beating strokes. Allow about 150 full strokes per minute. Pour batter into prepared 9½ x 5¼ x 2¾-inch loaf pan. Bake in moderate oven (350° F.) 40 to 60 minutes, or until done.

OUR FAVORITE CHOCOLATE CAKE

2 squares unsweetened
   chocolate, melted
3 tablespoons butter, melted
1 cup sifted cake flour
1½ teaspoons baking powder

¼ teaspoon salt
1 cup sugar
2 eggs, beaten
1 teaspoon vanilla
½ cup milk

Melt chocolate and butter and allow to cool. Sift together flour, baking powder and salt. Beat sugar and eggs into chocolate mixture and add vanilla; add flour alternately with milk, beating until smooth after each addition. Pour into prepared 8 x 8 x 2-inch pan and bake in moderate oven (350° F.) 30 to 35 minutes.

CHOCOLATE LAYER CAKE

2 cups sifted cake flour
2 teaspoons baking powder
½ teaspoon baking soda
½ teaspoon salt
½ cup butter or other fat

1 cup sugar
1 teaspoon vanilla
2 eggs
3 squares unsweetened chocolate, melted

1 cup milk

Sift together flour, baking powder, soda and salt. Cream butter until soft and smooth; gradually add sugar, beating until very fluffy; beat in vanilla and eggs, one at a time, then chocolate. Add flour alternately with milk, beating until smooth after each addition. Turn into prepared layer pans and bake in moderate oven (350° F.) about ½ hour. To substitute cocoa for chocolate, use ½ cup cocoa and sift with dry ingredients; add 1½ tablespoons butter. Yield: 2 layers (9 inch).

PARTY FUDGE CAKE

4 squares unsweetened chocolate
1¼ cups milk
⅓ cup firmly packed brown sugar
2¼ cups sifted cake flour

1 teaspoon baking soda
½ teaspoon salt
⅔ cup butter or other fat
1 cup granulated sugar
1 teaspoon vanilla
3 eggs, well beaten

Melt chocolate in milk in top of double boiler, beating with rotary beater until blended; add brown sugar, stirring until smooth; cool. Sift together flour, soda and salt. Cream butter until soft and smooth; gradually add granulated sugar, creaming until very fluffy; beat in vanilla and eggs. Add flour alternately with chocolate mixture, beating until smooth after each addition. Turn into prepared pan or pans and bake in moderate oven (350° F.): in 10-inch square pan, about 55 minutes; in 3 layer pans (8 inch), 25 to 30 minutes. Spread Fudge Frosting (page 716) on cake and press walnut halves over entire top surface. Yield: 1 square cake, or 3 layer cake.

Shadow Peppermint Cake—Prepare Seven Minute Frosting (page 711) with ¼ teaspoon oil of peppermint or 1 stick peppermint candy, crushed. Spread between layers and on top and sides of cake. For generous covering, prepare 1½ recipes. When frosting is firm but not hard, pour Bittersweet Veneer (page 714) over top, allowing it to run over edge and drip down on sides.

MAHOGANY CAKE

1 square unsweetened chocolate	¼ teaspoon vinegar
½ cup strong black coffee	½ teaspoon vanilla
¼ cup soft butter	1 cup sifted cake flour
¾ cup sugar	½ teaspoon baking soda
2 eggs	½ teaspoon salt

Melt chocolate in ¼ cup coffee over hot water; cool, stirring occasionally. Cream butter and sugar until light and fluffy; add 1 whole egg and 1 egg yolk and beat thoroughly. Beat in chocolate-coffee mixture; add vinegar and vanilla. Sift together flour, baking soda and salt; add half to butter-egg-chocolate mixture and beat until smooth. Add remaining coffee, then flour mixture, beating until smooth after each. Turn into prepared small square pan (7 inch) or 8-inch layer pan. Bake in moderate oven (350°–375° F.) 30 to 35 minutes. Cool and frost with a Lemon Icing (page 710) made with remaining egg white. Yield: 1 small square or round cake.

RICH CHOCOLATE CAKE

2¼ cups sifted cake flour	1 teaspoon vanilla
3½ teaspoons baking powder	3 eggs, separated
½ teaspoon salt	3 squares unsweetened chocolate,
1 cup butter or other fat	melted
1¾ cups sugar	¾ cup milk

Sift together flour, baking powder and salt. Cream butter until soft and smooth; gradually add 1½ cups sugar, beating until very fluffy; beat in vanilla and well-beaten egg yolks, then chocolate. Add flour alternately with milk. Beat egg whites until foamy; gradually beat in remaining ¼ cup sugar; fold into cake batter. Bake in moderate oven (350° F.) about 30 minutes. Yield: 3 layers (8 inch).

DEVIL'S FOOD CAKE

2 cups sifted cake flour	1 teaspoon vanilla
1 teaspoon baking soda	3 eggs, separated
½ teaspoon salt	2 squares unsweetened chocolate,
½ cup butter or other fat	melted
1½ cups sugar	1 cup sour milk or buttermilk

Sift together flour, soda and salt. Cream butter until soft and smooth; gradually add sugar, beating until fluffy; beat in vanilla and well-beaten egg yolks, then chocolate. Add flour alternately with sour milk; fold in stiffly beaten egg whites. Bake in moderate oven (350° F.) 30 minutes. Yield: 2 layers (9 inch).

FUDGE CAKE

2 cups sifted cake flour
1½ teaspoons baking powder
½ teaspoon baking soda
½ teaspoon salt
½ cup butter or other fat

1¼ cups packed brown sugar
1 teaspoon vanilla
2 eggs
3 squares unsweetened chocolate,
    melted

1 cup milk

Sift together flour, baking powder, soda and salt. Cream butter until soft and smooth; gradually add sugar, beating until fluffy; add vanilla and beat in thoroughly one egg at a time, then chocolate. Add flour alternately with milk. Bake in moderate oven (350° F.) 25 to 30 minutes. Yield: 2 layers (8 inch).

CHOCOLATE BOSTON CREAM CAKE

1½ cups sifted flour
1 teaspoon baking powder
½ teaspoon salt
¼ cup shortening
¼ cup sugar
¾ cup corn syrup

1 egg
2 squares unsweetened chocolate,
    melted
1 teaspoon vanilla
½ cup sour milk or buttermilk
½ teaspoon baking soda

Mix and sift flour, baking powder and salt. Cream shortening, add sugar and corn syrup. Add egg, chocolate and vanilla. Dissolve soda in sour milk and add alternately with flour, beating well after each addition. Turn into shallow loaf pan, and bake in a slow oven (300° F.) 45 minutes. Cool, cut in half, put together with white frosting.

CHOCOLATE CREAM CAKE

4 eggs
½ cup sugar
5 tablespoons sifted all-purpose
    flour
4 ounces dot semi-sweet
    chocolate

3 tablespoons coffee
1 recipe Chocolate Butter Cream
    (page 715)
1 recipe Cookie Wafers (page
    702)
confectioners' sugar

Place eggs and sugar in bowl in pan of hot water and beat with an electric beater or rotary beater until mixture is very stiff. Add flour and chocolate which has been melted with coffee, folding in gently. Turn at once into greased 8-inch spring form cake pan lined with greased waxed paper. Bake in moderate oven (350° F.) 45 minutes. Remove from oven, cool and cover with Chocolate Butter Cream. Place cooled Cookie Wafers around sides of cake. Decorate with pastry tube, making clusters of chocolate cream rosettes. Dust with confectioners' sugar. Refrigerate for at least 30 minutes. Yield: 10 portions.

GOURMET'S CHOCOLATE CAKE

4 eggs	3 tablespoons strong coffee
½ cup powdered sugar	Butter Cream Frosting (page
½ cup sifted all-purpose flour	715)
4 squares unsweetened chocolate	Chocolate Pellets (page 852)

Beat eggs until light; place bowl in bowl or pan of hot water. Gradually add sugar and beat continuously until very stiff and mixture forms peaks. Gradually fold in flour. Melt chocolate with coffee over hot water. Stir into cake batter just enough to blend. Turn into greased 8-inch spring form cake pan which has been lined with greased waxed paper. Bake in slow oven (325° F.) 45 minutes. Cool and remove spring form from cake. Frost with Butter Cream Frosting and decorate with Chocolate Pellets. Yield: 6 to 8 portions.

DARK CHERRY CAKE

1½ cups sifted flour	1 cup sour milk
1 teaspoon baking soda	1 4-ounce bottle maraschino
⅛ teaspoon salt	cherries
½ cup shortening	½ cup chopped walnuts
1 cup sugar	1 square unsweetened chocolate,
1 egg	melted

Mix and sift flour, soda and salt. Cream shortening, add sugar, and cream until fluffy; beat in egg. Add flour alternately with sour milk, beating until smooth after each addition. Add chopped cherries, juice from cherries, nuts and chocolate; mix well. Turn into greased shallow loaf pan and bake in moderate oven (350° F.) about 45 minutes.

CINNAMON CAKE

½ cup sifted flour	¾ cup melted shortening
1½ teaspoons baking powder	1 cup sifted all-purpose flour
¼ teaspoon salt	1 cup sugar
2 eggs	2 tablespoons cinnamon
milk	¼ cup sugar

Mix and sift first 3 ingredients. Break eggs into measuring cup and add milk to fill cup; add with shortening to 1 cup flour and sugar, beating until smooth. Add flour sifted with baking powder and salt and beat well. Turn into greased, shallow loaf pan and sprinkle with combined cinnamon and sugar. Bake in a moderate oven (325° F.) for 15 to 20 minutes.

AUNT CARRIE'S BONBON CAKE

1¾ cups sifted all-purpose flour
2 teaspoons double-acting
   baking powder
½ teaspoon salt
2 squares unsweetened
   chocolate, finely cut

5 tablespoons boiling water
½ cup butter or margarine
1½ cups sugar
1 teaspoon vanilla
4 egg yolks
4 egg whites
½ cup milk

Sift together flour, baking powder and salt. Combine chocolate and water. Stir until smooth and of custard consistency. Cream butter; gradually add sugar, creaming well. Add cooled chocolate and vanilla. Blend in egg yolks, one at a time. Beat for 1 minute. Add milk alternately with dry ingredients to creamed mixture, beginning and ending with dry ingredients. Blend thoroughly after each addition. (With electric mixer use low speed.) Beat egg whites until stiff but not dry. Fold gently but thoroughly into batter. Pour into prepared 8-inch layer pans. Bake in moderate oven (350° F.) 30 to 35 minutes. Cool layers, then fill with Bonbon Filling (page 724) and frost with Fudge Frosting (page 716). Yield: one layer cake (8-inch).

"MIX-EASY" DEVIL'S FOOD CAKE

2 cups sifted cake flour
1 teaspoon baking soda
¾ teaspoon salt
1⅓ cups sugar
½ cup shortening

1 cup milk
1 teaspoon vanilla
2 eggs, unbeaten
3 squares unsweetened chocolate,
   melted

Sift together flour, soda, salt and sugar. Cream shortening until soft. Add dry ingredients and ¾ cup of milk and mix until all flour is dampened. Then beat 2 minutes with electric mixer. Add vanilla, eggs, melted chocolate and remaining milk and beat 1 minute longer. Count only actual beating time. If mixed by hand, count beating strokes, allowing about 150 full strokes per minute. Pour batter into 2 layer cake pans (9 inch) or 13 x 9½ x 2-inch pan. Bake in moderate oven (350° F.) about 30 minutes for layers, or about 40 minutes for sheet cake. Yield: 1 layer or sheet cake.

PENN SPICE CAKE

3 cups sifted all-purpose flour
3 teaspoons baking powder
½ teaspoon baking soda
1 teaspoon salt
1 teaspoon ginger
1 teaspoon cinnamon
1 teaspoon allspice

½ teaspoon cloves
2 teaspoons nutmeg
¾ cup shortening
1 cup firmly packed brown
   sugar
3 eggs, separated
1 cup chopped raisins

1 cup sour milk

Sift together flour, baking powder, soda, salt and spices. Cream shortening until soft and smooth; gradually beat in brown sugar, beating until fluffy; add well-beaten egg yolks, beating thoroughly, then raisins. Add flour alternately with sour milk, beating well after each addition; fold in egg whites beaten stiff but not dry. Turn into prepared pan (7 x 11 x 1½ inches) and bake in moderate oven (350° F.) about 30 to 40 minutes. Spread with Caramel Fudge Frosting (page 717). Or spread with Lemon Frosting (page 710). Yield: 1 cake (7 x 11 x 1½ inches).

CHARLESTON SPICE CAKE

2 cups sifted all-purpose flour
1 teaspoon baking powder
½ teaspoon baking soda
¼ teaspoon salt
1 teaspoon nutmeg
½ teaspoon mace

1½ teaspoons cloves
½ cup shortening
1 cup sugar
3 eggs, well beaten
¼ cup molasses
1 cup milk

Sift together flour, baking powder, soda, salt and spices. Cream shortening until soft and smooth; gradually add sugar, beating until fluffy; beat in eggs. Add flour mixture alternately with combined molasses and milk, beating until smooth after each addition. Turn into prepared square pan and bake in moderate oven (350° F.) 35 to 45 minutes. Yield: 1 square cake (8 inch).

Pecan Spice Cake.—Beat ½ cup chopped pecans into butter-sugar-egg mixture and proceed as above. If desired, cut in squares and serve as a dessert with topping of whipped cream; or top with Cream Cheese Frosting (½ recipe, page 710). Yield: 1 square cake.

MAPLE CAKE

½ cup butter	½ cup milk
1 cup sugar	1 egg white, stiffly beaten
4 egg yolks	2½ cups maple syrup
1½ cups sifted cake flour	¾ cup egg whites, stiffly beaten
2 teaspoons baking powder	few chopped pecans

Cream butter, add sugar and beat until light and fluffy. Beat in egg yolks. Sift together flour and baking powder. Add to butter-sugar mixture alternately with milk. Fold in stiffly beaten egg white. Butter 2 shallow 9-inch layer cake tins; line bottoms with waxed paper and grease again. Divide batter into two tins and bake in moderate oven (350° F.) about 20 minutes, or until cakes are golden brown. Turn out on waxed paper and cool. Place maple syrup in pan and cook to thin thread stage (230° to 234° F.) Pour onto the ¾ cup stiffly beaten egg whites and continue beating until quite thick. Spread between layers and cover cake generously. Decorate with chopped pecans. Yield: 2 layers (9-inch).

BLACKBERRY JAM CAKE

3 cups sifted all-purpose flour	1 teaspoon cloves
2 teaspoons baking powder	⅔ cup shortening
1 teaspoon baking soda	1½ cups sugar
¼ teaspoon salt	3 eggs, well beaten
1 teaspoon cinnamon	1 cup blackberry jam
1 cup sour milk or buttermilk	

Sift together flour, baking powder, soda, salt and spices. Cream shortening until soft and smooth; gradually add sugar, beating until very fluffy, then beat in eggs and jam. Add flour mixture alternately with sour milk, beating until smooth after each addition. Turn into 3 prepared layer pans and bake in moderate oven (350° F.) 25 to 30 minutes. Put layers together and spread top with Butter Frosting (page 709). Yield: 3 layers (9-inch).

Berry Jam Cake—Substitute red or black raspberry or loganberry jam for blackberry jam. Put layers together and spread with Mocha Frosting (page 709) or Lemon Frosting (page 710).

APPLESAUCE CAKE

3 cups sifted all-purpose flour
2 teaspoons baking soda
¼ teaspoon salt
2 teaspoons cinnamon
1½ teaspoons cloves
2 cups chopped nuts

2 cups chopped raisins
1 cup chopped dates
½ cup shortening
¾ cup firmly packed brown
    sugar
2 eggs, well beaten

2 cups thick applesauce

Sift together flour, soda, salt and spices; mix about ½ cup with nuts and fruits. Cream shortening until soft and smooth; gradually add sugar, beating until fluffy, then beat in eggs. Add flour mixture alternately with applesauce, beating well after each addition; beat in fruit-nut mixture. Turn into prepared loaf pans and bake in moderate oven (350° F.) 35 to 40 minutes, or until done. Nuts and dates may be omitted, if desired. This cake will keep moist for several days if stored in closely covered cake box. Yield: 2 small loaves or 1 large loaf, 11 x 8 x 3 inches.

GINGERBREAD

2 cups sifted all-purpose flour
1 teaspoon baking soda
¼ teaspoon salt
1½ teaspoons ginger
1 teaspoon cinnamon

½ cup firmly packed light
    brown sugar
2 eggs, beaten
½ cup molasses
1 cup sour milk or buttermilk

½ cup shortening, melted

Sift together dry ingredients. Combine eggs, molasses, sour milk and shortening; gradually add to flour-sugar mixture, beating thoroughly. Turn into prepared 8-inch square pan and bake in moderate oven (350° F.) 35 to 45 minutes. Yield: 1 square cake (8 inch).

QUICK GINGERBREAD

1 cup sifted all-purpose flour
½ teaspoon baking soda
¼ teaspoon salt
2 teaspoons cinnamon
1 teaspoon ginger

¼ teaspoon nutmeg
1 egg, slightly beaten
5 tablespoons dark brown sugar
¼ cup dark molasses
½ cup sour milk or buttermilk

¼ cup shortening, melted

Sift together flour, soda, salt and spices. Combine egg, sugar, molasses, sour milk and shortening; gradually add flour mixture, stirring until mixed, then beat vigorously about 1 minute, or until smooth. Turn into prepared square pan and bake in moderate oven (350° F.) 30 to 40 minutes. Yield: 1 square cake (8 inch).

Tropical Gingerbread—Reduce cinnamon and ginger to ¾ teaspoon each and nutmeg to ⅛ teaspoon; add ⅛ teaspoon each cloves and allspice. Fold ⅔ cup shredded coconut into cake batter. Yield: 8 portions.

Cheese-Topped Gingerbread—When baked, cover top with cream cheese whip, made by stirring milk into 1 3-oz. package cream cheese until of desired consistency; then whip until light and creamy. Serve. at once. Approximate yield: 8 portions.

Gingerbread Tea Cakes—Bake in prepared muffin tins 20 to 25 minutes. Spread with Mocha Frosting (page 709). Yield: 8 cakes.

Gingerbread Dessert—Prepare gingerbread. Mash 1 3-oz. package cream cheese; add dash of salt and 1 cup drained, crushed canned apricots. Fold in ½ cup heavy cream, whipped; spread over warm gingerbread. Yield: 8 portions.

Gingerbread Banana Shortcake—When baked, cut gingerbread in half. Spread 1 cup heavy cream, whipped, and 3 bananas, sliced, between halves and on top. Yield: 8 portions.

Gingerbread Upside-Down Cake—Prepare batter. Melt ¼ cup butter or margarine in frying pan or cake pan; add ⅓ cup brown sugar and stir until sugar is dissolved. Arrange 7 to 9 cooked pear halves, hollow side down, in syrup. Cover with cake batter and bake as directed. Loosen cake from sides and turn out immediately; allow pan to rest over cake for a few seconds so that syrup will drain on cake. Serve warm. Yield: 8 portions.

STOW-A-WAY GINGERBREAD

2¼ cups sifted flour	1 cup sugar
1¼ teaspoons ginger	2 eggs
½ teaspoon cinnamon	½ cup molasses
½ teaspoon allspice	½ cup sour milk or buttermilk
½ cup shortening	1 teaspoon baking soda

Mix and sift flour and spices. Cream shortening and add sugar and molasses. Then beat in eggs, one at a time. Stir soda into sour milk and add alternately with flour, beating until smooth after each addition. Cover and store in refrigerator. Turn as needed into well-greased shallow loaf pan or muffin tins and bake in moderate oven (350° F.) about 25 to 30 minutes, or until done. Store remainder for several days, if desired. Yield: 1 loaf (11 x 7 x 1½ inches) or 18 large gingercakes.

FRUIT UPSIDE-DOWN CAKE

1 recipe Hot Water Sponge   ¼ cup butter or margarine
   Cake (page 670)   ½ cup brown sugar
         whole or chopped fruit (see below)

Prepare batter for Hot Water Sponge Cake; melt butter in 8-inch square
pan. Add brown sugar and stir until thoroughly mixed; remove from
heat. Arrange fruit in syrup, cut-side up, and cover with cake batter.
Bake in moderate oven (350° F.) 35 to 45 minutes. Loosen cake batter
from sides and bottom with spatula and turn out on cake plate. Let
pan rest over baked cake 1 minute to allow caramel syrup to drip on
cake. Serve with whipped cream, Hard Sauce (page 732), Sherry Sauce
(page 732), or Foamy Yellow Sauce (page 731); or sprinkle with rum,
brandy or Kirsch, if desired. Use any of the following fruits: 8 apricots,
halved; 2 cups sliced peaches or pears, fresh or canned; or 8 halves of
fruit; 4 slices canned pineapple and maraschino cherries; 12 halves
apricots and 6 cooked prunes, seeded and halved; any fruit with halves
of walnuts, pecans or blanched almonds. Yield: 1 square cake (8 inch).

ORANGE KISS ME CAKE

2 cups sifted all-purpose flour   2 eggs
1 teaspoon soda   1 large orange (reserve juice for
1 teaspoon salt   topping; grind rind and pulp
½ cup shortening   with raisins)
1 cup sugar   1 cup raisins, ground
                1 cup milk

Sift together flour, soda and salt. Cream shortening and sugar. Blend
in eggs, one at a time. Add ground orange and raisins. Add milk and
dry ingredients alternately to creamed mixture, beginning and ending
with dry ingredients. Blend thoroughly after each addition. (With
electric mixer use low speed.) Pour into prepared 13 x 9 x 2-inch pan.
Bake in moderate oven (350° F.) 30 to 35 minutes.

Topping

¼ cup sugar   1 teaspoon cinnamon
              ¼ cup walnuts, chopped

Drip orange juice (about ⅓ cup) over warm cake. Sprinkle with sugar,
cinnamon and nut topping. Decorate with orange slices. Yield: one
13 x 9 x 2-inch cake.

JEWEL CAKE

2 cups cranberries	¾ cup sugar
1 orange	1 package (14 oz.) gingerbread
¼ cup seeded raisins	mix
5 tablespoons butter, melted	heavy cream, whipped

Put cranberries and orange through food chopper, using finest knife; mix with raisins. Pour melted butter into 9-inch square pan and sprinkle evenly with sugar; spread fruit mixture over top and cover with gingerbread mix, prepared according to directions on package. Bake in moderate oven (350° F.) 35 to 40 minutes. Loosen cake from sides and bottom with spatula and turn out on cake plate. Serve with whipped cream. Yield: 9 squares.

DELICIOUS APPLE CAKE

4 medium-sized apples	1 teaspoon cornstarch
1 teaspoon lemon juice	1 to 3 teaspoons shredded
3 tablespoons sugar	coconut
½ teaspoon cinnamon or	1 recipe Fruit Upside-Down
nutmeg	Cake (page 651)

heavy cream, whipped

Pare and cut tart apples in thin slices and sprinkle with lemon juice; combine sugar, spice, cornstarch and coconut and sprinkle over apples. Prepare cake batter and turn into prepared 8-inch square pan. Press down well ¼ of apples into batter and cover with remaining apple mixture. Bake in moderate oven (350° F.) 35 to 40 minutes. Cut in squares and serve hot with whipped cream. Yield: 9 portions.

POUND CAKE

1 pound butter (2 cups)	1 pound sifted cake flour
1 pound sugar (2 cups)	(4½ cups)
10 eggs, separated	1 teaspoon baking powder
	(optional)

Cream butter until soft and smooth; gradually beat in sugar until light and fluffy. Beat egg yolks until thick and lemon-colored. Combine with butter and sugar mixture and beat hard until light and very fluffy. Sift flour with baking powder and add alternately with stiffly beaten egg whites, beating until very smooth and light after each addition. Add any flavoring desired. Turn into 2 loaf pans (8½ x 4½ x 2½ inches) lined with heavy waxed paper and buttered; bake in slow oven (325° F.) 1½ to 1¾ hours. The true pound cake has no baking powder. Add 2 tablespoons brandy if desired. Yield: 2 loaves.

OLD ENGLISH FRUITCAKE

5 cups sifted all-purpose flour
1 teaspoon baking soda
½ teaspoon salt
1 teaspoon cinnamon
½ teaspoon cloves
½ teaspoon mace
1 pound butter or other
   shortening
1 pound sifted brown sugar
8 eggs

½ pound each candied cherries,
   citron, orange and lemon peel,
   finely sliced
1 pound seedless raisins
1 pound currants, washed and
   dried
1 pound almonds, blanched and
   shredded
½ cup currant jelly
¾ cup honey

⅓ cup molasses

Sift together flour, soda, salt and spices. Cream butter thoroughly; add sugar gradually, beating until light and fluffy; beat in eggs, then fruits and nuts. Add jelly, honey and molasses and beat well; add flour mixture gradually, mixing well after each addition; turn into 2 paper-lined prepared tube pans. Bake in slow oven (250° F.) 3½ hours, or until cake is firm to the touch; a sheet of brown paper placed over the cakes during baking will prevent too rapid browning of the top surface. Cool in pan; remove paper, wrap in waxed paper and store in airtight can. Yield: 2 fruitcakes (5 pounds each).

MELLOWING THE FRUITCAKE

Add wine or brandy during the aging process of the fruitcake. If cake is stored in a tin box or the covered casserole in which it is baked, pour a small amount of Sherry or brandy over the cake at intervals for a week or ten days. Another method is to wrap the cake in a cheesecloth which has been saturated with the liquor. This curing may be applied to the ready-made fruitcakes that come packed in airtight tins. Store wrapped cake in the moist cold section or the fruit or vegetable compartment of refrigerator.

A piece of apple or orange placed on wax paper in the container helps keep the cake moist. If all the fruits given in the recipe are not available, substitute for the unavailable ones, but be sure to have 2¾ pounds of fruit in all.

DARK FRUITCAKE

1½ cups sifted cake flour	few drops orange, lemon and
2 teaspoons baking powder	almond flavoring
1 teaspoon salt	6 tablespoons orange juice
½ teaspoon nutmeg	¼ pound candied lemon peel
½ teaspoon mace	¼ pound candied orange peel
½ teaspoon cinnamon	¼ pound citron
¼ teaspoon allspice	½ pound candied pineapple
¼ teaspoon cloves	½ pound candied cherries
1 cup butter	½ pound dates
½ cup sugar	½ pound raisins
½ cup light honey	¼ pound broken pecans
5 eggs, well beaten	½ pound broken walnuts

½ cup sifted all-purpose flour

Sift together cake flour, baking powder, salt and spices. Cream butter until soft and smooth; gradually add sugar and honey, beating until light and fluffy; add eggs and flavorings, beating thoroughly. Add flour-spice mixture alternately with orange juice, beating until smooth each addition. Add chopped peels and fruits and broken nuts, dredged with all-purpose flour, to cake batter and mix well. Turn into well greased loaf pans or molds, paper-lined and buttered, filling them two-thirds full. Bake in a slow oven (300° F.) 1½ to 3 hours, or until done; cool and remove waxed paper. Approximate yield: 5 pounds fruitcake.

ORANGE FRUITCAKE

1½ medium oranges	1½ teaspoons baking soda
2¼ cups sugar	1 teaspoon salt
1 cup nuts	⅔ cup shortening
1½ cups seeded raisins	1 teaspoon vanilla
3 cups sifted all-purpose flour	3 eggs, well beaten

1 cup sour milk or buttermilk

Squeeze juice from oranges and add ¾ cup sugar. Cut orange skins in quarters and remove all of white pulp and membrane; put yellow rind, nuts and raisins through food chopper, using the finest knife. Sift together flour, soda and salt. Cream shortening until soft and smooth, gradually add remaining 1½ cups sugar, beating until very fluffy; beat in vanilla and eggs, then fruit-nut mixture. Add flour alternately with sour milk, beating well after each addition. Turn into 2 prepared loaf pans and bake in slow oven (300° F.) about 1½ hours. Remove and at once pour orange juice-sugar mixture over cakes. Cool in pans and allow to stand several hours or overnight before cutting. Yield: 2 loaves, 8½ x 4½ x 2½ inches.

SPICE FRUITCAKE

2 cups sifted all-purpose flour
2 teaspoons baking powder
½ teaspoon baking soda
½ teaspoon salt
½ teaspoon cinnamon
½ teaspoon nutmeg
¼ teaspoon ginger
¼ teaspoon allspice
¼ teaspoon cloves

½ cup chopped dried prunes
½ cup chopped dried apricots
½ cup chopped nuts
½ cup shortening
⅔ cup firmly packed dark
    brown sugar
2 eggs
⅔ cup sour milk or buttermilk
heavy cream, whipped
brandy

Sift together flour, baking powder, soda, salt and spices; mix ½ cup with prepared fruits and nuts. Cream shortening until soft and smooth; gradually add sugar, beating until fluffy; beat in thoroughly one egg at a time. Add flour mixture alternately with sour milk, beating until smooth after each addition, then beat in fruit mixture. Turn into prepared (8 inch) square pan; bake in moderate oven (350° F.) 35 to 40 minutes. Cut in squares and serve warm with whipped cream flavored with brandy. Finely cut preserved ginger may be added to cream, if desired. Yield: 9 portions.

LIGHT FRUITCAKE

2 cups sifted all-purpose flour
1 teaspoon baking soda
⅛ teaspoon salt
1 teaspoon cinnamon
½ teaspoon allspice
¼ teaspoon cloves
¼ teaspoon mace
1 cup seeded raisins
½ cup currants
½ cup minced candied orange
    peel

½ cup shredded citron
½ cup chopped maraschino
    cherries
½ cup blanched and chopped
    almonds
½ cup shortening
1 cup sugar
½ teaspoon orange extract
3 eggs, well beaten
½ cup molasses
½ cup sour milk

Sift together flour, soda, salt and spices; mix with prepared fruits and nuts. Cream shortening until soft and smooth; gradually add sugar, beating until fluffy; beat in flavoring and eggs, then molasses. Gradually stir in flour-fruit-nut mixture alternately with milk. Turn into 2 prepared loaf pans (buttered, lined with waxed paper and greased again). Cover tops tightly with waxed or greased paper and steam 1 hour; then bake in very slow oven (250° F.) about 1 hour, removing paper the last 15 minutes to dry surface. Yield: 2 loaves.

LAST–MINUTE FRUITCAKE

2 cups sifted all-purpose flour
1/8 teaspoon salt
1 teaspoon baking soda
1/2 teaspoon cinnamon
1/2 teaspoon allspice
1/4 teaspoon mace
1/4 teaspoon cloves
1/2 cup shortening
1/3 cup firmly packed brown
    sugar

1/3 cup honey
1/2 cup molasses
3 eggs, well beaten
1 cup seeded raisins, chopped
1/2 cup sliced candied orange peel
1/2 cup finely sliced citron
1 cup currants, washed and
    dried
1/2 teaspoon vanilla
1/2 cup milk

Sift together flour, salt, baking soda and spices. Cream shortening well, beat in brown sugar and honey, then molasses. Add eggs and beat until fluffy. Stir in fruit, then vanilla and milk. Mix well. Turn into prepared paper-lined tube pan and bake in slow oven (300° F.) 3 hours, or until firm to the touch. Cool. Remove from pan and tear paper carefully from cake. Wrap in clean waxed paper and store in stone crock or in tightly covered tin box. May be served within a week; moisten occasionally with brandy, if desired.

LIGHT GOLDEN FRUITCAKE

4 cups sifted all-purpose flour
4 teaspoons baking powder
1 cup shortening
2 cups sugar
2/3 cup orange juice
1 teaspoon grated orange rind
6 egg whites
1 cup golden seedless raisins

1/4 cup slivered dried apricots
1/2 cup candied cherries
1/2 cup slivered candied pineapple
1/2 cup sliced citron
1/4 cup sliced blanched almonds
1/4 cup shredded coconut
1/2 cup jelly, melted
brandy

Sift together flour and baking powder. Cream shortening until soft. Gradually add sugar and beat until light and fluffy. Add juice and rind. Beat egg whites until stiff but not dry. Fold into batter. Add remaining ingredients except jelly and brandy. Mix well. Line sides and bottom of 9-inch spring form cake pan with greased brown paper. Fill with batter. Bake in slow oven (300° F.) 2¾ to 3 hours, or until done. Spread with jelly and decorate as desired with candied fruits and blanched almonds. Return to slow oven for 20 minutes. Cool in pans. Remove and wrap in cheesecloth moistened with brandy. Store in air-tight container. Yield: 4-pound fruitcake.

FRUIT AND WINE CAKE

1 cup butter or margarine
2 cups granulated sugar
2¾ cups sifted all-purpose flour
½ teaspoon salt
1 teaspoon baking powder
1½ teaspoons cinnamon
½ teaspoon allspice
1½ teaspoons nutmeg
1 teaspoon mace
7 eggs, well beaten

½ cup Muscatel, Tokay or
  Angelica
2 cups raisins
1 cup shredded citron
½ cup shredded candied lemon
  peel
½ cup shredded candied orange
  peel
1 cup diced candied pineapple
¼ cup diced candied cherries

2 cups chopped nut meats
1 teaspoon almond flavoring

Cream butter until very soft. Add sugar gradually, beating until light after each addition. Mix and sift all dry ingredients together. Add eggs to butter-sugar mixture, beating until fluffy. Add wine, fruits, nuts and flavoring. Finally add dry ingredients. Turn into greased pans that have been lined with paper. Bake in slow oven (300° F.) until done. Place in pan of water in oven to prevent drying. Allow about 2 hours for cake in tube pan and about 1½ hours for loaf pans. Remove from pan, peel off paper and cool on rack.

To Store Fruitcake—Wrap in clean cloth moistened with wine, then in waxed paper. Store in pans in which cakes were baked. Place pans in airtight container. Sprinkle small amount of wine over cloth occasionally to keep moist. Store at least one week before cutting. If fruitcake is refrigerated it will cut easily with a sharp knife. Yield: one 4½-pound cake.

TOP-OF-STOVE CAKE

1 cup sifted flour
1½ teaspoons baking powder
3 tablespoons shortening

½ cup sugar
1 egg
¼ cup milk

½ teaspoon vanilla

Mix and sift flour and baking powder. Cream shortening, add sugar, and cream until fluffy; beat in egg. Add flour alternately with milk, beating until smooth after each addition; add vanilla. Turn into one section of a well-greased omelet pan, close pan and cook for 10 minutes over a low flame. Turn pan over and cook 10 minutes longer. Yield: 1 small cake.

UNUSUAL FRUITCAKE

1 pound mixed candied fruits (candied orange, lemon and grapefruit peel, citron and cherries)
¼ cup orange juice
3 cups sifted all-purpose flour
1 teaspoon salt
1 teaspoon cinnamon

1 teaspoon mace
1 teaspoon cloves
2 cups chopped nuts
3 cups seedless raisins
1 cup brown sugar
1 cup white sugar
2 cups water
½ cup jelly, melted
brandy

Prepare candied fruits by clipping into slivers or dice with scissors. Soak in orange juice 10 minutes. Sift together flour, salt and spices. Combine with candied fruits and nuts. Mix together raisins, brown sugar, white sugar and water in saucepan. Boil 5 minutes. Cool. Add to flour mixture and mix well. Line sides and bottom of 8½-inch tube pan with greased brown paper. Fill with batter and bake in slow oven (300° F.) 3 hours, or until cake tester inserted in center comes out clean. Brush top with jelly and decorate with candied fruits and blanched almonds. Return to oven 20 minutes longer. Cool thoroughly. Wrap in cheesecloth moistened with brandy. Store in airtight container. For several days moisten cheesecloth with brandy. Store in airtight container until ready to use. Yield: one 3-pound fruitcake.

TWELFTH NIGHT CAKE

3½ cups sifted cake flour
3 teaspoons baking powder
½ teaspoon salt
1 cup butter or other fat

2 cups sugar
5 egg yolks
½ cup orange juice
½ cup milk

3 egg whites

Sift together flour, baking powder and salt. Cream butter until soft and smooth; gradually add sugar, beating until light and fluffy. Add egg yolks one at a time, beating well after each addition. Add flour alternately with orange juice and milk. Fold in egg whites which have been beaten until stiff but not dry. Turn into a prepared 10-inch tube pan and bake in moderate oven (350° F.) 60 minutes. True to tradition, when cool and before frosting, push a bean and clove into one side of the cake and a pea into the other. Mark so the hostess will know which slices will contain the pea (for queen of the evening), the bean (for king of the evening), and the clove (for jester of the evening). Frost when cold. Yield: 1 cake.

CONFECTION FRUITCAKE

1 cup prunes
3 cups seedless raisins
1½ cups candied cherries
1 cup sliced preserved lemon peel
1 cup sliced preserved orange peel
2 cups sliced citron
½ cup honey
1 cup butter or margarine
1¼ cups granulated sugar

6 eggs, well beaten
3¼ cups sifted all-purpose flour
1½ teaspoons salt
½ teaspoon soda
1½ teaspoons cinnamon
1 teaspoon allspice
1 teaspoon mace
1 teaspoon ginger
½ teaspoon cloves
½ cup crushed banana
1½ cups chopped walnuts

1 tablespoon brandy extract

Boil prunes in water to cover 20 minutes. Drain and cool; slice from pits. Rinse raisins, drain and dry thoroughly. Cut cherries in halves. Combine all fruits, peels and citron with honey. Blend well, cover and let stand overnight. Cream butter and sugar together thoroughly. Blend in eggs. Sift together flour, salt, soda and spices and add to creamed mixture alternately with bananas. Blend in fruit-honey mixture, nuts and flavoring. Pour into pans lined with two thicknesses of greased brown paper and one of greased waxed paper. Bake in slow oven (300° F.) 2½ to 3¾ hours. When cool, decorate top with candied pineapple, cherries, citron and almonds. Wrap in cheesecloth well moistened with brandy or wine. This cake will store well and remain moist if it is sprinkled with brandy or wine each day for a week. Yield: one 6-pound cake (9-inch tube pan) or 2 loaves.

UNCOOKED FRUITCAKE

1 pound seeded raisins, cut fine
1 pound dates, cut fine
1 pound figs, cut fine
1 pound nuts, cut fine
grated rind of ½ orange
grated rind of ½ lemon
dash of salt

½ cup firmly packed brown sugar
1 teaspoon nutmeg
2 teaspoons cinnamon
½ teaspoon ginger
¼ cup orange juice
3 tablespoons brandy or rum

Combine fruit with nuts, rinds and salt and mix thoroughly. Combine sugar and spices and mix thoroughly with fruits. Add orange juice and brandy or rum and press firmly into buttered loaf pan lined with greased waxed paper. Smooth over top, cover with several thicknesses of waxed paper and keep in refrigerator several days before serving. Slice thin and use as fruitcake. Approximate yield: 2 loaves (8 inch).

GOLDEN STATE FRUITCAKE

2 cups seedless raisins
1 cup seeded raisins
½ cup dried apricots, slivered
1 cup pitted uncooked prunes,
    slivered
½ cup dried pears, slivered
1 cup candied cherries, halved
1 cup slivered citron
1 cup dates, cut in small pieces
2 cups chopped walnuts
2 cups sifted all-purpose flour
½ cup sifted cake flour
2 teaspoons baking powder

1 teaspoon salt
2 teaspoons cinnamon
1 teaspoon mace or nutmeg
1 teaspoon cloves
1 cup peanut oil
½ cup white sugar
½ cup brown sugar
½ cup corn syrup, honey or
    molasses
4 eggs, beaten
½ cup orange juice
½ cup orange marmalade
½ cup jelly, melted
brandy

Prepare fruits and nuts day before making cake. Sift together all-purpose flour, cake flour, baking powder, salt and spices. Combine oil, sugar, brown sugar, corn syrup and eggs. Add flour mixture alternately with orange juice. Add fruits, nuts and marmalade. Line bottom and sides of two 9½ x 5 x 2½-inch pans with greased brown paper. Fill with batter. Bake in slow oven (300° F.) 2½ hours, or until cake tester inserted in center comes out clean. Brush top with jelly and decorate as desired with candied fruits and blanched almonds. Return to oven 15 minutes longer. Cool thoroughly. Wrap in cheesecloth moistened with brandy. Store in airtight metal container. Moisten cheesecloth with brandy daily for a week. Store in airtight container until ready to use. Approximate yield: two (3-pound) fruit cakes.

PUFF CAKE

½ cup shortening
1 cup sugar
2 eggs, separated

1½ cups sifted flour
½ teaspoon vanilla
1 teaspoon baking powder

Cream shortening and add sugar, creaming until fluffy; beat in egg yolks. Add flour, beating until smooth after each addition; fold in the stiffly-beaten egg whites. Add vanilla and then baking powder, mixing well. Turn into well-greased tube pan and bake in a moderate oven (350° F.) 45 minutes, or until done. Yield: 1 small cake.

FIFTH GENERATION WEDDING CAKE

1 pound almonds
3 pounds currants
3 pounds raisins
1 pound mixed, sliced peel
2 cups Cognac
4 cups sifted all-purpose flour
2 teaspoons baking soda
3 teaspoons cinnamon
1 teaspoon cloves
½ nutmeg, grated
1 pound shortening
1½ cups firmly packed brown
  sugar
16 eggs
3 drops wintergreen
1 cup molasses
1 cup sour cream

Blanch and shred almonds; mix with fruits, peel and brandy and let stand in a closely covered jar 2 days. Sift together flour, soda and spices. Cream shortening until soft and smooth; gradually add sugar, beating until fluffy; beat in thoroughly one egg at a time, then wintergreen and molasses. Add flour mixture alternately with sour cream, mixing well after each addition; stir in brandied nuts and fruits. Turn into greased loaf pans, lined with waxed paper and again greased, filling them about ¾ full. Cover tightly with waxed or greased paper and steam 2 hours; then bake in very slow oven (250° F.) about 2 hours, removing paper the last ½ hour to dry surface. If kept covered with sugar and in an airtight can, this cake will be good on the 25th wedding anniversary. Approximate yield: 14 pounds fruitcake.

WEDDING CAKE

5 cups sifted cake flour
4 teaspoons baking powder
½ teaspoon salt
1 cup butter or other fat
4 cups sugar
¾ tablespoon vanilla
2 cups milk
10 egg whites

Sift together flour, baking powder and salt. Cream butter until soft and smooth and gradually add sugar, beating until very fluffy; add vanilla. Add flour alternately with milk, beating until smooth after each addition; fold in egg whites beaten stiff but not dry. Turn into 3 prepared layer pans of different sizes, filling each about ½ full, and bake in moderate oven (350° F.) 30 to 40 minutes. When cool, put layers together, pyramid style, with Foundation Boiled Frosting (page 713), spreading very smoothly. By forcing Decorative Boiled Frosting (page 713) through pastry tube, make a garland of white rosebuds around each layer and cover top with rosebuds. Over the top place a handle made by joining together the stems of small white flowers; stand the tiny bride and groom figures under this. Yield: 3 graduated layers, 12, 9 and 6 inches.

POPPY SEED CAKE

¾ cup milk
¾ cup ground poppy seeds
1 teaspoon grated lemon rind
½ teaspoon vanilla
¼ teaspoon salt

¾ cup butter or margarine
1 cup sugar
4 egg whites, stiffly beaten
1 teaspoon double-acting baking powder

2 cups sifted all-purpose flour

Pour milk over poppy seeds and add lemon rind, vanilla and salt. Blend and let stand 15 minutes. Cream butter with sugar and add poppy seed mixture. Fold in egg whites and baking powder that has been sifted with flour. Turn into 2 9-inch greased paper-lined layer cake tins and bake in moderately hot oven (375° F.) 25 to 30 minutes, or until done. Put together with Vanilla Cream Filling (page 720) and frost. Yield: 1 9-inch layer cake.

EASTER BASKETS

6 large sponge cup cakes
⅓ cup heavy cream, whipped
½ cup tinted coconut

gelatin eggs (strawberry, orange, lime or any color desired) or jelly beans

Cut thin slice from top of cup cakes, hollow out centers and build up edges with whipped cream. Sprinkle thickly with tinted coconut and fill centers with gelatin eggs, cut from a sheet of firm gelatin with cutter or measuring spoon. Or fill with jelly beans. Yield: 6 cakes.

MINT CAKES

2 large chocolate-covered peppermint patties
1 cup milk
1¾ cups sifted cake flour
3 teaspoons baking powder

1 teaspoon salt
1 tablespoon cocoa
⅓ cup butter or other fat
¾ cup sugar
½ teaspoon vanilla

3 eggs, separated

Melt patties over hot water; remove pan from water, stir in milk and cool. Mix and sift flour, baking powder, salt and cocoa. Cream butter until soft and smooth; gradually add sugar, beating until fluffy; beat in vanilla and egg yolks. Add flour mixture alternately with cold, mint-flavored milk, beating until smooth after each addition; fold in egg whites beaten stiff but not dry. Fill prepared muffin pans ⅔ full and bake in moderate oven (375° F.) 18 to 25 minutes. Spread with Mint Frosting (page 709). Yield: 14 cup cakes.

PINEAPPLE MERINGUE CAKE

½ cup sifted cake flour
¾ teaspoon baking powder
dash of salt
2 eggs, separated
¾ cup sugar

¼ cup butter or other fat
½ teaspoon vanilla
3½ tablespoons milk
blanched almonds, chopped
1 cup drained, crushed pineapple

½ cup heavy cream, whipped

Sift together flour, baking powder and salt. Beat egg yolks until thick and lemon-colored; gradually beat in ¼ cup sugar. Cream butter until soft and smooth, add vanilla and add to egg yolk-sugar mixture; stir in flour, then milk. Spread batter in 2 prepared 8-inch layer pans and chill. Beat egg whites until foamy but not stiff; gradually beat in remaining ½ cup sugar, beating until stiff; spread over layers. Sprinkle thickly with chopped almonds, pressing them into surface of cake. Bake in slow oven (300° F.) about 50 minutes. When cold, put layers together and cover top with mixture of pineapple and whipped cream. If fresh pineapple is used, shred 1 medium-sized pineapple with fork; sweeten to taste. When cold, fold in whipped cream. Yield: 2 layers (8 inch) or 8 wedges.

STRAWBERRY SHORTCAKE DE LUXE

½ cup sifted cake flour
⅔ cup egg whites (5 or 6)
¾ cup sifted sugar
⅛ teaspoon salt
½ teaspoon cream of tartar

½ teaspoon vanilla extract
¼ teaspoon almond extract
1 pint strawberry ice cream
whipped cream
whole strawberries

Sift flour 3 times. Beat egg whites until frothy; sprinkle salt and cream of tartar over top and continue beating until whites are just stiff enough to form peaks, but not dry. Gradually fold in sugar, sifting about ¼ cup at a time over surface. Turn into ungreased 10 x 5 x 3-inch loaf pan. Bake in moderate oven (350° F.) 25 minutes, or until done. Invert pan on rack and let stand 1 hour, or until cake is cool. Remove from pan; split into two layers. Fill with strawberry ice cream and garnish with whipped cream and whole strawberries. Yield: 6 portions.

JAY'S WHIPPED-CREAM CAKE

2¼ cups sifted cake flour
½ teaspoon salt
3 teaspoons double-acting
   baking powder
1½ cups sugar

3 egg whites
1 cup heavy cream
½ cup cold water
1 teaspoon vanilla extract
½ teaspoon almond extract

Sift flour twice with salt and baking powder. Add sugar and sift again. Beat egg whites until stiff but not dry. Whip cream until stiff and fold into egg whites. Add half of the flour mixture, a little at a time. Add remaining half alternately with water. Add flavorings. Pour into 2 8-inch greased layer pans and bake in a moderate oven (350° F.) 25 to 30 minutes. Cool. Spread with Whipped Cream Icing (page 715).

PINEAPPLE CHEESE CAKE

1½ tablespoons plain gelatin
6 tablespoons cold water
2 eggs, separated
½ cup sugar
⅓ cup pineapple juice
¼ teaspoon salt
1 cup strained cottage cheese
1 3-oz. package cream cheese
1 tablespoon lemon juice
1 teaspoon grated lemon rind

1 cup heavy cream, whipped
½ teaspoon vanilla
1½ cups crushed graham cracker
   crumbs
¼ cup melted butter
¼ teaspoon cinnamon
1 tablespoon sugar
1 small can (9-ounce) crushed,
   drained pineapple

Soften gelatin in cold water, about 5 minutes. Combine beaten egg yolks, ⅓ cup sugar, pineapple juice and salt. Cook in top of double boiler over hot water until thick and smooth, or until mixture coats the back of a silver spoon. Add softened gelatin and stir until dissolved. Blend together the cottage and cream cheeses. Combine with gelatin mixture. Add lemon juice and rind. Chill until partially thick. Beat egg whites until frothy; gradually beat in remaining sugar until stiff and smooth. Fold into cheese mixture with whipped cream and vanilla. Combine cracker crumbs, melted butter, cinnamon and 1 tablespoon sugar. Put all but ½ cup of crumb mixture on the bottom of a 7-inch spring-form cake pan. Top with drained, crushed pineapple. Pour in cheese mixture. Sprinkle remaining crumbs over top. Chill in refrigerator until firm. Just before serving, remove sides from spring-form pan. With a wide spatula gently transfer cake to serving plate. Approximate yield: 6 to 8 portions.

SPECIAL CHEESE CAKE

½ cup butter
1 (6 oz.) package zwieback, crushed
½ cup powdered sugar
4 eggs, beaten
1 cup sugar
¼ cup flour

¼ teaspoon salt
1½ teaspoons grated lemon rind
3 tablespoons lemon juice
½ teaspoon vanilla
1 cup heavy cream
1 pound (2 cups) cottage cheese

Cream butter and spread in bottom of 8-inch or 1½-quart spring form pan; add mixture of ½ of crushed zwieback and powdered sugar and press down or pack well. To eggs gradually beat in granulated sugar, salt, lemon rind and juice, and vanilla; stir in cream and mixture of cheese and flour; force through a fine sieve and beat well; turn into prepared spring-form pan and sprinkle with remaining crushed zwieback. Bake in very slow oven (250° F.) 1 hour; then turn off heat and leave cake 1 hour longer in oven. Serve as dessert. Yield: 1 (8-inch) cake or 6 to 8 portions.

CREAM CHEESE CAKE

Filling

1 cup sifted confectioners' sugar
¼ cup sweet butter

2 egg yolks
3 tablespoons heavy cream
1¼ pounds bulk cream cheese

Beat sugar and butter together in an electric mixer with medium speed or with a wooden spoon in a bowl, until smooth. Beat in egg yolks, one at a time, and add heavy cream. Beat until smooth and fluffy. Add cream chesee by pieces and blend well. Turn into 9-inch spring-form pan lined with following graham cracker crust. Refrigerate overnight. When ready to serve, run a spatula around edge of cheese cake and remove spring-form. Serve on pan set on tray or serving dish. Yield: 10 portions.

GRAHAM CRACKER CRUST

2 cups graham cracker crumbs
½ cup melted butter

2 tablespoons fruit juice
¼ cup sugar

Combine crumbs, melted butter, fruit juice or syrup and sugar and stir until well blended. Pat in layer on bottom of pan. Turn cream mixture on top and refrigerate. Yield: bottom crust for 9-inch spring-form pan.

CHEESE CAKE

1 pound creamed cottage cheese   1 cup sugar
¼ cup all-purpose flour   2 tablespoons lemon juice
1 cup zwieback crumbs   1½ teaspoons grated lemon rind
¼ cup powdered sugar   ½ teaspoon vanilla
¼ cup melted butter   ¼ teaspoon salt
4 eggs, separated   1 cup heavy cream, whipped

Force cottage cheese (at room temperature) through coarse sieve. Combine with flour, beating mixture to make it as light and fluffy as possible. Combine zwieback crumbs, powdered sugar and butter; pat all but ¼ cup onto bottom of buttered 8-inch spring-form pan. Beat egg yolks; add ½ cup sugar, lemon juice and rind, vanilla and salt. Fold in cheese mixture, whipped cream, egg whites stiffly beaten and remaining sugar. Blend mixture well and turn into pan. Sprinkle top with remaining crumbs. Bake in slow oven (250° F.) 1 hour and 15 minutes; turn off heat and leave cake in oven 1 hour longer. Remove and cool thoroughly. Remove spring-form and serve. Yield: 6 portions.

LINDY'S CHEESE CAKE

2½ pounds cream cheese   5 eggs
1¾ cups sugar   2 egg yolks
3 tablespoons flour   ¼ cup heavy cream
1½ teaspoons grated orange   ¼ cup sugar
   rind   1 cup sifted all-purpose flour
1½ teaspoons grated lemon rind   pinch of vanilla bean pulp
pinch of vanilla bean pulp or   1 egg yolk
  ¼ teaspoon vanilla extract   ½ cup butter

Combine cheese, sugar, flour, grated orange and lemon rind, and vanilla. Add eggs and egg yolks, one at a time, stirring lightly after each addition. Stir in cream. To make crust: Combine sugar, flour and vanilla. Make a well in center and add egg yolk and butter. Work together quickly with hands until well blended. Wrap in waxed paper and chill thoroughly in refrigerator, about one hour. Roll out ⅛-inch thick and place over oiled bottom of 9-inch spring-form cake pan. Trim off the dough by running a rolling pin over sharp edge. Bake in hot oven (400° F.) 20 minutes or until a light gold. Cool. Butter sides of cake form and place over base. Roll remaining dough ⅛ inch thick and cut to fit the sides of the oiled band. Fill form with the cheese mixture, bake in very hot oven (550° F.) 12 to 15 minutes. Reduce temperature to slow (200° F.) and continue baking one hour. Cool before cutting. Yield: 12 portions.

ANGEL FOOD CAKE

1 cup sifted cake flour	¼ teaspoon salt
1½ cups sifted granulated sugar	1¼ teaspoons cream of tartar
	1 teaspoon vanilla
1¼ cups egg whites (10 to 12)	¼ teaspoon almond extract

Sift together four times flour and ½ cup sugar. Beat egg whites and salt with rotary egg beater. When foamy, add cream of tartar and continue beating until eggs are stiff enough to form peaks, but not dry. Add remaining 1 cup sugar, 2 tablespoons at a time, beating with rotary egg beater or whisk after each addition until sugar is just blended. Fold in flavorings. Sift about ¼ cup flour-sugar mixture over top and fold in lightly; repeat until all is used. Turn into ungreased 10-inch tube pan. Bake in moderate oven (375° F.) 30 to 35 minutes. Invert pan 1 hour, or until cake is cold. Yield: 1 large cake.

Chocolate Angel Food Cake—Substitute 4 tablespoons cocoa for 4 tablespoons flour, mix with flour and sift 3 or 4 times; flavor with 1 teaspoon vanilla and omit almond extract. Yield: 1 large cake.

Marble Angel Food Cake—Add 2 tablespoons cocoa to 6 tablespoons flour; sift 4 times. Divide egg white-sugar mixture into 2 parts; to one part, fold in cocoa-flour mixture and to other, fold in remaining flour. Put by spoonfuls into ungreased 9-inch tube pan, alternating dark and light batters. Yield: 1 large cake.

Angel Food Loaf Cake—Halve all ingredients. Turn into ungreased 10 x 5 x 3-inch loaf pan. Bake in moderate oven (375° F.) 25 minutes, or until done. Yield: 1 large loaf.

MARSHALL CAKE TORTE

8 egg whites	2 cups sweetened fresh or frozen peaches, crushed pineapple or any fresh berries
1 teaspoon cream of tartar	
pinch of salt	
2 cups sugar	½ cup heavy cream, whipped
2 teaspoons mint or almond extract	

Beat egg whites until frothy and add cream of tartar and salt; gradually beat in sugar, sprinkling 1 tablespoon at a time over top of the egg whites. Add flavoring and beat until stiff and peaked. Pour into an ungreased 9-inch spring form pan. Bake in a slow oven (275° F.) 55 to 60 minutes. Allow to cool. With a spatula or knife, loosen cake by running knife around edge of pan. When thoroughly cool, remove sides of spring-form pan. Fill slight hollow that forms with fruit and top with flavored whipped cream. Approximate yield: 8 to 12 portions.

NUT TORTE

6 eggs, separated
1 cup sugar
1 cup chopped or ground
  walnuts or pecans
2 tablespoons graham cracker
  crumbs

1 teaspoon vanilla
1 cup sweet butter
1 cup confectioners' sugar
4 ounces chocolate
2 teaspoons sherry

Beat egg yolks, gradually adding the sugar. Add ground nuts and
cracker crumbs, then vanilla. Fold in stiffly beaten egg whites. Bake
in two greased, floured 9-inch pans in a moderate oven (350° F.) about
30 minutes. Cool.

Cream butter, add sugar and whip until fluffy. Melt chocolate in top
of double boiler, add to sugar-butter mixture, blending well. Spread
one layer of the torte with marmalade or strawberry jam to a thickness
of ¼ inch. Sprinkle with sherry. Place on top layer and cover top and
sides of cake with butter icing. Place in refrigerator and it will keep
at least two weeks, or without refrigeration for 2 to 3 days. Yield: 6
portions.

ZWIEBACK NUT TORTE

½ package zwieback
1 teaspoon baking powder
1 cup chopped walnut meats
4 eggs, separated

½ cup sugar
dash of salt
heavy cream, whipped, or
  marshmallow whip

Crush and roll zwieback; mix with baking powder and nuts. Beat egg
yolks until thick and lemon-colored; beat in sugar and salt and stir in
crumb-nut mixture; fold in thoroughly the stiffly beaten egg whites.
Turn into 2 prepared layer pans and bake in moderate oven (375° F.)
about 10 minutes; cool. Put layers together with whipped cream or
marshmallow whip. Yield: 2 layers (9 inch).

GINGER TEA CAKES

2 cups gingersnap crumbs
¼ teaspoon baking soda
¼ teaspoon salt

2 tablespoons sugar
⅔ cup sour cream, heated
1 egg, beaten

1 3-oz. package cream cheese

Roll gingersnaps fine and reserve 2 tablespoons of crumbs. To remaining crumbs add soda, salt and sugar and mix thoroughly; pour hot
sour cream over mixture and stir in egg. Turn into prepared muffin
pans and bake in moderate oven (375° F.) 18 to 25 minutes. Spread
with cream cheese and sprinkle remaining gingersnap crumbs over
cakes. Approximate yield: 1 dozen medium-sized cakes.

SPONGE CAKE

1 cup sifted cake flour	1½ tablespoons lemon juice
5 eggs, separated	½ teaspoon cream of tartar
1 teaspoon grated lemon rind	¼ teaspoon salt
1 cup sugar	

Sift flour 3 times. Beat egg yolks until thick and lemon-colored, add lemon rind and juice and continue beating until very thick. Beat egg whites with cream of tartar until frothy, sprinkle salt over top and continue beating until stiff enough to form peaks, but not dry; gradually beat in sugar, adding about 2 tablespoons at a time. Fold in well-beaten egg yolks, then gradually fold in flour, sifting about ¼ cup at a time over surface. Turn into ungreased 9-inch tube pan and bake in slow oven (325° F.) about 1 hour. Invert pan until cake is cold, or about 1 hour. Approximate yield: 1 large cake.

Black Walnut Sponge Cake—Add ½ cup finely chopped black walnut meats to sifted flour and mix well. Scatter over surface of egg white-yolk mixture in small amounts and fold in carefully.

Chocolate Sponge Cake—Substitute 4 tablespoons cocoa for 4 tablespoons flour; sift cocoa and flour 4 times. Substitute orange rind and juice for lemon rind and juice.

QUICK SPONGE CAKE

1 cup sifted cake flour	5 egg yolks
5 egg whites	1½ teaspoons grated lemon rind
¼ teaspoon salt	2 tablespoons water
¼ teaspoon cream of tartar	1½ tablepoons lemon juice
1 cup sifted sugar	

Sift flour three times. Place egg whites and salt in large mixing bowl and beat at medium to high speed until foamy. Add cream of tartar and beat until stiff enough to form peaks, but not dry. Continue beating, adding ½ cup of sugar rapidly, a tablespoon at a time. Beat only until sugar is just blended. Beat egg yolks with remaining sugar, lemon rind and water until very thick and light. Gradually beat in lemon juice. Add flour to egg yolk-sugar mixture and stir until blended. Fold into egg white mixture. Bake in ungreased 9-inch tube pan in moderate oven (375° F.) 30 to 35 minutes. Remove from oven, invert pan and let stand 1 hour, or until cake is cool. Yield: 1 cake.

DELICATE SPONGE CAKE

1 cup sifted cake flour   ½ teaspoon salt
1 cup sugar   ½ teaspoon cream of tartar
¾ cup egg whites (6 to 7)   4 egg yolks, well beaten
                   1 teaspoon vanilla

Mix flour and ½ cup sugar and sift three times. Beat egg whites until frothy, sprinkle with salt and cream of tartar and continue beating until stiff enough to form peaks, but not dry. Gradually beat in remaining ½ cup sugar; carefully fold in egg yolks and vanilla, then flour-sugar mixture, sifting about ¼ cup at a time over surface. Turn into ungreased 9-inch tube pan and bake in slow oven (325° F.) about 1 hour. Invert pan until cake is cold, about 1 hour. Yield: 1 large cake.

HOT MILK SPONGE CAKE

1 cup sifted cake flour   3 eggs
1 teaspoon baking powder   1 cup sugar
¼ teaspoon salt   2 teaspoons lemon juice
                 6 tablespoons hot milk

Sift together three times flour, baking powder and salt. Beat eggs until very thick and light (about 5 minutes). Add sugar gradually, beating constantly. Add lemon juice. Fold in flour, a small amount at a time. Add hot milk and stir quickly until thoroughly blended. Turn at once into ungreased 9½ x 5¼ x 2¾-inch loaf pan and bake in moderate oven (350° F.) 35 minutes, or until done. Remove from oven and invert pan 1 hour, or until cold. Yield: 1 loaf.

HOT WATER SPONGE CAKE

1 cup sifted cake flour   2 eggs, separated
1½ teaspoons baking powder   1 cup sugar
dash of salt   6 tablespoons hot water
                 1 teaspoon vanilla

Sift together flour, baking powder and salt. Beat egg yolks until thick and lemon-colored; gradually beat in sugar, then hot water, vanilla and finally flour; gently fold in egg whites beaten stiff but not dry. Turn into very lightly buttered square pan, layer pans or muffin pans and bake in moderate oven (350° F.): in square pan about 35 minutes; in layer or small muffin pans 20 to 25 minutes. Yield: 1 square (8 inch), 2 layers (8 inch), or 2 dozen cup cakes.

PECAN UPSIDE–DOWN SPONGE CAKE

1 recipe Hot Water Sponge
   Cake (page 670)
¼ cup butter
½ cup firmly packed brown
   sugar

1 tablespoon water
1 cup pecans, part chopped,
   part whole
heavy cream, whipped, or
   marshmallow whip

Prepare batter for Hot Water Sponge Cake; melt butter in frying pan, square or round pan, 2 inches deep; add brown sugar and water and stir until thoroughly mixed. Remove from heat, sprinkle chopped nuts, arrange whole pecans, flat side up, in syrup and cover with cake batter; bake in slow oven (325° F.) about 50 minutes. Loosen cake from sides and turn out immediately on cake plate; allow pan to rest over cake a few seconds so that all of caramel syrup will drain on cake. Serve warm with whipped cream. Yield: 8 portions.

WINE SPONGE CAKE

12 eggs, separated
1 cup sugar
1 cup sweet wine

1 cup sifted cake flour
½ teaspoon salt
1 teaspoon cinnamon

1 cup ground walnuts

Beat egg yolks until thick and add sugar, beating until well blended. Add wine, flour, salt, cinnamon and nuts. Mix until smoothly blended and then fold in egg whites beaten stiff but not dry. Turn into ungreased 10-inch tube pan and bake in slow oven (325° F.) 1 hour, or until done. Invert pan until cake is cold. Yield: 1 large cake.

GOLDEN SPONGE CAKE

2 cups sifted all-purpose flour
3 teaspoons baking powder
¾ teaspoon salt
9 egg yolks

1½ cups sugar
1 teaspoon grated orange rind
2 tablespoons lemon juice
¾ cup boiling water

Sift together flour, baking powder and salt. Beat egg yolks until thick and light colored; gradually add sugar, beating until very thick and light colored; then beat in orange rind, lemon juice and boiling water. Fold in flour and turn into ungreased tube pan. Bake in moderate oven (350° F.) 50 to 60 minutes; invert pan 1 hour before removing cake. Yield: 1 large cake.

DAFFODIL CAKE

1 cup sifted cake flour
1½ cups sugar
1¼ cups egg whites (10 to 12)
½ teaspoon salt

1 teaspoon cream of tartar
½ teaspoon vanilla
4 egg yolks, well beaten
½ teaspoon grated orange rind

Mix flour and ½ cup sugar and sift three times. Beat egg whites until frothy, sprinkle with salt and cream of tartar and continue beating until stiff enough to form peaks, but not dry. Gradually beat in remaining 1 cup sugar and carefully fold in flour-sugar mixture, sifting about ¼ cup at a time over surface. Divide batter into two equal parts: add vanilla to one part; fold well-beaten egg yolks and orange rind into other. Put by spoonfuls into ungreased 10-inch tube pan, alternating white and yellow batters. Bake in slow oven (325° F.) about 1 hour and 15 minutes. Invert pan until cake is cold, or about 1 hour before removing it from pan. Yield: 1 large cake.

Layered Yellow and White Sponge Cake—Turn yellow batter into ungreased tube pan and top with white batter; bake. Cover with Orange Butter Frosting (page 709).

BASIC JELLY ROLL

¾ cup sifted cake flour
½ teaspoon double-acting
  baking powder
¼ teaspoon salt
5 eggs, separated

¾ cup sugar
½ teaspoon vanilla extract
powdered sugar
jam or jelly
1 cup heavy cream, whipped

Sift together flour, baking powder and salt. Beat egg yolks until thick and lemon-colored. Gradually add sugar, beating until light and fluffy. Stir in vanilla. Fold in egg whites beaten stiff but not dry. Gently fold in flour mixture. Pour batter into 10 x 15-inch jelly roll pan that has been greased, lined with waxed paper and greased again. Spread batter evenly in pan. Bake in moderate oven (350° F.) 15 minutes. Invert over clean tea towel dusted with powdered sugar. Carefully remove waxed paper and roll cake lengthwise by gently lifting and pushing with the towel. Finish rolling with the open end of cake on the under side. Wrap the cloth tightly about the roll; cool on rack. Unroll cake, spread with jam, re-roll and garnish with whipped cream. Yield: 8 portions.

Orange Cream Roll—Spread with Orange Filling (page 722), roll, wrap and cool as directed. Yield: 1 jelly roll.

CHOCOLATE SPONGE ROLL

¼ cup sifted all-purpose flour
⅓ cup cocoa
¼ teaspoon salt
6 eggs, separated
½ teaspoon cream of tartar

1 cup sugar
1 teaspoon vanilla
1 cup heavy cream, whipped and
    sweetened

Sift flour, cocoa and salt together. Beat egg whites with cream of tartar until stiff but not dry. Gradually beat in ½ cup sugar. Beat egg yolks until thick and lemon-colored; beat in remaining ½ cup sugar, then sifted dry ingredients and vanilla. Fold into egg white mixture. Turn into 15½ x 10½ x 1-inch pan, lined with greased heavy paper. Bake in slow oven (325° F.) about 30 minutes; quickly turn from pan onto cloth lightly dusted with confectioners' sugar and remove paper from bottom of cake. Roll up cloth and cake together; cool. Unroll and spread with sweetened, whipped cream and roll up carefully. Spread top and sides with frosting. Yield: 10 portions.

Chocolate Nut Sponge Roll—Sprinkle ¼ cup finely chopped nuts over batter in pan just before baking.

CHOCOLATE PEPPERMINT ROLL

3 eggs
½ cup sugar
2 tablespoons water

¼ cup cocoa
½ cup sifted all-purpose flour
¼ teaspoon salt

1 teaspoon vanilla

Beat eggs until light colored. Add sugar gradually and continue beating. Add water and mix thoroughly. Sift cocoa, flour and salt; combine with first mixture. Add vanilla. Pour into well-greased shallow pan (15½ x 10½ x 1 inches), lined with well-greaesd heavy paper. Bake in moderate oven (350° F.) 15 minutes. Turn out on paper or towel sprinkled with confectioners' sugar. Remove paper. Cut off crisp edges. Spread with Peppermint Filling (page 712). Cut into 4 equal lengthwise and 4 crosswise sections. Roll each section like jelly roll. Sprinkle with confectioners' sugar. Yield: 16 small rolls.

MOLASSES ROLL

4 eggs, separated
½ cup molasses
1 teaspoon lemon juice
¼ cup sugar
¾ cup sifted all-purpose flour
2 tablespoons sugar

½ teaspoon salt
½ teaspoon baking soda
¼ teaspoon cinnamon
¼ teaspoon nutmeg
¼ teaspoon ground cloves
1 package vanilla pudding

Beat egg yolks until light, add molasses and beat thoroughly. Beat egg whites until stiff; add lemon juice and ¼ cup sugar gradually. Fold egg mixture into egg whites. Sift together flour, salt, soda, cinnamon, nutmeg and cloves and fold into the egg mixture. Turn into a shallow pan (10 x 15 x ¾ inches) lined on the bottom with greased waxed paper. Bake in slow oven (325° F.) 20 minutes. Turn out on a towel dusted with powdered sugar, roll up and cool. Unroll and spread with a vanilla pudding mixture. Roll up, dust with cinnamon and sugar. Approximate yield: 6 portions.

BASIC CHIFFON CAKE

2¼ cups sifted cake flour
1½ cups sugar
3 teaspoons baking powder
1 teaspoon salt
½ cup salad oil
5 unbeaten egg yolks

¾ cup cold water
2 teaspoons vanilla
2 teaspoons grated lemon rind
   (optional)
1 cup egg whites (7 or 8)
½ teaspoon cream of tartar

Sift together dry ingredients into mixing bowl. Make a well and add in order salad oil, egg yolks, water, vanilla and lemon rind. Beat with spoon until smooth. Measure egg whites and cream of tartar into large mixing bowl. Whip until whites form very stiff peaks. They should be much stiffer than for angel food or meringue. Do not underbeat. Pour egg yolk mixture gradually over whipped egg whites, gently folding just until blended. Do not stir. Pour into ungreased pan immediately. Bake in slow oven (325° F.) 55 minutes, then moderate oven (350° F.) 10 to 15 minutes for 10 x 4-inch tube pan and in moderate oven (350° F.) 45 to 50 minutes for 13 x 9½ x 2-inch pan, or until top springs back when lightly touched. Immediately turn pan upside down, placing tube part over neck of funnel. Let hang, free of table, until cold. Loosen from sides and tube with spatula. Turn pan over and hit edge sharply on table to loosen. Yield: 16 to 20 portions.

Note: For small cake, halve all ingredients but use 2 unbeaten egg yolks. Bake in (350° F.) oven 30 to 35 minutes for 8 x 8 x 2-inch or 9 x 9 x 1¾-inch square pans; in slow oven (325° F.) 50 to 55 minutes for 10 x 5 x 3-inch loaf pan and 9 x 3½-inch tube pan. Yield: 8 portions.

MODIFICATIONS OF BASIC CHIFFON CAKE

Orange Chiffon—Omit vanilla and lemon rind; substitute 3 table-spoons grated orange rind.

Cherry Chiffon—Reduce water to ½ cup and substitute ¼ cup mara-schino cherry juice for the remaining water; reduce vanilla to 1 tea-spoon; omit lemon rind. Mix together ½ cup very thinly sliced and finely chopped, well-drained maraschino cherries and ½ cup very finely chopped nuts. Sprinkle over top of batter, gently folding in with a few strokes.

Banana Chiffon—Reduce vanilla or lemon rind to 1 teaspoon; add ½ to ⅔ cup sieved fully ripe bananas (about 2 medium-sized) to the egg yolk mixture.

Pineapple Chiffon—Omit vanilla; substitute ¾ cup pineapple syrup (from canned pineapple) or unsweetened pineapple juice in place of water.

Marble Chiffon—Combine ¼ cup cocoa, ¼ cup sugar, ¼ cup boiling water and ¼ teaspoon red food coloring. Stir until smooth; cool. Omit lemon rind; prepare batter as directed and place half in separate bowl; pour cocoa mixture gradually over it, gently folding until blended. Im-mediately pour alternate layers of dark and light batter into ungreased pan.

Cocoa Chiffon—Combine ¾ cup boiling water, ½ cup cocoa and ¼ teaspoon red food coloring. Stir until smooth; cool. Prepare batter but decrease flour to 1¾ cups, increase sugar to 1¾ cups and egg yolks to 7. Decrease vanilla to 1 teaspoon; omit lemon rind. Add the cooled cocoa mixture to egg yolk mixture.

Chocolate Chip Chiffon—Increase sugar to 1¾ cups; omit lemon rind. Sprinkle 3 1-ounce squares unsweetened or sweetened chocolate, grated, over top of batter and gently fold in with a few strokes.

Butterscotch Chiffon—Omit sugar and lemon rind. Stir 2 cups brown sugar, firmly packed, into sifted dry ingredients.

Bit o'Walnut Chiffon—Omit lemon rind. Sprinkle 1 cup very finely chopped walnuts over top of batter and gently fold in with a few strokes.

Maple Pecan Chiffon—Reduce sugar to ¾ cup; stir ¾ cup brown sugar, firmly packed, into sifted dry ingredients. Substitute 2 teaspoons maple flavoring for vanilla and lemon rind. Sprinkle 1 cup very finely chopped pecans over top of batter and gently fold in with a few strokes.

Spice Chiffon—Sift 1 teaspoon cinnamon, ½ teaspoon each nutmeg, allspice and cloves with dry ingredients. If desired, mix in 2 table-spoons caraway seed. Omit vanilla and lemon rind.

Cookies, Small Cakes and Doughnuts

MOST cookies are not hard to make. Rolled or sliced cookie doughs should be chilled first to obviate adding extra flour, for the less flour used, the more tender the cookie. Nor is it necessary to grease the pans, except for fruited and molasses cookies which have a tendency to stick and burn. Drop cookies spread surprisingly on baking, hence should be placed at least two inches apart on the pan. With a variety of fancy cutters and a cookie press, a plain cookie mixture can assume many different shapes and forms. When shifting from all-purpose to cake flour, add 2 more tablespoons of cake flour for each cup called for in the recipe.

If cookies are brushed with egg white or beaten egg yolk before adding decorations, the surface develops an attractive glaze when baked. This also helps hold decorations in place while baking.

Decorative materials include dried fruits, citron and nuts; colored candies and sugars which lend a glistening effect if sprinkled on the cookies before baking; shaved chocolate, shredded coconut, tiny sprinklettes, rubyettes and crystallized flowers which can be sprinkled on the warm, moist cookie as soon as it is removed from the oven; and fruit pastes, softened marshmallows and frosting which can be used to put cookies together, sandwich-fashion, or for decorating after the cookies have cooled.

676

SUGAR COOKIES

2 cups sifted all-purpose flour (about)	½ cup butter or other fat
1½ teaspoons baking powder	1 cup sugar
½ teaspoon salt	1 egg
	1 teaspoon vanilla

1 tablespoon light cream or milk

Sift together 1½ cups flour, baking powder and salt. Cream butter until soft; beat in sugar, egg, vanilla and cream. Stir in flour mixture, then gradually add the remaining flour until dough is just stiff enough to roll; chill thoroughly. Place on lightly floured board and roll ⅛ inch thick; cut with floured cutter as desired and place on ungreased baking sheet. Sprinkle with sugar and bake in moderate to hot oven (375°–400° F.) 8 to 10 minutes. Store in closely covered cookie jar. Approximate yield: 4 to 5 dozen cookies.

Sour Cream Cookies—Reduce baking powder to ½ teaspoon; add ¼ teaspoon baking soda and ¼ teaspoon nutmeg and sift with flour; substitute ½ teaspoon lemon extract for vanilla; use ⅓ cup heavy sour cream instead of 1 tablespoon cream.

Butterscotch Cookies—Substitute 1 cup firmly packed brown sugar for granulated sugar.

Spice Sugar Cookies—Mix and sift ¼ teaspoon each cinnamon, allspice and cloves with flour and omit vanilla.

Chocolate Crisps—Mix and sift ½ teaspoon cinnamon with flour; add 2 squares chocolate, melted, to butter-sugar-egg mixture.

Molasses Date Cookies—Sift together 1 teaspoon cinnamon, ½ teaspoon ginger and ¼ teaspoon each allspice and cloves with flour, and stir in ½ cup chopped dates; substitute ½ cup molasses for ¼ cup of the sugar and 1 tablespoon vinegar for cream. Press nut meat half into center of each shape before baking, if desired.

Gingersnaps—Reduce baking powder to ½ teaspoon; add ¼ teaspoon baking soda and 1 teaspoon ginger and sift with flour; reduce sugar to ½ cup and beat ½ cup molasses into butter-sugar mixture; omit vanilla and substitute 2 tablespoons water for cream.

Maryland Sand Tarts—Roll dough thin and cut in desired shapes. Brush with 1 egg white, slightly beaten with 1 teaspoon water; sprinkle with mixture of ¼ cup sugar and 1 teaspoon cinnamon. Garnish with pieces of candied cherries and pineapple and blanched almonds.

Peanut Butter Cookies—Reduce butter to 2 tablespoons and cream with ½ cup peanut butter; substitute ⅓ cup milk for cream. Sprinkle shapes with ½ cup chopped peanuts.

Coconut Cookies—Add ½ cup shredded coconut to flour mixture, or sprinkle coconut over shapes.

Nut Cookies—Add ½ cup chopped nut meats to flour mixture, or sprinkle nuts over shapes. Use English or black walnuts, pecans, almonds, hickory or Brazil nuts, peanuts or cashews.

Fruit Cookies—Add ½ cup chopped fruit to flour mixture. Use raisins, currants, dates, figs, dried prunes or apricots. Garnish shapes with additional pieces of fruit, if desired.

Maraschino Cookies—Reduce sugar to ¾ cup, sift dash of nutmeg with flour and substitute 1½ tablespoons maraschino syrup for cream. Add ⅔ cup chopped cherries and ¼ cup chopped citron to butter-sugar mixture. Garnish shapes with additional fruit, if desired.

Candied Fruit Cookies—Add ¼ cup chopped candied orange, lemon or grapefruit rind, ginger, citron, cherries or pineapple to flour mixture. Garnish shapes with pieces of candied fruit, if desired.

Lemon Marshmallow Cookies—Reduce baking powder to ½ teaspoon and sift ¼ teaspoon soda and dash of nutmeg with flour; then stir in ¼ cup each chopped dates and chopped nuts. Substitute 1 teaspoon grated lemon rind for vanilla and ¼ cup lemon juice for cream. Cut in rounds. When baked, place marshmallow in center of each and return to oven to brown. It will take 1 pound marshmallows.

FILLED SUGAR COOKIES

For cookie doughs, use recipes given under Modifications of Sugar Cookies (page 677). Place filling in center of ½ of cut-out rounds, using 1 teaspoon for each; cover with remaining rounds and press edges together. Bake in moderate oven (375° F.) 10 to 15 minutes. Approximate yield: 2 dozen (2½ inch) filled cookies.

Apricot Surprises—Prepare dough for Sour Cream Cookies; roll thin and cut with 3½-inch round cutter. Place Apricot Filling in center of rounds, fold edges up and over to center to form tricorns and press together with pecan halves or candied fruit.

For *Apricot Filling*, mix together 2 cups apricot purée and ½ cup grape-nuts.

Caramel Cookies—Prepare dough for Sugar Cookies, roll thin and cut in desired shapes; put Caramel Filling between two. Decorate with sprinklettes, if desired.

For *Caramel Filling*, cook ¼ cup butter, ¼ cup firmly packed brown sugar, 3 tablespoons cream and 1 egg yolk over hot water until thickened, stirring constantly; add ½ teaspoon vanilla and cool.

Butterscotch Fruit Squares—Prepare dough for Butterscotch Cookies, roll thin and cut in 3-inch squares. Place fruit filling on half of each square, fold over and press edges together. Decorate with slices of candied cherries and angelica, if desired.

For *Fruit Filling*, mix together ⅔ cup drained, chopped canned figs, 1⅓ cups drained, chopped canned pears, ½ medium-sized orange, free from membrane and chopped, and ⅓ cup sugar; drain off any additional juice before using.

Chocolate Fruit Squares—Prepare dough for Chocolate Crisps, roll thin and cut in 2-inch squares; put Pineapple-Banana Filling between 2 squares and press edges together.

For *Pineapple-Banana Filling*, mix together ¾ cup grated pineapple, ½ cup sugar and 2 teaspoons cornstarch and cook until thick; cool and add 2 ripe bananas, mashed, and 1½ tablespoons lemon juice.

Cocoa-filled Cookies—Prepare dough for Butterscotch Cookies, roll thin and cut with 2½-inch round cutter; put Cocoa Filling between 2 rounds and press edges together.

For *Cocoa Filling*, melt ¼ cup butter, add 1 tablespoon milk and add mixture of 1 cup confectioners' sugar, 3 tablespoons cocoa and ⅛ teaspoon salt, stirring until well mixed. Add 1 teaspoon vanilla and ¼ cup chopped nuts. Cool.

Maraschino-filled Cookies—Prepare dough for Maraschino Cookies, roll thin and cut in desired shapes; put Raisin Filling between 2 shapes and press edges together.

For *Raisin Filling*, mix together ⅔ cup chopped raisins, ⅓ cup sugar, 1½ tablespoons flour, ¼ cup orange juice and 1½ tablespoons lemon juice; boil until mixture thickens, then cool.

Spice Nut Rounds—Prepare dough for Spice Sugar Cookies (page 677), roll thin and cut with 2½-inch round cutter. Put Honey-Nut Filling between 2 rounds and press edges together.

Honey-Nut Filling—Moisten ½ cup chopped nuts with honey and add ¼ teaspoon orange rind for flavoring.

SHORTBREAD COOKIES

2 cups butter or margarine   1 cup sugar
3 cups sifted all-purpose flour

Cream butter well; add sugar gradually and blend thoroughly. Add flour slowly and mix to a smooth dough. Roll out on lightly floured board about ¼ inch thick. Shape with a lightly floured cookie cutter. Place on ungreased baking sheet. Pierce each cookie several times with the tines of a fork to prevent its rising. Bake in moderate oven (350° F.) 15 to 20 minutes until golden brown. Yield: 50 cookies.

LEAF SUGAR COOKIES

1 cup sugar   3 cups sifted all-purpose flour
1 cup butter or margarine   1 teaspoon soda
1 egg   ¼ teaspoon nutmeg

Cream sugar and butter or margarine; beat in egg. Sift flour with soda and nutmeg and add to butter. Mix well and turn to floured board. Roll to ⅛-inch thickness. Lay over an oak leaf pattern, cut from cardboard, and with a sharp pointed knife outline edges. Sprinkle with granulated sugar. With spatula lift cookies from board to greased baking sheet. Bake in a hot oven (425° F.) 8 minutes. Yield: 3 dozen.

MOLASSES DOUBLE-DECKERS

3½ cups sifted all-purpose flour   ½ cup shortening
1 teaspoon salt   1 cup sugar
1 teaspoon baking powder   2 eggs, beaten
1 teaspoon baking soda   ½ cup dark molasses
2 teaspoons ginger   ⅓ cup boiling water

Sift together dry ingredients. Cream shortening with sugar, then add eggs and molasses. Blend. Add flour mixture alternately with water. When thoroughly mixed, roll out thin on a lightly floured board. Cut half of dough with round cutter. Use doughnut cutter to cut remainder. Bake on cookie sheet in moderate oven (350° F.) 8 to 10 minutes. Cool, put together with a creamy filling or an uncooked frosting. Yield: 3 dozen double cookies.

CINNAMON STARS

7 egg whites
2 cups granulated sugar
5 teaspoons cinnamon

2 cups finely chopped almonds
1½ teaspoons grated lemon rind
2 cups confectioners' sugar

Beat egg whites to a froth; gradually beat in mixture of granulated sugar and cinnamon, sifting about ¼ cup at a time over top. Beat mixture until it becomes very stiff (about 15 minutes in a mechanical mixer). Remove ½ cup of mixture; to the remaining mixture add almonds and lemon rind. Stir in thoroughly the confectioners' sugar. Roll ½-inch thick on well-sugared board; cut with star-shaped cutter. Brush tops with reserved mixture. Bake in moderate oven (350° F.) 20 minutes, or until lightly browned. Yield: 2 dozen cookies.

ALMOND CROISSANTS

½ cup butter or other fat
½ cup sugar
dash of salt
2 egg yolks
¼ cup finely chopped almonds

1 cup sifted all-purpose flour
 (about)
1 egg white
1 teaspoon water
chopped almonds

Cream together butter, sugar and salt; beat in egg yolks, then finely chopped almonds. Gradually stir in flour until dough is stiff enough to handle; chill thoroughly. Roll ⅛ inch thick on lightly floured board; cut with small crescent-shaped cutter and place on greased baking sheet. Brush with egg white and water beaten together until frothy; sprinkle with chopped almonds and bake in moderately hot oven (375° F.) 12 minutes. Yield: 1½ dozen cookies.

HAZELNUT RINGS

½ pound butter or margarine
1½ cups sugar
½ pound hazelnuts, ground

2 cups sifted all-purpose flour
½ teaspoon salt
2 egg whites, stiffly beaten

Cream butter or margarine with 1 cup sugar and hazelnuts, sift flour with salt and add slowly, mixing well. Dust pastry board lightly with flour, pat out a small piece of dough, cover with waxed paper and roll out. Cut rings with a doughnut cutter. Lift with spatula and place rings on greased, lightly floured tray. Using a pastry tube or a teaspoon, place a ribbon of meringue around the cookie ring, just wide enough so that an edge of the cookie shows on each side of the ribbon. To make meringue, fold remaining half cup of sugar into the stiffly beaten egg whites. Bake in a slow oven (300° F.) for about 12 to 15 minutes. Yield: 5 dozen rings plus 5 dozen centers.

CREOLE ANISE CAKES

1½ tablespoons aniseed   ½ cup sugar
½ cup water   ½ teaspoon salt
4 cups sifted all-purpose flour   1 cup lard
                  ¼ cup ice water

Simmer aniseed 5 minutes in ½ cup water and cool. Sift flour, sugar and salt together three times. Cut in lard until evenly mixed and the texture of coarse sand. Add cold aniseed and water mixture, stirring lightly with fork. Then add enough of remaining ¼ cup ice water to make particles hold together. Shape into ball, wrap in waxed paper. Chill. Roll ⅛ inch thick on lightly floured board; cut as desired and bake on ungreased baking sheet in moderate oven (350° F.) about 20 minutes, or until light brown. Yield: 10 dozen cakes.

GINGERBREAD MEN

5 cups sifted flour (about)   1⅛ teaspoons baking soda
1 teaspoon salt   1 cup shortening
¼ teaspoon nutmeg (optional) 1¼ cups sugar
½ teaspoon cloves   1 egg, well beaten
3 tablespoons cinnamon   1 cup light molasses
1 teaspoon ginger   ⅓ cup water

Sift together 1 cup flour, salt, spices and soda. Cream shortening, add sugar gradually, beating until light and fluffy. Add egg, then slightly warmed molasses. Stir water into mixture. Stir in sifted flour and spice mixture gradually. Add remaining flour, a cupful at a time, just until dough is soft and moist to the touch of the finger. Chill dough 6 to 8 hours. Remove dough, a small amount at a time. Roll out on lightly floured board ¼-inch thick for Santa Claus, donkeys, pigs and other animals; ⅛-inch thick for stars, trees and angels.

When a cardboard pattern is used, place it on the rolled dough, cutting around the outline with a small, sharp-pointed knife, folding back the outside dough as you work. With a pancake turner, transfer the figure to a buttered pan. Bake in a moderate oven (350° F.) 8 to 10 minutes. Yield: 75 to 100 figures, depending on size. Place cookies on rack to cool and dry before adding the fancy decorations.

BUTTERSCOTCH SLICES

3 cups sifted all-purpose flour
3 teaspoons baking powder
½ teaspoon salt
1 cup butter or other fat

1¼ cups firmly packed brown
    sugar
½ teaspoon vanilla
2 eggs

Sift together flour, baking powder and salt. Cream butter until soft; gradually beat in brown sugar, then vanilla and one egg at a time; stir in flour. Shape in rolls about 2 inches in diameter and wrap each in waxed paper; chill thoroughly in refrigerator. Cut chilled roll in ⅛-inch slices, place on ungreased baking sheet and bake in hot oven (400° F.) about 8 minutes. Yield: 8 to 9 dozen.

Butterscotch Creoles—Add 2 cups finely chopped dates and 1 cup finely chopped nuts to sifted dry ingredients.

Filbert Slices—Sprinkle chopped filberts over thin slices before baking.

Whole Wheat Slices—Substitute 4½ cups whole wheat flour for all-purpose flour; reduce baking powder to 2 teaspoons and add ½ teaspoon baking soda and 1 tablespoon ginger. Substitute ½ cup molasses for ¼ cup firmly packed brown sugar and omit vanilla. Bake thin slices in moderate oven (350° F.) about 8 minutes. Approximate yield: 10 dozen cookies.

Butterscotch Nut Slices—Add 1½ cups finely chopped nuts to sifted dry ingredients.

Chocolate Nut Slices—Add 1½ cups finely chopped nuts to sifted dry ingredients and 3 squares chocolate, melted, to shortening-egg mixture.

Coconut Orange Slices—Add 3 cups shredded coconut to sifted dry ingredients. Reduce brown sugar to ¼ cup, firmly packed, and use 1 cup granulated sugar. Omit vanilla and flavor with 1½ tablespoons grated orange rind and ¾ teaspoon lemon extract.

Tutti-Frutti Butterscotch Slices—Add ¼ cup finely chopped mixed candied fruits to sifted dry ingredients.

Mincemeat Refrigerator Cookies—Reduce baking powder to 2 teaspoons and add ½ teaspoon baking soda; reduce brown sugar to ½ cup, and shape rolls, 2½ inches in diameter. Cut chilled rolls in thin slices and put Date-Nut Filling between two, pressing edges together. Bake in moderate oven (375° F.) 10 to 15 minutes. Approximate yield: 3 dozen cookies.

Filled Refrigerator Cookies—Prepare dough for Butterscotch Slices and shape in rolls, 2½ inches in diameter. Cut chilled rolls in thin slices and put Date-Nut Filling between two, pressing edges together. Bake in moderate oven (375° F.) 10 to 15 minutes. Approximate yield: 3 dozen cookies.

For *Date-Nut Filling*, boil 1½ cups finely chopped dates, ½ cup sugar and ½ cup water about 5 minutes, or until thick, stirring constantly. Add 1 tablespoon each butter and lemon juice, and ½ cup finely chopped nuts; cool.

SOUR CREAM REFRIGERATOR COOKIES

3 cups sifted all-purpose flour	1 cup granulated sugar
1 teaspoon baking powder	¼ cup firmly packed brown
¼ teaspoon baking soda	sugar
1 teaspoon salt	2 eggs, well beaten
1 cup butter or other fat	1 teaspoon vanilla
½ cup heavy sour cream	

Sift together flour, baking powder, soda and salt. Cream butter; gradually add the sugars, creaming well. Add eggs and flavoring; then flour alternately with sour cream; chill. Shape in rolls about 2 inches in diameter and wrap each in waxed paper. Chill thoroughly in refrigerator. Cut chilled dough in ⅛-inch slices, place on ungreased baking sheet and bake in moderately hot oven (400° F.) about 8 minutes. Approximate yield: 9 dozen cookies.

THREE–IN–ONE SLICED COOKIES

Prepare dough for Sour Cream Refrigerator Cookies; divide in thirds and leave one part plain and choose two of the following variations for the remaining parts, or use all variations. Shape each, chill, slice and bake as directed.

Chocolate Refrigerator Cookies—To ⅓ cookie dough, add 1 square chocolate, melted.

Spice Refrigerator Cookies—To ⅓ cookie dough, add ½ teaspoon cinnamon, ⅛ teaspoon each allspice, ground cloves and nutmeg, ¼ teaspoon ginger and ½ cup finely chopped raisins.

Coconut Refrigerator Cookies—To ⅓ cookie dough, add ½ cup shredded coconut.

CREAM CHEESE DAINTIES

1 cup sifted cake flour
1/4 teaspoon salt
1/2 cup butter or other fat

4 ounces cream cheese
1/4 cup sugar
1 tablespoon caraway seeds

Sift together flour and salt. Cream together butter and cheese and blend in sugar; gradually stir in flour. Shape in 2-inch rolls; wrap each in waxed paper and chill thoroughly in refrigerator. Slice thin, sprinkle lightly with caraway seeds and bake in hot oven (400° F.) about 6 minutes. Approximate yield: 40 cookies.

PETTICOAT TAILS

1 pound butter
1 cup confectioners' sugar

5 cups sifted all-purpose flour
1 teaspoon vanilla

Cream butter until very soft. Add sugar and beat well. Add flour gradually, beating until smooth after each addition. Add vanilla. Chill dough until it can be formed into 2 rolls 1-inch in diameter. Wrap in waxed paper. Chill until firm. Slice very thin. Bake on ungreased sheet in hot oven (400° F.) 6 to 8 minutes, or until light brown. Cool before removing from sheet. Approximate yield: 2½ pounds wafers.

MOLASSES REFRIGERATOR COOKIES

2 cups sifted all-purpose flour
1/2 teaspoon baking powder
1/4 teaspoon salt
1/2 teaspoon cinnamon
1/2 teaspoon baking soda
1 teaspoon ginger

3/4 cup butter and lard, mixed
1 cup firmly packed brown
  sugar
1/3 cup molasses
1/2 teaspoon vanilla
1 egg

Sift together dry ingredients. Cream shortening until soft; gradually beat in brown sugar and molasses, then vanilla and egg. Beat in flour. Shape into rolls about 2 inches in diameter and wrap each in waxed paper. Chill thoroughly in refrigerator. Cut chilled roll in 1/8-inch slices; place on ungreased baking sheet and bake in moderate oven (350° F.) 6 to 8 minutes. Approximate yield: 50 thin cookies.

PEANUT BUTTER REFRIGERATOR COOKIES

1 cup shortening
½ cup peanut butter
2 cups brown sugar
3 eggs
4 cups cake flour
1 teaspoon soda

1 teaspoon cinnamon
¼ teaspoon each cloves and
nutmeg
1 cup salted peanuts, finely
chopped

Cream shortening thoroughly; blend in the peanut butter, then the sugar. Add well-beaten eggs. Mix and sift the dry ingredients, add the chopped peanuts and combine thoroughly with the creamed mixture. Form into rolls, wrap in waxed paper and let stand in refrigerator several hours or overnight. Slice thin, place on a baking sheet and bake in hot oven (400° F.) 8 to 10 minutes. Approximate yield: 150 cookies.

CREAM CHEESE MARMALADE CHIPS

½ cup shortening
½ cup cream cheese
¼ cup sugar

1 cup sifted cake flour
¼ teaspoon salt
orange marmalade

Cream together the shortening and cream cheese. Blend in sugar. Add flour and salt. Shape into rolls, wrap in waxed paper and chill thoroughly. Cut in thin slices and place on lightly buttered cookie sheet. Top each with a dab of orange marmalade. Bake in a hot oven (400° F.) 5 to 8 minutes. Approximate yield: about 2 dozen cookies.

STARLIGHT MINT SURPRISE COOKIES

3 cups sifted all-purpose flour
1 teaspoon soda
½ teaspoon salt
1 cup butter or margarine
(half shortening may be
used)
1 cup sugar

½ cup brown sugar, firmly
packed
2 eggs
2 tablespoons water
1 teaspoon vanilla
1 9-oz. package solid chocolate
mint candy wafers

walnut halves

Sift together flour, soda and salt. Cream butter; add sugars gradually, creaming well. Blend in eggs, water and vanilla; beat well. Add dry ingredients; mix thoroughly. Cover and refrigerate at least 2 hours. Enclose each chocolate wafer in about 1 tablespoon of chilled dough. Place on greased cookie sheet about 2 inches apart. Top each with a walnut half. Bake in moderate oven (375° F.) 10 to 12 minutes. Yield: 4½ dozen cookies.

HAZELNUT SLICES

1⅓ cups sifted all-purpose flour   1 egg white
⅓ cup sugar   ½ cup chopped hazelnuts
⅛ teaspoon ginger   (filberts)
½ cup butter

Sift flour, sugar and ginger together; cut in butter. Add egg white
and work to a smooth dough. Add nuts, shape into roll and wrap
tightly in waxed paper. Chill in refrigerator 2 hours. Slice ¼ inch
thick. Bake in moderate oven (350° F.) 12 to 15 minutes, or until
lightly browned. Yield: 40 cookies.

SPRITZ COOKIES

2½ cups sifted cake flour   1 teaspoon almond extract
½ teaspoon salt   2 egg yolks, beaten
1 cup butter   1 egg white
1 cup powdered sugar   1 teaspoon water
        coarse sugar crystals

Mix flour and salt. Cream butter until soft; beat in powdered
sugar; add almond extract and egg yolks. Gradually stir in flour
mixture; chill. Pack dough in cookie press; use various forms of
discs or nozzles to make shapes such as letter S, wreaths, bows, knots,
crescents, ribbons, etc.; press shapes on ungreased baking sheet; brush
with egg white and water, beaten together until frothy, and sprinkle
with coarse sugar crystals, colored or plain; or with chopped nuts or
sprinklettes. Bake in hot oven (400° F.) about 8 minutes, or until delicately browned. Approximate yield: 5 dozen cookies.

PINWHEEL COOKIES

Use recipe for Spritz Cookies; divide dough in half; add 2 squares
chocolate, melted, to one part and chill both parts. Roll each half in
rectangular sheets ⅛-inch thick, trimming edges if necessary. Moisten
plain sheet with milk, then place chocolate sheet on top; moisten with
milk and roll lengthwise as for jelly roll. Wrap each roll in waxed
paper and chill thoroughly. Cut in ⅛-inch slices and place on ungreased baking sheet; bake in hot oven (400° F.) 5 to 7 minutes, or
until delicately browned. Approximate yield: 5 dozen cookies.

CHECKERBOARD COOKIES

Use recipe for Spritz Cookies (page 687); divide dough in thirds; to one part add 2 squares chocolate, melted, and chill all dough thoroughly. Divide chocolate dough and one of the plain portions into 8 parts each; with fingers, roll pieces in thin rolls ¼-inch thick and flatten slightly with spatula to form square sides. Roll remaining plain dough into rectangular sheet as long as the rolls. Moisten center of sheet with milk and place 4 thin rolls in alternate colors side by side on top; then arrange remaining rolls in 3 similar layers with colors alternating to build checkerboard block, moistening each layer with milk. Fold plain dough around the block and cover with waxed paper; chill thoroughly. Cut in ⅛-inch slices and bake in hot oven (400° F.) 5 to 7 minutes, or until delicately browned. If easier to handle, double the number of small pieces of dough and make into 2 separate checkerboard rolls. Approximate yield: 5 dozen cookies.

CHRISTMAS ROCKS

1½ cups sifted all-purpose flour	⅔ cup shortening
1 teaspoon baking powder	½ cup firmly packed brown sugar
½ teaspoon baking soda	2 eggs
½ teaspoon salt	4½ cups chopped walnuts
1 teaspoon cinnamon	3 cups pitted dates, chopped
¼ teaspoon cloves	3 cups seeded raisins, chopped

Sift together flour, baking powder, soda, salt and spices. Cream shortening; gradually beat in brown sugar, then eggs, nuts and fruits. Stir in flour mixture. Drop from teaspoon on greased baking sheet and bake in moderate oven (350° F.) about 12 minutes. Yield 75 cookies.

Black Walnut Date Rocks—Substitute 1 cup chopped black walnuts for walnuts; reduce dates to 1 cup and omit raisins.

Nut Chocolate Chip Rocks—Use only 1 cup chopped nuts and 1 cup chocolate bits for dates and raisins.

BROWNIE OATMEAL DROPS

½ cup shortening, soft	⅓ cup cocoa
¾ cup brown sugar	1 teaspoon vanilla
1 egg	1 cup pancake ready-mix
½ cup milk	1 cup rolled oats, uncooked

Combine all ingredients in a bowl except oats. Beat with rotary egg beater about 1 minute. Fold in rolled oats. Drop by teaspoons on greased baking sheet. Bake in moderately hot oven (400° F.) 10 to 12 minutes. Yield: 3 dozen cookies.

ANGEL COOKIES

2 cups sifted all-purpose flour	1 teaspoon lemon extract
2 teaspoons baking powder	¼ cup finely chopped lemon rind
4 eggs	¼ cup finely chopped angelica
2 cups sugar	or citron

Sift together flour and baking powder. Beat eggs until very light and lemon-colored. Gradually add the sugar and beat until very thick and smooth. Fold in the flour and the lemon extract. Add the lemon peel, angelica or citron and mix well. Chill overnight, or until the dough is cold. Drop from teaspoon on greased baking sheet and bake in moderate oven (350° F.) 8 to 10 minutes, or until lightly browned. Store in tight tin box. Yield: 3 dozen cookies.

Cherry Angel Cookies—Substitute ¼ cup finely chopped candied cherries for angelica.

Toasted Almond Angel Cookies—Substitute ¼ cup almonds—blanched, shredded and toasted for angelica.

OATMEAL HERMITS

1½ cups sifted all-purpose flour	1 cup seeded raisins
2 teaspoons baking powder	½ cup butter or other fat
½ teaspoon salt	1 cup sugar
½ teaspoon cinnamon	2 eggs
2 cups rolled oats	½ cup milk

Sift together flour, baking powder, salt and cinnamon; stir in oats and raisins. Cream butter, gradually beat in sugar, then eggs; stir in flour mixture alternately with milk. Drop from teaspoon on greased baking sheet and bake in moderate oven (375° F.) about 15 minutes. Approximate yield: 3 dozen cookies.

OATMEAL CHOCOLATE CHIPS

1 cup shortening	1 teaspoon soda
¾ cup brown sugar	2 teaspoons hot water
¾ cup granulated sugar	3 cups rolled oats
2 eggs	1 pkg. (6-oz.) chocolate chips
1½ cups sifted all-purpose flour	1 teaspoon vanilla
1 teaspoon salt	1 cup nut meats

Cream shortening, add sugars, add eggs. Sift together flour and salt and add to mixture. Add soda, dissolved in (hot) water. Stir in oats, chocolate chips, vanilla and nut meats. Drop from teaspoon onto greased cooky sheet, bake in moderate oven (375° F.) about 12 minutes. Yield: 5 dozen cookies.

OATMEAL JAMBOREES

1 cup sifted all-purpose flour	¼ cup firmly packed brown
1 teaspoon baking powder	sugar
½ teaspoon salt	1 egg, beaten
1½ cups rolled oats	¼ cup molasses
½ cup seeded raisins	¼ cup jam or marmalade

½ cup shortening, melted

Sift together flour, baking powder and salt; stir in oats and raisins. Beat brown sugar into egg, then molasses, jam and melted shortening; gradually stir in flour-raisin mixture. Drop from teaspoon on lightly greased baking sheet and bake in moderate oven (375° F.) about 12 minutes. Yield: 2 dozen large cookies.

SPICY MOLASSES COOKIES

3 cups sifted all-purpose flour	¼ cup firmly packed brown
½ teaspoon baking soda	sugar
¼ teaspoon salt	½ cup molasses
½ teaspoon ginger	2 egg yolks, well beaten
½ cup shortening	1⅓ cups mincemeat

Sift together flour, soda, salt and ginger. Cream shortening and brown sugar, then beat in molasses and egg yolks; gradually stir in flour, then mincemeat. Drop from teaspoon on greased baking sheet and bake in moderate oven (375° F.) about 10 minutes. To use prepared mince-meat, follow directions on package. Yield: 4½ dozen cookies.

MOLASSES SNAPS

¼ cup fat	1 cup sifted all-purpose flour
⅜ cup sugar	½ teaspoon soda
½ cup mashed potatoes	¾ teaspoon ginger
¼ cup molasses	¾ teaspoon cinnamon

¼ teaspoon salt

Cream together the fat and sugar. Add potatoes and continue cream-ing. Mix in molasses. Sift together flour, soda, spices and salt. Stir into the first mixture. Drop the batter by tablespoonfuls onto greased baking sheets. Flatten to a thickness of ⅛ inch, using a greased flat-bottomed glass. Bake in moderate oven (350° F.) until cookies are lightly browned, about 15 minutes. Remove from baking sheet and cool. Approximate yield: 30 cookies.

VANILLA DROPS

2 cups sifted all-purpose flour
2 teaspoons baking powder
½ teaspoon salt
1 cup butter or other fat

1 cup sugar
1 teaspoon vanilla
1 egg
½ cup milk

Sift together flour, baking powder and salt. Cream butter until soft; gradually add sugar, creaming until fluffy. Beat in vanilla and egg; add flour alternately with milk. Drop from teaspoon on un-greased baking sheet and bake in moderate oven (375° F.) 8 to 10 minutes. Approximate yield: 50 cookies.

Butterscotch Drop Cookies—Substitute 1 cup firmly packed brown sugar for granulated sugar. If desired, add 1 cup chopped nuts.

Peppermint Chocolate Cookies—Add 2 squares chocolate, melted, to butter-egg mixture; omit vanilla and add a few drops of oil of peppermint or ¼ teaspoon peppermint extract. Drop from teaspoon on ungreased baking sheet; flatten with knife dipped in cold water and place pecan or blanched almond half in center.

CHOCOLATE–PEANUT BUTTER COOKIES

1 cup sifted all-purpose flour
1 teaspoon baking powder
¼ teaspoon baking soda
¼ teaspoon salt
2 tablespoons shortening

1 cup sugar
1 egg
½ cup peanut butter
1 square unsweetened chocolate,
    melted

¼ cup milk

Sift together flour, baking powder, soda and salt. Beat together shorten-ing, sugar and egg; then stir in peanut butter and chocolate; gradually stir in flour alternately with milk. Drop from teaspoon on greased baking sheet and bake in moderate oven (375° F.) about 15 minutes. Approximate yield: 2 dozen cookies.

MARMALADE DROP CAKES

3 cups sifted cake flour
½ teaspoon baking soda
½ teaspoon salt

½ cup shortening
1 cup sugar
2 eggs, well beaten

¾ cup orange marmalade

Sift together flour, soda and salt. Cream shortening; gradually beat in sugar and eggs; stir in flour, then marmalade. Drop from teaspoon on greased baking sheet, about 2 inches apart, and bake in moderate oven (350° F.) about 12 minutes; remove at once from pans. Approxi-mate yield: 4 dozen cookies.

SNACK DROP COOKIES

3 cups sifted all-purpose flour	1 cup shortening
2 teaspoons baking powder	1 cup sugar
¼ teaspoon salt	3 eggs, well beaten
1 cup seeded raisins	1 cup grated carrots
1 cup chopped walnuts	¾ teaspoon grated lemon rind

1½ tablespoons lemon juice

Sift together flour, baking powder and salt; stir in raisins and nuts. Cream shortening until soft; gradually beat in sugar, then eggs, carrots, lemon rind and juice; gradually stir in flour-nut mixture. Drop from teaspoon on lightly greased baking sheet and bake in moderate to hot oven (375°–400° F.) 12 to 15 minutes. Yield: 2 dozen cookies.

COCONUT CREAM JUMBLES

2 cups sifted cake flour	2 egg yolks
½ teaspoon baking soda	1 teaspoon grated orange rind
½ teaspoon salt	1 teaspoon grated lemon rind
¾ cup butter or other fat	1 tablespoon lemon juice
1 cup sugar	¾ cup sour cream

1 cup shredded coconut

Sift together flour, soda and salt. Cream butter; gradually beat in sugar, then egg yolks; stir in grated rinds and lemon juice. Add flour alternately with sour cream, beating well after each addition; stir in coconut. Drop from teaspoon on greased baking sheet and bake in moderate oven (375° F.) about 10 minutes. Approximate yield: 5 dozen cookies.

Chocolate Coconut Jumbles—Omit grated orange and lemon rinds and lemon juice and add 2 squares chocolate, melted, and 1 teaspoon vanilla. Approximate yield: 5 dozen cookies.

Sweet Cream Jumbles—Substitute heavy sweet cream for sour and 2 teaspoons baking powder for baking soda. Substitute chopped pecans for coconut, if desired.

FRUIT DROPS

1 cup sweetened condensed milk	2 cups shredded coconut
¼ teaspoon salt	1 cup chopped dates, uncooked
1 teaspoon vanilla	prunes or dried apricots

Combine ingredients and drop from teaspoon on greased baking sheet about 1-inch apart. Bake in moderate oven (350° F.) about 12 minutes, or until delicately browned. Yield: 2 dozen cookies.

PEANUT BUTTER NUGGETS

1 cup peanut butter	1⅓ cups (1 can) sweetened
1 teaspoon lemon juice	condensed milk
¼ teaspoon salt	1 cup chopped raisins

Mix together peanut butter, lemon juice and salt; gradually stir in condensed milk, then raisins. Drop from teaspoon on greased baking sheet and bake in moderate oven (375° F.) about 10 minutes. Approximate yield: 3 dozen cookies.

HONEY DROP COOKIES

3 cups sifted all-purpose flour	½ cup chopped citron
3 teaspoons baking powder	½ cup butter or other fat
¼ teaspoon salt	½ cup sugar
¼ teaspoon cinnamon	1 cup honey
¼ cup chopped almonds	2 egg yolks, well beaten
	1 teaspoon vanilla

Sift together flour, baking powder, salt and cinnamon; stir in almonds and citron. Cream butter; beat in sugar and honey; then egg yolks and vanilla; gradually stir in flour-nut-fruit mixture. Bake sample cookie to determine effect of honey on mixture. Some honey causes more spreading than others; add more flour if necessary. Drop batter from teaspoon on greased baking sheet and bake in moderate oven (350°–375° F.) 10 to 12 minutes. Substitute pecans for almonds, if desired. Approximate yield: 7½ dozen cookies.

BROWNIES

¾ cup sifted all-purpose flour	1 cup sugar
½ teaspoon baking powder	2 eggs, well beaten
½ teaspoon salt	½ teaspoon vanilla
1 cup chopped nuts	2 squares unsweetened chocolate,
⅓ cup shortening	melted

Sift together flour, baking powder and salt; stir in nuts. Cream shortening until soft; gradually beat in sugar, then eggs, vanilla and chocolate; stir in flour-nut mixture. Turn into buttered, 8-inch square pan and bake in moderate oven (350° F.) 30 to 35 minutes; cut in squares before removing from pan. Yield: 16 squares.

Fudge Brownies—Omit baking powder and bake in moderately slow oven (325°–350° F.) about 30 minutes. These fall slightly on removing from oven but are moist and fudge-like. Cut in squares before removing from pan. Approximate yield: 16 squares.

Chocolate Indians—Increase eggs to 3 and add ½ cup finely cut dates. Approximate yield: 25 squares.

Bran Fudge Squares—Reduce flour and nuts to ½ cup each and add ½ cup bran; increase chocolate to 4 squares and vanilla to 1 teaspoon. Yield: 16 squares.

Toasted Coconut Brownies—Sprinkle ½ cup shredded coconut over top of batter just before baking.

MIX–EASY FUDGE BROWNIES

½ cup butter or shortening	2 eggs
2 squares unsweetened chocolate	½ cup sifted all-purpose flour
	¼ teaspoon salt
1 cup sugar	½ cup coarsely chopped nuts

Melt butter and chocolate in saucepan over low heat. Add sugar and blend. Add eggs, one at a time, and beat well after each. Add remaining ingredients and mix well; pour into prepared 10 x 6 x 1½ inch pan. Bake in moderate oven (350° F.) 30 minutes. Yield: 9 to 12 pieces.

PEANUT BUTTER BROWNIES

1 cup sifted all-purpose flour	½ cup peanut butter
2 teaspoons baking powder	1 cup sugar
¼ teaspoon salt	1 egg, well beaten
½ cup chopped peanuts	2 squares unsweetened chocolate,
2 tablespoons shortening	melted

¼ cup milk

Sift together flour, baking powder and salt; stir in peanuts. Cream together shortening, peanut butter and sugar; beat in egg and chocolate; add flour-nut mixture alternately with milk. Turn into buttered shallow, 9-inch square pan and bake in moderate oven (350° F.) 25 to 30 minutes; cut in squares while warm. Yield: 25 squares.

DRIED FRUIT BARS

1 cup sifted all-purpose flour	1 cup sugar
¼ teaspoon double-acting baking powder	2 eggs, well beaten
	1 cup chopped nuts
½ teaspoon salt	1 cup dried fruit, sliced (dates,
¼ cup melted butter	apricots, figs, prunes)

Sift together flour, baking powder and salt. Mix in other ingredients in order given. Line a shallow pan (13 x 9 inches) with waxed paper and spread batter in it. Bake in moderate oven (350° F.) 25 to 30 minutes. Cool slightly; cut into bars 1 x 3 inches. Turn out on rack and peel off paper. When firm, roll warm bars in confectioners' sugar. Yield: 40 bars.

ALMOND STRIPS

3 eggs, separated   ½ teaspoon vanilla
¾ cup sugar   ¼ cup sifted all-purpose flour
                  ¾ cup ground almonds

Beat egg yolks until light; gradually beat in sugar and add vanilla;
stir in flour, then almonds. Fold in stiffly beaten egg whites and spread
about ¼ inch thick in buttered pan, 13¼ x 8¾ x 1¾ inches. Bake in
moderate oven (350° F.) about 25 minutes. Cool and cover with Boiled
Frosting (page 712); cut in 3 x 1-inch strips. Hazelnuts, Brazil nuts,
pecans, English or black walnuts, hickory nuts or cashews may be
substituted for almonds, if desired. Yield: 36 strips.

GINGERBREAD COOKIES

1 cup dark molasses   1½ teaspoons baking powder
½ cup shortening   ½ teaspoon baking soda
¼ cup milk   ½ teaspoon salt
4 cups sifted all-purpose flour   1½ teaspoons ginger
                  ¼ cup sugar

Heat molasses with shortening to boiling point; stir in milk and cool.
Mix and sift flour, baking powder, soda, salt and ginger; add all at
once to molasses mixture, mixing well; chill thoroughly. Turn out
on lightly floured board, roll into rectangular piece, ¼-inch thick,
and place on buttered cookie sheet, 17 x 14 inches. Rib surface with
fork, if desired, then mark in squares; or cut rolled dough with cookie
cutter. Sprinkle with sugar and bake in moderate oven (350° F.)
10 to 15 minutes. Yield: 2 dozen (3 inch) cookies.

CHOCOLATE MOLASSES SQUARES

1 cup sifted all-purpose flour   ½ cup sugar
½ teaspoon baking powder   ½ cup molasses
¼ teaspoon baking soda   1 egg
¼ teaspoon salt   2 squares unsweetened chocolate,
1 cup chopped walnuts   melted
½ cup shortening

Sift together flour, baking powder, soda and salt; stir in nuts. Beat
together shortening, sugar, molasses and egg; add chocolate; stir in
flour-nut mixture. Turn into buttered pan, 7 x 11 x 1½ inches, and
bake in moderate oven (350° F.) about 30 minutes; cool slightly and
cut in squares. Yield: 2 dozen squares.

BUTTERSCOTCH SQUARES

1½ cups sifted all-purpose flour
2 teaspoons baking powder
¼ teaspoon salt
1 cup chopped nuts

½ cup shortening
1 cup firmly packed brown sugar
2 eggs
1 teaspoon vanilla

Sift together flour, baking powder and salt; stir in nuts. Melt shortening; add to brown sugar; beat in thoroughly one egg at a time, then vanilla. Stir in flour-nut mixture; turn into buttered pan, 7 x 11 x 1½ inches, spreading mixture evenly. Bake in moderate oven (350° F.) 20 to 25 minutes; cut in squares while warm. Yield: 28 squares.

FRESNO SQUARES

1 cup sifted all-purpose flour
¼ teaspoon baking soda
¼ teaspoon salt
½ teaspoon ginger
1 cup seeded raisins

1 cup chopped nuts
¼ cup shortening
¼ cup firmly packed brown sugar
2 eggs
¼ teaspoon vanilla

½ cup molasses

Mix and sift flour, soda, salt and ginger; stir in raisins and nuts. Cream together shortening and brown sugar; beat in thoroughly one egg at a time, then vanilla and molasses; stir in flour-nut mixture. Turn into buttered, shallow, 9-inch square pan and bake in moderate oven (350° F.) about 30 minutes; cut in squares. Yield: 25 squares.

LADYFINGERS

½ cup sifted cake flour
⅛ teaspoon salt

⅔ cup confectioners' sugar
3 eggs, separated

½ teaspoon vanilla

Mix flour, salt and ⅓ cup sugar and sift three times. Beat egg whites until stiff and gradually beat in remaining ⅓ cup sugar; fold in vanilla and egg yolks, beaten until thick and very light colored. Carefully fold in flour-sugar mixture, sprinkling about 3 tablespoons at a time over surface. Press through pastry bag on ungreased paper-lined pan, making strips 4 x ¾ inches; dust with additional confectioners' sugar and bake in moderate oven (350° F.) 10 to 12 minutes. Or drop batter from teaspoon to make rounds. Yield: 2 dozen ladyfingers.

PETITS FOURS

French Almond Cake (page 1046)

Apricot Coating (page 715)

Fondant Frosting (page 714)

Decorative Boiled Frosting (page 713)

Petits fours require care and skillful technique to obtain that coveted French pastry effect. Prepare cake as directed; it should not be more than 1-inch high when baked; a sponge or pound cake may be used, if desired. Cut cold cake, bottom side up, in 1-inch strips crosswise; then cut in 1-inch squares, small triangles and oblongs, or cut in diamonds, circles, half circles, stars or other fancy shapes; use a sharp knife and wipe it with a damp cloth before cutting each piece. Coat cakes, one at a time, with apricot coating; insert fork in side of small cake and dip into coating, covering all but top, and arrange 4 in a row on wire cake rack, with uncovered surface down, placing cakes ½ inch apart; place rack on marble slab or over a plain surface covered with waxed paper. (This coating keeps the cakes moist, gives a gloss to the frosting and helps in keeping it from chipping off.) Pour fondant frosting from pan on center of cakes, moving from cake to cake, then back again to cover generously but gradually; it will require about 1 cup frosting for 4 cakes, and what runs off on table is scraped up into kettle and used again, with additional frosting, for other cakes. Shake rack gently to remove frosting which clings to it and place in warm place to set; when dry, remove cakes with spatula and trim frosting from bottoms; cakes are dry by the time next series of 4 is ready for frosting. Color fondant delicate shades with vegetable color paste.

To decorate cakes, make a cone of cooking paper or vegetable parchment and cut a tiny opening at tip, or use a pastry bag and tube with a small opening. Fill about ⅓ full with decorative boiled frosting and press out in fine lines to make scrolls, or make any desired design; frosting may be colored with vegetable color paste or with melted chocolate. Decorations such as nuts, candied orange peel, cherries, angelica, ginger, candied rose petals or violets may be used.

SPONGE TEA CAKES

Use recipe for Ladyfingers (p. 696) or ½ recipe for Sponge Cake (page 669). Turn batter into 8-inch square layer cake pan with bottom lined with waxed paper. Bake in slow oven (325° F.) about 20 minutes. When cold cut in rounds, squares, rectangles or diamond-shaped pieces. Cover with Butter Frosting (page 709) or Seven Minute Frosting (page 711); decorate as desired. Yield: 12 to 16 pieces.

MERINGUES

4 egg whites   **1 teaspoon cream of tartar**
¼ teaspoon salt   **1 cup fine granulated sugar**
                ½ teaspoon vanilla

Beat egg whites until frothy; sprinkle salt and cream of tartar over top and beat until stiff; gradually beat in sugar, sprinkling 2 tablespoons at a time over the surface; add flavoring and continue beating until stiff and peaked. With pastry bag or spoon, shape in mounds on greased baking sheet which has been covered with lightly buttered wrapping paper. Bake in very slow oven (250°–275° F.) 45 to 60 minutes, or until very delicately browned and dry. Remove from paper while warm. Approximate yield: 3 dozen large, or 5 dozen small meringues.

Kisses—These are small meringues. Shape mixture in small mounds; they may be shaped in pairs.

Creole Kisses—Fold 1 cup finely crushed nut brittle into meringue mixture; shape in small mounds.

Meringue Glacés—Shape mixture in large mounds. When baked, scoop out centers with spoon and place in oven to dry. Just before serving, fill shells with ice cream, crushed fruit or cream filling; serve with a dessert sauce (page 724) as desired.

Nut Glacés or Shells—Fold 1 cup finely chopped nut meats into mixture before shaping into large mounds. Use English walnuts, pecans, hickory nuts, toasted blanched almonds, pistachio nuts or cashews.

Date and Walnut Meringues—Fold 1 cup each chopped dates and broken walnut meats into meringue mixture. With teaspoon shape in small mounds.

Coconut Meringues—Fold 1 cup shredded coconut into meringue mixture. With teaspoon shape in small mounds.

Mushroom Meringues—With pastry bag shape mixture in mounds the size of mushroom caps; sprinkle with cocoa. Shape stems like mushroom stems. Bake, remove from paper and place caps on stems.

Strawberry Meringues—When removing baked meringues from paper, crush in at bottom and fill cavity with mixture of sweetened, crushed strawberries and whipped cream.

Maple Nut Meringues—Substitute 1 cup shaved maple sugar for granulated sugar and fold 1 cup ground pecans into meringue mixture. Shape in small mounds.

Meringue Nests with Peaches—Prepare 1½ times the recipe. Cover bottoms of medium-sized muffin pans with buttered unglazed paper. Pack with meringue, cutting with knife to remove air pockets. Bake 1 to 1¼ hours. Remove while warm and scoop out soft center from underside; then cool. Just before serving, fill with fresh peaches, sweetened with powdered sugar, and top with a hood of whipped cream. Substitute other fruits for peaches as desired. Approximate yield: 10 meringues.

GRANDMOTHER TANGEMAN'S MERINGUE COOKIES

1 cup butter or margarine	1 teaspoon double-acting baking
2 cups granulated sugar	powder
6 eggs, separated	2 cups blanched, sliced almonds
2 cups sifted all-purpose flour	¼ cup currant jelly

Cream butter with ½ cup sugar. Beat in egg yolks. Sift flour with baking powder and add, stirring in a little at a time. Cover bowl of dough and place in refrigerator for 1 hour or until firm enough to roll out (very important). Beat egg whites until stiff but not dry, fold in 1½ cups granulated sugar. Take a small piece of dough from the refrigerator—one piece at a time as this dough is hard to handle when soft. Turn onto floured pastry cloth, and we mean a pastry cloth, using a rolling pin covered with stockinet. Roll to the thinness of pie crust. Cut into 2-inch diamonds.

To each diamond add 2 teaspoons meringue, sprinkle with almonds thinly sliced lengthwise. Make a slight indentation in the center. Bake in hot oven (425° F.) for 5 to 7 minutes. Lower heat to 300° F. and bake 5 to 10 minutes to set meringue. Cool and add a dab of jelly in indented center of each cookie. Approximate yield: 5 dozen.

SWISS MERINGUES CHOCOLAT

Use ½ recipe for Meringues (page 698); mix 2 tablespoons cocoa with sugar. With pastry tube shape in form of a slender "S" on greased, baking sheet, covered with lightly buttered unglazed paper. The line of the meringue needs to be rather thick since the mixture does not swell in cooking. Bake in very slow oven (250°–275° F.) 20 to 30 minutes. When cool, remove very gently from paper. Approximate yield: 2 to 3 dozen meringues.

CHOCOLATE KISSES

½ cup sifted cake flour
¾ cup fine granulated sugar
4 egg whites

¼ teaspoon salt
4 squares unsweetened chocolate,
    melted
½ teaspoon vanilla

Mix and sift flour and ¼ cup sugar. Beat egg whites until frothy; sprinkle with salt and beat until stiff; gradually beat in remaining ½ cup sugar, adding 2 tablespoons at a time. Fold in flour-sugar mixture, sifting about ¼ cup at a time over surface; fold in chocolate and vanilla. Drop from teaspoon on greased baking sheet, covered with lightly buttered wrapping paper; bake in very slow oven (250°–275° F.) 40 to 50 minutes. Approximate yield: 2 dozen kisses.

CRANBERRY KISSES

4 egg whites
1¼ cups powdered sugar

1 cup chopped pecan meats
1 cup candied cranberries,
    chopped

Beat egg whites until stiff. Gradually add sugar, beating until mixture stands up in peaks. Fold in nut meats and cranberries. Drop from teaspoon on lightly buttered baking sheet and bake in slow oven (325° F.) 40 to 50 minutes. Remove from pan to a sheet of paper and cool. Approximate yield: 2 dozen small kisses.

ALMOND MACAROONS

1 cup Almond Paste (page 639)
¾ cup sugar

¼ teaspoon salt
3 egg whites

Rub paste until smooth; gradually work in sugar until well mixed; add salt; beat in thoroughly one egg white at a time; let mixture stand 20 minutes. With pastry bag shape in rounds on lightly buttered paper-covered baking sheet; wet tops by shaking a moist cloth over them and bake in slow oven (300° F.) about 30 minutes, or until dry on surface. When slightly cool, remove from paper and store in cool place overnight; they are much better on second day. Approximate yield: 2 dozen macaroons.

Coconut Macaroons—Add 1 cup shredded coconut to macaroon mixture.

Chocolate Macaroons—Increase sugar to 1 cup; fold ½ teaspoon vanilla and 2 squares chocolate, melted, into macaroon mixture.

Chocolate Coconut Macaroons—Add 1 cup shredded coconut to chocolate-macaroon mixture above.

CREOLE MACAROONS

½ pound almond meats
½ cup sugar
¼ cup water
½ cup chopped dates
4 egg whites, stiffly beaten

Blanch and chop almonds; boil in syrup made of sugar and water about 5 minutes; drain and reserve syrup. Mash nuts fine and return to syrup, add dates; fold into beaten egg whites. Drop from teaspoon on buttered baking sheet and bake in slow oven (300° F.) about 25 minutes. Approximate yield: 2 dozen macaroons.

CORN FLAKE MACAROONS

2 egg whites
½ teaspoon salt
1 cup sugar
¼ teaspoon almond extract
1 cup shredded coconut
2 cups corn flakes

Beat egg whites until frothy; sprinkle salt over top and beat until stiff; gradually beat in sugar, then flavoring; fold in coconut and corn flakes. Drop from teaspoon on greased baking sheet and bake in moderate oven (350° F.) 15 to 20 minutes. Place pan on damp cloth and remove macaroons immediately with spatula or knife. A heart-shaped or round cinnamon drop may be placed in center of each macaroon, if desired. Approximate yield: 3 dozen macaroons.

Rice Macaroons—Flavor with ½ teaspoon vanilla instead of almond extract, substitute crisp puffed rice for corn flakes and add ½ cup chopped nut meats.

Cake Crumb Macaroons—Substitute ⅔ cup cake crumbs for corn flakes. Coconut may be omitted, if desired.

MARGUERITES

Use recipe for Boiled Frosting (page 712) or Seven Minute Frosting (page 711); add 5 marshmallows, diced, to hot syrup just before pouring it over egg whites. Fold in ¼ cup shredded coconut and 1 cup chopped nuts. Spread on crackers and bake in moderate oven (350° F.) about 15 minutes, or until delicately browned. If syrup is made with brown sugar, omit corn syrup. Yield: 50 marguerites.

MARGUERITE TEA WAFERS

2 tablespoons powdered sugar
1 egg white, stiffly beaten
½ cup finely chopped walnuts

½ cup chopped, cooked prunes
½ teaspoon vanilla
24 round crackers (small)

Gradually beat sugar into egg white; fold in nuts, prunes and vanilla. Drop from teaspoon on small crisp crackers and bake in moderate oven (350° F.) about 15 minutes, or until delicately browned. Serve at once. Yield: 25 marguerite wafers.

COOKIE WAFERS

¼ cup butter
5 tablespoons sugar

1 large egg
¼ cup sifted flour

Cream butter and sugar until light and fluffy. Add egg and flour. Blend and place in pastry tube with opening the size of a dime. Pipe 1½-inch rounds onto well-greased cookie sheet. Bake in moderate oven (350° F.) 15 minutes, or until done. Yield: 1 dozen wafers.

ROLLED HONEY WAFERS

2 cups sifted all-purpose flour
¼ teaspoon nutmeg
½ teaspoon cinnamon
1 cup chopped almonds

1 cup butter or other fat
1 cup sugar
2 cups honey
2 eggs, well beaten

Sift together flour and spices; stir in almonds. Cream butter until soft; beat in sugar, then honey and eggs; stir in flour-nut mixture. Drop small portions from teaspoon on greased cookie sheet, about 2 inches apart, and bake in slow oven (300° F.) about 12 minutes, or until delicately browned. Quickly remove with spatula and roll at once, top side out, around handle of wooden spoon, or roll cone-shaped, or fit into a cup. Keep in covered container. Approximate yield: 80 wafers.

PECAN FUDGE FILLED WAFERS

⅓ cup butter or other fat
⅓ cup sugar
1 egg, well beaten

¼ teaspoon vanilla
¾ cup sifted all-purpose flour
Nut Fudge (page 836)

Cream together butter and sugar; beat in egg and vanilla and stir in flour. Spread ⅛-inch thick on greased cookie sheets; crease in 1½-inch squares. Bake in slow oven (325° F.) about 10 minutes, or until delicately browned. Cut squares apart with knife and while hot put two together with fudge. Approximate yield: 1 dozen double wafers.

DOUGHNUTS

DOUGHNUTS may be plump or slender, round or twisted. A good doughnut is uniform in shape, tender and *not* greasy.

Frying Pointers. The temperature of the fat used for frying must be gauged accurately. If the fat is too hot, the doughnuts will not be baked through; if too cold, the fat seeps in, resulting in a fat-soaked doughnut. A temperature of 360° to 370° F. is ideal—hot enough to brown a cube of bread in 60 seconds. Do not attempt to cook too many doughnuts at one time, because the fat becomes too cool for proper frying, and the cakes are likely to absorb too much fat.

DOUGHNUTS

3½ to 4 cups sifted all-purpose flour
4 teaspoons baking powder
1 teaspoon salt
¼ teaspoon nutmeg
¼ teaspoon cinnamon
1 cup sugar
2 eggs, well beaten
2 to 3 tablespoons butter, melted
1 cup milk

Sift together flour, baking powder, salt and spices. Gradually add sugar to eggs, beating until light; add butter; add flour mixture alternately with milk, stirring lightly until ingredients are combined. Turn out on floured board and shape lightly; roll ¼-inch thick and cut with floured doughnut cutter. Fry in hot, deep fat (360°–370° F.) 2 to 3 minutes, or until lightly browned, turning doughnuts when they rise to top and several times during cooking; drain on absorbent paper. Approximate yield: 2 dozen doughnuts.

Old-fashioned Doughnuts—Increase nutmeg to ½ teaspoon and add ¼ teaspoon mace; increase shortening to ¼ cup.

Orange Doughnuts—Use 1 teaspoon mace and 1 teaspoon orange extract, or 1½ teaspoons grated orange rind for flavoring. Sprinkle doughnuts with powdered sugar.

Black Walnut Doughnuts—Add ½ cup chopped black walnuts to batter. Roll doughnuts in sugar while hot.

Sour Milk Doughnuts—Reduce baking powder to 2 teaspoons and add 1 teaspoon baking soda; substitute sour milk or buttermilk for sweet milk; flavor with ¾ teaspoon nutmeg and add more flour, if necessary. Drop from spoon into hot, deep fat, or roll and cut with floured doughnut cutter. Yield: 2 dozen doughnuts.

Whole Wheat Doughnuts—Substitute ½ cup firmly packed light brown sugar for granulated sugar and use 1¼ cups unsifted whole wheat flour and 2¼ cups sifted all-purpose flour. Approximate yield: 2 dozen doughnuts.

Crullers—Increase shortening to ¼ cup, creamed; beat together shortening, sugar and eggs until light and fluffy. Roll ½-inch thick, cut in 8 x 1-inch strips and twist. Fry as directed. Approximate yield: 2½ dozen crullers.

Chocolate Doughnuts—Omit spices, increase sugar to 1¼ cups and add 1½ squares chocolate, melted, and 1 teaspoon vanilla to egg-sugar mixture. Add ½ cup chopped nuts, if desired. Approximate yield: 2½ dozen doughnuts.

Surprise Crullers—Roll dough about ⅛-inch thick and cut in rounds, 1½ inches in diameter. Place orange marmalade and seeded raisins on ½ of rounds and sprinkle lightly with cinnamon; cover with remaining rounds and press edges together firmly. Fry as directed, drain and roll while warm in powdered sugar. Approximate yield: 2 dozen crullers.

Potato Doughnuts—Reduce flour to 3 cups and increase shortening to ¼ cup, creamed. Add 1 cup mashed potatoes to egg-sugar-shortening mixture; if necessary, add more flour to make dough of proper consistency to roll. Approximate yield: 2½ dozen doughnuts.

NEW ORLEANS CALAS MODERNE

½ cup sifted all-purpose flour	½ cup sugar
3 teaspoons baking powder	2 cups cooked rice
½ teaspoon salt	3 eggs, well beaten
½ teaspoon nutmeg	½ teaspoon vanilla

Sift together dry ingredients. Combine remaining ingredients; add to flour. Test consistency of dough by dropping a spoonful into hot deep fat (375° F.) and fry until golden brown. Add a little more flour to remaining dough if cake does not hold its shape. Continue frying a tablespoon at a time. Drain on brown paper, sprinkle with powdered sugar. Yield: 3 dozen cakes.

GRANDMOTHER'S RAISED DOUGHNUTS

1 cup milk, scalded	4 cups sifted all-purpose flour
¼ cup shortening	¾ cup sugar
½ teaspoon salt	1½ teaspoons cinnamon
1 package dry granular yeast	¼ teaspoon nutmeg
¼ cup warm, not hot, water	⅛ teaspoon mace

3 eggs, well beaten

Place milk, shortening and salt in large mixing bowl and cool until lukewarm; add yeast dissolved in warm, not hot, water and stir well. Sift together flour, sugar and spices; gradually add enough to milk-yeast mixture to make a soft batter, beating thoroughly. Add eggs and remaining flour mixture to make a dough which can be handled. Knead well, cover and let rise in warm place about 1 hour, or until doubled. Turn out on lightly floured board; cover and let stand 10 minutes. Roll 1-inch thick and cut with floured doughnut cutter, or cut in rounds, or make into twists. Let rise on board, covered, until doubled in bulk. Fry in hot, deep fat (360°–370° F.) from 2 to 3 minutes, or until lightly browned. If dropped into hot fat, raised side down, the top side will rise while under side cooks, and doughnut will take up less fat. Drain on absorbent paper. Approximate yield: 2½ dozen doughnuts.

RICH CRULLERS

4¼ cups sifted all-purpose flour	1 teaspoon nutmeg
1¼ teaspoons baking soda	3 eggs
2½ teaspoons cream of tartar	1 cup sugar
½ teaspoon salt	1 cup heavy cream

Mix and sift flour, baking soda, cream of tartar, salt and nutmeg. Beat eggs until thick and light colored; gradually beat in sugar. Stir in cream. Add flour mixture, stirring until almost smooth. Turn out small porton on floured board; roll ¼-inch thick and cut with floured doughnut cutter. Fry in hot deep fat (360° F.), turning until golden brown. Drain on absorbent paper. Approximate yield: 3 dozen doughnuts.

RAISED CRULLERS

Use ½ recipe for Sweet Rolls (page 171); roll raised dough ½-inch thick, cut in 6 x 1 inch strips and let rise until doubled. Fry in hot, deep fat (360°–370° F.) 2 to 3 minutes, or until lightly browned; drain on absorbent paper. Approximate yield: 2 dozen crullers.

FRIED BREAD

Follow directions given for Raised Crullers (see above); use white bread dough, roll ½-inch thick and cut in 4 x ½-inch strips. Serve with butter and hot honey.

Frostings, Fillings
and Dessert Sauces

To MANY people the frosting on the cake is more important than the cake itself. It is the final touch that radiates good looks and appetite appeal. Frostings help to retain moisture and, when used with fillings, add richness, flavor and color to cakes.

A frosting may also serve as the filling. A fluffy, light frosting requires a tart or fruit filling. An uncooked butter frosting is appropriate for many cakes including sponge. Fluffy or boiled frostings are especially good on butter cakes, but offer less contrast for sponge types. Fudge frostings bring out the best flavor of chocolate as well as white butter cakes.

DIRECTIONS FOR FROSTING A CAKE

FROST a cake only when cold. Brush off all loose crumbs. Spread the bottom layers with frosting or filling; lay the second layer on top; hold in position with toothpicks if layers have a tendency to slip. (Remove when frosting is set.) Continue spreading with frosting of filling if more than one layer is used. To frost the top and sides of a cake, heap frosting around the edge of the top of cake. With a spatula, spread the frosting over the edge and sides of the cake. To swirl frosting, use a spatula with butter frosting and the back of a spoon with boiled frosting. If coconut is added, sprinkle it on the moist frosting.

707

To apply ornamental frosting, frost the top first and then the sides of the cake with a foundation frosting. Plain boiled frosting or a frosting made of confectioners' sugar may be used. If desired, an under coating or fruit glaze, such as Apricot Coating (page 715), may be spread on the cake before the foundation frosting is applied. The mild fruit flavor of the glaze enhances the flavor of the frosting, while the glaze further prevents a cake from drying out if it is to be kept for several days.

When the foundation frosting is thoroughly dry, half fill a pastry bag or tube with ornamental frosting. A butter frosting is satisfactory for this. Fold the bag over to keep frosting from oozing out and apply gentle pressure to pipe borders, festoons or rosettes on the cake. If a design is first sketched on paper and then etched into the cake with a pin, the decoration can be accurately gauged. Toothpicks at intervals are helpful in applying leaves, letters or other designs.

A cooked frosting that is too thin can be placed over hot water for a few minutes to evaporate moisture; if it is too thick, add a drop or two of hot water, beating until the frosting is of the right consistency to spread.

Cake decorating sets now on the market generally come with a complete set of directions for making flowers, leaves and other festive designs, writing names and greetings for special occasions.

Decorations should be simple. Citron may be cut into strips for stems of flowers, other slices into petals. Roses can be made by slicing candied cherries from the stem end to but not through the bottom. Spread each petal apart and place flat on the cake to form a rose, or place blanched almonds, pecan halves, or sliced Brazil and other nuts around a candied cherry—excellent for decorating fruit cake. Coconut, finely chopped nuts and chocolate shot are ornamental as well as edible. Delicately tinted frostings are often used for special occasions. An unusual effect can be attained by applying two layers of frosting that contrast in color.

BUTTER FROSTING

¼ cup butter or other fat	1 teaspoon vanilla
2 cups confectioners' sugar	dash of salt
3 tablespoons cream (about)	

Cream butter until soft; gradually stir in 1 cup sugar; then vanilla and salt. Add remaining sugar alternately with cream, beating until smooth after each addition, adding enough cream for proper consistency to spread. Approximate yield: frosting for tops and sides of 2 layers (8 inch), tops of 2 layers (9 inch), or 2 dozen cup cakes.

Mocha Frosting—Substitute strong coffee for cream and add 1½ tablespoons cocoa.

Parisian Frosting—Add a very small amount of vegetable coloring to make a delicate shade. Flavor as desired.

Chocolate Butter Frosting—Add 2 squares unsweetened chocolate, melted, to butter-sugar mixture after ½ of sugar has been added. Reduce vanilla to ½ teaspoon and substitute milk for cream, using just enough to make a creamy frosting.

Orange Butter Frosting—Substitute 2 tablespoons orange juice and 1 egg yolk for cream; flavor with 1½ teaspoons grated orange rind.

Strawberry Cream Frosting—Substitute powdered for confectioners' sugar and ⅓ cup fresh strawberry pulp (about) for liquid. About 1 tablespoon orange or lemon juice adds a piquancy. With canned fruit, decrease sugar.

Orange Cocoa Frosting—Sift ½ cup cocoa with sugar, substitute 6 tablespoons orange juice for cream; add ½ cup candied orange peel.

MINT FROSTING

2 large chocolate-covered peppermint patties	¾ cup confectioners' sugar
	1 tablespoon cocoa
1 tablespoon butter	2 tablespoons cream (about)

Melt patties over hot water; cool. Add butter and gradually stir in mixture of about ¼ cup sugar and cocoa; add remaining sugar alternately with cream, beating until smooth after each addition and adding enough cream for proper consistency to spread. Yield: frosting for top of 8-inch cake, or tops of 10 cup cakes.

LEMON FROSTING

1 egg yolk
1 tablespoon grated orange rind
1½ tablespoons lemon juice

dash of salt
2 cups sifted confectioners'
   sugar (about)

Mix together egg yolk, orange rind, lemon juice and salt; gradually stir in sugar until of proper consistency to spread. Approximate yield: frosting for tops of 2 layers (8 inch), or 1½ dozen cup cakes.

Orange Frosting—Omit grated orange rind and substitute 2 tablespoons orange for lemon juice.

Grapefruit Frosting—Substitute grapefruit for lemon juice.

Lime Frosting—Substitute ¼ teaspoon grated lemon for orange rind and lime for lemon juice. Tint a pale green with vegetable coloring.

LEMON ICING

1 egg white
1 teaspoon lemon juice

1 cup confectioners' sugar
   (about)

Beat egg white until frothy, then sprinkle with lemon juice and gradually beat in sugar until stiff enough to spread. Approximate yield: icing for top of 8-inch cake, or 10 cup cakes.

QUICK PEANUT BUTTER FROSTING

¼ cup butter
⅓ cup peanut butter
⅛ teaspoon salt

2¼ cups sifted confectioners'
   sugar
½ cup cold strong coffee
½ teaspoon vanilla

Cream butter, add peanut butter and salt; blend thoroughly. Add sugar alternately with coffee, a small amount at a time. Cream thoroughly after each addition until smooth. Add vanilla. May be stored in covered jar in refrigerator until ready to use. Approximate yield: frosting for tops and sides of 2 layers (8 inch).

CREAM CHEESE FROSTING

1 cup (8 oz.) cream cheese
2 tablespoons confectioners'
   sugar

juice of 1 orange
grated rind of ½ orange

Soften cream cheese and blend in remaining ingredients. Serve over spiced cakes or fresh fruit. Yield: enough for 2 layers (8-inch).

SEVEN MINUTE FROSTING

2 egg whites
1½ cups sugar
dash of salt

⅓ cup water
2 teaspoons light corn syrup
1 teaspoon vanilla

Beat together egg whites, sugar, salt, water and corn syrup in top part of double boiler; place over boiling water and continue beating with rotary beater about 7 minutes, or until frosting thickens and holds its shape when dropped from beater. Remove from boiling water, add flavoring and continue beating until stiff enough to spread. Approximate yield: frosting for tops and sides of 2 layers (9 inch), or 2 dozen cup cakes.

Fluffy Marshmallow Frosting—Beat 1 cup diced marshmallows into frosting before spreading on cake.

Coconut Frosting—Put layers together and cover cake with Seven Minute Frosting, sprinkling at once with 1½ cups shredded coconut while frosting is soft. Toast or tint coconut, if desired.

Fluffy Lemon Frosting—Omit corn syrup and substitute 2 tablespoons lemon juice for 2 tablespoons water; flavor with lemon rind.

Orange Seven Minute Frosting—Omit corn syrup and substitute 3 tablespoons orange juice for 3 tablespoons water; flavor with 1 teaspoon grated orange rind.

Burnt Sugar Frosting—Substitute 2 tablespoons Caramel Syrup (page 730) for vanilla.

Sea Foam Frosting—Substitute 2 cups brown sugar for granulated sugar and omit corn syrup.

Chocolate Seven Minute Frosting—Stir 3 squares unsweetened chocolate, melted, into frosting just before spreading on cake.

LORD BALTIMORE FROSTING

Use recipe for Fluffy Lemon Frosting above; when ready to spread, fold in ½ cup crushed toasted coconut, ½ cup toasted, chopped blanched almonds and 2 tablespoons chopped quince preserves or maraschino cherries. Approximate yield: frosting for tops and sides of 2 layers (9 inch), or 2 dozen cup cakes.

BUTTERSCOTCH NUT FROSTING

1 cup brown sugar   ⅛ teaspoon salt
⅓ cup granulated sugar   1 egg white
⅓ cup water   1 teaspoon vanilla
                ½ cup chopped nuts

Mix brown and granulated sugar with water and heat until syrup
threads when dropped from a fork (234° F.). Add salt to egg white
and beat until stiff, but not dry. Pour the syrup over egg white slowly,
beating until mixture will hold its shape. Fold in vanilla and nuts.
Yield: frosting for tops of 2 layers (9 inch).

PEPPERMINT FILLING OR FROSTING

1 cup granulated sugar   1 egg white
3 tablespoons light corn syrup   8 to 10 drops oil of
⅓ cup water   peppermint

Combine sugar, corn syrup and water in saucepan. Place over heat and
stir until dissolved. Cook until syrup reaches 238° F., or a soft ball is
formed when a small amount is dropped in cold water. Beat egg
white until stiff. Pour hot syrup slowly into egg white, beating constantly. Add peppermint. If filling becomes slightly hardened before
using, add a few drops hot water. Yield: filling for jelly roll or
frosting for tops of 2 layers (8 inch).

BOILED FROSTING

1½ cups sugar   2 egg whites
½ cup water   ¼ teaspoon cream of tartar
1 tablespoon light corn syrup   dash of salt
                1 teaspoon vanilla

Put sugar, water and corn syrup in saucepan and stir over low heat
until sugar is dissolved; boil, covered, about 3 minutes; then boil, uncovered and without stirring, until a small amount of syrup forms a
soft ball when dropped into cold water (238°–240° F.). Remove syrup
from heat; quickly beat egg whites with the cream of tartar until stiff
but not dry, then pour syrup in fine stream over egg whites, beating
constantly; add salt and flavoring and continue beating until frosting
is cool and of proper consistency to spread. On a rainy or humid day,
boil syrup to higher temperature. If frosting hardens before spreading, beat in a few drops of hot water. Approximate yield: frosting
for tops and sides of 2 layers (9 inch), or top and sides of 9 x 9 x 2-inch
cake, or 2 dozen cup cakes.

Marshmallow Cream Frosting—Add 3 tablespoons marshmallow cream to hot syrup; then pour in fine stream over stiffly beaten egg whites.

Ginger Frosting—Use ¼ cup firmly packed light brown sugar with 1 cup granulated sugar. Fold ½ cup well-drained and finely chopped preserved ginger into frosting when thick enough to spread.

Maple Frosting—Use 2 cups sugar, ⅔ cup maple syrup, add corn syrup and water and boil to soft ball stage (240° F.); then pour in fine stream over stiffly beaten egg whites.

Bisque Frosting—Use 2½ cups sugar, ½ cup corn syrup, ½ cup water and ¼ teaspoon salt and boil to firm ball stage (245° F.); pour in fine stream over stiffly beaten egg whites. Fold in ¾ cup almond macaroon crumbs and 2 tablespoons brandy when frosting begins to thicken. Spread at once on cake.

Apricot Frosting—Boil syrup to soft ball stage (240° F.) and add ½ cup apricot purée; then pour in fine stream over stiffly beaten egg whites. Cool before spreading on cake. Peaches, strawberries or other soft fruits may be substituted for apricots.

FLUFFY BOILED FROSTING

Use recipe for Boiled Frosting (page 712); reduce sugar to 1 cup and vary the egg whites from 1 to 3; flavor as desired. Use cold water test and thermometer for determining concentration of syrup. For 1 egg white, boil syrup to soft ball stage (236°–238° F.); for 2 egg whites, boil syrup to soft ball stage (238° F.); for 3 egg whites, boil syrup to firm ball stage (244° F.). Approximate yield: frosting for tops and sides of 2 layers (9 inch).

Foundation Boiled Frosting—Use 2 egg whites; add vegetable coloring to tint lightly, if desired. Spread on cake and let frosting dry out a little before decorating cake. Approximate yield: frosting for tops and sides of 2 layers (9 inch).

Decorative Boiled Frosting—Use 2 egg whites; add vegetable coloring, if desired. When of proper consistency to spread, stir in very lightly ¼ cup confectioners' sugar. This mixture should be firm enough to hold its shape when applied with a pastry tube. If frosting becomes too firm to use easily, add a small amount of unbeaten egg white. Approximate yield: 2 cups frosting.

LADY BALTIMORE FROSTING

1 recipe Boiled Frosting   ½ cup chopped figs
  (page 712)   ¼ cup chopped blanched almonds
½ cup chopped seeded raisins   ¼ cup chopped walnuts

Prepare boiled frosting, flavoring with ¼ teaspoon vanilla and ⅛ teaspoon almond extract. When of proper consistency to spread, add fruits and nuts. If preferred, add just enough frosting to fruits and nuts to make mixture that will spread easily and use as filling between layers. Spread remaining frosting over top and sides of cake. Seven Minute Frosting (page 711) may be used instead of boiled frosting; use raisins or figs and add ¼ cup candied cherries as desired. Approximate yield: frosting for tops and sides of 2 layers (9 inch).

FONDANT FROSTING

Use recipe for Fondant (page 839); melt 1 cup ripened fondant in top of double boiler; add just enough Simple Syrup (page 730) to make it of right consistency to spread, or about 2 tablespoons, beating until smooth. If too thin, add more fondant; if too stiff, add more syrup. Keep hot in double boiler and prepare a small amount at a time. Tint delicately with a vegetable color paste rather than a liquid color which may thin frosting; flavor as desired. Use for small cakes; place cakes on wire rack on a marble slab or over a strip of waxed paper and pour gradually on center of each cake to cover generously; scrape up frosting from underneath rack and use again. Approximate yield: 1 cup frosting, or enough to completely cover top and sides of 4 tiny cakes or Petits Fours (page 697).

BITTERSWEET VENEER

2 squares unsweetened   1 to 2 teaspoons butter
  chocolate

Melt chocolate over warm water; gradually stir in butter and blend. When slightly cool, pour over cake covered with frosting which has been allowed to harden; use Boiled Frosting (page 712). Seven Minute Frosting (page 711), or Marshmallow Frosting (page 711). For silhouette or shadow effect, permit chocolate to run over edge and down on sides of cake. Approximate yield: enough frosting to cover top of 8 or 9-inch cake.

APRICOT COATING

½ cup apricot jelly   ½ cup Simple Syrup (page 730)
                    rum, brandy or Curaçao

Melt jelly, add simple syrup and flavor with 1 or 2 teaspoons liquor.
Use as coating for fancy cakes such as Petits Fours (page 697), covering all but bottom of cakes. This coating will keep cakes moist, give
more lustre to frosting and keep it from peeling off. Approximate
yield: coating for 30 to 40 cakes (1 x 1 inch).

WHIPPED-CREAM ICING

1 cup heavy cream   ½ cup sugar
3 tablespoons Dutch-process
   cocoa

Whip cream until stiff. Combine cocoa and sugar and fold into
whipped cream. Spread between layers and over top and sides of cake.
Store cake in refrigerator until serving time. Yield. 2-layer 8-inch cake
to serve 8 large wedges.

CHOCOLATE BUTTER CREAM

¾ cup sugar   ¼ cup water or coffee
7 tablespoons water   2 cups butter, creamed
5 egg yolks, beaten   1 tablespoon dark rum
6 ounces dark sweet chocolate
   (Dot or Meiers')

Dissolve sugar in 7 tablespoons water; cook to soft-ball stage (234° F.).
Gradually add to beaten egg yolks and continue to beat until very stiff.
Melt chocolate with ¼ cup water or coffee. Beat into egg yolk mixture.
Blend in creamed butter and add rum to flavor. Yield: 3½ cups.

CREAMY CHOCOLATE FROSTING

2 squares unsweetened   1½ cups sugar
   chocolate   2 egg yolks, well beaten
½ cup milk   1 tablespoon butter
                    1 teaspoon vanilla

Heat chocolate and milk until chocolate is melted and beat until
smooth; gradually stir sugar into egg yolks, then chocolate-milk mixture and cook 8 to 10 minutes, or until thick, stirring frequently; add
butter and vanilla and cool. When lukewarm, beat until thick enough
to spread. Approximate yield: frosting for tops of 2 layers (9 inch),
or top and sides of 8-inch square cake.

QUICK CHOCOLATE FROSTING

2 squares unsweetened
    chocolate
1⅓ cups (1 can) sweetened
    condensed milk

1 tablespoon water
⅔ teaspoon almond extract
blanched almonds

Cook chocolate and milk in double boiler 5 minutes, or until chocolate is melted and mixture thickens, stirring until blended; add water and flavoring and cool. Spread on cake and decorate with almond halves, or sprinkle with ½ cup finely chopped almonds. Approximate yield: frosting for top and sides of 8-inch square cake, or 1 dozen cup cakes.

FUDGE FROSTING

4 squares unsweetened
    chocolate, melted
1⅓ cups milk
4 cups sugar

½ teaspoon salt
2 tablespoons light corn syrup
2 tablespoons butter
1 teaspoon vanilla

Add chocolate to milk and cook slowly until smooth and blended, stirring constantly; add sugar, salt and corn syrup, stirring until sugar is dissolved and mixture boils. Boil until a small amount forms a soft ball when dropped into cold water (234°–236° F.), stirring occasionally. Remove from heat, add butter and vanilla and cool. When lukewarm (110° F.), beat until mixture is creamy and thick enough to spread. If frosting stiffens while spreading, place over hot water to keep soft. Approximate yield: frosting for tops and sides of 3 layers (8 inch), or top and sides of 10 x 10 x 3 inch cake.

Chocolate Pecan Frosting—Substitute brown for granulated sugar and water for milk; omit corn syrup and increase butter to ¼ cup. Just before spreading, add 2 cups chopped pecan nut meats. For small cake, make ½ recipe.

French Fudge Frosting—Use 2 1-oz. squares dot chocolate, ⅔ cup light cream, 2 cups sugar, 2 tablespoons each light corn syrup and butter, and 1 teaspoon vanilla; omit salt. This is approximately ½ the recipe for Fudge Frosting.

BUTTERSCOTCH FROSTING

3 tablespoons butter
2 cups confectioners' sugar

1½ tablespoons milk
½ teaspoon vanilla

½ cup ground pecans

Brown butter and gradually stir in sugar; remove from heat, add milk and vanilla and stir until smooth; add ground pecans. Spread thickly over cake. Approximate yield: frosting for tops of 2 layers (8 inch), or top and sides of 8 x 8 x 2 inch cake.

RAISIN BUTTERSCOTCH FROSTING

¼ cup butter or other fat   2½ cups sifted confectioners'
½ cup brown sugar   sugar (about)
2 tablespoons water   1 egg white
        ½ cup chopped raisins

Melt butter and brown sugar together. Cook, stirring until mixture
bubbles. Add water and boil 1 minute. Cool. Add 1 cup of the confectioners' sugar and the egg white. Beat well. Add remaining sugar
and raisins. Yield: frosting for top and sides of 1 9-inch square cake.

CARAMEL FUDGE FROSTING

1½ cups firmly packed brown   2 tablespoons butter
   sugar   dash of salt
1 cup rich milk   ½ teaspoon vanilla

Bring sugar and milk to a boil, stirring constantly; boil until a small
amount forms a soft ball when dropped into cold water (234°–236° F.),
stirring occasionally. Remove from heat and add butter, salt and
vanilla. When lukewarm (110° F.), beat until mixture is thick enough
to spread. If frosting stiffens while spreading, place over hot water to
keep soft. For richer frosting, reduce milk to ½ cup and increase butter
to ⅓ cup, boiling butter with sugar mixture. Approximate yield: frosting for tops and sides of 2 layers (8 inch), or 2 dozen cup cakes.

Panocha Fudge Frosting—Boil syrup to soft ball stage (238° F.);
remove from heat and beat in ¼ cup butter in small amounts, beating
until creamy and of right consistency to spread. Add 1 cup chopped
nut meats and spread at once on cake.

Sour Cream Frosting—Substitute 1½ cups sour cream for milk and
omit butter. Add chopped walnuts to creamy frosting, if desired.

RICH CARAMEL FROSTING

2 cups granulated sugar   ¾ cup brown sugar
¾ cup light cream   dash of salt

Bring granulated sugar and cream to a boil, stirring constantly. Boil
until a small amount forms a soft ball when dropped into cold water
(238° F.), stirring occasionally; remove from heat. Melt brown sugar
slowly in iron skillet; stir rapidly into caramel syrup. Boil again to
238° F.; add salt and cool to lukewarm (110° F.); then beat until
creamy and stiff enough to spread. Add ½ cup chopped nuts to creamy
frosting, if desired. If frosting stiffens while spreading, place over hot
water to keep soft. Approximate yield: frosting for tops and sides of 2
layers (8 inch) or 2 dozen cup cakes.

PRALINE FUDGE FROSTING

2½ cups sugar
1 cup maple syrup
1 cup light cream

dash of salt
½ teaspoon vanilla
½ cup chopped pecans

Bring sugar, syrup and cream to a boil, stirring constantly; boil until a small amount forms a soft ball when dropped into cold water (236° F.), stirring occasionally. Remove from heat and add salt and vanilla. When lukewarm (110° F.), beat until mixture is stiff enough to spread; then add nuts. If frosting stiffens while spreading, place over hot water to keep soft. If desired, omit nuts and spread frosting on cake; while still soft, decorate with pecan halves or broken pecan meats. Approximate yield: frosting for tops and sides of 2 layers (8 inch), or 2 dozen cup cakes. Double the recipe for 2 layers (9 inch).

PECAN FUDGE FROSTING

½ cup firmly packed dark
   brown sugar
½ cup milk

1 tablespoon butter
½ teaspoon vanilla
½ cup finely chopped pecans

Heat sugar and milk, stirring constantly until sugar is dissolved and mixture boils. Boil until a small amount of mixture forms a soft ball in cold water (236° F.), stirring occasionally. Add butter and vanilla. Cool to lukewarm (110° F.); beat until creamy and mixture thickens. Stir in nuts. Spread between two wafers while they are still warm. If filling hardens too quickly, place pan over hot water. Use as frosting for cake, if desired. Approximate yield: filling for 2 dozen wafers, or enough for top of small cake.

BUTTERMILK COCONUT FROSTING

1 cup buttermilk
2 cups sugar

1 teaspoon vanilla
1½ cups shredded coconut

Combine buttermilk and sugar and boil to the soft ball stage (234° F.), stirring occasionally. Cool to lukewarm, add vanilla and beat to spreading consistency. Spread on layers and sprinkle with coconut. Yield: frosting for tops of 2 layers (9-inch).

MAPLE MARSHMALLOW FROSTING

Heat 2 cups shaved maple sugar and 1 cup light cream, stirring until sugar is dissolved. Then boil without stirring to the soft ball stage (238° F.). Remove from heat, add ½ pound marshmallows, shredded, and beat until of right consistency to spread. Yield: 3 cups frosting.

BAKED CHOCOLATE MERINGUE

¼ cup firmly packed brown   2 tablespoons cocoa
   sugar   1 egg white, stiffly beaten
              ¼ cup chopped nuts

Combine brown sugar and cocoa and gradually beat into egg white;
spread over cake batter which has been turned into shallow pan or
small muffin pans and sprinkle nuts over top. Bake in moderate oven
(350° F.) 20 to 25 minutes. Approximate yield: ¾ cup meringue, or
meringue for 8-inch cake or 9 medium-sized cup cakes.

Baked Coconut Meringue—Substitute ½ cup granulated sugar for
brown sugar; omit cocoa and nuts. Sprinkle with ½ cup shredded
coconut.

BAKED MARSHMALLOW COCONUT MERINGUE

Dip 24 marshmallows in water and cut in half; place on hot Quick
Gingerbread (page 649) and return to oven for 2 minutes to soften
marshmallows. Cover with coconut meringue and bake until browned.

BAKED LEMON MERINGUE

¼ cup sugar   2 eggs, separated
1 tablespoon cornstarch   1½ teaspoons grated lemon rind
¼ teaspoon salt   3 tablespoons lemon juice
¼ cup water   1 teaspoon butter

Combine sugar, cornstarch and salt in top part of double boiler; stir
in water and cook over boiling water 10 minutes, stirring until thickened. Add mixture of slightly beaten egg yolks, lemon rind and juice
and cook 2 minutes longer, stirring constantly; add butter and cool;
fold in stiffly beaten egg whites. Spread on warm, freshly baked cake
or cup cakes and bake in moderate oven (350° F.) about 15 minutes,
or until meringue is delicately browned. Approximate yield: meringue
for 8- or 9-inch square cake, or 1 dozen large cup cakes.

CONFECTIONERS' SUGAR ICING

Combine ¾ cup confectioners' sugar, 2 tablespoons hot milk, and ¼
teaspoon vanilla extract. Mix until smooth. Yield: icing for one coffee
cake.

HONEY TOPPING

Cream together ¼ cup butter or margarine and 2 tablespoons honey.
Add 1 unbeaten egg white. Mix well. Add 1 cup confectioners' sugar
and blend thoroughly. Yield: ½ cup topping.

CAKE FILLINGS

CREAM FILLING

¾ cup sugar	4 egg yolks
⅓ cup flour	2 cups milk, scalded
¼ teaspoon salt	1 teaspoon vanilla

Combine dry ingredients and mix with slightly beaten egg yolks; stir
in enough hot milk to make a thin paste. Then add paste to remaining
hot milk and cook over boiling water 5 minutes, stirring constantly;
cook 10 minutes longer, or until mixture is thickened, stirring occasionally. Cool and add vanilla. For a richer filling, add 2 tablespoons
butter to cooked cream. Approximate yield: 2¼ cups filling, or filling for 5 layers, or 2 dozen large éclairs or cream puffs.

Chocolate Cream Filling—Heat 2 squares unsweetened chocolate
with milk; when melted, beat with rotary beater until smooth. Increase
sugar to 1 cup.

Coffee Custard Filling—Add 2 tablespoons ground coffee to milk,
bring to a boil and let stand 5 minutes. Strain through fine sieve or
cheesecloth.

Creamy Custard Filling—Fold ½ cup whipped cream into cooled
filling.

Butterscotch Filling—Use ½ cup firmly packed brown sugar instead
of granulated sugar; add 2 tablespoons butter to cooked filling.

Caramel Filling—Substitute 2 tablespoons Caramel Syrup (page 730)
for vanilla; add 2 tablespoons butter to cooked filling.

Coconut Cream Filling—Add ½ cup shredded coconut to filling.

Pineapple Cream Filling—Add ½ cup crushed pineapple to cooled
filling. Flavor with 1 teaspoon lemon juice instead of vanilla.

Banana Cream Filling—Add 1 medium-sized banana, diced, to cooled
filling. Flavor with 1 teaspoon lemon juice instead of vanilla.

SOUR CREAM PRUNE FILLING

2 eggs, beaten	1 cup chopped, cooked prunes
¾ cup sugar	1 teaspoon grated lemon rind
½ cup sour cream	1 teaspoon vanilla

Mix together eggs, sugar, sour cream and prunes in top of double boiler and cook over boiling water 20 minutes, or until very thick, stirring constantly. Remove from hot water, add lemon rind and vanilla and cool. Approximate yield: filling for 2 layers (9 inch).

COFFEE PASTRY CREAM

1 egg	2 tablespoons cold water
1 egg yolk	½ cup strong coffee
2 tablespoons flour	¼ cup milk
¼ cup sugar	2 egg whites, stiffly beaten
1 envelope plain gelatin	2 tablespoons rum

Place egg, egg yolk, flour and sugar in a bowl and beat thoroughly; stir in gelatin which has been softened in cold water and dissolved over hot water. Mix coffee and milk and bring to boiling point. Pour over egg mixture slowly. Stir over heat until mixture boils, then stir over ice until it cools. Fold in egg whites and rum flavoring. Good in tart shells topped with fresh fruit, or piped through a pastry bag into stewed halves of apples. Yield: 2 cups cream.

LEMON FILLING

¾ cup sugar	¾ cup water
2 tablespoons cornstarch	3 tablespoons lemon juice
dash of salt	1 teaspoon grated lemon rind
1 egg yolk, slightly beaten	1 tablespoon butter

Combine sugar, cornstarch and salt in top of double boiler; stir in egg yolk, water and lemon juice and cook over boiling water 5 minutes, stirring constantly; cook 10 minutes longer, or until mixture is thick, stirring occasionally. Remove from hot water and add grated lemon rind and butter; cool. If desired, ½ cup heavy cream, whipped, may be folded in. Approximate yield: filling for 2 layers (9-inch), or cake roll, 14 x 10 inches.

ORANGE FILLING

½ cup sugar
2½ tablespoons cornstarch
dash of salt
1 egg yolk, slightly beaten

½ cup orange juice
1 tablespoon lemon juice
½ cup water
1 teaspoon grated orange rind

1 tablespoon butter

Combine sugar and cornstarch; add salt and slightly beaten egg. Add orange juice, lemon juice and water. Cook over direct heat until mixture starts to bubble, stirring constantly. Then cook over hot water 10 minutes longer, stirring occasionally. Add orange rind and butter. Cool.

Orange Date Filling—Add ½ cup chopped dates to Orange Filling.

Orange Coconut Filling—Add ½ cup shredded coconut or grated fresh coconut to Orange Filling.

LEMON BUTTER FILLING

¾ cup butter
3 eggs, beaten

¾ cup sugar
grated rind of 1 lemon

juice of 3 lemons

Combine butter, eggs, sugar, lemon rind and juice. Stirring constantly, cook over boiling water 5 minutes, or until it coats spoon and is smooth and thickened. Cool and turn into baked pastry or tart shells, or use as filling for cakes. Approximate yield: 1 cup filling.

NOUGAT FILLING

Mix ¾ cup sugar, ¼ cup cake flour and ⅛ teaspoon salt. Beat 1 egg slightly, add 1 cup water and add to sugar-flour mixture. Add to 2 squares unsweetened chocolate, melted, and cook over hot water about 10 minutes, or until thickened, stirring constantly. Add ½ teaspoon vanilla and ¼ cup chopped nuts; cool. Yield: 1½ cups filling.

FRUIT–NUT FILLING

½ cup chopped dates
¼ cup chopped walnuts

½ cup water
1 tablespoon orange juice

Cook together dates, walnuts and water until thick. Flavor with orange juice. Approximate yield: 1 cup filling.

BANANA FILLING

1 cup sugar   3 large bananas, mashed
¼ cup water   2 egg yolks, lightly beaten

Heat sugar and water until syrup forms 2 inch thread when dropped
from fork or spoon (234° F.) Combine mashed bananas with beaten
egg yolks and add syrup gradually, beating thoroughly. Place over
hot water and heat mixture through, beating well. Cool before spreading between layers. Approximate yield: 2 cups filling.

RHUBARB FILLING

1½ cups diced rhubarb   ¼ cup water
½ cup sugar   ½ cup heavy cream, whipped

Cook rhubarb, sugar and water about 20 minutes, or until rhubarb is
tender and mixture thick. When cold, fold in whipped cream and use
as filling for cream puff shells. Approximate yield: 1½ cups filling, or
filling for 1 dozen large cream puffs.

APPLE GINGER FILLING

½ cup heavy cream, whipped   2 tablespoons chopped, preserved
½ cup sieved, thick apple sauce   ginger

Fold into cream the combined apple sauce and ginger. Spread between
layers just before serving, or use as topping for cake squares. Approximate yield: filling for 2 layers (9 inch).

APPLE BUTTER FILLING

½ cup chopped nuts   ½ cup apple butter
                 1 cup heavy cream, whipped

Combine nuts and apple butter and fold into whipped cream. Approximate yield: filling for 2 layers (9 inch).

GENTLEMEN'S FAVORITE FILLING

2 apples   3 tablespoons lemon juice
1½ teaspoons grated lemon rind   1 cup sugar

Pare and grate apples, add lemon rind and juice, and sugar and cook
5 minutes, stirring constantly; cool. Approximate yield: filling for
2 layers (9 inch).

BONBON FILLING

1 cup sugar	⅛ teaspoon salt
6 tablespoons water	1 egg white
1½ teaspoons light corn syrup	½ teaspoon vanilla

Combine sugar, water, corn syrup and salt in saucepan. Cook over low heat, stirring until sugar dissolves. Cover saucepan and cook 2 to 3 minutes. Uncover; continue cooking until a little syrup dropped in cold water forms a soft ball (236° F.). Remove from heat. Beat egg white until stiff. Add hot syrup slowly, beating constantly. Blend in vanilla. Beat until filling is of desired consistency. Yield: filling for two 8- or 9-inch layers.

SUGAR CRUNCH FILLING

¼ cup sifted enriched flour	¼ teaspoon cinnamon
¼ cup brown sugar	2 tablespoons butter or
¼ teaspoon salt	margarine
2 tablespoons chopped nuts	

Blend flour, sugar, salt and cinnamon. Cut or rub in butter or margarine. Add chopped nuts. Mix well.

ORANGE SUGAR

Blend 1 tablespoon shredded orange rind and ¼ cup sugar. Yield: ¼ cup.

CINNAMON SUGAR

Blend 1½ teaspoons cinnamon and ½ cup sugar. Yield: ½ cup.

DESSERT SAUCES

DESSERT sauces complement many desserts that would otherwise be lacking in distinctive flavor. Rich desserts seem to require a light, delicate sauce of not too pronounced a flavor. Simple desserts are set off to advantage with sauces that contrast sharply with them in flavor. Hard sauces with butter foundation are favorites on steamed fruit puddings and certain fruit pastries. A simple foundation sauce, such as lemon or custard, can be transformed into a sauce of fluffy consistency by adding whipped egg white or cream. Leftover fresh and stewed fruits can be made into a sauce and their flavor heightened by the addition of a little wine or cordial. Wine and other flavorings should not be added to a hot sauce until just before the sauce is to be served.

CHERRY SAUCE

2 cups cherries, fresh or canned   ¼ cup water or cherry juice
   (drained)   ¼ to ½ cup sugar
           ¼ cup orange juice

Cook cherries in water until tender; if fresh, press through fine sieve; add sugar to sweeten and orange juice. Bing cherries are attractive left whole; omit orange juice and add brandy to taste, if desired. Approximate yield: 1 cup sauce.

SHERRIED CRANBERRIES

1 pound cranberries   1½ cups Sherry
2 cups sugar   ½ cup white seedless raisins

Wash and dry cranberries. Prick with a needle or pointed skewer to keep whole. Combine sugar and wine, stir over low heat until sugar is dissolved. Add cranberries and raisins and let simmer 5 minutes. Remove fruit and let syrup simmer until slightly thickened, or until syrup reaches 230° F. Return fruit to syrup. Chill. Serve either as a relish or a dessert topping. Approximate yield: 1 quart sauce.

GRAPEFRUIT SAUCE

¾ cup sugar   1 tablespoon grated grapefruit
2 tablespoons cornstarch   rind
¼ teaspoon salt   1 tablespon butter or margarine
1¼ cups grapefruit juice   1 egg yolk

Mix sugar, cornstarch and salt in a saucepan and gradually add hot grapefruit juice, stirring constantly until sauce is clear. Add rind and butter. Pour slowly over beaten egg yolk, stirring constantly. Serve hot over steamed pudding. Yield: 2 cups.

FRUIT APRICOT SAUCE

2 cans apricot nectar	¼ cup water
½ cup sugar	rum or brandy, if desired
2 tablespoons cornstarch	1 can fruit

Heat apricot nectar with sugar and thicken with cornstarch blended with water. Flavor with rum or brandy, if desired. Add 1 can of mixed canned fruits or portions of pears, peaches, Bing cherries and pineapple wedges, reserving some fruit for garnishing. Heat fruits in sauce and serve over slices of Easter Baba (page 178).

LINGONBERRY SAUCE

2 cups lingonberries or	¾ cup sugar
mountain cranberries	¼ cup water

Drain, pick over and wash; add sugar and water, bring to a boil and simmer 10 minutes. Serve hot or cold. It is often served as a Suzette sauce with Crêpes (see page 1043). For a thicker sauce for meats and poultry, increase sugar to 1 cup and add 1 cup grated tart apple to the berries. Approximate yield: 2 cups.

RHUBARB SAUCE

Cut rhubarb into 1-inch pieces, cover with boiling water and let stand, covered, 1 minute. Drain. Add ¼ cup sugar and ¼ cup water to each pound prepared rhubarb. Cover closely and simmer over low heat 10 minutes, or until tender. Do not stir.

ORANGE–LEMON SECTIONS

1 navel orange	water
1 lemon	⅔ cup sugar

Remove sections from orange and lemon (page 98); drain and add enough water to juice to make ¼ cup liquid. Bring sugar and water to a boil, stirring until dissolved, and boil 5 minutes; add fruit sections and boil gently 5 minutes longer. Chill thoroughly before serving. Approximate yield: ¾ cup sauce.

ORANGE MARMALADE SAUCE

1½ cups sugar	¼ teaspoon salt
1½ cups strained orange juice	3 tablespoons orange marmalade

Bring sugar, orange juice and salt to a boil, and boil to a thick syrup, or until thermometer registers 218° F.; add marmalade and cool. Store in covered container in refrigerator. Yield: 2½ cups sauce.

HOT JELLY SAUCE

1 cup currant jelly
½ cup boiling water

2 teaspoons finely chopped
orange peel

Beat ingredients together and serve hot. Any candied fruit peel may be used in this recipe. Approximate yield: 1¼ cups sauce.

MELBA SAUCE

1 cup fresh raspberries
½ cup currant jelly

1 tablespoon water
½ cup sugar

1 teaspoon cornstarch

If frozen raspberries are used, let stand in room to soften; add jelly and water and heat to boiling, stirring enough to prevent burning. Stir in mixture of sugar and cornstarch and cook 10 minutes, stirring until thickened and clear; rub through strainer and cool. Serve with a peach ice cream or vanilla ice cream served with peaches. Approximate yield: ¾ cup sauce.

CHERRY MUSH

4 cups sour cherries, pitted
sugar

4 tablespoons cornstarch
½ cup cold water

Cook cherries with sugar, added to taste, for 5 minutes, or until tender. Mix cornstarch with cold water; gradually add cherries slowly, stirring well, and cook over low heat, stirring until thick. Cover and simmer 10 minutes, stirring occasionally. Serve cold. If the mixture is to be served hot as a sauce for cottage pudding, only 2 tablespoons of cornstarch should be used. Approximate yield: 6 portions.

LEMON SAUCE

½ cup sugar
1 tablespoon cornstarch
¼ teaspoon salt

1 cup boiling water
1 teaspoon grated lemon rind
3 tablespoons lemon juice

2 tablespoons butter

Mix together sugar, cornstarch and salt; gradually stir in hot water, bring to a boil and cook 15 minutes, stirring until smooth, thickened and clear; stir in lemon rind and juice and butter. Approximate yield: 1¼ cups sauce.

Golden-Lemon Sauce—Before adding lemon juice and butter, stir hot mixture gradually into 1 egg yolk, slightly beaten, and cook 1 minute, stirring constantly.

Fruit Sauce—Substitute 1 cup hot fruit juice for water; reduce lemon juice to 1 tablespoon; omit grated rind. Use less or add more sugar, if necessary, according to sweetness of juice. This is an excellent way to use leftover canned fruit juices. A little of the fruit may be diced and added to sauce, if desired. Serve with Blanc Mange (page 769) or Cottage Pudding (page 776).

Orange Sauce—Reduce water to ¾ cup and lemon juice to 1 table-spoon; substitute grated orange for lemon rind; add ¼ cup orange juice. Add slightly beaten egg yolk for a richer sauce.

Lemon Coconut Sauce—Add 2 tablespoons brown sugar; omit grated lemon rind and increase lemon juice to ¼ cup; add ½ cup shredded coconut before serving. Serve, slightly cooled, on desserts or ice cream. Approximate yield: 1½ cups sauce.

SOUR CREAM SAUCE FOR FRUIT

¾ cup chilled sour cream	grated rind of 1 lemon
2 tablespoons sugar	½ teaspoon grated nutmeg

Combine sour cream, sugar, grated lemon rind and nutmeg. Serve separately as a sauce for fruits. Yield: Approximately ¾ cup sauce.

CREAMY CHOCOLATE SAUCE

1½ cups milk	1 tablespoon flour
2 squares unsweetened	dash of salt
chocolate	2 tablespoons butter
½ cup sugar	½ teaspoon vanilla

Heat milk and chocolate over boiling water; when chocolate is melted, beat with rotary beater until smooth. Combine sugar, flour and salt; gradually stir in milk-chocolate mixture and cook 5 minutes, stirring until thickened. Remove from heat, add butter and vanilla and serve hot or cold. Approximate yield: 1½ cups sauce.

HOT CHOCOLATE SAUCE

7 ounces semi-sweet chocolate	6 tablespoons coffee
1 square unsweetened chocolate	1 tablespoon salad oil
1 tablespoon rum or Crème de Menthe	

Melt chocolate with coffee over low heat. When melted, add oil and rum and blend well. Served hot over fruit or ice cream or on filled cream puffs. Approximate yield: ¾ cup sauce.

HOT FUDGE SAUCE

2 cups sugar
dash of salt
2 squares unsweetened
  chocolate

¾ cup milk
1 tablespoon butter
½ teaspoon vanilla

Combine sugar, salt, chocolate, milk and butter and heat slowly, stirring until sugar is dissolved and chocolate melted; boil until a small amount forms a very soft ball when dropped into cold water (234° F.). Remove from heat, add vanilla and beat slightly. Serve hot or warm; if it seems too thick, dilute with a small amount of cream. Approximate yield: 2 cups sauce.

Chocolate Mint Sauce—Omit vanilla and flavor with ½ teaspoon peppermint extract or ¼ cup crushed peppermint candy. Approximate yield: 2 cups sauce.

VANILLA SAUCE

1 cup milk
1 cup light cream

4 egg yolks
½ cup granulated sugar
½ teaspoon vanilla extract

Scald milk and cream with vanilla. Beat the egg yolks until light in top of double boiler; add the sugar and the combined hot milk and cream gradually, stirring constantly with a whip or spoon. Cook over hot water, stirring constantly until like a custard. Strain through cheesecloth or fine sieve and let cool. Yield: 1 pint.

CUSTARD SAUCE

2 eggs, slightly beaten
3 tablespoons sugar

dash of salt
2 cups milk
½ teaspoon vanilla

Combine eggs, sugar and salt in top part of double boiler, stir in milk and place over hot (not boiling) water. Cook, stirring constantly, until mixture coats the spoon. Pour into a bowl, add vanilla and chill. Approximate yield: 2 cups sauce.

Brandy Custard Sauce—Omit vanilla and add 3 tablespoons apricot or peach brandy and a dash of nutmeg. Approximate yield: 2 cups sauce.

MAPLE FUDGE SAUCE

1 cup sugar	¼ cup water
1 cup maple syrup	1 tablespoon butter

Bring sugar, syrup, water and butter to a boil and boil until a small amount forms a very soft ball when dropped into cold water (234° F.). Serve hot or cold. Approximate yield: 1¼ cups sauce.

CARAMEL FUDGE SAUCE

1½ cups sugar	1 tablespoon butter
1 cup boiling water	½ teaspoon vanilla

Melt sugar in heavy frying pan over low heat; when light brown in color, remove from heat, stir in water, add butter and boil until a small amount forms a very soft ball when dropped into cold water (234° F.). Remove from heat, add vanilla and beat slightly; serve hot or cold. Approximate yield: 1 cup sauce.

BUTTERSCOTCH SAUCE

¾ cup firmly packed brown sugar	1 cup corn syrup
	¼ cup butter
1 cup light cream	

Boil sugar, syrup and butter 5 minutes, stirring until sugar is dissolved; add cream and bring to a brisk boil. Serve hot or cold on ice cream, other desserts or sliced bananas; it thickens as it stands. Sauce may be kept for several days if stored in a covered container in refrigerator. For a thicker sauce, boil sugar-cream mixture to 234° F. Approximate yield: 3 cups sauce.

SIMPLE SYRUP

1 cup sugar	1 cup water

Boil sugar and water 10 minutes, stirring until sugar is dissolved. Use as needed for Fondant Frosting (page 714), or for ices and cold sweetened drinks. Store in covered jar in cool place. Approximate yield: 1 cup syrup.

CARAMEL SYRUP

1 cup sugar	½ cup boiling water

Melt sugar in heavy frying pan over low heat; when light brown in color, remove from heat and add water slowly. Boil 10 minutes, or until caramel is dissolved. Use as flavoring; store in covered jar in cool place. Approximate yield: ½ cup syrup.

FOAMY YELLOW SAUCE

⅓ cup butter or margarine   1 egg, separated
1 cup confectioners' sugar   ¼ cup orange juice

Cream butter until soft; gradually beat in sugar, then egg yolk and orange juice. Just before serving, fold in the stiffly beaten egg white. For variety, flavor with 1 tablespoon brandy, or substitute Sherry for orange juice. Serve with a steamed fruit pudding or minced pie (page 746). Approximate yield: ¾ cup sauce.

Foamy Cranberry Sauce—Substitute sweetened cranberry juice for orange juice.

Fairy Sauce—Omit orange juice and flavor with ½ teaspoon vanilla. Just before serving, fold in ¼ cup heavy cream, whipped, with the stiffly beaten egg white. Pile lightly into small bowl and dust with cinnamon. Approximate yield: 1¼ cups sauce.

FLUFFY DESSERT SAUCE

1 egg, separated   pinch of salt
¾ cup powdered sugar   ½ cup heavy cream, whipped
                 3 tablespoons brandy

Beat egg white until stiff; gradually add sugar, beating until mixture holds its shape; beat in salt and egg yolk. Fold in cream and brandy; chill thoroughly. Approximate yield: 1½ cups sauce.

FOAMY EGG SAUCE

3 eggs, separated   pinch of salt
½ cup sugar   almond extract
                 ⅛ teaspoon grated orange rind

Beat egg yolks until thick and light colored; gradually beat in sugar and add salt; flavor to taste and fold in stiffly beaten egg whites. Pile lightly in bowl and serve at once. Flavor with 2 tablespoons finely chopped preserved ginger and 1 teaspoon ginger syrup, 2 tablespoons Sherry, or 1 tablespoon brandy, if desired. Yield: 1½ cups sauce.

HARD SAUCE

⅓ cup butter	½ teaspoon vanilla, lemon or
1 cup confectioners' sugar	almond extract, cinnamon
1 tablespoon cream	or nutmeg

Cream butter until soft; gradually beat in sugar, then cream and vanilla, beating until fluffy. Brandy, rum, Sherry or Port, or maraschino cherry juice may be substituted for cream and flavoring. Pile lightly in serving dish and chill until cold but not hard. Approximate yield: ¾ cup sauce, or enough for 4 to 6 portions.

Apricot Hard Sauce—Cook ¼ pound dried apricots (page 105), drain and force fruit through strainer; substitute pulp (½ cup) for cream, beating it gradually into creamed butter and sugar; omit vanilla.

Strawberry Hard Sauce—Omit cream and vanilla; beat in gradually ½ cup mashed strawberries, then 1 egg white, beating until light. Blackberries, raspberries or blueberries may be substituted for strawberries.

Butterscotch Hard Sauce—Substitute ½ cup firmly packed brown sugar for confectioners' sugar; increase cream to 3 tablespoons and vanilla to 1 teaspoon. Beat in 1 egg yolk if a yellow sauce is desired.

Orange Hard Sauce—Substitute orange juice for cream, omit vanilla and add ¼ cup chopped candied orange peel.

Ginger Hard Sauce—Omit cream and vanilla and beat in 2 tablespoons ginger syrup and ¼ cup chopped preserved ginger.

Cinnamon Hard Sauce—Cream ⅓ cup butter until soft and smooth; gradually beat in 2 cups confectioners' sugar and ½ teaspoon cinnamon which have been mixed together, alternately with ⅓ cup corn syrup, beating until fluffy; chill thoroughly. Approximate yield: 1⅓ cups, or enough for 8 portions.

SHERRY SAUCE

1 cup sugar	2 cups boiling water
2 tablespoons cake flour	1½ tablespoons lemon juice
dash of salt	½ cup Sherry
	2 tablespoons butter

Mix sugar, flour and salt; gradually stir in boiling water and cook 5 minutes, stirring until thickened. Add lemon juice, Sherry and butter and heat thoroughly but do not boil. Serve hot or cold with vanilla or banana ice cream or other dessert. Approximate yield: 2½ cups sauce, or enough for 8 to 10 portions.

PORT SAUCE

1 cup sugar	2 egg yolks, well beaten
dash of salt	½ teaspoon grated lemon rind
dash of cinnamon	3 tablespoons lemon juice
1 tablespoon butter	½ cup wine, Port or Tokay

Mix together sugar, salt and cinnamon in top of double boiler and stir in softened butter; add egg yolks, lemon rind and juice and beat with rotary beater 10 minutes. Stir in wine, place over boiling water and beat until thick and frothy, stirring or whisking with beater; do not let it boil. Serve at once over hot or cold pudding such as plum or steamed puddings (page 785), or Blanc Mange (page 769). Approximate yield: ¾ cup sauce or enough for 6 portions.

MADEIRA BUTTER SAUCE

½ cup butter	½ teaspoon grated orange rind
⅓ cup Madeira or Port	½ teaspoon grated lemon rind

Heat ingredients slowly until very hot but do not boil; stir well and serve hot. If desired, 3 tablespoons brandy, whiskey or rum may be substituted for the wine. Approximate yield: ⅔ cup sauce, or enough for 4 to 6 small portions.

BRANDY–APRICOT SAUCE

½ cup sugar	¾ cup boiling water
1 tablespoon cornstarch	¾ cup apricot purée
½ cup Cognac	

Mix sugar and cornstarch; stir gradually into boiling water and cook 15 minutes, stirring until thickened and clear. Add apricot purée and brandy and heat thoroughly, but do not boil. Dried apricots may be used for purée; cook and force through sieve; serve hot sauce in pitcher. Approximate yield: 1¾ cups sauce, or enough for 6 to 8 portions.

KIRSCH WHIPPED CREAM

½ cup heavy cream	1 tablespoon shredded, blanched
¼ cup powdered sugar	almonds
dash of salt	2 tablespoons Kirsch

Put chilled cream, sugar and salt in deep bowl in pan of ice water and beat with rotary beater until thick; fold in almonds and Kirsch. Serve on fruit. Approximate yield: 1 cup, or enough for 6 portions.

DATE BRANDY PUDDING SAUCE

⅓ cup sugar	1 tablespoon butter
1 tablespoon flour	1 egg yolk, slightly beaten
dash of salt	2 tablespoons brandy
1½ cups boiling water	1 cup whole dates

Combine sugar, flour and salt. Add water slowly, mixing well, and cook over low heat, stirring constantly until mixture is thick and clear. Cover and cook 5 minutes. Add melted butter to egg yolk; beat until blended, then stir in hot sauce slowly, blending well. Serve warm, adding brandy and dates just before serving. Yield: 1½ cups sauce.

BRANDY SAUCE

1 egg, separated	dash of salt
¾ cup confectioners' sugar	½ cup heavy cream, whipped
	3 tablespoons brandy

Beat egg white until stiff; add sugar gradually, beating until sugar disappears; beat in salt and egg yolk. Fold in cream, add brandy and chill until cold, but not hard. Serve on hot or cold date-bread slice, or a steamed pudding. Approximate yield: 1½ cups sauce.

ZABAGLIONE

3 egg yolks	¼ cup Sherry, Marsala or
1 to 2 tablespoons sugar	Madeira

Beat yolks until thick and light colored; add sugar and beat until dissolved. Warm wine slightly; add to egg yolks and beat over hot water until thick and very light. Turn into serving glasses and top with a dash of cinnamon; serve warm or cold as a dessert. Or serve cold as a dessert sauce with lemon or chocolate soufflé, or over chilled fresh or canned peach or pear halves, or pitted bing cherries. Yield: 2 or 3 portions.

Pastries and Pies

PERFECT pastry is light, tender and flaky and "shatters" rather than crumbles when you bite into it. The surface is golden brown and delicately blistered, rather than smooth.

DO'S AND DON'TS FOR PASTRIES AND PIES

1. Hydrogenated fats, lard, chicken fat or butter may be used for making pastry. Lard has been found to make the shortest crust. Butter tends to make a brittle crust unless combined with another fat, but it is thought by some cooks to improve the flavor of pastry. Chicken fat is usually used for a meat or poultry pie crust.

2. Use enriched all-purpose flour for these recipes. If pastry or cake flour is substituted, add 2 tablespoons to each cup of flour, or use one part fat to four parts flour. Pastry or cake flour makes a very tender crust but one that is not flaky.

3. Fat should be hard when combined with the flour, yet not so brittle it is difficult to blend. The object is to coat small, uniform particles of fat with flour.

4. Too much liquid makes a hard, brittle, less tender crust; too little gives a crumbly crust, difficult to handle. The amount of liquid varies with the recipe but will average 2 to 4 tablespoons for each cup of flour.

5. In plain pastry, the fat can be cut in all at once before adding any liquid. In puff pastry, the fat is added in small amounts, being incorporated in layers in the rolled-out dough. These

735

layers help to hold in the steam and make the pastry flaky or puffy.

6. To make a flaky plain pastry: Cut half the fat into the flour until the mixture resembles coarse cornmeal. Then cut the other half into the fat-flour until the particles are the size of peas. The liquid should be added, a small amount at a time, always in a fresh unmoistened spot. When the dampened dough just holds together when pressed lightly, enough water has been added.

7. Pastry may be rolled as soon as mixed, but it is easier to roll and shape if the dough is refrigerated 10 to 15 minutes.

8. Before rolling, gently press dough into a ball. Roll the dough out on lightly floured board, rolling from the center in all directions, and occasionally turning the dough without lifting it, to prevent sticking. Just before the rolling pin reaches the edge of the dough, lift slightly to give an even crust.

9. Cut the pastry to fit the pan by placing the pie pan upside down on the rolled dough. With a knife or pastry wheel cut 1 to 1¼ inches beyond rim of the pan to allow dough for an attractive edging.

10. To seal edges of pie crusts, lightly moisten under edge with water. Lightly press upper crust into place. For freezing pastry, see page 904.

PLAIN PASTRY

2½ cups sifted all-purpose flour   ¾ cup shortening
1 teaspoon salt   ⅓ cup cold water (about)

Sift together flour and salt; cut in half shortening with pastry blender or two knives until evenly mixed and like coarse sand. Add remaining shortening and cut into size of peas. Add water in small amounts, stirring lightly with fork and tossing aside pieces of dough as soon as formed; use only enough water to make particles hold together. Place dough in waxed paper and press gently together; chill 10 to 15 minutes. Roll dough ⅛-inch thick on lightly floured board and use for pies and tart shells. Yield: pastry for two-crust (9-inch) pie, 2 shells (9-inch), or 14 tart shells (4-inch). For a two-crust (8-inch) pie, use 2 cups flour, ⅔ cup shortening, ¾ teaspoon salt, and about ¼ cup cold water.

Crumbly Pastry—Add 1 teaspoon baking powder and sift with flour. If a vegetable oil is used, reduce shortening to ½ cup and mix it into flour with fork; add only enough cold water to make particles cling together and proceed as for plain pastry.

Hot Water Pastry—Add ½ teaspoon baking powder and sift with flour; substitute ⅓ cup boiling water for cold water and beat into shortening. Gradually stir in flour mixture and proceed as directed.

Cornish Pastry—Add ½ teaspoon baking powder and sift with flour; use ½ cup shortening and proceed as directed. For meat pie, hunters' style, use half lard and half finely shredded suet for shortening.

Sour Milk Pastry—Add ¼ teaspoon soda and sift with flour; substitute thick sour milk for cold water, using just enough to hold the dough together.

Creamy Pastry—Add 1 tablespoon lemon juice and 1 egg yolk, well beaten, to ¼ cup cold water and proceed as directed.

Cheese Pastry—Add 1½ cups grated cheese; cut with ⅔ cup shortening into flour and proceed as directed. Use for wafers, straws, etc.

Cream Cheese Pastry—Reduce shortening to ½ cup, add ½ cup cream cheese and cut into flour and proceed as directed.

Nut Pastry—Add ⅔ cup ground nuts to flour mixture.

DEEP–DISH PIE
(Plain Pastry, page 736)

Place fruit (sliced, diced or whole) in baking dish, deep pie pan or individual baking dishes, heaping fruit slightly in center; sweeten to taste and moisten rim of dish with cold water. For 9-inch dish, use half of pastry; roll ⅛-inch thick to extend ½-inch beyond rim of dish to be covered. Fold over in half and cut several slits near center to permit escape of steam and place folded crust over half of filled dish; then unfold, adjust and trim crust, if necessary. Fold overhanging border under, press double edge against moistened rim of pan with floured fork and brush top with milk or cream. Bake in hot oven (425° F.) 40 minutes, or until filling is done and crust is browned. Apples, apricots, peaches and cherries are especially good fruits to use in pies of this type. For juicy fruits, add flour, cornstarch or quick-cooking tapioca. (See recipe for Fresh Fruit Pies, page 742).

TWO–CRUST PIE

Use slightly more than ½ of dough for under crust; roll ⅛-inch thick. Fold dough in half and place on pie pan, unfold and fit loosely, allowing crust to extend well over rim. Trim, leaving ½-inch border around rim of plate; fill and moisten edge of crust with cold water. Roll remaining dough ⅛-inch thick, fold over in half and cut several slits near center to permit escape of steam; place folded crust over half of filled lower crust, then unfold and adjust. Trim off edge around rim of pan; fold under crust over edge of top crust to seal; press edges of crusts together with floured fork. Bake in hot oven (425° F.) 40 to 50 minutes, or until filling is done and crust is browned. If a glazed crust is desired, brush top with milk, cream or white of egg.

LATTICE PIE

Roll half of dough ⅛-inch thick, fit loosely in pie pan, trim evenly, leaving a 1-inch overhanging border; fill lined pan. Roll remaining dough ⅛-inch thick, cut in narrow strips and arrange 7 or 8 strips over top; trim, moisten ends and press into dough on edge of pie pan. Then arrange same number of strips diagonally across first strips, making diamond-shaped openings. Trim, moisten ends and press into edge; moisten edge and press together. Or press into standing edge and flute. Bake as for two-crust pie.

PASTRY SHELL

Roll ½ of dough ⅛-inch thick, fit loosely in pie pan and trim evenly, leaving a 1-inch overhanging border; fold up and back to make an upright rim and flute with fingers. Prick crust thoroughly with fork. Anchor pastry onto rim of pie pan by pressing securely. Bake in hot oven (450° F.) about 15 minutes, pricking any large bubbles that may form during baking.

TART SHELLS

Roll pastry ⅛-inch thick and cut in rounds, allowing for depth of individual tart or muffin pans; fit over inverted pans, trim edges and prick thoroughly with fork. Place pans, pastry side up, on baking sheet and bake in hot oven (450° F.) 12 to 15 minutes, or until delicately browned. If large bubbles appear during baking, prick these with fork. Remove from pans and cool.

RICH FLAKY PASTRY

Use recipe for Plain Pastry (page 736); increase shortening to 1 to 1¼ cups. Cut ½ cup shortening into flour and roll dough in rectangular shape, ¼-inch thick. Cut remaining shortening in small pieces and spread ½ over half of dough, leaving a narrow margin. Fold in half to cover shortening and press edges together; then fold opposite sides to make 3 folds, one over and the other underneath. Roll pastry ¼-inch thick, spread with remaining shortening and fold as before. Reroll and fold again as directed. Chill thoroughly. Use for fine pastries or baked shells. Bake as directed. Yield: 2 pastry shells (9 inch), or 14 tart shells (4 inch).

SHORT PASTRY

1½ cups sifted all-purpose flour	pinch of salt
¼ cup sugar	6 tablespoons chilled butter
	4 egg yolks

1 tablespoon water

Sift flour onto board. Make a well in the center; place remaining ingredients in well. Mix center ingredients with fingers to a smooth paste; quickly work in the flour until blended. Roll out on floured board to fit a 9-inch pie pan. Line pan; trim and line with waxed paper. Place a layer of rice on paper. Bake in moderate oven (350° F.) 30 to 35 minutes. Yield: 1 9-inch pie shell.

SPICED PASTRY

2 cups sifted all-purpose flour	¼ teaspoon ginger
¼ teaspoon baking soda	¼ teaspoon cloves
¼ teaspoon salt	⅔ cup shortening
½ teaspoon cinnamon	¼ cup molasses

3 tablespoons fruit juice

Sift together dry ingredients, cut in shortening and add combined molasses and juice as for pastry; for fruit pie, use juice of fruit in pastry. Roll dough ⅛-inch thick and use for pies and tart shells. Chill; bake shells in hot oven (450° F.) about 15 minutes. Yield: pastry for two-crust (8 inch) pie, 2 shells (8 inch), or 12 tart shells (4 inch).

CORNMEAL PASTRY

1¾ cups cornmeal   1 tablespoon sugar
1 teaspoon baking powder   1 cup milk
1 teaspoon salt   3 tablespoons shortening, melted

Sift cornmeal, baking powder, salt and sugar together. Add milk and shortening and mix. Press half of the mixture into a well-buttered pie pan, distributing it as evenly as possible. Add any desired filling and cover with the cornmeal mixture, pressed into thin pieces, placed on top of the filling and joined together by pressing with the fingers. The filling must be relatively firm for a successful cornmeal top crust. This is excellent for meat pies. Yield: pastry for two-crust (9 inch) pie.

GRAHAM CRACKER PASTRY

20 graham crackers, crumbled   ¼ cup sugar
   (2 cups)   ½ cup butter
                 1 tablespoon water

Roll crackers very fine, stir in sugar and gradually add to softened butter, mixing thoroughly; stir in water. Press over bottom and sides of pie pan and bake in moderately slow oven (325° F.) about 10 minutes. Cool before adding cooked filling; use for any cream or gelatin filling. Yield: pastry for one-crust (9 inch) pie.

Graham Nut Pastry—Add ½ cup almonds, finely ground, to cracker-sugar mixture.

Zwieback Pastry—Substitute 1 package zwieback, finely ground, for graham cracker crumbs and omit water. Press into pie pan and use, without baking, for cream or gelatin pie.

Brazil Nut Pastry—Measure 1½ cups finely ground Brazil nuts and 3 tablespoons sugar. Mix well and press evenly over bottom and sides of pie pan. Use, without baking, for cream pie. Yield: pastry for one-crust (8 inch) pie.

Vanilla Wafer Pastry—Use only ¾ cup finely crushed vanilla wafers for crumbs and 7 whole vanilla wafers. Cover bottom of pie pan with crumbs and stand up whole wafers, cut in halves, around edge. Use, without baking, for cream or gelatin pie. Yield: pastry for 1 pie shell.

CHOCOLATE CRUMB CRUST

1 cup finely-crushed chocolate   2 tablespoons sugar
   crumbs   ¼ cup butter
1 tablespoon water

Crumble chocolate wafers to make crumbs and combine with sugar, butter and water. Press firmly ⅛-inch thick on bottom of 9-inch pie pan and fit whole wafers around edge in overlapping design. Yield: 1 9-inch bottom crust.

MERINGUE PASTRY

Beat 2 egg whites until frothy; add ¼ teaspoon each salt and cream of tartar. Beat until stiff but not dry. Gradually beat in ½ cup sugar and continue beating until meringue stands in stiff peaks when beater is lifted. Spread over bottom and sides, just to rim, of greased pie pan. Bake in slow oven (275° F.) 40 to 50 minutes. Yield: 1 8-inch shell.

PUFF PASTE

3½ cups sifted all-purpose   1 teaspoon salt
   flour   2 cups (1 pound) butter
1 to 1⅓ cups ice water

Sift together flour and salt and cut in ¼ cup butter until evenly mixed in coarse particles; add ice water in small amounts to dry material, stirring with fork and tossing aside pieces of dough as soon as formed; dough should be just moist enough to shape into ball; chill thoroughly. Cream remaining butter until soft and smooth and chill; divide dough in half and roll each into rectangular sheet ⅛-inch thick. Roll butter on lightly floured board into rectangular shape and place between two sheets of dough; press edges together. Fold opposite sides to make three folds, one over and the other underneath, and press edges together; fold other sides in same manner and chill about 1 hour. Pat dough straight with fold, then make quarter turn and pat again; roll in rectangular sheet, but do not permit butter to break through. Fold as directed; roll again in thin sheet, lifting paste to make sure that it does not stick to board; then fold and chill thoroughly. Repeat rolling, folding and chilling of dough three more times. If paste is not used at once, wrap in waxed paper and store in refrigerator; it may be kept several days before using. When ready to use, roll ¼- to ⅓-inch thick, cut as desired and place on baking sheet rinsed with cold water and drained thoroughly; prick shapes and chill. Bake in very hot oven (450° F.) about 8 minutes, or until paste has risen its full height; then reduce heat to moderate (350° F.) and bake 10 to 20 minutes, or until delicately browned. Yield: 2½ to 4 dozen fancy pastries.

Patty Cases—Roll paste about ¼-inch thick; cut in 3-inch rounds with lightly floured cutter. Cut out centers from ½ of rounds with small cutter; moisten underside of each ring with cold water and place on remaining plain rounds, pressing down lightly; then press in slightly the inside edge of ring to prevent uneven rising. Chill thoroughly. Bake small rounds for caps. Bake as directed. Yield: 18 patty cases.

Crescents—Roll paste about ⅓-inch thick; cut with floured small crescent-shaped cutter, chill and bake as directed. Use as garnish.

VERMONT BISCUIT PASTRY

Use recipe for Baking Powder Biscuits (page 149); prepare dough with ⅓ cup shortening, using half butter. Roll dough about ½-inch thick, cut with floured biscuit cutter and place rounds close together on stew; or cut several gashes in rolled dough to permit escape of steam, then fit on casserole and press dough on moistened rim. Bake in hot oven (450° F.) about 15 minutes. Yield: crust for 6 to 7 portions.

FRESH FRUIT PIE

3 to 4 cups prepared fruit
¾ to 1½ cups sugar
¼ teaspoon salt
2 tablespoons flour or 1 tablespoon cornstarch, potato

flour or quick-cooking tapioca
1 recipe Plain Pastry (page 736)
1 tablespoon butter
milk or cream

Combine fruit and dry ingredients, adjusting amounts of sugar and flour according to sweetness and juiciness of fresh fruit and mix thoroughly. Line pie pan with pastry, fill with fruit mixture and dot with butter; adjust top crust, or arrange lattice of pastry strips on top; brush with milk and bake in hot oven (425° F.) 40 to 50 minutes. For fruit, use blackberries, blueberries, elderberries, loganberries, raspberries, strawberries, cherries, grapes, peaches, plums, rhubarb, or a combination of fruits. If fruit is bland, add from 1 to 2 tablespoons lemon juice; and if fruit is dry, add water. Yield: two-crust (9 inch) pie.

CRANBERRY–RAISIN PIE

1 recipe Plain Pastry
   (page 736)
3 cups cranberries, cut in halves
1 cup raisins

¾ cup sugar
1 tablespoon flour
dash of salt
1 tablespoon butter

Line pie pan with pastry. Mix together fruits and dry ingredients and turn into pastry-lined pan; dot with butter and adjust top crust, or arrange lattice of pastry strips over top. Bake in hot oven (425° F.) 40 to 50 minutes. Yield: two-crust (9-inch) pie.

CANNED OR COOKED FRUIT PIE

3 cups drained, canned or cooked fruit	2 to 3 tablespoons flour, corn-starch, potato flour or
½ to ¾ cup juice	quick-cooking tapioca
½ to ¾ cup sugar	1 recipe Plain Pastry (page 736)
¼ teaspoon salt	1 tablespoon butter

Slice fruit if large fruit is used; add juice and combined dry ingredients, adjusting amounts of sugar and flour according to sweetness and juiciness of cooked fruit, and mix thoroughly. Line pie pan with pastry and fill with fruit mixture; dot with butter and adjust top crust, or arrange lattice of pastry strips on top. Bake in hot oven (425° F.) 40 to 50 minutes. For fruit, use apples, blackberries, blueberries, cherries, elderberries, gooseberries, peaches, pineapple, plums, raspberries and strawberries. Yield: two-crust (9 inch) pie.

Dried Fruit Pie—Wash dried fruit thoroughly in warm water, cover with hot water and soak about 2 hours; then simmer until fruit is plump and soft; sweeten to taste and use as cooked fruit. Use apples, apricots, prunes, peaches and raisins; combine apricots and prunes.

APPLE PIE

1 recipe Plain Pastry (page 736)	¼ teaspoon salt
6 to 8 tart apples	½ teaspoon cinnamon or nutmeg
¾ cup granulated or firmly packed brown sugar	½ teaspoon grated lemon rind
	1 tablespoon lemon juice
	2 tablespoons butter

Line 9-inch pie pan with pastry and fill with apples, pared and sliced thin; sprinkle with mixture of sugar, salt, spice and lemon rind, then with lemon juice and dot with butter. Moisten edge of crust, cover with top crust and press edges together; brush crust with milk or cream. Bake in hot oven (425° F.) 40 to 50 minutes. Yield: two-crust pie.

Apple Fruit Pie—Use 4 apples, diced, and add 1 cup each cranberries and raisins and ¼ cup water; cook until apples are tender. Add remaining ingredients and ¼ cup sugar, if not sweet enough.

Crab Apple Pie—Substitute 3 cups sliced, unpeeled crab apples for apples and omit cinnamon and lemon rind and juice. Add ⅓ cup raisins to sugar and sprinkle 1 teaspoon vanilla over top.

Black Walnut Apple Pie—Make Nut Pastry (page 737) with black walnuts. Use 3 cups sliced apples; substitute ½ cup honey for sugar and omit lemon rind and juice. Sprinkle cinnamon and 1 tablespoon water over top and dot with 1 tablespoon butter.

Applesauce Pie—Substitute 1 cup unsweetened applesauce for sliced apples; sweeten to taste and add salt, nutmeg and butter. Mix with custard mixture made from 2 eggs, well beaten, 2 cups milk and finely chopped rind of 1 lemon. Turn into pastry-lined pie pan and arrange lattice of pastry strips over top, or omit pastry strips, bake and top baked pie with sweetened whipped cream.

SPICED GOOSEBERRY PIE

3 cups gooseberries	½ teaspoon cinnamon
1½ cups sugar	½ teaspoon cloves
½ cup water	⅛ teaspoon nutmeg
2 tablespoons flour	1 recipe Plain Pastry (page 736)
dash of salt	1 tablespoon butter
marshmallows	

Cook gooseberries, 1 cup sugar and water until berries are tender. Combine remaining ½ cup sugar, flour, salt and spices; stir into cooked fruit and cool. Line 9-inch pie pan with pastry; fill with fruit mixture, dot with butter and arrange lattice of pastry strips on top. Bake in hot oven (425° F.) 30 to 40 minutes. When almost brown enough to serve, remove from oven, place a marshmallow in each diamond-shaped opening and return to oven to finish browning. Yield: two-crust (9-inch) pie.

RHUBARB LEMON PIE

1 recipe Plain Pastry (page 736)	1 tablespoon flour
3 cups diced rhubarb	1 egg, beaten
1 cup sugar	¾ teaspoon grated lemon rind
	1 tablespoon lemon juice
½ cup water	

Line pie pan with pastry and fill with diced rhubarb. Combine sugar and flour and stir in egg, lemon rind and juice and water; cook over boiling water until slightly thickened, pour over rhubarb and top with a lattice crust. Bake in hot oven (425° F.) 40 to 50 minutes. Yield: two-crust (9-inch) pie.

DEEP–DISH APPLE PIE

6 to 8 apples	⅛ teaspoon nutmeg
1 cup sugar	3 tablespoons water
½ teaspoon salt	2 tablespoons butter
½ teaspoon cinnamon	½ recipe Plain Pastry (page 736)

Pare, core and cut apples in thin slices; place in baking dish or deep pie pan and sprinkle with mixture of sugar, salt and spices. Pour water over filling and dot with butter; adjust pastry, rolled ⅛-inch thick, over top. Bake in hot oven (425° F.) 40 minutes, or until apples are tender. Yield: deep-dish (9-inch) pie.

Devonshire Pie—Use 1 quart raspberries and 1 pint red currants; combine 1 cup granulated sugar, 2 tablespoons flour and ⅛ teaspoon salt. Arrange fruits and sugar mixture in alternate layers, dot each with 1 tablespoon butter; cover with pastry. Bake as directed, reducing time to 30 minutes; cool. Just before serving, carefully lift off crust and cover with ⅓ cup heavy cream, whipped and sweetened with 2 tablespoons powdered sugar. Replace crust, dust with 1 tablespoon powdered sugar and serve at once. Yield: deep-dish (9 inch) pie.

Snow-topped Apple Pies—Place filling for Deep-dish Apple Pie in individual baking dishes, heaping fruit slightly in center. Cover each with crust and bake as directed, reducing time to about 30 minutes. Serve hot, topped with Frozen Cream Whip (page 808) or ice cream. Approximate yield: 6 individual pies.

MINCEMEAT

2 pounds lean beef	1 tablespoon salt
3 cups water	1 tablespoon cinnamon
1 pound suet	1 teaspoon allspice
4 pounds tart apples	1 teaspoon cloves
3 pounds seedless raisins	2 cups granulated sugar
1 pound currants	2 cups firmly packed brown sugar
1 cup diced candied orange peel	1 cup molasses
¼ pound citron, chopped	3 tablespoons lemon juice

1 pint cider or brandy

Use inexpensive cut of meat, or beef heart or fresh beef tongue; cut in small pieces, add water, bring to a boil and simmer, covered, 2 hours, or until tender; remove meat and measure 1½ cups stock. Put meat, suet, pared and cored apples through food chopper and place in large kettle; add raisins, currants, orange peel, citron, salt, spices, sugars, molasses and 1½ cups stock; simmer about 1 hour, stirring frequently to prevent burning; add lemon juice and cider the last 5 minutes of cooking. Cover closely and keep in cool place. Yield: 8 quarts.

HASTY MINCEMEAT

1 cup ground beef	1 tablespoon molasses
¼ cup chopped suet	1 teaspoon cinnamon
1½ cups chopped apples	½ teaspoon cloves
½ cup chopped raisins	½ teaspoon nutmeg
½ cup honey	½ teaspoon salt

Cook meat and suet in top of double boiler over hot water. Add remaining ingredients. Bring to boil over direct heat and simmer 5 minutes, stirring constantly. Allow to stand for an hour before using in mince pie. Approximate yield: 3 cups.

MINCE PIE

Use 3 cups mincemeat, prepared (see above) or commercial; moisten with leftover canned fruit juice, orange juice, cider or brandy if thick; add chopped apple, ½ cup raisins or currants if lacking in fruit and heat. Bake in hot oven (425° F.) 40 minutes. Yield: 1 two-crust (9-inch) pie. With commercial packaged mincemeat, follow directions for cooking given on package for best results.

CANDY APPLE PIE

2 large tart apples	1 cup sifted all-purpose flour
1 cup firmly packed brown sugar	¾ cup ground nuts
	½ cup butter
1 cup heavy cream, whipped	

Pare apples and cut in thin slices; arrange layer of sliced apples in bottom of greased baking dish, sprinkle with ½ cup brown sugar and add another layer of apples. Combine remaining ½ cup sugar, flour and ground nuts; gradually stir into butter, creamed until soft and smooth. Roll or pat out into shape the size of top of dish, then place over filling, press edges down and cut gashes to permit escape of steam. Bake in moderate oven (350° F.) about 1 hour. Serve warm with whipped cream. Yield: 6 portions.

PERSIMMON PIE

2 cups ripe persimmon pulp	1 tablespoon lemon juice
½ cup sugar	1 baked (8 inch) pastry shell
½ teaspoon cinnamon	1 cup heavy cream, whipped

Combine persimmon pulp, sugar, cinnamon and lemon juice and turn into baked pastry shell. Spread with whipped cream and serve at once. Yield: one-crust (8 inch) pie.

CUSTARD PIE

½ recipe Plain Pastry   ¼ teaspoon salt
   (page 736)   2 cups milk, hot or cold
4 eggs, well beaten   few gratings nutmeg, or
½ cup sugar   ½ teaspoon vanilla

Line 9-inch pie pan with pastry and make fluted standing rim. Combine eggs, sugar and salt; gradually stir in milk. Hot milk shortens the time for custard to form. Add flavoring. Pour into pastry-lined pie pan and bake in hot oven (450° F.) 10 minutes; then reduce heat to moderate (350° F.) and bake 25 to 30 minutes longer, or until knife inserted in side comes out clean. Cool. Yield: one-crust (9-inch) pie.

Custard Nut Pie—Increase sugar to 1 cup and add 1 cup finely ground nuts to custard mixture. On baking, nuts rise to top and make a delicious crust.

Coconut Custard Pie—Add 1 cup shredded coconut to custard.

Caramel Custard Pie—Increase sugar to ¾ cup; caramelize ½ cup of the sugar (page 730) and add to scalded milk.

Masquerade Custard Pie—Melt 2 squares unsweetened chocolate over slow heat; stir in ¼ cup each sugar and hot water, adding water in small amounts; cook until smooth. Pour over custard pie when just baked and continue baking in slow oven (300° F.) about 10 minutes. Garnish with cream, whipped and sweetened.

Maple Custard Pie—Use an 8-inch pie pan and substitute ¼ cup firmly packed maple sugar for sugar.

CRANBERRY CUSTARD PIE

½ recipe Plain Pastry   3 eggs, slightly beaten
   (page 736)   ¼ teaspoon salt
4 cups cranberries   dash of cinnamon
1½ cups sugar   1¼ cups milk, hot or cold

Line 9-inch pie pan with pastry. Put cranberries through food chopper, using finest knife; add 1¼ cups sugar and heat until sugar is dissolved, stirring constantly. Spread over bottom of pastry-lined pan. Combine eggs, remaining ¼ cup sugar, salt and cinnamon; gradually stir in milk. Pour custard mixture over cranberries and bake in hot oven (450° F.) 10 minutes; then reduce heat to moderate (350° F.) and bake 30 to 40 minutes longer. Yield: one-crust (9 inch) pie.

PUMPKIN OR SQUASH PIE

½ recipe Plain Pastry (page 736)
3 eggs, well beaten
1 cup sugar
1 teaspoon salt
½ teaspoon cinnamon
½ teaspoon nutmeg
½ teaspoon ginger
¼ teaspoon cloves
2 cups milk, hot or cold
2 cups strained cooked pumpkin or squash

Line 9-inch pie pan with pastry and make fluted standing rim. Combine eggs, sugar, salt and spices; gradually stir in milk, then pumpkin. Turn into pastry-lined pan and cake in hot oven (450° F.) 10 minutes; then reduce heat to moderate (350° F.) and bake 20 to 25 minutes longer, or until firm. Yield: one-crust (9 inch) pie.

Rich Pumpkin Pie—Substitute firmly packed brown for granulated sugar, reduce milk to 1½ cups and add ½ cup light cream.

Peanut Pumpkin Pie—Turn pumpkin mixture into pastry-lined pie pan, sprinkle ¼ cup finely chopped peanuts over top.

Pumpkin Nut Pie—Stir ½ cup grated coconut and ¼ cup finely chopped nuts into pumpkin mixture; sprinkle top with coconut.

STINA'S SPECIAL HOLIDAY PUMPKIN PIE

2 cups cooked, strained pumpkin
½ cup brown sugar
2 eggs, slightly beaten
½ teaspoon salt
1¼ cups light cream or evaporated milk
¼ cup molasses
2 tablespoons melted butter
3 tablespoons brandy or rye whiskey
1 teaspoon ginger
1 teaspoon cinnamon
¼ teaspoon nutmeg
1 cup chopped black walnuts
1 unbaked 10-inch pie shell
1 cup heavy cream, whipped

Combine pumpkin, brown sugar, eggs, salt, cream or milk, molasses, butter, brandy or rye, spices and nuts. Pour into pie shell. Bake in hot oven (400° F.) 10 minutes; reduce heat to moderate (350° F.) and bake 45 minutes, or until firm and knife inserted in center comes out clean. Cool and top with whipped cream flavored with few drops of almond and sprinkled with cinnamon and sugar. Yield: one-crust (10-inch) pie.

ALABAMA SWEET POTATO PIE

½ recipe Plain Pastry (page
736)
1½ cups mashed hot sweet
potatoes
3 eggs, slightly beaten
⅓ cup firmly packed brown
sugar

½ teaspoon salt
¼ teaspoon cinnamon
¼ teaspoon ginger
¼ teaspoon allspice
½ cup milk
¼ cup brandy
2 tablespoon butter, melted

Prepare pastry, using amounts for smaller recipe; line 8-inch pie pan with pastry. Mix together ingredients in order given; turn into prepared pie pan and bake in hot oven (450° F.) 10 minutes; then reduce heat to moderate (350° F.) and bake 25 to 35 minutes longer, or until knife inserted comes out clean. Yield: one-crust (8 inch) pie.

SOUR CREAM RAISIN PIE

½ recipe Plain Pastry (page
736)
2 eggs
1 cup sugar
1 cup sour cream

1 tablespoon flour
⅛ teaspoon salt
½ teaspoon nutmeg
½ teaspoon cinnamon
1 cup chopped raisins
½ cup chopped nuts

Line 9-inch pie pan with pastry. Beat together eggs and sugar; gradually stir in sour cream. Mix together flour, salt and spices; stir into raisins and nuts. Add to egg-cream mixture and turn into pastry-lined pan. Bake in hot oven (450° F.) 10 minutes; then reduce heat to moderate (350° F.) and bake 30 minutes. Yield: one-crust pie.

CALLIE'S PECAN PIE

3 whole eggs
2 tablespoons melted butter or
margarine
2 tablespoons flour
¼ teaspoon vanilla

⅛ teaspoon salt
½ cup sugar
1½ cups dark corn syrup
1½ cups broken pecan halves
1 unbaked (9-inch) pastry shell

Beat eggs; blend in melted butter, vanilla, salt, sugar and syrup. Sprinkle nuts over bottom of unbaked pie shell. Now gently pour over syrup mixture and bake in a hot oven (425° F.) 10 minutes. Reduce heat to slow (325° F.) and bake about 40 minutes. Yield: one 9-inch pie to serve eight.

LEEK AND COTTAGE CHEESE PIE

2 cups all-purpose flour   ¼ cup butter
2 teaspoons salt   ¼ cup milk
¾ cup warm water   2 eggs, beaten
½ cup oil (about)   ½ pound cottage cheese
4 large or 6 small leeks, sliced   ½ teaspoon black pepper

Make a dough of flour, 1 teaspoon salt and water. Roll and stretch
dough on floured board to a thin sheet. Sprinkle well with oil. Cut
into 12 squares. Make two piles of dough, 4 squares in one, 8 in the
other. Roll and stretch each pile into a thin sheet. Oil a 10-inch square
shallow baking pan and line with the large piece of dough. Sauté leeks
in butter 4 minutes. Add milk and simmer, covered, 5 minutes. Combine eggs, cheese, 1 teaspoon salt and pepper and add to leeks. Spread in
pan. Cover with remaining sheet of dough and sprinkle well with oil.
Bake in hot oven (400° F.) 30 minutes. Lower heat to 325° F. and bake
10 minutes longer. Serve with yogurt or buttermilk. Approximate
yield: 9 3-inch squares.

SOUR CREAM PIE

1 cup sugar   1 cup seedless raisins
½ teaspoon cinnamon   1 cup sour cream
½ teaspoon cloves   pinch of salt
2 eggs, beaten   2 tablespoons vinegar
            1 baked (9-inch) pastry shell

Mix all ingredients, stirring until the sugar is dissolved. Pour into
baked pie shell and bake in moderate oven (350° F.) 25 to 30 minutes.
Yield: 8 portions.

PINEAPPLE CHEESE PIE

1 cup cottage cheese   ¾ cup milk
1 cup sugar   1 teaspoon vanilla
¼ cup butter or margarine   1 No. 2 can crushed pineapple
½ cup flour   2 tablespoons cornstarch
2 eggs   1 unbaked (9-inch) pastry shell

Combine cheese and sugar; then add the soft butter. When well
mixed, add the flour and stir until thoroughly blended. Add eggs, one
at a time, stirring well after each addition. Slowly add the milk and
vanilla. Heat pineapple, add cornstarch mixed to a thin paste with a
little cold water and bring to a boil, stirring constantly. Cool; turn into
an unbaked pastry shell. Pour on the cheese mixture. Bake in a hot
oven (450° F.) 10 minutes; reduce heat to moderate (350° F.) and
bake 30 minutes, or until firm. Yield: one-crust (9-inch) pie.

CREAM PIE

1 cup sugar
½ cup flour or 4 tablespoons
cornstarch
½ teaspoon salt

2 cups milk, scalded
3 eggs, separated
2 tablespoons butter
1 teaspoon vanilla

1 baked (9-inch) pastry shell

Mix together ⅔ cup sugar, flour and salt; gradually stir in milk and cook over boiling water 10 minutes, stirring constantly until mixture thickens. Stir small amount into slightly beaten egg yolks; then gradually pour into thickened milk and cook about 2 minutes, stirring constantly. Add butter and vanilla and cool slightly; turn into baked pastry shell. Cover with meringue made by gradually beating remaining ⅓ cup sugar into stiffly beaten egg whites. Bake in moderately hot oven (400° F.) 5 to 8 minutes, or until delicately browned; chill. If made with 2 eggs, use ¾ cup sugar. If desired, omit meringue and serve with whipped cream, sweetened. Yield: one-crust (9-inch) pie.

Coconut Cream Pie—Stir ½ cup shredded coconut into cream filling; cover with meringue and sprinkle with ½ cup coconut.

Chocolate Cream Pie—Add 2 squares unsweetened chocolate to milk and heat until chocolate is melted; then beat until smooth; reduce flour to 5 tablespoons or cornstarch to 2½ tablespoons and proceed as for Cream Pie.

Chocolate Sponge Pie—Prepare Chocolate Cream Pie, folding meringue into cream filling. Bake as directed. Chill. Serve with sweetened whipped cream, using ½ cup heavy cream.

Butterscotch Cream Pie—Substitute firmly packed brown for granulated sugar and increase butter to 3 tablespoons.

Raspberry Cream Pie—Lightly stir 1 cup raspberries into cream filling before turning into baked shell; cover with meringue, brown.

Strawberry Cream Pie—Use 2 egg yolks in cream filling; turn into baked pie shell and arrange 1 cup strawberries, whole or halved, on filling. Cover with meringue made by beating 2 egg whites with ½ cup sugar, then folding in 1 cup strawberries. Chill in refrigerator.

SECRETS OF MERINGUE

Secrets of meringues are as follows:

1. Eggs will separate better if chilled, but will whip to a greater volume if the whites are at room temperature. So separate the eggs,

return the yolks to the refrigerator and let the whites stand about 30 minutes in the kitchen.
2. Whip to just the right amount of stiffness. Add a pinch of salt for each white of egg. Beat until the foam is relatively fine and forms rounded peaks when the beater is lifted from the bowl. Then add the sugar gradually, 2 tablespoons for each white of egg. Continue beating until the meringue is stiff but not dry.
3. Immediately place the meringue on a hot pie filling. There is less "weeping" as a result, than if spread over a cooled pie.
4. Bake at 425° F. for 4 to 4½ minutes. This causes less leaking than when baked at 350° F. Beading results from too long cooking.

MERINGUE TOPPING FOR PIES

2 egg whites
pinch of salt
¼ teaspoon cream of tartar
¼ cup sugar

Sprinkle egg whites with salt and cream of tartar. Beat until foamy and round peaks are formed when beater is lifted. Gradually add sugar, beating constantly until meringue is stiff but not dry. Spread with a spatula over hot pie fillings, being careful to touch crust around the edge of the pie. Bake in a hot oven (425° F.) 4 to 4½ minutes. Yield: topping for one 9-inch pie.

LEMON MERINGUE PIE

1⅞ cups sugar
2 tablespoons cornstarch
¼ cup cake flour
¼ teaspoon salt
2 cups boiling water
3 eggs, separated
2 teaspoons grated lemon rind
6 tablespoons lemon juice
2 tablespoons butter
1 baked (9-inch) pastry shell

Combine 1½ cups sugar, cornstarch, flour and salt; gradually stir in boiling water and cook 15 minutes, stirring constantly until mixture thickens, then occasionally. Mix together slightly beaten egg yolks, lemon rind and juice; add to thickened sugar-water mixture and cook 2 minutes, stirring constantly. Add butter. When slightly cool, turn into baked pastry shell and cover with meringue made by gradually beating remaining 6 tablespoons sugar into stiffly beaten egg whites. Bake in moderately hot oven (400° F.) 5–8 minutes. Yield: one-crust pie.

FLUFFY LEMON PIE

4 eggs, separated
1 cup sugar
1 tablespoon cornstarch
⅛ teaspoon salt

1 tablespoon water
2 teaspoons grated lemon rind
5 tablespoons lemon juice
1 baked (9-inch) pastry shell

Combine slightly beaten egg yolks, ½ cup sugar, cornstarch, salt, water, lemon rind and juice; cook over boiling water 15 minutes, stirring constantly until thick. Fold into meringue made by gradually beating remaining ½ cup sugar into stiffly beaten egg whites. Turn into baked pastry shell and bake in moderately hot oven (450° F.) about 5–8 minutes, or until delicately browned. Yield: one-crust (9-inch) pie.

MAGIC LEMON PIE

1 cup graham cracker crumbs
1½ cups sweetened condensed milk
½ cup lemon juice

1 tablespoon grated lemon rind
2 egg yolks
¼ cup cold water
2 egg whites
2 tablespoons sugar

Line an 8-inch greased pie pan with a mixture of graham cracker crumbs and ¼ cup sweetened condensed milk, packing well into place. Blend remaining condensed milk, lemon juice, grated lemon rind and egg yolks. Add cold water to egg whites and beat until stiff, adding sugar gradually. Pour lemon mixture into pie shell. Force stiffly beaten egg white through pastry bag with fancy tube. Pile meringue on top and bake in slow oven (325° F.) until brown. Chill well. Yield: 8 portions.

RAISIN EGGNOG PIE

1 cup seedless raisins
5 eggs
⅛ teaspoon salt
¾ cup sugar

3 tablespoons flour
1½ cups milk
1½ teaspoons plain gelatin
½ teaspoon nutmeg
1 baked (9-inch) pastry shell

Cover raisins with boiling water and allow to stand 5 minutes. Drain. Beat 3 egg yolks with 2 whole eggs, then beat in the combined salt, sugar and flour. Scald milk, add to egg mixture and cook over hot water until thickened. Stir in gelatin which has been softened in 2 tablespoons cold water, add raisins. Cool. Add nutmeg and fold in remaining egg whites, stiffly beaten. Turn into shell and chill.

NESSELRODE PIE

3 eggs, separated
1½ cups milk
¼ teaspoon salt
⅔ cup sugar
2 teaspoons plain gelatin
1 tablespoon cold water

2 tablespoons rum flavoring
¼ cup maraschino cherries,
  chopped
1 baked (9-inch) pastry shell
2 tablespoons sweet chocolate,
  shaved

Combine slightly beaten egg yolks, milk, salt and ⅓ cup sugar in top of double boiler. Cook over hot, not boiling, water until mixture thickens, stirring constantly; remove from hot water. Soften gelatin in cold water, add to hot mixture; stir until dissolved. Chill until mixture begins to thicken. Beat egg whites stiff but not dry; gradually beat in remaining sugar. Fold into gelatin mixture with rum flavoring and cherries. Pile into baked pastry shell, sprinkle with chocolate, chill until firm. Yield: one-crust (9 inch) pie.

MAGIC BLACKBERRY PIE

1 recipe Vanilla Wafer Pastry
  (page 740)
1 cup sweetened condensed milk
¼ cup lemon juice

1 cup blackberries
½ cup heavy cream, whipped
2 tablespoons powdered sugar
1 teaspoon vanilla

Prepare 8-inch pie pan with Vanilla Wafer Pastry. Combine condensed milk and lemon juice; add blackberries and turn mixture into prepared pie pan. Top with whipped cream, sweetened and flavored.

RASPBERRY CHIFFON PIE

1 envelope plain gelatin
¼ cup raspberry juice
1½ cups heavy cream
½ cup milk
¾ cup sugar
¼ teaspoon salt
2 teaspoons lemon juice

3 egg whites
pinch of cream of tartar
1 cup raspberries, fresh or
  drained frozen
1 cup chopped walnuts
Chocolate Crumb Crust
  (page 741)

Soften gelatin in raspberry juice 5 minutes. Dissolve over hot water. Combine cream, milk, sugar, salt and lemon juice. Blend in dissolved gelatin. Chill until slightly thickened. Fold in raspberries and walnuts. Beat egg whites with cream of tartar until stiff but not dry. Fold into fruit mixture. Pour into 9-inch pie pan lined with Chocolate Crumb Crust and chill. Approximate yield: 6 portions.

LEMON CHIFFON PIE

1 envelope plain gelatin
1/4 cup water
4 eggs, separated
1 cup sugar
1/2 teaspoon salt

1 1/2 teaspoons grated lemon rind
6 tablespoons lemon juice
1 baked (9-inch) pastry or Cream
    Cheese Pastry (page 737)
    shell

1 cup heavy cream, whipped

Soften gelatin in 2 tablespoons water. Combine slightly beaten egg yolks, 1/2 cup sugar, salt, lemon rind and juice and remaining 2 tablespoons water; cook over boiling water until mixture thickens, stirring constantly. Add softened gelatin, stirring until gelatin is dissolved; cool until mixture begins to thicken. Then gradually beat remaining 1/2 cup sugar into stiffly beaten egg whites and fold into lemon-gelatin mixture. Turn into baked pastry shell and chill until firm. When ready to serve, top with whipped cream. Yield: one-crust (9 inch) pie.

Lime Chiffon Pie—Substitute 1 teaspoon grated lime rind for lemon rind and 1/3 cup lime juice for lemon juice; add a few drops of Angostura bitters, if desired.

Pineapple Chiffon Pie—Reduce water to 2 tablespoons and sugar to 3/4 cup; use 3/4 cup drained, cooked, crushed pineapple, 1/4 cup pineapple juice and 1 tablespoon lemon juice for fruit and juice, and omit grated lemon rind.

STRAWBERRY CHIFFON PIE

1 envelope plain gelatin
1/4 cup cold water
1/2 cup boiling water
1 cup sugar

1 cup strawberry pulp, juice
1/4 teaspoon salt
2 egg whites
1/2 cup heavy cream, whipped

1 baked (8-inch) pastry shell

Soak gelatin in cold water 5 minutes. Add boiling water and stir until dissolved. Add 3/4 cup sugar, strawberry pulp and salt. Chill. When mixture begins to thicken, add egg whites beaten with remaining 1/4 cup sugar. Fold in whipped cream. Pour into baked pastry shell and chill. To serve, garnish with whipped cream and strawberries. Yield: one-crust (8 inch) pie.

SPICED CAKE TARTLETS

1 recipe Plain Pastry (page 736)   ½ cup raisins
½ cup currant jelly   ¼ cup minced citron
2 cups sifted cake flour   ⅔ cup shortening
¾ teaspoon baking soda   ¾ cup sugar
¼ teaspoon salt   2 eggs, well beaten
1 teaspoon cinnamon   ⅔ cup molasses
½ teaspoon cloves   ⅔ cup milk

Line medium-sized muffin pans with pastry; put 1½ teaspoons jelly in each. Mix and sift flour, soda, salt and spices; stir in raisins and citron. Cream shortening until soft, add sugar gradually, creaming thoroughly. Beat in eggs, then molasses. Stir in flour-fruit mixture alternately with milk; turn into prepared muffin pans, filling them ¾ full. Bake in hot oven (425° F.) 5 minutes; then reduce heat to moderate (375° F.) and bake about 15 minutes longer. Approximate yield: 15 tartlets.

FAVORITE RAISIN TARTLETS

1 recipe Plain Pastry (page 736)   3 tablespoons lemon juice
1 pound raisins   ¼ cup firmly packed
10 walnut halves   brown sugar

Prepare pastry, using amounts for smaller recipe; line tiny muffin pans with pastry. Put raisins and nuts through food chopper, using medium blade. Moisten with lemon juice and stir in ½ of brown sugar. Turn into pastry-lined muffin pans; sprinkle with remaining brown sugar. Bake in hot oven (425° F.) 15 to 20 minutes. Yield: 20 tartlets.

CHOCOLATE TARTS

2 squares unsweetened   ½ cup hot water
  chocolate   4 baked (4 inch) tart shells
1⅓ cups (1 can) sweetened   ½ cup heavy cream, whipped
  condensed milk   1 tablespoon powdered sugar

Melt chocolate over hot water, add condensed milk and cook 5 minutes, or until mixture thickens, stirring constantly. Then stir in hot water. Turn into baked tart shells; cool. Garnish with sweetened whipped cream. Chocolate may be grated over top, if desired. Yield: 4 tarts.

PEACH LINZER TARTLETS

1 cup sweet butter, softened	2 small egg yolks
½ cup sugar	2 teaspoons water
	3 cups all-purpose flour

Place butter and sugar in a mixing bowl and cream with the back of a wooden spoon. Add egg yolks and water and continue blending. Form a well of the mixture in the bowl and add the flour all at once. Pat very gently to form a soft dough; shape into a ball. Do not overwork as this toughens the pastry. Refrigerate wrapped in waxed paper for 1 hour. Roll out on lightly floured board ⅛-inch thick. Prick with tines of fork. Cut into 4-inch circles and place in small tart pans. Place squares of waxed paper in tart shell and weight with rice to prevent pastry bubbles. Bake 12 to 15 minutes, or until delicate brown, at 375° F. These tart shells will keep fresh and tender for several days if kept in a tightly covered container. The dough may be refrigerated or the shells frozen for long keeping.

To serve, fill with a custard cream and place on top a peach half that has been peeled and simmered in a sugar syrup until tender. (Make syrup by boiling 1 cup sugar with 1 cup water.) Cool peach and top with raspberry or strawberry jelly melted with 1 teaspoon water over heat. Garnish with whipped cream. Any other fruit may be substituted, such as apples, canned peaches, apricots or pears. Yield: pastry for 16 tarts.

BANBURY TARTLETS

1 recipe Plain Pastry (page 736)	1½ teaspoons grated lemon rind
1 cup chopped raisins	3 tablespoons lemon juice
1 cup sugar	1 egg, slightly beaten
	1 tablespoon cracker crumbs

Roll pastry ⅛-inch thick; cut in 4-inch squares. Combine ingredients in order given; place scant tablespoon on half of each pastry square. Wet edges with cold water and fold over to form triangle or rectangle, or turn up to form tricorn; press edges together with floured fork, prick top and chill. Bake in hot oven (450° F.) about 15 minutes. Approximate yield: 1½ dozen tartlets.

Cherry Turnovers—For filling, mix together 2 cups drained, pitted sour cherries, fresh or canned, ½ cup sugar, 2 tablespoons quick-cooking tapioca and 1 cup diced marshmallows. Roll pastry ¼-inch thick and proceed as directed.

Currant and Honey Turnovers—For filling, cook 1 cup dried currants in water to cover until plump and water is practically evaporated; mix with ⅓ cup sugar and 1 tablespoon each lemon juice, honey and butter. Roll pastry ¼-inch thick, cut in 4-inch rounds and proceed as directed. Approximate yield: 8 tartlets.

APRICOT RUM TARTS

1 recipe Spiced Pastry (page 739)
⅓ cup firmly packed brown sugar
2 tablespoons cornstarch
1⅛ cups apricot juice
2 tablespoons butter
12 canned apricot halves
2 3-oz. packages cream cheese
1 teaspoon rum flavoring
1 teaspoon milk
1 cup heavy cream, whipped

Use apricot juice for pastry. Line large muffin pans with pastry, flute edges and perforate shells with fork. Bake in hot oven (450° F.) about 15 minutes; remove from pans and cool. Combine sugar and cornstarch; gradually stir in apricot juice and add butter. Bring to a boil and cook 15 minutes, stirring constantly until mixture thickens. Add apricots and chill. Beat cream cheese until smooth, adding flavoring and milk; place about 2 tablespoons in each tart shell. Fill with fruit mixture and top with whipped cream. Yield: 12 tarts.

MINCEMEAT WHIRLS

1 recipe Baking Powder Biscuits (page 149)
2 cups mincemeat
¾ cup corn syrup
¾ cup water
cream

Roll biscuit dough in rectangular piece, ¼-inch thick; spread with mincemeat and roll as for jelly roll. Slice 1-inch thick and place flat in greased baking pan, and pour mixture of syrup and water in pan; bake in hot oven (425° F.) about 20 minutes; cool. Serve with plain or whipped cream. Approximate yield: 6 portions.

PEAR TURNOVERS

1 recipe Cream Cheese Pastry (page 737)
3 tablespoons butter
18 halves canned or cooked pears
6 tablespoons brown sugar

Roll pastry ⅛-inch thick; cut in 4-inch squares. Place pear half on half of each pastry square and fill hollow with 1 teaspoon brown sugar and ½ teaspoon butter; fold over to form triangle. Press edges together with floured fork, prick top and chill. Bake in hot oven (425° F.) 15 to 20 minutes. Yield: 1½ dozen turnovers.

TRANSPARENT TARTLETS

1 recipe Plain Pastry (page 736)	2 cups sugar
½ cup butter	5 eggs
	3 tablespoons lemon juice

Line medium-sized muffin pans with pastry. Cream together butter and sugar, then beat in one egg at a time. Stir in lemon juice. Turn into prepared pans and bake in hot oven (400° F.) 5 minutes; then reduce heat to moderate (350° F.) and bake about 10 minutes longer, or until firm. Approximate yield: 15 tartlets.

CREAM PUFF SHELLS

1 cup water	⅛ teaspoon salt
½ cup butter	1 cup sifted all-purpose flour
	4 eggs

Place water, butter and salt in heavy saucepan and heat; when boiling briskly, add flour all at once, stirring vigorously with a wooden spoon. Beat until mixture forms a smooth ball which leaves sides of pan clean, stirring constantly. Cool slightly. Beat in thoroughly 1 egg at a time; then continue beating until mixture is thick, smooth and glossy, and breaks off when spoon is raised. Shape at once, or wrap dough in waxed paper and store in refrigerator several hours or overnight before using. With pastry bag or 2 tablespoons, shape on greased baking sheet, putting shapes 2 inches apart to allow for spreading: for cream puff shells, make large rounds; for éclair shells, make 1 x 4½-inch strips; for miniature puff shells, make small designs such as 1-inch rounds, ½ x 1¼-inch oblongs, the letter "S," scallops, rings, crescents, stars and triangles. Bake large puff shells in very hot oven (450° F.) 15 minutes, then reduce heat to moderate (350° F.) and bake 20 to 25 minutes longer; bake miniature puff shells about one-half the time. Cut slit in side of each shell and fill as desired; sprinkle tops with powdered sugar, cover with frosting, or serve with a sauce. Yield: 1 dozen large puff shells, or 4 dozen miniature puff shells.

Cream Puffs—Fill round shells with Cream Filling (page 720), or one of the modifications (page 720), ice cream, whipped cream mixture or sweetened fresh fruit; sprinkle tops with confectioners' sugar, or top with whipped cream or a sauce.

Éclairs—Fill large oblong shells with Cream Filling (page 720) or one of the modifications; cover tops with Chocolate Butter Frosting (page 709) or Mocha Frosting (page 709).

Russian Puffs—Fill miniature puff shells with caviar or a Butter Spread (page 200). Use for cocktail or tea service.

Tea Puffs—Fill miniature puff shells with flavored whipped cream, Cream Filling (½ recipe, page 720), jelly or jam; cover with Chocolate Butter Cream or Butter Frosting (page 709).

FRIED PRUNE TURNOVERS

1 recipe Baking Powder Biscuits   2½ cups chopped cooked prunes
    (page 149)   ½ cup chopped nuts
                    1 tablespoon lemon juice

Roll biscuit dough ¼-inch thick; cut in rectangular pieces 4 x 2 inches. Mix together remaining ingredients; place 1 tablespoon filling on half of each piece, fold over and press edges together with floured fork. Fry in hot deep fat (375° F.) about 3 minutes, or until lightly browned. Cut rolled dough in squares or rounds as desired. Yield: 8 tartlets.

Fried Fruit Turnovers—Use 2 cups applesauce or other fruit sauce for filling. The sauce should be rather thick.

Fried Mincemeat Tartlets—Use 2 cups mincemeat for filling.

Fried Jelly Tartlets—Use tart jelly or jam, slightly beaten, for filling.

Fried Fruit-Nut Tartlets—Use Fruit-Nut Filling, page 722.

TIMBALE CASES AND ROSETTES

TIMBALE cases and rosettes are those fragile, deep-fried pastry cups which hold a mouthful of sweet or savory filling for garnishing a main dish, salad or dessert; or the rosettes can be dusted with confectioners' sugar and used as cookie confections.

ROSETTES OR "ROSETBAKKELS"

Use recipe for Timbale Cases (see above) adding 1 tablespoon sugar to batter; use rosette iron, being careful not to let batter come up over edge of iron. Use in same way as patties with whipped cream flavored with raspberry or other jams, or other creamy desserts. Or dust with confectioners' sugar before serving on a cookie plate. Store plain rosettes in tight container in dry place; if they soften, crisp by placing in moderate oven (350° F.) about 5 minutes. Yield: 40 rosettes.

TIMBALE CASES

1 cup sifted all-purpose flour   2 eggs, slightly beaten
½ teaspoon salt   ⅞ to 1 cup milk
1 tablespoon salad oil

Sift together dry ingredients, gradually stir in mixture of eggs, milk and oil, beating only until smooth; strain and let stand an hour if full of air bubbles; when ready to use, pour small amount into large cup for dipping. Set iron in deep fat and heat to 360° to 370° F., or until a cube of bread browns in 1 minute. Drain iron slightly on unglazed paper and dip into cup, covering only the sides of iron to about one-eighth inch of top. Lower into hot fat and fry 1 to 1½ minutes, or until delicately browned; remove from fat, loosen case from iron with a fork and drain on unglazed paper, inverting to drain inside; if fat is too hot or too cold, batter will not cling to iron. Repeat, adding batter to cup as needed. Timbale irons come in various shapes which can be used for vegetables, creamed entrées and desserts. Use a small flat-bottomed saucepan or kettle for frying to conserve fat. Approximate yield: 40 cases.

Desserts

It ISN'T just the children in the family who wait with great anticipation for dessert at mealtime. Grownups, too, have a sweet tooth and enjoy a mouth-watering dessert attractively served. The type of meal served usually determines the dessert; a substantial meal calls for a light dessert—perhaps fresh fruit and cheese—while a rich dessert is welcomed after a less hearty main course.

The right sauce for steamed or baked puddings, delicate garnishes for fluffy desserts, and interesting texture and color contrasts in fruit desserts add greatly to your success as a meal planner.

FRUIT BOWL

Fruits in season, washed, dried and thoroughly chilled, are always suitable. Fruit may be served on individual plates with fruit knife, fork or spoon. A finger bowl at each service will add to the comfort of guests and protect linen from stubborn fruit stains; or use a paper napkin at each place for simple family service.

FRUIT SUGGESTIONS

Strawberries marinated in rum, sprinkled with confectioners' sugar, served in coupé glasses, garnished with a soft meringue.

Strawberries marinated in Benedictine are served with sponge cake or lady fingers, topped with vanilla ice cream and black cherries. Various fruits—peaches, nectarines, pears and plums—marinated in rum or brandy may be substituted. These may be served flaming.

Fruits in tidbits, combined with pineapple or lemon sherbet and frozen rather soft, are delicious for hot summer days.

762

AMBROSIA

4 cups orange sections   milk from coconut
1 fresh coconut   sugar

Cut oranges into pieces, removing tough parts. Grate coconut and add
to oranges with the milk; add sugar to taste and mix lightly. Cover
and place in refrigerator until chilled. Approximate yield: 12 portions.

KUMQUAT SNOW

1 cup sliced kumquats   2 eggs, separated
1 cup orange juice   pinch of salt
4 tablespoons sugar   3 tablespoons orange marmalade

Separate skin and pulp of kumquats. Press juice from pulp into
orange juice. Cut skins into thin rings. Combine juice, 2 tablespoons
of sugar and slightly beaten egg yolks in top of double boiler and
cook until mixture coats the spoon, stirring constantly. Pour custard
over kumquat rings and chill. Gradually beat remaining sugar into
stiffly beaten egg whites; fold in marmalade and pour meringue in top
of double boiler. Cover and cook over simmering water 20 minutes.
Serve hot with chilled kumquat custard. Approximate yield: 4 portions.

RASPBERRY MIST

18 macaroons   ¾ pound white grapes
½ cup blanched almonds   1½ cups heavy cream
              3 cups raspberries

Put macaroons and almonds through food chopper together. Crush
white grapes through a potato ricer and pour juice over macaroons
and almonds. Whip ¾ cup cream until it begins to thicken and holds
its shape. Fold into macaroon mixture. Arrange in 6 sherbet glasses.
Cover with raspberries which have been crushed. Chill and serve with
remaining cream, whipped. Approximate yield: 6 portions.

COCOA PEARS

Peel the fresh ripe pears and sprinkle with citrus fruit or pineapple
juice to prevent them from turning brown. Hollow out the center
core neatly, using a teaspoon. Fill each pear half with a teaspoon of
cocoa and fasten together the two halves with toothpicks. Chill overnight. Serve with a Custard Sauce (see page 729) flavored with brandy.

PEACH CREAM DESSERT

6 slices sponge cake
1 cup heavy cream, whipped
1 tablespoon powdered sugar
½ teaspoon almond flavoring
6 canned peach halves, drained
¼ cup currant jelly

Cut sponge cake into slices; spread with cream, sweetened and flavored; top with peach half, and fill center of peach with jelly. Top with whipped cream. Yield: 6 portions.

PINEAPPLE DESSERT

1 cup diced fresh pineapple
2 cups hulled strawberries
8 marshmallows, cut in quarters
½ cup sugar

Combine ingredients; add more sugar, if desired, and chill. Approximate yield: 6 portions.

LEMON-PIE DESSERT

5 tablespoons cornstarch
pinch of salt
1 cup sugar
3 eggs, separated
1 cup boiling water
6 tablespoons lemon juice
1 tablespoon grated lemon rind
1 tablespoon butter or margarine
1 cup heavy cream, whipped

Combine cornstarch with salt and sugar. Beat egg yolks and add dry ingredients. Pour in boiling water, add lemon juice and rind and butter or margarine. Cook over slow heat, stirring constantly until thick and smooth. Fold in stiffly beaten egg whites. Cool; fold in whipped cream. Pour into mold lined with split ladyfingers. Chill overnight. Serve with whipped cream. Yield: 6 portions.

PEAR COMPOTE

1½ cups sugar
¾ cup water
3 tablespoons lemon juice
½ cup orange juice
1½ teaspoons grated lemon rind
1 tablespoon grated orange rind
2 teaspoons minced preserved ginger
12 canned pear halves

Heat sugar, water, fruit juices, grated rinds and ginger to boiling point; add pears and simmer 8 to 10 minutes. Chill. Yield: 6 portions.

BRAZILIAN COMPOTE

2 large raw sweet potatoes
1½ cups water
½ cup sugar
¼ cup honey

1 thinly sliced small lemon
½ stick cinnamon
3 tablespoons rum
1 No. 2 can pitted black cherries

Peel potatoes and cut in halves lengthwise. Scoop out centers, leaving a wall ½-inch thick. Combine water, sugar, honey, lemon and cinnamon in saucepan. Add potatoes. Bring to boiling and simmer until potatoes are tender. Add rum and simmer 5 minutes. Put potatoes on serving dish and spoon syrup into and over them. Chill, fill cavity with cherries and serve. Yield: 4 portions.

BAKED PEARS, GINGER SAUCE

6 large pears
⅓ cup sugar

3 tablespoons candied ginger
3 tablespoons ginger syrup

3 tablespoons water

Pare and core pears and cut into halves. Place them in a baking dish and fill center of each with sugar and finely cut candied ginger. Combine ginger syrup and water; add to pears and bake, covered, in moderate oven (350° F.) about 20 minutes, or until pears are tender. If necessary, add a little more water. Yield: 6 portions.

MERINGUE BUBBLES

3 egg whites
¼ teaspoon cream of tartar
pinch of salt
½ cup sugar

1 teaspoon almond extract
5 brandied whole peaches
¼ cup shredded coconut
½ cup toasted almonds

Beat egg whites until frothy. Add cream of tartar and salt. Beat until stiff but not dry. Gradually add sugar, one tablespoon at a time sprinkled over surface of egg whites, and beat well after each addition. Add extract and continue beating until stiff and peaked. Drain peaches thoroughly and remove stones. Refill with coconut. Grease a shallow baking pan and cut brown paper to fit. Place paper on greased pan and lightly butter the paper. Place 5 spoonfuls of meringue 2 inches apart on paper. Place one peach on each. Cover peach completely with remaining meringue. Insert almonds into meringue at right angles. Bake in a slow oven (325° F.) until golden brown. Yield: 5 portions.

DESSERT CHEESE TRAY

Crackers and cheese are appropriate to serve as a dessert. "Hostess" cheese trays or individual plates may be used. Provide two or more varieties of dessert cheeses (see suggestions below). On a large tray arrange the cheeses in the center with a suitable cheese knife for cutting and a cheese server. Arrange crisp, unsweetened crackers around the cheese. The tray may be passed at the table; or the hostess may serve portions of cheese and crackers on dessert plates.

DESSERT TRAY SUGGESTIONS

Concord grapes, smoked cheese, flaky crackers.

Unpeeled red apple slices, dipped in orange juice; blue cheese portions; whole wheat crackers.

Fresh fruit bowl; American Liederkranz cheese; thin slices of buttered pumpernickel bread.

Fresh, whole pears; American Gouda cheese; assorted crackers.

Assorted cocktail cheese spreads (pimiento, pineapple, relish, etc.); thin slices of buttered nut bread; Tokay grapes.

Cream cheese and chive wedges; thin slices buttered rye bread; tart plums.

Tiny, hot, buttered baking powder biscuits; cream cheese; jam.

Buttered raisin bread strips; pineapple cheese spread.

Fill 2 baked apples with cream cheese and water cress stuffing.

American Camembert cheese, chilled white grapes, butter wafers.

RENNET PUDDING

4 cups milk	½ teaspoon vanilla
6 tablespoons sugar	2 rennet tablets
dash of salt	2 tablespoons cold water

Heat milk until lukewarm. Add sugar, salt and vanilla and heat until dissolved. Do not heat more than enough to dissolve the sugar. Remove from heat. Dissolve rennet tablets in cold water and add to milk, mixing well. Pour into glasses and do not disturb until set. Then chill. Serve with any creamy sauce, stewed or canned fruit or cream; or serve with berries, sliced fruit or orange sections. Yield: 6 portions.

Chocolate Rennet—Melt 1 square unsweetened chocolate, add 2 tablespoons hot water and stir until smooth; add to warm milk and beat well.

Maple Rennet—Substitute maple sugar for granulated sugar, or use 2 tablespoons maple syrup with 4 tablespoons sugar. Brown sugar or caramelized sugar syrup may also be used.

SOFT CUSTARD

2 to 3 eggs, slightly beaten or 4 to 6 egg yolks	**3 tablespoons sugar**
	2 cups milk, scalded
⅛ teaspoon salt	**½ teaspoon vanilla**

Combine eggs, salt and sugar; gradually stir in hot milk and cook in top of double boiler over boiling water 5 minutes, or until mixture coats the spoon, stirring constantly. Add vanilla and cool quickly. Use as simple dessert or as a dessert sauce. Yield: 2 cups soft custard.

Almond Custard—Turn custard into sherbet glasses; chill. Just before serving, top generously with chopped toasted almonds.

Fruit Custard—Place fresh or canned fruit in sauce dishes, cover with custard and chill.

Soft Caramel Custard—Substitute 1 tablespoon caramel syrup (page 730) for 1 tablespoon sugar and omit vanilla.

Fairy Custard—Scald 2 cups thin cream and fold gently into 3 well beaten egg whites. Add a dash of salt, 3 tablespoons sugar and 1 teaspoon vanilla. Cook as directed.

Soft Coffee Custard—Substitute 1 cup strong coffee for 1 cup milk; omit vanilla, if desired, and add ¼ teaspoon cinnamon.

Soft Yellow Custard—Substitute 4 egg yolks for eggs.

FLOATING ISLAND

Prepare Soft Custard with 4 egg yolks (above); pour into sherbet glasses or sauce dishes and chill. Beat egg whites until stiff; gradually beat in ¼ cup sugar and flavor with vanilla; drop a spoonful into each dish and chill. Or drop meringue from tablespoon into boiling water, cover and cook about 5 minutes; place one meringue in each dish and chill. Use any one of the modifications. Yield: 6 to 8 portions.

BAKED CUSTARD

1 quart milk	¼ teaspoon salt
4 eggs, slightly beaten	½ teaspoon vanilla
¼ cup sugar	nutmeg

Scald milk. Combine eggs, sugar and salt; add milk slowly, stirring until sugar is dissolved; add vanilla. Turn into small custard cups, place in pan of hot water (about 160° F.); the water should come close to top of custard. Bake in moderate oven (350° F.) 25 to 30 minutes, or until firm. A knife point should come out clean when inserted part way into center. Sprinkle with nutmeg. Cool. Yield: 6 portions.

To make large custard—Use 6 eggs; turn into baking dish, place in pan of hot water and bake 1 hour, or until barely firm. Approximate yield: 6 portions.

Baked Honey Custard—Substitute ½ cup honey for sugar, omit vanilla and nutmeg and add ⅛ teaspoon cinnamon.

Caramel Custard—Add ¼ cup caramel syrup (page 730) to milk; sweeten to taste.

Golden River Custard—Place 1 spoonful of maple syrup in each individual custard cup. Fill cup with custard mixture, pouring against a spoon so as not to disturb syrup. Bake as usual and unmold to serve.

ORANGE SPONGE CUSTARD

3 cups cubed sponge cake	Soft Custard (page 767)
1 cup orange juice	dash of salt
	4 tablespoons sugar

Use stale sponge or angel cake; place in 6 buttered custard cups or 1 large casserole and pour orange juice over cake. Prepare custard with 4 egg yolks and pour over cake. Use egg whites remaining from custard for meringue: beat until stiff but not dry with salt and sugar. Pile lightly on desserts and bake in moderate oven (350° F.) 12 to 15 minutes, or until delicately browned. Serve hot or cold. Sprinkle shredded coconut over tops, if desired. Yield: 6 portions.

BLANC MANGE

3 tablespoons cornstarch   ½ cup cold milk
⅛ teaspoon salt   1½ cups scalded milk
⅓ cup sugar   ½ teaspoon vanilla

Mix cornstarch, salt, sugar and cold milk; stir slowly into scalded milk. Cook over hot water 10 minutes, stirring constantly until thick and smooth. Cover and cook 15 minutes longer, stirring occasionally. Add vanilla and turn into individual molds which have been rinsed in cold water. Chill until firm. Unmold and serve with maple syrup, cream or any sauce. Arrowroot, potato or rice flour may be substituted for cornstarch in same proportion. Use 2 tablespoons cornstarch to make a softer pudding. Approximate yield: 6 portions.

Caramel Blanc Mange—Add ¼ cup caramelized sugar syrup (page 730) to milk after scalding.

Chocolate Blanc Mange—Add 2 squares unsweetened chocolate to scalded milk and heat until chocolate is melted; then beat with rotary beater until blended and proceed as directed.

Coffee Blanc Mange—Substitute 1 cup strong coffee for 1 cup milk.

Fruit Blanc Mange—Surround mold with slices of fresh peaches or apricots, cherries or berries and serve with cream.

CARAMEL PUDDING

½ cup firmly packed brown   ½ cup cream
    sugar   ½ cup cold milk
2 tablespoons butter, melted   ¼ cup all-purpose flour
1½ cups milk, scalded   ⅛ teaspoon salt
2 eggs, well beaten

Add brown sugar to butter in heavy skillet and cook over low heat 5 minutes, stirring constantly. Add scalded milk and stir until sugar dissolves; add cream. Add cold milk slowly to flour and salt, mixing well. Add to brown sugar mixture and cook over hot water 15 minutes, stirring constantly. Stir small amount into egg, blend, then return to remaining hot mixture and cook 2 minutes longer, stirring constantly. Cool slightly, turn into serving dishes and chill. Approximate yield: 6 small portions.

WALTZING MATILDA'S HONEY PUDDING

3 slices bread, cubed   2 cups milk, scalded
1 tablespoon butter, melted   2 eggs, slightly beaten
¼ teaspoon salt   ½ teaspoon vanilla
½ cup brown sugar   ½ cup raisins
½ teaspoon cinnamon   ½ cup nuts, chopped
½ cup honey

Combine bread, salt, brown sugar, cinnamon, milk, eggs, vanilla, raisins and nuts. Blend well and turn into buttered bowl or mold in which honey has been poured. Cover pan or mold with waxed paper or aluminum foil and tie securely. Steam on rack in pressure saucepan 15 minutes at 15 pounds pressure. Serve with honey. Yield: 4 portions.

LEMON PUDDING

1 cup sugar   1 cup milk
1 tablespoon butter   6 tablespoons lemon juice
2 tablespoons flour   1 tablespoon grated lemon rind
3 eggs, separated   pinch of salt

Cream together sugar and butter. Sift in flour. Beat egg yolks and combine with milk. Stir into the sugar mixture. Beat until smooth. Add lemon juice and rind. Beat egg whites with salt until stiff. Fold into sugar mixture. Pour into greased casserole and place in pan of hot water. Bake in moderate oven (350° F.) about 35 minutes. Chill thoroughly in refrigerator. Yield: 6 portions.

FLOATING PEACHES

3½ tablespoons cornstarch   1 cup milk
2 tablespoons sugar   1 egg, slightly beaten
⅛ teaspoon salt   1 teaspoon grated lemon rind
1 cup syrup from canned   12 marshmallows
     peaches   6 canned peach halves, drained

Mix cornstarch, sugar, salt and ½ cup peach syrup. Mix remaining peach syrup with milk and scald. Stir in cornstarch mixture slowly and cook over hot water 10 minutes, stirring constantly until thick and clear. Mix small amount into egg, return to remaining hot mixture and blend. Add lemon rind and 6 marshmallows, cut in bits, and cook 5 minutes longer, stirring constantly. Turn into 6 glass custard cups, top with peaches, hollow side up; place remaining marshmallows in peach hollow and place under broiler until browned. Yield: 6 portions.

VANILLA CREAM

2 egg yolks
2 tablespoons sugar
1½ teaspoons flour

1 cup light cream
2 tablespoons heavy cream,
    whipped
1 teaspoon vanilla

Beat egg yolks until thick and light. Combine sugar and flour and gradually beat into egg yolks. Scald cream. Gradually add to egg mixture. Cook in top of double boiler over hot water until thickened. Cool. Fold in whipped cream and vanilla. Approximate yield: filling for 12 tarts.

FRENCH CREAM

¼ cup all-purpose flour
¼ cup sugar
½ cup cold milk
1 cup scalded milk

1 egg, slightly beaten
¾ teaspoon orange extract
2 drops Benedictine
12 ladyfingers, split

Mix flour and sugar, add cold milk slowly, mixing until smooth; add slowly to scalded milk and cook over hot water 15 minutes, stirring occasionally. Stir small amount into egg, then return to remaining hot mixture and cook 2 minutes longer; add flavorings and cool. Place ladyfingers upright in parfait glasses, sprinkle with a little additional Benedictine and fill glasses with French Cream. Yield: 6 portions.

TAPIOCA CREAM

2 eggs, separated
½ cup sugar
4 cups milk

⅓ cup quick-cooking tapioca
⅛ teaspoon salt
1 teaspoon vanilla

Beat egg whites until stiff; gradually add ¼ cup sugar and continue to beat until stiff but not dry. Set aside. Mix yolks with small amount of milk; add remaining milk, sugar, tapioca and salt. Cook, stirring constantly, until mixture comes to a boil. Pour small amount of hot mixture gradually on meringue and blend. Add remaining mixture, stirring constantly. Add vanilla. Cool; stir once after 15 to 20 minutes. Chill. Approximate yield: 6 to 8 portions.

Currant Jelly Tapioca—Arrange Tapioca Cream in alternate layers with currant jelly in parfait glasses, using just enough jelly to cover cream. Top with whipped cream.

Prune Tapioca—Fold in 1 cup steamed dried prunes, finely chopped. Any steamed dried fruit may be used.

Tapioca Parfait—Half fill parfait glasses with any bright colored gelatin, prepared according to package directions; chill, fill glass with tapioca and garnish with tiny cubes of gelatin.

Chocolate Tapioca—Add 2 squares unsweetened chocolate to 2 cups of the milk and heat until chocolate is melted; then beat with egg beater until blended and proceed as directed.

Tapioca Meringue Pudding—Do not add tapioca cream to meringue; turn hot mixture into baking dish, spread a thin layer of any preserve over top and cover with meringue. Bake in hot oven (425° F.) 4 to 4½ minutes, or until delicately browned.

Coffee Apricot Tapioca—Add 3 tablespoons coffee to 2 cups of the milk and heat to boiling; pour through fine strainer and proceed as directed. Omit vanilla and fold in ½ cup apricot preserves.

BAKED PEACH TAPIOCA

Use 1½ cups canned sliced peaches, 1 cup water and 1 cup peach juice, ¼ cup sugar, ¼ teaspoon salt, dash of nutmeg, 2 teaspoons lemon juice, 1½ tablespoons melted butter and ¼ cup quick-cooking tapioca. Mix and bake in moderate oven (375° F.) 30 minutes, stirring every 10 minutes. Apricots may be substituted for peaches. Yield: 6 portions.

BAKED CHERRY TAPIOCA

1½ cups canned sour cherries, drained	1½ tablespoons melted butter
2½ cups cherry juice and water	¾ cup firmly packed brown sugar
2 teaspoons lemon juice	¾ teaspoon salt
	dash of nutmeg
	⅓ cup quick-cooking tapioca

Combine ingredients in buttered casserole, mixing well. Bake in moderately hot oven (375° F.) 30 minutes, stirring every 10 minutes and again when removing from oven. Serve hot or cold with cream. Approximate yield: 6 portions.

CUSTARD BREAD PUDDING

6 slices bread	¼ cup sugar
¼ cup soft butter	½ teaspoon vanilla
4 eggs, well beaten	⅛ teaspoon nutmeg
1 quart milk, scalded	

Cut crusts from bread and butter one side. Combine eggs, sugar and flavorings; add milk slowly, stirring until sugar is dissolved. Turn into baking dish, top with bread, buttered side up. Place in pan of hot water and bake in moderate oven (350° F.) 45 to 50 minutes, or until firm. Approximate yield: 6 portions.

Individual Bread Puddings—Cut bread in cubes; place in 6 individual custard cups, add custard mixture and bake as directed 25 minutes, or until firm.

Strawberry Jam Bread Pudding—When making custard for bread pudding, use 3 whole eggs and 2 yolks, reserving 2 whites for meringue. Add ½ cup raisins, if desired. When pudding is done, spread with ½ cup soft strawberry jam or jelly and top with meringue made by beating 4 tablespoons sugar slowly into 2 stiffly beaten egg whites. Bake 4 to 4½ minutes in hot oven (425° F). Any tart jam or jelly may be used in this pudding.

Chocolate Bread Pudding—Add 2 squares chocolate to milk, heat until melted and beat with rotary beater until blended.

Coconut Bread Pudding—Sprinkle each slice of bread liberally with shredded coconut before moistening with custard mixture. Approximate yield: 6 portions.

OLD-FASHIONED BREAD PUDDING

1½ cups diced stale bread	½ cup sugar
3 cups milk, scalded	¼ teaspoon salt
2 eggs, beaten	½ teaspoon cinnamon
½ cup raisins, nuts or coconut	

Soak bread in milk in buttered baking dish. Combine eggs, sugar, salt and cinnamon; stir into bread mixture; add raisins and place in pan of hot water. Bake in moderate oven (350° F.) 45 to 50 minutes, or until knife comes out clean when inserted in center. Serve with Hot Jelly Sauce (page 727), or any hard sauce or cream. Yield: 6 portions.

LEMON MERINGUE PUDDING

½ cup water
1½ teaspoons grated lemon
 rind
¼ cup lemon juice

⅓ cup butter
1 cup sugar
2 eggs, separated
2 cups soft bread crumbs

Add water to lemon rind and juice. Cream butter, add ¾ cup sugar and beat well; beat in egg yolks and stir in crumbs and water-lemon mixture. Turn into buttered baking dish, place in pan of hot water and bake in moderate oven (350° F.) 30 to 35 minutes, or until firm. Beat egg whites until frothy, add remaining ¼ cup sugar gradually, beating until stiff. Spread on pudding and bake in hot oven (425° F.) 4 to 4½ minutes. Approximate yield: 6 portions.

CAKE CRUMB PUDDING

1 cup dry cake crumbs
½ cup milk (about)
4 egg yolks, beaten
1 cup sugar

¼ cup butter, creamed
1 cup peach preserves
1 cup chopped nuts
½ cup heavy cream, whipped

Soak cake crumbs in enough milk to moisten (amount depends on softness of crumbs). Mix egg yolks, sugar and butter; add cake crumbs, mixing well; then add preserves and nuts. Turn into buttered baking dish and bake in slow oven (300° F.) until firm. Serve with whipped cream. Approximate yield: 6 portions.

BAKED RICE PUDDING

¾ cup rice
1½ quarts milk
¾ cup sugar

¾ teaspoon salt
dash of nutmeg
¾ cup seedless raisins

Wash rice, add milk, sugar and salt and place in buttered baking dish. Bake, covered, in slow oven (250°–275° F.) 2 to 3 hours, stirring mixture well with fork several times during the first hour of baking. Add nutmeg and raisins and continue baking, stirring whenever a brown film forms on top. Yield: 6 to 8 portions.

RICE PUDDING

2 cups milk
1 stick cinnamon
¼ cup butter

⅓ cup sugar
4 eggs, slightly beaten
½ cup cooked rice

¼ cup raisins

Scald milk with cinnamon; remove cinnamon and add butter and sugar, stirring well. Add slowly to beaten eggs, mixing well; add rice and raisins. Turn into buttered baking dish and bake in slow oven (300° F.) 45 minutes, or until browned. Yield: 6 portions.

INDIAN PUDDING

5 cups milk
⅔ cup dark molasses
⅓ cup sugar
½ cup yellow cornmeal

1 teaspoon salt
¾ teaspoon cinnamon
⅜ teaspoon nutmeg
¼ cup butter

Scald 4 cups milk and add molasses, sugar, cornmeal, salt, spices and butter. Cook over hot water 20 minutes, or until mixture thickens, stirring constantly. Turn into baking dish, pour remaining cold milk over mixture. Bake in slow oven (300° F.) 3 hours without stirring. Serve warm with cream, hard sauce or ice cream. Yield: 10 portions.

APPLE BETTY

6 medium-sized cooking apples
1⅓ cups moist bread crumbs
¾ cup sugar

1½ teaspoons cinnamon
1½ tablespoons butter
2 tablespoons grated orange rind

⅓ cup water

Pare, core and slice apples; place half in casserole. Combine bread crumbs, sugar and cinnamon; sprinkle one-half over apples and dot with half the butter. Repeat with remaining apples, crumbs and butter. Sprinkle with orange rind; add water and cover. Bake in moderate oven (375° F.) 45 minutes. Serve with Hard Sauce (page 732) or Foamy Sauce (page 731). Approximate yield: 6 portions.

Pineapple Betty—Substitute 3 cups diced canned pineapple for apples; omit water.

Mincemeat Brown Betty—Use 1 cup mincemeat and 4 apples.

Rhubarb Brown Betty—Substitute 2½ cups stewed rhubarb for apples; omit water.

CRISPY BLUEBERRY BETTY

3 cups blueberries	4 slices French Toast (page 182)
¾ cup sugar	2 tablespoons confectioners' sugar
dash of salt	¼ teaspoon nutmeg
2 tablespoons lemon juice	Hard Sauce (page 732)

Wash and pick over berries; add sugar, salt and lemon juice and cook 10 minutes; turn into baking dish. Cut French toast in small squares and arrange over berries; sprinkle with confectioners' sugar and nutmeg. Bake in moderate oven (375° F.) about 30 minutes. Serve with hard sauce. Approximate yield: 6 portions.

CHEESE APPLE BETTY

3 cups sliced, peeled apples	½ cup brown sugar
1 quart corn flakes	½ cup grated American cheese
½ cup chopped almonds	½ cup melted butter
1 tablespoon lemon juice	

Place alternate layers of apples, corn flakes, almonds, brown sugar and cheese in casserole. Sprinkle with butter and lemon juice. Bake in moderate oven (350° F.) 30 minutes. Yield: 6 portions.

COTTAGE PUDDING

1¾ cups sifted all-purpose flour	¾ cup sugar
2½ teaspoons baking powder	1 egg
½ teaspoon salt	½ teaspoon lemon extract
¼ cup butter or other fat	⅔ cup milk
½ cup grape jelly	

Mix flour, baking powder and salt and sift 3 times. Cream butter until soft; add sugar gradually, beating until light; beat in egg and flavoring. Add flour alternately with milk, beating until smooth after each addition; turn into buttered square pan, 8 x 8 x 2 inches. Bake in moderate oven (350°-375° F.) 30 to 45 minutes, or until done. Cut in squares, split and spread grape jelly between and on top of layers; serve with whipped cream, if desired. Yield: 6 portions.

Cherry Pudding—Add 1 cup pitted large sweet cherries, drained, to batter. Serve with Hard Sauce (page 732). Use other fruit such as blueberries, sliced peaches or apricots.

Pineapple Topped Pudding—Place 2 cups canned shredded pineapple, drained, in buttered pan and sprinkle with 4 tablespoons brown sugar; cover with batter and bake as directed. Invert on large plate and serve with whipped cream.

APPLE SCALLOP

½ cup butter, or butter and   ¼ cup firmly packed brown
  other shortening   sugar
1 cup sifted all-purpose flour   4 cups sliced apples
              dash of cinnamon

Cut butter into flour and sugar mixture with pastry blender. Arrange apples in buttered baking dish, sprinkle with cinnamon and cover with flour mixture. Bake in moderate oven (375° F.) about 45 minutes, or until apples are tender. Yield: 6 portions.

BING CHERRY PUDDING

2 cups preserved black cherries   ⅔ cup sugar
1 cup sifted cake flour   2 eggs, well beaten
1½ teaspoons baking powder   ¼ cup milk
¼ teaspoon salt   ¼ cup hot water
¼ teaspoon cinnamon   1 teaspoon vanilla
¼ cup butter or margarine   whipped cream

Heat cherries and juice to boiling point. Sift together flour, baking powder, salt and cinnamon. Cream butter; add sugar and cream until light and fluffy. Add eggs and beat until blended. Add flour alternately with combined milk and water, beating until smooth after each addition. Add vanilla and blend. Place hot fruit in baking pan, turn in batter and bake immediately in hot oven (400° F.) 25 to 30 minutes, or until cake is done. Serve warm with plain or whipped cream. Blueberries, canned plums or any stewed fruit may be substituted for cherries. Approximate yield: 6 to 8 portions.

BAKED PERSIMMON PUDDING

1 cup persimmon pulp (about   1 cup sifted all-purpose flour
  3 large persimmons)   ½ teaspoon soda
2 eggs, well beaten   ½ teaspoon salt
1 cup milk   ¼ teaspoon cinnamon
1½ tablespoons melted butter   ¼ teaspoon nutmeg
              ¾ cup sugar

Mix persimmon pulp with eggs and add milk and butter. Sift together flour, soda, salt, spices and sugar. Pour pulp and milk mixture into sifted dry ingredients. Mix to a soft batter; add more milk if necessary. Pour the mixture into buttered 8 x 8 x 2 inch pan and bake in moderate oven (350° F.) 30 to 45 minutes. Cut into squares and serve warm with either plain or whipped cream topping. Yield: 6 portions.

BLACK CURRANT PUDDING

Stem 1 quart black currants, wash and place in shallow pan with empty cup inverted in center. Sprinkle 1 cup sugar mixed with 1 tablespoon flour over fruit. Prepare Baking Powder Biscuit dough (page 149) and roll about ½-inch thick to fit pan; make several gashes to permit escape of steam; place over fruit and press edges down on pan. Bake in moderate oven (375° F.) 45 minutes. Serve hot with juice collected in cup. Approximate yield: 6 portions.

APPLE ROLY POLY

Prepare Baking Powder Biscuit dough (page 149); roll ¼-inch thick. Spread with a mixture of 1 cup diced apple, ½ cup raisins, 1 teaspoon cinnamon, ½ cup sugar and ¼ cup firmly packed brown sugar. Roll as for jelly roll; cut crosswise in 2-inch slices, place in greased baking pan and add ¾ cup water. Bake in hot oven (400° F.) 30 minutes. Serve with Lemon Sauce (page 727). Approximate yield: 6 portions.

PEACH ROLL

Prepare Baking Powder Biscuit dough (page 149); roll ¼-inch thick. Pare and slice 6 peaches, place on dough and sprinkle with ½ cup sugar and 1½ tablespoons lemon juice. Roll as for jelly roll; place, seam down, on greased baking sheet. Brush with butter and bake in hot oven (400° F.) 25 to 30 minutes. Serve with Lemon Sauce (page 727). Approximate yield: 6 portions.

Blackberry Roll—Substitute 1 pint blackberries for peaches. Omit lemon juice and dust with cinnamon. Serve with whipped cream or Foamy Egg Sauce (page 731).

Blueberry Roll—Substitute 1 pint blueberries for peaches. Serve with Hard Sauce (page 732).

Apricot Roll—Substitute 1½ cups sweetened, cooked dried apricots for peaches; omit sugar.

Gooseberry Roll—Substitute 1 pint gooseberries for peaches; sweeten with ¼ cup firmly packed brown sugar and omit lemon juice.

SOUR CHERRY COBBLER

1½ cups sifted all-purpose flour ⅓ cup milk
2 teaspoons baking powder 1 egg, beaten
½ teaspoon salt 2 cups sweetened sour cherries
½ cup sugar 1 tablespoon quick-cooking
¼ cup butter   tapioca

Sift together flour, baking powder, salt and sugar. Cut in butter. Combine milk and egg; add to dry ingredients, stirring just until all flour is dampened. Pour cherries into baking dish and sprinkle with tapioca. Drop batter in 6 mounds on cherries. Bake in hot oven (450° F.) 15 minutes; then reduce heat to moderate (350° F.) and bake 30 minutes longer. Approximate yield: 6 portions.

APPLE PAN DOWDY

5 medium-sized tart apples ¼ teaspoon salt
3 tablespoons sugar ½ cup hot water
3 tablespoons molasses ½ recipe Baking Powder Biscuits
¼ teaspoon nutmeg   (page 149)
¼ teaspoon cinnamon

Pare and slice apples and place in casserole; add sugar, molasses, spices, salt and water; cover and bake in hot oven (400° F.) 20 minutes, or until apples are soft. Prepare drop biscuit dough with ⅓ cup each shortening and milk to make a soft dough. Turn out on apples, spreading evenly, and bake in hot oven (450° F.) 15 to 20 minutes. Serve hot with Hard Sauce (page 732). Approximate yield: 6 portions.

BISCUIT SHORTCAKE

Prepare Baking Powder Biscuit dough (page 149) with ⅓ cup shortening. Roll or pat dough ¼-inch thick and cut with floured 3-inch biscuit cutter. Place half of rounds in shallow baking pan, brush with melted butter and cover with remaining halves. Brush tops with butter and bake in hot oven (450° F.) 15 minutes. Separate halves, spread soft sides with softened butter and cover bottom halves with fruit; lay other halves on top, soft sides up, and cover with fruit. Serve with plain or whipped cream. For large cake, divide dough in half and pat each gently into an 8-inch layer pan. Bake and put together as for individual cakes. Or bake in one layer and split. Yield: 6 portions.

Fresh fruit such as berries, pitted cherries, sliced apricots and peaches, orange sections, sliced bananas or stewed fruits may be used. Use about 4 cups fruit and prepare as follows:

Strawberries and Raspberries—Crush 3 cups very slightly with fork, sweeten to taste and let stand in warm room 2 to 3 hours to draw out juices. Serve remaining berries, whole or split, on top.

Blueberries and Blackberries—Bring berries to a boil in hot syrup, using ½ to 1 cup sugar and ¼ to ½ cup water; cool.

Cherries—To pitted cherries add ½ to ¾ cup sugar and 3 tablespoons water and simmer 2 minutes, stirring until sugar is dissolved; cool.

Peaches and Apricots—Use 1 large peach or 3 apricots for one portion; peel, slice and sweeten to taste. Or simmer about 5 minutes in syrup, using equal amounts sugar and water; chill.

CAKE SHORTCAKE

Bake One Egg Cake (page 633) or Sponge Cake (page 669) in square loaf pan or cup cake pans; split while warm and place chilled sweetened fruit (see above) between layers and on top. Serve with whipped cream; garnish with fruit sections or whole berries.

WAFFLE SHORTCAKE

Use Cream Waffles (page 144), Nut Waffles (page 143), Coconut Waffles or Lemon or Orange Waffles (page 143), or Chocolate Waffles (below); brush with melted butter and spread jelly or jam on half of each waffle; fold other half over jelly and sprinkle top with confectioners' sugar. Or spread ice cream between and on top of 2 waffles; serve with crushed fruit and cream or chocolate sauce.

WAFFLES SUZETTE NOIR

2 teaspoons instant coffee
1 tablespoon boiling water
⅓ cup sugar
⅔ cup orange juice
1 tablespoon grated orange rind
½ tablespoon grated lemon rind
¼ to ½ cup brandy
¼ cup melted butter
2 tablespoons Cointreau or Curaçao
6 waffles
6 tablespoons confectioners' sugar

Dissolve coffee in boiling water, add sugar and orange juice and stir until dissolved. Add rinds and simmer 5 minutes. Add butter and liqueur. Pour over hot waffles and sprinkle with confectioners' sugar. Pour brandy on plate around waffles and ignite. Baste waffles with the flaming liquid. Yield: 6 portions.

CHOCOLATE DESSERT WAFFLES

2½ cups sifted cake flour   ¼ cup cocoa
4 teaspoons baking powder   2 eggs, separated
½ teaspoon salt   1½ cups milk
½ cup sugar   ¼ teaspoon vanilla
              ⅓ cup shortening, melted

Sift together dry ingredients. Combine well-beaten egg yolks, milk and vanilla; add to flour mixture, beating until smooth; add shortening and fold in stiffly beaten egg whites. Bake in moderately hot waffle iron. Serve with whipped cream or ice cream. Yield: 10 waffles.

DESSERT PANCAKES

1 cup sifted all-purpose flour   1 cup milk
1 tablespoon sugar   2 tablespoons melted butter
few grains of salt   1 cup spiced applesauce
3 eggs   cranberry sauce

Mix and sift flour, sugar and salt. Beat eggs and add to flour mixture. Add milk, stir until smooth. Add butter. Strain through a fine sieve. Let stand 2 hours. Melt ½ teaspoon butter in 7-inch skillet. Pour in a thin layer of batter. Cook over low heat until underside is golden brown. Turn and brown on other side (about 1 minute each side). Repeat until batter is used. Spread each pancake with applesauce and roll up. Top with a ribbon of cranberry sauce. Yield: 12 pancakes.

SOUFFLÉS

POINTERS for making puffy, golden soufflés are as follows: Use eggs at room temperature and separate them, beating the yolks until thick and lemon-colored, the whites until stiff but not dry (underbeaten eggs make a small, unstable soufflé, overbeaten eggs will cause a tough product).

The size, shape and preparation of the baking dish will influence the quality of a soufflé. A straight-sided dish gives maximum volume. For a 3- or 4-egg soufflé, use a 1½-quart dish; for a larger soufflé with more than 4 eggs, use a 2-quart dish. Butter or oil the bottom, but not the sides of the baking dish; the mixture will cling to the unbuttered sides and make a taller and more uniform product.

To bake a soufflé with a "top hat," just before baking cut around the mixture (about 2 inches from the edge) with a knife or spoon. The crust will break at this point and form a taller center. To bake a tall soufflé, tie a paper collar of waxed paper around the edge of the baking dish and bake slowly until firm to the touch and delicately browned.

The baking of a soufflé has much to do with its quality. It requires a slow to moderate oven and a long baking period. If baked at 300° to 325° F., the baking dish need not be placed in a pan of water. A soufflé made with 3 to 4 eggs will require 1¼ to 1½ hours; the product is likely to be somewhat dry but more stable than when baked at a higher temperature. At a temperature of 350° F., the dish usually is placed in a pan of water and baked 40 to 60 minutes for a more tender and moist soufflé. Always serve a soufflé in the dish in which it is baked.

VANILLA SOUFFLÉ

¾ cup Thick White Sauce (page 125)
3 eggs, separated
⅓ cup granulated sugar

1 teaspoon vanilla
¼ teaspoon almond extract
confectioners' sugar
½ cup heavy cream, whipped

⅓ cup toasted chopped almonds

Prepare white sauce, omitting pepper; stir in mixture of well-beaten egg yolks, granulated sugar and flavorings. Fold in egg whites beaten until they form fairly stiff but rounded peaks; turn into 1½-quart baking dish, buttered on bottom but not on sides, and sprinkle with confectioners' sugar. Place in pan of hot water and bake in moderate oven (350° F.) 50 to 60 minutes, or until firm. Serve at once from baking dish, or serve in sherbet glasses with sweetened whipped cream; sprinkle with almonds. Approximate yield: 6 portions.

Chocolate Soufflé—Stir 2 squares unsweetened chocolate, melted, into white sauce, reduce vanilla to ½ teaspoon and omit almond extract; proceed as directed but bake 1 hour. Serve with sweetened whipped cream; garnish with chopped nuts. Approximate yield: 6 portions.

VANILLA SOUFFLÉ À LA RITZ

3 tablespoons sweet butter   6 eggs, separated
1 tablespoon flour   ½ teaspoon vanilla
½ cup scalded milk   2½ tablespoons sugar
powdered sugar

Melt the butter in a saucepan, add the flour and let it become golden brown. Add the hot milk, stirring constantly, and cook 5 minutes. Add the egg yolks beaten with 2 tablespoons sugar. Add vanilla. Beat the egg whites very stiff and add remaining ½ tablespoon sugar. Carefully fold into yolk mixture. Place in a buttered and sugared soufflé dish and bake in hot oven (450° F.) for about 20 minutes. Sprinkle top with powdered sugar and serve immediately with Vanilla Sauce (page 729) plain, or with 2 tablespoons Grand Marnier liqueur added. Yield: 4 portions.

LEMON SOUFFLÉ

4 eggs, separated   ½ teaspoon salt
¼ cup hot water   2 teaspoons grated lemon rind
1 cup sugar   ¼ cup lemon juice

Beat yolks until thick; add water gradually and continue beating; add sugar gradually, beating thoroughly after each addition. Add salt and lemon rind and juice, and fold in stiffly beaten egg whites. Turn into 1½-quart dish, buttered on the bottom, and place in pan of hot water; bake in moderate oven (350° F.) 30 to 45 minutes, or until firm. Serve at once with Lemon Sauce (page 727). Approximate yield: 6 portions.

HOT LEMON SOUFFLÉ

2 tablespoons butter   grated rind and juice of 1 lemon
3 tablespoons flour   3 tablespoons sugar
pinch of salt   4 egg yolks
¾ cup milk   5 egg whites
confectioners' sugar

Melt butter, remove from heat and stir in flour. Add pinch of salt and gradually add milk, stirring constantly. Return to heat and cook until mixture is consistency of heavy cream, stirring constantly, but do not boil. Add lemon rind and juice and sugar. Add egg yolks and blend well. Beat egg whites until stiff and fold into cooled egg yolk mixture. Pour into well-greased straight-sided soufflé dish around which has been tied a 6-inch collar of greased waxed paper. Place in moderate oven (350° F.) and bake 30 minutes. Remove collar, dust with confectioners' sugar and serve immediately. Approximate yield: 6 portions.

BLACKSMITH SHOP CHOCOLATE SOUFFLÉ

3 tablespoons butter or
  margarine
3 tablespoons flour
¾ cup milk
4 ounces dark sweet chocolate
5 tablespoons strong coffee (or
  ½ water and ½ rum)

5 tablespoons granulated sugar
5 egg yolks
5 egg whites, stiffly beaten
confectioners' sugar
1 egg, separated
3 tablespoons granulated sugar
1 cup whipped cream

In a heavy saucepan melt the butter and quickly stir in the flour. Slowly add the milk, stirring constantly. Stir until the consistency of heavy cream but do not boil. Remove; add the chocolate melted over hot water with the cold coffee or rum and water. Add the sugar and egg yolks; blend well. Fold in the egg whites which have been beaten very stiff, using a folding motion with a spatula. Quickly turn into a greased soufflé dish dusted with granulated sugar. Tie a band of heavy waxed paper around the dish to increase the height to about 6 inches. Immediately bake 35 minutes in a moderate oven (350° F.). Carefully remove the paper, dust with confectioners' sugar and serve at once.

Sauce for Soufflé—Beat the egg yolk well, add 3 tablespoons sugar, fold in stiffly beaten egg white and cup of whipped cream. Yield: 4 portions.

EGGS À LA NEIGE

6 egg whites
1 cup granulated sugar

1 quart vanilla sauce
frozen raspberries

toasted, slivered almonds

Whip the egg whites very stiff and slowly add sugar. Put the mixture into a pastry bag and force egg-shaped pieces on a wet spoon. Dip each one off the spoon into boiling water and poach for a few minutes until firm. Remove with a slotted spoon and drain on a napkin. Place raspberries in dishes and place meringues on top. Cover with cold sauce and garnish with almonds. Yield: 6 to 8 portions.

PINEAPPLE SOUFFLÉ

⅓ cup butter
½ cup sugar

2 eggs, separated
1 cup soft bread crumbs

1 cup canned crushed pineapple

Cream butter and sugar and beat well; add beaten egg yolks, then bread crumbs and drained fruit. Fold in stiffly beaten egg whites and turn into 1½-quart dish buttered on bottom; place in pan of hot water and bake in moderate oven (350° F.) 35 minutes. Yield: 4 portions.

OLD ENGLISH PLUM PUDDING

¾ cup sifted all-purpose flour
1½ teaspoons salt
½ nutmeg, grated
¼ teaspoon cinnamon
⅓ teaspoon mace
⅓ teaspoon cloves
½ pound seeded raisins
¼ pound dried currants
¼ pound figs, chopped

2 ounces citron, chopped
2 ounces candied orange peel,
   chopped
½ cup dry bread crumbs
1 cup hot milk
¼ cup sugar
4 eggs, separated
½ pound suet, ground
½ cup brandy

Sift together flour, salt and spices; stir in fruits. Soak crumbs in milk
10 minutes. Beat sugar into well-beaten egg yolks and add suet and
soaked crumbs; stir into flour-fruit mixture. Add cider and mix well;
fold in stiffly beaten egg whites. Turn into buttered 1½ quart mold,
cover and steam 3½ hours. Approximate yield: 12 portions.

STEAMED QUAKER PUDDING

4 cups dry bread crumbs
1 cup milk
½ cup molasses
½ cup butter, melted
2 teaspoons cinnamon

¼ teaspoon cloves
¼ teaspoon allspice
1 teaspoon baking soda
1 cup seeded raisins, chopped
½ cup finely chopped citron

¼ cup all-purpose flour

Soak crumbs in milk 15 minutes; beat until smooth. Add molasses,
butter, spices and baking soda; beat well. Add fruit dredged with flour
and mix thoroughly. Turn into buttered 2 quart mold, cover and steam
3 hours. Serve hot with Hard Sauce (page 732) or a Sherry Sauce
(page 732). Approximate yield: 8 portions.

SUET PUDDING

1 cup ground suet
1 cup molasses
1 cup raisins
1 cup currants
3 cups sifted all-purpose flour

2 teaspoons baking powder
½ teaspoon salt
1 teaspoon cloves
1 teaspoon cinnamon
1½ cups milk

Combine suet, molasses, raisins and currants. Sift together dry ingredients; add to suet mixture alternately with milk, beating until
smooth after each addition. Turn into buttered 2 quart mold, cover
tightly and steam 5 hours. Serve with Lemon Sauce, Hard Sauce or
Foamy Egg Sauce (pages 727, 731, 732). Yield: 10 to 12 portions.

STEAMED CHOCOLATE PUDDING

1 cup sifted cake flour	1 egg
1 teaspoon baking powder	1 square unsweetened chocolate,
¼ teaspoon salt	melted
1 tablespoon shortening	1 teaspoon vanilla
½ cup sugar	½ cup milk

Sift together flour, baking powder and salt. Cream shortening; gradually beat in sugar, then egg. Stir in chocolate and vanilla; add flour alternately with milk, beating until smooth after each addition. Turn into buttered individual molds, filling them ⅔ full; cover and steam 45 minutes. Approximate yield: 6 portions.

HIGHLAND FEATHER CRUST PUDDING

2 cups sifted all-purpose flour	2 tablespoons butter
3 teaspoons baking powder	4 large apples, pared and sliced
¼ teaspoon salt	1 egg, beaten
½ cup sugar	¾ cup milk

Sift together flour, baking powder, salt and sugar; cut in butter; add apples. Combine egg and milk; add to flour-apple mixture, stirring just until flour is dampened. Turn into buttered baking pan, cover tightly with greased or waxed paper and steam 1¼ hours. Serve with Foamy Sauce (page 731). Approximate yield: 6 portions.

LEMON SNOWBALLS

1 cup sifted all-purpose flour	1 cup granulated sugar
1 teaspoon baking powder	3 tablespoons water
¼ teaspoon salt	1 teaspoon grated lemon rind
3 eggs, separated	2 tablespoons lemon juice

confectioners' sugar

Sift together flour, baking powder and salt. Beat egg yolks, add granulated sugar gradually, beating until thick and light. Add water, lemon rind and juice; stir in flour and fold in stiffly beaten egg whites. Fill buttered custard cups ⅔ full; tie greased paper over tops and steam 30 minutes. Turn from cups and roll in confectioners' sugar; serve with Lemon Sauce (page 727) or any fruit sauce. Yield: 6 to 8 portions.

DATE TORTE PUDDING

¼ cup sifted all-purpose flour	2 eggs, well beaten
½ teaspoon baking powder	½ teaspoon vanilla
⅛ teaspoon salt	1½ cups chopped dates
¾ cup sugar	1½ cups broken walnuts

Sift together flour, baking powder and salt. Beat sugar into eggs; add vanilla and stir in and nut mixture; then add flour mixture. Turn into buttered shallow glass baking pan; bake in slow oven (325° F.) 50 to 60 minutes. Serve with cream. Yield: 6 to 8 portions.

SWEET FRITTER BATTER

1 cup sifted all-purpose flour	2 tablespoons sugar
1 teaspoon baking powder	1 egg, slightly beaten
½ teaspoon salt	¾ cup milk
1 tablespoon butter, melted	

Sift together dry ingredients. Combine egg, milk and butter; stir into dry ingredients. Use as cover batter for fruits. Yield: 1 cup batter.

Cover Batter—Omit baking powder and sugar. Use as cover batter for vegetables and meats; or use for fruit fritters and sprinkle fried product with confectioners' sugar.

BLUEBERRY FRITTERS

1 cup sifted all-purpose flour	2 tablespoons sugar
1 teaspoon baking powder	2 eggs, separated
½ teaspoon salt	2 to 3 tablespoons water
¾ cup blueberries	

Sift together dry ingredients. Combine beaten egg yolks with water and add to dry ingredients, mixing only until smooth. Fold in stiffly beaten egg whites; add blueberries. Drop by spoonfuls into hot deep fat (350°–365° F.) and cook 2 to 5 minutes, or until browned; drain on absorbent paper. Serve with confectioners' sugar or Foamy Sauce (page 731) or fruit sauce. Diced banana, apple, peaches or any berry may be substituted for blueberries. If using cranberries, cook with ½ cup water and sugar until skins burst; drain and cool before using. Approximate yield: 6 portions.

PINEAPPLE FRITTERS

1 large pineapple   Sweet Fritter Batter (page 787)

Pare and core pineapple; cut in ¾-inch slices, then cut each in quarters. Dip in batter and fry in hot deep fat (370° F.) 3 to 4 minutes, or until golden brown; drain on absorbent paper. Serve with Lemon Sauce (page 727). Yield: 6 portions.

FRUIT DUMPLINGS

2 cups sifted all-purpose flour   1 tablespoon sugar
3 teaspoons baking powder   3 tablespoons shortening
½ teaspoon salt   1 cup milk
                1 cup fruit

Sift together flour, baking powder, salt and sugar; cut in shortening. Add milk, stirring quickly to make a stiff dough. Stir in 1 cup fruit such as seeded grapes or berries and drop from tablespoon into rapidly boiling salted water; cover and cook 12 to 15 minutes. Drain and serve with any desired sauce. Approximate yield: 6 portions.

Maple Dumplings—Omit fruit; cook dumplings in syrup made of 2 cups maple syrup and 1 cup water. Serve dumplings with syrup as sauce. Approximate yield: 6 portions.

Quince Dumplings—Omit fruit. Fill muffin pans half full of quince sauce or preserves and drop dumpling mixture on top. Bake in hot oven (425° F.) 15 to 20 minutes; or steam in steamer for 15 minutes. Serve with Lemon Sauce (page 727). Approximate yield: 6 portions.

BAKED APPLE DUMPLINGS

1 recipe Baking Powder   1 teaspoon cinnamon
   Biscuits (page 149)   1 tablespoon grated orange rind
6 medium-sized apples   ½ cup raisins
½ cup firmly packed brown   2 tablespoons butter
   sugar   1 egg white
dash of salt   confectioners' sugar

Prepare biscuit dough, using ⅓ cup shortening, or use plain pastry; roll ¼-inch thick and cut in 6-inch squares. Pare and core apples and place one in center of each square; fill cavities with mixture of sugar, seasonings and raisins and dot with butter. Bring opposite corners of dough together on top of apple, moisten edges of one side with water and seal; prick with fork. Brush with slightly beaten egg white and sprinkle with sugar. Bake in hot oven (450° F.) 10 minutes; then reduce heat to moderate (350° F.). Bake 20 minutes. Yield: 6 dumplings.

CHEESE BEIGNETS

½ cup cold water
3 tablespoons butter or
  margarine
⅛ teaspoon salt
½ cup all-purpose flour
2 eggs
½ teaspoon dry mustard

⅛ teaspoon red pepper
3 tablespoons grated Parmesan
  cheese
1 tablespoon grated American
  cheese
½ teaspoon double-acting
  baking powder

1 egg white, stiffly beaten

Combine water, butter and salt in heavy saucepan. Bring to a boil and add flour all at once, stirring vigorously with a wooden spoon. Beat until mixture forms a smooth ball that leaves the sides of pan clean. Place in a bowl. Beat in thoroughly one egg at a time; then continue beating until mixture is thick and smooth and breaks off when spoon is raised. Add mustard, red pepper, Parmesan and American cheese and baking powder. Fold in egg white. Drop by teaspoon into deep hot fat (375° F.) and fry about 5 or 6 minutes. Serve generously sprinkled with Parmesan cheese and paprika. Approximate yield: 30 small beignets.

MOLDED DESSERTS

Gelatin desserts require from 2 to 4 hours to set or form a gel. Those with greater acidity (having lemon juice, vinegar or other fruit juice) take a little longer to set. A rule for gel cookery is to use 1 envelope (equivalent to 1 tablespoon gelatin) unflavored (plain) gelatin to 2 cups liquid (this means total liquid including dissolved sugar). Up to 2 cups chopped or diced fruit may be added to 1 pint of liquid.

To Dissolve Plain Gelatin—Use one of the following methods: (1) Soak the dry gelatin in a small amount of cold liquid a few minutes. Add very hot liquid and stir until gelatin is dissolved. (2) Add the dry gelatin to total cold liquid, bring slowly to a boil and stir until dissolved. (3) Soak the gelatin in a small amount of cold liquid a few minutes; place over boiling water and stir until dissolved.

To Unmold Gelatin—Dip mold quickly in warm water almost to edge; remove, shake, cover with plate and invert. If gelatin does not come out at once, repeat.

RAGGEDY ANN TORTE

6 egg whites	1 teaspoon vanilla
dash of salt	1 tablespoon vinegar
¼ teaspoon cream of tartar	1 pint orange ice
1½ cups sugar	1 quart raspberry ice

3 oranges, sections removed

Beat egg whites until frothy, sprinkle salt and cream of tartar over top and beat until stiff. Gradually beat in sugar, then vanilla and vinegar. Turn into buttered 10-inch spring form and bake in slow oven (300° F.) 1 hour, or until firm. Invert pan to cool; the inside of cake will shrink, leaving a cavity. Remove sides of spring form and cut out center portion from torte and reserve this for top of dessert. Place orange ice in bottom of torte and raspberry ice on top; decorate with sections of orange and place center of torte on top. Yield: 10 to 12 portions.

GELATIN CUPS

Prepare several different kinds of flavored gelatin, following directions on packages; pour each in a shallow pan to make a ½-inch thick layer. When firm, serve in sherbet glasses with Custard Sauce (page 729).

Cubed Gelatin—Cut firm gelatin in cubes and pile one or more colors into each cup, or serve in combination with cubed fruit.

Flaked Gelatin—With fork break firm gelatin into bits, or force through ricer. Pile one or more colors into each cup in layers, or in combination with fruit.

SELF–LAYERED GELATIN DESSERTS

Canned sweetened fruits are heavier than the gelatin mixture and will sink to bottom; fresh fruits are lighter and float on top. For self-layering, add fresh and canned fruits, sliced or diced, to gelatin base:

Apples, nuts and canned cherries.
Bananas, canned peaches or apricots.
Blueberries, green grapes and canned peaches.
Cantaloupe or melon balls, green grapes, grapefruit.
Orange sections and canned pineapple.
Orange sections, grapefruit and chopped mint.
Canned pears, oranges, chopped pecans.
Halved and seeded grapes, canned peaches.

LEMON JELLY

2 envelopes plain gelatin
2 cups cold water
1 cup boiling water

¾ cup sugar
dash of salt
½ teaspoon grated lemon rind

¾ cup lemon juice

Soften gelatin in ¼ cup cold water 5 minutes; add hot water, stirring until dissolved; stir in sugar, salt, lemon rind and juice, and remaining 1¾ cups cold water; pour into mold and chill until firm. Unmold and serve with plain or whipped cream, custard sauce, berries, sliced fruit, or stewed fruit. Approximate yield: 6 to 8 portions.

Orange Jelly—Reduce cold water to 1 cup and lemon juice to ¼ cup and add 1½ cups orange juice; substitute 1 teaspoon grated orange for lemon rind.

Fruit Jelly—Substitute 1½ cups fruit juice drained from canned fruit for orange juice and add sugar and lemon juice to taste. When slightly thickened, fold in 1 cup diced or sliced fruit, then mold.

Lemon or Orange Whip—When gelatin is slightly thickened, beat with rotary beater until frothy.

Lemon Sponge or Snow Pudding—When gelatin is slightly thickened, beat with rotary beater until frothy, then fold in the stiffly beaten whites of 2 eggs.

Peach Nests—Pour gelatin mixture into shallow pan to make 1-inch thick layer. When firm, cut in 2- to 3-inch squares; hollow each out slightly to hold peach half, rounded side down. Place fresh cherries with stems in hollow and serve with Custard Sauce (page 729).

PRUNE MEDALLION PUDDING

1½ cups stewed prunes
¾ cup prune juice
1½ packages orange-flavored
    gelatin

1¾ cups hot water
dash of salt
¼ teaspoon cinnamon
2 tablespoons broken nuts

Pit and chop prunes, add juice. Dissolve gelatin in hot water, following directions on package; add prunes and seasonings and chill until slightly thickened. Turn into individual molds and chill until thickened. Unmold and garnish with nuts. Yield: 6 portions.

SCOTCH PUDDING

1 package strawberry-flavored   1 cup confectioners' sugar
   gelatin   2 cups blueberries
1 medium-sized casaba or   heavy cream, whipped
   honeydew melon   fresh mint

Prepare gelatin, following directions on package; cool. Cut melon into
sections, trim off rind, remove all seeds and cut pulp into small cubes.
Mix sugar with blueberries. Add fruit to cold gelatin, stirring carefully, so the effect will resemble a bright Scotch plaid. Turn into individual molds and chill until firm. Unmold; garnish with whipped
cream and mint. Yield: 6 to 8 portions.

APRICOT SPONGE

1½ tablespoons plain gelatin   16 dried apricots, cooked
¼ cup cold water   and sweetened
1 cup boiling water   1 tablespoon lemon juice
              6 egg whites, stiffly beaten

Soften gelatin in cold water 5 minutes; dissolve in hot water. Chill
until slightly thickened. Force 10 apricots through sieve. Add lemon
juice and fold into gelatin mixture; fold in egg whites. Turn into large
mold and chill until firm. Unmold. Garnish with remaining apricots
in juice. Approximate yield: 6 portions.

ORANGE SPONGE

1½ tablespoons plain gelatin   2 teaspoons grated lemon rind
1 cup cold water   ¾ cup sugar
2 tablespoons grated orange   1 cup orange juice
   rind   ½ cup lemon juice
              3 egg whites, stiffly beaten

Soften gelatin in ¼ cup cold water 5 minutes. Heat remaining ¾
cup water, add grated rinds and simmer 10 minutes. Add to gelatin
and stir until dissolved; add sugar and fruit juices and chill until
thickened. Fold in egg whites, turn into individual molds and chill
until firm. Unmold. Approximate yield: 6 portions.

COFFEE SPONGE

1 envelope plain gelatin	⅔ cup sugar
½ cup milk	¼ teaspoon salt
1½ cups hot coffee	3 eggs, separated
	½ teaspoon vanilla

Soften gelatin in milk; add to coffee, stirring until dissolved; add ⅓ cup sugar and salt. Beat egg yolks with remaining ⅓ cup sugar; add gelatin mixture and cook over hot water 5 minutes, stirring constantly until sugar is dissolved. Chill until slightly thickened. Fold in stiffly beaten egg whites and vanilla. Turn into 6 individual molds and chill until firm. Unmold. Yield: 6 portions.

SPANISH CREAM

1 envelope plain gelatin	3 eggs, separated
¼ cup cold water	⅓ cup sugar
1½ cups milk, scalded	1 teaspoon vanilla

Soften gelatin in cold water 5 minutes; add milk. Combine egg yolks and sugar, add gelatin mixture and cook over hot water 5 minutes, stirring constantly until sugar is dissolved. Cool and chill until slightly thickened. Add vanilla and fold in stiffly beaten egg whites. Turn into mold; chill until firm. Unmold and serve with chocolate or caramel sauce or whipped cream. Yield: 6 small portions.

Fruit Spanish Cream—Just before folding in egg whites, stir in 1 cup shredded canned pineapple, drained, 1 cup raspberries, 1 tablespoon lemon juice and ½ cup macaroon crumbs.

Chocolate Spanish Cream—Add 1 square unsweetened chocolate to milk and heat until chocolate is melted; beat with egg beater until blended.

Bavarian Cream—Just before folding in egg whites, fold in ½ cup heavy cream, whipped.

Russian Peach Cream—Just before folding in egg whites, fold in mixture of 1 tablespoon lemon juice, ¾ cup crushed peach pulp and ½ cup heavy cream, whipped. Chill until thickened; then beat well, fold in egg whites, turn into mold and chill until firm.

Ginger Cream—Just before folding in egg whites, add ½ cup heavy cream, whipped, 2 tablespoons preserved ginger, mashed, and 2 tablespoons preserved ginger syrup. Serve with whipped cream.

STRAWBERRY BAVARIAN CREAM

1 envelope plain gelatin	1 cup heavy cream, whipped
2 tablespoons cold water	¾ cup confectioners' sugar
1 cup crushed strawberries	ladyfingers
	6 whole strawberries

Soften gelatin in cold water 5 minutes; heat over hot water, stirring until dissolved. Add to strawberries, mixing well, and chill until slightly thickened. Fold in cream, sweetened with sugar, and chill mixture until thick enough to hold its shape. Line parfait glasses with ladyfingers, fill with gelatin mixture and top with a large berry. Chill. Approximate yield: 6 portions.

Apricot Bavarian—Substitute fresh apricot purée for strawberries.

Raspberry Bavarian—Substitute crushed raspberries for strawberries.

WESTERN BAVARIAN CREAM

1 envelope plain gelatin	¼ teaspoon salt
¼ cup cold water	¾ cup heavy cream, whipped
1 egg, separated	½ teaspoon vanilla
⅓ cup sugar	whipped cream
1¼ cups scalded milk	chopped nuts

Sprinkle gelatin over cold water and let stand 5 minutes. Beat egg yolk until lemon-colored. Melt sugar in heavy frying pan and heat until it is caramel-colored, stirring constantly. Add scalded milk with egg and softened gelatin and stir until dissolved. Add salt, whipped cream, vanilla and stiffly beaten egg white. Blend and pour into a chilled mold rinsed with cold water. Chill until firm and serve with Date Brandy Sauce (page 734) and garnish with whipped cream and nuts. Yield: 6 portions.

BAVARIAN CREAM

5 eggs, separated	¼ cup cold water
5 tablespoons sugar	1½ cups hot milk
4 teaspoons plain gelatin	1 cup heavy cream, whipped
	rum

Beat egg yolks with sugar until light and fluffy. Soak gelatin in cold water 5 minutes and add to yolk mixture. Add hot milk gradually and stir over low heat until gelatin dissolves and mixture thickens enough to coat a metal spoon. Remove from heat and stir until cool. Fold in stiffly beaten egg whites and 5 tablespoons whipped cream. Sprinkle with rum and chill. Garnish with remaining whipped cream and serve. Yield: 4 portions.

SAVOY TRIFLE

5 eggs, separated
¼ cup sugar
3 tablespoons all-purpose flour
confectioners' sugar

grape, red currant or guava
jelly
rum
Bavarian Cream (page 794)

Beat egg yolks with sugar until very light. Add flour and beat well. Fold in stiffly beaten egg whites. Pour batter into a greased 16 x 8-inch jelly roll pan which has been lined with greased waxed paper. Bake in moderate oven (350° F.) 15 minutes. Remove and dust with confectioners' sugar. Turn out on waxed paper and immediately peel off baked waxed paper. Roll like a jelly roll and chill in refrigerator 30 minutes. Unroll and spread thinly with jelly which has been whipped with a fork. Reroll tightly. Slice thin and place slices on bottom and sides of a dessert dish. Sprinkle with rum, fill with Bavarian Cream and garnish top with thin rounds of jelly roll. Yield: 6 portions.

CRANBERRY REFRIGERATOR CAKE

3 cups cranberries
1¼ cups water
⅓ cup seedless raisins
10 dates, finely cut

3 figs, finely cut
⅓ cup chopped walnuts
1 cup sugar
1 small sponge cake, sliced

Cook cranberries slowly in water until skins have popped; force through sieve. Add raisins, dates, figs and nuts and mix; simmer, covered, 5 minutes. Remove from heat and add sugar, stirring until mixed. Line a buttered mold with sponge cake, add a layer of cranberry mixture, then a layer of cake; repeat, finishing with cake. Chill. Unmold and serve with whipped cream. Yield: 6 to 8 portions.

PINEAPPLE–NUT REFRIGERATOR CAKE

1 cup butter
1½ cups confectioners' sugar
½ cup finely chopped nuts
heavy cream, whipped

1 cup drained shredded pineapple
2 egg whites, stiffly beaten
3 dozen vanilla wafers

Cream together butter and sugar, add nuts and pineapple and blend thoroughly; fold in egg whites. Line a cake pan with wafers, cover with fruit-nut mixture; add a layer of wafers and repeat until all ingredients are used, having a layer of wafers on top. Chill in refrigerator at least 12 hours. Serve with whipped cream. Yield: 6 to 8 portions.

PEACH REFRIGERATOR CAKE

½ pound marshmallows
½ cup orange juice
½ cup ginger ale
1 cup heavy cream, whipped

sponge cake or ladyfingers
6 to 8 peaches, sliced
½ cup chopped crystallized
ginger

Cut marshmallows in quarters, add to orange juice and stir over hot water until almost melted; cool slightly and add ginger ale. When slightly thickened, fold in ¾ cup cream, whipped. Line a spring form pan with waxed paper. Arrange layer of cake or ladyfingers on bottom, next a layer of peaches, then layer of marshmallows; repeat until there are 3 layers of cake and 2 of filling. Chill in refrigerator overnight. Unmold; garnish with remaining peaches and cream and ginger. Use fresh or canned peaches or apricots. Yield: 6 to 8 portions.

CHOCOLATE REFRIGERATOR CAKE

2 squares unsweetened
  chocolate
1⅓ cups sweetened condensed
  milk
1 egg, separated

⅓ cup chopped preserved ginger
2 tablespoons ginger syrup
½ teaspoon vanilla
ladyfingers, split
heavy cream, whipped

Melt chocolate over hot water, stir in condensed milk and cook until thickened. Stir 2 tablespoons chocolate mixture into beaten egg yolk; then add to remaining chocolate in double boiler and cook 3 minutes longer; cool. Stir in ginger, ginger syrup and vanilla and fold into stiffly beaten egg white. Line bottom and sides of mold or loaf pan with waxed paper, then with ladyfingers, round side out. Fill center with chocolate mixture and, if a loaf pan is used, arrange additional ladyfingers and chocolate mixture over top. Chill in refrigerator at least 4 hours. Unmold, slice and serve with slightly sweetened whipped cream. Approximate yield: 4 to 6 portions.

SWEET CHOCOLATE SPONGE

8 ounces sweet chocolate,
  grated
4 tablespoons strong coffee

1 tablespoon rum or whisky
5 egg yolks, beaten
5 egg whites, stiffly beaten

Melt chocolate over hot water with coffee. Stir in rum or whisky and beaten egg yolks. Cook until thickened, stirring constantly; cool. Carefully fold in egg whites and pour into individual serving dishes. Chill for 30 minutes in refrigerator. This dessert will keep for several days if closely covered. Yield: 6 to 8 portions.

RUM OMELET

3 eggs, beaten
1 teaspoon sugar

pinch of salt
1 tablespoon butter, melted

⅓ cup rum

Beat eggs until fluffy, then beat in sugar. Add salt, butter and 1 table-spoon of the rum. Pour into buttered frying pan and cook gently until omelet is done. Turn out on platter and pour around it remaining rum, which has been warmed in saucepan. Light this and bring omelet to table while burning. Sprinkle with sugar when serving, if desired. Yield: 2 portions.

SKYSCRAPER AFLAME

1½ cups maple sugar, shaved
2 tablespoons honey
1 teaspoon lemon juice (about)

12 hot French Pancakes (page 1043)
½ cup warm rum

Mix sugar, honey and lemon juice to taste and spread between hot pancakes, stacking them evenly on serving plate. Pour warm rum over all, ignite and serve flaming. Yield: 6 portions.

BAKED APPLES AGLOW

4 baking apples
2 teaspoons chopped walnuts
2 tablespoons minced dates

⅓ cup firmly packed light brown sugar
1 tablespoon confectioners' sugar

½ cup warm rum

Core apples and peel the upper third. Combine nuts, dates and sugar and fill apple centers with mixture. Place in baking dish, cover bottom with boiling water, cover the dish and bake in moderate to hot oven (375°–400° F.) 30 to 40 minutes, or until tender. Remove to individual serving plates, pour syrup from pan over them, sprinkle lightly with confectioners' sugar and pour rum over each one. Ignite rum and serve blazing. Yield: 4 portions.

Frozen Desserts

NOT MANY years ago, ice cream was "Sunday" fare and reserved for special occasions. Today, with modern freezing compartments, electric ice cream freezers and excellent mixes on the market, frozen desserts are a simple affair to make and serve.

Correct freezing procedures and the use of eggs, gelatin and cream, or evaporated milk in some recipes, will insure a firm, smooth, velvety textured dessert. Too much sugar may prevent the freezing of the mixture; ¾ cup sugar per one quart of cream is the usual allowance. Too heavy a cream mixture gives undesirable consistency. Gelatin needs to be used in very small amounts; too much makes a spongy product. Chilling a custard overnight increases the swell when frozen. Beaten egg whites and cream give a smooth texture when there is little or no stirring of the mixture. Fruits and nuts should be aded when the mixture is partially frozen to remain "suspended."

Hand Freezing the Mixture. The ice should be finely cracked. Ice and rock salt are used in the proportions 8 to 10 parts ice to 1 part rock salt. After the mixture is frozen, it is packed in ice and salt. The proportions vary, depending upon the type of mixture to be ripened.

Freezing Mousses, Parfaits and Puddings. Since these mixtures are frozen without stirring, any container, preferably of wood with provision made for draining off brine, may be used. Pack the mixture in the mold, filling it about three-fourths full. Cover tightly. Wind a piece of adhesive tape or a strip of cloth dipped in melted paraffin around the edge of the cover to prevent brine from seeping in, then bury the can in coarsely cracked ice and rock salt in the proportions 3 or 4 parts ice to 1 of salt. Freeze or "ripen" mousses and parfaits 3 to 4 hours. In freezing compartment of refrigerator or freezer, allow 3 to 4 hours.

Mousse mixtures, such as bisques and tortonis, may be molded in paper cups or other individual containers, placed in a large container, covered tightly and packed in ice and salt, or set, loosely covered, in the tray of an automatic refrigerator.

REFRIGERATOR FROZEN DESSERTS

SPECIAL recipes have been developed for automatic refrigerators and freezers. Always be sure to follow manufacturer's directions. If stirred once or twice during the freezing period, certain types of mixtures are smoother. The temperature of the freezing unit must be as cold as possible, since rapid freezing is essential for good texture by keeping ice crystals small. Most cream mixtures freeze in 2 to 4 hours. Sherbets, if very sweet, may require longer and they are likely to have large ice crystals.

PHILADELPHIA ICE CREAM

1 quart light cream   dash of salt
1 cup sugar   2 teaspoons vanilla

Heat cream until lukewarm; add sugar, stirring until dissolved. Add salt and vanilla. Cool and freeze (page 798). Modifications for Vanilla Ice Cream (below) may be used. Approximate yield: 3 pints.

PLAIN VANILLA ICE CREAM

2 cups milk   ⅛ teaspoon salt
¾ cup sugar   4 egg yolks, slightly beaten
1 tablespoon flour   2 teaspoons vanilla
             2 cups light cream

Scald milk over hot water, gradually add mixture of sugar, flour and salt and cook 5 minutes, stirring constantly; stir small amount into egg yolks, then return this to mixture in double boiler and cook 2 minutes, stirring constantly. Chill; add vanilla and cream and freeze (page 798). Approximate yield: 3 pints, or 6 to 8 portions.

Strawberry Ice Cream—Add ¾ cup sugar to 1 cup crushed strawberries or other berries and let stand 1 hour in warm room. Add to ice cream mixture just before freezing. Approximate yield: 2 quarts.

Chocolate Ice Cream—Add 2 squares unsweetened chocolate to milk or cream and heat over hot water until melted. Blend by beating with rotary beater and cool before adding cream to other ingredients.

Caramel Ice Cream—Add ¼ cup cold Caramel Syrup (page 730) after adding vanilla.

Pecan Brittle Ice Cream—Crush finely ½ pound pecan brittle; add to milk or cream and heat over hot water until brittle is dissolved; cool before adding other ingredients. Peppermint candy may be used.

Pistachio Ice Cream—Blanch and chop ¾ cup pistachio nuts and scald with milk or cream. Add 2 drops green vegetable coloring before adding cream to other ingredients.

Peach Ice Cream—Add ¾ cup sugar to 1½ cups sieved peach pulp and mix well; add to ice cream mixture just before freezing; add ¼ teaspoon almond extract. Approximate yield: 2 quarts.

Orange Ice Cream—Omit 1 cup milk or cream from ice cream mixture and add 1 cup orange juice just before freezing; omit vanilla.

Banana Ice Cream—Mash 3 ripe bananas with a silver fork, beating quickly to a smooth pulp; add to cold ice cream mixture and freeze. Approximate yield: 2 quarts.

CUSTARD ICE CREAM

3 tablespoons flour   3 egg yolks, slightly beaten
1 cup sugar   1½ cups heavy cream
3 cups milk   2 teaspoons vanilla

Mix flour and ¼ cup sugar; add milk slowly, mixing well. Cook over hot water 5 minutes, or until smooth and slightly thickened, stirring constantly. Stir hot mixture slowly into egg yolks and cook 2 minutes longer, stirring constantly; cool. Add remaining sugar, cream and vanilla and freeze (page 798). Yield: 3 pints.

FRENCH ICE CREAM

1 cup milk   5 egg yolks, slightly beaten
3 cups light cream   ⅛ teaspoon salt
1 cup sugar   2 teaspoons vanilla

Scald milk with 1½ cups cream. Mix sugar, egg yolks and salt; add scalded milk slowly, mixing well. Cook over hot water 5 to 8 minutes, or until mixture coats a metal spoon, stirring constantly. Cool; add remaining cream and vanilla and freeze (page 798). Approximate yield: 3 pints.

COFFEE ICE CREAM

1 teaspoon plain gelatin	⅛ teaspoon salt
1 tablespoon cold water	1 teaspoon flour
1 cup milk	1 egg, well beaten
1 cup strong black coffee	1½ cups heavy cream
⅔ cup sugar	½ teaspoon vanilla

Soften gelatin in cold water. Scald milk with coffee and add slowly to combined sugar, salt and flour, mixing well; cook over hot water 5 minutes, stirring constantly. Stir small amount into egg, return to remaining hot mixture and cook 2 minutes longer. Add gelatin and stir until dissolved. Cool, add cream and vanilla and freeze (page 798). Approximate yield: 3 pints.

Grape-Nuts Coffee Ice Cream—Add 1 cup grape-nuts to ice cream mixture just before freezing.

Bisque Ice Cream—Add 1 cup toasted macaroon crumbs to ice cream mixture before freezing.

Rum and Coffee Ice Cream—Add 2 tablespoons rum and 1 cup macaroon crumbs to ice cream mixture just before freezing.

Burnt Almond Coffee Ice Cream—Blanch, chop and toast 1 cup almonds and add to ice cream mixture just before freezing.

Coffee Marron Cream—Add 1 cup drained chopped marrons after ice cream mixture is partially frozen and freeze until firm.

Havana Cream—When ice cream mixture is partially frozen, add ½ cup chopped black walnuts and 1 cup chopped raisins and freeze.

RENNET ICE CREAM

1 rennet tablet	¾ cup sugar
2 tablespoons cold water	⅛ teaspoon salt
3 cups lukewarm milk	1 cup heavy cream
2 teaspoons vanilla	

Dissolve rennet tablet in cold water; add to milk, mix well and add remaining ingredients. Let stand in warm room until slightly thick, then freeze (page 799). Approximate yield: 3 pints.

LEMON ICE

1 quart water	1 tablespoon grated lemon rind
1 cup sugar	¾ cup lemon juice

Boil water and sugar 5 minutes; add lemon rind and juice; cool, strain and freeze (page 798). Serve in chilled sherbet glasses with poultry or game, or serve as dessert. Approximate yield: 3 pints.

Orange Ice—Make a syrup of 2 cups water and 1 cup sugar; add 2 cups orange juice and ¼ cup lemon juice; cool, strain and freeze.

Cranberry Ice—Make a syrup of 1 quart water and 2 cups sugar. Cook 1 quart cranberries until they pop; force through sieve; add to syrup, cool and freeze.

Grape Ice—Make a syrup of 3 cups water and 1 cup sugar; add 1 cup grape juice, ¼ cup orange juice and 3 tablespoons lemon juice; cool, strain and freeze.

Strawberry Ice—Make a syrup of 2 cups water and 1 cup sugar. Mash 1 quart ripe berries and force through sieve; add to syrup, cool and freeze. Raspberries may be substituted for strawberries.

Ginger Ale Ice—Make a syrup of 2 cups water and 1 cup sugar; cool, add 3 cups ginger ale and 3 tablespoons lemon juice and freeze.

Coffee Ice—Dissolve 1 cup sugar in 1 quart hot coffee; cool and freeze. Serve with whipped cream.

AVOCADO ICE

1½ large ripe avocados	¼ teaspoon salt
¼ cup honey	¼ teaspoon celery salt
	⅓ cup lime juice

Peel and remove seed from avocados; force pulp through sieve; add remaining ingredients and blend well. Pour into freezing tray of automatic refrigerator. Freeze 2 to 4 hours, or until firm, whipping once during freezing. Serve in sherbet glasses with lamb, turkey or game, or serve as dessert. Approximate yield: 6 portions.

LEMON SHERBET

1 quart water	1 tablespoon grated lemon rind
2 cups sugar	¾ cup lemon juice
	2 egg whites, stiffly beaten

Boil water and sugar 5 minutes, add lemon rind and juice and cool; strain and freeze to a mush-like consistency. Fold in egg whites and freeze until firm (page 798). Approximate yield: 3 pints.

Pineapple Sherbet—Substitute orange juice for half the lemon juice, and add 1 cup drained crushed pineapple.

Lemon Milk Sherbet—Substitute 1 quart milk for water; mix sugar, lemon rind and juice and add slowly to milk, stirring until sugar is dissolved. Strain and freeze until of mush-like consistency; fold in stiffly beaten egg whites and freeze until firm.

RASPBERRY SHERBET

1 teaspoon plain gelatin	1 cup sugar
¼ cup cold water	2 cups strained raspberry juice
1 cup boiling water	3 tablespoons lemon juice

Soften gelatin in cold water; dissolve in boiling water; add sugar and fruit juices, stirring until sugar is dissolved; strain, chill and freeze (page 804). Approximate yield: 1 quart.

Cranberry Sherbet—Substitute 1 pint cranberry juice; freeze.

Strawberry Sherbet—Substitute 2 cups strained strawberry juice, or 1 cup juice and 1 cup crushed berries; freeze.

Peach Sherbet—Substitute 2 cups sieved peach pulp; freeze.

REFRIGERATOR ICE CREAM

2 teaspoons plain gelatin	½ cup sugar
½ cup cold water	2 teaspoons vanilla
1¾ cups evaporated milk	1½ cups heavy cream, whipped

Soften gelatin in cold water and dissolve in hot milk; add sugar and vanilla, stirring until sugar is dissolved; cool. Turn into freezing tray of automatic refrigerator and chill until slightly thickened; fold gently into whipped cream. Return to freezing tray and freeze 1 hour, or until mush-like in consistency; turn into chilled bowl and beat until smooth, but not melted. Return to freezing tray and freeze until firm. Yield: 1 quart.

Frozen Strawberry Cream—Add 1 cup mashed, sweetened berries to cooled gelatin-milk mixture.

Frozen Orange Pecan Cream—Substitute orange juice for milk and increase cream to 2 cups. Fold in 1 cup chopped nuts before final freezing.

Frozen Chocolate Cream—Melt 2 squares unsweetened chocolate in milk; beat with rotary beater until blended. Increase sugar to ¾ cup.

Frozen Pecan Brittle Cream—Grind or crush ¼ pound nut brittle and fold into ice cream mixture before final freezing.

Frozen Pistachio Cream—Omit gelatin but add water in preparing ice cream mixture. Fold in 2 stiffly beaten egg whites, ½ cup finely chopped pistachio nuts, and ½ teaspoon almond before final freezing.

LIME SHERBET

1 teaspoon plain gelatin	1 tablespoon grated lime rind
¼ cup cold water	3 to 4 drops green coloring
2 cups sugar	¾ cup lime juice
3¾ cups hot water	2 egg whites, stiffly beaten

Soften gelatin in cold water for 5 minutes. Dissolve with sugar in hot water and add lime juice, grated lime rind and coloring. Let stand 5 minutes and strain. Cool and freeze to mush-like consistency in freezing tray of refrigerator. Remove to chilled bowl and whip until smooth. Fold in stiffly beaten egg whites. Return to tray and freeze until firm, about 2 hours. Yield: 1 quart.

MINT SHERBET

1 envelope plain gelatin	½ cup lemon or lime juice
1½ cups cold water	¼ cup minced fresh mint
¾ cup boiling water	green vegetable coloring
1 cup sugar	1 egg white

Soften gelatin in ½ cup cold water. Add to boiling water and stir until dissolved. Add sugar, remaining cold water, strained fruit juice and fresh mint. Add just enough coloring to tint mixture a delicate green. Turn into freezing tray of automatic refrigerator. When frozen to a mush, remove from sides and bottom into bowl, beat and add egg white beaten until stiff but not dry. Return to refrigerator to finish freezing. Yield: 6 portions.

LEMON ICE CREAM

1 tablespoon margarine or butter	⅛ teaspoon salt
	3⅓ cups milk
1 tablespoon flour	juice and rind of 3 small lemons

Melt butter in saucepan, stir in flour and salt to make a smooth paste. Gradually add 1⅓ cups milk and cook over low heat, stirring constantly until thickened. Cook 3 minutes longer. Add remaining milk; chill. Pour into a refrigerator tray; when freezing has started on sides and bottom, remove to chilled bowl, beat and add lemon rind and juice. Return to tray and freeze until firm. Yield: 1½ pints.

APPLE BLOSSOM ICE CREAM

2 eggs, separated	3 cups top milk or light cream
2 tablespoons sugar	¼ cup honey
1½ cups applesauce	⅛ teaspoon salt
¼ teaspoon cinnamon	1 cup heavy cream, whipped

Beat egg whites until creamy; add sugar gradually, continuing to beat until egg whites hold their shape. Combine applesauce, cinnamon, milk, honey, salt and beaten egg yolks; mix thoroughly; fold in egg whites. Fold in the whipped cream. Freeze in tray of automatic refrigerator. Approximate yield: 8 to 10 portions.

GRAPEFRUIT CREAM FREEZE

1 cup light cream	1 cup heavy cream, whipped
2 egg yolks	1 tablespoon grated grapefruit
pinch of salt	rind
6 tablespoons sugar	1 cup grapefruit juice
¾ cup crumbled macaroons	1 tablespoon lemon juice

Scald light cream in top of double boiler. Beat together egg yolks, salt and sugar. Add scalded cream slowly, mixing well. Cook over hot water, stirring frequently, until thickened or until mixture coats a metal spoon. Cool; fold in macaroons and whipped cream. Blend in the rind, grapefruit and lemon juices. Pour into freezing tray. Freeze 1 hour until mush-like consistency. Turn into chilled bowl and beat until smooth but not melted. Return to freezing tray and freeze until firm. Serve garnished with green-tinted grapefruit sections and sprinkled with chopped candied grapefruit peel. Approximate yield: 4 portions.

RED PLUM ICE CREAM

8 red plums	1 teaspoon plain gelatin
¾ cup sugar	2 tablespoons cold water
1½ cups water	2 tablespoons lemon juice
2 tablespoons corn syrup	1 cup heavy cream, whipped

Cook plums with sugar and water about 15 minutes, or until soft; remove stones and force pulp through sieve. Add corn syrup and gelatin, softened in cold water, and stir over heat until dissolved; cool. Add lemon juice and fold in cream; turn into freezing tray of automatic refrigerator. Freeze 2 to 4 hours, or until frozen to the desired consistency, whipping once during freezing. Yield: 6 portions.

FRUIT MOUSSE

1 cup strawberry, raspberry or   ½ cup confectioners' sugar
    other fruit pulp   2 cups heavy cream, whipped
                    1 teaspoon vanilla

Combine fruit pulp and sugar, mixing well. Fold into whipped cream; add vanilla. Mold, pack into ice and salt and freeze 3 hours (page 798); or turn into freezing tray of automatic refrigerator and freeze 2 to 4 hours, or until firm. Approximate yield: 1 quart.

The following fruits may be used:
    ½ cup sieved, stewed apricots and ½ cup mashed bananas.
    1 cup cinnamon-flavored, unsweetened applesauce.
    ½ cup drained, crushed canned pineapple and ½ cup sieved
        stewed rhubarb.
    1 cup mashed peaches.
    1 cup sieved stewed plums.
    ½ cup each mashed raspberries and peaches.

Grape Mousse—Substitute 1 cup grape jelly for fruit pulp; omit sugar.

Chocolate Mousse—Substitute ¾ cup commercial chocolate syrup for fruit pulp; fold sugar into cream.

Bisque—Fold 1 cup macaroon or graham cracker crumbs or ½ cup ground nut meats into any mousse mixture just before freezing.

Prune Cream Bisque—Use 1 cup cooked prune pulp, mashed, in mousse mixture. Fold in ¾ cup graham cracker crumbs and ½ teaspoon almond extract.

COFFEE-COTTAGE CHEESE MOUSSE

1 envelope plain gelatin   1¼ cups creamed cottage cheese
¼ cup cold strong black coffee   2 egg yolks, beaten
1 cup hot strong black coffee   ⅛ teaspoon cinnamon
2 tablespoons dark rum   3 egg whites
6 tablespoons sugar   ¼ teaspoon salt

Soften gelatin in cold coffee 5 minutes. Add to hot coffee with rum and sugar. Stir until gelatin and sugar are dissolved. Cool. Stir in cottage cheese, egg yolks and cinnamon; beat with rotary beater. Fold in stiffly beaten egg whites and salt. Pour into a mold rinsed with cold water. Chill until set. Before serving, unmold on serving platter and garnish with cottage cheese forced through a pastry bag, and fresh fruits. Yield: 6 portions.

MOUSSE AU CHOCOLAT

4 ounces bitter chocolate   1 cup sugar
6 egg yolks   6 egg whites, stiffly beaten
         1 pint heavy cream, whipped

Melt chocolate in top of double boiler over hot water. Beat egg yolks with sugar; fold in stiffly beaten egg whites. Add whipped cream, and blend well. Then add the melted chocolate and again blend. Turn into serving dish and refrigerate until thoroughly chilled. Yield: 8 portions.

PINEAPPLE MOUSSE

1 cup crushed pineapple   12 marshmallows
1 tablespoon water   2 cups heavy cream, whipped

Drain pineapple well. Add water to marshmallows and melt over hot water; cool and fold into whipped cream. Stir in pineapple. Turn into mold and freeze in ice and salt 3 hours (page 798); or turn into freezing tray of automatic refrigerator and freeze 2 to 4 hours, or until firm. Approximate yield: 1 quart.

BURNT ALMOND MOUSSE

5 egg yolks, beaten   1 cup sugar
1 cup maple syrup   1 cup chopped, roasted almonds
1/8 teaspoon salt   1 teaspoon vanilla
         1 quart heavy cream, whipped

Cook egg yolks, syrup and salt in top of double boiler, stirring constantly until thick. Cool. Caramelize sugar (page 730) and turn into pan that has been lightly buttered. When cold, pound into a fine mass. Combine custard, nuts, caramelized sugar and vanilla; fold in whipped cream. Turn into lightly buttered mold and freeze. Yield: 2¼ quarts.

QUICK PEPPERMINT CREAM

16 marshmallows   1 cup heavy cream, whipped
1 cup hot milk   1 cup crushed peppermint candy

Add marshmallows to hot milk and stir until dissolved; chill thoroughly. Fold marshmallow mixture into cream and beat until smooth and very light; fold in crushed peppermint candy. Turn into freezing tray of automatic refrigerator and freeze 2 to 4 hours, or until firm. Beat once during freezing period. Yield: 1 quart.

FROZEN CREAM WHIP

Whip 1 cup heavy cream until it begins to hold its shape; gradually beat in ¼ cup confectioners' sugar, dash of salt and ¼ teaspoon vanilla and fold in 1 stiffly beaten egg white. Turn into freezing tray of automatic refrigerator and freeze 2 to 4 hours. Yield: 1½ cups.

CHARLOTTE GLACÉ

1 envelope plain gelatin
¼ cup cold water
⅓ cup confectioners' sugar

2 cups heavy cream
1 teaspoon vanilla
ladyfingers

whipped cream

Soften gelatin in cold water 5 minutes; dissolve over hot water. Beat sugar into cream, add vanilla and stir in gelatin; turn into cylindrical mold, pack in ice and salt and freeze 3 hours (page 798). Unmold on chilled serving platter; garnish with whipped cream and ladyfingers. Approximate yield: 6 portions.

FROZEN CHARLOTTE

1½ teaspoons plain gelatin
¼ cup cold water
2 cups heavy cream, whipped

½ cup confectioners' sugar
1 cup finely chopped pecans
2 tablespoons wine

macaroons

Soften gelatin in cold water 5 minutes; heat over hot water until dissolved. Add to whipped cream, mixing well; fold in sugar, pecans and wine. Line small molds with macaroons, fill with gelatin mixture and place in freezing compartment of automatic refrigerator; freeze 2 to 4 hours, or until firm. Approximate yield: 6 portions.

MARASCHINO PARFAIT

¾ cup sugar
½ cup water
2 eggs, separated

⅓ cup maraschino cherries, diced
¼ cup maraschino cherry juice
2 cups heavy cream, whipped

Boil sugar and water to 230° F., or until it spins a thread. Add slowly to beaten egg yolks, beating constantly until cold. Stir in fruit and juice, then fold in stiffly beaten egg whites and cream. Turn into mold and freeze in ice and salt 3 hours (page 798), or turn into freezing tray of automatic refrigerator and freeze 2 to 4 hours. Yield: 1 quart.

TOASTED COCONUT PARFAIT

Boil ¾ cup sugar and ½ cup water to a syrup (230° F.); add gradually to 3 stiffly beaten egg whites, beating constantly until cold. Fold in 2 cups heavy cream, whipped, 1 teaspoon vanilla and ½ cup toasted coconut. Freeze. Yield: 1 quart.

MINT PARFAIT

½ cup Crême de Menthe or mint sauce
1½ pints vanilla ice cream

½ cup heavy cream, whipped and sweetened

Pour 1 tablespoon Crême de Menthe in bottom of each parfait glass. Add one or two scoops of ice cream. Pour another tablespoon Crême de Menthe over ice cream. Top each with whipped cream. If desired, garnish with maraschino cherries and fresh mint leaves. Yield: 4 parfaits.
If you don't have parfait glasses, Pilsener glasses serve as well.

MAPLE ALMOND PARFAIT

1 cup maple syrup
3 egg whites, stiffly beaten

2 cups heavy cream, whipped
½ cup chopped and toasted almonds

Heat maple syrup to boiling and pour slowly over egg whites, beating constantly; continue beating until mixture is cold. Fold in cream and almonds. Turn into mold and freeze in ice and salt 3 hours; or turn into freezing trays of automatic refrigerator and freeze 2 to 3 hours, or until firm. Approximate yield: 1 quart.

MOCHA BISCUIT

3 cups milk
1 cup double strength coffee
2 tablespoons flour

½ cup sugar
5 eggs, slightly beaten
1 teaspoon vanilla

Combine milk and coffee, mix flour and sugar and add milk-coffee mixture slowly, mixing well. Cook over hot water 15 minutes, or until smooth and slightly thickened. Stir a small amount into eggs, mixing well; return to remaining hot mixture and cook 5 minutes longer, stirring constantly; add vanilla; chill. Turn mixture into paper containers; freeze in trays of automatic refrigerator 2 to 3 hours, or until firm. Garnish with whipped cream. Sprinkle chopped nuts over tops, if desired. Approximate yield: 8 portions.

REFRIGERATOR MOCHA CREAM

1 teaspoon plain gelatin	½ cup sugar
½ cup milk	⅛ teaspoon salt
½ cup double strength coffee	1 square unsweetened chocolate
2 eggs, separated	¼ cup hot water
1 cup heavy cream, whipped	

Soften gelatin in ¼ cup milk. Scald remaining milk with coffee. Add slowly to beaten egg yolks, mixing well; add sugar and salt; cook over hot water 5 minutes, or until mixture coats spoon, stirring constantly. Add gelatin and stir until dissolved. Melt chocolate in hot water; add slowly to coffee custard, mixing well; cool. Fold in cream and stiffly beaten egg whites. Turn into freezing tray of automatic refrigerator and freeze 2 to 4 hours, or until firm, whipping twice during freezing. Approximate yield: 6 portions.

PEACH SURPRISE

2 diced canned peaches	3 egg whites, stiffly beaten
1 cup confectioners' sugar	½ cup heavy cream, whipped

Drain peaches and add sugar; fold in egg whites and cream. Turn into mold and freeze in ice and salt 3 hours (page 798); or turn into trays of automatic refrigerator. Freeze until firm. Yield: 1 quart.

NESSELRODE PUDDING

1½ cups milk	½ cup marrons glacés
¾ cup sugar	2 tablespoons marron syrup
3 egg yolks, slightly beaten	1 cup heavy cream, whipped
¼ teaspoon salt	¼ cup chopped candied fruits,
¼ cup Almond Paste (page 639)	assorted

Scald milk. Combine sugar, egg yolks and salt; add milk slowly, stirring until sugar is dissolved; cook over hot water 5 to 8 minutes, stirring constantly until mixture coats metal spoon; cool. Add almond paste, ¼ cup marrons pressed through a sieve, and marron syrup; fold in cream. Turn into freezing trays of automatic refrigerator and freeze 2 hours, or to a soft cream stage. Line a chilled quart melon mold with half the mixture; add remaining chopped marrons and chopped fruits to other half and fill mold. Cover and pack in ice and salt and freeze 3 hours (page 798). Yield: 1 quart.

FROZEN PLUM PUDDING

¼ cup currants
¼ cup seeded raisins
¼ cup finely shredded citron
12 maraschino cherries, chopped
3 tablespoons shredded dates

3 tablespoons shredded figs
½ cup maraschino cordial
3 tablespoons chopped blanched
  almonds
1 quart chocolate ice cream

Wash currants, add raisins and steam or simmer in small amount of water 5 minutes, or until plump; drain and cool. Marinate all other fruits in maraschino cordial 6 hours; combine fruits and nuts and mix into ice cream. Turn into freezing trays of automatic refrigerator and freeze 2 to 4 hours, or until firm. Approximate yield: 3 pints.

FROZEN MINT PUDDING

1½ teaspoons plain gelatin
2 tablespoons water
½ cup crushed white peppermint candy
¼ cup milk

2 eggs, separated
6 drops green vegetable coloring
¼ teaspoon salt
6 tablespoons sugar
1 cup heavy cream, whipped

12 plain chocolate cookies, crushed

Soak gelatin in water 5 minutes. Dissolve the candy in milk over boiling water. Beat egg yolks well; pour a little of the hot milk into them. Add to the rest of the hot mixture and cook until thick, stirring constantly. Add coloring and gelatin, stirring until dissolved. Cool until thick but not set. Add salt to egg whites and beat until stiff but not dry. Gradually add sugar, beating constantly. Fold into milk mixture. Add whipped cream. Put half the chocolate crumbs into two freezing trays. Pour in the prepared mixture; cover with rest of the crumbs. Freeze, without stirring, at coldest refrigerator temperature 3 to 4 hours. Yield: 8 portions.

FROZEN STRAWBERRY CUSTARD

1 quart strawberries
1¼ cups sugar
2 egg yolks, slightly beaten

1 teaspoon plain gelatin
2 tablespoons cold water
½ teaspoon vanilla

2 cups heavy cream, whipped

Wash and hull berries. Crush and add sugar. Let stand 3 hours. Press half the berries through cheesecloth. Add juice to egg yolks and cook over hot water 5 minutes or until slightly thickened, stirring constantly. Soften gelatin in cold water, add to hot mixture and stir until dissolved; cool. Add remaining berries and vanilla; fold in cream. Turn into mold, pack in ice and salt and freeze 3 hours (page 798), or turn into trays of refrigerator; freeze 2 to 4 hours. Yield: 3 pints.

JAVANESE FROZEN CREAM

2 cups milk
2 eggs, slightly beaten
¾ cup sugar
⅛ teaspoon salt

⅓ cup triple strength coffee
½ cup raisins
1 cup water
½ cup blanched almonds, ground
2 cups heavy cream, whipped

Scald milk. Combine eggs, sugar and salt; add milk slowly, stirring until sugar is dissolved. Add coffee and cook over hot water 5 to 8 minutes, stirring constantly until mixture coats metal spoon; cool. Simmer raisins in water 5 minutes; drain, cool and add to custard mixture; add nuts. Fold in cream and turn into freezing trays of automatic refrigerator; freeze 2 to 4 hours. Yield: 3 pints.

BAKED ALASKA

1 thin sponge cake
    (about 8 x 6 inches)

1 quart ice cream
5 egg whites
¾ cup sugar

Place sponge cake on several thicknesses of heavy paper on baking sheet; cover cake with ice cream, allowing the cake to extend ½ inch beyond edge of cream. Beat egg whites until stiff; gradually beat in ½ cup sugar and continue beating until the meringue is stiff. Spread over entire surface of cream and rim of cake and sprinkle surface with remaining ¼ cup sugar. Bake in hot oven (400° F.) about 5 minutes, or until lightly browned. Approximate yield: 6 to 8 portions.

Individual Baked Alaska—Scoop out crumbs from thick slices of sponge cake and fill shells with ice cream. Heap meringue on sides and tops and brown in hot oven. Fill centers with fruit sauce or nuts.

BOMBES

Peach Bombe—Line a melon mold evenly with a layer of vanilla ice cream 1-inch thick; fill center with peach mousse mixture; cover, pack in ice and salt and freeze 3 hours (page 798).

Almond Bombe—Line a melon mold evenly with a layer of vanilla or chocolate ice cream 1-inch thick; fill with Burnt Almond Mousse (page 807); cover, pack in ice and salt and freeze 3 hours (page 798).

SUNDAES

Banana Sundae—Peel and split ripe banana lengthwise and place on long, narrow dish; put ice cream in center and top with Cherry or Hot Jelly Sauce (pages 725–727) and chopped almonds.

Berry Sundae—Place alternate spoonfuls of ice cream and sweetened crushed berries in parfait glasses. Top with whipped cream.

Brandied Cherry Sundae—Top vanilla ice cream with Brandied Large Cherries (page 725).

Hot Fudge Sundae—Pour hot Butterscotch, Caramel, Chocolate or Maple Fudge Sauce (pages 729–730) over vanilla, coffee or chocolate ice cream. Sprinkle chopped walnuts, or chopped and toasted blanched almonds, or pecan halves over top.

Peach Melba—Place canned peach half in sherbet glass, fill center with vanilla ice cream and add 2 tablespoons Melba Sauce (page 727).

GRAPEFRUIT BAKED ALASKA

Prepare grapefruit halves for eating. Top each half with scoop of ice cream. Quickly cover with meringue made by stiffly beating egg whites with sugar, allowing 2 tablespoons sugar to each egg white. Lightly brown under broiler and serve immediately.

RAINBOW PIE

½ pint lemon sherbet	½ pint orange or lime sherbet
1 pint raspberry sherbet	1 9-inch baked pastry shell

Let sherbets stand at room temperature until slightly softened but not melted. Spread lemon, then raspberry and lastly, orange sherbets in pastry shell. (When cut, there will be three colorful layers.) Place in freezer until firm. Yield: 6 to 8 portions.

STRAWBERRIES ROMANOFF

2 quarts strawberries	½ cup Cointreau
½ cup sugar	1 quart vanilla ice cream

Wash and hull strawberries. Keep aside a dozen large berries. Cut remaining berries in half. Add sugar and pour over Cointreau. Let stand several hours. When ready to serve, whip ice cream slightly and spoon over fruit. Top each serving with a whole berry. Yield: 12 portions.

Sandwiches and Snacks

SANDWICHES and snacks can be called truly American favorites. No other country has adopted them with such enthusiastic gusto.

Rules for sandwich making are simple—you probably already know them. To remind you, we may say day-old bread cuts more easily than strictly fresh. Use a sharp, thin knife for the job, dipping it occasionally in hot water for greater efficiency. One family-size loaf yields 16 to 22 slices; a large sandwich loaf, 46 slices. Butter needs to be creamed for easy spreading; it may be softened with mayonnaise for savory sandwiches. Fillings should also be soft.

To keep sandwiches: Wrap in waxed paper or cellophane bags for two to three hours' keeping. For longer periods, wrap the paper-covered sandwiches in a damp towel and store in the refrigerator.

To freeze sandwiches, see material on bread freezing (page 897); defrost before using. Sandwiches will keep fresh in freezer up to 90 days.

The Lunch Box. The child's lunch box should contain sandwiches that are suitable to his needs. At least one savory sandwich that contains a simple protein such as chopped egg, chicken or ground roasted or broiled meat should be included. Peanut butter, cream cheese, dried fruits and nuts with their many variations are appropriate fillings to use. The man who carries his lunch requires at least two substantial sandwiches with a protein base; sweets may be included in the form of a sweet filling between slices of nut, orange or raisin bread; or as fresh or dried fruits, cake, or simple candies. Strong-flavored fish fillings are usually better appreciated at a picnic lunch. Salads can be packed in paper cups to accompany plain bread-and-butter sandwiches. All sandwiches should be wrapped in waxed paper, labeled if necessary and the box lined with a gay paper napkin.

FRUIT, CHEESE, NUT SANDWICH FILLINGS

Use for tea or fancy sandwiches, open or covered; crisp lettuce or water cress may be placed on bread if used soon after making.

Apricot and Nut Filling—Mash 1 cup stewed apricots; add ½ cup chopped nuts and 2 tablespoons heavy cream.

Date and Nut Filling—Chop dates and nuts and moisten with cream or mayonnaise.

Date-Fig Filling—Grind together dates, figs and raisins and moisten with Honey-Cream Dressing (page 622).

Orange Marmalade Filling—Combine orange marmalade with cream cheese; chop oranges if pieces are large.

Glacé Fruit Spread—Mix ½ cup minced glacé fruit, 1 tablespoon lemon juice, 1 cup cottage cheese and ½ teaspoon salt.

Cheese and Pineapple Spread—Mix 1 3-oz. package cream cheese with 1 cup crushed pineapple, 2 tablespoons pineapple juice, 1 tablespoon grated carrot and ⅛ teaspoon salt.

Almond-Celery Filling—Mix ½ cup each chopped almonds and celery and moisten with mayonnaise.

Peanut Butter and Honey Spread—Moisten peanut butter with honey to spreading consistency.

Cottage Cheese Spread—Mix 1 cup cottage cheese with ½ teaspoon salt, 2 tablespoons sour cream and 1 tablespoon chopped pimiento.

Cream Cheese-Guava Jelly—Spread with cream cheese moistened with cream, then with guava jelly.

Cream Cheese and Ginger—Mix cream cheese with minced preserved ginger and moisten with Cream Mayonnaise (page 621).

Spicy Cheese Spread—Mix ¼ cup each softened butter and Parmesan cheese, dash of cayenne and a few drops of Worcestershire sauce.

Sliced Cheese Filling—Slice American, Old English, processed or Swiss cheese, spread lightly with prepared mustard, if desired, and place between slices of bread; toast until browned and cheese starts to melt.

Cream Cheese-Honey—Spread with cream cheese moistened with milk, then with honey.

Orange Prune Filling—Peel and remove pulp from 2 small oranges; chop and add ¾ cup pitted, chopped dried prunes and ¼ cup chopped walnuts. Mix with a little mayonnaise.

Carrot, Nut and Pineapple Filling—Toss lightly together 1 cup grated raw carrot, ⅓ cup nut meats, finely cut, and 1 cup pineapple, drained and diced, and spread on whole wheat bread with mayonnaise.

Apple, Olive and Nut Filling—Put 2 small quartered and cored apples through the food chopper. Then add ¼ pound chopped nut meats, 2 stalks of chopped celery and 3 chopped stuffed olives. Season with salt and paprika and moisten with mayonnaise.

Maraschino-Cheese Spread—Mix finely chopped maraschino cherries with cream cheese and moisten with cherry liquor.

Peanut Butter-Bacon Spread—Moisten peanut butter with mayonnaise and mix with chopped crisp bacon.

Fruit Confection Filling—Use any of the fruit confection recipes (page 831); add mayonnaise until of consistency to spread.

Bacon-Honey Spread—Dice crisp bacon and add enough honey to form a spread.

SANDWICH SPREADS

See Canapé section (page 197) for butter, cheese, fish, meat and fruit spreads. There are fillings suitable for tea or fancy sandwiches and for more substantial ones.

EGG SANDWICH FILLINGS

Use for luncheon or picnic sandwiches or for lunch box; garnish as desired. Chop hard-cooked eggs, season with salt and pepper and use one of the following combinations:

Eggs, minced onion and Mustard Cream Mayonnaise (page 622).
Eggs, minced celery, pimiento and mayonnaise.
Eggs, chopped pickles and mayonnaise.
Eggs and Russian Dressing (page 623).
Eggs, chopped stuffed olives and Cooked Salad Dressing (page 624) or mayonnaise.
Eggs, diced crisp bacon, or chopped boiled ham and salad dressing or well-seasoned mayonnaise.
Eggs, canned salmon and chopped celery.
Eggs, mashed shad roe.
Eggs, chicken, tongue and Worcestershire sauce.
Eggs, caviar and onion.

VEGETABLE SANDWICH FILLINGS

Use crisp vegetables with mayonnaise or other salad dressings for fillings for tea or fancy sandwiches, or for tasty sandwiches with a luncheon dish. Prepare just before serving. Some suggestions follow.

Carrots—Grated and mixed with shredded cabbage or raisins.

Celery—Chopped and mixed with chopped nuts and mayonnaise.

Cucumbers—Sliced thin or chopped and mixed with onion or nuts.

Green Peppers—Minced and sprinkled lightly over buttered bread.

Radishes—Sliced thin. Use alone or with cucumber or green peppers.

Salad Greens—Lettuce, curly endive, water cress, tender spinach or young nasturtium leaves; use tender leaves, whole or shredded.

Tomatoes—Peeled and sliced thin, topped with finely sliced onion.

Veal Forcemeat—Grind any leftover veal, chopped nuts, pickle and stuffed olives. Add mayonnaise, season to taste. Mix lightly.

Corned Beef—Combine 1 cup ground or chopped corned beef with ¼ cup chopped water cress. Moisten with French dressing. Store in refrigerator. Yield: filling for 4 sandwiches.

OPEN SANDWICHES

Cut slices of bread in ¼-inch slices; then cut in fancy shapes such as hearts, diamonds, rounds, rings and shamrocks. Spread with creamed butter and any desired filling. Garnish with nut meats, stuffed olives, chives, water cress, parsley, pimiento, green pepper, hard-cooked eggs, anchovies, capers, caviar, bits of truffles, etc.

DAINTY SANDWICHES

Remove crust from thin slices of bread; put 2 together with creamed butter and any desired filling, spread well to the edge of bread. Cut in shapes such as: ½-inch strips for finger sandwiches, small rounds, oblongs, triangles, squares, stars, crescents, bridge-shaped pieces, etc.

ROLLED SANDWICHES

Remove all crust from loaf of fresh bread; spread cut side lengthwise, with creamed butter or other soft filling, and cut in ¼-inch slices lengthwise. Roll as for jelly roll and fasten with toothpicks. Wrap in waxed paper, then in damp towel; chill. Just before serving, cut in ¼-inch slices.

RIBBON SANDWICHES

Remove crusts from white and whole wheat or graham bread; spread cut ends of loaves with creamed butter or sandwich spread, using contrasting colors for each, if desired. Cut in ¼-inch slices and put 3 together with dark slice between 2 light slices or light slice between 2 dark slices. Wrap in damp cheesecloth or waxed paper, place under a weight and chill. Just before serving, cut in ¼-inch slices.

CHECKERBOARD SANDWICHES

Remove crusts from white and whole wheat loaves of bread; spread cut ends of each with creamed butter and cut in ¼-inch slices. Put 2 light and 2 dark slices together, alternating the colors; then cut, lengthwise, in ¼-inch strips. Lay 1 strip down flat on waxed paper and butter top side, place second strip on top, reversing it so that the dark strip is on top of the light one, checkerboard fashion. Repeat with 2 more strips, reversing it each time to alternate the colors as before. Wrap tightly and chill 2 hours. Remove paper and spread cream cheese, softened with cream, over top and sides; chill 1 hour. Serve on platter and cut in thin slices.

PINWHEEL SANDWICHES

Remove all crust from white and whole wheat loaves of bread; spread cut ends of each with creamed butter or other soft filling, using contrasting colors for each, if desired. Cut a very thin slice from each loaf and put the two together. Spread top slice with filling and roll as for jelly roll; fasten with toothpicks, wrap in waxed paper, then in damp cloth; chill ½ hour or more. Just before serving, cut in ¼-inch slices.

COTTAGE CHEESE–BACON PINWHEELS

1 loaf bread	2 tablespoons chili sauce
⅓ cup soft butter	¾ cup cottage cheese
⅓ cup minced cooked bacon	

Remove crusts from bread and cut in lengthwise slices. Blend together butter and chili sauce. Spread each slice first with chili sauce-butter mixture, then with combined cottage cheese and bacon. Roll each as for jelly roll, wrap in waxed paper and chill. Slice to serve. Approximate yield: 3 dozen pinwheels.

SANDWICH CAKE

1 loaf whole wheat bread	¼ pound liverwurst
1 loaf white bread	2 teaspoons anchovy paste
½ cup butter, creamed	1 8-oz. can crab meat
1 8-oz. can sardines	2 tablespoons French dressing
2 tablespoons lemon juice	1 cup butter, creamed
1 3-oz. package cream cheese	3 tablespoons anchovy paste
1 tablespoon grated onion or	cream cheese
chopped chives	hard-cooked egg
1 2-oz. jar black caviar	olive slices
red caviar	

Chill bread in refrigerator overnight. Remove crusts from both loaves
and cut each lengthwise in slices ¼-inch thick. Place 2 slices together,
side by side; place an 8-inch cake pan on top and trim bread to make
an 8-inch round slice. Repeat until 7 round slices are cut, alternating
light and dark bread. Butter each slice lightly. Place round slice of
white bread on chop plate and cover with a paste of sardines and
lemon juice. Top with a round of whole wheat bread (placed so
break in the center comes at right angles to the break in the slice
below); spread with a paste of cream cheese and onion or chives.
Repeat, alternating light and dark bread and spreading each round
slice with one of the following fillings: black caviar; liverwurst and
anchovy paste; crab meat and French dressing. Cover top and sides
of cake very thinly with a mixture of butter and anchovy paste. Place
in refrigerator until firm. Garnish with rosettes of cream cheese, slices
of hard-cooked egg and stuffed olives and sprinkle with red caviar.
Chill at least 2 hours and cut in thin wedges, using a very sharp knife.
Approximate yield: 25 to 30 portions.

GUAVA PECAN SANDWICHES

¼ cup guava jelly	¾ cup cream cheese
20 thin rounds of bread	2 tablespoons cream
¼ cup chopped pecans	

Spread guava jelly on rounds of bread; then spread with mixture of
cream cheese, cream and nuts. Approximate yield: 20 sandwiches.

SANDWICH LOAF

2 small cans deviled ham
½ teaspoon Worcestershire
    sauce
4 sweet pickles, minced
1 small can deviled chicken
¼ teaspoon dry mustard
1 tablespoon cream

2 pickled onions, minced
1 cup grated American cheese
1 tablespoon chili sauce
1 teaspoon prepared horseradish
½ pound cream cheese
½ cup sour cream
1 loaf (1 lb.) sandwich bread
mayonnaise

Combine ham, Worcestershire sauce and minced pickles for one filling; chicken, mustard, cream and minced pickled onions for another; and grated cheese, chili sauce and horseradish for a third. Blend cream cheese and sour cream to spreading consistency for the outside of the loaf. Remove crusts from bread and cut in 5 slices lengthwise. Spread each slice, except the top slice, with mayonnaise, with filling and then with mayonnaise again, spreading the first slice with all the chicken filling, the next with the cheese and the last with the remaining ham filling. Reassemble slices in loaf shape and frost generously with cream-cheese mixture. Wrap in waxed paper and damp cloth. Chill for several hours. Cut in wedges like a layer cake. To use leftover sandwiches on the second day bake them in a waffle batter. Drop a tablespoon of waffle batter in each quarter of a waffle iron, place a thin sandwich slice on top of each spoonful of batter, cover with batter and bake as an ordinary waffle. Serve plain or with sour cream.

FUNNY FACE SANDWICHES

Cut large circles from Boston brown bread or white bread. Make faces in half the circles by cutting out tiny eyes, nose and mouth with a sharp pointed knife. Spread remaining slices with sandwich filling of a contrasting color: a yellow cheese mixture for brown bread or ham spread for white bread. Press cut-out slice on top of filling, letting filling bulge up through the cut-out features.

CLUB SANDWICH

Toast 3 slices of bread; butter and cover 1 slice with crisp lettuce, letting it extend beyond edge. Arrange sliced white chicken meat or any desired meat on top, spread with mayonnaise and cover with second piece of toast. Spread top with mayonnaise, lay slices of crisp bacon, onion or tomato on top and cover with third piece. Garnish with parsley, pickles or olives. Cut in triangles and serve while toast is hot. For a smaller club sandwich, use 2 slices of toast.

Cheese Club Sandwich—Dip lettuce leaves in mayonnaise and substitute thin slices of American or Swiss cheese for meat. Shredded cabbage may be scattered over tomato on second layer.

Ham Club Sandwich—Use Russian dressing and substitute thin slices of baked ham for chicken. Use tomato slices on second layer.

Lobster Club Sandwich—Sauté canned lobster meat in butter 5 minutes, season with salt, pepper and Sherry and cook 2 minutes; use instead of meat.

Olive Club Sandwich—Substitute sliced hard-cooked egg for meat; sprinkle chopped ripe olives over tomatoes on second layer.

Three-Decker Sandwich—Spread cheese or any desired filling between two slices; cover top of sandwich with lettuce, spread with mayonnaise, with sliced tomato, anchovy fillet and toast on top.

VEGETABLE CLUB SANDWICH

Place 6 cooked asparagus tips between 2 slices buttered toast, spreading lightly with mayonnaise. Spread top of sandwich with mayonnaise and cover with chopped tomatoes, pearl onions and 2 slices of crisp bacon. Cover with third piece of toast and serve with pickles.

TOMATO AND BACON SANDWICH

Use 2 slices of white bread for each sandwich; toast, spread with butter and cover with crisp lettuce. Arrange slices of tomato on top, spread with mayonnaise and top with 2 slices crisp bacon. Cover with toast, cut in triangles and serve hot with dill pickles.

PICNIC SANDWICHES

Between halves of buttered hot or toasted biscuits serve one of the following: Broiled Hamburger (page 282) with sliced onion or Barbecue Sauce (page 475); broiled or grilled steak with tomato; broiled frankfurter with prepared mustard; broiled bacon with tomato slices; fried eggs with ketchup.

SAVORY BAKED BEAN SANDWICHES

1 cup Boston baked beans	½ small onion, minced
¼ cup chopped nut meats	2 tablespoons tomato ketchup
¼ cup chopped celery	¼ teaspoon salt

12 slices buttered toast

Mash beans and add nuts, vegetables and seasonings, mixing thoroughly; spread between slices of toast. Yield: 6 sandwiches.

ALL–GARDEN SANDWICHES

½ small cooked cauliflower   ½ cup cooked string beans,
½ cup cooked peas   cut fine
½ cup cubed cooked carrots   ½ cup cubed cooked beets
½ green pepper, chopped   French Dressing (page 618)

Separate cauliflower into very small pieces. Marinate each vegetable separately in French dressing. Chill thoroughly. Spread both slices of whole wheat or white bread with creamy mayonnaise, spread vegetables on the mayonnaise and close sandwich. Approximate yield: filling for 6 to 8 sandwiches.

TOMATO AND HERB SANDWICH

Cut French bread in half lengthwise. Spread with Garlic Butter (page 200) and fill with sliced tomatoes seasoned with salt, pepper and chopped fresh herbs. Cut in slices to serve.

SPANISH SANDWICHES

2 tablespoons chopped pimiento   1 cup grated cheese
2 tablespoons chopped onion   ½ teaspoon salt
1 tablespoon butter   dash of paprika
1 cup thick tomato pulp   1 egg, well beaten
             6 slices buttered toast

Sauté pimiento and onion in butter 5 minutes; add tomato pulp, cheese, salt and paprika and cook 5 minutes longer, or until cheese is melted. Stir small amount into egg; return to hot mixture and cook 2 minutes longer; serve on hot toast. Approximate yield: 6 portions.

SICILIAN SANDWICHES

4 slices bread   3 medium tomatoes, sliced
2 tablespoons butter   3 tablespoons India relish
¾ cup Cheddar cheese spread   4 strips bacon

Spread each slice of bread with butter, then with cheese spread. Arrange tomato slices over cheese and spread with India relish. Top each sandwich with 2 half slices of bacon; place under broiler until bacon is crisp and cheese melted. Serve hot. Yield: 4 sandwiches.

CHEESE AND BACON TRIANGLES

6 slices bread

6 slices American or Old English
cheese (packaged)
3 slices bacon, diced

Trim crusts from bread and cover with cheese; sprinkle bacon over cheese and place under broiler 6 minutes, or until cheese has begun to melt and bacon is crisp. Cut in triangles. Yield: 6 portions.

BACON–CHEESE TOAST ROUNDS

¾ cup grated American cheese   2 teaspoons chutney
⅓ cup minced crisp bacon   3 tablespoons chili sauce
3 tablespoons chopped pecans   salt
12 rounds buttered toast

Mix cheese, bacon, nuts, chutney and chili sauce and season with salt. Spread on toast rounds and place in hot oven (400° F.) 5 minutes, or until cheese is melted. Serve at once. Yield: 6 portions.

CHEESE DREAMS

Spread 6 slices of bread with peanut butter; top each with a slice of American cheese, then with another slice of bread. Sauté in butter until golden brown, cut in triangles and serve immediately. Approximate yield: 6 sandwiches.

HOT MEAT SANDWICHES

Heat slices of roast beef, pork, lamb, chicken or turkey in gravy made of meat drippings. Serve on buttered hot toast.

HOT BACON OLIVE SANDWICHES

½ cup ripe olives   3 tablespoons mayonnaise
2 slices bacon   salt
¾ cup grated American cheese   pepper
1 tablespoon chopped pickle   5 slices bread

Cut olives from pits into large pieces. Cook bacon until crisp, drain and chop. Blend olives, bacon, cheese, pickle and mayonnaise. Add salt and pepper to taste. Toast bread on one side under broiler. Turn and spread with cheese mixture. Broil until heated through and cheese melts. Yield: 5 portions.

LIVERWURST SANDWICHES

7 slices liverwurst
½ 3-oz. package cream cheese
3 hard-cooked eggs, chopped
3 tablespoons mayonnaise

dash of salt
dash of pepper
½ teaspoon chopped chives
butter

12 slices rye bread

Mash liverwurst; add cheese, eggs, mayonnaise, salt, pepper and chives and mix well. Spread between buttered slices of rye bread. Approximate yield: 6 portions.

HAM AND EGG SANDWICHES

1 cup chopped cooked ham
3 eggs, slightly beaten
½ teaspoon salt

⅛ teaspoon pepper
1 teaspoon minced onion
8 slices buttered toast

Mix ham, eggs and seasonings; drop from tablespoon into greased frying pan, spreading to make flat cakes, and brown on each side. Place between slices of toast. Approximate yield: 4 sandwiches.

DICED CHICKEN SANDWICHES

2 cups cubed cooked chicken
½ cup chopped celery
2 small gherkins, chopped
½ cup Cooked Salad Dressing
   (page 624)

1 teaspoon lemon juice
½ teaspoon salt
⅛ teaspoon pepper
12 slices whole wheat bread,
   buttered

Combine chicken, celery, gherkins, dressing and seasonings; spread between slices of bread. Yield: 6 sandwiches.

CRAB MEAT AND PIMIENTO SANDWICHES

Remove crusts from 12 slices of light or dark bread; spread 6 slices with mixture of 1 cup flaked cooked crab meat, 1 pimiento, finely chopped, ¼ cup chili sauce and a dash of salt and cover with remaining slices. Cut in triangles before serving. Yield: 6 sandwiches.

SALMON SANDWICHES

Mix 1 can salmon (about 1½ cups) with mayonnaise to moisten, add ½ cup chopped celery, 1 chopped cucumber and salt and pepper to season; spread on buttered bread covered with a crisp leaf of lettuce and top with second slice. Yield: filling for 10 to 12 sandwiches.

ITALIAN EGG–ANCHOVY SANDWICHES

3 hard-cooked eggs	mayonnaise
1 tablespoon minced celery	1 loaf cracked wheat bread
⅛ teaspoon paprika	1 jar rolled anchovies

Remove egg yolks and mash with celery, paprika and enough mayonnaise to moisten. Mince egg whites and moisten with mayonnaise. Cut bread as desired; spread ½ of each slice with egg yolk mixture and other half with egg white mixture. Top with a rolled anchovy. Approximate yield: 12 sandwiches.

ENGLISH MUFFIN SANDWICHES

Split English Muffins (page 180), spread with processed cheese and top with bacon slice; broil until bacon is crisp. Cheese Rabbit (page 134), creamed eggs or slices of roast or meat loaf with gravy may be served over toasted split muffins.

SNACKS AND TIDBITS

TINY pastry, biscuit, cracker and bread accompaniments for salads, soups, cocktails, or teas are often given the general term of snack or tidbit. They may not be more than a mouthful in size; they may be savory or sweet, salty or highly seasoned. Slender pastry and bread sticks, bits of puff paste, crackers and baking powder biscuits cut the size of a fifty-cent piece are favorite bases to use. Luncheon and supper snacks may be more generously proportioned. Many commercial products are available and convenient to keep on hand for ready use. For additional suggestions and recipes, see Appetizers (page 197) and Soup Garnishes (page 247).

TOASTED CINNAMON STICKS

Cut white bread in ½-inch slices, remove crusts and cut in 1-inch strips. Brush all sides with melted butter and roll in mixture of sugar and cinnamon, using ½ teaspoon cinnamon to ½ cup sugar. Bake in moderately hot oven (400° F.) 10 minutes, or until delicately browned, turning to brown all sides. Serve hot with fruit salad or with assorted hot breads.

TOASTED COCONUT CRESCENTS

Cut white bread in ½-inch slices, remove crusts and cut in crescent-shaped pieces. Brush well with sweetened condensed milk and roll in shredded coconut. Bake in moderate oven (350° F.) 10 minutes, or until coconut is delicately toasted. Serve with fruit salads.

TOASTED CHEESE STICKS

12 slices white bread
⅓ cup soft butter

½ cup grated cheese
cayenne

Trim ½-inch slices of bread, and cut in strips ½-inch wide; spread with butter; dip in grated cheese, sprinkle lightly with cayenne and heat in moderate oven (350° F.) 5 minutes, or until browned. Approximate yield: 4 dozen cheese sticks.

CHEESE SAVORY

1 clove garlic, halved
1 3-oz. package cream cheese
1 teaspoon minced chives
½ teaspoon chopped parsley

½ teaspoon anchovy paste
½ teaspoon Worcestershire
   sauce
dash of salt
dash of paprika

Rub inside of small bowl with garlic; then put remaining ingredients in bowl and mix well. Pack into small jelly glass and chill until firm. Remove from glass, cut in thin slices and serve on crisp crackers or toast rounds, as desired. Approximate yield: ½ cup or 6 portions.

ROQUEFORT CHEESE BALLS

¼ pound Roquefort cheese
3 tablespoons grated American
   cheese

¼ teaspoon paprika
1 tablespoon soft butter
1 teaspoon Worcestershire sauce

2 teaspoons chili sauce

Mix ingredients, beating well. Form into small balls and place in refrigerator to harden. Serve with crackers or salad. Approximate yield: 12 small cheese balls.

MAYONNAISE CHEESE PUFFS

Fold 1 cup mayonnaise into 1 stiffly beaten egg white. Pile on cheese wafers or canapé crackers spread with cheese. Toast under broiler 1 minute, or until puffed and delicately browned. Serve at once.

STUFFED SALAD ROLLS

Split finger rolls down the center, but do not cut through; butter and heat in hot oven (400° F.) 5 minutes. Fill generously with Salmon Salad (page 609), Egg Salad (page 123) or Chicken Salad (page 603). Garnish with mayonnaise and pimiento. Serve with sliced tomatoes.

SAUSAGE SNACKS

Prepare Baking Powder Biscuit dough (page 149) with ⅓ cup shortening; roll ¼-inch thick and cut in small oblongs. Parboil cocktail sausages 5 minutes; place one on each oblong, fold over, moisten edges with water and press together to seal. Bake in ungreased pan in hot oven (450° F.) 15 minutes, or until browned.

CARAWAY SEED SNACKS

Roll Plain Pastry (page 736) ⅛-inch thick, sprinkle with caraway seed and cut in small fancy shapes. Bake in hot oven (425° F.) about 10 minutes, or until delicately browned.

PASTELS

1½ cups sifted all-purpose flour	½ pound fresh shrimp, cooked
½ teaspoon sugar	(page 455)
dash of salt	1 teaspoon soy sauce
⅔ cup butter	1 teaspoon water
	1 egg, well beaten

Mix and sift together flour, sugar and salt; cut in butter until mixture resembles coarse cornmeal. Mash shrimp with a fork and stir into flour-fat mixture. Mix soy sauce and water, add slowly to shrimp mixture, tossing with a fork until a dough is formed. Turn out on lightly floured board and roll ½-inch thick; cut with small round cutter and brush with egg. Bake in slow oven (300° F.) 30 minutes, or until browned. Serve as canapé or as a salad accompaniment. Approximate yield: 2 dozen pastries.

Nuts and Confections

Nuts for cooking or eating come from many parts of the world and are simple to prepare for recipes. High in nutritive value, they may be occasionally used as a substitute for meat or poultry when combined with other foods. Best of all, nuts can be used for flavor and texture contrast in many desserts, candies and salads, or served salted as a cocktail accompaniment.

BLANCHED NUTS

Pour boiling water over shelled nuts and let stand 5 minutes, or until skins are wrinkled. Drain; rub with fingers to remove skins. Dry thoroughly on absorbent paper or in warm (not hot) oven before using or storing. Do not blanch more than 1/4 pound nuts at a time, for they become soggy on prolonged contact with water. Thin-skinned nuts such as English walnuts, pecans, etc., are used without blanching.

SALTED NUTS

Use any desired nuts; shell, blanch, if necessary, or wash in cold water and drain. Spread thin layer of moist nuts in shallow pan, sprinkle evenly with salt, using 1½ to 2 teaspoons salt to 1 pound nuts. Moisture on surface of nuts will cause salt to adhere. Heat in moderate oven (350° F.) about 20 minutes, stirring occasionally.

Buttered Salted Nuts—Dry nuts thoroughly, shake in bowl lightly rubbed with oil or melted butter, allowing about 2 teaspoons oil to 1 pound of nuts; sprinkle with salt and brown in hot oven (400° F.) 10 to 15 minutes. Drain on absorbent paper.

Sautéed Salted Nuts—Heat butter or oil (½ cup oil to 1 cup nuts) in small frying pan. Add enough dry, prepared nuts to cover bottom of pan and cook slowly, stirring constantly, until delicately browned. Remove with skimmer, drain on absorbent paper and sprinkle with salt.

828

Fried Salted Nuts—Fry dry, prepared nuts in hot deep fat (360°–370° F.) 4 to 6 minutes, or until brown. Drain, sprinkle with salt.

FRESH COCONUT

The fresh coconut, as it is commonly purchased, is a large, woody-looking brown nut, containing an inside covering of white meat about ½-inch thick and a small amount of "coconut milk" within the nut.

Coconut Milk—To drain the "milk" from the fresh coconut, force a hole through one of the "eyes" at the bud end.

Coconut Meat—Break the shell of the drained coconut with a heavy hammer; remove shell and cut off the brown skin. If shell is very hard, heat the drained coconut in a moderate oven (350° F.) about 20 minutes; cool and break.

Grated Coconut—Grate the white meat of the coconut as desired.

SUGARED NUTS

2 cups shelled nuts   ½ cup water
                1 cup granulated sugar

Blanch nuts, if desired; put in saucepan and keep in warm place. Combine sugar and water in another pan, stir until sugar is dissolved and boil, without stirring, until a small amount of syrup forms a soft ball in cold water (238° F.). Hold pan of nuts several inches above heat and shake vigorously while slowly pouring syrup over nuts. Occasionally stir nuts, then add remaining syrup drop by drop until all is used. Nuts should be evenly covered with coating of sugar. Store in closely covered tin box. Approximate yield: 2 cups nuts.

BRANDY BUTTER ALMONDS

¼ cup butter   2 cups blanched almonds
2¼ cups confectioners' sugar   ¼ cup almonds or pistachios,
¼ cup brandy   chopped

Cream butter and add sugar gradually, alternating it with brandy until both are used. Beat until smooth and well blended. Toast almonds in moderate oven (350° F.) 15 to 20 minutes, or until lightly browned, stirring occasionally to prevent burning. While nuts are warm, coat each one with sugar mixture, roll in chopped almonds or pistachio nuts, lay on shallow tray; let stand in cool place to harden. Yield: 4 cups.

SPICED NUTS

¼ pound nuts	1 teaspoon ginger
1 cup fine granulated sugar	½ tablespoon cloves
1 teaspoon salt	½ teaspoon nutmeg
2 tablespoons cinnamon	1 tablespoon water
	1 egg white

Freshen nuts by heating them a few minutes in oven. If almonds are used, blanch them first. Sift sugar, salt and spices together 3 times; add water to egg white and beat slightly. Dip nuts in egg white, then roll in sugar-spice mixture. Cover bottom of small baking pan with ½ of remaining sugar mixture, place nuts on top so they do not touch each other, cover with remaining sugar mixture. Bake in very slow oven (250° F.) about 2 hours. Remove from oven and shake excess sugar from nuts. Yield: ¼ pound nuts.

CANDIED CITRON

Cut citron in slices and cover with cold water. Bring to a boil and drain. Repeat three times and as many more as is necessary to extract the bitterness. For each pound of citron, make a syrup as follows: 1¼ cups sugar, 1 tablespoon corn syrup, 1¼ cups water and 1 lemon, thinly sliced. Add citron and cook until it is clear. Then drain on a rack and allow to dry. The pieces should be clear and tender.

CANDIED ORANGE PEEL

peel from 4 oranges   cold water   2 cups sugar

Remove peel from oranges in lengthwise sections, cover with cold water, bring to a boil and cook until soft. Drain, saving the water; scrape out white inner portion of peel with teaspoon and cut peel into thin strips with scissors. Dissolve sugar in 1 cup water in which peel was cooked, boil until syrup threads (232°–234° F.), add peel and cook slowly 20 minutes, or until most of the syrup has been absorbed. Drain, spread on waxed paper, let dry overnight and then roll in granulated sugar until well coated; shake to remove excess sugar. Store in tightly covered container. For a more moist peel, add 2 tablespoons light corn syrup to sugar in making syrup.

Candied Grapefruit Peel—Substitute 2 grapefruit for oranges. Boil peel in large amount of water 10 to 15 minutes; drain and repeat 3 times, cooking last time until tender. Use fresh water for syrup.

Candied Lemon Peel—Prepare as for Candied Grapefruit Peel.

FRUIT CONFECTIONS

Use a combination of dried fruits, or fruits and nuts; put through a food chopper or chop very fine. Mix well, moistening with fruit juice or condensed milk if necessary. Shape into small balls, roll in powdered or granulated sugar, ground toasted coconut, or nuts, or dip in chocolate (page 842). The mixture may also be shaped into rolls and sliced, or packed into loaf pan and cut into squares. The following combinations are suggested:

Apricot Candy—Chop ¾ cup dried apricots, ½ cup nuts, ¾ cup coconut; add 1 teaspoon each grated orange and lemon rind; moisten with 1 tablespoon lemon juice. Approximate yield: 50 small balls.

Children's Fruit Caramels—Chop ½ pound each dates, figs, raisins, coconut and nuts, and ¼ pound candied citron, orange or grapefruit peel. Pack into loaf pan; cut into squares and roll in sugar. Approximate yield: 50 pieces.

Chocolate Covered Roll—Chop 1 cup coconut, ½ cup walnuts and ½ cup raisins; add 1 cup peanut butter, dash of salt, 1 tablespoon cream and enough confectioners' sugar to make mixture easily handled. Pat out into ¼-inch sheet, spread with melted sweet chocolate, roll up into long roll and cut into thin slices. Yield: 3 dozen slices.

Date Sweets—Chop 1 pound dates, ½ cup walnuts and 2 tablespoons candied ginger. Approximate yield: 3 dozen small balls.

French Bars—Chop 1 cup each figs, seeded raisins, dates, and 12 maraschino cherries; combine with ½ cup shredded coconut, grated rind of 2 oranges, 2 tablespoons lemon juice and 1 tablespoon orange juice. Form into bar 1-inch square, cut into ½-inch pieces, roll in sugar and ground nuts. Approximate yield: 4 dozen slices.

Grape-nuts Fruit Roll—Chop 6 figs, ½ cup raisins, 12 dates and 12 dried apricots; add ⅔ cup grape-nuts, ¼ cup confectioners' sugar and 2 tablespoons lemon juice. Shape into rolls, 1½ inches in diameter, roll in sugar and slice. Approximate yield: 3 dozen slices.

Tutti-frutti Balls—Chop 1 cup each puffed rice or corn, seedless raisins, dates and figs, ½ cup each nuts and candied orange peel; mix with 2 teaspoons vanilla. Form into balls and roll in shredded coconut. Approximate yield: 4 dozen balls.

STUFFED FRUIT

Use prunes, dates or fresh whole figs; wash and dry if desired. If prunes are used, they may be steamed about 15 minutes, or until plump and soft. Make a cut along entire length of prunes and dates and remove pits; make an opening in each fig. Stuff with plain or salted nuts, peanut butter, preserved ginger, candied fruit peel, marshmallow, Fudge (page 835), Panocha (page 837), on Fondant or its modifications (page 839). The stuffing may or may not show. Pat fruit into original shape and roll in confectioners' or fine granulated sugar. Store in closely covered glass or metal container.

SPICED DRIED FRUIT

1¼ cups sugar	¼ teaspoon nutmeg
1½ teaspoons grated lemon rind	¾ cup water
1 teaspoon cinnamon	1¼ cups raisins or dried apricots
¼ teaspoon cloves	confectioners' sugar

Cook sugar, lemon rind, spices and water, stirring until sugar is dissolved and mixture boils; then continue cooking, without stirring, to soft ball stage (234° F.). Add fruit and cook slowly about 5 minutes, stirring just enough to separate fruit and keep syrup from scorching. Remove from fire; set in pan of hot water. Lift out fruit, a few pieces at a time, drain over kettle and drop in confectioners' sugar. Separate pieces of fruit and roll in sugar. Serve with salads or for tea. Approximate yield: 1¼ cups fruit.

CANDIED FRUIT

Use pitted cherries; pears, peaches and plums, pared, cored and sliced; sections of quinces, pineapple and citron, or whole figs or kumquats, simmered in water until just tender. Drain free from all juice. Combine 2 cups sugar, ⅓ cup light corn syrup and 1 cup water; heat to boiling, add prepared fruit and simmer gently until fruit is clear. For best results, cook only one kind of fruit at a time and do not have kettle crowded. Lift fruit from syrup with skimmer and drain on absorbent paper. · Dust with sugar and dry slowly in sun or very slow oven, adding more sugar if fruit seems sticky. Store between sheets of waxed paper in closely covered metal container. Water in which pineapple or figs, etc., is cooked may be used in making syrup. If canned fruits are used, drain thoroughly; use fruit juice instead of water in syrup and cook until it spins a thread (230°–234° F.) before adding fruit.

CANDIED FLOWERS

Use fresh rose petals or violets; wash and dry thoroughly. Cook syrup for Candied Fruits (page 832) until it spins a thread (230° F.); dip flowers into syrup, using hatpin or fine wire; then dust with sugar and dry. Or dip in melted Fondant (page 839), tinted as desired, and dust thickly with granulated sugar. See Bonbons (page 842).

CRYSTALLIZED MINT LEAVES

Coat both sides of fresh mint leaves with egg white beaten until stiff, using a tiny camel's hair brush. Dip each side in granulated sugar flavored with oil of spearmint (5 drops oil to ⅓ cup sugar.) Place on cake rack covered with waxed paper and let stand in warm place until dry. Serve with fruit cocktails, iced drinks and frozen desserts.

CACTUS CANDY

Remove spines and outside green layer of a small barrel cactus with sharp knife; cut in ½-inch slices and soak overnight in cold water. Drain; cut into 1-inch cubes. Cook slowly in syrup made with 3 cups sugar, ½ cup water, 2 tablespoons orange juice and 1 tablespoon lemon juice, until syrup is nearly all absorbed, watching carefully to prevent scorching. Tint syrup with food coloring, if desired.

GLACÉ FRUITS AND NUTS

1 cup sugar	⅓ cup light corn syrup
	½ cup water

Mix sugar, corn syrup and water in top part of small double boiler, cook over direct heat, stirring until sugar dissolves and mixture boils; then continue cooking, without stirring, to hard crack stage (300° F.), wiping sugar crystals from sides of pan with damp cloth. The syrup should be a delicate straw color. Remove at once from heat.

To dip nuts, drop several nuts into syrup. Dip them out, one by one, from syrup, using a fork; drain off syrup. With second fork, push nut onto buttered pan. If syrup becomes too thick, reheat carefully.

To dip fruits, use stoned cherries, strawberries, orange or grapefruit sections, bunches of currants, seeded grapes, figs, dates, etc. Dip as for nuts, taking care not to pierce fruit with fork and release juice. Glacé fruits and nuts do not keep well. Make them only in cold dry weather and use the same day, serving in tiny paper cups.

Marrons Glacés—Use large French chestnuts; blanch and boil until tender. Simmer in syrup made of 1 cup each sugar and water and dash of salt, until nuts look clear; drain in sieve. Add ¼ teaspoon lemon juice and ½ teaspoon vanilla to glacé syrup before dipping.

Taffy Apples—Wash and dry 6 red apples; insert wooden skewers in blossom ends. Use 1 cup sugar, ¼ cup corn syrup and 6 tablespoons water for syrup. When syrup has cooked, color a bright red with food coloring and flavor with oil of peppermint, clove or cinnamon, if desired. Hold apple by skewer, plunge into syrup, draw it out quickly and twirl until syrup runs down and covers sides evenly. Stand upright in rack so apple does not touch anything as it cools. Use the same day. Yield: 6 apples.

FUDGES

PERHAPS the first bit of cooking a child learns is that of fudge making. Quickly he learns just the right moment to turn the beaten fudge into the pan the moment it shows the first sign of hardening. If too soon, it will harden slowly, be coarse and grainy in texture; if too late, the fudge will be too hard, the surface dull and unattractive.

To avoid grainy fudge or fondant, follow directions carefully in recipe. If any crystals are splashed on the sides of the pan during cooking, wipe down with a piece of damp gauze wrapped around tines of a fork. Wash the spoon thoroughly between stirrings to prevent crystals forming.

Fudge is usually cooled to 110° F. (still hot but not uncomfortably so) before beating.

It is important to turn fudge into the modeling pan at the right moment when it shows the first sign of hardening. If turned out too soon, it will harden slowly and have a coarse, grainy texture. If too hard, the surface will be dull and unattractive.

A candy thermometer insures accurate temperatures and smooth, creamy fudges and fondants. When using it, be sure the bulb is immersed in the liquid but does not touch bottom or sides of the pan; read at eye level.

MAPLE FUDGE

1 cup maple syrup   dash of salt
1 cup sugar   ½ cup top milk or light cream
                ½ cup chopped nuts

Combine syrup, sugar, salt and milk; cook over low heat, stirring constantly until sugar is dissolved and mixture boils. Continue cooking, without stirring, until small amount of mixture forms a soft ball in cold water (238° F.). Remove from heat, cool to lukewarm (110° F.); then beat until thick and creamy. Add nuts and turn into buttered pan. When firm, cut in squares. Approximate yield: 18 large pieces.

CHOCOLATE FUDGE

2 squares unsweetened   2 cups sugar
    chocolate   dash of salt
⅔ cup top milk or light cream   2 tablespoons butter
                1 teaspoon vanilla

Add chocolate to milk and cook over low heat, stirring constantly until mixture is smooth and blended. Add sugar and salt and stir until sugar is dissolved and mixture boils. Cook, without stirring, until small amount of mixture forms a soft ball when dropped into cold water (236° F.). Remove from heat, add butter and vanilla without stirring; cool to lukewarm (110° F.), then beat until creamy. Turn at once into greased pan; when firm, cut in squares. Approximate yield: 18 large pieces.

Creamy Chocolate Fudge—Add 2 tablespoons light corn syrup with sugar; proceed as directed in recipe.

Cocoa Fudge—Substitute ⅔ cup cocoa for chocolate and increase butter to 3 tablespoons. Mix cocoa with sugar before adding milk.

Brown Sugar Fudge—Use 1 cup granulated sugar and ½ cup firmly packed brown sugar.

Chocolate Peppermint Fudge—Omit vanilla, flavor with 2 or 3 drops oil of peppermint; add ¾ cup broken, toasted almonds just before turning into pan.

Coconut Fudge—Add ½ cup shredded coconut just before turning into pan.

Fruit Fudge—Add ½ cup raisins, sliced figs or dates just before turning into pan.

Fudge Roll—Press warm fudge into sheet, cover with sheet of fondant, roll up lengthwise and wrap in waxed paper. When firm, cut in ¼-inch slices.

Ginger Fudge—Add ¼ to ½ cup finely cut crystallized ginger just before turning into pan.

Marshmallow Fudge—Add 1 cup marshmallows, cut in small pieces, just before turning into pan.

Marshmallow Fruit Fudge—Tear out centers from marshmallows and stuff with candied cherries. Arrange in buttered pan; pour fudge over marshmallows, covering them entirely. Cut so a marshmallow will be in center of each square.

Rich Chocolate Fudge—Add 2 more squares of unsweetened chocolate, increase light cream to 1 cup. Add ½ teaspoon salt. After beating fudge, add ½ pound pecans, broken, and turn at once into buttered pan.

Nut Fudge—Add ½ to ¾ cup chopped nuts just before turning into pan.

Peanut Butter Fudge—Substitute ¼ cup peanut butter for butter; add just before beating.

Tutti-frutti Fudge—Add ¾ cup candied fruits—cherries, pineapple, orange rind, etc.—just before turning into pan.

Two-toned Fudge—Press Fondant (page 839) into bottom of buttered pan; cover with fudge. When firm, cut in squares. Either fondant or fudge may be varied by the addition of nuts, fruits, etc.

CARAMEL HICKORY NUT FUDGE

3 cups sugar	1 cup light cream
2 tablespoons hot water	½ cup hickory nuts
1 teaspoon vanilla	

Melt 1½ cups sugar in heavy skillet, stirring constantly. When entirely melted, add 2 tablespoons hot water. Cook until smooth, stirring steadily. Place remaining 1½ cups sugar in saucepan, add caramel syrup, add cream, cook to soft-ball stage or 238° F. Cool thoroughly, beat until stiff; add nuts and vanilla, stirring well. Pour into greased pan and cool before cutting. Yield: 30 pieces one inch square. Or for packing, cut into half-pound blocks and wrap.

QUICK FUDGE

2 6-oz packages chocolate chips   1 teaspoon vanilla
¾ cup sweetened condensed   1 cup chopped nutmeats
   milk

Melt chocolate chips over hot water. Add condensed milk and stir until well blended. Remove from heat and add vanilla and nutmeats. Pour into waxed-paper lined pan. Allow to chill for a few hours. When firm, cut into squares. Approximate yield: 1¼ pounds.

SOUR CREAM FUDGE

2 squares unsweetened   ½ teaspoon salt
   chocolate   1 teaspoon vanilla
2 cups heavy sour cream   ¾ cup chopped nuts, raisins
1¼ cups firmly packed brown   or coconut
   sugar

Combine chocolate, cream, sugar and salt; cook over low heat, stirring constantly until sugar and chocolate are melted and mixture boils. Continue cooking, without stirring, until small amount of mixture forms soft ball in cold water (238° F.). Remove from heat, add vanilla; cool to lukewarm (110° F.) and beat until creamy. Add nuts and turn into buttered pan. When cool, cut in squares. Approximate yield: 18 large squares.

PANOCHA

1¼ cups firmly packed brown   ¾ cup top milk, milk or light
   sugar   cream
dash of salt   1 tablespoon butter
      ½ teaspoon vanilla
    ½ cup broken pecans

Combine sugar, salt and milk; cook over low heat, stirring constantly until sugar is dissolved and mixture boils. Continue cooking, stirring occasionally to prevent burning, until small amount of mixture forms soft ball in cold water (238° F.). Remove from heat, add butter and vanilla without stirring, cool to lukewarm (110° F.) and beat until creamy. Add nuts and turn into buttered pan. When cool, cut into squares. Peanuts, black walnuts, coconut, cut marshmallows, chopped dried fruits, candied orange peel or ginger may be substituted for pecans. Approximate yield: 18 large pieces.

Coffee Panocha—Substitute 1 cup double strength coffee for milk.

PERSIAN CREAMS

1½ cups firmly packed brown
    sugar
1 cup double strength coffee

3 squares unsweetened chocolate
3 tablespoons butter
1 cup nut meats

Combine sugar, coffee and chocolate; cook over low heat, stirring constantly until sugar and chocolate are melted and mixture boils. Continue cooking, without stirring, until small amount of mixture forms soft ball in cold water (238° F.). Remove from heat, add butter without stirring; cool to lukewarm (110° F.), then beat until creamy. Add nuts and turn into buttered pan. Cut in diamond-shaped pieces. Approximate yield: 18 large pieces.

BURNT SUGAR PRALINES

1¾ cups sugar
1 cup water
dash of nutmeg

1 tablespoon butter
1 cup pecan halves
½ teaspoon vanilla

Put ½ cup sugar in a heavy skillet and melt over low heat, stirring constantly until pale yellow in color. Turn off heat and let stand 5 minutes. Add remaining sugar and water. Stir carefully and then melt over moderate heat. Add nutmeg and butter. Cook, stirring occasionally until a little of the syrup forms a soft ball in cold water (236° F.). Remove from heat and let stand 3 minutes. Stir until mixture begins to look cloudy. Add pecans and stir until mixture begins to look creamy. If stirred too long, pralines will be thick. Drop mixture by spoonfuls onto waxed paper. Spread out and let harden. They will harden into a soft, slightly grainy base for the pecans. Approximate yield: 1 dozen 3-inch pralines.

Coconut Pralines—Burn sugar to a very pale caramel. Substitute 1 cup shredded coconut for pecans.

Chocolate Pralines—Add 2 squares unsweetened chocolate to sugar and water; flavor with vanilla.

Maple Pralines—Substitute maple syrup for burnt sugar.

HINTS FOR FONDANT MAKING

USE A candy thermometer and follow directions accurately. To cool a fondant mixture, place the pan on a rack. Before beating, cool to a lukewarm temperature (104° F.); then, with a wooden spoon, beat the syrup thoroughly until it becomes solid enough to handle (5 to 6 minutes) and work with the hands until it is smooth. Cover with a clean, damp cloth and store in a covered jar for at least 24 hours to ripen. To avoid grainy fondant, see below.

FONDANT

2 cups sugar 1 cup water
2 tablespoons light corn syrup

Put sugar, water and corn syrup in saucepan and stir over low heat until sugar is dissolved. Boil, covered, about 3 minutes to dissolve crystals that collect on sides of pan; then boil, uncovered and without stirring, until small amount of syrup forms a soft ball when dropped into cold water (238° F.), occasionally wiping off crystals from sides of pan with damp cloth. Immediately pour out on large platter, shallow tray or marble surface, wiped with damp cloth. When lukewarm (110° F.), work with spatula or wooden spoon until it becomes white and creamy; add ½ teaspoon vanilla, if desired; then knead until smooth. Store overnight or several days in tightly covered jar before using. Approximate yield: 1 pound.

Chocolate Fondant—Knead 2 squares unsweetened chocolate, melted, and ½ teaspoon vanilla into 1 cup fondant.

Coffee Fondant—Substitute double strength coffee for water.

Maple Fondant—Substitute ⅔ cup maple syrup for corn syrup and reduce water to ¾ cup.

Brown Sugar Fondant—Use 1 cup granulated and ½ cup firmly packed brown sugar; omit corn syrup.

Lemon or Orange Fondant—Mix juice and grated rind of ½ lemon or orange and spread on platter before pouring hot syrup on it. Long beating is required, since the juices and syrup do not readily combine.

QUICK FONDANT

2 egg whites 3½ cups confectioners' sugar
¼ to ½ teaspoon flavoring

Beat egg whites slightly, add sugar gradually, beating until stiff; then knead until smooth and creamy. Flavor to taste. Approximate yield: 1½ pounds fondant.

SIMPLE FONDANT CANDIES

Fondant is too sweet to be used alone successfully; it is much better when combined with fruit, nuts, etc., or used as centers for Stuffed Fruits (page 832), or Chocolates (page 842). Flavor and color as desired, kneading to distribute evenly; if nuts and fruits are added, they should not be too finely chopped and should be worked in just enough to blend; overmixing will discolor candy. Use dates, figs, raisins, shredded coconut, candied fruits, preserved ginger and nuts, alone or in combination. Some simple suggestions are:

Fondant Balls—Shape fondant into balls, flatten slightly and top with nut half or bit of candied fruit; or roll balls in toasted coconut shreds, ground nuts, cocoa or grated chocolate.

Cherry or Nut Bonbons—Mold fondant into tiny balls. Press between halves of split, candied cherries or nuts.

Red-hot Fancies—Mix ¼ teaspoon cinnamon and a bit of red vegetable coloring into 1 cup fondant; roll into flat cake, ½-inch thick, using rolling pin well dusted with confectioners' sugar. Cut into fancy shapes—diamond, heart, star, etc.—with tiny cookie cutters dipped in confectioners' sugar. Let stand in cool place 24 hours. Yield: 36 candies.

Fondant Loaves—Add fruit and nuts to fondant, pack into loaf pan; let stand until firm, then cut in slices. The following combinations are often used: coconut, candied pineapple, pistachio nuts; dates, figs, nuts; dried apricots, raisins, pecans; candied cherries, almonds, dates.

Neapolitan Loaves—Use 3 layers of different colors, or one or more modifications of Fondant (page 839). Add fruit and nuts, if desired.

FONDANT CENTERS

Prepare Fondant (page 839). Divide into several portions, adding flavoring, coloring and other ingredients such as chopped fruit or nuts, as desired; work with fingers until well blended. Shape each portion into 1-inch thick roll, cut into ½-inch pieces and shape into balls or ovals, flattening bases slightly. Keep centers small; dipping increases the size of the candies. Place on racks or trays covered with waxed paper and let stand several hours before dipping in melted chocolate or colored fondant.

PATTIES

Melt 1 cup fondant in top part of small double boiler over hot water (185° F). Add 1 to 2 drops flavoring and a tiny bit of vegetable coloring, if desired, stirring just enough to blend; if fondant is too thick, add hot water, drop by drop; if too thin, let stand 5 to 10 minutes to thicken. Drop from tip of teaspoon on waxed paper or lightly buttered flat surface to make small patties; or dip by tablespoons into lightly buttered small muffin or patty pans to make a layer about ¼-inch thick. When firm, invert on folded cloth and tap bottom lightly to loosen patties.

For **Peppermint Patties,** add oil of peppermint, leave fondant white, or color any delicate shade desired; for **Wintergreen Patties,** add oil of wintergreen and pink coloring; for **Mint Patties,** add oil of spearmint and green coloring; for **Cinnamon** or **Clove Patties,** add flavoring extract, color red; for **Lemon Patties,** add extract, color yellow.

Maple, coffee, and chocolate fondants may be made into patties. Patties may be partially or completely dipped in melted dipping chocolate (see Chocolates, page 842).

KISSES

Melt fondant as for Patties (above), adding coloring and flavoring as desired. For **Coconut Kisses,** add ⅓ cup shredded coconut; for **Nut Kisses,** add ⅓ cup chopped nuts; for **Fruit Kisses,** use candied cherries, candied pineapple and chopped figs, alone or in combination; flavor with lemon juice or fruit extract. Drop from tip of teaspoon on waxed paper; the mixture should be stiff enough to form little mounds. If too soft to hold shape, cool mixture before dropping.

TURKISH CREAM

2 cups sugar	2 cups chopped walnuts
½ cup water	¼ pound figs, diced
½ cup heavy cream	1½ cups seedless raisins
½ teaspoon vanilla	¼ cup diced candied pineapple
2 cups shredded toasted almonds	¼ cup candied cherries, cut in halves

Combine sugar, water and cream; cook over low heat, stirring constantly until sugar is dissolved and mixture boils; then cook, without stirring, until small amount of mixture forms soft ball in cold water (238° F.). Remove from heat, add vanilla and cool to lukewarm (110° F.); then beat until creamy. Melt candy over hot water, stirring constantly, and add nuts and fruit. Turn into buttered pan and cut in squares, or knead and mold in balls. Yield: 2 dozen squares.

Coconut Cream Candy—Omit fruits and nuts. When candy is cool, add 1 cup shredded coconut and beat until creamy. Turn at once into buttered pan and cut in squares, or drop by spoonfuls on buttered surface. Approximate yield: 18 squares.

CHOCOLATE CREAM BALLS

½ pound chocolate chips
2 tablespoons double strength coffee
½ cup butter

2 egg yolks
¼ cup heavy cream
½ cup cocoa or ground pistachio nuts

Place chocolate in top of double boiler and cook over hot water until chocolate is melted. Blend in coffee and cool. Cream butter, gradually add cold chocolate mixture, egg yolks and cream. Fill large bowl with ice cubes, place bowl of chocolate mixture in ice cubes and beat until mixture is firm enough to shape into balls 1 inch in diameter; roll in cocoa or nuts. Chill until firm. Yield: 2 dozen balls.

BONBONS

Use Fondant Centers (page 840), candied fruit or nuts. Melt fondant in top part of double boiler over hot water just below boiling point, adding flavoring and coloring as desired. Drop a center into fondant, rounded side down; cover completely with fondant and remove with fork or wire candy dipper, scraping bonbon on edge of boiler to remove excess fondant. Drop onto waxed paper, rounded side up, and twirl fork to give fancy twist to top of candy. Decorate with nut half or bit of candied fruit, if desired. If fondant becomes too thin, cool until it reaches desired consistency.

CHOCOLATES

Chocolate dipping is a difficult process and should not be attempted in the home unless the right equipment and the right ingredients are available. Use a special dipping chocolate, a 1- to 1½-quart double boiler, an accurate thermometer and a chocolate-dipping fork. Have trays or cake racks, covered with waxed paper, ready for dipped chocolates. Do not attempt chocolate dipping on warm or humid days.

Centers—Use Fondant Centers (page 840), balls made from Fruit Confections (page 831), nuts, dried fruits, candied fruit peel, etc.

Procedure—Grate or cut fine about 1 pound of dipping chocolate; place in top part of double boiler; place over warm water and stir constantly until chocolate is melted. Remove from hot water, fill bottom of boiler with cool water and stir until temperature of chocolate reaches 85° F. During dipping, the water in the lower part of the boiler should be about 85° F. Drop a center into chocolate, rounded side down, cover completely with chocolate and remove with dipping fork, scraping across edge of boiler to remove excess chocolate; drop onto waxed paper, rounded side up, and twirl fork to give fancy twist to top of candy. Decorate with nut half, if desired. When dipping chocolate hardens, scrape down sides of dish and remelt as before. Ends of blanched almonds, Brazil nuts or candied fruit peel may be dipped in chocolate, letting the chocolate cover about ⅓ of the nut or fruit. One pound dipping chocolate will cover 70 to 80 assorted centers.

Cautions—If chocolate is too soft, a wide base will form on dipped centers; if too thick, coating will not be smooth. Cover soft centers completely to prevent oozing. Cool chocolates quickly to avoid light spots. If chocolate is at the proper dipping temperature, the coated candy will harden immediately.

CARAMELS

1 cup sugar
½ cup light corn syrup
1½ cups heavy cream
1 teaspoon vanilla

Put sugar, corn syrup and half cup cream in a saucepan and cook over low heat, stirring constantly until sugar is melted. Then cook slowly to soft ball stage (234° F.), stirring constantly. Add another half cup cream and cook to soft ball stage again. Add remaining cream and cook to firm ball stage (246° F.); add vanilla. Turn into a small buttered pan (7 inch) and cool. Mark into squares and cut when cold.

Evaporated Milk Caramels—Substitute ¾ cup evaporated milk for ½ cup of the cream.

Maple Caramels—Omit corn syrup and add 1 cup maple syrup. Cook after last addition of cream to 248° F.

Chocolate Caramels—Cook 4 squares unsweetened chocolate with syrup.

Nut Caramels—Add chopped nuts after removing from heat.

Coconut Caramels—Add ¾ cup toasted, shredded coconut after removing from heat.

Fruit Caramels—Add ¾ cup finely cut figs, dates or raisins after removing from heat.

Caramel Curls—Cover a sheet of caramel with thin layer of marshmallows, melted over hot water; roll up like a jelly roll. Pull out into longer roll and slice off in small pieces. Wrap in waxed paper.

Layered Caramels—Pour thin layer of caramel into pan, cool, then pour in second layer of contrasting color and flavor. Add third layer, if desired, or use Nougat (page 845) or Divinity (below) between 2 layers of caramel. Cut in squares and wrap in waxed paper.

Chocolate-covered Caramels—Dip caramels in melted dipping chocolate (see Chocolates, page 842).

Nut Rolls—Cook caramel mixture to 245° F.; place pan over hot water to keep caramel from hardening. Have ready a roll of Fondant (page 839) about 3 inches long and ¾ inch in diameter. Dip quickly into hot caramel mixture, remove and drop into broken nuts spread on waxed paper, turning until well covered with nuts and pressing lightly to embed them. Wrap in waxed paper until ready to use; then slice with sharp knife. Toasted coconut may be substituted for nuts.

DIVINITY

2⅓ cups sugar
¼ teaspoon salt
⅔ cup light corn syrup
½ cup water
2 egg whites, stiffly beaten
1 teaspoon vanilla

Combine sugar, salt, corn syrup and water; cook over low heat, stirring constantly, until sugar is dissolved and mixture boils. Continue cooking, without stirring, until small amount of syrup forms hard ball in cold water (265° F.), wiping away crystals from sides of pan with damp cloth. Pour slowly over egg whites, beating constantly, and continue beating until candy holds its shape when dropped from spoon; mix in vanilla. Turn into buttered pan and cut in squares, or drop by spoonfuls on buttered surface. Approximate yield: 18 pieces.

Brown Sugar Divinity—Substitute ½ cup firmly packed brown sugar for 1 cup of granulated sugar.

Chocolate Divinity—Fold 2 squares melted unsweetened chocolate into candy just before turning into pans.

Maple Divinity—Decrease water to ¼ cup and add ½ cup maple syrup; proceed as directed.

Neapolitan Divinity—Divide candy into three parts; color one part pink and flavor with strawberry; add one square melted unsweetened chocolate to second part. Spread remaining white part on bottom of buttered loaf pan; add pink layer, pressing in place; spread chocolate layer on top. Press together and allow to harden; cut in slices.

Divinity Mallow Loaf—Add 12 marshmallows, cut in small pieces, and 1 cup chopped pecans. Turn into loaf pan lined with wet cloth, pat into shape and chill 3 hours in refrigerator. Lift out loaf, unwrap and cover entire surface with melted chocolate, using clean pastry brush.

Cherry Divinity—Color candy a delicate pink while beating it; add 1 cup sliced candied cherries.

Layered Divinity—Cover bottom of lightly buttered pan with a ½-inch layer of divinity. Pour similar layer of Fudge (page 835) or Panocha (page 837) over top. Cut in squares when firm.

NOUGAT

1 cup sugar	½ cup strained honey
½ cup water	2 cups toasted shredded almonds
3 tablespoons light corn syrup	½ cup blanched pistachio nuts
2 egg whites	1 teaspoon vanilla
	nougat wafers

Mix sugar, water and 1½ tablespoons corn syrup; bring to boiling point, stirring until sugar is dissolved; then continue cooking to hard ball stage (265° F.). When syrup is almost ready, beat egg whites until stiff but not dry; then add syrup slowly, beating constantly. Combine honey with remaining 1½ tablespoons corn syrup; while adding first syrup to egg whites, cook this second syrup to 265° F. At once add slowly to egg white mixture, beating constantly; add nuts. Place over hot water and cook until mixture dries, stirring constantly; if a little, taken out on a spoon, holds its shape when cold and is not sticky to touch, the candy is ready. Add vanilla; pour into pans lined with nougat wafers, cover with pan or board and press with heavy weight for at least 12 hours. Remove block of candy and cut in squares; wrap in waxed paper. Nougat wafers may be omitted if desired; turn candy into pan and when firm, cut in squares. Yield: 40 pieces.

NOUGAT MALLOW LOAF

3 cups sugar
¾ cup water
1 cup light corn syrup
3 egg whites
12 marshmallows

1 cup pecans, chopped
1 tablespoon vanilla or
   1 teaspoon peppermint extract
2 squares unsweetened chocolate,
   melted

Combine sugar, water and corn syrup. Cover and boil 3 minutes. Remove cover and continue boiling until mixture forms a hard ball (260° F.) when dropped in cold water. Beat egg whites until they stand in soft peaks. Gradually pour hot syrup in fine stream over egg whites, beating constantly. Beat until mixture becomes thick and white. Add marshmallows, nuts and vanilla. Beat with spoon until mixture appears dry and spongy. Pack into loaf pan lined with damp cheesecloth. Allow to stand 3 hours in refrigerator. Lift out, unwrap and paint entire surface with melted chocolate. When firm, cut large slices. Approximate yield: 2 pounds.

OLD–FASHIONED TAFFY

1 cup sugar
½ cup firmly packed brown
   sugar
2 cups molasses

¾ cup water
¼ cup butter
⅛ teaspoon baking soda
¼ teaspoon salt

oil of peppermint or vanilla

Cook sugars, molasses and water together until a small amount of mixture cracks when dropped in cold water (272° F.), stirring frequently toward end of cooking to prevent burning. Remove from heat, add butter, baking soda and salt, stirring just enough to mix. Pour into buttered large shallow pan and allow to stand until cool enough to handle. Oil fingers lightly and fold or gather taffy into ball. Pull candy, using tips of fingers, until it is firm, porous and light-colored, adding flavoring while pulling. Stretch out into long rope, twist slightly and cut with scissors (which are dipped frequently into cold water) into 1-inch lengths; wrap in waxed paper. Yield: 50 pieces.

WHITE TAFFY

2 cups sugar
½ cup light corn syrup

⅔ cup water
1 teaspoon vanilla

Combine sugar, corn syrup and water and cook until small amount of mixture will crack when dropped into cold water (272° F.); add vanilla. Turn onto buttered platter and let stand until cool enough to handle. Pull and cut as for Old-fashioned Taffy (above). Yield: 1 pound.

LOUISIANA MOLASSES CANDY

1 cup sugar
2 cups molasses
1 tablespoon vinegar
¼ cup water

½ teaspoon vanilla
1½ teaspoons margarine
¼ teaspoon baking soda
¼ teaspoon salt

Combine sugar, molasses and vinegar. Stir until sugar has dissolved, adding water if necessary. Cook slowly until small amount of syrup cracks when dropped in cold water (272° F.), stirring frequently toward end of cooking to prevent burning. Remove from heat; add vanilla, margarine, baking soda and salt, stirring just enough to mix. Pour into buttered shallow pan. Allow to stand until cool enough to handle. Proceed as for Old-fashioned Taffy (above). Yield: 50 pieces.

NUT STICKS

2 cups sugar
1 cup light corn syrup

½ cup coarsely chopped black
walnuts

Boil sugar and corn syrup together until a small amount of syrup will crack when dropped into cold water (272° F.). Then, without stirring, quickly pour onto buttered platter and spread nuts over top so they will sink into hot syrup. When cool enough to handle, pull as for Old-fashioned Taffy (page 846), working the nuts through the candy thoroughly. Approximate yield: 50 pieces.

Old-fashioned Stick Candy—Omit nuts. Flavor with 2 or 3 drops oil of peppermint or wintergreen. Divide in two portions, coloring one with red vegetable coloring. Pull each part separately, then twist red candy around white before cutting; cut in sticks or shape into canes.

RUM–BUTTER TOFFEE

1 cup sugar
¾ cup light corn syrup
¾ cup light cream

dash of salt
2 tablespoons butter
3 tablespoons rum

Combine sugar, corn syrup, cream and salt and cook, stirring constantly until sugar is dissolved. Continue cooking until mixture forms a firm ball in cold water (244° F.). Add butter and continue cooking, stirring very frequently, until mixture forms a hard ball in cold water (262° F.). Add rum and turn immediately into buttered shallow pan. When cool, mark into squares; when cold, break into squares with knife handle. Approximate yield: 100 pieces.

BUTTERSCOTCH

1 cup sugar

¼ cup molasses

1 tablespoon vinegar

2 tablespoons boiling water

½ cup butter

½ teaspoon vanilla

Combine sugar, molasses, vinegar and water; cook, stirring constantly until sugar is dissolved. Continue cooking, without stirring, until small amount of mixture forms hard ball in cold water (250° F.). Add butter and again cook to crack stage (272° F.), stirring only enough to prevent scorching. Add vanilla and pour into well-buttered pan. Proceed as for Toffee (above). Approximate yield: 1 pound.

ALMOND BUTTER KRUNCH

1 cup butter

1 cup sugar

3 tablespoons water

1 tablespoon corn syrup

⅓ cup chopped toasted almonds

¼ pound sweet or unsweetened chocolate*

¼ cup finely chopped blanched almonds

Melt butter, add sugar and stir until sugar is dissolved; add water and corn syrup and cook slowly, stirring occasionally to prevent burning, until a small amount of mixture is brittle when dropped in cold water (300° F.) Remove from heat, add toasted almonds, turn into buttered pan and mark into squares immediately. Melt chocolate in double boiler and when candy is almost cool, spread with chocolate coating and sprinkle with chopped almonds. If desired, turn candy over and coat other side with chocolate and nuts. Approximate yield: 12 pieces.

NUT BRITTLE

1½ cups sugar

¼ cup light corn syrup

dash of salt

½ cup water

1/16 teaspoon baking soda

2 tablespoons butter

¾ cup chopped nuts

Combine sugar, corn syrup, salt and water; cook, stirring constantly until sugar is dissolved and mixture boils. Continue cooking until small amount of mixture is brittle when dropped into cold water (300° F.). Remove from heat, add soda, butter and nuts, stirring just enough to mix. Pour in very thin sheet onto large buttered baking sheet; as candy cools, lift edges and pull as thin as possible. When cold, break into irregular pieces. If desired, brittle may be coated with melted chocolate as in Almond Butter Krunch (above). Approximate yield: 1 pound brittle.

Coconut Brittle—Omit soda; substitute 1 cup coconut for nuts.

Chocolate Nut Brittle—Use 1 cup sugar, ⅓ cup corn syrup, ⅓ cup cold water and dash of salt. Cook to 275° F.; omit butter and soda, add 1 teaspoon vanilla and fold in 1 square melted unsweetened chocolate and ½ cup broken nut meats. Approximate yield: ¾ pound brittle.

Cinnamon Fig Jibs—Use 1 cup firmly packed brown sugar, 1 cup corn syrup and ½ cup water. Cook to 285° F. Omit butter and soda; flavor with ¼ teaspoon cinnamon and fold in 1 cup shredded figs.

Grape-nuts Brittle—Substitute 1 cup grape-nuts for nuts.

CHOCOLATE BRITTLE

3 cups chocolate chips	½ cup water
1½ cups sugar	2 tablespoons butter
¼ cup light corn syrup	¾ cup nuts, finely chopped
dash of salt	(optional)

Place 1½ cups chocolate bits in shallow pan about 8 x 11 inches. Place in moderate oven (350° F.) 10 minutes, or until they appear soft. Remove from oven, let stand 2 to 3 minutes and spread in smooth coating over bottom of pan. Combine sugar, corn syrup, salt and water and heat, stirring constantly until sugar is dissolved. Continue boiling until mixture is brittle when dropped in cold water (300° F.). Watch carefully and stir frequently toward end of cooking. Remove from heat, add butter and nuts, if desired, and pour in thin sheet on top of chocolate. Cover with remaining chocolate bits, return to moderate oven for 7 to 8 minutes, remove from oven and spread as before, being careful not to press chocolate pieces into brittle. Let stand until firm. Break into irregular pieces. Approximate yield: 2 pounds.

PEANUT BRITTLE

1 cup sugar	½ cup chopped roasted peanuts
	dash of salt

Melt sugar in iron frying pan over low heat, stirring constantly until sugar is completely melted and golden brown in color. Remove from heat, add nuts and salt quickly, stirring just enough to mix. Pour into buttered pan in thin sheet; when nearly cold, mark in squares. Approximate yield: ½ pound brittle.

SPUN SUGAR

2 cups sugar   1 cup water
⅛ teaspoon cream of tartar   red vegetable coloring

Combine sugar, cream of tartar and water in top part of double boiler, stir until sugar is dissolved, cover and boil over direct heat 2 to 3 minutes; uncover and boil without stirring until syrup spins a long brittle thread (310° F.), occasionally wiping down sides of pan with damp cloth during cooking. Remove immediately from heat and set in cold place to stop further cooking; cool for 2 minutes. Tint syrup lightly with coloring, if desired. Place 2 clean smooth and oiled wooden sticks or broom handles about 2 feet apart on table with ends projecting about 1 foot from edge; place large sheet of clean paper on floor underneath. Dip sugar spinner (one may be made by cutting the looped wires of a wire whisk, leaving prongs free) or a fork into syrup, raise to allow threads to form and quickly spin threads back and forth from pole to pole. When sugar syrup becomes slightly thick, melt over hot water. As spun sugar accumulates, remove, shape into nests or pile on cold dish before spinning additional sugar. Spun sugar must be kept cold and dry and does not last more than two hours. Use as garnish for ice cream, piling cream in center of spun sugar nests. The syrup may be tinted as desired to harmonize with color of the ice cream.

LOLLYPOPS

1 cup sugar   ⅔ cup water
⅓ cup light corn syrup   6 to 8 drops oil of peppermint
            vegetable coloring

Combine sugar, corn syrup and water, cook over low heat, stirring constantly until sugar is dissolved and mixture boils. Continue cooking, without stirring, until a small amount of mixture is very brittle when dropped in cold water (310° F.), wiping away crystals from sides of pan with damp cloth. Cook slowly at last so syrup will not discolor. Remove from heat, add flavoring and coloring, stirring just enough to mix. Quickly drop syrup from tip of spoon on buttered flat surface, press end of wooden skewer into edge of each lollypop. When firm but still warm, loosen from surface to prevent cracking. Coloring and flavoring may be varied as desired. Faces or conventional designs made from nuts and fruits may be pressed into lollypops while still warm. Approximate yield: 10 to 12 small lollypops.

CEREAL PUFF CANDY

4 cups puffed cereal	1 cup molasses
1 cup seedless raisins	2 tablespoons butter or margarine
	1½ teaspoons vinegar

Mix puffed cereal and raisins in lightly buttered large bowl. Combine molasses, butter and vinegar and cook, stirring constantly until the syrup forms a hard ball when dropped into cold water (260° F.). Pour over puffed cereal, mixing quickly with a two-pronged fork until each kernel is coated. Spread out in a buttered shallow pan. Press down evenly and firmly. When cold, cut in squares. This candy should be eaten fresh since it does not keep crisp longer than a few days. Approximate yield: 1 pound candy.

MERINGUE CANDIES

Prepare ½ recipe for meringues (page 698). Using a pastry tube, drop ½-inch mounds onto lightly buttered cookie sheet, spacing them 2 inches apart. Bake in a slow oven (250° F.) until straw colored. When done, dip the tip of each meringue into bitter chocolate or colored frosting. Approximate yield: 3 dozen candies.

POPCORN BALLS

1 cup molasses	1 tablespoon vinegar
1 cup corn syrup	3 tablespoons butter
	10 cups popped corn

Combine molasses, corn syrup, vinegar and butter. Boil rapidly to hard ball stage (250° F.). Place popped corn in large bowl. Pour syrup gradually into the center of the corn; stir with fork and gather corn, well coated with syrup, into balls. Press between hands to pack hard. Yield: 8 to 10 balls.

Popcorn Chop Suey—Use 5 cups salted, popped corn, ½ cup shredded coconut and ½ cup shelled peanuts.

Crackerjack—Use 5 cups salted popped corn and 2 cups toasted shelled peanuts. Press lightly into a 1-inch layer in buttered pans. Approximate yield: 4 sheets (8 x 8 inch).

Raisin Popcorn Balls—Use 5 cups salted, popped corn and 1 cup steamed washed raisins.

Cereal Popcorn Balls—Use 4 cups salted popped corn and 2 cups puffed cereal.

Nut Popcorn Balls—Use 5 cups salted popped corn and 1 cup chopped walnuts, pecans or hickory nuts.

CHOCOLATE POPCORN BALLS

1 cup sugar
½ cup corn syrup
2 squares unsweetened chocolate

⅓ cup water
2 tablespoons butter or margarine
2 quarts salted popped corn

Combine sugar, corn syrup, chocolate and water and cook until a brittle mass forms when a bit is dropped in cold water (270°–290° F.). Add butter. Mix well and pour over popped corn. Mix and slightly cool. Press into balls. Yield: 12 medium-sized balls.

BAKED NUT CANDY

1 egg white
¼ teaspoon salt

½ cup firmly packed brown
sugar
½ teaspoon vanilla
1 cup nuts, finely chopped

Beat egg white until foamy; add salt. Beat in sugar gradually and continue beating until mixture is stiff; then fold in vanilla and nuts. Drop by spoonfuls on buttered baking sheet; bake in slow oven (225° F.) 1 hour. Approximate yield: 18 small patties.

NUT CLUSTERS

Add nuts, whole or halves, to melted sweet or dipping chocolate; mix lightly. Drop by spoonfuls on buttered surface.

CHOCOLATE PELLETS

4 ounces dark sweet chocolate,
grated

grated orange rind
preserved ginger, chopped

Melt chocolate over hot water. Flavor with orange rind and ginger, mixing well. Cut rounds of waxed paper 2½ inches in diameter and spread each round with chocolate. Chill until firm. Use to decorate cake or eat as candy. Approximate yield: 24 pellets.

The Joy of Home Freezing

OWNING a home freezer proves to be an exciting adventure for the American family today. It creates a new way of kitchen life. Food freezing is so simple and the results are so satisfying that not only the women of the household but the menfolk, as well, enthusiastically endorse this easy and effective way of food preservation.

WHAT YOU CAN EXPECT FROM YOUR FOOD FREEZER

1. *A Saving of Kitchen Hours:* If you get into the habit of never making only one recipe of anything, but instead learn to double, triple or use quantity cookery proportions, today's needs can be taken care of and the remainder frozen for effortless meals tomorrow.
2. *Freedom from Worry:* With planning and forethought, entire meals can emerge from the freezer in the frozen state to be defrosted and cooked within 30 minutes for those days when you return home a half hour before dinner or when company unexpectedly arrives.
3. *Money Savings:* Efficient freezer owners, today, testify that, with expert management, a freezer can be made to pay for itself within a matter of months. The more use you make of your home freezer, the bigger your savings. A complete turnover of food two or three times a year, foods bought in quantity at near-wholesale prices, cooperative buying, taking advantage

of "bargains" in foods, and freezing foods in season at their prime are some of the thrift measures these owners advocate.

4. *No Leftover Problems:* One homemaker we interviewed vowed that her freezer is worth its weight in dollars because she never has to worry about meal leftovers. Uneaten roasts, desserts, breads and baked goods—to name only a few foods—can go into the freezer to be used days later with no loss of essential goodness.

5. *Better Eating:* With the freezer as your storehouse, you'll find it easy to serve better meals to your family than has been your custom. Foods have no season in a freezer. Oysters can be eaten in July. Strawberries in January have a June-like flavor at June prices. A side of beef guarantees ready-to-eat choice steak at a bargain. Ice cream bought by the tub, in two- or three-gallon sizes, offers a delicious and nutritious dessert at a moment's notice. Fish and game trophies can be saved for holiday meals, losing little of their original fresh flavor in the freezer.

6. *Speed and Glamour:* Analyze a good meal and you will see that it can be described as an interesting blend of well-cooked and attractively served foods. Perhaps it will include one *pièce de résistance* as an appetite appeaser. Your freezer can help you serve glamorous meals in a speedy fashion. A beef stew takes on interest when served with a daffodil angel cake. A noodle casserole loses no caste when followed by Cherries Jubilee. Specialty foods can be prepared at your leisure, frozen, and be ready to add grace to your meals.

For instance, would you not like to serve Shrimp Arnaud, Shell Steak, Frozen Fruit Salad, Pecan Butterscotch Rolls, Chocolate Cake and Mint Ice within 30 minutes to the guests your husband unexpectedly brings home to dinner? Many women prefer to prepare and freeze their Thanksgiving and Christmas dinners days ahead so as to be relaxed and free from fatigue on the holiday.

7. *Twice-a-Month Shopping:* Shopping becomes easier and more

efficient with a food freezer. Bargains can be bought and frozen in quantity lots, day-old bakery goods combine thrift and convenience with no loss in flavor when held in the freezer. "Specials" in frozen commercial products can be bought in case lots and stored at considerable savings.

WHEN YOU BUY YOUR HOME FREEZER

THE QUESTION of size is one of the first considerations in buying a home freezer. The amount of space needed depends on the kinds and quantities of foods to be frozen and stored in a year and the rate of turnover. That in turn depends on such factors as size of family, their eating habits, amount of entertaining, source of foods and length of time between growing seasons.

Most home freezers range in size from 3 to 30 cubic feet of food-storage space. To convert size in cubic feet to capacity in pounds of food, multiply by 30 for family-size packages. Six cubic feet of freezer space per person will meet the requirements of most families. With most of the family's food to be stored in the freezer, 10 cubic feet per person may not be excessive. In the past, many freezer owners have made the mistake of buying too small a cabinet.

Some families may prefer two medium-sized freezers to one large model. One can be used primarily for freezing, the other for storage. A home freezer may supplement locker facilities or be used in conjunction with the two-compartment refrigerator.

COSTS AND OPERATING COSTS

THE PURCHASE price of a freezer is roughly dependent upon its size. As size decreases below 18-cubic-foot capacity, cost per cubic foot increases. As size increases, up to 30 cubic feet, cost per cubic foot decreases. To quoted purchase price, you may need to add freight, delivery and installation charges.

In estimating the running costs of owning a home freezer, interest on the investment may be included; the rate used should be based on the return that could be obtained from some other investment.

Depreciation costs, too, should not be overlooked. The life expectancy of a home freezer has been estimated at 10 years.

Annual cost of freezer repairs may be calculated at two per cent of the initial cost.

Cost of packaging materials runs around 2 cents a pound of food, even when outer wrappings are used again.

Operating costs vary, depending upon size and design, freezer location and local electrical rates.

In computing the total costs of a home freezer, the U. S. Department of Agriculture has published the following figures which represent a year's costs for home freezing exclusive of the cost of the food frozen. The example is based on the use of a $400, 12-cubic-food freezer (360-pound capacity), with no turnover of frozen food, and with turnovers of 50 and 150 per cent.

TABLE XXXIV
COST OF OPERATING A HOME FREEZER

Expenditure item:	360 lb. of Food	540 lb. of Food	900 lb. of Food
Amortization charges (3 percent interest, 10 years' life expectancy)	$46.89	$46.89	$46.89
Repairs (2 percent of purchase price) ..	8.00	8.00	8.00
Electricity—			
For freezing food (0.1 kw.-hr. per lb. at 3 cents per kw.-hr.)	1.08	1.62	2.70
For maintaining 0° F. (0.3 kw.-hr. per cu. ft. per 24 hr. at 3 cents per kw.-hr.)	39.42	39.42	39.42
Packaging (2 cents per lb.)	7.20	10.80	18.00
Total cost	$102.59	$106.73	$115.01
Cost per pound of food	.28	.20	.13

HOW TO SAVE MONEY WITH YOUR FREEZER

As you can see from the above table, the more times you fill your freezer during the year, the lower the cost per pound of food becomes. To make your freezer pay for itself, you will need to do careful planning. Whether, in the long run, your family food budget will be reduced or increased by use of the home freezer, will depend on whether the food is home-grown or purchased, kinds and quantities of food frozen and how you use the freezer. Obviously, it will not pay to freeze foods that are commonly available the year around and relatively inexpensive at all seasons.

The more you live out of your freezer, the more dollars-and-cents return you will have on your original investment. This calls for a well-thought-out freezing schedule based on a food-production plan that meets the family's needs. Best practice is a rapid turnover of food in the freezer. This means using the food in the freezer—often one of the hardest lessons for a freezer owner to learn.

Looking at table No. XXXIV, you will see that you will need to raise or buy foods at a savings of 28¢, 20¢ or 13¢ per pound (depending upon the number of times you fill the freezer) compared with current market prices, if your freezer is to pay for itself within the year. If you can do better than that, your freezer will be a source of money profit.

Families who can raise their own fruits, vegetables and meats easily can make their freezer a source of savings.

But even *Herald Tribune* readers who have only a tiny garden plot and who have to buy most of their foods report that they can save as much as $100 a year on their food bills by these thrifty habits of buying:

Ice cream bought in 2½-gallon tubs costs about two dollars less than if bought by the quart.

Meat can be bought directly from farmers or from locker plants at wholesale prices. Through cooperative buying, many families can cut their meat costs substantially.

Fruits and vegetables can be purchased from growers at wholesale prices. There is a trend now for frozen food packers of institutional size packages of fruits and vegetables to open retail outlets for consumers. With a minimum order, wholesale prices can be obtained. These fruits and vegetables may be stored in the 2- to 30-pound-size packages or may be re-packaged at home.

Assorted commercially frozen packages in lots of 12 to 24 can be bought at neighborhood stores with a savings of 10 per cent or more.

"Specials" of commercially frozen foods often can be bought by the case at near-wholesale prices.

Day-old bakery goods can be purchased at savings and frozen, with no loss of flavor. In fact, freezing seems to improve the quality of many pastry goods.

Fish may be purchased in wholesale lots, or caught fresh and frozen with little or no cost.

If you learn to cook in quantity proportions, using what you need for the current meals and freezing the remainder, you will find that you are saving both time and money.

Hoarded leftovers represent another way of saving pennies when used in a casserole, a meat loaf, or a salad.

WHERE TO PLACE THE FREEZER

FROM an operating standpoint, the freezer should be in a cool, dry, well-ventilated place. The higher the room temperature, the more the motor must run to maintain the freezer temperature. However, it is inadvisable to place the freezer where the temperature falls below 40° F. as the freezer mechanism may fail to function properly.

Dampness may damage not only the exposed parts of the freezer but also the motor. Circulation of air is needed to carry off the heat during freezer operation. Do not place in a niche with walls on three sides. Another requirement is a strong floor underneath the freezer which will weigh several hundred pounds when filled.

Convenience of location is important to the homemaker, but this is not of major importance because the freezer is opened only once or twice a day. From the standpoint of use, the kitchen or

utility room may be most convenient, but if space does not permit
a large freezer, the basement or garage may have to be used.

Before freezer and location are decided upon, it is wise to take
measurements to make sure that the freezer will go through
doors, around corners and narrow passageways to fit into the
desired space.

HOW TO RUN YOUR FREEZER

WHEN the freezer is installed, it is well to have a separate switch
so that a correct fuse can take care of a possible motor overload.
A small freezer may be plugged into a lighting circuit, but the
circuit must not be overloaded. Some large freezers require a 220-
volt circuit. Others should be wired directly into a 110-volt circuit
that supplies the freezer only. A tape to secure the plug prevents
accidental disconnection.

When to Defrost: Follow the manufacturer's directions for defrosting. A chest-type freezer requires less frequent defrosting
than the upright models. Ordinarily, you should not let the frost
build up more than one-fourth inch on the sides of the cabinet nor
allow it to collect around the lids and doors. Remove it as it
forms with a dull-edged metal scraper. A putty knife or thin
sheet of metal is also convenient. If frost is excessive, notify your
dealer and have the gaskets and hinges checked.

When to Clean: Clean your freezer once a year, experts say. Choose
a time when the food supply is low. Pack the food into a heavy
airtight box heavily lined with newspapers or into the frozen food
compartment of your refrigerator. Disconnect the freezer to allow
it to warm. Wash the interior with a solution of several tablespoons of baking soda in 1 quart of hot water. *Soap or caustic
solution must never be used.* Allow the freezer to dry, leaving all
the doors and lids open. When dry, close and turn on the power.

WHEN THE POWER FAILS

IT IS very important that you never open the freezer when the electric power is shut off, except to add dry ice or to remove the foods to another storage place. If the power is likely to be off more than 24 hours, place a quantity of dry ice in each compartment to prevent the foods from thawing.

Household equipment specialists say that a well-stocked freezer will hold foods at temperatures low enough to avoid danger of spoilage (40° F.) for 84 hours. With freezers one-fourth loaded, the time has proved to be about 47 hours.

An alarm device, a light or a bell, to call attention to a rise of storage temperature is important as a warning for repair work. Place the "bulb" that sets off the alarm against the back liner of the freezer and level with the top package layer.

REFREEZING FOODS

RESEARCHERS in food freezing say that foods may be refrozen if the food is thawed only partially (when ice crystals remain), or if the temperature of the freezer is not above 40° F. (refrigerator temperature). Do the refreezing quickly, but use this food carefully. Usually the odor of the food will serve as an indication of its condition. Discard any off-flavor or sour foods because they contain toxins that are deadly. Label the refrozen foods and examine before using. Cook promptly when defrosted and throw away leftovers.

HOW TO PLAN FOR YOUR FREEZER SPACE

GOOD management of freezer space requires experience and planning. Research has not yet determined optimum storage periods for various foods. But the more food you put through your freezer in a year's time, the shorter the storage period for each package and the more money you save on each pound frozen. Since the freezer space is limited, you must plan ahead to get full benefits.

First, decide what foods your family prefers frozen. If you are a beginner in food freezing, you may need to experiment a bit the first year. Short-season foods are good choices for year-long use from the freezer. It is unwise to freeze too many pounds of one food.

Next, estimate what your family will eat in the next year in terms of pounds of frozen food; then make out a freezing plan. It has been estimated that at least 390 pounds of food per person should be frozen each year for the best use of the freezer. About 30 pounds of food in family sizes can be stored in a cubic foot of freezer space. Two or three food turnovers will be necessary in the average-size freezer.

According to actual national food consumption, the 390 pounds of frozen food for each person in the family may be divided as follows: 125 pounds of fruits and vegetables; 115 pounds of meat; 60 pounds of pre-cooked items such as bakery goods and desserts; 30 pounds of ice-cream; 60 pounds of specialties—fruit juices, fish, game, and other foods desired.

DIRECTIONS FOR A FOOD RECORD

To CARRY through with your food freezing plan, you will need to keep a record to show foods you have on hand and the amounts you have used.

On a large piece of cardboard or heavy paper enter the amount of each batch of food you freeze in the column "Amount Frozen." At the end of the freezing period, enter the "Total Frozen." Place a mark for each food package in the month when you plan to use it. Then, as you use the food, cross off the marks. If more food than anticipated is needed in a particular month, check the packages in the following months. You may decide to turn those unused strawberries into jam rather than carry them through another season.

This chart may be attached to the inside cover of your freezer or to the wall above it. Tie a pencil on a string to the chart for easy use.

ORGANIZATION OF FREEZER SPACE

WHETHER your freezer is the cabinet or the upright type, you will need to be able to find the foods you want easily. Wire baskets, metal dividers and shelves are some of the commercial aids to organization. Perhaps a chart on the freezer cover will aid you in finding particular packages. Colored tapes, tags, twine and different colored wrapping papers are also helps to quick identification. Mesh bags are good for holding small packages that may become lost.

CARE OF FROZEN FOODS IN TWO-TEMPERATURE REFRIGERATORS

HOMEMAKERS who plan to store foods in the frozen food compartment of their electric or gas refrigerators need to check the temperature of that compartment carefully if foods are to be held more than a few days.

At 20° F. or higher, frozen foods deteriorate quickly. If the compartment maintains a steady 15° F., foods may be held satisfactorily 2 or 3 weeks, but peaches, asparagus and green beans will begin to show loss of quality in about 10 days at this temperature.

For longer storage of frozen foods, 10° F. or lower is required. And if foods are to be held more than four months, the storage compartment temperature should not exceed 0° F. Non-fluctuating temperatures are important for maintaining frozen foods at high quality.

Researchers do not advocate freezing more than three or four pounds of food at a time in refrigerator frozen food compartments that maintain temperatures between 0° F. and 15° F. Five pounds at a time may be frozen at 0° F. or lower.

In buying frozen foods, it is important for the consumer to buy freshly packed frozen foods since these will hold their moisture, flavor and color much better in the freezer or refrigerator frozen food compartment. Foods should be stored and thawed in their original wrappings. See page 860 for the defrosting and refreezing of frozen foods.

Defrosting of refrigerators containing frozen foods should be done very rapidly, and the frozen foods should be removed from the compartment and packed into the freezer or the refrigerator. Hot water placed in trays in the refrigerator freezing compartment will speed defrosting.

HOW TO PACKAGE FOODS FOR THE FREEZER

Packaged in special wrapping materials adapted for the freezer, high quality foods will maintain surprisingly well their original flavor, moistness and tenderness.

Improperly wrapped foods will dry out, turn rancid, acquire strange flavors and be tough when cooked because of the low humidity of the freezer as a storage place. You will have this experience if you wrap foods in ordinary wrapping paper, waxed paper, locker paper or waxed cartons. For successful freezer storage, *foods must be wrapped in moisture-vapor-proof materials and in containers especially adapted for freezing.*

Packaging must protect frozen food from loss of liquid through leakage (as when freezing fruits in syrups that never freeze solid), from absorbing and giving off odors (smoked products or fish should not taint other foods), and it must be durable. Since frozen foods often get a great amount of handling, the wrapping must resist cracking or puncturing.

Containers need to be liquid-tight. Containers designed for permanent use are available in glass, tin and plastic. A wide mouth enables one to remove the contents easily. Throw-away containers are of several types: bag-in-box, waxed cubes, waxed nesting tubs with slip-in lids, cylinders with slip-over lids, freezer bags of materials suitable for liquid and others designed for dry products.

Re-use of Containers: Containers may be used a second time if they are in good condition. Cellophane liners of bag-in-box type cannot be re-used, but the outside boxes may if not damaged. Heavily waxed cartons may be re-used if washed in lukewarm water, dried carefully and stored in a clean dry place so as to avoid mold. Lids must fit tightly.

Cellophane rolls and package liners need to be stored in cool, humid temperatures. Before using a second time, store 48 hours in refrigerator.

Directions for Packaging:

1. When wrapping food in cellophane or similar material, press as much air as possible out of the package before sealing. With aluminum foil, one may "mold" the foil around the food, making sure that the food is completely covered.
2. Some wrapping materials require heat-sealing to be absolutely moisture-vapor-proof—cellophane liners, for instance. This can be done with a warm, not hot, iron or a special heat-sealing iron resembling the old-fashioned curling iron. Too much heat will cause disintegration of the wrapping material. Be sure edges to be sealed are free from food particles.
3. Overwrap packages wrapped in cellophane or plastic materials in stockinette to prevent tearing and breakage. (Aluminum foil does not require stockinette.)
4. The "Drugstore Wrap" is good for irregularly shaped foods wrapped in cellophane or freezing paper. Place the food in the center of the wrapping material and draw the two opposite sides of the material up together, giving a fold at the top, over and over, until the material reaches the food. Fold the ends of the material up over the food and seal with freezer tape or heat sealer.
5. Foods that are packaged in containers must be given room to expand during the freezing process. Leave from $\frac{1}{2}$- to $\frac{3}{4}$-inch headspace for food with liquid; but fill almost to the top for food without liquid.

When Buying Containers: Select containers that fit the food and are suitable for family-size portions. You will also need to consider storage. Square-cornered containers store better than round ones, but many users prefer the convenience-in-use of the round type. Pints thaw quicker than quarts. Some packaging containers cannot be re-used.

Short-term Freezing: For convenience you may want to use your freezer like your refrigerator and store foods for only a limited time. *For 14 days or less, you will not need to store foods in moisture-vapor-proof materials.* Store wrappings, waxed paper or covered dishes are sufficent for these few days, but if held over too weeks, they must be properly packaged in moisture-vapor-proof wrappings to prevent drying out and loss of flavor.

BRINE SOLUTION

A 2% *brine solution* is made by dissolving 4 tablespoons of salt in each gallon of water.

FRUITS AND VEGETABLES FOR FREEZING

RESEARCH has shown that some varieties of all fruits and vegetables freeze better than others. Since growing conditions differ across the country and different varieties of fruits and vegetables are available in different localities, we have not specified suitable varieties for freezing in this cookbook. We suggest that you write to your state extension service, experiment station, or college of agriculture for information on the local varieties that give the best freezing results.

DIRECTIONS FOR FREEZING VEGETABLES

CHOOSE vegetables for freezing that you would select for eating at the table. The maturity of the vegetable has a great influence on its texture, taste and color when frozen. Pick at the peak of their goodness and remember, *the shorter the time from the garden to the freezer the better*. If delay is necessary, the vegetables should be packed in crushed ice or held in a refrigerator or chill room (32° to 40° F.) for not longer than a few hours.

Equipment for freezing vegetables: You will find it helpful if you assemble the needed equipment before you pick the vegetables. Have on hand:

1. Colander, wire basket of fine mesh or cheese cloth. (The French frying kettle with long-handled basket may be used. Two sets speed the process.)
2. Two large kettles, or one large steam kettle and a large pan (copper kettles should not be used). Kettles must be large enough to accommodate one or more gallons of water, as desired. A pressure canner may also be used.
3. Special funnel for filling cartons.
4. Trivet for steamer.

Steps in vegetable freezing:

1. Discard any vegetables that are not perfect for eating. Wash thoroughly. Prepare for cooking by shelling, cutting, peeling or slicing, as required. Except where stated in directions, it is not necessary to immerse vegetables in a salt brine solution.
2. Either preheat in boiling water or in steam. It is necessary to scald or blanch vegetables before freezing. Scalding stops the enzymes from changing the flavor and destroying certain vitamins; it also brightens the color of the vegetable and enables one to pack a greater quantity into the containers. Since research indicates that one has a choice of methods, we give detailed directions for both preheating in boiling water and preheating in steam. Preheating in boiling water is considered advisable for household use because it is possible to heat the vegetables uniformly and sufficiently to inactivate the enzymes. If vegetables or fruits are steamed, it is essential to steam in relatively thin layers in order to preheat all the product evenly. Steaming is advocated for some vegetables and fruits, because it gives a superior product.

a. *To preheat in boiling water:*

Pour water into the large kettle, allowing 1 gallon of water to 1 pound of prepared vegetable. Bring to a boil. Place prepared vegetable in colander, wire basket or cheesecloth and immerse in water. Bring water to a rolling boil again and start timing. Agitate vegetables by moving basket back and forth. Keep vegetables under water. Best results may be obtained by scalding only 1 pound of vegetables at a time.

b. *To preheat in steam:*

Use a 6- to 12-quart kettle fitted with a trivet and a tight cover, or a pressure cooker or canner. Pour 1½ to 2 inches of water into kettle and bring to a rolling boil. Place prepared vegetables in wire basket and place on trivet in kettle. Cover kettle. Bring water to full rolling boil again and start timing. (No pressure is needed.) Scald only 1 pound of vegetables at a time.

c. *Cool:*

Immediately pour the vegetables into a second container for cooling and draining, keeping the scalding basket in the boiling water to speed scalding of second batch of vegetables. As quickly as possible, plunge vegetables into about 2 gallons of cold running water having a temperature of 50° to 60° F., or into water to which ice has been added. Vegetables that are mashed or pressed through a sieve can be cooled in air or floated in a pan in cold water. Cool vegetables thoroughly to the temperature of the water. Usually this will take about twice the scalding time. Remove and drain vegetables.

d. *Package:*

A funnel will help to fill bag-in-box packages quickly and will help to avoid spillage on edges of liner which prevents perfect sealing.

e. *Freeze at once:*

Place cartons on quick-freezing surfaces in freezer. If unable to freeze at once, place in refrigerator, but do not hold longer than 3 hours.

The following charts give specific directions for each vegetable and the correct timing.

TABLE XXXV

DIRECTIONS FOR HOME FREEZING VEGETABLES

VEGETABLES	HOW TO PREPARE AND PACKAGE
Artichokes	Preparation: Pull off outside bracts and cut off tops of buds. Trim butt to a cone and submerge in water as quickly as possible. Heat treatment: Preheat in boiling water 7 minutes. Cooling: Cool in ice water or cold running water. Pack: Pack dry, without brine.
Asparagus	Preparation: Sort according to thickness of stalk. Wash thoroughly. Cut or break off tender portion of stalk. Leave spears in lengths to fit the package or cut in 2-inch lengths. Heat treatment: Preheat in steam: Small stalks—2 minutes. Medium stalks—3 minutes. Large stalks—4 minutes. *or* Preheat in boiling water: Small stalks—2 minutes. Medium stalks—3 minutes. Large stalks—4 minutes. Cooling: Cool promptly in ice water or in cold running water. Pack: Pack dry, without brine, or in 2-percent brine (see page 865).
Beans: Lima	Preparation: Shell, sort according to size, and wash. Heat treatment: Preheat in steam: Small beans—2 minutes. Medium beans—4 minutes.

TABLE XXXV—(*Continued*)

DIRECTIONS FOR HOME FREEZING VEGETABLES

Vegetables	How to Prepare and Package
Beans: Lima (*cont'd*)	Large beans—4½ minutes. *or* Preheat in boiling water (preferred): Small beans—2 minutes. Medium beans—3 minutes. Large beans—4 minutes. Cooling: Cool promptly in ice water. Pack: Pack dry, without brine.
Shell, green	Preparation: Shell beans. Do not wash them. Heat treatment: Preheat in steam: 1¾ minutes. Preheat in boiling water: 1 minute. Cooling: Cool in cold running water about 3 minutes. Pack: Pack dry, without brine.
Snap, green	Preparation: Wash in cold water, then remove ends. Leave whole, slice lengthwise, or cut into 1- or 2-inch pieces. Heat treatment: Preheat in steam: 4 minutes. Preheat in boiling water: 3 minutes. Cooling: Chill in cold water. Pack: Pack dry, without brine, or in 2-percent brine (page 865).
Soybeans, green	Preparation: Squeeze beans out of pods after heating and cooling. Wash in cold water, and drain. Heat treatment: Heat in pods 5 minutes in steam or in boiling water. Cooling: Cool pods in cold water. Pack: Pack dry, without brine.
Wax	Preparation: Wash in cold water, then remove ends. Leave whole, slice lengthwise into strips, or cut into 1- or 2-inch pieces. Heat treatment: Preheat in steam: Whole beans—3½ minutes. Cut beans—3 minutes. Strips—2 minutes. *or* Preheat in boiling water: Whole beans—2½ minutes. Cut beans—2 minutes. Cooling: Cool in cold running water. Pack: Pack dry or in brine (see page 865).
Beet greens	Preparation: Wash well. Remove tough stems and imperfect leaves.

TABLE XXXV—(*Continued*)

DIRECTIONS FOR HOME FREEZING VEGETABLES

Vegetables	How to Prepare and Package
Beet greens (*cont'd*)	Heat treatment: Preheat in boiling water: 2 minutes. Cooling: Cool in cold water. Pack: Pack dry, without brine.
Beets: Young	Preparation: Wash, place in boiling water ½ minute. Peel, slice ¼-inch thick or dice into quarter-inch cubes. Heat treatment: Preheat in boiling water: 2½ minutes. Cooling: Cool in cold water. Pack: Pack dry, without brine.
Mature	Preparation: Wash and leave whole. Peel and slice after cooking. Heat treatment: Preheat in boiling water. Cook until tender. Cooling: Cool in cold water. Pack: Pack dry, without brine.
Broccoli	Preparation: Wash, peel, and trim. Split lengthwise into pieces not more than 1½ inches across. Soak in solution of 4 teaspoons salt to 1 gallon cold water ½ hour. Heat treatment: Preheat in steam: 5 minutes. or Preheat in boiling water: 3 minutes. Cooling: Cool promptly in cold water. Pack: Pack dry, without brine.
Brussels sprouts	Preparation: Trim; remove outer coarse leaves. Wash thoroughly. Sort into small, medium, and large sizes. Heat treatment: Preheat in steam: Small—3 minutes. Medium—4 minutes. Large—5 minutes. or Preheat in boiling water (preferred): Small—3 minutes. Medium—4 minutes. Large—5 minutes. Cooling: Cool promptly in cold water. Pack: Pack dry, without brine.
Cabbage	Preparation: Trim outer coarse leaves from head. Cut into medium to coarse shreds or wedges, or separate head into leaves. Heat treatment: Preheat in steam: 2 minutes. or Preheat in boiling water (preferred): 1½ minutes.

TABLE XXXV—(*Continued*)

DIRECTIONS FOR HOME FREEZING VEGETABLES

Vegetables	How to Prepare and Package
Cabbage (*cont'd*)	Cooling: Cool in cold water. Pack: Pack dry, without brine.

Cabbage, Chinese	Preparation: Wash, cut crosswise into 1-inch pieces.
	Heat treatment:
	    Preheat in steam: 2 minutes.
	        or
	    Preheat in boiling water (preferred): 1½ minutes.
	Cooling: Cool in cold water.
	Pack: Pack dry, without brine.

Carrots	Preparation: Top, wash, peel. Small tender carrots may be frozen whole; others cut into ¼-inch cubes or thin slices, or Frenched.
	Heat treatment:
	    Preheat in steam:
	        Frenched—2 minutes.
	        Diced or sliced—3 minutes.
	        Whole, small—5 minutes.
	        or
	    Preheat in boiling water:
	        Frenched—2 minutes.
	        Diced or sliced—3 minutes.
	        Whole, small—5 minutes.
	Cooling: Cool rapidly in cold water.
	Pack: Pack dry, without brine.

Cauliflower	Preparation: Break or cut into pieces about 1 inch across. Wash well. Soak in solution of 4 teaspoons salt to 1 gallon water 30 minutes.
	Heat treatment:
	    Preheat in steam: 4 minutes.
	        or
	    Preheat in boiling water (preferred): 3 minutes.
	Cooling: Cool quickly in cold water.
	Pack: Pack dry, without brine.

Celery	Celery is not generally recommended for freezing. May be cooked and frozen for use in hot dishes.

Chard, Swiss	Preparation: Wash thoroughly in cold running water. Cut off large tough main stems.
	Heat treatment:
	    Preheat in steam: 3 minutes.
	        or
	    Preheat in boiling water: 2 minutes.
	Cooling: Cool in cold running water or in a large volume of cold water.

TABLE XXXV—(*Continued*)

DIRECTIONS FOR HOME FREEZING VEGETABLES

Vegetables	How to Prepare and Package
Chard, Swiss (*cont'd*)	Pack: Pack dry, without brine.
Collards	Preparation: Trim and wash thoroughly in cold running water. Heat treatment: Preheat in steam: 3 minutes. *or* Preheat in boiling water (preferred): 2 minutes. Cooling: Cool in cold running water. Pack: Pack dry, without brine.
Corn, sweet: Whole-kernel	Preparation: Husk, remove silk, wash, and sort ears according to size. Cut kernels from cob after preheating. Heat treatment: Preheat in boiling water: On the cob—4½ minutes. Cooling: Cool ears in cold water. Pack: Pack dry, without brine.
On cob	Preparation: Husk, remove silk. Wash and sort ears according to size. Heat treatment: Preheat in steam: Small ears—7 minutes. Medium ears—9 minutes. Large ears—11 minutes. *or* Preheat in boiling water (preferred): Small ears—7 minutes. Medium ears—9 minutes. Large ears—11 minutes. Cooling: Cool in cold water. Pack: Pack dry, without brine.
Eggplant	Preparation: Wash, peel, cut into ⅓- to ½-inch slices or cubes. Lemon juice: Dip in 3 teaspoons lemon juice per quart water. Dip again in lemon juice and water after heating and cooling. Heat treatment: Preheat in steam: 5 minutes. *or* Preheat in boiling water (preferred): 4 minutes. Cooling: Cool in cold running water. Pack: Pack dry, without brine.
Kale	Preparation: Wash young succulent leaves in cold running water. Remove large tough main stems.

TABLE XXXV—(*Continued*)

DIRECTIONS FOR HOME FREEZING VEGETABLES

Vegetables	How to Prepare and Package

Kale (*cont'd*)	Heat treatment:
	  Preheat in steam: 2 minutes:
	       or
	  Preheat in boiling water (preferred): 2 minutes.
	Cooling: Cool in cold running water.
	Pack: Pack dry, without brine.

Kohlrabi	Preparation: Cut off tops and roots; wash, peel, and dice in ½-inch cubes. Heat treatment: Preheat in boiling water: 1 minute. Cooling: Cool in cold water. Pack: Pack dry, without brine.

Mushrooms	Preparation:
	  Sort according to size. Wash thoroughly in cold water. Trim ends of stems and cut larger mushrooms into 4 or more pieces.
	  Citric acid: Before scalding dip 5 minutes in citric acid solution (see page 879).
	Heat treatment:
	  Preheat in steam (preferred):
	    Small, whole—3½ minutes.
	    Large, whole—5 minutes.
	    Slices—3 minutes.
	       or
	  Preheat in boiling water:
	    Small, whole—2 minutes.
	    Large, whole—4 minutes.
	    Slices—2 minutes.
	Cooling: Cool in ice water or cold running water and drain.
	Pack: Pack dry, without brine.

Mustard greens	Preparation: Wash young, tender leaves thoroughly in cold running water. Remove tough main stems.
	Heat treatment:
	  Preheat in steam: 1½ minutes.
	       or
	  Preheat in boiling water: 1½ minutes.
	Cooling: Cool in cold running water.
	Pack: Pack dry, without brine.

Okra	Preparation: Select young tender pods. Wash thoroughly, cut off stems so as not to rupture seed cells. Freeze whole or slice crosswise after scalding.
	Heat treatment:
	  Preheat in steam:
	    Small pods—3 minutes.
	    Large pods—4 minutes.

TABLE XXXV—(*Continued*)

DIRECTIONS FOR HOME FREEZING VEGETABLES

Vegetables	How to Prepare and Package
Okra (*cont'd*)	*or* Preheat in boiling water (preferred): Small pods—2 minutes. Large pods—3 minutes. Cooling: Cool rapidly in cold water. Pack: Pack dry, without brine.
Onions	Preparation: Peel, wash, slice. Heat treatment: Preheat in live steam: 3 minutes. Cooling: Cool in iced water. Pack: Pack dry, without salt.
Parsnips	Preparation: Top, wash, peel, cut in ½-inch cubes or lengthwise in slices ¾-inch thick. Heat treatment: Preheat in steam: Cubes—3 minutes. Slices—5 minutes. *or* Preheat in boiling water: Cubes—2 minutes. Slices—3 minutes. Cooling: Cool rapidly in cold water. Pack: Pack dry, without brine.
Peas: Field (blackeye)	Preparation: Shell peas, discarding those that are hard. Do not wash peas. Heat treatment: Preheat in steam: 3 minutes. *or* Preheat in boiling water (preferred): 2 minutes. Cooling: Cool rapidly in cold water. Pack: Pack dry, without brine.
Green	Preparation: Wash peas before or after shelling. Discard immature and tough peas. Heat treatment: Preheat in steam: 1½ minutes. *or* Preheat in boiling water (preferred): 1 minute. Cooling: Cool rapidly in cold water. Pack: Pack dry, without brine.
Peppers, sweet	Preparation: Wash, cut out stem, halve, remove seeds, slice if desired.

TABLE XXXV—(*Continued*)

DIRECTIONS FOR HOME FREEZING VEGETABLES

Vegetables	How to Prepare and Package
Peppers, sweet (*cont'd*)	Heat treatment: Blanching is not necessary but makes packing easier. Preheat in steam: Slices—3 minutes. Halves—4 minutes. *or* Preheat in boiling water: Slices—2 minutes. Halves—3 minutes. Cooling: Chill promptly in cold water. Pack: Pack dry, without brine or in brine (see page 865).
Pimientos	Preparation: Wash, remove seeds, and slice or cut as desired. Heat treatment: Preheating is not necessary but makes packing easier. Preheat in steam: 2 minutes. *or* Preheat in boiling water: 2 minutes. Cooling: Cool promptly in cold water. Pack: Pack dry, without brine or in brine (see page 865).
Potatoes	Preparation: For new potatoes: Select potatoes the size of walnuts. Scrub them vigorously in cold water to remove skins, or wash and scrape them. For French fries: Use mature potatoes suitable for French frying. Wash, peel, and cut into sticks ⅓-inch square. Heat treatment: Preheat in steam: New potatoes—5 minutes. Sticks—3 minutes. *or* Preheat in boiling water: Sticks—2 minutes. Cooling: Cool in cold running water 3 to 5 minutes. Pack: Pack dry, without brine.
Pumpkin	Preparation: Wash, cut into quarters or smaller pieces, and remove seeds. After preheating, remove pulp and mash or put through sieve. Heat treatment: Steam until soft. Cooling: Cool in air. Pack: Pack dry, without brine.
Rutabagas: Cubes	Preparation: Cut off tops, wash, peel. Dice into ½-inch cubes. Heat treatment: Preheat in steam: 2 minutes.

TABLE XXXV—(*Continued*)

DIRECTIONS FOR HOME FREEZING VEGETABLES

Vegetables	How to Prepare and Package
Rutabagas: Cubes (*cont'd*)	*or* Preheat in boiling water (preferred): 2 to 3 minutes. Cooling: Cool in cold running water. Pack: Pack dry, without brine.
Purée	Preparation: Cut off tops, wash, peel, cut in pieces, cook until tender, and press through a sieve. Pack: Pack dry, without brine.
Soybeans	See Beans, page 868.
Spinach	Preparation: Use only young tender leaves. Remove large tough stems. Wash thoroughly in running water. Heat treatment: Preheat in steam: 3½ minutes. *or* Preheat in boiling water (preferred): 1½ minutes. Cooling: Cool in cold running water. Drain and gently press out excess water. Pack: Pack dry, without brine.
Spinach, New Zealand	Preparation: Wash thoroughly in cold running water. Cut off large tough stems. Heat treatment: Preheat in steam: 2 minutes. *or* Preheat in boiling water: 2 minutes. Cooling: Cool in cold running water or a large volume of cold water. Pack: Pack dry, without brine.
Squash: Summer	Preparation: Wash, cut in ½-inch slices. Cut Zucchini into ¼-inch slices. Heat treatment: Preheat in steam: 5 minutes. *or* Preheat in boiling water: 4 minutes. For Zucchini, 2 to 3 minutes. Cooling: Cool rapidly in cold water. Pack: Pack dry, without brine.
Winter	Preparation: Wash, peel, cut into pieces, and remove seeds. After precooking, remove pulp and mash or press through a sieve. Heat treatment: Cook until soft. Cooling: Cool in air.

TABLE XXXV—(*Continued*)

DIRECTIONS FOR HOME FREEZING VEGETABLES

VEGETABLES	HOW TO PREPARE AND PACKAGE
Squash: Winter (*cont'd*)	Pack: Pack dry, without brine.
Succotash	Preparation: Prepare corn and beans separately according to directions given for each vegetable. After preheating and cooling mix equal proportions of kernel corn and lima beans, soybeans, or snap beans. Heat treatment: See Corn (page 871) and Beans (pages 868–869)—Lima, Soybeans, or Snap. Cooling: See Beans and Corn. Pack: Pack dry, without brine.

Sweet potatoes	Preparation:
	  Grade according to size. Wash. Peel after cooking and pack whole, sliced, or mashed.
	  Citric acid or lemon juice: Dip slices or whole potatoes for 5 seconds in solution containing 1 tablespoon citric acid or ½ cup lemon juice to 1 quart water.
	Heat treatment: Cook until tender.

Tomatoes:
  Whole, quarters,
    or slices
	Not satisfactory as frozen product.

Juice	Preparation: Wash, sort, trim; crush or grind tomatoes. Heat to boiling, press out juice using sieve or fine screen. Cool and pack in liquid-tight containers; leave ¾-inch head space.

Turnip greens	Preparation: Wash young tender leaves in cold running water. Cut off large tough stems.
	Heat treatment:
	  Preheat in steam: 100 seconds.
	or
	  Preheat in boiling water: 1½ minutes.
	Cooling: Cool in cold running water.
	Pack: Pack dry, without brine.

Turnips	Preparation: Wash, peel, and cut into ¼- to ½-inch cubes.
	Heat treatment:
	  Preheat in steam: 3 minutes.
	or
	  Preheat in boiling water (preferred): 2 minutes.
	Cooling: Cool in cold water.
	Pack: Pack dry, without brine.

1. A large kettle and one large pan.
2. Scoop for filling cartons and containers.
3. Packaging and labeling materials.
4. Cartons, jars, cans, all of which are liquid-tight.

DIRECTIONS FOR FREEZING FRUITS

FOR BEST freezing results select fruits ready for table eating; they should be of proper variety, of pronounced flavor, attractive in color, fully ripe and sound.

Certain procedures for processing are necessary to prevent undesirable changes occurring in the frozen product. Most fruits need to be packed in a sugar syrup or in sufficient dry sugar to draw the juice and to create a syrup that will cover the fruit. Ascorbic acid is added to fruits that darken easily to preserve their natural color.

To Make the Sugar Syrup:

A syrup for fruits of varying sweetnesses can be made by dissolving sugar in boiling water or combining clear light corn syrup with water. Syrups made by both methods must be cooled to 70° F. before adding the ascorbic acid and before packing with the fruit.

TABLE XXXVI

PREPARATION OF SUGAR SYRUP FOR FREEZING

PERCENTAGE OF SYRUP	AMOUNT OF SUGAR	AMOUNT OF WATER	AMOUNT OF CORN SYRUP	AMOUNT OF WATER
	Cups	*Cups*	*Cups*	*Cups*
20	1	4		
30	2	4		
40	3⅓	4	4	5
50	5	4	4	3
60	7	4	4	1½
65	9	4	4	1

Honey may be used in place of part of the sugar (up to 25%) in freezing fruit. Too much honey may cause a displeasing flavor. Enzyme-converted sugars, such as the commercial product Sweetose, may also be used in place of sugar according to individual taste.

Directions for Packing: Cover fruit in container completely with syrup to within ¾ inch of the top. Crush a piece of waxed or moisture-vapor-proof paper on top of the fruit to be submerged and seal or cover. (Cellophane liners will need heat-sealing. See page 864.)

Dry Sugar Pack: Place fruit and sugar in a large bowl and turn over and over with a large spoon until the sugar is absorbed and enough juice is formed to cover the fruit. Dilute ascorbic acid in water and add to fruit before packing into containers.

Dry Pack: Package the dry fruit without sugar or syrup into containers and seal.

USE OF VITAMIN C (ASCORBIC ACID)

Ascorbic acid (vitamin C) is available in the powdered and the tablet form. Research has not definitely determined the amounts that should be added to fruits that brown easily on exposure to air such as peaches, apples or apricots. A general rule for the homemaker is to add ¼ to ½ teaspoon ascorbic acid per quart of *chilled* fruit sugar syrup before packing with fruit. Dissolve the powder in a little water or add directly to the syrup. Stir gently to mix. Since vitamin C is lost on standing, use as soon as possible.

Tablets come in the 25-, 50- and 100-milligram sizes. Two hundred milligrams may be added to 1 pint of fruit. Crush and dissolve in a small amount of water.

Either the dissolved powder or tablets may be added to sugar in the dry sugar pack, allowing ⅛ to ¼ teaspoon ascorbic acid powder to one pound of fruit.

Commercial preparations containing ascorbic acid are also available.

To Label: College research authorities recommend that fruits be packed in leakproof containers and labeled with the name of the fruit, the processing date, and the use for which the fruit is intended—pie, dessert, jam. It may also be helpful to note the sugar percentage, and the results of the taste-tests may be written on the year's record.

TABLE XXXVII

DIRECTIONS FOR HOME FREEZING FRUITS

FRUITS	HOW TO PREPARE AND PACKAGE
Apples: Slices	Preparation: Wash, peel, and core. Slice medium-sized apples into twelfths, large-sized into sixteenths. Ascorbic acid in syrup pack: Add ascorbic acid to prevent darkening (see page 879). Ascorbic acid in sugar pack: Add ascorbic acid per pound sugar. Dissolve in ¼ cup water before adding to fruit (see page 879). Sodium chloride: Hold in 1-percent salt solution (2 tablespoons salt in 1 gallon water) until used. Heat treatment (for pie slices): Steam slices 1½ to 2 minutes. Cool in ice water. Pack: Sugarless pack: Pack dry. Add no sugar or syrup. (For steamed or sulfited apples only.) *or* Syrup pack: Slice directly into 25- to 50-percent syrup, depending on tartness of fruit. Press fruit down and use enough syrup to cover. *or* Sugar pack: Sprinkle 1 pound sugar evenly over 5 pounds fruit. Allow to stand a few minutes, then stir carefully until each slice is coated.
Juice	Preparation: Wash fruit, crush, press out juice. Ascorbic acid: Add 1½ teaspoons per 3 gallons of juice.

TABLE XXXVII—(*Continued*)

DIRECTIONS FOR HOME FREEZING FRUITS

Fruits	How to Prepare and Package
Applesauce	Core and slice apples. Add ⅓ cup water to each quart apples. Cook until tender. Cool and strain. Sweeten to taste.

Apricots:
  Halves and slices
	Preparation:
	  Sort, wash, halve, and pit. Peel and slice if desired.
	  Ascorbic acid in syrup pack: Add ascorbic acid per quart syrup (250 mg. per pint finished pack) to prevent darkening (see page 879).
	  Ascorbic acid in sugar pack: Use ascorbic acid per pound sugar used (185 mg. per pint finished pack). Dissolve ascorbic acid in ¼ cup water before adding to sugar (see page 879).
	Pack:
	  Syrup pack: Cover with 40-percent syrup.
	                  or
	  Sugar pack: Mix 1 pound sugar with 3 or 4 pounds fruit. Stir gently until sugar is partly dissolved, and pack.

Crushed	Preparation: Peel, pit, and coarsely crush apricots. Pack: Sugar pack: Thoroughly mix 1 pound sugar with each 5 pounds fruit.
Purée	Preparation: Pit, then press soft-ripe fruit through a sieve. Pack: Sugar pack: Mix 1 pound sugar with each 4 pounds fruit purée.

Avocados:
  Purée
	Preparation:
	  Peel, halve, and pit; mash pulp.
	  Add ascorbic acid: (see page 879).
	                  or
	  Lemon juice: Use 4 teaspoons lemon juice with pulp from two avocados.
	Pack:
	  Sugar pack: Mix 1 pound sugar with 4 pounds fruit purée.

Blackberries:
  Whole
	Preparation: Sort, wash, and drain carefully.
	Pack:
	  Sugarless pack: Pack without sugar or syrup.
	                  or
	  Syrup pack: Cover with 40- to 50-percent syrup.

TABLE XXXVII—(*Continued*)

DIRECTIONS FOR HOME FREEZING FRUITS

FRUITS	HOW TO PREPARE AND PACKAGE
Blackberries: Whole (*cont'd*)	*or* Sugar pack (for pie or jam): Add sugar in proportion of 1 pound sugar to 4 pounds fruit.
Crushed	Sugar pack: Add 1 pound sugar to 3 pounds berries; stir until sugar is well dissolved.
Purée	Preparation: Sieve washed berries. Pack: Sugar pack: Mix 1 pound sugar with 4 pounds purée.

Blueberries:
  Whole
	Preparation: Sort, wash, and drain.
	Heat treatment: Preheat in steam 1 minute.
	Pack:
	  Sugarless pack (for preheated berries):
	  Pack dry, without sugar or syrup.
	  Syrup pack (preferred): Cover with 40-percent syrup.

Crushed	Sugar pack: Mix 1 pound sugar with 3 pounds fruit.
Purée	Preparation: Press fully ripe berries through fine sieve. Pack: Sugar pack: Blend with sugar to sweeten.
Boysenberries: Whole	Same as Blackberries (see page 880).
Purée	Same as Blackberries (see page 880).

Cantaloupes:
  Slices, cubes, balls
	Preparation: Cut in half, remove seeds, and peel. Cut in slices, cubes, or balls.
	Pack:
	  Sugarless pack: Not recommended.
	or
	  Syrup pack: Cover with 30-percent sugar syrup.
	or
	  Sugar pack: Mix with sugar, using 1 pound sugar to each 4 pounds fruit. Stir until sugar is partially dissolved, and pack.

Crushed	Preparation: Crush in food chopper, using coarse knife; mix thoroughly 1 pound sugar with 3 or 4 pounds fruit.
Cherries, sour	Preparation: Stem, sort, wash thoroughly, drain and pit.

TABLE XXXVII—(*Continued*)

DIRECTIONS FOR HOME FREEZING FRUITS

Fruits	How to Prepare and Package
Cherries, sour (*cont'd*)	
For pie	Pack: Sugar pack: Add 1 pound sugar to each 4 pounds fruit.
For dessert	Syrup pack: Cover fruit with 60- to 65-percent syrup.
Crushed	Sugar pack: Crush coarsely and add 1 pound sugar to 3 pounds fruit.
Purée	Preparation: Crush, heat to boiling point. Press through a sieve. Pack: Sugar pack: Add 1 cup sugar to 6 cups fruit purée.
Juice	Preparation: Crush, heat just to boiling, and extract juice in jelly bag. Pack: Sugar pack: Freeze without added sugar or sweeten to taste.
Cherries, sweet	Preparation: Stem, sort, wash, and drain.
Whole	Ascorbic acid: Add to each quart of cold syrup to prevent darkening of cherries. Pack: Syrup pack: Cover with 40-percent syrup.
Pitted	Preparation: Ascorbic acid. Add powdered form (see page 879). *or* Add 500 mg. ascorbic acid, dissolved in 2 tablespoons cold water, to each 3 pints fruit. Mix with fruit before adding sugar. Pack: Syrup pack: Pack in 40- or 50-percent syrup.
Crushed	Sugar pack: Add 1 pound sugar to each 3 pounds fruit.
Purée	Sugar pack: For dessert purée: Mix 1 part 65-percent syrup with 2 parts by volume of Montmorency cherry purée, or with 3 parts by volume of Bing cherry purée.
Juice	Preparation: Crush, heat just to boiling, and extract juice in jelly bag. Pack: Sugar pack: Freeze without added sugar, or sweeten to taste.

TABLE XXXVII—(*Continued*)

DIRECTIONS FOR HOME FREEZING FRUITS

Fruits	How to Prepare and Package
Cranberries: Whole	Preparation: Stem and sort, discard imperfect and soft berries. Wash carefully and drain. Pack: Sugarless pack: Pack whole without sugar or syrup. *or* Syrup pack: Cover berries with 50-percent syrup. *or* Sugar pack: Add 1 pound sugar to each 4 pounds fruit.
Purée	Preparation: Cook berries, press through a sieve. Pack: Sugar pack: Add sugar to taste. Cool.
Sauce	See Prepared and Cooked Foods (see page 905).
Currants	Preparation: Wash in cold water.
Whole	Pack: Sugar pack: Add 1 pound sugar to each 3 pounds fruit. Stir gently until partly dissolved.
Crushed	Sugar pack: Add 1 pound sugar to each 4 pounds crushed berries.
Juice	Preparation: Crush and heat berries slightly to start flow of juice. Press hot fruit in a jelly bag to extract juice. Cool.
Dewberries	Same as Blackberries (see page 880).
Elderberries	Same as Blueberries (see page 881).
Figs: Whole or slices	Preparation: Wash, sort, and cut off stems. Peel; leave whole or slice. Pack: Syrup pack: Cover with 30-percent syrup.
Crushed	Preparation: Crush or coarsely grind figs. Pack: Sugar pack: Add 1 pound sugar to 4 or 5 pounds fruit.
Purée	Pack: Syrup pack: Mix 1 part 65 percent syrup with 3 parts, by volume, Calimyrna fig purée.
Gooseberries	Preparation: Sort, remove stems and blossom ends, and wash.

TABLE XXXVII—(*Continued*)

DIRECTIONS FOR HOME FREEZING FRUITS

Fruits	How to Prepare and Package
Whole	Pack: Sugarless pack (for use in pie): Add no sugar or syrup. Syrup pack (preferred): Cover with 50-percent syrup.
Grapefruit: Sections	Preparation: Wash and peel. Section, removing all membranes and seeds. Pack: Syrup pack: Cover with 30- to 40-percent syrup made partly with excess juice.
Juice	Preparation: Squeeze juice from fruit, trying to avoid any oil from rind. Handle rapidly and pack immediately.
Grapes: Whole	Preparation: Wash and stem. Leave seedless grapes whole, cut Tokays in half and remove seeds. Pack: Sugarless pack: Not recommended. Syrup pack: Cover with 40-percent syrup.
Purée	Preparation: Wash, stem, and press through a sieve. Ascorbic acid: Use dry by weight with a 1 to 4 sugar pack (see page 879). Pack: Sugar pack: Mix 1 pound sugar with 4 pounds fruit purée.
Juice	Preparation: Crush and heat grapes in top of double boiler to 140° to 145° F. Extract juice. Sweeten if desired. Remove tartrate crystals by freezing, thawing, and straining juice.
Huckleberries	Same as Blueberries (see page 881).
Loganberries: Whole	Same as Blackberries (see page 880).
Purée	Same as Blackberries (see page 880).
Melons: Persian, Honeydew, Crenshaw	Same as Cantaloupes (see page 881).
Nectarines: Halves, quarters, slices	Preparation: Sort, wash, pit, and peel if desired. Cut in halves, quarters, or slices.

TABLE XXXVII—(*Continued*)

DIRECTIONS FOR HOME FREEZING FRUITS

Fruits	How to Prepare and Package
Nectarines: Halves, quarters, slices (*cont'd*)	Ascorbic acid: Put fruit directly into 40-percent syrup containing ascorbic acid (see page 879). Pack: Syrup pack: Cover immediately with 40-percent syrup.
Purée	Same as Peaches (below).
Olives, ripe	Pack: Wash pickling brine from olives and replace with fresh 2-percent brine, or pack freshly cured olives without brine.
Oranges: Slices or sections	Preparation: Wash and peel; slice, or section by removing membranes. Pack: Syrup pack: Cover with own juice.
Juice	Preparation: Squeeze juice from fruit, trying to avoid any oil from rind. Handle rapidly and pack immediately.
Peaches: Slices	Preparation: Wash, sort, pit, peel, and slice. Ascorbic acid in syrup pack: Add ascorbic acid to each quart syrup (see page 879). Ascorbic acid in sugar pack: Add ascorbic acid, dissolved in ¼ cup cold water, to each 4 pounds fruit and 1 pound sugar (see page 879). Pack: Syrup pack: Put peaches directly into 40-percent syrup, using enough syrup to cover. Sugar pack: Add 1 pound sugar to each 4 pounds fruit and mix well.
Crushed	Sugar pack: Add 1 pound sugar to 4 pounds fruit.
Purée	Preparation: Peel, halve, pit, and press through a sieve. Ascorbic acid: (See page 879.) Pack: Sugar pack: Mix 1 pound sugar with 4 pounds fruit purée.
Pears: Halves, quarters, slices	Preparation: Wash in cold water, peel, core, and cut in halves or quarters. Slice or dice if desired.

TABLE XXXVII—(*Continued*)

DIRECTIONS FOR HOME FREEZING FRUITS

FRUITS	HOW TO PREPARE AND PACKAGE
Pears: Halves, quarters, slices (*cont'd*)	Ascorbic acid: Add to each quart cold syrup (see page 879). Pack: Syrup pack: Cover immediately with 40- to 50-percent syrup.
Purée	Preparation: Press through sieve. Ascorbic acid: (See page 879.) Pack: Sugar pack: Mix 1 pound sugar with 4 pounds fruit purée.
Persimmons:	Not recommended except as purée.
Purée	Preparation: Sort, wash, and cut into sections. Press through a sieve. Ascorbic acid: (See page 879.) Citric acid: (See page 879.) Pack: Sugar pack: Thoroughly mix 1 pound sugar with 4 pounds fruit purée.
Pineapple	Preparation: Pare, core, and remove other woody parts. Slice, dice, crush, or cut into wedges or sticks. Pack: Sugarless pack: Pack without sweetening, adding excess juice. Syrup pack: Cover with 30- to 40-percent syrup. Sugar pack: Mix 1 pound sugar with 4 pounds fruit.
Plums, prunes: Halves or quarters	Preparation: Sort, wash, halve, or quarter and pit fruit. Ascorbic acid in syrup pack: Use 1.5 to 2.3 gm. ascorbic acid to each quart syrup (¼ teaspoon to 1 to 1½ cups syrup). Pack: Syrup pack: Cover promptly with 40- to 60-percent syrup, depending on tartness of fruit.
Purée	Preparation: Use fully ripe fruit. Wash, halve, pit, and press raw fruit through a sieve. Ascorbic acid: (See page 879.) Citric acid: (See page 879.) Heat treatment: Heat just to the boiling point, adding only enough water to keep the fruit from burning. Cool and press through a sieve. Sweeten and pack.

TABLE XXXVII—(*Continued*)
DIRECTIONS FOR HOME FREEZING FRUITS

Fruits	How to Prepare and Package
Plums, prunes: Purée (*cont'd*)	Pack: Sugar pack: Add 1 part sugar to each 3 or 4 parts raw fruit purée. Mix thoroughly and promptly.
Juice	Preparation: Cover red fruit with water; cook until soft; strain. Cool juice 24 hours, filter and sweeten. Dilute with half water.
Raspberries: Whole	Preparation: Sort, wash carefully in cold water, drain thoroughly. Pack: Sugarless pack: Add no sugar or syrup. *or* Syrup pack: Cover with 40-percent syrup. *or* Sugar pack: Add 1 pound sugar to 4 pounds berries.
Crushed	Sugar pack: Add 1 pound sugar to 3 pounds crushed berries.
Purée	Preparation: Press through a sieve. Pack: Sugar pack: Mix 1 pound sugar with each 3 pounds fruit purée.
Juice	Preparation: Crush and heat berries slightly to start flow of juice. Press hot fruit in a jelly bag to extract juice. Cool.
Rhubarb: One-inch pieces	Preparation: Wash, trim, and cut into 1-inch pieces. Heat treatment: Preheat in steam: 1½ to 2 minutes. *or* Preheat in boiling water: 1½ minutes. Cool in cold water, drain. Pack: Sugarless pack: Pack raw without syrup or sugar. *or* Pack preheated rhubarb without sugar or syrup. *or* Syrup pack: Cover raw fruit with 40-percent syrup. *or* Sugar pack: Mix 1 pound sugar with 4 or 5 pounds raw fruit.
Purée	Preparation: Add 1 cup water to 2 pounds rhubarb and boil 2 minutes. Press through a sieve or grind. Mix 1 cup sugar with 6 cups purée.

TABLE XXXVII—(*Continued*)

DIRECTIONS FOR HOME FREEZING FRUITS

FRUITS	HOW TO PREPARE AND PACKAGE
Rhubarb: (*cont'd*) Sauce	Preparation: Cook in a 60-percent syrup, cool.
Juice	Preparation: Cut rhubarb in pieces 4 to 6 inches long, add 2 quarts water for each 10 pounds rhubarb, and just bring to a boil. Press hot fruit in jelly bag to extract juice. Cool. Sweeten to taste if desired.
Strawberries	Preparation: Sort and wash berries in cold water. Drain well and remove hulls. Berries may be cut in halves, sliced, crushed, or left whole.

Whole	Pack:
	  Syrup pack: Cover fruit with 50-percent sugar syrup.
	or
	  Sugar pack: Mix well 1 pound sugar with 4 pounds fruit.

Slices	Sugar pack: Mix gently with sugar in proportion of 1 pound sugar to 4 pounds berries.
Crushed	Sugar pack: Add 1 pound sugar to 4 pounds crushed fruit.

Purée	Preparation:
	  Press berries through a sieve.
	  Ascorbic acid: (See page 879.)
	Pack:
	  Sugar pack: Add 1 pound sugar to 4 pounds fruit purée.

Watermelon	Not recommended (may be frozen in balls).
Youngberries: Whole	Same as Blackberries (see page 880).
Purée	Same as Blackberries (see page 880).

DIRECTIONS FOR FREEZING MEATS

BEEF, pork, veal and lamb can be frozen with satisfactory results, provided they are of good quality and are carefully handled, frozen and stored. Choose healthy, well-conditioned young animals for the best quality meat.

Detailed directions for butchering and meat cutting may be obtained from the U. S. Department of Agriculture.*

Unless you live on a farm, no doubt you will buy animals on the hoof from a local farmer and ask your locker plant to do the slaughtering and preparation, or you will buy meat in quantity lots from the locker or butcher.

These precautions should be taken:

1. Buy the best grade of government-inspected meat, which assures you of high quality meat, free from disease.
2. Buy lean cuts of meat. Meat heavy with fat will not keep as long or as well in the freezer.
3. Check to see that the animal was cooled immediately after being slaughtered. Cooling should be done thoroughly in a room with a temperature of from 32° F. to 38° F. A large animal may require as long as 70 hours for complete cooling.
4. Cut meat into meal-size pieces depending upon the size of the family. Research authorities advise having the meat boned to conserve freezer space. Remove the rough edges from bones left in the meat to prevent holes being punctured in wrapping materials.
5. Package together enough steaks, meat patties, chops or cutlets for one meal. Pieces may be separated by placing two pieces of cellophane or freezer wrapping between the pieces of meat to facilitate separating them when thawing.
6. It is particularly important in meat wrapping to select materials that are moisture-vapor-proof and durable. Fragile wrappings such as cellophane require overwraps of stockinette or butcher paper. Freezer tape proves to be more efficient than string in tying the packages.
7. To preserve the meat's tenderness and juiciness, it is essential that it be wrapped so as to keep out air pockets and to keep

* *Farmer's Bulletins:* No. 1186, *Pork on the Farm—Killing, Curing and Canning;* No. 1415, *Beef on the Farm—Slaughtering, Cutting, Curing;* No. 1807, *Lamb and Mutton on the Farm;* No. 74L, *Boning Lamb Cuts.*

the package as airtight as possible. The drugstore wrap is advocated by freezing experts (see page 864) as forming the tightest seal when wrappings similar to cellophane are used. Aluminum foil and some plastic wrappings may be "molded" to the meat to maintain airtightness.

8. Smoked and cured meats must be wrapped and sealed carefully to prevent transmission of odors. Use moisture-vapor-proof wrappings. Whole or half hams have more moistness and better flavor if frozen whole. Bacon should be frozen in 2 or more pound packages unsliced. Since the addition of salt shortens the life of sausage, it should be added after the product is thawed. Spices may be mixed with the ground pork.

9. To prevent meat being held in storage too long, it is important to label carefully with the date of freezing. The label should give also the kind of meat, the name of the cut, and its weight or number of servings. Tags of different colors aid in quick identification.

10. Place meat immediately in freezing section of freezer, separating the packages so as to permit air circulation. Be careful not to overload freezer. Leave at least 24 hours. *Meat not frozen promptly or thoroughly is likely to spoil.*

11. Store the meat at a non-fluctuating 0° F. or below.

Aging or Ripening: To increase tenderness and flavor of some kinds of meat, it is advisable to age or ripen the meat after slaughter in cold storage (32° to 38° F.) at closely controlled temperatures.

Good quality beef (commercial to prime grades) will be more tender and flavorful if aged 4 to 9 days, before it is frozen. The time of aging will depend upon the fatness of the meat. Beef with little or no external fat may actually spoil rather than improve if held more than 5 days after cooling. At the present time, research seems to indicate that longer aging may tend to shorten the time that beef can be stored in a freezer at 0° F. without deteriorating in quality.

Lamb may be aged from 1 to 3 days after chilling. Good quality mutton may be improved by aging 2 or 3 days. Generally speaking, tenderness and flavor in lamb or mutton are not increased by any longer aging.

Pork, veal, poultry and fish should not be aged. Cut, process and freeze as soon as possible after chilling. Aging may cause serious and dangerous spoilage.

Yield from Meat: The percentage of carcass weight to live weight varies with the type and weight of the animal. Good grade beef should dress from 58 to 60 per cent: 1 beef of 600 pounds live weight should weigh about 330 pounds dressed.

Vealers of good grade weighing from 110 to 120 pounds usually dress 55 to 60 per cent.

Choice meat-type hogs ranging in weight from 180 to 230 pounds live weight will show a yield of 78 per cent dressed. A 200-pound hog will yield 156 pounds dressed, including 20 to 30 pounds of lard.

The dressed weight of lamb is usually 48 to 55 per cent of the live weight. A lamb of 80 pounds will yield about 40 pounds dressed.

DIRECTIONS FOR FREEZING POULTRY

FREEZING enables the family to have broilers, fryers or roasters the year around as desired, the quality very comparable with the fresh, if poultry of good grade and condition is used.

Form-fitting wrapping materials are especially important in packaging poultry to prevent freezer burn (drying out in storage). Pliable materials, aluminum foil, and bags designed for vacuumizing and shrinking to fit are best.

To De-feather: Plunge birds for 1 minute in hot water (130° F.). Rotate to allow water to penetrate through feathers to skin. Pick out feathers. Singe off pinfeathers, using pin picker if necessary. Wash the skin thoroughly in cold water.

To Cool: Immediately place birds in refrigerator for at least 12 hours.

To Clean: Cut off head and feet. Completely remove lungs. Draw, clean and wash chicken.

Broilers and fryers: With poultry shears or sharp knife, split bird from neck to tail along backbone. Remove entrails. Place halved birds together with two pieces of wrapping between the halves. Disjoint if preferred and wrap in moisture-vapor-proof materials.

Roasters: Remove most of the body fat so as to prevent rancidity. Remove entrails including crop. Wash thoroughly in cold water and drain.

Package liver, heart and gizzards in moisture-vapor-proof wrappings and insert in cavity of roaster, between halves of broiler or fryer or place in separate carton.

To Freeze: Immediately place in freezing section of freezer and leave for at least 24 hours. Store at 0° F.

Stuffed Poultry: Recent research indicates that poultry should not be stuffed and then frozen because of possible formation of harmful bacteria when frozen bird is defrosted and cooked. Freeze the unstuffed bird, thaw and stuff immediately before roasting. Refrigerate cooked stuffed bird at all times when not in use. Unstuffed poultry may be kept frozen up to 10 months.

Turkey: Follow directions for poultry. Prepare for roasting and truss. Insert in large bag of pliable material or use aluminum foil or cellophane and stockinette overwrap. Turkey may be frozen, thawed, then stuffed (preferred).

Defrosting: Allow 24 to 72 hours in refrigerator for defrosting of stuffed turkey. Remove outer wrappings but not the moisture-vapor-proof materials before thawing is complete. Proceed as for fresh stuffed turkey (page 893).

GAME BIRDS

FOLLOW the directions given previously for poultry. Promptly after killing, scald, pick, clean and wash. Freeze and store at 0° F.

SMALL GAME BIRDS

COOL animals as soon as brought in or killed. Skin, behead, eviscerate and carefully wash. Cut into pieces for cooking. Package in cartons or in moisture-vapor-proof wrappings. Freeze as for other meats.

VENISON

VENISON or other large game may be prepared and packaged the same way as beef or veal (see page 891).

FISH AND SHELLFISH

Fish: Place fish to be frozen in refrigerator or on ice as soon as possible. Clean, scale, behead, remove entrails and wash thoroughly. Cut up for cooking. Fillet or cut into steaks the large fish. Package in cartons or in moisture-vapor-proof materials. Freeze at least 24 hours in freezing section of freezer and store at 0° F. or below.

To Glaze Fish: Freeze unwrapped. Dip the frozen fish in ice water; place again in freezer to let an ice film develop over fish. Repeat the dipping and freezing until the fish are well coated in ice. Glazing may need renewing if fish stored several months. Wrapping will prevent the ice from being chipped.

Shellfish: Wash oysters, clams and scallops in salty water (2 tablespoons salt to 1 quart of water). Package in liquid-tight containers. Freeze immediately and store at 0° F. or below.

Crabs: Clean crabs thoroughly. Wash and steam or cook in salted water (½ teaspoon per quart water). Cool thoroughly and freeze immediately. Store at 0° F. or below.

Lobsters: Steam lobsters until cooked. Cool thoroughly. Pick edible meat from shells and package in moisture-vapor-proof material or in liquid-tight containers. Freeze rapidly and store at 0° F. or below. Lobster meat tends to toughen during storage.

Shrimp: Shrimp may be frozen uncooked. Break off heads, wash well and freeze in liquid-tight container. To freeze cooked, boil 5 minutes in salt water (12 ounces to 1 gallon of water). Shell, clean and package in liquid-tight containers. Freeze. Store at 0° F. or below. Cooked shrimp tends to toughen during storage.

HOW TO FREEZE EGGS AND DAIRY PRODUCTS

Eggs

BE CAREFUL not to choose cracked eggs, for they frequently contain bacteria. Break eggs into a clean bowl; smell each one to be sure it is fresh. Using a fork, beat just enough to break the yolks and to blend them with the whites. Pour eggs into containers of the size needed for particular use for the family; for example, eggs for scrambling for one meal; in lots of two or four for cakes, etc. Allow ½-inch for expansion. Small quantities of the eggs may be placed in individual moisture-vapor-proof bags or small cartons and all sealed in one large carton. Label with number of eggs or intended use for them. Freeze and store.

Egg Whites: Frozen egg whites may be used successfully in angel or white cake making. Separate the whites carefully from the yolks, package them in the amounts needed per recipe. Label and freeze.

Egg Yolks: Separate the yolks from the whites. Salt, corn syrup or honey will help prevent the texture of the yolks from changing in storage. For 6 egg yolks, use 2 level tablespoonfuls of sugar, honey or corn syrup, and 1 teaspoon of salt. Mark on label what is added.

Guide to Use: In general, 1½ tablespoons of egg white equal the white of 1 egg. One tablespoon of yolk equals an egg yolk.

Dairy Products

Butter: High quality butter or margarine may be stored with good results in a home freezer. Wrap in foil or parchment paper to exclude air and store in a waxed, sealed carton (the commercial butter cartons may be used). Store in pound or larger lots.

Cream: Pasteurized, rich cream may be stored at zero degrees. Use for making ice creams, puddings, etc.

Cheese: With rapid freezing, cottage and cheddar cheese may be frozen and stored with no loss in quality. Package in small sizes, ½-pound sizes, not more than 1¾ inches thick. Wrap tightly in moisture-vapor-proof material. Place near freezing surfaces. Store at zero degrees or lower and do not keep longer than four or five months.

TABLE XXXVIII

DIRECTIONS FOR HOME FREEZING BAKED GOODS

Food	How to Prepare and Package

Breads:
  Biscuits:
    Unbaked
	Formula: Use standard recipes. Use double-acting baking powder.
	Preparation: Roll and cut dough before freezing. Freeze as quickly as possible.
	Packaging: Stack one on another in airtight container. Place two sheets of waxed paper between layers.
	Storage: 1 month.
	Thawing and baking:
	  Bake on greased baking sheets: Thawed, 12 to 15 minutes at 425° F. Unthawed, 20 to 25 minutes at 425° F.

TABLE XXXVIII—(*Continued*)

DIRECTIONS FOR HOME FREEZING BAKED GOODS

Food	How to Prepare and Package
Breads: **Biscuits:** (*cont'd*) Baking before freezing	Formula: Use standard recipes. Preparation: Prepare and bake as usual. Cool, freeze immediately. Packaging: Place biscuits in cardboard boxes, wrap in moisture-vapor-proof material, heat-seal. Storage: 3 months. Thawing and heating: Thaw in wrapper in slow oven (250° F) 20 minutes.
Muffins: Unbaked	Formula: Use standard recipes. Preparation: Prepare as usual; fill paper baking cups two-thirds full. Freeze. Packaging: After freezing in paper cups, package within 24 hours. Nest cups and wrap in moisture-vapor-proof material or place in cellophane-lined cartons. Heat-seal or seal with tape. Thawing and baking: Thaw at room temperature 1 hour, bake same as fresh muffins.
Baked before freezing	Formula: Use standard recipes. Preparation: Prepare as usual, bake, cool. Freeze as quickly as possible. Packaging: Use moisture-vapor-proof material or bags and heat-seal. Place in cardboard boxes for added protection. Thawing and heating: Thaw in package at room temperature about 1 hour. Reheat in oven at 250° to 300° F.
Yeast bread: Unbaked	Formula: Use standard recipes. Preparation: After first rising, shape into loaves or flatten bulk dough to 1- or 1½-inch thickness. Grease all surfaces. Freeze immediately. Packaging: Wrap flattened dough in moisture-vapor-proof material with two sheets of waxed paper between layers of dough. Freeze loaves in pans wrapped in moisture-proof cellophane, heat-seal. Storage: Not over 2 months. Thawing and baking: Thaw wrapped dough in warm, moist place. Shape bulk dough into loaves. Let rise in pans in a warm place. Bake at 400° F. 30 to 40 minutes.
Baked before freezing	Formula: Use standard recipes. Preparation: Prepare and bake bread as usual. Cool quickly.

TABLE XXXVIII—(*Continued*)

DIRECTIONS FOR HOME FREEZING BAKED GOODS

FOOD	HOW TO PREPARE AND PACKAGE
Breads: (*cont'd*)	Packaging: Wrap in moisture-vapor-proof material. Heat-seal or seal with tape. Thawing and heating: Thaw in wrappings at room temperature. Use immediately.
Yeast rolls: Unbaked	Formula: Use plain or sweet, rich dough recipe. Preparation: Shape rolls after one rising. Grease all surfaces. Packaging: Place shaped rolls in shallow container or in paper baking cups, wrap with cellophane or metal foil, heat-seal. Freeze immediately. Storage: Not over 6 weeks. Thawing and baking: Thaw in warm, moist place, let rise until light, and bake at usual temperature.
Baked before freezing	Formula: Use standard plain or sweet-dough recipes. Preparation: Prepare and bake as usual. Cool quickly. Wrap and freeze immediately. Packaging: Wrap in moisture-vapor-proof material and heat-seal. Place in cardboard container. Thawing and heating: Reheat in sealed wrappings about 15 minutes in 250° to 300° F. oven. Use immediately.
Cakes: Plain: Unbaked	Formula: Use standard recipes. Formula: Use double-acting baking power if batter packaged in carton or jar. Cakes made with synthetic vanilla unpalatable after 6 months. Preparation: Prepare as usual. Pour batter into greased baking pan, package, and freeze immediately. Packaging: Wrap in moisture-vapor-proof material, seal by heat or with tape. Storage: 2 months. Thawing and baking: Loaf cakes: Thaw completely at room tempertaure. Bake as for freshly prepared batter. Layer cakes: Bake without thawing. Allow longer baking time.
Baked before freezing	Prebaked preferred to unbaked; has better volume. Formula: Use standard recipes.

TABLE XXXVIII—(*Continued*)

DIRECTIONS FOR HOME FREEZING BAKED GOODS

Food	How to Prepare and Package
Cakes: Plain: Baked before freezing (*cont'd*)	Preparation: Mix and bake as usual. Remove cake from pan. Cool thoroughly before wrapping. Freeze immediately. Packaging: Wrap in moisture-vapor-proof material, heat-seal, and store in cartons. Storage: 4 months. Thawing and heating: Loaf: Thaw in wrapper at room temperature 2½ hours, or with an electric fan 90 minutes, or in a 300° F. oven 30 minutes. Layer: Thaw in wrapper at room temperature 1 hour, or with an electric fan 40 minutes, or in a 300° F. oven 10 minutes.
Chocolate	Unbaked product better than prebaked. Formula: Use standard recipe.
Fruit Spice Gingerbread	Formula: Use standard recipe. Better to freeze unbaked rather than baked product. Formula: Use standard recipe. Gingerbread kept better than plain, spice, or chocolate cake.
Cup cakes: Unbaked	Formula: Use standard recipes. Preparation: Fill paper cups one-half to two-thirds full. Packaging: Pack cups in muffin pans or in a top-opening box, overwrap with moisture-vapor-proof material, heat-seal. Thawing and baking: Remove cups from package and thaw before baking.
Baked before freezing	Formula: Use standard recipes. Preparation: Fill paper cups one-half to two-thirds full. After baking cool the cup cakes. Packaging: Place cup cakes in a top-opening box overwrapped with moisture-vapor-proof cellophane, heat-seal. Thawing and heating: Thaw at room temperature 40 to 60 minutes, or with an electric fan 30 minutes, or in a 300° F. oven 10 minutes.
Sponge and angel food: Unbaked	Not as fine grained as baked frozen cakes. Formula: Use standard recipes. Preparation: Prepare batter as usual, pour immediately into baking pan.

TABLE XXXVIII—(*Continued*)

DIRECTIONS FOR HOME FREEZING BAKED GOODS

Food	How to Prepare and Package
Cakes: Sponge and angel food: Unbaked: (*cont'd*)	Packaging: Wrap pan in moisture-vapor-proof material, seal, freeze at once. Thawing and baking: Bake without thawing.
Baked before freezing	Formula: Use standard recipes. Preparation: Bake as usual. Cool thoroughly. Remove from pan. Packaging: Wrap in moisture-vapor-proof material, heat-seal. Place in box for greater protection. Thawing and heating: Thaw in wrappings: 2 hours at room temperature. 75 minutes with an electric fan. 15 minutes in a 300° F. oven.
Cake frostings and fillings	Formula: Recommended: Confectioners' sugar and fat. Cooked-candy type with honey or corn syrup. Fudge Fruit Raisin Penuche Apricot Nut Not recommended: Soft frostings. Boiled icings. Cream fillings. Thawing: Thaw in their original sealed packages in the refrigerator. If paper sticks to the frosting, loosen it before thawing. Keep iced cakes in the refrigerator until serving time.
Cookies: Bar	Little difference between freshly baked cookies, those baked before freezing, and those freshly baked from frozen dough.
Unbaked	Formula: Most recipes are successful. Preparation: Use standard procedures. Packaging: Bulk dough: Place in frozen-food containers of suitable size and shape. Shaped in pans: Place in baking pans, wrap in moisture-proof cellophane, heat-seal. Storage: 6 months. Thawing and baking: Thaw in unopened package or, if frozen in pan, bake immediately.
Baked before freezing	Formula: Most recipes are successful. Preparation: Cool thoroughly.

TABLE XXXVIII—(*Continued*)

DIRECTIONS FOR HOME FREEZING BAKED GOODS

Food	How to Prepare and Package
Cookies: Baked before freezing (*cont'd*)	Packaging: Pack in top-opening box or tubular carton with waxed paper between layers and in air spaces. Storage: 6 months. Thawing: Thaw in wrappings at room temperature.
Drop: Unbaked	Formula: Most recipes are successful. Preparation: Use standard procedures. Packaging: Pack dough in round or square frozen-food containers. Storage: 6 months. Thawing and baking: Thaw at room temperature until soft enough to be dropped by spoonfuls on greased baking sheet. Bake at 400° F. 10 minutes.
Baked before freezing	Formula: Most recipes are successful. Preparation: Mix and bake in usual way. Cool. Packaging: Pack in frozen-food containers with waxed paper crumpled around and between cookies. Storage: 12 months. Thawing: Thaw at room temperature in container.
Refrigerator: Unbaked	Formula: Use standard recipes. Preparation: Shape into roll or chill and slice. Packaging: Roll: Wrap shaped roll in moisture-vapor-proof material, seal with heat or tape. Slices: Place in layers in frozen-food containers with two layers waxed paper between layers. Storage: 6 months. Thawing and baking: Frozen in roll: Slice and bake as usual on greased cookie sheet. Frozen slices: Bake without thawing.
Baked before freezing	Formula: Use standard recipes. Preparation: Cool thoroughly before packing. Packaging: Pack in frozen-food container with waxed paper between layers and in spaces. Storage: 6 months. Thawing: Thaw at room temperature in wrappings.
Rolled: Unbaked	Formula: Rolled butterscotch cookies. Packaging: Pack bulk dough in airtight cartons.

TABLE XXXVIII—(*Continued*)

DIRECTIONS FOR HOME FREEZING BAKED GOODS

Food	How to Prepare and Package

Cookies:
  Rolled: Unbaked
  (*cont'd*)
	Storage: 1 year.
	Thawing and baking: Thaw at room temperature until soft enough to roll, bake at 350° F.

Pies:
  Fruit, general:
    Unbaked
	Better to freeze unbaked pies than baked pies.
	Formula: Use standard recipes.
	Filling: Fresh or frozen fruits (especially cherries) are better than canned fruits. Loose-pack frozen fruits may be used frozen, others are thawed slightly.
	Preparation: Prepare as usual but do not slit top crust before freezing.
	Packaging: Pack in glass, metal, or special paper pie plates. Cover with paper plate. Wrap in moisture-vapor-proof material. Heat-seal. If desired, cover with stockinette or paper box.
	Storage: 2 months.
	Thawing and baking: Remove wrappings, cut vent holes in top crust, and bake without thawing 20 minutes in a hot oven (450° to 475° F.), then at 375° until done.

Baked before freezing	Fruit pies freeze successfully. Formula: Use standard recipes. Either fresh or frozen fruit is recommended. Preparation: Prepare and bake as usual, cool. Packaging: Use glass, tin, or special paper pie plate, cover with paper plate, wrap in moisture-vapor-proof material, heat-seal. Cover with stockinette or paper box. Thawing and heating: Remove wrapper and heat at once in a 400° F. oven, or thaw at room temperature in the package.
Apple: Unbaked	Better to freeze pies unbaked than to prebake them. Formula: Use firmer varieties of apples, since apples soften on freezing. Use standard recipe for pastry. Preparation: Steam apple slices 1½ minutes, cool, and drain; or dip slices in ascorbic acid solution (1 teaspoon ascorbic acid to 1 pint water). Do not slit top crust. Packaging: Use glass, metal, or special paper pie plate. Cover with paper plate. Wrap in moisture-vapor-proof material. Heat-seal. Cover with stockinette, if desired. Thawing and baking: Place unwrapped pie in 425° F. oven 5 minutes. Remove and cut vents in top crust. Return to oven and bake 55 minutes longer.

TABLE XXXVIII—(*Continued*)

DIRECTIONS FOR HOME FREEZING BAKED GOODS

Food	How to Prepare and Package
Pies: Apple: (*cont'd*) Baked before freezing	Baked apple pie may be frozen satisfactorily. Formula: Use standard recipe. Preparation: Mix sugar and flour and sprinkle over fruit. Proceed as for fresh apple pie. Cool thoroughly. Packaging: Use glass, tin, or paper pie plate, cover with second plate, heat-seal in cellophane or in metal foil, wrap in ordinary wrapping paper. Thawing and heating: Unwrap, heat at 375° F. 30 minutes.
Berry: Unbaked	Preparation: Do not cut openings in top crust.
Baked before freezing	Preparation: Cool, freeze immediately. Thawing and heating: Thaw in a 400° F. oven 20 minutes.
Cherry: Unbaked	Preparation: Prepare pie as usual; seal edges well but do not slit top crust. Packaging: Leave pie in container in which it is to be baked; cover with paper plate, then wrap in moisture-vapor-proof material; heat-seal. Thawing and baking: Remove wrappings, cut vent holes in upper crust, and bake without thawing at 400° F. 1 hour.
Baked before freezing	Preparation: Prepare and bake as usual, cool, then freeze immediately. Packaging: Wrap in cellophane within 24 hours after freezing. Thawing and heating: Heat in oven.
Mince: Baked before freezing	Mince pies freeze well. Frozen unbaked mince pies are better than frozen prebaked. Formula: Use standard recipe. Preparation: Cool rapidly and thoroughly. Thawing and heating: Unwrap and heat at 375° F. 30 to 40 minutes.
Peach: Unbaked	Unbaked pies are superior to those baked before freezing. Preparation: Steam sliced fruit 1 or 2 minutes. Do not cut steam vents in crust. Thawing and baking: Cut vents in top crust and bake unthawed at 400° F. about 1 hour.

TABLE XXXVIII—(*Continued*)

DIRECTIONS FOR HOME FREEZING BAKED GOODS

Food	How to Prepare and Package
Pies: Peach: (*cont'd*) Baked before freezing	Formula: Use standard recipe. Preparation: Prepare as usual. Packaging: Wrap in moisture-vapor-proof cellophane, heat-seal, freeze, then wrap in stockinette.
Rhubarb: Unbaked	Storage: 4 months.
Fruit, deep-dish: Unbaked	Deep-dish pies prevent the most common cause of failure, soggy lower crust. Formula: Use standard recipe for apple, peach, cherry, or other fruit pie. Thawing and baking: Unwrap, prick top, bake without thawing, individual pies about 20 minutes at 450° F., large pies 15 to 20 minutes at 450°, then about 30 minutes at 375°.
Baked before freezing	Deep-dish pies prevent soggy undercrust, a common fault. Formula: Use standard recipe. Packaging: Wrap pie in baking tin in moisture-vapor-proof paper, place in paper carton.
Cream: Unbaked	Formula: Use standard recipes. Preparation: Use standard procedures. Packaging: Place in special paper pie plates; seal in cellophane before freezing or immediately after. Thawing and baking: Remove from package and bake without thawing.
Baked before freezing	Chocolate and lemon chiffon pies freeze successfully. Meringue toppings tend to toughen, separate, and stick to the wrapping. Formula: Use standard recipes. Preparation: Use standard procedure. Cool to room temperature. Packaging: Pack in metal, glass, or special fiber pie plates, cover with another pie plate, and wrap in moisture-proof material. Thawing and heating: Cream and chiffon pies may be eaten when partially thawed—20 to 30 minutes—or completely thawed—about 45 minutes.
Custard: Unbaked	Frozen unbaked custard pie is not satisfactory.

TABLE XXXVIII—(*Continued*)

DIRECTIONS FOR HOME FREEZING BAKED GOODS

Food	How to Prepare and Package

Pies:
  Custard: (*cont'd*)
    Baked before
      freezing
	Not recommmended.

Pumpkin: Unbaked	Better to freeze pumpkin pie unbaked than baked. Formula: Use varieties of pumpkin without coarse fibers. Preparation: Steam pumpkin until just soft enough to put through a sieve.

Pumpkin, squash,
    sweet potato:
    Baked before
      freezing
	Storage: Several months, provided pies are protected against drying out.

Pastry:
  Unbaked and
    baked
	Baked and unbaked shells and graham cracker shells can be frozen satisfactorily.
	Preparation: Roll out and fit dough into pie tins.
	Packaging: Wrap tightly in moisture-vapor-proof material, seal with heat or tape.
	Storage: Several weeks.
	Thawing and baking:
	  Bulk: Defrost overnight in refrigerator, or more quickly at room temperature, being careful not to let pastry become too warm.

Pie fillings	Pumpkin, mincemeat, and sweet potato pie mixes freeze well. Packaging: Pack in frozen-food containers. Thawing and baking: Partially thaw, add any extra ingredients, bake as usual, allowing extra baking time if not completely thawed.

TABLE XXXIX

DIRECTIONS FOR HOME FREEZING PREPARED AND COOKED FOODS

Food	How to Prepare and Package
Meats, poultry, fish:	
Fried meats and poultry	Thawing and baking: Fried meats do not freeze well because they lose crispness and develop warmed-over flavor. Preparation: Cover with gravy or sauce to retard rancidity.
Meat loaf and meat balls	Formula: Use standard recipes for ham loaf, beef loaf, liver loaf, and meat balls. Preparation: Use standard procedures; do not overcook. Cool quickly to room temperature, freeze immediately. Packaging: Pack in cartons with moisture-vapor-proof liners, heat-seal. Storage: 6 months. Thawing and heating: Heat in top of double boiler or in casserole in the oven.
Roast meats and poultry	Formula: Use standard recipes. Roast beef, pork, ham, chicken, turkey freeze satisfactorily. Preparation: Leave in large compact pieces whenever possible. If frozen in small pieces, cover with gravy or sauce to prevent stale flavor. Packaging: Frozen dry: Pack in moisture-vapor-proof material, seal, and cover with stockinette. Frozen in sauce: Pack in tub-type cartons or glass jars. Dressing: Wrap separately in moisture-vapor-proof material. Thawing and heating: Frozen dry: Thaw quickly in sealed original package in refrigerator, at room temperature, or by setting container in water. Serve cold or reheat. Frozen in sauce: Reheat meats packed in gravy in double boiler, in covered casserole, in steamer, or over direct heat. Dressing: Place stuffing before completely thawed in greased casserole; add small amount of water, cover, and heat in 350° F. oven.
Shrimp, cooked	Formula: Pack dry, with cocktail sauce, or as shrimp creole. Preparation: Boil unpeeled shrimp 10 to 20 minutes in a solution of 10 percent of their weight of salt. Boil peeled shrimp 5 to 10 minutes in salted water. Cool and freeze promptly. Packaging: Use high wet-strength moisture-vapor-proof packaging materials.

TABLE XXXIX—(*Continued*)

DIRECTIONS FOR HOME FREEZING PREPARED AND COOKED FOODS

Food	How to Prepare and Package
Meats, poultry, fish: Shrimp, cooked (*cont'd*)	Storage: Store at 0° F.: Unpeeled boiled shrimp, 6 months. Peeled boiled shrimp, 3 months. Shrimp cocktail, 6 weeks. Shrimp creole, 6 weeks.
Combination dishes: Creamed: General	Formula: Freeze almost any type of creamed dish except those containing hard-cooked egg white. Preparation: Avoid overcooking. Cool rapidly in pan of ice water. Packaging: Use wide-mouth containers.
Chicken	Formula: Cooked chicken and white sauce. Preparation: Prepare as usual. Avoid overcooking. Cool rapidly by setting pan of hot food in ice water. Packaging: Pack in freezer cartons with moisture-vapor-proof liners, heat-seal. Wide-mouth containers are best. Storage: 12 months. Thawing and heating: Put frozen block in double boiler over hot water, bring to boil, and heat 30 minutes.
Chicken à la king	Formula: Cooked chicken, white sauce, green pepper, mushrooms, pimiento, seasoning. Preparation: Simmer chicken until tender. Cook mushrooms and green pepper in fat 5 minutes, add flour, liquid, and seasonings. When thickened add chicken. Cool quickly by placing pan of hot food in ice water. Package and freeze immediately. Packaging: Use cartons with moisture-vapor-proof cellophane liners; heat-seal. Freezing: Freeze at 0° F. in air circulated with fan. Storage: 12 months. Thawing and heating: Put frozen block in double boiler over hot water; bring to boil and heat 30 minutes.
Fish dishes	Formula: Use standard recipes. Fish à la king, fish in cheese sauce, fish and rice, fish hash, clam fritters, fish chowder, fish in creole sauce. Newburg thermidor. Preparation: Prepare food as if it were to be served immediately. Packaging: Use lightly waxed fiberboard containers with heat-sealing moisture-vapor-proof cellophane liners. Storage: Store at 10° F. Fish à la king, 8 months. Fish chowder, 5 months. Fish and rice, 8 months. Creamed fish, 5 months. Fish hash, 5 months. Thawing and heating: Heat and serve.

TABLE XXXIX—(*Continued*)

DIRECTIONS FOR HOME FREEZING PREPARED AND COOKED FOODS

Food	How to Prepare and Package
Combination dishes: (*cont'd*) Beef, veal, and Brunswick stews	Formula: Use standard recipes for beef, veal, and Brunswick stews. Use ingredients of highest quality. Preparation: Prepare foods in usual way, but shorten cooking time for most of them. Package when stew reaches room temperature. Packaging: Use frozen-food containers. Storage: 6 months. Thawing and heating: Thaw in casserole in oven or in top of double boiler. Use reheated foods at current meal; holding and reheating not recommended.
Soups	Formula: Use standard recipes of practically any kind. Recommended: Split pea French onion Meat stock Navy bean Cream of noodle Black bean Cream of corn Asparagus purée Preparation: After soup is prepared by standard methods, cool quickly by placing pan in cold water. Packaging: Use watertight, moisture-vapor-proof containers. Storage: 6 months. Thawing and heating: Thaw cream soups in double boiler, clear soups in saucepan. Heat to serving temperature.
Vegetables: General	As a rule cooked vegetables lose color, aroma, and flavor, and taste somewhat like warmed-over vegetables. Formula: Avoid using root vegetables that have been stored for some time. Preparation: Boil in very small amounts of water, or steam; keep covered and cook short time. Cool quickly to room temperature before packaging. Set in pan of ice water or place in front of fan. Packaging: Pack in tub containers, jars, or heat-sealing cellophane-lined cartons.
Beans, baked	Formula: Use standard recipes. Preparation: Prepare beans in the usual way, cook until barely tender. Add pork, mustard, molasses, sugar, salt, and water. Bake 6 to 8 hours at 250° F. Chill quickly. Packaging: Pack in moisture-vapor-proof cartons. Storage: 6 months. Thawing and heating: Partially thaw at room temperature in package to prevent overcooking. Heat to serving temperature in casserole or double boiler.
Potatoes, scalloped	Add slightly more liquid to prevent drying out.

TABLE XXXIX—(*Continued*)

DIRECTIONS FOR HOME FREEZING PREPARED AND COOKED FOODS

FOOD	HOW TO PREPARE AND PACKAGE
Vegetables: (*cont'd*) Potatoes, French-fried	Formula: Use standard recipe. Select potatoes suitable for French-frying. Preparation: Fry in deep fat to light golden brown. Drain thoroughly on absorbent paper. Cool to room temperature. Packaging: Pack in moisture-vapor-proof frozen-food containers. Thawing and heating: Remove from package, place on baking sheet, reheat in hot oven (400° F.) 5 minutes.
Potatoes, mashed	Formula: Use standard recipe.

Succotash	Formula: Use either lima beans or mature, but not dry, shell beans. Use equal proportions of beans and corn.
	Preparation:
	    Corn: Remove the husks and silk, boil corn in salted water for 10 to 12 minutes in covered pan, or steam it. Cut kernels from cob.
	    Beans: Shell beans, cook in salted water to cover in covered pan until just tender.
	    Combine equal amounts of corn and beans with cooking liquors, and chill mixture rapidly.
	Thawing and heating: Heat with or without partial thawing in covered saucepan over low heat.

Sweet potatoes, candied	Preparation: Bake in oven or boil potatoes until soft. Cool, peel, slice, and dip in solution of 1 part lemon juice diluted with 8 parts water. Drain, roll in sugar. Packaging: Pack in airtight containers; seal.
Sweet potato puffs	Formula: Use standard recipe.

Vegetable purées:
General
	Formula:
	    Recommended:
	
	        Asparagus Beets Spinach
	        Beans, green Carrots Squash
	        Beans, lima Peas Sweet potatoes
	
	Preparation:
	    Cooking time:
	      Asparagus, 8 to 10 minutes.
	      Asparagus tips, 4 minutes.
	      Beans, green, 20 minutes.
	      Beets, 45 minutes.
	      Carrots (quartered), 20 minutes.
	      Peas, 8 to 10 minutes.

TABLE XXXIX—(*Continued*)

DIRECTIONS FOR HOME FREEZING PREPARED AND COOKED FOODS

Food	How to Prepare and Package

Vegetables:
  Vegetable purées:
    General (*cont'd*)
	Spinach, 8 to 10 minutes.
	Squash, 20 minutes.
	Squash, 30 to 40 minutes.
	Cool, purée, and freeze.
	Packaging: Use rigid moisture-vapor-proof containers. Pack solid without bubbles or air spaces.
	Storage: 1 year.
	Thawing and heating: Thaw at room temperature or in the refrigerator. Heat for serving.

Squash purée	Formula: Use only well-matured squash of "dry" types that show little tendency to flow when cooked and pulped. Preparation, Packaging, and Storage: Same as for Vegetable Purées. Thawing and heating: Thaw at room temperature or in the refrigerator or as heated for serving.

Salads:
  Fruit
	Formula:
	Recommended: Combine citrus fruits with non-acid fruits to prevent darkening.
	Not recommended:
	  Raw grapes become flabby.
	  Raw apples become pithy.
	  Nuts discolor and become bitter.
	  Crisp foods lose crispness.
	  Mayonnaise curdles.
	Packaging: Pack in waxed tubular containers with friction top.
	Thawing: Thaw in sealed original containers.

Meat and poultry	Formula: Cooked meats and poultry. Preparation: Cook, freeze, thaw; cut up and mix with other salad ingredients at serving time. Packaging: Pack in moisture-proof containers.
Vegetable	Formula: Few vegetable salads are suitable for freezing.

Sandwiches and sandwich fillings	Formula:
	Recommended:
	  Cheese. Tuna or salmon.
	  Hard-cooked egg yolk. Nut pastes.
	  Sliced meats or poultry. Peanut butter.
	  Ground meat or poultry. Olives, pickles.
	Not recommended:
	  Lettuce, celery, tomatoes, cucumber, watercress lose crispness, color, flavor.

TABLE XXXIX—*(Continued)*

DIRECTIONS FOR HOME FREEZING PREPARED AND COOKED FOODS

FOOD	HOW TO PREPARE AND PACKAGE
Sandwiches and sandwich fillings (*cont'd*)	Whites of hard-cooked eggs become tough. Fruit jellies soak into bread. Fruit jellies soak into bread unless spread with butter. Mayonnaise separates on freezing. Preparation: Freeze filling or complete sandwich. Packaging: Wrap in double thickness of heavy waxed paper for 1 week's storage; in moisture-vapor-proof material for more than 1 week's storage. Fold wrapping material tightly with drugstore fold. Storage: 2 weeks. Thawing: Thaw at room temperature about 3 hours.
Fruit: Baked apples	Formula: Varieties recommended: Cortland / Northern Spy Rome Beauty / Twenty-ounce Baldwin / Stayman Winesap Red Twenty-ounce Added ingredients: Sugar, cinnamon. Preparation: Remove core and score around middle of apple, fill core cavity with desired ingredients, bake. Cool quickly. Packaging: Use quart tub-shaped cups, bottoms lined with cellophane, three apples per container, each covered with two layers of cellophane, covered with lid. Thawing and heating: Reheat in 300° F. preheated oven.
Cranberry sauce	Preparation: Cook whole cranberry sauce, and package.
Pudding: Steamed	Formula: Use standard recipes. Preparation: Cool quickly. Packaging: Pack in moisture-vapor-proof paper or containers. Thawing and heating: Place while frozen, or after thawing at room temperature, in a steamer; heat to serving temperature.
Sauces	
Velva Fruit	It is better to make and store fruit purée for making into Velva Fruit at a later time. Formula: Recommended fruits: Apricots / Nectarines / Raspberries Cantaloupes / Peaches / Rhubarb Cranberries / Plums / Strawberries Grapes (Concord) / Prunes

TABLE XXXIX—(*Continued*)

DIRECTIONS FOR HOME FREEZING PREPARED AND COOKED FOODS

Food	How to Prepare and Package
Velva Fruit (*cont'd*)	Recipe: 6 cups fruit purée. 1½ to 2 cups sugar. 2 tablespoons lemon juice (omit for acid fruits). ¼ teaspoon salt. 2 tablespoons granulated gelatin. ½ cup water. Preparation: Make fruit purée; mix with sugar. Freeze as purée or make into Velva Fruit. For Velva Fruit: Add lemon juice and salt, add cool purée (70° F.) to soaked gelatin, stirring continuously. Packaging: Pack at once in moisture-vapor-resistant cartons. Fruit purée can be packaged in glass jars or tin cans (R-enamel cans for red or dark purées). Storage: Can be stored several months, but flavor and texture best a few days after freezing. Thawing: Thawing purée to make Velva Fruit: Place sealed container in cold or lukewarm (not hot) water, shake occasionally to speed thawing. A quart of purée will thaw in about 2 hours.
Meals, precooked	Choose foods that can be successfully reheated after freezer storage, will heat uniformly, and have about the same storage life. Formula: Typical menus: (1) Steak, French-fried potatoes, peas. (2) Beef stew, hot bread, asparagus. (3) Meat loaf, candied sweet-potatoes, spinach. (4) Corned-beef-hash patties, home-fried potatoes, string beans. (5) Ham steak, candied sweet-potatoes, turnips. (6) Breaded veal cutlet, home-fried potatoes, carrots. Food proved to be attractive as well as palatable. Preparation: All foods partially precooked. Packaging: Use special cardboard package enclosed in cellophane. Pack solid to eliminate air. Storage: Use before food with shortest storage life loses quality. Thawing and heating: Rate of heat penetration depends on nature of food, amount, and shape. Protein foods heat slowly. Mashed vegetables heat more slowly than loose vegetables.

TABLE XXXIX—(*Continued*)

DIRECTIONS FOR HOME FREEZING PREPARED AND COOKED FOODS

Food	How to Prepare and Package
Meals, precooked (*cont'd*)	Meat and poultry tend to dry out unless covered with gravy or sauce. Gravies tend to separate during thawing; to prevent separation, add raw starch to chilled gravy and mix. Cover with metal foil some foods that tend to dry out during reheating.

Canning and Preserving

CANNING has been greatly simplified today by the use of up-to-date equipment. No longer does it seem a formidable task. The labor and cost of equipment seem well justified when one enjoys the satisfaction of serving home-canned fruits, vegetables, jellies, jams and pickles to the family and to guests.

Only two important points need to be taken into account in canning. First, low-acid vegetables (all, except for tomatoes), meats, poultry and fish need to be canned in a pressure canner or cooker in order to destroy or inactivate injurious enzymes and microorganisms. Hot water bath or oven canning for these foods definitely is not recommended by all food authorities. On the other hand, tomatoes and fruits can be canned successfully by the hot water bath method. Oven canning is considered dangerous and inefficient.

Secondly, canning can be safe and successful if the right equipment is used and correct procedures are followed. If you have no pressure canner, team with someone who has. Or maybe you can go to a community canning center and use pressure equipment.

PROCESSING IN PRESSURE COOKER OR CANNER

FOLLOW manufacturer's directions for operation and care of a pressure cooker when these are available. Always have pressure canner ready for use before the canning season begins. Check the accuracy of the gauge which registers pressure within the canner. The weighted gauge needs no adjustment but must be thoroughly clean. The dial-type gauge needs to be checked for accuracy with a tested gauge which the dealer or your county home demonstration agent may be able to do for you. If not, pack the gauge as carefully as you would glass and send it to the manufacturer. If the gauge is off 5 pounds or more, get a new one. If it is off (high or low) from 1 to 4 pounds, make the following corrections for processing at 10 pounds steam pressure:

Gauge reads 1 to 4 lb. high	*Gauge reads 1 to 4 lb. low*
1 lb. high—Process at 11 lb.	1 lb. low—Process at 9 lb.
2 lb. high—Process at 12 lb.	2 lb. low—Process at 8 lb.
3 lb. high—Process at 13 lb.	3 lb. low—Process at 7 lb.
4 lb. high—Process at 14 lb.	4 lb. low—Process at 6 lb.

When ready to process, pour 2 to 3 inches of boiling water into the pressure cooker to cover bottom and prevent canner from boiling dry. Place hot-packed jars (as near boiling as possible) on rack with space between each for circulation of steam around and over the jars. Adjust and fasten the cover securely so that no steam escapes except through the petcock or weighted-gauge opening. Let steady jet of steam escape through the petcock or weighted-gauge opening for 7 to 10 minutes to drive out all air from the canner, leaving only steam inside. Then close the petcock or put on the weighted gauge. When pressure reaches 10 pounds, begin to count the processing time. Adjust the heat to keep the pressure constant. Uneven pressure may force liquid out of the jars. When time is up, turn off heat or remove the canner. Let pressure gauge return to zero. It will take from 20 to 30 minutes. Do not hasten cooling by fanning the canner or by pouring cold water on it. Wait from 2 to 3 minutes after gauge reaches zero before opening the petcock or removing the weighted gauge. Unfasten cover, tilt the far side up for the steam to escape away from you and remove. Complete the seal on each jar, if not self-sealing, as each is removed. Do not remove covers of jars to add more liquid or to replace any that may have boiled out during processing. Wash a pressure canner thoroughly after using. Do not put the lid in water but clean thoroughly. The petcock, safety valve (ball-and-socket type) or weighted-gauge opening and edges of lid and canner must be clean for canner to function. Store with cover inverted.

STEPS IN CANNING THE MODERN WAY IN GLASS JARS

FOR flavor, color, texture, and food values, foods should be canned while they are fresh and at their best. The fresher the fruits and vegetables the higher their vitamin content. Can only in quantities that can be easily handled; work quickly. Avoid delays by being thoroughly familiar with each step in canning; by having the equipment checked and ready for use before canning time; by knowing your jars and how to fill and seal them; by planning the work step by step. Cool jars away from drafts; check cold jars for leaks; label and store in a cool, dry and dark place.

1. Check pressure canner to be used (page 913). Assemble all small canning equipment: kettles, measuring spoons and cups, colander for easy washing, wire basket, cheesecloth, cutting boards, paring knives, spoons, wide-mouthed funnel, silver knife, jar tongs or lifter, holders and clean dishcloths.

2. Check all jars or cans; discard jars with cracks, chips or other defects; tighten loose wire clamps on jars and check size of glass lids; discard mason or screw-type tops with loose or cracked linings or spread or bent edges. Use new rubber rings of proper size; good rubber is soft, pliable and elastic. Use sealing lids only once; follow directions of manufacturer for specific jars.

3. Always wash jars, caps and rubbers in hot soapy water, rinse in hot water and sterilize jars by covering with boiling water and boil in a covered kettle for 20 minutes. Wash, then boil rubber rings in soda water for 10 minutes, adding 1 tablespoon baking soda to 1 quart of water for every 12 rings.

4. Keep sterilized jars hot until ready to can by letting them stand in boiling water. Keep screw tops, glass lids and rubber rings in a pan of warm water. Remove jars one at a time when ready to fill.

5. Prepare syrup in advance for fruits and have it boiling hot when filling jars. For vegetables, dairy or bag salt is preferred. Add 1 teaspoon salt to each quart of vegetables and cover with boiling hot cooking liquid.

6. Can only those foods that are in prime condition—fruits and vegetables, garden fresh or fresh from the market, and fresh, clean, cold, quality meats. Prepare only in quantities that can be handled easily. See specific recipes and Tables XLI–XLIII for directions. To wash fruit and vegetables, use a colander and lift them in and out of several waters, but do not soak them. Precook fruits in syrup or in juice. Sugar is not necessary but it helps to preserve color and flavor of fruit. Precook vegetables to shrink and drive out all air and shorten processing time. Meats are packed either precooked or raw; poultry, with or without bones.

7. Fit rubber ring on hot jar and fill quickly, leaving head space for expansion according to type of food—Tables XLI–XLIII, pages 921–930, footnote 4, page 930, pack but do not force. Cover with boiling hot liquid, add salt to vegetables (½ teaspoon to a pint). Run a silver knife blade down the sides to work out air bubbles. Wipe jar rim clean and seal partially or completely, depending on type jar used.

8. Place hot filled jars on rack in boiling water bath with water 1 to 2 inches over tops. Cover and begin to count processing time when water boils hard. Place hot packed jars on rack so they do not touch each other in pressure cooker with 2 or 3 inches of boiling water in cooker. When filled with jars, adjust and fasten lid securely with petcock open. Let steady jet of steam pour from open petcock for 7 to 10 minutes before closing it, to drive out all air. Begin to count processing time when pressure is at 10 pounds.

9. When time is up, turn off heat or remove pressure cooker. Remove lid of boiling water bath by tilting the far side of cover up for steam to escape. Remove jars one at a time and immediately complete seal, if necessary. For pressure cooker, let gauge return to zero, then wait a minute or two before opening petcock.

Remove lid carefully to avoid a steam burn. Lift out jars and completely seal the partially sealed jars.

10. Place jars on rack, apart and away from draft, to cool thoroughly overnight. On the following day, remove all screw bands. Do this by holding fingers firmly on lid while ring band is being unscrewed. Test each jar to see if each has a complete seal. Porcelain-lined top jars should be inverted to test for seal; leakage will be evident if seal is not perfect. Bail type—remove bail and lift cover with fingers. Metal top—remove metal ring, lift lid with fingers. Glass top—remove ring band and lift cover with fingers. If jar leaks, use at once or reprocess in another jar.

11. Label and store clean jars in a cool, dry, dark place.

12. Examine all canned foods for spoilage before tasting or serving. Destroy or burn spoiled low-acid vegetables and meats. Look for leakage, bulging of tin cans, bulging of rubber on glass jars, foreign odors, cloudiness of liquid or discoloration or softening of product. *Always boil home-canned low-acid vegetables and meats for 10 to 15 minutes before tasting or serving.* Fruits and acid vegetables (tomatoes) may be used at once when jar is opened.

CANNING IN TIN

TIN cans can be used in processing fruits, vegetables and meats with good results and a saving of time. Tin cans are either plain tin or enamel-lined. Plain tin cans are satisfactory for most fruits, vegetables and meats.

Enamel-lined cans are of two kinds: The sanitary, fruit or R-enamel-lined cans are used for red colored fruits and beets to preserve their color; also for pumpkin and squash to keep them from corroding the cans. The C- or corn enamel-lined cans are used for corn and succotash and sometimes lima beans and peas to prevent them from discoloring. Acid and fat may cause the C-enamel lining to peel off and make the products unattractive; acid fruits and tomatoes and meats and poultry should not be processed in C-enamel cans. Can sizes No. 2 (2½ cups), No. 2½

(3½ cups) and No. 3 (4 cups) are the most satisfactory for home canning. When ordering cans, always specify size, finish (plain, C- or R-enamel).

TABLE XL

SUGAR SYRUPS FOR CANNING FRUITS

TYPE OF SYRUP	SUGAR	WATER	SUGAR CONTENT (APPROX.)
	cup	*cup*	*per cent*
Light	1	3	25
Medium	1	2	33
Heavy	1	1	50

For different sized jars allow the following amounts of syrup: ½ to ¾ cup for pint jar or No. 2 can; 1 to 1½ cups for quart jar or No. 3 can.

USE OF ASCORBIC ACID IN CANNING

THE ADDITION of 300 milligrams of ascorbic acid (vitamin C) to a quart of apples, applesauce, pears, peaches, plums or sweet corn tends to prevent surface darkening and development of off flavor in the top layers of the canned food. The ascorbic acid itself is not detectable by flavor, odor or appearance and is not a preservative. For additional information see page 879.

APPLES

Use juicy apples. All-purpose apples such as Baldwins, Jonathans, McIntosh, Northern Spy, Spitzenberg, Wealthy and Winesaps are good for sauce and other cooking. Greenings make good sauce and Rome Beauties are excellent for baking. To prevent darkening of sliced apples, drop them into a weak brine (1 tablespoon each salt and vinegar to 2 quarts of water). Rinse and steam or boil in light syrup (above). Pack Applesauce (page 921) hot. For Baked Apples (page 86) omit spices or use sparingly. Pack hot, cover with hot liquid. Allow 2 to 3 pounds apples for each quart jar. Add 300 milligrams of ascorbic acid (vitamin C) to each quart.

BERRIES AND CURRANTS

(Except Strawberries)

Use blackberries, blueberries, dewberries, huckleberries, loganberries, raspberries and currants. Wash but do not soak; remove stems or caps. Prepare, pack and process (Table XLI, page 921). Allow 1½ to 2 quarts fresh berries for each quart jar.

CHERRIES

Wash and can cherries with or without pits. Remove pits by machine or by hand. (An inverted pen point in a holder removes pits easily and quickly.) Prepare, pack and process (page 921). If sugar is used, add just enough water to keep from sticking. Allow 1½ to 2 quarts cherries for each quart jar.

PEACHES AND APRICOTS

Select sound ripe fruit of uniform size; reserve undersized fruit for preserves. Apricots may be washed or wiped with a damp cloth and not peeled. To prevent discoloration, drop peeled and halved fruit into a weak brine solution (1 tablespoon each salt and vinegar to 2 quarts water). Rinse, prepare, pack and process (page 921). Allow 2 to 2½ pounds of fresh fruit for each quart jar. Add 300 milligrams of ascorbic acid (vitamin C) to each quart.

PEARS

Select sound ripe pears of uniform size. Pears are gathered while green and allowed to ripen in storage. Drop peeled halves or peeled whole small pears into a weak brine (1 tablespoon each salt and vinegar to 2 quarts water) to prevent darkening. Rinse, prepare, pack and process (page 921). Allow 2 to 2½ pounds fresh pears for each quart. Add 300 milligrams of ascorbic acid (vitamin C) to each quart.

PINEAPPLE

Select fully ripe fruit which is orange-yellow rather than green in color. When ripe, fruit is more fragrant, richer in flavor, less acid and less woody than the green fruit. Ripe pineapple can be stored for a month and longer at about 32° F., or in a cold dry place. To peel, slice or cut pineapple in pieces, see Pineapple (page 922). Prepare, pack and process. Allow 1 large pineapple for each quart jar.

PLUMS, PRUNES

Select plums that are ripe but not overripe. Some varieties are better than others for canning. All prunes are plums, but only those plums that can be dried without removal of pit are prunes. The Italian prune or plum (purplish-black) is one of the leading types. Prepare, pack and process (page 922). Allow 2 to 2½ pounds for each quart jar. Add 300 milligrams of ascorbic acid (vitamin C) to each quart.

RHUBARB

Rhubarb is an herb and not a fruit, but it is cooked as a fruit. Select young tender stalks; unless blanched, the stalks vary in color from green to a light red. Prepare, pack and process (page 922). Allow 1½ to 2 pounds for each quart jar.

STRAWBERRIES

Use fresh, plump, ripe berries. Wash thoroughly under running water. Prepare, pack and process (page 922). Allow 1½ to 2 quarts fresh berries for each quart jar.

TOMATOES

Select firm, field-ripened tomatoes with well-colored flesh, free from mold and decay. Cut away any green or hard portions. Prepare, pack and process (page 922). Allow 2½ to 3 pounds for each quart jar. For tomato juice, see Table XLI (page 922).

FRUIT JUICES

Use berries, cherries, plums or any juicy fruit, alone or in combination. Remove pits (if present) and crush fruit. Heat to simmering; strain through cloth bag. Sweeten, if desired; add from ½ to 1 cup sugar to 1 gallon of juice. Fill jars to within ¼ inch of top and bottles ½ inch from top. Process at once, just below boiling (180° F.) (page 922).

CANNING VEGETABLES

To prepare vegetables for canning and to process them, follow directions given in Steps in Canning in Glass Jars (page 916), Canning in Tin (page 918), and Table XLII (page 925). Use only fresh, young and tender vegetables from garden or store. Wash thoroughly. Precook, pack hot, fill with boiling hot cooking liquid or water, add 1 teaspoon salt to each quart of vegetables when packed. See Table XLII (page 925) and footnote 4 for head space to leave for each one in glass jars or tin cans. Remove air; adjust lids and seal tin cans. Process at once.

TABLE XLI

TIMETABLE FOR PROCESSING FRUITS AND TOMATOES [1]

FRESH FRUIT	PREPARING-PACKING FRUIT [2] (Pack as near boiling as possible, leave ½ inch head space and process at once)	SUGAR OR SYRUP [3] (Boiling hot)	BOILING-WATER BATH—212° F. [4] Pint or quart
			minutes
Apples, stewed	Pared, cored, sliced. Boil 5 minutes in syrup.	Light	15
sauce	Sweetened or unsweetened.	—	10
Apricots	Scald, plunge in cold water to peel; or leave unpeeled, whole or halved and pitted. Heat to boiling in syrup.	Light to medium	20
Berries (except strawberries) and currants	Wash, drain. If firm, add ½ cup sugar to each quart; cover and bring to boil. Shake pan to keep from sticking. Cover with hot liquid.	Sugar	15
	For soft berries and for red raspberries, fill jar with raw fruit, shake down for full pack. Cover with boiling syrup made with juice.	Light to medium	20
Cherries	With or without pits. Bring to boil in syrup or add ½ cup sugar to 1 quart, cover and bring to boil.	Medium or Sugar	10
Peaches	Scald, plunge in cold water, slip off skins. Halve and pit, or slice. Add ½ cup sugar to 1 qt. fruit. Cover and heat to boiling.	Sugar	15
	Drop less juicy fruit into boiling hot syrup and pack at once.	Light to medium	15
Pears	Peel, cut in halves and core. Drop into boiling hot syrup and pack at once.	Medium	15

TABLE XLI—(*Continued*)

TIMETABLE FOR PROCESSING FRUITS AND TOMATOES

FRESH FRUIT	PREPARING-PACKING FRUIT [2] (Pack as near boiling as possible, leave ½ inch head space and process at once)	SUGAR OR SYRUP [3] (Boiling hot)	BOILING-WATER BATH—212° F. [4] Pint or quart
			minutes
Pineapple	Peel, core, remove "eyes"; slice or cut in pieces. Add ½ cup sugar, cover and heat slowly 10 to 15 minutes. Pack hot, cover with juice.	Sugar	25
Plums, prunes	Prick skin, or cut in halves. Heat to boiling in syrup.	Light to medium	15
Rhubarb	Cut in ½ inch lengths; add ½ cup sugar to each quart and let stand until juicy. Bring to a boil and pack hot.	Sugar	10
Strawberries	Stem; add ½ cup sugar to each quart. Bring slowly to boil. Let stand overnight to plump berries. Bring quickly to boil to pack.	Sugar	15
Tomatoes	Scald, remove stem ends and peel perfect, ripe tomatoes. Quarter and bring to full boil, stirring constantly. Add 1 teaspoon salt to each quart.	—	10
Tomato juice	Remove stem ends of perfect tomatoes; cut in pieces and simmer until softened. Put through fine sieve. Add 1 teaspoon salt to each quart. Re-heat to boiling. Leave ¼ inch head space in jars; ½ inch in bottles.	—	15
Fruit juices	Follow recipe page 921.	Sugar	20 (180° F.)

[1] Based upon research by Agr. Research Admin., U. S. D. A. *Home Canning of Fruits and Vegetables,* AIS-64, Bur. Human Nutr. and Home Econ., July, 1947.

[2] For detailed information for preparation and amount of fruit needed for each quart, see specific recipes.

[3] For type of syrups see Table XL, page 919.

[4] Processing times apply to altitudes less than 1000 feet above sea level. For each 1000 feet above sea level, add 1 minute if time given is for 20 minutes or less; add 2 minutes for every 1000 feet if more than 20 minutes.

ASPARAGUS

Wash, trim off scales and cut tender stalks in 1 inch pieces. Cover with boiling water and boil 2 to 3 minutes. Pack hot, cover with cooking liquid and process. Allow 3 to 4 pounds for each quart.

SNAP BEANS

Wash, trim off ends and remove strings if stringy. Cut into pieces (½ to 1 inch) or cut lengthwise. Cover with boiling water and boil 5 minutes. Pack hot, cover with hot cooking liquid and process at once. Allow 1½ to 2 pounds for each quart.

LIMA BEANS

Can only young tender beans, freshly shelled. Cover with boiling water and bring to a boil. Pack hot, fill with fresh boiling water, leaving 1 inch head space in jar. Process at once. Allow 4 to 5 pounds beans (in pods) for each quart jar.

GREEN SOYBEANS

Cover pods with boiling water and leave 5 to 10 minutes for easy shelling. Cover shelled beans with boiling water and boil 3 to 4 minutes. Pack hot, cover with fresh boiling water, leaving 1 inch head space in jars. Process at once. Allow 4 to 5 pounds beans (in pods) for each quart jar.

BABY BEETS

Can only tender baby beets. Trim off tops, leaving 1 inch of stems. Wash and boil about 15 minutes or until skins slip easily. Skin and trim. Or peel beets before boiling them. Pack hot, cover with fresh boiling water. Process at once. Allow 2½ to 3 pounds fresh beets (without tops) for each quart jar.

CARROTS

Scrape and slice, cube or cut in strips young tender carrots. Boil, covered, 5 minutes in water to just cover. Pack hot, cover with boiling cooking liquid. Process at once. Allow about 2½ pounds fresh carrots (without tops) for each quart jar.

PEAS

Cover freshly shelled young, tender green peas with boiling water and boil 3 minues. Pack hot, cover with boiling liquid, leaving 1 inch head space in jars. Add ½ teaspoon salt to each pint. Process at once. Allow 2 to 2½ pounds unshelled peas for each pint jar.

CORN

Cut corn from cob of young tender corn, freshly picked. Cut so as to get kernel but not the husk. To each quart add 2 cups boiling water. Bring to a boil. Pack hot, leaving 1 inch head space in jars. Add 1 teaspoon salt to each quart and no more liquid. Add 300 milligrams of ascorbic acid (vitamin C) to each quart. Process at once. Allow 8 to 12 ears for each quart jar.

GREENS

Use freshly picked, tender greens such as Swiss chard, beet tops, spinach. Wash in many waters, lifting greens from water each time. Cut out tough stems and midribs. Steam or heat in a covered kettle with a small amount of water until wilted. Pack hot and loosely. Cover with hot cooking liquid, adding hot water if needed. Add 1 teaspoon salt to a quart. Process at once. Allow 2 to 3 pounds for each quart jar.

PUMPKIN AND SQUASH

Peel pumpkin and winter squash; do not peel summer squash; cut into 1 inch cubes. Bring to a boil in a small amount of water. Pack hot; cover with hot cooking liquid. Process at once. If mashed, do not add salt or liquid to packed jar. Allow 2 to 2½ pounds fresh pumpkin or squash for each quart jar.

SWEET POTATOES

Boil or steam until skins slip easily; skin. For wet pack, cut in pieces, pack hot, add 1 teaspoon salt to each quart and cover with boiling water. Leave 1 inch head space in jars. For dry pack, mash the potatoes, pack hot and do not add salt or liquid to filled jar. Process at once. Allow 2½ to 3 pounds for each quart jar.

SAUERKRAUT

Heat well-fermented sauerkraut in its own juice until simmering hot; do not boil. Pack hot; cover with hot juice. Process in boiling water bath.

TABLE XLII

TIMETABLE FOR PROCESSING VEGETABLES [1]

VEGETABLES	PRESSURE CANNER[2] 10 POUNDS PRESSURE—240°F.				CANNING IN TIN[2]	
	GLASS[4]		TIN			
	PINT	QUART	No. 2	No. 2½ OR No. 3	FOOD HEAD-SPACE	TIN CAN FINISH
	Minutes	*Minutes*	*Minutes*	*Minutes*	*Inch*	
Asparagus.......	25	35	20	20	¼	Plain
Beans, snap......	20	25	25	30	¼	Plain
limas.....	35	55	40	40	½	Plain C-enamel
soybeans..	60	70				
Beets, young.....	25	35	30	30	¼	R-enamel
Carrots, young...	20	25	20	25	¼	C-enamel
Corn, whole grain.	55	70	60	60	Full	C-enamel
Corn, cream style.	85	—	105	—	Full	C-enamel
Greens, tender leaves.........	45	70	60	—	¼	Plain
Peas, green......	40	40	30	30	¼	Plain
Pumpkin, cubed..	55	90	50	75	¼	R-enamel
mashed[4]	60	70	60	90	⅛	R-enamel
Sauerkraut.......	Process in boiling water bath 25 min.					
Spinach[5]	45	70	60	75	¼	Plain
Squash, summer..	30	35	20	20	¼	R-enamel
winter...	55	90	50	75	¼	R-enamel
Sweet potatoes, wet pack	55	90	60	90	¼	R-enamel
dry pack[4]......	65	95	80	95	Full	R-enamel

[1] For detailed information on preparation and amounts needed for canning quart, see specific recipes.
[2] Data on processing in pressure cooker and canning in tin based upon research by U.S.D.A. Bureau of Human Nutrition and Home Economics, released January, 1947. Foods are precooked, hot packed, and as near boiling as possible when processing starts. Processing times apply to altitudes less than 2000 feet above sea level. For every 2000 feet above sea level add 1 pound of pressure and process for the length of time given in the table (sea level).
[3] For starchy vegetables (peas, shelled beans and corn) in glass jars, leave 1 inch head space when covering with liquid. For other vegetables in table, leave ½ inch head space.
[4] Add no salt and no liquid.
[5] Reduce the usual amount of salt ½ for each size jar or can.

CANNING MEATS (LOW-ACID)

BEEF, veal, lamb, mutton, pork, rabbit and other game, chicken, duck, goose and turkey are all successfully canned at home. For processing large game, follow directions for beef; for game birds and small game mammals, follow directions for poultry. Can only fresh meat from healthy animals, slaughtered and handled in a strictly sanitary way. Refrigerate the meat at or near freezing until ready for canning. If frozen, can it as soon as it is thawed.

Meats may be processed by either the hot pack or the raw pack method. Fried meats are not satisfactory for canning; they are likely to be dry and hard and develop an "off" or disagreeable flavor in processing. Salt is not a preservative; its addition is optional. Canning by the pressure cooker method is the only safe way to process meats; the high temperature of 240° F. at 10 pounds pressure destroys or prevents the growth of harmful bacteria that cause spoilage. Pint or quart glass jars and plain tin cans, preferably with paper gaskets (No. 2, No. 2½ and No. 3) are satisfactory for canning meats. See Timetable for Processing Meats (page 930).

RAW PACK METHOD FOR MEAT
(Beef, Veal, Lamb, Pork)

Cut up meat as for Hot Pack (page 928); add salt to containers if desired.

Pack containers with raw lean strips; leave about 1 inch head space in glass jars; fill tin cans to top.

Place open jars or cans in large vessel of warm water with water about 2 inches from top of containers. Cover vessel and boil slowly until meat is steaming hot and medium done: about 75 minutes in glass jars; 50 minutes in tin cans. Center of jar or can should register 170° F. with meat thermometer. Press meat down in tin cans to ½ inch below top. Add boiling stock or water if needed to fill cans. Leave 1 inch head space in glass jars.

Adjust lids on glass jars and seal tin cans.

Process at once at 10 pounds pressure (240° F.). See timetable, page 930, for time to process each.

HOT PACK METHOD FOR MEAT
(Beef, Veal, Lamb, Pork)

Use loin and other cuts suitable for roasts, steaks or chops for canning large pieces; use less tender cuts and smaller pieces for stew meat. Cut meat from bone and trim away most of the fat; use bones for broth or soup. Cut large pieces into sizes that will fit into jars or cans with grain of meat running lengthwise.

Precook meat slowly in covered pan until medium done with just enough water or stock added to keep meat from sticking; stir or turn meat occasionally to heat evenly.

Keep hot sterilized jars in boiling water until ready to fill. If salt is desired add ½ teaspoon to each pint jar or No. 2 can, and ¾ teaspoon to No. 2½ can; add 1 teaspoon to each quart jar or No. 3 can before filling.

Pack strips of hot meat in hot jars or clean tins and leave about 1 inch head space in jars; ½ inch in tin cans. Cover with hot broth (fat removed) or water, leaving 1 inch head space in glass jars; fill tin cans to top.

Run silver knife along sides to work out air bubbles; adjust lids on glass jars; seal tin cans.

Process at once at 10 pounds pressure (240° F.). See timetable, page 930, for time to process each.

RAW PACK METHOD FOR POULTRY
(With Bone)

Cut up pieces of poultry, sort out meaty pieces, add salt to jars and cans if desired; pack into hot jars or tin cans as directed for Hot Pack with Bone (page 930).

To exhaust the meat, place the filled open jars or cans in large vessel of warm water with water about 2 inches from top of containers. Cover vessel and boil slowly until meat is steaming hot and medium done: allow about 75 minutes for glass jars; 50 minutes for tin cans. Center of jar or can should register 170° F. with meat thermometer.

Adjust lids on glass jars; seal tin cans.

Process at once at 10 pounds pressure (240° F.). See timetable, page 930, for time to process each.

RAW PACK METHOD FOR POULTRY
(Without Bone)

Remove bone but do not skin meaty pieces of poultry. Proceed as for Raw Pack—With Bone (page 930); allow 10 minutes longer for processing pint jars and No. 2 cans; 15 minutes longer for quart jars and No. 2½ and No. 3 cans (page 930).

HOT PACK METHOD FOR POULTRY
(With Bone)

Select plump stewing hens for best flavor. Disjoint or cut in pieces and sort into meaty and bony pieces; set giblets aside. Cook bony pieces for stock; cover with cold water and simmer until tender. Drain broth into bowl; skim off fat. Strip meat from bones and can as small pieces if desired.

Remove excess fat from meaty pieces, remove breastbone, saw off drumsticks. Pour hot broth or hot water over meat to cover and simmer, covered, until meat is medium done. When cut in center the pieces will show little or no pink color. Stir occasionally.

Add salt, if desired, to empty containers: ½ teaspoon to each pint jar and No. 2 can; ¾ teaspoon to No. 2½ can; 1 teaspoon to quart jar and No. 3 can. Adjust covers on jars and heat in pressure canner (see Canning Meats, page 930); tin cans (washed and rinsed) need not be heated.

Pack second joints and drumsticks with skin sides next to glass or tin; fit breast pieces into center; use small pieces for fitting into spaces. Leave 1 inch head space in glass jars, ½ inch in cans.

Cover meat with hot broth; leave 1 inch head space in glass jars; fill cans to rim. Work out air bubbles by running knife along side. Adjust lids on glass jars, seal tin cans.

Process at once at 10 pounds pressure (240°· F.). See timetable, page 930, for time to process each.

HOT PACK METHOD FOR POULTRY
(Without Bone)

Prepare and precook the meaty pieces, removing bones but not skin before or after cooking. Proceed as for processing poultry with bone, allowing 10 minutes longer for pint jars and No. 2 cans than for poultry with bone; 15 minutes longer for quart jars and No. 2½ and No. 3 cans (page 930).

CANNING RABBIT AND ALL SMALL GAME

Prepare the meaty pieces with or without bone, using bony pieces for stock. Pack and process as for poultry (page 928).

TABLE XLIII

TIMETABLE FOR PROCESSING MEATS [1]

MEAT[2]	PRESSURE CANNER—10 POUNDS PRESSURE—240°F.[3]							
	HOT PACK				RAW PACK			
	GLASS		TIN		GLASS		TIN	
	PINT	QUART	No. 2	No. 2½ No. 3	PINT	QUART	No. 2	No. 2½ No. 3
	Minutes	*Minutes*	*Minutes*	*Minutes*	*Minutes*	*Minutes*	*Minutes*	*Minutes*
Poultry With bone.....	65	75	55	75	65	75	55	75
Without bone...	75	90	65	90	75	90	65	90
Giblets [4].......	75		65					
Rabbit—same as for poultry.....								
Beef, veal, lamb, pork...........	75	90	65	90	75	90	65	90
Ground meat[5]....	75	90	65	90	—	—	100	135
Corned beef......	75	90	65	90				
Soup stock.......	20	25	20	25				

[1] Home canning of meat. Bur. of Human Nutrition and Home Econ. AWI–110. U. S. D. A.; Feb. 1945. Slightly revised, Jan. 1946.
[2] To prepare meats, follow recipes in section, page 927. Use plain tin cans with paper gaskets when canning in tin.
[3] Processing time applies to altitudes 1000 feet and less above sea level. For each 2000 feet above sea level, add 1 pound pressure and process for the length of time given in table.
[4] Can livers alone; can gizzards and hearts together.
[5] Raw pack is not practical in glass jars; too difficult to remove. Sausage with no sage and very mildly seasoned with onion or garlic and spices, can be processed like ground meat, hot packed. Precook thin cakes in slow oven (300° to 325° F.) until medium done: pack hot;

JELLIES

WITH improved methods for making jelly, much of the guesswork and uncertainty has been removed. Today even the inexperienced can learn to make a perfect jelly from a fruit containing adequate pectin or pectic substances or from commercial extractions of pectin.

Selection of Fruit. Tart apples, crab apples, cranberries, blackberries, currants, slip-skin grapes, gooseberries, sour plums and quinces contain sufficient pectin and acid to make good jellies. With other fruits such as apricots, peaches, raspberries and strawberries, either use a commercial pectin, following package directions exactly, or combine with another fruit high in pectin, adding lemon juice to fruits that are fully ripe or low in acid.

Select firm fruit, using a mixture of ripe and slightly underripe fruit. Wash and discard damaged portions. Remove stems and blossom ends from hard fruits such as apples, crab apples and quinces, but not the core and seeds as these contain pectic substances; cut in pieces or grind. Leave stems on currants and skins on grapes and plums; crush soft fruits to start flow of juice.

Extraction of Juice. Add required quantity of water (page 933) and cook until soft: 5 to 10 minutes for soft fruits; 20 to 25 minutes for hard fruits. Gooseberries are very high in acid and pectin; if green they will take more water (Table XLIV, page 934); if ripe and soft, use the amount indicated. Turn cooked fruit into a jelly bag of canton flannel or several thicknesses of cheesecloth and allow juice to drain; shift pulp occasionally to keep juice flowing. Juice may be squeezed through bag, if desired, but it will not be clear. A second and third extraction can be made from pectin-rich fruits such as crab apples, grapes and currants: return the drained pulp to kettle, barely cover with water, cook slowly about 25 minutes and again drain. This juice is usually kept separate from first extraction and made into jelly by itself.

Cooking Jelly. Measure juice (not more than 4 to 6 cups) into a deep kettle. If juice is lacking in acid, add 1 tablespoon lemon juice for each cup. Lemon juice is sometimes added to fully ripe fruits or fruits with insufficient acid when extracting the juice. Boil fruit juice rapidly 5 minutes; skim if necessary, then add required amount of sugar (page 933), stirring until dissolved; cook rapidly until jelly test is obtained. Long, slow cooking results in loss of flavor and darkening of color; it also breaks down the pectin and produces a gummy jelly.

Jelly Tests. Use either a candy thermometer or the "sheet" test. The thermometer at sea level should register 220° to 222° F. for a firm jelly; 218° to 219° F. for a soft jelly. To make the "sheet" test, lift a full spoon from the boiling syrup, hold it about 12 inches above the kettle and pour contents back into kettle. At first they pour like water; later the drops flatten out into a thin sheet, which, when the jelly reaches the finishing point, will shear away from edge of spoon, leaving it clean. Begin making this sheet test about 5 minutes after boiling the juice with the sugar. It should be repeated frequently until the test is successful two or three times in quick succession. The total time of boiling may vary from 10 to 20 minutes with different juices. Some juices low in acid and pectin make better jelly if cooked to 219° to 223° F.

Pouring and Sealing. Pour hot jelly into dry sterilized glasses, filling them to within ¼ inch of top. Cover jelly with a thin layer of hot but not smoking paraffin. On second day, cover with another thin layer of paraffin, turning glass to bring it well up on sides. The combined layers should not be more than ⅛ inch thick. Adjust tin lids or paste heavy paper over tops; label and store in cool, dark, dry place.

Two pounds of fruit yield about 2 cups of juice; with an equal quantity of sugar added to 2 cups of juice, this amount of fruit will make about 4 glasses (6 fluid oz. each) of jelly, or 3 glasses (8 fluid oz. each).

Storage of Jelly and Common Faults in Jelly. When stored for a while, jellies are likely to lose their flavor, aroma and bright color. For jelly at its best, make it occasionally from canned or frozen juice (unsweetened). Jellies will crystallize or become sugary if they contain too much sugar (higher than 65%). Grape jelly may contain tartaric acid crystals which are long and needle-like. If the juice is stored in the refrigerator overnight or for several days, then strained before making it into jelly, much of the acid in crystal form is removed. With too little sugar, jellies are likely to become thin, mold readily and even ferment. A damp storeroom may cause jellies to mold. Some jellies such as cranberry may have a tendency to "weep." It is more likely to take place in strongly acid fruits. The source and amount of pectin and the rate of setting of the jelly are thought to be causes for weeping jelly.

COMBINATION JELLIES

Two or more fruit juices may be combined to add variety of flavor, to supply pectin or acid deficient in one of the fruits, or to extend the juice of scarce or expensive fruits. Prepare juices separately, then mix in proportion desired and proceed as with any jelly. Some suggestive juice combinations with the proportion of sugar to use are: ½ each apple and cherry; ½ each apple and rhubarb; ⅓ each apple, blueberry and rhubarb; ½ each apple and black raspberry; ½ each apple and pineapple; ½ each apple and peach; ½ each apple and strawberry; ⅓ each apple, quince and cranberry; ½ each apple and blueberry; ½ each currant and red raspberry. Use approximately ¾ to 1 cup sugar for each cup of juice.

CRANBERRY AND GRAPE JELLY

1 cup cranberry juice
1 cup tart apple juice
1 pint Concord grape juice
2 cups sugar

Mix juices and bring to a boil; skim, if necessary. Add sugar; stir until dissolved and boil rapidly until jelly stage is reached and jelly sheets from edge of spoon. Pour into clean glasses. Cover immediately with layer of paraffin; when cool, follow by a second, thicker layer. Yield: 8 glasses (6 oz.).

TABLE XLIV

EXTRACTION OF JUICES FOR JELLY

FRUIT	WATER PER QUART PREPARED FRUIT	TIME OF COOKING	FRUIT	WATER PER QUART PREPARED FRUIT	TIME OF COOKING
	Cup	*Minutes*		*Cup*	*Minutes*
Apples	2, or to cover	20–25	Gooseberries	¼, or to cover	15
Crab apples	2, or to cover	20–25			
Blackberries	½, or none	5–10	Grapes,		
Cranberries	3	10–20	Concord	¼, or none	
Currants	¼, or none	10–15	wild	1	10–15
Lemons		60 or	Guava,	4	30
Grapefruit }	4	until	sour		
Oranges		soft	Plums, tart	½ to 1	15–20
			Quinces	1, or to cover	20–30

TABLE XLV

PROPORTION OF SUGAR TO FRUIT JUICE FOR JELLY

SINGLE FRUIT JUICE [1]	SUGAR PER CUP JUICE	COMBINATION OF JUICES	SUGAR PER CUP JUICE
	Cup		*Cup*
Apples [1]	¾	¼ apple + ¾ blackberry	¾
Crab apples [1]	¾–1	½ each apple, cherry	¾
Blackberries	¾–1	½ each apple, rhubarb	¾
Cranberries	¾	⅓ each apple, blueberry, rhubarb	1
Currants	¾–1	½ each apple, black raspberry	¾
Gooseberries	1	½ each apple, pineapple	¾
Grapes, Concord	¾–1	½ each apple, peach	¾
		½ each apple, strawberry	¾
Grapes, wild	1	⅓ each apple, quince, cranberry	1
Plums, tart [1]	¾–1	½ each apple, blueberry	¾
Quinces [1]	¾	½ each currant, red raspberry	1

[1] One tablespoon lemon juice may be added to each cup of juice if extracted from ripe fruit.

.934 •

RHUBARB AND STRAWBERRY JELLY

1 pound rhubarb   8 cups sugar
2 quarts ripe strawberries   1 bottle commercial pectin

Put rhubarb through food chopper, using finest knife. Crush strawberries thoroughly and blend with rhubarb. Drip through cloth jelly
bag and measure 3½ cups of juice; combine with the sugar in a large
kettle. Quickly bring to a boil and add fruit pectin, stirring constantly.
Bring to a full boil and boil hard ½ minute. Remove from heat, skim
and pour into clean glasses. Cover with layer of paraffin; when cool,
add a second, thicker layer. Approximate yield: 12 glasses (6 oz.).

ELDERBERRY JELLY

3½ cups elderberry juice   ½ cup lemon juice
7½ cups sugar   1 cup commercial pectin

Measure sugar and juice into large saucepan; add lemon juice and mix.
Quickly bring to a boil; at once add pectin, stirring constantly; then
bring to a full boil for ½ minute. Remove from heat, skim, pour
quickly into clean glasses. Cover immediately with a layer of paraffin;
when cool, follow by a second, thicker layer. Yield: 14 glasses (6 oz.).

HERB JELLY

Steeping the herb infusion is the first step in making herb jellies
with pectin base. Use this brew as a part or all of the liquid called for
in the recipe. Fresh herb infusions have a slight lingering harshness.
Those made from dried herb leaves are sweeter and sounder in basic
flavor. All herb jellies need the addition of vinegar. Best results seem to
be obtained from herbs grown in this country if essential oil is added
just as the mixture is taken from the heat. If added too soon, the
perfume, being volatile, is lost. When added later, an even blending
of the oil in the cooling liquid proves a difficult task.

HERB INFUSION

To ¼ cup chopped fresh herb leaves (stripped from the stalks) or
⅛ cup (2 tablespoons) dried leaves, crumbled, add 1 cup boiling water;
cover and simmer over very low heat 5 minutes. Strain. Use as base
in making herb jellies.

ROSE GERANIUM JELLY

crab apples
water
sugar

extract of rose geranium oil or
several small rose geranium
leaves

Wash and pick over crab apples. Cut in quarters, removing stem and blossom end. Almost cover with water and cook, covered, until apples are very soft. Drip through jelly bag. Measure and add 1 cup sugar for each cup juice. Cook rapidly to the jelly stage (222° F.), remove from heat. Skim and add rose geranium oil extract, or put leaf in bottom of hot sterilized glasses; pour a little jelly in each glass. Then return to first glass and fill with jelly. Cover immediately with layer of paraffin; when cold, follow by a second, thicker layer. If only one kind of herb jelly is desired, a handful of the fresh herbs, or a small amount of dried herbs may be added to the apples during cooking. The juices will be flavored with the herb. Or a few leaves of the herb can be steeped in the apple juice and then strained out before the sugar is added. Yield: 2 cups juice equals 3 small glasses of jelly.

MINT JELLY

½ cup vinegar
1 cup water
½ cup mint leaves

green coloring
3½ cups sugar
½ cup commercial pectin

Combine vinegar, water, mint leaves and enough coloring to give tint desired. Add sugar, stir, and bring to a boil. Add pectin at once, stirring constantly, and bring again to a full boil for ½ minute. Strain off mint leaves and pour into glasses. When cold, cover with paraffin. Approximate yield: 6 glasses (6 oz.).

PINEAPPLE MINT JELLY

1 cup unsweetened pineapple
    juice
¼ cup lemon juice

1¾ cups sugar
green vegetable coloring
½ cup commercial pectin

1 teaspoon spearmint extract

Measure juices and sugar into large saucepan. Add green coloring to desired shade and quickly bring to boil. Add pectin, stirring constantly. Bring to a full rolling boil for ½ minute. Remove from heat, add mint extract, skim and pour into glasses. When cool, cover with paraffin. Approximate yield: 4 (6 oz.) glasses.

JAMS

JAMS are made from crushed whole fruits such as berries, apricots, cherries, peaches, plums, and grapes, cooked with sugar to a soft, jelly-like consistency and containing almost no free liquid.

Cook no more than 3 to 4 quarts of fruit at a time. Wash fruit, crush or cut in small pieces, add small amount of water and cook 8 to 10 minutes. Best results are obtained by weighing both sugar and fruit, allowing ¾ to 1 pound sugar for each pound of fruit. Or measure fruit and add about ⅔ cup sugar for each cup of fruit; boil rapidly to jelly stage (220° F.), stirring occasionally to prevent sticking. Jam should sheet from spoon like jelly (page 932). Pour into sterilized glasses and cover at once with paraffin. Or pour into clean hot jars to overflowing and seal at once.

Less sugar may be used, but jam must then be canned open-kettle or processed before sealing. Pour hot jam into glass jars as for canning (page 916) and partially seal. Process 3 to 5 minutes in boiling water bath (page 921). Remove jars and complete seal.

JAM RECIPES
(Follow general directions above)

Berry Jams—Use 4 quarts raspberries, blackberries, blueberries, loganberries, gooseberries or currants. Partially crush in large kettle; heat slowly until juice flows freely; then boil rapidly until about ½ of juice has evaporated. Measure fruit; add ⅔ cup sugar for each cup fruit. For a less seedy jam, sieve part of hot fruit before adding sugar. Approximate yield: 14 glasses (6 oz.) or 10 half-pint jars.

Combination Jam—Use 1 quart sour cherries, pitted, 1 medium-sized pineapple, shredded, and 2 quarts strawberries, hulled. Boil cherries and pineapple 5 minutes, add strawberries and 7 cups sugar. Approximate yield: 14 glasses (6 oz.) or 10 half-pint jars.

Cranberry Jam—Put 4 cups fresh cranberries through food chopper. Add 1 cup water and cook slowly 3 to 4 minutes. Add 3 cups sugar and continue cooking, stirring frequently, until mixture is thick—about 20 minutes. Pack in hot sterilized jars and immediately cover with paraffin. Yield: 4 6-ounce glasses.

Spiced Elderberry Jam—Wash 2 quarts elderberries, pick from stems, grind and rub through coarse sieve to remove seeds. Add ¼ cup water to 2 quarts wild grapes. Cook until soft and rub through sieve. Add to elderberries. The mixture should measure 1 quart. Add 1 pound sugar, 1 cup vinegar, 1 teaspoon allspice, ½ teaspoon mace, ½ teaspoon ground cloves and boil rapidly until jam is thick and clear and sheets from spoon, stirring to prevent burning. Pour into hot sterilized glasses and cover immediately with paraffin . Yield: 4½ pints.

Grape Jam—Use 4 pounds Concord grapes; remove pulp from skins and put in separate kettles. Bring pulp to boiling point and press through sieve to remove seeds. Add skins to pulp and measure; add ½ to ¾ cup sugar to each cup fruit. Approximate yield: 8 glasses (6 oz.) or 6 half-pint jars.

Peach or Apricot Jam—Use 4 pounds peaches, peeled and stoned. Cook in 2 cups water; add 6 cups sugar. Yield: 12 glasses (6 oz.).

Plum Jam—Use 4 quarts damson or green gage plums, pitted. Cook in 4 cups water; measure and add ⅔ cup sugar for each cup fruit. Approximate yield: 12 glasses (6 oz.) or 8 half-pint jars.

Raisin and Cranberry Jam—Cook 1 cup seeded raisins with 4 cups water until liquid is reduced one-half. Add 4 cups cranberries and 2½ cups sugar. Approximate yield: 6 glasses (6 oz.) or 4 half-pint jars.

Red Raspberry Jam with Currant Juice—Crush 4 quarts raspberries, cover with 2 cups strained currant juice and let stand 10 to 15 minutes. Simmer 20 minutes; measure and add ⅔ cup sugar for each cup fruit. Approximate yield: 12 glasses (6 oz.) or 8 half-pint jars.

Strawberry Jam—Crush 1 quart strawberries, hulled, in large kettle; add 2¼ cups sugar. Heat quickly and boil rapidly until clear. This jam is not very thick. Yield: 4 glasses (6 oz.) or 3 half-pint jars.

PEACH JAM

4 cups prepared fruit	1 bottle liquid fruit pectin
¼ cup lemon juice	¾ teaspoon cinnamon
7½ cups sugar	½ teaspoon cloves
½ teaspoon allspice	

To prepare fruit—Peel and pit about 3 pounds soft ripe peaches. Grind. Measure 4 cups into a very large saucepan. Add lemon juice.

Add sugar and spices and mix well. Place over high heat, bring to a *full rolling boil* and *boil hard 1 minute*, stirring constantly. Remove from heat and at once stir in bottle fruit pectin. Then stir and skim by turns 5 minutes to cool slightly, to prevent floating fruit. Ladle quickly into glasses. Cover jam at once with ⅛ inch hot paraffin. Yield: 11 six-ounce glasses.

Spiced Peach Jam—Add cinnamon, cloves and allspice, or any desired combination of spices, to peaches before cooking. Proceed as directed.

Peach and Pear Jam—Peel and pit or core about 1½ pounds each fully ripe peaches and pears. Chop very fine or grind. Combine fruits and measure 4 cups into a very large saucepan. Add sugar, omit spices and proceed as directed.

Peach, Pear and Plum Jam—Peel and pit about 1 pound soft ripe peaches and ½ pound ripe pears. Grind or chop very fine. Pit (do not peel) about 1 pound fully ripe plums. Cut in small pieces and chop. Combine fruits and measure 4½ cups into a very large saucepan. Add sugar, omit spices and proceed as directed. Approximate yield: 12 six-ounce glasses.

PRESERVES

FRUIT preserves are whole fruits or pieces of fruit preserved in heavy sugar syrup. Hard fruits such as pears, pineapples, quinces are cooked in water until tender, the water drained off and used in making the syrup. Two-thirds to ¾ pound of sugar is added for each pound of fruit; for strawberries, use 1 pound sugar to each pound fruit. Berries and other juicy fruits are cooked in syrup from the start. Boil, stirring frequently and gently, until fruit is clear and tender and syrup is thick. Turn into hot sterilized jars and seal at once. To have plump preserves, let fruit stand in syrup several hours after cooking is completed. Reheat to boiling, pour into jars and seal at once.

PRESERVE RECIPES

Citron Melon Preserves—Select a slightly underripe melon, wash, and pare off the green rind. Cut the melon into half-inch slices and separate the inner and outer portions. These two portions must be handled separately throughout the preserving process because of the difference in their texture, and they should be packed in separate jars. Cut each portion into half-inch cubes and remove the seeds. Weigh the prepared fruit, and to each pound allow 1½ quarts of water, ¾ pound of sugar, ½ lemon thinly sliced, and, if desired, one or two pieces of gingerroot. Boil the citron melon in the water for about 25 minutes, or until tender. Add the sugar and boil for 1 hour. Add the lemon and the ginger and continue to boil until the syrup "sheets off" the spoon in the jelly test. Fill hot sterilized jars with the preserves and seal.

Citron melon preserves may be spread out to dry and later used in fruit cakes, or as a substitute for the commercial crystallized citron.

Green Tomato Preserves—Cook together 1 pound green tomatoes, thinly sliced; 1 lemon, thinly sliced; ¾ cup firmly packed brown sugar; and 1 tablespoon ground ginger, tied in a cloth bag. Remove ginger before pouring into jars. Approximate yield: 2 half-pint jars.

Peach Cantaloupe Preserves—Use 12 peaches, peeled, stoned and sliced; 1 cantaloupe, peeled, seeded and sliced; and pulp of 3 oranges. Measure fruit; add ⅔ cup sugar to each cup fruit, let stand several hours before cooking. Approximate yield: 5 half-pint jars.

Pear Preserves—Boil 4½ cups sugar and 2½ cups water together 8 minutes; add 2 pounds pears, peeled and cut in halves, 8 whole cloves, 12 raisins and 1 lemon, thinly sliced; cook until pears are clear and tender and syrup thick. Approximate yield: 2 half-pint jars.

Pear and Apple Preserves—Squeeze the juice from 1 lemon and cut peel in strips 1-inch long (⅓ cup peel). Add 1 cup water and cook until tender (30 minutes). Add cooked peel and liquid to 2 cups each pears and tart apples, peeled and chopped. Add sugar. Boil the mixture until thick (20 minutes). Stir frequently. Add lemon juice and cook until mixture thickens (about 2 minutes). Pour into hot, clean jars and seal. Approximate yield: 2 half-pint jars.

Pineapple Preserves—Prepare and slice 1 pineapple (page 104) and remove hard centers; cook in boiling water until tender. Drain, reserving liquid; weigh fruit. Use ¾ pound sugar for each pound fruit; dissolve sugar in 1 cup fruit liquid, add juice and grated rind of 1 lemon. Add pineapple when syrup boils.

Ripe Tomato Preserves—Use 5 pounds ripe tomatoes, peeled and cut in quarters; add 8 cups sugar and let stand overnight in crock or enameled kettle. Drain; boil juice until it threads. Add tomatoes and 2 lemons, thinly sliced. Approximate yield: 4 half-pint jars.

Quince Preserves—Use 1 pound quinces, pared, quartered and cored. Cook for 1 hour in syrup made of 1¼ cups sugar and 4 cups water; let stand 24 hours. Drain syrup, add 1 cup sugar, bring to a boil; add fruit and simmer until fruit is clear and syrup thickened. Again let stand overnight, drain, pack fruit in clean hot jars. Boil syrup until it sheets like jelly (page 932); pour over fruit and seal at once.

Strawberry Preserves—Use 2 quarts strawberries, hulled; add 4½ cups sugar; heat, stirring gently until mixture boils, then boil 6 minutes. Approximate yield: 2 half-pint jars.

Strawberry-Pineapple Preserves—Cook 1 cup shredded pineapple
with 3 cups sugar for 10 minutes; add 2 cups strawberries, hulled, and
cook about 20 minutes, or until thickened. Yield: 4 half-pint jars.

Watermelon Preserves—Select thick watermelon rind and trim off
the outer green skin and the pink flesh, using only the greenish-white
part. Cut into ½- or 1-inch cubes and weigh. For each 4 pounds of
the prepared rind, prepare 2 quarts of lime water. Let the mellon stand
in the lime water for 1 hour to make it crisp. Drain and place in clear
water for 1 hour. Drain and boil for 1½ hours in fresh water. Drain
again.

To each 4 pounds of the prepared watermelon rind weighed before the
lime-water treatment, allow 4 quarts of water, 4 pounds of sugar, 2
lemons thinly sliced, and, if desired, 4 small pieces of gingerroot. Boil
the lemon for 5 minutes in ½ cup of the water. Boil the rest of the
water with the sugar for 5 minutes to make a syrup. Add the watermelon and the gingerroot to the syrup. Boil for about 1 hour. When
the syrup thickens, add the lemon and the water in which it was
cooked. Continue to boil, stirring constantly, until the syrup is somewhat thick and the melon is clear. Pack at once into hot sterilized jars
and seal.

LIME WATER

ADD 1 tablespoon lime (calcium oxide) to 1 quart water. It is used
to give crispness to melon.

MARMALADES

MARMALADES are usually made from pulpy fruits rich in pectin
and acid, the entire fruit except core and seeds being used; one or
more citrus fruits are commonly used. Wash fruits thoroughly;
leave small fruits whole, cut larger ones in very thin slices. When
citrus fruits are used, water is usually added and mixture allowed
to stand overnight. Cook fruit in water until tender, add sugar,
about ¾ pound to each pound of mixture; continue cooking until
fruit is tender and syrup sheets from spoon (page 932), stirring
frequently. Remove from heat. Pour into hot sterilized glasses,
filling them to within ¼ inch of top. Cover immediately with
a layer of paraffin. When cool, add a second thicker layer as
directed for jelly (page 932); store in a cool, dry, dark place.

MARMALADE RECIPES
(Follow general directions above)

Amber Marmalade—Use 1 orange, 1 lemon and 1 grapefruit, each thinly sliced. Add 3 cups water to each cup fruit. Boil rapidly until tender; measure and add 1 cup sugar to each cup fruit and liquid. Approximate yield: 6 glasses (6 oz.).

Carrot Marmalade—Cook 6 carrots, scraped and finely cut, in small amount of water until tender. Add 3 oranges, thinly sliced, and rind and juice of 1 lemon. Measure; add ⅔ cup sugar for each cup mixture. Approximate yield: 6 glasses (6 oz.).

Cherry Marmalade—Combine 2 pounds pitted cherries, 3 cups sugar, 2 cups water; simmer 15 minutes and add grated rind and juice of 1 lemon and 1 orange. Approximate yield: 6 glasses (6 oz.).

Grapefruit Marmalade—Use 1 large grapefruit and 3 large oranges; cover with 3½ pints water; let stand overnight. Boil slowly until tender; add 3½ pounds sugar. Approximate yield: 8 glasses (6 oz.).

Green Tomato Marmalade—Use 3 pounds green tomatoes, finely sliced; 3 lemons, thinly sliced and boiled 5 minutes in ½ cup water and 3 cups sugar. Combine and boil rapidly until thick. Approximate yield: 8 glasses (6 oz.).

Mint Marmalade—Use 1 cup orange pulp, juice and grated rind of 2 lemons and ½ pound peppermint candy, ground or broken. Cook together until candy is melted and mixture thick. Yield: 3 glasses.

Orange Marmalade—Use 6 oranges, finely sliced or chopped. Add 3 cups water for each cup fruit; let stand overnight. Boil slowly until tender; add 1 cup sugar to each cup fruit. Yield: 8 glasses (6 oz.).

Peach Marmalade—Use 5 pounds peaches, pared, pitted and finely sliced; add 6¾ cups sugar and juice from ½-pint bottle maraschino cherries. Add chopped cherries before removing from heat. Approximate yield: 8 glasses (6 oz.).

Pineapple Apricot Marmalade—Use 1 pound chopped dried apricots, soaked overnight in 4 cups water, 1 can (No. 2) shredded pineapple, and 6 cups sugar. Yield: 12 glasses (6 oz.)

LIME MARMALADE

Wash 6 limes. Cover with cold water and simmer 2 hours, changing water 3 times. Cool fruit and slice very thin. Measure. For each cup of fruit, add 2 cups water and 2 cups sugar. Cook, stirring frequently, until thick, or about 45 minutes. Turn into hot sterilized jars and cover with paraffin. Approximate yield: 6 half-pint jars.

PAPAYA MARMALADE

10 cups sliced ripe papaya	grated rind of 2 lemons
1 cup shredded fresh pineapple	½ cup lemon juice
grated rind of 1 orange	2 tablespoons green ginger, grated
½ cup orange juice	8 cups sugar

Combine all ingredients except sugar and boil 30 minutes, or until thick. Add sugar and cook until clear. Stir frequently to prevent burning. Pour into hot sterilized jars. Immediately cover with paraffin. Approximate yield: 10 to 12 jars (6 oz.).

CONSERVES

CONSERVES are made from 2 or more fruits, one of them often a citrus fruit, with raisins, nuts or both added. Prepare fruit, slice, shred or cut in pieces; cook like Marmalade (page 941). Dip nuts in boiling water for a few seconds before adding them to the fruit. Add nut meats about five minutes before removing from heat; long cooking destroys their flavor. Walnuts sometimes cause a conserve to turn dark; this may often be avoided by blanching the nuts in boiling water 3 to 5 minutes, then cooling in cold water. Almonds should be blanched, left whole, shredded or coarsely chopped. Pour into hot sterilized jars and cover with paraffin or seal at once.

CONSERVE RECIPES
(Follow general directions above)

Cherry Conserve—Use 3 quarts pitted sour cherries, 1 cup seeded raisins, juice and grated rind of 1 orange and 1 lemon, and 7 cups sugar. When thick, add ½ cup chopped walnuts. Yield: 10 glasses (6 oz.).

Cranberry Conserve—Use 1 quart cranberries, chopped; ¾ cup dried currants; 1 cup seeded raisins; pulp and grated rind of 6 oranges; 2 tart apples, pared and finely cut; 1 can (No. 2) grated pineapple; 1 cup boiling water and 6 cups sugar. When thick, add ½ cup shredded, blanched almonds. Approximate yield: 8 glasses (6 oz.).

Damson Plum Conserve—Use 2 pounds plums, pitted and chopped; 1 orange, chopped and cooked 20 minutes in 2 cups water; ½ cup raisins and 3 cups sugar. When thick, add ¼ cup chopped walnuts. Approximate yield: 6 glasses (6 oz.).

De Luxe Conserve—Use 2 cups ground fresh pineapple and 5 cups raspberries. Add 6 cups sugar, mix and let stand 15 minutes, then cook until thick; add ½ cup chopped nuts. Yield: 6 glasses (6 oz.).

Gooseberry and Pineapple Conserve—Boil 1½ quarts prepared gooseberries in ½ cup water until skins burst; add 2 cups shredded pineapple and cook 10 minutes; then add 2 cups seeded raisins and 4 cups sugar. When thick, add 2 cups chopped pecans. Yield: 6 glasses.

Grape and Nut Conserve—Cook 6 cups bottled grape juice, 6 cups sugar, 6 oranges, chopped, 6 cups chopped raisins and grated rind and juice of 2 lemons. When thick, add 4½ cups chopped walnuts and 1 cup chopped filberts. Approximate yield: 12 glasses (6 oz.).

Medley Conserve—Use 4 cups stemmed currants, 5 cups prepared gooseberries, 2½ cups blackberries and 7 cups sugar. When thick, add 2 cups chopped walnuts. Yield: 10 glasses (6 oz.).

Peach Conserve—Cut 3 oranges in thin slices, stack and cut in quarters; boil 30 minutes in water to cover. Add 1½ cups peaches, peeled and cut in small pieces, and 4 cups sugar; when thick, add 1 cup shredded blanched almonds. Approximate yield: 4 glasses (6 oz.).

Peach and Ginger Conserve—Use 1 pound chopped dried peaches, soaked overnight in 4 cups water; 1 orange, thinly sliced; 1 cup seedless raisins; ¼ cup chopped crystallized ginger; juice of 1 lemon and 1 orange and 2 cups sugar. When thick, add ¼ cup chopped walnuts. Approximate yield: 6 glasses (6 oz.).

Peach Pecan Conserve—Use 14 large peaches, peeled, pitted and cut in small pieces, 4 pounds sugar and 1 tablespoon grated orange rind. When thick, add ½ pound chopped pecans. Yield: 8 glasses (6 oz.).

Rhubarb and Strawberry Conserve—Combine 2 cups diced rhubarb, 1 cup seeded raisins, pulp and grated rind of 2 oranges and 3 cups sugar; let stand overnight. Add 4 cups whole strawberries; when thick, add ½ cup chopped walnuts. Yield: 6 glasses (6 oz.).

Tomato Conserve—Use 4 pounds tomatoes, peeled, sliced and drained; ½ cup chopped preserved ginger; juice and grated rind of 1 lemon and 8 cups sugar. Approximate yield: 6 glasses (6 oz.).

RIPE PEACH CONSERVE

4 cups prepared fruit
1 medium orange
2 medium lemons
¾ cup water
1⁄16 teaspoon baking soda

7½ cups sugar
½ cup chopped maraschino
   cherries
½ cup finely chopped nutmeats
1 bottle liquid fruit pectin

To prepare fruit—Peel off the yellow rind of orange and one lemon with a sharp knife, leaving as much of the white part on the fruit as possible. Put yellow rinds through the food chopper twice; add water and baking soda to ground rind, bring to a boil and simmer, covered, 10 minutes. Cut off the tight skin of the peeled fruit and slip the pulp out of each section. Add pulp and juice and the juice of an additional lemon to the rind, and simmer, covered, 20 minutes longer. Peel about 1½ pounds fully ripe peaches. Pit and grind or chop very fine. Combine fruits.

To make the conserve—Add sugar, cherries and nuts to prepared fruit in large saucepan. Mix well. Bring to a *full rolling boil* over high heat and *boil hard 1 minute*, stirring constantly. Remove from heat and stir in liquid fruit pectin. Then stir and skim by turns for 5 minutes to cool slightly, to prevent floating fruit. Ladle quickly into glasses. Cover conserve at once with ⅛ inch hot paraffin. Approximate yield: 12 six-ounce glasses.

FRUIT BUTTERS

Use fleshy fruits such as apples, peaches, plums, grapes or tomatoes, alone or in combination. Wash, remove undesirable portions and cook in water to cover until tender. Rub through fine colander or sieve. If pulp is thin, cook until thick enough to heap or round up on spoon. Measure; add sugar, using about ⅔ cup or less for each cup fruit and spices. Sometimes spices are tied in cloth bag and removed before pouring. If cooked too long, spices lose their fragrance and flavor. Boil rapidly, stirring constantly to prevent scorching, until butter sheets from spoon (page 932). Pour into hot sterilized jars and seal. For less sweet butters, turn into jars and process 3 to 5 minutes in boiling water bath (page 921).

FRUIT BUTTER RECIPES

Apple Butter—Cook slowly 2 quarts peeled apple quarters in 2 quarts sweet cider about 2 hours; omit sieving and add 1½ cups sugar, 1½ teaspoons cinnamon, ½ teaspoon cloves and ½ teaspoon allspice. Approximate yield: 1½ quarts.

Grape and Apple Butter—Use 2 cups each sieved grape pulp and apple pulp; add 2 cups sugar. Approximate yield: 1½ pints.

Muskmelon Butter—Use 6 muskmelons, seeded and cut in small pieces. Add ½ cup sugar for each cup pulp and 1 teaspoon cinnamon. Approximate yield: 1½ pints.

Peach Butter—Use 4 pounds peaches, peeling only if very fuzzy; remove pits. Cook in 2 cups water; sieve, measure and add ⅔ cup sugar for each cup pulp. Add 2 teaspoons cinnamon and 1 teaspoon cloves, if desired. Approximate yield: 1½ quarts.

Plum Butter—Use 4 pounds plums; add ⅔ cup sugar for each cup pulp. Approximate yield: 1½ quarts.

OLD-FASHIONED PEACH BUTTER

5 pounds peaches   **2 pounds sugar**

Peel and slice the peaches. Cover with sugar and let stand overnight. Cook 3 hours over low heat; then pour into hot sterilized glasses and cover immediately with paraffin. Yield: 8 one-half pint jars.

PICKLES AND RELISHES

Most pickles are made from small or pickle-size cucumbers, prepared with salt and preserved in vinegar, with or without sugar and spices. Other vegetables such as beets, cauliflower, cabbage, gherkins, snap beans, tomatoes and onions may also be pickled. *Pickled fruits* are made with hard or fleshy fruits such as apples, crab apples, peaches, pears, cantaloupe, pumpkin and watermelon rind; they are cooked until clear in a pickling liquid. *Spiced fruits* differ from pickled fruits in that they are generally made from soft fruits; the finished product is almost a pulp and there is little free liquid. *Relishes* are made of finely chopped vegetables or the harder fruits, spiced, salted and preserved with vinegar. Certain relishes require no cooking, but most are cooked until rather thick.

Chutneys, hot, spicy and sweet, are made from fruits, vegetables or a combination of both, usually chopped and cooked until rather thick. *Ketchups* are made from vegetables, tomatoes or fruits and strained so that the finished product is a thick smooth sauce.

DILL PICKLES

Use a 5-gallon earthenware crock or keg for packing cucumbers. Place layer of dill plant and spices in bottom of jar, then 2 to 3 layers of washed small or medium-sized cucumbers, another layer of dill and spices and repeat until jar is almost full. Use 1½ ounces mixed pickle spice and 1 pound dill plant for a 5 gallon crock. Cover with brine (1 pound salt, 10 quarts water and ⅔ quart vinegar). Cover with layer of grape leaves and place weighted plate on top. Let stand 2 to 3 weeks, adding new brine when necessary to keep cucumbers covered. A cover over top ôf jar will lessen evaporation, reduce formation of scum at top of pickles, and prevent spoilage. Pickles may be stored in crock if kept in cool place. Remove scum and cover pickles with melted paraffin. For best results, pack pickles in clean glass jars, heat brine to boiling, cool slightly and pour over pickles, filling jars to top; seal at once and store in cool place. If desired, dill pickles may be prepared in 2-quart glass jars, reducing amount of dill, spice and brine as necessary. Allow 40 to 50 small cucumbers for a 5 gallon crock.

QUICK PROCESS PICKLES

Use small or medium-sized cucumbers; wash, drain and cover with weak brine (1 cup salt to each gallon water). Let stand 24 hours; then make into sweet or sour pickles.

BREAD AND BUTTER TYPE PICKLES

6 large cucumbers	1 cup sugar
3 onions	1 teaspoon celery seed
¾ cup salt	1 teaspoon mustard seed
4 cups water	¾ teaspoon turmeric
1 cup vinegar	½ teaspoon ginger
¼ teaspoon pepper	

Wash cucumbers, peel, if desired; peel onions. Slice thin and let stand in brine of salt and water for 3 hours. Drain, rinse under cold water. Combine remaining ingredients and bring to a boil; add cucumbers and onions and stir over low heat 2 minutes. Turn into jars, seal. Yield: 2½ pints.

SWEET CUCUMBER PICKLES

Use 12 medium-sized cucumbers, prepared as Quick Process Pickles (see above). Drain; cover with 1 quart vinegar, 1 cup sugar, 2 tablespoons whole black peppers, 1 teaspoon grated horseradish, 1 stick cinnamon, ¾ teaspoon mustard seed and ½ teaspoon whole cloves. Heat to boiling, boil 3 minutes, turn into jars, filling to overflowing, and seal at once. Approximate yield: 1 quart.

MIXED MUSTARD PICKLES

Use 2 cups whole small cucumbers; 2 cups sliced cucumbers; 2 cups string beans, broken in ½ inch pieces; 3 green peppers, chopped; 3 red peppers, chopped; 2 cups quartered small green tomatoes and 2 cups cauliflower flowerets. Cover with brine (½ cup salt to 1 quart water) and let stand overnight. Drain, rinse in fresh water, drain again and cover with mixture of equal parts vinegar and water. Let stand 1 hour, heat to boiling, drain, add mustard dressing and simmer 5 minutes. Fill hot sterilized jars to overflowing and seal at once. For **Mustard Dressing,** mix 4 tablespoons flour, 1 cup sugar, ½ teaspoon turmeric, 3 tablespoons dry mustard and ½ tablespoon celery seed; slowly add 1 quart vinegar and cook 5 minutes. Yield: 6 pints.

SOUR CUCUMBER PICKLES

Drain Quick Process Pickles (page 947), place in mixture of 1 part vinegar to 3 parts water, using enough to cover pickles completely. Simmer 2 to 3 minutes, pack into hot sterilized jars, fill jars to overflowing with boiling vinegar and seal at once.

PICKLED STRING BEANS

Select tender beans without strings, if possible. Keep them full length, but snip off ends and remove strings, if any. Soak beans overnight in enough brine to cover (¼ cup salt to each quart water). Drain, rinse in cold water and dry with cloth. Pack in sterilized jars, adding a few bits of chili peppers, mustard and celery seed. For each quart jar, allow about 3 cups vinegar, ¼ cup firmly packed brown sugar and small piece of horseradish root. Heat vinegar, sugar and horseradish to boiling and fill each jar to overflowing. Seal at once. Allow about 1½ pounds beans for each quart jar.

PICKLED ONIONS

Blanch small white onions in boiling water 1 to 2 minutes, dip in cold water, remove thin slice at root of each and slip off skin; pack onions in jars. For each quart jar of onions, prepare following syrup: tie 1 tablespoon mixed spices in cloth bag, dissolve 1¼ cups sugar in 1 cup vinegar, add spices, cover and simmer 40 to 60 minutes; then add enough boiling water to make 1 cup. Pour hot solution over onions, partially seal jars and process 30 minutes in boiling water bath (page 916). Allow about 1 pound onions for each quart jar to be filled.

PORTLAND GREEN TOMATO PICKLE

1 peck green tomatoes, sliced	2 tablespoons celery seed
12 white onions, sliced	1 tablespoon mustard seed
salt	1 cup mixed pickling spices
vinegar	4 red pepper pods, shredded

Arrange tomatoes and onions in layers, sprinkling each layer moderately with salt; let stand overnight. Drain and place in kettle, cover with vinegar, add remaining ingredients and simmer 10 minutes. Pour into hot sterilized jars and seal at once. Yield: 8 quarts.

CUCUMBER OIL PICKLES

Use 20 small cucumbers; slice very thin but do not peel. Cover with weak brine (¼ cup salt to 1 quart water) and let stand 2 or 3 hours. Drain, rinse in cold water and pack in 2 clean pint jars, adding to each jar ½ tablespoon mustard seed and 1 small onion, sliced. (The onion may be mixed with the cucumber, if desired.) Tie 1 teaspoon celery seed in cloth bag, simmer 20 minutes in 1½ cups vinegar; then add enough boiling water to restore vinegar to original volume; slowly stir in ⅓ cup olive oil. Pour over cucumbers; seal. Yield: 2 pints.

PICKLED PEACHES

Remove skins from 1 quart peaches. Boil 1 cup vinegar, 2¼ cups sugar, 1 stick (2 inches) cinnamon and ½ teaspoon whole cloves for 10 minutes; drop in peaches, a few at a time, and cook until tender. Transfer peaches to hot sterilized jars, fill to overflowing with hot syrup and seal at once. Approximate yield: 1 quart.

PICKLED MELON RINDS

Use rind of cantaloupe, watermelon, citron melon or ripe cucumber; place in salted water as rinds accumulate and make into pickles when convenient. Remove outer skin from rind and cut into medium thin slices; weigh and soak overnight in weak brine (2 tablespoons salt to 1 quart water). Drain and cook rind in fresh water until tender. When cooked, the rind may be soaked 5 to 6 hours in lime water (see page 941) for extra crispness if desired. For each 2 pounds prepared rind, use 4½ cups sugar, 2 cups water, 1 lemon, thinly sliced, 2 cups vinegar, 1 stick cinnamon, 1 teaspoon whole cloves and 1 teaspoon whole allspice. Boil together 5 minutes, add rind and cook until clear. Pack in hot sterilized jars, fill with syrup and seal at once. One-fourth cup preserved ginger may be cooked with rind, if desired, and removed before packing. Use 2 pounds prepared rind for 1 quart.

PICKLED PEARS

Peel 3 pounds pears, remove blossom end but leave stem on. If pears are firm, parboil 5 minutes in water to cover; drain and reserve liquid for syrup. To 1 pint liquid or water, add 1 pint vinegar, 1½ cups firmly packed brown sugar, 1 stick cinnamon, 2 blades mace, 2 pieces ginger root and 1 tablespoon whole cloves; boil 5 minutes, add pears and cook until transparent. Pack in hot sterilized jars, dividing spices among jars; seal. Substitute crab apples for pears. Yield: 3 quarts.

SPICED CRANBERRIES

5 pounds cranberries	2½ cups water
4½ cups firmly packed brown sugar	2 tablespoons ground allspice
	2 tablespoons ground cinnamon
1½ cups vinegar	1 tablespoon ground cloves

Wash and pick over berries; put through food chopper. Place in kettle with sugar, vinegar, water and spices, bring to a boil and continue boiling, stirring frequently, until thick. Pour into hot sterilized jars, filling to overflowing, and seal at once. Approximate yield: 5 pints.

SPICED GOOSEBERRIES

5 pounds gooseberries	2 tablespoons ground cinnamon
8 cups sugar	1 tablespoon ground cloves
2 cups vinegar	1 orange, grated rind and juice

Top and tail gooseberries, add remaining ingredients and let stand several hours. Bring slowly to boiling point and cook about 2 hours, or until thick, stirring frequently. Pour into hot sterilized jars, filling to overflowing, and seal at once. Approximate yield: 5 pints.

SPICED BLACKBERRIES

4 cups packed brown sugar	1 tablespoon whole cloves
2 cups vinegar	2 sticks cinnamon
5 pounds blackberries	8 whole allspice

Dissolve sugar in vinegar; add blackberries and spices tied in a cloth bag. Boil rapidly until thick. Remove spices, pour into hot sterilized jars, filling to overflowing, and seal at once. Yield: 5 pints.

BANANA RELISH

½ cup vinegar	12 cloves
2 tablespoons sugar	½ teaspoon cinnamon
	4 bananas

Combine vinegar, sugar, cloves and cinnamon and cook until sugar is dissolved and begins to thicken. Peel bananas, cut in halves, drop into syrup and boil hard 1 or 2 minutes. Remove from the syrup carefully, since they break easily. Chill and use as relish. Yield: 6 portions.

RIPE PLUM RELISH

3½ cups prepared fruit	½ teaspoon allspice
½ teaspoon cinnamon	6½ cups sugar
¾ teaspoon cloves	½ cup vinegar
	½ bottle liquid fruit pectin

Pit (do not peel) about 2 pounds fully ripe plums. Cut in pieces and chop fine. Add cinnamon, cloves, allspice, sugar and vinegar to fruit in saucepan and mix well. Place over high heat, bring to a *full rolling boil*, and *boil hard 1 minute*, stirring constantly. Remove from heat and at once stir in bottle fruit pectin. Then stir and skim by turns for 5 minutes to cool slightly, to prevent floating fruit. Ladle quickly into glasses. Cover relish at once with ⅛ inch hot paraffin. Yield: 10 six-ounce glasses.

PEPPER RELISH

12 red peppers, chopped	1 cup firmly packed brown sugar
12 green peppers, chopped	
12 onions, chopped	2 tablespoons salt
2 cups vinegar	2 tablespoons celery seed

Drain peppers and onions, cover with boiling water and simmer 15 minutes. Drain again and add vinegar, sugar, salt and celery seed. Boil 15 minutes and pour into hot sterilized jars, filling to overflowing, and seal at once. Approximate yield: 4 half-pint jars.

SPICED ORANGE SLICES

5 pounds (12) large oranges   1 pint vinegar
8½ cups sugar   2 sticks cinnamon
                1 tablespoon whole cloves

Cut oranges in ¼ inch slices; simmer, covered, in water to cover, about
½ hour, or until tender. Boil sugar, vinegar and spices 5 minutes;
add orange slices, about ½ at a time; cook, covered, about ½ hour, carefully removing slices when clear. Cover with the syrup and let stand
overnight; then drain and cook syrup until thick. Add orange slices,
heat to boiling, carefully pour into hot sterilized jars, filling to overflowing, and seal at once. Yield: 3½ quarts.

END–OF–THE–SEASON RELISH

2 quarts green tomatoes   1 peeled cucumber
1 quart ripe tomatoes   ½ cup salt
½ head cabbage   2 cups firmly packed brown
3 green peppers   sugar
3 red peppers   3 pints vinegar
3 stalks celery   1 teaspoon dry mustard
3 large onions   1 teaspoon paprika

Chop vegetables; place in kettle in layers, sprinkling each layer with
salt; cover and let stand overnight. Drain and press out all the liquid.
To vegetables add sugar, vinegar, mustard and paprika. Cook about
1 hour, or until transparent. Pour into hot sterilized jars, filling to
overflowing, and seal. Approximate yield: 4 quarts.

GARDEN RELISH

2 tomatoes, chopped, ¼-inch   2 tablespoons finely chopped
   dice   onion
¾ cup chopped celery   1 tablespoon French dressing
1 large cucumber, peeled,   2 to 3 tablespoons cider vinegar
   chopped   salt to taste
1 green pepper, chopped   black pepper to taste

Mix all ingredients and chill two hours until flavors are blended. Yield:
2 cups relish.

BEET RELISH

2 cups chopped peeled beets	½ cup sugar
2 cups chopped celery	2 cups vinegar
1 cup chopped onion	2 tablespoons salt
1 cup chopped sweet red pepper	3 tablespoons mustard seed
2 cups chopped cabbage	1 tablespoon celery seed

Mix ingredients and cook until vegetables are tender. Pour into hot sterilized jars, filling to overflowing, and seal. Yield: 3 quarts.

CORN RELISH

12 ears sweet corn	2 tablespoons salt
2 onions, chopped	¼ teaspoon pepper
2 sweet green peppers, chopped	1½ tablespoons dry mustard
1 sweet red pepper, chopped	1 cup sugar
1 cup chopped cabbage	2 cups vinegar

Cut corn from cob, but do not scrape the ear; mix with onions, peppers and cabbage and add remaining ingredients. Cook slowly 1 hour, stirring occasionally. Turn into hot sterilized jars, filling to overflowing, and seal at once. Canned kernel corn may be substituted for ear corn; use 6 cups, drained, and proceed as for fresh corn. Yield: 5 half-pint jars.

TOMATO KETCHUP

4 quarts tomatoes, peeled	2 teaspoons dry mustard
3 red peppers	1 teaspoon paprika
2 medium onions, cut fine	1 tablespoon whole allspice
2 tablespoons salt	1 tablespoon whole cloves
⅓ cup sugar	1 stick cinnamon
2 teaspoons celery salt	2 cups vinegar

Cook tomatoes, peppers and onions together until tender, without adding water. Press mixture through sieve or mill. To pulp, add salt, sugar, celery salt, mustard, paprika and whole spices, tied in a cloth bag. Cook rapidly 1 hour, add vinegar and cook until thick, stirring to prevent burning. Long, slow cooking gives an undesirable dark color. Pour into hot sterilized jars, filling to overflowing. If bottles are used, insert corks and dip in hot paraffin to seal. Yield: 3 quarts.

CHILI SAUCE

18 large tomatoes, chopped	3 tablespoons salt
6 large onions, chopped	5 cups vinegar
4 red peppers, chopped	1 teaspoon ground cloves
2 green peppers, chopped	1 teaspoon cinnamon
⅔ cup sugar	1 teaspoon allspice

Combine ingredients and cook slowly until thick. Pour into hot sterilized jars, filling to overflowing, and seal at once. Yield: 3 quarts.

GENEVA CHILI SAUCE

8 quarts (32 cups) tomato pulp and juice	4 onions
2 tablespoons celery seed	4 cloves garlic
2 teaspoons stick cinnamon	green peppers, if desired
½ tablespoon mustard seed	2½ cups sugar
1 teaspoon whole cloves	⅝ cup salt
1 teaspoon pepper corns	2–3 cups white vinegar or
	3–4 cups cider vinegar

Select sound, fresh red, ripe tomatoes. Wash and remove all green and yellow spots. Plunge the tomatoes into boiling water for a few seconds. Remove the skins and cores and cut up. Remove some of the juice so that it can boil down. Tie spices, onions and garlic in a cloth and hang it in the boiling tomato mixture. Boil spices and tomatoes until the tomato volume is reduced about one-half. About 6 minutes before removing from the fire, add salt, sugar, and vinegar. Pour the boiling hot chili sauce into sterile, hot bottles and seal immediately.

Note: If garlic and green peppers are used, add with onions and spices. For catsup, press tomatoes through a sieve to remove seeds.

ENGLISH CHUTNEY

3 green peppers, seeded	3 cups vinegar
1 medium-sized onion	1½ cups sugar
13 tart apples, pared	1½ tablespoons ginger
1½ cups seeded raisins	1½ cups tart grape jelly
1 tablespoon salt	¾ cup lemon juice
1 tablespoon grated lemon rind	

Put peppers, onion, apples and raisins through food chopper; place in large saucepan and add remaining ingredients. Simmer about 1 hour, or until quite thick. Turn into hot sterilized jars, filling to overflowing, and seal at once. Approximate yield: 4 pints.

CHERRY CHUTNEY

½ pound apricots, soaked
½ pound pitted dates
2 pounds sour red cherries, pitted
1 cup seedless raisins
2 cloves garlic, minced

1 small hot red pepper, dried or fresh
1 tablespoon salt
½ cup preserved ginger, cut fine
1 cup firmly packed brown sugar
½ cup honey

1 cup vinegar

Cut apricots and dates in small pieces with scissors. Add to cherries, raisins and minced garlic and chop coarsely. Remove seeds from red pepper and crumble or chop fine. Add to fruit with salt and ginger; let stand 1 hour. Add sugar, honey, 1 cup of liquid in which the apricots were soaked and the vinegar. Bring to a boil, let simmer very gently about 45 minutes, or until thick, stirring frequently. Turn into hot sterilized jars, filling to overflowing, and seal completely at once. Approximate yield: 3 pints.

SPICED ORANGE PEEL

1 quart orange peel, cubed
1½ cups vinegar

1½ cups sugar
4 sticks cinnamon

12 cloves

Scrape all flesh from orange peel and soak overnight in cold water. Cover with fresh water and bring to a boil. Repeat twice and cook peel until tender. Combine vinegar, sugar, cinnamon and cloves, bring to a boil, add peel and simmer 3 minutes. Pack into a sterilized hot jar to overflowing and seal completely. Yield: 1 quart relish.

WHOLE PICKLED GRAPES

whole bunches of grapes
1½ cups sugar
1 cup white vinegar

Select bunches of grapes of the same size and ripeness; any type of grape may be used; they should not be overripe. Wash carefully but leave grapes on the stems; pack bunches closely in hot sterilized glass jars, but do not crowd in packing, as the fruit must not be bruised. Boil sugar and vinegar 5 minutes, stirring until sugar is dissolved; pour over grapes to fill jars to overflowing; completely seal. These grapes have the appearance of fresh fruit and make an excellent relish to serve with meat or to use as a garnish for salads. Approximate yield: 1 pint.

PICKLED CHERRIES

1 quart cherries	vinegar
1 tablespoon salt	cold water

Select large, perfect, sour cherries; wash well, leaving the stems on. Pack into hot sterilized glass jar and add salt; fill the jar with equal parts of vinegar and cold water; seal and set away for winter use. This is particularly nice served with meat or in the hors d'œuvres dish. Approximate yield: 1 quart pickled cherries.

SPICED CURRANTS

5 pounds ripe currants	1 tablespoon cinnamon
1 cup water	1 tablespoon cloves
1 cup vinegar	6 cups sugar (3 lb.)

Simmer the currants and water together 15 minutes. Add vinegar, ground spices and sugar. Simmer 15 minutes. Pour into hot, sterilized jars and seal completely. Yield: 4 quarts.

SPICED PINEAPPLE STICKS

1 large pineapple	16 whole cloves
½ cup vinegar	1 stick cinnamon
3 cups sugar	1 teaspoon grated lemon rind

Cut peel from pineapple and remove eyes; remove sections lengthwise from core and cut into little sticks, 3 inches long and ¼ inch wide (page 104). Bring vinegar, sugar, spices and lemon rind to a boil, add pineapple sticks and boil 15 minutes, or until pineapple becomes transparent. Skim out sticks, place upright in hot, sterilized half-pint jars, fill to the top with boiling syrup and seal completely at once. Canned pineapple may be substituted for the fresh fruit. Approximate yield: 3 8-ounce jars.

BEET AND CABBAGE RELISH

2 cups vinegar	½ teaspoon pepper
1 cup sugar	½ cup prepared horseradish
2 teaspoons salt	2 cups chopped cooked beets
2 cups chopped raw cabbage	

Combine vinegar, sugar and seasonings; boil 5 minutes. Pour over vegetables, mix well and cook about 5 minutes longer. Turn into sterilized containers and seal. Approximate yield: 3 8-ounce jars.

APPLE PEPPER RELISH

2 sweet red peppers	1 tablespoon grated lemon rind
2 large sweet onions, peeled	1/3 cup lemon juice
3 cooking apples, peeled and	1 cup sugar
cored	1 teaspoon salt

Clean peppers and remove core and seeds; put with onions and apples through food chopper. Add lemon rind and juice, heat to boiling; add sugar and salt and boil 20 minutes, or until thick as honey, stirring occasionally. Fill hot sterilized jars to overflowing; seal completely or cover with paraffin. Approximate yield: 1 pint relish.

CUCUMBER KETCHUP

6 cucumbers, washed and peeled	1 teaspoon sugar
vinegar	1 teaspoon mustard seed
2 teaspoons celery seed	1 tablespoon chopped onion
1 teaspoon salt	(optional)
1/8 teaspoon cayenne	4 small dried red peppers

Chop or grind cucumbers very fine. Turn into double thickness of cheesecloth; let drip 1 hour, or until quite dry. Squeeze between 2 spoons to drive out any excess moisture. Measure liquid that has dripped from cucumbers. Three-quarters of this amount is the amount of vinegar required. (If 2 cups of liquid has dripped, the cucumber pulp will require about 1½ cups vinegar.) Discard cucumber liquid, or use for soup. Add seasonings to vinegar, bring to a boil; add cucumber pulp and simmer 5 minutes. Turn into sterilized half-pint jars, bury a hot red pepper in each jar and seal. Yield: 4 8-ounce jars.

PAPAYA RELISH

1 quart papaya, green or just	1 tablespoon salt
turning, chopped fine	1/2 teaspoon mace
1/2 cup chopped celery	1/2 teaspoon cloves
1/2 cup chopped onions	1 teaspoon celery seed
1 red pepper	1/2 teaspoon cinnamon
1 green pepper	1/2 teaspoon black pepper
	1/2 pint vinegar

Mix papaya with other ingredients and boil 5 minutes. Pour into hot sterilized jars to overflowing. Seal immediately. Yield: 3 to 4 pints.

Thrift and Time-Saving with Your Pressure Cooker

PRESSURE cooking is not new to you today, we know. Women across the nation have taken up this kind of cookery with great enthusiasm. But we are wondering if you are using your pressure cooker to the very best advantage. Used correctly, it can save you valuable time, effort and money.

Are you keeping your pressure cooker in a handy location, ready to go into action around the clock? With its help, in a matter of minutes you can prepare stewed fruits and cereals for breakfast; soups, stews, vegetables and desserts for luncheon; even a complete dinner in fifteen minutes or less at night.

Nutrition research authorities advise using the pressure-cooking method for the highest nutritive savings in vegetables and meats. In food freezing and canning, the pressure cooker and canner save much time and effort.

With intelligent use, your pressure cooker can cut down dollars on your food budget. More and more, we Americans are learning the secrets of European homemakers and chefs who utilize inexpensive cuts of meats and vegetables, in season, to make delicious soups, stews and ragouts. In our time-pressed mode of living, we shrink from spending hours cooking these dishes, no matter how truly good they taste. But with the pressure cooker, these long-cooking foods can be prepared in less than one-third of the time.

Many mothers today are finding the pressure cooker an effortless and money-saving way of preparing foods for babies and young children. The cooker can be used for sterlizing the babies' bottles, as well.

OPERATING YOUR PRESSURE COOKER

PRESSURE cooking is simple and safe provided you follow the manufacturer's directions for using the cooker. They are not complicated; and with a new type of pressure cooker on the market, you need only fill the pan, adjust the cover and set the dial; it pressure cooks for you automatically from start to finish.

If your cooker is the type that needs heat-regulating, you should keep these four steps in mind:

1. Exhaust the air in the pressure cooker by letting the steam flow through the vent for a full minute or as long as the manufacturer suggests.
2. Bring to the desired pressure and count the time from that point.
3. Regulate the heat under the cooker to keep the pressure steady.
4. Reduce the pressure completely before opening the cooker. Some models vent automatically, others may be vented at the range. Older models may need to be placed under the cold water faucet to reduce the pressure quickly. *In any case, follow the manufacturer's directions.*

A pressure cooker can be used with any type of range so long as the heat can be held steady—gas, bottled gas, electricity, wood, coal, kerosene, or canned alcohol. The electric pressure cooker operates on alternating current (AC) and is equipped with its own heating unit.

Pressure cookers today are so designed that a pressure higher than 15 pounds is automatically released through a safety vent. There is also a safety plug in every cooker top. This will "blow" if the vent becomes clogged. The plug can be easily replaced and may be purchased from your cooker dealer.

You'll find that some pressure cookers are adjusted to cook at three pressures; others operate at 15 pounds pressure only.

5 pounds pressure equals 228° F. and is recommended for canning tomatoes or fruits. Fresh peas, kernel corn and green lima beans are of better quality if cooked at this pressure, too.

10 pounds pressure equals 240° F. and is used for canning the non-acid vegetables. (See chapter for canning.)

15 pounds pressure equals 250° F. and is used in most of the recipes in this book.

SIMPLE RULES FOR PRESSURE COOKING

1. Study the manufacturer's directions for using your cooker. Pressure cooking is easy and safe, but like driving your automobile, requires that you follow a few basic rules.
2. Keep your pressure cooker clean. Inspect the vent opening in the cover to make sure that it is clear of foreign matter each time before using.
3. Do not fill the cooker more than three-fourths full with solid food in order to let the steam circulate with ease. *Under no circumstances should food touch the cover of the cooker.* Fill the cooker no more than half-full of soup, liquids or cooking cereal. By following these directions, you can avoid clogging of the vent and safety plug.
4. Unless you are making a stew or a soup, use only enough water or other liquid to come to the top of the rack in the bottom of the cooker, *not over it.*
5. Be accurate in your timing. Even an extra minute under pressure can ruin a product. Count the time from the second that 15 pounds pressure is reached.
6. Reduce the pressure quickly according to the manufacturer's directions. Never try to remove the cover on the cooker until

the steam pressure is entirely evaporated. Any difficulty in removing the cover indicates the presence of steam pressure. Remember that food left covered in the cooker will continue to "cook" even without direct heat.

7. Browned meats, poultry, fish or vegetables may be "dried off" in a hot oven or under the broiler for a crisp, dry texture. This will also take away any possible "steam-cooked" flavor.

8. When using recipes that give no pressure cooking time, divide the usual cooking time by 4.

9. Foods that take the same amount of cooking time may be cooked together in the cooker. Flavors will not be transmitted from one food to another (For example, cabbage may be cooked with any other food). Wrap loose foods in moistened parchment paper or place in dividers available to fit into cookers.

10. Wash cooker carefully after each use. Dry well and store with the cover upside-down on top of cooker or adjusted loosely. Never wash the gauge or indicator and be careful to guard this part of the cooker carefully because it is a delicate instrument.

Included in this chapter are a few recipes to use as a springboard to pressure cooking. Some of them have been adapted from our tried-and-true reader favorites with directions for cooking them in a pressure cooker. Others have been developed in our Home Institute kitchens.

SOUPS AND CHOWDERS

CHICKEN, beef and fish stocks form the basis for consommés and for many soups and chowders. Stocks are also used in stews, ragouts, aspics, salads and sauces. Pressure speeds the time of their making. They also have the advantage of storing well in the refrigerator. Cool quickly and place in a covered jar. Plain soup stock which does not contain meat or vegetables will keep 5 to 7 days in a refrigerator kept at 45 degrees.

HOW TO ADAPT SOUP AND CHOWDER RECIPES

IN OUR kitchens, our home economists have adapted soup and chowder recipes as follows: Estimate the amount of liquid in the recipe as compared with the size of your cooker. Remember that the cooker should not be filled more than half-full. Reduce the other ingredients in proportion. The seasoning may also be reduced one-fourth to one-third, since none is lost in evaporation. Be careful of whole seasonings like peppercorns and in using curry. If raw vegetables are to be added, you may need to reduce the pressure at the correct time, remove the cover and add, cooking the right length of time for the particular vegetable. Thicken soups and chowders at the end of the cooking process.

PRESSURE-COOKED CHICKEN BROTH, STOCK
OR CONSOMMÉ

1 fowl (and veal and chicken bones, if available)	2 leeks
	4 peppercorns
1 medium-sized onion, sliced	½ teaspoon celery seed or
1 stalk celery, sliced	1 cup celery leaves
1 medium-sized carrot, sliced	1 quart water
½ tablespoon salt	

Combine all ingredients in pressure pan and bring to 15 pounds pressure. Cook 30 minutes. Cool stock and skim off fat. Strain through a very fine strainer. Use the chicken in any recipe requiring boiled chicken. Reheat stock and dilute with equal quantity hot water; serve with any desired garnish or in recipes requiring chicken stock. If desired, ½ teaspoon meat extract may be added to step up flavor for consommé. Yield: 8 to 12 portions.

Pressure-Cooked Brown Soup Stock (Bouillon)—Follow directions for stock on page 221, browning the meat in marrow from bone, and simmering 10 minutes. Skim thoroughly, cover and bring pressure to 15 pounds. Cook 20 minutes. Remove any extra scum; add vegetables and cook 10 minutes longer at 15 pounds pressure. Strain stock through very fine sieve or several thicknesses of cheesecloth. Yield: 2 quarts stock.

MODIFICATIONS OF BROWN SOUP STOCK

Pressure-Cooked White Stock—Follow directions for White Stock on page 222 and cook in pressure pan by the method stated above.

Pressure-Cooked Lamb or Mutton Stock—Follow directions for Lamb or Mutton Stock on page 222, and cook in pressure pan by method stated above.

PRESSURE-COOKED FISH STOCK

Follow directions for making fish stock on page 222, placing all the ingredients in the pressure pan. Bring to 15 pounds pressure and cook 20 minutes. Strain through a very fine sieve.

OLD-FASHIONED SCOTCH BROTH

2 pounds neck of lamb	1 cup diced carrots
1 quart cold water	1 cup diced turnip
1 teaspoon salt	1 cup diced onion
¼ teaspoon pepper	½ cup finely minced lamb
2 tablespoons whole barley	2 tablespoons chopped parsley

Cut all fat from the lamb. Remove meat from the bones and cut into ½-inch pieces. Place lamb and bones in pressure pan with water, seasonings and barley. Bring the pressure to 15 pounds. Cook 10 minutes. Reduce pressure quickly. Strain. Add carrots, turnip and onion. Cover and bring to pressure again at 15 pounds. Cook 5 minutes longer. Serve garnished with lamb and parsley. Yield: 2 quarts broth.

POT-AU-FEU

2–2½ pounds shank or shin of beef (with bone cracked)	2 cups boiling water
	4 medium-sized carrots, quartered
2 tablespoons butter, margarine or bacon fat	½ pound turnip, diced
1½ teaspoons salt	4 small onions, peeled
⅛ teaspoon pepper	4 small potatoes, peeled
1 teaspoon sugar	2 leeks, cut in 1-inch pieces
2 bay leaves	grated Parmesan or Swiss cheese

Brown beef in hot fat in bottom of pressure pan. Season with salt and pepper. Add sugar, bay leaves and water. Cover and bring to 15 pounds pressure. Cook 25 minutes. Reduce pressure quickly. Add remaining vegetables. Bring pressure again to 15 pounds. Cook 5 minutes longer. Skim fat from top. Slice meat into thin strips, if desired. Serve very hot with grated Parmesan or Swiss cheese sprinkled on top and with toasted garlic French bread. Yield: 4 portions.

SPEEDY DANISH OXTAIL SOUP

Follow directions for Danish Oxtail Soup on page 1002, processing oxtails, seasonings, bouillon, bay leaf and thyme 16 minutes at 15 pounds pressure. Reduce pressure quickly and add sliced onion, carrot and chopped celery with leaves; process 3 minutes longer at 15 pounds pressure. Just before serving, add wine, lemon juice and curry. Serve very hot. Yield: 6 to 8 portions.

PRESSURE-COOKED FISH CHOWDER

Use ingredients listed in Fish Chowder, page 222, with the following changes in directions: Remove fins, skin and bones from fish and cut into ½-inch pieces. Do not parboil. Fry salt pork slowly in pressure pan until light brown. Remove and drain on absorbent paper. Add onions and sauté with the cut-up fish. Pour in boiling water, onion and potatoes. Cover and bring to 15 pounds pressure. Cook 4 minutes. Reduce pressure quickly. Add milk and cream; correct seasonings and heat thoroughly. Add crackers and butter. Sprinkle pork cracklings over chowder and serve at once. Yield: 6 portions.

SOUTHERN OKRA CHOWDER

1 cup diced bacon (1 pound)	1 cup canned corn
3 cups okra, sliced	½ cup minced onion
2 cups canned tomatoes	1 teaspoon salt
1 medium green pepper, diced	1 teaspoon minced parsley
1 cup lima beans, cooked	1 cup water

Sauté bacon in pressure pan until golden brown and crisp. Add remaining ingredients. Cover and bring to 15 pounds pressure. Cook 15 minutes. Yield: 6 to 8 portions.

AMERICAN CHOP SUEY

2 pounds lean pork, cubed	1 tablespoon flour
2 pounds lean veal, cubed	1 teaspoon salt
¼ cup olive oil	¼ teaspoon pepper
2 cups sliced sweet onion	¼ cup sliced fresh mushrooms
2 cups diced celery	2 cups water

Sauté meat lightly in hot olive oil in pressure pan. Add onion and celery and lightly brown. Stir in flour; add seasonings, water and mushrooms (if canned mushroms are used, include their liquor). Bring to 15 pounds pressure. Cook 10 minutes. Serve with cooked rice accompanied by soy sauce. Yield: 6 to 8 portions.

BRUNSWICK STEW

1 4-pound fowl	⅓ cup minced onion
2 cups water	1½ cups lima beans
½ pound beef brisket, cubed	1½ cups whole kernel corn
1½ teaspoons salt	1½ cups canned tomatoes
1 teaspoon paprika	2 cups diced potatoes
4 slices of bacon	1 teaspoon salt
	⅛ teaspoon pepper

Disjoint fowl and cook with 2 cups water in pressure pan 15 minutes at 15 pounds pressure. While chicken cooks, sprinkle brisket with salt and paprika; let stand until ready to use. Remove chicken from liquid, pour off liquid and reserve. Cut bacon into ½-inch pieces. Brown in pressure pan until crisp; add onion and sauté until golden. Add beef and brown. Remove chicken from bones. Cut chicken into serving portions and brown slightly. Add enough reserved chicken stock to cover meat. Cook 10 minutes at 15 pounds pressure. Reduce pressure quickly. Add vegetables. Cook 5 minutes at 15 pounds pressure. Thicken broth, if desired, with flour and fat using 2 tablespoons of each for each cup of broth. Yield: 6 to 8 portions.

RAGOUT OF VEAL PARISIENNE

4 pounds knuckle of veal	1 teaspoon salt
1 teaspoon sugar	¼ teaspoon pepper
3 medium-sized onions, sliced	½ teaspoon grated lemon rind
1½ cups boiling water or	¼ cup flour
vegetable water	¼ cup butter or margarine
	½ cup thick sour cream

Remove membranes from meat; remove meat from bones. Cut veal into serving pieces, but reserve bones to cook with meat. Melt sugar in bottom of pressure pan. When golden brown, add onion and stir until coated. Add meat, bones, liquid and seasonings. Bring to 15 pounds pressure. Cook 17 minutes. Reduce pressure quickly. Remove bone. Thicken ragout with flour and butter made into a paste. Blend in sour cream. Serve on platter surrounded with cooked white or wild rice. Yield: 4 to 6 portions.

PRESSURE-COOKED SAUERBRATEN

Use list of ingredients for Sauerbraten (page 292) and follow directions for marinating beef. Measure liquor drawn off; add water if necessary to equal 1 cup. Lightly brown meat in butter in pressure pan. Add spiced liquor and cover. Bring pressure to 15 pounds. Cook 45 minutes. Reduce pressure quickly. Remove meat to warm place. Thicken sauce with flour mixed to a smooth paste with water. Add tomato paste and Madeira; blend and pour over meat that has been cut in thick slices. Decorate with Potato Dumplings and parsley. Yield: 6 portions.

NEW ENGLAND BEEF POT ROAST

2 to 4 pounds pot roast of beef (round, chuck or brisket)
1/4 cup seasoned flour
1/4 cup chopped suet, or fat
1 medium-sized onion, sliced
1 1/2 teaspoons salt
1/8 teaspoon pepper
1/4 cup chopped celery
1/4 cup sliced carrot
2 tablespoons chopped parsley
1 cup hot water or beef consommé

See directions for buying pot roast (page 290). Remove excess fat from meat and dredge in seasoned flour. Brown on all sides in hot fat in pressure pan. Remove from pan and place on rack in pan, adding seasonings, vegetables and water or beef consommé. Cover and bring to 15 pounds pressure. Cook 11 minutes per pound. Remove to platter and thicken gravy with a blend of flour and water, boiling 3 to 5 minutes, stirring constantly. Serve with corn fritters, broccoli and spiced peaches. Yield: 6 to 8 portions.

STUFFED PORK CHOPS

4 pork chops, 1 inch thick
1 1/2 slices day-old bread, broken into small pieces
1/3 cup whole kernel corn
2 teaspoons finely cut green pepper
2 teaspoons minced onion
2 teaspoons finely cut celery
1/2 teaspoon salt
1/2 cup seasoned flour
2 tablespoons hot fat
4 medium potatoes
4 medium onions
4 medium carrots
1 teaspoon salt
1/2 cup water

Have pockets cut in pork chops. Combine bread, corn, green pepper, onion, celery and salt. Stuff into pockets of pork chops. Dredge in seasoned flour. Brown slowly on one side in hot fat in pressure saucepan. Turn chops. Place potatoes, onions and carrots on top of chops. Season, add water. Bring to 15 pounds pressure. Cook 15 minutes. Yield: 4 portions.

TONGUE SPANISH STYLE

1 beef tongue	½ cup fresh or frozen peas
2 cups water	½ cup cut green beans, fresh or
½ cup diced carrots	frozen
½ cup diced turnips	8 small onions
½ cup diced celery	8 cherry tomatoes or 3 large ones,
1 cup diced potatoes	quartered

2 tablespoons prepared mustard

Wash and dry off tongue. (If smoked tongue is used, see page 344 for preparation). Place tongue on rack in pan. Add water and bring to 15 pounds pressure. Cook 45 minutes. Reduce pressure quickly. Remove skin from tongue and keep warm. If more than 1 cup liquid remains, pour off excess. Place vegetables in pan, add 1 teaspoon of salt if fresh tongue is used. Bring to 15 pounds pressure. Cook 5 minutes. Serve tongue sliced on platter surrounded by vegetables. Thicken gravy with browned flour, using extra water from tongue to make additional gravy. Add mustard to gravy and blend. Yield: 6 to 8 portions.

HUNGARIAN GOULASH

½ pound beef, cut into 1 inch cubes	½ teaspoon paprika
	½ bay leaf
1 pound veal, cut into 1 inch cubes	½ teaspoon dried marjoram
	4 medium potatoes
2 tablespoons drippings	4 medium carrots, cut crosswise
1 large onion, sliced	4 small turnips
1 teaspoon salt	1 green pepper, cut fine
¼ teaspoon pepper	2 cups water

Brown meat with drippings in pressure saucepan. Add remaining ingredients. Cover and bring to 15 pounds pressure. Cook 15 minutes. Reduce pressure quickly. Yield: 4 portions.

HOT POTATO SALAD WITH FRANKFURTERS

5 potatoes cut into slices	¼ cup salad oil
1 pound frankfurters, cut into 1 inch pieces	¼ cup sugar
	1 teaspoon salt
⅓ cup finely chopped onion	2 tablespoons finely cut pimiento
½ cup vinegar	2 tablespoons minced parsley

Place potatoes, frankfurters and onions in pressure saucepan. Add vinegar, salad oil, sugar and salt which has been blended well. Cover and cook at 15 pounds pressure 3 minutes. Reduce pressure quickly. Garnish with pimiento and parsley. Yield: 4 portions.

PRESSURE–COOKED HAM

Scrub mild-cured ham and place rind side up on rack in large pressure cooker; or soak well-scrubbed strongly cured ham, home-cured ham, picnic or shoulder butts overnight or longer before cooking. Add about 2 cups water, or enough to cover bottom of cooker, clamp lid securely and heat, with petcock open, until steam has escaped for 5 minutes. Then close petcock; when pressure gauge registers 10 pounds, adjust heat to maintain this pressure until ham is cooked. It will require 12 to 15 minutes for each pound at 10 pounds pressure, or about 2½ hours for a 12 pound ham. Turn off heat and let pressure fall to zero; then wait 5 minutes, open petcock and take off lid. Remove rind, spread with desired sugar mixture and bake in moderate oven (350° F.) about 30 minutes, or until glazed, basting several times.

FLANK STEAK ROLL

Score a 3-pound flank steak and spread with dressing (page 485). Season with salt and pepper. Roll and tie securely. Brown on all sides in ¼ cup hot fat in pressure saucepan. Add ½ cup tomato juice and cook at 15 pounds pressure 40 minutes. The last 5 minutes reduce the pressure to zero quickly and add lima beans and sliced carrots, each wrapped in water-moistened parchment paper and tied bag like, and ½ cup water. Cook 5 minutes at 15 pounds pressure. Reduce pressure quickly. Approximate yield: 6 portions.

15-MINUTE DINNERS IN PRESSURE SAUCEPAN

BEEF STEW

2 pounds beef, cut into 2 inch cubes	½ teaspoon paprika
2 tablespoons fat	¼ cup minced onion
2 teaspoons salt	5 medium carrots, cut crosswise
¼ teaspoon pepper	5 medium potatoes
	1½ cups water

Brown meat in melted fat in pressure saucepan. Add remaining ingredients. Cover and bring to 15 pounds pressure. Cook 12 minutes. Reduce pressure quickly. To thicken gravy add 3 tablespoons flour blended with ½ cup cold water and cook until it is smooth and thickened, stirring constantly. Yield: 4 portions.

MEAT CABBAGE ROLLS

1 large head cabbage	1 cup cooked rice
1 pound ground beef	1 cup milk
2 teaspoons salt	2 tablespoons fat
¼ teaspoon pepper	2 tablespoons brown sugar

½ cup hot water

Dip cabbage leaves in hot water. Dry leaves on clean towel. Combine meat, salt, pepper, cooked rice and milk and mix well. Place a tablespoon of meat mixture in each leaf; roll cabbage leaf around meat and fasten with toothpick. Brown rolls lightly in hot fat in pressure saucepan. Sprinkle with brown sugar, add hot water, cover and bring to 15 pounds pressure. Cook 10 minutes. Reduce pressure quickly. Approximate yield: 4 portions.

STUFFED GREEN PEPPERS

6 green peppers	1 egg
1 pound ground beef	¼ cup milk
½ cup cooked rice	¼ cup chopped onion
1¼ teaspoons salt	1 can (No. 1) condensed tomato
¼ teaspoon pepper	soup

1 cup water

Wash peppers and remove seeds. Combine ground beef, rice, salt, pepper, egg, milk and onion. Stuff peppers lightly and place on rack in pressure saucepan. Add tomato soup and water. Cover and bring to 15 pounds pressure. Cook 12 minutes. Reduce pressure quickly. Yield: 6 portions.

HAMBURGER DINNER

1 pound ground beef	½ teaspoon salt
1 egg	¼ teaspoon pepper
½ cup fine bread crumbs	2 tablespoons hot fat
¼ cup minced onion	4 to 6 potatoes
¼ teaspoon herb seasoning, if	8 to 12 small onions or 12 to 18
desired	whole carrots

½ cup water

Combine beef, egg, bread crumbs, onion, herb seasoning, salt and pepper. Form into 4 to 6 patties. Brown well on one side in pressure saucepan in fat. Turn patties. Place potatoes and onions, or carrots, on top of patties. Add water and cook at 10 pounds pressure 10 minutes. Reduce pressure quickly. Season. Yield: 4 to 6 portions.

NEW YORK SPECIAL DINNER

2 tablespoons fat
½ to 1 pound ground beef
½ to 1 cup sliced onions
1 cup split quick-cooking green
    peas

2 teaspoons salt
1¼ cups canned tomatoes
1 teaspoon sugar
1 teaspoon Worcestershire sauce
1 cup water

Brown ground beef and onions in melted fat in pressure saucepan. Add remaining ingredients. Cover and bring to 15 pounds pressure. Cook 10 minutes. Reduce pressure quickly. Yield: 4 portions.

MEAT LOAF DINNER

1 pound ground beef
1½ teaspoons salt
⅛ teaspoon pepper
1 egg, beaten
2 slices dry bread, soaked in
    water

¼ cup chopped onion
¼ cup diced celery
2 tablespoons fat
5 medium potatoes
4 medium carrots, cut crosswise
½ cup water

½ cup tomato sauce

At least 30 minutes before cooking, combine beef with salt, pepper, egg, bread, onion and celery. Mix well, form into 4 small loaves, wrap in waxed paper and chill. Remove waxed paper. Brown in melted fat in pressure saucepan. Arrange vegetables around meat; add water and tomato sauce. Cover and bring to 15 pounds pressure. Cook 10 minutes. Reduce pressure. Yield: 4 portions.

5-MINUTE VEGETABLE DINNER WITH LAMB

1 small eggplant, halved
    lengthwise
lamb suet
1 pound breast or shoulder of
    lamb, diced
⅓ cup minced onion

1 teaspoon salt
¼ teaspoon pepper
1 cup potato balls
1 cup green beans
4 carrots, halved
½ cup water

Scoop out eggplant, leaving ½-inch rim. Place in cold water. Fry suet in bottom of cooker. Add lamb, onion, salt and pepper. Brown lightly and stuff shells. Put shells and vegetables on rack. Add water, adjust cover and bring to 15 pounds pressure. Cook five minutes. Reduce pressure immediately. Yield: 2 large portions.

5-MINUTE LIVER DINNER

2 pounds beef liver, cut into
   serving pieces
1 teaspoon salt
¼ teaspoon pepper
¼ cup flour

¼ cup butter or margarine
6 medium potatoes, quartered
2 cups lima beans
6 small onions
½ cup water

Roll liver in seasoned flour; brown in melted butter or margarine in pressure saucepan. Place on rack in pan and add remaining ingredients. Cover; bring to 15 pounds pressure and cook 5 minutes. Cool quickly. Yield: 6 portions.

5-MINUTE CHICKEN DINNER

1 small fryer, cut in serving
   pieces
½ teaspoon salt
¼ teaspoon pepper
flour

3 tablespoons fat or oil
¾ pound cabbage, cut in wedges
2 large ears of corn, halved
1 cup whole green beans
½ cup water

Roll chicken in seasoned flour. Brown in hot fat in pressure saucepan. Place on rack; add cabbage, corn, beans and water. Quickly adjust cover and bring to 15 pounds pressure. Cook five minutes. Reduce pressure immediately. Yield: 2 large portions.

5-MINUTE SALMON DINNER

1 1½-pound salmon slice, 1½
   inches thick
1 teaspoon salt
¼ teaspoon pepper
3 tablespoons butter

2 zucchini, halved
2 cups potato balls
4 small white turnips
4 carrots, halved
½ cup water

Rub salmon with salt and pepper. Lightly brown in melted butter in pressure pan. Place on rack and add remaining ingredients. Adjust cover. Bring to 15 pounds pressure and cook 5 minutes. Cool immediately. Yield: 4 portions.

5-MINUTE SPAGHETTI DINNER

1½ pounds beef, finely ground
½ cup olive oil or fat
1½ cups sliced onion
1 small clove garlic

½ cup diced green pepper
½ cup mushrooms (if desired)
2 6-ounce cans tomato paste
1 No. 2 can tomatoes

10 ounces spaghetti, cooked

Brown meat in oil. Add other ingredients except spaghetti. Cover and bring to 15 pounds pressure. Cook five minutes. Reduce pressure instantly. Serve on spaghetti cooked separately. Yield: 6 portions.

CHICKEN AND DUMPLINGS

1 chicken (4 to 5 lb.) cut into serving-sized pieces	1¾ cups sifted all-purpose flour
1½ cups water	2 teaspoons baking powder
2 teaspoons salt	¾ teaspoon salt
½ cup cold water	1 tablespoon shortening
	¾ cup milk

Wash chicken and dry on absorbent paper. Place in pressure saucepan with water and salt. If desired, add other seasoning. Cook at 10 pounds pressure 40 minutes. Reduce pressure quickly. Remove cover and test chicken for tenderness; cook longer, if necessary. Remove part of cooked chicken, leaving large bony pieces to support dumplings. Gradually add water to ¼ cup flour. Add broth and stir until well blended. Return to saucepan and bring to boiling. Sift together 1½ cups flour, baking powder and salt. Add milk and stir until just blended. Drop by tablespoonfuls onto boiling chicken. Cook, uncovered, 10 minutes. Cover and cook 10 minutes longer. Remove dumplings and chicken; arrange on hot platter and spoon gravy over top of dumplings. Yield: 6 portions.

PRESSURE-COOKED DUCKLING

If duck is to be used in salad, chop suey, duck à la king, duck pie or casserole of duck, it can be cooked quickly and satisfactorily in a pressure saucepan. Have meat dealer cut duck in quarters if it is to be cooked in a 6- or 7-quart cooker, smaller servings if the cooker is 4-quart size. Prepare duck for cooking. Place 1 cup water and rack in pressure saucepan. Place duck, together with giblets and neck, in cooker. Sprinkle with 1 teaspoon salt. Cook at 15 pounds pressure for 10 minutes. Let pressure come down gradually. Remove duck. Pour broth into suitable container. Allow fat to rise and pour it off. Use duck meat, duck fat and the broth as needed, or store in refrigerator for later use.

If duck is to be served barbecued or in any kind of special sauce, it may be pre-browned before cooking in the pressure saucepan. This improves the flavor. Have meat dealer cut duck in serving-size pieces. Prepare for cooking and braise in uncovered pressure saucepan or large frying pan. When duck is browned, cook in pressure saucepan as directed above. Reduce pressure as rapidly as possible. Pour off broth and fat. Add desired sauce to duck and simmer, uncovered, over low heat until the flavor of the sauce has permeated the duck meat. Serve immediately.

PRESSURE SAUCEPAN SAVORY BEEF

3 large onions, sliced	2 teaspoons salt
3 tablespoons hot fat	¼ teaspoon pepper
2 pounds beef chuck (or rump)	¼ teaspoon thyme
cut into small serving-size	1 cup boiling water
pieces	1 tablespoon ketchup
3 tablespoons all-purpose flour	2 tablespoons vinegar

Brown onions in hot fat in bottom of pressure saucepan. Add beef and
brown thoroughly. Combine flour, salt, pepper and thyme and stir into
beef and onions. Combine water, ketchup and vinegar and gradually
stir into meat mixture. Cook at 10 pounds pressure for 45 minutes. Reduce pressure. Stir well. If a thinner gravy is desired, add more hot
water. Approximate yield: 6 to 8 portions.

WHITE FRUIT CAKE

1½ cups sifted all-purpose flour	3 eggs
1½ teaspoons baking powder	¼ cup pineapple juice
½ teaspoon salt	2 cups chopped, mixed dried or
½ cup butter or margarine	candied fruits
½ cup sugar	4 cups water

Sift together 1 cup flour, baking powder and salt. Cream butter until
soft and smooth; gradually add sugar, beating until fluffy. Beat in thoroughly one egg at a time. Add flour mixture alternately with pineapple
juice, beating until smooth after each addition. Add fruit mixed with
remaining ½ cup flour and mix well. Turn into a greased mold (not
more than two-thirds full) and cover tightly with double thickness of
waxed paper (fasten with string). Place on rack with water in cooker.
Cover and allow steam to flow through vent 15 minutes, then bring to
15 pounds pressure. Cook 40 minutes. Yield: 1 small cake.

QUICK BROWN BETTY

1 cup dry bread crumbs,	juice and rind of 1 lemon
slightly browned	3 medium apples, sliced
¼ cup sugar	¼ cup butter, melted
½ teaspoon cinnamon	½ cup water

Combine bread crumbs, sugar, cinnamon, juice and rind of lemon.
Place alternate layers of apples and crumbs in buttered bowl or mold
fitting loosely into saucepan. Pour melted butter over ingredients,
cover mold with waxed paper and tie securely. Put bowl on rack with
water in saucepan. Cover cooker and bring to 15 pounds pressure.
Cook 15 minutes. Reduce pressure quickly. Yield: 6 portions.

QUICK INDIAN PUDDING

1 quart milk
1 cup yellow cornmeal
½ cup molasses
⅓ cup sugar
½ teaspoon salt

½ cup raisins
½ cup chopped nuts
2 teaspoons powdered ginger
2 tablespoons butter
1 cup hot water

Scald 3 cups milk in top of double boiler. Mix cornmeal with remaining cup of milk. Stir into scalded milk. Cook and stir over moderate heat until thickened. Add molasses, sugar, salt, raisins, nuts, ginger and butter. Pour well-mixed cornmeal mixture into buttered metal mold that fits into cooker. Add hot water. Place mold on rack. Cover and bring to 15 pounds pressure. Cook 15 minutes. Reduce pressure quickly. Serve with plain, whipped, or ice cream. Yield: 6 portions.

QUICK BREAD PUDDING

3 slices bread, cubed
1 tablespoon butter, melted
¼ teaspoon salt
½ cup brown sugar
½ teaspoon cinnamon

2 cups milk, scalded
2 eggs, slightly beaten
½ teaspoon vanilla
½ cup raisins
½ cup nuts, chopped

4 cups water

Combine bread, butter, salt, sugar, cinnamon, milk, eggs, vanilla, raisins and nuts. Mix well and turn into well-buttered bowl or mold that fits into saucepan. Cover mold with two thicknesses of waxed paper tied over the top; place on rack with the water in saucepan. Cover and bring to 15 pounds pressure. Cook 15 minutes. Reduce pressure quickly. Yield: 4 portions.

QUICK CUSTARD

3 eggs
¼ cup sugar
¼ teaspoon salt

2 cups scalded milk
1 teaspoon vanilla
¼ teaspoon nutmeg

1 cup water

Beat eggs, add sugar and salt. Slowly stir milk into egg mixture. Add vanilla and nutmeg. Pour into well-buttered individual custard cups. Cover with waxed paper and tie securely. Place cups on rack, add water and cook at 15 pounds pressure 4 minutes. Reduce pressure quickly. Yield: 6 portions.

QUICK ENGLISH PLUM PUDDING

½ cup sugar
2 eggs, well beaten
½ cup ground suet
⅓ cup milk
½ cup currants
½ cup raisins
1 cup flour

1½ teaspoons baking powder
½ teaspoon allspice
½ teaspoon cinnamon
½ teaspoon nutmeg
¼ teaspoon cloves
½ teaspoon salt
½ cup chopped walnuts

5 cups water

Combine sugar, egg and suet; add milk, currants and raisins and mix well. Sift together all dry ingredients and gradually stir into suet-fruit mixture. Add nuts. Turn into well buttered mold that fits into saucepan. Cover with two thicknesses of waxed paper tied over the top. Cover and allow steam to flow from vent 20 minutes, then bring to 15 pounds pressure. Cook 50 minutes. Reduce pressure quickly. Yield: 6 portions.

QUICK PRUNE PUDDING

½ cup sifted all-purpose flour
⅓ cup sugar
2 teaspoons baking powder
¼ teaspoon soda
½ teaspoon salt
¼ teaspoon cinnamon

⅔ cup chopped, cooked prunes
2 tablespoons butter
1 egg
⅓ cup chopped nuts
2 teaspoons grated lemon rind
1 cup boiling water

Sift together flour, sugar, baking powder, soda, salt and cinnamon. Add prunes, butter, egg, nuts and lemon rind. Stir until well blended. Divide batter into 3 well-greased 8-ounce jelly glasses. Cover glasses with jelly glass lids or three thicknesses of waxed paper and tie securely. Place on rack in pressure saucepan with 1 cup boiling water. Cook at 10 pounds pressure 45 minutes. Reduce pressure quickly. Cut puddings in half and serve warm with hot Lemon Sauce (page 727). Yield: 6 portions.

PRESSURE COOKED VEGETABLES

Fresh vegetables can be cooked in a very short time in a pressure saucepan. This method saves fuel as well as time and protects vitamins, minerals, appearance and in some cases, the flavor. To cook vegetables in a pressure saucepan, place ½ cup salted hot water and then the vegetable in pressure saucepan, cover, adjust cover. As soon as live steam escapes, seal and allow pressure to rise as quickly as possible and cook just the required time, no more. (Follow manufacturer's directions for using cooker.) When time is up, reduce pressure quickly. When pressure is down, remove vegetables, season and serve. If you are cooking two or more vegetables at a time, each may be wrapped in parchment paper. You need not defrost frozen vegetables before cooking them in a pressure saucepan but you do need to break them apart with a fork so that the heat penetration can be even. Place ½ cup boiling water or less in the cooker, add vegetables, adjust cover, exhaust air, adjust pressure gauge over vent, bring pressure up to 15 pounds and cook required time. Do not overcook by allowing vegetables to stand in cooker after processing.

Dried vegetables such as beans, peas and other legumes are an inexpensive form of protein. If cooked in a pressure saucepan they need to be washed, then soaked for an hour, drained and cooked at 15 pounds pressure 25 to 30 minutes.

Entertaining a Crowd

MANY TIMES you may be called upon to plan the food service for a crowd of people—either in your own home or as chairman of a club or church dinner committee. Entertaining should be as much fun for the hostess and the committee members as for the guests. A well thought-out plan for the food service and a schedule of work for the helpers enable one to serve fifty or more people easily and smoothly.

To help you with your plans, we have suggested here some menus for teas, holiday meals, suppers—indoors and out—luncheons and dinners that you may use as a springboard to your own meal planning. As you will note, we have included many recipes listed on the menus in this chapter, developed for approximately 24 or 48 servings. Expand these recipes, or divide them in two (in most cases), as the occasion warrants. A basic shopping list is given at the end of the chapter to help you plan your additional menus and marketing.

Italian Dinner
Antipasto *
Italian Spaghetti *
Stuffed Baked Tomatoes *
Cauliflower and Green Bean Salad *
Italian Bread Sticks   Italian Bread
Cheese Tray   Fresh Fruits
Coffee   Chianti

Outdoor Supper
Grilled Hamburgers *
Creamed Potatoes *
Sliced Tomatoes   Corn on Cob
Hamburger Buns   Butter
Cherry Cobbler *
Coffee

Dinner for Men
Chicken Liver Hors d'Œuvres *
German Sauerbraten Beef *
Potato Pancakes *   Red Cabbage *
Pumpernickel   Swedish Rye Crisp
Rich Apple Raisin Pie *
Coffee   Tea

Fish for Friday
Fish Fillets with Wine Sauce *
Shoestring Potatoes
Fresh-from-garden Salad Bowl
French Dressing
Toasted Parmesan Cheese Sticks *
Chocolate Roll *
Coffee

Spring Club Luncheon

Cream of Mushroom Soup
Tuna Fish Salad Ring *
Garnishes of Tomato, Cauliflower,
Olives, Pepper Rings
Buttered Zucchini and Baby White
Onions
Lemon Sponge Custard * or
Pecan Pie *
Coffee   Tea

Garden Luncheon

Tossed Garden Salad *
Cold Ham and Cheese Slices
Escalloped Corn
French Bread   Butter
Fruit Shortcake *

Summer Time Dinner Menu

Chilled Vichyssoise
Famous Curried Chicken on
Fluffy Rice *
Hot Buttered Cloverleaf Rolls
Spring Green Salad Bowl
Basil Dressing
Pineapple Icebox Pudding *
Coffee   Tea

Autumn Luncheon

Frosted Apricot Nectar
Chicken Turnovers *   Cream Gravy *
Green Beans and Mushrooms
Crisp Corn Sticks
Autumn Cranberry Salad Ring Mold *
Chocolate Fudge Pudding *
Coffee   Tea

Winter Club Luncheon

Hot Tomato Bouillon
Veal Birds en Casserole *
Carrot Soufflé   Buttered Green Peas
Arabian Peach Salad *
English Cheese Tart *
Coffee   Tea

Fare for Men

Smoked Ham Loaf *
Broiled Peaches with Rum
Celery   Olives   Radishes
Hot Garlic Bread
Mexican Corn and Peas
Escalloped Potatoes
Raspberry Whip *
Coffee

Plate Luncheon

Shrimp in Tomato Aspic *
in Lettuce Cups
Buttered Fresh Asparagus
Deviled Eggs
Hot Cheese Biscuits
Water Cress Sandwiches *
Banana Cream Cake   Coffee

Menu for Home Tea Party

Cucumber Sandwich Rounds *
Rolled Water Cress Sandwiches *
Petite Jelly Roll * or Madeleines *
Filled Cup Cakes with Chocolate
Frosting
Tea with Cream or Lemon
Mints   Nuts   Wafers

Tea Party for 200 People

Assorted Tea Sandwiches
Little Cakes
Tea with Cream or Lemon
Mints   Nuts   Candies
For the above menu for 200 people,
order 9 dozen sandwich squares, which,
cut into fours, equals 432 sandwiches,
about 2 to each guest. Little cakes may
be ordered by the pound; 12 pounds
will be sufficient.

ANTIPASTO

Prepare platters or trays with tiny anchovy canapés, garnished with rings of green pepper. In a circle around the canapés arrange overlapping thin slices of salami. Garnish with stuffed deviled eggs, stuffed ripe olives, celery sticks, tiny red whole peppers pickled.

CHICKEN LIVER HORS D'ŒUVRES

48 chicken livers
1 cup prepared mustard
1 cup finely chopped olives
48 slices bacon, cut in halves
2 cups dry bread crumbs

Rinse chicken livers in cold water and cut each in half; spread with mixture of mustard and olives. Wrap bacon around each piece, fasten with a toothpick and roll in crumbs. Bake in hot oven (425° F.) 10 to 15 minutes. Yield: 8 dozen portions.

FAMOUS CURRIED CHICKEN ON FLUFFY RICE

12 fowl (3½ lbs. each), cut in
  pieces
9 quarts boiling water
2 tablespoons salt
18 medium-sized onions, minced
36 stalks celery, minced
12 apples, minced
3 cups olive oil
1½ cups curry powder
1½ teaspoons pepper
1 tablespoon ginger
1 tablespoon Tabasco sauce
6 tablespoons Worcestershire
  sauce
1½ cups flour
3 cups cold water
6 fresh coconuts
3 quarts heavy cream
18 egg yolks, well beaten
36 cups boiled rice, molded in
  ring (page 507)

Add cleaned chicken to boiling water and simmer until tender, adding salt when half done; reserve stock, pick meat from bones and cut in smaller pieces. Sauté onions, celery and apples in olive oil until slightly browned; stir in curry powder and simmer 5 minutes; add remaining seasonings and chicken stock (6 quarts) and cook 20 minutes; stir in flour mixed with water and cook 5 minutes, stirring until thickened. Drain milk from coconut and add with chicken to vegetable-curry mixture, remove from heat and let stand 3 hours. When ready to serve, add cream and egg yolks and heat thoroughly, stirring constantly. Serve in hot rice ring with shredded fresh coconut. Yield: 50 portions.

VEAL BIRDS EN CASSEROLE

12 pounds veal steak, ½-inch thick

½ pound fat salt pork

4 cups soft bread crumbs

8 egg yolks

meat stock

1 tablespoon salt

1 teaspoon black pepper

½ cup Worcestershire sauce

flour

1 cup bacon fat

2 cups hot consommé

Wipe veal, cut off skin and fat and remove bone; pound meat until thin and cut into individual servings. Grind veal trimmings and pork; mix with bread crumbs, eggs, moisten with stock and add salt, pepper and Worcestershire sauce. Spread stuffing over each piece of veal, to within ⅛-inch of the edge, roll and fasten with toothpicks. Sprinkle with salt and pepper, roll in flour and sauté in hot bacon fat. Place in greased casserole or baking pan, cover and bake in slow oven (300° to 325° F.) about 1 hour, basting occasionally with bacon fat mixed with hot consommé. Serve with Brown Gravy (page 291) made from drippings in pan. Approximate yield: 50 portions or 100 veal birds.

TUNA FISH SALAD RING

10 envelopes unflavored gelatin

10 tablespoons lemon juice

10 tablespoons cold water

1¼ quarts boiling water

5 13-oz. cans tuna fish

2½ cups diced celery

2½ cups cabbage, finely shredded

2½ cups carrots, finely shredded

1¼ quarts mayonnaise

1¼ teaspoons salt

10 hard-cooked eggs

Soak gelatin in lemon juice and cold water. Soak 5 minutes. Add boiling water and stir until dissolved. Chill until about consistency of honey; then add fish, vegetables and mayonnaise. Slice eggs and use to line bottom of molds. Pour gelatin mixture into individual molds (3 oz.) or ring molds or rectangular pans and cut in squares. Chill well. Yield: 50 portions.

PAN GRAVY

8 ounces fat (meat drippings)

2 cups flour

1 tablespoon salt

1 teaspoon pepper

1 gallon water or meat stock

Melt fat; add flour and stir until smooth; add salt and pepper. Gradually add water, stirring constantly. Cook until smooth and thick.

Brown—Use 2½ cups flour and brown in the fat.

Cream—Substitute milk for water or stock.

Giblet—Use chicken drippings for the fat and chicken broth for the liquid. Add 1 quart cooked giblets, chopped.

CHICKEN TURNOVERS

3 quarts milk
4 slices onion
1 medium carrot
3 bay leaves
1½ cups butter or margarine

3 cups all-purpose flour
1 tablespoon salt
2½ pounds chicken, cooked and
  diced
1 recipe Pie Pastry (page 736)

Heat 1 quart milk, chopped onion, diced carrot and bay leaves. Strain and combine with remaining milk. Make a white sauce of butter, flour, milk and salt. Add diced chicken and mix well. Cool. Roll out pastry and cut in 5-inch rounds or squares. Place ¼ cup of chicken mixture in center of each pastry round. Fold over and press edges with a fork. Prick top. Bake in hot oven (400° F.) for 15 minutes, reduce to 350° F. and bake 15 minutes longer. Yield: 48 portions.

Note: Tongue or ham may be substituted for chicken.

GERMAN SAUERBRATEN BEEF

20 pounds pot roast (use
  chuck or round)
2 gallons water
2 quarts vinegar
1 pound brown sugar

½ cup pickle spices
4 medium-sized onions
2 cups celery leaves
4 medium carrots
½ garlic bud

Brown meat in fat and cover with above ingredients. Let stand 3 days to one week. Simmer until tender. Remove meat and strain liquid. Thicken stock for gravy. Add 1 cup sour cream or evaporated milk for each gallon of gravy. Yield: 50 portions.

GRILLED HAMBURGERS

12 pounds ground beef
6 eggs, slightly beaten
⅔ cup salt

2 cups chopped onion
2 cups dry bread crumbs
2 cups flour

½ pound shortening

Combine meat, slightly beaten eggs, salt, onion and crumbs. Shape into flat patties, one per serving. Dip in flour. Place in a large roasting pan in melted shortening and bake in a slow oven (325° F.) about 20 minutes. Yield: 50 patties.

ITALIAN SPAGHETTI

8 pounds of ground beef
16 small onions, chopped
1 cup chopped parsley
8 cups minced carrots
8 cups minced celery
4 pounds mushrooms, sliced
16 cloves garlic
1 cup butter or margarine
1 cup olive oil

4 teaspoons cloves
4 teaspoons cinnamon
salt and pepper
16 cups canned tomatoes,
   strained
16 cups stock or water
1 cup Italian tomato paste
9 8-oz. packages spaghetti
4 cups grated Parmesan cheese

Sauté meat and vegetables in butter and oil until almost tender; add seasonings, tomatoes, stock and tomato paste and simmer about 1 hour, removing garlic when flavor becomes pronounced. Cook unbroken spaghetti (page 499), place in ring on hot platter, fill center with heated sauce and pour some over spaghetti; sprinkle with cheese. Yield: 50 portions.

TOMATO ASPIC WITH SHRIMP

4½ envelopes plain gelatin
1⅛ cups cold water
1¼ quarts canned tomatoes
½ teaspoon Worcestershire
   sauce
¼ cup mild vinegar
1½ teaspoons salt
1½ teaspoons paprika
1½ tablespoons onion juice

½ tablespoon lemon juice
3 7-ounce cans shrimp or 1 quart
   cooked, clean fresh shrimp,
   diced
1 cup chopped celery
1 medium green pepper, finely
   chopped
3 heads lettuce
1 cup seasoned salad dressing
12 deviled eggs, halved

Stir gelatin into cold water and stand 15 to 20 minutes. Strain tomatoes and heat. Add gelatin and dissolve; add Worcestershire sauce, vinegar, paprika, salt, pepper; if desired, onion and lemon juice. Cool. When the mixture begins to congeal, add the diced shrimp, reserving a few whole shrimp for garnishing. Add celery and green pepper and turn into 24 individual molds rinsed with cold water and chill. When firm, unmold on crisp lettuce leaf and garnish with whole shrimp, mayonnaise and deviled eggs, the yolk put through a fancy pastry tube. Yield: 24 portions.

HAM LOAF

3 pounds smoked ham, ground
3 pounds fresh ham, ground
6 eggs, well beaten
4½ teaspoons Worcestershire
  sauce
¾ teaspoon black pepper,
  freshly ground

1½ quarts milk
¾ pound crackers
¾ cup brown sugar
1½ teaspoons dry mustard
1½ cups chili sauce

Combine and blend ham, eggs, Worcestershire sauce, pepper, milk and crackers. Turn into three greased loaf pans and sprinkle the top with brown sugar and mustard. Coat with chili sauce. Bake about 2 hours, or until done, in a moderate oven (350° F.). Line platters with canned peach halves, broiled with rum and brown sugar, prunes in center. Yield: 24 portions.

FISH FILLETS WITH CUCUMBER

12 double fillets of sole or
  halibut
2 slices bacon, cooked
1 small onion, minced
½ cup sautéed mushrooms

2 cups chopped cucumbers
3 cups soft bread crumbs
salt and pepper
1 tablespoon butter, melted
1 egg, slightly beaten

Wash fillets, dry and cut in halves. Spread with a thin layer of the following stuffing and roll; chop together bacon, onion, mushrooms and cucumbers. Add remaining ingredients and mix well. Place rolled fillets in baking dish and pour over ½ cup white wine and 1 cup water. Cover with waxed paper and a lid and bake in a moderate oven (350° F.) 30 to 35 minutes, or until the fillets are tender. Serve with White Wine Sauce (below), using left-over white wine from fish, and garnish with sautéed mushrooms and water cress. Yield: 24 fillets.

WHITE WINE SAUCE

⅓ cup butter
⅓ cup flour
3 cups clam juice
1 tablespoon tomato paste
¼ cup dry white wine

3 tablespoons butter
2 egg yolks
¼ cup heavy cream
2 cups cooked whole shrimp

Melt butter in saucepan and stir in flour off the heat. Gradually add the clam juice and tomato paste, stirring constantly until sauce comes to a boil. Bit by bit add 3 tablespoons butter. Add the egg yolks mixed with heavy cream and again bring to a boil, stirring constantly. Add cooked shrimp, wine and season to taste. Yield: 6 cups sauce.

TOSSED GARDEN SALAD

8 medium heads lettuce	2 medium-sized green peppers,
2 medium heads cabbage,	chopped
shredded	1 cup finely chopped onion
4 medium carrots, sliced	12 medium tomatoes
6 bunches radishes, sliced	2 tablespoons salt
6 bunches celery, sliced	2½–3 cups French dressing

Combine all ingredients and chill. Just before serving toss lightly with dressing. Serve in salad bowls. Yield: 50 portions.

CAULIFLOWER AND GREEN BEAN SALAD

Separate 4 pounds raw cauliflower heads into tiny flowerettes, wash, drain; combine with 4 pounds cooked green beans, strips of pimiento (3 cans), 8 ounces chopped onion and 36 ripe olives. Toss with 1 quart snappy French dressing and serve heaped on a bed of chicory (4 heads). Yield: 50 portions.

AUTUMN CRANBERRY SALAD RING MOLD

3 oranges (sections and rind)	4 cups sugar
3⅓ pounds cranberries	5 pints lemon gelatin (5 pkgs.)

Put oranges and cranberries through food grinder. Dissolve sugar in hot gelatin liquid. When gelatin begins to congeal, add ground oranges and cranberries. Pour into molds. Yield: 50 portions.

ARABIAN PEACH SALAD

1½ tablespoons whole cloves	1½ quarts drained, canned,
4½ cups canned peach juice	sliced peaches
1½ cups vinegar	2⅓ cups orange gelatin powder
3 cups sugar	or 7 pkgs. flavored gelatin
16 3-inch sticks of cinnamon or	
1½ ounces	

Tie cloves loosely in small cheesecloth bag. Combine peach juice, vinegar, sugar and stick cinnamon. Add cloves and bring to boil. Add peaches; simmer 10 minutes. Remove peaches and spices; add water to syrup to make 3 quarts. Dissolve gelatin in hot liquid. Chill until slightly thickened. Fold peaches into gelatin. Pour into individual molds (3 oz.) or rectangular pans to a depth of 1¼ inches. Chill until firm. Cut in squares. Serve on crisp lettuce. Garnish with mayonnaise. Yield: 48 portions.

CREAMED POTATOES

15 to 17 pounds potatoes	2 cups flour
2 cups shortening	2⅔ tablespoons salt
4 quarts milk	

Scrub potatoes and cook with skins on in rapidly boiling water or pressure saucepan. Remove skins and cut potatoes into 1½-inch slices. Place potatoes in large shallow roasting pan (8 x 12 x 2 inches). Cover with white sauce made by melting shortening with flour and salt in double boiler; add milk gradually and stir over hot water until thick. Keep potatoes hot (over hot water or in oven) until ready to serve. Sprinkle paprika lightly over potatoes just before serving. Yield: 50 portions.

RED CABBAGE

4 heads (12 pounds) cabbage, cut	3 apples, peeled and quartered
1½ dozen whole cloves	1 cup vinegar
2 pieces stick cinnamon	½ cup brown sugar
4 bay leaves	¼ pound butter or margarine
	2 large onions, peeled and sliced
2 cups water	

Shred cabbage. Add seasonings, onions and apples. Cook until tender (about 20 minutes). Yield: 50 portions (3-oz. or ½ cup).

POTATO PANCAKES

4 quarts potatoes, peeled and quartered	2 teaspoons baking powder
4 large onions	2 teaspoons salt
3 cups flour	¼ teaspoon pepper
	6 eggs, separated

Grind together potatoes and onions. Add dry ingredients. Separate eggs, add yolks and fold in beaten egg whites. Fry on hot griddle as needed. Approximate yield: 100 3-inch cakes, serve 2 per order.

CARROT SOUFFLÉ

12 cups carrots (cooked and put through ricer)	1 tablespoon pepper
2 tablespoons salt	2 tablespoons chopped onion
	18 eggs, beaten lightly
1½ quarts milk	

Combine all ingredients. Bake in ring molds set in water in slow oven (325° F.) for 1 hour. Turn out and fill with buttered peas. Approximate yield: 50 portions.

PETITE JELLY ROLL

5 eggs, separated   4 tablespoons sifted cake flour
4 tablespoons sugar   ½ teaspoon vanilla
                1 cup red currant jelly

Beat yolks until light and lemon-colored, adding the sugar gradually.
Fold in carefully the sifted flour, stiffly beaten egg whites and vanilla.
Grease two jelly roll pans (10½ x 15½ x ½ inches), cover with waxed
paper and grease again. Spread half of mixture in each pan, evenly on
top. Bake in 400° F. oven 10 minutes, or until golden brown on top.
Loosen edges from pans. Sprinkle tops of cake with granulated sugar.
Turn each onto large pieces of waxed paper and carefully pull off the
waxed paper on which each was baked. Roll waxed paper in with cake
and refrigerate 2 hours. Unroll and cut each cake in half lengthwise.
Spread each section with jelly and roll tightly, making a roll about the
width of a half dollar. Cover and refrigerate until serving time and
cut into thin slices. Yield: 10 dozen. *Note:* This recipe may be halved,
using 2 large eggs.

MADELEINES

1 vanilla stick   1 cup sugar
¼ cup water   1 teaspoon lemon juice
4 eggs, separated   grated rind of 1 lemon
                1 cup sifted cake flour

Soak vanilla stick in water. Beat egg yolks until thick and lemon-
colored. Gradually add sugar, lemon juice and rind. Add the vanilla
flavored water. Beat whites of eggs until stiff and fold in one-half of
the whites with the yolk mixture. Gradually add sifted cake flour and
fold in remaining egg whites. Bake in greased Madeleine shell tins for
about 10 minutes at 400° F. Yield: 6 dozen.

RASPBERRY WHIP

2 envelopes plain gelatin   2½ tablespoons lemon juice
¾ cup cold water   2½ cups fresh or frozen rasp-
¾ cup boiling water   berry purée
1 pound 2 ounces sugar   8 egg whites
   (2¼ cups)   1 pint heavy cream, whipped

Soak gelatin in cold water and dissolve in boiling water. Add sugar,
lemon juice and cool; add raspberry purée and blend. When mixture
begins to congeal, place in mixer bowl and beat until light and foamy.
Add beaten egg whites and turn into dessert dishes. Chill until firm.
Decorate with whipped cream forced through a pastry tube. Yield:
24 portions.

CHOCOLATE ROLL

7 eggs
1 cup sugar
7 ounces semi-sweet dipping
   chocolate
5 tablespoons coffee

1 tablespoon salad oil
4 oz. bittersweet chocolate,
   shaved
1 cup heavy cream, whipped
1 tablespoon rum
½ teaspoon vanilla

Separate eggs. Place yolks in bowl with sugar and beat until light and creamy. Add chocolate that has been melted down with coffee over low heat. Fold in egg whites beaten stiff but not dry. Blend so that no egg white is apparent. Oil 15½ x 10½ x 1-inch jelly roll pan, cover with waxed paper and oil again. Turn mixture into pan quickly and bake 15 minutes in 350° F. oven. Turn off heat and allow to remain in oven 5 minutes. Remove from oven and cover top with damp cloth wrung from cold water. Cool at room temperature, then place in refrigerator 30 minutes. Remove cloth. Loosen roll from tin. Dust top of roll with shaved chocolate. Turn onto waxed paper, peeling off waxed paper on which it was baked. Spread heavily with whipped cream flavored with rum and vanilla. Roll like a jelly roll and sprinkle with more shaved chocolate. Serve on wooden board. *Note:* This recipe is best made up for only 12 portions at a time. If additional servings are needed, remake recipe. Yield: 12 portions.

BANANA CREAM CAKE

1 pound 4 ounces cake flour
8 ounces fat (1 cup)
2 tablespoons double-acting
   baking powder
1 pound 8 ounces sugar

1 teaspoon salt
2⅓ cups milk
4 eggs
1⅓ cups milk
1 tablespoon vanilla

Combine flour, fat and baking powder in mixing bowl and mix 2 minutes on low speed, or beat well with rotary beater. Add sugar, salt and 1 cup milk. Mix 2 minutes at low speed and scrape down the bowl; mix 3 minutes longer. Combine eggs, 1⅓ cups milk and vanilla. Add to cake mixture, mixing 2 minutes on low speed. Scrape down and mix 2½ minutes longer. Turn into 6 paper lined, greased 8-inch layer pans. Bake 25 to 30 minutes in moderate oven (350° F.); cool and put together with whipped cream and sliced bananas; cover top with same. Yield: 3 layer cakes (24 portions).

CHERRY COBBLER

2½ cups sugar
½ cup cornstarch
3 cups cherry juice
12 cups cherries or 6 No. 2½
    cans

½ cup lemon juice
¼ cup butter or margarine
6 tablespoons water
⅔ cup flour
½ recipe for Pie Pastry (below)

Combine sugar and cornstarch and add to cherry juice. Stir over low heat until thick and clear. Pour over cherries. Add lemon juice and butter or margarine. Place in 4 baking pans (8 x 12 x 2 inches). Top with pastry. Prick small steam vents in it. Bake in a hot oven (425° F.) 20 to 25 minutes, or until pastry is lightly browned. Cut each pan 3 by 4 to make 12 servings. Yield: 48 portions.

PIE PASTRY

8 cups (2 lbs.) flour
1½ pounds shortening

1½ to 1¾ cups ice water
1½ tablespoons salt

Blend flour and shortening together with pastry blender, two knives, finger tips or at low speed (1 minute) on the electric mixer. Add slowly the water and salt, which have been combined. Use only enough water to make particles hold together. Mix with minimum handling to form a dough. Weigh out 5 ounces for bottom crust and 4 ounces for top crust. Let stand 10 minutes in refrigerator before rolling. Yield: 50 5-inch pastry rounds, or 50 pastry tarts, or 8 8-inch double crust pies.

FRUIT SHORTCAKE
Biscuit Rounds

10 cups biscuit mix   3 cups milk

Add milk to mix. Blend well. Knead gently on floured board. Roll about ½-inch thick. Cut into 3-inch biscuit rounds. Bake in hot oven (425° F.) 12 to 15 minutes. Yield: 50 rounds.

Fruit

6 quarts sweetened fruit   1½ quarts heavy cream, whipped

Spread fruit between and on top of split biscuit halves. Top with whipped cream. Yield: 50 individual shortcakes.

RICH APPLE RAISIN PIE

1/3 cup cornstarch	6 ounces butter or margarine
1 cup cold water	12 pounds apples, peeled and
2 pounds raisins	sliced
1 1/2 quarts water	2 pounds brown sugar
3 tablespoons lemon juice	1 teaspoon cinnamon
1 tablespoon orange rind	1 teaspoon nutmeg

1 teaspoon salt

Make a paste of cornstarch and 1 cup cold water; add to raisins. Add 1 1/2 quarts water, cook until clear over medium heat, about 15 minutes, add lemon juice, orange rind and butter. Weigh out 2 pounds of apples per pie. Pour 1 1/2 cups raisin mixture over apples. Sprinkle each pie with 1 cup Crumb Topping (see below). Bake in hot oven (400° F.) for 10 minutes, then at 375° F. for 35 minutes. Yield: 6 10-inch pies.

CRUMB TOPPING

3 cups all-purpose flour	1/2 teaspoon salt
3 cups sugar	3/4 pound shortening

1/2 teaspoon cinnamon

Blend together all ingredients. Yield: 6 cups topping.

PINEAPPLE ICEBOX PUDDING

1 1/4 pounds butter or margarine	18 egg whites, beaten until stiff
5 cups sugar	1 1/2 teaspoons vanilla
18 egg yolks, beaten	1 3/4 pounds graham crackers
2 No. 2 1/2 cans sliced pineapple	1 pound marshmallows

3/4 cup nut meats

Cream butter and sugar. Add beaten egg yolks, pineapple (drained and cut fine); fold in stiffly beaten egg whites; add vanilla and marshmallows (cut in small pieces). Combine graham cracker crumbs and nut meats. Arrange mixtures in alternate layers in pudding pans, with crumb mixture placed on bottom and top. Store in refrigerator at least 24 hours. Yield: 50 portions.

TOPPING MIXTURE

5 1/2 cups brown sugar	3/4 cup cocoa
5 cups white sugar	2 teaspoons salt

2 1/2 quarts boiling water

Mix sugars, cocoa and salt together. Sprinkle half of this mixture over each pan of batter. Pour 4 1/2 cups of boiling water over each pan. *Do not stir*. Bake as above. Yield: 48 portions.

CHOCOLATE FUDGE PUDDING

1¼ cups butter or margarine
4 cups sugar
3 tablespoons vanilla
3 squares unsweetened
  chocolate, melted

5 cups all-purpose flour
2 teaspoons salt
3⅓ tablespoons baking powder
2½ cups milk
3 cups walnuts, coarsely chopped

Cream butter until consistency of whipped cream. Add sugar gradually; cream well. Add vanilla and melted chocolate and mix until well
blended. Sift flour, salt and baking powder together twice. Add all of
flour, then all of milk. Mix until well blended. Add walnuts; mix.
Put batter into two pans (9 x 14 inches). Sprinkle Topping over mix-
ure. Bake in moderate oven (350° F.) for about 1 hour. This will separate into two layers, crust on top and chocolate fudge on bottom layer.
Serve crust side down with chocolate sauce on top. Garnish with
whipped cream. Yield: 50 portions.

PECAN PIE

2 cups butter or margarine
4 cups brown sugar
2 dozen eggs, beaten
4 cups dark corn syrup
4 cups light corn syrup

8 cups pecans
½ cup lemon juice
1 teaspoon salt
4 teaspoons vanilla
½ recipe Pie Pastry (page 988)

Melt butter; add sugar and beaten eggs. Add remaining ingredients
and blend well. Pour into unbaked pie shells. Bake at 375° F. for 30
to 35 minutes. Cut 6 servings per pie. Yield: 8 8-inch pies (48–50
portions).

LEMON SPONGE CUSTARD

1 cup butter or margarine
8 cups sugar
16 eggs, separated
2 cups flour

juice of 16 lemons
rind of 4 lemons
2 quarts milk
1 teaspoon salt

Cream butter, add sugar gradually, cream. Add well-beaten egg yolks,
flour, lemon juice and rind. Mix thoroughly. Add milk and salt. Fold
in stiffly beaten egg whites. Pour into greased baking pan or custard
cups. Set in hot water. Bake in slow oven (350° F.) for 45 minutes.
Yield: 48 portions.

ENGLISH CHESS TARTS

9 cups sugar
8 tablespoons butter or
  margarine
2 dozen eggs, separated
4 cups chopped nuts
4 cups chopped raisins
4 cups milk
2 teaspoons vanilla

1 recipe for Pie Pastry (page 988)

Mix sugar and butter. Beat together 8 egg whites and 24 yolks until thick and lemon-colored. Add to sugar and butter with remaining ingredients. Cook in top of double boiler over boiling water until thick and smooth, stirring constantly. Cool slightly, add vanilla and turn into baked tart shells. Top with meringue made by beating remaining egg whites until stiff but not dry, gradually adding remaining 1 cup sugar. Flavor if desired with vanilla. Bake in hot oven (425° F.) 4 to 4½ minutes or until meringue is delicately brown. Yield: 50 tarts.

STEEPED COFFEE

Mix 1 pound ground coffee, medium grind, 1 cup of cold water and 1 egg. Place in cheesecloth or muslin bag, allowing space for coffee to double in bulk. Drop bag into large kettle or boiler containing 2½ to 3 gallons freshly boiling water and bring to the boiling point (will require about 15 minutes). Remove bag, cover tightly and keep hot; it should be made just before serving. Approximate yield: 50 medium-sized cups.

URN COFFEE

For large quantities this method is often used. Use 1 pound coffee for 2 gallons water. Fill water jacket of urn with water until glass gauge registers ¾ full and heat just to the boiling point. Put coffee in basket or filter and pour briskly boiling water over it; cover and when water has dripped through, remove coffee container immediately. This coffee is strong enough for after-dinner or afternoon coffee serving. One pound coffee makes 40 medium-sized cups.

TEA FOR A CROWD

Pour 1½ gallons of vigorously boiling water over 1 pound of tea. Let steep for a full 10 minutes. Then strain into a storage crock or stainless steel container. The resulting concentrate can be used for making either hot or iced tea. *For hot tea:* pour one part of the concentrate into a serving pot and add seven parts of very hot water. *For iced tea:* dilute the concentrate with seven parts of cold tap water and serve in ice-filled glasses. (If tea is cloudy, add a small amount of boiling water to concentrate and it will be clear again.) This mixture may also be used as a base for a fruit punch, substituting fruit juices for a portion of the water. Yield: 200 servings.

ROLLED WATER CRESS SANDWICHES

Water cress sandwiches are made by slicing white bread very thin, removing crusts. Place slices on damp cloth and spread with butter or cream cheese mixture; lay on sprig of water cress with leaves left free beyond edges. Roll as tightly as possible, jelly-roll fashion, and fasten with toothpicks. Cover and refrigerate. Cut in two. Tie if desired with ribbon.

CUCUMBER SANDWICHES

Cucumber sandwiches are made by marking whole cucumber with fork tines in vertical rows. Then cut rounds very thin. Lay on buttered rounds of white bread and top with a bit of red caviar or pimiento.

TABLE XLVI

PURCHASING FOOD FOR FIFTY

Food	Approximate Size of Serving	Amount to Purchase for 50 Servings
Meat		
Beef: roast		
Rib, rolled, boned	2½ to 3 ounces cooked	17 to 20 pounds
Rib, standing	3 to 3½ ounces cooked	20 to 25 pounds
Chuck, pot roast	3 to 3½ ounces cooked	20 to 25 pounds
Beef: round steak	4 to 4½ ounces clear meat uncooked	17 to 20 pounds
Beef: stew		
Chuck and plate clear meat	5 ounces stew	10 to 17 pounds
Lamb: roast		
Leg	2½ to 3 ounces cooked	20 to 35 pounds
Shoulder, boneless	2½ to 3 ounces cooked	15 to 20 pounds
Lamb: stew		
Shoulder and brisket —clear meat	5 ounces stew	17 to 20 pounds
Pork: roast		
Loin, trimmed	2½ to 3 ounces cooked	20 to 25 pounds
Ham:		
Fresh	3 to 3½ ounces cooked	20 to 25 pounds
Smoked, tenderized	3 to 3½ ounces cooked	17 to 20 pounds

TABLE XLVI—(*Continued*)

PURCHASING FOOD FOR FIFTY

Food	Approximate Size of Serving	Amount to Purchase for 50 Servings
Veal: roast		
Leg	3 to 3½ ounces cooked	20 to 35 pounds
Shoulder, boneless	3 to 3½ ounces cooked	17 to 20 pounds
Veal cutlet	4 to 5 ounces uncooked	12 to 17 pounds
Meat cakes	4 to 5 ounces uncooked	17 to 20 pounds
	1 or 2 cakes	
Meat loaf or extended	4 to 4½ ounces cooked meat loaf	12 to 15 pounds
meat patties		
Bacon: medium	3 strips	5 to 6 pounds
Sliced, wide	2 strips	5 to 7 pounds
Canadian, sliced	2 or 3 slices	7 to 10 pounds
Liver	4 ounces cooked	13 to 17 pounds
Sausage:		
Links	3 links	17 to 20 pounds
Cakes	6 to 8 ounces raw meat	20 to 25 pounds
	2 cakes	
Wieners	2 wieners	12½ to 14 pounds
Fish		
Fresh or frozen fish	4 to 5 ounces	14 to 17 pounds
fillets		
Oysters:		
For frying, large	4 to 6 oysters	7 to 8 quarts
For scalloping, small		4 to 5 quarts
For stew, small	4 to 6 oysters	3 quarts
Poultry		
Chicken: Fryers	¼ fryer	35 to 40 pounds, dressed
		25 to 30 pounds, eviscerated
Fowl: Fricassee	4 to 6 ounces including bone	35 to 50 pounds, dressed
		25 to 35 pounds, eviscerated
Fowl: For dishes con-	1 to 2 ounces of clear meat	17 to 20 pounds, dressed
taining cut-up cooked		13 to 17 pounds, eviscerated
meat		
Turkey: Young Toms	2 to 2½ ounces of clear meat	35 to 50 pounds, dressed
or Old Toms		25 to 35 pounds, eviscerated
Vegetables		
Asparagus	3 ounces or 4 or 5 stalks	12 to 16 pounds
Beans: Green or Wax	2½ to 3 ounces or ½ cup	10 to 12 pounds
Beets	2½ to 3 ounces or ½ cup	12 to 14 pounds
Broccoli	2½ to 3 ounces	17 to 20 pounds
Brussels sprouts	2½ to 3 ounces	10 quart baskets or 12 lbs.
Cabbage:		
Raw	1 to 2 ounces	8 to 10 pounds
Cooked	2½ to 3 ounces or ½ cup	12 to 15 pounds

TABLE XLVI—(*Continued*)

PURCHASING FOOD FOR FIFTY

Food	Approximate Size of Serving	Amount to Purchase for 50 Servings
Vegetables (*cont'd*)		
Carrots:		
Cooked	2½ to 3 ounces or ½ cup	14 to 16 pounds
Raw, strips	2- to 3-inch strips	2 to 2½ pounds
Cauliflower	3 ounces or ½ cup	28 to 32 pounds
Celery:		
Raw		3 to 4 bunches
Cooked	2½ to 3 ounces or ½ cup	7 to 10 bunches
Eggplant	2½ ounces (1½ slices)	10 to 12
Lettuce	⅙ or ⅛ head	4 to 5 heads for garnish
		6 to 8 heads for salad
Onions	3 to 3½ ounces or ½ cup	14 to 16 pounds
Parsnips	2½ to 3 ounces	15 pounds
Potatoes:		
White	4 to 4½ ounces or ½ cup mashed or creamed	15 to 20 pounds
Sweet	3½ to 4 ounces	17 to 20 pounds
Rutabagas	3 to 3½ ounces or ½ cup	20 to 25 pounds
Spinach	3 to 3½ ounces or ½ cup	17 to 20 pounds
Squash:		
Summer	2½ to 3 ounces or ½ cup	13 to 16 pounds
Winter, mashed	3 ounces or ½ cup	25 to 30 pounds
Tomatoes		10 pounds fresh for slicing
Turnips (white)	3 ounces or ½ cup	15 to 20 pounds
Fruits		
Apples	½ cup sauce	15 to 20 pounds for sauce or pie
Bananas	1 small	15 pounds
Cranberries	¼ cup sauce	4 pounds for sauce
Lemons		25 to 30 lemons (1¼ quarts juice) for lemonade for 50 glasses
Oranges		4 to 6 doz. medium oranges (6 quarts juice) for 50 4-oz. glasses
Peaches	3 ounces or ½ cup	10 to 12 pounds for slicing
Pineapple	½ cup cubed	5 medium
Rhubarb	½ cup sauce	10 pounds
Strawberries	½ cup	10 to 13 quarts
	⅓ cup for shortcake	8 to 10 quarts
Miscellaneous Foods		
Bread		Usually allow 1½ slices per person to accompany meal
Butter		1 to 1½ pounds
Cheese:		
Brick		3¼ pounds sliced for sandwiches

TABLE XLVI—*(Continued)*

PURCHASING FOOD FOR FIFTY

Food	Approximate Size of Serving	Amount to Purchase for 50 Servings
Miscellaneous Foods		
Cheese: *(cont'd)*		
Cottage		6 pounds
Coffee		1 pound and 2½ gallons water for 50 cups
Cream:		
Heavy (40 per cent)	1 rounded tablespoon whipped	1 pint
Light (20 per cent) or top milk	1½ tablespoons	1¼ quarts
Fruit cup	⅓ to ½ cup	4 to 6 quarts
Fruit juice	½ cup or 4 ounces	2 cans, No. 10 or 6½ quarts
Honey	2 tablespoons	5 pounds
Ice cream:		
Brick		7 to 9 bricks
Bulk		2 gallons
Potato chips	¾ to 1 ounce	2 pounds
Puddings	½ cup	6 quarts
Rolls	1½	6 to 6½ dozen
Salad mixtures	½ cup	7 to 8 quarts
Salad dressing:		
Mayonnaise	1 tablespoon for each salad	3 to 4 cups (garnish) 1 to 1½ quarts for mixed salads
French		¾ to 1 quart
Soups	scant 1 cup	3 gallons
Tea	individual tea bags	50
		3 ounces bulk tea to 2½ gallons water and chipped ice
Dried prunes, apricots, etc.		6 to 7 pounds
Canned foods (in general)		2 No. 10 cans
Pickles: sweet		1½ quarts
Three-inch	½ pickle	1½ pounds
Macaroni or spaghetti		5 to 6 pounds
Rice		2 quarts
Jam		3 pints
Frozen Vegetables		
Asparagus tips	2½ ounces	10 pounds (4 40-oz. pkg.)
Beans, cut green	2¼ ounces	7½ pounds (3 40-oz. pkg.)
Beans, baby Lima	2¼ ounces	7½ pounds (3 40-oz. pkg.)
Beans, Fordhook	2¼ ounces	7½ pounds (3 40-oz. pkg.)
Broccoli	2½ ounces	10 pounds (4 40-oz. pkg.)
Cauliflower	2½ ounces	10 pounds (4 40-oz. pkg.)
Corn, whole kernel	2¼ ounces	7½ pounds (3 40-oz. pkg.)
Peas	2¼ ounces	7½ pounds (3 40-oz. pkg.)
Spinach	2½ ounces	10 pounds (4 40-oz. pkg.)

Popular Foreign Recipes

WE ARE indebted to the excellent cooks of many nations for a great enrichment of our American Cookery. To take the dishes of many countries into our own kitchens is a way of widening our appreciation of good food and of bringing about better international understanding.

Who has not enjoyed ravioli and gnocchi, contributed by the Italians, rice pilaff and kebab as prepared by the Greeks and Armenians; borsch and sour cream liked by the Russians; the fish puddings, bakkels and breads so popular on the Scandinavian tables; the Japanese sukiyaki; the Chinese casseroles; the hot peppery dishes of Spanish origin; the sauerkraut and sauerbraten beloved by the German people?

It is the trademark of the gourmet to know foreign foods and how to prepare them. Here are foreign recipes adapted to our American cooking methods and including ingredients easy-to-find in any well-stocked food grocery. All have been tested in our Home Institute kitchens.

Perhaps you will find it as interesting as we do to own a file of foreign foods with recipes, notes on ingredients and interesting bits of information about their use and origin.

INDIA COFFEE

Use purest straight Mocha coffee, ground very fine. Pour 4 cups freshly boiling water into pot, add 3 to 4 tablespoons coffee and bring to a full boil, stirring constantly. Add 1 tablespoon pure rose water and serve at once in small cups without cream.

AUSTRIAN ICED COFFEE

Half fill tall glasses with cracked ice, sprinkle powdered sugar over ice, as desired, and place 1 tablespoon whipped cream in each glass. Pour hot strong coffee into iced glasses.

CAFÉ BRÛLOT

rind of ½ orange cut in 5 or 6 pieces
2 sticks of broken cinnamon
thin peel of ¼ lemon

8 lumps of sugar
2 demitasses of Cognac
10 whole cloves
5 demitasses of double strength coffee

Place the ingredients, except coffee, in a metal bowl and light the burner under the bowl and stir constantly with the brûlot ladle (or a gravy ladle) until the contents are warm, then ignite. Burn about a minute, then slowly pour over the blaze 5 demitasses of freshly made double strength coffee. Ladle out at once into cups. Yield: 6 demitasses.

CAFÉ DIABLE

1 broken stick cinnamon
1 tablespoon whole cloves
1 tablespoon whole roasted coffee beans
1 teaspoon coriander seed

12 lumps of sugar
grated rind of 1 orange
½ cup brandy
1 quart hot coffee

Light flame beneath chafing dish and let bowl warm slightly before dropping in the cinnamon, cloves, coffee beans, coriander, sugar and orange rind. Let all warm together for a minute. Add brandy, about ¼ cup. Get the brandy hot, then touch it with flame. Ladle the liquid fire gently to mix, then add the hot coffee. Pour a little brandy into the ladle, burn a moment, dip this up and down in the coffee until the flames are extinguished. Add more brandy to the ladle and repeat the performance until another ¼ cup brandy has been used. Serve in after-dinner coffee cups or in diable cups. Approximate yield: 10 demitasses.

CAFÉ DIABOLIQUE

1 cup brandy or Cognac
40 whole cloves
2 sticks cinnamon, broken

rind of ½ orange, thinly sliced
8 teaspoons sugar
1 quart strong black coffee

Pour brandy into heatproof bowl; add spices, rind and sugar. Ignite 1 tablespoon of brandy in long-handled spoon and lower into bowl. Allow to burn a few minutes and add coffee slowly. Approximate yield: 15 demitasses.

ARABIAN COFFEE

4 tablespoons powdered, burnt
  Mocha coffee

2 cups boiling water
  pinch saffron
3 cloves

Place coffee in saucepan and pour boiling water over it. Simmer 5 minutes, keeping pan covered when not stirring. Add saffron and cloves. Pour coffee into the filter of a coffeepot (traditionally a copper jug or kettle) and let brew run through, keeping pot hot. Sweeten to taste. Yield: 2 cups.

TURKISH COFFEE

4 tablespoons coffee, pulverized
2 cups water

4 tablespoons sugar

Place coffee, sugar and water in a coffeepot. Heat and stir until mixture comes to a brisk boil and is very frothy. Remove from heat and let the froth subside; replace pan on a higher heat. Repeat this three times. Before serving, settle the grounds by adding a little cold water. If desired, add a few drops rose water. Approximate yield: 2 cups. Note: This can be made best with a lidless Turkish copper coffeepot.

CAFÉ AU LAIT

French Café au Lait—Make strong or double strength coffee by any method desired. Have ready an equal quantity of freshly scalded milk. Simultaneously pour coffee and milk in equal amounts into heated cups. If a richer drink is desired, add 1 tablespoon butter to each cup of milk, or top each cup with 1 tablespoon whipped cream.

CANAPÉ NORDAISE

2 smoked kippers
6 slices of bacon
white bread, toasted
3 egg yolks

2 tablespoons butter
1 cup light cream
3 tablespoons grated cheese
salt and pepper

Skin and bone kippers, cut in small fingers and wrap each in slice of bacon. Place on baking sheet and bake in moderate oven (350° F.) 10 minutes. Remove and arrange on thin slices of white toast the same size as the kippers. Place on hot flat dish and pour over the following sauce: Put egg yolks, butter, cream, cheese, salt and pepper to taste in top of double boiler and cook over hot water until mixture becomes thick, stirring constantly. Do not overcook or it will curdle. If it becomes too thick, add a little more cream. Pour sauce over kippers and brown quickly under broiler before serving. Yield: 4 portions.

ICED BORSCH

4 cups strong beef stock,
   clarified
1 bunch beets, peeled and
   grated
2 tablespoons tomato paste
1 tablespoon tarragon vinegar
3 tablespoons red wine

1 tablespoon Sherry
few whole peppercorns
salt and black pepper
1 envelope plain gelatin
   (optional)
½ cup heavy sour cream
1 teaspoon grated lemon rind

½ teaspoon minced garlic

Combine stock, beets, tomato paste, vinegar, wine, Sherry, peppercorns, salt and pepper to taste and gelatin. Heat slowly until gelatin dissolves. Remove from heat and let stand 15 minutes. Pour through two layers of cheesecloth or muslin which has been dipped in cold water and wrung dry. Soup may be served hot or cold. Combine cream, lemon rind, garlic and salt and pepper to taste. Mix well and serve separately as garnish for soup. Approximate yield: 4 portions.

BORSCH (RUSSIAN)

1 pound lean beef, cubed
1 soup bone
1 4-lb. fowl, cut up
3 carrots, chopped
3 small onions, sliced
3 stalks celery, diced
3 quarts water

1/4 teaspoon peppercorns
1/2 bay leaf
1 spray of thyme
2 bay leaves
1 sprig parsley
salt and pepper
2 beets, pared and chopped

heavy sour cream, whipped

Put beef, bone, fowl, carrots, onions, celery and water in large kettle and bring slowly to a boil. Tie spices and herbs in a small cloth bag; add with parsley to soup mixture and simmer, covered, 2 hours. Strain, setting meat aside, and season broth to taste; add beets and cook 15 minutes; strain and reheat. Serve with a topping of whipped sour cream. To serve cold, chill thoroughly. Approximate yield: 2 quarts.

SOUPE À LA OIGNON GRANDE MAISON

(Onion Soup)

3 large onions
1/4 cup bacon fat
1 1/2 teaspoon salt
1/8 teaspoon pepper

3 cups boiling water
1/2 French roll, sliced
1/4 cup beef or pork fat
grated Parmesan cheese

4 eggs

Blanch, peel and chop sliced onions fine; brown in hot bacon fat. When brown, add seasonings and boiling water. Bring to a boil and simmer 40 minutes. Meantime, slice French roll and spread with beef or pork fat and a little grated cheese; brown lightly in oven. Pour soup into marmites; put in 1 or 2 slices of roll. Send to table with two dishes for each person, one containing grated Parmesan cheese, the other a raw egg. The soup should be boiling when put into marmites and served at once so that when egg is dropped into it, it will set immediately. Yield: 4 portions.

POTAGE SANTÉ

4 large potatoes, sliced
2 onions, sliced
2 cups water
1 teaspoon meat concentrate
2 tablespoons fat
1 teaspoon salt
few grains cayenne
2 cups shredded fresh spinach
1½ cups stock

1 tablespoon lemon juice
1 tablespoon grated lemon rind
2 cloves garlic, minced
¾ cup light cream
⅛ teaspoon pepper
chili pepper
2 tablespoons heavy sour cream
1 egg yolk
1 tablespoon milk

finely shredded fresh spinach

Combine potatoes, onions, water, meat concentrate, fat, salt and cayenne. Simmer until vegetables are mushy. Add spinach and simmer 6 minutes. Add stock and cook, stirring constantly until mixture comes to a boil; simmer 4 minutes. Rub through a strainer. Return to saucepan, add lemon juice and rind, garlic, milk, pepper and chili pepper. Reheat slowly. Combine sour cream, egg yolk and 1 tablespoon milk; gradually stir it into hot mixture. Serve at once. Garnish with fresh spinach. Approximate yield: 6 portions.

FRENCH LOBSTER BISQUE

shells of boiled lobster
6 tablespoons butter
4 tablespoons rice flour
2 cups lobster stock
salt

cayenne
2 teaspoons tomato paste
1 tablespoon chopped parsley
1 cup light cream
¼ cup lobster meat, diced

croutons sautéed in cooking oil

Crush lobster shells until fine in a wooden bowl with a mallet, or with mortar and pestle, and combine with 4 tablespoons butter. Melt remaining butter in saucepan and, off the heat, add rice flour, blending well. Gradually add stock and return to heat, stirring constantly until thickened. Add salt and cayenne and simmer 10 minutes. Gradually beat in lobster butter with a wire whisk. To mixture add tomato paste, parsley, cream and lobster meat. Bring to boil over low heat and serve immediately with croutons. Approximate yield: 6 portions.

DANISH OXTAIL SOUP

3 pounds oxtails, cut in pieces   ¼ cup celery leaves
¼ cup flour   2 quarts well-seasoned bouillon
½ teaspoon paprika   1 bay leaf
3 tablespoons butter   ½ teaspoon dried thyme
½ onion, sliced   ¼ cup Madeira
1 carrot, sliced   2 tablespoons lemon juice
½ cup chopped celery   ¼ teaspoon curry powder

Dredge oxtails in combined flour and paprika. Cook in butter until
well browned on all sides. Remove oxtails. Add vegetables and fry
until golden brown. Combine oxtails, vegetables, stock, bay leaf and
thyme. Simmer until meat falls away from the bone (4 to 5 hours).
Remove stock from kettle and skim off fat. Add wine, lemon juice and
curry. Place oxtails in tureen, pour soup over them. Serve very hot.
Yield: 6 to 8 portions.

MADRILÈNE

2 cups chicken bouillon   1 cup chopped carrots
2 cups beef bouillon   1 medium-sized onion, chopped
2 cups canned tomatoes   ½ cup chopped leeks
salt and pepper

Bring bouillons and vegetables to a boil; cover and simmer 1 hour,
adding salt and pepper when partially cooked; strain and clarify
(page 220), if necessary. Approximate yield: 1½ pints consommé.

Jellied Madrilène—To 3 cups of Madrilène Consommé (page 1003)
use 1 envelope plain gelatin. Soften gelatin in 2 tablespoons water
about 5 minutes; add 1 cup hot soup and stir until gelatin is dissolved.
Then add remaining 2 cups cold soup, season to taste and pour into
bowl or bouillon cups; chill until firm or jellied. Approximate yield:
4 portions.

CONSOMMÉ MADRILÈNE

2 envelopes plain gelatin   2 tablespoons tarragon vinegar
5 cups beef stock   1 bay leaf
3 tablespoons tomato paste   1 teaspoon salt
2 tomatoes, sliced (skins on)   6 peppercorns
¼ cup red wine   3 egg whites, stiffly beaten

Soften gelatin in 1 cup stock 5 minutes. Add to remaining stock with tomato paste, sliced tomatoes, red wine, vinegar, bay leaf, salt and peppercorns. Add egg whites to soup. Heat to boiling, stirring constantly, over low heat. Remove from heat and let stand 10 minutes. Pour through a damp cloth. Chill until slightly thickened. Garnish with finely shredded tomato and chopped fresh mint. Approximate yield: 6 portions.

MINESTRONE MILANESE

½ cup dried kidney beans   2 cups shredded cabbage
¼ cup olive oil   2 cups sliced carrots
1 clove garlic, crushed   ½ cup rice
1 medium-sized onion, sliced   1 No. 2 can tomatoes
2 cups chopped spinach   2 quarts soup stock
1 tablespoon minced parsley   pinch of sage
2 stalks celery, diced   salt and pepper to taste
¼ cup grated Parmesan cheese

Soak beans overnight. Drain. Heat oil in soup pot. Add garlic, onion and fresh vegetables and sauté for 10 minutes, stirring constantly. Add beans, rice, tomatoes, stock and seasonings. Cover and simmer until beans and rice are tender and most of the liquid has been absorbed, about 1½ hours. Add cheese and mix thoroughly. Produces a thick, nourishing soup. Yield: 6 to 8 portions.

EGG FOO YUNG (CHINESE)

½ cup minced cooked ham   1 cup bean sprouts
½ cup minced onion   ¼ teaspoon salt
¼ cup sliced water chestnuts   5 eggs, well beaten

Combine ham, onion, water chestnuts (the Chinese "ling" or brown-skinned bulb of a rushlike plant) and bean sprouts; add salt and eggs, beating until thick. Drop from large spoon into frying pan covered with 1-inch layer of hot fat, and fry about 10 minutes, turning to brown both sides. Drain and serve hot. Approximate yield: 6 portions.

CHINESE EGG ROLL
Pancake Batter

1 cup sifted all-purpose flour   2 eggs, well beaten
½ teaspoon salt   1 cup water
              ¼ cup salad oil (approximately)

Combine and sift flour and salt. Combine eggs and water; add to the flour mixture blending until batter is smooth. (Batter will be very thin.) Heat an 8-inch skillet, grease lightly with oil. Cover bottom of skillet with a thin layer of batter, tipping pan to spread batter as thin as possible. Fry until lightly brown on one side only. Remove from pan and put aside to cool. Grease skillet before frying each pancake. Reserve 2 tablespoons of batter for sealing the rolls later.

Filling

2 tablespoons shredded carrots   1 teaspoon salt
2 tablespoons finely diced celery   ½ cup (¼ pound) finely diced
1 tablespoon finely diced   cooked shrimp
    scallions   ¼ teaspoon pepper
½ cup finely diced cooked meat   2 tablespoons salad oil
    (beef, pork, chicken or   1 teaspoon sugar
    ham)   salad oil for frying

Cook carrot and celery in small amount of boiling water for 4 minutes. Drain and cool. Add remaining ingredients except salad oil for frying; mix well. Place 1 tablespoon of filling in the middle of each pancake on the browned side. Roll the pancakes, folding in ends while rolling. Seal with remaining batter. Chill in refrigerator for 2 hours. Fry the rolls in a pan containing 3 inches of oil which has been heated to 370° F. Cook pancakes to a golden brown on one side for about 8 minutes, turn to brown on other side. Remove from pan. Drain on absorbent paper. Serve with hot mustard. Yield: 8 to 10 rolls.

Hot Mustard—Combine 4 tablespoons dry mustard and 3 tablespoons water; stir until smooth. Yield: ¼ cup.

POACHED EGGS—FRENCH STYLE

Eggs à la Grand Duc—Place fried croutons on serving plate; arrange poached eggs on top and garnish with asparagus tips. Serve with fresh mushrooms or truffles cooked in a rich Cream Sauce (page 466).

Eggs à la Mornay—Place poached egg on toast; pour Cream Sauce (page 466) over egg. Sprinkle with grated Parmesan cheese and place under broiler to melt cheese.

Eggs Richelieu—Spread toast with pâté de foie gras; place a poached egg on each slice and serve with Tomato Sauce (page 469).

Egg à la Portugaise—Place poached eggs on rounds of toast and serve with baked Stuffed Tomatoes (page 578), using a meat or fish filling and Brown Sauce (page 467) flavored with Sherry.

SALZBURGER NÖCKELN (AUSTRIAN)

Use recipe for Fluffy Omelet (page 120); omit milk and pepper and reduce salt to ⅛ teaspoon; add ¼ cup sugar and ¼ teaspoon vanilla, beating these into egg yolks. Drop by heaping tablespoons on buttered hot frying pan. The pan should be hot enough to brown soufflé in 1½ minutes. Turn over to brown the other side, reducing heat slightly; it should take about 3½ minutes to finish cooking; they are like uncooked meringues in the center. Serve at once on warm dish and sprinkle generously with confectioners' sugar; they fall slightly and must be eaten immediately. If cooked longer over low heat, they are more like an omelet. Approximate yield: 16 cakes.

CRÊPES DE BOEUF (FRENCH)

1 small onion, minced
2 tablespoons fat
1 cup finely chopped cooked
   beef
½ teaspoon salt
dash of pepper

1 cup sifted all-purpose flour
1 teaspoon baking powder
1 egg, beaten
1½ cups milk
butter
chopped parsley

Sauté onion in 1 tablespoon fat until browned, add meat, ¼ teaspoon salt and pepper, and cook 1 minute. Prepare griddle cake batter (page 141), using flour, baking powder, remaining ¼ teaspoon salt, egg and milk; beat in meat mixture. Cook as for large pancakes on greased hot griddle; spread with butter, sprinkle with parsley and roll tightly; serve piping hot. Approximate yield: 10 crêpes.

SUKIYAKI (JAPANESE)

2 cups canned bamboo sprouts
2 cups canned or cooked dried
    mushrooms
2 medium-sized white onions
1 bunch green onions
½ bunch leeks
2 stalks celery
2 pounds spinach or string
    beans

2 squares tofu (bean curd)
1 pound tender round steak
¼ cup shoyu sauce
½ teaspoon ajinomoto
    (Japanese seasonings)
2 tablespoons sugar
¼ cup mushroom liquor
½ cup salad oil
8 to 10 cups hot, cooked rice

Slice bamboo sprouts, mushrooms and white onions very fine; cut green onions, leeks and celery diagonally into 2-inch strips, using green tops of onions and leeks; shred the spinach or string beans and cut tofu in 1-inch cubes. Arrange separately in neat piles on large platters ready for cooking on grill; cut meat crossgrain in paper-thin slices and spread out on platter. For sauce, simmer shoyu, ajinomoto, sugar and mushroom liquor for 3 minutes. Brown onions slightly in hissing hot oil in heavy frying pan over charcoal brazier, spirit lamp or grill, at table; add vegetables and tofu (bean curd) and cook 1 minute; then add ½ of sauce. When hot, add meat, spreading it out thin; cook over low flame 15 minutes, stirring occasionally and adding remaining sauce as it is needed. Reduce heat and serve directly from pan on hot boiled rice in individual bowls, or break raw egg into each bowl and serve sukiyaki over it. Yield: 8 portions.

TEREYAKI (JAPANESE)

2 pounds beef steak (sirloin or
    hip) 1 inch thick
2 teaspoons ginger
2 cloves garlic, minced

1 medium onion, minced
2 tablespoons sugar
½ cup shoyu (soy) sauce
¼ cup water

Cut steak into serving pieces. Combine the remaining ingredients and pour over meat in a deep bowl. Allow to marinate 1 to 2 hours. Drain meat and broil 2 inches from source of heat for 15 to 18 minutes. Heat sauce, strain and pour over broiled steak. Yield: 6 portions.

DANISH BEEFSTEAK

2 to 2½ pounds round steak	3 tablespoons chopped suet
2 teaspoons salt	5 cups thinly sliced onions
¼ teaspoon pepper	⅓ cup butter

Season steak with salt and pepper and pound hard for several minutes, or until slightly flattened. Sear steak in suet in hot heavy frying pan; lower heat and cook 6 to 8 minutes longer, turning steak once for even cooking. Sauté onions in butter over low heat until soft and lightly browned. Serve over steak. Approximate yield: 6 portions.

BEEF À LA STROGANOFF (RUSSIAN)

2½ pounds lean beef, cut in strips	¾ cup tomato juice
½ cup butter or margarine	2 cups water or stock
1¼ cups chopped onions	⅔ cup Sherry
2¼ cups sliced mushrooms	salt
	pepper
¼ cup heavy sour cream	

Roll beef in flour; sauté in butter 5 minutes and place in a hot baking dish. Sauté onions in same butter until soft; place on beef and add mushrooms. Pour tomato juice, stock and Sherry over meat; season and bake in a moderate oven (375° F.) 30 minutes or until meat is tender. Serve on toast and top with sour cream. Yield: 4 to 6 portions.

ENGLISH BEEF STEW

2½ pounds shin beef	3 tablespoons chopped suet
¼ cup flour	1½ cups water
½ teaspoon salt	6 small onions, sliced
¼ teaspoon pepper	6 small carrots, diced
3 tablespoons butter	

Cut beef in 2 inch squares and roll in flour mixed with salt and pepper; sauté in suet until well browned. Transfer meat to heated casserole; add water to drippings in pan, bring to a boil and pour over meat. Cover and bake in slow oven (300°–325° F.) about 3 hours, adding onions and carrots, sautéed in butter, ½ hour before meat is done. Meat may be simmered in tightly covered kettle on top of stove. Approximate yield: 6 portions.

RICH GERMAN STEW

3 pounds chuck	3 large onions, sliced
¼ cup flour	1 teaspoon salt
3 tablespoons fat	8 whole cloves
2 cups water	4 tablespoons flour
¾ cup vinegar	water

1 recipe Dumplings (page 492)

Cut beef in small pieces, 1 to 2 inch cubes, dredge in flour and brown well in fat (chopped suet or drippings). Add water and vinegar, cover and simmer about 2 hours, or until tender, adding onions and seasonings ½ hour before meat is done. Thicken stock with a thin smooth paste of flour and water. Drop dumpling mixture from spoon into hot stew, cover and steam 12 to 15 minutes. Serve at once. Approximate yield: 6 portions.

DUTCH STEW

¾ pound beef	1 teaspoon salt
½ pound fresh pork	¼ teaspoon pepper
½ pound beef liver	¼ cup flour
2 quarts boiling water	¼ cup cold water
2 small onions, sliced	1 recipe Dumplings (page 492)

Cut meat in small pieces, add water and simmer, covered, 2 hours, adding onions and seasonings the last half hour of cooking. Thicken with flour and cold water mixed to a smooth paste. Drop dumplings by spoonfuls into hot stew and cook, covered, 15 minutes. Serve at once. Approximate yield: 6 portions.

IRISH STEW WITH DUMPLINGS

2 pounds lamb or mutton	1 medium-sized onion, sliced
water	1 teaspoon salt
1 cup diced raw carrots	¼ teaspoon pepper
½ cup diced raw turnip	½ bay leaf

½ recipe Dumplings (page 492)

Choose meat from shank, neck, shoulder, breast or flank; wipe with damp cloth and cut in small pieces. Cover with boiling water and simmer, covered, 2 hours; add vegetables and seasonings and cook ½ hour longer. Drop dumpling mixture by spoonfuls on top of mixture; cover tightly and cook 12 to 15 minutes; serve at once. Approximate yield: 6 portions.

SYRIAN EGGPLANT STEW

1½ pounds shoulder of lamb, cubed
2 tablespoons fat
1 eggplant
2 onions, quartered

2 large potatoes, quartered
1 8-ounce can tomato sauce
1 cup water
3 tablespoons tomato paste
1½ teaspoons salt

⅛ teaspoon allspice

Sauté lamb in fat until brown. Cut eggplant into 1-inch cubes. Add to lamb with remaining ingredients. Cover and simmer, stirring occasionally, until vegetables are tender, about 20 minutes. Taste for seasonings. Yield: 4 portions.

SPANISH LAMB STEW

2 pounds breast of lamb
2 tablespoons fat
2 quarts hot water
1 large onion, chopped
1 green pepper, chopped
½ cup rice

1 teaspoon salt
¼ teaspoon pepper
1½ cups canned tomatoes
1 cup canned peas
1 egg, beaten
1 teaspoon olive oil

½ teaspoon vinegar

Wipe lamb and cut in small pieces. Sauté in fat, add hot water and simmer, covered, 1½ hours; add onion, green pepper, rice and seasonings and simmer ½ hour longer, or until vegetables and rice are done, adding tomatoes and peas the last 10 minutes of cooking. Combine egg, olive oil and vinegar; add to stew, stirring until thickened; serve at once. Approximate yield: 6 portions.

KEBAB (ARMENIAN OR RUSSIAN)

¼ cup olive oil
¾ teaspoon salt
¼ teaspoon pepper
2 pounds of lean loin or leg of lamb, cut in 1½ inch cubes

2 firm tomatoes, cut in thick slices
2 large onions, sliced
1 green pepper, cut in 1½ inch squares

Combine olive oil, salt and pepper; spread over meat and vegetables and let stand in cool place 2 to 3 hours. Place meat and vegetables alternately on skewers and broil slowly under moderate heat, or in oven, until well browned and tender. Turn skewers occasionally to allow all sides to be browned. Yield: 4 portions.

BOTLAGON (ARMENIAN)

1 large eggplant, peeled and
   diced
2 green peppers, sliced

2 tablespoons chopped parsley
3 large potatoes, pared and diced
2 lbs. lamb shoulder, diced

4 large tomatoes

Prepare vegetables. Sauté lamb in its own fat until brown and then
turn into baking pan. Put prepared vegetables on top and cover. Cook
in slow oven (325° F.) 45 minutes. Then put sliced tomatoes on top
and increase heat (400° F.) and cook 15 minutes longer, or until
mixture is thick and rather dry. Slip under broiler for final browning.
Approximate yield: 6 portions.

DOLMEH–E–BEH (PERSIAN)

6 large or 8 small quince
1 tablespoon yellow split peas
water to cover
1 medium-sized onion, sliced
¼ cup butter or margarine
1 pound lean lamb, ground

1¼ teaspoons salt
¼ teaspoon pepper
¼ teaspoon allspice or cinnamon
water
½ cup vinegar
¾ cup sugar

Wash and core quince, but do not peel, leaving flower end intact. Parboil peas in water to cover. Sauté onion in butter or margarine until
golden brown. Remove onion and sauté meat in same pan, adding
peas, seasonings and spice. When meat is browned on all sides, stuff
filling into quince and place in covered pan with about 1 inch of
water. Cover and simmer until cooked. Cooking time will depend on
size and quality of the fruit. Just before quince are done, add combined vinegar and sugar and simmer 15 minutes. Yield: 4 to 6 portions.

BITOCHKY SMETANA (RUSSIAN)

1½ pounds veal, ground
4 medium-sized potatoes,
   cooked and chopped
1½ small onions, grated

1½ teaspoons salt
⅛ teaspoon pepper
1 egg, beaten
¼ cup butter

1¼ cups heavy sour cream

Mix together veal, potatoes, onions, seasonings and egg; shape in round
balls and fry in butter until well browned. Add ¾ cup sour cream and
simmer, covered, 15 minutes; just before serving, add remaining ½ cup
cream and bring to a boil. Yield: 12 balls, or 6 portions.

NORWEGIAN MEAT BALLS

2 pounds round steak	2 tablespoons flour
½ pound suet	2 eggs
1 teaspoon salt	2 cups light cream (about)
⅛ teaspoon pepper	1½ quarts beef stock
¼ teaspoon mace or nutmeg	butter
dash of ginger	Brown Sauce (page 467)

Grind meat and suet five times; stir in seasonings and flour. Beat in eggs, one at a time, and add cream gradually, beating until spongy and light. Shape into small balls, dipping teaspoon in cold water before shaping, and cook in beef stock about 5 minutes. Brown in butter and serve with brown sauce made from beef stock. Flavor sauce with Sherry, if desired, using 3 tablespoons Sherry to 2 cups sauce. These meat balls are usually made in quantity, cooked in stock, then canned and used as needed. If desired, brown the uncooked meat balls and cook in brown sauce about ½ hour. Approximate yield: 6 dozen small meat balls.

LAMB RAGOUT (AUSTRALIAN)

2½ pounds lamb loin, cut in serving pieces	hearts of celery or oyster plant (optional)
3 tablespoons butter	4 mushrooms, quartered
3 tablespoons Sherry or brandy	1 teaspoon meat extract
1 teaspoon minced garlic	2 tablespoons all-purpose flour
12 small onions, peeled	1½ cups stock
12 small carrots, pared	¼ cup red wine
12 small turnips, pared	salt and pepper
mixed herbs or 1 bay leaf	

Brown meat quickly in 2 tablespoons butter in large heavy skillet. Heat Sherry, ignite and pour over meat. Remove meat from pan and add remaining butter. Add garlic, vegetables and mushrooms and sauté until lightly browned, about 3 minutes. Remove pan from heat and stir in meat extract; blend in flour. Return to heat and gradually stir in stock; bring to a boil. Add wine, salt, pepper and herbs to taste. Return meat to sauce and cook, covered, about 30 minutes, or until tender. Approximate yield: 8 portions.

VEAL PAPRIKA (AUSTRIAN)

¼ cup butter or margarine
3 large onions, finely chopped
2 pounds leg of veal, cut into
 1-inch cubes
1½ tablespoons paprika

1 teaspoon salt
1 tomato, chopped
1 small green pepper, chopped
2 tablespoons water
2 tablespoons capers

1 cup heavy sour cream

Melt butter or margarine in heavy skillet. Add onions and cook until golden brown. Add veal cubes, paprika and salt. Cook until the meat browns, turning the mixture occasionally. When brown, add tomato, green pepper, and water. Cover; simmer for 45 minutes or until meat is tender. Add a small amount of water if necessary. Add capers and sour cream. Simmer for 5 minutes. Serve with buttered noodles or steamed fluffy dumplings. Yield: 6 portions.

VEAL SCALLOPINI SUPREME

4 veal cutlets, sliced thin
6 tablespoons butter or
 margarine
salt and pepper
4 chicken livers
4 mushrooms, sliced
½ cup cooked tongue or ham,
 shredded
4 tablespoons flour
cayenne

1 cup milk
½ teaspoon dry mustard
2 tablespoons grated Parmesan
 cheese
2 tablespoons light cream
2 to 3 tablespoons fat
1½ teaspoons tomato paste
½ teaspoon meat extract
½ cup light stock (chicken or
 veal)

Place veal slices between two pieces of waxed paper. Using either a wooden mallet or side of cleaver, beat them until about ⅛-inch thick. Remove from paper and brown quickly in 4 tablespoons butter. Season to taste with salt and pepper and arrange on greased baking sheet. Brown chicken livers in leftover butter, remove and slice. Brown mushrooms in pan, season and cook 3 or 4 minutes. Combine chicken livers, mushrooms, tongue and mix well. Place a spoonful of this mixture on each slice of veal. Cover with spoonful of cheese sauce made as follows: Melt remaining butter in saucepan. Off the heat stir in flour, blend and add salt and cayenne to taste and milk. Stir over heat until it comes to a boil. Add mustard, cheese and cream. Simmer 10 minutes, stirring frequently. Pour over veal and brown under broiler. Melt fat in saucepan. Stir in remaining flour, off the heat, and add tomato paste and meat extract. Return to heat, blend until smooth and season. Stir in stock and let simmer 10 minutes. Place veal in serving dish, pour sauce over; garnish with potato balls and mushrooms. Yield: 6 portions.

VEAL PARMIGIANA

1 pound veal cutlet, thinly sliced	¼ cup grated Parmesan cheese
1 egg, beaten	¾ cup bread crumbs
2 tablespoons water	⅓ cup olive oil
2 teaspoons salt	3 cups seasoned tomato sauce
¼ teaspoon pepper	1 pound Mozzarella cheese, sliced

Cut veal into serving-size pieces. Mix egg with water, 1 teaspoon salt and ⅛ teaspoon pepper. Mix Parmesan cheese with bread crumbs and remaining salt and pepper. Dip cutlets in egg mixture, then in bread crumb mixture. Sauté in hot oil in large skillet for 5 minutes on each side or until golden brown. Cover with tomato sauce and top with Mozzarella cheese; simmer 25 minutes. Place skillet under broiler, 2 inches from source of heat, for 5 minutes or until cheese is slightly browned. Yield: 4 portions.

ESCALLOPINE OF VEAL ARCHDUKE

1½ pounds shoulder of veal	1 teaspoon meat extract
1 tablespoon cooking oil	1 teaspoon lemon juice
3 tablespoons butter	¼ pound small white mushrooms
1 medium-sized onion, diced	½ cup heavy cream
1 medium-sized carrot, julienned	½ cup sour cream
	1 teaspoon mild prepared mustard
1 small bay leaf	1 teaspoon flour
½ clove garlic, minced	salt and pepper to taste

Cut veal in finger-sized pieces. Sauté in oil and 1 tablespoon butter in a heavy frying pan until lightly browned. Add onion, carrot, bay leaf and garlic. Sauté until lightly browned. Pour into a casserole. Add meat extract. Cover and simmer gently 25 minutes. Combine remaining butter and lemon juice in a frying pan. Add mushrooms and sauté about 5 minutes. Add to meat mixture. Combine heavy cream, sour cream, mustard and flour and blend until smooth. Add to casserole. Season with salt and pepper. Cook, stirring frequently, until it just reaches the boiling point. Serve immediately. Approximate yield: 4 to 6 portions.

PAUPIETTES DE VEAU FONTANGES
(Veal Birds with Peas)

2 pounds veal cutlet
6 chicken livers
7 tablespoons butter
8 large mushrooms, sliced
salt and pepper
8 thin slices smoked tongue
3 tablespoons Sherry

½ teaspoon tomato paste
½ teaspoon meat extract
4 tablespoons all-purpose flour
1 cup beef stock
1 bay leaf
2 cups pea purée
½ cup light cream

Slice veal thin, place slices between waxed paper and beat with wooden mallet or side of cleaver until very thin. Brown chicken livers in 2 tablespoons butter and remove from pan. Add 1 tablespoon butter to pan and sauté mushrooms 5 to 7 minutes. Shred chicken livers and add to mushrooms with salt and pepper to taste. Place 1 slice of tongue on each slice of veal and on top of tongue put a tablespoon of mushroom and chicken liver mixture. Roll up each slice, turning in the ends, and tie with string. Brown *paupiettes* quickly in 2 tablespoons hot butter. Heat and ignite 2 tablespoons Sherry and pour over meat. Remove *paupiettes* from pan. To pan, off the heat, add tomato paste, meat extract and 2 tablespoons flour. Blend until smooth. Add stock, season to taste and return to heat; bring to boil, stirring constantly. Add remaining Sherry and *paupiettes* and bay leaf. Cover and simmer slowly 20 to 25 minutes. Melt remaining butter in a saucepan, add remaining flour, blend well and brown slowly. When browned, add pea purée and cream; season with salt and pepper. Turn into serving dish. Remove string from veal birds and arrange them on pea purée. Strain sauce, pour over veal birds and serve. Approximate yield: 8 portions.

SPARERIBS REYKJAVIK (ICELAND)

3 pounds spareribs (2 racks)
2 cups prunes, soaked
3 apples, cut in eighths
1 teaspoon salt
dash of pepper

Wipe spareribs with damp cloth, skewer or tie together at small end. Cover lower rack with prunes and apples and tie firmly together. Place in baking pan, rub with salt and pepper and place in moderate oven (350° F.) 1¾ hours. Yield: 6 portions.

SZEKELY GOULASH (HUNGARIAN)

2 pounds lean shoulder of pork
  or fresh ham, cut in 2-inch
  cubes, without bone
1 medium-sized onion, sliced
1 clove garlic, minced
few caraway seeds
1 medium-sized green pepper,
  cut in 6 pieces
2 medium-sized tomatoes,
  quartered

1 small bunch fresh dill, chopped
1 tablespoon lard, melted
salt to taste
1 tablespoon Hungarian paprika
1½ pounds sauerkraut, washed
  and squeezed dry
¾ cup heavy cream
¾ cup sour cream
1 teaspoon flour

Place pork or ham, onion, garlic minced with caraway seeds, green pepper, tomatoes, dill and lard in casserole or heavy saucepan and cook partially covered on top of the range 1½ hours, or until tender, stirring frequently. Cook until the liquid is evaporated, then add salt to taste and the paprika. Add the washed and drained sauerkraut to the meat and blend. Combine heavy and sour creams and the flour. Blend and add to the meat. Simmer over very low heat for 10 minutes. Do not let stand, but serve immediately. Small boiled potatoes, a tossed green salad and a simple fruit dessert complete the menu for a typical Hungarian dinner. Yield: 4 portions.

POLENTA CON SALSICCIA (ITALIAN)
(Cornmeal with Sausage)

6 cups boiling water
2 cups yellow cornmeal
3 teaspoons salt
2 tablespoons olive oil
1 clove garlic, minced
1 pound sausage, Italian style,
  sliced

¼ cup chopped parsley
1 No. 2½ can (3½ cups)
  tomatoes
¼ teaspoon pepper
¼ cup grated Parmesan cheese

Pour boiling water into top of a 3-quart double boiler. Gradually pour cornmeal into water, stirring constantly to prevent lumping. Add 1 teaspoon salt and cook slowly over boiling water for 1 hour, or until of creamy consistency. Turn into greased 2-quart ring mold. Heat olive oil and garlic in skillet, add sausage slices; brown quickly. Add parsley, tomatoes, pepper and remaining salt. Cover, simmer for 1 hour. To serve, turn out polenta ring and fill center with sauce, sprinkle with cheese. Serve very hot. Yield: 6 to 8 portions.

Note: Browned mushrooms or ripe olives make a good accompaniment.

SAVORY LIVER MEXICANA

1 pound beef liver	½ cup chopped onion

Barbecue Sauce

3 cups tomato juice	¼ teaspoon nutmeg (optional)
1 tablespoon Worcestershire sauce	¼ teaspoon cloves (optional)
	1½ teaspoons salt
¼ cup brown sugar	2 tablespoons vinegar

Corn Bread Topping

1½ cups cornmeal	2 teaspoons baking powder
2 tablespoons flour	1 egg
2 tablespoons sugar	½ cup milk
1 teaspoon salt	2 tablespoons shortening, soft

Cut liver in small pieces; dredge in flour. Brown with onion in small amount of bacon drippings in large frying pan.

Combine ingredients for Barbecue Sauce and simmer 15 minutes. Pour over liver, cover pan and simmer another 15 minutes.

Corn Bread Topping—Sift together dry ingredients. Add egg, milk and shortening. Beat with rotary egg beater for 1 minute. Pour over barbecued liver in frying pan. Bake in moderately hot oven (400° F.) 20 to 25 minutes. Yield: 6 portions.

CHINESE CHOP SUEY

½ pound lean pork	2 tablespoons water
2 tablespoons fat	1 No. 2½ can bean sprouts, drained
1 cup dried celery	
¾ cup sliced onions	1 teaspoon salt
1 cup chicken bouillon	dash of pepper
¼ pound mushrooms, sliced	dash of paprika
1 tablespoon cornstarch	¼ teaspoon sugar

3 cups Boiled Rice (page 507)

Cut pork in small pieces and brown in fat; add celery, onions and bouillon, cover and simmer 20 minutes; add mushrooms and smooth paste made of cornstarch and water, and cook 10 minutes, stirring until thickened. Add bean sprouts and seasonings and heat thoroughly; serve hot with boiled or steamed rice. If desired, 2 tablespoons soy sauce may be added to chop suey and chicken broth or bouillon cubes substituted for chicken bouillon. Approximate yield: 6 portions.

CHINESE CHOW MEIN

⅔ cup chopped onion
½ cup chopped celery leaves
3 tablespoons fat
4 cups chopped celery
1 No. 2 can bean sprouts, drained
¼ cup flour
2 cups water

1½ teaspoons salt
⅛ teaspoon pepper
3 tablespoons soy sauce
2 cups cooked shrimp
1 No. 2½ can Chinese noodles
1½ cups shredded cooked chicken
2 hard-cooked eggs, sliced

Sauté onions and celery leaves in fat until golden brown; add celery and liquid from bean sprouts and simmer 20 minutes. Stir in flour, mixed with water to a smooth paste, and cook until thickened; add salt, pepper, soy sauce, bean sprouts and cleaned shrimp and simmer 15 minutes. Place noodles in shallow pan and heat in moderate oven (350° F.) about 15 minutes, stirring occasionally. Serve chow mein over noodles and top with chicken and eggs. Yield: 6 portions.

CHICKEN SAUTÉ CHASSEURS

¼ cup all-purpose flour
2 teaspoons salt
¼ teaspoon pepper
½ teaspoon thyme
1 2- to 2½-pound fryer, cut in 6 pieces
¼ cup butter or margarine
2 medium onions, chopped
¼ cup (¼ pound) sliced mushrooms

2 tablespoons lemon juice
1 teaspoon sugar
1 teaspoon salt
½ cup apple juice
2 medium tomatoes, diced (or 2 whole canned tomatoes, drained and diced)
2 tablespoons chopped parsley

Combine flour, salt, pepper and thyme in paper bag. Shake pieces of chicken in seasoned flour mixture until thoroughly coated. Melt butter or margarine in heavy skillet, and brown chicken thoroughly on all sides. Add onion and mushrooms. Cover and simmer 5 minutes. Mix lemon juice, sugar, salt and apple juice and pour over chicken. Add tomatoes. Cover skillet and simmer for 1 hour or until chicken is tender. Sprinkle with parsley. Serve piping hot. Yield: 4 to 6 portions.

CHOW YONG YOOK SI

¼ cup fat	1 teaspoon cornstarch
½ teaspoon salt	2 tablespoons water
1 cup thinly sliced onions	1 cup cooked lamb or mutton,
1 cup diced celery	sliced and cut in 1 inch
⅓ cup thinly sliced cucumbers	pieces
6 button mushrooms, thinly	1 teaspoon sugar
sliced	dash of pepper
1 pound (4 cups) Chinese	1 teaspoon soy sauce, or more if
cabbage, coarsely chopped	desired

Melt fat in large iron frying pan and add salt, onions, celery, cucumbers, mushrooms and cabbage. Sauté 2 minutes, turning constantly with a fork. Mix cornstarch and water until smooth and add with meat to sautéed mixture. Continue cooking 10 minutes; add remaining ingredients and cook another minute. Serve at once. Yield: 6 portions.

SUPREME OF CHICKEN PARISIENNE

3 whole breasts of chicken	2 tablespoons flour
(small), skin removed	1½ cups chicken stock
flour	1 small eggplant, peeled and
4 tablespoons butter	sliced thin
2 tablespoons dry Sherry	salt and pepper
½ teaspoon finely chopped	3 tablespoons cooking oil
garlic	4 tomatoes, peeled and sliced thin
1 teaspoon meat extract	finely chopped parsley or chives

Carefully remove breast bones from chicken. Dust chicken lightly with flour and brown quickly in 3 tablespoons hot butter in heavy skillet. Heat Sherry, ignite and pour over chicken. Sauté garlic in remaining butter 30 seconds over low heat in same pan; add meat extract and flour and stir until smooth. Remove from heat and gradually add stock, stirring constantly. Continue cooking until mixture begins to boil. Season to taste with salt and pepper and add to chicken. Cover and simmer 25 to 30 minutes.

Sprinkle eggplant well with salt. Allow to stand 30 minutes. Drain and brown well in hot oil. Remove eggplant from pan and add tomatoes. Fry tomatoes 1 minute only. Combine with eggplant and mix lightly; arrange on bottom of serving dish. Place chicken on top, pour over sauce and sprinkle with parsley or chives. Serve immediately. Approximate yield: 6 portions.

CHICKEN PIE, FRENCH STYLE

2 3-pound chickens
1 onion, sliced
1 carrot, sliced
1 stalk celery, sliced
salt and pepper
1 bay leaf
3 tablespoons butter
1¾ cups all-purpose flour
cayenne
1½ cups chicken stock

¼ cup light cream
2 cans mushrooms, finely chopped
3 hard-cooked eggs, sliced
3 tablespoons chopped fresh herbs
¼ cup shortening
3 egg yolks
3 tablespoons ice water (about)
3 tablespoons grated cheese
½ teaspoon paprika
1 teaspoon dry mustard

¼ teaspoon salt

Put chickens in saucepan with onion, carrot, celery, salt and pepper to taste, bay leaf and water to cover. Bring slowly to a boil and simmer 25 to 30 minutes, or until tender. Remove, reserving stock, and take meat from bones. Remove skin and cut meat in coarse shreds. Melt 2 tablespoons butter; blend in ¼ cup flour, salt and cayenne to taste; blend in stock. Stir over heat until sauce comes to a boil. Add remaining butter, cream and mushrooms, with a little of the mushroom liquid. When well blended, add chicken with eggs and herbs. Place in deep casserole, brush edge of dish with beaten egg and cover with following crust: Put remaining flour on board, make a well in the center and put in shortening, egg yolks, water, cheese, paprika, dry mustard and salt. Work center ingredients to a smooth paste with hands; work in flour. Roll to ¼-inch thickness and cover top of casserole. Trim crust, brush with beaten egg and bake in moderate oven (350° F.) 30 to 35 minutes, or until done. Approximate yield: 6 to 8 portions.

CHICKEN CACCIATORE (ITALIAN)

2 young fowl (3½ to 4 pounds each), cut up
½ cup flour
2 teaspoons salt
½ teaspoon pepper
2 cloves garlic, minced
1 cup cooking oil

2 cups tomato purée or paste
6 cups stewed tomatoes, canned or fresh, peeled
½ teaspoon dried rosemary, crumbled
1 bay leaf
½ cup Sherry

Dry and rub chicken with a mixture of flour, salt, pepper and garlic. Pour enough oil into deep skillet to cover the bottom. Heat and then brown each piece of chicken well. Place in deep, heavy kettle, add remaining oil, tomato purée or paste, tomatoes and seasonings. Cover and cook over very low heat 2 to 3 hours, or until chicken is tender. Fifteen minutes before serving add Sherry. Yield: 8 portions.

DUCK AND PINEAPPLE CANTON (CHINESE)

1 4-lb. duck
¼ cup shoyu sauce
1 tablespoon sugar
½ teaspoon salt
1 gingerroot, ground
1 clove garlic

¼ cup cooking oil
2 cups water
1 cup syrup from canned
   pineapple
2 tablespoons cornstarch
¼ cup water

2 cups diced pineapple

Wash duck and cut in pieces for stewing; dip in mixture of shoyu sauce, sugar, salt and gingerroot and add with garlic to oil in heavy frying pan. Sauté 15 minutes, or until well browned; add water and pineapple juice and simmer, covered, 1 hour, or until tender. Remove duck to hot platter and keep hot. Mix cornstarch and water to a paste, stir into hot liquid in pan and cook 10 minutes, stirring until thickened; add pineapple and cook 5 minutes longer. Turn sauce over duck and serve at once. Approximate yield: 6 portions.

BARCELONA STUFFED FISH

1 slice white bread, cubed
¼ cup milk
½ cup chopped mushroom caps
1 cup chopped spinach
½ cup chopped onion
½ pound codfish, chopped
1 large clove garlic, minced
¼ cup water
1 teaspoon salt
¼ teaspoon pepper
1 3-pound bass, dressed

4 large onions, finely sliced
3 carrots, finely sliced
¼ cup Sherry
1 tablespoon butter
¼ cup red wine
½ teaspoon salt
⅛ teaspoon pepper
2 hard-cooked eggs, finely
   chopped
1 teaspoon chopped parsley
1 teaspoon chopped chives

1 lemon, sliced thin

Soak bread in milk and drain. Combine with mushrooms, spinach, onion, codfish, garlic, water, salt and pepper. Bone bass (page 403). Fill cavity of bass with codfish mixture and sew or skewer cavity closed. Arrange sliced onions in bottom of 8 x 12 inch pan. Place fish on top of onions. Cook carrots in boiling salted water until almost tender. Drain. Combine carrots, Sherry, butter, red wine, salt and pepper. Cook over low heat until carrots are tender. Pour over fish. Cover with parchment paper or greased waxed paper. Bake in moderate oven (350° F.) 35 to 40 minutes. Place fish and sauce on platter. Sprinkle eggs, parsley, and chives over fish. Garnish platter with lemon slices. Approximate yield: 6 portions.

SALMON PARISIAN

3 pounds fresh salmon slices,
   boned and skinned, cut
   into 2 inch cubes
½ cup Burgundy or Claret
1 tablespoon Sherry
1 bay leaf
8 peppercorns
¼ teaspoon salt
8 large mushrooms, thickly
   sliced
2 tablespoons butter
5 tablespoons other fat
7 tablespoons flour

1 teaspoon meat extract
¼ teaspoon salt
dash of cayenne
¾ cup stock from fish
1½ cups light cream
2 tablespoons butter
¼ cup grated Cheddar cheese
½ teaspoon dry mustard
2 egg yolks
4 tablespoons light cream
2 tablespoons grated Cheddar
   cheese
1 tablespoon butter

Place salmon in greased shallow baking pan. Pour red wine and Sherry over fish. Add bay leaf, peppercorns and salt. Cover with waxed paper and tuck in around the edges. Bake in moderate oven (350° F.) 25 to 30 minutes; drain off stock, strain and use in sauce. Sauté mushrooms slowly in hot butter. When tender, arrange over cooked salmon. To make sauce, add other fat to butter in frying pan and blend in flour off the heat. Add meat extract, salt and cayenne. Gradually add stock and cream to flour mixture, stirring constantly until sauce begins to boil. Add butter, a small amount at a time, stirring constantly. Add cheese and mustard, stirring until well blended. Combine egg yolks with cream and gradually stir mixture into sauce. Pour over hot salmon. Sprinkle with cheese and dot with butter. Lightly brown under broiler just before serving. Approximate yield: 8 to 10 portions.

LOBSTER À LA MARSEILLES

1 1¼-pound lobster
1 tablespoon butter
1 small onion, finely chopped
4 large mushrooms

½ teaspoon salt
dash of pepper
1¼ cups canned tomatoes
lettuce

parsley

Boil or steam lobster (page 438); remove meat from shell and cut into small cubes. Add butter, onion, finely chopped mushroom stems, seasonings and lobster meat to 1 cup stewed tomatoes and simmer 3 to 4 minutes; turn into lobster shell. Peel and sauté mushroom caps and place on lobster. Place in baking pan, pour remaining ¼ cup tomatoes over top and bake in moderate oven (350° F.) 10 minutes. Serve on bed of lettuce and parsley. Yield: 3 to 4 portions.

LOBSTER CANTONESE STYLE (CHINESE)

1 large lobster	dash of pepper
1 teaspoon black beans, soaked	½ teaspoon sugar
(dow see)	1 teaspoon gourmet powder
2 cloves garlic	(mei jing)
4 ounces chopped, raw lean pork	1 cup stock or water
2 tablespoons butter	2 scallions, minced
½ teaspoon salt	2 teaspoons cornstarch

3 eggs, well beaten

Split lobster in half and cut through shell into 1-inch pieces. Wash black beans thoroughly; drain and crush with garlic. Add to lobster (unshelled) pieces and pork and sauté in butter 2 minutes, stirring constantly. Add salt, pepper, sugar, gourmet powder and stock; cover and cook 5 minutes. Add scallions and cornstarch mixed to a smooth paste with 2 tablespoons cold water. Cook 2 minutes; stir a small amount into eggs. Gradually add to cooked mixture, stirring constantly until slightly thickened. Approximate yield: 2 portions.

BOILED LOBSTER, FRENCH STYLE

2 teaspoons cooking oil	1 tablespoon tarragon vinegar
½ onion, sliced thin	2½ cups water
1 carrot, finely sliced	bay leaf
1 stalk of celery, finely sliced	peppercorns
¼ cup dry white wine	1 1½-pound lobster

Heat oil in saucepan and lightly brown onion, carrot and celery. Add white wine, vinegar, water, bay leaf and several peppercorns. Add dash of salt and bring to boil. Add lobster, cover and simmer 12 to 15 minutes, or until lobster is very red. Remove lobster and cool. Strain broth and use for lobster stock. Yield: 2 portions.

HOMARD PARISIENNE
(Cold Lobster with Mayonnaise)

2 large live lobsters	4 tablespoons Lobster Mayonnaise
2 cups mixed, diced, cooked	(page 1028)
carrots, beans and peas	2 hard-cooked eggs, chopped
2 tomatoes, peeled and diced	paprika

Cook lobsters (page 438) in boiling, salted water. Remove from heat and allow to cool in the water. Split lobsters in halves and carefully remove the meat from tails and claws. Fill shells with a mixture of cooked vegetables, tomatoes and 2 tablespoons mayonnaise. Cut lobster meat in slices and arrange on top. Pour over remaining mayonnaise. Garnish with chopped eggs and paprika and serve. Yield: 4 portions.

PILAF D'HOMARD
(Lobster Pilaf)

2 tablespoons oil	2 tablespoons grated Parmesan
4 tablespoons fat	cheese
1 onion, finely chopped	2 lobsters
1 clove of garlic, minced	4 tablespoons heavy cream or
2 cups rice	sour cream
4 cups strong stock (beef or	salt and pepper
fish)	paprika
1 bay leaf	¼ cup chopped chives (optional)

Heat 1 tablespoon oil and 1 tablespoon fat in a pan. Add onion and
garlic and cook until soft without browning. Add rice and cook slowly
7 minutes, stirring constantly. Cover with stock, bring to a boil, season
to taste with salt, pepper and paprika; add bay leaf. Cover and cook 25
minutes in a moderately hot oven (375° F.). Remove. With a fork
stir in cheese and 2 tablespoons fat. Line a well-greased, deep, round
mold with ⅔ of mixture and make a hole in the center. Wash lobsters
and split in halves. Remove the bag from behind the eyes and discard.
Heat remaining oil and fat in a large skillet and put in lobsters, split-
side down. Cover and cook slowly until a bright red. Remove meat
from shells and cut up coarsely. Mix with a little grated cheese and the
cream. Season and add chopped chives, if desired. Fill hole in center
with lobster mixture and cover with remaining rice mixture. Press
down gently. Turn out of mold onto a serving dish. Garnish with a
few lobster shells. Yield: 4 portions.

FRIED SHRIMP, ITALIAN STYLE

2 pounds jumbo shrimp, shelled	2 tablespoons minced parsley
and veins removed	1 teaspoon salt
2 eggs, beaten	¼ teaspoon pepper
1 cup bread crumbs	½ teaspoon dried basil
½ cup grated Parmesan cheese	olive oil and salad oil

Dip shrimp in beaten eggs. Roll in combined bread crumbs, cheese,
parsley, salt, pepper and basil. Allow to stand 5 minutes. Place equal
amounts of olive and salad oil in a heavy skillet to make a layer 1-inch
deep. Heat until hot but not smoking. Add just enough shrimp to fill
the pan; fry until golden brown on all sides. Cook remaining shrimp
in the same manner. Drain on absorbent paper. Approximate yield: 4
portions.

LOBSTER SARAMITO

1 2-pound live lobster	dash of cayenne
2 eggs	1 teaspoon brandy
1 pint heavy cream, whipped	1 truffle, chopped
1 teaspoon salt	lobster coral, chopped
⅛ teaspoon black pepper	small lobsters, cooked

When possible, have the fish dealer split the live lobster. To kill the lobster, insert a sharp knife between the body and tail shells. Place on back and make deep cut lengthwise from head to end of tail; open and remove stomach, dark vein and liver; discard. Remove coral, if present, and reserve. Remove flesh and force through a fine sieve. Place in saucepan with eggs and set over bowl filled with ice cubes. Add whipped cream slowly. Add seasonings, brandy and truffles. Turn into buttered 1-quart mold and sprinkle chopped, poached coral over top. Cover tightly and place in hot water to within 1 inch of top of mold. Poach slowly 20 minutes. Cool on ice 2 hours. Unmold on platter and garnish with cooked half lobsters and water cress. Yield: 4 portions.

TROUT MEUNIÈRE

4 large speckled trout, fresh or frozen	1 teaspoon tarragon vinegar
garlic	4 thin slices of lemon
salt and pepper	parsley or dill, finely chopped
flour	2 cucumbers, skinned and cubed
8 tablespoons butter	8 mushrooms, quartered
juice of 1 lemon	1 grapefruit, sectioned
1 onion, finely chopped	2 tomatoes, skinned and quartered
¼ cup white wine	paprika
1 tablespoon chopped fresh herbs	

Wash fish and dry well with cloth which has been rubbed with garlic. Season fish with salt and pepper and dust lightly with flour. Place in 3 tablespoons hot butter and shake pan while trout are browning to prevent sticking. Cook about 3 minutes on each side. Remove to hot platter and sprinkle with lemon juice. Serve with sauce made as follows: Sauté onion in 1 tablespoon melted butter. Slowly add wine, salt and pepper to taste, and herbs. Add vinegar and stir well. Place slice of lemon on each trout and pour sauce over trout. Sauté parsley or dill lightly in remaining butter. Add cucumbers and mushrooms and cook until lightly brown. Add grapefruit sections and tomato quarters and cook 1 minute. Arrange on platter around sauce-covered trout and garnish with paprika. Yield: 4 portions.

FILLET OF SOLE EN PAPILLOTE

8 fillets of sole	2 tablespoons Sherry
½ clove garlic, minced	¾ teaspoon salt
1¼ cups chopped mushrooms	¼ teaspoon pepper
3 tablespoons sour cream	2 apples, peeled and sliced
1 tablespoon chopped mixed	2 tablespoons sugar
fresh herbs	1 tablespoon chopped chives
½ cup butter	1 teaspoon chopped tarragon

Put 2 of the sole fillets through food chopper. Add ¼ clove garlic, ¼ cup mushrooms, sour cream and herbs and blend well. Place remaining fillets on board, spread with sole mixture, roll each as for jelly roll and secure with toothpick. Brush with 2 tablespoons melted butter. Arrange each fish roll on one end of a piece of greased parchment paper 8 x 5 inches. Sauté 1 cup mushrooms in 2 tablespoons butter. Add Sherry, ½ teaspoon salt and ⅛ teaspoon pepper. Cover top of each fillet with a layer of these mushrooms. Lightly brown apples in 2 tablespoons butter. Sprinkle with sugar. Arrange several slices of glazed apples on top of mushrooms. Cream 2 tablespoons butter. Blend in ¼ clove garlic, ¼ teaspoon salt, pepper, chives and tarragon. Place 1 teaspoon herb butter on top of apples. Fold free ends of paper over fillets and fold edges together to seal. Place on shallow baking pan and bake in hot oven (400° F.) 25 minutes. Cut crossing slits in paper and serve. Yield: 6 portions.

FILLET OF SOLE PARISIENNE

1½ cups shelled cooked shrimp,	¼ cup water
sliced	1 bay leaf
3 tablespoons butter, melted	3 peppercorns
1 tablespoon chopped parsley	1 teaspoon salt
3 tomatoes, sliced	3 tablespoons flour
10 fillets of flounder or sole	few grains of cayenne
½ cup dry white wine	¼ cup light cream

Combine shrimp, 1 tablespoon butter and parsley. Cook over low heat 1 minute. Add tomatoes. Arrange on serving dish. Arrange fillets in greased baking pan. Add white wine, water, bay leaf, peppercorns and ½ teaspoon salt. Cover with parchment paper and bake in moderate oven (350° F.) 15 minutes. Remove fillets and arrange on shrimp. Strain liquid and reserve. Combine remaining butter, flour, salt and cayenne; add liquid; cook and stir until mixture thickens. Add cream, heat, pour over fish. Yield: 10 portions.

FILET DE SOLE GRAND DUC

1½ pounds flounder fillets
2 peppercorns
½ teaspoon salt
¼ cup dry white wine
¼ cup water
stock from baked fish

1 recipe French White Wine
Sauce (page 1028)
1 recipe Hollandaise Sauce (page 473)
¼ cup sautéed mushroom caps
cooked asparagus (optional)

Place fillets in bottom of baking dish. Add peppercorns, salt, wine and water. Cover and place in slow oven (300° F.) 15 minutes. Drain off stock and reserve for French White Wine Sauce. Pour sauce over fillets in baking dish and spoon Hollandaise Sauce over top. Brown under broiler and garnish with mushroom caps and bundles of cooked asparagus, if desired. Yield: 4 to 6 portions.

HAISEH SAUCE (JEWISH)

2 tablespoons minced, uncooked beef
2 tablespoons minced carrot
2 tablespoons minced onion
2 tablespoons minced celery
2 tablespoons vegetable fat or shortening

2 tablespoons flour
2 cups beef stock
½ teaspoon salt
5 peppercorns
herb bouquet (page 1088)

Cook slowly beef, carrot, onion and celery in fat for 5 minutes; blend in flour and cook 3 minutes. Add beef stock gradually, stirring constantly; add salt, peppercorns and the bouquet and simmer 10 minutes; strain. Serve with beef. Yield 1⅔ cups sauce.

SAUCE MEXICANA

½ cup canned tomatoes
¼ cup chili sauce
2 tablespoons grated horse-radish
¼ cup vinegar

1 tablespoon prepared mustard
½ teaspoon salt
dash of pepper
½ teaspoon curry powder
2 tablespoons chopped parsley

½ teaspoon onion juice

Place all ingredients in saucepan and cook slowly until thickened; strain and cool. This sauce may be kept in refrigerator for a week. When ready to use, mix with tart mayonnaise dressing—1 part sauce to 2 parts mayonnaise. Serve with fish, fried oysters and cold meats. Approximate yield: ¾ cup sauce.

FILET DE SOLE FLORENTINE

6 fillets of sole or flounder
¼ cup dry white wine
¼ cup water
bay leaf
salt
peppercorns
2 pounds spinach, sorrel or
   lettuce, washed

1 tablespoon butter or bacon fat
3 tablespoons sour cream
1 recipe French White Wine
   Sauce (page 1028)
1 recipe Hollandaise Sauce
   (page 473)

Wash fillets, dry with a cloth and place in baking dish with white wine, water, bay leaf, salt and peppercorns. Cover and cook 15 minutes in moderate oven (350° F.). Place spinach in saucepan with butter or bacon fat and salt. Cook, covered, over high heat 7 to 8 minutes. Drain, chop fine and add sour cream and salt and pepper to taste. When ready to serve fish, arrange spinach on bottom of hot serving dish, shaping into a slight mound; smooth down the top with spatula. Lay baked fillets in a row and cover with White Wine Sauce mixed with Hollandaise. Brown under broiler and serve immediately. Approximate yield: 6 portions.

SOLE DURAND

2 cups finely sliced carrots
2 cups finely sliced turnips
1 cup finely sliced onion
2 cups white wine
¼ cup chopped mixed herbs
½ cup butter or fat

1 small whole sole
6 tomatoes, skinned, pipped and
   shredded
1½ teaspoons lemon juice
½ cup light cream
salt and pepper to taste

¼ cup chopped parsley

Place carrots, turnips, onions, 1 cup white wine, half the herbs and 2 tablespoons butter in a pan. Cover and cook until liquid is evaporated, without browning. Wash, trim and place sole in oven-proof dish. Put vegetable mixture around fish with tomatoes. Sprinkle with remaining herbs and pour over remaining wine. Cook in moderate oven (350° F.) 20 minutes, basting frequently. Remove from oven and strain liquor from saucepan. Reduce liquor from sole to half. Add lemon juice. Beat in cream slowly and season. Bring slowly to a boil. Remove from heat and add, bit by bit, remaining butter and parsley. If desired, thicken with a little potato or all-purpose flour blended with water. Pour sauce over sole and place in hot oven 2 to 3 minutes before serving. Yield: 4 portions.

FRENCH WHITE WINE SAUCE

2 tablespoons butter or
  margarine
3 tablespoons flour
salt and cayenne

¼ cup light stock (fish or
  chicken)
¼ cup dry white wine
¼ cup water

¼ cup light cream

Melt butter and stir in flour off the heat. Season to taste with salt and cayenne. Gradually add stock and wine mixed with water, stirring constantly. Season to taste and cook 2 minutes. Stir in cream and heat, stirring occasionally. Do not boil. Yield: 1 cup sauce.

MAYONNAISE D'HOMARD
(Lobster Mayonnaise)

2 cups rice
3 tomatoes, shredded
2 tablespoons chopped parsley

Spicy French Dressing (page 619)
pieces of cold boiled lobster
French Mayonnaise (below)

Boil rice, drain and rinse in cold water. Place in a bowl and add tomatoes and parsley; mix well. Mix with Spicy French Dressing and arrange in a long serving dish. Place lobster meat on top. Pour over French Mayonnaise. Yield: 4 portions.

FRENCH MAYONNAISE

2 egg yolks
1 teaspoon salt
pinch of coarsely-ground
  pepper
pinch of dry mustard

2 tablespoons vinegar or lemon
  juice
1½ cups cooking oil
2 tablespoons light cream
tomato pulp

Put egg yolks, salt, pepper, mustard and 1 tablespoon vinegar or lemon juice in a bowl and blend. Slowly beat in oil, ½ teaspoon at a time. As mixture thickens, add remaining vinegar. When thoroughly mixed, add cream and tomato pulp. Yield: 2 cups.

TURKISH PILAU

3 cups cooked rice (page 507)
2 small tomatoes, quartered
¼ cup chopped onion

1½ cups stock or water
2 cups chopped, cooked mutton
3 tablespoons buttered crumbs

Combine rice, tomatoes, onion and stock; arrange in alternate layers with mutton in greased casserole; cover with crumbs. Bake in moderate oven (350° F.) 25 to 30 minutes. Yield: 6 portions.

RICE MEXICANA

1 cup rice
½ clove garlic, minced
1 small onion, chopped
2 tablespoons fat
2 teaspoons salt

½ medium-sized green pepper, chopped
2 teaspoons chili powder
1 cup canned tomatoes
2 cups beef stock

Wash rice; sauté with garlic and onion in hot fat until browned. Add salt, green pepper, chili powder, tomatoes and stock; cover and simmer 20 to 30 minutes, or until rice is soft, removing cover during last 5 minutes to finish evaporation and let mixture dry out. One-half pound chopped beef may be cooked with rice, if desired. Yield: 6 portions.

NOODLES ANTOINE

1 8-oz. package of thin noodles
1 cup cottage cheese
1½ cups sour cream
1 clove garlic, minced
¾ cup finely chopped onion

1 teaspoon Worcestershire sauce
dash of Tabasco
1 teaspoon salt
⅛ teaspoon pepper
½ cup grated Parmesan cheese

Cook noodles in boiling salted water until tender. Mix cottage cheese, sour cream, garlic, onion, Worcestershire sauce, Tabasco, salt and pepper. Drain noodles, add to sauce mixture and turn into a greased casserole. Bake in a moderate oven (350° F.) for 30 minutes. Ten minutes before removing dish, sprinkle with Parmesan cheese. Yield: 6 portions.

SPAGHETTI SAUCE ITALIAN STYLE

½ cup olive oil
2 cups boiled, sliced fresh mushrooms
2 cloves garlic, finely crushed
¼ teaspoon crushed red pepper seeds

1 large green pepper, minced
1 pound chopped beef
2 large cans plum tomatoes
1 can tomato paste
salt

Heat olive oil in deep well cooker and add mushrooms, garlic, red pepper seeds, minced green pepper and chopped beef. Simmer 5 minutes, stirring frequently. Add plum tomatoes and simmer for 45 minutes. Add tomato paste and blend. Add salt to taste. Cover and simmer at least 30 minutes more, stirring occasionally to prevent sticking. This is enough sauce for 2 pounds of spaghetti. Yield: 12 portions.

LASAGNE ROLLS

1 pound lasagne	1 pound hamburger
4 tablespoons olive oil	2 eggs
2 garlic cloves, chopped	3 cans Ragù sauce
½ pound mushrooms, sliced	½ teaspoon salt
½ pound Italian sausage	few grains pepper
4 chicken livers, chopped	1 2½-oz. jar Parmesan cheese

Place lasagne, one at a time, in 6 quarts boiling salted water to which 1 tablespoon oil has been added, to prevent lasagne from sticking together. Cook 20 minutes. Drain. Sauté garlic and mushrooms in 2 tablespoons oil about 3 minutes, or until brown. Remove sausage meat from casing. Add to mushroom mixture, remaining oil, chicken livers, hamburger and sausage, break meat into small pieces with fork, stir and sauté until brown. Beat eggs; add 6 tablespoons Ragù sauce, salt, pepper, 2 tablespoons cheese and meat mixture. Mix well. Place 1 lasagne ribbon on flat platter; spread with thin layer of meat mixture. Roll up jelly-roll fashion; stand up in baking dish, continue until all is used. Cover with remaining Ragù sauce and sprinkle with remaining cheese. Bake in moderate oven (350° F.) 20 minutes. Yield: 6 to 8 portions.

SPAGHETTI OR MACARONI SUPREME

3- to 4-lb. chicken, disjointed	1 pound mushrooms
½ cup butter	2 8-oz. packages spaghetti or
1 teaspoon salt	macaroni
pinch of sage	3 tablespoons flour
½ cup celery tops	evaporated milk
1 small onion, chopped	½ cup dry Sherry
1 cup boiling water	⅔ cup grated Romano cheese

Sauté chicken in 3 tablespoons butter, turning to brown all sides; add salt, sage, celery tops, onion and boiling water. Cover; simmer until chicken is tender, about 45 to 50 minutes, adding more water if necessary. Cool. Remove chicken from bones. Save stock. Cut mushrooms in thick slices; sauté in 2 tablespoons butter; add cooked chicken. Prepare spaghetti, according to directions on package. Drain; keep hot. Melt remaining butter; blend in flour. Measure chicken stock; add enough evaporated milk to make 3 cups. Gradually add to butter and flour mixture; cook, stirring constantly, until thick. Add Sherry and cheese; heat. Add chicken mixture; heat. Place spaghetti on platter; pour over sauce. Serve immedritely. Yield: 4 to 6 portions.

SPAGHETTI WITH MEAT BALLS

2 cloves of garlic, halved
¼ cup olive oil
1½ pounds ground beef
1½ quarts canned puréed
   tomatoes
1 cup water
½ teaspoon basil
¼ teaspoon orégano
¾ teaspoon pepper
   grated Parmesan cheese

6 ozs. lean pork, cut in 3 pieces
½ teaspoon dried mint
¼ cup grated Parmesan cheese
¼ cup bread crumbs
1 teaspoon salt
2 small eggs
2 tablespoons water
salt
2 pounds spaghetti

Sauté garlic in 2 tablespoons oil until lightly browned. Add ½ pound ground beef and sauté gently until cooked but not browned. Add puréed tomatoes, 1 cup water, ¼ teaspoon basil, orégano and ½ teaspoon pepper. Add pork and cook slowly, partially covered, 2 hours, stirring occasionally. Combine 1 pound ground beef, mint, ¼ teaspoon basil, grated Parmesan, bread crumbs, salt and remaining pepper. Add eggs and water and mix until blended. Shape into small balls and brown on all sides in remaining olive oil. Add to sauce during last half hour of the cooking time. Cook spaghetti in boiling salted water until tender. Drain and rinse. Serve with sauce and meat balls. Top with grated Parmesan cheese. Yield: 4 to 6 generous portions.

ITALIAN SPAGHETTI SUPPER

½ cup olive oil
4 medium-sized onions, sliced
1½ green peppers, finely diced
2 cloves of garlic, minced
3 cans tomato paste
2 cans water
2½ pounds ground chuck steak

1 clove minced garlic
1 onion, finely chopped
1 egg
¾ cup dry bread crumbs
salt and pepper
2 tablespoons olive oil
3 8-ounce packages spaghetti

Heat oil in heavy skillet; add onions, green pepper and garlic. Sauté slowly until light brown. Reduce heat; add tomato paste and water (use tomato paste cans for measuring). Cook, stirring constantly, for 5 minutes. Combine ground steak, minced garlic, chopped onion, egg and bread crumbs; shape into balls 2 inches in diameter. Heat 2 tablespoons of oil in frying pan and brown meat balls. Add to sauce. Simmer 2 to 3 hours, stirring frequently. Serve over spaghetti. Yield: 4 to 6 portions.

ITALIAN SPAGHETTI À NAPLES

1 cup coarsely cut chicken
  livers
½ cup chopped onion
2 tablespoons chopped parsley
1 cup minced carrots
1 cup minced celery
½ pound mushrooms, sliced
2 cloves garlic
2 tablespoons butter
2 tablespoons olive oil

½ teaspoon cloves
½ teaspoon cinnamon
salt and pepper
2 cups canned tomatoes,
  strained
2 cups stock or water
2 tablespoons Italian tomato
  paste
1 8-oz. package spaghetti
½ cup grated Parmesan cheese

Sauté livers and vegetables in butter and oil until almost tender; add
seasonings, tomatoes, stock and tomato paste and simmer about 1
hour, removing garlic when flavor becomes pronounced. Cook unbroken
spaghetti (page 499), place in ring on hot platter, fill center with heated
sauce and pour some over spaghetti; sprinkle with cheese. Calf's liver
or any meat may be substituted for chicken livers. Yield: 6 portions.

NAPOLI SPAGHETTI

1 8-oz. package spaghetti
6 slices bacon, diced
1 onion, sliced
3 cups canned tomatoes
½ teaspoon salt

⅛ teaspoon pepper
¼ teaspoon allspice
¼ teaspoon mace
dash of cayenne
½ bay leaf

Cook spaghetti (page 499). Sauté bacon until crisp, add remaining
ingredients and simmer 50 minutes. Add spaghetti and keep hot for
10 minutes before serving. Approximate yield: 6 portions.

SPAGHETTI À LA BRAZILERIO

1 8-oz. package spaghetti
4 slices bacon, diced
2 medium-sized onions, sliced
1⅓ cups canned tomatoes
2 green peppers, chopped

1 clove garlic, chopped
¼ cup sliced stuffed olives
1 teaspoon sugar
salt and pepper
½ cup grated Italian cheese

Cook spaghetti (page 499). Sauté bacon until crisp; remove from pan
and sauté onions in the bacon fat until golden brown; add tomatoes,
pepper and garlic and simmer 10 to 15 minutes. Add spaghetti, bacon,
olives, sugar and salt and pepper to taste. Heat thoroughly; serve on
platter and sprinkle with cheese. Yield: 6 portions.

SPAGHETTI À L'ASTA

1 clove garlic, chopped
1 No. 2 can tomatoes
2 teaspoons celery salt
1 teaspoon sugar
1 teaspoon cinnamon
1 teaspoon cloves
1 teaspoon ginger
1 large onion, chopped

dash of cayenne
1 cup beef stock
1 cup finely chopped chicken
   livers
1 cup chopped mushrooms
3 tablespoons butter
1½ tablespoons flour
1 8-oz. package spaghetti

½ cup grated Parmesan cheese

Simmer garlic, tomatoes, celery salt, sugar, spices, onion and cayenne ½ hour; add beef stock. Sauté livers and mushrooms in butter until lightly browned; stir in flour; then add tomato mixture slowly and simmer 15 minutes, stirring constantly. Cook unbroken spaghetti (page 499); mix thoroughly with sauce. Sprinkle each serving generously with cheese. Approximate yield: 6 portions.

AMSTERDAM SPAGHETTI

2 cups prepared canned spaghetti
   or spaghetti with tomato
   sauce

2 cups canned sauerkraut
6 slices bacon

Put alternate layers of spaghetti and sauerkraut in greased baking dish; cut bacon slices in halves and arrange on top. Bake in moderate oven (350° F.) 30 minutes, or until bacon is crisp. Yield: 6 portions.

GNOCCHI ROMANA

2 cups water
1 teaspoon salt
dash of cayenne pepper
½ cup farina
1 egg, beaten

1 teaspoon dry mustard
½ cup grated cheese
1 tablespoon butter
¼ cup grated American cheese
2 tablespoons melted butter

Bring water to boil with salt and cayenne. Gradually add farina, stirring constantly. Cook until very thick and mixture comes clean away from side of pan (about 15–20 minutes), stirring well with a wooden spoon. Remove from heat and stir in egg, mustard, ½ cup cheese and butter. Blend well. Spread ½-inch thick on shallow pan and place in refrigerator to chill. When firm, cut into rounds with 2-inch cookie cutter. Place on shallow baking pan, sprinkle with ¼ cup cheese and brush with melted butter. Place under broiler until cheese is melted and lightly browned. Arrange overlapping on hot platter. Yield: 4 to 6 portions.

SPINACH GNOCCHI

2 cups water
1 teaspoon salt
dash of cayenne pepper
⅔ cup white or yellow cornmeal
1 egg
1 teaspoon dry mustard

½ cup grated cheese
1 tablespoon butter
½ cup finely-chopped cooked
    spinach, drained
¼ cup grated Cheddar cheese
2 tablespoons melted butter

Bring water to boil with salt and cayenne. Gradually add corn-meal, stirring constantly. Cook until very thick, stirring constantly with a wooden spoon. Remove from heat and stir in egg, mustard, cheese, butter and spinach. Blend well and heat for 2 minutes. Spread ½ inch thick on shallow baking pan. Place in refrigerator to chill. When firm, cut into rounds with 2 inch cookie cutter and place on baking pan. Sprinkle with cheese and brush with melted butter. Broil until cheese is melted and golden brown. Arrange overlapping on hot serving platter. Approximate yield: 4 to 6 portions.

GNOCCHI PARISIENNE

2 cups water
½ cup shortening
1 teaspoon salt
dash of cayenne
2 cups flour

1 teaspoon dry mustard
4 tablespoons Gruyère cheese
3 eggs
2 cups water
½ teaspoon salt

Combine water, shortening, salt and cayenne. Bring slowly to boiling. Sift flour and mustard. Remove hot mixture from heat. Quickly add flour and cheese and beat until smooth with a wooden spoon. Blend in eggs. Fill pastry tube with this mixture. Heat remaining ingredients but do not boil. Press gnocchi through tube in 1 inch lengths and drop into hot water. Cook until just firm. Drain and serve with Mornay Sauce (page 469). Approximate yield: 6 to 8 portions.

SPANISH BEANS

2 cups dried beans
salt
1 cup chopped smoked ham

½ pound sausage meat
1 green pepper, minced
½ clove garlic, minced

Wash, soak and simmer beans (page 527) until tender. Season to taste with salt. Fry ham and sausage, remove from pan and add to beans. Drain off all but 2 tablespoons of the fat; fry pepper and garlic lightly and add to beans; bring again to a boil and simmer 20 minutes. Approximate yield: 6 portions.

RED KIDNEY BEANS PAYSANNE

1 cup chopped onion
3 tablespoons bacon fat or
   butter
1 slice of smoked ham, cut
   ½-inch thick, diced
1 tablespoon flour
½ cup consommé

1 cup claret
pinch of cayenne
1 teaspoon salt
2 No. 2½ cans kidney beans,
   drained
6 slices bacon
¼ cup toasted bread crumbs

¼ cup Parmesan cheese

Sauté onion in hot fat and add diced ham. Stir in flour and add combined consommé and claret. Heat to boiling and add cayenne, salt and beans. Turn into casserole and place slices of bacon on top of beans. Bake 20 to 30 minutes in 400° F. oven and add the combined bread crumbs and cheese the last 5 minutes. Yield: 6 portions.

AZTEC BAKED BEANS

3 cups canned red kidney beans
1½ cups canned tomatoes
1 pimiento, minced
¼ cup deviled ham
1 medium-sized onion, minced
¾ teaspoon salt

dash of pepper
¾ teaspoon dry mustard
¾ teaspoon curry powder
1½ tablespoons molasses
1½ tablespoons sugar
6 strips thinly sliced bacon

Mix all ingredients except bacon; turn into greased casserole, arrange bacon on top and bake in moderate oven (350° F.) about 30 minutes, or until bacon is crisp. Approximate yield: 6 portions.

MEXICAN ASPARAGUS

2 green peppers, minced
1 large onion, minced
1 clove garlic, minced
2 pimientos, minced

6 tablespoons oil or butter
2 tablespoons vinegar
½ teaspoon salt
2 pounds hot boiled asparagus

6 poached eggs

Sauté green peppers, onion, garlic and pimientos in oil until browned. Add vinegar and salt. Arrange hot asparagus and eggs on platter; pour sauce over. Yield: 6 portions.

HARICOTS VERTS PARISIENNE
(Green Beans Parisienne)

1 pound green beans	salt to taste
3 tablespoons butter	cayenne to taste
1 teaspoon lemon juice	¼ cup water

Cut beans in very thin slices diagonally. Slowly bring to a boil in cold water; drain. Melt butter in heavy pan; add lemon juice, salt, pepper and water. Add beans. Cover and cook slowly, stirring occasionally, until tender, about 20 minutes. Drain and serve. Yield: 4 portions.

VIENNESE SNAP BEANS

1½ pounds snap beans, cut in julienne strips	¼ cup minced onion
	½ cup fresh dill, minced
1 tablespoon butter	½ teaspoon salt
1 tablespoon flour	dash of pepper
1 sprig parsley, minced	2 tablespoons sour cream

1 teaspoon vinegar

Cook string beans in boiling salted water 20 minutes, or until tender. Drain, saving ¾ cup of liquid. Melt butter and stir in flour. Add parsley and onion, then gradually the bean stock. Stir until smooth and slightly thickened. Add dill, let simmer 5 minutes. Add string beans and remaining ingredients. Yield: 6 portions.

SPROUTS À LA BRIGOULE

1 quart Brussels sprouts	¼ cup chopped celery
½ cup chopped carrots	1½ cups bouillon
¼ cup chopped onion	3 tablespoons butter
½ cup chopped, cooked chestnuts (page 543)	salt and pepper
	2 thin slices lemon, cut in quarters

Cook Brussels sprouts (page 535); arrange in greased casserole; add vegetables and chestnuts to bouillon and cook 10 minutes; add butter, season to taste and add lemon. Pour vegetable mixture over sprouts and bake in moderate oven (350° F.) 30 minutes. Yield: 6 portions.

ITALIAN CELERY

Melt 2 tablespoons butter, add 1 tablespoon minced ham, ½ cup meat stock, bring to a boil, then pour over 1 beaten egg yolk mixed with 2 tablespoons grated cheese; cook until sauce thickens slightly; add 2 cups cooked celery (page 541). Pour over 6 rounds buttered toast, place in hot oven about 1 minute and serve. Yield: 6 portions.

SAUERKRAUT MIT APFEL

To 2 cups sauerkraut add ¼ cup fat, ¼ cup water, 3 apples, peeled, cored and quartered, 1 medium-sized onion, sliced, and cook until tender. Add ½ teaspoon salt, 1 tablespoon sugar, ½ teaspoon caraway seeds and 2 small potatoes, grated; cook 5 minutes longer. Approximate yield: 6 portions.

RUSSIAN SAUERKRAUT

Simmer 6 dry mushrooms in small amount of water until just tender; drain, reserving ⅓ cup liquor. Add mushroom liquor and 1 cup sour cream to 2 pounds sauerkraut; simmer about 20 minutes, add chopped mushrooms and cook 5 minutes longer. Approximate yield: 6 portions.

POLISH CABBAGE

1 cup diced onion	½ cup milk
1 cup sliced mushrooms	½ cup water
3 tablespoons butter or oil	2 teaspoons salt
2½ cups thinly sliced raw potatoes	¼ teaspoon white pepper
	½ teaspoon caraway seeds
6 cups coarsely chopped raw cabbage	

Sauté onion and mushrooms in butter 10 minutes. Add potatoes, cabbage, milk, water, salt, pepper and caraway seeds. Simmer, covered, 15 minutes, stirring occasionally. Approximate yield: 1 quart.

EGGPLANT IMAN BAILDI (TURKISH)

1 large eggplant	1 cup finely chopped onion
12 slices of tomato	salt and pepper
	olive oil

Pare eggplant and slice. Parboil 10 minutes. Remove with a skimmer and place in layers in a casserole with a slice of tomato on each slice of eggplant. Fill interstices with onion. Season and add oil barely to cover. Bake in a moderate oven (350° F.) 30 minutes. Serve cold. Yield: 6 portions.

EGGPLANT PARMESAN

1 medium-sized eggplant	2 tablespoons shortening
1 egg, beaten	1 8-oz. can tomato sauce
¼ cup milk	1 tablespoon minced parsley
½ cup dry bread crumbs	pinch of orégano
½ teaspoon salt	1 bay leaf
oil	¼ cup grated Parmesan cheese
1 clove of garlic, minced	¼ pound Mozzarella cheese, sliced

Pare eggplant and cut in ¼-inch slices crosswise. Dip into combined egg and milk, then into combined bread crumbs and salt. Sauté in hot oil until golden brown on both sides. Sauté garlic in shortening until light brown. Add tomato sauce, parsley, orégano and bay leaf. Simmer slowly 15 minutes. Place alternate layers of eggplant, Parmesan cheese, tomato sauce and Mozzarella cheese in greased casserole. Top with Mozzarella cheese. Bake in moderate oven (350° F.) about 20 minutes, or until cheese is melted. Approximate yield: 4 to 6 portions.

IRANIAN EGGPLANT

1 large eggplant, peeled	2 cups canned tomatoes
2 tablespoons shortening	1 cup seedless raisins
1 pound ground beef or lamb	1 cup pistachio nuts
½ cup sliced onions	salt and pepper

Cut eggplant in ½ inch slices. Lightly brown in hot fat. Remove eggplant and lightly brown meat and onions. Add tomatoes and heat to boiling. Place alternate layers of all ingredients in well-greased baking dish, seasoning well between each layer. Bake in moderate oven (350° F.) 30 minutes or until liquid is absorbed and top is brown. Serve over hot rice. Approximate yield: 4 to 6 portions.

GREEK FAKAIS (LENTILS)

2 pounds dried lentils	1 to 2 cups oil (optional)
8 quarts water	salt, if necessary
1 ham bone	½ teaspoon pepper
10 cloves garlic, minced	vinegar

Pick over lentils, carefully removing all foreign material. Wash well and soak overnight. Drain, add fresh water, ham bone and garlic. Simmer uncovered six hours, adding more water only if necessary. If ham bone is not fatty, add 1 cup of oil or more to taste, and simmer 1 hour more. Add salt and pepper to taste. Serve with a dash of vinegar. Yield: 4 quarts or 16 portions.

SPINACH FLORENTINE

Arrange bed of well-seasoned cooked spinach in serving dish; place poached eggs on top and pour Hollandaise Sauce (page 473) or Cheese Sauce (page 470) over top.

SALENYIA GRIBI (RUSSIAN)

Chill 1 pound sautéed whole mushroom caps, pack in a jar and add 2 cups vinegar which has been simmered 10 minutes with 4 whole cloves, 12 peppercorns, 1 tablespoon salt, and 2 tablespoons olive oil. Cover closely and let stand in a cold place 3 days. Yield: 1½ cups.

CALABAZAS CON ELOTE (MEXICAN)
(Zucchini with Corn)

4 tablespoons salad oil
1 medium onion, chopped
1 lb. (4 medium-sized) zucchini squash, washed and cut in ¼-inch rings
1 12-oz. can (1½ cups) whole kernel corn
3 medium-sized tomatoes, cut in eighths
2 teaspoons sugar
1 teaspoon salt
½ teaspoon chili powder
¼ teaspoon pepper

Heat oil in large skillet. Add onion and sauté 3 minutes, or until tender. Add squash and sauté 5 minutes, turning often. Add remaining ingredients and cook, stirring occasionally, over moderate heat for 10 minutes, or until squash is just tender. Yield: 6 portions.

FINNISH CUCUMBER SALAD

5 small cucumbers
salt
1 small bunch fresh dill
1 cup sour cream
1 clove of garlic, crushed
salt and black pepper
¼ teaspoon sugar
2 tablespoons fresh tomato pulp
2 tablespoons tarragon vinegar
¼ cup salad oil

Peel cucumbers and slice very thin. Place in bowl and sprinkle liberally with salt; let stand 30 minutes, drain and rinse in cold water; drain. Finely chop dill and add to sour cream with garlic, salt and pepper to taste, and sugar. Mix in tomato pulp and add vinegar and oil slowly, stirring constantly. Blend in cucumber slices and serve very cold. Yield: 4 portions.

TORTILLAS (MEXICAN)

1 cup cornmeal   1 teaspoon salt
1 cup flour   warm water

Mix cornmeal, flour and salt; add water to make a stiff dough. Set
dough aside 20 minutes. Wet hands in water and mold balls of dough
the size of hens' eggs, and pat into paper-thin cakes. Bake on a lightly
greased griddle; brown both sides. Usually filled, rolled and served with
a seasoned sauce. Yield: 12 tortillas.

PIZZA

2 lbs. sifted all-purpose flour   2 cups drained canned tomatoes,
1 tablespoon salt   cut up
1 envelope dry granular yeast   16 fillets drained anchovies,
2¼ cups warm, not hot, water   cut up
2 tablespoons olive oil   ½ teaspoon orégano
2 cloves garlic, minced   ¼ teaspoon black pepper
   (optional)   salt
1½ cups finely diced onion   ½ teaspoon dried basil
½ cup olive oil   2 tablespoons chopped fresh mint
1½ cups finely diced Provolone   or 2 teaspoons dried mint
   cheese   ¾ cup freshly grated Parmesan
                                        cheese

Sift flour and salt together onto a board. Soften yeast in ¼ cup warm,
not hot, water 10 minutes. Make a well in the center of the flour. Add
softened yeast and 2 tablespoons oil. Work in with the fingers, gradually adding remaining water. Work together until well blended. Knead
until smooth and elastic. Place in a large bowl; brush with oil, cover
and let stand in a warm place until doubled in bulk. Punch down
dough. Divide in half to make two pizzas. Pat out each portion of
dough into a large rectangle. Place each onto an oiled shallow metal
tray 12 by 17 inches. Continue to pat with fingers and gently stretch
until dough is size of tray. Sprinkle with 2 tablespoons oil. Sauté
garlic and onion in ¼ cup oil until browned. Drain and spread over
each portion of dough. Add Provolone cheese, tomatoes and anchovies.
Sprinkle with orégano, black pepper, salt, basil and mint. Top with
grated Parmesan cheese. Drizzle over 2 tablespoons olive oil. Bake in
hot oven (400° F.) 30 minutes, or until the edge of the crust is golden
brown. Cut each pie into 8 pieces. Serve warm. Approximate yield:
2 large pizzas, or 16 pieces.

MEXICAN ENCHILADAS

½ cup sifted flour
1 cup cornmeal
1 teaspoon baking powder
2 teaspoons salt
1½ cups milk

1½ cups grated cheese
1 onion, minced
4 to 8 fresh chili peppers
1 quart boiling water
3 tablespoons flour

6 eggs

Mix together flour, cornmeal, baking powder, salt and milk. Bake into large thin pancakes on a hot oiled griddle. Place ¼ cup cheese and some onion on each and place in warming oven. Simmer peppers in water 15 minutes. Press through sieve. Add flour mixed to a paste with ½ cup cold water and cook until thickened. Fry eggs; place one on each cake and top with pepper sauce. Yield: 6 portions.

CHEESE BLINTZES (JEWISH)

1 cup sifted all-purpose flour
¼ teaspoon salt
1 tablespoon sugar
6 tablespoons melted butter or
    margarine

1 cup milk
2 eggs, well beaten
1 cup sour cream

Combine and sift flour, salt and sugar. Add 2 tablespoons melted butter or margarine and milk to eggs. Add the egg-milk mixture to the flour mixture blending well until batter is smooth. (Batter will be very thin.) Heat an 8-inch skillet, grease lightly. Cover bottom of skillet with a very thin layer of batter, tipping pan to spread batter as thin as possible. Fry until lightly browned on one side only. Remove from skillet. When pancakes are cool, place 2 tablespoons cheese filling in center of each pancake on the browned side. Fold over edges to the middle and fry in remaining butter or margarine until golden brown. (Or place blintzes in baking pan (10 x 6 x 2 inches), pour remaining butter or margarine over them and bake at 350° F. for 15 minutes or until golden brown.) Serve with sour cream. Yield: 10 to 12 blintzes.

Cheese Filling

1 lb. dry cottage or farmers'
    cheese
½ cup sugar
2 teaspoons vanilla extract

¼ teaspoon salt
1 egg
1 tablespoon all-purpose flour
1 teaspoon cinnamon

Combine all ingredients and mix thoroughly.

PIROG RUBLONOYE MYASO (RUSSIAN)

(Meat Pastries)

1 pound hamburger	1 tablespoon chopped parsley
1 medium onion, chopped	Pirog Dough
1 teaspoon salt	1 teaspoon beaten egg
¼ teaspoon pepper	1 cup sour cream

Brown meat in skillet without added fat. Add onion and cook until tender. Pour off excess fat. Add salt, pepper and parsley. Roll Pirog Dough on floured board into a large rectangle (10 x 8 x ¼-inch). Place dough on greased baking sheet. Place meat filling down center of dough in long strip about 4 inches wide. Fold dough over filling, pinch edges together, then pinch the ends together. Brush with egg. Allow to rise 30 minutes. Bake at 375° F. for 20 minutes. Serve hot with sour cream. Yield: 4 to 6 portions.

Pirog Dough

1 package dry granular yeast	2 tablespoons melted butter or
¼ cup warm, not hot, water	margarine
1 egg, well beaten (save 1	1 teaspoon salt
teaspoon)	1¼ cups sifted all-purpose flour

Dissolve yeast in warm, not hot, water. Add egg, butter or margarine and salt. Beat in flour until well blended. Turn out on floured board, knead for 5 minutes. Place in greased bowl, cover and let rise in warm place for 1 hour. Punch down and roll out.

KUCHEN

1¼ cups milk, scalded, cooled	3 egg yolks, well beaten
1¼ teaspoons salt	6 cups sifted all-purpose flour
1 cup sugar	(about)
1 package dry granular yeast	¾ cup shortening, melted
¼ cup warm, not hot, water	1 egg white, slightly beaten
1 tablespoon water	

Follow standard method of mixing, kneading and rising on page 164. Add egg yolks to liquid mixture before first addition of the flour. When dough is double in bulk and is ready for shaping, roll into rectangle ½ inch thick and fit into 2 greased square pans or 1 large pan; cover and let rise in warm place until double in bulk. Then brush with mixture of egg white and water, or sprinkle with chopped nut meats or currants if desired, and bake in moderately hot oven (375°–400° F.) 20 to 25 minutes. Yield: 2 square (9-inch) cakes.

NORWEGIAN CHRISTMAS BREAD

1 recipe Kuchen (page 1042)
1 teaspoon crushed cardamom
    seeds

3 eggs, beaten
1½ cups seedless raisins
⅔ cup sliced citron

Add cardamom seeds and 3 whole eggs to kuchen instead of 3 egg yolks; add additional flour, as necessary, to form a dough stiff enough to knead. When dough has doubled in bulk, add raisins and citron, and knead until mixed; shape into loaves, place in greased bread pans, cover and let rise in warm place until doubled in bulk. Bake in moderate to hot oven (375°–400° F.) 40 to 50 minutes. From 6 to 8 hours are needed for making this bread with 1 pkg. of yeast. Yield: 2 loaves.

SWEDISH CARDAMOM BREAD

Use recipe for Norwegian Christmas Bread (above); increase cardamom seeds to 1 tablespoon and omit raisins and citron. Shape into long, narrow loaves; sprinkle with additional seeds before baking.

SWEDISH RYE BREAD

Use recipe for White Bread (page 163). For 2 loaves, add 2 tablespoons molasses, 2 tablespoons dark corn syrup and ¾ cup rye flour. Bake at 375° F.

CRÊPES SUZETTES
(French Pancakes)

½ cup sifted cake flour
1 egg
1 egg yolk

1 tablespoon oil
½ cup milk
1 tablespoon melted butter

Combine flour and eggs, oil and milk. Beat until smooth. Chill for 30 minutes. Brush the bottom of small heavy frying pan with butter when very hot. Cover bottom of pan with a very thin layer of batter. Tilt pan so that batter quickly covers bottom of pan evenly. Cook until golden brown on one side, then turn and cook on other side. To keep hot, store one on top of other on cake rack and cover with inverted bowl. If pancakes are made several hours ahead, reheat in oven. To serve: fold twice or roll and serve with hot Suzette Sauce (page 1044). Approximate yield: 6 to 8 pancakes (5 inch).

SUZETTE SAUCE

6 lumps sugar
1 orange
1 lemon
¼ cup sweet butter

¼ teaspoon vanilla
¼ cup powdered sugar
¼ cup brandy or
¼ cup Cointreau

Rub lumps of sugar on outside of orange and lemon for flavor and color and squeeze juice from orange. Place butter in hot chafing dish, add prepared lump sugar, orange juice and vanilla and reduce heat. Cook until sauce is reduced to a heavy syrup. Fold crêpes in quarters, sprinkle with powdered sugar and pour brandy or Cointreau over them. Ignite and serve 3 with sauce to a portion. Or pour ¼ cup Curaçao or Grand Marnier over crêpes, ignite and serve. Approximate yield: 6 portions.

BABA AU RUM (FRENCH)

2 cups sifted all-purpose flour
1 cake compressed yeast or
    1 pkg. dry granular yeast
¼ cup warm, not hot, water
4 tablespoons warm milk

3 eggs, well beaten
⅓ cup melted butter
1½ tablespoons sugar
¼ cup dried currants
dash of salt

Place sifted flour in a bowl. Make a hollow in the center and pour in the yeast which has been softened in the warm water (cool to lukewarm for compressed yeast). Work a little flour into it; cover and let stand in a warm place about 5 minutes. Then add eggs and mix well and quickly. Work with spoon or knead on lightly floured board for 5 minutes. Return to bowl, cover and let stand 45 minutes. Stir in butter, sugar, currants and add a dash of salt. Work in well, turn out on lightly floured board and knead with the finger tips, very gently, until all the fat is absorbed and the dough is satiny. The dough is very soft and difficult to handle. Place in a small buttered tube pan or Turk's head pan, filling not more than ½ full. Cover and let rise almost to the top. Bake in a moderate oven (375° F.) 40 minutes, or until done. Turn out on cooling rack and spoon rum syrup over the top so that it is slowly and evenly absorbed by the cake. Approximate yield: 6 portions.

Rum Syrup—Combine ½ pound loaf sugar or 1 cup granulated sugar with ½ cup water and simmer 1 minute, or until completely dissolved. Cool slightly and stir in ⅓ cup rum.

SPICED MATZOTH

6 matzoth   2 tablespoons sugar
2 tablespoons butter, melted   ½ teaspoon salt
3 eggs, well beaten   ½ teaspoon cinnamon
                   ¼ teaspoon nutmeg

Brush matzoth or Jewish bread with butter, then with beaten eggs; sprinkle with sugar-salt-spice mixture. Bake in moderate oven (375° F.) 10 to 15 minutes, or until crisp. Yield: 6 portions.

GERMAN COFFEE CAKE

1 cake compressed yeast or   ¾ pound melted butter or
    1 package of dry yeast   margarine
½ cup warm, not hot, water   ⅔ cup sugar
4 cups all-purpose flour   1 teaspoon salt
1 cup milk   6 egg yolks

Crumb Mixture

2 cups all-purpose flour   ¼ teaspoon cinnamon
¼ pound confectioners' sugar   ¼ cup melted butter or
¼ cup brown sugar   margarine
pinch of salt   ¼ cup melted shortening

Dissolve the yeast in the warm, not hot, water (cool to lukewarm for compressed yeast). Sift 2 cups flour into bowl. Scald and cool the milk. Make a hole in the flour—pour in milk along with the dissolved yeast. Stir into a smooth batter. Cover and let rise in warm place until doubled in bulk. Add one half pound melted butter or margarine, sugar, salt and egg yolks. Stir in balance of flour until well blended. Place ½-inch layer of dough into each of two pans approximately 8 inches square. Cover and let rise in warm place until doubled in bulk. Sprinkle coffee cake with remaining melted butter and cover with crumb mixture.

To make crumb mixture, sift flour with dry ingredients, add melted butter and shortening until little balls or crumbs are formed, sprinkle over coffee cakes. Bake in moderate oven (350° F.) for 25 minutes. Yield: 2 cakes.

CRÊPES AU KIRSCH

3 eggs, separated
2 tablespoons sugar
¼ teaspoon salt
½ cup melted butter

1 cup milk
½ cup sifted all-purpose flour
½ cup confectioners' sugar
½ cup Kirsch

Beat yolks well; add sugar, salt and 2 tablespoons melted butter. Add milk and flour, beating until smooth. Stir mixture into stiffly beaten egg whites and spoon small portions of the batter into a greased 6-inch frying pan. When slightly browned, turn and brown other side. Roll and place over heat in chafing dish. When 4 or 5 crêpes are made, sprinkle liberally with sugar, melted butter and Kirsch. Light liqueur and burn until it goes out. Add other pancakes as they are cooked and repeat additions of butter, sugar and Kirsch, serving as needed. Approximate yield: 6 portions.

FRENCH ALMOND CAKE

1¾ cups sifted all-purpose flour
½ cup butter
1 cup powdered sugar
2 teaspoons vanilla

¼ cup almond paste (page 639)
2 tablespoons milk
4 eggs, slightly beaten
2 egg yolks, slightly beaten

Sift flour several times. Cream butter until soft and smooth; gradually add sugar, beating until fluffy; add vanilla. Mix almond paste with milk, beating with fork until smooth; add to butter-sugar mixture; then gradually beat in eggs and egg yolks. Fold in flour in small amounts, turning the bowl half around with each addition and in same direction. Turn batter into prepared 10 x 6 x 1½-inch pan, lined with heavy paper and again buttered. Bake in moderate oven (350° F.) 40 minutes. Let stand 5 minutes before removing from pan. Cut in very small shapes (1½ inches)for Petits Fours (page 697); cut in small circles, half-moons, stars, or other fancy shapes and frost as desired; or cut in layers, split each, put together as a 4 layer cake with Cream Filling (page 720) and cover with frosting as desired. Yield: 1 sheet (10 x 6 x 1½-inch).

DUTCH APPLE CAKE

2 cups sifted all-purpose flour   ¾ cup milk
3 teaspoons baking powder   ¼ cup butter, melted
½ teaspoon salt   ⅓ cup firmly packed brown
2 tablespoons sugar   sugar
⅓ cup shortening   ½ teaspoon cinnamon
1 egg, well beaten   ½ teaspoon nutmeg
          2 cups thinly sliced apples

Sift together flour, baking powder, salt and sugar. Cut in shortening.
Combine egg and milk and add to flour mixture, stirring quickly to
make a soft dough. Mix butter, brown sugar and spices; spread over
bottom of 8-inch square pan. Cover with apple slices. Turn dough
over apples and pat out to cover top. Bake in moderate oven (350° F.)
1 hour. Serve with cream. Approximate yield: 6 portions.

DOBOS TORTE

4 large eggs   1 recipe Chocolate Butter Cream
¾ cup granulated sugar   (page 715)
1 cup sifted all-purpose flour   ½ recipe Caramel Sauce (page
                                      730)

Beat eggs thoroughly; gradually beat in sugar until very stiff—it must
hold its shape. Carefully fold in flour. Grease 3 cooky sheets. Lightly
dust with flour. Using an 8-inch round cake pan draw 6 circles in flour
—dusting on cooky sheets and spread batter thinly within circles. Bake
in hot oven (400° F.) 5 minutes. Remove from oven. Do not bake
longer as cake will become tough. Take up carefully and trim edges
with a paring knife, using pan as a guide. Top all but one baked ring
with Chocolate Butter Cream and sandwich together. Reserve some
of chocolate for decorating. Place remaining circle on greased cooky
sheet and pour Caramel Sauce over. Cool slightly and with wet knife
make decorative markings in caramel. Place layer on top of other
layers. Decorate with remaining Chocolate Butter Cream, using pastry
tube. Chill thoroughly before serving. Yield: 8 to 12 portions.

FRENCH CRULLERS

¼ cup sugar
½ teaspoon salt
¼ cup shortening

1 cup water
1 cup sifted all-purpose flour
3 eggs

1 teaspoon vanilla

Place sugar, salt, shortening and water in heavy saucepan and heat; when boiling brisky, add flour all at once, stirring vigorously with a wooden spoon. Beat until mixture forms a smooth ball which leaves sides of pan clean. Place in a bowl. Beat in thoroughly one egg at a time; then continue beating until mixture is smooth and shiny and breaks off when spoon is raised. Add vanilla. Chill. Force through a pastry tube in the shape of rings onto strips of oiled waxed paper. Carefully turn the paper upside down so that the crullers will drop into deep fat. Fry at 380° F. until golden brown on all sides. Drain. Cool. Brush with Confectioners' Sugar Icing (page 719). Yield: 10 crullers.

VANILLA KIPFEL

1 cup butter or margarine
¼ cup granulated sugar
½ teaspoon salt
2 cups sifted all-purpose flour

2 cups ground almonds (no need to blanch)
1 cup powdered sugar
⅛ teaspoon vanilla-bean pulp

Cream together butter or margarine, sugar and salt, using the hands; add flour, a little at a time, stirring in thoroughly. Add almonds. Take 1 teaspoonful of mixture at a time, roll in palm of hand to form crescent. Lay in rows on a greased cookie sheet and place in hot oven (400° F.) to keep the crescents from running. After 2 minutes reduce heat to slow (300° F.). Bake to a pale yellow, about 10 minutes. Cool and roll in powdered sugar mixed with vanilla. Yield: 6 dozen crescents.

MOORISH DATE COOKIES (NORTH AFRICAN)

¼ cup butter or margarine
½ cup honey
1 egg
½ teaspoon lemon extract
½ teaspoon almond extract

1 cup sifted cake flour
½ teaspoon salt
¼ teaspoon baking soda
⅛ teaspoon cream of tartar
1 cup finely chopped dates

1 cup finely chopped walnuts

Combine butter or margarine and honey. Blend well. Add egg and extracts. Beat thoroughly. Combine and sift dry ingredients. Add gradually to creamed mixture, blending well after each addition. Fold in dates and nuts. Drop from a teaspoon 1 inch apart on greased baking sheet. Bake at 425° F. for 6 to 8 minutes. Yield: 3½ dozen cookies.

ALSATIAN GÂTEAUX DE NOËL

1 cup sifted all-purpose flour	1½ tablespoons melted butter
½ teaspoon cinnamon	2 tablespoons finely chopped
½ teaspoon cocoa	citron
½ teaspoon ginger	¼ cup finely chopped figs
2 eggs	2 tablespoons chopped nuts
1 cup sugar	2 teaspoons grated lemon rind

Sift together flour, cinnamon, cocoa and ginger. Beat eggs until light and lemon-colored. Gradually add the sugar, beating until smooth and thickened. Stir in butter. Add flour gradually, mixing well. Add fruits, nuts and rind and mix well. Wrap in waxed paper and chill overnight. Drop from teaspoon on greased baking sheet. Bake in moderate oven (350° F.) 10 minutes, or until done. Cool. If desired, cookies may be iced with a plain white icing and sprinkled with colored sugar. Approximate yield: 30 small cookies.

BOHEMIAN CHRISTMAS COOKIES

1 cup butter	4 cups sifted flour (about)
¾ cup powdered sugar (about)	2 tablespoons water
6 egg yolks	1 cup confectioners' sugar
3 tablespoons cream	1 cup chopped blanched almonds

Cream together butter and ⅔ cup powdered sugar; beat in 4 egg yolks and cream. Gradually stir in flour until dough is just stiff enough to roll; chill. Sprinkle board lightly with mixture of flour and powdered sugar combined in equal parts; place dough on this and roll ¼-inch thick. Cut with star-shaped cutter, place on ungreased baking sheet and bake in moderate oven (350°–375° F.) 15 to 20 minutes. When cold, spread with icing made by beating together the 2 remaining egg yolks and water and adding confectioners' sugar to mixture. Sprinkle almonds over iced cookies. Yield: 4 to 5 dozen small cookies.

ALMOND CAKES (CHINESE)

1 teaspoon almond extract	1½ cups sugar
2 cups shortening	1½ teaspoons salt
4 cups sifted all-purpose flour	blanched almond halves

Blend almond extract into shortening, creaming until soft. Gradually work in flour, then sugar and salt. Knead to a paste. Form into a thick roll, then cut in ½-inch slices. Arrange on ungreased cooky sheet, press an almond half into center of each and bake in a slow oven (300° F.) about 30 minutes. Approximate yield: 20 cakes.

KRINGLES (GERMAN)

2 cups sifted all-purpose flour (about)
2 teaspoons baking powder
¼ teaspoon salt
½ cup shortening

1 cup granulated sugar
1 egg, well beaten
½ tablespoon caraway seeds
3 tablespoons brandy
¼ cup confectioners' sugar

Mix and sift 1½ cups flour, baking powder and salt. Cream together shortening and sugar; beat in egg, caraway seeds and brandy. Stir in flour mixture, then add remaining flour until dough is stiff enough to handle; chill thoroughly. Roll ⅛-inch thick on lightly floured board, cut in desired shapes, place on ungreased baking sheet and sprinkle with confectioners' sugar. Bake in moderate oven (375° F.) 10 to 15 minutes. Approximate yield: 4 dozen cookies.

DANISH VANILLA COOKIES

2½ cups sifted all-purpose flour
½ teaspoon baking powder
1 cup sugar

1 cup butter
2 egg yolks, slightly beaten
1½ teaspoons vanilla

Sift together flour, baking powder and sugar; cut in butter until well mixed. Stir in egg yolks and vanilla and work dough until smooth; chill. Roll thin on lightly floured board and cut as desired, or force through a cookie press on ungreased baking sheet. Bake in moderate to hot oven (375°–400° F.) 10 to 12 minutes. For more festive cookies, brush shapes with slightly beaten egg white and sprinkle with chopped nuts or plain or colored sugar. Approximate yield: 4 to 5 dozen cookies.

ENGLISH BRANDY SNAPS

¾ cup butter
¾ cup sugar

½ cup molasses
2 teaspoons ginger

1½ cups sifted all-purpose flour

Heat butter, sugar and molasses until blended. Add ginger. Remove from heat, add flour, beating until smooth. Drop from tip of spoon on greased baking sheet, about 2 inches apart. Bake in slow oven (300° F.) about 12 minutes. Quickly remove from pan and roll at once, top side out, over handle of a wooden spoon. Keep in covered container. Approximate yield: 4 dozen wafers.

COLOMBOS (ITALIAN)

1 cup sifted all-purpose flour
1 teaspoon baking powder
dash of salt
¼ cup shortening

¼ cup sugar
1 egg yolk
2 tablespoons milk (about)
caraway seeds or currants

Mix and sift flour, baking powder and salt. Beat together shortening, sugar and egg yolk; stir in flour, then just enough milk to form a stiff dough. Knead well and chill; roll ⅛-inch thick, cut with bird-shaped cutter and place on ungreased baking sheet. Mark eyes with caraway seeds or currants. Bake in moderate oven (375° F.) about 12 minutes. Approximate yield: 1½ dozen cookies.

MANDELKRANSER (SCANDINAVIAN)

1½ cups butter
4 cups sifted all-purpose flour
1 cup finely chopped, blanched
   almonds

2 eggs
¾ cup sugar
1 teaspoon vanilla

Cut butter into flour until well mixed; stir in almonds. Beat eggs until light; gradually beat in sugar and add vanilla. Gradually stir in flour-butter mixture; chill. Force through pastry tube, using large star-shaped opening; cut in three-inch lengths and bring ends together to form rings. Place on ungreased baking sheet and bake in moderate hot oven (365°–400° F.) 8 to 10 minutes. Yield: 7 dozen cookies.

TURKISH CRESCENTS

1 cup sifted all-purpose flour
1 tablespoon sugar
¼ teaspoon salt
2 egg yolks

⅔ cup butter or other fat
¾ cup sieved cottage cheese
½ cup chopped nuts
honey

Sift together flour, sugar and salt. Combine egg yolks, butter and cottage cheese. Add flour. Pat small portions out thin on floured board and cut into triangles. Moisten nuts with honey; add a little orange rind, if desired, place small amount in corner of each triangle, roll and curve into crescent shape. Brush with milk and bake in moderate oven (350° F.) about 15 minutes. Yield: 18 crescents.

SWISS BIRTHDAY COOKIES

1 cup light cream
2 eggs, beaten

1 teaspoon salt
2 cups sifted all-purpose flour
½ cup butter

Combine cream, eggs and salt. Mix well. Add flour to make a soft dough. Turn onto floured board, dot with butter and work into dough. Butter should be firm but soft. Place dough in refrigerator until firm enough to roll out. Roll out ⅛-inch thick. Cut in any desired shape. Slash each cookie through the center with a ½-inch gash. Fry in hot fat (375° F.) until browned. Drain on absorbent paper. Roll in granulated sugar while hot. Reheat to serve. Yield: 3 dozen cookies.

OLYKOEK

Use ½ recipe for Sweet Rolls (page 171); cut off small pieces of light dough and enclose brandied raisins or raisins and citron in center of each when shaping into small balls. Let stand until doubled. Fry in hot, deep fat (360°–370° F.) about 3 minutes, drain and roll in powdered sugar while warm. This is an early American favorite; the epicures of New Amsterdam soaked the olykoeks in Santa Cruz rum and served them with whipped cream. Yield: 2 dozen olykoeks.

MEXICAN TEA CAKES

1 cup butter
½ cup confectioners' sugar
1 teaspoon vanilla

2¼ cups sifted all-purpose flour
¼ teaspoon salt
confectioners' sugar for rolling

Cream butter and sugar together. Add vanilla. Sift flour and salt together and add to the creamed mixture. Chill in refrigerator for a few hours. Roll into small balls about an inch in diameter. Bake on a buttered cookie sheet in a hot oven (400° F.) 14 to 17 minutes. As soon as tea cakes are removed from oven, roll them in confectioners' sugar. Cool on a wire rack and then roll in sugar again. Approximate yield: 2½ dozen cookies.

PFEFFERNUESSE

4 cups sifted all-purpose flour	1 teaspoon aniseed
1 teaspoon baking soda	¼ pound candied orange peel
½ teaspoon salt	½ pound citron
1 tablespoon cinnamon	2 tablespoons butter
1 teaspoon cloves	2½ cups powdered sugar
1 teaspoon nutmeg	5 eggs, separated
¼ teaspoon black pepper	1½ teaspoons grated lemon rind
1 tablespoon crushed	¼ cup milk or water (about)
cardamom seeds	1 cup confectioners' sugar

Sift together flour, soda, salt and spices; stir in seeds, then ground orange peel and citron. Mix together butter and sugar; add well-beaten egg yolks and lemon rind and beat thoroughly. Gradually stir in flour-fruit mixture; fold in stiffly beaten egg whites. Chill 1 hour; then shape in small balls the size of hickory nuts. Place on cloth and let stand, uncovered, overnight at room temperature. In the morning brush balls with thin confectioners' icing made by gradually stirring milk into confectioners' sugar. Place on ungreased baking sheet and bake in moderate oven (350° F.) 15 to 20 minutes. Store in tightly covered tin container. Approximate yield 7½ dozen cookies.

Pfeffernuesse are hard cookies which will remain crisp and fresh for a long time when properly stored. If they soften, crisp by heating them in a moderate oven (350° F.) 5 to 10 minutes.

BASIC RECIPE FOR STRUDEL

3 cups all-purpose flour	1 egg, beaten
1 tablespoon cooking oil	1 cup lukewarm water

Place flour on marble slab or pastry board. Make a well in center of flour; place oil and egg in depression. Work flour gently into oil and egg and gradually add water to make a soft dough. When all flour is added, throw the ball of dough with force against table top for about 10 minutes until dough is very elastic. Add a very little extra flour, only enough to give dough a smooth surface. Turn out on lightly floured board and brush surface of dough with oil. Cover with a bowl and let stand in warm place 1 hour. Cover table with a clean cloth, lightly floured. Roll out dough into 12-inch square; brush generously with oil. With well-floured hands, loosen dough and stretch gently and evenly until it extends over table top and hangs down 3 or 4 inches all the way around. (It should be thin enough to see through.) With scissors, trim off edges after pastry has been allowed to dry a little while. Brush surface generously with oil.

APPLE STRUDEL

2 cups dry bread crumbs	grated rind of 1 lemon
1 cup butter or cooking oil	½ cup chopped walnuts
4 pounds apples, peeled, cored and sliced	½ cup seedless raisins
	½ cup currants
2 tablespoons vanilla extract	2 teaspoons cinnamon
4 tablespoons brown sugar	1 teaspoon allspice
1 recipe Basic Strudel Dough (page 1053)	melted butter
	confectioners' sugar
heavy cream	

Sauté bread crumbs in hot butter. Combine apples, vanilla and brown sugar and blend well; let stand 30 minutes. Drain off liquid. Place bread crumbs along one end of strudel dough; put apple mixture on top of bread crumbs. Add lemon rind, walnuts, raisins, currants, cinnamon and allspice. Fold over sides, then one end, to enclose filling, and roll like a jelly roll. Place on well-greased baking sheet and brush liberally with melted butter. Bake in moderate oven (350° F.) 35 minutes, basting frequently with melted butter. Cool slightly and sprinkle with confectioners' sugar; slice and serve with heavy cream. Approximate yield: 6 portions.

DANISH PASTRY

Use 2 cups sifted pastry flour, ¼ teaspoon salt, 1 cup shortening and 1 cup riced cold potatoes. Follow direction for Plain Pastry (page 736), stirring in potatoes last. Yield: pastry for two-crust (9-inch) pie.

BOUCHÉES

Roll Puff Paste (page 741) about ⅛-inch thick; shape as for patty shells, making them much smaller—1½ to 2 inches in diameter.

VOL-AU-VENT

Roll Puff Paste (page 741) about ⅓-inch thick; cut two large ovals or rounds, using floured mold or knife. Brush outer top edge of one with cold water; cut off a ¾-inch wide band around edge of remaining oval and place this ring on plain oval, pressing lightly; then press in very lightly the inside edge of ring to prevent uneven rising. Prick several places with fork and chill thoroughly. Roll remaining piece ¼-inch thick and cut shape for cover. Bake in hot oven (450° F.) about 8 minutes, then reduce heat to moderate (350° F.) and continue baking 20 to 30 minutes. Cover with paper if paste browns too quickly.

SAVORY STRUDEL

1 recipe Basic Strudel Dough (page 1053)
1½ cups dry bread crumbs
¼ cup bacon fat
1 small cabbage, shredded
1 large onion, finely chopped
4 hard-cooked eggs, finely chopped
½ cup sour cream
oil
2 teaspoons minced garlic
1 tablespoon chopped fresh dill
grated Parmesan cheese
paprika
Hot Mustard Sauce (page 477)

Sauté bread crumbs in 2 tablespoons bacon fat. Spread in a long strip at one end of strudel dough. Sauté onion in remaining bacon fat until soft. Combine with cabbage, eggs and ¼ cup sour cream. Place on top of bread crumbs and add remaining sour cream, spreading over surface. Sprinkle remaining dough with 1 tablespoon oil and fold over the three sides to form a rectangle. Begin rolling by picking up the cloth on which the filled end of the strudel is placed and, holding it taut, roll strudel into long, thin roll. Brush with remaining oil as you roll it up. Place on greased baking pan, brush again with oil and bake in moderately hot oven (375° F.) 40 minutes, basting frequently with oil during baking period. When done, remove from oven, brush with oil and place on wooden board for serving. Sprinkle with cheese and paprika. Serve with Hot Mustard Sauce. Approximate yield: 8 to 10 portions.

FRENCH SWEET PASTRY

2 cups sifted all-purpose flour
4 egg yolks
¼ cup sugar
salt
¼ pound butter or margarine, chilled
½ cup rice
dry bread crumbs

Place flour in a heap on pastry board and make a well in the center. Place egg yolks, sugar, salt and butter, cut into pieces, in well. With one hand quickly work center ingredients together. Move remaining flour over center of mixture and work in with one hand. Knead dough until elastic. Lightly flour board and roll out pastry ⅛-inch thick to lightly overlap a flan ring (a square or round metal frame). Place flan frame on baking sheet. Line flan with pastry. Trim off overlapping rim by running rolling pin across edge of flan. Line pastry with waxed paper and weight with uncooked rice. Bake in moderate oven (350° F.) 12 to 15 minutes or until golden brown. Remove waxed paper and rice. Sprinkle bottom with bread crumbs and fill with desired mixture. Yield: pastry for 1 square or round flan mold.

PASTRY HORNS

2 cups all-purpose flour
1 cup butter or margarine
1 egg

2 tablespoons cold water
1 teaspoon lemon juice
1 teaspoon grated lemon rind

Sift 1 cup flour onto a board. Work in butter or margarine with hands until well blended. Wrap in waxed paper and chill ½ hour. Sift remaining flour onto board and make a well in the center. Add egg, water, lemon juice and rind and work together quickly with fingers until a smooth, soft dough is formed. Roll out on lightly-floured board into a rectangle ⅛-inch thick. Roll out the chilled butter dough to the same size and place on top of egg dough. Fold into thirds lengthwise; then into thirds widthwise. Wrap in waxed paper and chill 1 hour. Repeat rolling, folding and chilling two more times. Roll out ⅛-inch thick and cut into strips ¾-inch wide. Wrap each strip around metal tubes and place on a cooky sheet. Bake in moderate oven (350° F.) about 20 minutes. Cool and store in an airtight container. Fill with flavored whipped cream forced through a pastry tube. Approximate yield: 12 to 14 pastries.

FRENCH LEMON MERINGUE PIE

juice of 2 lemons
grated rind of 2 lemons
¾ cup sugar
¾ cup butter (6 ounces)
3 eggs, beaten
½ teaspoon salt

1 baked pie shell lined with
   1 recipe Sweet Pastry
   (page 1055)
3 egg whites
¼ teaspoon cream of tartar
6 tablespoons sugar

Combine lemon juice and rind, sugar, butter, eggs and ¼ teaspoon salt in top of double boiler over hot water over medium heat. Stir constantly with wooden spoon until mixture begins to thicken and coats spoon. Place in bowl of crushed ice and stir constantly until mixture is consistency of whipped cream. Pour into baked pastry shell and top with meringue made as follows: Beat egg whites until stiff, adding cream of tartar and remaining salt. Gradually fold sugar into egg whites until thoroughly blended. Spoon meringue into pastry bag fitted with fancy tube and cover pie. Sprinkle top of meringue with sugar and place in hot oven (425° F.) 4 to 4½ minutes, or until lightly browned. Yield: 6 portions.

SAVORY DOUGH

¾ cup sifted all-purpose flour | 2 tablespoons grated Parmesan
2 eggs | cheese
¼ cup iced water | 1 teaspoon paprika
⅓ cup chilled butter | ½ teaspoon salt

Place flour on pastry board. Make a well in center and add remaining
ingredients. Work together all ingredients quickly with hand. Knead
lightly but thoroughly and roll out to ⅛-inch thickness on lightly-
floured board. Place flan ring (round or square metal frame) on baking
sheet and line carefully with pastry. Cover center of ring with waxed
paper and place a handful of rice on top of paper to hold in place. Bake
until half done (about 20 minutes) in moderate oven (350° F.). Remove pastry from oven and discard waxed paper and rice. Sprinkle
with bread crumbs and fill with mixture. Yield: pastry for flan of 4
portions.

BAKLAVA (TURKISH)
Pastry

1 teaspoon salt | ½ cup shortening
2 cups sifted all-purpose flour | 2 eggs, well beaten

Combine salt and flour. Cut shortening into flour until mixture looks
like cornmeal. Add eggs to dry ingredients and mix until thoroughly
dampened. Turn out on waxed paper. Knead for 2 minutes. Roll into
ball and allow to rest 30 minutes.

Filling

2 cups blanched ground almonds or pistachio nuts | 1 teaspoon cinnamon
½ cup brown sugar, firmly packed | ½ teaspoon nutmeg
1 cup melted butter or margarine | pastry
grated rind of 1 lemon | 1 cup honey
 | 1 cup water
 | grated rind of 1 orange

Combine nuts, sugar, butter or margarine, and spices. Blend well.
Divide pastry into 8 pieces. Roll very thin on floured board. Place a
layer of pastry in the bottom of a greased pan (8 x 8 x 2 inches). Spread
3 tablespoons of filling over pastry. Place second layer of pastry on top
of filling. Continue making layers of pastry and filling, ending with
pastry on top. Boil honey, water and rinds together for 5 minutes.
Pour 3 tablespoons of syrup over Baklava. Bake at 350° F. for 35 to 40
minutes. Pour remaining syrup over the baked pastry and allow to cool
before cutting into 2-inch squares. Yield: 16 2-inch squares.

QUICHES LORRAINE

4 slices bacon, finely shredded
2 eggs
1 egg yolk
½ teaspoon paprika
salt

cayenne
¾ cup hot milk
2 tablespoons grated Parmesan
cheese
1 recipe Savory Dough (page 1057)

Fry bacon until crisp. Combine eggs, yolk, paprika, salt and cayenne. Beat well and mix with hot milk. Add cheese and bacon with bacon fat. Blend well and put into half-baked savory pastry shell. Sprinkle top with paprika. Finish baking in slow oven (300° F.) 15 to 20 minutes. Remove and cool slightly before serving. Yield: 4 portions.

BRÛLÉ

2 cups sugar
½ cup boiling water
2 tablespoons cornstarch

1½ cups milk
2 egg yolks, slightly beaten
1¼ cups heavy cream, whipped

Place sugar in heavy frying pan and cook over moderate heat until melted and pale yellow in color; stir in water and cook until dissolved. Mix cornstarch to a smooth paste with ½ cup milk and add remaining milk; add caramel syrup and cook over hot water 15 minutes, stirring until mixture is thickened. Stir small amount into egg yolks, then return to remaining hot mixture and cook 2 minutes longer; cool, fold in cream and turn into freezing trays of automatic refrigerator; freeze 2 to 4 hours, or until firm. Yield: 1 quart.

NORWEGIAN PRUNE PUDDING

2 cups chopped cooked prunes
1 cup prune juice
½ cup sugar

4 tablespoons cornstarch
dash of salt
prune pits
2 tablespoons lemon juice

Bring prunes and juice to a boil. Combine sugar, cornstarch and salt; gradually stir into prune mixture and cook 15 minutes, stirring until thickened, then occasionally. Crack 12 or more pits, chop kernels and add with lemon juice to pudding mixture. Turn into individual molds or large mold and chill thoroughly. Serve with whipped cream or Custard Sauce (page 729), as desired. Yield: 4 to 6 portions.

DULCE COCADA (MEXICAN)

1 large coconut

4 eggs, well beaten

1 cup sugar

½ cup light cream

1 cup coconut milk

Remove shell and brown skin from coconut, reserving milk; grate the white meat. Combine eggs, sugar and cream; stir into coconut meat. Add the coconut milk and turn into greased baking dish. Bake in a moderately slow oven (325° F.) 30 to 45 minutes, or until set. Chill before serving. Approximate yield: 6 portions.

HAWAIIAN PAPAYA FREEZE

1 cup sugar

½ tablespoon lemon juice

1½ cups orange juice

1 cup papaya pulp

2 cups rich milk

Mix sugar, fruit juices and papaya pulp and chill thoroughly; gradually stir into milk and freeze (page 798) in an ice cream freezer. If papaya is out of season, use one cup papaya marmalade and omit sugar. Approximate yield: 1½ quarts.

PETITS POTS DE CRÈME CHOCOLAT

1 pound grated sweet chocolate

1 pint milk, scalded

8 egg yolks

Add chocolate to hot milk and cook, stirring constantly, until it is melted and the boiling point is reached. Pour mixture over slightly beaten egg yolks and stir until smoothly blended. Strain through a fine strainer; pour into custard cups. Refrigerate until cold. Serve with heavy or whipped cream. Yield: 8 portions.

CHANKELE (ALSATIAN)

6 eggs

1¼ cups confectioners' sugar

¾ cup ground almonds

2 cups sifted flour

Beat eggs until light; add sugar gradually and beat until thick. Stir in almonds and enough flour to make a soft dough. Turn dough onto a floured board and form into little rolls, the shape of a finger or a small candle (chankele) and fry in hot deep fat (370° F.) 2 minutes, or until golden brown. Drain, cool and roll in additional confectioners' sugar. Approximate yield: 12 dozen chankele.

TURKISH PASTE

3 envelopes plain gelatin
½ cup cold water
4½ cups sugar
½ cup boiling water

dash of salt
3 tablespoons lemon or lime juice
green vegetable coloring
confectioners' sugar

Soften gelatin in cold water 5 minutes. Cook sugar and hot water over low heat, stirring constantly until sugar is dissolved and mixture boils; add salt and gelatin and simmer 20 minutes. Remove from heat; add lemon juice and color a delicate green. Let mixture stand until it thickens slightly, stir and pour 1-inch thick in pan that has been rinsed with cold water. Chill overnight; cut in cubes with warm knife and roll in confectioners' sugar. Flavoring and color may be varied as desired. Approximate yield: 40 pieces.

MARZIPAN (ITALIAN)

½ pound almonds, blanched
2 egg whites
1¾ cups confectioners' sugar
(about)

orange or lemon juice
rose water or vanilla
1 egg white
confectioners' sugar
vegetable coloring

To prepare almond paste, grind almonds in food chopper, using finest blade; repeat 3 or 4 times, or until very fine. Beat egg whites until foamy, gradually stir in sugar, then nuts; knead until smooth and creamy, adding sugar if not stiff enough and orange or lemon juice, drop by drop, if too stiff. Knead in 2 or 3 drops of rose water for flavoring, or add vanilla. Work paste gradually into egg white beaten until frothy, adding confectioners' sugar, as needed, to knead and mold. Divide and color lightly with vegetable coloring to imitate fruits and vegetables and flavor as desired. Mold into shapes. Dip one end in dipping chocolate or decorate with angelica for more elaborate candies. Marzipan may be made by combining equal amounts of commercial almond paste and fondant. Approximate yield: 1 pound.

FOREIGN WORDS AND PHRASES

Agneau (*F*) Lamb.

À la (*F*) In mode or fashion of.

À la broche (*F*) Cooked on a skewer.

À la carte (*F*) Foods prepared to order.

À la mode (*F*) In a normal fashion.

Allemand(e) (*F*) German; concentrated white *velouté* sauce, thickened with cream and egg yolk, and seasoned with nutmeg and lemon juice.

Anglais(e) (*F*) English; à l'anglaise usually means cooked very simply.

Antipasto (*I*) Usually assorted vegetables, fish or cold cuts, constituting hors d'œuvres or appetizers.

Apéritif (*F*) Any dry fortified wine such as vermouth or dry sherry.

Asperge (*F*) Asparagus; **asperges en branches** means plainly boiled.

Au gratin (*F*) Sprinkled with crumbs and/or cheese and baked brown.

Au jus (*F*) Served with natural juices or gravy.

Au lait (*F*) With milk.

Au naturel (*F*) Plainly cooked, or without cooking.

Béarnaise (*F*) Yellow sauce of vinegar, egg yolk and spices.

Béchamel (*F*) Cream sauce usually with veal stock base and vegetables; named after a celebrated cook.

Beignets (*F*) Fritters.

Bel Paese (*I*) Soft cows' milk cheese from Italy.

Beurre (*F*) Butter; **au beurre fondu**— with melted butter; **au beurre roux**— with browned butter; **beurre noir**— browned melted butter sauce.

Blanc(che) (*F*) White.

Blanquette (*F*) White meat in cream sauce.

Bœuf (*F*) Beef.

Bordelais(e) (*F*) From Bordeaux, usually with red wine.

Borsch (*R*) Russian soup with beets as main ingredient.

Bouchée (*F*) Small pastry shell filled with creamed mixture.

Bourgeoise (*F*) Average family; **à la bourgeoise**—in family style.

Brie (*F*) Soft French or French-style cheese.

Brioche (*F*) Light, sweet yeast bread, characteristically French.

Brochette (*F*) Skewer; **en brochette**— broiled and served on skewer.

Brut (*F*) Natural, no added sugar; usually used with Champagne.

Byrrh (*F*) A tonic wine similar to Dubonnet.

Café (*F*) Coffee; **café au lait**—coffee with hot milk; **café noir**—black or after-dinner coffee.

Carte (du jour) (*F*) Bill of fare for the day.

Champignons (*F*) Mushrooms.

Chantilly (*F*) With whipped cream.

Chapon (*F*) Capon.

Chartreuse (*F*) A liqueur; a food mixture enclosed in fancy case or mold.

Chaud-froid (*F*) Hot-cold. A cold jellied food.

Chou (*F*) Cabbage.

Confiture (*F*) Jam.

Cordon Bleu (*F*) Famous French cooking school; a fine cook.

Crème (*F*) Cream.

Crevettes (*F*) Shrimps.

Demi-tasse (*F*) A small cup of coffee; in this country, after-dinner coffee; in France, **café noir** is after-dinner coffee.

En coquilles (*F*) In the shell; in shell-shaped ramekins.

En papillottes (*F*) In paper frills.

Entremets (*F*) Main dish, side dish, savory or sweet.

Escargots (*F*) Snails.

Escoffier (*F*) Famous chef.

Espagnole (*F*) Brown sauce of butter, flour and meat juice.

Estragon (*F*) Tarragon.

Farci (*F*) Stuffed.

Fines herbes (*F*) Sauce, soup, or other food with herbs.

Flambé (*F*) A food served with lighted spirits poured over.

Flan (*F*) Custard or open tart.

Fraises (*F*) Strawberries.

Frijoles (*M*) Mexican beans cooked with oil, tomatoes and chili.

Froid (*F*) Cold.

Fromage (*F*) Cheese.

Galantine (*F*) Food stuffed in sausage.

Gâteaux (*F*) Small cakes.

Grenouilles (*F*) Frogs.

Grillé (*F*) Grilled or broiled.

Haricots (*F*) Beans.

Homard (*F*) Lobster.

Hors d'œuvres (*F*) Relishes, usually served at the beginning of a meal.

Huîtres (*F*) Oysters.

Jambon (*F*) Ham.

Jardinière (*F*) Diced, mixed vegetables.

Julienne (*F*) Vegetables cut in thin strips.

Jus (*F*) Juice.

Kirsch (*G*) Cherry; a cherry cordial.

Knackebrod (*Scand.*) Whole rye, flat, hard bread.

Kuchen (*G*) Cake.

Lait (*F*) Milk.

Laitue (*F*) Lettuce.

Langue (*F*) Tongue.

Lapin (*F*) Rabbit.

Lyonnaise (*F*) Cooked with chopped onions and parsley.

Maigre (*F*) Without meat (fasting).

Maître d'hôtel (*F*) Head of food service; maître d'hôtel butter—mixture of butter, lemon juice, parsley, salt, etc.

Milanaise (*F*) Spaghetti or macaroni with tomato sauce, etc.

Noir(e) (*F*) Black.

Normand(e) (*F*) From Normandy.

Œuf (*F*) Egg.

Oiseaux (*F*) Birds.

Paillette (*F*) White sauce.

Pain (*F*) Bread.

Pâté (*F*) Pie or pastry, paste.

Pâté de foie gras (*F*) Goose liver paste.

Pâtisserie (*F*) French pastry.

Petite marmite (*F*) A strong consommé with beef, chicken and vegetable; small casserole, or kettle.

Petits fours (*F*) Small cakes.

Pièce de résistance (*F*) The main dish in a meal, as a roast.

Pois (*F*) Pea.

Poisson (*F*) Fish.

Pomme (*F*) Apple.

Pomme de terre (*F*) Potato.

Potage (*F*) Soup.

Poulet (*F*) Chicken.

Réchauffé (*F*) Reheated.

Rémoulade (*F*) Yellow sauce of eggs, vinegar, mustard and spices.

Riz de veau (*F*) Calf's sweetbreads.

Rôti (*F*) Roast.

Rôtisserie (*F*) Restaurant that specializes in meals broiled or barbecued.

Salade (*F*) Salad.

Salmis (*F*) Hash (game) with thick rich sauce.

Salpicon (*F*) Minced poultry or meat.

Sauternes (*F*) Pale, sweet wines.

Smörgåsbord (*Scand.*) Hors d'œuvres.

Sorbet (*F*) Frozen punch.

Soubise (*F*) Flavored with onion.

Spumoni (*I*) Fancy Italian ice cream.

Tamale (*M*) Cooked cereal and meat served in corn husks.

Tarte (*F*) Pie.

Truffe (*F*) A fungus, similar to mushrooms; seasoning and garnish; truffle.

Veau (*F*) Veal.

Velouté (*F*) White sauce with white stock.

Vert(e) (*F*) Green.

Viande (*F*) Meat.

Vichy (*F*) Mineral water.

Vinaigrette (sauce) (*F*) Oil, herbs, vinegar, hard-cooked eggs and pickles.

Vol au vent (*F*) Large puff pastry shell.

Wurst (*G*) Sausage.

Abbreviations used:
F = French, G = German, I = Italian, M = Mexican, R = Russian, Scand. = Scandinavian.

Wines, Cocktails and Liqueurs

WINE has been traditionally linked with food for many centuries. It has added immeasurably to the enjoyment of good food just as discriminating dining has encouraged the selection of great wines.

Wines are either dry or sweet, with gradations between, but the term "dry" does not mean sour. "Dry" means the opposite of sweet without meaning sour. The majority of wines are called *still* wines to differentiate them from the sparkling or effervescent-type wines. A wine is "fortified" when it is strengthened by the addition of distilled spirits, usually brandy. There are five main types.

APPETIZER WINES

APPETIZER wines are favored for before-meal or cocktail use. The main appetizer wines are Sherry and Vermouth. They range from extra-dry to semi-sweet, to make them suitable for before-meal serving.

RED TABLE WINES

TABLE wines are usually dry, to accompany main course dishes. Most red table wines are completely dry and with their rich, sometimes tart and even astringent flavors, blend admirably with red meats, pastes and highly seasoned foods. The most popular dry red table wines are Claret and Burgundy. The alcoholic content of red table wines is from 10 to 14 per cent. There also are some sweet red table wines, usually called "sweet red wine."

WHITE TABLE WINES

WHITE table wines vary from extremely dry and tart to sweet and full-bodied, with delicate flavor that blends best with white meats, fowl and seafoods. They must be served well chilled. In color they range from pale straw to deep gold and in alcoholic content from 10 to 14 per cent. The most popular white table wines are Sauternes, Chablis and Rhine.

DESSERT WINES

THE sweet, full-bodied wines served with desserts and as refreshments in the afternoon or evening are called dessert wines. Their alcoholic content is usually from 18 to 20 per cent. They range from medium-sweet to sweet and in color from pale gold to red. The four popular types are Port, Muscatel, Tokay, white Port.

SPARKLING WINES

SPARKLING wines are table wines which have been made naturally effervescent by a second fermentation within closed containers. Their alcoholic content ranges from 10 to 14 per cent by volume. The most popular types are Champagne and sparkling Burgundy.

FRENCH WINES

BORDEAUX WINES. The Bordeaux area, from which come many red and white wines, is divided into several districts. The Médoc division produces most of the great Clarets. Claret (from the French "clairet" meaning "of light color") is an English term applied loosely to all red Bordeaux wines. The Graves district is famous for its white wines and a few very fine red wines. Sauternes is the area noted for its splendid sweet white dessert wines. Saint Émilion and Pomerol, are renowned for their Clarets.

The Clarets of the Graves District have more body but not the delicacy of those of the Médoc. The Clarets of the Saint Émilion and Pomerol are the fullest bodied of all.

White Graves, for the most part, are dry in comparison with other white Bordeaux wines such as Sauternes. They are slightly flinty in flavor, make excellent table wines and are admirable with fish. Sauternes are widely imitated. True Sauternes are medium sweet or sweet and are generally considered dessert wines. Château d'Yquem is the most famous of the Sauternes. Barsacs are medium-sweet, interchangeable with medium-sweet Sauternes.

Burgundy. The Burgundy wine region is really three separate districts. The most famous, known as the "True Burgundy," is the Côte d'Or (Golden Slope). South of the Côte d'Or is the district of the Maconnais and Beaujolais, producing light red and white wines, while halfway between the Côte d'Or and Paris is the village of Chablis which gives its name to the wine produced from the grapes which grow on a thousand acres surrounding it. The Côte d'Or is divided into sections, the Côte de Nuits to the north, from which come superb, full-bodied, full-flavored red Burgundies, and the Côte de Beaune, stretching southward, yielding light, more delicate red wines and the great white Burgundies, of which Le Montrachet is the outstanding. Some of the great red wines are Romanée-Conti, Romanée-St. Vivant, Chambertin, Clos de Vougeot from the Côte de Nuits, Le Corton, Beaune-Greves and Pommard-Rugiens from the Côte de Beaune.

Sparkling Burgundy. A sparkling wine which has always enjoyed much favor in America, it is usually made in the same manner as Champagne. Although white and pink (Œil de Perdrix) sparkling Burgundy is produced, it is the deep red variety that is most popular. Sparkling Burgundy is sweeter than Champagne.

Chablis. Chablis comes from the district of Chablis. It is a dry, pale golden wine somewhat flinty in flavor and makes excellent table wine; it is often served with oysters and shellfish.

Champagne. Champagne comes from a delimited area (fixed by law) in the Department of the Marne. It is generally sparkling, light or pale amber in color and is a blend of grapes from different vineyards. Each Champagne house has its secret blending formula so that the quality and grade of Champagne may vary with each house. A dry or extra-dry Champagne is usually served with fish or throughout a meal. Medium-sweet or sweet Champagne, the latter sometimes labeled "demi-sec," is considered an excellent dessert wine. Since the added sweetening makes it possible to mask inferior wine, it is important to be able to identify as reliable and authentic the house that makes the Champagne; the date is considered less important as a guide to quality. The characteristic sparkle is the result of the secondary fermentation which takes place in the tightly covered bottle and which cannot escape until the bottle is opened.

Alsace. On the French side of the Rhine, in the ancient province of Alsace, lie the vineyards which produce light, fresh, tangy wines with a flowerlike bouquet known as Alsatian or French Rhine wines. Instead of place names customary in other wine regions, the wines take their names from the grape variety which produces them. Best-known Alsatian wines are Riesling — dry, fresh; Gewuerz Traminer—less dry, more flowery bouquet; Sylvaner—medium dry, soft. One of their most charming qualities is freshness and fruit, most pronounced when the wine is young.

Other well-known French wines include the fine red and white wines of the Côtes du Rhone, including Côte Rotie, red; Hermitage, red and white; Châteauneuf-du-Pape, red; and Tavel, a light, fresh pink-rose-colored wine. In the valley of the Loire and in the midst of the famous château country, much red and white wine is made. The best are the rather sweet white petillante (creamy or crackling) wines of Anjou and Saumur. They also use the Champagne method for producing a pleasant sparkling wine called sparkling Vouvray.

GERMAN WINES

THE German wine regions of fame are the valleys of the Rhine and Moselle Rivers. Although some minor red wines are produced, it is for her distinguished white wines that the country is known. The principal difference between Moselle and Rhine wines is body. Moselle wines are light, fresh, dry wines with a sparkling tang and flowery bouquet. Rhine wines have more body, are usually softer and when made from specially selected or late picked grapes can be quite sweet. Famous Moselle wines are Piesporter, Zeltinger and Bernkasteler, the district in which lies the renowned Bernkasteler Doktor vineyard. Rhine wines of repute come from Rudesheim, Johannisberg, Nierstein, Oppenheim, Forst and Deidesheim. Liebfraumilch includes a blend of Rheinhessen wines.

ITALIAN WINES

ITALY is a country that is liberally laced with vineyards. Some of the wines take their names from the variety of grape from which they come, others from the district. They may be considered authentic if the label bears the "national export label" prescribed by the government—not necessarily evidence of quality.

Some of the finest Italian wines come from the Piedmont area of which Barolo and Barbera are famous red wines. Within the district of Tuscany in an area called Chianti are a few of the most famous of Italian wines. Chianti is usually exported in native straw-covered flasks or *fiascos*. Orvieto, a dry or slightly sweet wine also bottled in straw-covered flasks, is native to Umbria. Asti Spumante is the best known sparkling wine of Italy. It has a pleasant muscat flavor and is on the sweet side. Sicily is noted for certain sweet wines, including Albanello, a heavy, sweet white wine which may also be dry; Malvasia, a sweet, deep golden wine, and Marsala, usually sweet and rather heavy. The dry Italian wines, red or white, do good service as table wines; the sweet wines are favored for dessert.

Vermouth. As an apéritif and ingredient of cocktails, both Italian and French Vermouths are widely used. It is a white wine, blended, fortified and aromatized by the addition of various herbs and spices such as cardamom, camomile, bitter orange peels and certain flowers. Italian Vermouth is generally sweeter and slightly darker than French Vermouth.

WINES OF SPAIN

Mention of Spain brings to mind Sherry and Malaga before all other Spanish wines. There are, however, a few excellent red and white wines such as Rioja and Valdepeñas. It is a little difficult to judge the quality of wines from the label; the date is usually omitted. But by trying a number of them, one may be pleasantly surprised in a selection of palatable and comparatively inexpensive Spanish table wines. Of the sweet dessert wines, Malaga, Muscatel and Malvasia are well-known.

Sherry. Sherry owes its character to the white, chalky soil on which the grapes are grown in the district around Jerez de la Frontera. Sherry is a wine made from wines blended with painstaking care and aged in the cask. The term "solera" sometimes found on the bottles is a part indication of the progressive blending of Sherries of the same variety but of different ages—and of the aged-in-the-wood quality of the Sherry. Some Sherries are dry, others sweet and they are usually classed accordingly.

Fino Sherry is pale, very dry and delicate. Vino de Pasto is also pale and dry. Amontillado is a pale, dry, or medium-sweet Sherry possessing a delicate bouquet. Oloroso or Amoroso is a sweet Sherry. The golden or brown Sherries, sometimes sold as Solera, are sweet and somewhat heavy and make fine dessert wines.

PORTUGUESE WINES

Port. From a specified area in Portugal, the Alto Douro region, comes the only true authentic Port in the world.

Tawny Port is a blend of wines aged in the wood. The descriptive name, tawny, comes from the characteristic tawny or bronze coloring it acquires during the aging. Ruby Port is generally a blend of tawny Port with fresh, young wines. Port is distinctly an after-dinner wine, served in the best tradition with cheese or nuts. Vintage Port is unblended wine of a superior year allowed to age in the bottle for upward of 15 years, developing a heavy crust.

Madeira. Madeira wine ranges from dry to sweet and from pale amber to red brown. The sweet, deep-colored wines are excellent afternoon or dessert wines, whereas the dry Madeiras are the perfect accompaniment to a soup such as turtle.

SOUTH AMERICAN WINES

SOUTH AMERICA has three important wine-producing regions: Argentina, fifth wine-producing country of the world, Peru and Chile. The wines of Argentina generally carry the names of European-type wines, Sherry, Port, Claret, since they are, for the most part, produced from European vines. Peru also produces wines from European grape varieties, although not much of it is exported. Of all South American countries, the wines of Chile are best in quality and are mostly of Rhine type. Volcanic soil is responsible for much of this high quality. Chilean wines are labeled in order of quality, so that it is fairly easy for the consumer to determine what grade of wine he is purchasing—Gran Vino para Banquetes, Gran Vino and Reservado.

NORTH AMERICAN WINES

BECAUSE California has such a wide variety of soils and climate, almost every well-known type of European grape can be grown there. Some authorities believe that the San Francisco Bay region, with Alameda and the famous Livermore and Napa Valleys, produces California's best light wines. The State of California produces the largest quantity in America—about 84 per cent.

North American wines are also produced in New York, Ohio, New Jersey, Michigan and Missouri, with New York leading in production. These wines are from grapes native to North America and they cannot be crossbred successfully with the European grapes. Northern New York State, with its Finger Lakes District, is especially famous. Red and white wines are made here.

LIQUEURS

LIQUEURS are sweet, aromatized alcoholic beverages, often referred to as cordials. They are used with coffee following dessert and in the cooking of many dishes. Among the more famous liqueurs are: Chartreuse and Bénédictine—liqueurs originally made in the famous French monasteries after which they are named; Curaçao, manufactured largely in Holland from a variety of orange grown in the Dutch West Indies; Anisette, which takes its name from aniseed, one of the principal ingredients; Kirsch, from the German word for cherries from which it is made; Kümmel, consumed widely in Germany and made from various herbs including caraway; Strega, an orange-flavored liqueur from Italy; Cointreau and Grand Marnier, both made from orange and Cognac; Crème de Menthe from mint and Cognac; and many fruit liqueurs including Crème de Cassis and Apricot and Peach brandies.

HOW TO KEEP WINES

THE ideal storage place for wines in quantity is a dark, dry cellar, well ventilated, free from vibration and draft and maintained at a temperature of about 55° F. The shelves in which the wine is kept should be far removed from water or heating pipes of any kind and from electric wiring. Store all wines on their sides to keep the corks moist and prevent the entrance of air.

Decanting. Very old wine, or red wine that has thrown a sediment, may require decanting. Stand bottles upright an hour before decanting. Stop pouring when sediment appears in the neck.

WINE GLASSES

A 4-ounce stemmed glass of neutral shape is the most suitable all-purpose glass. If Sherry and dessert wines are served in a glass of this size, the serving, of course, should not exceed 1½ to 2 ounces. Only four kinds of glasses are needed to serve all kinds of wines. They are the 2½-ounce tulip-shaped dessert wineglass, equally suitable for appetizer wines; a tulip-shaped table wineglass of 5 to 8 ounce capacity; and a Champagne glass for sparkling wines. The standard Champagne glass has a 5 ounce capacity and is either tulip- or saucer-shaped. Hollow-stemmed Champagne glasses are usually preferred by Americans, because the wine bubbles vigorously through the stem. (The bubbles are started by a tiny rough spot at the bottom.) Hollow-stemmed ware is difficult to wash. Saucer- and tulip-stemmed Champagne glasses are preferred in Europe. To this selection of three kinds of glasses may be added special cone-shaped glasses for Sherry, which are impressive but unnecessary. Liqueurs or cordials are usually served in 1-ounce liqueur glasses; Cognac may be served in small or 1½-ounce liqueur or pony glasses, and very fine old brandy, in 18-ounce brandy inhalers or Napoleons.

WINE IN COOKING

WINE is often the element of difference between tasteless and tasty dishes. The same factors that make wines harmonize with foods on the table—their ability to balance the sweetness, acidity, saltiness and bitterness of foods and to supply aroma, acidity and smoothness for foods which lack those qualities—account for its use in cooking. Wine should lend background for natural food flavors. In fact, a dish cooked with wine should not taste solely of wine. The alcoholic content of the wine is lost when subjected to heat. Wine imparts distinction to the simplest foods. Any wine is suitable for cooking use. Wine which has turned sour can be used in salad dressings and in tart sauces.

TABLE XLVII

GUIDE TO WINE SERVICE

COURSE	KINDS OF WINE	TEMPERATURE
Appetizers (Hors d'oeuvres, etc.)	Sherry Vermouth	Optional from 50° to 60° F. Chill an hour or more in refrigerator, or serve at room temperature.
Soups	Sherry (Preferred with clear soups) or White table wine (Dry Sauternes Hock, or Rhine wine, Chablis, Riesling, Moselle, etc.)	Same as above 45° to 50° F. Chill 2 or 3 hours or longer in refrigerator
Fish or shellfish	Any white table wine or Dry Champagne	45° to 50° F. 4 hours or longer in refrigerator.
Poultry	Any white table wine or Dry Champagne With turkey, serve either red or white table wine	45° to 50° F. 40° F.
Wild duck or Game	Red table wine (Claret, Burgundy, Cabernet, Chianti, Barbera, Zinfandel, etc.)	Room temperature. Remove cork to allow wine to "breathe"; leave wine at room temperature for about 2 hours while it is warming gradually.
Red meats	Any red table wine	70° F. room temperature.
Cheese	Any red table wine, or Port	70° F. room temperature.
Dessert or fruits	Sweet dessert wines (Port, Tokay, Madeira, Marsala, not-too-dry Sherry) Sweet Sauternes Sweet Champagne	Optional—from 50° to 70° F. 40° to 50° F. Chill 3 or 4 hours. 40° F. Chill 4 or more hours.

CHAMPAGNE FRUIT CUP

3 ripe pears   3 peaches
1 small melon   1 pint lemon ice
                Champagne

Pare and dice fruit and place in Champagne glasses. Top with lemon ice. Fill glasses with Champagne and serve. Yield: 6 portions.

PINEAPPLE WITH MADEIRA

1 medium-sized pineapple   1 cup sugar
                1 cup Madeira

Pare and dice pineapple; place in serving dish, sprinkling each layer with sugar. Add wine and chill. Yield: 6 portions.

GREEN TURTLE SOUP

1 green turtle (2 to 4 lb.)   cayenne
consommé, veal or chicken   ¼ to ½ cup Sherry
   stock   2 hard-cooked eggs, chopped
black pepper   6 slices lemon

Select a green turtle; it is the top shell that makes the green gelatinous stock; prepare and cook 1 to 3 hours, or until legs are very tender (page 461). Measure turtle stock and add consommé or stock to make 1 quart; cut meat in small cubes. Bring stock to a boil and season with pepper and cayenne; add turtle meat and heat thoroughly but do not boil. Pour at once into heated tureen, add Sherry, chopped eggs and lemon slices and serve at once. (Canned green turtle soup mixed with Sherry may be purchased; place in refrigerator for several hours to jell, or serve hot.) Approximate yield: 1½ quarts, or 6 portions.

BURGER'S BURGUNDY

1½ pounds ground beef   ¼ teaspoon pepper
1½ teaspoons salt   1 cup Burgundy or Claret

Combine ground beef, salt, pepper and ½ cup wine. Blend well; shape into 6 cakes 1-inch thick. Preheat broiling compartment and pan to moderate (350° F.). Place cakes on pan 2 inches from source of heat. Broil 5 minutes, or until browned; turn to broil second side. Season and remove from pan. Add remaining wine to meat juices. Heat to boiling, season and serve over cakes. Yield: 6 portions.

LOBSTER THERMIDOR

2 live lobsters (3 pounds each)
½ cup chopped onion
3 tablespoons butter
¼ cup dry wine
2 tablespoons flour
dash of cayenne
pinch of salt

¾ cup milk
3 tablespoons light cream
4 tablespoons grated Parmesan
   cheese
1 teaspoon dry mustard
½ teaspoon paprika
2 tablespoons butter

Cook lobsters according to directions, page 440. Split cooked lobsters in half lengthwise. Remove large and small claws. Crack large claws and remove meat. Remove all lobster meat from body and cut into 1-inch pieces. Clean and wash body shells. Cook onion in butter 2 to 3 minutes; add wine and simmer until evaporated. Stir in flour, cayenne and salt. Gradually add milk and cook over low heat until smooth and thickened, stirring constantly. Add cream and 2 tablespoons cheese, mustard, paprika and lobster meat. Turn into prepared shells, sprinkle with remaining cheese and dot with butter. Broil until brown, or about 3 minutes. Sprinkle with paprika and garnish with small claws before serving. Yield: 4 portions.

WINE FRUIT COMPOTES

1. Sprinkle melon balls (watermelon, honeydew, cantaloupe) with confectioners' sugar, add California Port, Angelica or Sauternes to about half cover the balls, and chill thoroughly, stirring once or twice. Serve piled in sherbet glasses, topped with mint.

2. Sweeten berries or other fresh fruits with white wine syrup. Boil equal parts sugar and water to a heavy syrup; remove from heat, add ⅓ as much white table wine (California Sauternes or Rhine); cool. Pour over fruits and chill.

SYLLABUB

1 pint heavy cream
½ cup confectioners' sugar
1 teaspoon vanilla

¼ cup sweet Madeira or
   Sauternes or peach or
   apricot brandy

Whip cream until it begins to hold its shape; gradually beat in sugar. Carefully stir in flavoring and wine so that it does not curdle, and serve at once. Heap in glasses and serve with Shortbread (page 680) or Ladyfingers (page 696). For a more stable syllabub, gradually beat sugar into 2 egg whites; fold in whipped cream, vanilla and wine. Approximate yield: 8 portions.

CHAMPAGNE PUNCH

3 quarts fresh or frozen peach
   slices
1 fifth of brandy
2 quarts strong tea
1 fifth of light rum
1 quart soda water
2 quarts champagne

Let peaches stand overnight covered with brandy in bowl. When ready to serve, place a cake of ice in punch bowl and pour in tea, rum, soda water and champagne over peaches and brandy. Yield: 40 3-ounce glasses.

SPEEDY CHAMPAGNE PUNCH

2 bottles of white wine, chilled
2 quarts sparkling water,
   chilled
2 bottles of champagne, chilled
1 fifth of brandy, chilled

Place a large cake of ice in the punch bowl. Pour in wine, sparkling water, champagne and brandy. Stir, garnish with raspberries and float mint leaves on surface. Yield: 70 champagne glasses.

FOR A BOTTLE OF WINE

4 pounds any fruit (cherries,
   tart plums, peaches, blackberries, beach plums, elderberries)
4 quarts boiling water
4 oranges, sliced
4 lemons, sliced
4 pounds sugar
1 envelope dry granular yeast or
   1 cake compressed yeast
¼ cup warm (not hot) water
1 slice toast

Wash fruit and crush it or cut it fine. Add boiling water and let cool. Add sliced oranges and lemons and let stand 4 days. Strain and add sugar, stirring until sugar is dissolved. Sprinkle yeast (crumble yeast cake) into warm water and stir until dissolved. Place toast in yeast solution until all liquid is taken up. Float toast in fruit juice mixture for 4 days, then remove it; strain and then bottle the wine, corking it loosely until fermentation stops. Pour off, leaving sediment in the bottom of the bottles, and put through cheesecloth, or for very clear wine, put through filter paper. Rebottle; cork tightly. The wine will be ready to drink in about 3 months.

SORBET DELICIOUS

1½ cups sugar	½ cup lemon juice
3 cups water	1 cup grape juice
1½ cups orange juice	½ cup Claret or Sherry

Boil sugar and water 15 minutes; add fruit juices and wine; strain and cool. Pour into refrigerator tray and freeze 2 to 3 hours, or until of thick consistency, stirring once every hour. Yield: 6 to 8 portions.

TIPSY CHARLOTTE

1 envelope plain gelatin	1 large stale sponge cake
½ cup cold water	1 cup Sherry or Port
1 pint cream	1 cup almonds
½ cup sugar	butter
1 teaspoon vanilla or almond	angelica and cherries

Custard Sauce (page 729)

Soften gelatin in cold water 5 minutes. Heat cream almost to boiling, add softened gelatin and sugar and stir until dissolved; cool and flavor, then chill. Sponge cake should be at least 2 days old; mark off ¾ inch band around edge of cake and cut off top within this band in a 1-inch thick piece. Scoop out the middle, leaving the sides and bottom ¾ inch thick; pour ½ cup wine in spoonfuls over side so that all may be evenly moistened. When gelatin mixture is slightly thickened, beat until fluffy; turn at once into cake shell. Replace top and pour remaining ½ cup wine over it. Chill in refrigerator 2 or 3 hours. Blanch almonds and while still hot, cut in lengthwise shreds; toast in moderate oven (350° F.) with a little butter. Stick them into the finished cake and decorate with angelica and cherries. Serve with custard sauce. Approximate yield: 10 to 12 portions.

COCKTAIL ACCOMPANIMENTS

WHEN the cocktail is served as an appetizer before a meal, accompaniments should be simple things such as biscuits, wafers or savory snacks. These should be diminutive in size to do no more than whet the appetite. Tiny canapés or simple hors d'œuvres are often served with cocktails and take the place of a first course (melon or oysters) at the table. In place of cocktails before a meal, many people prefer an "apéritif" such as Vermouth, dry Sherry, Byrrh,

San Raphael or Dubonnet, the two last being light, aromatized wines. With these, a plain or slightly sweet biscuit is preferred to a salty or sweet biscuit. Tiny grilled cocktail sausages are relished by some with Sherry or Vermouth.

MIXING COCKTAILS

MOST of the following recipes for cocktails are proportioned for one. Amounts may be increased proportionately. Most cocktails are served in 2½, 4 or 5 ounce glasses. The Old-Fashioned cocktail is traditionally served in a broad, almost straight tumbler; highballs, in 8 or 10 ounce, and rickeys in 10, 12 or 14 ounce glasses.

Measuring terms vary in different localities. In this cook book, a "dash" means 3 drops; a "pony," 1 fluid ounce or about 2 tablespoons; a "jigger"—1½ to 2 fluid ounces, or about 3 to 4 tablespoons; a "split"—½ pint or 1 cup; a "twist" or "curl" of lemon peel—a thin slice of outer rind cut with a curved knife. The term "part" is equivalent to a measure which may mean more or less than a jigger depending upon individual taste. A silver or glass cocktail shaker or a large tumbler is ideal for shaking or mixing drinks. There is no inflexible rule about mixing drinks; some are stirred, some shaken. Usually, cocktails containing wine as a principal ingredient are stirred, but there are exceptions to the rule. Use a glass rod or silver spoon for stirring.

GIN COCKTAILS

Stir with cracked ice, strain and serve in cocktail glass.

Martini—One part French Vermouth, 3 or 4 parts dry gin; garnish with an olive and add a dash of orange or Angostura bitters.

Bronx—Muddle a quarter of an orange in a glass, add 3 parts gin to 1½ parts French and 1½ parts Italian Vermouth. Shake well.

Alexander—Two parts gin, 1 part Crème de Cacao and 1 part cream. Stir or shake. Cognac may be substituted for gin.

Orange Blossom—One part orange juice and one-half part gin. Shake.

Grapefruit Cocktail—One part grapefruit juice, 1 part dry gin and 1 teaspoon powdered sugar. Shake.

RUM COCKTAILS

Shake with cracked ice, strain and serve in cocktail glass.

Bacardi—One part lemon or lime juice, 1 part grenadine and 2 parts Bacardi rum.

Daiquiri—One part lemon or lime juice, 3 parts Cuban rum and 1 teaspoon powdered sugar.

Planter's Punch—One part lime juice, 3 parts Jamaica rum, 2 teaspoons powdered sugar and dash of bitters. Strain into a tall glass half filled with cracked ice, garnish with maraschino cherry, a sliver of pineapple, a slice of orange and a sprig of mint. Serve with a straw.

WHISKY COCKTAILS

Stir with cracked ice, strain and serve in cocktail glass.

Manhattan (dry)—One-fourth part French and one-fourth part Italian Vermouth, one-half part Rye and a dash of bitters. For **Old Manhattan**, use Italian for French Vermouth, add maraschino cherry.

Whisky Sour—One part lemon juice, 2 parts Rye and 1 teaspoon powdered sugar. Shake.

GIN RICKEY

Put cube of ice in medium-sized glass, add juice of ½ lemon or 1 lime and 1 jigger of gin, and fill glass with carbonated water. Stir and garnish with sprig of mint, if desired. Rum, Bourbon, or Rye may be substituted for gin.

MISCELLANEOUS COCKTAILS

Stir or shake with cracked ice, strain and serve in cocktail glass.

Dubonnet Cocktail—One part Dubonnet, 1 part dry gin and twist of lemon peel. Add more gin if desired very dry.

Coq Rouge—One part lemon or lime juice, 1 part Cointreau, 1 part gin and 2 parts rum.

Applejack Special—One part Applejack, 1 part grapefruit juice and dash of grenadine.

Frosted Mint Cocktail—One part French Vermouth, 1 part Crème de Menthe, 1 part gin, powdered sugar and sprig of fresh mint for garnish. Serve in glass frosted with sugar (page 213).

TOM COLLINS

Put 1 tablespoon sugar and juice of 1 lemon or 2 limes in tall glass; add 1 jigger gin and fill one-third with cracked ice; stir and add carbonated water.

MULLED PORT

½ nutmeg	sugar
2 cups Port	4 eggs, separated

Grate the nutmeg into the wine, add sugar if desired, cover and heat just to the boiling point. Remove from heat and let cool slightly. Beat egg yolks until thick and lemon-colored. Blend with a little cold wine and then gradually with the hot wine. Pour it back and forth in two containers several times until it is light and thoroughly mixed. Place it over low heat and stir constantly until mixture coats a metal spoon. Do not let it boil. Pour into cups and top with beaten egg white, if desired. Serve with slightly sweetened wafers. This eighteenth century brew is light and especially adapted for service in the afternoon. Yield: 4 portions.

OLD–FASHIONED

½ lump sugar	lump of ice
2 dashes bitters	slice of pineapple
1 teaspoon water	slice of orange
1 jigger rye	maraschino cherry

Put sugar in 6 ounce or Old-Fashioned glass, add bitters and water and crush or muddle to dissolve sugar; add whisky, ice and fruit, as desired; stir with glass rod.

MULLED BLACKBERRY JULEP

1 bottle blackberry julep	2 sticks cinnamon, broken
2 tablespoons sugar	⅛ teaspoon nutmeg
6 whole cloves	thin rind of 1 lemon

⅛ teaspoon nutmeg—to be sprinkled on top

Heat well, but do not boil, the wine, sugar, cloves, cinnamon and ⅛ teaspoon nutmeg. Add lemon rind and taste for sweetness. Add nutmeg and serve in pottery wine cups. Yield: 8 to 12 portions.

MINT JULEP

1 tablespoon sugar syrup   bourbon
12 tender young mint leaves   finely crushed ice
2 to 3 dashes of Angostura   mint leaves
   bitters

Place julep glass in refrigerator to chill thoroughly. In a bar glass place syrup, mint leaves and bitters. Bruise the mint gently with a muddler; stir lightly a few minutes to blend all ingredients. Add 2 ounces bourbon. Pack julep glass with crushed ice. Strain and add mint mixture. With a long bar spoon churn the contents up and down a few minutes. Add more ice and enough bourbon to within ¼ inch of top of glass. Repeat churning until glass frosts. Garnish with mint leaves. Serve with straws. Yield: 1 mint julep.

TOM AND JERRY

6 egg whites   1 cup brandy
6 egg yolks   ½ teaspoon cinnamon
½ cup sugar   ½ teaspoon nutmeg
1 cup Jamaica rum   3 cups boiling water

Beat egg whites, then beat egg yolks with sugar. Add whites to yolks and fold until blended. Add rum and brandy. Add cinnamon and nutmeg. Stir into this gradually 3 cups boiling water. Serve in earthenware mugs with a dash of nutmeg. Yield: 6 portions.

FARMER'S BISHOP

whole cloves   granulated sugar to taste
6 oranges   ½ gallon sweet cider
1 quart apple brandy   ground cinnamon
                          nutmeg

Stick oranges full of cloves. Bake in moderate oven until they soften and the juice begins to exude. Place hot oranges in well-warmed punch bowl and pour over them warm brandy and sugar to taste. Set fire to brandy and in a few minutes, extinguish the flame by adding sweet cider that has been heated but not boiled. Stir in cinnamon and nutmeg to taste. Serve in punch cups. Approximate yield: 25 portions.

SQUIRE'S WINE PUNCH

12 cubes sugar
6 lemons
12 oranges
1 quart tea
4 bottles 1929 Graves
(white Bordeaux)
1 bottle Cognac

1 pint rye
6 ounces Benedictine
6 ounces maraschino or
cherry liqueur
8 ounces Italian Vermouth
½ pound sugar (about)
4 bottles Champagne
fresh fruits and mint

Rub twelve cubes of sugar against the skin of an orange, scraping off the sugar as it absorbs oil from skin. This is known as oleo-saccharine. Use this oleo-saccharine to sweeten ½ pint lemon juice and 1½ pints orange juice. To this add prepared tea, previously made and chilled, the wine, Cognac, whisky, Benedictine, maraschino or cherry liqueur and Vermouth. Add sugar to taste and a large piece of ice. Stir until very cold. Just before serving, add the Champagne, fresh fruits and mint. Approximate yield: 80 to 100 portions.

HOLIDAY GLÜGG

1½ pounds seedless raisins
1½ cups sugar
1 tablespoon broken cinnamon
bark

1 tablespoon whole cloves
2 dozen cardamom seeds
1 gallon red Burgundy wine
⅘ quart brandy or bourbon

Cover raisins with water, about 3 cups; add sugar, cinnamon and cloves. Crack cardamom seeds, drop in with shells. Simmer, covered, for 2 hours or until the raisins swell. If necessary add more water from time to time. Remove from heat, add wine, bring almost to simmer, but not quite, and keep hot at about 160° F. for 2 hours. Cool; leave spices in the brew overnight. Drain. Squeeze raisins to get out every last drop of wine. Pour into bottles until ready to use. Reheat when ready to serve, adding brandy or bourbon. Yield: 4 quarts Glugg.

NEW YEAR'S EGGNOG

6 eggs, separated
¾ cup sugar
1½ cups Cognac

½ cup rum
4 cups milk
4 cups heavy cream
nutmeg

Beat egg yolks until thick and light-colored, add sugar and continue beating until well blended; slowly add brandy and rum, then the milk and cream. Beat egg whites until stiff; fold into egg yolk-brandy mixture. Grate nutmeg lightly over each glass. Yield: 24 portions.

NEW YEAR'S PUNCH

3 cups sugar
3 cups lemon juice
2 cups shredded pineapple
1 pint strawberries
1 pint strong green tea

2 tablespoons Curaçao
1 quart Champagne
1 quart white wine
1 quart carbonated water
ice

Dissolve 2 cups sugar in lemon juice; sprinkle remaining sugar over shredded pineapple and whole, hulled strawberries and allow to stand until sugar is dissolved. Put chilled green tea, Curaçao and wines into punch bowl, stir in sweetened lemon juice, fruits and carbonated water; place a large block of ice in the bowl and serve ice cold. Approximate yield: 5 quarts, or 40 small glasses.

MAY WINE

10 bottles Rhine wine
6 tablespoons white Maraschino
6 tablespoons Cognac
1½ pounds confectioners' sugar

6 tablespoons tea leaves
3 quarts sparkling water
ice
strawberries

Combine Rhine wine, Maraschino, Cognac and confectioners' sugar and stir until dissolved. Place tea in cheesecloth bag and steep in the mixture. Remove and add the sparkling water and pour over ice block in the large punch bowl. Float strawberries in punch and serve at once. Three quarts of Champagne may be substituted for water, tea and sugar, if desired. Approximate yield: 90 punch glasses.

WASSAIL BOWL

4 apples
¾ cup sugar
¼ cup water

3 cups ale or porter
3 cups apple cider
1 teaspoon allspice

Core apples, sprinkle with ¼ cup sugar, add water and bake in moderately hot oven (375°) 30 minutes or until tender, basting several times with syrup in the pan. Combine ale, cider, remaining sugar and allspice and place over low heat, stirring until sugar is dissolved. Do not boil. Pour over roasted apples in the punch bowl. Approximate yield: 6 portions.

Herbs and Spices

ANYONE with a tiny patch of cultivable ground, a rock garden or sunny window box can rediscover the delights of growing "pot" and salad herbs. Many of them come dried and packaged ready for use. A few of the more commonly known herbs, like chives, parsley and mint, are available fresh in many markets.

How to Cook with Herbs. Use herbs sparingly since their aromatic oils are very strong. Do not use them in several dishes at the same meal—use them for variety and accent only. Blend judiciously for different purposes; have a leading flavor and combine two, three or four less pronounced flavors with it. Never emphasize more than one of the very strong herbs in a blend, except perhaps for sausage. Blends should be so subtle that only the expert can tell which herbs are used. Chop savory leaves very fine. For some purposes, grind them in a mortar. The more the cut surface is exposed, the more completely the aromatic oil can be absorbed. Blending or heating with butter or other fats is the best way to draw out and extend the flavor of the aromatic oils. It's well to remember when using herbs in recipes that one tablespoon of freshly chopped herbs is equal to ½ teaspoon of dried or ¼ teaspoon of powdered herbs. Soaking dried herbs in a few drops of water or lemon juice for 15 minutes before using helps to point up the flavor. For soups and gravies, add sprigs of fresh herbs tied in tiny bunches or use ground herbs in cheesecloth bags. Remove them after they have served their purpose. Herbs left too long in soups or gravies will impart unpleasantly strong flavors. They are best added a short time before the cooking is finished.

Herbs may be grouped as very strong, fairly strong and delicate in flavor. The very strong herbs are: Rosemary, sage and winter savory. The fairly strong herbs are: Basil (sweet), balm (lemon), mint, marjoram (sweet and pot), thyme, dill, fennel and tarragon. The delicate herbs are: Summer savory, chervil, parsley, chives. The delicate herbs are excellent for general use.

Herb Bouquets. To season soups, stews and sauces make bouquets of dried herbs (bouquet garni). Prepare a quantity of them at one time and store until ready to use. Making them is simple. Cut small cheesecloth bags about 1½ to 2 inches square and fill these with mixtures of dried, crushed herbs. Store the bouquets in tightly covered and labeled containers. The bags are added to the soup, sauce or stew toward the end of the cooking period. They should remain long enough for the soup (or sauce) to achieve a fine herbal aroma and should then be removed. Do not let them stand indefinitely in the soup or it will become bitter and over-seasoned. Use only once, then discard.

The cooking term *fines herbes* is applied to a selection of fresh herbs chopped fine and either sprinkled over the food as it cooks or combined with the sauce or gravy.

Fines herbes may be made by chopping finely a combination of the following: ½ onion, 2 scallions, 2 sprigs parsley or chervil, ½ leek and 1 tablespoon fresh marjoram. You may prefer another combination of your own.

To prepare herb butter minced tender leaves of fresh chives, fennel, chervil, tarragon and marjoram and a few crumbs of dry bread are ground with a pestle in a mortar with a drop or two of brandy, or an aromatic liqueur. This is then blended with butter and forced through a fine sieve. (The crumbs and liqueur help distribute and hold the flavor of the herbs in the butter.) The mixture is chilled and rolled into balls with wooden butter paddles. A ball of herb butter is placed on piping hot steak or broiled fish and allowed to melt into it, or the mixture is used as a savory cracker or sandwich spread.

Mixed Herb Vinegar. Take leaves of balm, mint, marjoram, savory and tarragon, stalks of chives and chervil, add a few shallots and a little basil. Fill jar one-third full, cover with a fine quality vinegar. Cover tightly and let stand for 2 weeks. Strain, bottle, label and store in a cool place. Use these herb vinegars for flavoring salad dressings, soups, fish sauces, pickles, etc.

HOW TO USE HERBS AND SPICES IN COOKING

Appetizers

Tomato Juice—A dash of mace or marjoram, basil or tarragon or finely chopped parsley.
Cranberry Juice—A tiny dash of ground cloves.
Avocado—Freshly ground pepper, onion juice, onion salt, chili powder season the mashed avocado pulp, wedges or halves.
Stuffed Celery—Paprika for appearance and flavor.
Smoked Salmon—Paprika, black pepper.
Cream Cheese Spread—Onion juice, onion salt, celery seed.
Ham Spread—Onion juice, onion salt, celery seed.

Soups—In general the following herbs may be used: Basil, bay leaf, caraway seeds, chervil, chives, cloves, coriander seeds, marjoram, mint, parsley, peppercorns, rosemary, savory, tarragon (especially with tomato), thyme (particularly with onion).

Creamed Chicken or Tomato—Mace, paprika.
Creamed Tomato or Pea—Cloves, paprika (a dash of nutmeg in split pea soup), tarragon.
Vegetable—Thyme, savory, garlic.
Chowder—Poultry seasoning, thyme, bay leaf.
Consommé—Ground allspice, thyme, or sage.
Vichyssoise—Chervil.
Mulligatawny—Curry powder, mace, cloves.
Chicken—Nutmeg.
Lamb Broth—Mace, curry powder.
Oyster Stew—Light touch of mace, nutmeg, cayenne and dash of paprika.
Bean Soup—Cloves, thyme, mustard.
Beef—Cloves, allspice, garlic, bay leaf, dash of nutmeg.
Mock Turtle—Basil, bouquet.

Meats—Fines herbes may be used with most broiled, baked or braised meat: anise, basil, bay, chervil, chives, horseradish, lemon balm, mace, marjoram, mint (with lamb), parsley, peppercorns, rosemary, sage, savory and thyme.

Roast Beef—Onion or garlic rubbed into meat before cooking; rosemary; thyme sparingly.

Pot Roast—Cloves, allspice, bay leaf, garlic, ground ginger (sometimes rubbed on meat before cooking), marjoram, savory.

Boiled Beef—Cloves, bay leaf.

Hamburger—Onion, allspice, poultry seasoning, savory, marjoram, basil, rosemary, occasionally pickling spice, thyme sparingly.

Beef Stew—Celery seed, bay leaf, pepper, nutmeg, thyme sparingly, occasionally pickling spice, basil, rosemary.

Ham—Whole cloves.

Chicken—Rosemary, onion, mace or nutmeg, curry, poultry seasoning, basil, chervil, sage, tarragon, thyme.

Lamb—Garlic, freshly ground pepper, marjoram.

Meat Loaf—Celery, onion, cloves, allspice, parsley, ground pepper, garlic, poultry seasoning, marjoram, sage, savory, thyme.

Croquettes—Poultry seasoning, sage, celery seed.

Sweetbreads—Onion juice, mace, white pepper, paprika.

Cooked meat—Curry.

Spareribs—Garlic, chili powder, bay leaf, paprika, marjoram, savory, thyme.

Fish—In general basil, bay leaf, chervil, chives, dill, fennel, lemon balm, marjoram, mint, parsley, peppercorns and tarragon are used; whole allspice, mustard, Worcestershire sauce, onion, celery, curry and pickling spice (steamed fish).

Stuffings—Poultry seasoning is generally used in combination with onion, parsley, and celery, but if there is none available, use the following combination: onion, sage, thyme, pepper and mustard.

Eggs—In general good herb combinations are basil, chervil, chives, marjoram, parsley, rosemary and tarragon.

Omelets—Basil, chervil, marjoram, tarragon and occasionally rosemary.

Vegetables—Besides the specific herb musts below, basil is particularly good with tomatoes, potatoes and peas; bay leaf with tomatoes; marjoram and mint with peas, carrots and green vegetables; rosemary and sage with vegetable-cheese dishes; tarragon is usually used with vinaigrette vegetables and thyme is particularly good with scalloped dishes.

Beets—Cloves, bay leaf.
Kidney Beans—Chili powder, bay leaf.
String Beans—Sage, savory, basil, bay leaf, whole cloves.
Cabbage—Onion, celery seed, curry.
Rice—Curry.
Cauliflower—Poppy seeds, celery seed.
Swiss Chard—Onion, salt, marjoram.
White Potato—Paprika, parsley, basil, dill.
Squash—Cinnamon, marjoram.
Onions—Celery seed, cloves.
Tomatoes—Allspice, celery, basil, marjoram, sage, tarragon, bay leaf.
Sweet Potatoes—Nutmeg, cloves.
Baked Beans—Pepper, mustard, allspice.
Corn—Paprika, pepper, chili powder.
Eggplant—Allspice, bay leaf, sage.
Kale—Nutmeg.
Red Cabbage—Allspice (especially with apples).
Succotash—Nutmeg.
Spinach—Nutmeg, marjoram, mint.
Lima Beans—Cayenne, celery, onion, savory, basil, chives.
Carrots—Thyme, marjoram, mint.
Peas—Thyme, rosemary, tarragon, basil, marjoram, mint.

Sauces—Bay leaf, chervil, chives, curry powder, horseradish, mace, parsley, saffron (particularly to impart a yellow color), tarragon (in vinegar or white sauce and in French dressing) may be used.

Cream Sauce—Onion juice, celery, mace or nutmeg (with chicken and veal), cayenne, mustard, paprika and parsley.
Brown Sauce for Meats—Onion juice, garlic, allspice, pepper.
Fish Sauce—Béarnaise, Tartar Sauce, etc.—Tarragon, chives.
Tomato Sauce—Onion, garlic, celery, celery seed, cloves, black pepper and basil.
Mushroom Sauce—Onion, nutmeg, pepper.

Salads and Salad Dressings—Among the many herbs, both fresh and dried, that can be used in salads are: Anise (leaves), basil, borage, burnet, chervil, chives, fennel, lemon balm, mint, parsley, rue, sorrel and tarragon.

Coleslaw—Generous amounts of celery seed, pepper, paprika, caraway seeds.
Tomato Aspic—Bay leaf, celery salt, onion juice, cloves, cayenne, basil and tarragon.
Cottage Cheese—Onion, marjoram, sage, thyme, chives.

Pear Salad—Add ginger to the dressing.
Cooked Salad Dressing—Pepper, mustard, paprika.
Spiced Vinegar—Savory, cloves, mace, allspice, pepper, chives, celery seed and bay leaf.
Fruit Salad Dressing—Ground mustard, nutmeg.
French Dressing—Curry, freshly ground pepper, chervil, savory, basil, marjoram, tarragon.

DUNKING TRAY

1 cup mayonnaise	¼ teaspoon savory
¼ cup chili sauce	¼ teaspoon oregano
2 tablespoons horseradish	cucumber strips
1 teaspoon chopped chives	carrot strips
1 teaspoon dill seeds	flowerets of cauliflower
½ teaspoon tarragon	sliced dill pickles

shrimp on toothpicks

Mix mayonnaise, chili sauce and herbs. Place in bowl in center of a large platter. Arrange vegetables and shrimp in alternate groups around sauce. Approximate yield: 6 to 8 servings.

BOUQUET GARNI

3 cloves	½ teaspoon dried basil
1 bay leaf	½ teaspoon dried thyme

Tie herbs in cheesecloth bag; boil with 2 cups stock or tomatoes 5 minutes to flavor; remove and discard bag.

BIBLIOGRAPHY

Alkire, Lura Jim and Schuler, Stanley, *Home Freezing for Everyone*, M. Barrows & Company, Inc., New York, 1950.

Allen, Ida Bailey, *Pressure Cooking*, Garden City Publishing Co., New York, 1947.

American Home Economics Association, *Handbook of Food Preparation*, Washington, D. C., 1950.

Amidon, Edna P., Bradbury, Dorothy E., and Drenckhan, Vivian V., *Good Food and Nutrition for Young People and Their Families*, John Wiley and Sons, Inc., New York, 1946.

Burright, Ora Blanche, *A Source Book on Foods*, Pioneer Women Publishing Company, Oklahoma, 1948.

Carrol, Leone R., *Pressure Cookery*, M. Barrows and Co., Inc., New York, 1947.

Cereal Institute, Chicago, Ill., Miscellaneous Publications.

Committee on Preparation on Factors, National Cooperative Meat Investigations, *Meat and Meat Cookery*, Chicago, Ill., 1942.

Dahnke, Marye, *The Cheese Cookbook*, A. A. Wyn, New York, 1950.

Draper, Dorothy, *Entertaining Is Fun*, Doubleday & Co., Inc., New York, 1941.

Halliday, Evelyn G. and Noble, Isabel T., *Hows and Whys of Cooking*, The University of Chicago Press, Chicago, Ill., 1946.

Harvard Schools of Public Health and Medicine, Miscellaneous Publications.

Hughes, Osee, *Introductory Foods*, The Macmillan Co., New York, 1942.

Justin, Margaret M., Rust, Lucile Osborn and Vaile, Gladys E., *Foods, An Introductory College Course*, Houghton Mifflin Co., New York, 1940.

Lowe, Belle, *Experimental Cookery*, John Wiley and Sons, Inc., New York, 1943.

Lowenberg, M. E., *Food for the Young Child*, Collegiate Press, Inc., Ames, Iowa, 1934.

MacLeod, Grace and Taylor, Clara Mae, *Rose's Foundations of Nutrition*, The Macmillan Co., New York, 1944.

Mazza, Irma G., *Herbs for the Kitchen*, Little, Brown and Co., Boston, 1947.

Monroe, Day, Kyrk, Hazel and Stone, Ursula B., *Food Buying and Our Markets*, M. Barrows and Co., New York, 1938.

Monsch, Helen and Harper, Marguerite K., *Feeding Babies and Their Families*, John Wiley and Sons, Inc., New York, 1942.

Nason, Edith H., *Introduction to Experimental Cookery*, McGraw-Hill Book Co., New York, 1939.

National Livestock and Meat Board, Chicago, Ill., Miscellaneous Publications.

National Research Council, Food and Nutrition Board, Washington, D. C., Food and Nutrition Charts.

New York State College of Agriculture and Home Economics

CROSBY, MARION W. AND HARRIS, KATHERINE H., *Purchasing Food for Fifty*, Bulletin 803, Cornell University, Ithaca, N. Y., 1950.

FENTON, F. AND DARFLER, J., *Foods from the Freezer*, Bulletin 692, Cornell University, Ithaca, N. Y., 1946.

HUNTER, M., BRIANT, M. AND PERSONIUS, C., *Cake Quality and Batter Structure*, Bulletin 860, Cornell University, Ithaca, N. Y., 1950.

MASTERMAN, N. K. AND LEE, F. A., *The Home Freezing of Farm Products*, Bulletin 611, Cornell University, Ithaca, N. Y., 1950.

MASTERMAN, N. K., *Using the Home Freezer*, Bulletin 658, Cornell University, Ithaca, N. Y., 1944.

PIMENTEL, M., HODGSON, R. AND BRIANT, A., *Cake Mixes: Home-Made*, Cornell University, Ithaca, N. Y., 1950.

SHABEN, L. AND HURD, L., *How to Prepare and Cook Poultry*, Bulletin 785, Cornell University, Ithaca, N. Y., 1950.

POST, EMILY, *Etiquette*, Funk and Wagnalls Co., New York, 1937.

Production and Marketing Administration, War Food Administration, *Fresh Fruit and Vegetable Supplies*, 1943.

PROUDFIT, FAIRFAX T. AND ROBINSON, CORINNE H., *Nutrition and Diet Therapy*, The Macmillan Co., New York, 1947.

ROBERTS, L. J., *Feeding the Family*, 4th edition, The Macmillan Co., New York, 1940.

SHERMAN, HENRY C. AND LANFORD, CAROLINE SHERMAN, *An Introduction to Foods and Nutrition*, The Macmillan Co., New York, 1943.

SHERMAN, HENRY C., *Food and Health*, The Macmillan Co., New York, 1947.

SPACKLING, HELEN, *Setting Your Table*, M. Barrows and Co., New York, 1941.

STANLEY, LOUISE AND CLINE, JESSIE ALICE, *Foods, Their Selection and Preparation*, Ginn and Co., New York, 1935.

TRESSLER, DONALD K., EVERS, CLIFFORD, F. AND LONG, LUCY, *Into the Freezer and Out*, Avi Publishing Co., New York, 1946.

TRESSLER, DONALD K., "Storing Frozen Foods in Domestic Refrigerators," *Practical Home Economics*, January, 1951, p. 27 ff.

United States Department of Agriculture

Bureau of Animal Industry, Agric. Research Admin.
Freezing Meat and Poultry Products for Home Use, AWI–75 (1944).

Bureau of Human Nutrition and Home Economics, Agric. Research Admin.
Family Food Consumption in the United States, Misc. Publ. 550 (1944).

Food for the Family with Young Children, AIS–59 (1946).

Food Values in Common Portions, AIB–36 (1951).

Freezing of Fruits and Vegetables, AIS–48 (1946).

Home Canning of Fruits and Vegetables, AIS–64 (1947).

Home Canning of Meat, AWI–110 (1945).

Home Freezers, Their Selection and Use, Misc. Publ. 687 (1949).

Home Freezing of Fruits and Vegetables, Home and Garden Bulletin No. 10 (1951).

National Food Guide, AIS–53 (1946).

Tables of Food Composition in Terms of Eleven Nutrients, Misc. Publ. 572 (1945).

U. S. Grades for Beef, Leaflet 310 (1951).

DAWSON, E. H., GILPIN, G. AND REYNOLDS, H., *Procedures for Home Freezing of Vegetables, Fruits and Prepared Foods,* Agricultural Handbook No. 2 (1950).

STIEBLING, H. K., MONROE, DAY, EVANS, CALLIE M. and others, *Family Food Consumption and Dietary Levels, Five Regions,* Farm Series, Misc. Publ. 405 (1941).

STIEBLING, H. K. AND RHIPARD, E. F., *Diets of Families of Employed Wage Earners and Clerical Workers in Cities,* Circular 507 (1939).

United States Department of Interior

Fish and Wildlife Service

How to Cook Fish, 106FL (1947).

How to Cook Oysters, Test Kitchen Series No. 3 (1947).

WARD, ARTEMAS, *Encyclopedia of Food,* Baker and Taylor Co., New York, 1929.

Wheat Flour Institute, Chicago, Ill., Miscellaneous Publications.

Wine Advisory Board, *The Wine Industry and Wine Growing and Types,* San Francisco, Calif., 1946.

Index

❖❖

INDEX

Desserts, gelatin—*Continued*   PAGE

cups 790
   cubed 790
   flaked 790
   self-layered 790
ginger cream 793
gooseberry 778
jelly,
   fruit 791
   lemon 791
   orange 791
kumquat snow 763
lemon, snowballs 786
   whip 791
lemon-pie 764
meringue bubbles 765
molded 789–796
Norwegian prune 1058
orange whip 791
peach
   cream 764
   nests 791
   roll 778
pear compote 764
pears
   baked, ginger sauce . . . 765
   cocoa 763
pineapple dessert 764
pudding
   Bing cherry 777
   black currant 778
   bread 773
   cake crumb 774
   caramel 769
   chocolate, steamed . . . 786
   cottage 776
    cherry 776
    pineapple topped . . . 776
   creamy 771–772
   date torte 787
   Highland feather crust . . 786
   honey, waltzing Matilda's . 770
   Indian 775
    quick, in pressure saucepan . 974
   lemon 770
    meringue 774
    snow 791
   persimmon, baked . . . 777
   plum, English
    Old 785
    quick, in pressure saucepan . 975
   prune
    medallion 791
    quick, in pressure saucepan . 975
   Quaker, steamed 785
   rice 774–775
   Scotch 792
   suet 785
raspberry mist 763
rennet pudding 766
   chocolate 766
   maple 767
rum omelet 797
Russian peach cream . . . 793
Savoy trifle 795
shortcakes 779–780
skyscraper aflame 797
soufflés 781–784
sour cherry cobbler . . . 779
Spanish cream 793
   chocolate 793
   fruit 793
sponge
   apricot 792
   chocolate, sweet . . . 796
   coffee 793
   lemon 791
   orange 792
strawberries 762
tapioca 771–772

Desserts—*Continued*   PAGE

vanilla cream 771
waffles
   chocolate dessert . . . 781
   suzette noir 780
wines to serve with . . . 1072
see also Fruits
Desserts, frozen
   baked Alaska 812
    grapefruit 813
    individual 812
   bombes 812
   brûlé 1058
   charlotte 808
   cream whip 808
   custard, strawberry . . . 811
   glacé, charlotte 808
   ice creams . . . 799–801, 803–805
   ices 802
   Javanese cream 812
   mocha biscuit 809
   mocha refrigerator cream . 810
   mousses 806–807
   parfaits 808–809
   peach surprise 810
   peppermint cream, quick . . 807
   puddings 810–811
   rainbow pie 813
   refrigerator creams . . 803–805
   sherbets 802–804
   strawberries Romanoff . . 813
   sundaes 812–813
Devil's food cake 643
   mix-easy 646
Devonshire pie 745
Dewberries, freezing procedure for . 884
Diet, good 5–10
Dill
  -cheese canapés 202
   pickle stuffing 485
   pickles 947
   sauce for cold fish . . . 472
Dinner menus 12–15
   fish for Friday 977
   Italian 977
   for men 977, 978
   summertime 978
   evening wedding . . . 978
   oven 14
Dinners
   fifteen-minute, in pressure sauce-
    pan 968–970
   five-minute, pressure-cooked . 970–971
   table settings for . . . 27, 28
   three-layered 288
Divinity 844–845
   brown sugar 844
   cherry 845
   chocolate 844
   layered 845
   mallow loaf 845
   maple 844
   Neapolitan 845
Dobos torte 1047
Dolmeh-E-Beh (Persian) . . . 1010
Doughnuts 703–705
   black walnut 703
   chocolate 704
   frying 703
   grandmother's raised . . 705
   old-fashioned 703
   orange 703
   potato 704
   sour milk 704
   temperature and time-table for . 72
   whole wheat 704
Doughs
   basic sweet 171
   modifications . . . 172–173
   savory 1057

PARMESAN 1038

RECIPES FROM FOREIGN COUNTRIES

1154

INDEX